Bt
28.00

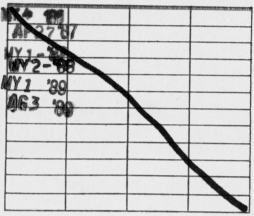

DATE DUE

MY 17			
AP 27 87			
MY 1 -			
MY 2 - 88			
MY 1 '89			
AG 3 '80			

THE LEGISLATIVE STRUGGLE

A Study in Social Combat

THE
LEGISLATIVE STRUGGLE

A Study in Social Combat

Bertram M. Gross

GREENWOOD PRESS, PUBLISHERS
WESTPORT, CONNECTICUT

Library of Congress Cataloging in Publication Data

Gross, Bertram Myron, 1912-
  The legislative struggle.

    Reprint of the ed. published by McGraw-Hill, New
York, in series: McGraw-Hill series in political
science.
    Includes bibliographical references and index.
    1. Legislation--United States. 2. United States.
Congress. I. Title.
[JK1096.G7 1978]   328.73   77-18784
ISBN 0-313-20205-2

Reprinted with the permission of Bertram M. Gross

Reprinted in 1978 by Greenwood Press, Inc.,
51 Riverside Avenue, Westport, Conn. 06880

Printed in the United States of America

10 9 8 7 6 5 4 3 2 1

TO

Nora, David, Larry, Sammy, and Teddy

PREFACE

There are at least three motives behind the writing of "The Legislative Struggle."

First, while serving as a staff adviser to various Senate committees and later as an official in the Executive Office of the President, I long ago learned that many people felt the need for a book which could serve as a guide in the handling of concrete legislative problems.

True, many books were available on the organization, rules, and history of Congress, on the case histories of individual laws, on proposals for congressional reform, and on governmental operations as a whole. But none had ever attempted to deal in practical terms with the full gamut of problems that arise from questions of whether and when to seek legislative action to the final issues revolving around Presidential signature or veto.

Ignorance is not tolerated as an excuse for breaking the law. Yet ignorance accounts for the failure of many Americans to do their share in making the law. Baffled by the complexities of the lawmaking process, the average American finds it difficult to weigh the promises or appraise the accomplishments of the congressional candidates who seek his vote. He is easy prey for legislative double talk. When he is bestirred to petition the lawmakers directly, the result is often pathetic. The wastebaskets of Congressmen overflow with mail of the wrong kind to the wrong person on the wrong subject. The office buildings of Washington are filled with organizations that have never penetrated to the inner sanctum; their efforts for the most part end in futility. The lobbies of Capitol Hill teem with lawyers, public-relations men, and ex-government officials who accomplish little except to wrest large fees from gullible individuals, associations, and corporations.

Nor is the average public official given the clue to the mystery by virtue of his office. Many a well-meaning administrator, for want of knowledge concerning currents and soundings, has steered a government program on the legislative rocks. In fact, the expanding science of public administration is yielding large numbers of administrators, all well fitted for a world run entirely by administrators, but having little or no understanding of relations with legislators. Many a judge, too, in rendering a decision, will talk learnedly about "legislative intent," although his interpretation of the statute in question may be based upon an utterly naïve conception of how laws are born.

Some members of Congress never learn the secret of how to advance a legislative project. Many go through extended legislative battles without any clear
idea of the forces that make for victory or defeat.

Second, through many years of behind-the-scenes work on legislation, I
have often been urged to reveal what really happened on measures with which
I have been connected.

The motive for doing this has always been compelling. For many years I
had worked intensively on all sorts of legislative matters—developing ideas
for legislation, drafting bills, arranging for committee hearings, interrogating
witnesses, assisting in floor action, sitting in with legislative committees and
conference committees in "marking up" bills and writing committee reports,
preparing agency views on legislation, presenting agency budgets to the appropriations committees, participating in the process of Presidential clearance
of legislative measures, and helping to prepare Presidential messages to Congress. I worked closely with Democrats and Republicans in both Houses of
Congress, with government officials in the White House, the departments, the
independent agencies, and state and local governments, and with representatives of corporations, labor unions, trade associations, and other private organizations. I became intimately involved with problems of legislative strategy
and tactics. On a number of occasions, I experienced the unique thrill of seeing measures that I had initiated or collaborated on—such as the Employment
Act of 1946, the Contract Settlement Act, the Surplus Property Act, the War
Mobilization and Reconversion Act, the resolution setting up the Joint Committee on the Reorganization of Congress, the Defense Production Act and
the National Capital Planning Act—approved by the Congress.

In all these situations I found that more things went on than were dreamed
of by the most diligent observers, let alone by the general public. In his book
"Congress Makes a Law," Stephen K. Bailey has described the legislative
process as a drama played behind closed curtains. "It is much as though the
citizenry were seated in a huge auditorium, allowed printed programs, but
kept in total ignorance of what was happening on the stage. To the handful
of citizens who have watched the show from the wings, this separation of
players from audience is a dual tragedy: a tragedy for the players who might
profit from audience reaction, a tragedy for the members of the audience who
miss both entertainment and vitally needed education." In the drama of lawmaking there are as many competing directors and stage managers as there
are would-be Hamlets. Nor are all the participants themselves privileged to
see and hear the entire performance. Most of them give their orders or strut
their bit and then take their places on the other side of the curtain to await
the denouement. From his place in the wings Bailey proceeds to tell the story
of the Employment Act of 1946, one of the dramas in which I played an
active role. It seemed only natural that one of the characters should become
an author.

But these two motives would scarcely have been sufficient by themselves. Far more important has been my growing belief in the need for a new and more realistic concept of the legislative process. I wrote the book mainly to develop such a concept—one that would emphasize people in action as the essence of legislative activity; that would analyze the role in the legislative process not only of members of Congress but also of Presidents and executive officials, judges, private organizations, and political parties; that would recognize the similarities between the legislative process and other governmental and social processes; and that would contribute to the development of better understanding of social behavior as a whole.

My basic aim has thus been to develop a theoretical structure, a systematic method of thinking about legislation. Yet I have always believed that if a theory does not work in a practical situation, it is a bad theory. I am, therefore, hopeful that the intellectual framework will stand up under the weight of practical application. If it does and if it therefore serves to promote more intelligent and more widespread participation in the writing of our laws, the effort will be amply rewarded.

In writing this book I have drawn extensively upon firsthand personal experience and upon secondhand experiences gleaned from discussions with other participants in the legislative process. I have also relied heavily upon the *Congressional Record,* congressional committee hearings and reports, and other publicly available records of legislative activity. My debt to other writers who have dealt with legislation is particularly great. The following have been the most helpful:

Arthur F. Bentley, "The Process of Government" (Bloomington, Indiana: Principia Press, 1949 reissue).

David B. Truman, "The Governmental Process" (New York: Knopf, 1951).

Woodrow Wilson, "Congressional Government" (Boston: Houghton Mifflin, 1885).

Stephen K. Bailey, "Congress Makes a Law" (New York: Columbia University Press, 1949).

Robert Luce's quartet: "Legislative Procedure," "Legislative Assemblies," "Legislative Principles," and "Legislative Problems" (Boston: Houghton Mifflin, 1922, 1930, 1930 and 1935, respectively).

Roland Young, "This Is Congress" (New York: Knopf, 1943).

George Galloway, "Congress at the Crossroads" (New York: Crowell, 1946).

James M. Burns, "Congress on Trial" (New York: Harper & Bros., 1949).

Joseph P. Chamberlain, "Legislative Processes: National and State" (New York: D. Appleton–Century, 1936).

Harvey Walker, "The Legislative Process" (New York: The Ronald Press, 1948).

Floyd M. Riddick, "The United States Congress: Organization and Procedure" (Washington, D.C.: National Capitol Publishers, 1949).

I must also express my indebtedness to those courageous friends who read carbon copies of the manuscript at various stages in its six years of growth and gave me the benefit of their advice and counsel. The hardiest of these souls are Ralph Goldman, of the American Political Science Association Cooperative Research Project on Convention Delegations, who assisted in reducing the first draft to a more suitable length; Stephen K. Bailey, of Wesleyan University; Arthur F. Bentley; Kurt Borchardt, of the House Committee on Interstate and Foreign Commerce; Kenneth Hechler, of Princeton University and the White House staff; Fritz Morstein Marx, of American University and the Bureau of the Budget; and Eve Zidel and Nora Gross, who wielded powerful vetoes by refusing to type anything that did not live up to their standards.

I am also grateful for the encouragement I have received from so many of my colleagues in the American Political Science Association. Participation in the Association's Committee on Political Parties and in the short-term special committees on Congressional Reapportionment and Soldier Voting has brought me into contact with some of the outstanding minds in American social science and has helped to deepen my understanding of governmental processes.

There may be those who believe that I have written too freely about confidential matters. My intention has been to write nothing that could be personally embarrassing to anyone. If there have been any deviations from this course, they have been accidental.

There are those whose writings on legislation and related matters have received too little attention in the text. For this I blame the rigorous limitations of space.

BERTRAM M. GROSS

ARLINGTON, VA.
JANUARY, 1953

CONTENTS

PART II.   COMBAT ON THE LEGISLATIVE TERRAIN

THE LEGISLATIVE STRUGGLE

A Study in Social Combat

Chapter 1

THE TWOFOLD CHALLENGE: AN
INTRODUCTION

EVERY YEAR the legislative process in Washington grinds out a bewildering variety of products. On the slight preeminence known as Capitol Hill, members of the Senate and the House of Representatives sponsor thousands of bills covering almost every conceivable subject. Many of these are unceremoniously ignored. Many become the focal point for energetic lobbying and propaganda, closed-door confabs, public hearings, and the making or unmaking of records, reputations, and election issues. Some win quiet acceptance in both houses. Others give rise to impassioned debate and voting, the forming and re-forming of political lines, or sharp disagreement between the two chambers.

Out of all the hubbub and confusion emerges a steady flow of bills to be signed by the Presiding Officer of the Senate and the Speaker of the House and carried by messenger up Pennsylvania Avenue to the White House. A few are stricken down by vetoes. Most are signed by the President and sent to the nearby National Archives where they are numbered, filed, and subsequently printed in the latest volume of an endless series entitled "United States Statutes at Large." These statutes embody decisions establishing a Federal budget which represents a huge share of the national income, regulating vast sectors of industry, agriculture, and labor, and extending the network of our economic, military, and political links with the rest of the world. They are the law of the land—to be administered for better or worse by the President and assorted bureaucrats; to be interpreted by the courts; to be praised, cursed, ignored, or supported by the American people; and sooner or later to be amended by other laws.

How do these laws really come into being? Why are these passed, and others not? Why was this clause voted down, and the proviso approved?

Does the national legislative process operate properly? How might it be improved?

These two sets of questions are not easy to answer. The legislative process is one of the methods of untying the Gordian knots created by the growing complexities of a highly organized capitalist society. Any attempt to describe

1

it must recognize that it is closely interwoven with the full fabric of American life. Any effort to appraise and improve it must recognize that its weaknesses reflect underlying maladies, its strong points America's underlying strength. Yet for these very reasons the two sets of questions present a tempting challenge. Even partial success in discovering how the legislative process really operates would cast a penetrating light upon *homo americanus,* his folkways and mores, his place in today's sun. By grappling with proposals for improvement of the legislative process we can put ourselves in a better position to reflect upon his social ideals and ethics, to understand how his group life and conflicts determine the substance that fills the "interstices of democracy," and to help steer his path through the remaining decades of a troubled century.

THE PROBLEMS OF DESCRIPTION

Even in the physical sciences description is difficult. Every forward step in chemistry, physics, and biology has meant new challenges, new vistas for description and explanation. To meet these challenges and explore these vistas, physical scientists constantly must create new theoretical conceptions and new hypotheses that can be used to explain and organize the facts of physical life. They must develop new experiments and forms of observation to test their theories and hypotheses. They can rarely achieve complete certainty about anything fundamental. Progress is from one degree of possibility to a higher degree, with every basic theory being supplanted eventually by a new one that seems to provide a better explanation of reality.

In the social sciences observation is more difficult. Measurement is less frequently relevant. Controlled experiments are generally impossible, for the laboratory of the social scientist is society itself, and what happens in it is beyond his puny power to control. The intrusion of social and ethical values tends to blur the difference between "is" and "should be" and impedes the formulation of theories and hypotheses that can most fruitfully explain social processes. Hence the entire problem of social-science description and explanation is fraught with pitfalls.

The Inadequacy of a Formal Approach

One way to approach the problem of describing the legislative process is to look at the rules, procedures, and organizational structures. You will find some of them in the Constitution, many more in the Senate Manual, in the Rules of the House of Representatives, and in erudite tomes about Congress and the legislative process. If the rules really showed how the legislative process works, the inquiring analyst would have no choice but to grit his teeth and plow ahead through the heavy mass of detail. But the rules are merely fragmentary sources for finding out how some of the persons involved in the legislative process behave, claim to behave, or are expected to behave. One might just as well expect to learn about American and English literature by reading a dictionary. The only difference is that lawmakers break the rules of lawmaking far more frequently than writers depart from the spelling and definitions of the dictionary.

A slightly more sophisticated variant of this approach is to start with the assumption that the members of Congress make our laws. This assumption is buttressed by the first sentence in the first section of the American Constitution: "All legislative powers herein granted shall be vested in a Congress of the United States, which shall consist of a Senate and House of Representatives." It is reinforced by the fact that every bill introduced in Congress starts with the words: "Be it enacted by the Senate and House of Representatives of the United States of America in Congress assembled . . ." and, if passed, is then referred to as an "Act of Congress." [1] Yet the Constitution itself gives the President important legislative powers and functions: recommending, approving, disapproving. This practice, from the first weeks of the First Congress, has involved executive officials in the most intimate details of the legislative process. Judges also play an important role in the making of statutes; every interpretation of the Constitution or of an existing statute has a direct bearing upon the production of new statutes. All the agencies of government—Congress, the executive branch, the judiciary, and even the so-called "independent" boards and commissions, often referred to as the "fourth branch of government"—take part in the legislative process. You cannot learn much about it if you assume that the existence of separate agencies of the Federal government means that one of them has an exclusive franchise to operate the legislative process.

Nor is it very helpful to concede that all the branches of government help cook the legislative broth and therefore to assume that laws are made by government officials alone. Political parties are not a formal part of the government structure but they are a part of the legislative process. There is no place in the *Congressional Directory* or the Government Manual for interest groups and pressure groups, but there is a very real place for both in the process of lawmaking. Early in this century, one of the greatest of American political

---

[1] A law, of course, is not merely an act of Congress. No bill can become law without some act by the President also. When the first bill to be enacted under the Constitution was debated in Congress, the proposal was made that the President's name be included in the enacting clause. This proposal made no headway, probably because it called to mind the preamble used in England: "Be it enacted by the King's most Excellent Majesty, by and with the advice and consent of the Lords Spiritual and Temporal and Commons, in this present Parliament assembled. . . ." Senator Maclay wrote in his Journal: "This imitation of monarchy died a-borning." "Journal of William Maclay" (New York: Appleton-Century-Crofts, 1890), May 5, 1789, pp. 18–19.

writers, Arthur F. Bentley, pointed out the danger of trying to understand government by looking at government alone:

A discussion of the work and defects of a state legislature carries one nowhere as long as the legislature is taken for what it purports to be—a body of men who deliberate upon and adopt laws. Not until the actual lawmaking is traced from its efficient demand to its actual application, can one tell just where the real law-creating work is done, and whether the legislature was Moses the law-giver or merely Moses the registration clerk.[2]

Bentley's comment applies just as well to the national legislative process.

A Realistic Approach

Another approach to the problem of description is to start with the recognition that the process of government is one of struggle as well as of cooperation. "There is no political process that is not a balancing of quantity against quantity. There is not a law that is passed that is not the expression of force and force in tension. There is not a court decision or an executive act that is not the result of the same process. Understanding any of these phenomena means measuring the elements that have gone into them." [3] From this viewpoint the production of statutes is far from a dull and static application of formal procedures to an issue of public policy. It is a dynamic process which, like any large-scale military operation, follows no rigid pattern. At every turn there are difficult choices to be made either on broad strategy or on daily tactics. The rules and procedures are the codes of battle. The agencies of government are instruments in the organization and disposition of contending forces. A statute is merely one of the things that can happen as a result of the struggle: a compromise, an armed truce, a prelude to the next conflict, or, more rarely, an all-out victory for one side.

It would be possible to describe this process with more euphemistic words, such as "adjustment" or "bargaining." Both could probably be interpreted in a manner that would give the full flavor of group conflict. Yet "adjustment" overemphasizes the end result of given conflicts and does too little justice to the motives and methods of the actors in the drama. "Bargaining," while bet-

[2] Arthur L. Bentley, "The Process of Government: A Study of Social Pressures" (Bloomington, Ind.: University of Chicago Press, 1908; reissued, Principia Press, 1935 and 1949), p. 163. Until recently, this book has been one of the neglected classics in the literature of social science. See this author's review of the 1949 reissue in *American Political Science Review*, Vol. 44, No. 3, September, 1950. "The Governmental Process," by David B. Truman (New York: Knopf, 1951), restates Bentley's approach in more up-to-date terms. An excellent application of this approach to the history of a single legislative contest is made by Earl Latham in "The Group Basis of Politics: A Study in Basing-point Legislation" (Ithaca, N.Y.: Cornell University Press, 1952).

[3] Bentley, *op. cit.*, p. 202.

ter oriented toward the activities of the participants, is too narrow a concept. Just as "competition" has long since proved itself as one of the most expressive terms in economics, "struggle" is the most useful term with which to describe the process of government. In this struggle men and women tend to align themselves in various groupings rather than operate as isolated individuals.

All phenomena of government are phenomena of groups pressing one another, forming one another, and pushing out new groups and group representatives (the organs or agencies of government) to mediate the adjustments. It is only as we isolate these group activities, determine their representative values, and get the whole process stated in terms of them, that we approach to a satisfactory knowledge of government.[4]

Individuals, it must be recognized, are of great importance—but their importance stems from their actual or potential relationship to groups. They are the bedrock materials from which groups are organized. They supply the ideas and leadership needed for successful group operations or, for that matter, even for rudimentary group organization. This does not mean that individual ability and personality are unimportant; they are often decisive factors. It means that individual leadership can be understood only in its relationship to group activities.

It is for this reason that Part I of this book is entitled "The Contestants." Without giving primary attention to people and to types of people, government becomes a lifeless landscape instead of the vital and human drama that it really is. The contestants in the legislative process are, in the first place, persons like the rest of us. They become *special* persons, with *special* criteria of choice, as a result of their membership in certain groups or kinds of groups; for example, the legislature itself, a political party, a privately organized association or "pressure group," one of the other branches of government, etc. They act as members of one or another of these groups, and frequently this action becomes a formalized part of the legislative process. More frequently their actions must be described as "informal" and "typical," at all times difficult to extricate from the maze of legislative pushing and pulling. A shift of the eye will move our attention from the individuals as group members to the groups themselves.

There are all sorts of groups engaged in this struggle: organized groups and potential groups, formal ones and informal ones, private organizations, political parties, government agencies, and blocs or factions within any of them. Some of these are transitory; others are hoary with age. Some are local in character; others are large and sprawling groups with supply and communication lines extending like a network across America and into many other countries.

Group conflict has often been described in terms of economic classes. James Madison took this approach in his famous Federalist Paper, No. 10:

[4] *Ibid.*, p. 300.

A landed interest, a manufacturing interest, a mercantile interest, a moneyed interest, with many lesser interests, grow up of necessity in civilized nations, and divide them into different classes, actuated by different sentiments and views. The regulation of these various and interfering interests forms the principal task of modern legislation, and involves the spirit of party and faction in the necessary and ordinary operations of the government.[5]

Oliver Wendell Holmes made a similar observation early in his juristic career:

The more powerful interests must be more or less reflected in legislation. The objection to class legislation is not that it favors a class, but either that it fails to benefit the legislators, or that it is dangerous to them because a competing class has gained in power, or that it transcends the limits of self-preference which are imposed by sympathy. . . . But it is no sufficient condemnation of legislation that it favors one class at the expense of another; for much or all legislation does that. . . .[6]

It would be a serious oversimplification, however, to assume that all the important groups are highly organized "classes" in the Marxist sense of the term. Only a few have class consciousness. Many of the most cohesive groups have very narrow purposes far removed from the idea of class domination of American society. Instead of standing alone in tight isolation, most of them develop close relations with other groups, forming an intricate pattern of clusters and coalitions. Some are interested mainly in the process of mediating between conflicting groups. Few make exclusive claims upon the loyalties of their members; overlapping membership is the rule rather than the exception. Nor can the purposes of many groups be fitted into a watertight set of compartments such as economic, political, sectional, religious, or nationalistic; most of them tend to represent a combination of two or more of these.

The most generalized method of describing the purpose of all these groups is to regard the struggle as one to win a larger share of power or maintain their present share. From this viewpoint the term power must be regarded in its broadest sense as including (1) political power of the formal type, (2) control of worldly goods of all types, machinery, know-how, and the monetary claims to any of these forms of wealth, and (3) the power to impress one's ideas upon a larger part of one's community, win security, and obtain deference. Political scientists tend to concentrate on the production and distribution of power; economists on the production and distribution of wealth; but neither special approach should obscure the fact that the basic struggles in society are power contests.

If the entire process of government can be described as one of group struggle for power, how does the legislative process differ from the administrative

---

[5] "The Federalist" (New York: Modern Library Series, Random House, 1937), p. 56.

[6] Oliver Wendell Holmes, "The Gas Stokers' Strike," *American Law Review*, Vol. 7, 1873, pp. 583–584.

process and the judicial process? When viewed at a high enough level of abstraction, there is little or no difference. Both the contestants in the struggle and their objectives are generally the same. At a more specific level of description, however, the difference is that the legislative struggle is fought on a different battlefield. This calls for a more specialized use of general weapons and a development of specialized strategy, tactics, rules, procedures, and organizational forms.

From this viewpoint, an analysis of the formalized aspects of the legislative process becomes tremendously significant. It is every bit as important as is the analysis of the terrain to a historian whose task it is to record a great military engagement. Many of the fundamental conflicts in the legislative struggle are fought over the procedures and forms of government. Formal changes can be of great influence upon the course of the victories won, the defeats suffered, the compromises fashioned, and the truces solemnized. It is for this very reason that the participants in the legislative struggle concern themselves with the most minute details of rules, procedures, and organization. This, too, explains why proposed changes in the rules, procedures, and organizational forms are bitterly contested and why many "improvements," which abstract logic would seem to require, simply never take place.

The Obstacles to a Realistic Approach

It is the realistic approach upon which the activities of the more effective leaders in legislative conflicts have always been based. With few exceptions, they approach the task of legislation as one of social engineering, of the organization of power for the purpose of attaining a specific objective. To operate on any other assumption would mean a waste of their time.

Yet the fact that someone operates on the assumption that the legislative process is one of group struggle does not mean that he is consciously aware of this assumption or capable of accurately describing it. This is a basic obstacle to a realistic look at government. There are undoubtedly many participants in this struggle who are sincerely carried away by the river of words written or uttered about the legislative process by themselves, their associates, or their opponents.

We have in this world many lawyers who know nothing of law making. They play their part, and their learning is justified by their work. We have many lawmakers who know nothing of law. They too play their part and their wisdom—though they may not be able to give it verbal expression—is nonetheless real. But the practical lore of neither of these types of men is a scientific knowledge of society nor by putting the two layers together do we make an advance. It is they themselves we must study and know, for what they are, for what they represent.[7]

[7] Bentley, *op. cit.*, p. 164.

Furthermore, the more one is embroiled in the legislative struggle or any other form of social combat, the more he knows that everything he says is a weapon that can be used on his behalf or, if he is not on his guard, can be used against him. Hence the proclivity of every group spokesman to describe his activities as being above the realm of narrow partisan interests and wholly and unselfishly dedicated to the welfare of everybody. Hence the habitual insistence of persons in all branches of government that they are above the madding throng and wholly dedicated to advancing the national interest irrespective of the pressures exerted upon them.

Another obstacle is the blunt fact that the legislative struggle is unbelievably complex. Many of the most sophisticated and acute observers can participate in a legislative battle without ever succeeding in obtaining a clear idea of the forces that make for victory or defeat. Two of the persons who were in the center of the conflict involved in the Atomic Energy Act of 1946 put it this way:

> The historian who attempts to recreate this drama is appalled by the confused and chaotic nature of the action. The scene that confronts him resembles the description of the Battle of Borodino in Tolstoy's "War and Peace." The hosts gather, impelled by some impulse deeper than they comprehend, seeking a goal they do not altogether understand. The struggle that ensues takes on a life of its own, independent of any individual's will or direction. The conflict swirls and eddies and becomes not one but scores of battles, each appearing crucial to its participants. The field is a confused jumble of motion, the whole is obscured in smoke, and even the commanding generals have little understanding of developments, much less any effective control of them. The motives of the contestants are frequently obscure; the action is extended over weeks or months, rather than hours; there are sometimes not two but several armies engaged; alliances are shifted in the heat of battle; and in the end the issue is not decided on the field at all but in some clandestine meeting among rival leaders.[8]

This quotation illustrates the difficulty of following the course of only one of the battles that took place in 1946. During the same year, as in any year, there was not one but scores of Borodinos. To describe the legislative struggle as a whole in any year would be to give a complete cross section of American society.

A third obstacle in the description and explanation of governmental and legislative processes arises from the tendency to confuse realism with cynicism. Charges of "cynicism" and "immorality" have been levied against Machiavelli; yet few writers have contributed more to our understanding of political realities. In the present account of the legislative process there will be ample opportunity for similar charges. For example, the objectivity with which judges do and *do not* arrive at decisions is discussed. The "myth" of objectivity is distinguished from the realities in language that may be vigorous for the sake

[8] James R. Newman and Byron S. Miller, "The Control of Atomic Energy" (New York: McGraw-Hill, 1948), p. 9.

of emphasis. Similar editorialization and use of examples and language appear throughout this book. The object is *not* to be cynical and destructive but to state an observation with force and to give a slant upon the truth which stems from many years of personal participation in the processes being described. After all, most of our laws, rules, and "understandings" about the processes of government are really myths and fictions whose acceptance, tongue in cheek or otherwise, is necessary for making national and group life and disputes bearable for all.

The Problem of "Should Be"

One of the major differences between the physical and the social sciences is that in addition to dealing with "has been," "is," and "may be," the latter focuses directly on "should be" also. In the physical sciences social values may affect the selection of one's field of specialization. In the social sciences they are part of any field one selects. To neglect their consideration is to deal with the material in an incomplete fashion or else to have one's normative judgments traipse around in the guise of factual observations.

No Absolute Standards

One of the most persistent of all ideas about social change is the delusion that intelligence or education can provide objective solutions to problems of public policy. As standard-bearers of the one and purveyors of the other, social scientists should therefore, it is claimed, be able to advise on maladjustments in the social organisms as authoritatively as physicians handle diseases of the body. If capable social scientists disagree or even line up in dramatically opposite camps, the reason is given that someone's methodology is out of joint, a "mature discipline" has not yet been developed, or that the foundations have not furnished enough money to support essential research.

The effort to establish absolute standards, of course, is made every day. It is a habitual part of every propaganda campaign, one that is used in the legislative struggle itself every time the claim is made that this or that bill is the ultimate method of saving freedom and democracy or making the Government efficient. Yet if rules, procedures, and organizational structures are merely the more formalized methods through which the legislative struggle is conducted, they can be judged only in terms of their function as instruments in the struggle. A rule or procedure can be "good" only in the light of its utility in facilitating the efforts of given groups to achieve given objectives. It can be "bad" only because it frustrates, or inadequately facilitates, such objectives. To regard it as good or bad in itself would be a rejection of the realistic approach to the problem of description.

If the realistic approach to the legislative process is accepted, one can then obtain absolute standards of judgment only by regarding as absolute the aims and views of one social group, or cluster of groups, among the contestants in the legislative struggle. This is entirely justifiable and indeed praiseworthy—but one deludes himself when he thinks that his own social standards are capable someday of revealing themselves in a blaze of glory to everyone else and of commanding the same broad acceptance as the proposition that two plus two makes four. Conflicting standards of judgment are inherent in the structure of the democratic society; every reconciliation of conflicting standards is usually merely the prelude to a new clash in the future. The only final decisions are made on the basis of power in one form or another. Once they are made, it is then the province of historians to carry on endless debates on whether Might made Right.

There are those to whom one or another set of abstract forms of government is enshrined as a moral absolute and who, if these abstractions are seriously deprecated, find themselves tottering on the edge of moral cynicism and emptiness. The trouble here is a lack of self-recognition, for the deep attachment to abstract forms is itself a reflection of group values and affiliations.

There are also those who stick to abstractions in the effort to avoid substantive controversy and to be constructive without seeming to leave the confines of the ivory tower. Yet the abstractions themselves, if they are at all meaningful, are in some way tied in with the partisan controversies of one's era. From the time of Plato and Aristotle to the present, the greatest writers on government have been protagonists of one or another social viewpoint and have dealt with governmental forms as instruments for achieving their objectives.

The Author's Standards

It is entirely possible to regard "should be" judgments of the legislative process as themselves data to be scientifically described. One can analyze the motivations behind a proposal, its probable effect, and the reasons for resistance to it. In this manner one can best understand the significance of various proposals for change and relate normative judgments to the process of group conflict.

Yet it is impossible to decree a divorce of head from heart in order to describe these judgments and proposals in a purely objective manner. No matter how carefully one may seek to balance the scales, he can scarcely avoid weighing the scales on the side he favors. Even the selection of the proposals to be explained, the order in which they are discussed, and the amount of attention given to each tend to reflect personal biases. True objectivity consists not of trying to withhold judgment but of recognizing one's biases. Straightforward analysis requires an effort to state these biases as candidly as possible.

A full statement of the author's personal values would require another book. For the present purposes it is probably sufficient to list several of the author's "inarticulate major premises." One is deep-rooted support for those who speak and act to provide the underprivileged, the underorganized, and the under-represented with a greater share of material goods and of power to affect the decisions that shape their lives. Another is an instinctive support for govern-mental operations designed to provide more adequate opportunities for indi-vidual growth and security and to help prevent the scourges of depression, inflation, and war. Still another is the placement of a high moral value upon the diversity and pluralism of American society, as distinguished from the deadliness of any society in which one group achieves complete domination. This is coupled with strong attachments to certain group values and allegiances and a strong propensity—nourished by an overfondness for the excitements of combat and by years of self-restraint in the civil service—to advance these views through all available channels of academic, nonpartisan, political, un-official, and official activity. Finally, as a guide to such activity, is the convic-tion that power without idealism is barbarity and that idealism without power is futility.

THE METHOD OF PRESENTATION

One method of attacking the twofold problem of description and prescrip-tion would be to jump directly into the middle of things and deal with such matters as the birth and drafting of legislative proposals.

Yet these activities can scarcely be seen in three-dimensional reality unless one focuses upon the people and groups who bring about the birth, do the drafting, and carry on the legislative process in all its many phases. It is, there-fore, more meaningful to begin at the beginning and to introduce rather fully the actors in the drama.

This is done in Part I, "The Contestants: Reality and Reform." Two chap-ters deal with the private organizations (Chaps. 2 and 3), two with the political parties (Chaps. 4 and 5), and two with the government agencies (Chaps. 6 and 7). The first chapter in each pair presents a descriptive survey and a discussion of the role of each set of actors in the legislative drama. The second chapter in each pair presents a survey of reform proposals relevant to each type of contestant. As a result of this related handling of description and prescription, it is hoped that the subsequent account of the legislative struggle in process will take on sharper meaning.

At the end of Part I comes "The Contestants and Their Power" (Chap. 8).

Here the effort is made to indicate the sources of the power exercised by the various contestants in the legislative struggle and to indicate how this power may be extended through various sorts of combinations.

Part II, "Combat on the Legislative Terrain," attempts to capture the movement and vigor of the legislative struggle. It points up the basic decisions that need to be made by the various contestants in it and tells of the long and muddy marches which are the daily lot of those actively involved. Shall a bill be introduced into the congressional hopper, or shall some other arena of social combat be selected (Chap. 9)? Whence and when shall it originate (Chap. 10)? What words and ideas shall go into the design of a bill as a combat vehicle (Chap. 11)? How and by whom shall the legislative troops be organized and led (Chap. 12)? How shall the arsenal of propaganda and pressure best be employed (Chap. 13)? What are the strategies and the tactics of the infighting that occurs in congressional committees (Chaps. 14–16)? What happens as the battle front moves onto the floor of Congress (Chaps. 17–18)? After Congress registers its approval of a bill, how does the legislative struggle sweep on to the choice to be made by the President (Chap. 19)? And, finally, having gone over the battleground that is Congress, what comments may be made regarding the improvement of the rules of on-the-ground legislative warfare (Chap. 20)?

In each of these chapters generalizations and examples are liberally mixed together. To describe the legislative process through a series of case studies would not have permitted sufficient interpretation. An abstract presentation of different phases of the process would hardly present it in its full flavor and variety.

While Part II describes scores of problems that are faced by participants in the legislative process, it should not be thought for a moment that all or even most of them arise in connection with an individual bill. Also, there is a danger of reading into the picture a more conscious awareness of strategies and tactical considerations than really exists. Most contestants deal with the majority of problems on the basis of habit and rote and engage in active calculation on only a handful of problems.

Part III provides a brief conclusion devoted to a general appraisal of the potentialities for future change in the legislative process (Chap. 21).

Much of the material presented in these chapters is relevant to the legislative process in the states. Occasional references are made to state experiences. However, the analysis deals directly with the national process only.

In the preparation of these chapters, considerable use has been made not only of the publicly available records concerning legislative activity, but also of personal experiences that can scarcely be documented by references to other sources. Other writings dealing directly or indirectly with the legislative process have also been drawn upon extensively. The major references which the author would recommend as most pertinent to a general understanding of the legislative process are as follows:

1. Arthur F. Bentley, "The Process of Government" (Bloomington, Ind.: Principia Press, 1949 reissue).
2. David B. Truman, "The Governmental Process" (New York: Knopf, 1951).
3. Woodrow Wilson, "Congressional Government" (Boston: Houghton Mifflin, 1885).
4. Stephen K. Bailey, "Congress Makes a Law" (New York: Columbia University Press, 1949).
5. Robert Luce's quartet: "Legislative Procedure," "Legislative Assemblies," "Legislative Principles," and "Legislative Problems" (Boston: Houghton Mifflin, 1922, 1930, 1930, and 1935, respectively).
6. Roland A. Young, "This Is Congress" (New York: Knopf, 1943).
7. George Galloway, "Congress at the Crossroads" (New York: Crowell, 1946).
8. James M. Burns, "Congress on Trial" (New York: Harper, 1949).
9. Joseph P. Chamberlain, "Legislative Processes: National and State" (New York: Appleton-Century-Crofts, 1936).
10. Harvey Walker, "Legislative Process; Lawmaking in the United States" (New York: Ronald, 1948).
11. Floyd M. Riddick, "The United States Congress: Organization and Procedure" (Washington, D.C.: National Capitol Publishers, 1949).

PART I

*THE CONTESTANTS: REALITY
AND REFORM*

Chapter 2

THE PRIVATE ORGANIZATIONS

THE SIMPLEST method of classifying the groups that take part in the legislative struggle is to divide them into private organizations, parties, and government agencies. The first term covers such private groups as the American Federation of Labor and the General Motors Corporation, the Baptist church and the American Wild Life Institute. The second refers to the Democratic and Republican parties, the various minor parties, and the wings and factions in all of them. The third covers the Congress, the executive branch, the judiciary, and local and foreign governments.

Yet the formal quality of this classification should not lead one to overlook certain fundamental similarities. The term "group"—whether it applies to a private organization, a party, or a government agency—merely provides a way of talking about people acting in concert. When we say that a corporation has started a propaganda campaign, a party has drawn up a platform, or a government agency has spent its funds wastefully, we are talking in each case about the actions of individual persons. There is no such thing as an organization, party, or agency consciousness or philosophy apart from the individuals who make up the group. "Collective consciousness and behavior," as Allport has pointed out, "are simply the aggregation of those states and reactions of individuals which, owing to similarities of constitution, training, and common stimulations, are possessed of a similar character." [1] Each group represents an organization of individual opinions. It is the welter of diversified sets of opinions which is the reality behind the much-abused term "public opinion." As John Dickinson observed many years ago: "The larger number of members of any political society have no opinion, and hence no will, on nearly all the matters on which government acts. The only opinion, the only will, which exists is the opinion, the will, of special groups." [2]

The person who has a degree of responsibility in one of these groups may seem to represent—and in a way does represent—much more than himself.

[1] Floyd Henry Allport, "Social Psychology" (Boston: Houghton Mifflin, 1924), p. 6.
[2] John Dickinson, "Democratic Realities and Democratic Dogmas," *American Political Science Review*, Vol. 24, February, 1930, p. 291.

Essentially he is a human being and, despite the halo of importance that may encircle his brow, he is subject to the same drives, impulses, and failings as are other human beings.[3] Each type of group provides both leaders and members with an opportunity to solve inner conflicts by losing themselves in a "cause" and building the sense of security that can be derived only from working in cooperation with others. Each can be subdivided into smaller groups that lead and larger ones that follow.[4] Each opens up avenues toward personal advancement—whether that advancement be measured in terms of profit, power, prestige, or any combination of these. All tend to serve as vehicles for pursuing the immediate interests of their leaders and members rather than what others may conceive of as their "ultimate" interest or the "national" interest.[5] This tendency cannot be disputed on the ground that "material" interests, measured in terms of money, are often far weaker than such "nonmaterial" interests as the drive to achieve greater power, status, admiration, or self-respect; these latter interests are often the most immediate and compelling of all.

There is a profound difference between interests as such and organized groups. An interest by itself has neither eyes, voice, nor motive power. If, at a given moment, it should be to the immediate interest of domestic sugar producers to prevent the importation of Cuban sugar, the mere existence of that interest does not mean that anything will be done. Rather, it indicates a potentiality for the organization or operation of some group based upon the desire to restrict the importation of Cuban sugar. It provides an opportunity for private organizations, politicians, and government officials to organize sugar growers and in one way or another to do something about their interest. For almost every underlying interest of any importance there are competing organizations seeking to build upon that interest, or competing organizers seeking to start a group of some sort. The more pronounced these interests and the more deeply they are felt, the greater is the probability that an organization may be built to represent a large portion of those who share the interest in common. Yet the complete organization of people with common

---

[3] The Great Man, of course, usually succeeds in concealing this fact from most people, particularly himself. The aura of semidivinity often becomes so impressive that not even his closest associates—with the possible exception of wife, mistress, or psychiatrist—realize how much he resembles other human beings.

[4] The classic description of the oligarchic tendencies within social groups is found in Robert Michels, "Political Parties" (Glencoe, Ill.: The Free Press, 1949 ed.).

[5] ". . . if the conduct of human beings was determined by no other interested considerations than those which constitute their 'real' interest, neither monarchy nor oligarchy would be such bad governments as they are. . . . It is not what their interest is, but what they suppose it to be, that is the important consideration with respect to their conduct. . . . As Coleridge observes, the man makes the motive, not the motive the man." John Stuart Mill, "Considerations on Representative Government" (New York: Macmillan, 1947 ed.), pp 183–184.

interests rarely takes place. Organizers and leaders have their limitations. Many people with interests in common tend to be lethargic or concerned mainly with other problems. As a result, organized groups are usually but an imperfect organization of underlying interests.

"Pressure Groups" and the Legislative Process

In recent years it has become customary, both in colloquial language and in the learned writings of political science and economics, to refer to private organizations as "special-interest groups" or "pressure groups."

Yet both these terms have an invidious connotation that impairs their utility in objective analysis. The "special interests" or the "vested interests" are organizations one looks upon with disfavor as contrasted with organizations with which one sympathizes and therefore regards as laboring in the "public" or "national" interest. "Pressure groups," similarly, usually turn out to be those which exert pressure in the "wrong" direction. Those which exert the "right" kind of pressure are educational bodies working on behalf of the majority of the people.[6]

Neither term, moreover, is a precise label. Both refer to characteristics shared by parties and government agencies. The Republican party and the Department of Agriculture, for example, have as many special interests as the United States Chamber of Commerce and, in their own way, also make use of pressure techniques. Hence, the most serviceable label is simply "private organizations."

Who They Are

"Americans of all ages, all conditions, and all dispositions, constantly form associations. They have not only commercial and manufacturing companies, in which all take part, but associations of a thousand other kinds—religious, moral, serious, futile, extensive or restricted, enormous or diminutive." [7]

If private organizations of this type played a significant role in the young capitalist society observed by De Tocqueville, they became even more significant with the growth of American civilization during the subsequent century. Through them, people organize to make a living, achieve social status, provide for material aid and self-protection, and engage in cultural, religious, and self-expressive activities. They have become a dominant part of the

[6] A splendid attack on the invidious connotation of "special interests" is contained in Dickinson, *op. cit.*, p. 292.

[7] Alexis de Tocqueville, "Democracy in America" (New York: Oxford, 1947 ed.), p. 319. It is an interesting commentary on the ambiguity of the term "public" that De Tocqueville habitually refers to these associations as "public" associations. "Public" is used to distinguish both the general public from the government and government agencies from private agencies.

structure of American society, relegating the family group to a somewhat more subordinate position and providing an indispensable foundation for the organization of political parties and government agencies.

The most powerful and the most intimately developed organizations are those composed of businessmen. The basic business grouping is the corporation, "a means whereby"—to quote the classic study on the modern corporation—"the wealth of innumerable individuals has been concentrated into huge aggregates and whereby control over this wealth has been surrendered to a unified direction." [8] Many corporations are "holding companies" rather than organizations directly engaged in business operations; through the pyramiding of stock ownership they control the business activities of many lesser corporations. The largest corporations are vast economic empires with financial resources greater than those of most states. Also, in almost every phase of manufacturing, mining, transportation, construction, distribution, foreign commerce, and finance, there are firmly established trade associations; most of these are controlled by the management of the larger corporations among their membership. Finally there are the peak associations, such as the National Association of Manufacturers and the United States Chamber of Commerce, which purport to act on behalf of business as a whole. In these organizations, as well, the dominant influence is that exercised by certain corporate members.

Next in importance come the organizations in the farm and labor fields. There are special associations for individual agricultural-commodities groupings, such as milk, fruit and vegetable, cattle, wheat, cotton, wool, and sugar. Many of these are quite similar to the trade associations on the business front. This similarity derives not only from the fact that farmers are business entrepreneurs but also from the extensive agricultural holdings of insurance companies and other nonagricultural business organizations. Nationally, there are at least four major peak farm organizations: the American Farm Bureau Federation, the National Grange, the Farmers Educational and Cooperative Union (usually referred to as the National Farmers Union), and the National Council of Farmer Cooperatives.

Labor unions also are organized by individual lines of business activity. Some are associations of craftsmen, such as machinists, bricklayers, and electricians. Others—and the trend has been increasingly in this direction—are industrial unions covering such fields as coal mining, steel, shipbuilding, and textiles. Most of these are affiliated with one of the two major national groups: the American Federation of Labor or the Congress of Industrial Organizations. A number of unions, such as the Brotherhood of Railroad Trainmen, maintain an independent and unaffiliated status. Most of the craft unions in the railroad in-

[8] Adolf Berle and Gardner Means, "The Modern Corporation and Private Property" (New York: Macmillan, 1937), p. 2.

dustry, including both independents and A.F.L. affiliates, are represented in the Railway Labor Executives Association.

There are also hosts of other private organizations that may not measure up to the business, farm, and labor groups in general significance but are nevertheless an integral part of American life. In the religious field there is a vast array of organized churches, church societies interested in causes that go far beyond the purely religious, and church affiliates for both women and younger people. Veterans are organized into two huge groups: the American Legion and the Veterans of Foreign Wars, and into a number of smaller and competing bodies. There are also separate veterans' organizations for each war in which the United States has taken part, for various categories of veterans— overseas, wounded, and disabled—and for veterans of different religions. There are special organizations for Negroes, Italians, Irishmen, and other nationality or racial groups; for women, youth, the aged, and the physically handicapped. There are professional groups like the American Bar Association, the American Medical Association, the National Education Association, and the American Political Science Association. There are organizations which speak the views of the Left, such as Americans for Democratic Action, and others which advance the philosophy of the Right, such as the Committee for Constitutional Government. There are organizations established for the sole purpose of serving as fronts, allies, preceptors, scouts, and trial-balloon testers for other groups who stay behind the scenes and pull the strings.

Private organizations defy any ready-made classification. Many of those that might be regarded as primarily economic organizations engage in cultural activities. Nationality and minority groups usually have clear-cut economic objectives. A sense of fervor and consecration that merits description by the term "religious" can be found in many organizations completely outside the formal church groups. Almost all have political objectives of one sort or another. Even the categories "reactionary," "conservative," "liberal," and "radical" are hard to apply. American society is fluid rather than highly stratified. At any one time most of these organizations contain conflicting currents within them, and the strength of these currents varies with the shifting trends in the economic development of the country and in the business cycle, with the pendulum swing between war and peace, and with the unpredictable influence of leaders and organizers.

Upon first examination the difference in the way these groups organize—entirely apart from social objectives—appears bewildering. The variations in type of membership, in the election of officers, in the relationship between central offices and local units, and in the discharge of legislative, executive, and judicial functions are every bit as great (and as fascinating) as those between the governments of nations. Underlying these differences, however, are at least three striking similarities. First, each is subject to internal struggles over positions of leadership, particularly between the "ins" and the "outs," but also among the "ins" and among the "outs." Second, the loyalty of most leaders and members of each group is shared with other groups; overlapping group membership has the dual effect of promoting internal conflict and serving as a "balancing force in the politics of a multigroup society such as the United States." [9] Third, each represents a combination of formalized structure which tends to become crystallized in constitutions and bylaws and of informal arrangements that are never recorded in the rules and seldom meet the eye. Recognition of these traits is fundamental to an understanding of the role of private associations in the legislative struggle.

Their Role in the Legislative Struggle

In other countries private organizations have at times been formally given a central position in the structure of the state. The separate houses or "estates" of legislative bodies have themselves been the vehicles for group organization. Thus, to pick an extreme example, the early Swedish constitution provided for five separate houses, one for the great landlords, one for the bishops, one for the landed gentry, one for the representatives of the burghers of the town, and one for representatives of the farmers and peasants. In the development of fascism during the period between World Wars I and II a basic principle called for turning over governmental functions to organizations of private businessmen. In Italy these bodies were known as "corporations" and they were supposed to represent labor as well as business. In Germany the central role was given to the cartels and the peak associations.

In the United States the formal position given to private associations has been either temporary or incidental. For a brief period under the NRA codes, vast governmental authority was vested in trade associations. This period was brought to a halt by a unanimous Supreme Court decision in which the judges, while declaring that the code-making authority conferred on the President was "an unconstitutional delegation of legislative power," also took time out to criticize the role of private groups.[10] Both executive agencies and congressional committees have from time to time set up advisory committees composed mainly of the official representatives of business, agricultural, la-

---

[9] David B. Truman, "The Governmental Process" (New York: Knopf, 1951), p. 520. For an interesting discussion of overlapping membership and its implications, see all of Chaps. 6 and 16.

[10] ". . . would it be seriously contended that Congress should delegate its legislative authority to trade or industrial associations or groups so as to empower them to enact the laws they deem to be wise and beneficent for the rehabilitation and expansion of their trade or industries? . . . The answer is obvious. Such a delegation of legislative power is unknown to our law and is utterly inconsistent with the constitutional prerogatives and duties of Congress." *Schechter Poultry Corporation v. United States*, 1935.

bor, or professional organizations. In the case of certain executive agencies, some of these committees have at times been given a formal veto power over governmental decisions.[11]

The informal role of private organizations, however, has been so intensive that observers constantly—and ruefully—refer to "government by pressure groups." Private organizations make themselves felt in the political parties by influencing the selection of candidates and the drafting of campaign platforms, by campaign contributions, and by electioneering. At times, their leaders become personally active in political parties. They play an important role in influencing appointments to executive and judicial positions and to congressional committees. They organize "blocs" in Congress: farm blocs, mining blocs, labor blocs, and others. Occasionally their leaders themselves win posts in the Government, or, what amounts to almost the same thing, members of Congress or executive officials are given official positions of leadership in private organizations. On matters of public policy in which they are interested they collect facts and statistics, develop new ideas and angles, and draft proposed bills and regulations. The larger organizations hire experts, technicians, and contact men (these are the lobbyists) who sometimes come to know more about their subject than anyone else in the country, even including the specialists in the executive branch of the Government. Finally (and it is this point of their activity which is most conspicuous) they conduct campaigns to achieve their objectives at all stages of the legislative process—from the decision on whether or not to have a bill to the time of Presidential signature or veto.

Hardly a year goes by without a hue and cry being raised against the lobbyists who represent private organizations. In February, 1947, for example, Representative Adolph Sabath of Illinois made a nationwide broadcast in which he demanded a sweeping investigation of lobbies, lobbyists, and propagandists. "When I first came to Congress 40 years ago," he declared, "I found the ever-present railroad lobby, the banking lobby, the shipping lobby, and, most vicious of all, the power lobby, and others too numerous to mention. Not only are all those lobbies still operating, but scores more have joined the battle of pressures. . . ."[12] Later in the same year, in a message sent to Congress after he had reluctantly signed the Rent Decontrol and Housing Act, President Truman attacked the real-estate lobby as "subversive of representative government" and called for a congressional investigation.[13]

Behind both these attacks was a disagreement with the objectives of specific pressure groups. The fact that Representative Sabath was really opposed to

[11] Under the Hospital Survey and Construction Act of 1946, for example, the Surgeon General is required to prescribe certain regulations "with the approval of the Federal Hospital Council." Most of the members of the Federal Hospital Council, set up in the same Act, are representatives of hospital and health organizations.
[12] *Congressional Record* (daily edition), Feb. 26, 1947, pp. A753–A754.
[13] *The New York Times*, July 1, 1947.

only certain types of lobbies was revealed in a somewhat piquant statement later in the same broadcast. "The detrimental effect on the country of all these skilled and ruthless private-interest pressure groups has forced veterans, consumers, law, women, and even religious groups to counteract these other poisonous influences and work for the public interest." [14] President Truman's blast was more sophisticated, being aimed only at the lobbies opposing rent control and public housing. The fact that neither of the two requests for investigations was granted is testimony to the weakness of the pressure groups favored by Messrs. Sabath and Truman. Historically, lobby investigations themselves come into being largely as the result of lobbying. The 1913 investigation of the National Association of Manufacturers was the product of the American Federation of Labor's campaign for the Clayton Act. Senator Nye's investigation of munitions makers was a triumph for the women's peace societies. Senator Black's probe of the private-power lobby was strongly backed by the public-power lobby. Senator La Follette's civil-liberties investigation was strongly backed by the labor lobby.

The methods by which private groups influence legislation have also been under constant attack. In 1910, revelations of bribes accepted by Congressmen in exchange for votes resulted in the Corrupt Practices Act. Secrecy of operation, allegedly unethical operations within the law, exaggerated claims as to an organization's effectiveness or the number of people for whom it speaks— all these have been struck at through efforts to bring the facts before the public view. Investigations by congressional committees have been one method. Another has been the requirement of registration with a designated public officer. In 1940, as a defense measure, all representatives of foreign governments were compelled to register with the Department of State. The Legislative Reorganization Act of 1946, in a rather loosely worded passage, provided for the quarterly filing of financial statements with the Secretary of the Senate and the Clerk of the House by persons who receive or spend money for the principal purpose of influencing legislation. In an equally ambiguous section any person "who shall engage himself for pay or for any consideration" for the purpose of attempting to influence legislation is to register quarterly with the Secretary of the Senate and the Clerk of the House.

The private associations as such—as distinguished from their representatives and their methods of operating—have also been subjected to criticism. Stuart Chase has penned the following indictment: "Pressure groups have long been the despair of patriots. They have been responsible for some of the darkest days in Washington. . . . They continually pervert, twist and halt the path of progress in the Republic." [15]

[14] *Congressional Record* (daily edition), Feb. 26, 1947, p. A754.
[15] Stuart Chase, "Democracy under Pressure" (New York: Twentieth Century Fund, 1945), p. 9.

Yet no competent observers have ever gone so far as to suggest that direct action be taken to abolish the role of private associations in the legislative process. To do so would mean an attack on traditional American conceptions of the right of petition and free speech and of other civil liberties. Furthermore, the inevitable tendency is toward increased specialization and more marked concentration of economic power. One of the accompanying factors, both cause and result, is the growing strength of private associations, particularly business and labor organizations. One of the automatic by-products is the broadening of governmental activities and a steadily more active role by private organizations in the processes of government. Aside from registration requirements to provide more public information about them, the only feasible way to counteract objectional activities of private groups is to develop counterpressures on the part of other contestants in the legislative struggle. This means a strengthening of certain organizations at the expense of others. Or it means stronger political parties or government agencies. But parties and government agencies cannot become significantly stronger without the support of private organizations. Hence, these two latter alternatives imply no fundamental subordination of private associations but only another way of changing organizational alignments and modifying the channels through which they affect the governmental process.

THEIR FUTURE ROLE IN SOCIETY

The importance of private organizations in the legislative process derives from their general role in American society.

Deep fears have often been expressed concerning the continuation of conflict among private groups and the dire consequences that could result from its intensification. In the light of these fears, various ideas have been developed concerning the possibilities for a larger role for individuals, for a more cooperative relationship among groups, or for government planning as an escape from the tyranny of private pressures. While each of these ideas goes far beyond the legislative process, and even beyond the sphere of government as a whole, their consideration is nonetheless vital to an analysis of the legislative structure.

The Dangers in Group Conflict

There are three types of "dire consequences" that can be seen from a continuation—particularly if in sharpened form—of the conflict among private groups: deadlock, violence, and dictatorship. Moreover, there is genuine justification for believing that any or all of these three might come to pass, although it must be recognized that dark visions of each or all are an inevitable part of the sales kit of anyone with a panacea to peddle.

In a sense, the possibility of deadlock—or, to use a closely related term, stasis —is inherent in the democratic process of peaceful group conflict. When few victories are ever complete, when power is widely dispersed among many "veto groups," when every solution is a compromise that is objectionable to many, and when every settlement itself creates new problems, you have the makings of a stalemate. In the sphere of American economic organization, for example, as organized labor increases its strength and stands on a more equal plane with organized business groups, the opportunities for one-sided victories by the business community become slimmer and the potentialities for deadlock become greater. This is one of the great risks whenever the weak become stronger.

This kind of deadlock, of course, is not limited to the conflicts between organized business and organized labor. A prime example of deadlock can be found in the controversy over Federal aid to education that has been going on for many years. The proponents of Federal aid for public schools have been able to prevent legislation that would provide aid to parochial schools. Yet apart from certain emergency programs for schools in defense areas, their antagonists have been able to stymie legislation that would provide aid for any school. Similar examples could be given in the field of civil rights and natural resources. Perhaps the most dramatic example is found in the problem of dealing with inflationary trends. At any time when government expenditures are sharply rising, and particularly when an increasing volume of goods is being diverted away from civilian use into building up the armed forces, almost any major group in society is in a strategic position to stymie a stabilization effort. If businessmen insist on profiteering, there is little that can be done about wages or farm prices. If farm groups insist on getting as much as they can while the getting is good, the problem of holding the dike against inflation at other points becomes much more difficult. If labor tries to get as much as it can, it might wreck efforts to deal with businessmen and farmers. This kind of deadlock leads to protracted inflation. In the field of foreign affairs, similar deadlocks can lead to a fluctuating foreign policy that puts our representatives in a difficult position in dealing with other nations.

Widespread violence is less of a likelihood in America than deadlock, but it is always a possibility. Behind the peaceful struggle among the groups that compose society there always lies the possibility that any group or cluster of groups may resort at times to some form of force. Americans with a knowledge of the history of their country can never forget this fact. America's own Civil War came after many years of repeated efforts to adjust differences between the North and the South through the legislative process. One compromise after another failed and bloodshed ensued. We have also seen the use of violence as a method of preventing labor organization and as a weapon used on both sides during the course of strikes. "The essential and central problem of representative democracy," according to Laski, "is the question of what 'the better' classes can do when some claim is made which, in their judgment, they cannot 'safely' concede." [16] During the Roosevelt New Deal, thunderous talk of violent action could often be heard on the extreme right. Yet potentialities for violent action are usually present in some form on all sides, for there is almost always some limit beyond which no group can be forced without its contemplating the most drastic of countermeasures.

The third danger is closely related to the other two. After a period of protracted deadlock on issues of importance to many people, dictatorship becomes a method of getting things done. While it must use violence either as a method of achieving power or as a threat against dissidents, an effective dictatorship can provide an outward appearance of peacefulness.

It is difficult for Americans to take the danger of dictatorship very seriously. True, there are a few states in which dictatorial groups have taken control of state and local governments and suppressed opposition by the use of one or another form of violence. Yet these are rare exceptions, and short-lived at that. When we look at the world about us, the possibility seems more real. There are innumerable examples of domination of whole nations by small groups which have seized the reins of government and literally annihilated all sources of effective opposition. Also, the international military situation always threatens the continuation of normal relationships within American society. In time of war or near war, dictatorial or at least semidictatorial forms of government become more and more expedient as a means of organizing mobilization activities and protecting against internal divisions that might undermine national security.

As one reflects upon these three "dire consequences," one is tempted to join with Justice Holmes in proclaiming "I have no faith in panaceas and almost none in sudden ruin." And, indeed, a measure of skepticism is undoubtedly warranted. Yet ruin in any of these forms can come on slow and silent feet. Preventives ought to be discussed regardless of their avowed inadequacies. The discussion can serve to test and summarize the brief descriptive account of American private associations in the legislative process and sharpen our perceptions of trends into the future in this area of political behavior. Retaining Justice Holmes's skepticism about panaceas and sudden ruin, one may observe three recommended escapes from the dangers of group conflict: a return to individualism, the substitution of group cooperation instead of conflict, and governmental planning.

[16] Harold J. Laski, "Parliamentary Government in England" (New York: Viking, 1947), p. 7.

Back to the Individual

If there are dangers for society in organized groups, why cannot we hope for more from individuals as such rather than from organizations?

This question has a persistent appeal. It is answered in affirmative tones by those who plead for "return" to laissez-faire economics. Yet this is a call for a return to a nonexistent society. The so-called days of *laissez faire* were days when group organization and group conflict were also essential parts of the social structure. For Adam Smith, the mythical beauties of the free market constituted valuable propaganda in the campaign for private business organizations against state-fostered monopolies. The early days of so-called free and competitive private enterprise in America were days when organized groups used state subsidies of one form or another—particularly protective tariffs and land grants—to extend their power and strengthen their organization. The "break-them-down approach" of the Sherman Antitrust Act has itself been merely a part of the campaign against certain business organizations by other, and sometimes weaker, business groups, by farm organizations, and by labor organizations. The attack upon the extension of labor organizations is itself a part of the campaign of business organizations. The modern call for a rebirth of "rugged individualism" usually comes from propagandists or from powerful private organizations who use this symbol in campaigning activities against any threatening sources of opposition.[17]

The overwhelming probabilities for the future are all on the side of more organization of social relationships rather than less. In fact, it is only through an acceptance of group struggle and participation in the process that anyone with conviction concerning the path this struggle should take can make progress toward carrying his convictions into practice.

The yearning for individual action as opposed to group action is evidenced also in the recurrent idea that the way out for the dog-eat-dog battle of the major groups in society is for disinterested thinkers to work out a solution for our problems. Perhaps the most classic presentation for this viewpoint is found in a book by Stuart Chase.

> Sometimes I have a clear picture of the way the Agenda for 1950 could be presented to the people. I see, perhaps, a hundred leading Americans, men and women, meeting in some high, quiet place to prepare it. They are not the kind of people who are active in Me First groups. They are scientists, judges, teachers, university people, philosophers of business, lovers of the land, statesmen; and they think in terms of the whole community.[18]

[17] If a return to rugged individualism should ever really take place, the result would probably be a breakdown in moral values and an increase in all varieties of corruption.

[18] Chase, *op. cit.*, p. 133.

These thoughtful citizens, dreamed Chase, would get together amid the beauty and remoteness of Sun Valley and would draft a program for America. A delightful prospect! Particularly for the participants! But the keenest minds in America could get together and prepare a general program for America or even a little program dealing with a single problem and, unless the participants represented important groups in the social conflict, or had guidelines for conveying their ideas to these groups, their proposals would be neglected. In so far as the proposals really tied up with interests of organizations with power, they would themselves be another incident in the group struggle. Actually many conferences of this type have taken place and no more can be expected from them than the production of occasional reading matter, propaganda for one side or another, or a rather purified version of the round-table conference approach discussed in the next chapter.

Individuals have a major role in group conflict. There can be no doubt about this, but their role is in the process as leaders, subleaders, and followers —not outsiders. The only active role that individuals can play is in the guidance or direction of the efforts of this or that group or set of groups.

A still more rarefied emphasis on the individual is found in the hope that somehow or other the forces of Intelligence, of Reason, or of Science will bring order out of chaos. During the first years of disillusionment that followed in the wake of World War I, James Harvey Robinson urged "the liberation of Intelligence" as the first and most essential step in dealing with "the shocking derangement of human affairs which now prevails in most civilized countries. . . ." [19]

Walter Lippmann enlarged upon the idea by proposing a network of government "Intelligence Bureaus" manned by experts with lifetime tenure and insulated against the pressures of either congressional committees or department heads.[20] Since then, the dramatic achievements of physical scientists have suggested to many that these achievements might be transferred to the field of human relations and group conflict.

If intelligence and science are viewed as abstract forces apart from either individuals or groups, then they are the products of dreamy-eyed mysticism and deserve little further discussion. If they are viewed as characteristics or power of individuals in splendid isolation, they can have as little effect as the men on Stuart Chase's mountaintop. If they are viewed as qualities and characteristics of individuals who serve as leaders of groups, then they are meaningful— and of tremendous potency. But one simple fact cannot be forgotten: intelli-

[19] James Harvey Robinson, "The Mind in the Making, the Relation of Intelligence to Social Reform" (New York: Harper, 1921). See Chaps. 1 and 2, pp. 3–29.

[20] Walter Lippmann, "Public Opinion" (New York: Macmillan, 1922). See Part 8, "Organized Intelligence."

gence, science, and reason can be used by both or many sides. By themselves they do not necessarily weight the scales in favor of a milder form of conflict any more than more effective armaments or generalship can be regarded as weighting the scales in favor of less bloody warfare.

Groups without Conflict

Once the fact of large groups in society is taken for granted, then the thought occurs that some means might be developed for escaping the dangers of deadlock, violence, or dictatorship, by promoting more amicable relations among them.

At one extreme one finds one of the greatest pipe dreams of all time: Karl Marx's vision of a classless society in which, with the instruments of production taken over by the proletariat, there would no longer be any basis for economic class war. In the Marxian scheme of things, this has the double merit of picturing "pie in the sky" after the fighting on the barricades is over, and of serving as the basis for Marx's theory of the "withering away of the state," which has provided an intellectual appeal to the anarchists and other anti-state theorists whose support was sought by Marx and his followers. From the strict Marxian standpoint, as interpreted by Lenin and his followers, this state of grace is no alternative to, but rather a consequence of, violence and dictatorship.

Even from the point of view of evolutionary, as contrasted to revolutionary, socialism, the classless-society prospect makes little sense. The socialization of the means of production, even if carried to the full extreme, as in the Soviet Union, can merely change the economic conditions under which groups emerge and the struggle for power takes place. Max Nomad has stated this from the class-struggle point of view in terms more logically consistent than those used by Marx and Lenin:

> The permanent change of masters and the accompanying striving of the masses in the direction of an ever greater *approach* towards equality in the enjoyment of the good things of life forms the basic content of the historical process. That process knows of no millennium when full harmony has been achieved once for all eternity. There is no "happy ending" just as there is no "final revolution" that will eliminate all further class struggles.[21]

The major American variant is found in the vision of cooperation among the leaders of organized groups. This vision takes many forms. At times it appears in the administrative terms of a national economic council or some other piece of machinery which will bring group leaders together. But such

[21] Max Nomad, "Masters—Old and New," in V. F. Calverton (ed.), "The Making of Society" (New York: Modern Library, 1937), p. 893.

machinery, as indicated in the next chapter's discussion of proposals for formal group representation in the structure of government, can do no more than bring people together, as in a back alley or a boxing ring; it cannot determine how they behave when they get there.

An extremely interesting variant is found in the writings of Edwin G. Nourse, who has repeatedly pictured the tremendous potentialities that could come from the exercise of more economic wisdom by the leaders of business, labor, and agriculture. Nourse pictures a future in which each of them "will seek to make their best contribution to maximize total production and then will cooperate in those patterns of distribution that will do most to keep the productive process going with both vigor and efficiency." [22]

This is all very well and good as far as it goes. But it does not go very far. First of all, there are different views, even among the most expert of experts, of what the best contribution of various groups might be, either toward the maximization of total production or the development of sound distribution patterns. Economics cannot resolve these matters; it can only provide refined technical instruments for the development and presentation of one or another point of view. Any philosophy capable of translating itself into reality must be backed by power, and power can come only from direct participation in group conflict.

The vision of more cooperation and less bitterness in the struggle among the groups that make up society is a valuable one. It provides a goal which can probably be regarded as the only substitute for the three dangers of deadlock, violence, or dictatorship. But it is too valuable a goal to be dissipated by suggesting that it can be obtained by administrative gadgetry, sermonizing, or learning more about textbook economics. It can come only through development of the group struggle itself, for the vicissitudes of this struggle create the conditions that promote cooperation and make it possible. From the world viewpoint, the emergence of threats to national survival creates conditions under which—depending upon the degree of the threat—there is more inclination toward amicable and cooperative domestic group relationship. From the internal viewpoint, the expansion of real national income to a point where there will be much more for all groups can also create conditions under which the law of the jungle will recede into the background, and group collaboration can become more feasible. Yet this development itself is the cart and not the horse, for it can be obtained only through the organization of sufficient power to oppose those groups in the economy who prefer scarcity to abundance and to put into effect concrete programs that will achieve the desired goal of genuine economic growth.[23]

[22] Edwin G. Nourse, "The 1950's Come First" (New York: Holt, 1951), p. 179.

[23] For a fuller statement by this author on Nourse's viewpoint, see his "The 1950's Come First," a book review, *American Political Science Review,* Vol. 45, No. 3, September, 1950, pp. 867–874.

An interesting approach toward development of group cooperation has been presented by Stuart Chase on the basis of human-relations studies undertaken in many fields of social science. In a book written eight years after the presentation of his "mountaintop" proposal referred to a few pages back, he accepts the existence of group combat and group tensions as a major factor to be reckoned with and offers the following five principles upon which group agreement can be based:

1. The principle of participation
2. The principle of group energy
3. The principle of clearing communication lines
4. The principle of facts first
5. The principle that agreement is much easier when people feel secure [24]

As more knowledge on human relations is added to the storehouse, Chase maintains we can become "better prepared to meet the two chief tasks which have always faced mankind: coming to terms with nature, and coming to terms with our fellows."

Here again we find observations which are extremely useful but suffer serious limitations. The greatest limitation flows from Chase's failure to recognize that agreement among people also depends upon the development of objectives for group action and that such objectives usually conflict in some manner with objectives of others. Still more specifically, there is nothing like a common enemy and a "clear and present danger" to make people work together in genuine cooperation. When these facts are kept in mind, it then becomes apparent that the limited set of principles offered by Chase is of value not as a means of eliminating group combat and tensions, but as a means of organizing group action as a part of social combat.

Government Planning [25]

Government planning often comes to the fore as an antidote for the jungle conflict between competing groups of American society, and, more specifically, as a means of bringing order and purpose into the legislative process. Toward

---

[24] Chase, "Roads to Agreement" (New York: Harper, 1951), pp. 235–240.

[25] The following are leading books in the growing literature on government planning: Herman Finer, "Road to Reaction" (Boston: Little, Brown, 1945); Friedrick Hayek, "The Road to Serfdom" (Chicago: University of Chicago Press, 1944); John Jewkes, "Ordeal by Planning" (New York: Macmillan, 1948); Karl Mannheim, "Freedom, Power and Democratic Planning" (New York: Oxford, 1950); John P. Millet, "The Process and Organization of Government Planning" (New York: Columbia University Press, 1948); Theo Surányi-Unger, "Private Enterprise and Governmental Planning" (New York: McGraw-Hill, 1950); Barbara Wootton, "Freedom under Planning" (Chapel Hill, N.C.: University of North Carolina Press, 1945); and Ferdinand Zweig, "The Planning of Free Societies" (London: Secker and Werburg, 1943).

the end of the troubled 1930's, for example, Rexford G. Tugwell called for an integration of all forces of society, maintaining that "the articulation of the whole is the emergent need of society" and that the planning arts are "the only available resource in the crisis." [26] In Donald Blaisdell's pioneering study, "Economic Power and Political Pressures," the strengthening of planning is listed—along with lobby registration, the development of advisory councils, and the improvement of government administration—as a major method of coping with the economic and political power of private organizations.

For many years there has been an unending stream of suggestions for new departures in government planning. In scope, these range from proposals to deal with the totality of economic life to proposals dealing with such specific problems as defense mobilization, the prevention of depression, the control of inflation, the scheduling of public works, or the development of river-valley basins. Some center upon planning by officials of the executive branch, others upon planning in Congress, others upon the development of new planning agencies apart from both the executive branch and Congress, and still others favor more ambitious planning by local and state governments. Some propose the vast extension of governmental functions, while others are aimed at more adequate performance of present functions. Many such proposals are hidden under words that have proved less controversial than the word "planning"—words like "coordination," "integration," "general policy making," or "programming." The fact that the Government has long been involved in many planning activities in no way diminishes the interest which exists in new proposals.

Practically all conceptions of government planning are subject to two divergent interpretations. According to one interpretation, planning provides escape from the pressure and propaganda activities of private organizations. This view is buttressed by the techniques of planning themselves, which emphasize the compilation of fact and the application of professional skills. It is supported by the arguments of many technicians who, undoubtedly, like to view their skills as sufficient to produce inevitable conclusions and as enabling government to close its ranks against group pressures. Some plans are so breath-taking in their scope and imaginative quality that they stir up semi-religious emotions of order and balance and seem to place the planning process upon a pinnacle far removed from the sordid aspects of social combat. This is the idealistic interpretation of planning, one which, if not counterbalanced by powerful injections of realism, leads to useless plans and frustrated planners.

In the second interpretation, planning is a method of organizing power to achieve given objectives. Schattschneider illustrated this more realistic viewpoint very aptly in a discussion of planning for full employment:

[26] Rexford G. Tugwell, "The Fourth Power" *Planning and Civil Comment,* April–June, 1939, p. 2.

. . . what is required is that an organized and systematic attempt be made to use political methods to produce an amplitude of power to do all that needs to be done. Power is emphasized because all plans and policies for the maintenance of high-level employment imply power; without the power to do something about it, planning is a mere form of wishful thinking. All planning and all policies imply power. However, power in turn implies politics; for it is the business of politics to produce power.[27]

The production of power, in turn, involves the obtaining of support, either directly or indirectly, from various groups in society. Obviously support by governmental agencies is indispensable; a planning agency with no allies within the Government is indeed an orphan. As Schattschneider has pointed out at great length, the mobilization of power through political parties is also relevant. Private organizations, too, must be brought into the planning process in one manner or another. This is why the more successful type of planners talk about "participation" and "public relations." They realize the necessity not only of selling their plans to private groups, but of drawing them into the entire operation so that their responsible support can be assured. Some plans, of course, rely to an important degree upon the support of relatively unorganized groups or groups which come into being intermittently. But this merely means that the character of the relationship between planning and private organizations varies from time to time, not that the relationship is nonexistent.

One of the reasons why the idea of planning has been so controversial is the fact that it becomes so intensively involved in conflicts between private organizations. Planners inevitably take sides, and inevitably in a democratic society there are competing plans and competing planners. Planning often means concrete shifts in power—gains for some and losses for others. Those who are afraid of losing power wail about their loss of "freedom," which becomes a more euphemistic term for describing power they wish to preserve. The push and pull of private interests operates upon both plans and planners. Few successful plans are developed without a careful eye toward balancing the interests and groups that might be affected by the plan. In other words, the plan becomes a tentative or semifinal resolution of conflicts between various groups, including private organizations. If the process of group conflict is not sufficiently reflected in the development of the plan, it will make itself felt rather sharply when the time comes to take action upon the plan. At this stage the pressures will either tear the plan to pieces or modify it. Planners who seek to prevent this contingency can avoid complete failure only by dealing with basic group conflicts in the early stages of the planning process.

Planning can be an escape from the pressure and propaganda activities of private organizations only if it degenerates into the development of paper plans which are politically unrealistic or if it is backed up by that dictatorial

[27] E. E. Schattschneider, "Party Government and Employment Policy," *American Political Science Review*, Vol. 39, No. 6, December, 1945, p. 1149.

use of force which threatens or perpetrates acts of violence to suppress the activities of private groups. On the other hand, planning is an indispensable method for democratically organizing private groups—not to suppress their differences and create a barren uniformity, but to achieve certain objectives that are unattainable without a more rationally developed power structure. More extensive planning is needed for purposes of military defense, of providing more efficiently the governmental services which are needed, of providing more effective representation for the weaker and less organized groups in the country. But always the questions must be asked, planning for what, planning for whom, planning by whom, and even planning against whom?

It has often been suggested that the basic approach of government to problems created by the power of private organizations should be to support the weak against the strong so that they can contend on a more equal basis. Actually, the activities of government agencies of necessity must affect the distribution of power in one way or another. It is natural, therefore, for weaker groups to seek governmental support and for governmental agencies to strengthen themselves by relations of this type. This is illustrated by government action which has facilitated the organizational activities of union labor, supplemented the organizational activities of farmers through financial assistance, or provided financial support for banking institutions.

Government planning often becomes a means of doing all this on a broader scale. Some plans would turn increased power over to business organizations. Other plans would enhance the power of weakly organized groups or provide representation for the interests of those who come together to express themselves on only few occasions other than at the ballot box during national elections. "Government planning" along the latter lines has succeeded in making the term a *bête noire* to the minds of many conservative citizens.

Quis custodiet ipsos custodes? This is the recurring question that all proponents of planning must meet. Who will plan for the planners? If government planners are to obtain the power needed to carry out their plans, what protection is there against an overwhelming concentration of power in their hands?

The question is not one that can be answered in abstract terms. The problem has relevance only as it bears upon the kind of planning that is proposed and the present and potential distribution of power in existing societies. If one thinks in terms of all-powerful governmental planning, there can be no satisfactory answer. The "guardians" will do as they please until they fall out among themselves, are stricken from power by an internal revolt, or become weak as a result of clashes with other nations.

If one thinks of limited planning, the answer depends upon the nature of the limitations or—to put the matter in other words—the actual distribution of power between competing forces in society. "Guardianship will emerge," writes David B. Truman in the last sentence of his book, "out of the affiliations of the guardians." [28] Through this extremely suggestive phrase Truman points out that the overlapping groups to which the planners themselves may have loyalties are a protection against planning that might go too far in the interests of any one group or coalition. One might well carry the matter a little further and add that guardianship will also emerge "out of the group conflicts in society." The process of group combat itself—harsh and cruel though it may be—provides a check-and-balance system of protection far more powerful and meaningful than the constitutional arrangements envisaged by the Founding Fathers against the harshness and cruelties of unguarded guardians.

[28] Truman, *op. cit.*, p. 535.

Chapter 3

THE PRIVATE ORGANIZATIONS: REFORMING
THEIR METHODS

IF THE process of group combat is so central to "guarding the guardians," clearly its procedures and practices are vital to the preservation of a democratic legislative system. The behavior of private groups and organizations, therefore, has been of particular interest to those who would either preserve or change these procedures and practices. Generally their interest has been grounded upon a fear of the growing power of Big Business, Big Labor, the Farm Lobby, and other groups. It has been nurtured by the realization that every group has specialized interests of its own and cannot be depended upon to use its power in behalf of other groups or, to use a term which usually serves as a method of referring to the interests of a particular congeries of groups, the "general welfare."

The specific proposals that have been advanced concerning private organizations may be divided into three groups. The first deals with certain aspects of their legislative campaigning activities. The second deals with the question of whether they should be given a more formal status within government itself. The third deals with the dangers inherent in group conflict and various admonitions to the effect that private organizations should either vanish from the scene or behave themselves.

THEIR CAMPAIGNING ACTIVITIES

The campaigning activities of private organizations are extremely extensive. They include the organization of group support, the application of pressure, the dissemination of propaganda, and all the arts of leadership that are needed to make these elements effective. The major proposals thus far presented deal with the existence of financial bonds between private organizations and government officials, contributions to the campaign funds of candidates for Congress and the Presidency, the activities of lobbyists, and the control of the major channels of communication.

Financial Bonds with Government Officials [1]

American history is full of recurring exposés of how private groups have purchased government favors—including favorable action on legislative proposals—by lining the pockets of government officials. The extent of such direct financial bonds between private groups and government officials has probably declined sharply over the decades, particularly as nonfinancial bonds have come into being to take the place of the direct financial nexus. V. O. Key has observed:

> It may be that bribery . . . occurs on a large scale only in a relatively chaotic society in which new interests are forging upward, rapid realignments of wealth are being formed, the introduction of new inventions, social and technological, is rapidly upsetting the old economic order, society is relatively unstratified, or old class alignments are being shifted and re-formed. . . . The rise of the propaganda and public-relations experts of the pressure groups in some ways contribute toward the reduction in the reliance on corrupt techniques. Results, formerly secured by bribery or kindred methods, may be secured by more or less legitimate methods. [2]

Yet it would be a mistake to assume that direct financial connections will decline steadily to the point of becoming inconsequential. The more intensive organization of society in fact multiplies the interest of many private groups in the buying of favors, and does nothing of itself to diminish the widespread tendency to use hook or crook to advance one's own personal interests if one can get away with it. Nor has wealth in the United States become, as many radical commentators have charged, so consolidated and so powerful that it can rely on the more accepted forms of influence alone. Furthermore, corruption itself is not merely tolerated but, as Robert C. Brooks pointed out several decades ago, it is justified by many on the grounds that it is good for business, that "it may be more than compensated for by the high efficiency otherwise of those who engage in it," [3] that it is a useful technique of getting things done.

Accordingly, proposals are continuously being made for dealing with the problem. The more important proposals deal with such matters as codes of ethics, disqualification requirements, the disclosure of outside sources of in-

[1] One of the most useful documents on this subject, as indicated by the frequent quotations and references on the following pages, is "Ethical Standards in Government," a report of the Douglas subcommittee of the Senate Committee on Labor and Public Welfare, 82d Cong., 1st Sess., 1951. See also, "Establishment of a Commission on Ethics in Government," Hearings before a subcommittee to study S. Con. Res. 21, 82d Cong., 1st Sess., 1951.

[2] V. O. Key, Jr., "Politics, Parties, and Pressure Groups" (New York: Crowell, 1942). The chapter on pecuniary sanctions, from which this quotation is taken, has been omitted from the 1947 edition of this book, probably because the rash of exposés in the aftermath of World War II suggested that this thesis on the decline of bribery might call for reexamination.

[3] Robert C. Brooks, "Corruption of American Politics and Life" (New York: Dodd, Mead, 1910). This is an excellent sociological and political analysis of this field.

come, bribery and corruption laws, and larger rewards through the government service itself.

Codes of Ethics. Early in 1951 dramatic exposés of highly questionable activities by executive officials led to the repeated suggestion that codes of ethics should be established for the public service, which would be comparable to those that have been commonly accepted in medicine, law, and other professions. In fact, a number of members of Congress began to prepare sample codes governing members of Congress themselves.

After long hearings on the subject of ethics in government, a Senate subcommittee headed by Senator Douglas recommended the creation of a Commission on Ethics in Government. Without the leadership and assistance of a high status commission, the subcommittee did not believe the work of formulating the needed ethical codes would go forward as it should. The subcommittee also listed the following arguments on behalf of ethical codes:

(1) They would clarify new or complex situations where the application of basic moral principles is far from obvious; (2) they would anticipate issues so that difficulties could be foreseen and basic policy decided when rational consideration is possible (*i.e.*, the rules of the game must be approved before play begins); (3) the enhancement of the influence of the more progressive elements of the group who will tend to bring the whole group up to higher standards; (4) they would be a basis for discipline if the group had enough leadership and pride to act; (5) they would furnish a basis for instructing new members of the group as to their professional obligations (Hippocrates required all of his disciples to take the oath); and (6) they would instruct the public as to what it should expect of the principal elements in the realm of public affairs.[4]

An additional argument, not mentioned by the subcommittee, but one of great importance, is that ethical codes can include principles of conduct which are extremely difficult or even impossible to enforce, and which therefore cannot practicably be included in more formalized requirements.

It is obvious, of course, that codes of this type can provide no ironclad protection against undesirable financial bonds between private groups and government officials. They could be neither applicable to all situations that develop nor susceptible of rigorous enforcement. Furthermore, high standards of personal conduct are bound to come into conflict with contradictory standards which are widely held.

Disqualification. It has long been customary to disqualify executive officials from the handling of governmental affairs that directly affect their personal financial interests, and former government officials from conducting relations with government agencies on matters which they had previously handled when in the government service. The Douglas subcommittee proposed that, in the case of executive officials, disqualification provisions of this type be considera-

---

[4] "Ethical Standards in Government," p. 35.

bly extended. It urged that nonsalaried officials who are brought in from industry should not be assigned to positions that require them to deal with their former industries. It called for the permanent "disbarment" of former Federal officials from appearing before executive agencies in connection with any cases which they had previously handled during their period of government service. It recommended "disbarment" for a two-year period of all former officials who wish to appear before an agency with which they formerly worked on any cases whatsoever.

In the case of members of Congress, a disqualification provision has been in existence in the Rules of the House of Representatives since 1789. Rule VIII provides that every member of the House "shall vote on each question put, unless he has a personal or pecuniary interest in the event of such question." Yet only in the rarest of instances has a Speaker of the House ever decided that, because of personal interest, a member could not vote. Nor have members of the House asked that this rule be enforced or extended to cover committee as well as floor action.

Disclosure. Another method of dealing with financial relations between private groups and government officials is found in the highly controversial proposal that Congress should add "glass pockets to the appurtenances of office." In sponsoring a proposal for the registration of the amounts and sources of Congressmen's incomes, Senator Wayne Morse of Oregon put the case as follows:

I believe a legislator's viewpoint may be influenced—no matter how honest he is— by his own personal interests. Therefore I believe the public has a right to know from whom and from where we get our money. My own actions show that I do not think it improper for a senator to receive money over and above his salary. I lecture and write for fees. Neither do I say or believe that sources from which my colleagues receive money are improper. That's not the point. The point is that the people have a right to know what influences the attitudes of their representatives. They need to know this in order to decide whether we truly represent them.[5]

Four years later, in a special message to Congress, President Truman presented the same proposal in broader terms, asking that disclosure requirements cover not only members of Congress, but also the Federal judiciary, top executive officials, and the top officials of the national political parties.

If an official of an executive agency knew that he would have to disclose the fact that he accepted a gift or loan from a private company with which he has public business, or if a Member of Congress who is on a committee concerned with a certain industry knew that he would have to disclose the fact that he accepted a fee from a company in that industry, I believe the chances are that such gifts or fees would not be accepted.[6]

[5] Quoted in editorial by James C. Derieux, *Collier's,* Sept. 20, 1947.
[6] White House press release, Sept. 27, 1951.

A veil of secrecy, of course, will always cover the full facts on the financial relations between government officials and private organizations. Income flowing to a wife or brother or to a firm of which one has been a member will always be difficult to pin down. Understandings concerning future rewards in the form of personal employment are too tenuous to be uncovered ahead of time. Moreover, the recording of certain facts on outside sources of income—no matter how comprehensive they might turn out to be—would by no means destroy or even significantly curtail the relations between government officials and private groups. It would probably result in still more use of the less direct financial relationship. Nor would it by itself throw a "spotlight of publicity" on these officials. It would merely make certain facts available for interpretation and use by various contestants in the legislative struggle. These facts would probably be used in most cases by those groups in society with the weakest financial resources and might often be used with great effectiveness.

Penalties for Bribery and Corruption. In addition to the many other points covered in its report, the Douglas subcommittee recommended a thorough study of changes needed in the provisions of the Criminal Code dealing with bribery and corruption. To facilitate such a study the subcommittee included in its report a draft of a bill to amend the criminal laws.

One of the major changes in the proposed bill would strengthen the Criminal Code by broadening the definition of "bribe" to include "other considerations just as useful to bribers as hard cash," such as any "emoluments, fee, profit, advantage, benefit, position, future position, employment, future employment, opportunity, future opportunity, advancement, or future advancement." Another provision would cover public officials who "receive things of substantial value not for doing things which come within their official capacity, but for using their influence with other persons in the government." Also, bribers would be treated as harshly as the bribed. Just as the latter are subject to disqualification from henceforth holding an office, honor, or trust under the United States, the former would be henceforth prohibited from participating in any substantial business activity with the Federal government. Existing penalties would be sharply increased. In the case of employees of executive agencies, administrative sanctions were recommended by the subcommittee so that, entirely apart from any criminal action, employees who had used their official position for purposes of personal profit or who had accepted bribes of any sort could be promptly dismissed without extended hearings or appeals procedures.

Action along these lines would face innumerable obstacles. In so far as members of Congress are concerned, the enforcement of criminal provisions is particularly difficult. Administrative officials are naturally loath to risk tangling with members of Congress. This is particularly true inasmuch as "Congress adheres pretty faithfully to the theory that mistakes will happen, and when a member slips on the banana peel of mischance and lands all sprawled out before the gaze of his countrymen, the disposition is to form a circle about him and hide his confusion." [7] Bribery and corruption, moreover, are extremely hard to prove. The line between minor foibles and crimes is, in this area, extremely hard to draw. The difficulty is made worse by the existence of what Brooks has called "auto-corruption" and "smokeless sin," the one involving no direct associates in a legitimate transaction and the other being of a nature that attracts no attention and can rarely be found out. The difficulty is also compounded by the fact that the greater felonies are often legalized. As stated in the old English quatrain:

> The law locks up both man and woman
> Who steals the goose from off the common,
> But lets the greater felon loose
> Who steals the common from the goose.

Larger Rewards through Government Service Itself. Another approach toward weakening financial bonds between government officials and private organizations is found in action that would increase salaries and retirement benefits.

As far back as 1945, the Heller Report advocated $25,000 per year for members of Congress. A closely related proposal called for retirement benefits after age fifty-five of $1,000 for each full year of congressional service, up to a maximum of $10,000 a year. One of the reasons given—euphemistically phrased—was: "In providing such security, the country at least partially safeguards the legislative function from possible deficiencies resulting from efforts of members to protect themselves against the time when they are not reelected." [8] Many similar proposals have been made for increasing the financial rewards and economic security of employees in the executive branch.

From the viewpoint of wealthier groups, action along these lines is intended to make government posts more attractive to men who might otherwise gravitate toward well-paying private jobs, although, for men of real wealth, a few thousand dollars more or less in one's salary is a minor matter. In the case of persons from the lower-income groups, higher government salaries might serve as a counterbalance against the influence of wealthy interests. In either case, the extraordinary expenses involved in being a member of Congress, even with salary increases, will probably continue to make difficult a life of luxury from the rich man's viewpoint.

[7] H. H. Wilson, "Congress: Corruption and Compromise" (New York: Rinehart, 1951), p. 245.

[8] Robert Heller, "Strengthening the Congress" (Washington, D.C.: National Planning Association, January, 1945), p. 35. Since the issuance of this report, salaries of members of Congress have been raised and a retirement system has been established, but both salaries and benefits are considerably below the levels proposed in the report.

Yet substantial opposition to proposals of this type can always be expected. Higher salaries and retirement benefits, whether in the executive or congressional branches, are anathema to those who see in them one more step toward an all-powerful state and an overheavy Federal budget. Efforts to raise congressional remuneration must always reckon with the potential embarrassment faced by members of Congress who publicly vote for an increase in their own pay or retirement benefits in the face of the frequent denunciation of such proposals by a few members of Congress who proudly proclaim their desire to serve their country irrespective of remuneration.

Contributions to Political Campaigns [9]

A special type of financial bond between private groups and government officials is found in campaign contributions. Candidates for Congress and the Presidency need money in order to conduct their election campaigns. Many private groups are always eager to meet this need in the hope that their contributions may yield a substantial return in the form of support for the legislative objectives.

Accordingly, repeated efforts have been made to deal with this problem by various prohibitions, by requirements for the registration of facts concerning campaign contributions and expenditures, and by various forms of public financing of political campaigns.

Prohibitions. The prohibitions thus far brought into effect have dealt with three aspects of campaign financing: sources of contributions, amounts of contributions, and expenditures. Corporations and unions have been prohibited from contributing money to political campaigns. It has been made illegal to intimidate Federal employees into contributing to campaign funds. The amount any person can contribute to an individual candidate or campaign has been limited to $5,000. In so far as expenditures are concerned, candidates for the Senate operate under a $25,000 ceiling, candidates for the House of Representatives under a $10,000 ceiling, and national-party committees under a ceiling of $3,000,000 during any calendar year. Campaign expenditures by both corporations and unions have been prohibited. Naturally, the direct purchase of votes has long been illegal.

It is doubtful whether any provisions of law have ever been so systematically evaded as the above prohibitions. It is certain that no provisions of law have ever been so thoroughly evaded by political leaders and government officials. The prohibitions on sources of contributions are evaded by the device of having the money flow from individuals and groups associated with corporations

[9] Although the literature on this subject is vast, the following references will serve to provide background for proposals in this field: Key, *op. cit.*, 1947 ed., Chap. 15, "Party Finance"; Louise Overacker, "Presidential Campaign Funds" (Boston: Boston University Press, 1946); and James K. Pollock, "Party Campaign Funds" (New York: Knopf, 1926).

or unions, rather than from the corporations or unions themselves. The limitations on personal contributions are evaded by having the money given in smaller sums by various members of a family, rather than in one large sum. The limitations on expenditures are evaded by the development of a large number of campaign committees.

Many changes are obviously needed. Among those recommended are more rigorous enforcement of the present prohibitions; recognition that the existing ceilings on personal contributions and on expenditures are unrealistic, not only because the value of the dollar has declined, but also because new methods of mass communication and development of larger constituencies have made campaigning more expensive; and discontinuance of all prohibitions, with the exception of those on political assessment and vote buying.

Disclosure. Present prohibitions are accompanied by registration provisions designed to deal with contributions and expenditures through the disclosure method. Yet the wholesale evasion of the intent, if not the letter, of the requirements is so great as to suggest that more is concealed than disclosed.

Many proposals have been developed for strengthening registration provisions. The following list synthesizes the most constructive of these proposals:

1. Include campaigns for nominations as well as for elections
2. Include loans as well as gifts
3. Include contributions to, and expenditures by, all campaign organizations
4. Provide for more adequate reporting before primaries, conventions, and elections
5. Develop more uniform methods of reporting
6. Provide a central repository for the filing of statements
7. Provide for the prompt auditing, compilation, and analysis of this material and for its publication within each state as well as in Washington

In reflecting upon the significance of these proposals, it should be kept in mind that dollar contributions to political campaigns are by no means an accurate indication of the power exerted by contributors upon electoral or legislative decisions. Small contributions, strategically placed, may win more power than large contributions that flow haphazardly or are not actively followed up. The flow of campaign contributions may reveal nothing whatsoever of the campaigning done directly by business, labor, religious, and other organizations or of the many campaign resources stemming from the prerogatives of office and enjoyed exclusively by incumbents running for reelection. In many cases, the "spotlight of publicity" upon large campaign contributions might turn out to be merely a feeble glimmer competing with hundreds of other flashes, sparked by groups seeking advantage in the legislative process.

Public Support. Back in 1907, President Theodore Roosevelt sent a message to Congress in which he suggested that the Federal government subsidize most of the "proper and legitimate expenses of each of the great national parties." [10]

[10] *Congressional Record*, 60th Cong., 1st Sess., Dec. 3, 1907, p. 78.

The purpose of this proposal was clearly to free candidates from overdependence upon contributions from private organizations and to provide more equality in campaign resources. It has always enjoyed a widespread appeal. The Douglas subcommittee on Ethics in Government, for example, concluded that "some form of public support is justified" and that it "would be less expensive than the indirect costs of allowing candidates and parties to be solely dependent upon the support of well-heeled special interests." [11]

In a few states candidates are given free or low-cost space in publicity pamphlets which are printed and distributed to all voters by the state governments. Senator Benton of Connecticut and others have proposed that the franking privilege be made available to *all candidates* for Congress. A still more significant proposal would provide political candidates with a limited amount of free television and radio time.

It is suggested that the Federal government could appropriate the money and transfer specified sums to the television and radio stations. Or the Federal Communications Commission could require its licensees, as a condition for receiving access to the airways, to provide a certain amount of free political time—and this approach might be associated with indirect subsidy in the form of tax concessions.[12] An extremely indirect form of Federal assistance could be provided through action to reduce campaign costs, since newspapers often charge political candidates higher advertising rates than commercial advertisers, and television and radio stations habitually raise the rates for political candidates. Another minor form of public assistance could be provided through the indirect method of allowing candidates, in computing their Federal income taxes, to deduct up to a fixed amount of their personal campaign expenses as an expense of doing business. At present, because of a bare 5 to 4 decision of the Supreme Court, this is not allowed.[13] Attention should also be given to the possibility of allowing individuals to deduct from taxes up to a certain amount of money spent in campaign contributions. A final method of diminishing the dependence of political candidates upon funds supplied by private organizations would be to increase, by systems of regular dues payments, the amount of funds made available through party sources themselves.

Lobbying [14]

Legislative provisions dealing with lobbying differ from campaign laws in that they have been on the statute books for a shorter period of time and con-

---

[11] "Ethical Standards in Government," p. 63.

[12] "Establishment of a Commission on Ethics in Government," pp. 464–468.

[13] *McDonald v. Commission of Internal Revenue,* 63 Sup. Ct. 96 (1944).

[14] The following items are particularly relevant: Hearings of Select Committee on Lobbying Activities of the House of Representatives, 81st Cong., 2d Sess., 1950; this same committee's "General Interim Report," H. Rept. 3138; "Report and Recommendations on Fed

tain neither prohibitions nor ceilings. Yet the experience with these requirements since their enactment in 1946 has been similarly disillusioning and has led to many proposals for more effective disclosure of facts concerning lobbying and for a number of prohibitions.

Disclosure. The information on organizations, individuals, contributions, and expenditures under it, printed four times a year in the *Congressional Record,* is a miscellaneous array of undigested facts, often extremely misleading. Only a meager reflection is given of activities of the richer, multipurpose organizations like the National Association of Manufacturers or the American Federation of Labor, whose influence on legislation is far greater than that of special groups set up to work on legislation alone.

If all the problems of coverage, accuracy, and compilation were solved, the question might well be asked: What would be the use of this highly complex mass of information?

The answer hardly lies, as some of the ardent advocates of disclosure have maintained, in the possibility that large numbers of people who might be described as "the public" will have time or interest to read, understand, react to, or act upon this information. Nor does it lie in the possibility that disclosure requirements will inhibit large-scale lobby operations; the probability is rather that the bulk of legislative campaigning by private organizations would go on as always, with somewhat more attention paid to techniques of channeling funds and activities in a manner that would evade disclosure.

The best answer to the question, as with the disclosure of facts concerning political contributions, probably lies in the potential use to which the disclosed information can be put by various participants in the legislative process, including not only members of Congress and executive officials, but also the leaders of private organizations and the lobbyists themselves. The information would be of greatest use to those participants in the legislative process whose sources of intelligence are meager and whose power might be buttressed by facts of this type concerning other participants. In short, the information could, to some extent, serve to deprive some participants, particularly the stronger ones, of the advantages achieved through more complete secrecy and add a minor increment to the power of the weaker participants.

The suggestion has often been made that the disclosure operation be extended to cover private attempts to influence executive action. It is argued not only that administrative decisions are important but also that legislative decisions are often influenced via executive officials. The Buchanan Committee dealt with this matter merely by proposing that Congress authorize investiga-

---

eral Lobbying Act," H. Rept. 3239; "Report and Recommendations on Federal Lobbying Act, Minority Views," H. Rept. 3239, pt. 2. Also, Belle Zeller, "The Federal Regulation of Lobbying Act," *American Political Science Review,* Vol. 42, No. 2, April, 1948, pp. 239–271.

tions of various private attempts to influence executive action.[15] The Douglas subcommittee, as part of its work on the problem of ethics, suggested that anyone spending more than $10,000 a year in connection with representation before the Government be required to file expenditure details with the agency involved.[16]

It has occasionally been suggested that the registration system be extended to cover the legislative activities of Federal executive officials themselves. In rejecting this proposal, the Buchanan Committee commented that "Congress, through the proper exercise of its powers to appropriate funds and to investigate conditions and practices of the executive branch, as well as through its financial watchdog, the General Accounting Office, can and should remain vigilant against any improper use of appropriated funds and any invasion of the legislative prerogatives and responsibilities of the Congress." [17]

Regulation. In so far as regulation is concerned, three proposals can be mentioned briefly—and quickly dismissed.

One is the idea that misrepresentation in legislative propaganda, like misrepresentation in drug advertisements, should be prohibited. Though superficially appealing, this proposal is rendered both unfeasible and undesirable by the fact that the distinction between "good" and "bad" and "true" and "false," in the realm of legislative propaganda, is almost entirely subjective.

The second is the proposal that contingent-fees contracts with respect to legislative activities be prohibited. The use of such arrangements is objected to by many members of Congress because of their dislike of any remuneration system which seems to brand their actions as the "effect" and the activities of specific individuals or groups as the "cause." Yet if working to influence legislation is a legitimate form of employment or business activity, as all observers seem to agree it is, it is difficult to find any sound basis for special public regulation of the methods or amounts of remuneration. If exorbitant contingent fees are charged, one can always go to a court of equity.[18]

The third is the proposal that former members of Congress be denied access to the floor of the Senate and the House if they appear there as lobbyists. Although access to the floor is a minor form of access to power and not one which necessarily confers a major advantage upon any ex-member of Congress, a change in the rules would seem unquestionably in order. Congressional reluctance to change the rules probably stems from the desire of incumbent mem-

---

[15] "Report and Recommendations on Federal Lobbying Act," p. 35.

[16] "Ethical Standards in Government," pp. 49–50.

[17] "Report and Recommendations on Federal Lobbying Act," p. 36.

[18] There are a number of cases on record in which courts have refused to enforce contingent-fees contracts calling for exorbitant fees. By sleight-of-hand reasoning these cases are sometimes used in backing up the argument that contingent-fees contracts in the field of legislative influence should be made illegal.

bers themselves, when no longer in office, to be able to visit the scenes of their former glory, whether to indulge in nostalgia or to carry on personal business.

Control of the Major Channels of Communication [19]

As major weapons in the arsenal of social combat, newspapers, television, radio, and cinema are mainstays of the argumentation and propaganda which are vital to the wars of words and influence in the legislative process, particularly in a democratic society. Throughout his career each legislator time and again must decide whether or not to try to break into the headlines, whether or not, when, and where he should be seen and heard inside the legislature and out, whether or not his appeals for personal or policy support should be made "on the stump," over television, in the magazines, or by book and pamphlet, and to which audiences. Usually these choices and the accessibility to him of the communications media are influenced by his relations with private and party organizations or by his status as a public official. Nor is the legislator the only one in the legislative process to make use of the major channels of communication. Leaders and members of the private organizations, the parties, and the other government organizations are equally significant as users.

Yet it is too readily forgotten that the owners and operators of the media are themselves a group as well as members of a variety of other groups and that they have their own interpretations of their private interests and those of the public. Each of these channels of communication rests upon business enterprises involving heavy investments and substantial financial backing. In each there has been a well-defined tendency toward concentration of power into major units and the development of close financial bonds with the more powerful business groupings in the country.

As a result, many individuals and groups have outlined standards which they would like communication enterprises to conform with and have proposed various forms of private or governmental action to compel adherence to these standards or change the pattern of control.

Standards. In its 1923 Code of Ethics, the American Society of Newspaper Editors listed "independence of private interests" as a major standard. Although the code in which it was embodied has probably been something of a dead letter, the concept itself has shown great staying power and widespread appeal.

[19] One of the most valuable of the many books written on this subject—one that will serve as an admirable starting point for anyone who is interested in penetrating further into this fascinating subject—is "A Free and Responsible Press: A General Report on Mass Communication" by the Commission on Freedom of the Press (Chicago: University of Chicago Press, 1947). The other volumes in this series provide rich source materials on newspapers; radio, motion-picture, magazine, and book industries; freedom of the press; and international communications.

A more broad-gauged approach is found in the following five standards developed by the Commission on Freedom of the Press:

"1. A truthful, comprehensive, and intelligent account of the day's events in a context which gives them meaning

"2. A forum for the exchange of comment and criticism

"3. The projection of a representative picture of the constituent groups in the society

"4. The presentation and clarification of the goals and values of the society

"5. Full access to the day's intelligence" [20]

The great advantage of this approach is that it fully recognizes the pluralistic character of American society. Instead of fastening its hopes upon the spurious standards of independence from private interests, it suggests that all interests in society should have access to the major channels of communication. It is based upon a conception of "freedom of the press" which insists that in the freedoms enjoyed by communication enterprises lie reciprocal responsibilities, and that those who have something worth saying should be free to have a public hearing.

A major response to the promulgation of these standards has been to point out that by and large the performance of the American communication industries in the United States is far superior to that of other countries. Another is to indicate that the public is being given what it wants, and that anyone is unrealistic who seeks to impose standards of performance which are far different from those of the average men and women of the country. The critics of the communication industries, however, have not been convinced. Many of them would agree with the Commission on Freedom of the Press when it stated that while the communication industry "has displayed remarkable ingenuity in gathering its raw material and in manufacturing and distributing its finished product" and that "extraordinarily high quality of performance has been achieved by the leaders in each field of mass communications," the industry as a whole "is not meeting the needs of our society." [21]

Codes of Conduct. Most of the communication industries have adopted minimum codes designed to protect against indecency and other flagrant violations of the mores of the community. Yet these codes rarely attempt to set forth goals of public responsibility or ideal performance. The Commission on Freedom of the Press, therefore, attempted to outline in ideal terms the responsibilities of the communication industries. Without asking them to do what can be done more properly by other private groups or more effectively by the Government, the Commission recommended that each of the communication

[20] Commission on Freedom of the Press, "A Free and Responsible Press," Chap. 2, "The Requirements," pp. 20–29.

[21] *Ibid.*, p. 68.

enterprises develop ideal codes of conduct similar to those of the established professions of law and medicine.

Among the other recommendations set down by the Commission were those advocating "That the agencies of mass communication assume the responsibility of financing new, experimental activities in their field . . . that the members of the press engage in vigorous mutual criticism . . . that the press use every means that can be devised to increase the competence, independence, and effectiveness of its staff . . . that the radio industry take control of its programs, and that it treat advertising as it is treated by the best newspapers." [22]

Organization of Weaker Interests. Under the heading of "What can be done by the public" the Commission on Freedom of the Press recommended three lines of action that would tend to provide somewhat greater access to the major channels of communication by the weaker interests in society. The Commission called for greater use of the major communication channels by schools and other nonprofit institutions, for the creation of "academic-professional centers of advanced study, research, and publication in the field of communications," and "the establishment of a new and independent agency to appraise and report annually upon the performance" of the communication industries.[23]

One of the most discerning critics of radio performance, Jerome Spingarn, has urged a localized form of the national agency advocated by the Commission on Freedom of the Press.[24] He emphasizes that the air waves belong to the public and that the public ultimately pays all of radio's bills. He therefore urges that community radio councils be established not only to protest unbalanced radio programs but also to advise community groups on how to use the radio in a competent, interesting fashion. Whatever potentialities there may be in this approach seem to lie in more attention to radio and other channels of communication by existing organizations formed for other purposes. This is borne out by the experience of various religious, racial, and national groups which have been formed for other purposes but which have been extremely effective at times in forcing communication enterprises to eliminate material which they regard as offensive.

Government Control. There are four major methods through which the Government, apart from any direct communication activities of its own, can control the major channels of communication: antitrust action, the enforcement of certain performance standards, censorship, and antilibel sanctions.

Among those who advocate central economic planning or who cater to the whims of large concerns, it is often fashionable to cast sly aspersions upon the value of antitrust action. These aspersions are usually based upon the

[22] *Ibid.,* pp. 90–96.
[23] *Ibid.,* pp. 96–102.
[24] Jerome Spingarn, "Radio Is Yours," Public Affairs Pamphlet, No. 121 (New York· Public Affairs Committee, 1946).

rather obvious fact that a broadside effort to break down bigness and to prevent newspapers from owning radio stations and other forms of joint ownership would clearly be a backward step. Nevertheless, antitrust action, used selectively, can be an invaluable tool. It can open up opportunities for new enterprises which otherwise would not be able to come into being or survive in the face of concentrated competition. It can be used to prevent overpowering concentrations of control in the hands of a few interests and to break down restrictions on the extension of new services or the use of new technological improvements.

Antitrust action can be particularly effective when backed up by economic assistance to smaller enterprises. Morris Ernst has proposed special tax exemptions for small communications enterprises to assist them in building up the capital needed for effective competition with larger groups. In connection with small newspapers and magazines, he has proposed sliding scales of postal rates which would favor smaller companies.[25]

The most ambitious attempt to establish standards of performance for any communication industry is found in the "blue book" of the Federal Communications Commission. The Commission indicated that in considering the renewal of licenses of broadcast stations, it would give particular consideration to various "service factors relevant to the public interest." One of these service factors was "the carrying of sustaining programs" (which in many cases consist of programs dealing with the pros and cons of public issues), while another was "the carrying of programs devoted to the discussion of public issues." [26] As a result of vigorous resistance from the radio industry, the Commission has walked gingerly, as though on eggshells, in carrying out these policies.

A specific method through which the Commission tried at one time to develop a policy of equal treatment was its "Mayflower decision" prohibiting editorializing by radio stations. This was defended on the ground that it prevented undue power over public-policy decisions on the part of those few individuals who are given a franchise to use the air waves and of the large advertisers who support them. If it did not prevent indirect propaganda, at least it prevented direct and open propagandizing. If it prevented the expression of views by a minority of liberal broadcasters, it also prevented a great social imbalance from developing through giving more freedom of action to the great majority of conservative broadcasters. Finally it was argued that the requirement that a station licensee must not be an advocate is inseparable from the policy that stations present all sides of controversial issues.

[25] Morris Ernst, "The First Freedom" (New York: Macmillan, 1946), pp. 254–255, 258–259.

[26] Federal Communications Commission, "Public Service Responsibility of Broadcast Licensees," pp. 12–36, 39–40.

The Commission formally dropped its anti-editorializing policy in 1949 after it was vigorously attacked on many scores. In its place it repeated its policy standard that a reasonable percentage of broadcasting time be devoted to the discussion of public issues, and set forth the requirement that "such programs be designed so that the public has a reasonable opportunity to hear different opposing positions on the public issues of interest and importance in the community." Commissioner Hennock dissented from this decision on the ground that "The standard of fairness . . . is virtually impossible of enforcement by the Commission." [27]

The difficulties in enforcing such standards upon the radio industry are illustrated by the rather remarkable fact that scarcely anyone has seriously proposed the extension of the same principles to the other communications industries. Probably the only such proposal has come from J. B. S. Hardman, an editor of a trade-union newspaper, who proposed that a Free Press Authority be set up to regulate the entire network of communication channels. One of the major functions of the Authority would be to ascertain the relative strength of majority and minority opinions and to compel where necessary adequate expression of minority views.[28] According to Chafee, this proposal "offers to a government the most magnificent opportunity to fetter the press which has ever existed in English-speaking countries." [29]

Censorship is one of the most powerful instruments of control that any government can use. In any full-blown dictatorship the power of censorship is an indispensable weapon, one that assures that views other than those of the group in power have no opportunity to be presented through the major channels of communication. In the past there has been little danger of censorship in America. Yet every war has produced censorship in one form or another. The possibility of partial military mobilization over long periods of time holds the threat of at least partial censorship in some areas. This is a problem that will require serious attention in future years.

Libel laws are a means of self-defense for individuals and groups who feel they have been seriously hurt by statements concerning them made through some channel of communication. The Commission on Freedom of the Press criticized present libel proceedings as "expensive, difficult, and encumbered with technicalities," and therefore proposed, as an alternative, "legislation by which the injured party might obtain a retraction or a restatement of the facts by the offender or an opportunity to reply." [30] The Commission also in-

[27] *Federal Communications Commission's revised ruling* (1 *June*, 1949) *in the matter of Editorializing by Broadcast Licensees* (FCC-49-769 36009).

[28] J. B. S. Hardman, in Harold L. Ickes (ed.), "Freedom of the Press Today" (New York: Vanguard, 1941), pp. 130–131.

[29] Commission on Freedom of the Press, "Government and Mass Communications," Vol. 2, p. 696.

[30] "A Free and Responsible Press," pp. 86–87.

dicated its opposition to proposals that have been made in various states for group libel laws, insisting that libel actions should be confined to civil suits brought by individuals who can prove that they were specifically damaged by false statements. Otherwise, according to the Commission, libel laws could be used to suppress legitimate public controversy among various social groupings.

Government Communication Activities. The most direct form of government participation in communication activities is the conversion of a communication industry into a government monopoly. In England, for example, the British Broadcasting Company, a government corporation, owns and operates the radio broadcasting facilities of the country.

In the United States nothing so far-reaching has been seriously proposed. Outside the radio industry, not even limited forms of Government operation have been suggested. In radio the only serious approach toward Government-owned radio stations for domestic broadcasting has been made by Jerome Spingarn who proposes that the Government establish three stations which would set yardsticks by which to judge private stations.[31]

Government informational activities represent the most effective and acceptable form of direct communication on the part of the government. For the most part, these activities use the established channels of communication; the only major production facility owned by the Government is the Government Printing Office, which produces a wealth of specialized literature that is generally noncompetitive with commercial newspapers and magazines. The Commission on Freedom of the Press favored activities of this sort as a method through which government could improve the level of communications.

We recommend that the government, through the media of mass communication, inform the public of the facts with respect to its policies and that, to the extent that private agencies of mass communications are unable or unwilling to supply such media to the government, the government itself may employ media of its own.[32]

THEIR PARTICIPATION IN GOVERNMENT [33]

Since private organizations play an inescapable role in the processes of government, the question is sometimes raised as to whether or not they should be given a more directly recognized type of participation. The geographical basis of representation in Congress, it is pointed out, is not capable of reflect-

[31] Spingarn, "Is Your Radio On Now?" *Ladies' Home Journal,* May, 1948, p. 61.

[32] "A Free and Responsible Press," pp. 88–89.

[33] For general material on this subject, see the following: Avery Leiserson, "Administration Regulation" (Chicago: University of Chicago Press, 1942) ; Lewis Lorwin, "Advisory Economic Councils" (Washington, D.C.: Brookings Institution, 1931) ; and Fritz Nova, "Functional Representation" (Dubuque, Iowa: Wm. C. Brown, 1950).

ing the multiple interests of a highly differentiated society. It is therefore
suggested that the extralegal structure of private organizations, particularly
those representing national economic interests, should be incorporated in some
manner into the structure and processes of government, either by placing private groups or their representatives in positions of formal power or casting
them in advisory roles.

Positions of Formal Power

Here one finds an interesting combination of totally impractical ideas
for the reconstruction of government as well as ideas firmly grounded in the
practicalities of power politics.

On the impractical side are various proposals—more frequently offered in
other countries, less frequently in America—for organizing Congress, or at
least one house of Congress, along economic, rather than geographical, lines.[34]
One such proposal suggests that for a state with 6,000,000 population and 20
seats in the House of Representatives, the members of the House might be
selected from economic groups in the following manner: [35]

Category	Population	No. of Members
Agriculture	2,100,000	7
Mining	600,000	2
Manufacturing	1,500,000	5
Transportation	300,000	1
Retail distribution	600,000	2
Professional service	600,000	2
Public service and utilities	300,000	1
	6,000,000	20

Other proposals, more along the lines of the corporate state theories used
by the theorists of Italian Fascism during the 1920's and 1930's, would supplement the present structure of Congress with a new body set up along functional lines. Inspired by the NRA experience, one writer envisions the creation
of a "commonwealth of industry" based upon the trade associations as the unit
of organization. The many units would then be organized into six supertrade
associations. Each would send two representatives to a National Economic
Council. With this structure we could then have self-government by industry,
with far less intervention and control by the Government than under the
NRA.[36] Another writer proposes a system of Federal charters for trade, pro-

[34] For a general discussion of proposals of this type see William A. Hobson, "Functional
Representation," *Encyclopaedia of the Social Sciences,* Vol. 6, pp. 518–520.

[35] Harvey Walker, "Legislative Process; Lawmaking in the United States" (New York:
Ronald, 1948), p. 134.

[36] Benjamin A. Javits, "The Commonwealth of Industry" (New York: Harper, 1936),
passim.

fessional, labor, farm, and consumer organizations. "These autonomous legal entities will have elected in a democratic manner several hundred delegates to a Supreme Council that shall have been permanently established in Washington to cooperate with the President and Congress in making social and economic plans to govern our society. . . ." [37]

There have also been various proposals for bringing conflicting economic groups directly into individual agencies of government. "The principal groups in our free society should get together to solve their mutually dependent problems instead of either neglecting them or leaving them to a centrally constituted governmental bureaucracy to try and solve." [38] This philosophy, varied at times by leaders of some segments of organized labor, is developed in more specific terms in the industry council plan which Philip Murray submitted to President Roosevelt in behalf of the Congress of Industrial Organizations in December, 1940.[39] Under this plan defense mobilization would be put under the direction of a "National Defense Board" consisting of an equal number of representatives of industry and labor unions, over which the President or his designee would be the chairman. The major administrative agencies would be industry councils representing management and organized labor in each industry, with a government representative to serve as chairman.

In discussions of such proposals, the technical difficulties in setting up a system of this type are usually pointed out. "The principal difficulty would be the determination of the action to be taken in cases of divided economic interest. . . . Divided residence is rare. Divided economic loyalties would not be unusual." [40] On a more substantive level, Key refers to "the anarchy of groups that would arise with the delegation of public authority to private associations." [41]

Among the more workable proposals are those that arise when the functions of government are being extended into areas previously handled by private groups, particularly in time of national emergency. Such proposals often call for some method of fusion between these groups and the Government. This can be done through "delegating" powers to a private association, making the private group a quasi-government agency, or placing its representatives at key positions in the Government.

A special approach is the formal participation of opposing groups within the governing body of an agency. During both World War II and the mobilization program following the invasion of Korea in 1950, it was felt that much

---

[37] Michael O'Shaughnessey, "Economic Democracy and Private Enterprise" (New York: Harper, 1945), pp. 38–39.

[38] Clinton S. Golden and Harold J. Ruttenberg, "The Dynamics of Industrial Democracy" (New York: Harper, 1942), pp. 329–330.

[39] *Ibid.*, pp. 343–347.

[40] Walker, "The Legislative Process" (New York: Ronald, 1948), p. 135.

[41] Key, *op. cit.*, p. 149.

was to be gained by bringing the management-labor bargaining process directly into the structure of the Government. This was done by setting up tripartite boards to develop wage policies and handle labor disputes. These boards consisted of labor representatives, business representatives, and public members who served as mediators between the other members. This approach has the effect of maintaining or strengthening the power of the private groups involved, which is why it is so frequently advocated by business and professional organizations. It also supplies the Government with skilled and experienced manpower and an opportunity to avoid head-on conflicts with certain powerful groups. This is the reason why it is frequently welcomed by Government.

Advisory Positions

"Could representatives of the more important occupational and cultural groups," asks Galloway, "be brought together in some council or federation which would provide a forum for the reconciliation of inter-group controversies and advise Congress on their areas of agreement?" [42]

Proposals for advisory councils bringing together the representatives of divergent groups have enjoyed a remarkably wide vogue. In fact, proposals of this type have probably been as frequent in America as proposals for thoroughgoing functional representation systems have been in other countries. One of the earliest was offered by Senator Robert M. La Follette of Wisconsin who, in 1931, introduced legislation that would have set up a National Economic Council. The Council would have been composed of 15 persons appointed by the President from lists submitted by industrial, financial, agricultural, transportation, and labor organizations. A similar proposal was advanced by Senator Bulkley of Ohio in 1935. In subsequent years the idea received recurring support from national leaders who hoped that some such device would ameliorate the pushing and pulling among divergent groups. It was given a prominent place among the conclusions reached by the chairman of the Temporary National Economic Committee.[43]

In 1944 in the War Mobilization and Reconversion Act, a national group of this type was finally established. The War Mobilization and Reconversion Board was composed of three leaders of farm groups, three leaders of labor groups, three businessmen, and three representatives of the public at large. In actual practice, many of the high hopes held out for such an agency were frustrated. First of all, since its deliberations took place behind closed doors, as they necessarily had to be, the Board's activities did little or nothing to bring private pressures out into the open. Second, it was found while the members

[42] George Galloway, "Congress at the Crossroads" (New York: Crowell, 1946), p. 309.
[43] Final print of the TNEC, Mar. 31, 1941, p. 48.

might at times agree when recommending policies to adjust competing interests, they often failed to obtain the support of their organizations. Third, by the time the Board expired in 1947, many of its members had wearied of attending meetings. By and large, its experience showed that the best to be expected from such a group was an opportunity to exchange information on current problems and test reactions to possible solutions.

Another function for groups of this type is suggested by the following quotation from one of the most irreverent and penetrating analysts of governmental processes:

Where a separate institution has arisen in order to represent an ideal by separating it from the practical situation, it is never able to reach any conclusion leading to practical action. Its failure to reach such a conclusion is part of its function because the debate convinces everyone that nothing could be done about the practical situation without further study and prayer.[44]

Proposals are always being made that private organizations take part in advisory operations in connection with *individual fields* of government activity. But in such cases there is rarely any thought that by so doing the role of private groups in the processes of government can somehow be improved. Rather, advisory committees of one sort or another are recognized as an invaluable method of organizing support for specific projects. From the point of view of the private groups that take part they are recognized as a potential device for enhancing a group's status and power and wielding more decisive influence upon governmental decisions. In fact, many a so-called "advisory committee" has been the real locus of power in governmental operations. Hence, proposals to place private groups in advisory positions are frequently adopted as a normal part of both the administrative and legislative processes of government rather than as techniques of reform and improvement.

Avery Leiserson has offered an interesting set of conditions to govern interest-group representation in executive agencies:

Generally three preconditions may be stated as necessary adjuncts to any plan providing for representation of organized groups. There should be an independence of administrative initiative which serves as a compelling incentive for affected groups to co-operate. Second, either through the terms of the grant of authority or in specific declarations of policy, the statute should make it clear that administrative responsibility is wider in scope than any one group interest. Third, administrative officials should be able to calculate consequences of particular group proposals and to secure modifications of these proposals if necessary so that they will be acceptable to other groups. Obviously this concept of administrative ability includes the capacity of persuading particular interests to appreciate the necessity of accepting and conforming

[44] Thurman Arnold, "The Folklore of Capitalism" (New York: New York University Press, 1937), p. 363.

to a positive program of public welfare, which almost inevitably embodies something other than the groups' original demands.[45]

Whether in formal or in advisory capacities, the private organizations will continue to have a major influence upon governmental and legislative action. They will continue to campaign in behalf of their conceptions of their own and the public interest. As agreements and disagreements unfold among these private groups so will the proposals for reforming their behavior and limiting their choices. At times these proposals will be weapons in the armories of distinct groups; less often they will transcend all lesser group interests in order that the larger community may survive.

[45] Leiserson, *op. cit.*, pp. 284–285.

Chapter 4

THE POLITICAL PARTIES

POLITICAL parties in America [1] have never been entirely respectable. In his famous farewell address, George Washington warned against "the baneful effects" and "horrid enormities" of the party spirit. We still hear about the "mire of party politics." "Nonpartisan" is usually used as a term of approval, in contrast with the evils of partisanship. "Politician" is a term of disapproval, and a "statesman," in the words of Speaker "Uncle Joe" Cannon, is a politician who has been dead a long time. According to Schattschneider, so many writers have explained democracy, sovereignty, laws, constitutions, suffrage, representation, liberty, and so on, without reference to parties, that the parties at one time became "the orphans of political philosophy." [2]

Yet parties have always been with us. In the prerevolution days the colonial leaders divided into Whigs and Tories, much along the same lines as in England. Washington's condemnation of parties was sound Whig doctrine. The revolution against the British was organized by party formations. The Committees of Correspondence, organized under the lead of the Virginia House of Burgesses, were the predecessors of our state central committees. [3] At the Constitutional Convention and throughout the bitter struggle over ratification, rival party groups were already emerging. In subsequent years they

substantially abolished the electoral college, created a plebiscitary presidency and contributed greatly to the extra-constitutional growth of that office. . . . As the political entrepreneurs who have mobilized and organized the dynamic forces of American

[1] For basic material on political parties see Wilfred E. Binkley, "American Political Parties" (New York: Knopf, 1947); Committee on Political Parties, American Political Science Association, "Toward a More Responsible Two-party System," *American Political Science Review*, Vol. 44, No. 3, Part II, Supplement, September, 1950; Pendleton Herring, "The Politics of Democracy" (New York: Rinehart, 1940); Arthur N. Holcombe, "Our More Perfect Union" (Cambridge, Mass.: Harvard University Press, 1950), Chaps. 4 and 5; V. O. Key, Jr., "Parties, Politics and Pressure Groups" (New York: Crowell, 1947); E. M. Sait, "American Parties and Elections" (New York: Appleton-Century-Crofts; rev. ed. by Penniman, 1948); E. E. Schattschneider, "Party Government" (New York: Rinehart, 1942).

[2] Schattschneider, *op. cit.*, p. 10.

[3] Henry Jones Ford, "The Rise and Growth of American Politics" (New York: Macmillan, 1898), p. 8.

public life, these parties have presided over the transformation of the government of the United States from a small experiment in republicanism to the most powerful regime on earth, vastly more liberal and democratic than it was in 1789. They have supervised or adapted themselves to the conquest of a continent, the transformation of the economic system, the absorption of the largest immigrant population in the history of the world, a series of economic crises, and the rise of the modern administrative state, to mention only a few of the developments in which the parties have participated.[4]

ORGANIZATION AND ACTIVITIES

Who They Are

It is easy for anyone to make a list of the political parties in America. The two major parties, Democratic and Republican, and the more widely advertised minor parties, Communist and Socialist, come quickly to mind. By glancing at a local ballot or reading the papers at the time of a Presidential election, one can pick up the names of lesser-known minor parties. But knowing the names of the parties tells us very little about them. To find out who the parties really are, one must discover what groups of people comprise them, how these groups differ from other social groupings, and how they differ among themselves.

A popular conception of a political party is that it is made up of all voters who participate in a party primary or support a party candidate. The leaders who comprise the party organization—or "machine"—are merely the agents of the party voters. This concept is actively promoted by party leaders, much as the managers of a large corporation often promote the idea that their corporation is really the property of widows, orphans, and everyone else who owns a share of stock. Yet, as Schattschneider has pointed out, this is precisely what parties are not.

Whatever else the parties may be, they are not associations of voters who support the party candidate. That is to say, the Democratic party is not an association of the twenty-seven million people who voted for Mr. Roosevelt in November, 1940. To describe the party as if it were this sort of association of voters is to produce confusion, and, moreover, to be victimized by a promotional device so old that it should deceive no one. The concept of the parties as a mass association of partisans has no historical basis and has little relation to the facts of party organization. . . . Would it not be to our advantage to abandon the whole concept of party membership, the mental image of the party as an association of all partisans, and to recognize frankly that the party is the property of the "organization"? [5]

The major party organizations are built along similar lines. Each is a cluster or confederation of separate organizations. The most numerous of these are

[4] Schattschneider, op. cit.
[5] Ibid., pp. 53–54, 61.

local party groups organized on a geographical basis to conform to the pattern of local governmental units. State groups are made up of the leaders of the local machine. These groups are invariably made up of officeholders, would-be officeholders, and individuals hoping for other forms of personal benefit from their labors on behalf of the organization. The formal structure of local and state groups consists of an intricate network of geographical committees and of party clubs and societies. The actual control is more apt to be found in the hands of a small informal group. Invariably there is a leader—the "boss" —who may or may not have a formal position in the party and who may be a local or state official, a member of Congress, or a completely nonofficial power. The essence of control is the power to pick the party candidate for office. Since the growth of the primary system (which is essentially a method of resolving differences between opposing groups seeking control of the party organization), this has come to mean the power to mobilize sufficient votes in party primaries.

The local and state machines, which are the basic party units, come together in various national groups. First, there is a national committee which is a loose alliance of state and local leaders brought together to perform certain functions with respect to the Presidential elections. Second, there are party organizations in the Senate and House respectively: caucuses or conferences, steering committees and policy committees, party leaders and whips, and congressional campaign committees. These organizations, composed of members of Congress whose political roots are found in local and state organizations, assign party members to committees, consult on the legislative agenda and on legislative policy, and work on campaigns for reelection to Congress.

In the case of the Administration party, there is a third element in the cluster, namely, the President and his associates. The President, by virtue of the powers of office, is invariably the leader of his party. He can hand-pick the chairman of the national committee and run the national office as his personal organization. Depending upon circumstances, he can exercise varying degrees of influence on the local and state party organizations and on the party organizations in Congress. In the case of the anti-Administration party, the Presidential candidate defeated in the last election is called the "titular leader." But the title has little meaning, and leadership is apt to be divided among the local and state organizations and the Senate and House leaders. In both parties, all the various clusters are brought together every four years in a National Convention for the purpose of selecting candidates for President and Vice-President.

Organizationally, the minor parties differ from the major parties in that they usually have a single national body which exercises firm control over its entire operations. This is a corollary of the fact that their local organizations are extremely weak and are seldom able to elect local or state officials or members of Congress.

Many organizations that are called parties scarcely merit the name. Note V. O. Key's description of the Democratic party's organizations in the South:

. . . the Democratic party in most states of the South is merely a holding-company for a congeries of transient squabbling factions, most of which fail by far to meet the standards of permanence, cohesiveness, and responsibility that characterize the political party. The restriction of all significant political choices in the South to the Democratic primaries enables the South to maintain its constancy to Democratic presidential candidates, but it has not enabled the South to maintain social groupings equivalent to political parties within the Democratic party. In the conduct of campaigns for the control of legislatures, for the control of governorships, and for representatives in the national Congress, the South must depend for political leadership, not on political parties, but on lone-wolf operators, on fortuitous groupings of individuals usually of a transient nature, on spectacular demagogues odd enough to command the attention of considerable numbers of voters, on men who have become persons of political consequence in their own little bailiwicks, and on other types of leaders whose methods to attract electoral attention serve as substitutes for leadership of a party organization.[6]

Parties, Private Organizations, and Government Agencies

How do parties differ from private associations and government agencies? This question cannot be answered without first understanding how much they resemble these other groups. Viewed from one perspective, the parties are themselves private associations closely allied with other associations whose interests they represent in one way or another and from whom they derive indispensable support. Viewed from the perspective of their role in manning the key positions in government, they can be regarded as part of the government structure itself. In fact, the people who man the parties are largely the leaders of other private organizations and of government agencies, plus a certain amount of specialized party personnel who make the machinery run. Nor is the existence of machines and bosses and the use of patronage and other favors anything peculiar to parties. No organization, including private associations and government agencies, can be effective without the development of machines and bosses of some sort or can be held together without the ability to provide specific benefits to its supporters.

The most distinguishing function of a party organization is that it serves as a vehicle for winning or maintaining control of the key positions in government through participation in the electoral process. Whether the purpose of winning control is to obtain personal advantage or to carry out certain policies is not particularly relevant; in fact, both motives are usually insepa-

[6] V. O. Key, Jr., "Southern Politics in State and Nation" (New York: Knopf, 1949), p. 16.

rably entwined. The important thing is that the group needs to select the persons who occupy the key positions. To achieve this objective, party organizations engage in two kinds of activity. First of all, they nominate candidates. Schattschneider regards the nominating process as the most important activity of the party. Although other groups influence the nominating process, it is the nomination of candidates that brings a party together more than anything else.

The nomination may be made by a congressional caucus, a delegate convention, a mass meeting, a cabal, an individual, or a party election. The test is, does it bind? Not, how was it done? Unless the party makes authoritative and effective nominations, it cannot stay in business, for dual or multiple party candidacies mean certain defeat. As far as elections are concerned, the united front of the party, the party concentration of numbers, can be brought about only by a binding nomination. The nominating process thus has become the crucial process of the party.[7]

Second, parties play a specialized role in campaigning for candidates. They do not monopolize political campaigns, for the campaign activities of business, labor, and farm groups often dwarf the activities of party organizations. But they do supply the basic machinery through which other groups take part in election campaigns; they do provide an organization which is interested more in the electoral process than anything else; and they do provide a connective tissue that brings electoral considerations into the processes of government between elections.

Parties, of course, are not the only groups interested in winning or maintaining control of the key positions in government. The leaders of the most powerful and ambitious private organizations have similar objectives. But they seek to fulfill this by working in cooperation with party groups, particularly in matters relating to elections. The fact that they may control a party, or even two parties, does not mean that they themselves have become parties. They would become parties only if they converted their own organizations into vehicles for seeking power rather than using a specialized organization for this purpose. This is rarely done. In England, for example, where organized labor provides the basic support for the Labour party, there is a clear organizational distribution between the Trade Union Congress and the Labour party. In America the purpose of the various political organizations set up by the A.F.L. and the C.I.O. is to influence and support the activities of party organizations rather than to supplant them.

Despite their conflicts, the parties have numerous common characteristics. First, all parties that unite to work in terms of political power develop a community of interest among the members of the party organization. They become self-help societies oriented toward achieving major personal advantage for the leaders and minor personal advantage for the rank and file. It is this

[7] Schattschneider, *op. cit.*, p. 64.

factor which makes the party always something more than a mere representative of other groups and interests.

Second, any party that is interested in winning majority support throughout the country must appeal to a wide variety of competing groups and interests. In a sense, it must try to become all things to all men. The local groups must give representation to the interests that are strongest locally. Nationally, it must find means of accommodating local party groups with divergent interests and outside support from divergent interests.

Third, there is always a strong tendency for nonparty organizations to work through competing parties. By so doing they can achieve their objectives better, no matter which party wins out. Finally, there are many areas of the country where, by reason of historical traditions and economic and social structure, there is only one party which ever has much of a chance to win elections. In those areas, competing groups all tend to work through the dominant party, thus contributing to intraparty diversity and interparty similarity. All these forces militate against any black-and-white differences between the major parties and tend to make the major point of variance the fact that one is made up of "ins" and the others of "outs."

Yet the contrast between the two major parties in America has rarely been simply one of "ins" versus "outs." The two major parties have never been based upon an identical combination of groups and interests. At times the major differences have been merely reflections of divergent sectional and national interests among business groups or among agricultural groups. At other times. depending upon the changing character of American society and upon the political strategy adopted by group leaders, the differences have been more striking. When Jefferson's Republican party was waging its campaign against the Federalists, the conflict was mainly between agricultural and business interests. In recent years, with the growing strength of organized labor, the business interests are finding their best expression through the modern Republican party and the labor interests through the Democratic party. In both cases, however, it would be a great oversimplification to define the opposing parties in terms of single competing interests. There were certain agricultural groups supporting the Federalists and there are certain labor groups supporting the Republicans today. No party can be properly identified except in terms of a complete analysis of the various groups and subgroups from which it derives support. Moreover, such an analysis must be made not only in terms of business, agriculture, and labor but also in terms of all the other groups and interests into which the people of the country are divided.[8]

[8] As examples of detailed analyses of the group bases of political parties see Charles A. Beard, "The Economic Origins of Jeffersonian Democracy" (New York: Macmillan, 1916) ; Arthur N. Holcombe, "Political Parties of Today" (New York: Harper, 1924) ; and Key, "Politics, Parties and Pressure Groups," Chap. 9.

Their Legislative Activities

One of the minor myths about American government centers around the role of political parties in the legislative process. Each party, so the story goes, formulates the principles to which it is devoted and selects candidates to carry these principles to the people at election time. The people then decide by majority vote which party is to be entrusted with the reins of government. The victorious party, with a popular mandate behind it, is then responsible for putting its program into action. On the legislative front, the ties of party loyalty, supported by disciplinary measures, bridge the separation between the Presidency and the Congress and bring the two into cooperative action to carry out party policies. If these policies are not carried out, it is because the party leaders have blundered or because they were never really sincere in their campaign pledges. When the next elections roll around, the opposing parties once again present their case to the people and once again the people make their choice.

The presentation of party policy is just not this simple. Party candidates appeal to voters not only in terms of policy but also in terms of their personalities—their winsome smile, their family life, their sense of humor, and goodfellowship. When they deal with policies, neither candidate nor platforms can, in the very nature of things, cover the entire gamut of major legislative issues, deal with the detailed intricacies of any of them, anticipate the new issues that may arise between elections, or separate the national from the local or the international. They must necessarily deal mainly in abstract terms which, depending on one's point of view, may be regarded as "fundamental principles" or "glittering generalities." [9] Even apart from the problem of vagueness and ambiguity, there is the problem of conflicting commitments. Presidential candidates often take positions that differ from the national platform on which they run. The national platform is not regarded as binding upon candidates for Congress, who may refuse to support certain provisions or directly oppose them. At mid-term elections, the major parties have not been accustomed to the promulgation of national platforms, and each candidate for the House or Senate is even more on his own. Most candidates make private commitments that are never publicly broadcast and may, either directly or through unofficial spokesmen, make contradictory commitments to conflicting groups.

The electoral process is not this simple either. Millions of citizens of vot-

[9] A perfect example is the following plank in the Republican party platform of 1944: "We pledge the establishment by Federal legislation of a permanent Fair Employment Practices Commission." This sounded like a clear-cut, unqualified commitment. However, when legislation to establish a Fair Employment Practices Commission came up in Congress shortly after the 1944 election, it became evident that one of the major issues in this area was not whether such a commission should be established but rather whether such a commission should have regulatory powers or confine itself instead to educational activities.

ing age stay away from the polls. In 1940, 1944, and 1948, the percentage of potential voters, twenty-one years of age and over, who voted in the Presidential elections was, respectively, 62, 56, and 54. One reason for the stay-at-homes is apathy—as evidenced by the fact that the figures for the congressional elections of 1942, 1946, and 1950, when the excitement of a national campaign was lacking, were still lower: 34, 39, and 43. Another reason is found in the many barriers that still exist between the people and the polls. These range from poll taxes, discriminatory literacy tests, and threats of violence against Negroes to onerous residence and registration requirements, polling places that are open for an insufficient number of hours or are geographically inaccessible, and inadequate absentee provisions.

Furthermore, each vote actually cast is not given equal weight. This is not merely a matter of the use of fraudulent and corrupt practices, which seem to be a persistent, though immeasurable, part of the political scene. By constitutional requirement, two Senators are elected in each state regardless of population. The districts from which members of the House of Representatives are elected are of varying size and are frequently gerrymandered to distort the actual vote. Presidents are elected not by popular vote but by the antiquated electoral-college system which can at times give the Presidency to a candidate with less than the greatest number of popular votes and which on all occasions gives extra weight to every vote cast in the "doubtful states." Finally, there are many areas of the country in which one party is so strong that there are really no election contests worth the name. In some of these areas, one-party control of the elections is duplicated in the party primaries, where one party group dictates the party candidates, and opposition in the primaries by competing groups is usually futile.

Thirdly, the parties seldom have full hold upon the reins of the Government. One party may win the Presidency but lose out in the Senate or the House of Representatives. At mid-term elections the opposition party may win a majority in Congress, or in one house, without even getting a chance to capture the White House. If a party has nominal control of both the White House and the Congress, there is still the possibility that a majority of the members of the Supreme Court may declare its legislation unconstitutional. But these are merely the more obvious obstructions to party control. Of much greater significance is the fact that formal party control—even though it may cover all branches of the Federal government, including the Supreme Court—is often merely a façade behind which one finds bitterly antagonistic groups and interests. In recent years, for example, the Democratic party has had formal control of the Government, and again and again we have seen Democratic Presidents, both Roosevelt and Truman, go in one direction on major legislative issues, while Congress, controlled by a coalition of conservative Republicans and Democrats, has gone in another direction. Under such circumstances, within Congress itself, party leadership is also weak. "Steering committees seldom meet and never steer," generalized ex-Senator James Byrnes.[10] When policy committees meet, the Senate and House groups may move in opposite directions—as in 1946 when the Senate Policy Committee approved the Wagner-Ellender-Taft Housing Bill and the House Republicans fought it. The chairman and ranking members of legislative committees reach their positions of power through seniority and are neither responsible to, nor necessarily a part of, party leadership. Party caucuses or conferences invariably reveal deep splits on legislative issues among a party's members. Hence, they are only infrequently convened on matters of policy; when they are, decisions are seldom regarded as binding.[11]

In the great majority of legislative struggles the major parties are observers on the side lines. When attempts are made to enroll them as combatants, they prove adept at preserving their neutrality. If drawn in momentarily, the next moment they may be back on the side lines. When they really get into a legislative struggle, it is usually at an advanced stage in combat, rarely before the battle positions of conflicting contestants have been crystallized. Sometimes a tacit bipartisan understanding yields a party battle staged like a professional wrestling match. Spokesmen for opposing parties will grunt and groan through a series of phony routines, applying holds that are dramatic to the spectators in the gallery but harmful to nobody and ending up with a preordained finale. Most "bipartisan" policies, moreover, are nothing of the sort. Instead of being agreements reached on the basis of negotiations between authorized representatives of the two parties and ratified by appropriate party organs, they are usually policies on which at least one party has officially taken no position, and on which there has never been any official party negotiations. They are bipartisan only in the sense that they are supported by individuals in both parties.

[10] James L. Byrnes, "Streamlining Congress," *The American Magazine,* February, 1945.

[11] Statistical interpretations of party loyalty in terms of congressional votes can be very misleading. The line-up on floor votes often fails completely to indicate the actual influences brought to bear by members of Congress, particularly in committees. (See discussion in Chap. 18.) Nevertheless, statistical tabulations on "party loyalty" are constantly being attempted. For example, see the *Congressional Quarterly,* which publishes its own party-loyalty tabulation for important issues at every congressional session; Key, "Southern Politics in State and Nation," Chaps. 16 and 17, on Senate and House voting behavior of Southern Democrats, non-Southern Democrats, and Republicans; Robert A. Dahl, "Congress and Foreign Policy" (New York: Harcourt, Brace, 1950), pp. 45–50; Julius Turner, "Responsible Parties: A Dissent from the Floor," *American Political Science Review,* Vol. 45, No. 1, March, 1951; and—an incisive analysis by an extremely competent newspaperman— Richard Strout, "The Elephant, the Donkey and the Tariff," *Christian Science Monitor,* Sept. 17, 1949 (Magazine), p. 5. The earliest systematic study of this sort was prepared by A. L. Lowell, "The Influence of Party upon Legislation in England and America," *Annual Report of American Historical Association,* 1901, Vol. 1.

It would be a great mistake, however, to come to the conclusion that the political parties have no role in the legislative struggle. They always have a certain role, no matter how limited. The party organization always provides a certain degree of connective tissue among the party leaders and followers in Congress, the executive branch, and the Federal courts. Some legislative matters become genuine party issues. On many legislative matters the struggle between divergent party factions becomes a crucial part of the legislative process. In nominating candidates, the parties select a small group of men from whom key contestants in the legislative struggle will be drawn, thereby defining the choices that are submitted to the voters. If these men sometimes appeal for votes mainly on the basis of character, charm, and other personal traits, it is nevertheless true that there is no sharp line to be drawn between personality and policy. The nomination of a solid, stolid candidate with a safe-and-sane family and religious background is often merely another way of entering a campaign on the basis of safe-and-sane, standpat conservatism. The drafting of party platforms is part of the push-and-pull process that lines up the conflicting forces in the legislative process. The inclusion of a specific legislative objective in a major party platform can give crucial impetus to a legislative campaign. Inclusion in a minor party platform often serves as a trial balloon for ideas that are subsequently taken over by a major party.

Although elections are a far cry from legislative referenda, they unquestionably have legislative implications. While they never comprise all the elements that are weighed, they always tilt the legislative scales in one direction or another—if only in the direction of speed as opposed to sluggishness. The conduct of electoral campaigns is itself a method of organizing people into groups. From the viewpoint of group structure it is one of the lowest forms of organization, just a few notches above the organization of participants in a parade or of customers for a certain brand of cigarettes or breakfast cereal. From the viewpoint of the group struggle, however, it is a far more important operation, one which has come to be identified with democratic government itself. It not only brings divergent groups together for the purpose of pooling their resources for mutual advantage, but also opens up the processes of government to under-represented interests. Electoral campaigns are a method of organizing the unorganized. Just as the advertising firm that seeks a mass market for a cigarette or breakfast cereal cannot be content with merely keeping present customers, the political party conducting an election campaign must seek to organize the support of those who have been inactive, undecided, or even followers of a rival party.

It would also be a mistake to think that any one description can precisely describe the legislative role of the political parties. At any one time, there may be stronger party control in one house and weaker party control in the other, stronger party control within one party and weaker within the other. At one time, the role of the parties may be relatively unimportant; at another it may become exceedingly important. The factors that determine these variations are the economic, social, and cultural development of the country, the diverse changing interests of the American people, and the manner in which these interests are organized by the leaders not only of the political parties but also of the private associations and government agencies.

THE PARTY "SYSTEM"

A discussion of party "systems" can be extremely misleading if it gives the impression that we can legislate or otherwise decree a "one-party system" or a "two-party system" into being. The number of parties that operate in any area, their role in government, and the differences between them—these are the result of group conflicts, social traditions, and the strategy and tactics used by the various participants in the social struggle.

Ideas concerning the kind of party system that is desirable are understandably influenced by one's substantive goals in life and one's ideas concerning the best methods of attaining these goals. Those who are satisfied with governmental policies and their own position in the power structure will tend to be more or less satisfied with whatever party line-up exists. Those who want to "change the world" or "get ahead in the world" are apt to think differently. As Holcombe aptly observes: "There will always be ambitious politicians and discontented factions watchfully waiting for opportunities to break up the established factional combinations and bring about a new alignment of the major parties in which their own prospects of influence would be greater." [12]

The Number of Parties

The simplest way to discuss the number of parties that may be regarded as desirable is to start with zero and move up the line to one-party domination, the two-party system, and a multiparty setup.

No Parties. The idea that we should have no parties at all was rather strongly presented early in American history by the Federalists. This, however, is merely another way of saying that the dominant political group at that time looked with disfavor upon the development of a strong opposition. Both among the Founding Fathers and their Whig counterparts in England, the most vocal opponents of parties as such were members of a dominant group which developed the habit of attacking opposing groups on the ground that they were fomenting partisanship.

In many local communities in America there has developed a "nonpartisan" approach to local politics. The nonpartisan theory is that local elections should

[12] Holcombe, *op. cit.,* p. 145.

be fought strictly on the basis of the ability of the rival candidates and not by parties as such. At times, however, this point of view becomes an attack on national parties, with some recognition of the partisan functions of local private organizations. Usually a nonpartisan movement is strong where the "nonpartisans" have developed an organization, loose though it may be, which is essentially a local party and which has probably developed an alliance with the weaker of the established parties as a means of beating the dominant or formerly dominant "machine."

In some communities, the nomination of local candidates by the local wings of the national parties is prohibited by law, an arrangement which is ardently sought by many nonpartisans. If such prohibitions effectively eliminated party candidates, they would in fact confer a political monopoly on the nonpartisan organizations and create a local one-party system. In practice, however, the regular parties take part in supposedly nonpartisan elections by informally sponsoring candidates and by entering into all sorts of alliances and understandings with other groups and factions.

The opponents of nonpartisanship at the local level charge that it introduces an anarchic note into local government and that it weakens the two-party system nationally. The proponents maintain that nonpartisan local officials can be just as responsible as party representatives and that the national two-party system is not affected, and may even be strengthened, by local nonpartisanship. The specific character of the influence upon national parties varies substantially from one community to another.

One-party. If the idea of no parties has been frequently talked about but never carried into practice, the idea of one-party domination has often been carried into practice but—in America at least—is rarely advocated. Even in the one-party states and congressional districts, those who benefit from and participate in the quasi monopoly enjoyed by the dominant party usually talk glibly about the virtues of a two-party system and justify such a position by pointing out that a second party, weak though it may be, exists. Or else they claim that internal conflicts over the nomination of candidates by the dominant party sometimes approach the dimensions of two-party conflict.

The most open defense of a one-party system comes from the Russians. One of the leading Soviet theorists, G. F. Aleksandrov, argues first that in capitalist countries such as the United States or in England the major parties "do not differ in principle on many quite important contemporary questions." Hence, there is really no genuine two-party system in these countries. Secondly, he argues that under a two-party system, each party really tries to obtain all the elected posts held by the opposition. The only reason two-party systems persist is that neither party has succeeded in carrying out its objectives. The Communist party of the Soviet Union has merely succeeded in doing what the bourgeois parties in England and the United States have tried to do but without success.[13]

The answer to this argument, of course, is that in neither England nor the United States has either party tried to suppress its rivals through the use of force and violence, as the Communist party has done in Russia. In both countries, moreover, there are matters on which the two major parties disagree as well as matters on which they agree.

One-party domination can mean one of three things. It can mean a social structure in which the dominant group has few rivals of any importance and power. It can reflect the suppression of political competition and rivalry through trickery, disenfranchisement, or open violence. It can serve as a façade for inner-party conflict which develops to the point where it may at times become almost as meaningful as direct competition between rival parties.[14]

Two-party. The two-party system is one of the most revered of all the sacred cows in American thought. The defense of the two-party system has become an emotional undertaking akin to the protection of the Constitution and the home. This emotion is based upon the solid interest of party leaders who oppose the formation of new parties which might split their own support rather than that of their rivals. It is also based upon conservative opposition to the radical ideas often associated with the minor parties. Some of the most vocal defenders of the two-party system are those who are active leaders of the dominant party in states where there is no meaningful opposition to one-party domination. Under these circumstances the second party often becomes a useful tool and ally of the top-dog party. From the liberal standpoint, too, there is good reason to support the idea of a two-party system so long as it provides an instrument for carrying liberal ideas into action through a political party capable of winning not only the Presidency but also a genuine liberal majority in Congress.

Perhaps the most forcibly presented argument in favor of the two-party system stems from the manageable number of leadership alternatives that it presents for selection by the electorates. The "yes-no" range of choice thus provided is generally about all that millions of voters can handle effectively by way of the ballot box. Two parties, rooted as they are in single-district systems of representation operating on the "winner-take-all" principle, are also

[13] G. F. Aleksandrov, "The Pattern of Soviet Democracy" (Washington, D.C.: Public Affairs Press, 1948), pp. 22ff.

[14] "One-party states, however, vary in the degree to which their factual systems approach the nature of a two-party system. North Carolina, for example, is in reality quite as much a two-party state as some non-southern states, while Arkansas and South Carolina present examples of one-party factionalism in almost pure form. . . ." Key, "Southern Politics in State and Nation," p. 299. The chapter from which this quotation is taken (pp. 298–311) provides a penetrating analysis of this entire subject.

supposed to absorb some of the more disruptive shocks of intergroup political strife as a result of their tendency to limit these choices and of their need to be broadly representative of the population as a whole.

Many Parties. Like one-party domination, the idea of a multiparty system in the United States is something that is rarely advocated. Even the proponents of minor parties and new parties (and the number of such proponents seems to be declining) base their political thinking upon the hope that someday they will become major parties. It is generally recognized that a multiplicity of parties leads to internal instability. The major recognition given to the multiparty setup in American political thought lies in the observation that minor parties represent a germinating center for ideas that are often picked up and used by the major parties.

Party Government

"Why not try party government?" writes E. E. Schattschneider. "The potentialities of the party are very great. Moreover, party government is good democratic doctrine because the parties are the special form of political organization adapted to the mobilization of majorities. How else can the majority get organized? If democracy means anything at all, it means that the majority has the right to organize for the purpose of taking over the government."[15]

The case for party government is also justified on a number of other grounds. The political party, it is argued, is the only instrument that can present alternatives to the voters and give them meaningful choices on Election Day. It is the only body capable of bridging the separation between the branches of government or even of bringing consistency to the policies of the executive branch. It is far better that party activities be brought out into the open through party government rather than have party bosses hold the strings from behind the scenes where they cannot be held accountable for their actions. Finally, it is felt that party government provides a means for realizing in America a political system akin to that of cabinet government in England, which has been fondly regarded by many political scientists as the best of all systems.

These arguments are somewhat unrealistic. First of all, no majority organizes expressly for the purpose of taking over the government. Parties are organized not by majorities but by small groups of leaders. While one group of leaders may win majority support in an election, this does not mean that the people who voted for these leaders can be described as a party organization. Further, there is a danger in placing too much reliance on the theory that a mandate at the polls can be specific enough to serve as a charter for the development of national policy. When elections deal with principles they can deal with them

[15] Schattschneider, *op. cit.*, p. 208.

only in general terms and cannot serve as a guide in the development of all important details. Many issues of national policy simply cannot be brought to focus in election contests.

Moreover, the sheer bulk of conflicts in American society is so great that the parties could be expected to carry the entire burden of government only by developing a concentration of political power which, in the views of most individuals and most groups, would be highly undesirable. If the parties should ever become the arena for the reconciliation of the major conflicts in American life, this would be a far cry from bringing governmental operations out into the open. While it would clearly identify the importance of the party leaders, such a change would transfer into the secret sessions of the parties and of the party bureaucracies many of the conflicts that now receive much more airing in the halls of Congress as well as in the activities of various executive agencies.

A final question might be raised as to the accuracy of the term "party government" as a description of the British system of *cabinet* government. True, the British Cabinet is usually composed of the leaders of the majority party in the House of Commons. Yet to conclude from this observation that the British have "party government" is to minimize the influence of the King, the House of Lords, the Civil-Service bureaucracy, and the private organizations which, in England as in America, wield a huge influence upon the operations of government.

Tweedledum and Tweedledee

There is another school of thought which, although more realistic than that of the party government advocates, is equally sterile as a guide to action. In 1944 Pendleton Herring wrote a brilliant description of the operations of American government. Looking at the party system, he expressed considerable satisfaction with the lack of clear-cut lines of demarcation between the Republican and Democratic parties: "If all those wanting change," he wrote, "were able to gang up and force through a sweeping party program, while all those of the party against change were expected to stand by until an election occurred two or three years hence, the pent-up feeling and the resulting clash would probably blow the dome off the Capitol." [16] A few years later, this theme was stated in even stronger terms by one of the early New Dealers, David Cushman Coyle, who abhorred "the ghastly choice of a communist-infiltrated 'liberal' party versus a fascist-infiltrated 'conservative' one." [17] Herbert Agar has written a vivid history of American government for the

[16] Herring, *op. cit.*, pp. 113–114.

[17] David Cushman Coyle, "Reorganizing Congress," *Virginia Quarterly Review*, Winter, 1947.

purpose of illustrating his thesis that parties without programmatic unity are the price we pay for union.[18]

The most complete statement of the tweedledum-tweedledee thesis comes from Arthur Holcombe.

Perhaps the best party system would be one in which each of the major parties was as nearly as possible a fair sample of all the important factional interests in the country. Under such a party system the voters would possess the greatest freedom of choice between the candidates for important offices on grounds of merit and fitness. Under the existing system much freedom of choice is restricted by the necessity of choosing between the parties as well as between the candidates. Perhaps under a new party alignment each of the major parties might be a truer sample of the whole body of people than is either of the present major parties.[19]

There are obvious virtues in this approach. It emphasizes acceptance of "reality" rather than impractical departures. It is well suited to those who are essentially conservative or to those who, if liberal, prefer to take their liberalism in very small doses. It is well geared to the goals of those who prefer middle-class domination of the political scene and are wary about the implications of a growing labor movement and labor's emerging political power. Finally, it provides a formula which, if followed faithfully and never abandoned, would prevent America from coming under the sway of a dictatorial government of either the Right or the Left.

The approach also has many defects. It minimizes the significant differences that have often developed among the parties, particularly during the 1930's and the 1940's. The differences between the two major parties are rarely clean-cut, but nevertheless existent. Those who ask for a straight tweedledum-tweedledee line-up would probably be interested more in a return to some "good old days" than in a maintenance of the *status quo.*

Another defect in this approach is the automatic inference that party conflict must lead to intolerable stresses upon society. While Agar seems to claim that the Civil War resulted from the fact that the parties began to have meaning in the ten years before 1860, it is also possible to maintain that the weakness and decentralization of the parties contributed to the outbreak of hostilities between the states. Roy Franklin Nichols places a major share of the blame for the Civil War upon the disruption of the Democratic party.[20] Agar lends credence to this interpretation in a passage which, clashing with his own major thesis, bewails the fact that neither Pierce nor Buchanan were able to invoke the "mighty spell" of party loyalty.[21]

18 Herbert Agar, "The Price of Union" (Boston: Houghton Mifflin, 1950), pp. 689–690.

19 Holcombe, *op. cit.,* p. 145.

20 Roy Franklin Nichols, "The Disruption of American Democracy" (New York: Macmillan, 1948).

21 Agar, *op. cit.,* pp. 354–355.

Whether or not social conflict is fanned by the operations of a party with clear-cut positions on major issues depends, of course, on what these issues are. It also depends upon the dynamics of party relationships at a given time and the quality of leadership evidenced by party rivals. A case might well be made, for example, that a Democratic party with more internal unity on liberal programs would have the effect not of fanning sharper conflicts with the Republican party, but of bringing about a softening and liberalization of conservative forces in America. The growth of the Labour party in England has by no means meant that a communist-dominated party has faced a fascist-infiltrated party, nor has it tended to blow the dome off the House of Commons. Rather, it has placed the business interests and the Conservative party in a position where they long ago discovered the expediency of taking more progressive positions on many fronts. This is the basic explanation of the fact that the British Conservatives have often proved themselves far more liberal than the New Deal or Fair Deal wings of the Democratic party in the United States.

A case can also be made that a more unified Democratic party would operate to the right rather than to the left of the Democratic party's present liberal wing. The price of unity would unquestionably be paid in terms of a rapprochement with the Southern middle-of-the-roaders. This would mean that the Democratic party would have to forgo many of the more advanced positions taken by its Northern liberals but, in return, would be in a better position to obtain legislative action on moderately advanced policies. Stronger parties, therefore, might well lead to the development of two parties, one liberal and one conservative, but both with definite leanings toward the center. This has already been the path of development in both England and Sweden, where strong and rather well-disciplined parties have opposed one another for many years and where the political atmosphere has been characterized by relative stability and peacefulness.

More Party Responsibility

In its report of September, 1950, the Committee on Political Parties of the American Political Science Association steered away from the idea of "party government" which had been earlier advocated by the chairman of the committee, E. E. Schattschneider. It also disassociated itself from the tweedledum-tweedledee school. In contrast, it brought forth a middle-of-the-road concept that, without becoming monolithic in character, each of the two major parties ought to become more "responsible." Responsibility was spelled out in terms that emphasized the inevitability of gradualism, that is, of changes by small degrees. The report calls for a stronger party system in which the parties, first, "are able to bring forth programs to which they commit themselves," and, second, "possess sufficient internal cohesion to carry out these programs." It also called for an organized party opposition as well as for parties with greater resistance to pressures, more internal party loyalty, and more opportunities for discussion of party policy among the various leaders throughout the party. The report recognizes that there are and must be both nonpartisan and bipartisan issues and that the process of adjustment between conflicting groups cannot be entirely channeled through the parties.

The great value of this approach is that it projects a party system ideally suited to the needs of many groups. For the liberal Democrats it provides a rationale for liberalizing the South and developing a genuine two-party system in that region. For the conservative Republicans it provides a rationale for suppressing or combating the activities of the "me-too" liberals in Republican ranks. From the point of view of those who are interested in developing a more consistent approach in foreign affairs, it suggests a structure in which American policies on foreign affairs and national security could be more firmly grounded upon party decisions.

The limitations upon this approach are two in number. First, there is the question of feasibility. The desire of party leaders to appeal to the broadest possible section of the American electorate, the interests of private organizations in getting support within both parties, the strategic advantages that are often obtained by party disunity—these and other factors are considerable obstacles in the path of any who seek to make either one of the major parties a more responsible organization.

Second, any program implies concrete action to strengthen one or another party. It is not quite accurate to say that action to strengthen the responsibility of the Democratic party sets an example which forces the Republican party to be more responsible. The dominant consideration in political combat is to strengthen one's supporters and divide one's opponents. This inevitably leads to the use of coalition-party strategy. The legislative combat on domestic legislation has been characterized for many decades by crystallization, with varying degrees of clarity and precision, of a bipartisan conservative coalition and a bipartisan liberal coalition. Politics of this type are unquestionably here to stay and are by no means inconsistent with the development of more responsibility within any one major political party.

Chapter 5

THE PARTIES: PROPOSALS FOR CHANGE

WHILE MOST of its proposals follow the "more responsible parties" orientation, the report "Toward a More Responsible Two-party System" of the Committee on Political Parties of the American Political Science Association serves as an excellent jumping-off point for general consideration of normative and reform attitudes toward the role of political parties in the legislative process.

Proposals have been made for changes *outside* Congress as well as *inside*. These are pointed up here because it is believed that the relevance of party developments outside the arena called Congress is not so far removed as some would think. The operations of local primaries, national conventions, and other agencies of the national party have their effect upon the legislative struggle, later if not sooner.

PROPOSALS FOR CHANGES OUTSIDE CONGRESS

The Local Primaries

The local primaries operate at the roots of party life. Through them, candidates for Congress are nominated and the basic decisions are thus made on the variety of people and viewpoints that may be represented within the congressional ranks of each party.

Objections to Primaries as Such. A wide variety of arguments has been leveled against the primary system. While it was first advocated as a method of attacking or controlling local party machines, it has become evident that local party bosses can often succeed in dominating the local primaries. Moreover, the primary contests cost money and, combined with the campaigning necessities of the election itself, make candidates for Congress all the more dependent upon contributions from private organizations. Finally, the primary system represents a serious obstacle toward the development of unified national parties. Anybody who can succeed in winning a primary contest is automatically the candidate of the party no matter how much he may disagree with the party's national position.

There are many advocates of party responsibility who have, therefore, long yearned for the abandonment of the primary system and who would prefer to see the central party organizations picking party candidates for Congress as is done to a large extent by the English parties. They feel that as long as the present system is maintained, any Administration party which is sincerely interested in winning the support of dissident members of Congress is compelled by the force of circumstances to place major reliance upon patronage, the allocation of funds for local projects, and favorable handling of constituents' complaints. This undermines the Civil-Service system, prevents the independent exercise of Executive judgment in choosing administrators and employees, and introduces an arbitrary or capricious note into the determination of Executive policy.

Yet open opposition to the direct primaries is rare indeed. The number of reasons that can be added up against the primary system never seems to provide enough support for a frontal attack. One of the most vocal advocates of stronger national parties satisfies himself with a wistful eying of the English system where "nominations are made informally, privately, and simply" and "once a candidate has been adopted by the local party association in a constituency he is entitled, in practice, to be the party candidate permanently until he retires voluntarily, whether he is elected to Parliament or not." [1] In fact, the Committee on Political Parties concluded: "[The direct primary] is a useful weapon in the arsenal of intra-party democracy. No workable substitute has been found for it and it probably can be adapted to the needs of parties unified in terms of national policy." [2]

The only seriously entertained proposals concerning the primary system in America deal not with its possible abandonment but with possible adaptations. Among these, the major proposals relate to whether or not the primary should be "open" or "closed," whether or not they should be preceded by a preprimary designation of official candidates, and whether or not national party leaders should intervene in local primary contests.

Open versus Closed Primaries. The American Political Science Association report contains a useful summation of the debate concerning open versus closed primaries:

In an open primary the voter is not required to register his party affiliation ahead of time or to disclose it when he applies for a primary ballot. He receives the ballots of all parties, and in the secrecy of the polling booth makes his decision. Party affiliation is thus a "some time" thing which may be changed from primary to primary. In more than three-fourths of the states some variation of the closed primary is used, voters

[1] E. E. Schattschneider, "Party Government" (New York: Rinehart, 1942), p. 99.

[2] Committee on Political Parties, American Political Science Association, "Toward a More Responsible Two-party System," *American Political Science Review,* Vol. 44, No. 3, Part II, Supplement, September, 1950, p. 71.

being required either to register their affiliations beforehand or to declare their affiliation, subject to challenge, when they apply for ballots at the primary.

Supporters of the open primary argue that it preserves the full secrecy of the ballot, prevents intimidation, and avoids disfranchising the independent voter, who is unwilling to declare himself a member of one or another. In support of the closed primary it is urged that party members should be willing to "stand up and be counted," that it prevents raids in terms of participation by members of other parties, and that it is impossible to develop party responsibility if nominations may be controlled by those with no continuing allegiance to the party.[3]

The report favors the closed primary,[4] but two qualifications seem essential. First, the closed primary can be used in many states as a method of buttressing the power of a state organization which is strongly at odds with the national organization of the same party. Secondly, given favorable circumstances, a well-organized and well-financed group of party leaders can and have been known to operate effectively in an open primary or even under systems where party labels themselves are completely abandoned.

Preprimary Designations. One of the earliest proposals for improving the party system came from Charles Evans Hughes in 1910. Hughes proposed that party committees be given the duty of recommending candidates for nomination.

If such a party committee did its duty well there would be no necessity for a double campaign. Its choice would be ratified on primary day without contest. . . . If it ignored the sentiment of the party voters, if it appeared that some ulterior or sinister purpose had been served, if the candidates, or any of them, which it selected were unworthy, then there should be opportunity for the party members, immediately and without difficulty, to express themselves in opposition and on primary day to have a chance to show whether or not the designation of the organization party was approved.[5]

In similar vein, the report of the Committee on Political Parties states that "the formal or informal proposal of candidates by preprimary meetings of responsible party committees or party councils is a healthy development." The statement itself indicates that there has been considerable action along the lines of the Hughes proposals.

Joseph P. Harris has proposed a fundamental revision of the present direct primary system, one which rests largely upon preprimary designations. The political parties under the Harris plan would be authorized to hold conferences or conventions before the primaries and recommend candidates to be voted on at the primary election. The names of the candidates so designated,

---

[3] *Ibid.,* p. 71.

[4] *Ibid.,* pp. 71–72.

[5] Charles Evans Hughes, "The Fate of the Direct Primary," *National Municipal Review,* Vol. 10, 1921, pp. 23–31.

together with any other candidates for whom petitions might be filed, would then appear on a single ballot. The candidates who received a majority of all votes cast for the office in the primary would be declared elected. If no one received a majority, the two highest candidates would compete at the regular election.[6] In many cases, therefore, the preprimary designating process would in effect become the primary, and the primary would be converted into the final election.

National Intervention in Local Primaries. The Committee on Political Parties also strongly endorsed "the principle that it is proper for a nationally representative party organ to discuss possible nominees for office which are of national rather than local concern."[7] In contrast, the guiding principle of the major national parties seems to be never to intervene in local primary contests or, if on rare occasions such action seems imperative, to do so surreptitiously. The results of President Roosevelt's ill-fated attempt to purge anti-New Deal Democrats in the 1938 congressional primaries are recalled whenever the matter is raised. Yet with the growing emphasis on national issues and national campaigning via television and radio, the principle favored by the Committee on Political Parties will probably gain ground.

Another proposal would have all congressional primaries held after the party conventions. When a local primary is held before a party's Presidential candidate is selected and its campaign platform promulgated, there is somewhat less chance that the platform decisions of the convention may be regarded as binding. With the nomination already in his pocket, a party candidate is free either to disavow his party's pledges or pay them only lip service. If all primaries were held after the political conventions, then the platforms could be used as principles to which candidates for the congressional nomination would be required to pledge themselves as a condition of national support.

The National Conventions

The national conventions of the major parties operate at the highest level of party life. Through them, four men are nominated from whom the next President and Vice-President of the United States will be selected, and the one occasion is provided on which the heterogeneous groups that make up each party can meet each other face to face.

Objections to Conventions as Such. The national conventions of the major parties have been on the receiving end of far more open attack than have the local primaries. Its hurly-burly atmosphere, its unwieldy size, and its unrep-

[6] Joseph P. Harris, "A New Primary System," *State Government,* Vol. 21, No. 7, July, 1948.

[7] "Toward a More Responsible Two-party System," p. 73.

resentative composition have led many critics to agree with Ostrogorski, whose final word, after describing the operations of the national party convention, was: "God takes care of drunkards, of little children, and of the United States." [8]

After emerging victoriously from the ordeal of a major national convention and the subsequent campaign, Woodrow Wilson included in his first annual address to Congress a recommendation for dropping the convention as an instrument for nominating a Presidential candidate:

> . . . I urge the prompt enactment of legislation which will provide for primary elections throughout the country at which the voters of the several parties may choose their nominees for the presidency without the intervention of nominating conventions. I venture the suggestion that this legislation should provide for the retention of party conventions, but only for the purpose of declaring and accepting the verdict of the primaries in formulating the platforms of the parties. . . . [9]

This proposal has received little serious attention. The most that has happened as a result of the efforts of those who agreed with Wilson has been the development in a number of states of preferential primaries, through which convention delegates are given a mandate of sorts whom they should support when they arrive at the convention. The major use of these preferential primaries has been to serve as a battleground for preliminary skirmishes between contenders for the nomination at the convention itself.

Many observers have leaped to the defense of the national convention. Pendleton Herring maintains that the national convention "is admirably suited to testing the talents of our politicians. It demands organizational skill and manipulative genius—both of which qualities are exceedingly useful in democratic government." And again: "The party convention is one institutional expression of human beings competing by their wits and emotions for some of the prizes available under popular government." [10] Conventions are also a unifying force in national politics. They bring people together from all parts of the country and attract national attention to the problems and personalities in the coming Presidential election.

Here the reform situation is much like that of the local primaries. Despite all the criticism, both open and latent, no one seriously proposes any more to abolish the national convention. Those proposals that merit consideration are therefore aimed at the improvement of the institution.

More Frequent Meetings. The first proposal, made by the Committee on

[8] Moisei Yakovlevich Ostrogorski, "Democracy and the Organization of Political Parties" (New York: Macmillan, 1902), Vol. II, p. 279.

[9] First Annual Address to Congress, Dec. 2, 1913.

[10] Pendleton Herring, "The Politics of Democracy" (New York: Rinehart, 1940), pp. 238–239.

Political Parties, is that the national conventions "should meet at least bien-
nially instead of only quadrennially as at present, with easy provisions for
special meetings." [11]

There is considerable weight behind this recommendation. One of the most
important factors making for futility in party platforms is the fact that it is
impossible to project meaningful policies—even though they are, at best,
compromises—over a period as long as four years. No matter how much effort
and skill are channeled into the writing of a party platform, the march of
events will inevitably render its major provisions irrelevant in one or two years.
National conventions in the mid-term election years would not only serve to
bring party platforms up to date but would also lend more national significance
to the mid-term congressional elections. In 1950, a mid-term election year, both
the Democratic and Republican national parties held various regional conferences which served as instruments for underscoring the views of both parties on
current issues of national policy. To many observers, these conferences appeared to be important steppingstones toward a subsequent system of full-
fledged biennial conventions.

In attacking the conventions as both unwieldy and unrepresentative, the
committee also proposes an entirely new structure. "Much better results could
be obtained," the report suggests, "with a convention of not more than 500–
600 members, composed mostly of delegates elected directly by the party voters
on a more representative basis (300–350 members), a substantial number of
ex-officio members (the national committee, state and party chairmen, congressional leaders—probably about 150 altogether), and a selected number of prominent party leaders outside the party organizations (probably
25)." [12]

From the viewpoint of political dynamics the most important part of this
package is the proposal that delegates be elected on a more representative basis.
The other changes in composition represent no significant shift in political
power. A representative apportionment of delegates among the states, however,
based more upon the number of party voters in each state and less on the
apportionment of Presidential electors, would have the effect of providing
greater power at the Democratic Party Convention for the urban centers and
lesser power at the Republican National Convention for delegates from the
Southern states.

The National Agencies

The problem of developing a strong national organization to guide national
election campaigns and to provide leadership between national conventions

[11] "Toward a More Responsible Two-party System," p. 38.
[12] *Ibid.*, p. 38.

has also received considerable attention. Four proposals along this line deserve discussion.

Party Councils. It has been proposed that each major party establish a Party Council to serve as the major organ of party leadership between national conventions. This proposal was first made many decades ago by Charles E. Merriam, who suggested a Party Council of about 600 members,[13] an agency which would be larger than the abbreviated national conventions that have been proposed by others. The Committee on Political Parties trimmed down Merriam's proposals and offered instead a Party Council of 50 members. This Party Council would be made up of representatives of five main groups: "the national committee (probably 5, chosen by the committee); the congressional party organizations (5 from each House, chosen by the respective organizations); the state committees (10, chosen on a regional basis by the regional groups, if any, otherwise by the national convention); the party's governors (5, chosen by them); and other recognized party groups, such as Young Republican and Young Democrats' groups as well as the party following at large (20, with the majority chosen by the national convention and the remainder by the particular groups)."[14] The President and some cabinet officers designated by him would serve as ex-officio members of the Party Council of the Administration party. In the case of the anti-Administration party the ex-officio positions would go to the Presidential candidate or, as the case may be, the defeated Presidential candidate and his running mate.

The merit of proposals of this type is that they underscore the desirability of developing working relationships between party leaders operating in separate and disconnected areas. The national committees of the major parties cannot by themselves perform this function, inasmuch as they are both organized strictly on the basis of representing state organizations. The weakness of these proposals is that they underestimate the possibility of accomplishing the same objective through making better use of the national committee and its national-headquarters organizations. From time to time various officers of both national committees have, in fact, attempted to develop closer working relations with House and Senate party members, the party's state organizations, and various national leaders of the party. A more effective effort along these lines could achieve the same objectives as are sought by the proposals for a formalized Party Council.

A major obstacle to effectiveness, however, is the understandable opposition that most Presidents have evidenced toward the clustering of other, and potentially rival, party leaders into a potent organization. There is little doubt that an organization of this type might trim a President's wings. Nor is this

[13] Charles E. Merriam with Harold F. Gosnell, "The American Party System" (New York: Macmillan, 1949), 4th ed., pp. 356–360.
[14] "Toward a More Responsible Two-party System," p. 43.

merely a personal question of the President versus Party. A stronger national-party organization might well become the vehicle of a somewhat different aggregation of group interests and purposes than of the President himself.

In the case of the anti-Administration party there is an obstacle of an entirely different sort. The "titular leader," as the defeated Presidential candidate is euphemistically called, is rarely recognized as a *de facto* leader. There are so many rivals for nomination at the next Presidential Convention that the centrifugal forces within the party are extremely strong. Under those circumstances the chances of pulling the party together into a tighter national party are exceedingly slim. It has occasionally been proposed that the national-leadership vacuum in the anti-Administration party be remedied by giving a place of high honor and dignity—say, a nonvoting seat in the United States Senate—to the defeated Presidential candidate. Yet it is hard to see how a device of this sort would go very far toward making up for the power and prestige lost by a candidate's defeat or toward dampening the aspirations of Senators, governors, and other ambitious party leaders.

The National Committees. It has also been proposed that "the members of the national committee reflect the actual strength of the party within the areas they represent." [15] This could be done by having each member of a national committee cast a vote equal to the total party vote in areas he or she represents. This would reduce the voting power of those members of the national committee from the states with smaller populations and with lesser support among the voters. This proposal, however, seems to be based upon the presumption that the national committees decide on important matters by casting ballots. This is done only in rare instances when representatives of dissident state organizations are refused seats on the national committee. For the most part the national committees do not deal with policy decisions. If the national committees should become more active, naturally the problem of representation and voting methods would become more acute. However, it is doubtful whether any formalized change in the basis of representation would ever be feasible. Probably the best method of activating the national committees and of introducing a more representative quality into their work would be to use them as instruments for bringing together party leaders from Congress, the executive branch, and other spots in the party structure.

The National Headquarters Staff. A third proposal is that each of the major parties maintain rounded staffs on a permanent basis. The Committee on Political Parties pointed out:

Staff development at party headquarters provides the essential mechanism to enable each party to concern itself appropriately with its continuing responsibilities. The availability of professionally trained staffs in particular makes it more readily possible for the party leadership to grasp issues clearly, to see trends and problems in

[15] *Ibid.*, p. 39.

perspective, and to consider the far-flung interests of the party as a whole. . . . What is needed is a much stronger full-time research organization adequately financed and working on a year-in, year-out basis.[16]

Expenditures of National Committees. It has been proposed that the legal ceiling of 3 million dollars upon the annual expenditures of the national committees should be repealed. "Repeal of these restrictions," comments the committee, "would make it possible for a national body to assume more responsibility in the field of party finance." [17] If this proposal should eventually be adopted, it would be interesting to note the extent to which funds, as a result, flow in greater volume toward the national committees and in lesser volume to independent-party and nonparty committees. In either case there is little likelihood that the source of the funds and the interests of those who put up the money will in any way be modified.

Proposals for Changes inside Congress

In Congress the parties operate year in and year out within a major center of national attention. Here their weaknesses, particularly those relating to the legislative process, are most apparent. As a result, the bulk of attention on party reform has tended to center on such matters as the structure of congressional party leadership and the role of the parties in the struggle for committee power and congressional time.

Congressional Party Leadership

This rather complex subject can best be discussed if reference is first made to (1) the party leaders, (2) the party-leadership committees, and (3) caucuses and conferences.

The Party Leaders. In what was probably the only complacent portion of its entire report, the Committee on Political Parties gave its hearty endorsement to the informal meetings between the President and the Big Four, that is, the Speaker of the House, the Majority Leader of the House, the Vice-President, and the Majority Leader of the Senate. The committee argued that the Big-Four meetings "have provided an essential tie between Congress and the executive branch" and that "it would be an error to attempt to supplant the relationship between the Big Four and the President by some new body to carry on the same function." [18]

The committee also endorsed the occasional doubling of the Big Four into an eight-man group including the leadership of the anti-Administration party

[16] *Ibid.*, pp. 50, 81.
[17] *Ibid.*, p. 75.
[18] *Ibid.*, p. 58.

and recommended that this should be done more frequently on bipartisan issues.

Moreover, the committee took the position that both the Speaker of the House and the Majority and Minority Leaders should be regarded as spokesmen for one or the other party as a whole. It specifically endorsed Presidential interest in the selection of these leaders. This is in sharp contrast to the attitude of Vice-President Garner on Roosevelt's intervention in the effort to obtain the election of Senator Alben Barkley as Senate Democratic Leader in 1937: "It is an encroachment on the prerogatives of members of the legislative branch no President of the United States ought to engage in." [19]

The Party-leadership Committees. "Each house should establish a Majority Policy Committee," advised Heller, "composed of the chairman of each major standing committee and let the chairman be the majority leader, and a minority policy committee composed of ranking minority members." [20] The obvious theory here is that since committee chairmen and ranking minority members occupy positions of greater strategic strength, the best way to obtain strong party-policy committees is to establish them from among these gentlemen. One might just as validly maintain that the way to get weak party-policy committees is to place in them members of Congress who are in the best position to go their own way and fight established party policies. The Joint Committee on the Organization of Congress seemed to follow the second line of reasoning. [21]

The Committee on Political Parties dealt with this problem by recognizing the existing proliferation of party leadership in committees and then calling for the consolidation of existing party-leadership committees into four committees with specific powers both with respect to the committee structure and to legislative schedules. A related recommendation suggested that "the four party leadership committees meet jointly at the beginning of every session as a Joint Committee on the President's Program. Such a committee could consider the entire program embodied in the President's three principal annual messages and furnish guidance to the general line of action on the part of the various legislative committees." [22]

Caucuses and Conferences. "Whether they be called caucuses or conferences," suggested the Committee on Political Parties, "more frequent meetings of the party membership in each House should be held. Otherwise, there can be no real discussion of party positions and no real participation in or check upon the decisions of the party leadership. Without such discussion

[19] Bascom N. Timmons, "John N. Garner's Story," *Collier's,* Feb. 28, 1948.

[20] Robert Heller, "Strengthening the Congress" (Washington, D.C.: National Planning Association, January, 1945), pp. 13–14.

[21] Joint Committee on the Organization of Congress, H. Rept. 1011, 79th Cong., 2d Sess., Mar. 4, 1946.

[22] "Toward a More Responsible Two-party System," p. 60.

and participation, efforts to make party operations more responsible will be futile." [23] There is no doubt that strong party leadership needs caucuses or conferences as a means of mobilizing the support of their members. Where leadership is weak, however, or where there is a fundamental split among party membership, these meetings of party members may accomplish little except to fan the flames of dissension.

The question has often been debated furiously whether or not a decision arrived at at these meetings of party members should be regarded as binding upon the party membership when the matter later comes up on the floor of either house. On the one hand, it has been pointed out that through the instrumentality of a binding caucus decision a bare majority of a majority-party caucus may comprise only 51 per cent of a party having only 51 per cent in the entire house and yet may dictate the decision of that house.[24] It has also been charged that binding caucus decisions would transfer the deliberative processes of Congress from the more leisurely and less secret committee and floor sessions to the cloistered haste of the caucus room. On the other hand, it is claimed that unless party members subordinate their views to those of the majority of the party membership, effective party leadership in Congress will continue to be impossible.

The tendency of party leaders in both houses and in both parties is to dodge this issue, calling few caucuses and only occasionally attempting to develop binding decisions. They have resolved the problem at various times by regarding a caucus decision as binding only when there is a two-thirds vote in favor of a particular proposition. The Democratic House Caucus rules allow members to evade a decision when they regard it as unconstitutional or when it conflicts with clear instructions from their constituents or clear promises made by them during their election campaigns.

Parties and the Struggle for Committee Power

The formal structure of party-leadership committees is far less important than the extent to which the party leadership can affect the structure of committee power. Some of the most important proposals concerning party leadership in Congress, therefore, relate to the role of the parties in determining the party line-up on committees, assigning members to committees, and selecting committee chairmen.

Party Line-up on Committees. Woodrow Wilson believed that it was a mistake to have both parties represented on legislative committees. He felt that the majority party should take full responsibility for committee work and

[23] *Ibid.*, p. 60.

[24] See the attack on the closed caucus in Glenn Haines, "Your Congress" (Washington, D.C.: National Capitol Press, 1915), pp. 75–86.

that members of the minority party should be excluded. At the other extreme, it has occasionally been proposed that the two parties be given equal representation on the committees. In the case of an occasional subcommittee, joint committee, or congressional commission, this practice has been adopted.

As a practical matter, however, the problem boils down to a series of decisions by majority-party leaders regarding the additional margin of seats they will assign to their party members on this or that committee. Certain mathematical limits are set by the size of each committee and by the fact that, with the exception of only a few minor committees, each Senator may serve on only two committees and each Representative on only one. A party with a slender majority is thus unable to achieve a substantial committee majority in all committees and must therefore carefully select the points at which to concentrate its strength. In the interests of party responsibility, therefore, it would seem desirable to weaken the limitations on committee service as a means of strengthening party representation within the committees.

A large margin of majority members on a committee, however, does not necessarily provide a means of party control. In some cases party leaders can rely upon sympathetic viewpoints in the ranks of the other party and dominate a committee with a one-member margin only. In other cases, a large nominal margin will be completely negated by the existence of vigorous dissidents within the party ranks.

Assignments to Committees. Of all the proposals to give party leaders more definite responsibility with respect to committee assignments, the first to originate in Congress and win considerable congressional support was the proposal which George Norris and his insurgent colleagues fashioned back in 1910 when they were planning their revolt against Speaker Cannon. The Republican rebels attached to the resolution that stripped Speaker Cannon of many of his powers a provision converting the House Rules Committee into a joint-party-leadership body with the power and the duty of appointing the members of all the legislative committees of the House. The Democrats opposed this provision, however, and in order to obtain their support, which was essential to the success of the anti-Cannon campaign, Norris was forced to remove the constructive part of his resolution and limit it to a negative restraint on the powers of the Speaker.[25]

Norris's old idea is revived in the recommendations of the Committee on Political Parties. In keeping with its recommendation on the consolidation of the various party-leadership committees, it urged that the function of preparing slates of committee assignments be handled by the party-policy committees themselves rather than by any special committee or committees.[26]

[25] "Fighting Liberal, The Autobiography of George Norris" (New York: Macmillan, 1946), pp. 114–119.

[26] "Toward a More Responsible Two-party System," pp. 62–63.

Although the committee indicated that slates of committee assignments should be presented to party caucuses or conferences for approval or modification, it did not deal directly with the fact that the rules call for election of committee members by the entire membership of each house. Thus, a small minority within a party's ranks may hold on to positions of considerable committee power by the tacit threat of joining with the other party in taking control of the committee structure. A truly logical system of party responsibility would, therefore, dispense with the requirement that committee assignments be voted upon in each house and would leave the matter entirely up to each party caucus or conference.

Selection of Chairmen. The practice of selecting committee chairmen on the basis of seniority has been a consistent target for criticism. Yet it is generally conceded that it is easier to criticize the seniority system than to devise a workable substitute. The Joint Committee on the Organization of Congress came to the conclusion that on this question, as with the powers of the House Rules Committee, it would be impossible to iron out the conflicting views among the committee members.

Writing a year later, George Galloway dealt with the matter as follows:

. . . the best method of selection in the final analysis would be the appointment of committee chairmen by the majority leaders in each house . . . They should also be empowered by the party caucus to remove chairmen who refuse to cooperate in the execution of the party's legislative program. In this way, the line of party responsibility and accountability for legislative action would be clearly drawn. . . .[27]

The Committee on Political Parties took a similar position. In so doing, it conceded that "advancement within a committee on the basis of seniority makes sense, other things being equal" and opposed the idea that seniority as such should be abolished.

It also recognized that as long as party dissidents succeed in getting regularly reelected to Congress, it will be extremely difficult to amass enough power to dislodge them from important committee posts.[28]

Parties and the Struggle for Congressional Time

Another index of the power of congressional party leaders is their ability to affect the scheduling of floor operations. For those who seek a strengthening of party leadership, therefore, proposals to give the party leaders a greater role in the struggle for congressional time are almost as important as proposals to give them greater power over the congressional committee structure.

The House Rules Committee. Along with the seniority system and the Sen-

---

[27] George Galloway, "Congress at the Crossroads" (New York: Crowell, 1946), p. 194.
[28] "Toward a More Responsible Two-party System," pp. 61–62.

ate filibuster, the House Rules Committee ranks as a major target for those who criticize congressional operations. Critics of the Rules Committee have often made the unwarranted assumption that traffic direction in Congress can somehow or other be separated from policy decisions. "It seems to me," testified Representative Herter of Massachusetts, "the Rules Committee job is more that of a traffic director than one to pass on the merits of the bills that have been heard very completely by the individual committees." [29]

Legislative traffic in Congress cannot be compared to that of automobiles on a highway, where the right of way is generally given without examination of a vehicle's destination or cargo. The applicable simile is that of a railroad system. An examination of the merits of bills reported from committees is as much a part of the decision to recommend consideration on the floor as such an examination is a part of decisions by legislative committees.

One proposal is to cut down the powers of the Rules Committee. This could be done by regarding as "privileged" any bill which has a unanimous committee endorsement, or by requiring that all committee-reported measures be given some sort of rule by the Rules Committee. This objective could also be attained by organized revolts against, and amendments of, the rules proposed by the Rules Committee.

A second approach, advocated by the Committee on Political Parties, is to substitute open party control for control by the Rules Committee or by individual chairmen. The committee pointed out that there are many ways to do this. At one extreme, the Rules Committee could be abolished and its functions be taken over by two party-leadership committees in the House of Representatives acting jointly. Or else the majority leaders might be allowed the choice of either using the Rules Committee as its instrument or bypassing it.

A short-lived change in rules during the life of the Eighty-first Congress allowed the committee chairmen to bypass the Rules Committee under certain circumstances. But this reform, in taking power away from the Rules Committee, transferred more power to committee chairmen rather than to the party leaders.

Legislative Scheduling. In the House, there are scheduling problems outside the sphere of the Rules Committee. In the Senate, as contrasted with the House, the problem is one of looseness in legislative scheduling. The Committee on Political Parties has dealt with this question by stressing the inseparability of policy and steering functions and advocating a comprehensive scheduling operation by the party-leadership committees: "Scheduling should include not only what measures are to be taken from the calendar for floor action but also the general scheduling of major hearings. Schedules should be openly explained on the floor in advance. They should apply to all issues, not just party

[29] Hearings before the Joint Committee on the Organization of Congress, 79th Cong., 1st Sess., p. 104.

issues." [30] A specific proposal along these lines was offered some years ago by former Senator Myers of Pennsylvania.[31]

Party leaders have usually been aloof to proposals of this type. The task of holding things together is already so difficult, particularly in the Senate, that the thought of a more ambitious effort is a little disconcerting. Some of them have probably felt that their ability to control the floor schedule depended upon surprise action and that a more openly handled scheduling operation would weaken them. There has probably also been a feeling that the end-of-the-season log jam which results from inadequate scheduling during the course of a session places them in an unusually strategic position to decide what shall and what shall not be considered.

Discharging Committees. The strongest invective of the incumbent leaders of a majority party is always reserved for proposals to liberalize the House discharge rule. The majority leaders of the House usually argue that a discharge rule allowing less than a majority to bring a bill out of a committee would break down party discipline.

One of the greatest defenders of the discharge rule has advocated that, instead of requiring an affirmative vote of the majority of the House membership, "no more than an ordinary majority of those voting should be required." While this proposal appears to be "antiparty," Hasbrouck justifies it on the very ground that it would tend to strengthen the two-party system. Hasbrouck also suggests that if existing parties cannot adapt themselves to new conditions, the new rule "would provide a parliamentary outlet for the forces of change." [32]

A liberalized discharge process could be used effectively as a means of getting action on a party measure that has been bottled up by a bipartisan coalition. It can also become a protection against an overconcentration of party power. "If we generally develop a more responsible party structure in the House of Representatives, then we would not only have conditions under which you could afford to have a better discharge system, but we would need a method of making the party leadership more accountable to the members." [33]

[30] "Toward a More Responsible Two-party System," p. 64.

[31] S. Con. Res. 62, 80th Cong., 2d Sess.

[32] Paul Hasbrouck, "Party Government in the House of Representatives" (New York: Macmillan, 1927), pp. 212, 216–217.

[33] Bertram M. Gross, "Organization and Operation of Congress," Hearings before the Senate Committee on Expenditures in the Executive Departments, 82d Cong., 1st Sess., p. 283.

Chapter 6

THE AGENCIES OF GOVERNMENT

ANOTHER of the many fictions concerning politics is the idea that government agencies are above the daily conflict among competing groups and interests. If private organizations and political parties, having special ends in view, stir up conflicts, government is said to appear on the scene to serve the national or public interest and to make peace. This idea has considerable psychological value in winning acceptance of government decisions and is of obvious utility to the officials of government agencies themselves. Yet to realize how fictitious this is, one should go back to James Madison's famous Federalist Paper, No. 10. "What are the different classes of legislators," he asked ruefully, fresh from his experience in the Virginia House of Delegates, "but advocates and parties to the causes which they determine?" [1] He might well have asked the same rhetorical question about the other officers of government. During his lifetime he saw the Federal courts packed with advocates of Federalist doctrines and as Chief Executive himself became an advocate of causes which he helped to determine.

In the present era of "Big Government," it has become increasingly evident that each part of the vast and complex structure of government has a dual role as a contestant in the struggle among competing groups. On the one hand, it reflects or represents various nongovernment groups and interests which provide its basic support. On the other, it develops specialized interests of its own, for government is the one group in the world furthest from being a single homogeneous mass; it is rather a conglomeration of assorted groups divided by an endless series of inner conflicts. If the function of many of these groups is to serve as mediator, there is almost always one or more rival groups eager and willing to impose a rival brand of mediation.

THE MEMBERS OF CONGRESS

The stock Congressman, for many cartoonists, wears a broad-brimmed hat, a potbelly in front, a shaggy mane of hair behind, and delights in demagoguery.

[1] "The Federalist" (New York: Modern Library Series, Random House, 1937), p. 56.

He is elected through the machinations of a corrupt political boss. He acts in accordance with instructions from people who pull the wires.

Although it would be a comforting thought to brand this character as pure myth, a few days in the congressional galleries and committee hearings will always uncover a number of Congressmen who seem to be modeled after the cartoon character. Yet these are far from being typical. In fact, there is no such animal as a typical or average member of the Congress. Congress is made up of people—96 Senators and 435 Representatives—people whose characteristics and practices are infinitely varied. This is one of the reasons why Congress—to drop the distinctive "the" which is invariably used by members of Congress—has always been and always will be a favorite target for jokes, jibes, and lampoons.

Background

Although these people are not a cross section of American life, they are closely associated with important social groupings. Most of the lawyers, businessmen, bankers, and farmers in Congress—and these are the great majority [2] —maintain their occupational pursuits. If some withdraw from an active role, others, particularly lawyers and insurance men, expand their activities as a result of the contacts made through their official positions. Many members of Congress serve as officials of trade associations, farm groups, and organizations set up to obtain some specific kind of legislative measure. Many more obtain substantial remuneration from speeches and lecture tours arranged by friendly outside groups. The basic bonds, of course, are the political relationships between the individual member and his constituency. This means close ties not only with a party machine but also with the more important private organizations in the state or district. Are members so close to local interests that they have little direct concern with the great national and international issues? "Sometimes we wish to vote for measures of national good," confessed Representative Charles L. Gifford of Massachusetts in a speech acquainting new members with the problems faced by the average Representative, "but somehow there are people back home pulling the strings, are there not? . . . Sometimes we have that appalling decision to make: shall I vote for my country as a whole

[2] A statistical justification of this observation is found in the table entitled "Occupational Distribution of the Membership of the 79th Congress, 1st Session," in George Galloway, "Congress at the Crossroads" (New York: Crowell, 1946), p. 349. In the 79th Congress, the table indicates, lawyers alone accounted for 55 per cent of the House and 65 per cent of the Senate. The affinity thus suggested between the legal profession and the function of legislation is based to a large degree upon the fact that lawyers often have (1) flexible working schedules into which political activity can be readily (and often profitably) inserted, (2) business connections which can be helpful in raising campaign funds and experience in representing the interests of others, (3) experience that is as serviceable to constituents as it is to clients.

or must I vote to protect my own particular district? Which should I represent? Your conscience must be your guide. But you can almost always subdue your conscience, you can always educate your conscience." [3]

It should be remembered, however, that most local organizations are interested in issues which have a broad geographical significance. Some of these are regional issues, as in the cases of textile manufacturers who want higher tariffs and the tobacco growers who seek more ample foreign markets. The bulk of the more powerful local groups is associated with national organizations whose viewpoint is anything but geographically restricted. Thus, a member of Congress cannot sink political roots in his locality without concerning himself with many national and international issues. A Southern Senator may obtain strong financial support from Northern industrial interests. A Northern Representative may have to win the support of national labor bodies before obtaining sufficient backing from organized labor at home.

Burdens

The tasks expected of Congressmen are exceptionally onerous. During the sessions of the Eighty-first Congress, for example, there were 921 public and 1,103 private bills that became law, 455 recorded votes on the floor of the Senate, and 275 recorded votes on the floor of the House. In addition, every member had hundreds of decisions to face in unrecorded votes, committee sessions, correspondence, and other individual legislative activities. In no other walk of life and in no other branch of government, with the single exception of the President's office, are men called upon to make so many decisions so quickly. And every decision, it must be remembered, is not merely an intellectual exercise; it is the Congressman's answer to the private, party, and governmental groups who are competing with one another to pressure and persuade him to act in accordance with their wishes. But legislative activities are not the only part of a Congressman's duties. The members of Congress not only make laws but also participate in the country's greatest public forum. They investigate public conduct and survey the administration of specific laws. Senators confirm hundreds of appointments in the executive and judicial branches. Members of both houses are vitally interested in the character and distribution of other Presidential appointments. In addition, constituents expect all sorts of help in obtaining jobs, settling cases before administrative agencies, and obtaining Federal funds for various local projects. In 1940, Representative Luther Patrick of Alabama made a speech on the floor of the House in which he described the burden of placating constituents:

A congressman has become an expanded messenger boy, an employment agency, getter-out of the Navy, Army, Marines, ward heeler, wound healer, trouble shooter,

[3] *Congressional Record*, Jan. 27, 1947, p. 668.

law explainer, bill finder, issue translator, resolution interpreter, controversy oil pourer, gladhand extender, business promoter, convention goer, civic ills skirmisher, veterans' affairs adjuster, ex-serviceman's champion, watchdog for the underdog, sympathizer with the upper dog, namer and kisser of babies, recoverer of lost baggage, soberer of delegates, adjuster for traffic violators—voters straying into Washington and into toils of the law—binder up of broken hearts, financial wet nurse, good samaritan, contributor to good causes—there are so many good causes—cornerstone layer, public building and bridge dedicator, ship christener—to be sure he does get in a little flag waving—and a little constitutional hoisting and spread-eagle work, but it is getting harder every day to find time to properly study legislation—the very business we are primarily here to discharge, and that must be done above all things.[4]

Another task that absorbs the time of most members of Congress is running for office. The exceptions, of course, are those members from one-party districts who are so firmly entrenched that they have no real opposition in the primaries. By the time a member of the House takes his seat at the beginning of any Congress, the date of the primaries for the next election in his home district is only about fifteen months away. Members of the Senate have more breathing time, but any Senator who is lulled into a false sense of job security by reason of his six-year tenure is courting disaster. A Senator's political fences extend across a whole state and need constant tending.

Finally, much time is taken up by conflicts among congressional competitors for a place in the sun: between Senators who want to be nominated as Presidential candidates; between Representatives from the same state who want to be Senators; between Senators from the same state who want to achieve preeminence at home; and between members of both houses from all states who are competing to perform public service, to obtain power, prestige, and publicity, or to enhance their personal finances.

The burdensome character of the congressional job is made still more difficult by the survival of an old tradition that, except in time of war, Congress should meet for only a portion of the year and then adjourn. After four or five months of every session, there develops a deep-seated and persistent yearning for adjournment. Their motives are to secure relief from the strain; to get close to the grass roots; to carry on investigations or political campaigns; or to prepare for the legislative battles of the next session. Although a few energetic individuals in Congress always complain publicly that Congress shirks its duty by going home and leaving its business unfinished (which it always does), most members are impatient with any congressional action that might delay adjournment. In fact, once adjournment is in sight, the legislators start to fold their tents and quietly steal away. It is sometimes difficult to get a quorum for the act of adjournment.

[4] *Congressional Record,* 76th Cong., 3d Sess., p. 3028.

Behavior

Congressmen react to their burdens in different ways. Some take every decision seriously; the result is ceaseless overwork and nervous strain. Some react like the doctor so familiar with human anatomy that nothing upsets his equanimity. A blasé shell is their protection. They can take part in the most heated debates without real inward concern over the outcome. Many choose special fields and give only perfunctory interest to the rest. Some become creative participants through the introduction of innumerable bills, while others have no interest whatsoever in introducing measures or, if they do, in trying to get them enacted. Some glory in the excitement of floor debate and examination of witnesses at public hearings, while others labor only behind the scenes. A growing number resort to expert assistance for advice on technical matters, although the more old-fashioned members still shun staff assistance as a confession of ignorance. Some develop faculties of comprehension and analysis unequaled elsewhere in public life, while others operate on an intellectual level akin to that of the Crustacea. Some become inveterate straddlers; others specialize in meeting certain issues squarely.

Most, of necessity, acquire an intensive interest in learning the other man's viewpoint and develop thereby high proficiency in bargaining, yielding, and working out compromises. For self-protection practically every member learns how to evade decisions, to blur issues, and to crawl back after being pushed out on a limb. At times, all members act as the direct agents of powerful groups without bothering to exercise personal discretion, a line of action which has the merit—not to be scorned in a hectic world—of ease and simplicity. On other occasions, they rely on their own discretion.[5] At times they yield to pressure or propaganda and accept the views of others—a line of action which is facilitated by the sheer impossibility of having personal views on all the issues that arise in Congress. On other occasions they stand by personal convictions that have been firmly bred into them by their cultural background and lifetime associations. The extent to which personal discretion and conviction enter

[5] A long-standing controversy centers around the question of whether a legislator should be an instructed agent of his constituents, bound by an "imperative mandate," or a representative who, in the words Edmund Burke used in his famous speech to the Electors of Bristol, will sacrifice his "unbiased opinion, his mature judgment, his enlightened conscience" to no set of men living. The first alternative is often advocated by groups who feel their interests are being neglected, the latter by those who resent specific outside influences. In the early days of the French Estates and English Parliament, the monarchs often demanded that the members be uninstructed so that they might be free to vote for the king's policy, while the rising opposition groups usually favored binding mandates from their constituencies. Actually, the issue is not a real one, for every agent must use discretion and every representative must be flexible in opinions and judgments. The dispute over the abstract question of how a legislator should behave usually resolves itself into a contest between groups with opposing substantive interests.

into the life of the individual member varies with the character of the issue, the political and legislative situation at any given time, and the personality of the individual member.

There is a Senate at the northern end of the Capitol; a House at the southern end.

As bodies they are strangers to each other. Save for conference committees, they might as well sit at the opposite extremes of the continent, or at different times of the year. The leaders confer once in a while, no doubt, but for the rank and file there is neither acquaintance nor interest. Rarely does a Senator deign to enter the House. Rarely does a Representative go to the other end of the Capitol from motives other than those of curiosity, unless he has occasion to consult a Senator from his own State in some personal or political matter.[6]

One of the few institutional forces that join the two houses together is congressional rivalry with the executive branch, especially the President. But this is counterbalanced by an undercurrent of institutional hostility between the House and the Senate. Members of the House are jealous of the powers exclusively reserved to the Senate: confirmation of Presidential nominations and the ratification of treaties. They are also jealous of Senators' greater influence over patronage, greater access to channels of publicity, and habitual domination of joint committees. Senators, in turn, frequently resent House prerogatives on the initiation of revenue and appropriations measures. Members of each house are often conspicuously patronizing toward the other house —an attitude which itself promotes conflict. "The Senate," Speaker Thomas B. Reed is alleged to have said, "is a nice, quiet sort of a place where good Representatives go when they die." Countless wisecrack variations on this theme are coined every year.

There are a number of interesting organizational differences between the two houses. In the House, with its larger membership, the very need to get action by a large group of men has called into being a tighter degree of control than in the Senate. Its rules and traditions tend to promote expeditious action at the expense of the personal prerogatives of individual members. In the Senate the emphasis is more toward a deliberative atmosphere and personal privilege. This attitude stems not only from the tradition that Senators are "ambassadors of the sovereign states" but from the fact that the Senators themselves, facing reelection only once every six years, have more time at their disposal.

When the Constitution was drawn up, it was thought that the House would be closer to the people and therefore the more liberal body, while the Senate would be the more conservative influence. The story is told that Washington described the difference between the two houses by saying, "We pour legislation into the senatorial saucer to cool it." Since the constitutional amend-

[6] Robert Luce, "Legislative Procedure" (Boston: Houghton Mifflin, 1922), p. 141.

ment providing for the choice of Senators by popular vote instead of by the state legislatures, this concept has completely broken down. There have been many periods in which the Senate has been the liberal body and the House the saucer to cool the senatorial tea.

Organized labor has had less influence, and conservative business and farm groups more influence, in the House. While every Senator represents a combination of both rural and urban areas, many Representatives represent only rural areas, areas in which there are no organized labor groups of any consequence and in which the dominant farm groups frequently work in close cooperation with business groups. The districting of seats has been controlled by the state legislatures, which usually allocate more congressional seats to rural areas than is warranted by the size of the rural population. In Ohio, for example, one rural congressional district contains only 166,932 people, while one district of the city of Cleveland contains 908,403 people. This discrepancy is not accidental; it results from the fact that the state legislatures themselves are organized on the basis of overrepresentation for rural areas and are used by conservative farm and business groups to achieve a similar structure in the House of Representatives.[7]

It is misleading to talk about Congress as a whole. It is just as misleading to think of either house as acting under the direction of its formal leadership. The highest official of the Senate—despite his two high-sounding titles of "Vice-President of the United States" and "President of the Senate"—is little more than a figurehead. The first Vice-President, John Adams, spoke for all Vice-Presidents when he lamented that "My country has in its wisdom contrived for me the most insignificant office that ever the invention of man contrived, or his imagination conceived." The President pro tem of the Senate, who serves when the Vice-President is absent or has moved into the White House, is somewhat more of a senatorial leader because he is chosen by members of the Senate themselves rather than superimposed upon them by a national election.

The real direction of the Senate, in so far as there is direction, is found in the positions of party leadership and in the chairmen and ranking members of committees. The ceaseless tug of war within each party, however, often makes it difficult, if not impossible, to determine exactly who is really the Majority Leader. Party leadership is divided between the Majority Leader, the chairman of the majority steering committee, the chairman of the majority policy committee, and the chairman of the majority caucus or conference. During the Eightieth Congress Senator Robert A. Taft, who served as chairman of both the policy and steering committees of the Republican party, was the acknowledged leader on domestic policy, while Senator Arthur Van-

[7] On this, see Arthur N. Holcombe, "The Middle Classes in American Politics" (Cambridge, Mass.: Harvard University Press, 1940), p. 100.

denberg, President pro tem of the Senate, was the acknowledged leader on foreign policy. Senator Wallace White, although elected as Majority Leader, had the name but not the power.

In the House of Representatives the top official is the Speaker, who is elected by the majority party at the beginning of each session. While the Speaker is always a far more significant figure in congressional life than the Vice-President, he is no longer the czar he was before 1911, the year in which a coalition of Democratic and Republican progressives forced a revision of the rules to clip the wings of Speaker "Uncle Joe" Cannon. The Speaker shares his leadership not only with the Majority Leader and Whip, the majority caucus and conference, and whatever steering or policy committees may be set up, but also with the powerful House Rules Committee and the members of the more important legislative committees.

The legislative committees of both houses, in turn, are founded upon a Balkanization of power that outshines any of the crazy-quilt patterns ever developed in the Balkans.[8] While each party contrives to get its due share of representation on every committee, there is no clear-cut centralization of the appointive power in the hands of the party leadership. Even when committee members hold their positions as a result of party decisions, there is no real sense of accountability. The Republican or Democratic members on a given committee are seldom regarded as responsible to the Republican and Democratic parties. This practice favors those members of Congress who manage to get reelected often and is thus of particular benefit to the dominant groups and interests in one-party areas of the country.

The real legislative leadership in Congress lies with those who have behind them the strongest array of organized backing by groups outside Congress, that is, private organizations, party groups, and executive agencies. If this backing is given to a majority party leader or a committee chairman, we then see examples of party or committee leadership. If it is achieved by a President—and on some issues Presidents are in a unique position to organize such backing—then the President becomes the leader of Congress. The secret of success is usually the organization of a coalition—in most cases a coalition between like-minded members of both the major parties, and, in all cases, a coalition of supporting private and governmental organizations. Sometimes such coalitions are of fleeting duration, coming into being for action on one or two bills. Sometimes they represent long-term understandings and arrangements and cover a broad variety of mutual interests. The shifting nature of these coalitions is further explained in part by the altering views taken by the leaders of organized groups and by the changing distribution of group strength among the senatorial and congressional districts.

The manner in which the individual members of Congress balance the in-

[8] The structure of committee power is discussed at length in Chap. 14.

terests of conflicting groups is of central importance. Only a small number of members have such strong backing from one set of interests that they can afford complete consistency. For most members the price of survival is for the member to try to do something for every organized interest in his constituency, even though his actions seem inconsistent when judged on the basis of abstract principles. Hence the wry witticism so often heard in the halls of Congress: "There comes a time in the life of every member when he must rise above conviction." Hence, too, the spectacle of outstanding liberals at times working hand in glove with the most conservative interests in the country and that of deep-dyed reactionaries occasionally behaving like liberals.

THE EXECUTIVE OFFICIALS

"The third house of Congress" is a metaphorical phrase variously applied to congressional conference committees, the Supreme Court, the Washington lobbyists, and the press. If its purpose is to indicate the extent of direct and continuous activity in the legislative struggle, it is particularly applicable to the executive branch of the Federal government. In the President and the people around him, in the high officials of the many agencies and bureaus, and in the vast staff of miscellaneous administrators and experts we find an aggregate of people who not only far outnumber the members of Congress and their employees but also spend an incalculably greater total of man-hours in the production of bills and statutes.

Presidents

A President, of course, is many men. "The 'President Roosevelt' of history, for example," as Bentley said with reference to Roosevelt I, "is a very large amount of official activity, involving many people. Any other 'President Roosevelt' of public life, physical, temperamental, moral, is but a limited characterization of that activity." [9] The same observation might be made concerning Roosevelt II or any of his successors, the only difference being that Presidents are now a still larger amount of activity involving a much larger number of people.

In pictorial and formal terms, these people can be described as a series of concentric circles. At the center are the members of the White House staff, which has grown considerably in recent years. Next come the top officials of the Bureau of the Budget, the Council of Economic Advisers, the National Security Resources Board, and the National Security Council.[10] Then come

[9] Arthur F. Bentley, "The Process of Government" (Bloomington, Ind.: Principia Press, 1949 reissue), p. 176.

[10] For an interesting discussion of the Executive Office of the President in which these agencies are located see F. Morstein Marx (ed.), "Federal Executive Reorganization Reexamined: A Symposium," *American Political Science Review,* Vol. 40, 1946, pp. 1124ff.

the heads of the Departments, who collectively comprise the Cabinet and meet with the President regularly, and the officials of the other agencies, boards, and commissions. On the outermost rim, in the informal sense, are the members of Congress, party officials, personal friends, and various leaders of industry, agriculture, labor, and other private organizations.

These circles, however, are constantly undulating and overlapping. "Our twentieth century President," writes a White House correspondent, "is like a fortress under constant siege." [11] Every now and then various besiegers succeed in penetrating into the inner circles. The President, for his part, usually sets up circles of his own, picking this selected group for one purpose and that group for another, playing one off against the other, never allowing anyone else to capture too much power. It is this shadowy set of groups that is often called the "Kitchen Cabinet," a colorful phrase indicating that the members of the formal Cabinet are frequently overshadowed in importance by people who are much closer to the President. The phrase should not lead one to regard the President's closest intimates as a compact and nonfluctuating body. Most of them serve only for fixed purposes, and all of them run the risk of being charged off as expendable at any moment and being summarily removed from the throne room and propelled into the outer darkness.

In function also the President is many men. He is the single living symbol of the national government; and everything connected with him, his family and the house he lives in and works in, rivals Hollywood as an object of public attention, discussion, and gossip. He is Commander in Chief of the Army and Navy. He conducts our foreign relations. He is the head of a major political party. He is supposed to administer laws and interpret them in the process. In addition to all this he is a legislative leader—in fact, the most important single legislative leader in the Government. Except in wartime, Presidents are now judged more by the quality of the legislation they propose or succeed in getting enacted than by their records as Executives.

In part, the President's legislative activities are based squarely on the provisions of the Constitution. Under the Constitution the President "shall give to the Congress Information of the State of the Union and recommend to their Consideration such Measures as he shall judge necessary and expedient." He may convene special sessions of either or both houses to consider his legislative proposals. He may wield a limited veto over measures adopted in Congress—a power which can be exercised not only in a negative and defensive fashion but also as an affirmative and aggressive weapon in the legislative struggle.

Upon this foundation has been erected an elaborate structure of Presidential recommendations for legislative action. The President now sends three general messages to Congress at the beginning of every year. They are (1) a

[11] Merriman Smith, "A President Is Many Men" (New York: Harper, 1948), p. 9.

State of the Union Message outlining the general nature of his program for Federal action, including legislation; (2) an Economic Report which includes legislative proposals supposedly geared to the maintenance of maximum employment, production, and purchasing power; and (3) a Budget Message which contains his proposals for appropriation acts, both in general terms and in specific legislative language. He sends to Congress every year scores of special messages dealing with individual legislative matters, many on his own initiative, others in conformance with the requirements of individual statutes. He makes many legislative proposals through both correspondence and conferences with official congressional leaders, chairmen of congressional committees, and many individual members. Veto messages themselves often become vehicles for alternative proposals.

In great part, also, a President's legislative activities are based on functions and powers unmentioned in the Constitution (although most became quite familiar to those Founding Fathers who later became Presidents). Among these is a President's ability to influence congressional action through the manipulation of patronage, the allocation of Federal funds and projects, and the handling of constituents' cases in which members of Congress are interested. Still more important is the power which he enjoys as leader of his party and chief election campaigner and by reason of occupying a strategic position for promoting broad coalitions of social groups and interests.

Every President is a complex combination of strength and weakness. Even those who seem to enjoy the greatest power and to be most suited temperamentally for its aggressive exercise have proved utterly unable to cope with many situations. For one thing, a President is like an Oriental potentate who has a harem of a thousand wives. While he is theoretically free to give attention to all of them, there are only so many hours a day and so many days a year. Although the President and the people around him usually do their best to cover the water front, the time always comes quickly when they must make the choice between exercising their powers of office on important matters or risking a nervous breakdown.[12] Then again there is an institutional rivalry between Presidents and members of Congress, many of whom can best develop public stature by demonstrating their ability to "clip the President's wings." "There can be no doubt," writes Harold Laski, "that in its own eyes, Congress establishes its prestige when it either refuses to let the President have his own way, or compels him to compromise with it."[13] This institutional analysis can

[12] "Men of ordinary physique and discretion cannot be Presidents and live if the strain be not somehow relieved. We shall be obliged always to be picking our chief magistrates from among wise and prudent athletes,—a small class." Woodrow Wilson, "Constitutional Government in the United States" (New York: Columbia University Press, 1911 ed.), pp. 79–80.

[13] Harold J. Laski, "The American Presidency: An Interpretation" (New York: Harper, 1940), p. 116.

easily be carried too far. In fact, it has been carried too far by many writers on American government, particularly Laski, who, despite his background as a Marxian, seems to regard the institutional factor as the whole story and to neglect the significance of social groups able to use the members of one government agency against the members of another.

The battle line-up and the disposition of contesting groups always have a material effect on a President's strength. Bentley writes:

> If group interests tend in a certain direction and are checked in their course through Congress, they will find their way through the presidency. If the group interests take permanently a form which makes Congress an inadequate agency for them, then the presidency will consolidate its power. If, on the other hand, the shifting of interests or the change in Congress makes the latter agency adequate, then the presidency's power will readjust itself accordingly. . . . If the executive yields to a group organization gathering force from without, before the legislature yields, it will gain in power as compared to the legislature, until the legislature yields in its turn.[14]

Binkley puts it this way: "It can be set down as a fundamental principle that whether Congress or the executive is dominant in the government depends upon which of the two, in a given period, is the more adequate medium of governmental control for the dominant interests of the nation." [15]

The manner in which various groups express themselves through the Presidency or the Congress is closely connected with the electoral system. The underrepresentation of the urban population in Congress tends to make Congress a more adequate medium for farm groups and for the business groups which have succeeded in obtaining the support of farm organizations against their fellow urbanites, the organized workers.

The clash of President and Congress is intensified by the striking differences between the ways in which pressures play upon the Congress on the one hand and upon the President on the other. For example, important elements such as labor, racial and certain other groups are peculiarly weak in urging their desires upon Congress. Consequently they quite naturally and properly seek to exert a leverage on the government through their voting strength as balances of power in presidential elections. Indeed, here is a counterbalance against the immense advantage the interests of property and production hold in Congress due to the under-representation of urban voters in Congress and to the fact that the practice of seniority in determining control of the House of Representatives reduces considerably the power of the urban voters. Such is the predominance of rural constituencies that the majority of Congressmen can ignore the desires of the urban masses with impunity while the President does so only at his peril.[16]

---

[14] Bentley, *op. cit.*, pp. 351, 358–359.

[15] Wilfred E. Binkley, "The President and Congress," *Journal of Politics,* Vol. 11, February, 1949, p. 69.

[16] *Ibid.*, p. 76.

Other Executive Officials

Entirely apart from whatever services they may render as part of the Presidential team, the officials of the various executive agencies are inextricably involved in the legislative struggle. In the daily process of administering legislation, they run into countless problems that can be solved only through amendments or new legislation. They constitute a vast reservoir of information and know-how needed in the legislative process. Success in obtaining the funds upon which their agencies exist depends upon their ability to justify favorable appropriation legislation every year. And so the officials of the various agencies can be found spending large portions of their time in preparing recommendations for legislation, writing detailed reports in support of legislation, presenting testimony before congressional committees, and actively organizing support for their legislative efforts.

A bogeyman has been created of a vast Executive bureaucracy with such power and influence that the President can use it to dominate Congress and obtain whatever legislation he wants. One reason that this is not so is that no President has ever been able to avoid or overcome serious conflicts between the heads of the various agencies. From the days of the historic battles between Secretary of the Treasury Alexander Hamilton and Secretary of State Thomas Jefferson we have seen rival agency heads pitted against one another. Many of these have been able to go their own ways irrespective of Presidential direction, thumbing their noses at the President, yet surviving. The Army Corps of Engineers is the prize example of successful insubordination.

Almost without exception, the Corps has disregarded the orders of its Presidents. It has set itself above its commander-in-chief. It calls itself "the consulting engineer to and contractor for" the Congress, and it considers itself an arm of the legislative branch. Franklin D. Roosevelt, generally regarded as a strong President, lost every round he fought with the Corps. Although the Champ swung angrily and often, he never laid a glove on the Army Engineers. . . . The Corps has the whole-hearted support of the so-called "Rivers and Harbors Bloc," led largely by men from the lower Mississippi area. . . . Staunchly behind the "Rivers and Harbors Bloc" is the National Rivers and Harbors Congress—an organization dedicated to the principle that no stream is too small for a Federal handout, no levee tall enough, no channel deep enough, no harbor improved enough. It is a comprehensive lobby group, an involuted sort of affair which includes among its membership representatives and senators— the lobbied—as well as the contractors, and state and local officials—the lobby.[17]

Many Cabinet members and heads of agencies regard themselves as more responsible to certain members of Congress than to the President. When Rep-

[17] Robert de Roos and Arthur A. Maass, "The Lobby That Can't Be Licked," *Harper's Magazine*, August, 1949.

resentative Carl Vinson was chairman of the House Naval Affairs Committee he spoke fondly—and not wholly inaccurately—of "my Navy" and referred to Cabinet members as "the best (or worst) Secretary of the Navy I ever had." [18] Within the Departments, also, one finds firmly established heads of bureaus and divisions who within their own walls are lords of the manor and have learned through many years of experience how to evade or act counter to instructions from their superiors. "Matters of routine organization are of primary importance and if you ever want to run the United States of America," writes a newspaperman who had a splendid opportunity to observe Washington agencies during World War II, "never mind about the top jobs, take over the spots at the operating level and you'll really have your hands on the controls. . . . In any government organization, the operating man is likely to find himself in possession of an effective veto power over the policy man." [19]

Each agency and each part of an agency tends to develop a special interest of its own, with its people ever alert to see how they can best strengthen their personal positions. This tendency is immeasurably strengthened by the fact that many agencies themselves are established only in response to the pressure of private organizations and their representatives in Congress and can continue in existence only by working with and serving such groups. Alliances of this type are fortified by requirements for senatorial confirmation of Presidential appointments, by limitations on the President's power to remove the members of so-called "independent" boards and commissions, and by statutory provisions placing the appointive power for various second-level positions with the President rather than with the agency heads. As a result of these diverse and often conflicting allegiances, there are more checks and balances within the executive branch itself than the Founding Fathers ever dreamed of when they wrote the Constitution.

THE JUDGES

Although the legislative, judicial, and administrative processes of government are all interrelated parts of one complex struggle between competing groups and interests, there is a tendency among lawyers and law-school teachers to regard the courts as the end of the road and legislative activity as merely a preliminary action that provides materials used by the judges.

Yet from the viewpoint of the legislative process, judicial decisions are often merely incidents in the production of statutes. If it is true that one can never be positive concerning the meaning of a statute until a controversial question

[18] Jim G. Lucas, "Vinson the Invincible," *Washington Daily News*, Oct. 17, 1949.
[19] Bruce Catton, "The War Lords of Washington" (New York: Harcourt, Brace, 1948), pp. 232–233.

of interpretation has been settled by the courts, it is also true that those who disagree with a court interpretation can, and often do, immediately proceed to obtain a reversal of court action by an amendment of the original statute or by a new law. A judicial decision can serve the purpose of terminating efforts to obtain action through legislation and diverting efforts to other means. This occurs in matters of interpretation as well as when the Federal courts overthrow a law on the ground that it is unconstitutional. Decisions of executive officials in the administration of a law have a direct bearing upon the legislative process, but it is probably true that a larger proportion of judicial decisions have a more direct impact on the legislative process.

But does this mean that the judges are actually contestants in the legislative process? The theory that government officials can be neutral and objective mediators between contesting forces is nowhere more full-blown than with respect to the Federal judiciary. It is buttressed by three specialized fictions which often seem to have as much force in modern times as that once enjoyed by the concept of the divine right of kings. The first, which has been developed by the judges themselves with the valiant aid of the courtroom lawyers, is the idea that judges are able to grasp and interpret the intent of the legislators. The second fiction is that, with the Constitution as its finely drawn yardstick, the judges declare a law unconstitutional only when it goes beyond the legislative powers given to the Federal government under the Constitution. The third is that when a man is appointed to a life-term position, he is thereby immunized against the virus of personal ambition and insulated against the influence of group allegiances and pressures.

Yet in the misleading judicial jargon, "the intent of Congress" is little more than a method of rationalizing the views of the judges themselves. Every statute leaves broad room for interpretation. The issues litigated before the courts are usually ones which never arose during the course of the legislative process, were scarcely considered by the legislators, or upon which the Congress as a whole would certainly never have had an "intent." In fact, many issues which are determined "in accordance with the intent of Congress" were in the first instance deliberately left unsolved because any effort to resolve them in Congress would have made too many people unhappy.

The yardstick theory with respect to matters of constitutionality is still more hollow. Members of the Constitutional Convention had very little "intent" that was applicable to the problems of later decades. They were wise enough to write a document which could be flexibly interpreted. They even left it wide open as to whether or not the Supreme Court itself could declare a Federal statute unconstitutional. Although Alexander Hamilton's Federalist Paper, No. 78, explained the Constitution as giving the Supreme Court this power, the explanation itself was a matter of creative interpretation. Not a single word in the document deals directly with the matter. The Supreme

Court's power to overthrow a Federal statute is itself a prime example of extra-Constitutional action which is taken in the name of the Constitution.

As for lifetime tenure,[20] it is interesting to note that in most other contexts security against replacement is usually regarded as providing stronger entrenchment for a given social viewpoint. This is true with respect to those members of Congress who, coming from one-party areas, face no real opposition in the primaries. It is too seldom realized that similar realities lie behind the lifetime tenure of judges. A result of the constitutional provision that "Judges, both of the supreme and inferior Courts, shall hold their Offices during good Behavior" has undoubtedly been to maintain a group of people who could protect the interests of property against officers of the Government chosen through more popular methods and who are thereby more susceptible to the influence of the less propertied groups.

Many aspects of the judicial branch are inevitably partisan. It is impossible for a man to rise to the point of being considered for appointment to the bench without entering in a prominent fashion into partisan struggles, whether as a corporation lawyer, a member of Congress, an Attorney General, or a law-school professor. If appointed to a lower court, he may well play his cards so as to lead toward a subsequent seat on a higher court. If appointed to the Supreme Court, he can scarcely help realizing that the Supreme Court is often regarded as a reservoir of potential Presidential candidates. If he has no ambition for future political advancement, he cannot help but regard his position as an opportunity to translate into action the social convictions he has developed during the course of his lifetime. Few justices can avoid developing a vested interest in the judicial branch and becoming partisans in the competition of roles among judges, Congressmen, and executive officials.

There have always been and will always be sharp conflicts within the judicial branch: the circuit courts reversing the district courts, the supreme courts reversing the circuit courts, and the members of the Supreme Court perpetually squabbling among themselves. There have always been and will always be dramatic instances of a court taking one position at one time and then later on executing a dramatic about-face. This may be lamented by those who would like to find somewhere in our governmental system a firm and unchanging Rock of Gibraltar.[21] But it cannot be otherwise. What Robert Jack-

[20] The impeachment of judges is so rare that it is questionable whether reference to it in a broad discussion of the role of the judicial branch as a limitation on lifetime tenure merits more than a footnote.

[21] Jerome Frank suggests that one of the major reasons why people seek unrealizable certainty in the law is because "they have not yet relinquished the childish need for an authoritative father and unconsciously have tried to find in the law a substitute for those attributes of firmness, sureness, certainty and infallibility ascribed in childhood to the father." "Law and the Modern Mind" (New York: Tudor Publishing Co., 1935), p. 21.

son wrote about the Supreme Court before he became a member is applicable to the entire judicial branch:

> The ultimate function of the Supreme Court is nothing less than the arbitration between fundamental and ever-present rival forces or trends in our organized society. . . . Conflicts which have divided the Justices always mirror a conflict which pervades society. In fact, it may be said that the Supreme Court conference chamber is the forum where each fundamental cause has had its most determined and understanding championship. . . .[22]

The Local and Foreign Governments

When the Constitution was drafted it was contemplated that state governments would have indirect participation in the work of the Federal government through their role both in the ratification of constitutional amendments and in the designation of the members of the Senate. Participation of this type still continues. With the popular election of Senators, though, the influence of the state legislatures is concentrated in the House, the composition of which is materially affected by the manner in which the states set up their congressional districts.

Yet beyond these formal functions, the states have become exceedingly active in influencing the course of national legislative action. Within their given fields, organizations such as the American Association of State Highway Officials and the Conference of State and Territorial Health Officers have been able to determine the character of national legislation, even in the face of Presidential opposition. The Council of State Governments serves as an active vehicle for advancing the interests of the state governments as such.

The influence of state agencies, however, is complicated by the growth of urban governments and the steadily increasing power of organizations such as the United States Conference of Mayors. The state and local groups join arms in fighting to have Federal funds for local projects spent through local rather than Federal agencies, but they are in continuous conflict as to whether Federal aid for localities is to be channeled through state agencies or made available directly to the cities.

To an advancing degree, the actions of both "unfriendly" and "friendly" nations have a major impact upon American policy. When a major power takes an aggressive step that seems to threaten American interests, it obviously exercises a powerful influence on behalf of increased armament appropriations. In addition, the major powers, without exception, take direct steps of intervention in our legislative process. The Russians see to it that their supporters in America agitate vigorously against legislative action that opposes

---

[22] Robert Jackson, "The Struggle for Judicial Supremacy" (New York: Knopf, 1941), pp. 311–312.

Russian interests. The anti-Russian countries play an equally active role. The Washington embassies and legations of foreign governments are traditionally the organizing centers for these activities. Embassy and legation officials hire the services of American lawyers, research agencies, and lobbyists; organize support of nationality groups, American affiliates of international church bodies, American corporations with international business interests, and American affiliates of foreign corporations; and generally develop sources of legislative influence in the same manner as any domestic group or local government.

Midway between foreign governments and the American government stands a large array of international agencies, such as the International Bank for Reconstruction and Development, the Food and Agriculture Organization, the International Labor Organization, and the United Nations. Their functions depend to a high degree on legislative ratification of Executive agreements and Senate ratification of treaties. Often their major financial sustenance is derived from American appropriations, relying to a large extent upon the legislative activities of the various agencies of the Federal government and the business, farm, and labor groups with a direct interest in their world-wide activities.

Chapter 7

GOVERNMENT AGENCIES: RELATIONSHIPS
AND REFORMS

As ONE LEAVES the area of private organizations and political parties and considers proposals for changes in government agencies, he finds those that deal with the election of Congressmen and Presidents, the relations among the various branches of the Federal government, and the relations between the administrative and legislative processes.

THE ELECTORAL SYSTEM

The electoral system has an obvious bearing not only upon the choice of members of Congress and of Presidents but also upon their behavior. It affects the scope of their interests, the sources of their political support, and their attitude toward specific issues and conflicts. Changes in the electoral system, therefore, are often regarded as an important method of strengthening or impairing the position of various contestants in the legislative struggle. In a democracy, of course, the system for elections provides the ultimate sounding board for the attitudes of the community regarding the character of its political leadership and many of the basic orientations of its public policy. Here, too, the meaning of elections for the legislative struggle is profound. The discussion that follows will serve merely to make the reader aware of the range of this impact and of the areas of controversy regarding changes.

The Election of Members of Congress

Apportionment and Districting. The basis of representation in the Senate constitutes the most obvious violation of the democratic ideal that voters should have equal representation in an elected legislature. The justification for the unequal basis of representation in the Senate is that at the Constitutional Convention it was conceded to the smaller states as a matter of expediency, that it placed the senatorial representation of the smaller states in a privileged position that they would not willingly abdicate, that the present setup could scarcely be circumvented short of a veritable national emergency, and that the unequal basis of representation in the Senate has never produced and is never likely to produce such an emergency.

When one looks at the House of Representatives, one finds another series of representation problems with which it is easier to grapple. Every ten years in the light of the population shifts that have taken place between the states, Congress faces the very practical question of how to decide upon the number of seats assigned to each state. If the population of each state were an exact multiple of the average-sized House district, there would be no problem on the apportionment of seats among the states. The average-sized district would be divided into the population of a state, and the resulting figure would be the number of seats to which the state would be entitled. Population changes, however, never conform to meet mathematical patterns. The ratio of population to representatives will never divide exactly into the population of each state. There is always a fraction left over. Many complex mathematical formulas have been developed to allocate these fractions one way or another. Schmeckebier lists 16 different formulas, and many more probably could be devised.[1] The major contenders among the competing mathematical formulas are the methods of major fractions and of equal proportions. The latter method was written into the apportionment legislation of 1941.

However, disputes concerning the apportionment of House seats among the states sometimes tend to distract attention from the much more important problem of districting within each state. The tendency, as indicated in Chap. 6, is for redistricting within states to lag seriously behind the population shifts which enlarge the population of urban districts and decrease the population of rural districts. The political effect is to maintain political influence in rural districts far beyond that warranted by their population.

In 1950, as an outgrowth of the recommendation of its Committee on Political Parties, the American Political Science Association set up a special committee to study the problem.

The committee's basic proposals were as follows:

1. "That the standard requiring districts to be 'compact and contiguous,' found in the 1911 apportionment statute and omitted in the 1929 statute, should be included in a new law.

2. "That the statute should include a standard limiting to a certain percentage the deviation of any district within the State, upward or downward, from the average of all districts for the State; and that an effort should be made to keep the deviation of any district from the average of all districts for the State within a limit of 10%; but in any event such deviation should not be permitted to exceed 15%. [The practical effect of this recommendation would be to allow districts to vary over a range of about 100,000—that is from about 300 to 400 thousand.]

[1] Laurence F. Schmeckebier, "Congressional Apportionment" (Washington, D.C.: Brookings Institution, 1941), Chaps. 3–5, pp. 12–85.

3. "That the evasion of the above standards by electing Congressmen-at-large be prohibited." [2]

The committee then appraised various sanctions that might be used to force the states to live up to these standards. It then proposed a procedure designed to help bring the matter to a head in Congress:

First, the States should be required to do their own redistricting soon after Congress passes the Apportionment Act; this would give Congress ample time to consider whether this action by the States complies with the statutory standards of approximate equality.

Second, the President should transmit the results of State redistricting to Congress and to all the States, with information showing how any particular State has violated the statutory standards of approximate equality. Since the President's statement will appear in the press, unequal districting will be subjected to the powerful sanction of publicity.

Third, Congress may then take such action as it deems proper. Congress may order the State to do the job over again. Or Congress may redistrict the State itself.

The committee recognized that these sanctions applied more to districts of unequal size than to gerrymandered districts. Because it felt that precise standards on what is and is not gerrymandering are impossible, the committee recommended no specific action on the subject. The essence of the committee's proposals was adopted by President Truman in his regular decennial message dealing with apportionment.[3] Their adoption would tend to lead to a House of Representatives with a greater number of Congressmen from urban constituencies, a lesser number from rural constituencies, and a new power balance among the groups covered within the rural-urban rubrics.

Smaller or Larger Districts. In 1951, one proposal was to increase the size of the House from 435 to 509. This would have preserved the existing number of seats for all states with declining populations and would have rewarded faster-growing states with an additional 74 new seats. The compromise proposal would have enlarged the House to 450 seats, thereby reducing in part the individual losses that otherwise loomed over states with declining populations. In defense of these proposals, the argument is always made that smaller districts will allow individual members to maintain closer personal relationships with their constituents. It is also stated at times that greater membership will help the House of Representatives to handle its steadily growing burden.

Basically, however, proposals of this type constitute methods of avoiding sound apportionment and redistricting. They are effectively answered in the report of the Committee on the Reapportionment of Congress.[4]

[2] Committee on Reapportionment of Congress, "The Reapportionment of Congress," *American Political Science Review*, Vol. 14, No. 1, March, 1951, pp. 153–157.

[3] Message of Jan. 9, 1951.

[4] "The Reapportionment of Congress," p. 153.

In the course of a polemical debate with Friedriek Hayek over economic planning, Herman Finer proposed that the membership of the House of Representatives be increased to about 750.[5] According to William Y. Elliott, the forty-eight states should be brought together into a much smaller number of regional "commonwealths," each of which would be represented in a national House of Representatives on the basis of population. The broadening of the area in which a candidate might stand for office "would tend to defeat the purely local character of representatives." Furthermore, the recognition of "sectional areas as the primary bases of a new Federal system . . . would revive our groping federalism and stay the present march of centralization in Washington." [6]

Multimembered Districts. In some other countries, particularly in France, there has been continuous controversy on the merits of the single-member district versus the multimember district. Single-member districts, it is pointed out, give an unfair advantage to the majority party and greatly handicap the development of any third parties. For this very reason they are defended by the proponents of the two-party system.[7]

The use of multimembered districts (districts from which two or more of the legislative body are to be chosen at the same election) always raises the question of whether elections should be held on the basis of a general ticket or of proportional representation. Under the first alternative, the party with the highest number of votes on its side will send its complete slate to the legislature. Under the second alternative, all parties will send representatives to the legislature in proportion to their voting strength.

During the first fifty years of the American Republic these were live issues. Close to the middle of the nineteenth century, however, this problem was solved by requiring each state to establish congressional districts. This system has served well and it should be continued. The only departures that are made from this system occur on certain occasions when state legislatures dodge redistricting by providing for Congressmen at Large. As suggested by the Committee on Reapportionment of Congress in the report referred to above, this practice should be prohibited.

Terms of Office. The most far-reaching proposal for changes in the terms of office would synchronize Presidential elections and congressional elections. One advocate of complete realignment writes:

The four-year term of office for all Congressmen, Representatives and Senators alike, would afford, as a rule, an opportunity for the Administration to pursue its

[5] Herman Finer, "Road to Reaction" (Boston: Little, Brown, 1945), p. 213.

[6] William Y. Elliott, "The Need for Constitutional Reform" (New York: McGraw-Hill, 1935), pp. 182–208.

[7] See E. E. Schattschneider, "Party Government" (New York: Rinehart, 1942), pp. 69–84 for a useful analysis of the "single-member-district-system-plus-plurality-elections."

projects and plans untrammeled by partisan prejudice, pettiness, and opposition, thereby making possible a constructive, more nearly unified policy; and at the same time would place the responsibility for the management of affairs where it belongs— squarely on the shoulders of the leaders in power.[8]

In so far as the shortening of senatorial terms is concerned, this approach has received little favorable attention in Congress. The case for extending the terms of members of the House of Representatives, however, is more popular. Members from contested districts have scarcely any breathing space between elections. Four-year terms would unquestionably give them more time to devote to the legislative process. The proposal is particularly attractive to those who see in the mid-term elections a barrier to effective Presidential and party leadership, but under present political circumstances the desire of House members for longer terms of office is scarcely strong enough to override the strong opposition in the House to any increase in Presidential power. Furthermore, scores of members of Congress have been elected on the same day that Presidents were and have found it unnecessary to stand together with the President during the election campaign.

The Election of Presidents

How the Votes Are Counted. Many arguments have been made for abolishing the electoral-college system of electing our Presidents, on the ground that the electors selected in each state are not only useless but also dangerous. In some elections, as has happened occasionally, electors might switch their votes. They might withhold them. They might involuntarily create national problems by dying before the day arrived to cast their votes. They might become storm centers of litigation over electoral qualifications.

A more important target of criticism—one that would remain even if electors as such were eliminated—is the bloc-voting or "winner-take-all" system of electoral votes. Under this system the total amount of electoral votes of every state goes to the candidate who has received the largest number of votes, and the candidate with less than a plurality gets no electoral votes whatsoever. This enhances the political power of "swing" groups in the most populous states, since large masses of electoral votes can be moved *in toto* into one column or the other. It provides little incentive for voting or for Presidential campaigning in the so-called "safe states," for here the vote for a minority candidate can rise from 10 to 49 per cent of the total without making one bit of difference in the electoral vote by which the Presidential contest is decided. Moreover, through this disenfranchisement of minority voters within each state,

[8] Pearl Olive Ponsford, "Evil Results of Mid-term Congressional Elections and a Suggested Remedy" (Los Angeles: University of Southern California Press, 1937), p. 70.

it becomes possible, on occasion, for a candidate with the greatest number of popular votes to lose the election.

Theoretically, no constitutional amendment is necessary in order to break down this bloc-voting system. The Founding Fathers wrote nothing in the Constitution suggesting that the electoral vote in any state be given in entirety to the candidate obtaining the plurality. Under the Constitution, the states decide how their electoral votes are allocated. During the first years of the Republic the votes were divided among the congressional districts in each state. The bloc-voting system developed in 1800 when a number of Federalist states adopted it as a method of reducing the voting power of Jefferson's supporters. The Jeffersonians countered by trying to amend the Constitution to prevent Federalist use of this device. Failing to obtain a two-thirds majority in Congress, they then adopted the bloc-voting system themselves in the Jeffersonian states in order to reduce the voting power of the Federalists. During the subsequent years, the bloc-voting system became frozen into the electoral system through legislation in every state.

The effort to change the voting method used in Presidential contests by use of a constitutional amendment has been the greatest lost cause in the history of all efforts to amend the Constitution. From 1800 to 1950 almost 400 resolutions to change the system were introduced in the Congress. The proposals are of three basic types: The first is to have a direct popular vote, the most democratic method of electing a President. The adoption of this type is generally regarded as beyond the realm of probability. The fact that it would involve substantial shifts in political power alone would make it unfeasible. The second type is to return to the district system. This would go a few steps in the direction of distributing the electoral vote more in accordance with the popular vote. In one-party states, however, where the minority party often fails to capture even one congressional seat, it is unlikely that the district system would effect any significant change. It would also extend into Presidential elections the influence of gerrymandering. The third type is to allocate the electoral vote in each state in accordance with the number of voters. Thus, in a state with ten electoral votes, a candidate who obtains 40 per cent of the votes cast would be credited with four electoral votes. This proposal has sometimes been confused with proportional representation but it is entirely different. Proportional representation applies only to elections in which two or more persons are elected on the basis of the voting strength behind each candidate. In this case there is still only one person to be elected and no minority representation is possible. It has also been charged that this proposal would give great additional power to minority parties. Yet, in exchange for a paper showing on the final tally sheets, the minority parties would in fact be nudged out of the balance-of-power positions in what are now pivotal states.

An interesting suggestion on how to steer electoral-college reform through the shifting shoals of opposition has been designed by Samuel Huntington who has suggested that the Lodge-Gossett reform be combined with a constitutional amendment requiring congressional districts of approximately equal population.[9]

A subordinate, though fascinating, question of electoral-college reform is whether or not a full majority of the total vote, rather than a mere plurality, should be required as a condition of election. Recent proposals for a proportional system of allocating the electoral vote within each state, therefore, have provided that no candidate could become President without winning a given percentage of all electoral votes—usually 40 per cent. A closely related problem is the present provision for having the election determined in the House of Representatives if no candidate obtains the required number of electoral votes. It is often proposed, therefore, that any election in the House of Representatives be made by the vote of the entire membership only. A still more attractive proposal is that the selection be made by the membership of both houses of Congress voting together as a unit.

Number of Terms. In 1950, with the ratification of the Twenty-second (anti-third-term) Amendment to the Constitution, the venerable two-term tradition, so decisively broken by Franklin D. Roosevelt, came back into its own.

What effect the anti-third-term amendment may have remains to be seen. It will probably make it more difficult for a second-term President to obtain legislative support in Congress. On the other hand, it may turn out that a President, whose nomination at the next convention is thus forestalled, may yet exercise a strategic influence over the selection of his party's Presidential candidate and thereby maintain considerable power during his second term. There is also the possibility that in some cases the new prohibition will encourage the growth of contenders for party leadership. When a President can be reelected repeatedly, there is always the danger that the functions of the party leadership will devolve upon his shoulders alone.

A hoary proposal which still seems to have a long life ahead of it is that Presidents be limited to one term of six years each. One of its latest proponents is Harold Laski.[10] Others have been Representatives Hobbs and Gossett, whose minority views attached to the House Judiciary Committee report on the anti-third-term amendment argued that a single term of six years "would eliminate, as far as it is possible to do so, political considerations from the execution of office." [11] This is much like eliminating water as a consideration in the life of a fish.

[9] Samuel Huntington, "Electoral Reform: Congress and President" (unpublished paper, Harvard University, February, 1951).

[10] Harold J. Laski, "The American Democracy" (New York: Viking, 1948), pp. 122–124.

[11] "Proposed Amendment to the Constitution of the United States Relating to Terms of Office of the President," 80th Cong., 1st Sess., H. Rept. 17, Feb. 5, 1947.

Succession and the Vice-Presidency. Since death itself plays a role in the selection of Presidents, many minds have pondered over the question of how to get Vice-Presidents who are best equipped to take over when tapped by the finger of fate.

There is little reason to change the present constitutional provisions regarding the Vice-President. An elected Vice-President is certainly better than one who is appointed. A designated successor is certainly better than a period of interregnum and possible chaos during which a new election would be held.

It is often argued that the party conventions should nominate Vice-Presidential candidates who are highly qualified to serve as President and who have more to offer than an appeal to various groups whose support is needed for the Presidential campaign. Yet the necessities of politics will inevitably continue to produce "balanced tickets" made up of Presidential and Vice-Presidential candidates with differing points of view on national issues.

It is also suggested that the Vice-President become the key link between the President and the Congress. Some Vice-Presidents have already served in this capacity and others will undoubtedly play a similar role. Yet, in many cases, political differences between the President and the Vice-President make such a relationship impossible.

A more formidable suggestion calls for legislation to designate the Vice-President "as the President's chief assistant in the over-all direction of the administrative branch." The Vice-President might even be given the task of planning the annual budget and transmitting it to Congress. Finally, the President would be expected to invite the Vice-President to sit regularly with the Cabinet and to transfer various administrative duties to him by Executive order. With these additions to Vice-Presidential prestige and responsibility, the national conventions would probably be induced to nominate more first-rate men to serve as Vice-Presidential candidates.[12]

What about the line of succession in the event of the death of both the President and Vice-President? Here a convincing argument can be made for remedial action. Under legislation passed in 1947, the Speaker of the House and subsequently the President pro tempore of the Senate are next in the line of succession. This is a very unsatisfactory arrangement. The Speaker of the House might be a member of an opposing party, as was in fact the case when the law was passed. The present law should be amended to restore the previous arrangement whereby various high-ranking Cabinet officers are designated as the next in line.[13]

[12] Clinton Rossiter, "The Reform of the Vice-Presidency," *Political Science Quarterly*, Vol. 43, No. 3, September, 1948, pp. 383–403.

[13] Joseph E. Kallenbach, in "The New Presidential Succession Act," *American Political Science Review*, Vol. 41, No. 5, October, 1947, pp. 931–941, points out the need for clarifying the question of how Presidential disability should be established and of what procedure should be followed in the event that Presidential or Vice-Presidential candidates die be-

The Voters

Behind the members of Congress and the President stand the men and women whose votes placed them in office or almost elected their opponents. Since large numbers of eligible voters customarily stay away from the polls, the case is often urged that larger turnouts are needed.

The Case for More Voters. In abstract terms of general principles, the case for more voters is a very appealing one. President Truman in December, 1950, wrote to the president of the American Political Science Association:

> The strength of democracy stems from popular participation in the government and popular support of our free institutions. Unfortunately, in the past ten years we have seen a marked decline in the percentage of eligible voters who go to the polls. This is a serious matter which challenges the interest of all citizens, regardless of party affiliation.[14]

Still on the level of abstract principle, the case is occasionally made against a large turnout at the polls. Francis G. Wilson has suggested that a high percentage of participation in voting would be a symptom of dangerous social struggles.

> In a society in which only fifty percent of the electorate participates, it is clear that politics does satisfy in a way the desires of the mass of individuals in the state. As the percentage of participation rises above, let us say, ninety percent, it is apparent that the tensions of political struggle are stretching to the breaking point the will toward the Constitution.[15]

In support of this thesis, it can be pointed out that mass participation in European elections has resulted from struggles that threatened—sometimes successfully—the very structure of democracy.

Calculations as to the implications of increases in voting have entered into all the historic conflicts over extension of suffrage. The removal of property-owning and taxpaying qualifications was the outcome of a long struggle for more political power on the part of Western settlers and lower-income groups. The drive for woman suffrage, finally consummated in the Nineteenth Amendment to the Constitution, was opposed not only by men who wanted to preserve their masculine prerogatives but also by liquor interests sensitive to feminine hostility to their business and by corporations fearful that women with votes would add to the strength of labor organizations. The still-continuing

---

tween Election Day and the formal casting of electoral ballots. These and related questions should probably become a specific subject for study by an expert committee or a special congressional commission.

[14] *American Political Science Review*, Vol. 45, March, 1951, p. 165.

[15] Francis G. Wilson, "The Inactive Electorate and Social Revolution," *Southwestern Social Science Quarterly*, Vol. 16, No. 4, 1936, pp. 73–84.

struggle over Negro suffrage has been characterized by opposition, particularly from the black belt counties of the Deep South, to the idea of more political power in the hands of Negro leaders. It has also been accompanied by less outspoken opposition to the idea of greater political activity by the lower-income elements generally, whether white or Negro. Practically all proposals for the extension of suffrage have been opposed by leaders of entrenched political organizations with anxieties about how an increased electorate might affect their power.

The available evidence seems to indicate that the greatest number of stay-at-homes on Election Day are to be found among lower-income groups. "In breaking the native-white group down into its economic constituents," reported Edward Litchfield in his classic study of voting in Detroit between 1930 and 1938, "it was learned that its laxness during non-presidential years was confined entirely to the lower and middle-income groups." As for Presidential elections, "The participation data revealed the existence of a direct relationship between income and the amount of participation. The higher the income the higher the percentage of participation. . . ." [16] It is therefore evident that the largest increment of additional votes is to be found among the lower-income groups generally and particularly among lower-income women and Negroes. Any party which successfully appeals to these elements of the population will thereby win a major advantage in election contests. On the other hand, any party which depends for the bulk of its support upon the lower-income groups will usually be seriously hurt by a low turnout at the polls.

Above all, it should be kept in mind that the size of the vote is not a causative factor. It is rather a reflection—in statistical and therefore in limited terms —of the concrete achievements of competing organizations, each one of which is presumably concentrating on getting out the vote for its candidates. To analyze the meaning of the turnout at a given election, therefore, one must look at its composition.

The composition of the vote in any election, in turn, is a result of the political struggle that has taken place before the election. To some extent, the character of this struggle is determined by social conditions. It is also determined by the character of the campaigning. Not only do allegiances shift but many American voters have little or no allegiances. Attractive candidates, skillful campaigning, and organizational unity can do wonders in winning conservative support for Democrats or liberal supporters for Republicans.

Methods for Widening Participation. Whether or not it seems doctrinally

[16] Edward Litchfield, "Voting Behavior in a Metropolitan Area" (Ann Arbor, Mich.: University of Michigan Press, 1941), p. 66; see also G. M. Connelly and H. H. Field, "The Non-voter—Who He Is, What He Thinks," *Public Opinion Quarterly*, Vol. 8, 1944, pp. 175–187; and Julian L. Woodward and Elmo Roper, "Political Activity of American Citizens," *American Political Science Review*, Vol. 44, No. 4, December, 1950, pp. 872–885.

sound to have more people vote at a particular time or in a particular situation in a democracy such as ours, the compulsions to widen participation in the community's decisions are ever present and will remain so as long as opportunity remains for new leaders to arise through the social structure and for the poor and the disenfranchised to obtain more than a modicum of education. Growth in participation comes in two ways: (a) by making more individuals and groups eligible to vote through the enactment of new suffrage laws or the enforcement of the old ones; (b) by facilitating participation by those already eligible.

Despite constitutional provision to the contrary, a whole array of formal and informal restrictions on the exercise of suffrage rights by Negroes has developed throughout the Southern states. To penalize these restrictions, it has been recommended that the electoral vote of each state be geared to the actual number of voters instead of basing it upon population. It has been estimated that this would initially cut Southern representation in the House of Representatives by at least 50 per cent. Another line of attack has been the drive to eliminate poll taxes. Thus far the number of poll-tax states has been reduced from eleven to six. Less progress, however, has been made in dealing with discriminatory registration practices.

New laws have been proposed for extending the suffrage to residents of the District of Columbia, to Indian citizens of New Mexico and Arizona, and to eighteen-year-olds (now in effect in Georgia). There have been efforts to relax naturalization laws allowing aliens, regardless of race, color, or national origin, to become citizens and acquire the right to vote. Resident requirements for voting tend automatically to disenfranchise many hundreds of thousands of persons at every election (one extreme estimate puts the figure at 11 million) because of the highly migratory character of the American population. McGovney has suggested that a national standard for the residence requirement be established.[17]

Many persons who are eligible to vote fail to do so because of inconvenience and other difficulties, many of which result from a positive disinterest among certain local groups to facilitate the voting function. Among the recommendations along these lines have been: permanent registration; improved voting hours; more accessible voting places; easier absentee voting, particularly for the increasing numbers of men and women serving in the armed forces; and the use of the short ballot to prevent "voter fatigue."

The participation problem has also been viewed as one in developing incentives for voting. More and better education is a fundamental step in this direction. Broadening the tax base is considered one way to make people aware of their stake in government. Compulsory voting is another device de-

[17] Dudley O. McGovney, "The American Suffrage Medley" (Chicago: University of Chicago Press, 1949), pp. 181–182.

signed to lead *all* the voters to polling booths, thereby compelling a larger number of them to think and choose. Short of compulsory voting, however, perhaps the greatest incentive to voting lies in the character and vigor of the party battle.

RELATIONS AMONG THE THREE BRANCHES

It is a striking paradox of American life that the provisions of the United States Constitution outlining the tripartite structure of our national government are viewed with awe and reverence by almost everyone except students of government. The result has been a long series of proposals to eliminate the separation between Congress and the executive branch, provide for closer cooperation between them, or modify the legislative veto of the Supreme Court.

Congressional-Executive Merger

The Case against the Constitution. Misconceptions about the British parliamentary system have played a large role in American government and political science. The Founding Fathers thought that the British system at that time was based upon the "separation of powers" described by Montesquieu. They failed to realize that with the development of the Cabinet's power, there had come into being a fusion between executive and legislative agencies.

In 1867 Walter Bagehot weighed the American Constitution and found it wanting. "The English Constitution, in a word, is framed on the principle of choosing a single sovereign authority, and making it good; the American, upon the principle of having many sovereign authorities, and hoping that their multitude may atone for their inferiority." [18]

Woodrow Wilson expressed the same thought in still stronger language:

The best rulers are always those to whom great power is intrusted in such a manner as to make them feel that they will surely be abundantly honored and recompensed for a just and patriotic use of it, and to make them know that nothing can shield them from full retribution for every abuse of it.

It is, therefore, manifestly a radical defect in our Federal system that it parcels out power and confuses responsibility as it does.[19]

The major case made against the Constitution is that the President and the Congress are independent bodies, with the election and tenure of neither directly dependent upon the will or the action of the other. The result, it is maintained, is to prevent both democracy and effectiveness in the processes of gov-

[18] Walter Bagehot, "The English Constitution," in "World's Classics," No. 330 (New York: Oxford, 1949 ed.), p. 202.
[19] Woodrow Wilson, "Congressional Government" (Boston: Houghton Mifflin, 1925), pp. 284–285.

ernment. Since there is no one central organ of acknowledged leadership, it is impossible to place responsibility for what is or is not done. There is no logical channel through which majority sentiment can be organized. In the absence of majority control, it follows that there is no crystallization of an effective minority to present minority viewpoints and protect minority rights. Congressional activities, therefore, and particularly congressional debates, lack the essential drama to bring them forcibly to public attention and educate the people on political issues. Congress feels compelled to resist attempts at Presidential leadership and to win a place in the sun by public demonstrations of its ability to frustrate or humiliate executive officials.

Moreover, when deadlocks develop at any time other than immediately prior to a Presidential election, there is no method of resolution. With elections occurring at fixed dates rather than at the call of the legislative or executive bodies, it is impossible to take a fundamental legislative issue directly to the people. By the time elections roll around, the issues that have developed since the previous election and the records of men and parties alike tend to be forgotten by everyone except a few powerful pressure groups. Knowing that they need not be prepared at any moment to wage an election campaign and, if successful, assume control of the Government, the political parties have little incentive to concern themselves with basic policy issues. They, therefore, yield command of the legislative battlefield to the pressure groups. Under such conditions, there is no source of control to focus the legislative process on the many matters appropriate to it and to keep it from becoming involved in matters which should be handled rather through administrative or judicial processes. There is no leadership to schedule legislative operations, operate expeditiously, provide for the organization of relevant facts and opinions on proposed measures, or take responsibility for seeing that the laws produced are precisely and intelligibly drafted and consistent with one another.

To a lesser degree, a case has also been made against the separation between the two houses of Congress, between the Supreme Court and the rest of the Federal government, and between the Federal government and the states.

Proposals for British-type Systems. Woodrow Wilson had argued that "Congress must be organized in conformity with what is now the prevailing legislative practice of the world. English precedent and the world's fashion must be followed in the institution of Cabinet government in the United States." [20] The first complete proposal for the reconstruction of the American constitutional system was made by William MacDonald. He wrote:

> If the United States is to have a responsible government, it can only be done by such changes of the constitution as will give to Congress the control of policy. This

[20] Woodrow Wilson, "Committee or Cabinet Government?" *Overland Monthly,* Vol. 3, No. 1, January, 1884, p. 25.

can only be done, in the first place, by creating a ministry or administration—the particular term is not important—which shall represent the majority and which shall give way to another ministry or administration when the majority no longer supports it; and, in the second place, by stripping the President of the control of policy which he now has.[21]

A still more far-reaching reconstruction of the Government has been proposed by Henry Hazlitt. Hazlitt has argued that a popularly elected President would be a potential source of too much power and might impair the leadership of the Cabinet. The President, therefore, would be elected directly by Congress for a term of from five to ten years. The Cabinet would be responsible to the House alone. The Senate would have no direct legislative powers. It would have "the role merely of delaying, revising, forcing the House to reconsider, and telling the people unpalatable or unpopular truths. . . ."[22] There have also been a number of proposals for constitutional structures lying somewhere in between the English system and the American. William Y. Elliott has proposed that the President be given the power to dissolve Congress at least once during every four-year Presidential term. This, he argued, would provide the President with enough power to keep Congress in line and harmonize Executive-congressional operations.[23]

Thomas K. Finletter has made another set of interesting proposals. Using as a starting point Elliott's proposal for giving the President power to dissolve Congress, he argues that there should be no limitation on the number of times that a new election of Congress might be called by the President. He also proposes that in every case the dissolution work both ways, with the President, as well as the members of Congress, being required to face an election. It is also proposed that consultation between the two branches of government be institutionalized by the creation of a joint Executive-legislative Cabinet.[24]

C. Perry Patterson has developed an elaborate plan for placing Executive power in the hands of Congress without any change in the schedule of fixed elections or, for that matter, in the written Constitution itself. He points out that within the framework of the written Constitution there have been many great and revolutionary changes in the actual structure of the Government. The unwritten Constitution now makes the President tantamount to a dictator. New changes in the unwritten Constitution could provide us with responsible government in the hands of Congress. This involves the creation in Congress of "a

[21] William MacDonald, "A New Constitution for a New America" (New York: B. W. Huebsch, 1921), pp. 60ff.

[22] Henry Hazlitt, "A New Constitution Now" (New York: McGraw-Hill, 1942), pp. 176–177, 217.

[23] William Y. Elliott, "The Need for Constitutional Reform" (New York: McGraw-Hill, 1935).

[24] Thomas K. Finletter, "Can Representative Government Do the Job?" (New York: Reynal & Hitchcock, 1945).

body of political leaders who will be responsible to the party system and who will initiate legislative policy, and, thereby, serve as a check upon the President by means of the party system in Congress. They cannot be Presidential puppets subject to his dismissal at will. They must be responsible to the Congress through the party organization." This joint committee of both houses of Congress would rule the congressional roost as well as the executive departments. Bicameralism would be reduced to a fiction. The President would become little more than a ceremonial head of state.[25]

The Defects in This Approach. Whether these proposals are desirable or not can be questioned on a number of counts.

First, these proposals are based upon an unrealistic ideal of what government should be like. They are geared to the conception—to use Woodrow Wilson's words—that we should make self-government "a straightforward thing of simple method, single unstinted power, and clear responsibility. . . ." Yet this is a dubious standard for a complex, pluralistic society. One might just as well ask that all future wars be straightforward conflicts, decisively fought upon one front alone.

Second, these proposals are based upon an excessively generous—indeed, romantic—idea of the virtues of the British parliamentary system. The formal structure described by Bagehot and Wilson is delightfully logical. Yet it has not been able to prevent years of instability and confusion during those periods when no one party has been able to obtain a clear majority in the House of Commons. It has not been able to solve the problem of the tremendous gap between Cabinet Ministers, who are supposed to make policy, and the civil-service bureaucracy which has a quasi monopoly of knowledge and thereby often holds the reins of government. In fact, British commentators, similarly dissatisfied with the British system, have also looked admiringly across the seas and proposed measures borrowed from American examples.

Finally, proposals of this type, if adopted, would do little to achieve the objectives sought. If one thinks that they would make elections more meaningful, let him look at city and county governments where there is usually little separation between the legislative and the executive agencies. Nor is there any reason to believe that some form of parliamentary system in the United States could have any significant effect upon party alignments. In fact, James M. Burns maintains—and with considerable validity—that the parliamentary system in America might serve to break down the ties that hold the major parties together and promote the formation of a number of minor parties constantly negotiating alliances with each other for the formation of one Cabinet or the overthrow of another. He describes the power of dissolution, which has customarily been regarded as a method of enforcing the power

---

[25] C. Perry Patterson, "Presidential Government in the United States" (Chapel Hill, N.C.: University of North Carolina Press, 1947).

of the national government, as "a method applying party discipline, not a cause of that discipline." He also points out that to the extent that centralized government power is found in Britain it is the result not so much of the constitutional system as of the fact that Britain is a more homogeneous country with stronger traditions of class leadership and orientation toward the central government.[26]

Congressional-Executive Collaboration

"The letter of the Constitution wisely declared a separation," wrote Franklin D. Roosevelt in one of his earliest messages to Congress, "but the impulse of common purpose declares a union." [27] The search has led to proposals for various devices and joint organizations that would bring together executive officials and members of Congress, permit consultation and cooperation between the two branches of government, and allow Executive participation from the floor of Congress.

Joint Organizations. The most formidable proposal along these lines, first proposed by Corwin and subsequently advocated by Senator Robert La Follette, Jr., Finletter, and many others, is that the President should "construct his Cabinet from a joint legislative council to be created by the two Houses of Congress and to contain its leading members." [28] Under this proposal the President would become neither a prime minister who is supposed to resign when defeated in Congress nor a figurehead like the king in Great Britain or the president in other countries with parliamentary systems. According to Corwin, arrangements of this type would mean that we would no longer have to depend upon the accidents of crisis or personality to obtain genuine Presidential leadership.

[26] James M. Burns, "Congress on Trial" (New York: Harper, 1949), pp. 144–162. Cf. Ralph M. Goldman, "Party Chairman and Party Faction, 1789–1900" (doctoral dissertation, University of Chicago, 1951), pp. 672–673: "The absence of a meaningful minority leadership in the American system makes all comparison with the parliamentary model of doubtful value in theory or in practice. The privileged status of the Opposition Leader in a parliamentary system is quite as important to that kind of party system as is the Prime Minister. . . . The American system merely has its Residual [National Committee] Chairman. . . ."

To meet this need, Paul T. David has suggested that the defeated Presidential candidate automatically become minority leader, established in Washington with a $50,000 per annum allowance and nonvoting privileges in Congress, until replaced at any time by a minority party national convention or by action of the national committee under rules set out by the national convention. (*Washington Post,* Nov. 24, 1952, p. 8.)

[27] "Public Papers and Addresses of Franklin D. Roosevelt" (New York: Random House, 1938–1950).

[28] Edward S. Corwin, "President, Office and Powers" (New York: New York University Press, 1948), pp. 361–364.

A less pretentious proposal was presented by Leon H. Keyserling in his 1945 prize-winning essay on Post-war Employment Policy. Keyserling suggested the creation of an American Economics Committee composed of three Senators, three Representatives, and three members of the President's Cabinet, together with six representatives of industry, agriculture, and labor, which would "find an American Economic Goal, reflecting America's optimum productive capacity, national income and employment, and correlating these with an 'optimum standard of living within the reach of all American families.' " [29] This proposal was sidetracked by the subsequent framing of the Employment Act of 1946 and by the creation of the President's Council of Economic Advisers, an agency which Keyserling subsequently headed. The drafters of this statute believed that better cooperation could be obtained among the various representatives of the two branches of government if separate planning organizations were established in each and that a joint body could neither provide necessary staff services to the President nor effective economic leadership in Congress.

More specialized proposals have often been made for joint agencies in specific areas. William Y. Elliott has proposed an organization of Cabinet committees which would "bring in responsible leaders of Congress, and, in particular, the chairmen of important committees into the policy-formulating stages on all government policy." [30] These Cabinet committees would cover six crucial areas: national defense and foreign policy, fiscal policy, labor and social welfare, physical resources and development, commercial policy, and government organization.

This approach has been given particular attention by those concerned with foreign policy. Nathaniel Peffer, for example, has proposed the creation of a joint foreign policy council which would include the President, the Secretary of State, the Secretaries in charge of the Armed Forces, the Secretary of the Treasury, and the Chairmen and the two ranking minority members of the foreign affairs committees in the Senate and the House of Representatives.[31]

Rebuttal to Peffer has been provided by Harold Laski.

Whether its status be that of the convention of the Constitution or of a change made by formal amendment, the subordination of the President implied would make his position intolerable. He could not, in any case, sit in a "cabinet of foreign affairs" where four of his Cabinet officers, all of whom owed their appointments to him, were able to argue against him, to intrigue against him, even to vote against his views; very

[29] L. H. Keyserling, "The American Economic Goal: A Practical Start toward Post-war Full Employment" (mimeographed).

[30] Hearing before the Joint Committee on the Organization of Congress, 79th Cong., 1st Sess., pp. 961–962.

[31] Nathaniel Peffer, "America's Place in the World" (New York: Viking, 1945), p. 216.

early in the evolution of this committee he would clearly require from his Cabinet Members, as a condition of their appointment, that they act solely under his direction.[32]

Yet Laski's skilled polemics should not lead one to think that joint commissions can serve no purpose whatsoever. There are many specific purposes which can be well served by joint bodies representing both branches of government. The Temporary National Economic Committee made economic history in the assembling of important information and in educating people on economic problems. The Hoover Commission on the Organization of the Executive Branch succeeded in paving the way for a number of other reorganization operations that could probably not otherwise have been effectuated. Both these joint bodies, it should be noted, were set up for specific purposes and for limited periods of time.

Consultation and Cooperation. A less formal approach toward the problem of congressional-executive cooperation can be found through the devices of consultation and cooperation. Here one deals with something that is harder to concretize. Consultation and cooperation can be taking place, even though "outsiders" may be complaining that they are not. On many occasions, when observers are taking it for granted that there is consultation and cooperation, there may be a complete vacuum with respect to both.

There are at least four formal methods of promoting consultation and cooperation among the branches of government. One is the formal inclusion of members of Congress in various official bodies or delegations constituted by executive officials. In the field of foreign affairs considerable use has been made of this technique. Another is regular meetings between executive officials and congressional committees. "Excellent relations between the State Department and the foreign affairs committees of both Houses resulted," Kefauver and Levin have observed, "when Secretary of State Cordell Hull took the latter groups into his confidence on the big issues of planning for postwar world organization." [33]

A third method is staff collaboration. "We propose," wrote Kefauver and Levin, "that quarters for liaison staffs for each Federal department and major agency be provided on Capitol Hill." [34]

A fourth method, to use Roland Young's words, is through "having the administrators give Congress more complete and more regular reports on their activities." [35]

[32] Laski, *op. cit.*, p. 524.

[33] Estes Kefauver and Jack Levin, "A Twentieth Century Congress" (New York: Duell, Sloan & Pearce, 1947), pp. 145–149.

[34] *Ibid.*, p. 149.

[35] Roland A. Young, "This Is Congress" (New York: Knopf, 1943), p. 255.

Although all four of the formal methods referred to above have their place in consultative and cooperative relationships among members of Congress and executive officials, there is probably even a much greater role for the use of informal relationships. Genuine consultation is an intimate affair. If it is formalized there is always a danger that it will be postponed until a very late stage in any proceedings and regarded mainly as the perfunctory performance of a ritual. Furthermore, genuine consultation upon major issues is possible only with friends. One can cooperate with opponents but by no means in the same fashion as with one's allies. Informal methods have the advantage of allowing greater selectivity in the making of contacts while more formal methods sometimes bring together people who are animated by little or no common purpose.

Certain prerequisites for successful consultation and cooperation deserve to be mentioned at this point. One of these is time. Many good intentions to consult with members of Congress have been obliterated by an avalanche of hard work and new problems. Another is the ability on the part of an executive official to make up his own mind rather than to be dominated by the last pressure that makes itself felt. It presupposes a capacity to reject advice and at the same time maintain the respect of those whose advice is rejected.

Executive Participation on the Floor of Congress. During the Civil War a Congressman from Ohio proposed the establishment of a system having the heads of executive departments occupy seats on the floor of the House and participate, without voting, in floor activities. This proposal, while never acted upon by either house, has always had a contingent of earnest adherents. It has been hailed by Young, Heller, and Kefauver as one of the best methods of developing constructive relations between the executive and legislative branches. It would, according to them, provide members of Congress with a firsthand opportunity to learn about executive operations. It would prevent department heads from neglecting congressional opinion and require them always to be prepared to defend their operations before Congress.

Laski has argued that the question-period system, while well-suited to a parliamentary form of government, as in England, would "not meet the real problems created by the presidential system." He believed it would give undue prominence and authority to the members of the Cabinet who, in America, are merely the President's appointees and have no recognized status in their own right.[36]

The proponents of this scheme have attempted to counter the objections that have been raised by suggesting the use of various safeguards.[37]

[36] Laski, "The American Presidency" (New York: Harper, 1940), p. 108.
[37] See Robert Heller, "Strengthening the Congress" (Washington, D.C.: National Planning Association, 1945), p. 27. A still more elaborate set of safeguards and conditions is contained in a special memorandum by Herman Finer, entitled "Questions to the Cabinet in the British House of Commons; Their Applicability to the United States Congress," a memorandum

In checking through the dispute on this proposal one cannot help wondering what all the shooting is about. Questions are continuously being submitted to the officials of the executive branch by members of Congress. Many of them are answered in letters that are printed in the *Congressional Record* or in statements that are otherwise made available to the public. A large number of questions are presented to executive officials at committee hearings at which a detailed line of interrogation can be developed, where the opportunities for orderly procedure are much greater than they would be in a larger body and where the spotlight of publicity is probably as strong as it is on comparable debates on the Senate or House floor. In fact, as indicated earlier in the quotation from L. S. Amery, there are many people in England who would like to see a greater use of specialized committees in the British House of Commons in order to enable the members of Parliament to learn more from administrators about what is going on in the various executive departments.

The Supreme Court's Veto

The atmosphere of discussion concerning the relations between Congress and the executive branch is relaxed in contrast to the atmosphere surrounding the recurrent conflicts over the Supreme Court legislative veto. Here the lines are drawn in conflicts over specific and hotly contested cases, and the air is full of vigorous constitutional polemics.

The case for change has invariably been directed against Supreme Court action in overthrowing Federal statutes. There has been little interest in depriving the Court of its power to overthrow state laws. Most critics of the Court would agree with Justice Holmes's observation on this point: "I do not think the United States would come to an end if we lost our power to declare an act of Congress void. I do think the Union would be imperiled if we could not make that declaration as to the laws of the several States." [38]

Nor has there been any demand for alteration in the Court's power to legislate through its interpretation of Federal statutes. The road is always open for changing these interpretations through new legislation. But when a Federal statute is declared unconstitutional, then there is little recourse left to those whom the Court has frustrated. They must either amend the Constitution or else must force the Court to reverse itself, and either of these courses is extremely difficult.

In abstract terms, the case against the Supreme Court's veto—to quote one of the most conservative critics of the Court—is based upon the "danger that the Supreme Court could become a third legislative body more powerful than

---

submitted on request to the Joint Committee on the Organization of Congress, Joint Committee Print, 79th Cong., 2d Sess., "Suggestions for Strengthening Congress," pp. 49–58.

[38] "Law and the Court," in "Speeches" (Boston: Little, Brown, 1918), p. 102.

Congress and beyond its reach, or beyond the reach of the people." [39] In the more concrete terms used by liberal critics, the case against the Court is based upon the well-documented charge that the majority of the Court has too often served as the protector of propertied interests and as the uncompromising opponent of desirable Federal intervention in the national economy. In the eyes of most observers, however, these charges need to be qualified by the fact that the Court has come to be regarded, to use Charles Beard's phrase, as "the last safeguard for civil liberties." [40]

The gentlest method of dealing with the problem has been to suggest self-restraint on the part of the judges. Justice Marshall himself was the first to make this point: "A just respect for the Legislature requires that the obligation of its laws should not be unnecessarily and wantonly assailed." The traditional method of dealing *roughly* with the Court has been through special efforts to pack it. The size of the Court has been changed by statute seven times. It has been reduced in size twice in order to prevent Presidents from filling vacancies. It has been increased in size five times in order to give Presidents more vacancies to fill. In his famous 1937 attack upon the Court, Franklin D. Roosevelt tried to increase the Court a sixth time but failed. He also failed in the effort to provide for compulsory retirement at the age of seventy though he succeeded in making voluntary retirement more attractive. An effort to pack the Court, no matter what the specific techniques may be and no matter how they may work themselves out in practice, is at least a method of producing self-restraint on the part of the judges. In fact, when allied with organized opposition to given Court decisions, it has probably been the most effective instrument for combating the Supreme Court's legislative veto.

There are two other lines of approach, however, which deserve mention. The first is to amend the Constitution for the purpose of directly affecting the Court's operations. During the 1937 Court fight, Senator O'Mahoney of Wyoming proposed an amendment to provide that the Court could declare a statute unconstitutional only by a vote of at least 6 to 3. Another proposal, offered during the same year, by Senator Wheeler of Montana and Senator Bone of Washington, was to provide that the Court's veto, like a Presidential veto, could be overridden by a two-thirds majority in Congress. Another has been directly to enlarge the scope of the interstate-commerce clause and to limit the scope of the due-process clauses of the Fifth and Fourteenth Amendments. Yet it must be recognized that each of these proposals was a diversionary approach offered for the major purpose of providing a constructive position for those who opposed the Roosevelt program of court reform. Those who proposed amendments of this type in 1937 during the Roosevelt battle subsequently abandoned them.

[39] Hazlitt, *op. cit.*, p. 220.
[40] Charles A. Beard, "The Republic" (New York: Viking, 1943), p. 237.

The second approach is to amend the amending process itself, thereby opening up the way for specific amendments to override specific Court vetoes. Henry Hazlitt has suggested the adoption of the amending process used in Australia. "Amendments to the Constitution of that country may be proposed by a vote of an absolute majority of both the Senate and the House of Representatives. The proposed amendments are then submitted to a direct vote of the people and adopted if they are approved by a majority of the voters in a majority of the States." [41] Other variations have been played upon this theme.

The major case for changing the amending process is that the Constitution is not flexible enough. Yet this argument has weight only if one focuses exclusively upon the written document and the formal process of amendment. In actuality, the Constitution has been undergoing a constant process of change since the time it was written. These changes have been brought about through court decisions, legislation, administrative action, and the development of informal usages and traditions. In fact, some of the most specific of all the Constitution's provisions, such as those dealing with the electoral college, the sending of concurrent resolutions to the President for signature or veto, the size of a quorum, and the recording of Yeas and Nays, have been construed in a manner that constitutes thoroughgoing revision. Formal amendment is merely one—and the least used—of all the methods for revising the Constitution. The availability of many other methods of accomplishing the same objective is a decisive factor in preventing development of any widespread interest or organized effort directed toward easing the amending process.

The Legislative versus the Administrative Process

A final series of general proposals deals with the relationship between administrative and legislative processes. According to many of them, the legislative process would be significantly improved if a better line of demarcation were drawn between the two processes and if the areas of choice permitted to participants and contestants were thereby narrowed. According to others, members of Congress would be able to do a better job with their legislative activities if they approached the administrative process in a different manner.

The Scope of the Administrative Process

Despite a considerable volume of debate as to how much discretion should be allowed within the administrative process, this is not a problem that can be handled by generalizations. This can be demonstrated by an examination of five oft-repeated "principles."

Details through the Administrative Process. The first can be briefly phrased

[41] Hazlitt, *op. cit.*, p. 261.

as follows: "Details should be handled through the administrative process rather than through legislation."

But how to determine what is and is not detail? One man's detail is apt to be another man's burning issue. Decisions on details are sometimes the key to making decisions on "large" policy, without which any purported policy decision might be vague and meaningless. Furthermore, there are many details which can best be handled through the legislative process and which, if not handled thus, will haunt the waking and sleeping days of administrative officials and seriously impair administrative operations.[42]

Broad Policy through the Legislative Process. The second general principle, which is the side of the coin opposite the one discussed above, can be stated in this manner: "The broad general policies of government should be handled through the legislative rather than the administrative process."

This point of view enters in an interesting fashion into the Hayek-Finer controversy over economic planning. Hayek points out that the legislative process can scarcely be used to solve such important economic questions as "how many pigs are to be raised or how many busses are to be run, which coal mines are to operate, or at what prices shoes are to be sold." But if these decisions are handled through the administrative process, he maintains, the result is a breakdown in representative government and a long step forward on the road to serfdom.[43] Government, therefore, should not get involved in such matters, but should confine itself to fixing general rules determining the conditions under which resources are to be used rather than directing their use. Finer, on the other hand, defends large-scale governmental intervention in the economy, but justifies it on the ground that the full framework of economic planning can be constructed through a set of democratically adopted statutes. "The legislature," he writes, "is the heart of the planning process, for it is here that the less authoritative and less definite programs of the parties enter for definition and authorization." [44] Both Hayek and Finer, in effect, advocate "the rule of law," the one regarding it as an alternative to, and the other as the framework of, economic planning.

At times, of course, administrative officials create difficult problems for themselves and the programs they are administering by attempting to handle too many questions themselves instead of channeling them into the legislative process. Two competent observers write:

[42] Charles Hyneman, "Bureaucracy in a Democracy" (New York: Harper, 1950). Chap. 5, "Giving the Bureaucracy Its Job," is one of the few efforts in political-science literature to discuss in broad terms how far legislation should go in prescribing details. The chapter also contains a useful bibliographical note listing various writings that have dealt with some aspects of the problem (pp. 91–93).

[43] Friedrick Hayek, "The Road to Serfdom" (Chicago: University of Chicago Press, 1944), pp. 72–87.

[44] Finer, *op. cit.*, p. 213.

In administrative–legislative relationships the administrator who has a sense of delineation between legislative and administrative functions unerringly feels this sense; and if he respects it, he will be well received. The administrator who lacks faith in democratic methods and hesitates to lay vital issues before the legislative group for final judgment also reveals himself, and he is and should be poorly received.[45]

It is in this sense of delineation rather than any abstract rule that guidance must be found for the participant in the governmental process.

The Administrative Process in Time of Crisis. "In time of crisis and emergency, it is necessary to shift the handling of many problems from the legislative process to the administrative process." This is the third general principle.

There is little doubt that in time of crisis the President and other executive officials must take many drastic steps without waiting for legislative authorizations. Laws that are adopted under such circumstances, moreover, must give executive officials tremendously broad discretion.

This point of view has been presented in persuasive detail by Clinton Rossiter. According to Rossiter, the need for giving executive officials dictatorial powers in time of crisis should be clearly recognized beforehand so that plans can be made to assure its temporary character. He, therefore, suggests eleven criteria to which such dictatorships should be expected to conform in order to be "constitutional." [46]

In time of emergency, the ordinarily perplexing problem of choice between the administrative and the legislative routes multiplies in difficulty. There are matters of both detail as well as general policy that may be handled best through legislation. In the delegation of broad discretion to executive officials, there remains the ever-challenging question as to precisely how much and what powers are to be given to whom. In periods of semiemergency these questions become particularly pressing. In periods of intense crisis, they become critical, the chief problems, in many respects, depending upon the extent to which military authorities should be allowed to declare martial law and upon the extent to which other administrative officials are to be given the authority to restrict the customary civil liberties of individuals—too rigorous curtailment of civil liberties may help the "temporary" dictatorship to remain in power after the end of the crisis which called it into being!

The Administrative Process and Foreign Affairs. "The conduct of foreign affairs is the function of the President and the executive branch."

This fourth principle has often been justified on the legalistic ground that the conduct of foreign relations is an Executive function which has been vested by the Constitution in the President. Yet this is a barren approach to

[45] Jarle Leirfallom and L. J. Metcalf, "Legislation—From an Administrator's Viewpoint," *Public Welfare,* Vol. 6, No. 2, February, 1948.

[46] Clinton Rossiter, "Constitutional Dictatorship" (Princeton, N.J.: Princeton University Press, 1948), pp. 288–314.

the problem. The only monopoly that the President enjoys in the field of foreign relations is a monopoly of "the function of international intercourse." Whether in exercising this monopoly he should serve as the maker of foreign policy or as an instrument of communication is a question that can be resolved only in terms of specific circumstances and specific alignments of power.

The impressive case for administrative as opposed to legislative action in the field of foreign affairs is the frequent need for speed and flexibility. New situations are constantly developing in this field, situations to which policy must be adjusted, without taking time out to initiate legislative action or even in some circumstances to explain the development to many people in the United States. Many of the problems a President faces are of an emergency character, and he can ill afford to cater to minority interests which might attempt to hold up action if he sought decisions through the legislative process.[47]

Furthermore, the President and his representatives need a free hand in negotiations. They are constantly dealing with officials of other nations who can make decisions promptly and they also must be prepared to play a fluid role in the give-and-take process of diplomatic negotiations. This is particularly true about United States participation in the United Nations.

Yet there is also something to be said on the other side. Decisions on foreign policy have a major impact on domestic affairs. It has become increasingly true that the hand that writes our foreign policies rules the country. The excessive use of administrative discretion in this area could thus go a long way toward displacing the legislative process in other areas. It could put the future of the country in the hands of a small group of Government officials whose interests and allegiances are closely tied up with business, military, and diplomatic considerations, and who are often only remotely susceptible to pressure from other equally legitimate interests or to genuine Presidential control.

Safeguards over Administrative Discretion. "More matters can be handled through the administrative process if adequate safeguards are established over the use of administrative discretion."

It is interesting to note that almost all of the safeguards that are proposed in this connection are two-edged swords. They can be put to use not only to facilitate broad administrative discretion but also to prevent it.

Many of these safeguards are of long-standing vintage, having been used for decades and invariably being looked to when new problems of discretion and control are raised. One is the vesting of administrative discretion in multi-headed agencies, presumably responsible to Congress rather than to the Chief Executive. Another is to provide for extensive judicial review of administrative decisions either through the regular courts or special courts established to handle particular programs. Still another is to establish procedures for ad-

---

[47] This point of view has been fully presented in Thomas A. Bailey, "The Man in the Street" (New York: Macmillan, 1948).

ministrative operations such as requirements for notification in connection with public hearings, consultation with advisory committees, and, in the case of certain agencies, the formal separation between the personnel serving as "prosecutors" and "judges." Each of these approaches has been the focal center for a tremendous amount of debate and discussion concerning Government organization. There is an abundance of learned literature for and against each of these approaches, and a wealth of variations on each.

A more recently proposed "safeguard" is some form of "legislative veto" through the use of concurrent resolutions. Corwin, for example, asks how the line can be drawn between legislative "delegation" and "abdication," and answers his question as follows: "Only, I urge, by rendering the delegated powers recoverable without the consent of the delegate; and for this purpose the concurrent resolution seems to be an available mechanism, and the only one." [48]

It is pertinent to note in passing, however, that reorganization proposals are important weapons in the social struggle. They provide methods for the "outs" to attack the "ins," for the "ins" to consolidate their power, and for almost any type of public or private group to extend or contract governmental operations that they favor or dislike. They provide, above all, a method of pursuing these aims in the name of economy, efficiency, accountability, and other abstract principles that may have little or no connection with the real objectives that are sought.

Congressional Participation in the Administrative Process

In addition to their various activities discussed earlier in this chapter under the heading of "Congressional-Executive Collaboration," and in connection with such quasi-legislative measures as concurrent resolutions, members of the Congress can participate in the administrative process in three ways. They can influence the appointment or removal of executive officials. They can supervise, scrutinize, or investigate the administrative process. They can serve as "errand boys" on behalf of constituents with business before executive officials. Proposals meriting careful attention have been developed in connection with each of these points.

Appointments and Removals. ". . . Congress should restrict senatorial approval of presidential appointments to those officers enumerated in the Constitution. The power to appoint to all positions of a purely administrative character should be lodged in the heads of the respective agencies and the positions should be placed in the competitive classified service." [49]

The effect of proposals of this type unquestionably would be to strengthen the position of the President and other executive officials in both the adminis-

[48] Corwin, *op. cit.*, p. 160.

[49] George Galloway, "Congress at the Crossroads" (New York: Crowell, 1946), p. 237.

trative and legislative processes. It would tend to weaken the capacity of various members of Congress as well as private organizations to use senatorial confirmation as a weapon for opposing executive officials or for undermining party programs.

In so far as removals from executive offices are concerned, the constitutional provisions for impeachment give the members of Congress a weapon which is too burdensome for use. Those who advocate a parliamentary system of government in the United States point out that members of Congress would then have a sharper weapon, at least with respect to the Chief Executive. Others have from time to time suggested that the Constitution be amended in order to make the impeachment process easier. Frequently, lesser executive officials can readily be forced from office by the organized opposition of members of Congress in strategic positions.

During the nineteenth century there were a number of conflicts, particularly during the Presidential term of Andrew Johnson, over the Senate's power to prevent the President from removing an official whose appointment had been subject to Senate confirmation. A Supreme Court decision in 1926 favored the President. "The friction accompanying the controversy over the question," reported Luce, "has naturally led to proposals for amending the Federal Constitution in this particular. Nearly a score of amendments have been introduced, looking to restricting the power of the President." [50] Various statutory restrictions also have been devised with respect to the President's power of removal. The legislative process can be used to install members of regulatory boards and commissions for fixed terms of offices and to fix the grounds upon which they may be removed by the President, conditions which tend to prevent removals except under the most unusual circumstances.[51] A rather unique restriction was written into the Budget and Accounting Act of 1921. Under the provisions of this law, the Comptroller General cannot be removed except by joint resolution.

Preventing the removal of certain executive officials often can be achieved through informal means. Many a bureaucrat maintains his position because of the support of one or more members of Congress who occupy influential positions. Sometimes this support is based upon the backing of private organizations to whom the executive official in question has demonstrated a friendly and cooperative attitude. Many officials in this position enjoy a hidden form of permanent tenure, and any superior officer who tries to unseat them must reckon with a storm of reprisals.

Supervision, Scrutiny, and Investigation. One of the most popular and longstanding theories concerning the relations between the administrative and legislative processes depends upon the proposition that members of Congress,

[50] Robert Luce, "Legislative Problems" (Boston: Houghton Mifflin, 1935), p. 134.
[51] See *Humphrey's Executor v. United States,* 295 U.S. 602 (1935).

preferably through their committees, have an important function to perform in keeping their eye upon administrative operations. Woodrow Wilson maintained that "even more important than legislation is the instruction and guidance in political affairs which the people might receive from a body which kept all national concerns suffused in a broad daylight of discussion." [52] It is useful to analyze these particular activities into three forms or degrees, as follows: supervision, scrutiny, and investigation, each closely related to the others but distinct in certain respects.

"Supervision" connotes a continuing and informed awareness on the part of a congressional committee regarding executive operations in a given administrative area.

As the powers exercised by the bureaus and commissions are those that have been delegated to them by Congress, Congress should be kept constantly and systematically informed regarding the use to which those powers are being put. If the government agency and the congressional committee could not agree regarding the desirability of a particular regulation or regarding some other policy followed by the agency, then the committee could call the matter to the attention of the whole Congress and offer its recommendations.[53]

"Scrutiny," on the other hand, implies a lesser intensity and continuity of attention to administrative operations. Scrutiny is an exercise of supervisory powers with the flexibility that may be achieved through informal understandings among committee members and executive officials, or, as in the case of the appropriations committees, through "policy guides" which are written into committee reports and which executive officials are expected to follow.

The difficulty which members of Congress may encounter in making a careful distinction between supervision and scrutiny was mirrored in an interesting phrasing problem encountered during the preparation of the Legislative Reorganization Act of 1946. "Without effective legislative oversight of the activities of the vast executive branch," stated the report of the Joint Committee on the Organization of Congress, "the line of democracy wears thin. . . . We feel that this oversight problem can be handled best by directing the regular standing committees of the Senate and House, which have such matters in their jurisdiction, to conduct a continuous review of the agencies administering laws originally reported by the committees." [54] In a subsequent paragraph, "continuous review" was referred to as a "supervisory function."

To get away from the word "supervision," which implied a degree of control not contemplated by all the members of the committee, other words, e.g., surveillance, scrutiny, were used in the section of the Legislative Reor-

[52] Wilson, op. cit., p. 297.

[53] Editorial in The New York Times, Jan. 16, 1939.

[54] Report of the Joint Committee on the Organization of Congress, 79th Cong., 2d Sess., Mar. 4, 1946, p. 6.

ganization Act assigning this function to the standing committees (Sec. 136).[55] But the flight from Latin to French and Anglo-Saxon did not resolve the difficulty. The term "surveillance" was challenged on the floor of the Senate by Senator Donnell of Missouri.[56] As a result, the key word in the text was changed from "supervision" to "watchfulness." "Oversight" was left, however (probably by oversight), in the title of the section and stands as a mute reminder of the difficulty faced in making this distinction. This difficulty could probably have been resolved if the word "scrutiny" had been offered as a substitute.

The provisions of the Legislative Reorganization Act with respect to the scrutiny of administrative operations are extensive. The watchfulness mandate was given to every legislative committee and the two appropriations committees. The two Committees on Expenditures in the Executive Departments were given the responsibility of "studying the operation of government activities at all levels with a view to determining its economy and efficiency." Thus provision was made for a six-way scrutiny. To help in discharging this responsibility each committee was authorized to hire a certain number of staff employees. All Senate committees were given the power to subpoena witnesses and documents. Yet this comprehensive approach is still more of a proposal than a fact. "This feature of the Act has met with only partial success to date," George Galloway has observed. "Many standing committees have been too heavily burdened with their legislative duties and limited staffs to keep very close watch upon the executive agencies within their jurisdiction." [57]

The distinction between congressional scrutiny and a congressional investigation is that the former is a more passive process of looking at the facts that are readily available, and the latter involves a more intense digging for facts. If there are many who believe that we need more of the former, there are probably just as many who maintain that we can get along with less of the latter.

Luce has written one of the most vigorous and comprehensive indictments of congressional investigations:

Prosecution turned into persecution, the ruthless sacrifice of reputation, the vindictive display of prejudice, the mean debasement of partisanship, the advancement of personal fortunes through the use of scurrilous publicity—these are some of the features that make the whole thing a stench in the nostrils of decent men. . . .

The net result of the practice is more harm than good. It interferes sadly with legislative time, especially when overburdened legislators are taken away from legitimate duties for weeks and weeks. . . .

[55] The author of this book feels that he must shoulder part of the blame for the use of the term "surveillance," since it—and, in fact, the entire phrasing of the section—was borrowed from Sec. 2 of the Contract Settlement Act of 1944 which he himself had drafted.

[56] *Congressional Record*, 79th Cong., 1st Sess., p. 6445.

[57] Galloway, "The Operation of the Legislative Reorganization Act of 1946," *American Political Science Review*, Vol. 40, No. 1, March, 1951, pp. 59–60.

It is costly. . . .

It conduces to trial by newspaper. . . .

Worse yet is the effect on the public mind, by encouraging the dangerous belief that all public servants are knaves. . . .

Indeed, what purpose of inquiry is normally legislative unless it involves the making of a law? To that degree and no further can legislative audit, whether by full assembly, or by committee, be justified.[58]

One line of change suggests the delegation of investigations to executive agencies [59] or to special investigating commissions appointed by the Chief Justice of the United States Supreme Court.[60] Another line suggests that there is "greater need for forward-looking inquiries than for backward-looking ones," [61] and Congress should more frequently make "searching investigations into matters of great economic and social significance." [62] Senator Kefauver has expressed the view that the purposes of congressional investigations should be limited. Speaking against the continuation of the Senate Crime Investigating Committee which he had headed, Kefauver stated that "it is not the province of a legislative committee, in my opinion, to pile on cumulative evidence time and time again. I think the byproduct of arousing public opinion is very important, (but) that alone is no justification for having investigations." [63]

The most frequent and most important proposals for reform relate to the adoption through statute, rule, or voluntary acceptance of minimum standards of procedure. In an excellent summation of these proposals, Galloway lists a grand total of 41 possible safeguards. After carefully exploring the question of whether any such safeguards are really needed, he comes to the well-considered conclusion that "a code of fair conduct for all investigating groups might well be adopted by the House and Senate as part of their standing rules. . . . In the Federal Administrative Procedure Act, Congress had provided a code of procedure for administrative agencies. This action should now be matched by the enactment of a code for its own investigators." [64]

"Errand-Boy" Work. If members of Congress spent less time in running errands for their constituents, it is frequently argued, they would have far more time to devote to their legislative duties. One approach to this objective

[58] Luce, *op. cit.,* pp. 446–447.

[59] Nelson M. McGeary "The Developments of Congressional Investigative Power" (New York: Columbia University Press, 1940), pp. 115–160.

[60] Lindsay Rogers, "When Congress Fumbles for Facts," *New York Herald Tribune,* Mar. 29, 30, 31, 1950.

[61] Fritz Morstein Marx, "Congressional Investigations: Significance for the Administrative Process," *University of Chicago Law Review,* Vol. 18, No. 3, Spring, 1951, p. 517.

[62] Heller, *op. cit.,* p. 29.

[63] *Congressional Record* (daily edition), Apr. 24, 1951, p. 4387.

[64] Galloway, "Congressional Investigations: Proposed Reforms," *University of Chicago Law Review,* Vol. 18, No. 3, Spring, 1951, pp. 478–502.

is to provide members with better staff assistance in their personal offices, in the committees to which they belong, and through the Library of Congress.

Another is to provide more information services for constituents. This can be done by channeling requests for information or assistance to congressional committees dealing with the subject matter of any inquiry, to agency liaison offices, or to general information services set up for the use of Congress. Another suggestion is that each state establish special offices in Washington to help represent the interests of private individuals of the state before the various executive agencies.

The American Political Science Association's Committee on Congress has suggested "that Congress might well formulate a Charter of Congressional Freedom from trivial errands. . . ."

. . . we suggest that the Charter of Congressional Freedom might well prohibit any person from trying to enlist the aid of a legislator in getting a government job below the grade of presidential appointments or in seeking a promotion. . . .

We suggest that Congress forbid its members to intervene in individual cases, contenting themselves with passing the criticism of undue delay on to the appropriate legislative committee.[65]

But before one sets aside the ideas of political scientists as impractical, consider the strange formulation trotted out by a "practical" politician, Representative Robert Ramspeck of Georgia: "I am suggesting that we adopt a constitutional amendment which would prohibit a member of Congress, or Senator, from contacting the executive branch of the Government except in regard to legislation." [66]

If one maintains his hold upon the world of reality, he may well ask himself a number of questions. If the time spent in errand running were cut down, is there any assurance that the vacuum would be filled by attention to legislative duties? In a society which is constantly imposing greater burdens upon the Government, is it reasonable to suppose that the burden on members of Congress can be lightened? Is it not more reasonable to suppose that the burden will constantly grow and that the problem for members of Congress is how to select the matters on which they expend their energies and how to obtain sufficient staff services to help them do a good, instead of a halfway, job? And is errand running something necessarily apart from a member's legislative work? Can it not give him valuable experience on many matters which are dealt with in more general terms in legislative measures? Would he not remain relatively ignorant concerning the practical

[65] Committee on Congress, American Political Science Association, "The Reorganization of Congress" (Washington, D.C.: Public Affairs Press, 1945), pp. 66–67.

[66] Hearings before the Joint Committee on the Organization of Congress, 79th Cong., 1st Sess., p. 296.

problems involved in many legislative proposals if it were not for his work in representing the interests of individual constituents?

A final question is whether or not the errand-boy work of members of Congress may not be of positive value to the administrative process. John Stuart Mill argued that the British Parliament had a major function in serving as "the Nation's Committee of Grievances." [67] In America this function has been well described by Pendleton Herring:

More and more will the Senator, and even more especially the Representative, come to serve as a mediator between his constituency and the operations of government within it. He is in a strategic position to observe how governmental functions actually impinge upon his constituents. He is in a position to advise his constituents how to receive maximum benefits from what the government stands ready to give them and how to make their views felt about desirable fields for governmental action. He is in a position to discover areas where governmental activity should be withdrawn or modified. He is in a position to advise administrative officials how their actions affect the people of his district. Such advice may come as a welcome supplement to the information the administrator receives from his subordinates, from field reports, or from personal inspection, affected as they are by the interests, aspirations, and limitations of the persons making them.[68]

[67] John Stuart Mill, "Considerations on Representative Government" (New York: Macmillan, 1947), p. 172.

[68] Pendleton Herring, "The Politics of Democracy" (New York: Rinehart, 1940), p. 383.

Chapter 8

THE CONTESTANTS AND THEIR POWER

POWER [1] MAY be defined as the ability to influence people through persuasion, compulsion, or—as is usually the case—a combination of the two.

The power displayed by the contestants in the legislative struggle is not easy to measure. The distribution of power is constantly shifting. We have no voltage or kilowatt standards that can readily be applied on a quantitative scale. Also, just as every nation tries to keep its military strength a secret, the wielders of legislative power have erected an elaborate camouflage system. Researchers in social science have barely scratched the surface in penetrating the barriers and in measuring the power of individual groups in specific group conflicts.

Fortunately, a vector analysis of the power exerted by each of the contestants in the legislative process is not essential to the purposes of this book (although a full analysis of power relationships in individual legislative situations would be invaluable). It is enough at this point to indicate the basic factors that serve as the source of any group's power and to show how such power can be multiplied by combining with others. At a later point the effort will be made to show how the power of the various contestants in the legislative process is used to influence the outcome of specific legislative conflicts.

[1] "There is no reasonably adequate study of the nature of social power. The majority of the works on the theme are devoted either to proclaiming the importance of the role of power, like those of Hobbes, Gumplowicz, Ratzenhofer, Steinmetz, Treitschke, and so forth, or to deploring that role, like Bertrand Russell in his *Power*. . . ." Robert MacIver, "The Web of Government" (New York: Macmillan, 1947), p. 458. While MacIver's comment is unquestionably justified, interesting discussions of the nature of social power are to be found in Robert Bierstedt, "An Analysis of Social Power," *American Sociological Review*, Vol. 15, No. 6, December, 1950; Guglielmo Ferrero, "The Principles of Power" (New York: Putnam, 1942); Herman Heller, "Political Power," *Encyclopaedia of the Social Sciences*, Vol. 12 (New York: Macmillan, 1934), pp. 300–305; Benjamin Kidd, "The Science of Power" (New York: Putnam, 1918); Harold Lasswell, "Politics: Who Gets What, When, How" (New York: McGraw-Hill, 1936); and Charles Merriam, "Political Power" (New York: McGraw-Hill, 1934).

THE SOURCES OF POWER

The various factors that are combined to give any group its power can be divided into four closely interrelated categories: (1) wealth, (2) numbers, (3) leadership and organization, and (4) strategic position.[2] Upon examination, each of these turns out to be a vastly complex area in itself.

Wealth

The importance of wealth as a source of power is quite obvious. Over the course of centuries the wealthier groups in any nation have always been among the dominant forces, if not *the* dominant ones. In America the growing concentration of economic power in the hands of a few has consistently, and correctly, been regarded as placing greater political power in the same hands. Throughout the world the case for the nationalization of basic industries has been based mainly upon the desire to wrest political power from the present owners and give it to the state or, in more accurate terms, a competing group.

In fact, there is good reason to believe that the strength of the famous "profit motive" as an important factor in economic behavior derives from the contribution that economic gains can make to the satisfaction of the desire for more power.

In the age of capitalism, supported by democracy, the rich man is happy whenever his money can give him great influence over his economic inferiors and over public affairs. . . . Biographical studies that speak of the lives of our contemporary plutocrats demonstrate how much of the dynamic force of great industrialists and merchants, directed at reaching the pinnacle of wealth, is basically subordinated to the end of acquiring authority over men and establishing themselves as autocrats of finance.[3]

[2] A somewhat similar breakdown is given in Bierstedt, *op. cit.*: "Power would seem to stem from three sources: (1) numbers of people, (2) social organization, and (3) resources. . . . Given the same social organization and the same resources, the larger number can always control the smaller and secure its compliance. . . . A well-organized and disciplined body of marines or of police can control a much larger number of unorganized majority. . . . Of two groups, however, equal or nearly equal in numbers and comparable in organization, the one with access to the greater resources will have the superior power. . . . Resources may be of many kinds—money, property, prestige, knowledge, competence, deceit, fraud, secrecy and, of course, all of the things usually included under the term 'natural resources.' . . . Power appears only in the combination of all three—numbers, organization, and resources."

One difficulty with this analysis is that the term "resources" is stretched so far that it includes qualities or techniques of leadership that are more logically tied up with social organization rather than with wealth per se. Also, the analysis fails to recognize that a social group can derive power from their occupation of a strategic position.

[3] Robert Michels, "First Lectures in Political Sociology" (Minneapolis, Minn.: University of Minnesota Press, 1949), de Grazia translation, p. 93.

When a given cause of action holds forth the promise of increasing profits but threatens a decrease in power, it is apt to be rejected.

In addition to its direct value as a means of persuasion and compulsion,[4] wealth has the great advantage of providing the wherewithal to obtain other sources of power. To win followers, build an organization, and achieve strategic positions costs money. Generally speaking, the more money available for these purposes, the better the job that can be done. The size of their assets, reserves, and current profits, therefore, is one of the clues to the power of business organizations; the size of their treasuries and dues payments is an indication of the power of labor organizations. Similarly, the size of agency appropriations and the degree of control exercised over agency expenditures are respective guides to the power of executive officials and of members of Congress.

Yet care should be taken not to overemphasize, as most Marxians do, the power potential of wealth.

The economic strength of any group or class is no longer, as it tended to be under feudal conditions, the measure of its political strength. The relative ease with which powerful economic interests have been defeated in the political arena, the many encroachments of government, by taxation and regulation, on the prerogatives of wealth, the progress of "social legislation" all along the line, and the manner in which various governments, without any proletarian revolution, have taken over such important sectors of capitalistic enterprise as railroads and public utilities, demonstrate the inadequacy of the Marxian thesis to comprehend the complex relationship between economic and political power.[5]

Nor should wealth itself be too glibly equated with economic power, a term which is used to describe power that is to a large degree based upon wealth. The economic power of a nation, a corporation, a union, or a government agency cannot be derived solely from its physical or monetary assets. These are transmuted into power only after being combined with numbers, organization and leadership, and strategic situations.

Numbers

> Rise like Lions after slumber
> In unconquerable number . . .
> Ye are many—they are few.[6]

[4] In the full sense of the term, "wealth" includes not only the more ordinary forms of machinery, goods, and materials but also such "persuasive" forms of property as policemen's blackjacks and atomic bombs. The four factors listed as the sources of power are therefore suitable to the analysis of power not only in situations in which, as with the legislative process, relatively peaceful methods are used but also in conflicts between policemen and racketeers or between nations locked in mortal combat.

[5] MacIver, op. cit., p. 92.

[6] Percy Bysshe Shelley, "The Mask of Anarchy."

With these ringing words, Shelley tried to inspire the workingmen of England to an exercise of their potential power. In fact, this theme has been central to the efforts of every organizer of the underprivileged. There is tremendous strength in the sheer number of followers any group may have.

Even to a small group, numbers are essential. An individual in isolation is weak, and it is only as a number of individuals get together that the possibilities of power emerge. In primitive societies the larger tribes tended to become the more powerful because, given no great disparities in the effectiveness of weapons, a fight can be won by the side with the greatest number of bodies. Even under conditions of modern warfare, "manpower resources" are not to be sneezed at, which is why many militaristic nations have adopted policies to encourage population growth. When disputes are settled by peaceful rather than by violent means, "counting noses" is a widely used technique. It is by a show of numbers in one form or another that elections are won, Supreme Court decisions made, and bills enacted.

Numbers can also provide access to other sources of power. They can provide a source of wealth, if only through dues payments or tithes. They provide the raw materials for organization and leadership. They can lead to a monopoly of certain types of skills or services, thereby putting a group in a highly strategic position.

Organization and Leadership

That the mercantile and manufacturing classes, with all the advantages given them by their wealth, their intelligence, and their habits of co-operation, should have been vanquished by the agricultural masses, may be ascribed partly to the fact that the democratic impulse of the War of Independence was strong among the citizens who had grown to manhood between 1780 and 1800, partly to the tactical errors of the Federalist leaders, but largely also to the skill which Jefferson showed in organizing the hitherto undisciplined battalions of Republican voters. Thus early in American history was the secret revealed, which Europe is only now discovering, that in free countries with an extended suffrage, numbers without organizations are helpless and with it omnipotent.[7]

Only through organization can the full advantage of wealth or numbers be exploited. Indeed, a high degree of organization can often compensate for serious deficiencies in either wealth or numbers. As Ludwig Gumplowicz long ago pointed out:

. . . it is not the size of the social group which determines its power. The lords were always in a minority, and in modern states with millions of inhabitants the power rests with the "upper ten thousand." The intimacy of the union and the resultant organiza-

[7] James Bryce, "The American Commonwealth" (New York: Macmillan, 1907), 3d ed., Vol. II, p. 10.

tion and discipline together with mental superiority complement numerical inferiority giving the minority preponderancy. The minority applies the strategical maxim: march as individuals, strike as one.[8]

In more recent times, the striking power of well-organized minorities has been dramatically demonstrated by the successes of the bolshevist parties in Russia and China. One of the guiding principles of Lenin, Stalin, and Mao Tse-tung has been to draw a sharp line between a mass following, which is to be encouraged, and a revolutionary party, which through tight entrance requirements and successive purges, is to be kept down to a small, compact core of "true believers."[9]

Organization, in turn, is the product of leadership. To some extent, it is the residue left behind by former leaders. Formalized structures, conventionalized procedures, habits of thought—these are the heritage received from leaders of the past. But it is the leaders of the present who must pour new wine into the old bottles, or at least try to prevent the old wine from turning sour.

A powerful organization calls for a variety of leadership skills. Leaders must be perceptive enough to gauge accurately the community of interest upon which people can be brought to act in concert. They must be imaginative enough to create or use the ideals and symbols—the "credenda and miranda" of power, as one writer has put it [10]—that can inspire enthusiasm and loyalty. They must define the objectives of group action, choose the weapons, and develop staff services in the fields of intelligence, planning, and public relations. They must nurture every source of power, extend their group's power through combinations of various sorts, and negotiate the compromises that spell victory or defeat in individual engagements.

Leadership capacity is deeply affected by an organization's general characteristics, including its followers and the problems it faces. It is also the result of such personal qualities as vitality and endurance, decisiveness, persuasiveness, responsibility, and intellectual capacity.[11] Whether an organization can get or maintain leaders with these qualities depends to a large extent on the character of its internal struggle for control. If any one clique goes too far in eliminating rivals and ensconcing itself in control for a long enough period of time, the inevitable result is a hardening of the arteries and a senescence of organizational strength. At the other extreme, if turnover is too rapid, no set of leaders will have sufficient time to become familiar with their tasks and win the confidence of their followers.

[8] Ludwig Gumplowicz, "The Outlines of Sociology" (American Academy of Political and Social Science, 1899, translated by Frederick W. Moore), p. 143.

[9] This useful term is taken from Eric Hoffer, "The True Believer" (New York: Harper, 1951), a profoundly suggestive study of mass movements.

[10] Merriam, op. cit., Chap. 4.

[11] These five leadership qualities are taken from Chester Barnard, "Organization and Management" (Cambridge, Mass.: Harvard University Press, 1948), Chap. 4.

Strategic Positions

At the famous Greek mountain pass of Thermopylae, Leonidas and his band of 300 Spartans held up the advance of the vast Persian army of Xerxes. The entire field of social combat is studded with mountain passes which give organized groups splendid opportunities for both defense and attack. The more complex any situation is, the greater the possibilities of achieving vast power by occupying one or more of these strategic spots or by obtaining access to, and influence over, those who occupy them.

The Government is full of strategic positions. Members of Congress who sit on important committees wield tremendous power within their areas of operation. The same is true for executive officials who have their hands on the controls of a given program and of staff subordinates who have almost monopolistic control of operating facts and procedures. The power of the President's position, of course, comes from the fact that he tends to be the center of the whole works and can play some part—greater or less—in almost any contest. The strategic position of the political parties lies in their virtual monopoly of the machinery of nominations.

Outside Government, the tremendous power of bankers and financiers flows to a large extent from the fact that they are in a position to influence business operations over a tremendous area without incurring a commensurate degree of personal risk. Business managers, unions, farm organizations—each have a strategic position in the process of production and distribution. Business managers have a unique strategic advantage resulting from the community of interest among business managers in general and the managers of newspaper, radio, television, and motion-picture businesses in particular—a community of interest which is nourished by the purchase of advertising space and time and by other financial interrelations. The power of professional organizations, particularly in the legal and medical fields, flows not only from their quasi monopolies of specialized services but also from the access their leaders usually have to influential people outside the professional world.

Strategic positions, however, are only a source of generalized power. The American Medical Association can swing considerable weight to the subject of Government health policies, but its closest friends in Government would not give it much attention on foreign policy. During World War II, when William Green, president of the A.F.L., tried to get Representative Clarence Cannon of Missouri to vote for farm subsidies to bring farm prices down, Mr. Cannon put Mr. Green in his place: "I have always followed Mr. Green on labor bills," he told the press. "But this is not a labor bill. This is a farm bill. On this bill I will follow the farm leaders." [12]

[12] Quoted in an editorial, *New York Herald Tribune*, Nov. 25, 1943.

The Extension of Power through Combinations

The most profound strategic problems in modern warfare, those that are more the province of statesmen than of generals, relate to the forming of combinations. As a basis for initiating World War II, Adolf Hitler developed the Anti-Comintern Axis, a combination composed mainly of Germany, Italy, and Japan. For the purpose of defense and then of counterattack, Roosevelt, Churchill, and Stalin developed a cooperative effort between the United States, England, Russia, and minor allies.

All the contestants in the legislative struggle operate in the same way—the weak in order to build up their power, the strong in order to extend their power and to maintain it. To some extent the formation and dissolution of alliances can be described in the words of James M. Burns: "Like dancers in a vast Virginia reel, groups merge, break off, meet again, veer away to new combinations." [13] To a much greater extent, there is no pattern and less chance in the manner in which partners come together. In agriculture, the cotton, wool, and tobacco interests have traditionally worked together to ob-tain special legislation. As the lobbyist for the National Wool Growers' Association told a reporter: "It may not be nice to say, but the way you get bills passed is—'you scratch my back and I'll scratch yours.' " [14] The textile manufacturers and the textile unions traditionally cooperate in opposing the reduction of tariffs on textile imports. One of the traditional aims of organized labor has been to form a farmer-labor coalition against business interests. In turn, business interests have aimed—and have often hit the mark—at forming a business-farmer coalition against organized labor.[15] Both groups compete for the

[13] James M. Burns, "Congress on Trial" (New York: Harper, 1949), p. 33.

[14] Tristram Coffin, "No Speech Ever Changed a Vote," *New Republic,* July 14, 1945.

[15] "Nor are all constituents of the farm bloc farmers. There is a powerful voice of business —both big and little. Partly through mutual dislike for organized labor, and partly because of inherent conservatism, the alliance of agriculture and business grows stronger. . . .

The United States Chamber of Commerce, which maintains a temple-like structure across Lafayette Square from the White House, has had an agricultural division for years. . . .

A second point at which industry and the farm bloc converge, though in a minor way, is the National Highway Users Conference, 'a fact-finding, information-giving, and coordinat-ing agency, acting in behalf of the development of highway transportation in the public interest.' . . .

A third item of significance in the effort of industry to hold the moral support of agri-culture, sometimes making it a silent partner in farm-bloc proceedings, is the program of the National Industrial Information Committee. Sponsored by the National Association of Manufacturers and composed of the cream of New Deal enemies, the committee functions under the following officers: national chairman, J. Howard Pew, president of the Sun Oil Company; vice-chairman, Ernest T. Weir, Chairman of the Board of National Steel Corpo-ration, and the other vice-chairman, C. M. Chester, chairman of the board of General Foods Corporation." Wesley McCune, "The Farm Bloc" (New York: Doubleday, 1943), pp. 8–10.

support of the veterans, the church, women's organizations, and the other organized groups.

Presidential and executive officials carry this principle even further. The secret of Franklin Roosevelt's power in Congress lay in his ability to bring together behind his proposals Southern Democrats, Northern liberals, the bosses of the big city machines, organized labor, and important blocs of agricultural and business interests. The decline in his power, with respect to practically all domestic measures initiated after his first term in office, stemmed from the formation of a conservative coalition between the Republicans and the Southern Democrats backed by a solid and growing bloc of business and farm interests. Irrespective of political configurations, any President who can get a sufficiently strong coalition of group interest behind a given legislative proposal can succeed in obtaining its passage by Congress. In the same way any department or bureau in the executive branch of the Government which can organize sufficient backing for its own proposals can thumb its nose at the President and more or less have its own way in Congress. This has been demonstrated repeatedly by combinations among the army engineers, the power interests, and certain members of Congress.

The increments of power obtained through combinations, however, are not always "net." The account books will usually show some offsetting factors. At the least, combinations reduce the ease and simplicity with which groups can act and react, extending the area of essential consultation and calculation. They also may require the sacrifice of certain objectives or techniques that might be objectionable to one's allies. It is likely that group power can be extended through combinations only at a discount. While these discounts will vary in size, even when they seem comparatively small, they are an integral part of the power structure of society.

The exchange of legislative support has been persistently held up to scorn as a procedure that threatens the public interest. In its more fleeting forms, it has been branded as "logrolling," a procedure alleged to endanger democratic processes. Yet in any society with more than two groups it is inevitable that every group will try to supplement its inherent sources of power by tapping the power of other groups. In fact, the process of swapping support—with all that it involves in the bringing about of mutual understandings and adjustments and whether it implies a temporary relationship or a long-standing coalition—can be regarded as an essential part of the democratic process.

Logrolling is, however, in fact, the most characteristic legislative process. When one condemns it "in principle," it is only by contrasting it with some assumed pure public spirit which is supposed to guide legislators, or which ought to guide them, and which enables them to pass judgment in Jovian calm on that which is best "for the whole people." Since there is nothing which is best literally for the whole people, group arrays being what they are, the test is useless, even if one could actually find legislative judgments which are not reducible to interest-group activities. And when we have reduced the legislative process to the play of group interests, then logrolling, or give and take, appears as the very nature of the process. It is compromise, not in the abstract moral form, which philosophers can sagely discuss, but in the practical form with which every legislator who gets results through government is acquainted. It is trading. It is the adjustment of interests. . . . There never was a time in the history of the American Congress when legislation was conducted in any other way.[16]

Whether one looks with favor upon any specific combination, whether one regards it as an "unholy alliance" or "a united front in a common cause" depends entirely upon one's own interests and allegiances.

[16] Arthur F. Bentley, "The Process of Government" (Bloomington, Ind.: Principia Press, 1949, reissue), pp. 370–371.

PART II

COMBAT ON THE LEGISLATIVE TERRAIN

Chapter 9

TO HAVE OR NOT TO HAVE A BILL

THE LEGISLATIVE process is only one of the methods through which the contestants in the social struggle pursue their objectives. The concentration of attention on it in this book should not obscure the fact that the most crucial conflicts are often fought on other battlegrounds. In an era of "Big Government," the administrative process has assumed major significance. There are also the processes of judicial action, constitutional amendment, and state and local government. There is the entire field of private action outside the sphere of government. And finally, there are the processes of changing the leadership of government through electoral action or through the most extreme forms of social combat, revolution, and war.

Since the social struggle spills over into all these fields, any attempt to describe the legislative process as though it were the entire universe of struggle, without looking at the manner in which contesting groups weave in and out of the legislative battleground, would give a narrow and distorted picture. "To have or not to have a bill" [1]—that is a question whose pros and cons are repeatedly being weighed by the leaders of private organizations and political parties and by government officials. It is more a question of strategy than of law or of constitutional requirement. It is like the problem of choosing the section of an island on which to establish a beachhead. There are many shores to choose from, each with its peculiar advantages and disadvantages. There is even the possibility of bypassing the island completely. No abstract laws of military science can either guide the generals or provide a basis for an observer to predict exactly how individual generals will behave. Similarly, it would be idle to seek some neat formula by which one could automatically explain decisions on having or not having a bill. In describing how these decisions are made, one must proceed by appraising the alternative choices that lie before legislative strategists and by indicating both the advantages and disadvantages of the legislative terrain.

[1] For purposes of convenience, the word "bill" is used to refer to any type of legislative measure, whether a bill or a resolution. A full distinction between the various types of measures is provided in Chap. 11.

THE AREA OF CHOICE

There are certain objectives that can be achieved only through the production of Federal statutes and others that can be achieved only through administrative or judicial decisions. There are some things that can be done only by the Federal government, and others only through other organizations. In addition, there is also a broad area of overlapping, an area in which it is entirely possible for contesting groups to embark on two or more courses of action at the same time or else choose between them on the basis of their relative advantages and disadvantages. This area of choice exists because of the flexibility and adaptability of various processes. What rules exist are mostly vague and open to many varieties of interpretation. Contestants with sufficient "know-how" and resourcefulness can often concoct effective devices for their circumvention. Contestants with sufficient power behind them can, in fact, break the rules with impunity. When this is done often enough, the old rules break down and new precedents take their place.

The existence of choice, of course, is a relative matter; it shifts from one situation to another. For many contestants in the social struggle, there is no choice whatsoever; the battleground is picked for them by the action of opponents and competitors. For stronger groups, the area of choice is far broader than for weaker people faced with identical problems; the ability to make choices is itself a good measure of power. For all groups, strong and weak, the availability of alternatives is limited by habit; many of the obstacles to the use of one process as opposed to another flow entirely from an inability to break with customary methods of operation.

The Overlap with the Administrative Process [2]

General Overlapping. The existence of a significant overlap between the legislative process and the administrative process has been touched upon. In the course of the legislative struggle, questions are always arising as to whether or not fundamental policy decisions shall be left to executive officials [3] or shall

---

[2] For general books which deal with the administrative process and throw some light on the overlap between legislative and administrative processes, see James Hart, "An Introduction to Administrative Law" (New York: Appleton-Century-Crofts, 2d ed., 1950); James M. Landis, "The Administrative Process" (New Haven, Conn.: Yale University Press, 1938); and Herbert A. Simon, Donald W. Smithburg, and Victor A. Thompson, "Public Administration" (New York: Knopf, 1950).

[3] This is often referred to as "the delegation of legislative power," a concept stemming from the old and outworn idea that any uniform rule is "legislative," the administrative role being little more than the clerical application of the rule. It is also associated with the old warning of John Locke that "the legislative cannot transfer the power of making laws to any other hands, for it being but a delegated power from the people, they who have it can-

be by legislative provisions. The geographical distribution of Federal funds can be left entirely up to executive officials, as in the case of the lending operations of the Federal Public Housing Authority, or it can be provided for in accordance with statutory formulas, as in the case of Federal aid to states for the construction of roads and hospitals. The Interstate Commerce Commission may be given broad power to regulate freight rates, while the Agriculture Department may be bound by statutory "parity" formulas in the determination of prices at which farm products are to be supported. Legislation can be used equally either for overthrowing policies and rules established by administrators or for writing them directly into the law. In the course of the administrative process, in turn, many decisions are made which can be legitimately regarded as a substitute for or alternative to legislative action. The appointment of a conservative official to administer a liberal law, or vice versa, can have the same effect as legislative action to amend the law or nullify it. Hence the great importance in the administrative process both of patronage—particularly that form of patronage which stems from an ideological interest in seeing the appointment of people with one's own point of view—and of Senate confirmation of Presidential appointees.[4] Also, congressional investigations and pressure campaigns are habitually used to accomplish through the administrative process what might otherwise be attained through legislation—and used by those who are most intimately connected with the legislative process.

Nevertheless, there are always a large number of cases where the overlapping between the legislative and administrative processes is far from obvious. The relationship between the two has become a subject that is enlivened by endless disputes concerning the alleged propriety of one process being used on matters that are heatedly claimed as the exclusive province of the other. There have been few periods in American history when public life has not been marked by charges from members of Congress that the President or executive officials have exceeded their legitimate powers and have trespassed in the legislative domain. Similarly, there are always continuous laments within the executive branch (though less outspoken, for fear of congressional reprisals) concern-

---

not pass it on to others." "On Civil Government," Book II, Chap. 11. This latter maxim has often been used to support opposition to statutes conferring broad discretion on executive officials. As far back as 1916 the death of this maxim was acknowledged by Elihu Root when he voiced the view that, as a result of the rapid growth of executive agencies, "the old doctrine prohibiting the delegation of legislative power has virtually retired from the field and given up the fight." "Addresses on Citizenship and Government" (Cambridge, Mass.: Harvard University Press, 1916), p. 534. This does not mean, of course, that the doctrine cannot be brought back from the grave as justification for a Supreme Court decision, as in fact happened in the 1935 decision overthrowing the National Industrial Recovery Act.

[4] Senate confirmation is herein regarded as part of the administrative process itself; it would be stretching our words too wide to include in the legislative process the Senate resolutions dealing with Presidential nominations. The type of measures to be regarded as falling within the legislative process is discussed fully in Chap. 11.

ing the usurpation of administrative functions by legislation. To a man from Mars these arguments would sound exceedingly strange, for the charge is always that somebody or some people do not have the power to do what they have already done.[5] These charges of usurpation, however, are usually nothing but a means of arguing or agitating against action which is opposed on substantive grounds. Their effect is to becloud—though actually they document—the fact that the area of overlapping is extremely broad.

Within the entire area of overlapping between the legislative and administrative processes there is an important distinction between essentiality and possibility. The fact that a given objective can be achieved through administrative action and that a new law is not essential does not imply that it is not possible or desirable to achieve the identical objective through legislation. After Pearl Harbor, the Roosevelt Administration could have operated its price-control machinery under the War Powers Act, as was done with the rationing and priorities programs. For reasons of expedience, however, it chose to seek special price-control legislation. In 1943, President Roosevelt set up the Office of War Mobilization by Executive order. A year and a half later a law was enacted changing the name of the agency to the Office of War Mobilization and Reconversion and somewhat broadening its duties, an action that could have been achieved by an Executive order of the President. In the case of the disposition of surplus war property, new legislation was not necessary and the first view of the Roosevelt Administration was that surplus property should be disposed of under existing powers. However, a combination of pressures within Congress forced the Administration to change its mind and the result was the Surplus Property Act of 1944.

To indicate how extensive this area of overlapping really is, let us now look at the area where it is generally assumed that legislative action is indispensable and then at the area that on first thought would appear to be the exclusive province of administrative action. In both cases we will find ample illustrations of the age-old maxim—probably more applicable to the processes of government than to anything else—that there are many ways of skinning a cat.

The "Exclusively Legislative." It is generally regarded as axiomatic that

---

5 In ordinary usage, and in the terminology of the previous chapter, the fact that someone has done something is proof that he had the power to do it. But the term "power" is also used in a specialized sense to refer to the rightful use of power. It's as though one said that heavyweight champion Joe Louis does not have power to lick a flyweight pugilist; what would be meant, of course, is that by the rules of the game heavyweights are supposed to fight heavyweights only (at least in the ring). The trouble comes with the presumption that rules can be tight with respect to the subjects with which any given process of government is supposed to deal. In some form or other, all the contestants in the social struggle take part in all the processes of government. The differences among the processes flow more from variations in the role of these various contestants than from any inherent limitations on the scope of the processes or the real powers of any of the contestants.

legislative action is required for the appropriation of funds from the Federal Treasury. Yet the device of setting up a Federal corporation has been developed for the purpose of avoiding, among other things, the annual appropriation process.[6]

While an appropriation may be used to provide the capital stock of a corporation, the initial legislation may also allow the corporation to borrow much larger amounts by selling securities to the Secretary of the Treasury or to private investors; these funds may be used then on a revolving basis. Once legislation of this type has been enacted there may be little or no need for its administrators ever to obtain appropriations; and subsequent requests for legislation may be limited to increases at irregular intervals in the ceilings set upon the borrowing and lending.

It is also regarded as axiomatic that a President cannot make a treaty without Senate ratification (which is a form of legislative action) or declare a war without congressional assent. And in both these cases the axiom corresponds accurately with the formalities of government; the administrative process cannot be used for anything called a treaty or called a declaration of war. But the administrative process can be used to achieve similar or identical ends through other means. The Atlantic Charter, promulgated by President Franklin D. Roosevelt and Prime Minister Winston Churchill, was a dramatic example of purely Executive action. Less dramatic but often fully as important in the arena of international power politics are Executive decisions to recognize this or that government, withdraw this or that ambassador, send a military mission to this country, or direct a Government lending corporation to make a loan to that country. As for military action, a President is Commander in Chief of the armed forces and as such can threaten, or participate in, war by moving military forces into foreign seas or territories. In an age of atomic or bacteriological warfare, moreover, no President would wait for a formal declaration of war before ordering our armed forces to retaliate against an enemy that had struck America. A formal declaration of war can always follow later. In fact,

[6] "The most significant privilege enjoyed by a full-fledged government corporation is its freedom from the customary rules about finance. . . . The government corporation furnishes a method of modifying these principles. A subscription by government to the capital stock of a corporation or an allocation of funds to the corporation removes the money from the Treasury and from annual appropriation control. The funds may be utilized until exhausted whether it takes one year or ten. Earnings of the corporation since they may be corporate funds rather than public revenues, need not be covered into the Treasury but may be retained in the custody of the corporation. They may then be spent at the discretion of the officers of the corporation, though only within the limits of corporate purposes fixed by the charter. If the corporation is engaged in a self-sustaining function, its revenues would enable it to operate on its own resources more or less indefinitely without annual subjection to the presidential and congressional power of the purse." V. O. Key, Jr., "Government Corporations," in Fritz Morstein Marx (ed.), "Elements of Public Administration" (New York: Prentice-Hall, 1946), pp. 244–245.

the exigencies of modern warfare may even make it necessary, in order to avert irreparable losses, for the President to order American forces to strike the first blow.[7]

Is legislation needed to confer on Government agencies new powers or responsibilities not already provided for under the Constitution and existing statutes? History is full of cases in which Executive officials, without waiting for legislative authorization, have taken actions never dreamed of under the Constitution or existing statutes. If the occasion is serious enough and if there are enough supporting interests and groups, Executive officials will often go far into uncharted seas. Was Franklin Roosevelt within his rights when he gave Great Britain 50 overage destroyers in exchange for a ninety-nine year lease of air and naval bases on British islands off the Atlantic Coast? While good lawyers wrote convincing briefs on both sides of the matter, the fact remains that the deed was done. Does the President have power to seize the coal mines or the steel mills when a prolonged strike has threatened to prostrate the economy? If such a strike lasts long enough, any President would take this action even if, like President Truman, he had vigorously opposed legislative action conferring upon him this specific power. In fact, most Presidents in recent decades feel that they are breaking no rules of the game if they take action which is not expressly forbidden by the Constitution or by statute.

This applies even to a relatively unaggressive President like Taft who went beyond specific authorization to bring into the public domain a large tract of land in California in which oil had been discovered. He assuaged his critics and his conscience by subsequently asking Congress for legislation to ratify his action, a procedure that is often used to solidify the administrative actions of Executive officials.

A more aggressive President like the first Roosevelt was less interested in legislative ratification. He wrote:

I decline to adopt the view that what was imperatively necessary for the Nation could not be done by the President unless he could find some specific authorization to do it. My belief was that it was not only his right but his duty to do anything that the needs of the Nation demanded unless such action was forbidden by the Constitution

[7] In a bitter attack against the foreign policy of Franklin D. Roosevelt, Charles A. Beard complained that "The theory that the President has the power to determine foreign policy, support his policy by arms, and, without appealing to Congress for war authority, strike a designated enemy, has received approval in certain military, naval and civilian circles of the U.S." . . . and that "propaganda in universities, colleges and schools has deeply implanted in the minds of the rising generation the doctrine that the power of the President over international relations is, for all practical purposes, illimitable." Charles A. Beard, "President Roosevelt and the Coming of the War—1941" (New Haven, Conn.: Yale University Press, 1948), pp. 584, 590. Yet what Beard really objected to was the substantive character of the Roosevelt foreign policy. The words he uses are merely another illustration of the good old American habit of seasoning substantive arguments with charges of usurpation.

or by the laws. Under this interpretation of executive power I did and caused to be done many things not previously done by the President and the heads of the Departments. I did not usurp power, but I did greatly broaden the use of executive power. In other words, I acted for the public welfare, I acted for the common well-being of all our people, whenever and in whatever manner was necessary, unless prevented by direct constitutional or legislative prohibition. I did not care a rap for the mere form and show of power; I cared immensely for the use that could be made of the substance.[8]

Furthermore, it should be noted that there are many situations in which administrative action can be used in direct violation of clear-cut legislative or constitutional prescriptions. In fighting the Confederacy, Abraham Lincoln clearly broke the rules of the game when he took money from the Treasury without an appropriation, raised the size of the Army and Navy beyond their statutory limits, and suspended the writ of habeas corpus in various areas.[9] In time of war, martial law can be used to suspend the Bill of Rights itself. The history of Supreme Court decisions on questions of this type shows a strong probability that a majority of the Court will decline to rule against Executive action which seems justified by the situation and which enjoys sufficient support throughout the country.

Finally, administrative action can be used to repeal statutory provisions by the simple method of inaction. As Corwin has pointed out,

any particular statute is but a single strand of a vast fabric of laws demanding enforcement; nor—simply from the nature of the case—can all these be enforced with equal vigor, or with the same vigor at all times. So the President's duty to "take care that the laws be faithfully executed" has come to embrace a broad power of selection among the laws for this purpose; and that this power is today without statable limits the history of the Sherman Act alone is sufficient proof. In a word, the President's very obligation to the law becomes at times an authorization to *dispense with* the law.[10]

[8] Theodore Roosevelt, "Autobiography" (New York: Scribner, 1925), pp. 388–389.

[9] Lincoln justified his action as follows: "My oath to preserve the Constitution imposed on me the duty of preserving by every indispensable means that government, that nation, of which the Constitution was the organic law. Was it possible to lose the nation and yet preserve the Constitution? By general law life and limb must be protected, yet often a limb must be amputated to save a life, but a life is never wisely given to save a limb. I felt that measures, otherwise unconstitutional, might become lawful by becoming indispensable to the preservation of the Constitution through the preservation of the nation. Right or wrong, I assumed this ground and now avow it. I could not feel that, to the best of my ability, I had ever tried to preserve the Constitution, if to save slavery or any minor matter, I should permit the wreck of the government, country, and Constitution altogether." John G. Nicolay and John Hay, "Abraham Lincoln: A History" (New York: Century, 1890), Vol. X, pp. 65–68.

[10] Edward S. Corwin, "The President, Office and Powers" (New York: New York University Press, 1948), p. 149.

This applies to appropriation acts as well as other types of legislation. Although an appropriation is a mandate to spend, Executive officials can refuse to spend. Thus, the military appropriation bill for fiscal year 1950 appropriated funds for a fifty-eight-group Air Force, rather than the forty-eight-group Air Force backed by the Truman Administration. Although he was opposed to this provision, President Truman signed the measure instead of vetoing it. But at the time of signing it, he announced his intention of not spending the extra money. In a statement to the press he said:

Increasing the structure of the Air Force above that recommended in the 1950 Budget would be inconsistent with a realistic and balanced security program which we can support in peacetime and would interfere with orderly planning for the three services based on a unified strategic concept. I am therefore directing the Secretary of Defense to place in reserve the amounts provided by the Congress in H.R. 4146 for increasing the structure of the Air Force.[11]

The "Exclusively Administrative." At the other extreme, it is commonly supposed that only the administrative process can be used for hiring and firing, dealing with the minutiae of organization and administration, and handling individual cases as opposed to general rules. Yet entirely apart from considerations of desirability, it is blunt fact that the legislative process can be used for each of these purposes. A bill can provide that certain officials meet given statutory requirements. When it is obvious that an incumbent official does not meet these requirements, its passage is equivalent to forcing resignation. By a reduction in the appropriations for a certain division or for a certain type of agency activity, whole groups of employees can be pushed out of government service or, at least, forced to look for other jobs. The only effective limitation on this device, one that can readily be circumvented, is that officials to be fired should not be mentioned by name.[12]

[11] White House press release, Oct. 29, 1949.

[12] In the notorious case of Lovett, Watson, and Dodd, a 1943 appropriation act prohibited all future employment of these three individuals by any agency of Government, except to positions for which they had been confirmed by the Senate. With no dissents, the Court ruled as follows: "Legislative acts, no matter what their form, that apply either to named individuals or to easily ascertainable members of a group in such a way as to inflict punishment on them without a judicial trial are bills of attainder prohibited by the Constitution. . . . When our Constitution and Bill of Rights were written, our ancestors had ample reason to know that legislative trials and punishments were too dangerous to liberty to exist in the nation of free men they envisioned. And so they proscribed bills of attainder. Section 304 is one. Much as we regret to declare that an Act of Congress violates the Constitution, we have no alternative here." (*United States v. Lovett*, 328 U.S. 303.) For a detailed review of this case, see Laurence E. Seibel, "Personal Liberties and the Appropriation Power of Congress," *George Washington Law Review*, Vol. 14, February, 1946, pp. 337–353. Seibel points out that despite judicial decisions, specific individuals could be eliminated from the Government service by a return to the system, used in the first few years

Legislative action can also extend into the minutiae of organization and administration. Appropriations for certain Departments allocate funds so closely to individual bureaus and divisions that the head of the Department has practically no leeway whatsoever to make organizational shifts in his own agency. Many an agency must obtain a special provision of law in order to buy a new car, enlarge its printing budget by $1,000, or subscribe to a few additional technical journals. Legislation for flood control and irrigation projects usually goes still further toward narrowing administrative discretion; individual dams are habitually listed by name together with the sum of money to be spent on each.

Until recently, whenever an army truck collided with Farmer Jones's cow on a country road, the War Department was unable to compensate the farmer for the damages. The poor farmer, if able to survive the deluge of red tape descending from the Adjutant General's office, would very likely call on his Congressman for help. The result would be a private bill for the relief of Farmer Jones. The multiplicity of such private claims, together with similar bills dealing with the grievances of individuals, resulted in the introduction of more than 3,700 private bills during the Seventy-ninth Congress, more than a third of all bills introduced. Almost 900 of these were enacted into law, more than half of all the Federal laws produced during 1945 and 1946. In an effort to relieve the Congress of this burden, the Legislative Reorganization Act of 1946 broadened the discretion of administrative agencies by allowing them to settle private claims up to $1,000. It also extended the jurisdiction of the United States district courts over claims of this nature. Nevertheless, the legislative route is still wide open, and the continued congressional consideration of multitudinous private bills indicates that neither aggrieved individuals nor members of Congress are averse to this overlapping of the legislative and administrative processes.

The Overlap with Other Processes

The area of choice is by no means limited to the overlap between the legislative and administrative processes. The social struggle is punctuated by innumerable instances of groups being faced with a choice of either using the legislative process or going to the courts, trying to obtain a constitutional amendment, seeking action by state or local governments, or carrying on their activities through private and nongovernmental channels.

The Judicial Process. In so far as questions of interpretation are concerned, the position of the judicial process in relation to the legislative process is that

---

of the Republic, of listing the names of those to be paid under an appropriation, ". . . a forerunner of further repressive legislation in the field of personal liberties."

of the inner circle of two concentric circles. There is nothing that can be done through a judicial decision that could not also be accomplished through legislative action. It could be argued that a judicial decision deals with an individual case rather than a general rule. The answer is that legislation can provide the general rule covering the individual case. A long history of judicial decisions on the Sherman Antitrust Act is one of judicial actions that were equivalent to a detailed series of amendments in the statute itself. The results of any of these decisions could have been attained by prior legislative action. Any of these decisions could have been subsequently reversed by legislative action.

One of the best illustrations of the overlapping between the legislative and judicial processes is to be found in the recent history of railroad legislation. In 1945 the major railroads of the country were attacked by antitrust suits on two major points. The state of Georgia brought an original suit before the Supreme Court charging Northern and Southern railroads with conspiring to maintain a freight-rate system which discriminated against Southern shippers. The Department of Justice launched a similar attack in a Federal district court in Nebraska, charging discrimination against the West. The railroads decided that a passive defense in the courts was not enough; they launched a counteroffensive by backing a bill to exempt the railroads from the antitrust laws and legalize any rate agreements that the railroads may make subject to certain vague controls by the Interstate Commerce Commission. The two efforts proceeded side by side for a number of years. But in June, 1948, the passage of the Bulwinkle bill exempted railroad rate-making practices from the antitrust laws, thus cutting the ground out from under the Supreme Court case. During the early debates on this measure, Senator Alben Barkley, then Senate Majority Leader, bewailed the use of legislation as a means of undercutting the judicial process. He complained:

> The introduction of such bills seems to have become a habit here. I think it is a vicious practice; I think it is a vicious habit; it ought never to have been indulged in. This measure involves the same principle as that involved in the insurance cases. It involves the same sort of situation as existed last week when the Senate passed a bill taking away from the courts its jurisdiction of passing on the tidelands controversies.[13]

\ A similar, though less lusty, complaint was voiced by President Truman two years later in his veto of the measure.[14] Yet Truman's opposition was not strong enough to stop the congressional supporters of the railroads from overriding his veto. In doing what Truman found "inappropriate" and Barkley, "vicious," they violated none of the rules of the game.

On questions of constitutionality, the relationship of the judicial process to

[13] *Congressional Record*, 79th Cong., 2d Sess., July 27, 1946.
[14] Veto message, June 10, 1948.

the legislative process is one of overlapping rather than concentric circles. The judicial process can be used to annul state and local laws that are beyond the jurisdiction of the national legislative process. The legislative process, on its part, obviously extends far beyond acts of negation and annulment. The area of overlapping—and it is a fairly extensive one—covers all those cases where the Supreme Court can overthrow a Federal law on the ground of unconstitutionality. In such cases, direct legislative repeal is an obvious alternative to judicial action.

Constitutional Amendment. The problem of choice often arises as one of whether a given objective can be achieved through legislation or whether it is first necessary to enlarge the powers of the Federal government through a constitutional amendment.

One of the most historic battles of this type centered around the issue of the income tax. In 1895 legislation was enacted imposing a 2 per cent tax on all incomes over $2,000. A year later a bare majority of five members of the Supreme Court ruled the law unconstitutional. Despite widespread assault, the courts succeeded in blocking off use of the legislative process for two decades until finally, during the Wilson Administration, the Sixteenth Amendment to the Constitution gave Congress and the President specific power to pluck the previously forbidden fruit.

In more recent decades, however, the tendency has been for the Supreme Court majority to sanction the use of the legislative process without prior amendment of the Constitution. An excellent example is found in the history of efforts to have the Federal government prohibit child labor, under the interstate-commerce or the taxing clauses. In 1916 a Supreme Court majority overthrew a Federal anti-child-labor statute on the ground that it exceeded the powers given to the Federal government under the Constitution. As a result, the proponents of this reform embarked on the long and weary path toward having the constitutional amendment approved by two-thirds of the Congress and three-fourths of the state legislatures. Although the first of these objectives was achieved in 1924, it proved impossible to obtain favorable action by enough states. In 1933 the legislative route was again assayed, this time through one of the provisions of the National Industrial Recovery Act. When this Act was itself declared unconstitutional in 1935, it again appeared as though the arduous task of obtaining an amendment to the Constitution must once again be resumed. Yet the opposition within the state legislatures was still strong. In 1937, more than twenty years after the first effort had been blocked, another attempt to use the legislative process was tried. The vehicle was the Fair Labor Standards Act which, in the words of its advocates, consisted of "a floor for wages, a ceiling for hours, and a break for children." In 1941 the Court finally withdrew from the contest by reversing previous rulings and upholding this statute.

Similar decisions in one field after the other have overthrown judicial limitations upon legislative action. In fact, the use of the legislative process coupled with a favorable decision by a Supreme Court majority is not only an alternative to the process of constitutional amendment; for all intents and purposes it constitutes the major way in which we go about amending our Constitution.

State or Local Action. The extent of overlapping between the national legislative process and the processes of state and local governments has been largely determined by the Supreme Court's changing conception of constitutional limitations upon what can be accomplished through Federal action.

There was a time when almost any Federal legislation attempting extensive regulation of industry would be overthrown by a court on the ground that it was an exercise of power reserved to the states and not expressly dedicated to the Federal government. In 1933, for example, the Agricultural Adjustment Act established a system of acreage control as a method of avoiding "overproduction" of farm products and keeping farm prices from falling too low. In 1935, when one Supreme Court decision after another torpedoed New Deal statutes, the Roosevelt Administration tried to protect the Triple A through a set of amendments toning down the original Act. Despite this protective action, a thunderous decision in January, 1936, declared the Act null and void on the ground that the power to regulate agricultural production was a power reserved to the states.[15]

On the heels of the Supreme Court's 1936 decision, President Roosevelt promptly announced his Administration's determination to continue the agricultural adjustment program or "its equivalent." With the cooperation of farm leaders, a new bill was drawn up which regulated acreage control to soil conservation and provided for administration through the states rather than by the Federal government directly. The bill became a law on March 1, less than three months after the Court had ruled that this objective could not be achieved by legislation. This time the acreage-control program weathered all assaults by appeals in the courts. By 1938 the power to regulate agriculture through Federal legislation was so fully accepted by the Court that the Roosevelt Administration was able to obtain a new act superseding the 1936 statute and vastly expanding the Government's activities in the control of agricultural production.

By a long series of decisions in other cases the Court has interpreted almost every form of Federal regulatory action as falling within the province of the constitutional provision authorizing Congress to regulate commerce among the several states. One might go so far as to say that the commerce power has been interpreted so broadly and interstate commerce now affects so many aspects of our economy that it appears very unlikely that future Federal legislation dealing with economic problems will be declared unconstitutional. This

[15] Hoosac Mills decision.

series of decisions has been accompanied by the growing use of Federal grants to state and local governments. By the grant-in-aid device, Federal legislation can provide indirectly for many activities—such as aid to education—in areas where any proposal for direct Federal operations would evoke a storm of organized and unbeatable opposition.

The issue of states' rights versus a powerful Federal government has become, as Wendell Willkie pointed out in 1944, not an issue but a relic.[16] In the same way, the constitutional reference in the Tenth Amendment to powers that are "reserved to the States respectively, or to the people" is hopelessly out of date, for there is no limit on what the Federal government can do through legislation, given sufficient support among private organizations and the members of Congress, executive agencies, and the Supreme Court. The old quip that the British Parliament can do everything but make a woman a man and a man a woman is now almost fully applicable to the national government in the United States.

Private Action. With respect to a large portion of private conflicts, there is little if any recourse to national legislation. This is particularly true of breaches of contract between private parties, where the obvious method of carrying the conflict into public channels is the use of the courts. Yet the more significant any private conflict becomes, the greater are the possibilities that one or another contestant can attempt to gain his objectives through national legislation. In fact, the legislative process is to a large extent a reflection of conflicts between private organizations. The history of labor legislation, for example, is mainly a story of the attempts of both organized labor and employers to attain through the legislative process advantages which they have sought through the nongovernmental processes of collective bargaining. In the same way business and agricultural organizations have not been content to rely upon market competition but have sought legislative action to fortify their position in the business struggle. Thus, the airlines have consistently attempted through legislation to prevent railroads and shipping companies from entering the field of air transportation.

Ballots or Bullets. Both the electoral process and its violent counterpart, revolution, are methods of effectuating changes in the top leadership of government. As such they are not on the same plane of relevance as the legislative process, since they deal with the shift of power from group to group rather than with any group's use of power. Nevertheless, there is a real area of overlapping between these and the legislative process. In the course of the legislative struggle choices are always arising as to whether given ends can be attained through legislation or whether it is not necessary first to effectuate a change in the personnel of government. The extent to which these choices arise and the character of the choice depend not upon any rules or traditions but upon how

[16] Quoted in *The New York Times,* June 12, 1944.

much shift in power and resources is contemplated. Generally speaking, if one aims at a minor shift in power and resources, the legislative process is adequate to the task—although even in such circumstances the defeat or reelection of even one Congressman who is in a strategic position may be helpful. If a greater shift in power and resources is sought, such as legislation which takes long strides toward increasing the power of either organized labor or organized business, legislative action may be impossible until there has been an electoral change in the Presidency or in the composition of Congress. If an extremely radical shift is contemplated, such as the expropriation without compensation of the means of production or the placing of political power in the hands of a fascist dictatorship, then resort to violence would probably be needed as an adjunct of, a preliminary to, or a substitute for, legislative action.

ADVANTAGES IN THE LEGISLATIVE PROCESS

Among the obvious considerations in the minds of those who ponder whether or not to travel on the legislative highway are the smoothness of the road and the amount of assistance they are likely to obtain along the wayside. When it is believed that a large number of Senators or Representatives will be friendly to a given proposal, there is more reason to seek its embodiment in a bill. Thus, during World War II, business groups that regarded themselves as unduly injured by the "hold-the-line" philosophy of the Office of Price Administration made a habit of floating anti-OPA bills and amendments among their many friends in Congress. When there is slight chance of developing support in Congress, this is reason to drop the idea entirely or use some other avenue. The opponents of early New Deal legislation, for example, made no attempts to seek repeal through legislative action, confining their efforts largely to appeals before the Supreme Court.

Considerations of this type involve an analysis of the disposition of opposing forces and of the best use of one's own available resources. But there are other important considerations that flow more directly from the character of the legislative process itself. To carry the military metaphor one step further, one might say they involve a topographical analysis of the terrain. Apart from the strategic location of friends, enemies, and neutrals, there are unquestioned advantages to be found in the legislative terrain itself. Some of these relate to the mere act of having a bill irrespective of whether the bill ever blossoms into a statute. Some relate to the value of a statute, even under circumstances where the identical objective could be achieved through other processes.

The Importance of a Bill

As a Publicity Device. Introducing a bill in Congress is one of the time-honored methods through which a Senator or Representative can improve his position with constituents and interest groups. In fact, the great majority of bills are not seriously regarded by their congressional sponsors. The process of introducing a bill is easy and painless. It is not even necessary to obtain recognition on the floor. Proposed measures need merely be given to a page boy or carried over to the Bill Clerk in either house. No clearance is needed through any party or congressional machinery. The act of introduction constitutes no commitment as to whether its sponsor will ever lift a finger to advance its progress on the legislative highway. If no action is ever taken on a bill, it is no discredit to the sponsor; most bills die in committee. If there is a chance that it might strike a spark among enough groups to become a going proposition, then there is nothing lost in taking the gamble. The sponsor is in the same position as a millionaire who puts a few dollars on a long shot in a horse race or takes a flier on the stock market. There have even been cases when a member of Congress has introduced a bill for the dual purpose of placing himself in a strategic position to exercise decisive influence to *prevent* its enactment, thereby maintaining the favor of its opponents as well as of its supporters.

One of the reasons why the introduction of a bill can serve as a real favor to an interest group or government agency is its unquestioned value as an educational and propaganda instrument. A bill provides a very concrete symbol to serve as a rallying point for a campaign, whether the purpose be to set up a world government or to increase the pensions of the widows of Spanish-American War veterans. Its official format and trappings give it an important public-relations value. There is nothing like a bill to show that you mean business. It is a good thing around which to organize a campaign, to refer to in a speech, or to mail with a pamphlet. From the viewpoint of those interested in making a living through the conduct of a legislative campaign it is a way of obtaining employment with private organizations, members of Congress, or executive agencies. From the viewpoint of a sponsor, a bill is a good way to supplement a speech and to get a better break in the press or on the radio.

As a Counterweight. A bill is an ideal instrument for warding off charges of negativism and demonstrating that you have a constructive position. It is hard to fight something with nothing. During the Eightieth Congress many of the Senators who were leading the fight against the Taft-Hartley Labor-Management Relations Act introduced an alternative bill of their own. From the political viewpoint, they simply could not afford to be put in a position where it would be charged that they were always against legislation in the labor field and never had any constructive proposals to offer. In the same way, the Senators who led the fight against the Truman Administration's health-insurance legislation could not afford to be in the position of being against the people's health. The logic of the situation called for an alternative measure, and the result was the National Health Bill introduced by Senator Taft and others.[17]

Sometimes following the principle that "you can't fight something with nothing" requires little more than an informal proposal. In January, 1949, for example, Senator Paul Douglas of Illinois was confronted with the problem of what to do about a Veterans Economic Development Corporation Bill which had been referred to a Senate banking and currency subcommittee of which he was chairman. The bill was something of a legislative monstrosity. It proposed to set up a new and heavily financed government corporation which would provide for veterans various services already being made available to broader segments of the population by the Reconstruction Finance Corporation, the Veterans Administration, the Housing and Home Finance Agency, the Departments of Agriculture and Commerce, and many other agencies. The bill was bitterly opposed by all these organizations and by the Bureau of the Budget. Nor did it commend itself to those who were concerned with cutting down special preferential treatment for veterans and developing instead a broad and more balanced array of governmental services. The key proponent of the bill, Colonel Richmond Harris, working in conjunction with the Veterans of Foreign Wars, had brought together a formidable amount of paper support for the measure. Nineteen Senators had been cajoled into serving as sponsors, including the Vice-President-elect, Senator Alben Barkley, and the chairman of the full Banking and Currency Committee, Senator Burnet Maybank of South Carolina. In fact, Senator Maybank had already announced his intention of reporting favorably on the bill to the floor in the near future. Confronted with this situation, Senator Douglas was naturally reluctant to place himself in a position of direct frontal opposition to the measure in the subcommittee. Yet he was equally reluctant to go along on a measure that ran counter to his best judgment and which was so strongly opposed by the executive agencies. The way out of the dilemma was the preparation in draft form of a substitute measure which directed existing governmental agencies to take special precautions against the possibility that the interests of veterans might be neglected in the administration of their programs. To give the bill additional substance, a provision was inserted expanding the lending resources of

[17] "The bill is a political measure only, an assist to Senator Taft's Presidential campaign. It records him as favoring a national health program, which should get him a lot of lay votes, and it assures organized medicine that he wants the program left entirely to its control, which lines up one of the most powerful pressure groups in the United States in his support." Bernard De Voto, "Doctors along the Boardwalk," *Harper's Magazine,* September, 1947, p. 222.

the Reconstruction Finance Corporation. Senator Douglas then sent the draft bill around to various people for comment. This action served to complicate what was previously a straightforward but one-sided issue ("muddied the waters" is the phrase the Veterans of Foreign Wars probably used). As a result of the difficulties involved in reconciling the two drafts, action on the initial proposal was indefinitely postponed.

As an Intellectual Stimulus or Expression. The introduction of a bill is one of the best ways of getting attention in the highly competitive market place of ideas. A bill can serve as an ideal trial balloon for executive officials who are wary of taking a given course of action—particularly if the bill can be planted in Congress in such a manner as to leave the officials who originated the idea free from any responsibility for its preparation. Irrespective of reactions to a bill, the very fact that one or more members of the Congress may introduce it can itself serve to indicate potential support for a given course of action. Furthermore, the availability of the legislative process for the launching of new ideas is one of the factors that helps to protect the Government against hardening of the arteries. In every large governmental organization, there are occasions when people of the highest ability and the greatest creativity find themselves traveling up a dead-end street. Whenever they attempt to get their views before the attention of responsible officials of the highest echelons they find themselves boxed in by intervening superiors who refuse to pass papers along and who issue peremptory instructions on the importance of keeping one's mouth shut. Many a repressed bureaucrat has escaped these restrictions by passing on his ideas in legislative form to a Representative or Senator, either directly or through the intermediary of a private organization. This is all highly irregular, of course, and deserves to be frowned upon by all who believe that the Government should be operated in accordance with organizational blueprints. But in balance it probably adds considerably to the vitality of governmental processes.

Another fundamental advantage of the legislative route is its value in the formulative stages of a program. Since the executive branch of the Government has grown faster than its machinery for the coordinated formulation of executive policies, the only clearinghouse that operates regularly between the multitudinous departments and bureaus is the Legislative Reference Division of the Bureau of the Budget. Under these circumstances sometimes the only possible way to get government agencies working together is by having a draft bill circulated or having a bill introduced unofficially through a friendly Congressman. Agency reactions to it can then be brought together through the Budget Bureau clearance process.

Apart from their need for coordination machinery, many ideas can never be properly crystallized unless they are put into bill form and are thereby subjected to public analysis. The experts who prepare a memo within a government agency can usually coast along on the knowledge that it will be subjected to the criticism of no more than a limited number of officials. When the same men draft a bill, however, they know that their handiwork must be able to withstand the slings and arrows of a far wider circle. They must weigh more precisely the effect of their proposals upon conflicting interests and gauge more accurately the total implications of any course of action that is recommended. This aspect of the legislative process is important irrespective of whether or not the ideas embodied in a bill are finally enacted into law.

In Expediting Executive or Judicial Action. The legislative process can also expedite executive or judicial action. In 1943 Senators Maloney, Taft, and Scrugham introduced a bill aimed at stimulating more attention by the war agencies to questions of civilian supply. During the hearings before the Senate Banking and Currency Committee, testimony brought out many important defects in the operations of the civilian-supply division of the War Production Board. While the chairman of the War Production Board, Donald Nelson, opposed the measure, he took vigorous action independently to achieve the objectives of the bill by strengthening the WPB's civilian-supply division. The bill went through the Senate, but by the time it got to the House it was evident that the case for it had disappeared.

One of the great legislative battles in recent years was centered around President Franklin Roosevelt's highly controversial "court-packing" bill. The purpose of this measure was to change the character of the Supreme Court's decisions by adding more Roosevelt appointees to the bench. Roosevelt lost the legislative battle. But he clearly won the war; for the conflict that developed over the legislation was credited with being instrumental in bringing about the Supreme Court's dramatic reversals in decisions on New Deal legislation.

In Election Campaigns. The use of the legislative process can also be a vital factor in electoral campaigns. Perhaps a classic example is the anti-inflation program which President Truman sent to the Eightieth Congress in November, 1947. Among other proposals of a more or less technical nature, Truman called for the reimposition of price control on a selective basis. There was considerable doubt in the minds of its proponents as to whether or not a price-control act could be administered and enforced—but no doubt whatsoever that enactment of a price-control law by the Eightieth Congress was inconceivable. Nevertheless, by pressing for the inconceivable, the President succeeded in dramatically divesting himself of any responsibility for inflationary price increases, thus putting the Republican leaders of the Eightieth Congress squarely on the spot. By so doing he created an invaluable campaign issue, one that probably meant a large number of additional votes from housewives and low-income families generally. If he had not pressed the legislative fight for price control so vigorously, it is possible that Dewey would have been elected President in November, 1948.[18]

The Importance of a Law

There is something very compelling about a Federal law. It is a document that presumably has the force of the American government behind it. As a pronouncement that has had the approval of a large number of the elected representatives of the American people, it has an aura of prestige and sanctity about it.

To appreciate the attraction exercised by the hope of attaining a law, it is not enough to think of cases where legislation is sought in order to provide an "Open sesame" to the Federal Treasury or a key to a toolbox of Federal powers that would otherwise remain securely locked. Even more revealing are the legislative battles themselves which have centered around objectives that could have been achieved through another route.

As a "Mandate." The struggle over the Employment Act of 1946 was one of the most sharply fought legislative battles during President Truman's first year in the White House. The key provisions of this legislation, in the form first endorsed by the Truman Administration, consisted of a resounding declaration of the Government's responsibility to "assure continuing full employment" and a procedure whereby for the first time the President of the United States would transmit to Congress at the beginning of every regular session a comprehensive economic program. Neither of these provisions necessarily called for legislation. The only objective of the bill that could not have been achieved by Executive action was the provision setting up a Joint Congressional Committee to study the President's economic program, and this could have been accomplished by a simple concurrent resolution of Congress. The opponents of the bill were quick to point this out, contending that the objectives of the provisions could be achieved through Presidential action alone.

Representative Carter Manasco made this the first point in his cross-exam-

[18] The fight over price control in the 80th Congress had an interesting epilogue in 1949. Shortly after the Truman election victory, when it became evident that prices were leveling off, Truman was left in the paradoxical position of having campaigned vigorously for something that was no longer a pressing necessity. Nevertheless, if the fight for price control had been suddenly dropped like a hot potato immediately after the election, the President would have opened himself to charges of insincere campaigning. Accordingly, although the case for the reimposition of price control was no longer as valid as when he had first made it, he renewed his request in his messages to Congress in January, 1949. No sooner had he done so than prices began to turn down of their accord and his proposal fell on even more barren ground in the Democratic 81st Congress than it had in the Republican 80th Congress. Yet the introduction of price-control legislation in 1949 had the merit of helping to keep the record straight.

ination of Harold Smith, Director of the Budget, who was the Administration's leadoff witness in the hearings before the House Committee on Expenditures in the Executive Departments.[19] The Budget Director, however, had anticipated this attack in his prepared statement. His line of defense was as follows:

Some critics say that no law is needed to authorize the President to transmit estimates of the Nation's Budget and recommendations for a coordinated program. They say that the President can transmit and, as a matter of fact, has transmitted estimates of the Nation's Budget and policy recommendations under existing power and authority. It is true that recent Presidential Budget Messages have moved in the direction of the requirements of this bill. This proves, not that the bill is superfluous, but that it is in line with present needs and developments. The appraisals and recommendations required by this bill are of such importance that, in my judgment, they should be transmitted not merely at the discretion of the President, but should become part of his statutory responsibility.

Behind this argument lay a realization that any President, in moving along the lines contemplated by the proposed measure, would much prefer to operate under the provisions of a statute rather than on his own initiative. In the former case he would be merely complying with a procedure agreed to by the Congress. In the latter, he would always run the risk that congressional leaders would attack him for trying to foist upon them some new and foreign kind of economic planning.

The Budget Director's defense, however, was not a complete one. In countering Representative Manasco's question, he confined himself to the procedural aspects of the bill.

A central Administration purpose of the legislation was to obtain specific congressional endorsement of the concept that the Government has a very high degree of responsibility in stabilizing the national economy. It was felt that an endorsement of this type, while having no legal value in the narrow sense, would serve as a psychological springboard from which the Administration could launch many of its individual economic programs dealing with social security, health, resource development, monopoly, taxation, and other economic matters. Conservative groups throughout the country claimed that enactment of the bill with its original strong declaration of policy would lead people to expect too much from the Federal government, and would undermine the foundations of capitalistic free enterprise in America. This point of view made considerable headway in Congress, and by the time the bill became law the declaration of policy was toned down to a carefully qualified statement that aroused very little public expectation of aggressive Government action.

A still more clear-cut example of the value of a legislative mandate was provided in 1944 by the Fulbright and Connally resolutions on foreign policy.

---

[19] "Full Employment Act of 1945," Hearings before the House Committee on Expenditures in the Executive Departments, 79th Cong., 1st Sess., Sept. 25, 1945.

Both these resolutions consisted of reiterations of policy statements previously made by President Roosevelt and Secretary of State Cordell Hull. Neither added anything to the substance of American foreign policy as proclaimed by the executive heads of the Government. Nor did they have much legal significance. Nevertheless, they proved invaluable in laying the basis for public understanding of the need for international cooperation and for subsequent congressional acceptance of the Administration's work in the formation of the United Nations.

As an Aid in Administration. Richard E. Neustadt, an acute and informed observer, writes:

Generally speaking, an administrator who wants to undertake a new program gains by prior Congressional sanction quite as much as Congress gains by demonstrating its authority. The more specific the sanction the better. It backs up the administrator. It lightens his load of counter pressures. The fight for Congressional approval enables him to test in advance the forces behind him and in his way. The terms on which approval is obtained give him a blueprint of the alignment of interests with which he will have to deal.[20]

Another example is supplied by James M. Landis:

Frequently the administration is faced with the need to exercise a power that lies within the limits of its statutory grant; but the subject matter happens to be of such great public concern that it is desirable to have the more direct democratic processes of our government participate in the decision. An illustration from another field may serve to give point to this problem. Under the statutory authority that had already been granted to him, the President had the power to commit the nation to large expenditures in connection with the Florida Ship Canal. The project, however, partly because of the amount of expenditure that it entails and partly because it had for various reasons already become the subject of political debate and conflicting allegiance, differed considerably from the regular public works projects to which the President was authorized to allocate public monies. For these reasons it was an act of political wisdom to put back upon the shoulders of the Congress the basic question as to the desirability of allocating the money necessary for the development of this project.[21]

The lack of a specific legislative mandate can often impair the effectiveness of an executive agency involved in conflicts with other agencies. At an important point in the development of the war production program, for example, the War Production Board officials became convinced that it was necessary to cut back the War Department's plans for building new plants. They pointed out that the Department's construction program would drain needed materials and labor out of current industrial production, and insisted that more emphasis should be placed on better utilization of existing plant facilities. The generals

[20] Richard E. Neustadt, "Presidential Clearance of Legislation" (unpublished doctoral dissertation, Harvard University, June, 1950).

[21] *Op. cit.,* pp. 76–77.

not only protested the WPB's authority to order a curtailment of War Department activity; they made the case that the chairman of the War Production Board received his authority merely on the basis of an Executive order of the President. The War Department, in contrast, received its authority directly from an appropriation act which authorized it to spend money as it saw fit. The importance of this argument cannot be weighed on any legal scales. The fact of the matter is that, to any bureaucrat, statutory authority flowing directly from legislation is regarded far more highly than authority flowing through the intermediate office of the President. This was one of the reasons why legislation was sought, through the War Mobilization and Reconversion Act, to provide a basis for the coordinating functions of the Office of War Mobilization and Reconversion.

As a Basis for Appropriations. A new legislative mandate can always be of value in enhancing the chances of executive agencies in obtaining increased appropriations from Congress. At every session many bills are introduced authorizing or directing this or that agency to undertake activities that it has always been empowered to undertake. To the outside observer these bills seem meaningless. The purpose, however, is usually to mobilize additional support for increased appropriations. The original legislation creating the Bureau of Mines, for example, clearly authorized it to engage in research on all aspects of fuel resources. Yet, during the Eightieth Congress, Interior Department officials arranged to have introduced in Congress a synthetic-liquid-fuels bill providing for up to 30 million dollars to be spent by the Bureau of Mines in experimentation on methods of deriving synthetic liquid fuels from coal and oil shales. With the support of the legislative committees dealing with Interior Department affairs, the bill became law. As a result, the Bureau of Mines was able to obtain Budget Bureau support for a budget request for this purpose and a subsequent appropriation. Without this substantive legislation, which in fact served to restrict the authority of the Bureau of Mines (inasmuch as it set a ceiling on expenditures for synthetic-liquid-fuels research), it is doubtful whether funds for this purpose could have been obtained without a few more years of agitation.

During its brief tenure of existence between 1941 and 1946, the Fair Employment Practices Committee was engaged in a continuous struggle for survival against Southern Democrats who sought to cut off its appropriations. At the outset, funds for the FEPC were obtained from the reserve made available to President Roosevelt for unrestricted wartime expenditures. In 1944, the Southern Democrats wrote into the Independent Offices Appropriations Act a provision forbidding the use of any appropriations whatsoever to pay the expenses of any agency created by Executive order after it had been in existence for a year, unless "the Congress has specifically authorized the expenditure of funds" for this purpose.[22] If the FEPC had received a specific appropriation in the first place, it would have been in a stronger position. Once it was forced to seek its funds through appropriation acts rather than from the President's own funds, it then suffered from the fact that it was an agency operating under an Executive order only, rather than under a statute. Accordingly, a vigorous effort was made to enact legislation giving the FEPC a statutory basis. While this legislation also had the purpose of strengthening its powers and extending its tenure into the postwar period, its most immediate purpose was to help in the struggle for appropriations. All these purposes were frustrated, however, for the bill never became a law, and the agency was terminated by an appropriation provision in 1945 which gave the agency funds for the purposes of liquidation only.

DISADVANTAGES IN THE LEGISLATIVE PROCESS

The advantages discussed above are all relative rather than absolute. In any particular situation there are likely to be as many disadvantages in the use of the legislative process as there are advantages, some relating to the hazards of the process itself and some to the futility or disutility of any statute that may eventuate. This necessitates a careful weighing of potential gains and losses rather than automatic decision on a priori grounds.

Here again it is important to point out that appraisals of the legislative terrain cannot be disassociated from judgments made in terms of the disposition of forces. A beachhead which may be beautifully adapted to the landing of large numbers of troops and motorized equipment may also afford an ideal opportunity for opposing forces, if they can reach the vicinity, to crush the attackers.

The Uphill Grind

Delays. The legislative highway is neither short nor easy. Rather it is a long, uphill grind over dangerous terrain with booby traps and pitfalls all along the way. Traffic congestion alone can mean protracted delays. The number of twists and bends in the road is almost endless. At every turn in the road action can be held up by new points of view, new facts, new attacks, new grouping of forces, complex amendments, and alternative proposals. Moreover, the road may be blocked by the opposition of a small minority of Senators and Representatives in strategic positions. Sometimes even a single member can completely stall the progress of a bill either in committee or on the floor. Roland Young has pointed out that this time element is one of the reasons why executive officials often choose the administrative rather than the legislative process.

[22] Public Law 358. June 27, 1944.

Instances continually recur where the position of the President would be bolstered by securing the consent of the Congress to a proposal. This procedure would give Congress a real opportunity to deliberate on and to decide many crucial political problems. And being a political body, Congress should decide these problems. In making decisions, however, the element of time is important, and Congress is not now organized so that it can be relied on to give a quick answer to a problem.[23]

Boomerangs. Another danger is the ever-present possibility that the very act of seeking legislation of one type may stimulate legislative action of the opposite kind. Consider the attitude taken by organized labor toward new labor legislation during the decade between the passage of the Wagner National Labor Relations Act and the Taft-Hartley Labor-Management Relations Act of 1948. It was not long after the passage of the first Act that the leaders of organized labor realized that certain amendments were necessary. Nevertheless, they formed an almost unbroken united front in opposing any and all proposals for an amendment. They steadfastly maintained this position despite a growing outcry on the part of management that organized labor should take a more positive attitude and map out the legislative changes that they would be willing to see made. There is no doubt that this standpat attitude deprived labor leaders of considerable public support that they might have obtained through a more positive and cooperative attitude. They knew, however, that if they should once approve a set of acceptable amendments, the floodgate would be opened and there would be no way to prevent a deluge of destructive amendments. This approach, however unpalatable from the viewpoint of public relations, was clearly grounded on accurate understanding of the legislative facts of life. It yielded concrete results for labor during the legislative work on the 1947 statute, for this stubborn opposition to all legislation unquestionably was an important factor in the Senate's action in toning down considerably the provisions of the bill as it passed the House of Representatives.

One of the most informed observers of the governmental processes finds a disinclination among executive officials to use the legislative process. He writes:

Government agencies hesitate to seek modifications from Congress. They will rather indulge in improvisations and patiently endure the oddest kinds of legal limitation. The reason is obvious. They never know what will emerge from the legislative mill once it begins to turn. Except for the most important questions on which broad public discussion and understanding may be brought to bear, the administrative tendency is to limp along on the existing legal basis, no matter how unsatisfactory it may be. It is regarded as better than to arouse sleeping dogs.[24]

An illustration of the unpredictability of what may emerge from the legislative mill is to be found in the behind-the-scenes maneuvering on the Civilian

[23] Roland A. Young, "This Is Congress" (New York: Knopf, 1946), p. 24.
[24] V. O. Key, Jr., "Legislative Control," in Marx (ed.), *op. cit.*, p. 351.

Supply Bill, referred to earlier in this chapter. The introduction of this measure in the first place was encouraged by various assistants of Donald Nelson who saw in it an opportunity to provide a legislative foundation for the operations of the War Production Board. To their chagrin, however, the congressional sponsors of the measure listened to other advisers and wrote into the bill instead a provision taking the civilian-supply functions away from the War Production Board and setting them up in a new agency. If Donald Nelson's assistants had had any premonition that this might develop, they never would have encouraged the project in the first place and it is probable that the legislation would never have been introduced.

This observation needs supplementation on two scores. Executive disinclination to arouse sleeping dogs can be a means of either frustrating an organized majority of Congress or of preventing an organized minority from dominating a government program. Also, this attitude on the part of executive officials is by no means exclusive to officialdom. It often reflects a strong disinclination on the part of the leaders of some private organizations and of certain members of Congress themselves to use the legislative process.

Another boomerang is the possibility that seeking legislative action may close other routes. In cases where there is a legal doubt concerning the power of the executive branch to achieve a given objective, the act of seeking clearcut legal authority tends to imply the inadequacy of existing authority. Failure to obtain clarification may be regarded either as conclusive evidence that the doubt should be resolved against the executive branch or that the desired course of action is contrary to the views of the majority of Congress. This danger was undoubtedly one of the factors that led President Franklin Roosevelt to handle on his own the destroyer deal with Great Britain rather than request enabling legislation.

Hollow Victories

A Federal law is after all only a piece of paper with a number, a great many words, and three names signed at the bottom. Whether or not it has any really compelling force behind it depends on the precision with which it is drawn, the will and ability of those who are supposed to administer it, the extent to which the right people know about it, and the amount of organized or potential support it commands. Although many laws are the product of a significant and continuing aggregation of groups and forces, there is, however, as Bentley has pointed out,

a great deal of "grand-stand-play" law on the federal statute books. . . . There is also much dead-letter law, forgotten by the law officers of the government as well as by the people, which in the terminology of this book is not real law at all, but merely occupies a favored position, so that with less formality it can again become law if popular initiative or federal attorneys in a representative capacity choose to invoke it.[25]

The day that the Interstate Commerce Act was enacted was an occasion for rejoicing among the farmers and shipping interests, who felt they had won the battle against the malpractices of the railroads. Today the hollowness of this victory is clear. Instead of operating as an agency to control the railroads in the public interest, the Interstate Commerce Commission serves largely as an instrument to protect the railroads. Every time amendments to the interstate commerce legislation have been enacted giving the Commission more regulatory authority, the Commission has exercised its discretion to refrain from using its new powers. Specific instructions which would have resulted in reduction of freight rates or elimination of discriminations have met with interminable delays.[26]

The entire history of antitrust legislation points up the fact that the passage of a statute may produce little more than words on a piece of paper. The original Sherman Antitrust Act stood for years without any real attempt to enforce it. Bentley analyzed the production of this law as follows:

> The enactment of the Sherman law represented a certain stage in a certain group struggle. The presidency stood aligned with the groups which opposed the enactment of such a statute—the fact that a president's signature was appended to the law does not alter this situation. . . . As time went on, the presidency, through certain of the department heads, took gradual steps toward representing the interests in favor of the law. In recent years we have seen the law invoked more vigorously than before, till now we may say in this matter that the presidency is representing the groupings that favor the law much more than those against it. The more or less comes into operation because of the complexity of the agencies united in the presidency.[27]

A more up-to-date appraisal would show that at various times in subsequent years it once again became a meaningless scrap of paper.

In the case of some legislation—and this is true of course of the Sherman Antitrust Act—the responsibility for enforcement does not lie only with executive officials; private parties can also appeal to the courts. But there is a broad realm of statutory law in which judicial action is irrelevant and in which executive officials can completely nullify the enactment. In cases where the effectiveness of the law calls for subsequent appropriations, the refusal of adequate appropriations can carve the innards out of a statute. The Employment Act of 1946 provides another example of the same thing. Its passage was a great victory for all those who believed that the Federal government

[25] Arthur F. Bentley, "The Process of Government" (Bloomington, Ind.: Principia Press, 1949 reissue), p. 353.

[26] On relations between the ICC and the railroads, see Samuel P. Huntington, "Clientalism in Administrative Politics" (unpublished doctoral dissertation, Harvard University, 1951).

[27] Bentley, *op. cit.*, p. 354.

must assume a high degree of responsibility for the stabilization and expansion of the national economy. While the commitment to maintain full employment was weaker than in the original Full Employment Bill, it did represent a long step forward in the enunciation of the Government's economic responsibilities. Yet the bill can well be compared to a check for a large amount signed by a man who has little money in the bank and no intention of making any immediate deposits. Its passage was immediately followed by a series of measures which wrecked the Government's stabilization machinery and precipitated the serious 1946–1948 inflationary boom. Nor did the bill's provisions for congressional machinery meet with any more respect in the initial years than its declaration of policy. The legislation clearly provided that on a given date, shortly after Congress receives the President's Economic Report, the Joint Congressional Committee on the Economic Report should submit to both houses "its findings and recommendations on the major recommendations of the President." Yet when President Truman sent his first Economic Report to Congress, the Joint Committee, all of whose members had voted for the legislation, cavalierly ignored the "mandate of the people." On the appointed day, the Committee brought forth a *pro forma* report that included neither findings nor recommendations but merely pointed out that the President's proposals were of a controversial nature.

Chapter 10

LEGISLATIVE PARENTHOOD

IT IS a few seconds after the noon hour.

The Presiding Officer raps his gavel sharply. The early comers here and there in the chamber lower their eyes, bow their heads, and the Chaplain invokes the blessings of God upon the United States Senate.

The moment the prayer is over there is a confused bustle. A motion is made to approve the Journal for the previous day without reading it. One clerk mumbles an announcement about a conference report that has been disapproved by the House. Another reads the title of a measure that has been received from the President. A half-dozen Senators seek recognition from the Chair.

As these events follow one another in rapid succession, a Senator at one of the desks in the back snaps his fingers. A page boy leaps to his feet and in a second is at the Senator's side. A moment later the boy lays a typewritten document in a tray beside the Bill Clerk, a somber official who sits on the lowest tier of the three-decked rostrum.

The Bill Clerk writes a number on the first page of the manuscript, notes with approval the Senator's suggestion for committee referral, and sets it down in another tray whence, with a dozen or more companions, it will soon be whisked away to the Government Printing Office. A bill has been born!

A similar act of parturition, with only the most minor differences in procedure, takes place each day that the House of Representatives meets. Between the two houses from five to six thousand bills are born every year, or from ten to twelve thousand every session.[1] Any attempt to trace the origins

---

[1] This estimate is based on the ten-year span from 1937 to 1946. It is surprising to note, however, that during the first ten years of this century, about three times as many bills were introduced during each Congress. In part, the decline in the birth rate is probably due to the increasing ability of the administrative process to achieve objectives that formerly were sought more exclusively through legislation. The decline may also reflect a diminished number of private relief bills. A definitive explanation will not be possible until bills are counted in a manner that identifies both private relief bills and duplicate bills. Some observers have estimated that 40 per cent of all bills introduced represent duplications within and between houses and that, of the 60 per cent remaining, one quarter are private relief bills. See Richard Neustadt, "Presidential Clearance of Legislation" (unpublished doctoral dissertation, Harvard University, June, 1950).

of even one of these bills would involve a tangled network of people, groups, motives, and conflicts. It would mean peering back into the dim past, for "legislation unquestionably generates legislation. Every statute may be said to have a long lineage of statutes behind it." [2]

In general, however, there are typical problems that are encountered in the birth process; problems of legislative parenthood, of drafting original bills, and of preparing amendments. A description of these problems cannot give the same sense of growth and dynamics that can be obtained from a story of one bill's birth, but it can supply a broad view of the birth process itself.

GODPARENTS AND PARENTS

It is a wise child, the saying goes, who knows his own father. In the case of a bill, wisdom is not always enough to identify the real parents. Sometimes nothing short of omniscience will do.

Since the sponsor of any bill has his name publicly inscribed on its first page, it is one of the polite traditions of Capitol Hill to refer to him as its author or drafter, because it is easier to label a bill by the sponsor's name than by using its number or formal title. The press and radio follow this tradition. Yet a bill's sponsor often has taken no hand whatsoever in developing the conception behind it. In most cases he did not draft the specific language. Occasionally, he knows little or nothing about the bill. "In 1890 a bill was passed," wrote an old-time Senator in his autobiography, "which was called the Sherman Act for no other reason that I can think of except that Mr. Sherman had nothing to do with framing it whatever." [3] While the memoir-writing Senator may have been guilty of some exaggeration, there are countless other cases that more readily fit the description.

In analyzing the genesis of a bill, therefore, sponsorship and authorship must be considered separately. Both are essential to the birth of a bill, but just as with a child's father and mother, each has a different function to perform.

The Sponsors

In countries operating under the Cabinet-Parliament system, the administrative arm of the government can introduce legislative proposals by its own action. In England, for example, all major bills are introduced in the House of Commons by members of the Cabinet. In America, however, the separation of agencies precludes formal sponsorship by the Administration. While any-

[2] Woodrow Wilson, "Congressional Government" (Boston: Houghton Mifflin, 1925), p. 297.

[3] George F. Hoar, "Autobiography of Seventy Years" (New York: Scribner, 1903), Vol. II, p. 363.

one from the President to the lowliest lobbyist may prepare a draft for a bill, only a Senator or Representative can introduce it in Congress.

Personal Responsibility of Congressmen. The act of sponsorship carries with it a certain degree of personal responsibility. It is one way of registering a member's point of view—for the benefit of his constituents or a pressure group. It often involves a member of Congress in a host of supplementary activities—answering correspondence on a bill, defending his viewpoint before Congress, and discussing it with proponents and opponents. Sometimes it entails a very high degree of political leadership, a function just as important to the legislative process as the draft of a measure. "If Mr. Sherman had not written a line of the law or contributed a single idea in the course of its enactment, he would be entitled to more credit than any single man in Congress because he alone carried the bill through Congress." [4] In recording the history of the Employment Act of 1946, Stephen Bailey shows that the original measure was prepared for Senator Murray by staff assistants working with executive-agency economists. Yet, fundamentally, Bailey points out, it was Murray's "spark of will which transformed an idea into a specific legislative proposal." [5] The National Labor Relations Act, the Social Security Act, and the United States Housing Act of 1937 are all complicated statutes that were drafted by experts inside and outside the Government. Yet it was Senator Robert F. Wagner of New York who not only introduced the bills which evolved into these statutes but who also became the focal point for the campaign on their behalf. It was Wagner who was always there at the right time to defend each bill in committee, to protect it on the floor, to negotiate with congressional opponents, to handle relationships with the President, to rebut attacks, and to handle (but not necessarily devise) parliamentary maneuvers.

In contrast with his activities on these measures, all of which very properly became known as "Wagner Acts," Senator Wagner's action on behalf of the Urban Redevelopment Bill, introduced during the Seventy-eighth Congress, was limited to the mere act of introduction. On this bill, following the Senator's name, there appeared the words "on request," a device used occasionally to allow a member of Congress to sponsor a bill without necessarily committing himself to its principles. In this particular case the request was made by various real-estate organizations which opposed an extension of public housing but favored the use of public funds for private redevelopment of blighted areas. The limited type of sponsorship was a result of Senator Wagner's obvious interest in assuring real-estate interests that he favored the private redevelopment of blighted areas and at the same time not allowing himself to be regarded as favoring this program as a substitute for public housing. Shortly

---

[4] W. S. Kerr, "John Sherman" (Boston: French, 1908), p. 206.

[5] Stephen K. Bailey, "Congress Makes a Law" (New York: Columbia University Press, 1949), p. 41.

thereafter, in the Wagner-Ellender-Taft Housing Bill, the Senator joined in sponsoring a measure that combined both approaches.

Sponsorship Power. In the early days of the century, exposés of state legislatures pointed to the introduction of many "strike" bills, bills that could injure a given business enterprise or industry and which were introduced for the purpose of obtaining "protection money." While the strike bill has no direct counterpart in modern legislative practice, nevertheless the principle behind it is not dead. Sponsorship brings with it a certain degree of personal power. The sponsor of a bill is often in the position of exercising a controlling influence over its future. Government officials, members of Congress, and leaders of private organizations will seek him out and ask for amendments. Many will offer various types of inducements to him to seek more rapid action on his bill or to try to hold up action. There are even cases where close observers have been convinced that a member of Congress has introduced a bill for the express purpose of killing it. Although it would be difficult to substantiate a charge of this type in the case of any particular bill, the logic of the situation is clear. No one can be more effective than the sponsor of a bill in counseling against precipitate action or in paving the way toward amendments that would defeat its very purpose—particularly if he should happen to be chairman of the committee to which the bill is referred.

The choice of sponsors, therefore, is one of the primary problems facing anyone who seeks legislative action. An obvious consideration, of course, is whether a member of Congress will regard his sponsorship lightly or whether he will really assume an important degree of leadership.

Choice of Sponsor. A valuable asset in obtaining favorable action on a bill is to have as its sponsor a member—or even better, the chairman—of the committee to which it is referred. The lack of proper committee connections by the sponsors of a bill may mean that it will not even get a hearing. This was the case for many years with the social-security legislation introduced in the Senate by Senators Wagner and Murray, neither of whom were members of the Senate Finance Committee. In the case of the Atomic Energy Act of 1946, for example, Senator Brien McMahon of Connecticut was chairman of the Special Senate Committee on Atomic Energy at the time when he introduced the original bill. This was an invaluable factor in obtaining favorable action by the Congress. In 1937, before the Wagner-Ellenbogen slum clearance and low-rent housing bill could be acted upon in the House, Representative Ellenbogen had to yield the role of House sponsor to Representative Steagall who was chairman of the committee handling it and who demanded the honor of sponsorship as the price of his support.

Party connections are also important. It is usually more effective to get a member of the majority party as the sponsor of a measure. Bills introduced by minority members seldom travel far. In 1944, Senator Maloney, a middle-of-the-road Democrat, succeeded in getting his resolution for a Joint Committee on the Organization of Congress approved by Senator McKellar, head of the Rules Committee subcommittee to which it was referred. Senator La Follette, who became chairman of the committee when Maloney died, would never have succeeded in getting the resolution past McKellar.

In 1947, shortly after the Republicans won a majority in Congress, Representative Hebert of Louisiana, a Democratic member, introduced a bill setting up machinery in the District of Columbia for treating alcoholism as a disease instead of as a crime. The measure attracted national attention as the "Hebert bill." At this point the Republican chairman of the subcommittee handling the subject, Representative Miller of Nebraska, introduced an identical bill. Representative Hebert protested vigorously. "The leadership told me to introduce this bill in my name," retorted Representative Miller at a subcommittee session. "I personally hesitated about doing this but I was told by the leadership to do it. We are the majority party and we are going to be responsible for all good legislation. . . . If it is a good bill we will reintroduce it in our name. We are going to take the cream. You fellows have had your way long enough." [6]

A sponsor's ability as a fighter for his bill or as a symbol evoking certain kinds of group support is also of the greatest importance. Although Senator Wagner was not a member of the Senate Labor Committee, his dogged perseverance and his prestige among organized labor were vital factors in the enactment of the National Labor Relations Act. Although Senator Norris was a member of the minority party after the 1932 election, his deep convictions and understanding regarding TVA legislation were instrumental in its passage in 1933. In 1946, although handicapped by being a member of the minority party and not on the Foreign Relations Committee, Senator Morse led the successful fight for Senate ratification of the World Court Resolution.

Multiple Sponsorship. Although sponsorship by one member is all that is required for introduction, the practice of obtaining multiple sponsorship has developed. In its simplest form this involves cosponsorship by a Senator and Representative in order to obtain a focal point for activity in both houses at the same time. Multiple sponsorship is also used as a method of obtaining the support of key members. Some Senators and Representatives will be interested in working for a measure only if their names are on it. In other cases multiple sponsorship is a valuable symbol of bipartisan support. The sponsorship of the Ball-Burton-Hatch-Hill Resolution by two Republicans and two Democrats symbolized bipartisan support for American participation in an international organization. The sponsorship of the Wagner-Ellender-Taft Housing Bill joined a liberal Northern Democrat, a conservative Southern Democrat, and a conservative Republican, one of the outstanding examples of

[6] Drew Pearson, "Washington Merry-Go-Round," *Washington Post*, Mar. 24, 1947.

sponsorship as a form of legislative strategy. In the case of the Full Employment Bill there was a serious problem in regard to the Senate committee to which the measure would be referred. Had it gone to a committee with an unfriendly chairman, it might have been buried quietly. This contingency was protected against by the fact that among the Senate cosponsors of the measure appeared the chairmen of each of the three committees to which the bill might have been referred. An additional motive was to "take out insurance against competition" on the part of those who were preparing a rival bill. The only committees to which the rival bill could have been referred were the committees of which the three chief sponsors were chairmen.[7]

Occasionally multiple sponsorship is used to build up mass support. In the case of the G.I. Bill of Rights, over 90 members of the Senate were included as its sponsors. In the case of a 1947 housing bill, multiple sponsorship was used to obtain the prior support of the committee to which the measure was referred. Its sponsor stated:

> I call attention to the rather unique fact that this bill is signed and endorsed by every member of the Banking and Currency Committee, of both political parties, which to my mind suggests the scriptural comment, "Behold, how good and how pleasant it is for brethren to dwell together in unity!" [8]

A similar though less successful attempt was made by Representative Patman, the House sponsor of the Full Employment Bill, who built up a bloc of 116 "coauthors and cosponsors."

Multiple sponsorship is frowned upon by many old-timers in Congress who believe in preserving the fiction that the sponsor of a measure is, or should be, its author. Obviously, the extension of multiple sponsorship reduces this tradition to absurdity. Moreover, some members of Congress feel that multiple sponsorship impairs the publicity value for each individual sponsor.

In the House of Representatives, opposition to multiple sponsorship is expressed in the rules themselves, which provide that the name of only one sponsor can be printed on a bill. This provision is consistently evaded, however, by introduction of identical bills by several members. Representative Patman evaded it and at the same time saved on printing costs by making up a list of his 116 "coauthors and cosponsors" and having it printed in the *Congressional Record*.

The Authors

"Who drafted this bill?"

This question is often asked—sometimes as a matter of historical curiosity,

[7] Bailey, *op. cit.*, p. 55.

[8] Senator Charles W. Tobey, *Congressional Record* (daily edition), Nov. 20, 1947, p. 10776.

sometimes as a matter of back-room gossip, more often in order to find a culprit. It is seldom possible to find a factual answer. As Woodrow Wilson said: [legislation] "is an aggregate, not a simple production. It is impossible to tell how many persons, opinions, and influences have entered into its composition." [9]

Complex Backgrounds. The ideas found in most bills have long and complex histories. Their origin is buried in evolving needs and interests, in similar theories evolved by many different people, and in passing through the hands of many "idea brokers" and organizations. Many bills are little more than slightly modified versions of old measures, combinations of old measures, or minute insertions in a long-standing legislative framework.

The process of drafting, moreover, is a continuous one, with amendments and substitutes being offered from all directions at every intersection on the legislative highway. Even at the initial stage, it is usually a conglomerate process with broad participation by many authors. When a private lawyer prepares a bill for a private organization, he usually takes pains to consult widely with various government officials. Many bills are prepared in executive agencies to carry out the views of members of Congress. Preparation of bills in Congress is often merely an assembly job on various parts prepared elsewhere. The bill that became the Contract Settlement Act of 1944, for example, included sections and provisions that were prepared in the War Department, in the Antitrust Division of the Justice Department, in the Bureau of the Budget, by the American Arbitration Association, by the Aeronautical Chamber of Commerce, by a lawyer who represented a major railroad in an important court suit arising out of World War I contracts, and by congressional staff members. Sometimes "congressional preparation" of a bill involves nothing more than a careful checking, somewhere in Congress, of a draft prepared elsewhere.

It is only natural that people associated with one phase of this conglomerate operation very sincerely may regard themselves as the center of the universe and not realize how many other authors are involved. In the development of the Federal Reserve Act, Woodrow Wilson's close adviser, Colonel House, certainly regarded himself as a major force behind the scenes. At least, this was the interpretation of Charles Seymour, editor of Colonel House's intimate papers. Yet to Senator Carter Glass, Colonel House's version of the authorship of the Federal Reserve Act was a scandalous lie. Glass wrote an entire book [10] to set the record straight and to show the real authors of the Act to be Woodrow Wilson, Carter Glass himself, and Glass's staff assistant on the House Banking and Currency Committee, H. Parker Willis.

In writing the history of his activities during the early days of the New

[9] Wilson, *op. cit.,* p. 320.

[10] Carter Glass, "Adventures in Constructive Finance" (Garden City, N.Y.: Doubleday, 1927

Deal, Raymond Moley tells how the House version of the Securities Act of 1933 was prepared by James M. Landis and Benjamin V. Cohen under the general direction of Felix Frankfurter.[11] A broader view of the authorship of this legislation came some years later from Middleton Beaman, legislative counsel of the House, who testified that he, his assistant, and the members of a House subcommittee under the chairmanship of Representative Rayburn of Texas played an important part in the drafting of the measure.[12]

Stephen Bailey's history of the Employment Act of 1946 is probably the most extensive effort yet made to show how many authors are involved in the process of bill drafting.[13] His account shows that the scores of people in the executive agencies, both houses of Congress, and private organizations were among the authors. Yet even here there are great gaps in the effort to track down the full story of authorship. An interview with Representative Will Whittington of Mississippi indicated that Whittington solicited drafts from the United States Chamber of Commerce, the Committee for Economic Development, and Secretary of the Treasury Fred Vinson. "With the aid of these drafts," Bailey reports, "Whittington pieced together a substitute bill which was finally submitted to the full committee for consideration." [14] But Bailey was still unable to discover the precise origin of the original proposal for a Council of Economic Advisers—whether it came from one of these sources or from Whittington himself.

A complicating factor in any effort to find the author is the fact that many authors, like ghost writers, cover up their tracks. Anyone who advertises his role in preparing a bill for a Senator or Representative runs the risk of undercutting the status and prestige of the member of Congress and of precluding himself from future working relationships with him. A passion for anonymity seems to be as much a qualification for authors of legislative proposals as it is for Presidential assistants. Such a passion often develops in the minds of draftsmen whose yearnings for deference can be assuaged through the vicarious experiences of the sponsors and through the limited personal prestige gained among those who know where the work was really done.

Taboos. Moreover, there are all sorts of taboos concerning the question of who should and who should not draft legislative proposals. Authorship by the Chamber of Commerce or the Congress of Industrial Organizations is often regarded as bordering on the sinful. When it was learned that the Republican National Committee had hired a lawyer to participate in the drafting of the

[11] Raymond Moley, "After Seven Years" (New York: Harper, 1939), pp. 180–181.

[12] Hearings before the Joint Committee on the Organization of Congress, 79th Cong., 1st Sess., p. 422.

[13] An unusual companion piece of this type of political research is Seymour Z. Mann, "Congressional Behavior and Labor Policy" (unpublished doctoral dissertation, University of Chicago, 1951), which traces the intricate history of the Taft-Hartley Act.

[14] Bailey, *op. cit.*, p. 166.

Taft-Hartley Act, a hue and cry of protest arose from the opponents of the Act.

Protests of this type are based, of course, not so much upon theoretical principles concerning who should draft a bill but rather upon objections to the substance in a bill and the influence wielded by the drafters. Where there is broad agreement upon the substance of the bill, these taboos tend to be forgotten. The Railway Labor Disputes Act of 1926, for example, originated with a group of railway-management executives and railway labor leaders who formed a drafting committee in 1924 and engaged Donald Richberg to prepare a bill for them. When the bill was introduced in Congress, its origin was not merely admitted; it was stressed. In fact, the argument was made in both houses that it should be approved in the very form in which it was introduced, since railway management and railway labor would feel obliged to abide by it if there were no important changes.

Middleton Beaman once tried to draw a line between who is responsible for the policies in a bill and who writes the words. He also suggested that the important thing is not where a bill has been prepared but whether the legislation, when enacted, expresses accurately the intention of Congress in passing it. "If it meets that test 100 per cent, it makes no difference where it comes from, whether it comes from Heaven, from an executive department, or is written in our office or some other place." [15]

The preparation of a bill is essentially a strategic phase of the legislative struggle nonetheless. It is not merely a method of recording policy or general principles that have been previously formulated. It is part and parcel of the process of policy formulation. It is a job of formulating general principles in a precise form and of making a long series of choices between alternative methods of building upon them. Moreover, bill drafting represents an important act of taking the initiative in formulating issues in a manner most consistent with one's own views and interests. Coming in with the first draft of a bill is like beating the other fellow to the draw. The ability to draft effectively is thus a vital element in the power picture. It has almost as much meaning for the legislative process as nominations have for election campaigns.

All this does not imply that technical advisers on the preparation of bills, such as the lawyers in the Senate and House Office of the Legislative Counsel, are necessarily partisans in the legislative struggle. To a considerable extent they deal only with the surface technicalities of bills prepared by others. Much less often do they do a complete job of bill drafting. But in either case they need be no more partisan than the editorial writer who works for the publisher of two papers in the same town and writes Republican editorials for the morning paper and Democratic editorials for the evening paper. "We have constantly worked, as some of you gentlemen know," Beaman testified, "for both

[15] Hearings before the Joint Committee on the Organization of Congress, 79th Cong., 1st Sess., p. 421.

sides on the same question at the same time, without any suspicion on the part of either that we are betraying their secrets to the other. . . . What we want to do is to express precisely the intent of our client, whether it be a committee or an individual member." [16]

Executive Drafting. The executive official faced with the question of whether or not to submit a bill draft to Congress is often in the position of being "damned if he does and damned if he does not." If he does, he is apt to be charged with attempts to usurp congressional prerogatives and dictate congressional action. "Are you aware also of the extreme unwisdom of irritating Congress," wrote President Theodore Roosevelt to a friend, "by fixing the details of a bill concerning which they are very sensitive instead of laying down a general policy?" [17] On the other hand, if an executive official does not prepare a draft, he is apt to be criticized on the ground that his proposals are too vague and that too great a burden is placed on the meager technical resources of Congress.

It is certainly true that a proposal for legislative action has little meaning unless embodied in a draft of a bill. When President Truman called a special session in November, 1947, to ask for anti-inflation legislation, members of Congress who previously had been in the forefront of protests against executive drafting criticized the Truman Administration for not having submitted draft legislation to Congress. "If the President wants to tell the people that he stands for a certain thing," observed Senator Homer Ferguson of Michigan, "he ought to come out with his proposal. He ought to come to the House and Senate with a message. And he ought to provide a bill if that is exactly what he wants." [18] Representative Joseph Martin of Massachusetts, the Republican Speaker of the House, construed the absence of Administration drafts as evidence that the President really did not want the powers which he had requested.

Generally speaking, there has been an increasing tendency to accept executive initiative in bill drafting. The various departments are regularly expected to prepare specific drafts of legislation affecting their interests.[19] Even in the field of taxation, where congressional prerogatives have long been jealously

[16] *Ibid.,* pp. 414–418.

[17] J. J. Bishop, "Theodore Roosevelt and His Times." Quoted by Wilfred E. Binkley, "President and Congress" (New York: Knopf, 1947), pp. 210–211.

[18] Homer Ferguson, "What Is Your Congress Doing?" *University of Chicago Round Table,* No. 483, 1947, p. 4.

[19] "Most of the bills affecting the Department of Justice, for instance, are prepared in the Department of Justice and are sent up either to the Chairman of the Judiciary Committee or to the Speaker, and then the Chairman of the Committee, or someone on the Committee suggested by him, introduces the bill. That is the usual procedure." Statement by Representative Earl Michener of Michigan. Hearings before the Joint Committee on the Organization of Congress, 79th Cong., 1st Sess., pp. 456–457.

guarded, the legislative committees usually look to executive officials for leadership in the formulation of initial proposals. "This is particularly true," one of America's leading tax experts has pointed out, "when increases in taxes are in prospect." [20]

Most executive proposals are now cleared in advance through the Legislative Reference Division of the Bureau of the Budget, acting as the agent of the President.[21] This procedure aids in the process of executive planning and helps to eliminate or modify jurisdictional conflicts among executive agencies—although many executive officials sidetrack the clearance process by surreptitiously passing draft bills along to friendly members of Congress.[22] In general, however, the procedure has served to enhance the role and power of the Bureau of the Budget. On minor matters the tendency has been for Budget Bureau officials to make the final decision as to whether a bill should be accepted as "in accord with" or as "not inconsistent with" the program of the President, or branded as "not in accord." More important matters come directly to the attention of the President, White House staff, the CEA, and other officials. The Budget Bureau clearance process nevertheless places Bureau personnel in a highly strategic position for influencing the direction of the President's ever-changing legislative program.

It has also become customary for each President to have a key list of "must bills." Many of these measures are drafted in the White House or the Executive Office of the President. To assist in the handling of these measures, specialized personnel has been developed in the White House staff. President Franklin D. Roosevelt established the position of Special Counsel to the President, first filled by Judge Samuel Rosenman, and later by Clark Clifford and Charles Murphy. President Truman expanded this function by employing additional staff members to concentrate upon legislative drafting, review, and clearance.

Presidential participation in drafting, however, does not mean that the President himself transmits the bill to Congress. The Economic Stability Bill of 1949, for example, was drafted by a working group in the Executive Office of the President and then discussed in detail at a series of Cabinet committee meetings. Yet the final draft of the measure was presented to the Congress by the Secretary of Agriculture rather than by the President, thereby relieving the President of responsibility for a multitude of details.

No matter how an executive bill is transmitted to Congress, whether by the President or the head of an agency, whether officially or through the back

[20] Roy Blough, "The Federal Taxing Process" (New York: Prentice-Hall, 1952). See Chap. 5, "The Executive and Tax Legislation," for a detailed review of executive participation in the drafting of revenue measures.

[21] Neustadt, *op. cit.* See in particular Chap. 3, "Current Operating Methods," which includes four remarkably informative case studies.

[22] *Ibid.*, pp. 118–119.

door, it usually commands a certain amount of respect merely on the ground that it has been prepared by an executive agency. This respect is not merely grounded on an appreciation of the familiarity of executive draftsmen with their materials; it also flows from the recognition that an executive draft represents a power potential. It holds a promise of support both by influential executive officials and by the private organizations with which these officials are allied.

Drafting Skills. Far more prevalent than the fiction that sponsorship implies authorship is the notion that any good lawyer can draft a bill. Actually, an excellent lawyer may butcher the draft of a bill. Bill drafting has been one of the neglected phases of law-school training. In fact, the legal profession as a whole has done very little to advance the art of draftsmanship. There are no up-to-date manuals on the legal aspects of the problem, nor has American jurisprudence developed any theoretical handling of legislative drafting that in any way approaches Jeremy Bentham's work in nineteenth-century England.

In any case, bill drafting calls for more talents than can be obtained through abstract legal training, no matter how excellent it may be or become. It calls for an intensive knowledge of administrative regulations, judicial decisions, existing law, and other proposed laws in the field where the work is being done. It requires an understanding of the realities behind the legal forms; above all, it requires an ability to appraise the line-up of interests and the relative strength of conflicting pressures and to assist in the formulation of basically political decisions. It calls for flexibility and dexterity in the use of language, both to convey meaning and, where necessary, to avoid meaning; both to avoid emotional connotations and, where necessary, to arouse emotion. In short, it calls for a wide range of talents and skills in law, administration, economics, politics, and public relations.

Drafting Teams. Since all these qualities are rarely found in one person, the best drafting is done on a teamwork basis. The Bretton Woods Agreement, for example, was drafted by a team composed of Treasury Department lawyers, economic and political advisers of the Treasury and State Departments, and the legislative counsels of the Senate and the House. Occasional checks were made with the three members of Congress who were scheduled to introduce the legislation, Senators Robert F. Wagner of New York and Charles Tobey of New Hampshire, and Representative Jesse Wolcott of Michigan. Under President Truman's Administration the technique of setting up working teams or "task forces" to formulate new bills has been widely used. Sometimes Congress establishes committees of its own for the specific purpose of drafting a bill or of supervising the drafting process. When the movement for reorganization of Congress was getting under way during the last years of World War II, strenuous opposition was expected from many members of Congress, particularly from those who had a strong personal stake in the present committee structure and who might be expected to object to any reshuffling of committees. It was felt that the best way to obtain an effective bill, therefore, was to have one drafted by members of Congress themselves. It was for this purpose that the Joint Committee on the Organization of Congress was established in 1945. Its staff director, George Galloway, went to work in drafting a measure with the assistance of the Office of Legislative Counsel in both the Senate and the House. A year later, this Joint Committee brought forth a bill which, with certain changes, became the Legislative Reorganization Act of 1946.

TIMING THE OFFSPRING

As in the case of planned parenthood, the choice of time is a vital element in all phases of the legislative struggle. The entire fate of a bill may hinge upon how its supporters or opponents time a campaign on its behalf and their actions with respect to committee handling, floor operations, or Presidential approval or veto. The time question initially arises in connection with the problem of whether or not to use the legislative process. It continues to be a question at every stage of the process. The manner in which it is answered determines the number and the variety of legislative measures and has an obvious bearing upon the type of legislation enacted during any period.

Timing in the Narrow Sense

In the narrow sense, the choice of time involves selecting which part of a Presidential or congressional term would be best for initiating legislative action, and whether or not action should be initiated in one house of Congress before the other.

Between Elections. An ever-present consideration in timing is the problem of the proximity of elections. A Presidential election year is usually regarded as providing an unpropitious occasion for proposing action on measures unpalatable to large groups of voters, such as a widespread increase in taxes. Military leaders had this factor in mind when they persuaded President Truman to send a special message to Congress in 1947 proposing universal military training. They feared that during the election year of 1948 it would be impossible to obtain sufficient congressional support for so stringent a measure. As it turned out, no action was obtained in either year, although Truman added a personal appeal to the Joint Session of March 17, 1948. It was on the same theory that during both 1947 and 1948 no major proposals for the reorganization of the executive branch were made from any source, even though reorganization was ardently advised by many groups. Instead, the Republican leaders and the Truman Administration both supported the resolution which set up the Hoover Commission to study the subject during 1948 and bring in legislative proposals in 1949 after the Presidential election was over.

Another narrow aspect of the timing problem is whether to introduce a bill at the beginning, middle, or end of the two-year period during which a Congress meets. Usually there is a flood of legislative proposals in the early days of the Congress, a flood which tapers off slowly, becomes a steady stream, and then narrows into a trickle toward the end of the two-year period. In most cases, early introduction is the best policy. On certain questions it is imperative. This is particularly true of any measures which are likely to be combated by a filibuster in the Senate or by delaying tactics in the House. At the end of the session, when there are so many competing demands on congressional time, it is much more difficult to deal with dilatory tactics. The early days of a given Congress, when the calendars are relatively free, provide the ideal circumstances under which to handle problems of this type. In the case of amendments to the House rules, these are feasible only on the first day of any Congress when the House adopts the rules to guide it during the following two years.

Finally, there is an end-of-the-season technique for rushing through controversial measures. This was used consistently by the Roosevelt Administration in obtaining extensions of price-control and war-powers legislation. By holding off extensive requests until the last moment, Roosevelt was able to side-step a large amount of debate and obtain many of his objectives at a minimum cost in harmful amendments.

Which House First? One by-product of a bicameral legislature is that it affords a choice among introducing a bill in both houses of Congress at the same time, introducing it first in one house and then in the other, or limiting introduction to one house only. The first of these alternatives is clearly the most advisable in the case of measures that are being pushed forward toward rapid enactment. It also serves the purpose of facilitating a broader campaign than can be carried on when a bill is introduced in one house only. Often the fact that a bill is introduced in one house only is merely indicative that it lacks significant support and is not considered seriously as a legislative vehicle.

On the other hand, there are many instances when the sponsors of legislation have chosen one house as the springboard, postponing until a more favorable time introduction of companion measures in the other house. Sometimes it is felt that the best way for a bill to reach the Senate is in the form of a measure already approved by the House, or vice versa.

The Flow of the Tides

Long-range Cycles. The history of American legislation reveals cyclical trends almost as sharp as the rise and fall in the level of business activity and employment. During the New Freedom era of Woodrow Wilson, reform legislation reached boom levels with the Clayton Act, the Federal Reserve Act, the Federal Trade Commission Act, and the legislation establishing an income-tax system under the Sixteenth Amendment. In the conservative administrations of Harding, Coolidge, and Hoover, legislation of this type sank into a deep slump. With the New Deal of Franklin Roosevelt, it staged a sensational comeback and reached heights never before dreamed of in America. Then, as the New Deal lost its grip and war broke out in Europe, the cycle once more turned downward.

War itself brings on another type of cycle. During the emergency there is a pronounced tendency to look to the President rather than legislation as a source of decision. The aftermath of a war brings a violent shift. The emergency powers of the President are curtailed, and even though the executive officials may be left with a larger residue of power than they ever before enjoyed, there is a renewal of emphasis upon legislative rather than executive solutions to the problems of the day.

Trends of this type have a direct effect on the type of legislation that is introduced. When the outlook for reform legislation seems black, it is natural to postpone its introduction until some more auspicious moment. During periods of prosperity the productivity of ideas for economic reform is low. In depression there is a plethora of proposals for legislative action to benefit disadvantaged groups.

Some legislative measures, of course, have little relation to the economic and political climate. Year in and year out the departments and pressure groups bring in their bills designed to expand a bureau in order to take away certain rights from the Indians and give others back to them; change the status of reserve officers in the Navy; or provide for another attack on hoof-and-mouth disease near the Mexican border. Yet whenever an idea for legislation calls for drastic changes in the *status quo,* there is a natural disposition in favor of waiting until the time is ripe. After the passage of the Employment Act of 1946, many of those groups which had backed the original full-employment proposals felt it was necessary to call for a much higher degree of economic planning. The National Catholic Welfare Conference, for example, issued a circular calling for formation of labor-management councils in each industry as a means of planning a full-production and full-employment program. Other proposals aimed at providing a full-fledged framework of economic planning for America were discussed among labor and left-wing organizations. None of these, however, were embodied in legislative proposals. The feeling seemed to be that the time was not ripe and that until the economic and intellectual atmosphere changed, proposals of this type would evoke more criticism than support. The same delaying attitude was evidenced by business groups whose thinking ran in the direction of reinstituting, as a means toward economic stabilization, the type of controls over production and floors under production that had been experimented with under the NRA.

Catching the Flood Tide. The ability to accurately appraise legislative cycles is of particular importance to a President, whose prestige may suffer from an untimely proposal. The best example of Presidential concern with timing is Franklin Roosevelt's cautious handling of the neutrality versus intervention issue during the years preceding Pearl Harbor. In 1935 Roosevelt signed the neutrality legislation which prevented shipment of munitions to either side in a foreign conflict. Early the next year, however, as civil war broke out in Spain and German troops occupied the Rhineland, it became increasingly apparent that Nazi and Fascist aggression held the seeds of future world conflict. From then on, it is evident that the Roosevelt Administration desired to move away, as fast as possible, from the isolationist stand represented by the Neutrality Act toward a system of collective security. In October, 1937, the President made his famous speech calling upon peace-loving nations to quarantine the aggressors. As described by Roosevelt himself many years later,[23] this speech "was hailed as warmongering; it was even ridiculed as a nervous search 'under the bed' for dangers of war which did not exist." From then on, Roosevelt moved very carefully. Often, in fact, he retreated toward isolationism as though in an effort to catch the tide of public opinion. It was in September, 1939, when Hitler's armies had invaded Poland and there was no doubt that his objective could be achieved, that Roosevelt asked again, this time in clear-cut fashion, for legislation repealing the arms embargo and permitting munitions shipments to countries invaded by the aggressors.

This period of slow searching for the right time stands out in sharp contrast to the situation at the beginning of the Roosevelt Administration in 1933. If ever there was a tide in the affairs of men that, taken in the flood, led on to fortune, this was it. Practically any legislation that Roosevelt might have proposed, short of the socialization of industry, would have been timely. Bill after bill was transmitted from the White House to the congressional leaders and promptly brought back for Presidential signature. Soon, however, the magic "one hundred days" came to an end. The flood tide subsided, and from then on the Administration's proposals had to be paddled strongly against the current.

A similar period came into being on December 7, 1941, when the Japanese bombed Pearl Harbor. The Administration immediately proposed, and Congress approved, legislation giving the President greater war powers than any President had ever before enjoyed in American history. Two years later when Roosevelt proposed compulsory labor service, he was faced with strong opposition in Congress and eventual defeat in the Senate. One may assert from

---

[23] "Public Papers and Addresses of Franklin D. Roosevelt" (New York: Random House), 1939 Vol., p. 28 of Introduction.

the point of view of the necessities of war mobilization that compulsory labor service was not needed that early in the game. From the viewpoint of legislative strategy, however, the discretionary power to clamp on compulsory labor controls whenever necessary might well have been granted if the request had been made before the country had recovered from the initial shock of Pearl Harbor.

The wise legislative strategist recognizes that the legislative tides do not run according to fixed schedule. There are too many fluid factors in the legislative process. Sudden changes in international affairs or in the economic cycle may occur overnight. Pressure groups and politicians often shift positions in an unpredictable fashion. The introduction of a measure itself is a factor which may, under certain circumstances, affect the climate that surrounds it.

Swimming against the Tide. On many occasions the wisest course of action is to swim against the tide. There was certainly no more unfavorable climate for public-power proposals than that existing in the 1920's when Senator George Norris of Nebraska first proposed government utilization of the abandoned Muscle Shoals project in Tennessee. For many years, every effort he made to obtain enactment of his proposals met with defeat. Yet every defeat made him stronger. Finally, in 1933, the combination of widespread unemployment and the Roosevelt Administration tipped the scales in his favor, and legislation was finally enacted setting up the TVA. The same approach was taken by Senator James E. Murray of Montana in 1945 when he introduced his bill to set up the Missouri Valley Authority, a measure which was more of an option on the future than a bid for immediate action. The Murray approach was that the only way to develop a situation in which the enactment of Missouri Valley legislation would be timely was to propose the measure long in advance of its feasibility. The same theory applies even more aptly to the Wagner-Murray-Dingell bill for compulsory health insurance, also first introduced in 1945. Not only was this measure politically inexpedient at the time of proposal; but because of the shortage of hospital facilities and medical personnel it would have been administratively unworkable if enacted. Nevertheless, the bill itself and the campaign on its behalf provided a great stimulus toward the expansion of hospital and other facilities. When the tide of social reform once again starts to rise, the odds should favor early enactment of legislation setting up a more unified development program in the Missouri Valley and some form of government-promoted health insurance.

One great advantage of swimming against the tide is that it provides a long period of maturation and growth. It puts all parties to the legislative struggle on notice. It provides all the contestants with an opportunity to make a careful appraisal of gains and losses and to work out new combinations and coalitions. It gets people accustomed to new ideas and new modes of action. so that when action finally comes, it is more acceptable and more practicable. Chamberlain writes:

Most of the great mass of regulatory legislation of the past decade, popularly dubbed New Deal legislation, had a well-defined prenatal history extending back several years before it was espoused by the Roosevelt administration. This is true not only of the more conventional fields such as banking, railroads, and taxation, but of the newer areas of social security, holding company regulation, and securities control. Congressional attention to these new fields had not been absent prior to the time the President made his specific recommendations. The normal process has been fairly uniform: an initial reference by one or a few individuals, then a gradually increasing volume of comment accompanied by numerous specific proposals coming from widely divergent sources. In some cases legislation results in a very short time, but more frequently the initial flurries of interest will subside, to be revived from time to time until finally culminating, perhaps with the help of the President, in a law. The long germination period detectable in the genesis of most laws is of the utmost importance: it constitutes one of the most valuable contributions that a legislative body can make.[24]

[24] Lawrence H. Chamberlain, "The President, Congress and Legislation" (New York: Columbia University Press, 1946), pp. 462–463.

Chapter 11

THE ART OF DRAFTING

IT IS impossible to devise any rigid set of rules to guide the drafting of legislative proposals.[1] Legislative drafting is an art. It cannot be formalized.[2] The authors of a bill are continuously faced with important choices. Each must be decided in the light of the purposes to be achieved and the specific legislative situation.

A bill is not merely a proposal for action; it *is* itself a form of action. It involves the setting of an objective, as the first stage in the push-and-pull process of bargaining. It is a proposal for some change in the distribution of power and wealth. In the determination regarding these types of action lie the major substantive problems faced in the drafting of a bill.

THE SUBSTANCE OF A BILL

The Asking Price

When a person thinks of selling a house, three different figures usually come to mind. First, there is the price that he would like to get. Here the sky may be the limit, but let us say he daydreams hopefully about $20,000. Second, there is the price he guesses he may have to settle for in the end—say $15,000. Then there is the asking price. If he asks $20,000 he runs the risk of frighten-

[1] For general material on the preparation of legislation, see Ernst Freund, "Abstract of Statutory Precedent Material Collected and Available for a Manual of Legislative Drafting," Appendix C of "Fiscal Report of the Committee on Legislative Drafting" (*Reports of the American Bar Association,* Vol. 46, 1921); Sir Courtenay Ilbert, "Legislative Methods and Forms" (New York: Oxford, 1901), and by the same author, "The Mechanics of Law Making" (New York: Columbia University Press, 1914); Chester Lloyd Jones, "Statute Law Making" (Boston: Boston Book Co., 1912); Thomas L. Parkinson, "Legislative Drafting" (New York: Academy of Political Science, 1912); and by one of the Parliamentary Counsel to the Treasury, "The Making and Form of Bills," *Parliamentary Affairs,* London, Spring, 1949.

[2] It is possible, however, to list in an orderly form the problems that are met in the drafting process, as is attempted in a general way throughout the rest of this chapter. The most intensive listing of rules that has thus far been made—and it needs revision to extend it and bring it up to date—is found in Freund, *op. cit.*

ing off would-be purchasers. If he asks $15,000 there is little room left for bargaining. The chances are that he will ask for about $17,000 or $18,000.

The framers of a bill face the same problem. In the case of appropriation bills or bills to authorize future appropriations, the considerations are identical. Where bills deal with policies that cannot be measured in quantitative terms, the problem is still very similar. In both cases the primary substantive problem in the initial drafting process is how to strike a mean between what one really wants and what one could ultimately agree to take.

This is not a problem that is easy to approach in a systematic manner. Not many participants in the legislative struggle know what they really want. Those who do have a great strategic advantage. Some merely follow the general principle of wanting as much as they can get—a principle which is so elastic as to have little guiding value. Moreover, wants are highly subjective and difficult to measure; they depend upon a long series of conjectures as to what is desired by group leaders, members, and supporters. Similarly, it is not easy, before the process of legislative tug of war gets under way, to predict what end product may be accepted. Short-run political trends are every bit as baffling as short-run economic trends. He who starts with an unqualified commitment to the battle cry of "unconditional surrender" may end up eager to accept "peace without victory." Furthermore, within limits, the amount you can expect to get often depends upon how much you initially ask for.

Figure Flexibility. The determination of an asking price, therefore, tends to be an arbitrary judgment based upon past relationships and current intuitions. The wisdom in any particular asking price lies less in any inherent value than in one's ability to indicate that it is less than was really desired and at the same time to leave elbowroom for subsequent compromises. The entire process of preparing the Government's appropriation requests fits into this pattern. Since it is usually taken for granted that the Bureau of the Budget makes substantial reductions in agency requests for appropriations, it is easier to justify any agency request that appears in the President's Budget Message. At the same time, the Budget Bureau itself never cuts too far. It leaves room for further cuts to be made in the process of legislative action on appropriation bills.

The preparation of the Marshall Plan by the Truman Administration is another illustration of the pattern. An indication as to the amount of aid desired by the Administration was given in an early trial-balloon speech by a State Department official who suggested the need of 20 billion dollars over a four-year period. At the Paris Conference of European nations, a preliminary report was drafted which indicated the need for closer to 30 billion dollars over the same number of years. Emissaries of the State Department then flew to Paris to advise the Conference that such a preview would scare off members of the Congress. The report was revised to call for 19 billion dollars in American aid. A Citizens' Committee, headed by the Secretary of Commerce, then went to work on the problem of preparing a formal recommendation to the President and to Congress. In their report of November, 1947, it was suggested that the volume of aid be set at between 12 to 17 billion dollars over a four-year period. The practical problem involved in devising this figure was how to allow leeway for bargaining with Congress and at the same time how to avoid the undesirable international complications that might result from too sharp a congressional cut in the Administration's asking price. This problem was solved by planning on very little leeway in the amount to be made available the first year but leaving the door open to congressional limitations on the number of years over which aid will be given.

Ideological Flexibility. The drafting of the Full Employment Bill presents an example in qualitative rather than in quantitative terms. This measure represented a middle ground between what its backers really wanted and what they thought they could get. On the one hand they were interested in the full philosophy represented by Franklin Roosevelt's Economic Bill of Rights, a document that established as a goal not only full employment but also better housing, better education, better health, and other aspects of a constantly rising standard of living. Yet the Full Employment Bill dealt only with the employment goal and scrupulously avoided any suggestion of having the Government assume responsibility for a constantly rising standard of living. It was strictly limited to the purpose of providing employment opportunities for "all Americans willing and able to work." On the other hand, the original bill asked for far more than any of its backers thought could be obtained. Rather than limiting itself to a declaration of the Government's responsibility to promote full employment, it set forth an unqualified responsibility of the Government to "assure" continuing full employment. To have asked for more, in the opinion of the sponsors, would have been to transcend the realm of practical consideration. To have asked for less would have been to draft a bill that would lack the inspirational qualities needed to obtain popular backing.

Evasion or Postponement. One of the fascinating things about the legislative process is the manner in which the problem of the asking price, like many other problems, can be evaded or postponed. The Maternal and Child Health Bill, introduced by Senator Pepper and others in the Seventy-ninth Congress, provided for Federal grants to enable states to give free medical services to all children and to all maternity cases. In essence, it meant that health services for all children and mothers would be provided on the same free basis as public education. Estimates as to how much money would have to be appropriated in order to carry out such a program indicated a figure of close to one billion dollars a year. Sponsors of the measure were thereby faced with a dilemma. On the one hand, the billion-dollar figure was so large that, if presented to a conservative Congress, it would have forestalled consideration of the measure. On the other hand, any figure of less than a billion dollars would have broken down the principle of the bill and would have invited a limitation that would restrict such services only to those who could not pass a means test. This dilemma was avoided by the simple expedient of leaving all figures out of the measure and merely using the language "There are hereby authorized to be appropriated such funds as might be necessary to effectuate the purposes of this Act."

A similar example occurred in the framing of the Sherman Antitrust Act. The aim of the bill was to make unlawful "agreements in restraint of trade." The big problem, however, was how much ground was covered by the term "agreements in restraint of trade." A broad definition would have made the Act more stringent. A narrow definition would have made it relatively unambitious. The dilemma was solved by the simple expedient of not defining the term at all and leaving its interpretation to the courts and to future legislation.[3]

The Distribution of Power and Wealth

Inseparably allied with the problem of how much to ask for are the questions "for whom?" and "from whom?" The greater the number of groups for which one asks benefits, the broader his potential support and the more ambitious his demands may become—although this must be counterbalanced by the fact that the more numerous the portions cut from any piece of pie, the smaller each portion must become. The fewer the groups over which one proposes to establish controls or take resources, the less widespread the resistance will be —although a more aggressive approach may be needed in order to develop enough support to counterbalance the inevitable opposition. In this sense, the handling of "how much?", "for whom?", and "from whom?" is essential not only to the process of preparing a bill but also to the organization of support for it at various stages in the legislative process.[4]

For Whom and from Whom? In the case of the farmer whose cow has been killed by an army truck, the question of "for whom?" is relatively simple. A relief bill asking for damages will provide for a minor transfer of money from the Federal government to a single recipient (although it may be based upon prior understandings concerning a split with the lawyer who handles the bill). On bills of a public character, distribution patterns become much more complex. In the preparation of legislation dealing with Federal aid to education, a major issue has been whether all of the pie goes to public schools or some to

[3] George F. Hoar, "Autobiography of Seventy Years" (New York: Scribner, 1903), Vol. II, p. 364.

[4] This is discussed at greater length in Chaps. 12 and 13.

religious groups. There is also the question of whether aid should be provided for colleges and universities, how it should be distributed geographically, and how much of their own the recipients should be expected to put up. These questions, in turn, open up a multidimensional series of alternatives, each of which favors some groups more than others.

On the other side of the ledger, the Government is continuously faced with the problem of maintaining an inflow of financial resources. It has long been an axiom among those concerned with taxation that the goose will squawk no matter where the feathers are pulled from it. Most private organizations are intensely concerned with having the tax burden shifted as much as possible to others than themselves. In fact, there are few common interests that promote vigorous group activity as much as a common interest in avoiding onerous taxes —particularly on the part of those with substantial resources.[5] Government officials are naturally concerned with distributing the burden in such a way as to confine the squawking to those who are less able to follow squawks with action. A similar problem of "from whom?" is faced in the development of nationwide regulatory measures. The drafters of price-control measures during and immediately after World War II, for example, were faced with the ever-recurring question of what parts of the economy would fall under control and what parts would be exempted.

Governmental Machinery. In the case of most legislative proposals, there are many choices as to which officials are to get more power or funds or, perhaps, be deprived of present power or funds. These choices are no less substantive because they deal with governmental machinery. They are every bit as political as the problems involving the distribution of power and wealth among private organizations. In fact, the decisions on who does what inside the Government are often the answer to the problem of who gets or loses what outside the Government. Hence the tremendous emphasis in legislative struggles upon the details of governmental machinery and the writing of legislative provisions to gear into the existing personnel of Federal agencies rather than in terms of abstract organizational blueprints.[6]

The first problem in deciding "for whom?" within the structure of the Government is: Which Federal officials should get the increased power or funds provided for in a bill? Should they be given directly to the President? If so,

[5] The development of parliamentary institutions in England, for example, was closely associated with the opposition of the country gentry and the burghers to onerous taxes levied by the king. In colonial America, onerous taxes levied by the English led first to the campaign of "No taxation without representation" and then, with other factors, to the Revolutionary War itself. For a full review of this problem in present-day America, see Roy Blough, "The Federal Taxing Process" (New York: Prentice-Hall, 1952), particularly Chap. 2, "Tax Programs and Pressure Groups."

[6] Hence, too, are those public-administration experts who dream of the day when governmental reorganization plans can be divorced from politics doomed to eternal despair.

should he be left free to turn them over to subordinate officials in whatever manner he sees fit? Or should the channel through which the President is to operate be spelled out in the bill? If the power and funds are not to be handed to the President directly, should they be given to the head of an agency that is directly under Presidential control or to a bureau within such an agency? Or should they be given to a so-called "independent board or commission"? Where public works programs are involved, should the projects be built directly by the Federal government? If not, to what extent should funds be channeled to state governments as contrasted with city governments? In either case, how much control should Federal officials be expected to exercise?

And what about relationships with private organizations? An administrative agency can be required or authorized to consult with those who are affected by its activities. More specifically, advisory committees may be established in the bill itself. If so, who are the members to be appointed? Are they to have a semi-independent status of their own, with a chairman of their own choosing? Or are they to operate merely at the beck and call of the administrative agency? Are they to be limited to advisory functions or are they to be given powers and funds of their own?

Then there is the problem of legislative provisions with respect to the courts and the Congress. A bill may subject administrative decisions to a thorough and complete review by the courts. Or it may limit the function of the courts to overthrowing an administrative decision only on the ground that it is "arbitrary and capricious." It may confine judicial review to "questions of law" as distinguished from "questions of fact." [7] Occasionally, judicial machinery may be specially augmented in order to handle the burden of appeals that is anticipated.

A long-standing method of congressional review is the requirement of reports to Congress. Recent legislation has required reports ranging from once a year down to every sixty days. Special reports may be required as an antecedent or a concomitant to a given type of executive action. A special committee can be set up to keep tabs on administrative operations as was provided in the Atomic Energy Act of 1946. Or certain types of executive action may be made susceptible to congressional veto within a given period of time, as was done in the 1945 and 1949 legislation giving the President power to reorganize executive agencies.

Specificity versus Discretion. There is also the vital problem of how much substance should be contained in the bill itself and how much discretion should

[7] The fluidity and usages of these distinctions have been well stated by John Dickinson: "It would seem that when the courts are unwilling to review, they are tempted to explain by the easy device of calling the question one of 'fact,' and when otherwise disposed, they say that it is a question of 'law.'" "Administrative Justice and the Supremacy of Law in the United States" (Cambridge, Mass.: Harvard University Press, 1927), p. 55.

be left to executive officials and the courts. "Modern legislation," it has been said, "should seek to steer a clear course between the Scylla of attempting to anticipate every possible situation and the Charybdis of expressing no policy more definite than some such empty formula as public interest, convenience, or necessity." [8] This ideal is but rarely approximated. When those who support a given bill seriously doubt that the executive officials will do what is desired, the most natural inclination in the world is to spell out the duties of executive officials as fully as possible. This accounts for the extensive use of legislation to deal with the minutiae of organization and administration as already discussed in Chap. 9. At the same time it is particularly difficult to spell out general policies in terms that make them more than an empty formula.

Yet in the process of bill drafting, as in every other phase of the political struggle, all is not always what it seems. Sometimes the most elaborate façade of detail merely hides a tremendous blank-check delegation of power and resources. In the Contract Settlement Act of 1944, paragraph (d) of Sec. 6 listed various costs that would be allowable in the calculation of compensation to war contractors for work done under terminated contracts. It also listed a number of items that "shall not be included as elements of cost." Yet at the end of the section was a provision to the effect that whenever the application of these principles would be impracticable "the contracting agencies may establish alternative methods and standards." In other words, the guides for administrative action with respect to cost items, as with similar standards in many other statutes, had no force whatsoever; they were written into the bill for the sole purpose of supplying window dressing and of giving some members of Congress an illusory feeling of concrete achievement.

Policy Declarations. Declarations of general policy often may seem to be useless ornaments. They are sneered at by many members of Congress who think that all a statute should attempt to do is authorize, direct, or prohibit. Yet increasing weight has been given to policy declarations. Regarding the utility of preambles and textual provisions which describe the necessity for a particular piece of legislation, James M. Landis writes:

In part this recital takes the place of the old-fashioned preamble, the passing of which many men wise in the law have deplored. Despite the occasional cavalier and cynical treatment of these recitals by the courts, they do help to create the frame of reference within which the administrative is to operate, and to pose the objective that was intended to be reached. It is worth remembering that, at the time of the passage of the Securities Exchange Act of 1934 and the Public Utility Holding Company Act of 1935, representatives of the exchanges and the utilities were considerably disturbed at certain of the recitals. As a result they spent no little effort in an attempt to change some of the language of what professedly is nonoperative phraseology. The years

[8] James Hart, "The Exercise of Rule-making Power," Report of the President's Committee on Administrative Management, p. 316.

have proven that from their standpoint they were right; for both the trend in meaning given the operative provisions of the legislation and the character of subsequent administration was determined, in large measure, by the form and content of the recitals.[9]

THE FORM OF A BILL

What kind of legislative measure should be drafted? How much ground should be covered in one measure? How can it be put together in such a fashion as to stand up under attack? To what extent should deception be used to mislead the opposition? These are the major problems of form that are faced by the sponsors and authors of a bill.

Obviously, they are far from unrelated to the question of the asking price and of the distribution of power and wealth. The two sets of questions must always be considered together, for almost any decision on what may be arbitrarily classified as "substantive" has implications for the form of a measure, and vice versa.

The Type of Measure

The preparation of legislative measures involves choices between various forms of resolutions, between appropriation bills as contrasted with other legislative bills, and between treaties as distinguished from executive agreements. Amendments themselves are also available for use, but there are so many specialized problems involved in amendments that the subject is discussed in a separate section at the end of this chapter.

There are three forms of resolutions: a simple resolution prepared for action in one house of Congress only, a concurrent resolution, and a joint resolution. A Senate or House resolution is the method whereby each house handles its own rules of operating procedures and instructs its committees to engage in studies or investigations. A Senate or House resolution is often used as a method of calling upon the President or an executive agency to submit to either house a report on a given subject. While such a resolution does not have the force of law, it is usually complied with by the President or the appropriate agency. The Federal Trade Commission Act, however, puts the force of law behind a Senate or House resolution directing the Federal Trade Commission to embark upon an investigation.

A concurrent resolution is one that is approved by both houses of Congress but is not sent to the President for signature. It, therefore, does not have the force of law; it merely expresses the intent of the two houses of Congress. In

[9] James M. Landis, "The Administrative Process" (New Haven, Conn.: Yale University Press, 1938), pp. 66–67.

recent years there have been many attempts to use the concurrent resolution as a means of congressional control of the executive branch. In many of the wartime statutes enacted during World War II, Congress was given the authority, through concurrent resolution, to terminate war powers.[10] In the Reorganization Act of 1945 it was provided that a reorganization plan prepared by the President would not go into effect if, within a given number of days, a concurrent resolution of disapproval were passed by both houses of Congress. In the Reorganization Act of 1949 this approach was carried still further by a provision that a Presidential reorganization plan would be ineffective if a simple resolution of disapproval were adopted in either house of Congress.

A joint resolution is, for all intents and purposes, the same as a bill. It is often used in making minor changes in past legislation or in endorsing executive agreements. When so used, it is signed by the President and has the full force of law. It is also used as the vehicle for proposing constitutional amendments, in which case it is not sent to the President for signature or veto.

Theoretically, there is supposed to be a clear distinction between an appropriation bill and all other bills. The former is supposed to be confined to the provision of funds authorized by other legislation. It is not supposed itself to contain new or general "legislation." The rules of each house contain provisions allowing a point of order to be made from the floor against "legislation" in appropriation bills. If the point of order is sustained, the offending item is stricken. Legislative bills, on the other hand, are not supposed to provide funds but merely to authorize subsequent appropriations. Nevertheless, there is a broad borderline area in which either type of measure can be used. If an appropriation act embodies certain prohibitions and limitations on the use of funds, it can be just as effective as substantive legislation. A good example is the appropriation-bill provision enacted during the Eightieth Congress forbidding funds to be used for the employment by the Federal government of members of unions asserting the right to strike. Whether or not this amounted to "legislation" depends entirely upon one's point of view. The advantage of the appropriation-act approach is that an appropriation measure invariably gets passed by Congress in one form or another. Presidential veto is rare. Moreover, the appropriation process is an ideal avenue for those who are afraid of public attention and who want to avoid a full airing of the issues involved. A regular bill, in turn, can be used to direct an agency to use for slightly different purposes money that has already been appropriated. This can have an effect very similar to providing a new appropriation. In the case of government corporations, there is little resort to appropriation bills, and nonappropriation measures are habitually used to make more funds available.

[10] For an interesting historical discussion of the use of concurrent resolutions see Howard White, "Executive Responsibility to Congress via Concurrent Resolutions," *American Political Science Review,* Vol. 36, 1942

In the field of international relations, there is a clear-cut choice between a treaty and an executive agreement. The former requires a two-thirds majority of the Senate and is not considered in the House.[11] The latter has grown up as a method of attaining an international agreement without having to run the gauntlet of the two-thirds requirement in the Senate. Some executive agreements are handled on the basis of Presidential action only—as was the case with the Atlantic Charter and the Declaration of the United Nations. Others are submitted to both houses of Congress in the form of a bill or joint resolution and require merely a majority vote. Because of the difficulties associated with attaining a two-thirds majority in the Senate, the tendency has been to submit international agreements in the form of executive agreements whenever possible. In fact, the latter vehicle has been used more frequently than the former.

During the course of World War II, for example, one of the major tactics of President Roosevelt and Secretary of State Cordell Hull was to avoid the two-thirds requirement for treaty provisions. Their first step was to initiate a series of purely executive agreements which were not to be submitted to Congress in any form. Members of the Senate Committee on Foreign Relations became alarmed at this prospect and a subcommittee was elected to negotiate with Hull.

Between them they sought to develop an understanding with the Secretary that would permit the participation of Congress in the negotiation of post-war pacts. In turn, the State Department would receive the authority of the national legislature for negotiating such agreements. The Compromise eventually developed by Senator Green and Assistant Secretary Sayre relied upon the use of the joint resolution. Adoption of a resolution of this character would require only a majority vote in the two houses of Congress. This arrangement would by-pass the minority obstruction in the Senate, while permitting both houses to have a hand in pact-making.[12]

Kenneth Colegrove and others have objected to this use of executive agreements on the ground that it is an evasion of the constitutional limitation of

[11] When the Constitution was written, there was important motivation behind the two-thirds requirement on treaties. New England interests were anxious to protect their fishing rights in the North Atlantic and feared that the majority of the other states might yield these rights in a treaty with England. The representatives of the four Southern states, on the other hand, were interested in navigation on the Mississippi and in the future of New Orleans. This dispute became so heated that consideration was even given to dividing the states into three groups rather than joining them in one union. As part of the over-all settlement of this dispute, the two-thirds provision previously contained in the Articles of Confederation was continued in the Constitution itself.

[12] Kenneth Colegrove, "The American Senate and World Peace" (New York: Vanguard, 1944), p. 94. Other interesting examples are found in the stories of the annexation of Texas and Hawaii, accomplished not by treaty but by congressional joint resolution, as told by Senator George Wharton Pepper. "Family Quarrels: The President, The Senate, The House" (New York: Baker, Voorhis, 1931), pp. 41–42.

treaty making and that no executive agreement can have the sanctity of a
treaty. Nevertheless, the availability of the method is hardly a matter of dispute. As Quincy Wright wired to a House committee considering proposals
for amending the treaty provisions of the Constitution: "President now has
authority, if supported by Congress, to make international agreements on any
subject within the delegated powers of Congress." [13]

The Scope

The draftsmen of the bill introduced in 1947 to abolish the Jackson Hole
National Monument had no concern with the problem of scope. There was
only one monument to be abolished. There were no related subjects which
by any stretch of the imagination could have been appropriately dealt with
in the same measure. But the draftsmen of the Taft-Hartley Labor-Management
Relations Act faced an entirely different situation. They were dealing with an
extremely broad and complex field in which there were dozens of points that
might properly be dealt with in one bill and dozens of others that might be
reserved for separate handling.

Omnibus Measures.[14] The drafters of the Legislation Reorganization Act of
1946 were quick to see the many advantages in an "omnibus bill," a term
used to describe a bill composed of many parts, each of which might also stand
on its own two feet. The bases for their drafting work were the recommendations contained in a report of the Joint Committee on the Organization of
Congress. In all, there were thirty-eight recommendations, divided into eight
different categories. There was ample material for from eight to thirty-eight
separate bills. The members of the committee decided, however, to have one
omnibus measure. The wisdom of this decision was borne out by the results.
First of all, the big bill made a big splash. Its very size endowed it with a
significance that could never have been achieved by a less ambitious measure.
A set of separate measures introduced simultaneously might have had the
same initial impact, but public interest would certainly have been weakened
and dissipated in the attempt to follow each separate measure on its tedious
way through the congressional mill. The omnibus device served, therefore, as
a means of both creating and sustaining public interest. It also served to shield
and make less objectionable two of the most controversial provisions in the
bill—the simplified committee system and the salary raises for members of
Congress.[15]

[13] Hearings before subcommittee number 3 of the Committee on the Judiciary, House of
Representatives, 78th Cong., 2d Sess., p. 145.

[14] For a full discussion of proposals for omnibus appropriations bills, see Chap. 20.

[15] Another illustration of how controversial provisions can be shielded by less controversial
provisions is found in Marriner Eccles' vivid story of the three titles of the Banking Act of
1935, "Beckoning Frontiers" (New York: Knopf, 1951), pp. 196–199.

The omnibus approach also provides the opportunity to execute a hidden ball play. The broader the scope of the measure, the more chance there is of its carrying along to enactment provisions that would otherwise stand no chance of being enacted into law. At the hearings of the Joint Committee on the Organization of Congress, before the drafting of the committee's bill, Professor Fred A. Fairchild of Yale University appeared on behalf of the United States Chamber of Commerce and proposed that a Joint Congressional Budget Committee be established to set annually an over-all ceiling upon appropriations. This recommendation was set forth in the Joint Committee's report and became the basis for a brief and harmless-looking provision in the legislative reorganization bill. It so happened that this provision was drafted in a manner that endowed it with tremendous significance by requiring the President every year to keep expenditures below a ceiling set forth in a concurrent resolution. It would have had the serious effect of depriving the President of any veto power on measures to cut appropriations, thereby strengthening the position of "economy-minded" business interests with active representation in Congress. If this provision had been handled separately, it would have been subjected to careful analysis and would probably have been revised considerably before reaching the Senate floor. Embedded in a broad omnibus measure, however, this provision never received the attention it deserved—either in committee, on the floor, or by the Bureau of the Budget and other executive agencies affected by it. It was not until the bill passed the Senate and reached the desk of the Speaker of the House that the administration had a chance to present its views fully and, at the eleventh hour, have the provision changed.

The combination of separate elements in an omnibus measure also provides the basis for winning the support of diverse interests and pressure groups. In 1933 the National Industrial Recovery Act gave business exemption from the antitrust laws, gave labor the right to organize and bargain collectively, and gave city and state governments the benefits of a large-scale public-works program. The consolidated appeal contained in the measure was one of the major factors in its rapid enactment. A broad bill also provides its backers with a flexibility which is extremely useful in maneuvering. An omnibus bill can contain extra provisions which, like a ship's ballast, can help keep a bill afloat in its long journey through stormy congressional seas. Without resulting in mortal injury to the bill, they can be dropped in a manner that will appease the opposition. In the case of the legislative reorganization bill, for example, the provision calling for a director of congressional personnel was certainly not a fundamental part of the measure but it proved to be useful ballast on the Senate floor when Senator La Follette of Wisconsin agreed to have it deleted at the request of Senator Kenneth McKellar of Tennessee. This flexibility also provides the opportunity to plan the referral of a bill to a friendly committee. If the health-insurance provisions of the Truman Administration's health-insurance bill had been handled separately, the bill would have been referred to the unfriendly Senate Finance Committee. To avoid this, an omnibus measure was prepared which included not only health insurance but also a lengthy title on the public health service. Through this device, it was possible to have the bill referred to the Senate Labor Committee whose chairman was one of the bill's sponsors and who quickly arranged for public hearings.

Narrow Measures. In many situations, a narrowly drafted bill is far more appropriate than an omnibus measure. The bills to exempt railroads, newspapers, and insurance companies from the antitrust laws have all been handled separately. If they had been combined into one measure, the amount of public attention that would have been attracted would have been a great impediment. As it was, the backers of each separate bill made their case for one particular type of exemption. None of them had to assume the onerous burden of defending a measure that would have been attacked as utterly wrecking the American antitrust tradition.

Another consideration is the fact that a number of bills dealing with various phases of the same subject provide an opportunity for a number of Congressmen to serve as the chief sponsors. There is something about being the sponsor of a bill which cannot be gained merely by having the Congressman's name appear on a list with other sponsors. During the Eightieth Congress, private-utility companies gave their strong support to seven different measures, each dealing with various aspects of public-utility regulation and public-power activities.

A narrowly conceived bill can often slip through the crevices of congressional opposition at a time when a broad measure is stalled in its tracks. In 1946 the Case labor-relations bill was vetoed by the President and the veto was upheld in the House of Representatives. The President's veto message, however, did not take issue with the antiracketeering provisions of this omnibus measure. As soon as the veto was upheld, the antiracketeering provisions were handled separately and were quickly enacted into law.

The valley-authority movement has thus far developed on the basis of separate bills. There have been bills to set up a Missouri Valley Authority, to establish a Columbia Valley Authority, and so forth. While Representative John Rankin of Mississippi has introduced an omnibus measure providing for seven TVA's, there has been little support for this approach. It has been felt rather that each river-valley problem should be approached on its own terms, with a special measure aimed at developing the largest possible amount of local support. However, in a period of depression and unemployment, there might develop potential support for drastic action. Under such conditions, the type of bill introduced by Representative Rankin might prove to be the most effective.

Finally, the smaller the scope of a bill, the easier it is to prepare. A narrow bill can be prepared with less drain upon the resources of its backers and with infinitely more speed. Every additional provision means new drafting problems, new pressures to be weighed, and new compromises to be formulated.

Design for Combat

In an item-by-item count, the great bulk of legislative action would seem to consist of purely routine correction and uncontested enactments. Much that goes uncontested in the present would likely have been bones of violent contention in a past day before one or another precedent was established or area of consensus came into being. Other uncontested measures may actually be "out-of-court" settlements, or they may be compromises destined to fail because their sponsors are unwilling to offend powerful groups. If it were possible, however, to separate the relatively few "important" measures from the overwhelming number of "unimportant" ones, it would be found that each of the important bills is a fighting document designed for combat almost as literally and carefully as any tank or artillery piece intended for a battlefield. At the very least, each significant bill is devised to capture a certain amount of attention. At the most, it is aimed at standing up under the shock of attack throughout the legislative, administrative, or judicial processes. From this standpoint, the manner in which a bill is organized and the kind of language that is used are of considerable interest.

Subdivision. The first problem of organization is subdivision. The section is the basic unit of a bill. Each section may be divided into subsections; each subsection into paragraphs; each paragraph into subparagraphs. The various sections can be assembled into titles or even into separately lettered parts of titles. Although there can be no general rule as to where the line can be drawn between any of these segments, experience has proved that a bill's provisions can be understood best if no segments are allowed to become too long and if the various segments are grouped together in a balanced and logical fashion. Draftsmen will often give major emphasis to the strong points in a bill by putting them at the very beginning or by spelling them out with far more language than might otherwise be necessary. More controversial points, on the other hand, can be tucked away at the end in brief and unobtrusive language. Detachability is also a major consideration. "If its several parts are too tightly dovetailed together, if it is so constructed that a modification of one part necessarily involves numerous modifications of other parts, an amendment made in the course of debate may throw it hopelessly out of gear." [16] The careful draftsman, therefore, often erects his structure along the

[16] Ilbert, *op. cit.*, p. 110.

lines of a large, rambling, one-story building rather than of a skyscraper. When this is done, almost any part can be removed without irreparable injury to the other parts. This has the extra advantage of allowing more room for the addition of new provisions. In a particularly complex bill it has also proved helpful to have a subtitle for each section—sometimes even for subsections— and a table of contents listing all the subtitles.

Titles. Increasing use is being made of special sections providing for what is called a "short title." While the regular title which appears before the enacting clause is usually too long for ready reference, the short title provides a convenient label. For example, the regular title of the bill which finally became the Full Employment Act of 1946 was "To establish a national policy and program to assure continuing full employment in a free competitive economy, through the concerted efforts of industry, agriculture, labor, State and local governments, and the Federal Government." Quite a mouthful! But Sec. 1 of this bill ran as follows: "This Act may be cited as the 'Full Employment Act of 1945.'" This short title was invaluable in dramatizing the measure. The charge was often made that the bill was misnamed, since the short title gave the impression that enactment of the legislation would automatically provide full employment. Be that as it may, a more subdued and less challenging title would have served to weaken the chances of obtaining any legislation of this type whatsoever.

Statements of Purpose. Another labeling device is to preface a bill with a preamble or statement of purposes. Such a statement can be invaluable in setting forth the need for a certain type of legislation and the values to be derived from it. It can also serve as a handbook of arguments on behalf of the measure and refutation of the charges made by its opponents. An interesting example is the set of whereases which Senator Vandenberg brought forth as a prelude to the 1947 legislation to aid Greece and Turkey. The major argument against this measure, and against the Truman doctrine on which it was based, was that it side-stepped the United Nations. Senator Vandenberg therefore devised language which indicated why aid to Greece and Turkey was needed and offered a set of six whereases justifying the legislation, the last of which was as follows:

Whereas the United Nations is not now in a position to furnish to Greece and Turkey the financial and economic assistance which is immediately required; and Whereas the furnishing of such assistance to Greece and Turkey by the United States will contribute to the freedom and independence of all members of the United Nations in conformity with the principles and purposes of the Charter: Now, therefore. . . .

The prefatory language used in this legislation is rather unusual since it appeared before, rather than after, the enactment clause and, technically, was not even a part of the statute itself. It is more customary to use for this purpose the various declarations of policy appearing in early sections of a measure.[17]

Relation to Existing Legislation. With respect to the language of a bill itself, a primary fact to be reckoned with is the prior existence of a tremendous body of related language in statutes, administrative rules and regulations, and judicial decisions. Hence the general character of most bills is commonly "the insertion of a new part in a long-worked machine."[18] A good example is the Interstate Commerce Act which was first passed in 1887 and has since been directly amended by almost fifty separate statutes and indirectly affected by many other acts of Congress. The Act as amended now encompasses about 230 pages. The index to it, including reference to supplementary legislation as prepared by the Interstate Commerce Commission itself, covers more than 150 pages. This labyrinthine body of existing law hangs over the head of anyone who attempts to draft a new measure dealing with the regulation of transportation. It makes it well-nigh impossible to formulate a transportation bill that can be fully comprehensible in its own terms. A similar situation exists with respect to bills dealing with taxes and other long-tilled fields of public policy.

An important decision that must always be faced, therefore, is whether a bill should be drafted in the form of amendments to existing law or as a new measure with or without provisions repealing certain elements in the old law.

The method of amendment has the advantage of apparent simplicity. It focuses attention upon the proposed change. But it has technical difficulties, other sections of the law may be affected, and later give rise to litigation and judicial interpretation as to implied repeals. A new law offers the advantage of unity of purpose and language, has the difficulty of exaggerating the importance of the change to be made.[19]

The dilemma is often solved by a combination of both approaches.

At times the use of the straight amendment approach is adopted because it has a propagandistic value. An opponent of the Taft-Hartley Act made the following observation:

It has already been pointed out that key provisions in the act nominally took the form of an "amendment" to the Wagner Act. Why call it an "amendment" when it is a radically different law? The answer is that it was politically wise to do so, because the sponsors knew that large masses of workers would bitterly resent a repeal of the

[17] Statements of this kind may be introduced with such phrases as "It is the policy (or purpose) of the Congress . . . ," ". . . of the Federal Government . . . ," or ". . . of the people of the United States. . . ." At times they are preceded by "findings."
[18] "The Making and Form of Bills," p. 182.
[19] Harvey Walker, "The Legislative Process" (New York: Ronald, 1948), p. 355.

Wagner Act, hence the misleading designation of "amendment" to the Wagner Act, implying that the Wagner Act essentially was retained.[20]

To the extent that amendments are used, another dilemma arises to confront the draftsman. On the one hand, he can merely refer to the previous act, thereby making it almost impossible for anyone to understand the nature of the amendment without looking up the previous act in the statute books. On the other hand, he can reproduce an amended form of the appropriate section of the statute that is being altered. This sometimes has the effect of not indicating in any precise manner the nature of the change. A closely related problem is the extent to which portions of past statutes are to be incorporated by reference without directly repeating the language that is incorporated. This device has the advantage of indicating that what is proposed to be enacted has already received approval in other circumstances. It also serves as a method of accomplishing major objectives in an unobtrusive manner or even in a manner that will prevent many people from finding out what is really being proposed.

Intelligibility. It is sometimes thought that the test of good drafting is whether the product is intelligible to a lay reader. To some extent this is symptomatic of the great illusion that in a democratic society every intelligent citizen should be able to understand every issue of public policy. It may also represent something of a vestigial remnant of Jeremy Bentham's old dream of a comprehensive code that would be "designed for all understandings, and particularly for the less enlightened class." [21]

The germ of truth behind this approach lies in the fact that there is always a certain amount of leeway with respect to using more words or less words, more Anglo-Saxon words or more polysyllabic Latin derivatives, more involved language or more simple language. Some draftsmen still produce unnecessarily torturing language, reminiscent of the "tortuous and ungodly jumble" of the English law in pre-Bentham days. A striking example of this was pointed out by Representative Kitchin back in 1918 when he was defending the legislation that first provided for the Office of the Legislative Counsel in Congress:

Take the excess- and war-profits-tax title. No tax feature of the bill was at first more complicated and so hard to arrange and simplify. . . . I venture the assertion that not in the knowledge or observation of any gentlemen here was a complicated proposition put into a clearer or more understandable form and terms than are the provisions in the bill relating to this tax. . . . Mr. Beaman put into about five lines

---

[20] Elias Lieberman, "Unions before the Bar" (New York: Harper, 1950), p. 323.

[21] Jeremy Bentham, "The Theory of Legislation" (New York: Harcourt, Brace, 1931), p. 157.

of this bill what it took a page in the existing excess-profits-tax law, and what it took two or three pages of the English law to state and provide.[22]

Many draftsmen seek, and often attain, the goal of writing legislative provisions so clearly that they cannot be clarified by a paraphrase.

Nevertheless, complex policies cannot be written in a simple fashion. To attempt simplicity in most legislation "is likely to be as profitless as to attempt to turn a Yale lock with a penknife blade." [23] A bill dealing with tax reform, for example, no matter how great an attempt may be made to make the language intelligible, can be understood only by tax experts. The draft which Representative Kitchin found so "understandable" was probably unreadable for, and unread by, most members of Congress. Furthermore, precision itself is a goal which often conflicts with intelligibility. Sometimes the only way to state a thing in clean-cut terms is to use more words, highly technical words, and an intricate exposition of ideas. An effort to achieve a draft that is appealing to the reader may result in creating, beneath the surface appearance of easy intelligibility, one complex ambiguity after another.

Another standard that has sometimes been used to judge the quality of draftsmanship is the ability to write legislative language that leaves no room for interpretation by the courts. One writer on the subject has said:

It is of prime importance in choosing language for statutes to remember that if the language of the law is clear and plain, courts of justice have no authority, because of evil consequences which would result, to give it a construction different from its natural and obvious meaning. . . . If the bill is exact, it leaves no room for judicial legislation under the guise of an effort to ascertain the legislative intent.[24]

Few bills of any real significance in complex fields of public policy could possibly live up to this standard. Adequate coverage of all conceivable situations is impossible. Although the treatises on the statutory construction of laws provide valuable information on how various judges have construed language in the past, they provide no firm basis whatsoever for predicting how they will do so in the future.

Ultimate precision in the use of language is a sheer impossibility. A word, as Justice Holmes pointed out, "is not a crystal, transparent and unchanged" but "the skin of a living thought and may vary greatly in color and content

---

[22] *Congressional Record,* 56th Cong., 2d Sess., 1918, pp. 701–702. Mr. Beaman's services had been made available to members of Congress on a demonstration basis by the Legislative Drafting Research Fund of Columbia University. The demonstration proved the utility of having trained draftsmen attached to Congress, and provisions to set up the congressional service with Government funds were written into the Revenue Act of 1918.

[23] "The Making and Form of Bills," p. 182.

[24] Jones, *op. cit.,* p. 110.

according to the circumstances and the time in which it is used." [25] There is a definite limit upon how much of an agreed-upon meaning can be read into the words of any statute. Beyond that limit the field is wide open for creative construction by administrators and judges. In many situations, moreover, the real art of draftsmanship is found not in the ability to state things precisely, for to do so might lose too many votes, but to state things with sufficient generality—or with sufficient ambiguity, if you will—to gain or maintain the necessary support to secure enactment and to provide administrators and judges with the leeway needed to meet new situations.

The Use of Deception

Deliberate intent to deceive is an inescapable element in any conflict. The legislative conflict is no exception to this rule. The bargaining process itself requires a certain amount of deception. Ultimate objectives are concealed. Opponents are prevented from learning the next moves that are to be taken. Sows' ears are talked of as if they were silken purses. It would be miraculous, therefore, if legislative drafting did not on occasion include an important element of deception as to the meaning of a bill's provisions.

The drafting of a bill offers endless opportunities for deception. First, within the framework of a legislative proposal the simplest sentence composed of the simplest words is often far different from what it seems to be. The meaning of most bills can be ascertained only by appraising the interrelationships among a large number of highly complex sentences. A flat prohibition against certain types of activity may be modified by a phrase or proviso in another section or even converted into an open encouragement of the identical activity. Secondly, as indicated earlier, innumerable tricks of concealment are possible in the drafting of provisions amending previous acts or in incorporating parts of them by reference.[26] When provisions of this type are inserted at the end of a long measure or buried within language that attracts attention for unrelated reasons, there are relatively few persons who will take the trouble to find out what they really mean. "You are going to find out that there is more in this bill than may meet the eye," Representative Hartley is quoted as having boasted during a defense of the Taft-Hartley Act.[27]

In addition to the standard tricks of the trade, the substantive ideas in many measures are so complex as to provide endless opportunities for technicians to pull the wool over the eyes of laymen. When such opportunities are fully ex-

[25] *Towne v. Eisner,* 245 U.S. 418 (1917).

[26] Concealment is not something that has recently been invented. It is said that Caligula wrote his laws in very small characters and hung them on high pillars to ensnare his people.

[27] Lieberman, *op. cit.,* p. 315. "This was no idle boast," Lieberman adds, "for the law contains many hidden anti-labor traps calculated to have far-reaching effects on the rights and strength of labor unions in the United States."

ploited, the story of what was done can be unraveled only through an extended explanation.

The United States Housing Act of 1937 provides a first-rate example. When this Act was in the drafting stage, provisions were inserted allowing local housing authorities to obtain loans from the Federal government at an interest rate of 3 per cent and to repay the Government over a period as long as sixty years. In addition, the Government was to give the local housing authority an annual subsidy for the purpose of bringing the rents down to a level that could be afforded by low-income families. Each annual subsidy payment was limited to 3½ per cent of the total cost of any housing project. In order to find out what the net cost would really be to the Government, the average reader of the Act subtracted from the 3½ per cent the Government would pay out the 3 per cent that the Government would get back in the form of an interest payment. This indicated a net loss to the Government of ½ of 1 per cent a year. He then multiplied ½ of 1 per cent by sixty years and came to the conclusion that the Government's net subsidy amounted to 30 per cent of the cost of construction. Since the previous housing program under the Public Works Administration had provided for a capital grant of 40 per cent of the cost of construction, the obvious conclusion was that this new proposal was indeed very moderate.

The bill passed with a substantial majority in both houses. Subsequently, however, many members of Congress, prodded by the real-estate lobby, started to pay a little more attention to the mathematics of this subsidy arrangement. They discovered what would be obvious to a banking expert, the fact that the only way to know the annual charge on repaying a loan is to consult an amortization table. It so happens that any amortization table will show that the annual payment needed to repay a $100 loan over a sixty-year period is $3.50 or 3½ per cent. In other words, the Government's 3½ per cent subsidy to local housing authorities was exactly the amount needed to repay both interest and principle on total cost of any housing project. So far as a local housing authority would be concerned, therefore, the Housing Act of 1937 allowed a 100 per cent subsidy— not 30 per cent—on the cost of the construction. From the viewpoint of government financing, this arrangement seemed better than a lump-sum capital grant, since it spread the 100 per cent subsidy over a period of sixty years, adding only a minor charge to the Federal budget in any single year. From the point of view of low-income families this arrangement was also quite effective. Any smaller subsidy would have meant a rent beyond their means and would have denied access to the housing projects to those who were most in need of decent housing.

If the full implications of this formula had been clear before enactment of the statute, the probability is that the amount of subsidy would have been reduced considerably. On the other hand, the revelation a few years later as to the real meaning of the Act's provisions unquestionably added fuel to the high flames that were lit by the opponents of any type of public housing. In 1939, when President Roosevelt asked for additional funds for the low-rent public-housing program, one speaker after another on the floor of the House denounced the subsidy provisions of the 1937 Act, and the Roosevelt proposal was buried under an overwhelming vote of disapproval.

As this illustration suggests, deception of any kind always runs the risk of leading to serious repercussions. Self-restraint is the safest course in this matter. Jeremy Bentham might well have applied to legislative drafting his comment concerning business practices, "that, if there were no such thing as honesty, it would be a good speculation to invent it, as a means of making one's fortune." [28]

THE ARSENAL OF AMENDMENTS

As an observant judge once remarked, "Laws seem to be born full-grown about as often as men are." [29] It is a rare bill that is regarded by anyone, even its proudest authors and staunchest backers, as a finished document to be approved or voted on in the form in which it is introduced. Most bills are regarded by everyone as open to amendment at any time. Occasionally, the amendments are even offered to bills that have no chance of obtaining consideration by a committee. Sometimes the sponsors of a bill will amend their own measure even before it obtains consideration by a committee. If the committee-consideration stage is reached, proposals for amendments fly thick and fast. On the floor, the key maneuvers and the major votes usually relate to amendments rather than to the bill as a whole. The only purpose of a conference committee is to produce amendments that will reconcile the differences between the two houses.

There are many differences between an amendment and a bill. A bill can be vetoed by the President. An amendment cannot be vetoed, since the President has never been given the power, enjoyed by many state governors, to reject a portion of a bill. Amendments, moreover, get less public attention. They usually deal with what seem to be minor details. They are hard for the press or any outside observers to understand. Sometimes they pile up one on top of another in a manner that defies comprehension by anyone except a small handful of members of Congress, experts, and lobbyists.

Amendments for the Offensive

Amendments are peculiarly suited to certain types of offensive fighting. The historic method of opposing a strongly backed measure is to propose crippling

[28] Bentham, *op. cit.*, p. 64.
[29] Judge Dean, *Waters v. Wolf*, 162 Pa. 167.

amendments. This was the strategy used by Senator Henry Cabot Lodge and his small group of irreconcilables in their fight against the League of Nations. Rather than make a frontal attack upon the Versailles Treaty itself, they proposed one reservation after another. They thereby drew public attention away from the major issue, split and confused the Senate supporters of the treaty, and by the time the final vote came, had succeeded in developing a measure that was no longer acceptable to President Wilson.[30] Senator Borah himself took the lead in developing a similar attack some years later against a resolution for American affiliation with the World Court.[31] In this case the Senate accepted the resolution with Borah's reservation, but the League of Nations balked.

More recently, the same strategy was followed in the 1946 struggle on the extension of price-control legislation. The major opponents of price control concentrated their attention upon writing into the extension measure a long series of amendments exempting various commodities and providing for various formulas that would facilitate price increases. The result was what Price Administrator Chester Bowles called a "booby-trap bill."

A striking variant of this approach occurs when members of Congress offer or support amendments which run directly counter to their own views and are intended to make a bill more, rather than less, undesirable. In writing about his experiences in the House of Representatives, former Representative Jerry Voorhis of California tells how this strategy was used by the prolabor group in the House. After the antilabor bloc had succeeded in writing into a pending bill amendments that made it more and more unacceptable to the prolabor group, "the prolabor groups would decide that their best strategy was to 'make the bill as bad as possible so it would be easier to vote against it.' Thus there would be only a handful of the middle group opposing the amendments. And when the final vote came it was almost impossible for a conscientious member to support the bill. . . ."[32]

One of the most effective types of crippling amendments deals strictly with matters of administration and enforcement. When a new function for a Department is proposed, a favorite device is to offer an amendment switching the administration to another agency that is either unfriendly to the program or is incapable of administering it. Another tactic is to provide for such extensive powers of judicial review as to tie up the administrators in unending litigation. Still another is to reduce fines for evasion of any prohibition to an inconsequential sum of money.

[30] The essence of this strategy was frankly outlined by Senator Lodge in his "The Senate and the League of Nations" (New York: Scribner, 1925).

[31] "Senator Borah had learned a valuable lesson from Lodge," comments Karl Schriftgiesser in "This Was Normalcy" (Boston: Little, Brown, 1948), pp. 232–233.

[32] Jerry Voorhis, "Confessions of a Congressman" (Garden City, N.Y.: Doubleday, 1947), p. 98.

During the 1946 and 1947 conflicts on labor legislation, opponents of the Case bill and the Taft-Hartley Act often used the technique of threatening retaliatory amendments. When the Case bill reached the Senate, an amendment was proposed by Senator Byrd requiring unions to give a public accounting of their financial operations. Senator Taylor countered this amendment with a retaliatory proposal that would require members of the Senate to register the amounts and sources of their outside income. While it is difficult to judge whether the Taylor threat was a decisive factor, the Byrd amendment did not succeed. Subsequently, during the drafting of the Taft-Hartley Act, Senator Pepper threatened to propose an amendment increasing regulations upon business for every provision that increased government controls over labor unions. While in this case the threat was never fully carried out, it is conceivable that if an adequate set of retaliatory amendments of this type had been prepared, Senator Pepper might have succeeded in toning down some of the labor controls in the Taft-Hartley Act.

Amendments of this type are often strictly propagandistic in character. One of the earlier advocates of prohibition repeal, for example, habitually made a telling point by repeatedly offering appropriations amendments providing tremendous sums for enforcement of the prohibition laws. During the 1920's, the elder Senator La Follette "showed up the reckless trend of the entire Harding-Coolidge-Hoover era when he sarcastically suggested that all acts of Congress should carry a rider saying that 'this Act shall not apply to any individual or corporation worth $100,000,000 or more.' " [33]

Defensive Amendments

Amendments are also basic to the defense of any proposal. During the Case bill debate, for example, Senator Pepper concentrated his attack upon provisions of an amendment introduced by Senator Byrd to control the operation of union health and welfare funds. Since his attack uncovered many weaknesses in the Byrd proposal, Senator Byrd himself offered numerous modifications upon his own amendment.

The variety of defensive amendments that may be used is well illustrated by the following report on the strategy of a measure's sponsors after it had sustained its first major attack:

At the conclusion of the hearings on S. 1944 it was obvious to those who had shared in its drafting that some revision would be necessary. Certain amendments were called for because of deficiencies in the bill which had become evident either before or at the hearings. Other amendments seemed desirable because thereby criticism could be met without requiring substantial sacrifices in objectives. Still others,

[33] Schriftgiesser, *op. cit.*, p. 130.

though regretted, seemed inescapable if the opposition to the bill were to be reduced to a point where it could be overcome.[34]

On many occasions the sponsors of a bill will offer strengthening or perfecting amendments before any critic has an opportunity to uncover defects. In this category falls the amendment to the School Lunch Bill of 1946, introduced by Representative Hall, providing that all school lunches subsidized through Federal funds should be handled on a nonprofit basis. Another perfecting amendment introduced from the floor in the case of measures providing for the expenditure of Federal funds is the antidiscrimination amendment frequently recommended by the National Association for the Advancement of Colored People. This amendment usually requires that any services promoted through Federal aid be equally available to Negroes as well as to whites, without prohibiting the use of funds by institutions that segregate Negroes from whites.

Riders

A highly specialized type of amendment, one that has little or nothing to do with the purposes of the bill to which it is offered, is the "rider."

In 1918, when the agriculture appropriation bill was before Congress, the "drys" succeeded in attaching to it an amendment providing for wartime prohibition of intoxicating liquors. In 1925, when a post-office appropriation bill was up for consideration, Senator Walsh of Massachusetts offered an amendment dealing with campaign expenditures, later known as the Corrupt Practices Act. In 1937, Senator Tydings of Maryland attached the Resale Price Maintenance Act to an appropriation bill for the District of Columbia. In each of these cases, the sponsors of the rider succeeded in side-stepping regular committee consideration. Because the riders were attached to appropriation bills on which essential government operations depended, the President had no choice but to approve the legislation.

But appropriation bills are not the only vehicles to which riders may be attached, nor is passage of the rider the only objective. Late in the 1946 session of the Senate, when the Tidelands Oil Bill was being debated, Senator Morse of Oregon offered as an amendment the anti-poll-tax bill that had already been approved by the House. A Senator promptly asked that the amendment be ruled out of order because it was not germane. The point of order was denied. For a while it seemed that a Southern filibuster against the anti-poll-tax rider would kill off hopes of action on the oil legislation. But the trouble-

[34] David F. Cavers, "The Food, Drug, and Cosmetic Act of 1938: Its Legislative History and Its Substantive Provisions," *Law and Contemporary Problems*, Vol. 6, No. 1, Winter, 1939, p. 10.

some rider was disposed of by being laid on the table, and a few minutes later the oil bill was passed. Earlier in the same session a similar ruse was used to defeat a bill raising the minimum-wage level. Senator Russell of Georgia won Senate acceptance of a rider which revised the parity-price formula in a manner wholly unacceptable to the Administration. The amended bill was passed by the Senate. By the time the bill reached the House it became evident that the Senate would accept no bill without the farm-parity amendment and the President would approve no bill that contained :t. So the bill was allowed to die.

Any bill which seems destined to achieve final passage tends to attract those who want a "free ride." Samuel Clemens found this out during the course of his labors on behalf of copyright legislation to protect authors against the unauthorized publication of their writings. "See here, Uncle Joe," he complained to Speaker Cannon, "does every fellow who comes here get hitched up to a train he does not want to pull?" [35]

[35] L. White Busbey, "Uncle Joe Cannon" (New York: Holt, 1927), p. 271.

Chapter 12

CAMPAIGN LEADERSHIP AND GROUP SUPPORT

WHILE SOME of the myths about government are the product of naïveté, others shine with a slick veneer of sophistication. Among the latter is the stereotype picture of myriad lobbyists swarming through the halls of Congress trying to influence legislative decisions. On one side, according to this conception, stand the members of Congress trying to see the issues and make up their minds on competing claims. On the other side are the lobbyists conducting never-ending campaigns for or against this or that bill.

Yet if the total bulk of legislative campaign activities were to be compared to an iceberg, the portion handled solely by professional lobbyists—both those acting on behalf of private organizations and those representing government agencies—would be only a fraction of the segment appearing above the surface of the water. A full-fledged legislative campaign covers not only all phases of the legislative process from drafting to Presidential signature or veto, but also a broad range of variegated activities.

The initiative and the continuing coordination of the activities of a legislative campaign require the most skillful exercise of campaign leadership if they are to be effective. A legislative campaign necessitates the organization of group support. Leadership and its group support will be dealt with in the present chapter. In the chapter that follows it will be seen how leaders and supporters utilize and are affected by the production and dissemination of propaganda and by the development and application of political pressure.

While the lobbyists usually take some part in these aspects of legislative campaigning, the people they speak to and the people they speak for—whether members of Congress, Presidents, executive officials, or leaders of private organizations—are also campaigners. The great difference between the professional lobbyists and the others is that the former include a greater proportion of the foot soldiers and lieutenants and a lesser proportion of the generals.

CAMPAIGN LEADERSHIP

Of the various sources of power spelled out in Chap. 8 leadership is the active, energizing element. It is leadership which transmits wealth, people, and strategic situations into power, extends such power through organization of support, and puts it to use through the dissemination of propaganda and the application of pressure.

It is pertinent, therefore, to give special attention at this point to the strategy and tactics of leadership and to the organizational foundations of this leadership.

The Strategy and Tactics of Leadership

Strategy can be defined as the development of a basic campaign plan. Tactics can be defined as the application of such a plan at specific points.

Again, this is a distinction which is far from absolute. One man's strategy is another man's tactics. In both strategic and tactical operations, one must calculate alternatives without a precise quantitative measurement of the risks involved and must, in the final analysis, act on hunch.[1] In both, one faces identical problems of defining objectives, developing and executing a combat plan, and negotiating settlements.

Objectives. "First things come first, and I can't alienate certain votes I need for measures that are more important at the moment by pushing any measure that would entail a fight." [2] It was with words such as these that Eleanor Roosevelt's husband customarily countered when she attempted to have him give all-out support to certain types of civil-rights legislation. Presidents, however, are not the only legislative strategists with *must* lists. The major contestants are always in a position where they can win any one objective by concentrating all their resources upon it—but at the expense of sacrificing all other objectives. Every active participant in the legislative struggle must decide what he is going to sacrifice in order to obtain the objectives that count the most. "Pursue one great decisive aim with force and determination," wrote one of the greatest of military strategists, Carl von Clausewitz.[3] Unless this is done, one's resources are bound to be dribbled away in profitless efforts.

It is simpler, of course, if "the great decisive aim" is a clearly-spelled-out, long-range goal. Yet in many situations the "great decisive aim" has to be altered and redefined on the basis of almost continuous improvisation. Objectives are factors that unite or divide one's supporters. In a campaign based upon a loose coalition of sharply divergent groups, any attempt to establish

[1] In "The Theory of Games and Economic Behavior" by John von Newmann and Oskar Morgenstern (Princeton, N.J.: Princeton University Press, 1944), the case is made that in every problem of strategy there can be only a single optimum policy and that it would be irrational to act otherwise. While this theory sounds appealing, the closer one gets to action in given situations, the less applicability it has.

[2] Eleanor Roosevelt, "This I Remember" (New York: Harper, 1949), p. 162.

[3] Carl von Clausewitz, "Principles of War" (Harrisburg, Pa.: Military Service Publishing Co., 1942), p. 19.

fixed and nonflexible objectives would be inconsistent with the maintenance of maximum strength. The broad legislative campaigns of the New Deal and of the Fair Deal both fall into this category.

The scope of any group's objectives, apart from the various priorities that may be applied to them, has a direct bearing upon its decisions to support or oppose candidates for elective (and appointive) posts. Limited-purpose groups often judge members of Congress and executive officials by a single standard, that is, the position taken on one legislative issue. The broader a group's objectives become, the more difficult it is to use a single standard. In the same way a President, whose legislative objectives are invariably multiple despite the changing priorities of the "must list," can never afford to use a single standard. In the distribution of Presidential rewards and punishments he can never forget that even the rebellious Senator who opposes him on most things might be a valuable source of support on a few vital things.

Combat Plans. The development and execution of a combat plan call for attention to special problems associated with given objectives, to strategic positions, to the use of weapons, to intelligence operations, and to bluffing. All these elements are affected by the psychological make-up of leaders. No matter what the objectives may be, sound strategy calls for a full appraisal of strategic positions already occupied or that might be attained in the future. Many opportunities for successful operations can be lost if the possibilities of fully exploiting the former are neglected. Much energy can be wasted in propaganda and pressure that is not carefully directed toward winning support at specific points of influence. Some points of influence—such as committee chairmen, party-policy committees, and the highest officials of executive agencies and private organizations—are obvious. In many other cases—as with individual Congressmen, technical experts, office assistants, and secretaries—their utility is harder to detect or may be nonexistent unless special operations arise into which they may fit.

The use of weapons is also important. There are times when more use of propaganda is needed, others when only direct pressure will suffice. There are some supporting groups that can use only limited forms and media of influence. There are others that, in certain situations, can be called upon to use a variety of weapons. An interesting illustration of skill and restraint in the choice of campaign methods is found in the efforts of the National Association of Real Estate Boards to weaken Senator Taft's support of public-housing legislation. "The quiet and easy way you are handling your political contacts there is quite disturbing to the Senator," wrote a Washington official of the group to the Columbus, Ohio, real-estate board. "The more subtle you can be, the more effective you are. You do not need to exert a public-relations campaign in the press or radio. That helps the Senator. The behind-the-scenes operations with his political cronies are what counts. In my opinion, this is no time for public opinion pressure. It is time for political infighting without fanfare." [4]

Throughout any campaign the strategist-tactician must develop sources of intelligence that keep him minutely informed concerning the lay of the land, the progress of the battle in all theaters of operation, and the plans of his opponents. Only thus can one know *where* to get "fustest" with the "mostest." A good intelligence operation concentrates not so much on learning about public opinion in general but upon the views and intentions of people with power. It is not limited to the analysis of generally available information but penetrates to the innermost recesses of supposedly confidential meetings and conferences.

On the other hand, the strategist-tactician must try to keep opponents from seeing the whole picture. This calls for surprise and diversion. "It is the very essence of politics to set up diversions. . . ." [5] It also calls at times for the deliberate creation of confusion and, more frequently, for deliberate bluffing. Yet if these tactics are to be effective, they cannot be carried too far. As in poker, the opposition must be misled into thinking that most of the time one's moves can be predicted. Moreover, to be safe, one must usually act upon the assumption that in at least some cases one's bluffs will be detected.

As Von Clausewitz has pointed out, the success of any combat plan is greatly affected by the emotional drives of leaders. "A powerful emotion must stimulate the great ability of a military leader, whether it be ambition as in Caesar, hatred of the enemy as in Hannibal, or the pride in a glorious defeat, as in Frederick the Great." Such emotions are needed to maintain "confidence and firmness of convictions" in the face of daily obstacles. They are needed if one is to heed the admonition "Be audacious and cunning in your plans, firm and persevering in their execution." [6] Von Clausewitz might well have added that the more successful leaders know how to arouse and keep aroused similar emotions in their followers.

Settlements. In military combat, physical force always presents the possibility of achieving the desired objective without compromise by destroying the opponent. But none of the weapons found in the arsenal of legislative strategy are based upon physical force. Power, therefore, is less sure, decisions less decisive. No victory is ever total, no defeat unmitigated. As a consequence, the art of compromise is essential in negotiating legislative settlements and in reacting to settlements in the negotiations of which one has not taken a direct part. The skilled leader who wants one loaf of bread will usually ask

---

[4] "Housing Lobby," Hearings before the Select Committee on Lobbying Activities of the House of Representatives, 81st Cong., 2d Sess., Part 2, p. 885.

[5] E. E. Schattschneider, "Politics, Pressures and the Tariff" (New York: Prentice-Hall, 1935), p. 289.

[6] Von Clausewitz, *op. cit.,* pp. 67, 69.

for two, accept half a loaf rather than nothing at all, and be willing to allow his opponents a few crumbs. Whether a compromise is praised as wise or damned as opportunistic or whether a compromiser is accepted as a realist or accused as a traitor depends upon where the observer stands and how much value he places upon the *quid* and the *quo*. In any case, accusation of betrayal or opportunism are an inevitable part of legislative dynamics.

"I'll never yield on a matter of principle," rings out a familiar battle cry. But principles are usually the first things to be yielded, for the simple reason that they are so rarely a clean-cut expression of fundamental high-priority interests. Because they are sometimes willing to sacrifice principles which are not directly related to basic interests but are rather propagandistic devices for the extension of support, the most effective leaders in the social struggle often appear to be totally unprincipled men. In a world of sharp divisions and dispersed power, they may even have to yield on basic interests. What to yield on and where to stand firm are questions that cannot be intelligently answered until one is able to sense the limits of the obtainable. Franklin Roosevelt was not a lesser man because he made compromises with "Southern Bourbons" and big-city bosses and compacts with Darlan and Stalin but a greater man because he was often able to use such lesser deeds for achieving higher objectives that would otherwise have been unattainable.

Limitations on Strategy and Tactics. Although the above discussion covers all the major factors that enter into the strategic and tactical thinking of more skilled and experienced leaders, it should not be inferred that they enter into all or even most strategic and tactical calculations. Campaign leaders, like everyone else, have their limitations. Some are experts in one type of operation, at a loss in others. Many are eternal amateurs or professional bunglers.

The complexity of American society, moreover, militates against the successful execution of too many pat and well-laid plans. No one individual or group can hold all the strings in one hand all the time. The limits within which legislative campaigns can be effective, no matter how expertly conceived they may be, are defined by the social and economic trends of any period and by the shifting dispersion of power among conflicting groups and interests.

Campaign leaders are often criticized for not having performed the impossible. The facts of life indicate that the most devoted and skillful head can still be broken against a stone wall. Leadership is an essential source of power but not a substitute for power.

In turn, leaders are often praised for strategic wisdom which they do not possess or which may not have been put to any genuine test. The possession and customary exercise of power help in the development of leadership, which in turn can lead to an augmentation of power. The weakest groups participating in the legislative struggle seldom develop the skillfulness and resourcefulness evidenced by the leaders of the large private organizations and government agencies and by the members of Congress who have formidable aggregations of power behind them.

The Organizational Foundations of Leadership

Throughout the entire process of social combat, leadership and organization are closely interrelated. Leaders face the task not only of mobilizing resources but also of dealing with organization itself as a foundation of leadership. High among the problems involved here are those of specialization, of centralization versus decentralization, and of money.

Specialization. The leadership of a legislative campaign involves many kinds of knowledge and activity. It calls for skills in such specialized fields as law, public administration, public relations and publicity, economics, statistics, and governmental procedures. It also calls for the more important abilities to get along with people, influence people, and think in strategic and tactical terms —abilities that have little relation to one's formal training and are often found where one might least expect them to exist.

The full array of needed skills is usually available to large organizations— such as Federal agencies and the national business, farm, and labor organizations—whose purposes extend beyond the legislative process and whose staffs include large numbers of specialized personnel. This is why some of these organizations can conduct the most large-scale and far-flung of legislative campaigns and still show only a small budget allocated directly to legislative work.

Many organizations have separate legislative units. Labor unions and businessmen's associations customarily have "legislative departments" or "legislative representatives." Presidents usually have at least one top assistant specializing in legislative matters, and in recent years the Bureau of the Budget has developed a legislative reference division. Yet specialized units of this type rarely succeed in handling the functions of leadership.[7] Many campaign problems call for the direct attention of the top leadership. Most campaigns require some participation by all branches of an organization. The function of a special legislative unit usually becomes one of advising the top leadership and helping it in the task of mobilizing the rest of the personnel in the organization.

Separate legislative units are sometimes set up outside the formal framework of an organization. In 1939, for example, the American Medical Association collaborated in the creation of the National Physicians Committee, a cam-

[7] For a detailed analysis of the legislative-leadership functions exercised by the Bureau of the Budget and the White House staff, see Richard Neustadt, "Presidential Clearance of Legislation" (unpublished doctoral dissertation, Harvard University, June, 1950).

paign organization whose main objective was to defeat legislative proposals for national health insurance. It would have been beneath the dignity of a professional organization like the A.M.A. to conduct this type of campaign entirely on its own. Subsequently the bulk of the work was turned over to a private publicity firm. In 1946 an opposing organization, the Committee for the Nation's Health, was established to spearhead the campaign on behalf of national health insurance. Previously the campaign work had been handled separately by the congressional sponsors of health-insurance legislation, a few small organizations of doctors who favored this approach to medical service, and the Social Security Board. The Committee for the Nation's Health provided a vehicle for doing a more organized and thorough job than had been done before. Both these organizations had the advantage of being able to concentrate on one single issue in contrast with their affiliated groups, most of which had many irons in the fire. Specialized organizations of this type are of particular value to executive agencies that, for fear of criticism or for lack of funds, prefer to remain behind the scenes rather than conduct active campaigns on their own. For example, during the Eightieth Congress the Committee on the Marshall Plan and the Committee on Peacetime Selective Service played an invaluable role in spearheading the legislative campaign on behalf of the Economic Cooperation Act and the Selective Service Act of 1948.

Specialized campaign organizations can also be hired on a fee basis. Many law firms and public-relations firms provide ready-made organizations for use in legislative campaigns, the former concentrating on bill drafting and the organization of government support, the latter on legislative propaganda and the mobilization of private-group support.

Centralization versus Decentralization. As in any other organizational operation, the leaders of a legislative campaign must always steer a course between one extreme of too little central control and the other of overtight centralization. Some degree of central planning and control is vital. Without it, action taken on one front may totally negate action taken on the other. Without it, objectives cannot be carefully defined, combat skillfully led, or settlements approached in a responsible manner.

Even within organizations that appear to be tightly knit, there is a tendency for those who deal with instruments of power to "go into business for themselves." Unless they can be controlled, they may end up in control. "The Army has lost all control over its chief lobbyist on Capitol Hill, Brig. Gen. Robert Moore," runs a story which illustrates situations that frequently occur. "He has so many friends in Congress that he ignores his bosses in the Pentagon and does as he pleases. When the Army passed over his promotion, Moore's Congressional friends made him a general anyway by writing it into the Appropriation Bill." [8] In many other cases legislative representatives have ig-

[8] Drew Pearson, "Washington Merry-Go-Round," *Washington Post*, Oct. 1, 1951.

nored an organization's views on the vital questions of basic objectives and strategy and have shifted their loyalties to whatever groups seemed to offer the most in personal rewards.

Central control, however, need not be formalized or institutionalized. Informal steering committees and little cabinets will do the job. In fact, they sometimes do the job much more effectively, particularly if formal responsibility is placed publicly on some other group existing on paper only and serving as a "front" to absorb the heat of combat.

The members of a central group are never wise enough to know all the answers or dexterous enough to hold all the strings. In any campaign, large or small, the effort to impose too much direction from a central point merely cuts down the initiative and creative urges of those on the periphery. Von Clausewitz writes:

> The concerted attacks of the divisions and army corps should not be obtained by trying to direct them from a central point. . . . The true method consists in giving each commander of an army corps or division the main direction of his march and in pointing out the enemy as the objective and victory as the goal. . . . We therefore assure the cooperation of all forces by giving each corps a certain amount of independence, by seeing to it that each seeks out the enemy and attacks him with all possible self-sacrifice.[9]

This principle is doubly significant in social combat, where almost every corps whose support is needed has already a certain amount of independence and is bound to assert it, come what will.

Money. While high salaries, sumptuous headquarters, and a large number of employees do not necessarily imply effectiveness, the best campaigns are run by those with enough financial resources to procure the wheels that are needed and keep them greased. A key to the N.A.M.'s effectiveness is the size of its budget. During 1945, according to its financial report for that year, its total income was over $3,600,000. In addition, its members, affiliated bodies, and sympathizers may be regarded as sources of indirect revenue. According to one student of the organization's activities, "the 1936 outdoor advertising campaign for which the Association paid $50,000 would have cost $1,250,000 had not free billboard space been furnished. Similarly, free newspaper space and donated radio time were valued at more than $2,000,000." [10] An accurate estimate of the total financial resources at its command would be impossible to compute. Little help for this is to be obtained from the financial data filed with Congress under the lobby-registration provisions of the Legislative Reorganization Act of 1946. The Act does not provide information on the total budget of pressure groups. It asks only for reports concerning expenditures

[9] Von Clausewitz, *op. cit.*, pp. 25–26.

[10] Alfred S. Cleveland, "NAM: Spokesman for Industry?" *Harvard Business Review,* Vol. 26, No. 3, May, 1948.

for the "principal purpose" of influencing legislation. However broadly or narrowly this may be interpreted (and no accurate definition or standard interpretation has been provided), it can scarcely be construed as covering expenditures for the mobilization of group support and for the more general type of legislative propaganda and pressure activities. In 1949, in a report filed along with a protest against the interpretation that it was required to file at all, the N.A.M. reported legislative expenditures of about $117,000—approximately 1.5 per cent of the organization's total expenditures.[11]

Fund raising is an integral part of any legislative campaign. Pressure groups spend a considerable part of their time in the collection of regular dues and in the solicitation of contributions from members and sympathizers. The most important and most intricate devices for the collection of funds allow for the deduction of contributions from tax payments to the Federal government, thereby providing for an indirect government subsidy. Since contributions to research organizations are tax-exempt, many legislative campaign organizations set up separate affiliates which handle their research functions and can be financed through tax-exempt funds. Others rely on the difficulty of enforcing restrictions on deductions from income taxes [12] and, even though they are on shaky legal ground, succeed in convincing contributors that contributions can be deducted.[13] Business concerns are allowed to deduct any "ordinary and necessary" expenses for doing business. This includes regular dues to pressure-group organizations, as distinguished from special contributions, depending upon the circumstances and the judgment of the Bureau of Internal Revenue and the Board of Tax Appeals. It is also construed to include fees to law firms and public-relations firms, expenditures for institutional advertising, and even for entertainment of government officials.

[11] On Jan. 28, 1948, the N.A.M. brought civil suit against the Attorney General before a special three-judge Federal court in Washington. N.A.M. asked the court to declare sections of the Federal Regulation of Lobbying Act unconstitutional as well as inapplicable to N.A.M. The court declared, on Mar. 17, 1952, that Secs. 303 through 307 of the Act were unconstitutional because (1) the crime established in the Act is not defined with sufficient precision, (2) the Act infringes upon free speech, and (3) the "principal purpose" of a lobby is not sufficiently distinguished from an "incidental purpose." Further congressional action on lobbying will probably await a final ruling by the Supreme Court.

[12] The regulations of the Bureau of Internal Revenue provide that "Sums of money expended for lobbying purposes, the promotion or defeat of legislation, the exploitation of propaganda, including advertising other than trade advertising, and contributions for campaign expenses are not deductible from gross income."

[13] See statement on this contained in a letter from John M. Pratt, Administrator of the National Physicians Committee, to a correspondent who claimed that organization had no right to solicit contributions on the ground that they were deductible from income taxes: "It is generally accepted that 'the proof of the pudding is in the eating.' On this basis, financial contributions to the National Physicians Committee are tax exempt for contributors." "National Health Program," Hearings before the Senate Committee on Education and Labor, 79th Cong., 2d Sess., Apr. 17–24, 1946, p. 884.

The source of funds for legislative campaigns by the executive agencies is the legislation itself. Here the major organizations in the Federal government, particularly the defense establishments, are at a great advantage since their huge budgets allow ample room for the personnel and public-relations expenditures needed in legislative campaigns and include vast amounts of contract expenditures that can be allocated throughout the country in a manner designed to influence individual members of Congress. In 1919 an attempt was made to prohibit legislative campaigns by executive officials. A rider to a deficiency appropriation act provided that

hereafter no part of the money appropriated by this or any other Act shall, in the absence of express authorization by Congress, be used directly or indirectly to pay for any personal service, advertisement, telegram, telephone, letter, printed or written matter, or other device, intended or designed to influence in any manner a Member of Congress to favor or oppose, by vote or otherwise, any legislation or appropriation by Congress, whether before or after the introduction of any bill or resolution proposing such legislation or appropriation; but this shall not prevent officers and employees of the United States from communicating to Members of Congress on the request of any Member or to Congress, through the proper official channels, requests for legislation or appropriations which they deem necessary for the efficient conduct of public business.[14]

It is not difficult to see why there have been no prosecutions or violations of this legislative restriction. It is relatively easy for an executive official to arrange for requests by friendly members of Congress for the submission of formal recommendations for legislative action. The only effect of this restriction has been to impel executive officials to conduct their legislative campaigns cautiously and at times surreptitiously.

THE ORGANIZATION OF GROUP SUPPORT

The very birth of most bills is tied up with group support—in the form either of direct activity to obtain sponsorship or of the sponsors' efforts to estimate potential support. But if they are to make much progress in the legislative process, bills need far stronger backing than is required merely to bring them into being. Just as artillery must be moved into place or an air force readied before an assault upon an enemy stronghold, so group support must be lined up at various points to provide the sources of propaganda and pressure bombardment.

At times, because of a peculiar line-up among contesting forces or because of large previous investments in organizational activities, this support comes more or less automatically. In most cases, however, truly significant support will be forthcoming only if a direct effort is made to develop the most help-

[14] Statutes at Large, Vol. 41, pt. 1, ch. 6, 66th Cong., 1st Sess., 1919.

ful pattern of such support and to cope with a number of difficult problems in organizational relations and management.

Patterns of Support

The initiation of a legislative campaign does not take place in a vacuum. It is merely another incident on the vast battleground of social combat. The initiators operate within an existing alignment of forces. Here stand friends and allies, here a variety of neutrals, here opponents. The obvious steps in developing an effective pattern of support, therefore, are to organize and solidify the support of friends and allies, to win over—or at least prevent opponents from winning—the neutrals, and to split the opposition. Success in these steps, moreover, may transcend the importance of any single bill. The tightening of group lines or a realignment of forces can have profound implications for the outcome of election campaigns, the general course of governmental action, and the direction of economic and cultural change. In fact, a bill or even an entire legislative program is often viewed merely as a means of forging a new coalition to serve in a strategy transcending the legislative process.

Friends and Allies. It might seem that the organization of support among those with interests in common is an easy task. And it is indeed true that unfurling a banner and sounding some clear bugle notes will usually summon a few loyal and eager souls to battle. But to build a solid phalanx around the banner is much harder. Group leaders, particularly the more powerful ones, tend to be busy and overworked. The rank and file tend to be apathetic, even where their most immediate interests are involved.

Considerable effort is needed to build support vertically within a given grouping and keep it at a high level of intensity. Thus a central, and perhaps the crucial, element in the American Medical Association's campaign against national health insurance has been the organization of the medical profession itself in opposition. When the liquor industry is threatened by regulatory legislation, the first step in defense is to line up every company and see that they pass the word down the line to their department heads, factory superintendents, salesmen, suppliers, and customers. When business leaders oppose higher taxes or prolabor legislation, the same pattern is developed on a larger scale. In conducting their campaign against the enactment of the Taft-Hartley Act, and subsequently for its repeal, the national leaders of organized labor spent a large part of their resources whipping up intense resentment against the legislation on the part of local officials, shop stewards, and rank and file members. In developing the campaign for the Brannan Plan, one of the big problems faced by Secretary of Agriculture Charles Brannan was the mustering of support by bureau officials and regional office personnel within the Department of Agriculture itself.

The horizontal organization of support among friendly groups also calls for persistent effort. Common interests must be discovered, nourished, and exploited. Otherwise they cannot lead to common action. One of the chief functions of the "peak" organizations in the business community is to develop unified action among the thousands of separate business groupings. The key to effective campaigning by a labor movement which is organizationally divided is the development of broad support among the rival labor organizations for identical objectives. In the campaign which resulted in the passage of the Employment Act of 1946, "the lining up of a strong phalanx of political forces was considered to be politically necessary and in truth it is doubtful if S. 380 would ever have passed, even in modified form, without active support of these liberal organizations." [15] The lining-up process was not limited to private organizations. The executive agencies of the Government and both houses of Congress were scoured from top to bottom to discover new sources of strength for the full-employment phalanx. In contrast, the legislative campaign for a Fair Employment Practices Commission has always suffered from an inability to mobilize sufficient support among Negro organizations themselves, the very groups with the largest stake in the fair-employment program.

Negro organizations, notwithstanding the very considerable contributions of some of the groups discussed, fell short of making a contribution to the movement which was commensurate with their organizational strength and their vital stake in the issue. Rivalry for leadership among Negroes, organizational and ideological struggles, general lack of faith in the National Council for a Permanent FEPC, and distrust of its motives split and debilitated Negro strength. Some small solace can be found in the fact that important Negro groups have rarely been successfully united and activated in political movements requiring extended planning and work. Still FEPC offered a better than average opportunity for united action which was not capitalized upon.[16]

Neutrals. A difficult dilemma is always faced by those who attempt to win friends among groups who would otherwise be neutral. On the one hand, new allies may mean added strength against opponents. On the other hand, the broader one's support becomes, the less one can get depth of agreement and the more one must compromise. The recruitment of support from some one group may create difficult tensions among other supporters and may even alienate them completely. A point usually is reached where additional support is not worth either the additional effort needed or the repercussions that might result. There is, therefore, a principle of marginal utility that cannot be

[15] Stephen K. Bailey, "Congress Makes a Law" (New York: Columbia University Press, 1949), p. 76.

[16] Louis Coleridge Kesselman, "The Social Politics of FEPC" (Chapel Hill, N.C.: University of North Carolina Press, 1948), p. 224.

ignored. The emphasis must be on selectivity and upon a careful weighing of the price to be paid against the benefits that might be received.

There is a tendency among most groups to aim at sources of support that will put them in a "middle-of-the-road" position. This is viewed as a means of distinguishing them from "extremists" on both sides, of putting them in a balance-of-power position, and of facilitating future moves toward developing support on either side. Even those groups that appear to be located at the ultimate extreme have the same interest in balance. The theoreticians of Communist parties, for example, have always inveighed against the twin dangers of "rightist opportunism" and "infantile leftism." This illustrates the barrenness of ranging groups arbitrarily on a one-dimensional line from "right" to "left" —even if, as has been at times suggested, the straight line is transformed into a circle. The infinite variety of in-between positions can be illustrated only by depicting groups as deployed over the length and breadth of a field.

There is a marked tendency toward neutrality and inactivity on the part of groups which are not directly affected by a given issue. Schattschneider has dealt with this tendency by a useful distinction between primary interests and secondary interests. He refers to primary interests as "resolute minorities . . . surrounded by vast marginal aggregates whose impulses to action were almost never able to formulate themselves. The politics of the tariff are apparently predicated on the belief that slumbering and smouldering interests would remain passive while a few men who knew what they wanted acted with decision." [17] The extent to which secondary interests can be activated obviously depends largely upon the ability of primary interests to prod them out of their slumber.

The loose alliances running under the name of national political parties make a special point of staying neutral on the bulk of legislative issues. Their interest in mobilizing a majority vote in national elections makes them wary of taking any position that might antagonize influential groups. The internal logic of a legislative campaign, however, leads the campaigners to an effort to win the support of both parties. Before the 1948 party conventions, for example, the Committee for the Nation's Health set itself the task of committing "both political parties to the insurance principle as the basis of major health legislation." To achieve this objective they saw to it that the case for the health-insurance principle was presented to President Truman and other leaders of the Democratic party, to leading liberals in the Republican party, and to the platform-drafting committees of the Republican and Democratic parties in 1948. While this objective was not attained before the 1948 election, it is interesting to note that the farm organizations, in contrast, succeeded in obtaining almost identical commitments in the platforms of both parties.

[17] Schattschneider, *op. cit.*, p. 122.

Interestingly enough, the effort to build a bipartisan support is not inconsistent with efforts to develop a partisan alignment at the same time. Supporters of the original full-employment bill proclaimed it a nonpartisan measure and bid for, and partially obtained, the support of Republicans. Yet they also attempted to make it a party issue among Democrats, accusing Democratic opponents of disloyalty to the party.

Splitting the Opposition. Divide and conquer is a time-honored maxim of social combat. In its campaign on behalf of the Taft-Hartley Act, business leaders attempted to divide the labor movement's drive against the Act by exempting railway labor organizations from many of its provisions hoping thereby to split off the railway labor unions. The major tactic in the campaign for the Brannan Plan was to divide the American Farm Bureau Federation and the National Grange by winning over and activating a number of favorably disposed state organizations within these two major farm groups. The supporters of the original Full Employment Bill made a special point of trying to split the business opposition to the legislation. "The qualified support of a small number of influential businessmen like Beardsley Ruml and Ralph E. Flanders made it possible for the sponsors of the bill to claim that '. . . small businessmen want full employment. . . . Enlightened big businessmen want full employment.' " [18] No attempt was made to win business support generally. This would have been regarded as a waste of time. In fact, it was felt that a key to splitting the business opposition was to carefully identify that section of business leadership which was the main enemy of the legislation and to concentrate a heavy attack upon them.[19]

The difficulties of splitting a business opposition have been demonstrated on many occasions. Marriner Eccles made the effort in connection with the Banking Act of 1935. "It seemed for a while that a policy of concessions as a price of reducing banker opposition would pay off, but it turned out that the 5-man committee and the conciliatory Executive Council of the ABA were generals without troops. They could not carry the majority of the nation's bankers with them." [20]

A representative of independent oil producers who testified before a congressional committee on the tariff told of the difficulties he found in getting business executives to take an "independent" position:

I want to say to you that most of the executives of the so-called middle-sized companies and some of the almost major class, even though they are independents, supposed to be independent companies, are afraid to espouse this cause. They are intimidated. They are in favor of a tariff but won't come out in the open. They assured me privately that they are in favor of it but they are afraid of the big boys.

[18] Bailey, *op. cit.*, p. 76.
[19] *Ibid.*, p. 77.
[20] Marriner Eccles, "Beckoning Frontiers" (New York: Knopf, 1951), pp. 201–202.

They cannot go back to New York and borrow the money that they need for developing their properties and carry on their business. At least they think they cannot and are afraid to talk.[21]

Government organization itself provides a splendid opportunity for the divide-and-conquer strategy. Any private organization opposing a legislative proposal originating in an executive agency inevitably tries either to promote interagency or intra-agency squabbles or to create an executive-congressional conflict. The former provides a springboard for bewailing "executive confusion," the latter arousing indignation in Congress toward "executive dictatorship." The ease with which this is so often accomplished arises from the divergent interests underlying governmental activities and is a basic reason why executive officials, even Presidents, often find it impossible to obtain unified agency support for a legislative proposal. The Presidential task of organizing broad interagency support for a legislative program is just as much a three-in-one job of organizing friends, winning over neutrals, and splitting the opposition as any similar task among nongovernmental groups.

The greatest of all opportunities for a divide-and-conquer strategy lies within the political parties. Here one deals with aggregations supported by interests even more divergent than those behind government agencies. Despite abstract talk about the two-party system and the importance of party responsibility, when it comes down to specific issues and campaigns, nobody really wants rigid party lines. A President, for example, who is trying to unify his own party must necessarily try to divide the opposing party. Hence party conflict in the legislative arena becomes a matter of coalition strategy. Both Franklin Roosevelt and Truman suffered from the fact that the opponents to their legislative programs succeeded in maintaining a deep split within the Democratic party ranks. Yet they themselves, while trying to heal this split, were always eagerly looking for sources of support within the Republican party.

Types of Groups. A campaign based upon the support of executive agencies only or that of private organizations only usually cannot go very far. The more effective combinations and coalitions are those bringing together all types of groups—private organizations, political parties or factions, members of Congress, the executive branch, and the judiciary. An interesting example is the National Rivers and Harbors Congress, a private organization which sparkplugs the annual legislative campaign for rivers and harbors appropriations. This organization, according to its own literature, "is the country's oldest and largest water organization and occupies semi-official status by reason of its close liaison with the governmental agencies, legislative and executive, responsible for public works." Its president and most important officials are members of Congress, both Democrats and Republicans, with strategic positions

---

[21] United States Senate Lobby Investigation Hearings, 71st Cong., 2d Sess., Part 7, p. 3110.

on the legislative committees handling rivers and harbors projects. The closest possible cooperation with officers of the Army Corps of Engineers serves as a means of bringing together representatives of power companies, contractors, coal operators, oil interests, landowners, and railroads. Which of these participants in the rivers and harbors coalition pull the strings and which are the puppets is not only an irreverent question but an irrelevant one. They all pull strings and they all use one another.

Nor can a powerful pattern of support be built if overattention is given only to large and powerful organizations. Small groups of minor importance if operating by themselves can make a major contribution to a legislative campaign. Often they may turn out to be the only ones able to develop a special type of propaganda or to apply pressure on someone in a strategic position. Similarly, individuals who occupy no strategic position in their own right may provide access or entree to individuals and groups of considerable power. Hence, every lobbyist worth his pay attempts to win friends among the lower-level employees, including secretaries and clerks, in private organizations and government agencies.

Organizational Problems

Mixing Ingredients. In making a cake, everything can go wrong if the ingredients are mixed in the wrong order. The same principle applies to the far more difficult task of social engineering involved in organizing mass pressures into a bloc capable of obtaining a given objective on Capitol Hill. On the labor front, for example, it is the practice to seek A.F.L. support before C.I.O. support, for reasons that while the C.I.O. is not so much afraid of the A.F.L. measures, the A.F.L. will shy away from any measures which they regard as sponsored by their energetic rival.[22]

As a corollary to this principle, it sometimes becomes essential to avoid bringing all the supporters of a given legislative objective into close contact with one another. If strange bedfellows become an essential of an effective campaign, an important never-ending problem arises to prevent all the occupants from knowing who else is in the bed. Thus the broad support for the Marshall Plan could hardly have held together if the more radical labor supporters of the proposal had realized how much support it enjoyed on the part of conservative bankers and businessmen. In fact, one of the devices in developing labor support for the Marshall Plan was to build up a bogeyman of conservative opposition.

Limited-purpose Organizations. Every organization has certain primary objectives. If it strays too far afield, there is always a danger it will spread itself

[22] Bailey, *op. cit.*, p. 80.

too thin. The Railway Labor Executives Association, for example, although sympathetic toward the majority of the campaigns waged by organized labor, has an established policy of sticking to its own knitting, campaigning only for those legislative measures that are of the most direct and immediate concern to the railroad workers it represents. It gives sympathy to its labor-union colleagues, but rarely active support.

To win over limited-purpose organizations of this type to a legislative coalition calls not only for high-class salesmanship but also for the shaping of one's legislative objectives to appeal more directly to the organizations whose support is desired. Mutual aims must be hammered out and divergent objectives must be compromised.

Formalization of Support. The formalization of an organization's support also presents a problem. In some cases, the executive board or the legislative representative is given wide discretion with respect to the formation of legislative alliances. In other cases, an organization's support for a legislative campaign can be obtained only through formal action by its convention or by a referendum of its total membership.

Often special subsidiary campaigns are needed to win formal support. In the early stages of the campaign for the Full Employment Bill, for instance, considerable hostility toward the measure was shown by key officials in the C.I.O. national office—despite the bill's closeness to major objectives of organized labor. If the matter had been left in the hands of these hostile officials, C.I.O. support might never have been forthcoming, and the effort to organize liberal support might have ended in frustration. The sponsors of the legislation dealt with this problem by sending the bill with explanatory material to a complete list of individual C.I.O. unions, state-industrial-union councils, and regional directors. The enthusiastic responses to this communication lit a hot fire under the national leaders who slowly and somewhat reluctantly found seats on the band wagon.

Special Machinery. To bring groups together, new machinery is often needed. Where formal support by key groups is impossible or untimely, unofficial support often can be obtained by recruiting group leaders as sponsors or officers of new organizations. Some of these are merely paper organizations which are expected, like Joshua's army before the walls of Jericho, to make enough noise and commotion to convince people that a great army is on the march. Others are designed to organize previously unorganized areas or to tap hitherto unexploited sources of funds. Examples of these are the National Foundation of Home and Property Owners which was established to collaborate in obtaining the legislative objectives of the National Association of Real Estate Boards and the National Association of Home Builders. According to one publicist:

The Foundation is a new catch-all group sired by NAREB to recruit people of its turn of mind who are not in the business of buying and selling real estate. Its membership partly duplicates the rolls of established real estate organizations but the Foundation will admit anybody who holds clear title to a chicken coop or cemetery lot.[23]

Another example is the National Council for Permanent FEPC. This group performed services which no other organization interested in FEPC legislation could possibly handle.[24]

Sometimes special machinery is needed not so much to bring groups together or to organize campaigns as to serve as a clearinghouse for information on the progress of certain measures. The cooperation of church lobbies with other groups, for example, "is facilitated by clearing-house organizations, such as International Legislation Information Service, and Civil Liberties Clearing House." The last-named serves about 75 "non-Communist national organizations interested in the protection and fostering of our civil liberties." [25]

Devices that are particularly appropriate for use by executive agencies are the convening of *ad hoc* conferences and the formation of advisory committees. In May, 1948, with the approval of President Truman, the Federal Security Agency convened a "National Health Assembly" in Washington, D.C. This assembly brought more than 800 representatives of organized groups, including the professional medical organizations, behind every point in the Administration's health program, except national health insurance.

One of the most elaborate advisory committee arrangements, for exclusively legislative purposes, was the one created by the War Department as part of its campaign for peacetime universal military training. Representative Arthur Miller of Nebraska, in a critical speech, has described this effort as follows:

It would seem the military has established a so-called Army Advisory Committee which has for its goal the establishing of these committees in at least 600 representative communities, with an approximate membership of 9,000 civilians. The purpose of these advisory committees, according to a memo signed by Col. James Pierce, issued August 26, 1946, was "preparing a favorable reception for Army policy and discovering the things that hamper Army policy; to advise the Army on all community attitudes which are based on adverse reactions to acts, facts, and policies of the Army; to provide channels for the dissemination of facts and policies of the Army in a manner so that the public will understand and be completely informed." [26]

[23] Alexander L. Crosby, "The Real Estate Lobby," *The American Mercury,* March, 1947, p. 288.

[24] Kesselman, *op. cit.,* pp. 66–67.

[25] Luke Ebersole, "Church Lobbying in the Nation's Capital" (New York: Macmillan, 1951), p. 99.

[26] *Congressional Record,* 80th Cong., 2d Sess., Jan. 19, 1948, p. 319.

Advisory committees have also been used on occasion directly by members of Congress. Thus, advisory committees have been set up by the House Ways and Means Committee on revenue legislation, by the Senate's Finance Committee on social-security legislation, and by the Senate Interstate Commerce Committee on basing-point legislation. In most of these cases the purpose has been dual—to assist in the formulation of a program, and to provide an organizing center for the development of support.

Chapter 13

PROPAGANDA AND PRESSURE

THIS CHAPTER will discuss how the dissemination of propaganda and the application of pressure become tools for the campaign leaders in the achievement of group support and of legislative decisions.

THE DISSEMINATION OF PROPAGANDA

Propaganda acquired its bad reputation in this country during the 1920's when countless writers and scholars exposed the lies which the propaganda machines of both sides disseminated throughout World War I. In addition, "propaganda" is disliked in a democratic society because people feel naïvely that their decisions should be made by themselves and not by someone else. The feeling is naïve because decisions result from past experiences, many of which are usually culturally determined; but it is certainly in keeping with the belief of our society that man, if he only will, can shape his own destiny.[1]

Propaganda is habitually used to refer to *someone else's* efforts to win favorable opinion. One's own efforts are described in terms of "education." Propaganda connotes deception or distortion, as contrasted with "information."

In the sense that propaganda may be defined as an effort to persuade people to favor certain objectives or do certain things, there is no reason why it should necessarily have a derogatory connotation. All the participants in the legislative struggle, from the Catholic church to the Communist party, engage in propagandistic endeavors. Without it they would be at a disadvantage in the organization of group support or the application of pressure. There is effective propaganda and ineffective propaganda. There is honest and deceitful propaganda. There are those who command vast propaganda resources for producing propaganda and those whose output is very meager. Whether specific propaganda activities are judged "good" or "bad" depends on many types of value judgments. The very drafting of legislative measures is part of the propaganda process, although only a small part. The major concern of legislative propagandists is to develop both indirect and direct methods of persua-

[1] Leonard W. Doob, "Public Opinion and Propaganda" (New York: Holt, 1948), p. 242.

sion, to fashion a convincing case, and to disseminate it through the various media of communication.

The Indirect and the Direct

When one thinks of legislative propaganda there inevitably comes to mind such direct operations as the full-page ads, radio orations, and illustrated pamphlets used to defend or attack a pending bill. There are, however, many degrees of direction and indirection in the field of propaganda. Probably the most effective legislative propaganda is the kind which never mentions any specific issue.

Through the considered use of word-symbols over a couple of generations; through the attention paid by business and big commercial agriculture to rural opinion; through the concerted drive of business organizations to convince the public-at-large that "What is good for business is good for America," the conservative pressures helped to shape the prepossessions which a majority of our national legislators brought with them to the Seventy-ninth Congress. This educational campaign pays enormous dividends.[2]

Goodwill broadcasts by labor, church, and business organizations, "institutional advertising" by large companies,[3] the emphasis upon one or another set of values in schools and churches—all these are of indirect propaganda utility.

Nor is this utility accidental. Bailey refers to the "considered use" of word symbols. Church and school leaders often consciously attempt to influence people's attitudes in certain broad directions. The strategic importance of indirect propaganda can be inferred from the care with which various organizations attempt to commandeer church and school channels. The National Association of Manufacturers, for example, sends to clergymen of all faiths, as well as to seminaries, a regular publication entitled "Understanding." Its subtitle is "A Publication Devoted to Cooperation between Clergymen and Businessmen." It has also organized a nationwide schedule of "Business-Industry-Education days."

The B-I-E project is based on having one of the familiar "teacher institute" days set by a community's education officials, but instead of attending an "institute" the teachers tour local business companies in groups, see the city's industry at work, hear executives explain company objectives and problems at luncheon, then all dine

[2] Stephen K. Bailey, "Congress Makes a Law" (New York: Columbia University Press, 1949), p. 149.

[3] "Some of the institutional commercials emitted by large manufacturers like the Ford Motor Company are devoted much less to their products than they are to heaping praise upon the over-all wisdom of management, of private ownership, and of our present economic system." Doob, op. cit., p. 477.

together to listen while some of the industrial leaders review the benefits of the American free enterprise system to community and nation.[4]

It is activities of this sort that lay the groundwork for *direct* propaganda on *specific* measures. Indirect propaganda provokes less sales resistance than persuasive efforts of a more specific character. Much direct propaganda, on the other hand, does little more than provide the on-hand supply of ammunition for use by those who already have been made ideologically receptive as a result of many years of influence by indirect propaganda.

Often, the alertness of various powerful groups to the impact of indirect propaganda has led them into forceful action against literature which they regard as potentially dangerous. According to Schriftgiesser, the Pennsylvania Society for the Encouragement of Manufactures and the Mechanic Arts, during the tariff battles of the 1820's, tried to advance the cause of protectionism by "a campaign to remove the textbooks of Adam Smith and J. B. Say, his French disciple, from the schools and colleges, and even hired a German propagandist and economist, one Friedrich List, to write a substitute for these subversive texts." [5] Similar campaigns by business groups have not been unknown in subsequent years—although the object of more recent purge efforts has been literature that departs from the now hallowed concepts of Adam Smith.

In some cases, direct propaganda is almost entirely dispensed with or else directed in a quiet fashion toward only a few carefully selected groups. During the Seventy-ninth Congress the Trademark Act was put through with no public hearings and hardly a word of comment in the press with the exception of certain business and legal publications. General publicity would have militated against it. This method also was used with bills to exempt railroads and newspapers from antitrust laws. By contrast, occasionally a direct propaganda campaign is developed loudly on behalf of one measure to divert attention from simultaneous efforts to slide through a "sleeper" bill. Thus, during the last years of World War II, a vociferous public attack was conducted by business organizations against the existing war-contract-renegotiation legislation. While administration officials and liberal groups ran to the defense of contract renegotiation, the business groups very quietly succeeded in obtaining the enactment of unpropagandized tax legislation that meant far more to them than any possible changes in contract renegotiation.

Building One's Case

Interests. The secret of effective propaganda is the ability to make a case in terms of the interests of those whom one wants to persuade. This means

---

[4] *N.A.M. News,* Feb. 4, 1950, p. 7.

[5] Karl Schriftgiesser, "The Lobbyists" (Boston: Little, Brown, 1951), p. 7.

sensing what really interests people as contrasted with what someone thinks these "true interests" are or should be. The propagandist who proceeds on the assumption that people can be sold a program that clashes with what they strongly regard as their direct and immediate interest succeeds in little more than deluding himself.

In appealing to the interests of any group, a basic problem is *to demonstrate* that a given legislative proposal will really serve the group's interests. Pure and simple assertion that it will do so will not convince all the people all the time. Many will be bound to assert the contrary. Furthermore, since many legislative proposals are likely to have bad effects as well as good effects, it is necessary to demonstrate that the former are outweighed by the latter. Hence, a full bill of particulars is usually necessary—not because it will be an important or even a major part of a propaganda campaign, but because without it the inevitable criticisms cannot be effectively anticipated and because some people in every group insist upon grubbing into the details. A full bill of particulars usually presents the expected effects of the proposal if it is enacted, discusses alternative approaches, and indicates the precise benefits that might be obtained.

Almost every successful propaganda effort of a major character will contain carefully slanted appeals to a large variety of groups. "Something in it for everyone" is a motto that applies to legislative propaganda as well as to political platforms. At times, of course, separate appeals to divergent interests must be handled separately. Thus, a campaigner for public power may address a business organization one evening on the value of public power to American businessmen and the next evening address a labor or consumer audience on its value as a bulwark against predatory private-business interests.

Similarly, a bill which has been worked out with the bankers and whose original title indicated that its purpose was "to relieve the banks" can be taken by a Franklin D. Roosevelt (as actually happened) and slanted toward a much larger group by calling it a bill to set up a Home Owners' Loan Corporation.

In an era of mass communication, however, it is dangerous to assume that what is said to one group may not be heard by another. Hence, it becomes essential to develop a propaganda approach that has direct appeal to people with divergent interests. Here there is an obvious dilemma: the more one appeals directly to different groups in terms of their immediate interest, the greater is the danger that one's language is meaningless or offensive to some other groups. The favored device for escaping through the horns of this dilemma is to emphasize a broadly desirable objective, such as Recovery or National Security, and de-emphasize the means of attaining the objective. People who will fight to the bitter end among themselves about method can often be united on objectives. Long-range or abstract conceptions, as indicated in subsequent sections of this chapter, can be particularly exciting—so long as they skirt the risk of being so fantastic as to look like "pie in the sky."

The Public Interest. One of the major elements in the art of legislative propaganda is the development and presentation of arguments to the effect that a given point of view will advance "the public interest." Roy Blough, in describing testimony given before congressional committees on tax legislation, observes:

> The purpose of arguments is to persuade the policy-maker that the public interest would be promoted by the adoption of a tax proposal which would financially benefit its advocates. . . . When the witness for a taxpayer interest group appears at hearings before the Congressional Taxing Committee, he does not merely say, and often does not say at all: "Please adopt our proposal because it would benefit us." It is always assumed that each witness thinks he and his group would be benefited by the action he proposes. The argument is usually on a high plane of public welfare. The witness may indeed point out that his industry is subject to an unusual hardship, but even in this case the testimony usually goes beyond the private benefit to consider the public interest. Witnesses do not argue that their proposals would benefit personally the members of the committee, except as these are part of a much larger general group.[6]

Thus, many of the most crucial legislative debates are fought out verbally at the level of conflicting conceptions of the public welfare. If each party to the conflict feels sincerely that his conception of the public interest is sound and that the opposition viewpoint really serves a "narrow interest" or "vested interest," this demonstrates not the accuracy of his observation but rather the intensity with which he adheres to his own conception of the public interest. Mere assertion is never sufficient. A good case on the public-interest aspect of any proposal calls for a full rationale. Blough has made an excellent analysis of the rather limited number of thought patterns that are used in developing rationales on behalf of tax legislation by reducing "public-interest" arguments on taxes to the following 10 propositions: (1) The proposal will increase (decrease) revenue; (2) The proposal will enlarge (diminish) tax fairness; (3) The proposal will promote (destroy) a high and stable level of production and employment; (4) The proposal will encourage (discourage) an important industry or business group; (5) The proposal will repress (promote) socially undesirable consumption; (6) The proposal will improve (make worse) the distribution of wealth and income; (7) The proposal can readily be (cannot be) administered in a complete and uniform manner; (8) The proposal will simplify (complicate) the compliance problems of taxpayers; (9) The proposal will increase (decrease) a "wholesome" tax consciousness; and

[6] Roy Blough, "The Argument Phase of Taxpayer Politics," *University of Chicago Law Review*, Vol. 17, No. 4, Summer, 1950, pp. 605–606.

(10) The proposal will enlarge (contract) the rights and financial independence of the states.[7]

When arguments such as these—which could well be paralleled by similar thought patterns in other fields—are interlarded with copious statistics, quotations from authority, and statements of personal experience, they can be impressive indeed.

Goals, Ideals, Principles. A striking example of long-range goals developed in this context is contained in "The Nation's Health—a Ten-year Program," [8] prepared by the Federal Security Agency's National Health Assembly. This report proposes the following goals:

"1. Twenty years of life added to the average expectancy of individuals at birth

"2. Conquest of certain disastrous epidemics, which have been virtually eliminated as a threat to health in this country

"3. A generation of stronger, better-fed children; and a larger body of knowledge on the child—his physical, mental, and social development—from before birth to the age of six than we have about any other period of human life

"4. A vast storehouse of knowledge about the prevention and treatment of diseases

"5. A sharp reduction in the death tolls from many diseases that were high on the mortality lists of the past"

This is language that everybody can understand. It affects one's life, livelihood, and expectation of survival. It provides a favorable background of ideals within which to propose and debate specific measures to build hospitals, medical centers, train doctors, dentists, and nurses, extend medical research, and provide improved methods of payment for medical care.

In President Truman's Economic Reports to Congress long-range goals of tremendous propaganda value have often been set forth. One of the best illustrations is found in the January, 1950, Report:

Within five years we can achieve an annual output in excess of 300 billion dollars. . . . Expansion to a 300 billion dollar economy within five years would place 30 to 45 billion dollars more per year in the hands of consumers for buying the needs and comforts of life. It would provide opportunity for profitable business investment in plant, equipment, and housing which might run 3 to 6 billion dollars per year above the 1949 level. It would enable farmers to sell about 10 per cent more food for domestic consumption.[9]

Few things move people so deeply as their ideals. Through the ages millions of men and women have died in struggles for ideals—ideals that are often

[7] *Ibid.*, pp. 606–610.

[8] A report to the President by Oscar R. Ewing, Federal Security Administrator (Government Printing Office, September, 1948).

[9] Economic Report to Congress, January, 1950, pp. 6–7.

beyond their understanding and more often unattainable during their lifetime. The greatest of all campaigns are those in which both leaders and followers would sacrifice themselves on behalf of an ideal which they consider greater than themselves. This does not mean that self-interest and ideals are incompatible or contradictory. As Merriam has pointed out, "sacrifice is indeed a form of personal interest" [10] and, at times, those personal interests that are of overwhelming weight are the ones that flow from deep inner frustration, resentment, and hatred.

Nothing attracts people's thinking processes more than a principle. When real-estate propagandists spoke out for the quick removal of rent controls after World War II, they did not say: "Decontrol is needed so that the people I represent can have more money with which to buy more luxuries for themselves and their families and enhance their feelings of prestige and power." They talked rather in terms of abstract principles of housing economics, principles which learned minds labored arduously to devise. A "principle" has a double advantage. On the one hand, it conceals or blurs the direct interests of the propagandists. On the other hand, by stating the case in general terms, it suggests great potentialities of benefit to those on the periphery whose support is being sought. If the general principle advanced under certain conditions should subsequently have implications detrimental to one's own interests, it can then be turned upside down, put on the shelf for use at some later date, or reinterpreted to meet new conditions.

Thus, in the early day of the Republic, business interests propagandized on behalf of a strong central government. But when political conditions changed and when it became evident that a strong central government threatened their interests, they somersaulted completely and became advocates of states' rights. In times of depression, Keynesian economists have developed the principle that public expenditures, particularly for public works, should be varied upward and downward to compensate for the fluctuations in the business cycle.[11] Conservative interests tend to oppose this principle when it means larger expenditures but to leap warmly to its support in times of prosperity when it holds forth the hope of lower expenditures. Liberals tend to desert it when it would lead to a reduction in public spending for social purposes which they value highly.

Symbols. The case for a bill, program, or point of view can be completely lost if presented in terms of a multitude of separate statements. Ideals and principles themselves are sometimes excessively complex. The best way to

[10] Charles Merriam, "Political Power" (New York: McGraw-Hill, 1934), p. 246.

[11] Depending upon their social values, group allegiances, and specialized professional interests, competent and intelligent economists will discuss this principle in many sharply divergent fashions. "Objectively correct" views on public policy aspects of economics, it becomes evident, are a delusion. See this author's review of "The 1950's Come First," *American Political Science Review,* Vol. 45, September, 1951, pp. 867–874.

wrap up many facts and emotions in one package and to make ideals and principles glow with meaning is through the use of symbolism. Contestants in the social struggle have therefore invested heavily in the development of symbols.[12] During the nineteenth century the symbol used most often in attacking someone else's legislative objectives was "unconstitutional." Although still used, this symbol has lost much of its force. Much more effective is the stigma in such terms as "communistic," "socialistic," "red," "radical," "alien," or "un-American."

In buttressing his demands for larger subsidies for silver, one of the Senate leaders of the "Silver Bloc" offered the following alternative to the country: "The Nation must adopt bimetallism or face bolshevism." [13] In attacking the original Full Employment Bill, Merwin K. Hart, president of the National Economic Council, charged that "The real origin of this bill is found in the Constitution of the Union of Soviet Socialist Republics, which states (Art. 118) that its citizens have 'the right to work,' that is, are guaranteed the right to employment and payment for their work in accordance with its quantity and quality." [14] The proponents of the measure, in referring to their opposition, often replied along the following lines: "Those who argue that continuing full employment means regimentation are themselves sowing the seeds of economic and political revolution. No hostile foreign agent could do more to wreck the fabric of our society than to tell our people that unemployment is the price we pay for free enterprise." [15]

Other negative symbols are "political" and "partisan," terms that seem most frequently used by partisan politicians themselves in attacks upon the programs of those with whom they disagree. "Objective," "nonpartisan," and "scientific" are terms used just as frequently—and usually interchangeably—by all sides. These latter symbols appeal deeply to everyone's dream that somewhere in this world of endless struggle and shifting values can be found a firm source of authority. "Impartial experts" are used by all sides in a legislative controversy. One of the best of all propaganda devices is to set up a board composed of "men of unimpeachable integrity and objectivity whose disinterested views will command the respect of everyone." During World

[12] The use of the symbols "civilian control" and "military control" in the conflict over the Atomic Energy Act of 1946, for example, has been carefully analyzed by one of the participants in the struggle. Byron Miller, "A Law Is Passed—The Atomic Energy Act of 1946" *University of Chicago Law Review*, Vol. 15, No. 4, Summer, 1948, pp. 817–819. See also James R. Newman and Byron S. Miller, "The Control of Atomic Energy" (New York: McGraw-Hill, 1948).

[13] Allen Seymour Everest, "Morgenthau, the New Deal and Silver" (New York: King's Crown Press, Columbia University Press, 1950), p. 15.

[14] "Full Employment Act of 1945," Hearings before a subcommittee of the Senate Committee on Banking and Currency, 79th Cong., 1st Sess., p. 890.

[15] "Assuring Full Employment in a Free Competitive Economy," report from the Senate Committee on Banking and Currency, 79th Cong., 1st Sess., S. Rept. 583, p. 22.

War II Bernard Baruch served as a one-man board of this type and the famous Baruch Reports on rubber and postwar adjustment were of inestimable propaganda value to the Roosevelt Administration. In the battle over the Atomic Energy Act of 1946 the atomic scientists were a major factor. "Those Men Who Made the Bomb . . . were awesome creatures indeed to have built the bomb." The fact that few people could understand what they were talking about made them all the more formidable.

When the Council of Economic Advisers was established, its members often reiterated the thesis that they were objective and professional economists.

There are important values to be derived from having an independent group of economists in a position of high visibility in the government. One result of this posi-tion is a dramatic impact on the public, the Congress, and administrators, of the importance of economics as such, and of economic stabilization and growth.[16]

The great bulk of all legislative measures is wrapped up in such symbols as "our democratic institutions," "the American way of life," "national inter-est," "public interest," "our great traditions," "the ideals for which our fa-thers died," "national unity," "peace," and "national defense." Some groups concentrate on building up special symbols. The N.A.M. has made extensive use of the phrase, "the American individual-enterprise system," or in abbre-viated form, "free enterprise." New Deal propaganda during the period before World War II made similar use of the term "the forgotten man." Later Henry Wallace tried—not too successfully—to develop the symbol of "the common man" and "the century of the common man."

The propagandists are also careful to use symbols of the most timely char-acter. Before Pearl Harbor, Congress was flooded with bills, enactment of which, it was claimed, would build the first line of defense. The first line of defense ranged, it seemed, from recreation and maternity care to the Coast Guard and the FBI. Toward the end of the war, a customary rubric was "post-war planning." When there was wide expectation of serious postwar unem-ployment, the prevention of unemployment or the provision of full employ-ment was a customary angle. When serious unemployment failed to materialize and instead rising prices became the major domestic problem in the postwar period, almost all economic measures were portrayed as weapons in the fight against inflation.

A bill that itself has recently become law can serve as a symbol to back up future legislation. Thus the major case in selling the British Loan to the American public was that it was needed to make a success of the previously

[16] Roy Blough, "Political and Administrative Requisites for Achieving Economic Sta-bility" (paper presented at American Economic Association, Hotel Commodore, New York City, Dec. 28, 1949).

approved Bretton Woods International Monetary Agreement. In turn, a major part of the case for the Marshall Plan was its value in making the British Loan a success. And part of the case for the Point IV Program of American aid to underdeveloped countries was that it was needed to carry out the objectives of the Marshall Plan.

It is the practice for one group to appropriate the symbols of its opponents. Measures promoted by labor groups and measures calling for greater Federal intervention in the private economy are often described as "promoting free enterprise." Antilabor measures are described as helping to "balance the budget." Huey Long was once quoted as saying, "If fascism ever comes to America, it will come in the name of Democracy." This might well be paraphrased by suggesting that if socialism ever comes to America, it will come in the name of promoting private enterprise. The obvious danger in using the symbols of the opposition, of course, is the possibility that the stolen symbols may sink the stealer.

Some measures, of course, almost defy application of a simple symbol to them. The proposal for a Missouri Valley Authority, for example, has multiple objectives: conservation, irrigation, flood control, power, and navigation. Realizing the difficulty the average person has in grasping so many separate ideas, the propagandists on behalf of this measure have concentrated on trying to sell the administrative concept of a single Federal planning agency located in the Missouri Valley itself. They have attempted to fuse substantive content into this essentially abstract idea, heralding the valley authority as a new form of decentralization that will help democratize American government. Its opponents, in turn, have charged that Federal valley authorities are but another step in the aggrandizement of the Federal bureaucracy and the destruction of local initiative. Both sides put the case in rather abstract terms. More specific symbols were used in the battle over the Taft-Hartley Labor-Management Relations Act of 1948. Organized labor pitched its general propaganda campaign on the theme that it was a "slave-labor bill." In turn, the business organizations behind the Act described it as a measure to combat "labor monopoly."

Defense and Attack. A portion of the time spent in legislative campaign propaganda is always devoted to answering the "unfounded attacks" and "distortions" of opponents. Some campaigners prefer not to answer attacks directly but to do it without making a positive reference to the specific attack. A favorite device is to have the reply emanate from a presumably disinterested source. But just as in warfare, the best method of defense is attack. In the fight for the original Full Employment Bill the offensive was taken at the outset by Senator Murray's testimony before the Senate Banking and Currency Committee linking the opposition to "a small but vocal minority who are against the full employment bill because they are against full employment." [17] This was in sharp contrast to the band-wagon approach, previously taken by most friends of the bill, that "everybody is for full employment." It immediately put the opponents of the bill on the defensive, forced them in self-protection to endorse the objectives of the measure, and gave a psychological advantage to the bill's proponents. In contrast, one of the reasons for the Office of Price Administration's repeated defeats in Congress during World War II was the fact that it spent too much time defending itself. Only sporadically and halfheartedly did it take the offensive and wage a direct case against the opponents of price control.

A difficult decision that faces all legislative propagandists who are campaigning on behalf of a specific measure is whether to present the measure as a basis for discussion or to adopt a more aggressive, change-not-a-line approach. In the early stages of the campaign on its behalf, the original Full Employment Bill was presented as a basis for discussion. "Sound legislation can be developed only by clarifying the differences between conflicting schools of thought," stated Senator James E. Murray.[18] This approach served to develop a friendly attitude on the part of those who liked some things about the bill but objected to others. Seven months later, however, when the bill was brought up in executive sessions of the Senate Banking and Currency Committee, the sponsors produced a revised version and, when the bill was reported from the Committee, the Majority Report argued that "the bill, as reported, adequately meets all valid criticisms . . . no further changes are needed." Referring to proposals for amendments that had been made within the Committee, it stated that "if the bill is not to be converted into a meaningless scrap of paper, it is essential that such amendments be rejected."

Propaganda Media

The great bulk of propaganda relies on use of the printed word. All the tools and tricks known to public-relations experts—from press releases and press conferences to "leg art" and stunts—are used to assault the editors, reporters, and article writers of newspapers and magazines. The National Association of Manufacturers prepares model advertisements for use by local businessmen. These advertisements are described in the *N.A.M. News* of November 1, 1947, as follows: "Your Association has compiled a 'package' of scientifically tested ads with top attention-getting and 'play-back' qualities for use by the regional office staffs in stimulating supplemental advertising in local

[17] "Full Employment Act of 1945," Hearings before a subcommittee of the Senate Committee on Banking and Currency, 79th Cong., 1st Sess., July–September, 1945, p. 16.

[18] "Assuring Full Employment in a Free Competitive Economy," report from the Senate Committee on Banking and Currency, 79th Cong., 1st Sess., S. Rept. 583, p. 2.

media on this key subject of profits." Lesser organizations often arrange to deluge local newspapers with well-prepared "letters to the editor."

Hundreds of labor unions issue papers of their own which keep their members informed on labor's legislative campaigns. The American Legion sends a weekly clip sheet to every community newspaper in the United States and also publishes the *American Legion Monthly* and the *National Legionnaire,* a newspaper which is normally printed every two weeks. Through the provision of a regular weekly news and picture service, it also nourishes about 300 papers that are published by its state, district, county, and post organizations. The N.A.M. does a unique job of preparing specialized periodicals for important groups. In addition to "Understanding," mentioned above, it publishes the following: "Farm and Industry," which "goes primarily to county agricultural agents, to land grant college presidents and deans and to both national and local leaders in the Grange and Farm Bureau"; "Program Notes," which is sent to the program-committee heads of women's clubs as well as to national women leaders; and "Trends," which is circulated "primarily among teachers from the secondary school to the college level." [19]

Frequent use is also made of up-to-the-minute bulletins designed to inform supporting organizations of the latest developments in a legislative campaign and advise them on campaign maneuvers. An interesting example is a mimeographed bulletin entitled "Strategy on Health Legislation" issued by the Committee for the Nation's Health on May 12, 1947. It read in part as follows:

Battle Lines Drawn

With the introduction of the National Health Insurance and Public Health Act, the legislative battle lines for 1947 are visibly drawn.

The issue is between this Bill and the Taft "Health" Bill, which poses as a "substitute" for it—between an adequate, comprehensive health program and a stop-gap measure offered as a sop to divert the demand for a real solution. . . .

The Task This Year

1. Defeat the Taft "Health" Bill. Fight it on the charity issue. Fight it on the administrative issue. Fight it as a sop which doesn't provide nearly enough to accomplish even its own limited purposes.

2. Boost by contrast the health insurance principle by backing the National Health Insurance Bill. Commit both political parties to the insurance principle as the basis for major health legislation.

3. Enact constructive health legislation of a limited nature consistent with our broad national health program.

Many organizations issue legislative pamphlets and leaflets. Under the auspices of the National Physicians Committee, "from 12 to 15 million

[19] *N.A.M. News,* Oct. 4, 1947.

pamphlets were circulated in the attack on the previous Wagner-Murray Dingell bill, which passed into innocuous desuetude, and many millions of pamphlets are now being circulated through drug stores, supply houses, hospitals, and other medical agencies." [20] Government agencies customarily publish informational brochures making an attractive case for one or another government program. Government documents of this type are usually written in a restrained mood, and their official status gives them a prestige value that cannot be achieved in more out-and-out campaign propaganda.

A favorite device used by both private organizations and government agencies is the reprinting from the *Congressional Record* of speeches by members of Congress. In addition to having an air of authority about it, a reprint from the *Congressional Record* often represents the quickest or cheapest method of printing campaign material. Committee hearings, committee reports, and other congressional documents are also often used. Some of the most valuable propaganda on behalf of national health insurance was contained in a series of committee prints issued during 1946 at the request of Senator James E. Murray in the form of reports to the Senate Committee on Education and Labor. These reports, which were compiled in the Federal Security Agency, included a scholarly memorandum entitled "Need for Medical Care Insurance," questions and answers on the Health Insurance Bill, and the more important statements made for and against the measure.

Occasionally books will be written for the express purpose of serving as legislative campaign propaganda—as with "The American Individual Enterprise System," [21] prepared by the Economic Principles Commission of the National Association of Manufacturers to provide a theoretical justification of the N.A.M.'s general program. A major weapon in the fight for the Taft-Hartley Labor-Management Relations Act was a report entitled "A Labor Policy" prepared by two economists of the Brookings Institution. Documents of this type have a double value. In addition to having the appearance of objectivity (from the viewpoint of the authors, presumably, this is much more than appearance), they provide valuable ammunition for use in other propaganda efforts.

Most of the propaganda carried by radio, television, and moving pictures is of a generalized nature, dealing with broad social values rather than with specific legislative programs. Nevertheless, the broad legislative objectives of business organizations are regularly broadcast by newscasters and commentators. Occasionally a labor organization will sponsor a commentator or even erect a radio station of its own to present its views. Every legislative campaign organization is eager to present its views on the various radio forums and debates and to make other uses of radio time. Government officials make fre-

20 *Journal of the American Medical Association*, Feb. 3, 1946.
21 (New York: McGraw-Hill, 1946.)

quent use of the air waves. President Franklin Roosevelt's "fireside chats" were among the most potent propaganda weapons of the "New Deal." Motion-picture propaganda for direct legislative objectives is usually in the form of educational shorts and documentaries.[22] Some of these, such as army shorts on national defense, are customarily played at local movie houses. Most of them, however, are distributed through organizations.

With all the attention that is given to the newer media of mass communication, one should not lose sight of the value of persuasion through personal contact. Other media of propaganda operate more or less in a blunderbuss fashion. Persuasion through personal contact is the only way to deal effectively with specific individuals in strategic positions. There is no other more effective medium of propaganda for use between the leaders of various groups and organizations. Only in this manner, furthermore, is it possible to handle the involved psychological problems resulting from the desire for deference and the fear of being neglected or sidetracked. Nor should it be assumed that in personal contacts major emphasis is necessarily placed upon argumentation and appeals to reason or to emotion. Purely personal interactions, the development of mutual fondness, the discovery of other interests in common—all these can be of inestimable importance. Personal charm itself, in all its innumerable manifestations, is an invaluable influence.

Another of the most effective means of propaganda can be found in "persuasion by participation." Many people never can be won over to the support of a given proposition unless they are consulted at the very outset and asked to play a major role either in formulating the proposition or in criticizing preliminary formulations. This approach is of particular value at the drafting stage. Failure to develop sufficient personal consultation prior to the introduction of a bill can spell serious trouble at later stages. This is borne out by the following commentary on the handling of the Food, Drug and Cosmetic Act of 1938:

Viewed in retrospect it seems probable that the progress of the legislation would have been facilitated if no attempt had been made to introduce a bill in the special session and, instead, the draft had been made available upon its completion to industrial and consumer groups to obtain their reactions and suggestions. Some of the revisions which were later forced by industry opposition could have been made before the beginning of the regular session in January, 1934. The course followed served to arouse suspicion and hostility which thereafter could never be completely

[22] "By and large, film producers in democratic countries have intentionally avoided pictures which can be labelled propagandistic because they have thought of their medium as a vehicle of entertainment. This means, in turn, that the propaganda content of pictures has been mostly unintentional." (Doob, *op. cit.*, p. 504.) Doob means, of course, that the direct propaganda is mostly unintentional. That the indirect-propaganda content of major film productions is intentional is illustrated by the producers' argument that broader distribution of American films abroad will popularize the "American way of life."

allayed. Opposition there inevitably would have been, but it is doubtful that, if the other procedure had been followed, this opposition would have gained the impetus that it did.[23]

A tried-and-tested propaganda device is the convening of special conferences on individual legislative measures. "These conferences," writes Ebersole, "appear to have one or all of three main functions: the political education of constituents and their leaders, furnishing information to public officials, and the organization and promotion of political action."[24] They also serve as a method of getting newspaper attention—particularly when "big-name" speakers can be scheduled to perform.

THE APPLICATION OF PRESSURE

"Turn on the heat, boys." A President is putting it bluntly to his legislative lieutenants. Or a strategist for a labor union is laying out the next steps toward getting a bill out of committee. Or a Representative, meeting in an anteroom off the House floor with congressional colleagues and representatives of government agencies and private organizations, is appealing for action before the vote is taken on a crucial amendment.

The listeners know the difference between turning on the heat—or pressure —and using the gentler methods of influencing action. The former involves rewards and punishments. It involves the promise or threat that *if* such and such is done, or not done, such and such steps will be taken—or are in process of being taken. The latter relies on the more subtle approach of appealing to interests, ideals, and principles without recourse to rewards and punishments.

In practice, of course, the distinction between the two becomes blurred. Both are used to mobilize group support, and both, in turn, become weapons in the hands of supporters. Both can be used alike for blanket bombardment and for pin-point assaults to influence individuals (although when individuals are propagandized, the usual term is "persuasion"). The two are usually as close as the velvet glove to the iron fist.

Rewards and Punishments

Types. As with propaganda, the pressure that matters most is the indirect variety. In any society, people grow up under a cloud of cultural coercion and restraint. Some things are safe to do or think; others are taboo. By experience

[23] David F. Cavers, "The Food, Drug, and Cosmetic Act of 1938: Its Legislative History and Its Substantive Provisions," *Law and Contemporary Problems,* Vol. 6, No. 1, Winter, 1939, p. 7.

[24] Luke Ebersole, "Church Lobbying in the Nation's Capital" (New York: Macmillan, 1951), p. 100. Ebersole gives a number of interesting examples of conferences and "seminars" conducted by religious organizations. See pp. 100–103.

and example one learns that there is a predictable pattern of rewards and punishments. No matter how much one may rebel this pattern leaves its mark. Many a legislator speaks truly when he claims that he will vote his conscience, come what may, no matter how strong the outcries and threats from his constituents. The thing he may overlook is the fact that the same indirect pressures that molded the consciences of his constituents also molded his own conscience and even helped to put him into office.

Direct pressure does not always appear in the more obvious forms. People want to be liked. They are eager for approval, deference, and prestige. No one, not even the most conspicuously placed of public officials, is so thick-skinned as not to wince under criticism and disapproval. Deference is a potent reward, disapproval a potent punishment.

In its most effective form, direct pressure deals with people's employment. No President or member of Congress can afford to disregard the threats or promises of those who are in a position to affect their continued employment in elective office. Campaign contributions, endorsement and support, and labors to bring out the vote are decisive pressure weapons. Outside the field of elective office, as well, the promise of future employment or the threat of unemployment are also important influences. Business groups are continuously dangling before the noses of government officials the prospect of future employment, a prospect that leads one to avoid stepping on the toes of possible future emplòyers. Patronage also enters the picture. Although it is much less of a weapon than in the days before the growth of the civil-service system, the President and executive officials can often get certain things done by offering or withholding congressional patronage. Private patronage is probably just as widespread. When economic activity declines, the offices of members of Congress become employment centers. Under such circumstances business concerns with direct interest in pending legislation find it to their advantage to find jobs for the constituents of friendly members of Congress.[25]

From a broader viewpoint, the offering of rewards and the threatening of punishments is the very essence of the process of forming a coalition or of making "a deal." Government officials can use their strategic positions to promote or impede public projects for this or that area, contracts for backers and friends, and the favorable handling of cases and claims brought forward by constituents. They can assert their influence at this or that stage in the varying processes of government. Private organizations also have powerful pressure weapons. Businessmen can expand plants or close them down, raise or lower prices, tolerate competition or push competitors to the wall, deal amicably with labor unions or force a strike. Labor organizations can boycott nonunion goods, slow down production, or go out on strike.

[25] The use of "business patronage" in state government is discussed by William V. Shannon in "Massachusetts: Prisoner of the Past," a chapter of Robert S. Allen (ed.), "Our Sovereign State" (New York: Vanguard, 1949), pp. 50–51.

Actions of this type have important implications for the legislative process. In President Wilson's Administration the Adamson Eight-Hour Law was passed under the threat of a general railroad strike. It was also asserted by many that during the period preceding passage of the Taft-Hartley Labor-Management Relations Act certain parties to the controversy precipitated various strikes for the express purpose of assisting the campaign for the law's enactment.

The most extreme pressure, of course, is violence. In other countries legislators have again and again been forced to take their stand under threat of the firing squad or the hangman's noose. In America, happily, such events have not come to pass, although occasional steps in this direction have been made in a number of states. Nevertheless, the implied threat of violence is always in the background. The power of any government rests upon its capacity to suppress revolt and law evasion by direct force. It is also true that the power of many private groups rests in the assumption that if they are pushed too far by national law they may resist by force.

Bribery (see page 38). One of the oldest forms of pressure is direct bribery. In the early days of our Government, votes were bought and sold openly. In his Journal about Senate activities during the First Congress, Senator William Maclay wrote: "In the Senate chamber this morning Butler said he heard a man say he would give Vining one thousand guineas for his vote, but added, 'I question whether he would do so in fact.' So do I, too, for he might get it for a tenth part of the sum." [26] In describing the legislative operations of Alexander Hamilton and his New York banker associates, Maclay commented on the fact that most votes were carried by a majority of only one. The reason for this, Maclay commented wryly, is "the fact that Hamilton and his New York *junto* do business on the principles of economy, and do not put themselves to the expense of hiring more than just the number necessary to carry their point." [27]

Although the incidence of corruption is hard to estimate, observers of the political scene seem agreed that it has declined. The trends have been both from cupidity to probity and from cupidity to timidity. Both givers and receivers have learned to operate more cautiously. In one form or another, bribery still exists—although it would be difficult to uncover many cases that could be sustained before a court of law. "I never have to bribe anybody," a lobbyist has been quoted by a Washington columnist. "It's a bad practice. I just show them how to make a little money. . . ." [28]

[26] "Journal of William Maclay" (New York: Appleton-Century-Crofts, 1890), p. 209.
[27] *Ibid.*, p. 310.
[28] Drew Pearson, "Washington Merry-Go-Round," *Washington Post*, Oct. 24, 1947. For an interesting compilation of cases concerning members of Congress who learned "how to make a little money," see H. H. Wilson, "Congress; Corruption and Compromise" (New York: Rinehart, 1951).

Since most members of Congress maintain some form of business activity in order to pay for homes, offices, and assistance in their constituencies and in Washington, it is relatively easy for business opportunities to be channeled in their direction. It is because there are so many other things that bribes can be called and so many people, including colleagues and relatives, to whom they can be given, that the ominous prohibitions against bribery in the Corrupt Practices Act and the Criminal Code have so little meaning.

Methods. The application of direct pressure is as much an art as the exercise of persuasion. If used too blatantly it may defeat its own purposes. The great bulk of legislative pressures occurs in a hidden or implied form. This is particularly true in the case of campaign support or opposition where, entirely apart from reasons of diplomacy, the issues are so complex that it is dangerous for legislative campaigners to commit themselves too quickly. Moreover, people must be handled with kid gloves. If they are to be pressured into taking a given form of action, they dislike the humiliation involved in being compelled to change positions in public. Rationalizations and face-saving devices are invaluable aids in the application of pressure. The velvet touch of persuasiveness is of the essence.

One of the most effective legislative campaign organizations has stated the case for sweetness and light as follows:

Never threaten your Congress with loss of your vote. Understandably, such threats only irritate Congressmen, so avoid demands and bullying tactics. Avoid haranguing and the attitude that your belief is incontrovertible.

Yours is a selling job, so apply the same common rules of salesmanship that you use in everyday work. Convince your Congressman you have thought about the issue, and that you are sincere in your position.[29]

An interesting contrast to this approach is provided by the following statement made by William Z. Foster, chairman of the Communist party of the United States, in a speech exhorting the unions to action against pending labor legislation:

Every union everywhere should adopt resolutions and indignation, union committees should visit Representatives and Senators, mass lobbies should be sent to Washington, protest meetings should be held, citizens' committees should be organized, and if necessary, one-day local protest strikes should be prepared.[30]

Channels for Direct Pressure

Personal Contact. Only an infinitesimal amount of direct pressure takes place in the lobbies off the floor of the Senate and the House of Representatives.

[29] "How to Work with Congress" (Washington, D.C.: The Realtors' Washington Committee of the National Association of Real Estate Boards), p. 8.
[30] *The New York Times,* Jan. 23, 1946.

Discussion in the lobby is necessarily brief, hurried, and conspicuous. Most of the Washington pressure work is done not in the lobbies, but at committee hearings (which will be discussed in detail in Chap. 14) and in government offices. There is hardly a day in the week, particularly while Congress is in session, that hundreds of representatives of private organizations, executive officials, and members of Congress are not using direct pressure, coupled with propaganda, to advance their legislative interests.

According to Senator Harry Cain of Washington,

. . . there is probably more lobbying going on in nearby country clubs than in the corridors of the Capitol. . . . Here is an intangible manifestation of the political lobby —it is the social lobby—the plethora of elaborate cocktail and dinner parties, sports, junkets and related activities that provide entertainment.[31]

Executive officials in influential positions probably receive as many invitations to social affairs and miscellaneous forms of entertainment as members of Congress. The value of the social lobby lies not so much in the influence of entertainment upon a man's thinking as in the opportunity it provides for obtaining access to someone who is extremely busy during working hours. It is not a "wine, women, and song" kind of influence. It often brings people together for serious consideration of mutual problems. Wesley McCune writes:

A luncheon club, conducted with informality, may be as productive in lining up support for a unified program as are twice as many hours in congressional office buildings. One such group, called the Farm Hands, meets weekly at the Harrington Hotel to compare notes on the past seven days' grist of announcements and gossip. The forty or more farm representatives, food-trade spokesmen, congressmen, publicity men, journalists, and department officials who keep the club going are one vehicle of the farm bloc. It is they who carry much of the ammunition up front for all-out assaults.[32]

Occasionally personal contact is expanded to group contact in the form of mass lobbying and marches on Washington. During World War II the Consumer Advisory Committee of the Office of Price Administration organized large delegations of housewives to lobby members of Congress on behalf of OPA. In 1945 the C.I.O. brought in large delegations from each of the industrial states to put pressure on their congressional delegation on behalf of a three-point program: expanded unemployment compensation, liberalized minimum-wage provisions, and the Full Employment Bill. Marches on Washington are less frequent. The two great historical marches were those of Coxey's Army at the turn of the century and the famous Bonus March of 1932 on behalf of veterans' legislation. It was a threatened march on Washington which induced President Roosevelt to set up the FEPC by Executive order. Yet

[31] Statement quoted in *Washington Star*, June 9, 1947.
[32] Wesley McCune, "The Farm Bloc" (New York: Doubleday, 1943), pp. 11–12.

when it came to the problem of obtaining congressional action to make the FEPC permanent, the leaders of the Negro organizations decided against another march on Washington for fear that it would serve unduly to antagonize members of Congress.

The People Back Home. Perhaps the most effective channel of personal contact is through "the people back home." One railroad representative has observed:

All of us have long recognized that the only effective way to influence congressional action is to convince the influential men in each congressional district that the public interest and the interest of the railroads coincide. I have the impression that most of the congressmen, particularly those living in the smaller states and in rural districts, depend for their support upon a comparatively few men in each county in their respective districts. If we could reach the men upon whom a congressman depends for advice and assistance in his political campaign, we could go far toward having the problem solved.[33]

The N.A.M. advises every industrialist and businessman to "map out a sound public-relations program designed especially to keep its Congressman informed of the part industry is playing in the home life of its community."[34] The more successful legislative Representatives stay in the background and concentrate upon developing a general program for contact work with government officials. "I plan the strategy and direct the moves," Purcell Smith, legislative representative of the National Association of Electric Companies, has been quoted as saying, "but it is our company executives who carry the ball."[35] A legislative report of the Citizens' Committee on Displaced Persons, describing direct lobbying in Washington "as an essential but proportionately minor part of the task," advises that "it would be best to concentrate on local instrumentalities. . . ."[36]

Petitions and Memorials. One of the oldest methods of attempting to influence a legislature is the presentation of petitions. In England the legislative process itself was born when the first Parliaments began to petition the king for changes in the law and when, with the reign of Henry IV, individuals and localities began to petition Parliament in turn to petition the king. In America the petition became a major instrument of influence upon the colonial legislatures and "the right to petition the government for a redress of grievances" was written into the Federal Constitution and most of the state constitutions. The use of written petitions, however, has greatly declined. Luce writes:

[33] *United States v. The A.A.R. et al.,* Govt. Brief, Part II, Exhibit G. 207, p. 125. Quoted in John G. Shott, "The Railroad Monopoly" (Washington, D.C.: Public Affairs Institute, 1950), p. 86.
[34] Walter Chamblin, Jr., "Know Your Congressmen" (New York: National Association of Manufacturers, 1944).
[35] Robert S. Allen, "King of the Lobbyists," *New Republic,* Feb. 9, 1948.
[36] Quoted in *Congressional Quarterly Notebook,* Vol. 6, No. 18, May 5, 1948, p. 159.

Everybody in public life knows perfectly well how easily petition signatures are obtained, how carelessly they are given, how little weight they really deserve. The result is that when they reach an American legislative body, they get scant courtesy. . . . One earnest word spoken to a Representative by a constituent whose judgment inspires confidence is worth a yard of petition signatures.[37]

Another old tradition is the presentation of memorials from state legislatures. In the days when the states loomed much larger on the national scene and when Senators in fact were deemed to be delegates from sovereign state legislatures, the memorial was an important channel of contact. While still used, it also has waned in importance. Robert Luce, who served in the Massachusetts state legislature as well as in Congress, writes:

Anyone who has served in a State Legislature knows, for example, how scant the attention there given to proposals for memorializing Congress or otherwise affecting Congressional action. These proposals usually prevail with little or no debate. Somehow the legislators feel no responsibility for positions taken in regard to them. Inasmuch as many members of Congress have served in State Legislatures and understand all about this, it is not surprising that the hundred and more memorials sent by the Legislatures to every Congress are ignored. They are that much waste paper.[38]

Letters and Telegrams. But memorials are not the only form of waste paper that descends upon Washington. The waste-paper baskets of members of Congress and executive officials are kept ever full with form letters and form telegrams. Many of these communications are futile because misdirected. Letters from a Negro organization to a Senator from Mississippi can hardly influence the actions of the recipient. Form post cards, canned letters, and telegrams are seldom influential. They tend to call to mind the deluge of fake and inspired telegrams used by utility organizations in the 1934 campaign against the New Deal's holding company bill and exposed by the Senate investigation led by Senator Hugo Black of Alabama. The more seasoned legislative campaigners usually try to follow the advice of former Representative George Outland of California: "One thoughtful letter will outweigh half a dozen which simply say 'vote for this' or 'vote against that.' One spontaneous outburst on your own stationery is worth a hundred mimeographed letters of newspaper clippings in some write-your-Congressman drive."[39] They concentrate on planning for spontaneity. As part of its campaign on behalf of rent control in 1947, the National Association of Consumers evolved a form letter to Senators which told in detail about the writer's personal financial problems and advised its correspondents to make slight alterations of fact and wording.[40]

[37] Robert Luce, "Legislative Principles" (Boston: Houghton Mifflin, 1930), pp. 530–531.
[38] *Ibid.*, p. 483.
[39] "Write to Your Congressman, but Do It Right," *The Reader's Digest,* Vol. 48, June. 1946.
[40] Quoted in *The Wall Street Journal,* June 18, 1947.

In "How to Work with Congress" the National Association of Real Estate Boards, an outspoken opponent of rent control, sent its members these explicit instructions on how to write to members of Congress:

Whenever possible, make your letters apply to a local situation. Tell specific instances of how legislation affects or would affect your business. Give facts, figures, and sources of information. Avoid confusing Federal with State legislation.

Be brief as possible, but tell your story, simply and naturally. Come directly to the point. Don't bury your requests. Identify, as fully as possible, the legislation about which you're writing. Don't refer merely to the "Jones Bill." Rep. Jones may have introduced several bills, so give the resolution or bill number if possible.

Don't just state that you oppose or favor a certain measure, but also give your reasons for opposing or favoring it. Most Congressmen are more interested in your reasons than in your position.

If you are writing in behalf of an organization, be sure to state your position with the organization, the number of members, and your authority to commit the membership on the issue at hand.[41]

At crucial stages in the legislative struggle, a careful effort is usually made to pick the specific points at which communications can be most useful and to canvass those correspondents who might be most influential. The following letter from a representative of the A.F.L. to labor organizations in California provides a useful illustration:

Within the next few days a joint conference of the United States Senate and Congress will draft an anti-labor bill, based upon the Taft and Hartley legislation. This bill undoubtedly will be adopted by both Houses. We have every reason to believe President Truman will veto the bill; however, from present indication, the Congress will pass the bill over the President's veto by an overwhelming majority.

In the Senate we are informed that the A.F. of L. needs the support of 7 or more Senators to block the passage of the bill over a veto. Senator KNOWLAND is one of the Senators needed. It is essential that a sufficient number of telegrams, letters and telephone calls be made to Senator KNOWLAND in an attempt to influence him to refuse to override the veto. Thousands of letters from business men are arriving daily, requesting the adoption of this antilabor legislation. However, communications and contacts from members are very light. The united A.F. of L. is, therefore, requesting each union to have each officer, executive board member, and business agent take it upon himself to get 5 persons to wire, write or telephone Senator KNOWLAND within the next week, requesting him to vote against passage over a veto.

In Los Angeles County, A.F. of L. unions have over 5,000 members who are officers in the above capacities. If each of these officers got 5 persons to respond, Senator KNOWLAND will have received word from at least 25,000 citizens. If each officer leaves it to the others, Senator KNOWLAND will receive no correspondence. This is a program that must be carried out. It is a last-ditch attempt to avoid sabotage of the free trade-union movement. Please act immediately.

[41] Op. cit., p. 7.

We will appreciate copies of letters or telegrams sent, or a reply from each officer when he has accomplished the above outlined task.[42]

This letter inadvertently fell into the hands of Senator Knowland himself who inserted it in the *Congressional Record*. In view of the fact that the groups favoring the Taft-Hartley Act undoubtedly used similar methods, it is a credit to Senator Knowland that he merely inserted this letter in the *Congressional Record* without comment rather than using it as a springboard for accusing the A.F.L. of unscrupulous tactics.

Sometimes the sheer bulk of correspondence received on a legislative measure may, if not outweighed by corresponding bulk on the opposite side, have decisive influence. One of the most important issues in the conflict on atomic-energy legislation was military control (as provided for in the May-Johnson bill in the House of Representatives) versus civilian control (as provided for in the McMahon bill in the Senate). A hastily organized group of atomic scientists led a correspondence campaign in protest against the May-Johnson bill.

Professional societies, women's clubs, church federations, labor unions, veterans' groups, and university students adopted resolutions of protest. Letters and telegrams poured into the White House and Congressional offices; the Senate special committee alone received over 75,000 messages, of which the overwhelming majority opposed the provision.

This storm aided the administration, by this time committed to the principle of an exclusively civilian commission, in its effort to keep the May-Johnson bill bottled up in the House. Thus, the issue was brought to a focus in the Senate special committee, where the compromise ultimately incorporated in the act was hammered out.[43]

[42] *Congressional Record*, 80th Cong., 1st Sess., p. 6326.
[43] James R. Newman, "America's Most Radical Law," *Harper's Magazine*, May, 1947.

Chapter 14

THE STRUGGLE FOR COMMITTEE POWER

A LARGE GROUP of people cannot get much work done without some specialization of labor. The 81 members of the First Congress realized this when they met in 1789. After a bill had been considered on the floor, they would usually appoint a special committee to work out the details. Once these committees made their reports, they passed out of existence. At least 350 were born and died during the Third Congress.[1]

As the legislative burden grew heavier and more complex, however, the select-committee system began to bog down. It proved impossible for the Senate and the House themselves to find time to discuss many bills before referring them to a committee. Moreover, select committees proved weak vehicles for the communication of propaganda and pressure between Congress and the executive branch. They lacked the technical proficiency desired by the first Secretary of the Treasury, Alexander Hamilton, in order to establish his control of Congress. They lacked the stability needed by the Jeffersonians to resist Hamilton and later, when Jefferson became President, to carry out their own executive policies.

As a result, more and more use was made of "standing" committees set up to handle all measures in a given field. Less and less effort was made to instruct the committees in advance. By the early 1820's the revolution was complete. Under Henry Clay the standing committees became the automatic recipients of legislative proposals and the focal points of legislative power. By 1885, there had already been ample justification for Woodrow Wilson's pungent

[1] For general material on congressional committees, see Ralph V. Harlow, "The History of Legislative Methods in the Period before 1925" (New Haven, Conn.: Yale University Press, 1917); Lauros G. McConachie, "Congressional Committees" (New York: Crowell, 1898); Ada C. McCown, "The Congressional Conference Committee" (New York: Columbia University Press, 1927); Gilbert Y. Steiner, "The Congressional Conference Committee: 70th to 80th Congresses" (Urbana, Ill.: The University of Illinois Press, 1951). For material on individual congressional committees see Eleanor E. Dennison, "The Senate Foreign Relations Committee" (Stanford, Cal.: Stanford University Press, 1942); and Albert C. F. Westphal, "The House Committee on Foreign Affairs" (New York: Columbia University Press, 1942). For material on committees in state legislatures see C. I. Winslow, "State Legislative Committees" (Baltimore, Md.: Johns Hopkins Press, 1931).

description of the standing committees of Congress as "little legislatures" and of American government as "government by the standing committees of Congress." [2]

Today every bill is automatically consigned to a legislative committee before which it comes, in Lord Bryce's words, "as a shivering ghost stands before Minos in the nether world." [3] The committee members can lock it in "dim dungeons of silence whence it will never return." [4] Or, as is done less frequently, they can arrange for hearings. After hearings, they can let it languish in the files or can report it to the floor. If the latter instance, they can determine the form in which it will be considered by the Senate or House and can exercise great influence on the floor decision. If a bill passes both houses in a form unacceptable to one or the other, its fate is then largely in the hands of a joint conference committee made up of members of the two legislative committees which considered it in the first place.

Hence the real legislative infighting takes place at the committee stage. The legislative contestants are engaged in a ceaseless struggle for positions of committee power. They try to utilize committee hearings as a means of furthering their objectives, to obtain the potent backing of a favorable committee decision, to obtain control of conference committees, and to resist any counter-pressures that operate through the formalized channels of either or both houses.[5]

"Power is nowhere concentrated . . . ," observed Wilson. "It is divided up, as it were, into forty-seven seignories, in each of which a Standing Committee is the court baron and its chairman lord-proprietor." [6]

To understand how power is divided up among committees, it would be futile to map the seignories and list the court barons in any particular year. A few years later both map and list would be out of date. The pattern of committee power is always in flux. The committee system (if something so inchoate can be called a "system") can be understood only by examining the process of struggle and change itself as manifested in the structure and personnel of the committees.

[2] These terms and many others that have become common phrases in American political science come from Woodrow Wilson's "Congressional Government" (Boston: Houghton Mifflin, 1925).

[3] James Bryce, "The American Commonwealth" (New York: Macmillan, 1907), 3d ed., Vol. I, p. 157.

[4] Wilson, op. cit., p. 69.

[5] For an idealistic interpretation differing from the above, see E. Jordan, "Theory of Legislation" (Indianapolis: Progress Publishing Co., 1930), p. 364.

[6] Wilson, op. cit., p. 92.

THE COMMITTEE STRUCTURE

Anyone who has tried to thread his way through the labyrinthine tangle of agencies and bureaus in the executive branch of the Federal government must be prepared to find at least as much complexity, if not more, in the structure of the standing committees of Congress.

Nor is the similarity accidental. The growth of both executive agencies and legislative committees stems from the same factors: the need for specialized organizations to deal with the ever-expanding burdens of the Federal government; the demand for recognition by powerful organizations; and the interest of Congressmen and executive officials in building instruments of personal power or prestige.

The Birth and Death of Committees

It is far easier to create a new legislative committee of Congress than it is to set up a new agency in the executive branch. All that is needed is a simple resolution. The area in which consent must be obtained is therefore far smaller than it would be if a law itself were needed, as is usually the case with executive agencies.[7]

The decision to establish a new standing committee is occasionally worked out ahead of time on the basis of compromise and accommodation between the affected members in either house. These understandings have been eased by the implicit understanding on many occasions that a new committee would not be overactive. Many committees, in fact, have had little function other than to provide additional office space and clerical personnel for the chairman. In 1900 the House Committee on Coast and Insular Survey was set up "for the sole purpose of becoming a burial ground for legislation sponsored by the Navy Department to take over the Coast and Geodetic Survey." This committee "proved an effective defense of the Coast and Geodetic Survey from the inclusion on the part of the Navy Department" without ever making a report.[8]

More often, however, new committees can be born only after a knockdown struggle. In the first decades of congressional history, the creation of new standing committees was slowed down by the opposition of those who pre-

[7] The only legislative committee of Congress established under law is the Joint Committee on Atomic Energy set up under the Atomic Energy Act of 1946. The provisions of the Legislative Reorganization Act of 1946 dealing with the legislative committees of both houses were defined "as an exercise of the rule-making power of the Senate and House of Representatives respectively and as such shall be considered as part of the rules of each House *respectively* or of that House to which they specifically apply." Sec. 101(a).

[8] George H. Haynes, "The Senate of the United States" (Boston: Houghton Mifflin, 1938), Vol. 1, footnote, pp. 281–282.

dicted—and rightfully so—that they would detract from the power of each of the individual members.[9] Once the system of standing committees became firmly established, every proposal for a new one threatened the power and influence of members of one or more existing committees.

The issue of whether or not to establish a new committee is often a struggle over specific legislative policies. Thus, before the Civil War, efforts to set up a Committee on Education and Labor were fought by Southerners, who viewed it as a threat to the slave-labor system in the South. It was impossible to establish this committee until the South had been defeated in the Civil War. Similarly, the abolition of the House Appropriations Committee in 1885 and the creation of eight new committees to take over its functions were the culmination of a decade's conflict over legislative policy on the tariff and internal improvements.

In recent years, the difficulties of establishing new committees have become greater than ever before. During the 1940's only two new legislative committees were created: the House Committee on Un-American Activities and the Joint Committee on Atomic Energy. In both these cases the method used was first to set up a special committee with no standing-committee functions. Once public recognition was won for the work of the special committee, all that remained was the formality of converting the special committees into standing committees.[10]

If the birth rate of standing committees is low, the death rate is still lower.

[9] In 1805, for example, when the House Committee on Rules proposed the creation of a standing committee on public lands, one member who voted against it voiced his fear that a "standing committee, vested with the entire business connected with the public lands, should gain such an ascendancy over the sentiments and decisions of the House, by the confidence reposed in them, as to impair the salutary vigilance with which it became every member to attend to so interesting a subject." *Annals of the Congress of the United States*, 9th Cong., 1st Sess., p. 286.

[10] It is doubtful that these two committees could have been created without resort to special forms of strategy. In January, 1945, when the routine motion of adopting the rules that prevailed during the previous Congress was put before the House, Representative John Rankin of Mississippi, in a surprise maneuver, moved to amend the previous rules by creating a permanent Committee on Un-American Activities. The motion could not be referred to a committee since the House was not yet organized. So it was discussed at once on the floor of the House and was adopted. If Rankin had waited until later and handled his resolution in the ordinary manner, the natural opposition of a number of standing committees with jurisdiction in the same area, combined with that of the liberal members of Congress who objected to the Committee's activities, would probably have resulted in its burial in committee. The Joint Committee on Atomic Energy was established through a relatively minor provision in the broad legislation dealing with atomic energy. If the Senate Special Committee on Atomic Energy had sought instead to create a joint committee by sponsoring a concurrent resolution (and a concurrent resolution is the usual vehicle for setting up a joint committee), the proposal would have run the risk of being killed in the House Military Affairs Committee.

The creation of every new committee necessarily implies the creation of new vested interests in its perpetuation. Many a committee has survived for years and years after all its purposes, save the provision of extra office space and personnel for its chairman, have utterly vanished.

Over the long run, of course, this trend becomes self-defeating. The time always arrives when the number of committees is so great that in the interests of economy and effectiveness, large-scale consolidation becomes imperative. This happened in 1921 when the many individual committees on appropriations and expenditures were merged into two sets of committees on appropriations and expenditures. The most recent amalgamation took place when the Legislative Reorganization Act of 1946 reduced the number of Senate committees from 33 to 15, cut the number of House committees from 48 to 19, and wiped out a large number of special committees that threatened the jurisdiction of standing committees.[11]

In 1946 the obstacles to pruning the luxuriant committee growth were exceedingly great. The strategy for overcoming them lay in the use of an omnibus bill containing many provisions of direct benefit to the members of Congress, such as higher salaries, a retirement program, and more staff assistance. The fact that the amalgamation program as a whole reduced the number of chairmanships then held by the liberal members of Congress probably served as a

[11] The standing legislative committees of Congress, as of January, 1953, were as follows:

Senate:

Agriculture	Interior and Insular Affairs
Appropriations	Interstate and Foreign Commerce
Armed Services	Judiciary
Banking and Currency	Labor and Public Welfare
District of Columbia	Post Office and Civil Service
Finance	Public Works
Foreign Relations	Rules and Administration
Government Operations	

House of Representatives:

Agriculture	Interstate and Foreign Commerce
Appropriations	Judiciary
Armed Services	Merchant Marine and Fisheries
Banking and Currency	Post Office and Civil Service
District of Columbia	Public Lands
Education and Labor	Public Works
Expenditures in the Executive Departments	Rules
	Un-American Activities
Foreign Affairs	Veterans' Affairs
House Administration	Ways and Means

Joint Committees:

Atomic Energy

factor in winning support among the conservative majority in both houses and among the conservative pressure groups that joined in supporting the entire measure.

Only part of the picture is in the full committees. Each full committee has the power to subdivide itself into any number of subcommittees without recourse to permission from the house of which it is a part.[12] This power is customarily exercised by the committee chairman.[13] The tendency, therefore, is for subcommittees to sprout up in great numbers regardless of what is done with the full-committee structure.

Immediately before the Legislative Reorganization Act of 1946 went into effect, there were 140 subcommittees in Congress.[14] A few months after it went into effect, a special count revealed 146 subcommittees, thereby suggesting that the reshuffling had produced a more complex rather than a less complex system.[15] A later count shows that in 1950 there were 131 standing subcommittees: 66 in the Senate and 65 in the House.[16] Unfortunately for the ambitious enumerator, there are no public records that regularly provide a full list of all subcommittees. In fact, some subcommittees have neither name nor formal status and some are set up only as special bodies for the purpose of considering individual bills.

The members of subcommittees enjoy much more power than is generally realized. By refraining from acting on a measure, they can considerably delay action on it, if not kill the measure completely. Many subcommittees, like the 24 subcommittees of the two committees on appropriations, exercise great influence in their own right and are subject to scarcely any review by the full committee of which they are nominally a part.

The Flexibility of Committee Jurisdiction

Since the birth of the standing-committee system, there has never been a period in the history of Congress which has not been enlivened by jurisdictional

[12] A formal resolution on behalf of a subcommittee is needed for the purpose of obtaining additional funds or staff personnel.

[13] This power was challenged in one of the court trials arising from postwar investigation by the National Defense Investigating Committee of the Senate. The appellant claimed that a subcommittee could be established only by formal resolution of the full committee. But the court thought otherwise. ". . . the evidence shows that it is the unvarying practice of the Senate to follow the method of creating and appointing subcommittees which was employed in this instance." *Bennett V. Meyers v. United States,* U.S. Court of Appeals, Decision of Nov. 8, 1948.

[14] Hearings before the Joint Committee on the Organization of Congress, 79th Cong., 1st Sess., 1946, pp. 1040–1043.

[15] *The New York Times,* Apr. 14, 1947.

[16] George B. Galloway, "The Operation of the Legislative Reorganization Act of 1946," *American Political Science Review,* Vol. 45, No. 1, March, 1951, p. 43.

conflicts between rival committees or by the spectacle of individual committees reaching out for more and more territory to control.

In part, this is due to the complexity of the subject matter that comes before Congress. The problems of legislative policy are so interrelated that it would be a sheer impossibility to devise a jurisdictional pattern that eliminated overlapping areas. Even if this miracle could be achieved, new subjects would always arise that were not foreseen in the original pattern.

Jurisdictional conflicts are also due to the efforts of pressure groups and executive agencies to have legislation they want enacted referred to a friendly committee and legislation they oppose referred to a hostile committee. In addition, they arise from the interest of individual members of Congress, particularly committee and subcommittee chairmen, in expanding their personal power and prestige.

The jurisdiction of a committee is determined by two variable factors. The first, and most important, is the subject matter of the bills referred to it. The second is the subject matter on which it chooses to report. As indicated in Chap. 10, careful draftsmanship can often help to steer a bill toward one or another committee. The proper choice of sponsors and a friendly attitude on the part of the Presiding Officer will also contribute. In the Senate, the traditional respect for the prerogatives of the individual Senator has meant that considerable attention is paid to the sponsor's wishes concerning the committee to which his bill should be referred.[17] In the House of Representatives, on the other hand, the wishes of individual sponsors have seldom been an important factor. Discretionary power, except in those cases where the Speaker takes a direct personal interest, has been exercised almost entirely by the House Parliamentarian. In the case of referral to subcommittees, the word of the committee chairman is invariably accepted as final in both houses.

Sometimes an open jurisdictional struggle on the floor of the Senate or House occurs. In 1894, for example, the bill to impose a tax on oleomargarine was referred to the Committee on Ways and Means which had jurisdiction over taxation. This committee, however, was unfriendly to the proposal. The chairman of the Committee on Agriculture, on behalf of his committee, moved that the bill be transferred to his committee. The dairy interests rolled up a majority of 169 to 58 on behalf of the motion.[18] Since then the Committee on Agriculture has always retained jurisdiction over oleomargarine taxation in the House.

There are few restrictions on what a committee chooses to report to the floor. A bill dealing with one subject clearly within a committee's jurisdiction can be

[17] Vice-President Garner was frequently quoted as saying that, so far as he was concerned, he would *always* refer a bill in accordance with the sponsor's wishes. Although the Presiding Officer's discretion was considerably modified by the Legislative Reorganization Act of 1946, this tradition has not been eliminated.

[18] *Congressional Record,* 53d Cong., 2d Sess., Feb. 26, 1894, pp. 2422–2423.

amended in committee to deal with other subjects that would otherwise be under the jurisdiction of other committees. In committee operations possession is often nine points of the law, and possession can often be determined not by what bills are referred to a committee but by the subjects on which a committee may decide to conduct a study or hold a hearing.

The only formal limitations on what a committee may report relate to appropriations. Committees other than the appropriations committees may report bills containing authorizations for subsequent appropriations but are not allowed to report measures which actually appropriate funds. Likewise, the rules forbid appropriations committees from including legislative provisions in their appropriation measures. While the first of these restrictions is always lived up to, the second is habitually violated. In both houses the appropriations committees are prone to include legislative riders in appropriation measures and these violations of the rules are often upheld on the floor.

Often the maneuvering for committee jurisdiction is so intricate that it is extremely hard for any observer to follow the ball, let alone to know who may be calling the signals. The story of jurisdiction over reconversion legislation is an interesting example. The first round in this struggle started during World War II when the referral of a bill to establish an Office of War Mobilization was won by the Military Affairs Committee. Senator Harley Kilgore of West Virginia, a member of this committee, then succeeded in establishing and heading up a War Mobilization subcommittee to which this bill was referred. Somewhat later, Senator James E. Murray succeeded in setting up and becoming chairman of a War Contracts subcommittee, obtaining jurisdiction, at first, over legislation dealing with terminated war contracts and thereby freezing out the Naval Affairs Committee. Then the Murray subcommittee achieved jurisdiction over the disposition of surplus property, an area formerly covered by the Committee on Executive Expenditures. It then took over the field of reconversion legislation and with it the war mobilization legislation formerly considered by the Kilgore committee. "By April, 1944, Murray's War Contracts subcommittee had managed to get control of every important piece of proposed legislation dealing with reconversion and postwar problems." [19]

With the support of both the War Contracts subcommittee and the War Mobilization subcommittee, the full Military Affairs Committee went into the entire subject of unemployment compensation. Encouraged by the representatives of all sections of organized labor, its members had legislation drafted to provide emergency unemployment benefits for the millions of workers and returned veterans who, it was then felt, would be rendered unemployed at the end of the war. The purpose was to bring forth more liberal legislation on this subject than could be expected from the more conservative Finance Committee.

[19] Stephen K. Bailey, "Congress Makes a Law" (New York: Columbia University Press, 1949), p. 33.

The Finance Committee, however, did not sit idly by. In a surprise maneuver it brought an unemployment-compensation bill to the floor of the Senate before the Military Affairs Committee was able to report. The Military Affairs Committee, in turn, promptly reported an omnibus measure dealing not only with unemployment compensation but also very comprehensively with demobilization problems and the establishment of an Office of War Mobilization and Reconversion. When the Finance Committee bill was taken up, the Military Affairs Committee bill was offered as a substitute. The Finance Committee then suddenly broadened its scope far beyond the jurisdiction conferred by the bills that had been referred to it and produced a substitute omnibus measure dealing in a different manner with all the items covered in the Military Affairs Committee bill. This measure was offered as a substitute for the Military Affairs Committee substitute and was adopted by the Senate.

In the House of Representatives the Ways and Means Committee won jurisdiction on the ground that it dealt with social security despite the fact that the bill merely authorized Federal loans to state unemployment compensation systems and did not provide for new taxes. With slight modifications in the Ways and Means Committee and the conference committee, the Finance Committee measure became the War Mobilization and Reconversion Act of 1944.

The cure for jurisdictional tangles has been the goal of many congressional reform movements. One of the recommendations of the Joint Committee on the Organization of Congress was that "the jurisdiction of each reorganized committee be clearly defined so that overlapping and duplication will be eliminated." [20] Accordingly, the Legislative Reorganization Act of 1946 went into great detail in specifying the exact subject matter to be covered by each full legislative committee. This represented a marked change from the past when the jurisdictions of full committees were described in the rules of each house merely by a few general words that never attempted to clarify separate subject-matter areas. The Act also tightened up the Senate rules against the inclusion of legislative provisions in bills reported by the appropriations committees.

Nevertheless, the 1946 legislation did not provide—and could not have provided—a final answer to the jurisdictional problem. This was made clear in the 1947 conflict over proposals to unify the armed services. In the House, this legislation was referred to the Committee on Executive Expenditures which, under the rules, was supposed to handle the entire field of governmental reorganization. In the Senate, a sharp conflict developed between members of the Committee on Executive Expenditures and the Armed Services Committee. The latter claimed jurisdiction on the ground that unification was a problem that dealt exclusively with the armed services. They obtained jurisdiction by winning a majority vote on the floor of the Senate. In 1948, another case oc-

[20] "Organization of the Congress," Report of the Joint Committee on the Organization of Congress, 79th Cong., 2d Sess., S. Rept. 1011, p. 5.

curred when a measure to repeal the tax on oleomargarine was finally forced out of the House Committee on Agriculture by a discharge petition and was adopted by the House. It was then sent to the Senate where traditionally the subject had always been handled by the Finance Committee. Here the butter interests tried a jurisdictional maneuver that had previously been successful in the House. Senator Arthur Vandenberg of Michigan, the President pro tem of the Senate, referred the bill to the hostile Senate Agricultural Committee, but the advocates of repeal challenged his decision and succeeded in reversing him by a 40 to 37 vote on the floor.

The Committee People

We too often tend to think of agencies of government as abstract entities. We too often forget that government "structure" is merely a way of bringing people together to do various things. In the case of congressional committees particularly it should be remembered that committees are people. The struggle for committee power is essentially a struggle to decide who shall be the members of the various committees, who shall be the chairmen, and what kind of staff resources shall be available to whom.

The Members

The assignment of members of Congress to the various legislative committees must be viewed from three vantage points. In strictly formal terms, each house elects members for all its committees.[21] Actually, the formal process of election applies to little more than the assignment of newly elected members to committees and occasionally the transfer of members from one committee to another. By traditional practice, a member who has once served on a committee is regarded as entitled to continue to serve on it so long as he keeps his congressional seat. There is also a tradition that the members with the greatest seniority in either house have a right to any vacancies that develop on the more important committees, such as those dealing with appropriations, taxation, and foreign affairs.

Looked at another way, committee assignments are the responsibility of the major political parties (see pages 87–89). The party with a majority in either house "organizes" the committees in that house. The floor votes by which the members of committees are "elected" usually represent automatic acceptance of lists previously developed by each party. Although the majority party of either house could theoretically exclude the minority party from

[21] Until 1910, the Speaker of the House of Representatives had the power to assign members to House committees. In 1910–1911, however, the famous "revolution" against Speaker "Uncle Joe" Cannon took away the Speaker's power of committee appointments.

membership on legislative committees, it is part of the tradition of Congress that minority members be appointed to every committee.[22] This is usually done in a manner that provides a minority party with committee representation roughly proportionate to its numerical strength in the House as a whole.

Nevertheless, there is room for variation. Thus, in the Eightieth Congress, the Democratic minority received 6 out of 13 committee positions on 11 of the Senate's legislative committees. In three other committees, where majority-party control was regarded more highly, Democrats received only 5 out of 13 posts. On the Appropriations Committee the Democrats received 8 out of 21 positions. The extent of this variation has been limited in recent years by the provisions of the Legislative Reorganization Act which, with only minor exceptions, limits each Senator to membership on two standing committees and each Representative to membership on only one standing committee. When a majority party's margin is not very great, this provision means that the price of a safe majority on some committees is acceptance of a bare majority on other committees.

From a third and more realistic point of view, however, the parties are not actually responsible for committee assignments. Although each party caucus in each house has a Committee on Committees, this group is usually different in membership from the top policy committee of the party in each house. Among the House Democrats, the function of the Committee on Committees has been traditionally performed by the Democratic members of the Ways and Means Committee, a group which, by virtue of the seniority tradition, is to a considerable extent self-perpetuating and which is not directly amenable to control by party leadership or the party caucus. Nor is the national leadership of either party expected to concern itself with the pattern of committee assignment. Even a newly elected President with tremendous popular prestige and with the direct influence that patronage can give him during the first months in office can seldom have more than a very minor effect upon committee assignments. Personal deals and behind-the-scenes horse trading between the party members in each house would probably add up to more than Presidential influence. In the case of the anti-Administration party, the national-party organization outside Congress has no function whatsoever in this field.

This situation creates many favorable opportunities for the use of influence by strong private groups. The farm organizations, for example, have usually succeeded in having the membership of the agriculture committees in both houses limited almost entirely to Senators and Representatives from pre-

[22] Both Thomas Jefferson and Woodrow Wilson objected to representation of minority parties on legislative committees. Jefferson felt that "the child is not to be put to a nurse that care not for it. It is therefore a constant rule that no man is to be employed in any matter who has declared himself against it." (Jefferson's Manual, Sec. 26.) "It is plainly the representation of both parties on the Committees," wrote Wilson, "that makes party responsibility indistinct and organized participation impossible." Op. cit., p. 97.

dominantly agricultural areas. "Until I took my place near the bottom of the committee table," writes former Congressman Jerry Voorhis concerning his assignment to the Agriculture Committee, "I had not realized certain significant facts about the makeup of the committee . . . the committee represented the 'five basic commodities.' The main interests of the overwhelming majority of the committee were—and still are—summed up in 'cotton, tobacco, wheat, corn, and hogs.' " [23]

The interest of the N.A.M. in committee structure is evidenced by its self-satisfied statement on the organization of the House Labor Committee after the Republican victory in the congressional elections of 1946.

> The House Labor Committee completed its organization this week. Its makeup rather well insures the kind of bill the leadership will decide is needed. Not one of the Republicans is regarded as a laborite, and at least half of the ten Democrats are conservatives. Only a little over two years ago, organized labor had such strong representation on the House Labor Committee that any bill which labor favored could be reported favorably—any bill it opposed, bottled up in committee.[24]

Labor, on its part, has long shown the same interest. Speaker "Uncle Joe" Cannon was once accused by Samuel Gompers, head of the A.F.L., of packing House committees with members more friendly to business interests. "Gompers' grievance," commented the Speaker to a newspaperman, "is not that I packed the committees; oh, no; he thinks he was badly treated because I wouldn't pack the committees as he wanted them packed." [25]

The struggle to "pack" or "unpack" a committee is carried on through both parties. The choice of the minority members assigned to a committee can provide the basis for a coalition that can be used effectively to carry a fight against a majority or ultimately to organize a dominant coalition. During the New Deal, conservative Republicans on many committees in combination with conservative Democrats succeeded in overruling many New Deal proposals. In 1947, the liberal Republicans and the liberal Democrats on the Senate Labor and Public Welfare Committee combined to overrule Chairman Taft in the preparation of the Taft-Hartley Act. Although this liberal coalition was subsequently outvoted on the floor, there is little doubt that the final version of the Taft-Hartley Act would have been much more stringent had it not been for the concentrated power of prolabor Senators within the Senate Committee.

In assigning members to major committees, considerable weight is usually given to seniority. Newer members are often assigned posts on the less important committees. The longer a member of Congress serves, the better his chances

[23] Jerry Voorhis, "Confessions of a Congressman" (Garden City, N.Y.: Doubleday, 1947), p. 132.

[24] N.A.M. News, Jan. 18, 1947.

[25] The Boston Globe, May 2, 1909.

of obtaining the committee assignments he values the most. Since those with the highest seniority cannot be given all the important assignments, choices must be made. These choices are often difficult ones for more than purely personal considerations. An interesting illustration is found in the maneuvers to fill a Republican vacancy on the Senate Foreign Relations Committee at the beginning of the Eighty-second Congress.

Normally the Foreign Relations post would have gone to Senator Morse of Oregon, who had urgently requested representation for the West Coast and had the explicit backing of Senator Vandenberg. But Vandenberg was ill in Michigan, and Taft and Wherry were determined that the liberal and internationalist Morse should not be appointed. Since places on major committees are allotted strictly according to seniority, the conservatives were able to cook Morse's goose by proposing Senator Capehart of Indiana, who outranks Morse. The liberals countered with Senator Aiken of Vermont, who outranks Capehart. The conservatives next advanced Senator Brewster of Maine, who outranks Aiken. The liberals came back with Senator Tobey of New Hampshire, who outranks Brewster. That was when the fun really started.

Tobey already was the ranking Republican on the Banking and Currency Committee and the Interstate and Foreign Commerce Committee. Brewster did not have any top rank on any committee, although he was second to Tobey on Interstate and Foreign Commerce. Delicate negotiations were now begun, with Brewster trying to obtain an assurance from Tobey that if he went to Foreign Relations, he would withdraw from Interstate and Foreign Commerce, leaving Brewster top Republican there. Tobey for his part offered to renounce Foreign Relations if Brewster would do the same, thus clearing the way for Aiken. Brewster and the conservatives did not like this and redoubled the pressure on Tobey to take the Foreign Relations post if he wanted to, but to retire from the Interstate and Foreign Commerce Committee.

Refusing to do any favors for Brewster, Tobey quietly retired from the Banking and Currency Committee, applied for the Foreign Relations post and got it, and held on to his ranking position on Interstate and Foreign Commerce.[26]

The selection of subcommittee members is entirely divorced from the party structure in either house of Congress. Here again, as with the creation of subcommittees and the assignment of bills to subcommittees, the word of the committee chairmen is law. This gives the chairmen considerable discretion in determining whether bills are handled in a friendly or unfriendly fashion. By careful selection, a subcommittee with a conservative majority can be pieced together out of a full committee with a liberal majority. A subcommittee with a liberal majority can be carved out of a bill committee with a conservative majority. In 1945, for example, when the Full Employment Bill was referred to the Senate Committee on Banking and Currency, Senator Robert F. Wagner of New York set up a Full Employment subcommittee to hold hearings on the measure and prepare a report for the full committee. He did this with

[26] Willard Shelton, "Civil War in the G.O.P.," *The Nation*, Jan. 27, 1951, pp. 75–76.

great care, taking pains to see that the conservative members of both parties were represented but at the same time guaranteeing a clear numerical majority that favored the principles of the measure.

The Chairmen

To become chairman of a committee, a Senator or Representative must be assigned to the committee in the first place. If he is reelected enough times, and if he lives long enough, and if his party comes into power, sooner or later he is bound to become a chairman. Once chairman, he is regarded as having the right to continue in his chairmanship so long as he continues to be reelected and continues to live. This is the famous—or rather, infamous—seniority system. Luce comments:

> It is a dangerous system, for sooner or later the man who has started at the tail end of a committee, if reelected enough times, will knock at the door of the chairmanship. He may be unqualified to preside over meetings or at hearings. He may have no capacity for defending committee reports on the floor. He may be a man whose reputation for honor is questioned—there are black sheep in every legislative flock.[27]

The seniority system has often been mistakenly attacked on the ground that it puts too much power in the hands of old men. This argument misses the real implications of the seniority system. Age alone does not cause diminution of mental vigor, alertness, and leadership ability. Nor does it mean that a man becomes more conservative. Some of the outstanding liberals in Congress have been old men who have fought valiantly despite the other handicaps of age. Witness Senator Norris, Senator Wagner, Senator Murray, and Representative Sabath.

The significant effect of the seniority system is that it tends to concentrate political power in the hands of members from "safe and solid" areas of the country, areas where there is very little real competition between the two major parties. This tends to insulate committee chairmanships from the real meanings and mandates of national electoral conflicts. It tends to undermine the ability of party leaders to carry out campaign pledges. Above all, it tends to bring a greater number of conservatives than of liberals into committee chairmanships.

In 1948, President Truman won the Presidential election on the basis of a liberal party platform and a campaign which attacked conservative control of the Eightieth Congress. On the basis of this campaign, the Democratic party won control of both houses of Congress. The liberal and middle-of-the-road Democratic contingent was augmented greatly, outnumbering the hard core

27 Robert Luce, "Legislative Procedure" (Boston: Houghton Mifflin, 1922), pp. 120–121.

of Southern conservatives. Yet, in the Senate, the seniority tradition gave at least three out of four of the committee chairmanships to the anti-Truman Southerners. The chairmanships of the Senate committees on appropriations, finance, foreign relations, armed services, and the judiciary, for example, were turned over to men who had unquestionably demonstrated their opposition both to the Democratic party platform and to the pledges given to people by the President during the course of his election campaign. In the case of the Senate Banking and Currency Committee, the result of the election was to take the chairmanship away from a liberal Senator, Charles Tobey of New Hampshire, who often favored the President's program, and give it over to a chairman, Senator Burnet Maybank of South Carolina, who had demonstrated opposition toward many fundamental aspects of the President's program.

Immediately after the 1948 election, many people asked the question: "Why don't the Truman Democrats dislodge the anti-Truman Democrats from committee chairmanships?" This is not a question that can be answered easily. There are many factors, including many personal strategies, that are not readily discernible to the outside observer. One of the most important causes of inaction, however, was the blunt fact that the Truman Democrats had a majority only among the Democrats in each house of Congress. They did not enjoy a full majority in either house. The anti-Truman group was in a balance-of-power position and, if aggressive action had been taken against them by the Administration's supporters, they might have joined with their fellow conservatives among the Republican members and put the conservative coalition into formal control of Congress. This ultimate possibility, enhanced by the fact that the rules themselves call for the selection of committee chairmen and committee members by the vote of each house of Congress rather than by party caucuses, was a nightmare that often preyed on the minds of the Truman Democrats.

Seniority rights, however, are not always clear-cut. By one standard they are measured in terms of the length of consecutive service *on a given committee*. By another standard, they are computed in terms of the number of consecutive years served *in the House*. The seniority tradition itself is not sufficiently refined to resolve this ambiguity. An opportunity is thus provided for the various contestants in the legislative struggle to throw their weight in one direction or another. At the beginning of the Eighty-first Congress, Senator James E. Murray of Montana ranked fourteenth among the Senate Democrats. By this standard he was entitled to a chairmanship of one of the 15 standing committees. However, he did not rank first in seniority on any one committee. The weight of the conservative pressures succeeded in denying him a committee chairmanship during the entire Eighty-first Congress.

Another limitation on the seniority principle is the tradition that the member of Congress who successfully proposes the creation of a new committee has a right to the chairmanship. It was on the basis of this tradition that Senator Brien McMahon of Connecticut succeeded in winning the chairmanship of the Senate Special Committee on Atomic Energy. In addition, the Atomic Energy Act of 1946, which provided for a Joint Committee on Atomic Energy, was based upon a measure proposed by Senator McMahon. When the Joint Committee on Atomic Energy was created and the members of the Senate Special Committee were appointed as the Senate representatives of the joint body, Senator McMahon therefore had a double claim to the chairmanship of the new joint committee.

There is far less rigidity in the selection of subcommittee chairmen. Here the decision is entirely in the hands of the full-committee chairmen. In parceling out the more important subcommittee chairmanships, the chairman will usually regard seniority as one factor to be taken into account. But he will also give weight to considerations of policy and personal relationships and feel free to make all sorts of deals. In the Senate where the number of members on each committee is much less than in the House, and where more attention is given to the personal prerogatives of individual members, it is possible for even a newly elected member to win a subcommittee chairmanship.

The Staff

Staff assistance is a vital element in the pattern of committee power. The effectiveness of committee members depends to an important degree on the quality and amount of staff assistance at their command. Likewise, staff aides are often moving forces in their own right. They are delegated important functions with respect to the planning of hearings, the handling of contacts with pressure groups, and the preparation of bills, amendments, and reports. Having direct access to committee members, they are in a strategic position to exercise an influence upon committee decisions.

Only part of the committee-staffing picture can be seen by looking at the official records on congressional employees. Staff assistance for legislative committee work is customarily provided both by executive agencies and private organizations. Organizations conducting legislative campaigns offer this assistance to friendly members of Congress, knowing that it is one of the best ways of advancing their objectives. In many instances, members of Congress request such staff services of them.

In the case of pressure groups, this request is usually made to enable the member to perform more effectively in the interest of the group involved. In the case of the executive agencies, however, the purpose is not necessarily so narrow. Staff assistance from executive agencies is often requested not merely to help serve the ends of interested agencies but also to serve the specific interest of the member or committee making the request. When the same party is in control of the executive branch as in Congress, influential members of Congress, particularly committee chairmen, regard it as a personal prerogative to obtain the assignment of executive personnel from executive agencies to work under their direction. In a limited sense, this is a form of patronage. In a broader sense, there has developed the conception that a committee has a right to assistance from the executive agencies, a right which has in many instances been formalized by statute or congressional resolutions.

In 1921 the Budget and Accounting Act instructed the Comptroller General, at the request of any committee having jurisdiction over revenue, appropriations, or expenditures, to "direct assistants from his office to furnish the committee such aid and information as it may request." (Sec. 312(b).) Similarly, the Atomic Energy Act of 1946 authorized the Joint Committee on Atomic Energy "to utilize the services, information, facilities and personnel of the departments and establishments of the Government." (Sec. 15(c).) Customarily, resolutions providing a special study or investigation either by a legislative committee or a special committee contained language "authorizing" the use of executive services and personnel. The validity of such authorizations, however, is impaired by the fact that a resolution, not having the force of law, cannot authorize executive agencies to use their funds for the purpose of providing services to congressional committees. The Comptroller General has on occasion ruled such use of executive funds illegal and has established certain conditions governing the assignment of executive personnel to congressional committees. Yet these conditions are rarely enforced, for the simple reason that most executive assignments to legislative committees are unofficial.

This entire matter became a subject of contention in the Senate of 1945 when a number of conservative members realized that the full exercise of this right by a number of liberal committee chairmen was a powerful force in the campaign for liberal reconversion legislation. Senator Kenneth Wherry of Nebraska, a staunch Republican conservative, started a campaign to forbid the assignment of executive personnel to Senate committees except on a reimbursable basis. He succeeded in attaining approval of a requirement that the names of all executive personnel assigned to Senate legislative committees be printed monthly in the *Congressional Record*. His efforts also led to a provision in the Legislative Reorganization Act of 1946 forbidding the formal assignment of executive personnel "except with the written permission of the Committee on Rules and Administration of the Senate or the Committee on House Administration of the House of Representatives, as the case may be." (Sec. 202(f).) One effect of Wherry's effort was to weaken the campaign for liberal reconversion legislation. Another was to force executive assignments to congressional committees to be handled in a more subterranean fashion. Still another was to strengthen the case for the employment of professional legislative staffs on the congressional payroll.

For many decades, the theory of congressional staffing seemed to be that each member of Congress was a statesman capable of handling all legislative problems himself. Under this theory any proposal for the formal provision of professional staff services to Congress would be an implied slur upon the capacities of the members themselves. Accordingly, the official staffing of Congress was limited to clerical help in the committees and secretarial help in the offices of the individual members. The only modifications were the creation of the Legislative Counsel's Office to perform technical services on bill drafting and of the Legislative Reference Service in the Library of Congress to perform elementary research services.

The Legislative Reorganization Act of 1946 made a complete break with this tradition. It authorized every standing committee of Congress to hire up to four professional staff members in addition to their clerical staffs. These staff members were to be appointed "by the majority vote of the committee . . . without regard to political affiliations and solely on the basis of fitness to perform the duties of the office." They were to be "assigned to the chairman and ranking minority member of such committee as the committee may deem advisable." In practice, the appointment of professional staff members has been left largely in the hands of committee chairmen and the ranking minority members.

Moreover, two competing patterns have emerged. By one a clear division is made between those staff members assigned to the majority and those assigned to the minority. By the other, staff members are assigned neither to majority nor minority but to the various subjects covered by the committee. "There is no particular reason to assign any of them (staff experts) to the minority or the majority," stated Senator Robert A. Taft during discussion on the floor of the Senate. "They are experts on particular subjects and we have five important subjects within the jurisdiction of the Committee on Labor and Public Welfare, so I think those professional assistants ought to be looked upon as experts performing for the entire committee. . . ."[28] Obviously, this pattern is useful in denying staff services to the ranking minority members or any of the minority members of a committee.

The services provided by the professional staffs of committees cannot be described by any general formula. In some cases staff members make a valiant effort to stand apart from the legislative struggle and provide objective assistance to both sides. When this happens, they pass into the background whenever a really "hot" issue comes up. The genuine staff work, which is necessarily controversial, is thereby left to the staffs of executive agencies and private organizations. In other cases, staff members are required to take sides or do so of their own choosing. When this happens the more imaginative ones are in a better position to mobilize and direct the staff operations of friendly agencies

[28] *Congressional Record*, Jan. 27, 1947, p. 638.

and organizations. The others tend to serve as transmission belts—with some leeway for initiative and judgment—between members of Congress and non-congressional groups.

The Legislative Reorganization Act also expanded the Legislative Counsel offices in both houses. It provided for a well-paid staff of professional experts in the Legislative Reference Service.[29] The Senate version of the Act also would have provided a highly paid administrative assistant to each member of Congress. Members of the House objected to this provision and it was stricken from the final legislation. In a subsequent appropriation act, however, members of the Senate Appropriations Committee picked up this issue and succeeded in inserting a provision which gave each Senator a $10,000-a-year assistant. This assistant was supposed to work on administrative matters, thereby freeing his Senator to devote more time to legislative matters.[30] The net effect, however, has been to provide members of the Senate with more staff assistants in the handling of their committee work.

[29] Under the Act, these experts are to cover the following fields: agriculture; American government and public administration; American public law; conservation; education; engineering and public works; full employment; housing; industrial organization and corporation finance; international affairs; international trade and economic geography; labor; mineral economics; money and banking; price economics; social welfare; taxation and fiscal policy; transportation and communications; and veterans' affairs. (Sec. 203(b)(2).)

[30] This is an amusing survival of the theory that on "legislative" matters a member of Congress needs no assistants.

Chapter 15

THE HEARINGS: STAGING AND PERFORMANCE

"CONGRESS in session," commented Woodrow Wilson, "is Congress on public exhibition, whilst Congress in its committee rooms is Congress at work." [1] This oft-quoted description was written at a time when committee hearings were convened in executive session. Today, with relatively few hearings held behind closed doors, Congress at work on committee hearings is also Congress on public exhibition.

In fact, the committee hearings outrank the floor sessions of Congress—or, for that matter, the policy conference of any other government agency—in the sheer scope and volume of public operations. They provide a means through which members of Congress can educate themselves on the issues involved in a bill. They serve as a clearinghouse for information needed by all the contestants in the legislative process. They provide a springboard for propagandistic and pressure activities. They serve as a testing ground on which preparatory battles can be fought before a measure moves on to a subsequent stage of committee decision. In the case of major legislation it is usually impossible without full and intensive hearings to produce a measure that can stand up on the floor of Congress or prove its value after enactment.

A hearing, like a play, must be staged. The stage managers—that is, the committee and subcommittee chairmen and their staffs—must make a number of important behind-the-scenes decisions, which will be discussed in the following sections. The performance may then proceed.

THE STAGING

Silent Murder or a Hearing

The first decision is whether to have a hearing at all.

Occasionally a committee may act on a bill without having a hearing. This happened in the development of the Legislative Reorganization Act of 1946. Long hearings on the subject were held by the Joint Committee on the Or-

[1] Woodrow Wilson, "Congressional Government" (Boston: Houghton Mifflin, 1925), p. 79.

ganization of Congress. A comprehensive bill was drafted subsequently. But the committee members called no hearings on the bill itself. To have done so would have risked postponement of action until a subsequent session of Congress. Similar maneuvers are used to help prevent the mobilization of effective opposition. In 1948, for example, the House Ways and Means Committee voted suddenly one day to report legislation intended to exclude salesmen and other "independent contractors" from the Social Security Act.

Some decades ago committee action without hearings was the rule.[2] In recent years it has become an exception. The general rule now is that a committee will not report a bill without a hearing and that the denial of a hearing is considered a bill's death sentence.

In American courts a man is presumed innocent until proved guilty. In congressional committees and subcommittees, the ordinary bill is presumed unworthy of attention and automatically sentenced to an ignominious death until enough pressure is brought to give it a hearing. Sometimes the weight of the pressure is against a hearing. For a number of years the coal-mine operators succeeded in preventing hearings in the House of Representatives on legislation for tighter mine-safety regulation.[3] The opposition of committee or subcommittee chairmen is especially potent. Thus, Senator Henry Cabot Lodge, chairman of the Senate Foreign Relations Committee, saw to it that no hearing was ever given to the American-French Treaty which President Wilson forwarded to the Senate in conjunction with the Versailles Treaty.

A strong enough campaign, however, can override a chairman's desire to prevent a hearing. In 1947 the railroad lobby succeeded in having the chairman of the Interstate Commerce Committee in the House order a hearing on legislation which was opposed by the railroad labor unions. But the latter groups then staged a counteroffensive and overrode the chairman.

When the committee assembled, Congressman "Bob" Crosser, Ohio Democrat, "raised the question of consideration." That means the veteran Cleveland progressive was asking the committee members to vote whether they wished to continue hearings on the bills, or whether they desired to turn to other business. . . . Under parliamentary law, Crosser's "question" was not debatable, so the clerk called the committee roll. Only six members voted to continue the hearing, and twelve against doing so. As a result, the proceedings came to a sudden close.[4]

In the case of a measure that is reasonably sure of being eventually enacted into law in one form or another, all factors usually favor giving a green light to hearings. The advocates and opponents of specific provisions are eager to establish in the hearings a basis for action in subsequent stages in the legisla-

[2] *Ibid.*, p. 83.

[3] For example, see Drew Pearson, "Washington Merry-Go-Round," *Washington Post*, July 6, 1947.

[4] *Labor*, May 24, 1947.

tive process. Members of the committee are anxious to familiarize themselves with the issues involved.

Many groups can get a hearing on almost any measure they want to, particularly if it is referred to a committee on which they have a friend or two in a strategic position. According to McCune, the farm lobbyists were always able to rely on Senator "Cotton Ed" Smith of South Carolina "to convene his committee on Agriculture and Forestry for any purpose—even to hold hearings on bills assigned to other committees. In convening the committee at the drop of a lobbyist's suggestion, Smith is likely to bark to the clerk: 'Call up those butt-heads and tell 'em we're going to have a meeting tomorrow.' " [5]

However, the decision to hold a hearing in no way implies subsequent congressional action. Many hearings merely serve to appease groups that are clamoring for legislative action. A hearing has the virtue of itself giving direct satisfaction of "blowing-off-steam" activity and can often serve as an alternative to subsequent legislative action. Moreover, as indicated below, a hearing can also be staged in such a fashion as to delay or prevent legislative action.

Timing the Show

The most obvious problem of timing is "How soon should hearings be held after the introduction of a measure?" Appropriation-bill hearings usually start in the House of Representatives at the beginning of each session. In fact, the Subcommittee on Independent Appropriations has often started hearings a month before the regular session. On emergency measures, particularly those requested in special Presidential messages, hearings usually are begun quite promptly—sometimes within twenty-four hours.

On the great bulk of measures, however, the chairmen of full committees and subcommittees have a genuine opportunity for the exercise of broad discretion. In the case of the Versailles Treaty Senator Henry Cabot Lodge, chairman of the Senate Foreign Relations Committee, planned a strategic delay before initiating hearings. This was generally interpreted at the time as part of his campaign against the measure. In the case of the Full Employment Bill, Senator Robert F. Wagner, chairman of the Senate Banking and Currency Committee, deliberately postponed hearings for a period of six months after the introduction of the bill. The purpose was to allow time for the organization of group support behind the measure and for the planning of a well-staged set of hearings.

A second problem is "Which committee should begin hearings first?" When two committees in one house are engaged in a jurisdictional struggle, the tendency is for each one to try to beat the other to the draw. The same question also comes up with respect to choosing between House and Senate committees

[5] Wesley McCune, "The Farm Bloc" (New York: Doubleday, 1943), p. 38.

handling identical or similar measures. Each participant in the legislative struggle generally attempts to have hearings started in whichever committee is most favorable to his particular viewpoint. Thus, in the case of the Full Employment Bill, the proponents of the measure succeeded in having hearings begun before the friendly Senate Committee on Banking and Currency. The Senate committee hearings then served as a basis for organizing a stronger presentation and defense of the measure before the hostile House Committee on Expenditures in the Executive Departments.

Coordination with other hearings on related subjects is a rare consideration. Each congressional hearing is run as a separate sideshow only remotely connected with something else members of Congress may be doing. Except for recurrent efforts to keep committee hearings from being held during floor sessions [6] there have been few attempts to develop a general schedule for hearings.

A third problem is "How long should the hearings be?" On minor bills, committee time is of necessity rationed very sparingly. In an atmosphere of dire emergency hearings tend to be brief. The National Industrial Recovery Act, one of the most far-reaching statutes ever to be enacted in American history, was the subject of only three days of public hearings in each house. On major measures, particularly those of a more complex, controversial, or novel character, relatively long hearings are—short of crisis conditions—usually unavoidable. Thirty-one days of hearings were held by the House Committee on Interstate and Foreign Commerce in connection with the Public Utilities Holding Company Act of 1935.

Occasionally long-drawn-out hearings are sought for the express purpose of delaying legislative action. Whenever hearings have been held for proposals on national compulsory health insurance, the American Medical Association and other opponents of this legislation have seen to it that every local medical society in the country demands to be heard. The cumulative effect of long-drawn-out testimony has been to delay the time when proponents of the legislation may move to win affirmative action by the committee. In the House of Representatives where the rules call for a quorum of committee members, dilatory quorum calls may be used for the same purpose. This was done in the case of the Taft-Ellender-Wagner Housing Bill during the Eightieth Congress.

When hearings finally began, the committee set a precedent by scrupulously observing the House rules. Indeed, the rules were so carefully heeded that the commit-

---

[6] The Legislative Reorganization Act of 1946 provided that "No standing committee of the Senate or the House, except the Committee on Rules of the House, shall sit, without special leave, while the Senate or the House, as the case may be, is in session." (Sec. 134(c).) However, permission to hold committee hearings while the Senate or the House is in session is given rather freely.

tee made no discernible progress whatsoever. Day after day, a conscientious member would point out that a quorum was lacking or that the committee was meeting when the House was in session. . . . Congress adjourned at the end of July and S. 1592 was defunct.[7]

Occasionally an effort is made to hold a "quickie" hearing on a major bill for the purpose of attaining quick congressional action before the opposition has an opportunity to mobilize. Thus a few days after the introduction of the May-Johnson bill on atomic energy, Representative Andrew J. May, chairman of the House Committee on Military Affairs, "opened and closed public hearings on October 9, 1945 and rushed executive committee sessions designed to report the bill out promptly." [8]

This action was only partially successful. Immediately the scientists' organizations, on behalf of civilian rather than military control of atomic energy, demanded more careful consideration of the problem.

Led by such outstanding men as Drs. Condon, Szilard, and Urey, they descended upon Washington insisting that a single day's hearings limited to favorable witnesses was a shocking abuse of legislative discretion in dealing with such a momentous and largely uncomprehended subject. When their request for further hearing was initially refused, they met informally with a large caucus of congressmen, then used the hearings of a Senate subcommittee considering science legislation as a sounding board for airing the defects of the May-Johnson Bill. Simultaneously, they were calling on prominent private citizens, editors and publishers, on leading figures in the Administration, and on influential senators and representatives. Their efforts so moved Mr. May that he reopened hearings—for a single day.[9]

Open or Closed Doors

As indicated earlier, congressional committees hold a vast number of public hearings on legislative measures at every session of Congress. In fact, the Legislative Reorganization Act of 1946 inserted a provision in the rules requiring committee hearings to be open to the public except "where the committee by majority vote orders an executive session." [10]

A careful peek behind the curtain, however, shows that there are also many closed hearings. In 1947, for example, an able reporter made a tally of his own and concluded that almost half of all committee hearings were secret. "In the first 20 days of March," he wrote, "113 House hearings on the public's

[7] Alexander L. Crosby, "The Real Estate Lobby," *The American Mercury,* March, 1947.

[8] Byron S. Miller, "A Law Is Passed—The Atomic Energy Act of 1946," *University of Chicago Law Review,* Vol. 15, No. 4, Summer, 1948, p. 805.

[9] *Ibid.,* p. 805.

[10] Sec. 133(f). This provision also excepted executive sessions from "marking up bills or for voting." Sessions of this character, however, are entirely different from hearings. They always take place in executive session.

business were held behind closed doors. In the same period 137 hearings were public. A fairly complete list of Senate Committee hearings in the same period showed 47 closed and 56 open." [11] But it is doubtful whether this tally reports the full story. There are many differences of degree between a door that is wide open and a door that is tightly closed. Many hearings that are nominally public are "quickie" operations called on short notice and with no effort to inform all interested parties. Moreover, there are limits on the number of hearings that an overworked press corps can cover. Many public hearings are attended by no one but a handful of witnesses. As far as providing public information goes, they might just as well have been secret in the first place.

Closed hearings are well adapted for favoring "insiders" or weighting the scales against "outsiders." This is probably the reason why the subcommittees of the House Appropriations Committee invariably hold closed hearings on appropriations measures. The reason given is that open hearings would be an invitation to pressure operations by private organizations. It is difficult to conceive, however, how private organizations could be any more interested in Government appropriations than they have always been in the past.

At times, paradoxically enough, the best way to guarantee full news coverage for testimony is to have it presented at a closed hearing. What would be a fairly dull story as it transpired in open hearings can become an exciting piece of headline news if it represents an inside tip on what happened at a hush-hush meeting.

Closed hearings can also be used to prevent unfavorable publicity. Executive officials often ask for the opportunity to testify at executive sessions so that they can deny opponents on the congressional committee the opportunity to use their appearance as an excuse for questioning and speech making that would make the headlines and destroy any useful effect of their own testimony. Secrecy is also a method of sidestepping outside critics. "I can't see that any useful purpose could be served," stated Representative Bertrand Gearhart, in defending closed hearings on the 1948 extension of reciprocal trade agreements, "by listening to spokesmen for a bunch of ladies' sewing societies reading statements on the legislation that have been prepared by the State Department." [12] To those interested in promoting the State Department's program on reciprocal trade, however, the utility of allowing the ladies to make public statements was obvious.

The result of efforts to keep hearings closed sometimes produces a backwater of adverse publicity—particularly when there is a split within the committee itself. When the House Ways and Means Committee decided to close the door on its 1948 hearings on the extension of the Reciprocal Trade Act, ranking minority member Representative Doughton of North Carolina led a public

---

[11] Charles T. Lucey, *The Washington Daily News*, Mar. 24, 1947.
[12] *The New York Times*, Apr. 30, 1948.

attack on the Republican members,[13] and much of the press echoed his charges that the Republicans were using "star-chamber" methods.

There is no doubt, however, about the utility of closed hearings as a means of promoting a more intimate give-and-take between witnesses and committee members. Many witnesses will speak much more freely at a closed session. Many committee members will behave quite differently when the emphasis is more upon exploring the issues than upon offering opportunities for publicity. Closed hearings are particularly useful in gathering facts for use in the subsequent staging of an open hearing.

But the closing of committee doors offers no real protection against subsequent publicity of confidential information. After a closed hearing on a legislative measure, almost everybody in attendance—committee members, witnesses, and staff aides—is solicited for "leaks" by reporters and representatives of various contestants in the legislative struggle. This is why the executive officials dealing with foreign affairs and the national defense seldom present really confidential information at the many closed meetings in which they participate. The chief benefit for them in closing the doors is that their testimony is thereby surrounded with an aura of high significance.

The Dramatis Personae

"Anytime a bill is presented to the Congress," a small businessman once complained at a Senate hearing, "I can close my eyes and visualize who will appear. They will be about the same people who usually testify for or against a bill. You never have any new blood." [14]

One reason why the same people testify over and over again at one hearing after another is the broad range of interests of those groups that play the largest role in the legislative struggle. During any month, selected at random, the Secretary of Commerce may appear before a dozen committees on a dozen different bills. During the same month, the legislative representative of the National Grange may be just as active. Even where these groups are not themselves anxious to testify, their power and status create a considerable interest on the part of others in finding out what their views may be on pending measures. Another reason is that the job of representing these key groups is largely turned over to a limited number of staff experts or top officers. The former are often the only people in an organization who really have sufficient facts at their finger tips to qualify as informed witnesses. The latter, by virtue of their positions of prominence, provide an essential element of prestige and dignity.

[13] *Congressional Record*, 80th Cong., 2d Sess., pp. 6502–6507.

[14] Testimony of Harry Golden, Hearings before a subcommittee of the Senate Committee on Banking and Currency, 79th Cong., 1st Sess., S. Rept. 380, Aug. 23, 1945, p. 381.

Occasionally a private organization will bring in "grass-root" witnesses. This has the great advantage of adding freshness and variety to a committee hearing. In his vivid book, "Missouri Compromise," which is replete with graphic pictures of committee testimony, Tristram Coffin tells how a welder from Schenectady was brought before a Senate committee to defend price control during the period immediately following World War II.[15] His testimony was brief, human, and moving. "It's a very healthy thing for the Committee to have you here. Nothing is finer than for common people to bring these matters to Congress," remarked one of the Senators. To bring common people before Congress, however, is not easy. It involves transportation and hotel costs. Time must be spent in familiarizing them with the legislative situation and advising them on how to behave before a congressional committee. Hence most grass-root witnesses are brought to Congress by the uncommon people—or, to use more exact language—by organizations representing the more affluent members of the population.

Sometimes, somewhat sparingly, a committee will itself go to the common people. While working on the Agricultural Adjustment Act of 1938, the Senate Agriculture Committee held a series of "gallus" or field hearings throughout the country. Subcommittees of the House Education and Labor Committee did the same in 1949 in developing the case for Federal aid to education in localities affected by wartime activities. These hearings enabled the committee members to meet with lots of "new blood." They also served to stimulate local interest in the measures under consideration.

On important and highly controversial measures a committee may receive many more requests to testify than can possibly be honored. This may simply result from the large variety of interested groups. Or it may be the product of deliberate campaigns to pack or protract the hearing. In either case, the committee members are faced with a problem of rationing the available time. In most instances this responsibility is left in the hands of the committee or subcommittee chairmen. Many of these, in turn, delegate the job to staff assistants.

One way to ration is to set up a schedule that favors friends and supporters. A striking example is found in the health hearings that opened before a Senate subcommittee in May, 1947. "More than nine-tenths of the allotted time," charged Senator James E. Murray, "has been given over to organizations almost all of which represent doctors and hospitals, less than one percent of the people who would be affected by this legislation." This pattern was developed by a staff member who sent out a special news letter to physician and hospital groups in advance of committee plans suggesting that they take steps to request an opportunity to appear. At the same time, the same staff member led the proponents of health insurance up a blind alley by informing them that no schedule for hearings had yet been determined. As a result, the first four weeks of the health hearings were given over to one side and three subsequent days allotted to the other side.[16]

To protect against incidents of this type, special subcommittees are occasionally set up for the sole purpose of serving as a rationing board. In the 1949 hearings on labor relations, the Senate Committee on Labor and Public Welfare decided that the hearing time should be divided equally between the majority and minority members and gave a Democratic Senator (Murray) responsibility for allotting the majority's time and a Republican Senator (Morse) the responsibility of allotting the minority's time.[17]

Where witnesses with a particular point of view are denied an opportunity to testify before one committee, it is sometimes possible to achieve the same objective through another committee. In 1949, for example, the House Judiciary Committee held a brief one-day hearing on the basing-point legislation. Representative Wright Patman of Texas felt that an insufficient opportunity had been granted to the opponents of this measure.

As chairman of the House Select Committee on Small Business, he undertook himself to hold the hearings on S. 1008 which he said had been denied to him and to small business groups. And for five days, witnesses made appearances before the Small Business Committee or sent statements attacking S. 1008. Professional economists, representatives of small business organizations, wholesale and retail distributors, the National Farmers Union, the American Trucking Association, Inc., and staff of the Federal Trade Commission made a record of protest of 300 pages, the theme of which was that S. 1008 would weaken the anti-trust laws, cancel recent gains in the clarification of the laws, create more confusion and litigation, make it easier for violators to justify infractions, and harder for the Federal Trade Commission to halt such infractions.[18]

Some committees solve the rationing problem merely by trying to divide the time equally between proponents and opponents. Occasionally an ambitious schedule is prepared for the purpose of dividing up the testimony by various aspects of subject matter that may be involved. This was attempted by the House Ways and Means Committee in the hearings that preceded its 1949 recommendations for expanding the social-security system.

Sometimes the amount of time given to any group is not nearly as important as the order of appearance. Many witnesses engage in considerable pulling and hauling for the purpose of being allowed to appear early or late among the list of witnesses. An early appearance allows one to come before a committee while the members are still fresh and untired. It also helps win more prom-

[16] This story is told in a vivid and frankly partisan manner by Nelson Cruikshank in "Playing Politics with Health," *American Federationist*, June, 1947, pp. 24–26.

[17] This arrangement was crystallized and publicized in a resolution in the Daily Digest section of the *Congressional Record*, Feb. 19, 1949.

[18] Earl Latham, "The Group Basis of Politics" (Ithaca, N.Y.: Cornell University Press, 1952), pp. 137–138.

inent attention from the press and radio. A later appearance, on the other hand, often makes it possible to make a careful appraisal of the situation and prepare more definitive answers to questions that may arise.[19]

The juxtaposition of two witnesses whose views are not compatible is a good way to create drama. It also serves to underline conflicts. During the Republican-controlled Eightieth Congress, Republican members of the Banking and Currency Committees in the two houses found that they could undermine the President's proposed anti-inflation program by bringing in one after the other Secretary of the Treasury John Snyder and Marriner S. Eccles of the Federal Reserve Board. It was hoped that the two would take strikingly divergent positions, a hope that partially materialized.

Sometimes the problem is merely one of excluding cranks and crackpots. Announcing hearings on the nomination of Dean Acheson as Secretary of State, for example, the Senate Foreign Relations Committee stated that it would hear all "respectable and creditable" persons. Sometimes unrespectable and discreditable persons who appear on the scene are disposed of by allowing a personal appearance of one or two minutes or by merely inserting their statements in the record of the hearings.

No one has an abstract right to be heard before a congressional committee. Representatives of minor political parties, for example, are often excluded. In denying the American Labor Party an opportunity to testify at the 1947 hearings of the Joint Committee on the Economic Report, the Committee staff director stated that it is often the consensus of committee members "that we ought not to invite as witnesses representatives of any political party, as such. The hearings are set up to deal with the economic question and every effort is being made by the Committee to keep them to a non-partisan basis." [20]

Occasionally all nongovernmental witnesses are ruled as ineligible to appear. This happened at the 1948 hearings of the House Ways and Means Committee. It is only in rare cases, however, that a representative of any substantial organization is ever denied the right to be heard. This is particularly true if the organization has a close friend or two among the committee membership.

It should not be thought, however, that committees are always flooded with requests to testify from people who are interested in a pending measure. Many potential witnesses are reluctant dragons. Sound strategy often calls for withholding testimony entirely or for delaying until the most auspicious moment. In the development of the Clayton Antitrust Act, long hearings were held be-

---

[19] For an illustration of how delay in appearing can work to a witness's disadvantage see Marriner Eccles, "Beckoning Frontiers" (New York: Knopf, 1951), pp. 205–207. Eccles tells in great detail how Senator Glass, as chairman of the Senate Banking and Currency Committee, delayed for almost a month Eccles' appearance on the Banking Act of 1935 until the views of opposition witnesses "had been firmly fixed in the public mind. . . ."

[20] *The New York Times*, Sept. 15, 1947.

fore the House Judiciary Committee from December, 1913, to April, 1914, but one can leaf through a thousand pages of oral testimony without finding a word from a single government witness. This was probably the result of a wait-and-see attitude on the part of President Wilson. Chamberlain writes:

> It may well be that the decision to keep the Administration position unrecorded during the formative stage was a deliberate one dictated by the strategic needs of the occasion. . . . When it became apparent that the stringency of regulation envisioned in the proposed bill was impossible of realization, Wilson was able to disclaim responsibility for it and demand sweeping changes in the direction of moderation.[21]

Similarly, the United States Chamber of Commerce, although solicited for testimony at the 1945 Senate hearings on the Full Employment Bill, succeeded in dodging all requests and deferring testimony until hearings began in the House.[22]

It follows, therefore, that it is also wise strategy on the part of other contestants in the legislative struggle to try to have reluctant dragons brought into the hearing room. The purpose may be merely to elicit support from timid witnesses who would like to stay on the fence instead of taking a position. Or the purpose may be to bring opponents out in the open rather than allow them to carry on their opposition entirely behind the scenes. It may even be to put opposition witnesses on the spot by having them subjected to antagonistic questioning by committee members. No matter what the purpose, it is only rarely that testimony dodgers are brought before legislative hearings through the use of their committee subpoena powers.[23] In most cases, the method used is to extend a written invitation and use the threat of adverse publicity against a witness who refuses to accept. When subpoenas are used in connection with legislative testimony, it is usually at the instigation of the witness himself. During World War II, for example, many government officials found that by having a committee subpoena them as witnesses they could achieve a dual objective of making their case in public and also of maintaining a record of being opposed to the washing of dirty linen in public.

[21] Lawrence H. Chamberlain, "The President, Congress, and Legislation" (New York: Columbia University Press, 1946), p. 39.

[22] See Stephen K. Bailey, "Congress Makes a Law" (New York: Columbia University Press, 1949), pp. 138–143.

[23] Under the Legislative Reorganization Act of 1946, every standing committee of the Senate was given subpoena power to require the attendance of witnesses and the production of documents. This was part of an effort to merge legislative with investigatory functions and thereby reduce the need for special investigating committees. House committees must obtain this power by special resolution.

The President's Spokesmen

There is one important contestant in the legislative struggle whose name never appears on the list of *dramatis personae*—the President of the United States. It is not merely that Presidential testimony before a congressional committee would be a task too time-consuming for the busiest man in the country; it is also that it would be beneath a President's dignity to subject himself to committee interrogation. Nor has any member of Congress seriously proposed that a President come before his committee as a witness. If there are compelling reasons for a meeting—and there are at times—between a President and a committee, then it is Mahomet who will go to the mountain. In August, 1919, for example, members of the Senate Committee on Foreign Relations wanted more information on the Versailles Treaty proposed by President Wilson. "They therefore instructed me," wrote Senator Lodge, "to ask the President whether he would receive the Committee. He replied in the affirmative, appointed the day and invited the Committee to lunch with him after the conversation had been held." [24]

The question has often arisen, however, as to who should appear before a congressional committee to explain the President's position on specific matters. In a sense, all agency heads are representatives of the President. For this reason increasing efforts have been made during recent years to check agency testimony to see if it conforms with "the President's program." [25] Yet in an equally important sense, every executive agency representative is also on his own, because a President needs to be as free as possible to shift his own position at some subsequent stage of the legislative process.

A more delicate problem arises in connection with the President's closest associates in the White House and the Executive Office. It has generally been the Presidential practice to extend the shield of protection to cover members of the White House staff whether they be shadowy men with a passion for anonymity or more prominent figures, such as the President's Counsel or the Assistant to the President. Officials in various parts of the Executive Office of the President, however, often come before congressional committees to expound the President's program in authoritative terms. This has been done as a matter of course by the Director of the Budget. In the case of the Council of Economic Advisers, there has been some degree of controversy. The first members of the Council of Economic Advisers split publicly on this question. The chair-

[24] Henry Cabot Lodge, "The Senate and the League of Nations" (New York: Scribner, 1925), p. 158.

[25] See Richard E. Neustadt, "Presidential Clearance of Legislation" (unpublished doctoral dissertation, Harvard University, June, 1950) for a realistic appraisal of these efforts during the period from 1921 to 1949. In particular, see section on "Use and Effect of Clearance Phraseology," Chap. 3, pp. 192–196.

man, Edwin G. Nourse, objected to Council appearances before congressional committees on the following grounds:

. . . if the precedent of such appearance is established, the time would come sooner or later when Council members would be asked to testify on matters on which the President has seen fit to take a position definitely contrary to their advice. This would present Council members with the alternative of arguing for the President's position regardless of their own professional convictions, or, on the other hand, of arguing against a policy recommended by the President.

The other two members, Leon H. Keyserling, vice-chairman, and John D. Clark, stated

that both the President and the members of the Joint Committee although occupying "political" office, are strongly predisposed to draw upon objective economic analysis in fulfilling their defined functions under the Employment Act. They feel that, because the Council was established to assist the President in the preparation of his Economic Reports, the intent of the act will best be served if the Council extends cooperative professional assistance to the Joint Committee as, in its turn under the act, it comes to consider the fundamental materials contained in the President's Economic Reports as transmitted to the Congress.[26]

With Nourse's resignation in 1949 this issue was resolved in favor of Council testimony before the Joint Committee on the Economic Report on behalf of the President's general program. There still remained, however, the ever-recurring problem of choosing the specific measures on which the Council members might appropriately appear as the President's representatives.

Executive Reports and Documents

A widespread committee practice is to request written reports on pending bills from executive agencies. This is usually done before a hearing takes place. This practice provides committee members with valuable detailed information. It also helps in the decisions on whether or not to have a hearing and on how a hearing should be planned. In most cases these requests go in a routine fashion to all interested agencies. One variant from the norm is to present detailed questions along with the request for an agency's views. Another is to avoid requesting reports from agencies whose views might be regarded as hostile.

The preparation of agency reports to congressional committees is an important and far-flung operation within the executive branch. Agency officials usually welcome the opportunity to express their views and lay the groundwork for possible testimony in the future. They also recognize that the preparation of these reports is itself a vital part of the policy-formation process.

[26] Edwin G. Nourse and Bertram M. Gross, "The Role of the Council of Economic Advisers," *American Political Science Review,* Vol. 13, No. 2, April, 1948, pp. 290–291.

In fact, it is so vital that the work of the Bureau of the Budget in clearing and coordinating agency reports to congressional committees has become one of the outstanding examples of coordination activities in the executive branch. Agency reports often play a determining role in the legislative struggle. This is particularly true when the reporting process is used as a means of developing a rallying point for agencies, private organizations, and members of Congress.

A perfect illustration of this is found in the history of the school-construction legislation in 1949. Neustadt writes:

> In May of 1949, a letter from the (Budget) Director to the Chairman of Senate Labor Committee set forth the considerations which should govern legislative action in the field of school construction. In so doing he outlined a middle course among the conflicting programs and approaches with which the Committee was confronted. The agencies generally fell in behind the Bureau's line. The rival interest groups joined hands on it. The Senate sponsors of a variety of measures united to support and advance it.
>
> None of this was accidental. The Bureau's letter was the product of three months of appraisal and discussion with the interest groups, the agencies concerned, the White House staff and key members of the Senate. The line which the Bureau took was that worked out informally by a group, composed of a key Senator's secretary, the strategist of a vital interest group and the Presidential assistants most concerned, in addition to its Budget members. The line was mutually satisfactory. It was acceptable to the Budget's technical staff. The agencies could live with it. The risks were removed and the results rendered reasonably certain before the words were spoken.[27]

Occasionally members of a legislative committee are interested in obtaining executive documents that are classified as secret or confidential. In these situations subpoena power may be used. Here again, as with the problem of obtaining witnesses, the great utility of a subpoena is that it provides an excuse for executive officials to make available documents that they want to make available, but with a public display of reluctance. Many officers of government agencies, and of private organizations as well, have collaborated in preparing the details of subpoenas that require them to produce certain very specifically designated documents and letters. When a congressional subpoena meets with strong resistance by agency officials, however, there is no guarantee that it will succeed in producing even a single sheet of paper. The judicial and penal sanctions that ordinarily stand behind a subpoena are simply not applicable to members of a coordinate branch of the Federal government. This was illustrated in March, 1948, when congressional committees attempted to obtain confidential employee loyalty files from a number of government agencies. President Truman immediately directed all executive officials who might receive congressional subpoenas for these files to refer them to the

27 Neustadt, *op. cit.*, pp. 200–201.

White House.[28] Although it is probable that some of these files were "leaked" to some members of Congress by minor officials, none were obtained through the subpoena technique.

Joint Sessions

The suggestion has often been made that there be more joint hearings between parallel committees of the Senate and the House of Representatives. This suggestion is not the brain child of political scientists alone. It comes from tired and harried legislative representatives who would like to simplify their lives by killing two birds with one stone. It also comes from ambitious folk who would like to stage one big show rather than two small ones.

Joint sessions of this type, however, are extremely rare. The few experiments that have been made merely serve to demonstrate the tendency of Senators to steal the play from Representatives and monopolize the limelight. This tendency is enforced by the fact that the problem of who should be chairman of a joint hearing is usually resolved in favor of a Senator, and the problem of where it will meet is usually resolved in favor of a meeting room in the Senate Office Building or on the Senate side of the Capitol. Senators, therefore, tend to like joint sessions but their inclinations in this direction are usually frustrated by the corresponding disinclination of Representatives.[29]

Within each house somewhat more use is made of joint sessions between committees dealing with related subjects. This practice has been extensively developed to give expression to the community of interests between members of appropriation committees and the members of legislative committees. Designated members of the Armed Services Committees, for example, meet in conjunction with the appropriations subcommittees handling appropriations for the armed services.

PERFORMANCE AT THE HEARINGS

The blustering committee chairman shakes his fist at an intimidated witness. . . . A press agent places a midget on J. P. Morgan's lap. . . . A mysterious "Madam X" tells all. . . .

Incidents like these, confined largely but not exclusively to congressional investigations, have given many people a wrong impression about congressional hearings. It is a rare hearing that is either a sensational spectacle or an outrage upon commonly accepted principles of good taste or fairness. Although

---

[28] President's Directive of Mar. 13, 1948.

[29] It is nonetheless true that joint hearings on *ad hoc* basis are easier to arrange than it would be to operate a formal structure of joint legislative committees.

the performance at legislative hearings runs a broad gamut from America at its best to Congress at its worst, the sum total of public hearings held every year is an invaluable part of American political life. To the onlooker, the legislative hearing is "an indispensable key to the puzzles of that vast onward sweep of legislation in the full arena of the House. Here he sees the headsprings of law." [30] To the advocate, it is a crucial point of direct touch with members of Congress.

For the member of Congress, it is one of the principal means of learning the points and bases of conflict. Senator Paul Douglas of Illinois has stated this in language of general applicability.

If one reviews the Senatorial day, it becomes evident that there is not much chance for a Senator to undertake a profound or cloistered study of a problem. The research personnel in the departments may be of some help to him. His own staff will be of greater help. But in the final analysis, he must learn for himself what is true or false. And he can only find that out in the committee hearings.[31]

Congressional Attendance

Most members of Congress have the feeling that they are always being cut into little pieces by competing demands for their time. This is particularly true of members with important committee assignments, difficult personal projects, or high ambitions. It applies more to Representatives whose constituencies are near Washington than to those whom geography protects from inundations of personal visits. It is more true for Senators than for Representatives. It is more applicable during the hectic closing days of any session.

As a result, it is very unusual to have full committee attendance at public hearings. Advance commitments to attend have little meaning. Until a hearing actually starts, there is no telling who will actually show up. Often a member will rush into a hearing for the sole purpose of making a brief appearance. He will thumb through a witness's prepared statement, ask a question or two, and then, murmuring regrets to the chairman, hastily depart.

Not infrequently one can see more committee staff members at a hearing than members of the committee themselves. Occasionally staff members may in fact run a hearing in the absence of members—although this practice is usually confined to the taking of preliminary evidence in connection with committee investigations. At times a member's staff assistant may attend the hearing on his behalf.

When a person is defending himself in court on charges of perjury before a congressional committee or of failure to comply with a committee subpoena, an obvious point of defense is to attempt to prove that the committee or

[30] Lauros G. McConachie, "Congressional Committees" (New York: Crowell, 1898), p. 63.
[31] *The New York Times Magazine*, Mar. 20, 1949.

subcommittee was acting illegally because of the absence of a quorum.[32] However, most of these questions arise in connection with congressional investigations rather than in hearings on specific legislative proposals. Small committee attendance is only rarely a legal problem. In practical, everyday terms, its effect is to detract from a hearing's significance as a method of getting ideas across to committee members or of obtaining general publicity.

The various contestants in the legislative struggle, therefore, have a direct interest in rounding up committee members, particularly their friends and supporters. This effort is not limited to committee members. Attendance can be augmented by members of Congress who do not themselves belong to a given committee. Most committees, as a matter of courtesy, allow any other member of Congress who so chooses to sit with them at a public hearing.[33] One of the great weaknesses of the Democratic Administration after World War II was the failure to organize the active participation by Administration supporters in Congress in committee hearings on Administration bills. This reflected in part the weaknesses of the private organizations supporting the Democratic Administration. On the other hand, the opponents of the Administration's legislative program were usually extremely active in mobilizing congressional attendance on the part of Republican and conservative Democrats. This, in turn, reflected the energy and resources of the private organizations on their side of the fence.

The Testimony

In advising businessmen how to testify before congressional committees the National Association of Manufacturers once selected as a model the 1939 testimony of petroleum-industry representatives before the Temporary National Economic Committee. The N.A.M. document stated:

[32] This point was raised in the Meyers case, in addition to the question of the subcommittee's legality. The U.S. Court of Appeals agreed with the appellant in part: "On October 6, 1947, however, only two Senators were present at the hearing. Since they were a minority of the subcommittee, they could not legally function except to adjourn. For that reason, the testimony of Lamarre given on that day cannot be considered as perjury nor can appellant be convicted of suborning it." But the court then pointed out the following: "But practically all Lamarre's testimony was given on October 4, when a quorum was present. The proceedings of that day contain the perjurious statements described in all three counts, and his examination on October 6 was largely repetitious." United States Court of Appeals for the District of Columbia Circuit, No. 9797, *Bennett E. Meyers, Appellant, v. United States,* Nov. 8, 1948.

[33] The appropriations committees allow participation by other members of Congress only on the basis of the subcommittee relationships worked out with parallel legislative committees. A few other committees from time to time have also insisted that other members of Congress can take part in their proceedings only as witnesses and not as participants on the committee side of the table.

For weeks the petroleum group studied the TNEC members and watched their conduct of witnesses. When the oil men appeared, they knew the likes and dislikes of each committee member, and they pulled out an organ stop that appealed to everyone on the committee. Even the committee members were high in their praise of what the oil industry had done. And most important of all, it ended the clamor to enact legislation drastically regulating the oil industry.[34]

The oil-industry testimony was based upon more than a mere study of "the likes and dislikes of each committee member." It was the product of a large research organization mobilized in advance under the general direction of the American Petroleum Institute for the specific purpose of developing and documenting the industry's case. It was replete with charts, tables, and statistics, some of which helped to get the industry's points across and some of which gave the industry's presentation that degree of incomprehensibility which is best calculated to impress a not-too-sophisticated listener. Moreover, it is probable that the oil-industry witnesses were not only coached in advance but were also the beneficiaries of dress rehearsals at which their colleagues pretended to be congressional inquisitors.

In these respects the oil-industry testimony was not much different from testimony of any other large and well-financed organization. The appraisal of individual committee members, the use of research techniques, the presentation of elaborate charts and tables, careful advance coaching—these are all elements that go into the preparation of testimony. Although witnesses with meager resources behind them cannot do much along these lines, it is a rare witness indeed who will come before a congressional committee totally unprepared. The organizations that play a serious part in the legislative struggle have learned that a witness who has not organized his case beforehand will, at best, be wasting his time and, at worst, be a lamb led to slaughter.

The Legislative Reorganization Act of 1946 requires witnesses to submit written statements in advance of appearance so that these can be summarized by committee staff members. (Sec. 133(e).) In this way, it was thought, "the tedious oral repetition of oral testimony could be avoided, much valuable time would be saved, and the conduct of committee hearings could be greatly expedited." [35] This requirement, however, is not generally observed. Many witnesses never finish preparing a final draft of their prepared statements until the very last moment. They are not always eager to provide hostile committee members or their staff representatives with an advance inkling of the approach to be taken. When advance statements are submitted, committee staffs often neglect

[34] Walter J. Chamblin, Jr., "Know Your Congressmen" (New York: National Association of Manufacturers, 1944), p. 8.

[35] "Organization of Congress," Report of the Joint Committee on the Organization of Congress, 79th Cong., 2d Sess., S. Rept. 1011, p. 11.

entirely the preparation of digests, or solicit their preparation by the witnesses themselves.

Some witnesses glue their eyes to the text of their prepared statements and deviate not an inch. More expert witnesses, however, ask leave to have their prepared statements inserted in the *Record* and then speak more informally. Some will even plan ahead of time to leave their strongest points out of prepared testimony (particularly if it should be made available to committee members in advance) and save them for more effective use in informal talking.

Informality and spontaneity, of course, are often the product of advance labors. In the preparation of business witnesses against the Full Employment Bill, for example, two research workers prepared mimeographed documents to serve in the preparation of testimony. One of these documents contained a section called "Items for Ridicule." According to Bailey, one of the items suggested several "spontaneous" witticisms.[36]

President Franklin D. Roosevelt, it seems, often lectured his Cabinet members on how to handle themselves before congressional committees. He said:

> We must confine ourselves again to our own business and we must be factual. There has been altogether too much going before committees of Congress and talking about somebody else's work and venturing all kinds of opinion evidence which only is the opinion of the person who happens to give it. . . . In all our testimony before Congress and in all our answers to questions, let us stick to our own last and let us be factual about it. That is one of the most important things that has been said in a long time.[37]

A more extended lecture has been given to businessmen in the "Know Your Congressmen" pamphlet of the National Association of Manufacturers. The five "do's" in the pamphlet are worthy of quotation:

> "1. Before flatly opposing a bill, see if there is not some way of offering a compromise that would be acceptable.
>
> "2. Avoid demagoguery before a committee. It is resented.
>
> "3. The best witness is the man who is doing the job—not somebody to whom he has told the story and who is paid to represent him.
>
> "4. Get directly to the facts. Committees are not much interested in long discussions about the trends of the time.
>
> "5. Get your story told to the committee itself. Any material inserted in the committee record is of little value unless you take the trouble to motivate it yourself."

The four "don'ts" that follow are also of great interest:

> "1. Don't get 'smart.'
> An engineer testifying on a bill made a sneering reference to the Antitrust Act.

---

[36] Bailey, *op. cit.*, p. 138.
[37] Excerpt from Proceedings, Twenty-eighth Meeting, National Emergency Council, Dec. 17, 1935.

He was asked to tell what he knew about the Antitrust Act and was forced into a display of ignorance that destroyed the value of his testimony on the bill.

"2. Don't get off the subject.

A member of a Congressional committee diverted an important business witness into a discussion of the German tariff system, and the witness never got back from Germany.

"3. Don't assume a superior attitude.

It never pays to have a chip on your shoulder. Congressmen are experts at knocking them off.

"4. Don't get pugnacious and stand on your rights.

You haven't any. You only have such privileges as the committee may give you."

Pugnaciousness has its place, however. Sometimes the only effective way of dealing with a domineering interrogator is to hit back instead of merely turning the other cheek. One of the best practitioners of this approach was Harold Ickes who, as Secretary of the Interior, developed a highly effective technique. In 1946, Ickes testified on health insurance on behalf of a private organization with which he associated himself after his departure from the Government. Senator Forrest Donnell of Missouri tried to make the case that Ickes was unqualified to testify because he had not read each section of the bill. Ickes answered with a stinging reply that put Donnell in his place and won for Ickes the support and respect of other committee members. He said:

Well, I was prepared for that question because I understand that is a customary question from the Senator. I have not. I have read a carefully prepared digest of it, and I did not know—I have been appearing before congressional committees for some 13 years—and I did not know that it was a necessary prerequisite to have read carefully a bill, because I have appeared before so many committees the members of which had not read the bill.[38]

In contrast with this display of pugnacity, many witnesses maintain attitudes of deference bordering on the obsequious. When asked stupid questions, they will answer with respect rather than tolerance. When asked difficult or embarrassing questions, they will emphasize their willingness to cooperate and act in conformance with the "doctrine of apparent frankness" (a term coined by a high Government official during World War II to describe his agency's attitude when dealing with congressional committees). When slapped in public, they will turn the other cheek.

Facts are so important that many witnesses will answer factual questions in statistical terms without really being sure of their ground. This is risky business when there is a chance that one's bluff may be called. The risk is minimized, however, by the opportunities that exist for making a revision of the

38 "National Health Program," Hearings before the Senate Committee on Education and Labor, 79th Cong., 2d Sess., S. Rept. 1606, Part 1, p. 401.

written record before it is printed. To protect themselves on points of fact, many heads of private companies and government agencies will never appear before a congressional committee without being surrounded by a battery of experts who can ply them with notes on questions that arise or who, when asked, can speak directly on a given question.[39] The more experts surrounding a witness, however, the less chance there is of his building up an impression of personal familiarity with his case. Some witnesses, therefore, prefer to take their chances on factual details and appear unattended.

The Interrogation

Seated together in a group facing the witnesses across a committee table, committee members make a most impressive appearance. They enjoy something of the same institutional dignity that surrounds a group of judges in a courtroom. They feel important, too. This can be corroborated by anyone who has sat as a committee member at a public hearing. It is publicly demonstrated by the demeanor of committee interrogators.

And they are important! The behavior of a committee member can make one witness's testimony an outstanding success. He can throw a monkey wrench into the well-laid plans of another witness and convert his presentation into a dismal failure. This was illustrated by the brief hearings on the atomic energy legislation in 1946 by Representative Andrew May of Kentucky when he was still chairman of the House Committee on Military Affairs. "The witnesses favoring civilian control," writes an observant reporter, "were skillfully hushed. Those on the other side were led on with gracious smiles." [40]

Committee interrogation, like cross-examination in a courtroom, is an art in itself. An effective interrogation must be based upon a clear understanding of the objectives to be achieved and a grasp of the basic facts that are involved in the matter at hand.

A friendly interrogation will often start by questions that build up the character and competence of the witness. It will give the witness a chance to make a prepared statement before any questions are asked him. A good example of a rapprochement between the interrogator and the witness is found in the 1948 hearings on basing-point legislation before a subcommittee of the Senate Committee on Interstate and Foreign Commerce.

Harmony prevailed in the relations between the subcommittee, its chairman, and all other witnesses. With the skill of a conductor on the podium, Capehart led wit-

[39] A witness is customarily allowed to bring advisers with him. The question of whether a witness should be allowed to be accompanied by legal counsel is one that has arisen only in connection with the activities of a few investigating committees.

[40] Coffin, op. cit., p. 233.

ness after witness (once their prepared statements were out of the way) through a series of questions that made it appear that enterprisers were confused by the existing law, that they had no place to go in the government for a definitive answer, and that it was necessary for Congress to come to their rescue and write legislation on the subject. He was his own best witness, and he spoke to the record through many voices.[41]

An unfriendly interrogation is quite different. It may very well start with questions that demonstrate the incompetence or unreliability of the witness. It may then go into the character of the organization which he is representing. In interrogating witnesses who favored national health insurance at a long series of hearings from 1946 to 1949, Senator Forrest Donnell of Missouri habitually asked for facts concerning membership and strength of the organizations represented. He also asked—and in many instances this was extremely damaging—for the facts concerning how and when an organization formally authorized a position in favor of health insurance. This line of interrogation revealed that many witnesses were appearing without the formal support of the organizations in whose name they purported to speak.

Customarily, a witness is allowed to make some sort of preliminary statement before questions are fired at him. This practice gives every witness a distinct initial advantage. Sometimes, however, a hostile committee member will deny a witness this opportunity by initiating a substantive interrogation before he can make a preliminary statement or by breaking in upon the statement without allowing him to finish. If the witness succeeds in making an effective point, the interrogator may then change the subject. In the questioning of an organized-labor spokesman who opposed his position on basing-point legislation, Senator Capehart sidetracked the witness's prepared presentation and "undertook to swoop him off into the imperium of speculation." [42]

A friendly committee member will sometimes give a witness a list of questions in advance. A hostile committee member would never do so. As Senator Fall stated to President Wilson, "If you were on a stand and I were cross-examining you as a witness, I would prefer not to let you see the whole series of questions." [43] As with courtroom examinations, committee interrogators often take great delight in carefully laying a trap for a witness and taking him by surprise.

There is no one source of the questions asked. Many spring extemporaneously from the minds of the committee members. Sometimes these are the most per-

[41] Latham, *op. cit.*, p. 106.

[42] *Ibid.*, p. 117.

[43] From transcript of White House Conference between President Woodrow Wilson and members of the Senate Committee on Foreign Relations, Aug. 19, 1919. Lodge, *op. cit.*, App. 4, p. 346.

tinent of all. Sometimes the committee member "gets tripped up by his im-provisations in committee sessions and feels like a fool because of it," [44] or per-haps, while feeling wise, looks idiotic. Some questions are handed to committee members during the course of a hearing by their staff assistants, by reporters or spectators, or even—in a manner that provides an indirect form of cross-examination—by other witnesses. Many witnesses lay the ground for favor-able questioning by friendly members by submitting lists of prepared ques-tions in advance. These may even be interlarded in a witness's prepared testi-mony so that the committee member can interrupt with a helpful question at a desired point. Occasionally, when the subject matter is important enough to warrant it, a witness and a committee member will get together ahead of time to develop a prepared dialogue and may even rehearse it like actors pre-paring a play.

On matters calling for a high degree of preparation on details, a committee chairman will sometimes allow the interrogation to be handled by members of the committee staff. A staff member who takes on this task, however, always runs the risk of drawing thunder and lightning upon his head if he steals too much of the limelight from committee members or antagonizes any outside groups. Or else he may get in bad with committee members who agree with former Senator James F. Byrnes' dictum that "only members of the committee should be allowed to interrogate witnesses." [45]

The Record

One could compile a good-sized library every year, far more than any one pair of eyes could possibly read, merely by collecting the printed record of congressional hearings. There was a time when the publication of committee hearings was regarded as an infringement of parliamentary procedure. In 1885 Woodrow Wilson observed:

> There is a conclusive objection to the publication of the proceedings of the Com-mittees, which is recognized as of course by all parliamentary lawyers, namely, that those proceedings are of no force till confirmed by the House. . . . It is made a breach of order for any member to allude on the floor of the House to anything that has taken place in committee, "unless by a written report sanctioned by a majority of the Committee." [46]

This procedural objection has long since vanished from the scene. In its place has arisen in the minds of many witnesses and members of Congress an exaggerated regard for the significance of the fine points contained in a pub-

[44] Paul H. Douglas, "Report from a Freshman Senator," *The New York Times Magazine,* Mar. 20, 1949.

[45] James F. Byrnes, "Streamlining Congress," *American Magazine,* February, 1945.

[46] Wilson, *op. cit.,* pp. 83–84.

lished record. This is partly due to the fact that lawyers mistakenly attribute to the written record of a congressional hearing the same legal importance that is more properly ascribed to the record in a courtroom proceeding. They often labor over fine points that are subsequently read and appreciated by no one but themselves.

The real significance of published records of a committee hearing is that they provide a valuable source of information and propaganda. The publication of a statement in a committee report gives it a certain amount of dignity and status. The record is also used as a means of publishing various supplementary memoranda and reports that could not otherwise be readily published or made freely available. Furthermore, committee members can always get a thousand or two thousand copies for free distribution and these can be made available to interested organizations and agencies. At times published hearings on bills or at least some sections of them are so valuable for informational and propaganda purposes that additional copies are ordered from the Government Printing Office for more widespread distribution. The utility of the published hearings generally is diminished by the fact that hearings are seldom organized and edited in a manner that promotes readability. This obstacle, however, is overcome at times by the addition of such editorial aids for the reader as subheads in a text, indices, and so forth.

The published record is not always an accurate reflection of what actually went on at a committee hearing. Both witnesses and committee members are usually given an opportunity to correct their remarks. Theoretically, they are supposed to catch only errors made by the transcribers and improve upon the grammar of an extemporaneous discussion. In practice, this opportunity is habitually used to change the meaning of what was actually said and even to add entirely new material. In addition, the chairman of the committee often makes and allows others to make many off-the-record statements. When this happens, the official reporter rests for a moment. On these occasions some of the juiciest bits of testimony and interrogation are recorded only in the memories of those in the committee room at the time.

Nor is the transcribed record of a committee hearing always published. Economy is the reason that is often given; the publication of hearings costs money. The better reason, however, is a disinclination to tell what has been happening. In 1949, for example, the Senate Committee on Rules and Administration held a "quickie" hearing at which representatives of the Democratic party organizations in the counties immediately adjoining the District of Columbia requested that a pending amendment to the Hatch Act be broadened by the addition of a section that would allow Federal workers in the vicinity of the District of Columbia to take part in local party activities. This proposal was vigorously opposed by other groups in the vicinity of the District of Columbia, particularly in Arlington County. The publication of the printed transcript would have made it easier for the opponents of this proposal to mobilize their forces. Accordingly, the transcripts were never published.

For many years the hearings of the House Committee on Appropriations were never published until after an appropriations bill had come up for consideration on the floor of the House. This had the effect of giving the members of the House Appropriations Committee a monopoly of information. In protest against this practice, the following provision was inserted in the Legislative Reorganization Act of 1946: "No general appropriation bill shall be considered in either House unless, prior to the consideration of such bill, printed committee hearings and reports on such bills have been available for at least three calendar days for the Members of the House in which such bill is to be considered." This requirement has not always been followed by the House Appropriations Committee. Nor is the principle contained in the provision necessarily respected by other committees.

Chapter 16

DECISIONS IN COMMITTEE

"LEGISLATION, as we nowadays conduct it," wrote Woodrow Wilson, "is not conducted in the open. It is not threshed out in open debate upon the floors of our assemblies. It is, on the contrary, framed, digested and concluded in committee rooms." [1]

Although it would be stretching the point to write off floor action as negligible in importance in the legislative process (and in the severity of his attack upon the committee system, Wilson did some stretching), the bulk of congressional decisions on legislative matters is unquestionably framed and digested in committee rooms. The decisions made on the floor of either house by and large represent ratification or modification of committee decisions. Even when floor changes occur, mild or drastic, they are usually the outgrowth of views formulated in committee by a minority group of committee members. The shaping and making of decisions in committee bring our attention to executive sessions of committees, committee reports, and committee voting methods. A very special kind of committee to be examined is the conference committee. Further, there are certain formal devices for bringing influence to bear upon committee choices, and these too shall be noted.

SHAPING DECISIONS IN COMMITTEE

The Executive Sessions

A high navy official was once asked by a Presidential staff member to explain the Navy Department's position on a proposed amendment to an Administration bill dealing with the national defense. "This is no time for us to take a stand," the navy man replied. "We'll develop our position when we go down to the Hill and meet in executive session to help the committee mark up the bill."

This incident illustrates the fact that the executive sessions of congressional committees are centers of vital decision making. Public hearings are merely a

[1] Woodrow Wilson, "The New Freedom" (Garden City, N.Y.: Doubleday, 1913), p. 125.

preliminary. The decisions are made after the hearings are over and the doors are closed. It also points up the fact that the activity in process behind committee doors is often far more significant than that policy-making process behind the closed doors in the executive branch. The nonpublic character of executive sessions promotes the free interplay of ideas among committee members. Compromises and alternatives can be shaped in a fluid environment that could never be approximated at a public meeting.

The executive session also confers a special position of power upon every participant, each one of whom shares the oligopoly of information which is created by the nonpublic character of the meetings. Each participant is in an especially effective position to convey information to outsiders—whether they be the President and other Administration officials, the leaders of private organizations, or other members of Congress—for use in the conduct of their respective campaigns.

These opportunities are seldom allowed to go unnoticed. An "executive session" is far from being a "secret" session. One member may leave the committee room and immediately phone the President or a White House Secretary to ask that the "heat" be put on at a place where it is sorely needed. Another member may move directly from the committee room to a meeting of representatives of government agencies and private organizations called to discuss the next steps in their legislative campaign. Sometimes, through either a legal or an unofficial action, the whole story of conflicts within the committee may be given to the press.

In some instances official statements on the progress of committee decisions are given out at regular intervals. The practice of the House Ways and Means Committee, when working on a major bill, has been described as follows:

> Statements are customarily issued to the press at the end of every session of the Committee by the chairman. Thus, all decisions of the Committee, even of a tentative character, are publicly known almost as soon as they are taken. In one sense, this helps make the decisions final, since there is a certain reluctance to reverse the vote after announcement has been made to the public.[2]

One of the major campaigns in the development of the Atomic Energy Act of 1946 centered around the debate on civilian versus military control which developed at the executive sessions of the Special Senate Committee on Atomic Energy. The disclosure of an amendment presented by Senator Vandenberg "was the signal for a direct offensive by the scientists, the conference of organizations, the emergency committee of prominent individuals, and the many friends of civilian control in the communications fields and elsewhere."[3] Dur-

---

[2] Roy Blough, "The Federal Taxing Process" (New York: Prentice-Hall, 1952), p. 72.

[3] Byron S. Miller, "A Law Is Passed—The Atomic Energy Act of 1946," *University of Chicago Law Review*, Vol. 15, No. 4, Summer, 1948, p. 811.

ing the same series of executive sessions, committee members "sought advice from leading scientists in close touch with the scientists' organizations and made a determined effort to produce a section which would preserve the maximum secrecy consistent with dissemination of enough data not to hamper research." [4]

When hard and fast lines are drawn among the committee members, it is only natural for opposing groups to meet separately before the committee sessions. On those relatively rare occasions when a decision of this character follows party lines, the Republican and Democratic members may meet separately. Upon conclusion of the public hearings by the Senate Finance Committee on the Tariff Bill of 1929–1930, "the Republican members met as a party group, privately, to rewrite the House bill, and having arrived at a party decision on the bill in secret, went into a regular session of the Finance Committee and by a strictly partisan vote adopted the amendments agreed upon and reported the revised bill favorably to the Senate." [5] The rarity of this method of operation is not only a reflection of the looseness of party operations in Congress but also a contributing factor toward the development of intimate relations between members of opposing parties.

A committee chairman is in a strategic position to influence the operations of an executive session. He can call meetings at a time inconvenient for members whom he would see absent. By delaying the calling of a session, he can provide time for the application of pressure to certain members, or for the preparation of new drafts, or merely for killing time. Unless there is serious objection among his committee colleagues, he can give positions of privilege and potential influence to representatives of government agencies or private organizations by inviting them to the sessions. He can direct the preparation of staff memoranda, drafts, and other documents.

The first problem confronting an executive session is the decision as to what measure will serve as the starting point of discussion. This is not as easy as it might seem. Many bills are skeleton measures introduced to serve as a springboard for hearings, while the period during which the hearings are held is used for the preparation of a more adequate measure. By the time an executive session begins there may be many alternative drafts before the committee. When the Senate Special Committee on Atomic Energy began its 1946 executive sessions, for example, there were three measures before it: a bill introduced by its chairman, Senator Brien McMahon of Connecticut, a bill submitted by Senator Ball of Minnesota, and the May-Johnson bill which was the first measure that had been introduced on the subject and had the support of the

[4] *Ibid.*, p. 812.
[5] E. E. Schattschneider, "Politics, Pressures, and the Tariff" (New York: Prentice-Hall, 1935), p. 35.

War Department. After a preliminary skirmish, Senator McMahon succeeded in having the committee decide to use his bill as a working guide.[6]

"Reading the bill" is a customary procedure in executive sessions. Once various members have had a chance to make general comments on this or that point, the chairman will usually start with the first section and read the measure line by line. When another draft is before a committee, the reading process is sometimes facilitated by a "comparative print." This consists of a large broad-paged booklet in which one column gives the sections of one bill and the other column gives comparable sections of the alternative measure.

The reading of a bill at an executive session is a valuable intellectual discipline. It usually brings the committee members face to face with many points they never before had the time to understand. It brings out hidden meanings that would otherwise lie undiscovered. It is also a grueling operation. The finest points may take up a whole day's discussion. The reading and rereading of a major bill may stretch over many weeks of meetings. The following is a description of this phase of the work of the House Ways and Means Committee:

If the measure is a major one, the opening session of the Committee is likely to be given over to general remarks by various members of the Committee. The remarks may approach speeches in length and character. . . . After one or more sessions of this preliminary shake-down character, a procedure for discussion and decision is adopted. From then on, the various subjects under consideration are taken up for discussion in a more or less pre-determined order. However, since each subject considered by the Committee is usually related to every other subject, the Committee in its early sessions appears to be moving very slowly towards reaching decisions. This slowness is desirable and is more apparent than real, for after the Committee has thought its way through to an understanding of the problems and a perspective of their inter-relations, discussion moves rapidly toward tentative decisions.[7]

The Committee Reports

The most decisive form of action that a committee can take on a bill is inaction. This negative form of action almost invariably means the death of a measure. Nor is the corpse consigned elsewhere for burial. When committee members kill a bill by inaction, they do not discharge themselves of the measure and report it to the floor. Nor do they even prepare a written report stating why and wherefore.

Occasionally committee members will merely report a measure to the floor with no recommendation for either favorable or adverse action. This is something less than burial but also less than genuine endorsement. Or the mem-

6 Miller, op. cit.
7 Blough, op. cit., pp. 72–73.

bers of a committee may report a bill to the floor but very specifically reserve the right of committee members to propose amendments when the measure comes up on the floor. This strategy was used by Senator Aldrich in 1907 in connection with the report on the Hepburn Act to strengthen the interstate commerce legislation by the Senate Committee on Interstate Commerce. Its purpose was to deprive the measure of the prestige of the full committee endorsement and to sow the seeds for a floor attack on the bill through amendments capable of mustering widespread support.

An entirely favorable report on the other hand may be nothing but a grandstand play. In 1949 when the House Committee on Interstate and Foreign Commerce reported the O'Hara bill to curb the powers of the Federal Trade Commission, both the proponents and the opponents of the measure agreed that no attempt would be made to call the measure off the calendar and have it taken up for consideration on the floor of the House. The reporting of the bill, therefore, constituted in reality a device for doing nothing.

A committee report almost always invites amendment. These may be of a minor and perfecting nature. They may be "small and immaterial variations intended for the purpose of inducing the House to believe that they had matured the subject well. . . ." [8] They may make major changes or additions. Or else, the committee may, to use the stylized language of a congressional report, "report an amendment in the nature of a substitute."

Once a committee has reported a measure, it need not let go of the subject. Before or during floor consideration, committee members will often come forth with another report offering various proposed changes. Thus, in reporting the Versailles Treaty in September, 1919, the Senate Committee on Foreign Relations proposed four reservations and then reserved "the right to offer other reservations if they shall so determine." Two months later Senator Lodge reported a resolution of ratification and fourteen reservations which included in modified form the four that had been recommended earlier.

When subcommittees report to a full committee, they do so usually in the form of presenting merely the bill itself with any amendments that are being proposed. Sometimes a written report will be prepared but more for the purpose of submitting a proposed draft for the full committee's final report than for the purpose of making a public statement describing the grounds for its action.

The reports of full committees, however, invariably consist not only of the bill and amendments but also of a written report which is given the same calendar number as the reported bill. These committee reports play an important role in the legislative struggle. They serve as campaign documents for use not only in floor debate but in the organization of group support and the development of propaganda. They are useful as a means of exerting pressure

[8] Address by Rep. Hardin, *Annals of the Congress of the United States,* 14th Cong., 1st Sess., Jan. 24, 1816, pp. 747–748.

upon executive officials and of creating a record of "congressional intent" for the purpose of influencing subsequent judicial decisions. The participants in the legislative struggle, therefore, regard the preparation of committee reports as a vital operation. The quality of these reports, no matter what standard may be used in judging them, is a reflection of the ability and resourcefulness of the various contesting groups. The more detailed committee reports are usually prepared by executive officials and representatives of private organizations, with staff members and members of Congress playing a role in the direction of the work. Some of the most vigorous statements on the necessity of congressional independence from the bureaucrats and the pressure groups are to be found in committee reports prepared by executive-agency and pressure-group officials.

One of the recommendations of the Joint Committee on the Organization of Congress was "That a complete and understandable digest of a bill, together with legislative changes made by the bill, written in nontechnical language, accompany the committee report of each bill; and that this digest include a supporting statement of reasons for its passage, of the national interest involved, its cost, and the distribution of any benefits." [9] This recommendation was eliminated from the final version of the Legislative Reorganization Act of 1946. However, the growing tendency has been for reports to contain reasonably full explanations of whatever action is recommended. Experience has proved that information of this type is essential in the prosecution of a legislative campaign and that a committee report is one of the best ways to propagate it. From time to time, however, there will crop up conspicuous examples of a committee report that completely glosses over very important parts of the legislation it is proposing. This usually develops in a situation where there is no dissension within the committee and no clearly organized opposition discernible in the future.

When there is no disagreement among members of the committee, the committee's report will be tagged with neither the term majority nor minority. When there is disagreement, a number of alternative courses are open. With committee members in agreement upon a committee report, one or more members may submit and have printed in document form their "additional or supplemental" views. Or one report may be clearly labeled the majority report and another the minority one. There have even been occasions when the majority group in a committee issued "additional views" to put themselves on record in favor of a principle which they were not altogether willing to embody in a specific legislative proposal.

It is often completely impossible to tell from a committee report exactly what position each member of the committee has taken. A majority report is sometimes printed with only the name of the chairman attached to it. Other

[9] Organization of the Congress, 79th Cong., 2d Sess., S. Rept. 1011, Mar. 4, 1946, p. 8.

members are therefore free to indicate at any future date that they really did not go along with the rest of the committee. Even when there are both majority and minority reports, many members may fail to sign. Moreover, techniques have been developed whereby members can stand clearly on both sides of a given issue. In 1950, for example, the Senate Judiciary Committee reported the Mundt-Ferguson bill outlawing Communist activities by a vote of 12 to 1. Senator Harley Kilgore of West Virginia was one of the 12, but when he was publicly described by a newspaper writer as favoring the measure, he wrote a special letter to the editor of a Washington paper explaining that while he had voted to report the bill out, he was really against it. "As I explained at the time, I voted to report out the bill but reserved the right to oppose it when it was called up for action on the floor of the U.S. Senate. After the legislation was reported out, I wrote to Senator Pat McCarran, Chairman of the Judiciary Committee, and expressed grave doubts about this proposed legislation." [10]

The designation of the committee member who is responsible for preparing a report is handled along hierarchical lines. A committee chairman will often take over the preparation of a report. He may turn it over to the chairman of the subcommittee that handled the legislation in the first instance. Or he may go down the line of seniority and select a ranking member to sponsor the report. One of the most interesting examples of tactical discretion in the selection of the committee member who makes the report occurred in connection with the action of the Senate Committee on Interstate Commerce in 1907 on the Hepburn Act. Skipping over the various Republican Senators who best qualified for the task, Chairman Aldrich moved that the report be made by "Pitchfork" Ben Tillman, who was not only a Democrat but also a bitter personal enemy of President Theodore Roosevelt. Aldrich's motion was welcomed by all the members of the committee who saw in it a hope of splitting the ranks of those who supported the proposed reform.[11]

The Committee Voting

As indicated above, the committee reports do not always give a full record of how committee members have voted on the final product. They are even less informative, however, about the process of voting during strategic points in the committee's work. In some cases, of course, there is very little voting at all. Decisions are made on the basis of nods, assents, mutual understandings, and friendly accommodations among members and their representatives. At other times, a chairman may bypass some of his colleagues and deny them

[10] *The Washington Star,* Apr. 22, 1950.
[11] It so happened that President Roosevelt and Senator Tillman succeeded in overcoming their distaste for each other and cooperated in a successful effort to have the measure enacted.

the opportunity to vote. While the most conspicuous examples of this have occurred in the activities of various investigating committees, the same incidents occur with somewhat less regularity in the operations of legislative committees.

On highly controversial issues, there will often be a long-drawn-out series of votes within the committee. The opposition may start by offering a test amendment at the very outset, the line-up upon which will indicate the relative strength of opposing groups. The voting process is very simple. The chairman will go down the list of committee members, call each member's name, and record the vote beside it. The committee clerk will often keep a whole set of tally sheets and file the tally sheets away when the voting process is completed. It is an unwritten rule that these tally sheets should not be made public. When intracommittee votes are publicized, loud protests may be voiced. During the 1951 debate over the extension of price control, Senator Moody disclosed that during the executive sessions of the Banking and Currency Committee, Senator Capehart had voted for an amendment that would have removed all price and wage controls. "I do not know why the Senator brings up that matter on the floor," protested Senator Capehart, "and whether it is necessary to have persons snooping to see whether a Senator holds up his hand. I wish to say that I do not like such tactics, and I do not think the Senator should make such statements." [12]

A member does not necessarily have to be present to have his vote recorded. Frequent use is made of proxy voting. Much of the strength of committee chairmen in the voting process lies in the fact that they are in an ideal position to obtain proxies from colleagues who are dependent upon them for favors. Some committee chairmen have standing arrangements with other committee members to obtain their proxies in any matters that may come up when they are out of town. Sometimes the voting conflicts within a committee can be handled almost entirely by two members on opposing sides, each one with a pile of proxies in his pocket or on the table in front of him. These proxies may be from people who are out of town, too busy to attend, or sick in bed. It is a well-known fact that for a number of years when Senator Carter Glass of Virginia was too sick to attend any sessions of the Senate or Senate committees, his proxy was invariably handled by Senator Robert F. Wagner of New York. Wagner's opponents invariably charged that Glass's proxy was being cast in favor of proposals that Glass himself would unquestionably have opposed. However, they never succeeded in having a committee vote to overrule this use of Glass's proxy. Nor were they particularly interested in winning this point because from time to time during the same period there were two members on the committee from the Republican side who were also physically indisposed and whose proxies were given to the Republican Senators.

[12] *Congressional Record* (daily edition), June 25, 1951, p. 7205.

People with proxies do not always use them but rather try to accomplish their objectives through persuasion and compromise before they use the blunderbuss weapon of the proxy. The only formal limitation on the use of the proxy is a seldom invoked requirement that no bill shall be reported unless a majority of the committee has actually been present for the vote. Even when there is such a majority present, however, the decisive votes can readily be cast through proxies on behalf of the absent members of the committee. When the quorum requirement is enforced, it serves as an effective device for delaying action. During the long executive sessions of the House Military Affairs Committee on the Atomic Energy Act of 1946,

the bill encountered such parliamentary obstacles that its chances of stillbirth rose alarmingly. House rules designate a majority of the committee's roster as a quorum and require a quorum for formal action if the point is raised. Several members of the committee were off in Bikini, others were ill or out of town, leaving it within the power of eight or nine members acting in concert to prevent a quorum. The same Republican group then followed the practice of coming to meetings, counting noses, and, if a quorum were present, taking turns leaving the committee room; This process continued for several days despite powerful objections from the public, from the Administration, and from the Speaker of the House.[13]

Although these delaying tactics finally broke down, the use of the quorum calls to prevent votes served as a means of advancing the policies favored by the quorum callers.

DECISION MAKING IN THE CONFERENCE COMMITTEE

Every bicameral legislature needs some means whereby its two branches can iron out their inevitable disagreements on policy matters. In the United States this need has been met through the creation of *ad hoc* conference committees selected to deal with individual measures.

Since the members of a conference committee invariably come from the legislative committees which have handled a measure, conference committees must be viewed as an extension of the standing-committee system. They are by-products of the structure of committee power in existence at a given moment. Since conference-committee bills cannot be amended in either house but must be accepted or rejected in toto, the conference committees represent committee power in its most concentrated form. "For practical purposes, in most cases, it is impossible to defeat the legislation proposed by this conference committee. Every experienced legislator knows that it is the hardest thing in the world to defeat a conference report."[14]

[13] Miller, *op. cit.*, p. 814.

[14] George B. Galloway, "Congress at the Crossroads" (New York: Crowell, 1946), p. 99.

To Have or Not to Have a Conference

After losing a point of order against the conference committee report on the Transportation Act of 1940, Senator Bennett Champ Clark of Missouri introduced this resolution in rueful protest against the practice of allowing conference committees to write the basic legislative decisions: "All bills and resolutions shall be read twice and, without debate, referred to conference."

Jesting though he was, his proposal had the virtue of highlighting the tendency to make frequent use of conference committees. The differences between measures approved by each of the two houses are often of crucial importance to individual members of Congress, private organizations, and executive officials. Conference committees become the only practical method of settling these differences. In fact, the realization ahead of time that a conference committee will eventually be set up creates a natural tendency to postpone serious conflict on the floor of each house and pass the buck to the conference committee. When this occurs, almost everything that takes place in committee and on the floor before the appointment of conferees tends to be in the nature of byplay, rehearsal, and preliminary maneuvering.

Often the proponents of an important amendment will refrain from advancing their views on the floor lest a defeat endanger their chance of obtaining the same ends at the conference committee stage. Thus, during Senate consideration of the Displaced Persons Act in 1948, Senator Howard McGrath of Rhode Island indicated that he had an over-all substitute in readiness but that he would not offer it. He was very frank in explaining his reasons for this behavior: "In order not to allow anyone to be able to say that the Senate had already turned down many provisions that are found in the substitute bill, and thereby make it ineligible for consideration in conference, the Senator from New Mexico (Hatch) and myself have reluctantly come to the conclusion not to call up our substitute during the course of this debate." [15]

On the other hand, members of Congress will often accede to amendments that they really oppose on the theory that the place to kill the objectionable proposal is in the conference committee. During the Senate consideration of the Atomic Energy Act, Senator Joseph O'Mahoney of Wyoming offered a floor amendment providing that no one having a part in the development of the bomb project could subsequently benefit by any claim or by location on the public domain deriving from his participation in the project. Senator Milliken of Colorado went along with O'Mahoney's proposal but explained his position as follows: "So, merely to get it out of the way, and although I am in complete disagreement with the theory of the Senator from Wyoming but

[15] *Congressional Record*, 80th Cong., 2d Sess., p. 6900.

not with the ethics involved, I am willing to accept the proviso in the hope that the conference will eliminate the amendment." [16]

The extent to which legislative strategy is based upon the eventual possibility of settling controversies in conference committee, and the immediate character of such a strategy, depend to a large extent upon the distribution of power between and within the two houses. During the Seventieth Congress, for example, the progressive Republicans in the Senate, working in collaboration with many Democrats, produced Senate bills that were much more liberal than the regular Republican organization could tolerate. The formal Republican party position, on the other hand, crystallized in the House. The progressive Republicans usually had less representation in the leadership of Senate committees, and therefore less representation in conference committees. As a result of these circumstances, the conservative Republican viewpoint often came forward in the conference-committee bills, which were then enacted into law. A striking case of this was the Merchant Marine Act of 1931, which contained the very subsidies for private shipping interests that had been opposed at an earlier stage by the progressive Republicans in the Senate.

Similarly, the conference committee can be used to liberalize a measure. During the development of the Public Utility Holding Act of 1935, the Senate passed a bill which contained a strong version of the famous "death-sentence" clause, while the House passed a measure which weakened this provision considerably. Speaker Sam Rayburn refrained from a substantive debate on the issue on the floor of the House. "My position is this," he said. "I should like to see this bill in conference. I have pointed out a great many things in both bills. I think there are frailties in the House measure and also in the Senate measure, but I think we can do a better job in conference than we can here." [17] According to Raymond Moley, who seems to have been close to many of the decisions on legislative strategy adopted during the first term of the Franklin Roosevelt Administration, many legislative campaigns were planned in this manner. In discussing the Securities Act of 1933, Moley says: "This was the first appearance of the strategy that Cohen and Corcoran were to use so often in the years thereafter—ramming a too-severe bill through one House and then using it for trading purposes in the other." [18]

"Blind-fold," writes Luce, "the House puts its interest in the hands of its conferees." [19] Luce's protest is based upon the fact that one house will often ask for a conference without either waiting to see whether the other house will accede to the changes it has made, or, if the changes have been made in the

[16] *Congressional Record*, 79th Cong., 2d Sess., p. 6093.
[17] *Congressional Record*, 74th Cong., 1st Sess., July 2, 1935, p. 10635.
[18] Raymond Moley, "After Seven Years" (New York: Harper, 1939), p. 181, note 12.
[19] Robert Luce, "Legislative Procedure" (Boston: Houghton Mifflin, 1922), p. 404.

other house, without waiting to analyze them carefully and consider the possibility of accepting them.

Yet it is not quite the act of a blind man to do something that has been taken for granted all along. As pointed out above, the intention to have a conference is often accepted by all parties from the very beginning of a legislative campaign, particularly in the case of major measures and measures of an intricate nature. In addition, there are strategic gains in quick action to set up a conference committee. Toward the end of a session, any serious effort to avoid a conference committee through the possibility of accepting a bill as approved by the other house might, under certain circumstances, provoke enough delay to make the enactment of a measure impossible. The members of the house that asks for a conference place themselves in a strategic position also by virtue of the fact that the other house is expected to consider a conference report first. The asking house is thereby put in the position of having the last word.

Situations occasionally arise, however, where even major differences are glossed over in the effort to avoid a conference. Toward the end of a session, initiation of the conference process sometimes threatens sufficient delay as to prevent action. Thus, in the last days of the Seventy-ninth Congress, the Senate yielded completely on House amendments made to the Legislative Reorganization Act of 1946. The House, in turn, yielded to the Senate on legislation to extend social-security benefits for railroad employees.

The conference process may be opposed by those who have reason to believe that disagreement between the two houses would eventuate in a measure going to a conference dominated by members with an objectionable point of view. At the end of the Seventy-ninth Congress, the House yielded to the Senate on the Case bill, which was the precursor of the Taft-Hartley Act. Here the motivation was to avoid a conference committee, the majority of which would have come from two committees dominated by prolabor opponents of the measure. This bill was vetoed by President Truman and the veto was sustained. But if the conference committee had been established, the conferees might have prolonged their deliberations to the point where the veto stage would never have been reached.

The Selection of Conferees

The selection of conferees is even more important than the selection of committee members and committee chairmen, for it is the conferees who often write the final version of a law. In fact, it is because the positions of power established in the standing committees usually carry over into the conference committees that the struggle for power in the legislative committees in each house is often so intense.

Nominally, the conferees from each house are chosen respectively by the presiding officer of the Senate and the Speaker of the House. In actual practice, however, these officials invariably accept the recommendations of the chairmen of the two committees that handled the measure originally.

On the most important measures, a committee chairman will usually head up his list with his own name and that of the ranking minority member. Where a subcommittee has exercised major responsibility, as in the case of appropriation bills, he will often step aside in favor of the subcommittee chairman, who in turn invariably starts off by selecting himself and the ranking minority member of the subcommittee. In the selection of the additional members great weight is given to seniority. On only the rarest occasions will a conferee be appointed who was not a member of the legislative committee that worked on the measure.

In so far as party line-up is concerned, the minority party is always well represented. The ratios usually run 2 to 1, 3 to 2, or 5 to 3. Wherever there is a division along party lines, this practice puts a dissident member of the majority party in a particularly strategic position. By joining with the opposition party, one dissident member can often swing the balance of power.

In so far as size is concerned, committee chairmen have an important degree of latitude. Since the conferees of each house vote as a unit, there is no formal ceiling on the number of conferees that can be chosen from either house. The chairman may select two major-party members and one minority member, or he may set a ratio of 3 to 2, or 5 to 3. This gives him the same leeway in selecting men for or against the viewpoint that he normally exercises in the selection of subcommittees. During the 1948 Senate conflict on the Displaced Persons Act, Senator Wiley of Wisconsin, who was chairman of the Senate Judiciary Committee, selected three Senators as conferees—Revercomb, Ferguson, and Kilgore. This action was taken just as Senator Wiley was departing hastily for his home state. The haste probably explains his failure to realize that Ferguson and Kilgore had both been strong supporters of the more liberal approach with which Wiley himself disagreed and which had already been voted down in the Senate. Upon returning to Washington, therefore, Senator Wiley succeeded in adding to the conferees Senators Donnell and Eastland. These two new conferees, joining with Revercomb, were then able to outvote Ferguson and Kilgore and prevent any liberalization of the measure in the conference committee.

There is no reason to believe that conferees appointed by one house are necessarily interested in defending the bill approved in that house, although this is a general expectation. In fact, if one wanted to stretch the point a little, one might whimsically claim that any similarity between the views of the House or the Senate and those of the conferees representing the House or the Senate is purely coincidental. Many members come to a conference committee eager to defend the views represented in the bill passed by the *other* house or to strike out provisions inserted in their own house. Some are intent upon striking out identical provisions appearing in both bills or upon inserting provisions that appear in neither. Many conference committees include members who voted against the bill in their own house and are equally opposed to the version adopted by the other house and are fully committed to having no legislation whatsoever. During the Senate debate on the Agricultural Adjustment Act of 1938, Senator McNary of Oregon referred to "an unbroken rule of mine that when I oppose a bill I refuse to act as a conferee." [20] McNary's rule has interest because of its rarity. When most members of Congress oppose a bill, they view an opportunity to serve as conferees as a chance to help make the measure less objectionable to themselves or to make it so much more objectionable to others as to enhance the chances of a Presidential veto.

Theoretically, either house may change its conferees if they fail to defend adequately the measure passed by the house or if they prove unable to work out an agreement with the conferees selected in the other house. Actually, this is practically never done. Occasionally, the conferees from one house will, in a situation of deadlock, go back to their house and ask that a new set of conferees be appointed. This invariably leads to the reappointment of the same members, in effect, a device whereby the conferees obtain a vote of confidence which strengthens their position at the bargaining table.

Conference Action

The activities of conference committees are shrouded in secrecy—even more so than the executive sessions of the standing committees in each house of Congress.

Conferees have almost never been known to hold public hearings.[21] Only rarely are the representatives of private organizations allowed to appear at conference-committee sessions. Attendance by representatives of executive agencies is carefully limited. The great bulk of contacts between conferees and outside organizations takes place on a personal basis rather than through the medium of the conference committee itself. Attendance by staff assistants to committee members is usually kept to a minimum. In at least one instance the House members of a conference committee refused to allow their Senate colleagues to continue bringing along an adviser who had been assigned from an

[20] *Congressional Record,* 75th Cong., 3d Sess., Feb. 11, 1938, p. 1818.

[21] One of the few references to formal hearings on the part of conference committees is found in De Alva S. Alexander, "History and Procedure of the House of Representatives" (Boston: Houghton Mifflin, 1916), p. 284. "In one case formal hearings, attended by witnesses and attorneys, aided in eliminating difficulties." But Alexander gives no reference on the case. If a formal record was kept, it was probably never published.

executive agency.[22] There are probably less "leaks" from conference committees than any other brand of secret meeting in the nation's capital. Whatever leaks do take place are usually in the form of information privately piped to colleagues in Congress and supporters in private organizations and executive agencies. Finally, the reports and explanatory statements issued by the conferees rarely give a full and complete explanation of the action taken.

Behind the closed doors of conference committees takes place some of the hardest bargaining and fiercest battling to be found in the entire legislative process. The participants feel that the final language of any law that may be passed is now being written and are eager both to press any minor advantage and to make the final settlements on issues that can no longer be postponed. Their basic weapon is their ability to obtain the support or acquiescence of a majority in their own house. To some extent, the strength of this weapon depends upon the voting line-up on the bill as it originally passed or any instructions that might have been sent along with it. It also depends upon their ability to go back to their house and win consent to a measure that flies in the face of previous floor votes or baldly violates instructions.

Dilatory tactics are another "weapon" in conference-committee battles. Major gains can be won by any group of conferees that is in a position to sit tight and yield little while their opponents are being pressed for speedy action. This is most effective at the end of a session when just a day's delay may mean no opportunity for final action on a conference-committee report. The threat of dilatory tactics on the floor of either house also has implications for a conference committee. This is particularly true of a Senate filibuster. In 1938, Senator Royal Copeland reported to the Senate on how the Senate conferees succeeded in striking from the measure a House amendment which would have labeled whisky "misbranded" if distilled from anything but grain. "I told the House conferees," he said, "that some of the most able filibusters in the Senate

---

[22] The adviser in this case was Benjamin Cohen of the famous Corcoran-Cohen team. Cohen had been brought to early conference committee meetings on the Public Utility Holding Act of 1935. The House conferees disliked his effective work on behalf of the Senate version of the "death-sentence clause." They reported to the House "That a conference has been prevented by the unyielding refusal of the managers on the part of the Senate to hold same under conditions consistent with the proper conduct of an executive session and free from the presence and participation of an outsider, who was not an employee of Congress and who is objectionable to the managers on the part of the House." By a vote of 183 to 172 the House backed up its conferees in a demand for Mr. Cohen's exclusion. It is interesting to note that during the debate preceding this vote, one of Mr. Cohen's defenders asserted that "with respect to every one of the supply bills that have been passed after conference for the last twenty years the House conferees have taken with them to the conference any experts they chose, and likewise, the managers on the part of the Senate have had their experts with them in the conference." *Congressional Record,* 74th Cong., 1st Sess., July 29, 1935, p 12012.

were so opposed to this amendment that we could not accept it, and it was stricken from the bill." [23]

When the conferees emerge from a session on major legislation, they know they have been through a tense experience. Representative Wolcott of Michigan in reporting upon the conference committee that produced the Housing Act of 1937 states:

When I first came to Congress, I was told that all major legislation was a matter of compromise. I did not know quite what that meant until I took part in some conferences with the Senate on legislation. I did not fully realize what it meant until a conference on this bill, when, after spending eleven and a half hours yesterday giving and taking, adding and subtracting, sparring for advantage back and forth, we finally succeeded in coming to an agreement.[24]

Conferees habitually report back to their respective bodies in tones of despair and fatigue. "It was this bill or nothing," is a refrain echoed again and again in the personal explanations of conferees. In explaining his concurrence to the conference report on the Displaced Persons Act of 1948, Representative Chelf argued that: "we had a gun barrel at our heads . . . it was either this compromise or nothing . . . We did not raise any white flag—had it not been for the time element and immediate adjournment slapping us in the face, I would have hung the jury until Gabriel blew taps on his trumpet. I would never have compromised. I would have demanded the Fellows bill." [25]

One of the best expressions of the weariness usually felt by conferees is made by Representative Carter Manasco when he reported on the Surplus Property Act of 1944: "We thought that the bill as it passed the House was a much better bill than the bill we agreed to, but in 3 weeks' time, when you go up against men who have ideas different from your own, you finally get worn down. I have talked surplus property all day . . . I am tired of it and I want to get rid of it." [26]

The question is often raised as to whether the Senate or the House is stronger in conference committees. Roland Young has answered this question with the assertion that "the Senators are better bargainers than the Representatives in securing both appropriations and legislation." [27] Steiner, in his book on the operations of conference committees, disputes this point of view and after a consideration of 56 pieces of legislation comes to the conclusions that "the influence of the House of Representatives has been found to outweigh that of the Senate to a considerable extent. Thirty-two instances were found wherein House influences dominated the final version of a bill; Senate superiority was

[23] Congressional Record, 75th Cong., 3d Sess., June 10, 1938, p. 8738.
[24] Congressional Record, 75th Cong., 1st Sess., Aug. 21, 1937, p. 9636.
[25] Congressional Record, 80th Cong., 2d Sess., June 18, 1948, p. 8859.
[26] Congressional Record, 78th Cong., 2d Sess., Sept. 18, 1944, pp. 7850–7851.
[27] Roland A. Young, "This Is Congress" (New York: Knopf, 1946), p. 233.

found in fifteen cases, while an apparently even break obtained in nine situations." [28] Nevertheless, everything else being equal, the Senators are in a better bargaining position. Of course, everything else is never equal. The major strength of any set of conferees lies in forces beyond themselves and, in fact, outside of either house of Congress. The power line-up in a conference committee can only be appraised in terms of the major social groupings that are actively campaigning on the measure or may be regarded by the conferees as potentially interested in the decisions to be reached. These groups often have more influence on one house than on the other and more on some conferees than on others. Moreover, in the unfolding of any legislative battle, they often change their strategy and objectives as a measure moves from one house to another and then to a conference committee.

New Provisions in Conference Bills

The rules of Congress have almost always contained provisions limiting conferees to the disagreements between the two houses and prohibiting them from bringing in entirely new provisions. These rules have consistently been side-stepped, however, by having one house strike out everything after the enacting clause and offering an amendment in the nature of a substitute. When this happens, everything is technically under disagreement and the conferees are thereby free to start from scratch and write an entirely new measure.

An attempt was made in the Legislative Reorganization Act in 1946 to strengthen the rule by a specific prohibition against the inclusion by conferees in a conference report of "matter not committed to them by either House." [29] However, the same section also provided that the conferees may "include in their report in any such case matter which is a germane modification of subjects in disagreement." This limitation is not much of an obstacle toward the inclusion of new material, for when a subject is in disagreement, almost any change is germane.

In 1938 a Civil Service Retirement Act came from the House with provisions for annuities at the age of sixty, averaging $1,155. The Senate bill provided for annuities averaging $1,090. The conference bill provided for an average annuity of $1,402. In defense of the conference bill, Senator Robert Taft stated:

It is true that the provision of the conference report results ultimately in a condition somewhat more favorable to the annuitant than resulted from the bill passed either by the House or by the Senate bill, and I think the Senate conferees would have a perfect right to say, "We will take this amendment in some modified form, whether such modified form is more favorable to the employees or less favorable."

[28] Gilbert Y. Steiner, "The Congressional Conference Committee: 70th to 80th Congresses" (Urbana, Ill.: The University of Illinois Press, 1951).
[29] Sec. 135(a).

That does not seem to me to make the report subject to a point of order. One may question the wisdom of the conferees in doing that, but it seems to me there may be circumstances which would lead the Senate to say, "Well, if you are going to change it, we think this is the fair way to change it." So I can see no violation of the La Follette–Monroney Act.[30]

Taft's view was accepted and the bill was approved by voice vote.

When the support for a measure is shaky, however, then it is wise to refrain from introducing new materials. In the development of the Employment Stabilization Act of 1931, the House conferees foresaw that a point of order might be made and sustained against the insertion in the conference bill of a provision for six-year advance planning of public works. Accordingly, the bill was allowed to die in conference. The conference bill was introduced as a new measure. It was then quickly acted upon and passed.

The rules also appear to prohibit conferees from dropping provisions that have previously been agreed upon in both houses. But here again, conferees with adequate support behind them have demonstrated that they have wide latitude whenever the bill adopted by one house is a complete substitute for the one approved in the other house. In the development of the Agricultural Adjustment Act of 1938, Senator McNary and Representative Boileau succeeded in having the Senate and the House respectively adopt an amendment to protect northern dairy-farming interests against the rapid expansion in southern dairy farming. The provision was dropped in the conference committee and a point of order was offered against the conference report on the floor of the Senate. Vice-President Garner ruled against the point of order and explained his action as follows: "It is the reasoning of all the parliamentarians who have ever considered this rule, so far as the Chair can ascertain from all the precedents, that the philosophy should be that where one House passes an entirely new bill as a substitute for the bill of the other House, there is very little limitation placed on the discretion of the conferees, except as to germaneness." [31] He was sustained by a vote of 48 to 31.

Nor do the provisions of the Legislative Reorganization Act of 1946 make any substantial change in this situation. In 1947, when the conference report on the Taft-Hartley Act reached the House, Representative Hoffman of Michigan made a point of order against the section dealing with anti-Communist affidavits. He pointed out that the conference bill had not only inserted new matter but had also eliminated the anti-Communist affidavit as a prerequisite to certification by the National Labor Relations Board for collective-bargaining purposes, a provision that had been previously agreed to in both houses. Overruling the point of order, Speaker Martin explained that "When either branch of Congress strikes out all after the enacting clause of a bill of the other there

[30] *Congressional Record,* 80th Cong., 2d Sess., p. 1740.
[31] *Congressional Record,* 75th Cong., 3d Sess., Feb. 11, 1938, p. 1821.

is unusually wide latitude permitted for the conferees to work on to secure a meeting of the minds between the two bodies." [32]

FORMAL INFLUENCES ON COMMITTEE DECISIONS

There is no longer any formal control of committee decisions of the type in existence during the early years of the Republic when committees were set up on the *ad hoc* basis to work out details of measures that had already been agreed upon in general terms on the floor of the House or Senate. Floor control of committee action is now rendered almost impossible by the large and amorphous character of each house as contrasted with the relatively compact character of any committee.

Yet it would be a great error to describe legislative committees of Congress as totally independent, as laws unto themselves. For one thing, members of legislative committees are subjected to a high degree of outside pressure and persuasion from private organizations, executive officials, and other members of Congress. Whether a member of Congress bends like putty under these influences or performs creatively in fashioning an adjustment between competing interests, he operates within an environment that has a marked effect upon his actions. "Independent" is probably the least descriptive adjective that could be used to describe him or his associates.

The formal procedural machinery at times becomes a vehicle for influencing committee decisions. The term "at times" is used advisedly because the formal machinery of the legislative process has no motive power in its own right. It becomes important only when used by forces inside and outside Congress that have their own sources of initiative. The term "influence" is also used advisedly; the word "control" would be an exaggeration. The degree of influence depends upon the amount of power enjoyed by those who use the machinery.

"Instructions" by Resolution

Under the rules of Congress it is perfectly possible for the Senate and the House to pass motions "instructing" legislative committees to do this or that. In actual practice, however, motions to instruct are of only two kinds. The first is a floor motion to recommit a bill to committee with instructions that it bring forth a new bill of a different type. This type of motion is little more than a polite way of applying the kiss of death to a measure on the floor and is discussed in connection with floor operations in Chap. 17. The second is the motion to recommit a bill to conferees with instructions that they bring forth an amended bill. This is the only method of getting a conference bill amended.

[32] *Congressional Record,* 80th Cong., 1st Sess., June 4, 1947, p. 6382.

One of the most effective uses of this latter method occurred in the battle over the Transportation Act of 1940. Representative Harrington had succeeded in having the Committee of the Whole adopt an amendment to the original House bill which would prevent railroad consolidations that might create unemployment among railroad workers. No record vote was attained on this amendment on the floor of the House after the Committee of the Whole had reported. The conferees then dropped this amendment. A motion was then made to recommit the conference bill with instructions that the conferees insist upon the Harrington amendment and two other amendments that had also been made in the Committee of the Whole. This motion was carried by a vote of 209 to 182. Three months later another conference report was brought to the House which included the Harrington amendment but completely eliminated another amendment that had been covered in the motion of instructions. This other amendment had been previously agreed to by both houses in identical form. The second conference report was approved after considerable argumentation in both houses.

Instructions to conferees may also be given before the conference committee starts its work. Such instructions have no binding force, for conferees may violate them without being subjected to a point of order. Moreover, during the course of a conference, the issues may shift in such a way as to render any previous instructions meaningless.

Strenuous objections are usually raised whenever anyone proposes detailed instructions in advance of a conference. When the Senate appointed conferees on the Selective Service Act of 1940, for example, Senator Clark of Missouri moved to instruct the Senate conferees to agree to one House amendment and to refuse to recede at all on one provision of the Senate measure. Senator Burke of Nebraska opposed this motion on the ground that it would not be desirable for the Senate conferees to go to the conference

bound by any alleged statement made by the chairman of their conferees that they were going to do a certain thing, and with the Senate conferees pledged in advance along a certain line . . . they would meet together with the two bills, the Senate conferees, of course, giving full weight to all the provisions in the Senate bill and the House conferees to their own measure, and then bring back to the respective Houses the best possible bill.[33]

Senator Barkley added that Senate managers "would be woefully handicapped" by instructions that forced them to come back to the Senate and get further instructions before they could negotiate a compromise. The motion to instruct was defeated.

A rather unique form of preconference instructions was developed in the battle over the Transportation Act of 1940. When the House bill came to the

[33] *Congressional Record*, 76th Cong., 3d Sess., p. 11785.

floor of the House, Representative Harrington and his labor supporters suspected that the conferees would drop his amendment for preventing unemployment among railroad workers. Accordingly a petition was circulated reading as follows:

The undersigned members of the House of Representatives respectfully petition that the Harrington amendment inserted in the Wheeler-Lea Bill, S. 2009, by vote of the House be retained in the conference report. Secondly, we urge and insist in the event you do not retain the Harrington amendment in the conference report that the Harrington amendment be reported in disagreement so that a separate vote on same may be obtained in the House.[34]

The Harrington amendment and other provisions that had been inserted in the Committee of the Whole were dropped in the conference bill. The entire bill was then recommitted with instructions that the deleted provisions be inserted. Three months later a new conference report was brought back which included the Harrington amendment. Thus, the petition device proved a useful one, among other techniques, in developing the campaign on behalf of railroad labor.

"Instructions" by Statute

Perhaps the closest analogy to the ancient system of floor instructions to committees is found in the appropriations process. Appropriations committees are regarded as operating under a framework established by legislation. Their instructions are contained in the statutes authorizing appropriations. These instructions are ironclad when they set a ceiling upon the amount of money that subsequently can be appropriated for a given purpose. The appropriations committees will never report a bill that allocates money in excess of a statutory limit. Ways may be found to achieve the same objective through another method; for example, the appropriation of funds to be channeled to a similar purpose, or the authorizing of a public-debt transaction. But the appropriations committee will never report—and neither house will ever approve—an appropriation measure that directly violates a statutory ceiling.

Attempts have often been made to formulate legislative authorizations that can be regarded as firm commitments to appropriate specified sums of money. But ever since the appropriations function was taken away from the legislative committees and given to the appropriations committees, these attempts have not been successful. Members of appropriations committees have always insisted—and with considerable logic—that, unless there is no real job for the appropriations committees to perform, there is no sense in having separate appropriation bills. And there would be little or no job to perform if measures other than appropriation acts were to contain instructions for specific appropria-

[34] *Congressional Record,* 76th Cong., 3d Sess., p. 5869.

tions as well as ceilings or general authorizations for whatever sums may be subsequently determined necessary and desirable. When one of the appropriations committees brings forth a bill containing a figure lower than the ceiling in the enabling legislation, it usually produces a vehement denunciation of the committee's action as an attempt to "undermine the integrity of legislative committees," [35] or "nullify the action and will of the two Houses and the President." [36]

These arguments are usually countered along the following lines:

If Congress enacts legislation authorizing an appropriation, is it absolutely binding upon the Appropriations Committees of the two houses and are the Appropriations Committees thereafter foreclosed from looking into the question? . . . I think the time has come when both houses of Congress will have to determine whether or not the Appropriations Committees are merely rubber stamps, or whether they have a duty to look into every appropriation.[37]

The above position has usually emerged victorious. In terms of the actual amounts appropriated, however, the victory of this principle has often been counterbalanced—or one might even say facilitated—by appropriations-committee action to raise the figure in question to the desired level. Whether this is done or not depends upon the amount of power behind the drive for an increased sum, not upon any automatically binding force found in enabling legislation.

On rare occasions a law may contain instructions to specific committees concerning their future legislative activities. When the Revenue Act of 1950 was in its later stages, a sharp controversy arose between those who opposed and those who favored the inclusion of excess-profits-tax provisions. The former fortified their position by promising action on excess profits at a later date and, as a way of making this promise concrete, the following subsection was written into the law:

The House Committee on Ways and Means and the Senate Committee on Finance are hereby directed to report to the respective Houses of Congress a bill for raising revenue by the levying, collection, and payment of corporate excess profits taxes with retroactive effect to October 1, or July 1, 1950, said bill shall be reported as early as practicable during the Eighty-first Congress after November 15, 1950, if the Congress is in session in 1950 after such date; and if the Congress is not in session after November 15, 1950, said bill shall be reported during the first session of the Eighty-second Congress, and as early as practicable during said session.[38]

[35] Representative Clifford R. Hope of Kansas in debate on agriculture appropriation bill, *Congressional Record*, 80th Cong., 1st Sess., Vol. 93, pp. 5874ff.

[36] Senator Carl A. Hatch of New Mexico in debate on Greek-Turkish aid appropriation, *Congressional Record*, 80th Cong., 1st Sess., p. 5482.

[37] Senator Homer Ferguson of Michigan in debate on Greek-Turkish aid appropriation, *Congressional Record*, 80th Cong., 1st Sess., pp. 5482–5483.

[38] Sec. 701(a).

The instructions were complied with faithfully. An excess-profits-tax bill was reported out during December, 1950, and the final legislation was in fact retroactive to July 1, 1950.

Discharge Action

Floor action to "discharge" a bill from a committee that has been refusing to report it out is a blunderbuss weapon through which a majority on the floor of either house can attempt to influence committee decisions. In the Senate any member theoretically can move to discharge a bill from a committee and a majority vote will do the job. Actually, such motions are practically never made. It is always more feasible to seek the same objective through a motion to take a bill out of one committee and refer it to another. In the House it takes a petition signed by a large number of members—currently 218—to bring such a motion up for a vote.[39]

During the twenty-year span from the beginning of the Seventy-first Congress to the end of the Eightieth Congress, 252 discharge petitions were filed in the House but only 29 of these obtained enough signatures to be printed on the calendar. Only 15 bills were discharged from committees.[40] Although most of the bills that were discharged from committees during this period were passed by the House, only one of them, the Wages and Hours Act of 1937, became law—and this was a measure that was discharged from the Rules Committee rather than from a legislative committee.[41] The indirect effect of the discharge operations in the House, however, has probably been greater than this record indicates. The threat of a discharge maneuver has often served to

[39] See Floyd Riddick, "The United States Congress: Organization and Procedure" (Washington, D.C.: National Capitol Publishers, 1949), pp. 241–253, for a detailed historical summary of various changes in the number of names required on the petition. The discharge rule was first adopted in 1910 as part of a coalition attack on the House leadership. The most recent change took place in the 74th Congress when the Democratic leadership succeeded in having the number of names required on a discharge petition raised from 145 to 218.

[40] *Ibid.*, p. 256.

[41] ". . . it seems quite unlikely that any legislation of the type of the wage and hour bill would have been enacted at that session if it had not been for Senator Pepper's victory in the Florida Democratic Primary. The House Labor Committee had already reported out a new bill but it was resting in its usual pigeon-hole in the Rules Committee. Senator Pepper's victory, after a campaign in which the Bill had been an issue, served to open the floodgates, and when the petition to discharge the Rules Committee was opened for signature the required number of names were secured in two hours and 20 minutes. The favorable poll of the Institute of Public Opinion undoubtedly had its effect, also." Louise Stitt, *Law and Contemporary Problems*, "Legislative History of the Fair Labor Standards Act," Vol. 6, No. 3, Summer, 1939, pp. 471–472.

accelerate committee action and even to force committee members to beat a discharge petition to the draw.

There are three disadvantages in the discharge approach. First, a bill that is discharged cannot be perfected through the use of minor amendments and the perfecting process is thrown open on the floor of the house. Second, the members of a committee can beat a discharge petition to the draw by amending the measure in a substantial fashion and then reporting quickly. Third, members of a committee can anticipate this action by reporting a bill out with an unfavorable recommendation and a strong report urging its defeat.

Discharge petitions often serve little purpose other than to allow members of Congress to convince various organizations that they are trying to put up a real fight. For many years in succession discharge petitions have been filed to force out of the House Ways and Means Committee legislation to put into effect the Townsend Plan for old-age pensions. In 1939, this effort forced members of the Ways and Means Committee to counter with an unfavorable report on the Townsend bill. But by 1950 the operation had become a routine affair. An inquiring Washington reporter diagnosed the failure of the discharge petitions as follows:

"As new names go on top of his petition, the old names strangely drop off the bottom. Some party regulars who sign, to add another string to their political bow, are gently 'persuaded to withdraw.' " [42]

In the 1948 struggle over legislation to turn over tideland oils to the states, a dramatic maneuver was attempted by Senator Sheridan Downey of California. The House had already approved a bill to accomplish this objective but the members of the Senate Judiciary Committee were stalling. When the House bill came to the Senate, Downey took advantage of an obscure Senate rule which, on the objection of a single Senator, would keep a House-approved bill on the calendar instead of allowing it to be referred to a committee. The same bill had already been passed by the Senate as well as by the House in the previous year and its enactment was held up only by Presidential veto. Thus, Downey was confident that a majority vote could easily be mustered to support his move. "If the Judiciary Committee does not report the bill in time for the Senate to express its will upon it," explained Downey, "the Senate will then have two methods by which to proceed—either a motion to discharge the committee, or, if this bill is still upon the calendar, a motion to make it the business of the Senate." [43] A few weeks later the Senate Judiciary Committee reported the measure favorably by a close vote of 6 to 5. Because of the imminent end of the session and the certainty of a Presidential veto, the committee bill was allowed to die on the calendar instead of being brought up for a vote.

[42] Robert C. Albright, "Townsend Plan Skeleton Is Rattling," *The Washington Post,* Apr. 2, 1950.

[43] *Congressional Record* (daily edition), May 3, 1948, p. 5297.

This, however, does not minimize the importance of the Downey maneuver as a method of forcing committee action.

Leadership Influence

The distinction should always be kept in mind between the formal *techniques* of influencing committee action and the formal *leadership agencies*—the President, the Speaker of the House, the President of the Senate, the majority and minority leaders, and the majority and minority policy or steering committees —that have prerogatives to influence congressional action.

Motions to instruct or discharge, as formal techniques of directly influencing committees, are usually used by groups other than the leadership agencies. In fact, they often become instruments in the hands of those who seek to weaken, frustrate, or circumvent the formal leadership of Congress. The official leaders of Congress, on the other hand, make only occasional use of these direct techniques. The procedural methods available to them are for the most part of an indirect character. Presidents influence committee action, through the use, or threatened use, of the Presidential veto. This is discussed in detail in Chap 18. The Speaker of the House and the President of the Senate can influence committee action through decisions on the referral of bills as explained in an earlier section of this chapter. The Speaker may also hold up action on a bill that has been passed by the Senate. This was done by Speaker Sam Rayburn in 1946 when he refused to refer the Senate version of the Legislative Reorganization Act to the appropriate committee until agreements had been negotiated to make a number of specific changes in which he was interested. The power of floor recognition is still another technique available to the Speaker for the purpose of influencing committee action.

In so far as party leadership and party-leadership committees are concerned, there are three principal circumstances under which they can affect committee decisions. The first is the selection of committee members and chairmen. When party leadership can determine the personnel of committees, committees become in large part the servants of party leadership. But, as explained in an earlier section of this chapter, the structure of congressional-committee power is usually in the hands of party leadership only in a nominal sense.

The second is control of the floor schedules. To the extent that party leaders can decide which bills may or may not come up for discussion and action on the floor, they can indirectly affect the substantive provisions of committee bills. Favored measures can be given the green light. Unfavored measures can be allowed to die on the calendars. Naturally, the more crowded the calendars are, the more effective this technique becomes. In the House of Representatives the Rules Committee has long enjoyed a high degree of monopoly over this function. In fact, the House Rules Committee has become a leadership institution which often rivals or even outshines and counterbalances the Speaker and the party leaders.[44] An interesting example of how this committee can affect the details of committee action was provided at the end of the Seventy-ninth Congress when the House Ways and Means Committee reported a social-security bill containing equalization provisions to favor areas of the country in greatest financial need. The majority of the House Rules Committee refused to grant this measure a rule unless the equalizations provisions were deleted. The Ways and Means Committee made the amendment and the rule was obtained.

The third is the use of party caucuses to bind all party members to support or oppose a specific action. This device is used infrequently. Because of internal party divisions, caucuses are not held very often and when they are held, it is generally for the purpose of discussing issues rather than reaching a firm party line. Furthermore, the caucus is only rarely used on matters that are directly before a congressional committee. Most caucuses are concerned with measures that have already been processed by committees. Caucus influence, therefore, is necessarily of an indirect character.

An attempt to establish a formal procedure for directly influencing committee action was made in the Employment Act of 1946. Under this legislation, a Joint Committee on the Economic Report would issue reports to "serve as a guide to the several committees of the Congress dealing with legislation" affecting employment, production, and purchasing power. To enhance the prestige and expand the work program of this group, provisions were made for reference to it at the beginning of each year of the President's annual economic program. Although the Committee has issued many reports, there is no evidence to indicate that they have really served "as a guide to the several committees of the Congress." On February 11, 1948, for example, the Joint Committee issued a report recommending allocation powers for the use of grain as part of a program to cope with inflationary trends. In the House of Representatives, the vice-chairman of this Joint Committee, Representative Wolcott of Michigan, was himself the chairman of the committee handling this proposal. However, Wolcott's own committee never even held hearings on the measure and allowed it to die a swift death.

---

[44] With all the criticism that has been heaped upon the head of the Rules Committee in recent years, it is interesting to note that early in the twentieth century there were those who viewed it as the great solution to the problem of effective leadership in the House. "Here," stated McConachie, "is the new central instrument for equitable and economical distribution of the annual revenue among the great governmental interests. . . . Here is a revival and perpetuation of that unity of lawmaking which characterized those first years when the Committee of the Whole on the State of the Union held the primacy for the formulation of laws. A better century has begun, wherein the American House of Representatives will express more readily and truly the more easily known will of the people." "Congressional Committees" (New York· Crowell, 1898), pp. 206–207.

This listing of the formal techniques available to official leadership agencies should not obscure the fact that these agencies have many informal weapons at their disposal. Essentially, these are the same weapons used by many other participants in the legislative struggle: the organization of group support, the production and dissemination of propaganda, and the development and application of pressure. In fact, the ultimate power of formal leadership agencies to influence committee action depends fundamentally upon the extent to which they become part of a legislative campaign. Official leaders have often been charged with incompetence, deviousness, or downright insincerity for their failure to get committees to do things which, under the existing line-up of social forces, no leaders could ever get them to do. In the same way, various leaders have been branded as "czars" or "dictators" when they have merely served as the instruments for achieving what no one could have prevented.

The power of leadership does not lie in office alone. It lies in the men who are involved and the forces with which they work. At times, the leaders seem to have complete control. Henry Clay, as Speaker of the House, it has been said, "framed his committees so as to force an English war." [45] During the Civil War, Lincoln dominated congressional decisions as had no President before him. During the years immediately after the Civil War, when the frustrated Andrew Johnson took over the Presidency, Thaddeus Stevens, the leader of the Republican radicals, "ruled not only the South but the National Government, through a junto or 'directory,' as Johnson correctly charged. From 1866 to 1868, the year of his death, Stevens, as a sort of prime minister for Congress, virtually ruled in place of the repudiated President, even holding the country's moneybags in his hands." [46]

In the early days of the Republic, according to Harlow, "committees became in a way the specialized agents of the majority, just as they were of the House, and of the executive." [47] According to Harlow, "The real work of legislation was put into shape, not in the legislature, but in secret session of the majority party. In this organization, unknown to the Constitution and beyond the reach of the rules of either chamber, the executive could work with the party following in Congress, and secure the adoption of a pre-arranged program." [48]

And yet one can readily select other periods in history when on a great bulk of legislative measures this picture would be the opposite of the true one. It is unrealistic to talk about the power of leadership in any fixed and static sense. Sometimes it flows through the leaders and sometimes around them. The leaders sometimes seize control and sometimes fail to attain it and sometimes never

[45] Hubert Bruce Fuller, "The Speakers of the House" (Boston: Little, Brown, 1909), p. 273.
[46] Matthew Josephson, "The Politicos" (New York: Harcourt, Brace, 1938), p. 38.
[47] Ralph V. Harlow, "The History of Legislative Methods in the Period Before 1825" (New Haven, Conn.: Yale University Press, 1917), p. 208.
[48] Ibid., p. 145.

try. Moreover, in any given year, the power of leadership over congressional committees shifts from issue to issue. There are all sorts of delicate changes in the structure of power which make it impossible to discuss leadership influence or control in terms of static reference to 1910, to 1946, or to any other specific period, or in terms of Clay, Stevens, or Cannon. The history of leadership influence can be discussed only through full examination of the legislative campaigns as they unfold at specific periods of time, truly a vast and challenging field for historical and political research.

Chapter 17

THE RANGE OF CHOICE ON THE FLOOR

A GOOD WAY *not* to find out what is happening on the floor of either house is to check on the regular order of business.[1] The regular order merely provides a point of departure from which special business is taken up out of order. Few members in either house ever keep track of such recondite information as what the regular order, if followed, would lead to next. To make matters still more like the topsy-turvy world of Alice-in-Wonderland, one of the key devices for departing from the regular order is to recess at the end of the day instead of adjourn. This means that the so-called "legislative day" has not ended. Rather, it keeps on going. Hence when the body meets the next calendar day, there is no need to take up the first items on the regular order of business. It is perfectly proper under the rules for a legislative day to last weeks.

Nor are the rules themselves much of a guide. In both houses they are frequently suspended, evaded, or broken. This is particularly true of the Senate. "Rules are never observed in this body, a President pro tempore of the Senate

---

[1] Under Rule XXIV of the House, the regular order runs as follows:

First.   Prayer by the chaplain.
Second.   Reading and approval of the Journal.
Third.   Correction of reference of public bills.
Fourth.   Disposal of business on the Speaker's table.
Fifth.   Unfinished business.
Sixth.   The Morning Hour for the consideration of bills called up by committees.
Seventh.   Motions to go into Committee of the Whole House on the State of the Union.
Eighth.   Order of the day.

While the Senate rules are not so specific, they provide the basis for an order of business somewhat as follows:

First.   Morning Hour.
           Prayer by the chaplain.
           Reading and correction of the journal.
           Presiding Officer presents business to the Senate.
           Presiding Officer calls for morning business.
Second.   Call of the Calendar.
Third.   Unfinished business.
Fourth.   Motions to proceed to the consideration of executive business.

337

once observed. "They are only made to be broken. We are a law unto ourselves." [2] In the House, new rules have been written to evade rather than
change old rules. A good example is the use of fictions concerning operations
on the floor of the House. In order to get around certain requirements on
quorums and record votes, the House can meet not only as the House but
also in three masquerades—as the Committee of the Whole, the Committee of
the Whole House on the State of the Union, and "in House as in the Committee
of Whole."

Like the Constitution, the rules of Congress need interpretation. They tend
to be what the presiding officers say they are. The source for their rulings
are the precedents of the House and Senate,[3] which are comparable to the
decisions of the Supreme Court. Moreover, as complex as they are, the rules
have not been fashioned to deal with all situations. Traditions and usages,
leavened with recurring innovation, fill many a gap.

The first step in understanding floor action is to find out how the participants
in the legislative struggle handle rules, precedents, and usages in getting bills
to the floor and how, once a bill is on the floor, they choose among the alternative types of decisions available to them.

GETTING TO THE FLOOR

"The running of trains on a single-track railroad may be likened to the
passage of measures through the House," an able observer once wrote in language that is equally applicable to both houses. "The freight gives way to a
local passenger train, which sidetracks for an express, which in turn sidetracks
for the limited, while all usually keep out of the way of a relief train. Meantime, when a train having the right of way passes, the delayed ones begin to
move until again obliged to sidetrack. . . ." [4]

To make the simile still more apt, one should assume that this railroad has
no fixed schedule of priorities. One should think of many trains being run by
canny engineers who will try to hold back on some occasions and to plow
ahead on others. One should then visualize a tremendous number of trains
lined up in the railroad yard, with their crews eager to devise means of

---

[2] J. J. Ingalls, *Congressional Record*, 44th Cong., 2d Sess., Dec. 18, 1876, p. 266.

[3] The House precedents have been compiled by Asher C. Hinds and Rep. Clarence Cannon,
respectively, in "House Precedents" and "Cannon's Procedure in the House of Representatives" (U.S. Government Printing Office). The Senate precedents, however, are the private
property of the Senate Parliamentarian, who keeps them in a card index. The last available
analysis of Senate precedents is Henry H. Gilfrey's, "Precedents, Decisions on Points of
Order, with Phraseology, in the United States Senate, 1789–1913," which was published by
the Government Printing Office in 1914.

[4] De Alva S. Alexander, "History and Procedure of the House of Representatives" (Boston: Houghton Mifflin, 1916), p. 222.

getting a favorable signal and with gangs of switchmen roaming the yards making efforts to assure that certain trains are permanently sidetracked. Finally, one should realize that every week new trains are lined up in the yards and that every week brings closer the end of the Congress when the yards and tracks are all completely cleared and the entire process of lining-up starts over again.

While the term "legislative graveyard" is probably best suited to describe the standing committees of Congress, where about nine out of ten bills die for lack of committee action, the death rate at the calendar stage is far from negligible. As a result of congestion, accidental collision, or purposeful maneuvering, from one to three out of ten bills reported by committees die silently at the end of every Congress. Even bills that have been passed by one house run the risk of dying on a calendar of the other house. Conference-committee bills, however, are invariably brought up for action.

When to Get There

On some measures there is little problem of deciding upon the best time to obtain floor consideration. "Never" is the best time for a bill one wants to kill. "Any time" is the best for a bill that is in serious danger of dying on the calendar. For measures on which the continuation of vital government activities depends—legislative vetoes that must be approved within a given number of days, crisis bills, or bills that have been reported at the end of a Congress—the best time is "the sooner the better."

With the competition for floor time as keen as it is, however, the best time is often impossible to achieve and the participants in the legislative struggle are faced with the problem of judging between second, third, and fourth choices. On other types of measures the margin of choice is still greater. Between the extremes of "never," "any time," and "the sooner the better" there is a broad area of choice and maneuver.

At what point during a session of a Congress is it most desirable to bring a bill to the floor? Early consideration has distinct advantages. The first weeks of a Congress provide the best occasion to fight off a filibuster. Early consideration allows time to handle sharp attacks and to deal with proposed amendments. Consideration near the end of a session provides an ideal opportunity to kill a measure by insisting on protracted discussion in the Senate even though such discussions are not carried to the extreme of a filibuster. It also provides an opportunity to slip measures through unnoticed. During the last hectic days of a session, when members are tired out and anxious to leave, many a bill can be passed that could never hope to receive favorable consideration during the middle of the session.

Delay toward the end of a session also provides an ideal opportunity for avoiding a conference committee by forcing compliance by the other house. An interesting example of this tactic is the 1947 legislation providing for an elected government in Puerto Rico. In response to the desires of local Republicans in Puerto Rico, Senator Robert Taft was eager to have the legislation include a provision for Presidential appointment of members of the Puerto Rico Supreme Court. This provision was not in the bill which passed the House. It was left out of the bill in the Senate committee because of the danger that it would send the bill to conference and a conference delay would prevent action at the First Session of the Eightieth Congress. Therefore, when the bill came up on the Consent Calendar somewhat earlier in the session, Senator Taft objected to its consideration. At the very last moment of the last day, however, he called it off the calendar himself, moved the amendment, and had the bill passed in the form he wanted it. It was then sent to the House of Representatives which concurred without asking for a conference because there were only a few minutes remaining before the session was to be adjourned.

Delay also proves useful—paradoxically enough—on matters of great urgency. By keeping a bill off the floor for a required length of time, an important measure may be transformed into an urgent one, urgency may be transformed into emergency, and emergency may be made into crisis. Delays of this sort are particularly useful in the case of measures to renew expiring programs. When there is still ample time for action before the expiration date, the opponents of renewal are in a stronger position. On the very eve of an expiration date, however, tables are often completely turned and the proponents are in a dominating position. This has been illustrated again and again in the extension of various control operations such as rent control, export control, and mandatory priorities and allocations initiated during World War II. In these cases the strategy of delay necessarily ties in with the timing of committee action.

Another consideration is timing of floor action in relation to elections and primaries. Congressional elections always take place in November of even-numbered years, usually at the end of the second regular session of every Congress. Primaries are strung out from February to September of the same years. Here again the question of timing relates to the introduction of measures, committee action, and floor action. Floor action is particularly important for members who face difficult primary or election contests. What one says or does on the floor of either house is important news to people back home. It is, therefore, natural for many members to be interested in timing floor consideration in a manner that will be most helpful to themselves. In some cases this involves keeping measures on the calendar until the strategic moment. In others, when the contemplated matter might prove distasteful to constituents, it involves early floor consideration (in the hope that dissatisfied constituents will forget by the time elections roll around) or postponement until after the elections. A typical example of the latter was the Truman Administration's efforts to prevent excess-profits-tax proposals from being considered on the floor of Congress before the 1950 elections. The best way to handle the matter, President Truman was reported as saying at a press conference, would be to wait until after "the election jitters were over."

There is also the problem of relating action in one house to action in the other house. It is sometimes extremely advantageous to call a bill up for consideration first in the house in which it stands a better chance of favorable action. In 1950 President Truman sent to Congress a reorganization plan to curtail the powers of the General Counsel of the National Labor Relations Board. The Administration and organized-labor groups favored this plan and attempted to have a resolution of approval brought up first in the House of Representatives where it had more support, and subsequently in the Senate, where it had less support. The object was to confront the Senate with a House-approved measure. This strategy was frustrated by the insistence of the chairman of the House Appropriations Committee in bringing up an appropriations measure first and by the diligence of the antilabor organizations in speeding up Senate action. The Senate disapproved the plan before the House could get around to acting upon it and since the disapproval of one house is sufficient as a legislative veto, the matter ended there.

Labor groups have often sought House action first for an entirely different reason. In the case of legislation restricting the rights of organized labor, they have usually felt that the liberal forces in the Senate would be in a stronger position if they came into the game later and acted to modify House-enacted provisions. This route was followed again and again in the long series of bills that culminated in the Taft-Hartley Act. The fact that it would tend to give the Senators an upper hand is evidenced by Representative Hartley's frequent but futile insistence that House action should be delayed until after the Senate had passed a bill.

At one point during the history of the struggle over FEPC legislation, factional controversies broke out around the question of "Senate or House first?"

The National Council (for a Permanent FEPC) felt that success in the House would be comparatively easy to achieve, but that Southern opposition in the Senate was the major stumbling block and unless overcome first, the work on the House of Representatives would go for naught. The left-wingers, conversely, agreed with the American Jewish Congress and several other groups which urged the "House-first" approach. . . . The National Negro Congress asserted in this connection: "It is well known that any bill which has passed one House of Congress has the better chance of passing the other. Hostility in the Senate has been so marked as to make approval of the House almost a necessity before passage by the Senate can be expected." [5]

[5] Louis C. Kesselman, "Social Politics of FEPC" (Chapel Hill, N.C.: University of North Carolina Press, 1948), p. 158.

The above questions are in many ways similar to those faced in the introduction of measures and the scheduling of committee operations. There are others, however, that are more directly geared to the specific terrain of floor consideration. One problem relates to whether one bill should be called up before or after another measure. There are occasions when the best time to consider one subject is in the lull immediately before the consideration of a major measure which will monopolize attention for days or weeks. There are other situations in which the best time to seek action is after a major conflict has been fought and before all the participants can recover from battle fatigue. When two committees have reported rival bills, the advantage often goes to the first brought up for consideration. As in the case of the involved struggle over the War Mobilization and Reconversion Act already referred to, the measure which comes up first is in the favored position. The proponents of the second bill are then put in the position of having to offer primary floor amendments. The supporters of the first measure can then come back with secondary amendments. Since tertiary amendments cannot be offered under the rules, proponents of the secondary amendments are in the position of having the crucial votes taken on their proposals on ground of their own choosing.

Still another problem is providing time for preparation. A bill is sometimes reported from a committee before a formal committee report has been prepared. Still more frequently bills are reported and committee reports submitted before their key supporters have readied their formal talks, prepared formal floor statements, acquainted themselves with the kinds of problems that might arise on the floor, or mapped out their floor strategy. Under these circumstances, a certain amount of delay is essential to adequate presentation.

Another problem relates to floor attendance. One of the most humorous events ever to take place on the floor of the Senate occurred in 1946 when Senator Wayne Morse noticed that, as a result of a protracted harangue by Senator William Langer, all the other members of the Senate except the Presiding Officer, Langer, and himself had left the floor. Taking advantage of this situation, he asked unanimous consent that the anti-poll-tax bill be called off the calendar. "I believe that we are in a position to save the Senate a great deal of time," he quipped, "inasmuch as the Senator and I are about the only members of the Senate now present on the floor." [6] The highly controversial anti-poll-tax bill would then and there have passed the Senate had not some Senate employees who were friendly with the Southern Democrats collared a Democratic Senator and rushed him to the floor to voice a quick objection.

A less playful but somewhat similar maneuver was attempted by Senator McCarran of Nevada in 1949 when he moved to disagree to the House-amended version of the basing-point bill. McCarran had earlier promised the opponents of this legislation, many of whom believed the House version to be more

[6] *Congressional Record*, 79th Cong., 2d Sess., Apr. 18, 1946, p. 3971.

acceptable than any bill that might emerge from a conference committee, that he would inform them before he called the House version up for consideration. On July 26, however, he suddenly called the bill up, moved that it be sent to conference, and secured agreement without objection. "It was my understanding," Senator Long of Louisiana subsequently protested, "that we were to be notified before a motion was made to send that bill to conference. . . . I thought we were to be notified and I was on my way to the Senate chamber at the time the motion was made." [7] McCarran explained his action by pointing out that various opponents of the bill, including Senator Kefauver of Tennessee, were on the floor when the motion was made. Senator Kefauver retorted by charging that McCarran had made his motion in a low tone of voice. "It is true that the junior Senator from Tennessee was on the floor at the time," he added, "but he was talking to the distinguished Presiding Officer at the moment and did not hear the motion. For that matter, several other Senators who are interested in the matter did not hear the motion, either." [8] The issue was then fought out on a motion to reconsider the Senate's action. This was a highly favorable situation for McCarran. Under the Senate rules, a motion to table a motion to reconsider is not debatable, and McCarran thus had the decisive power to shut off debate at any time. If notice had been given in the original motion or if it had been made in a louder voice, the debate would have taken place under circumstances that would have allowed Long, Kefauver, and their colleagues to stall action indefinitely by protracted discussion. The motion to reconsider failed.

A similar tactic was attempted when the conference bill came to the Senate later in the year. Here the effort was made to have the conference bill called up for consideration and acted upon so quickly that its opponents would not realize what had happened. Earl Latham gives this story in detail:

With the submission of the conference report to the Senate, the opponents of S. 1108 had picked up another ally—time. The Senate was in the last days of the First Session of the Eighty-first Congress, and the Congressmen wanted to expedite their business in order to get home. O'Connor was reported to be confident that he had enough votes to push the bill through. The pressure was so great that the sponsors of the conference report actually managed to slip it through the Senate in a Saturday night session with what Douglas described as "supersonic speed." The action was recalled by the timely attentiveness of Douglas and Long. The Senator from Illinois said that he and Long were standing close to the Chair, but even could not hear the question which was stated, and "we were startled by the almost instantaneous announcement that the report had been agreed to." [9]

[7] *Congressional Record*, 81st Cong., 1st Sess., July 26, 1949, p. 10150.
[8] *Ibid.*, p. 10151.
[9] Earl Latham, "The Group Basis of Politics" (Ithaca, N.Y.: Cornell University Press, 1952), p. 153.

The opponents of the conference bill then succeeded in having its consideration postponed until the beginning of the next year.

How to Get There

How to bell the cat? This is often more difficult than judging the most desirable time to do it.

In the House of Representatives, with its large membership, there has evolved the following exceedingly complex system of rules and usages governing the methods of calling a bill up for consideration: (1) All bills that might be brought before the House are generally classifiable into six types. (2) Some of these bills are highly privileged, others not. (3) Some can be brought up on special days only. (4) Any other bills must be brought up by special orders of the House.

In the smaller-sized Senate, the members work things out with a minimum degree of formality.

Classification of House Bills. All bills that are reported out by committees are divided into (a) public bills dealing with appropriations or revenue, (b) other public bills, and (c) private bills. These three sets of bills are listed in the order in which they are reported. The lists are called, respectively, the "Union Calendar," the "House Calendar," and the "Private Calendar." Any bill on the first or second of these calendars may, if there is no objection, be placed on a fourth list called the "Consent Calendar." A fifth list is the "Discharge Calendar." As explained in Chap. 16, any bill still in committee can be listed on this calendar when a petition with the required number of signatures has been filed with the Clerk of the House. A sixth list is for those bills which come from the President with a veto message, from a conference committee, or, after previous passage, from the other house in amended form. These bills are referred to as "on the Speaker's Table," a calendar by another name.

This process of classification is largely automatic. The only variations for the first three lists are borderline cases. Here the decisions are made by the Clerk of the House. Any member is free to have any bill already on the Union or House Calendars placed on the Consent Calendar. This apparently broad discretion is limited by the fact that subsequently a single objection can prevent it from being taken off the calendar. Controversial bills are thereby excluded and the problem of judgment and choice relates to deciding whether or not to place on the Consent Calendar bills that are slightly controversial. In so far as the Discharge Calendar and the Speaker's Table are concerned, there are no choices and no borderline cases.

Privileged Bills in the House. Special attention is given to revenue-raising bills from the Ways and Means Committee, general appropriation bills from the Appropriations Committee, rivers and harbors bills from the Public Works Committee, and certain bills from the Public Lands and Veterans' Affairs Committees. These committees have the "right to report at any time" on such measures and this right has come to mean consideration at the same time the report is made. This places considerable power over the timing of floor consideration in the hands of the chairman and the dominant group in these four committees. When there are competing claims among these committees, the Speaker uses his power of recognition to favor one or the other. "Any time," however, really means at any time except when business of high precedence is being considered or motions of higher precedence are offered.[10]

Still more highly privileged are measures on the Speaker's Table. Veto messages are promptly presented to the House when received, and action to sustain or override the veto is immediately in order. Consideration can be avoided only by a motion to lay on the table, postpone action, or refer the bill back to a committee. Conference bills can be presented to the House for action at almost any time deemed desirable by the House conference and the party leadership. A request to take up a House bill that has been amended by the Senate is usually coupled with a unanimous consent request to concur or to disagree and ask for a conference. This request must be made by the appropriate committee. If there is objection, the bill can then be called up under a special order from the Rules Committee. Senate-passed bills similar to bills already on the House Calendar can also be called up by the appropriate committee. This means that fast Senate action is one of the best ways to expedite floor consideration in the House.

Special Days in the House. All the bills on the Consent, Private, and Discharge Calendars are specially favored in that specific days of the month are set aside for their consideration. Bills on the Consent Calendar can be taken up on the first and third Mondays of every month, bills on the Private Calendar on the first and third Tuesdays, and bills on the Discharge Calendar on the second and fourth Mondays.

These bills are favored in a limited sense only. When the Consent Calendar

[10] The precedence of business in the House is as follows: "1. Reception of messages. 2. Oath. 3. Quorum. 4. Presentation of conference reports. 5. Adjournment. 6. Entering motion to reconsider. 7. Organization of House. 8. Impeachment. 9. Journal. 10. Election cases. 11. Vetoed bills. 12. Electoral vote. 13. Adjournment or recess of Congress. 14. Privilege. 15. Change of reference to calendars. 16. Calendar Wednesday. 17. Call of Private Calendar. 18. Change of reference to committees. 19. Consideration of conference reports. 20. Reconsideration. 21. Report from Committee on Rules. 22. Special orders. 23. Suspension of rules. 24. Propositions coming over with previous question ordered. 25. Resolutions of enquiry. 26. Amendments in disagreement. 27. Motions to go into Committee of Whole for consideration of revenue and appropriation bills. 28. Bills privileged under right to report at any time. 29. Census. 30. Motions to discharge committees. 31. District Monday. 32. Consent Calendar. 33. Senate bills on Speaker's Table similar to bills on House Calendar. 34. Disposition of Messages." Cannon, *op. cit.*, p. 241.

is ready the Speaker asks: "Is there objection to the present consideration of the bill?" A single objection means that the House moves on to the next bill on the list. Every member thus has a personal veto to use at his discretion.[11] Moreover, the majority and minority leaders customarily assign a few members as "official objectors" to serve as watchdogs and to voice objections, when desirable, on behalf of the party or of absent party members. Accordingly, there is a considerable amount of horse trading and maneuvering surrounding the use of objections. To get a member, for example, to withdraw his objection to bill A, it is sometimes necessary for the sponsor of bill A to withdraw his objection to bill B so that the sponsor of bill B will withdraw his objection to bill C which is close to the heart of the original objector to bill A.

Bills on the Private Calendar are subject to the same procedure. In addition, on the second of the two days per month allotted to this calendar, the Speaker may at his own discretion dispense with this item entirely and recognize members offering motions for other privileged business.

There are two possible obstacles to calling up for consideration a bill that has been listed on the Discharge Calendar. First, under the rules a bill must have been on the Discharge Calendar seven legislative days in order to be called up when Discharge Day rolls around. During this interval the bill can be reported in amended form—and the amendments can make it substantially different— by the committee that had previously failed to act. In this event, the bill would have to be called up from another calendar. A more devious form of circumvention is also possible through the extreme device of recessing the House so that seven legislative days will not be allowed to occur before Discharge Day. This strategy was successfully used in 1934 when the House leadership was eager to stave off action on the Lemke-Frazier farm bill. The Speaker ruled that seven legislative days had not elapsed, even though nine actual days had gone by.[12] His ruling stood unchallenged. By the time of the next Discharge Day, the House had adjourned.

The second obstacle is that the signatures on the petition will not by themselves guarantee consideration of the bill. These signatures must be translated into a majority vote when the actual motion to discharge is made. This calls for a continued campaign. When the motion came up in 1950 to force the discharge of legislation to restore curtailed postal services, Representative Miller of California sounded the call as follows: "I ask the members who have had

---

[11] It is interesting to speculate on what might happen in the House if some member should someday choose to make frequent use of this veto. Theoretically, he could force less extensive use of the Consent Calendar, or else wrest innumerable concessions from other members on matters in which he was personally interested. Practically, however, every member has such a personal vested interest in having certain measures brought up from the Consent Calendar without objection that he will object to consideration of someone else's bill only when there are clear and present pressures favoring such a step.

[12] *Congressional Record,* 73d Cong., 2d Sess., June 11, 1934, pp. 11063–11065.

the courage to sign this discharge petition to stick with their first and sound decision." [13] The 249 to 81 record vote to take up the bill was testimony to the effectiveness of the postal-clerk campaign that underpinned the gentleman's rallying cry.[14]

There are two other days on which certain bills have a special chance to be considered: District of Columbia Day and Calendar Wednesday. The purpose of the former, which occurs on the second and fourth Mondays of each month, is to provide for the concentrated handling of the many measures rendered necessary by the lack of local self-government in the nation's capital. It is used only when the members of the District of Columbia Committee desire.

The purpose of the latter is to give the various standing committees a chance to call up bills that are not highly privileged in themselves or that have not been given a green light by the Rules Committee.[15] Under it, the committees are called in alphabetical order, and debate on any measure is for all practical purposes limited to one Wednesday. Because of the pressure of urgent business and because of the awkwardness of a procedure under which any given committee may not be called upon for a dozen or more Wednesdays, this procedure is rarely attempted. Moreover, attempts to use it can be frustrated by adjournments and dilatory tactics. A classic example occurred in 1945 when Chairman Mary Norton of the House Labor Committee was trying to obtain consideration of FEPC legislation.

[13] *Congressional Record*, 81st Cong., 2d Sess., Aug. 14, 1950, p. 12449.

[14] An additional obstacle was faced in this case. Since it was the Rules Committee that was being discharged, the result of the above vote was to bring before the House a special order outlining the manner in which the postal-services bill would be considered. This resolution provided that upon the following day Rep. John Walsh of Indiana, the leading proponent of the bill from the Committee on the Post Office and Civil Service (the chairman of the committee had opposed the measure), would be recognized by the Speaker to call up the measure. Rep. Walsh at this moment happened to be on his way to Wisconsin for a radio speech. Without his presence, the rule would be inoperative. This came as a rude shock to Walsh, who had not known that he would have to be on the House floor—and, in fact, the rule was probably designed by Rules Committee members who knew Walsh was away and hoped to catch him off guard. At the last moment, however, Walsh found out what had happened and succeeded in making an airplane connection that brought him back in time to save the day.

[15] The first Calendar Wednesday rule was adopted under Speaker Cannon's guidance in 1909 as a sop to the Republican insurgents. They, in turn, attacked it as inadequate and as threatening to defeat real reform in the rules. "A homeopathic dose of nothingness," George Norris branded it. (*Congressional Record*, 60th Cong., 2d Sess., p. 3150.) Shortly thereafter the Cannon organization itself tried to weaken the Calendar Wednesday rule by bringing up a census bill early on a Wednesday. There ensued a historic debate on whether or not a privileged bill could interfere with Calendar Wednesday. The Republican insurgents and certain Democrats were now in the position of defending the new procedure. It was the overruling of the Speaker's ruling on this matter, by a vote of 163 to 112, that made the first crack in the structure of the Cannon organization and gave Norris the signal for the introduction of his famous resolution to depose Cannon as chairman of the Rules Committee.

On Tuesday, September 25, when the customary request was made for unanimous consent to suspend next day's Calendar Wednesday, she objected. . . . On Wednesday, September 26, however, within fifteen minutes after the session began, William M. Whittington (Dem.-Miss.) moved the adjournment of the House, which was carried by a vote of 74 to 31, thus ending the calendar and legislative day. The friends of FEPC thus learned: Calendar Wednesday could not be utilized unless a firm, stable and continuous majority was at hand to defeat all dilatory motions. . . .[16]

In the Spring of 1946, the effort was repeated. This time the opponents of the FEPC legislation interspersed repeated adjournment motions with dilatory quorum calls that rendered the House almost incapable of legislative action. The FEPC forces finally mustered up a firm majority against adjournment and succeeded in having the call of committees initiated. The Labor Committee, however, was seventeenth on the list and the hope of its ever getting to the top of the list was a vain one. The FEPC strategy was therefore shifted toward getting action through a discharge petition.

At an earlier stage the question of whether to use Calendar Wednesday was a burning issue among the various organizations supporting FEPC legislation. Representative Marcantonio of New York City and others proposed the Calendar Wednesday approach. Rival groups regarded it as a snare and a delusion. For example, the head of one C.I.O. union wired his local unions as follows:

The flimsy charge of Marcantonio that failure to use Calendar Wednesday is solely responsible for inability to get HR 2232 to the floor of the House of Representatives is further evidence of the divisive tactics commonly practiced by those whose endorsement is the kiss of death. The use of Calendar Wednesday was fully explored by proponents of the bill and the consensus was that it would involve more time than the petition method. A bill brought to the floor in this manner must be disposed of in that particular day. Mr. Marcantonio is an expert parliamentarian and was well aware of all these implications.[17]

Special "Rules" in the House. For the first hundred years in the history of the House, any member was theoretically entitled to move that a bill be called off a calendar out of numerical order. Actually, this could not be done unless a member was recognized by the Speaker, who thereby exercised considerable control over the calling up of nonprivileged bills. Gradually, this control came to be exercised through the Rules Committee, which had been chaired by the Speaker since its creation in 1860. By the Fifty-first Congress the Rules Committee was formally given the function of submitting highly privileged resolu-

[16] Will Maslow, "FEPC—A Case History," *University of Chicago Law Review*, Vol. 13, June, 1946, pp. 421–422.

[17] Quoted in Louis C. Kesselman, "The Social Politics of FEPC" (Chapel Hill, N.C.: University of North Carolina Press, 1948), p. 160.

tions—or rules—giving the right of way to any bill of its own choosing. With these rules customarily being adopted, the majority of the Rules Committee had in effect the power to direct an important portion of the legislative traffic in the House.

At times it has seemed as though this power has moved into the hands of the chairman of the Rules Committee. "It makes no difference what a majority of you decide," Rules Committee Chairman Phillip Campbell once told his committee colleagues: "If it meets with my disapproval, it shall not be done; I am the Committee; in me repose absolute obstructive powers." [18] Yet any such obstructive power—and, of course, it could never be absolute—derives from much more than the chairmanship alone. For many years Chairman Adolph Sabath, a New Dealer and Fair Dealer, enjoyed very little power, since the majority of his committee was made up of conservative Southern Democrats and Republicans.

The strategic position given the majority of the Rules Committee has been formally augmented or diminished on many occasions, as changes in the rules have given varying power to the Rules Committee, the Speaker, other party leaders in the House, or the chairmen of the legislative committees. The so-called overthrow of Speaker Cannon in 1910–1911, by diminishing the role of the Speaker, automatically enhanced the position of the Rules Committee and of majority party leaders other than the Speaker. Recurrent fortification of the discharge procedure and Calendar Wednesday strengthened the legis-lative committees against the Rules Committee and other leaders, although at times they have been used by the party leaders against the Rules Committee.

The last major changes in the rules of the House occurred at the beginning of the Eighty-first and Eighty-second Congresses. In 1949, eager to get action on measures that had loomed large in President Truman's 1948 election cam-paign, a group of Truman supporters succeeded in having the rules amended to provide a method of obtaining a special rule even when the Rules Committee refused to act. It provided that when the Rules Committee had delayed action for twenty-one days on a reported bill, the chairman of the committee which had reported it, if recognized by the Speaker, could offer a resolution on Dis-charge Calendar days to call the bill up for consideration. This shifted a portion of the traffic control power from the Rules Committee to the committee chair-men and the Speaker. Since recognition to obtain the floor cannot be automatic, particularly when other members are also striving for recognition, it also put a degree of power back in the hands of the Speaker. During the following months, the anti-Truman Democrats planned a counterattack. In January, 1951, with the support of the great majority of Republicans, they wiped out the two-year-old reform and brought back the previous rule.

If a member of the House (other than a committee chairman operating under

[18] Phillip Campbell, *The Searchlight*, Vol. 6, No. 12, 1922, pp. 5–6.

the twenty-one-day rule adopted in 1949) wants to obtain a special order of the day to call up a bill for consideration, he is not allowed to present a resolution that can be adopted by majority vote. The only courses open are to seek a suspension of the rules, which requires two-thirds approval, or make a unanimous consent request. In either case, previous arrangements usually must be made with the Speaker to win his consent to recognition and the approval of both majority and minority floor leaders must be obtained.

Motions to suspend the rules (which are in ord r only on the first and third Mondays, the days of the Consent Calendar) are infrequently made, since members who can obtain a two-thirds majority can usually obtain either a special order from the Rules Committee or unanimous consent. Yet the Rules Committee staff will occasionally bring in a special order calling up a bill under suspension of the rules on some day other than the first or third Mondays. The reason for this is that the suspension of the rules procedure can serve as an effective gag rule, since under it debate is strictly limited and no amendments may be offered.

Unanimous consent requests to call up bills are made more frequently. They are used both for the handling of emergency bills and for getting quicker action on minor bills than would be possible by waiting for Consent Calendar day.

The Senate System. The classification of bills is much simpler in the Senate than in the House. As contrasted with the House's five calendars and the Speaker's Table, the Senate has only two calendars. One is the Executive Calendar, on which treaties and nominations are listed; the other is the Calendar of Business, on which are all other bills awaiting Senate action.

As in the House, certain bills are highly privileged. These include vetoed bills, conference bills, Senate bills with House amendments, revenue bills, and appropriation bills (but all appropriation bills, not merely general ones).

Unlike the House, the Senate has no elaborate system of special days. Bills are brought up in two ways, either by taking bills off the Calendar of Business in order or by special action to take up bills out of order. The Calendar of Business may be called at almost any time.[19] Under this procedure—which in some ways is comparable to the House's use of the Consent Calendar and Private Calendar—the Clerk calls off the bills in the order of their appearance on the calendar.

As in the House, official objectors are designated by each party. Objections are usually raised by asking that a bill be passed over—in which case it will come up again at the same place in the calendar. Sometimes an objection will be made merely to delay consideration until a little later the same day. The 1950 legislation to amend the Hatch Act, for example, came up at a time when

[19] Although the call of the calendar is the regular order of business on Mondays at the conclusion of morning business, the calendar also may be called on other days. Usually the party leaders arrange to have it come about twice a month.

Senator Tydings, who wanted to offer an amendment, was not on the floor. "Mr. President, it is my understanding that the Senator from Maryland (Mr. Tydings) intends to offer an amendment to the measure," stated Senator Lucas, the majority leader. "I would respectfully suggest that the bill go to the foot of the calendar until we can confer with the Senator from Maryland." [20] Without objection, the bill went to the foot of the calendar. As a result, the bill came up again in the same afternoon, whereas if it had merely been passed over and left at the same place in the calendar, it might not have come up until the next day the calendar was read.

But an objection does not necessarily prevent consideration. Any member can move to take up the bill. If he wins a majority vote, the measure is then before the Senate despite any objection. [21]

There is nothing in the Senate comparable to the House Rules Committee. The Majority Policy Committee takes the lead in preparing a list of bills to be taken off the calendar. The minority leadership is informally consulted. Special action is then proposed to bring individual bills before the Senate. The most ordinary form of special action is a unanimous-consent agreement. This is required in order to take up a bill during the Morning Hour or while unfinished business is still before the Senate. When not required, it is conducive to cooperative working relations between the party leaders and to the development of an atmosphere in which everyone is expected to perform certain favors for others.

Unanimous consent, of course, is not always feasible. Hence, the rules provide that a motion to call up a bill may be made at almost any time by any Senator. A majority vote is all that is needed under the rules to pass it. The simplicity of the rules on this point, however, is deceptive. A determined minority can stage a filibuster to prevent a vote on such a motion. This happened in the Eightieth Congress during the special session called by President Truman after his nomination at the Democratic National Convention. One of his declared purposes in calling the special session was to obtain passage of the anti-poll-tax bill that had been passed by the House and reported out by the Senate committee. Taking him up on this issue, the acting Republican leader of the Senate, Senator Wherry of Nebraska, moved to call the anti-poll-tax bill off the calendar. A filibuster by Southern Democrats prevented the motion itself from being voted on.

A filibuster on a motion to take up a bill can be prevented by offering the motion during the Morning Hour before 2 P.M. During this period a motion to take up a bill is undebatable. Yet a Morning Hour can take place only at the beginning of a new legislative day. When the Senate takes a recess instead

[20] *Congressional Record*, 81st Cong., 2d Sess., Aug. 9, 1950, p. 12254.

[21] This would not apply, of course, if the calendar is being read under a unanimous consent agreement to take up bills without objection.

of an adjournment at the end of a calendar day, there can be no morning hour on the next day and all motions to take up bills are debatable.

THE QUESTIONS FOR DECISION

Anyone who has analyzed the voting records of members of Congress knows full well that decision making on the floor of Congress is not simply a matter of accepting or rejecting a bill. The questions that come up for decision may involve complex amendments, rejecting a bill or amendment by indirect means, or the reconsideration of whatever action had been taken earlier. By emphasizing procedural complications, the emergence of clear-cut issues or readily evident indications where each voting member really stands are circumvented.

In the Senate there is more fluidity for this than in the House. On controversial matters it is impossible to predict what types of action may be proposed; almost anything can happen. In the House, floor operations are under tighter control. When a special order is adopted, it often constricts the gamut of action. Motions that are not highly privileged have little chance of being brought before the House. The Speaker will often ask, "For what purpose does the gentleman rise?" If the Speaker does not approve of a motion which the gentleman may want to offer, the gentleman will probably not get the floor. Yet, at times, despite these restrictions on action, the House as well as the Senate finds itself in a situation where a majority of its members and most outside observers have lost track of accumulating amendments and motions and only a handful of members are in a position to unravel the tangled skein of questions before the body.

Amendments

Committee amendments enjoy a privileged status in both houses. Amendments proposed by the majority of a committee are always given central attention on the floor. If a complete substitute is reported—in the form either of an amendment or a new bill—it displaces the original bill as the primary object of discussion. Committee minority amendments are also in a strong position. Both majority and minority amendments are usually buttressed by committee reports and by the full background of hearings, executive sessions, and concentrated campaigning and maneuvering that lie behind the reports.

Amendments offered from the floor by noncommittee members, in contrast, are often attacked on principle. One will find in the *Congressional Record* innumerable instances of members of Congress—usually members of the committee whose bill is up for consideration—strongly asserting that "the place to write a bill is in the committee, not on the floor." [22]

22 In "Considerations on Representative Government" (New York: Macmillan, 1947 ed.) John Stuart Mill developed in considerable detail the thesis that a representative assembly

The theoretical case against floor amendments can be substantiated in many ways. Although floor amendments may be every bit as important as the bill which is proposed, they are often objected to on the ground that they do not provide enough time or appropriate circumstances for careful study and consideration. Nor should one suppose that just because an amendment is offered from the floor it is necessarily a proposition more "open" in character than if it were presented in committee.

Amendments are supposed to be presented in writing, but there is no requirement that they be printed before they are voted upon. The Senate, however, authorizes members to have amendments printed before they are actually offered so that these advance drafts can be circulated to whomever the individual member wants to keep informed. The House does not allow this practice. In both houses, in fact, many amendments are often discussed and voted upon without much of an opportunity for many members fully to analyze their content or to prevent "hidden ball plays."

At times a committee bill may be snowed under by a large number of unintelligible or even contradictory amendments. Action is sometimes taken to recommit such a bill to the committee in which it originated in the hope that the committee can bring order out of chaos. Or the bill is passed with fervent expressions of hope that the other house or the conference committee will rectify the most obvious errors. On the other hand, there are innumerable advantages in the offering of floor amendments. The most important is that the process of offering amendments from the floor tends to some extent to enlarge the circle of insiders in a larger group. It can bring out facts and issues that might otherwise go unnoticed. The very possibility of having to defend a bill against floor amendments forces committee members to give more thorough consideration to the original provisions of the bill and to prepare more intensive explanations of the reasons for this or that provision. Moreover, the line-up of forces on the floor of the Senate or the House is often much different from the line-up in individual committees. This means that certain groups can have hope of obtaining their ends only on the floor.

A floor amendment provides a member of Congress with a good opportunity to attract attention and build up his record. A member who offers an amendment to an important bill can sometimes move much more into the limelight than by introducing a score of bills that are never acted upon. From the

is qualified only to pass or reject a measure, not to alter it. He felt that the work of both original drafting and subsequent amendment could be properly handled by a small expert body. Although British practice has not gone this far, bills brought before the House of Commons by the Cabinet—which is in an important sense the central leadership committee of the House—are not subject to as many floor amendments as are committee bills in the U.S. Congress. In the case of appropriations, no amendments in the House of Commons are allowed to raise the total level of appropriations beyond that recommended in the Cabinet's budget.

strategic viewpoint, moreover, floor amendments provide ideal instruments for consuming time and postponing final decision on a bill. Amendments that succeed in narrowing the support enjoyed by a measure are an ideal way of building up a final coup de grâce. Both sides in a contest find that a vote on even a minor amendment may provide an ideal method of testing the strength of opposing forces and of serving as a guide to subsequent floor strategy.

In the Senate, the amending process is wide open. Rarely is an amendment ever ruled out of order for reason that it is not germane. Even under the tightest unanimous consent agreements, there is usually full opportunity for the presentation of amendments. In the House, the offering of amendments is hardly as open. Amendments to a bill taken off the Consent and Private Calendars or taken up on Calendar Wednesday are never in order. Beyond this fixed limitation, many important legislative struggles center around the procedural issue of whether or not amendments are to be allowed. The Speaker has considerable personal discretion in ruling amendments out of order on the ground that they are not germane.

The Rules Committee also takes action often to directly limit amendments themselves. The Agricultural Adjustment Act of 1933 was considered under a ruling which not only waived all points of order and limited general debate to four hours but also prevented the offering of any amendments whatsoever. Many tax bills are passed under rules that provide that no amendments may be in order "except those offered by direction of the Committee on Ways and Means, and such amendments shall not be subject to amendment." Sometimes all amendments are out of order except certain specified ones. The 1940 act which extended the Sugar Act of 1937 allowed only those amendments "proposing the extension of the provisions of Section 207 of the Sugar Act of 1937." These authorized amendments are usually committee amendments.

Rules of this type are often the subject of bitter controversy. The 1947 debate over the rule dealing with the legislative budget resolution of that year is illustrative. Representative Sabath, ranking minority member of the Rules Committee attacked the rule as "the most drastic gag rule ever submitted to the House since the days of Uncle Joe Cannon's Czaristic control of Congress . . . it deprives you of your rights under the Constitution under the rules of the House." [23] The Republican chairman of the Rules Committee defended this rule by bringing in a full list of similar rules proposed by Democrats during previous years. "I believe the record will disclose," he maintained, "that the Democratic leadership during those many years brought in many closed rules, and the Democratic members, without exception, voted solidly for those closed rules." [24]

[23] *Congressional Record* (daily edition), Feb. 20, 1947, p. 1253.
[24] *Ibid.*, p. 1252.

One of the most illuminating comments on such debates was made by Representative Rankin of Mississippi in connection with a closed rule on a bill to stabilize commodity prices. "The average member of the House," observed Mr. Rankin, "does not want to be gagged on a measure he is against, but he does not mind being gagged on a measure he is for." [25]

In the case of tax bills, "gag rules" are usually an accepted way of doing business in the House of Representatives. Roy Blough summarizes House practices on revenue measures as follows:

Although revenue measures have priority without a rule, the Ways and Means Committee usually asks the Rules Committee for a "closed" rule which limits debate and forbids amendments to the bill except those sponsored by the Ways and Means Committee. . . .

Restriction of amendment is defended on the ground that amendments made without careful regard to the numerous inter-relations among sections of the Code would result in conflicting provisions and an unworkable law. Moreover, the bill is presumed to represent a balanced program and balance might be seriously affected by amendments. An unemphasized consideration is the fear that superficially attractive but impractical or basically undesirable provisions would be adopted on the floor. . . . Occasionally when sentiment in the House is sharply divided on some issue the rule permits amendment as to that issue alone. [26]

In some respects the offering of an amendment is comparable to the introduction of a bill. Sponsors must be selected, and, at times, cosponsors lined up. A floor amendment may be printed and announced long before the measure at which it is aimed comes up for consideration. In the case of tax measures which are not introduced in original form in the Senate, Senators have often been known to announce and publicly discuss the amendments they plan to propose long before the Senate committee has reported a measure or even before the House has acted. In many other respects there are special tactical problems involved in the offering of amendments on the floor. On certain occasions, a bill is read section by section when the time comes for approval or disapproval. This is done in the case of appropriation bills in both houses. When this is done, an amendment relating to a given section can be offered only at the appropriate time.

There is also the problem of picking the particular stage in the consideration of a measure at which an amendment is to be offered. During the 1921–1922 depression, for example, farm-bloc Senators developed a full strategy for talking on behalf of a farm-relief bill during the hottest days of July. Administration opponents of the bill succeeded in sidetracking them to an im-

[25] *Congressional Record* (daily edition), Dec. 19, 1947, p. 11846.
[26] Roy Blough, "The Federal Taxing Process" (New York: Prentice-Hall, 1952), pp. 76–77.

portant degree by the surprise offer of an Administration substitute. The method by which this substitute was brought before the Senate is related by Karl Schriftgiesser:

> Although Vice-President Calvin Coolidge had quietly encouraged the supporters of the bills to believe that, on the crucial day, he would first recognize one of them, when that day came he slyly evaded his promise by not appearing in the chamber. In his place was Senator Curtis of Kansas, who immediately recognized Senator Kellogg of Minnesota. This clever, tactical manipulation allowed Kellogg to present an administration substitute measure, of which he was the apparent author.[27]

Sometimes the air is so thick with amendments that even the most skilled parliamentarians have difficulty in keeping track of what is happening. An amendment to a pending measure can itself be amended. Although a third-degree amendment is not in order, additional changes can be proposed by offering a substitute for the first amendment. An amendment is then in order to the substitute itself. Four separate proposals for change may thus be in the air at one time.

The order in which these proposals is considered may have a direct bearing on the outcome, since the one which is taken up first may pave the way for other amendments or close the door against them. In both houses, the vote is first taken on an amendment to an amendment. Votes are then taken, respectively, on the amendment to the substitute, on the substitute, and the original amendment itself (although by this time the original amendment may have been significantly changed). In many situations this puts the supporters of the amendment to the amendment in a strategically favorable position, since their proposal must be voted upon first. This is a position which can best be won by the committee majority which had the bill reported to the floor, for all they have to do is wait for an opposition amendment and then regain the initiative by offering a counteramendment.

Sometimes an amendment may be printed and announced but never offered. Or it may be delayed until an occasion arises for proposing its attachment to another measure. Or it may be offered and then, in the light of opposition or because of some informal understanding, may be withdrawn by its sponsors.

Rejection by Indirection

In most cases a bill or an amendment is either passed or defeated. If the former occurs, it can happen in only one way: by actual approval. But in the latter case, members of Congress may avail themselves not only of an outright negative vote but also of five other weapons of rejection. These weapons— recommittal, tabling or postponing, striking out the enacting clause, points of

[27] Karl Schriftgiesser, "This Was Normalcy" (Boston: Little, Brown, 1948), pp. 104–105.

order, and dilatory action—can be used either to force amendments as the price of approval or to defeat a bill or its amendments as conclusively as though it had happened by a direct negative vote.

Recommittal. For the most part, recommittal is merely a delicate way of writing out a death sentence. Lingering doubts may exist as to the future awakening of the corpse but this does not usually detract from the finality of the action.

The recommittal action becomes somewhat puzzling to uninformed observers when the motion to recommit includes certain instructions to the committee. During any typical session motions are offered to recommit one bill for further study, another for a report by a given time,[28] another for the deletion of a specific clause, another for the making of specific amendments. One might get the impression that this is a method of having certain changes made. In the great bulk of the cases, however, the purpose is either to kill the bill or, in the event that not enough votes are available for this purpose, to obtain a record vote on the position presented in the recommittal motion.

This latter alternative is highly popular. It will be noted that a motion to recommit with instructions that certain changes be made provides an ideal method of expressing a negative position on a pending measure. First of all, it is negative in a constructive fashion; it is a way of indicating not blind opposition but opposition *unless* some change is made. At the same time, it expresses more than it is possible to say with an amendment alone, since, in a way, it covers the bill as a whole and the desired amendments. In the House of Representatives, as spelled out more fully in a subsequent section of this chapter, a motion to recommit is often the only way of getting a record vote on amendments.

To a restricted degree, bills may be recommitted at an interim stage before passage. In the case of conference bills, recommittal is a step in the push and pull between the floor majorities of the two houses. In the case of ordinary bills, the purpose may be to have certain changes made in committee that cannot be efficiently handled on the floor, or to arrange for a more relaxed negotiation among competing interests, or to shift the locus of power. It is the last of these that is usually uppermost when a bill is recommitted to another committee than the one from which it was reported. When the Sherman Antitrust Bill was reported from the Senate Finance Committee, those who sought certain amendments adopted the strategy of having it referred to the Senate Judiciary Committee first. They "loaded the bill with a series of humorous amendments, whereupon Senator Sherman who had successfully combatted repeated proposals that the bill be turned over to the Judiciary Committee for revision,

---

[28] In the House, a recommittal motion can call for a report "forthwith," but cannot specify a given date. In the Senate, a report can be requested "forthwith" or at any specific future date.

was no longer able to prevent such reference." [29] The bill was completely rewritten in the Judiciary Committee and was then passed without change by the Senate.

Tabling or Postponing. Theoretically, action to table a question leaves a grain of hope. A question laid on the table may sometimes be taken off the table. Actually, there is little hope of this, because the motion to table is highly privileged and the motion to take off the table is not. A motion to table also has the peculiar virtue of stopping debate, for in both houses the motion is undebatable. This provides a powerful weapon of restriction upon the continuation of debate, but—and this is an all-important qualification—by its very nature, it can be used only by those who are opposed to the pending question. Even in the Senate a filibuster can be stopped by moving to table the measure, although the stopping of debate in this manner would merely represent surrender to the filibuster.

In 1950 Senator Langer of North Dakota expressed his opposition to the pending bill repealing the tax on oleomargarine by offering as amendments the various civil-rights bills dealing with fair employment practices, poll taxes, and lynching. The obvious purpose was to embarrass those supporters of the pending measure who also supported these civil-rights measures. Defenders of the pending bill countered Langer's strategy by moving to table his amendments instead of trying to vote them down directly. This made it easier for the civil-rights supporters to oppose Langer, and subsequently all of his amendments were tabled.

During this same session when a bill to suspend tariff duties on metal scrap was being considered, Senator Wiley offered an amendment curbing Russian fur imports. Senator George succeeded in having it tabled. This killed two birds with one stone. He stopped debate on a rather irrelevant matter and he succeeded in preventing himself and his colleagues from being recorded as directly opposed to an anti-Russian position.

In the House a motion to table is too deadly an instrument to be used very frequently with respect to amendments. Under the House rules a successful motion to table an amendment carries with it to the table all other amendments that are pending and the bill itself. In the Senate a similar rule was in effect many decades ago. Senator Hoar tells in his autobiography how he had changed this so that a successful motion to table an amendment would carry with it only the amendment.[30]

In both houses the motion to table is frequently used with respect to questions other than a bill or an amendment. It is an ideal method, for example,

[29] John D. Clark, "The Federal Trust Policy" (Baltimore, Md.: Johns Hopkins Press, 1931), p. 29.

[30] George F. Hoar, "Autobiography of Seventy Years" (New York: Scribner, 1903), Vol. II, p. 99.

of stopping debate on motions to reconsider and on appeals from decisions of the Chair. In both houses, also, an effect equivalent to tabling can be achieved by postponing a question indefinitely or to a "day certain." But since motions to postpone are debatable and less privileged than motions to table, they are used but infrequently.

Striking Out the Enacting Clause. A somewhat whimsical way of killing a bill is to strike out the "Be it enacted, etc." clause. When such a motion is successful, the effect is just the same as though a vote had been taken to strike out every other word or all the consonants in every word. A typical example occurred during the Eighty-first Congress when Representative Stefan of Nebraska succeeded in having the enacting clause stricken out of a bill which would have authorized the contribution to international relief funds of the money which was earned by conscientious objectors during World War II and was still in the hands of the Government.

The motion to strike out the enacting clause has the minor effect of converting a negative action into a positive motion. As with recommitting and tabling, it puts its supporters in the position of taking the offensive rather than of just voting against something. Of probably much greater importance is the fact that a motion to strike out the enacting clause is in order during the reading of a bill for amendments in the House. In other words, this particular amendment—even though it has the effect of amending a bill out of existence—can come up at a time when amendments only are being considered for action in the House.

Points of Order. When appropriation bills are being considered, a point of order can often be raised against specific provisions of a "legislative" character. In the case of conference bills, points of order may be raised against various provisions on the ground that they contain new material not included in either the House or the Senate version.

If a point of order is sustained by the Chair, the provision against which it was raised is thereby deleted without any direct voting on the floor. However, the decision of the Chair may be appealed and a direct vote can thereby overrule the Chair. In this case the effect is the same as if the point of order had been rejected by the Chair in the first place.

In the House, the Rules Committee often brings out rules to protect bills against points of order that may be raised in an effort to strike out certain provisions of the bill or to defeat certain committee amendments. An interesting rule of this type was brought forth in the case of the Independent Offices Appropriation Bill for Fiscal Year 1948. This rule provided that during the consideration of the measure,

all points of order against the bill or any provisions contained therein are hereby waived; and it shall also be in order to consider without the intervention of any point of order any amendment to said bill prohibiting the use of the funds appropriated in such bill or any funds heretofore made available, including contract authorizations, for the purchase of any particular site or for the erection of any particular hospital.[31]

The purpose of this provision was to protect certain budget cuts which had been made in committee through the insertion of legislative provisions and to make it easier for members to propose other cuts from the floor.

Dilatory Action. Dilatory action for the purpose of rejecting a measure is one of the oldest of legislative weapons. It has the double virtue of providing a method for avoiding a clear showdown vote and for eliminating the risks involved in having a measure actually brought up for decision.

In the Senate, dilatory action is easier than in the House. Since dilatory amendments in the Senate are rarely ruled out of order, prolonged senatorial talking, as explained in detail later in this chapter, is extremely hard to stop.

But in both houses the strategists of delay have available many opportunities, particularly if they are well versed in rules and occupy positions of strategic advantage on various legislative and party-leadership committees. They can raise intricate points of order at various points in the course of business. They can appeal the decisions of the Chair and develop full discussions on each appeal. They can use every possible excuse for forcing a roll-call vote, which itself may take fifteen minutes in the Senate and forty-five minutes to an hour in the House. They can slow up the whole process of floor action by forcing recesses or adjournments.

Without a quorum—which, under the Constitution, is a majority of the members—neither house is supposed to be able to transact any business. This requirement is habitually winked at and a considerable amount of business is taken care of in each house without a quorum being present. Nevertheless, any member who can obtain the floor can "suggest the absence of a quorum" and thereby obtain a roll-call vote to determine how many members are really present. The history of the House has been punctuated by many efforts to prevent action by prevention of a quorum. Speaker Clay held that the constitutional provision concerning "a majority of the House" meant one-half of all possible members plus one. By thus pushing to the highest limit the number of members needed for a quorum, it became more feasible for a given number of absentees to prevent a quorum. By the time of Speaker Cannon, however, this limit was reduced by five separate qualifications, each one of which was the result of a bitter parliamentary battle. A quorum now consists of a "majority of those members chosen, sworn and living, whose membership has not been terminated by resignation or by the action of the House."

A still more historic conflict centered around the strategy of refusing to answer a roll call even when present. In many of the legislative battles concerning elections in the South after the Civil War "the Democrats found their most

[31] *Congressional Record,* 80th Cong., 1st Sess., June 17, 1947, p. 7166.

effective weapon in refusing a quorum; in practicing that peculiar art of meta-physics which admits of corporeal presence and parliamentary absence. Even parliamentary law has many fictions; but it seemed a self-contradiction to assert that a member may be present for obstruction and not present for business." [32] In a famous ruling in 1890 Speaker Thomas B. Reed took it upon himself to count those who were present but who had refused to answer when their names were called. Despite violent protests from the Democrats, Reed held firm. Im-mediately, members tried to rush from the chamber and found to their dismay that Speaker Reed had ordered the doors bolted. On one occasion an irate Southerner kicked open a door in order to escape the count. In the course of a few years, however, even the Democrats accepted the "Reed rules" and the only way to obtain a vanishing quorum was to vanish.

In recent decades a long series of quorum calls has often served to produce protracted delay. The roll will be called; it will be found that less than a ma-jority is present; the names of the absentees will then be called again, while late-comers straggle in; in some cases the sergeant-at-arms will be sent to round up absentees. By the time a full quorum has been reached, many members will have vanished through the doorways and once again the tedious process may be initiated.

One of the major protections against a vanishing quorum in the House is the institution of the Committee of the Whole. By meeting in the guise of "the Com-mittee of the Whole" the House can thereby dodge the constitutional require-ment for a quorum. Under the House rules a hundred members—less than half the number required in the House as such—are all that are needed to make up a quorum of the Committee of the Whole.

Reconsideration

The motion to reconsider is one of the few motions known only in American legislative bodies. In most other countries the tradition has always been that a matter should be voted upon only once. This position was shared by Thomas Jefferson who regarded reconsideration as offering an opportunity for a minor-ity to achieve a surprise victory. In one of his letters, Jefferson explained how reconsideration came into being during the Continental Congress. Since the Continental Congress had to serve as the executive body in the direction of the American Revolution, its members renounced the old parliamentary practice of regarding a legislative decision as immutable and adopted the more flexible method of reconsidering their decisions freely.[33] After the adoption of the Con-stitution, the new Congress maintained the same practice.

[32] Hubert Bruce Fuller, "The Speakers of the House" (Boston: Little, Brown, 1909), p. 219.

[33] Letter to M. deMeusinier, in Thomas Jefferson, "Writings," Ford ed., Vol. IV, p. 149.

A continuing controversy has revolved around the question of who is entitled to move reconsideration. Can it be someone who voted in the minority and wants another chance? Or must it be someone who voted in the majority and has then switched? This question came up in the very first session of the Senate when Senator Maclay of Pennsylvania made a point of order against a motion to reconsider offered by someone who had previously voted in the minority. He was overruled by Vice-President John Adams. Later in the same session, however, Adams reversed himself and ruled on the other side of the issue. After many long controversies Maclay's position is the one which has been generally accepted in both houses.

In actual practice, however, anyone who can get the floor for the purpose can move to reconsider. All that one on the losing side need do is to follow the course of the voting and, when he finds that the vote is definitely against him, switch to the other side. He is then technically on record as having voted with the majority and can move to reconsider.

Another interesting question is how long after the original action is taken can a motion to reconsider be offered. In 1820 when the original Missouri Compromise passed the House, Representative John Randolph moved reconsideration. Speaker Henry Clay ruled the motion out of order "until the ordinary business of the morning, as prescribed by the rules of the House, should be disposed of." Clay then quickly hurried the bill over to the Senate and when Randolph offered the motion again a little later, Clay announced that the bill was no longer before the House and that reconsideration was no longer possible. At present, a motion to reconsider is in order in the House at any time on the same or succeeding day. Two succeeding days of actual session are allowed in the Senate. If the bill has already been forwarded to the other house or to the President, a request may be made for the return of the papers.

A *pro forma* motion to reconsider is usually moved immediately after a measure has been passed. The motion is then habitually voted down or tabled by voice vote. This serves to protect an enacted measure against a sneak surprise attack by its opponents at a later hour or day when its proponents are not on the floor in sufficient numbers. It also has the effect of eliminating any real opportunity for reconsideration.

A genuine motion to reconsider as distinguished from a *pro forma* motion can lead to one of three results. The first is complete failure, as when Senator Kilgore moved to reconsider the Spanish-loan amendment to the Omnibus Appropriation Bill for fiscal year 1951 and saw his motion tabled. The second occurs when the motion to reconsider is carried but when reconsideration itself leads to no change in the original decision. This happened in the case of the same appropriation bill for which Senator Douglas used the reconsideration technique as a means of making a second but futile attack against the funds appropriated for merchant-marine construction. The third possibility is complete victory. When the appropriation bill just mentioned was being considered, the Senate rejected by a division vote an amendment offered by Senator Smith of New Jersey to exempt funds for international-children's-welfare work from a pending 10 per cent across-the-board reduction in the size of the appropriation. Senator Neely of West Virginia offered a motion to reconsider this vote. Senator Wherry of Nebraska moved to table Senator Neely's motion. The tabling motion lost. The motion to reconsider was then passed by 43 to 42. The original amendment of Senator Smith then came before the Senate again and this time was passed by a record vote of 44 to 41.

Chapter 18

ACTION ON THE FLOOR

ONE OF the oldest stories about Congress concerns the little boy who was taken to Washington by his father. For a few days in succession he and his father visited the galleries and saw the chaplain open the sessions with a prayer. After viewing this ceremony a number of days, the boy asked, "Why does the minister come in every day and pray for Congress?" The father replied, "You've got it all wrong, son. The minister comes in every day, looks over Congress, and then prays for the country."

To anyone who views Congress in floor session as Congress at work, a visit to the Senate or House gallery indeed suggests that the country's future is in jeopardy. Floor attendance is usually small. Members will casually stroll in and out. Speakers will use language that sounds formal or stilted. Other members will read newspapers without listening to nearby orators. They will intersperse discussions on one subject with multitudinous irrelevancies. Long periods of time will be filled up by quorum calls and roll calls.

But casual gallery visits provide little basis for finding out what is happening. Floor action is irregular. It fluctuates between deadly dullness and high drama, routine ratification of committee action and momentous decisions. Moreover, it is often of an extremely refined character. Like an East Indian dance, in which the flick of an eyebrow has profound meaning, a harmless-looking minor motion may have tremendous implications. A dreary speech on an irrelevant subject or a bit of frivolous horseplay may provide a smoke screen for behind-the-scenes maneuvering and campaigning. A dramatic clash between opposing members may be nothing but a meaningless performance of stereotyped routines.

THE TALKING

When King John of England, a few years before the Magna Carta, summoned knights of the shire to the first meeting of "the King's Council in Parliament," the reluctant knights knew full well that what he wanted to do was talk over new taxes before he levied them. The French language was known well enough for all of them to be familiar with the words *parler* and *parlement*. And ever since, talking has been properly regarded as an essential part of the parliamentary process.

It is a customary practice among journalists to lampoon the talking on the floor of Congress as useless babbling. Even among serious students of society there are always some who carry on in the vituperative tradition of Thomas Carlyle, who once referred to the members of the House of Commons as "six hundred talking asses." At the other extreme, the glorification of congressional debate as the ideal method of informing the nation and clarifying issues has been a customary theme among political scientists. Idealists find that congressional debate rarely meets their standards and promptly leap to the conclusion that most of it, therefore, is dross. Neither the skeptic nor the idealist provides a sound approach for realistically describing the talk recorded in the *Congressional Record*. An intimate examination of its purposes and its organization reveals a variety and complexity that can be understood only by using many additional scales of measurement.

Its Purposes [1]

During the early nineteenth-century debates on the Missouri Compromise, a Representative from Buncombe County, North Carolina, was pleading for a chance to talk, despite the fact that other members were impatiently calling for a vote. He explained that he wanted merely to "make a speech for Buncombe." His frank admission of purpose gave American speech two new words: "buncombe" and its shortened form "bunk."

In a very real sense, most floor speeches on pending legislation are buncombe. Their purpose is to build a record for the ultimate consumption of specific audiences whose support or approval is valued. The principle is the same whether a Senator from Nevada is aiming at a news story to enhance his reputation among the folks back home or is seeking the approbation of a

[1] The analysis in this section has much in common with the approach taken on the subject of public debate in Thurman Arnold, "The Folklore of Capitalism" (New York: New York University Press, 1937). The key points in Arnold's analysis are as follows: "Public debate is necessarily only a method of giving unity and morale to organizations. It is ceremonial and designed to create enthusiasm, to increase faith, and quiet doubt. It can have nothing to do with the actual practical analysis of facts. . . . The notion that legislation becomes more expert because of prolonged public discussions of proposed measures is an illusion which follows the notion that public debate is addressed to a thinking man through whose decisions organizations have group free-will. All prolonged public discussions of any measure can do is to reconcile conflicts and get people used to the general idea which the measure represents. . . . Public argument never convinces the other side, any more than in a war the enemy can ever be convinced. Its effectiveness consists in binding together the side on which the arguments are used. . . ." Pp. 379–381.

business leader in Chicago who is a past or potential campaign contributor. It is the same when a member of Congress, either from soaring ambition or a natural interest in personal prestige, plays for a nationwide audience. In no case, however, does the motive of building a personal record necessarily imply either a lack of sincerity on the part of the speaker or an absence of meaningful content in the speech. In fact, the most effective buncombe is both sincere and informative.

Does floor talk play a role in legislative campaigns? Certainly it is not the decisive weapon it seems to those who equate oratorical ability with influence. Speech making alone, no matter how eloquent, cannot by itself organize group support, supplant other forms of propaganda, or apply significant pressure. By the time a bill comes to the floor, the things that Congressmen say generally reflect a well-developed line-up of forces, and the opposing lines are generally drawn tightly enough to resist major changes that may be attempted through speech making alone. One of the ablest orators who ever strode the floor of the Senate was Claude Pepper of Florida. Yet despite his spellbinding, his speeches on behalf of advanced social legislation never brought him into a position of genuine leadership in the Senate. Senator Arthur Vandenberg, however, became an outstanding shaper of foreign policy during the period immediately following World War II. A sterling speaker, his oratory was no whit superior to Pepper's. The difference between the two lay in the relative weakness of the organized forces behind Pepper and the relative strength of those behind Vandenberg.

Nevertheless, it would be a mistake to accept too readily the sweeping oversimplification of Senator Carter Glass: "In the twenty-eight years that I have been a member of one or the other branches of Congress, I have never known a speech to change a vote." [2] There are three distinct purposes (other than that of preventing a vote, a subject discussed separately in the previous chapter) that speech making may serve in a legislative campaign.

The first is to provide a medium of communication between those who are lined up on the same side of a question. The signals passing between leaders and followers are by no means always given behind the scenes. Floor statements are often the quickest and most effective methods of passing the word around among other members of Congress, strengthening the cohesiveness of a group, or fanning the enthusiasm of supporters.

The second purpose is to win additional votes. On most important bills there are usually a number of members who are not able to make up their minds how to vote until the last minute. When the floor amendments raise puzzling new questions and cut members adrift from past commitments, this number may be quite large. Under such circumstances, a well-oriented speech

[2] Quoted in George H. Haynes, "The Senate of the United States" (Boston: Houghton Mifflin, 1938), Vol. I, p. 382.

or series of speeches can often directly influence fence sitters to jump in one direction or another. The most effective speech sets forth an appealing and defensible line of argument, one that can be taken over by a listener and adapted to his own uses. When backed up by a possible exchange of favors among Congressmen and by vigorous campaigning by noncongressional forces, speech making can help in the process of getting members to change their votes, if not their minds also. It can provide both factual guidance and propaganda leadership for other campaigners.

By delaying the final vote, speeches can also provide time for stepping up the tempo of a broad campaign. In early 1945, for example, the Roosevelt Administration succeeded in having the House pass a bill for compulsory control of the civilian labor force. It also succeeded in lining up a majority of votes in the Senate. But before the Senate could vote on the measure, Senators Joseph O'Mahoney and Wayne Morse took the floor of the Senate and launched a vehement and lengthy attack against the measure. During the course of their speech making, labor and business organizations mounted a sharp offensive against the Administration's position. Within a week's time so many Senators had switched into the opposition camp that the Administration leaders dropped the bill like a hot potato rather than risk a resounding public defeat. A similar maneuver was attempted in 1947 when President Truman vetoed the Taft-Hartley Act. Senators Wayne Morse and Glen Taylor staged a delaying action on the motion to override the President's veto. Their motives, they explained, were to give the country a chance to understand and ponder the reasons given by the President in his veto message. While they spoke, leaders of the Administration and of organized labor tried to convince enough Senators either to vote against overriding the veto or else to abstain from voting. This time, when the speaking ended, the campaign failed. Although the speech making was every bit as eloquent as it had been on compulsory-labor service, the power that could be amassed during the speech-making process was not nearly as strong.

The third purpose of speeches in Congress is to help lay the basis for future campaigns. Some of the best floor talks are made by those who are on the losing side and have no immediate hope of winning. Speeches help keep the colors flying. For the winning side, they help in the task of keeping the campaign alive until victory is won in the other house, in the conference committee, or at the stage of Presidential signature. For either side, when a bill is due to become law, they help prepare the ground for carrying on the contest in the administrative and judicial arenas. An innocent-sounding explanation of a section or clause, totally ignored by most members of Congress when first made, may later be used as proof of "congressional intent" and become highly important in administrative or judicial decisions.

However, the contribution of floor speeches to the building of personal records and the conducting of legislative campaigns is not always needed. A strongly entrenched member need not worry much about his record. A steam-roller campaign can gain little from talk on the floor. In fact, too much talking can have the effect of raising troublesome questions and attracting too much attention from latent sources of opposition. Many of the most influential members of Congress are men of few words. This lesson was learned by Speaker Joseph Cannon during his early days in the House. His maiden speech, a long and elaborate defense of a bill to amend the postal code, stirred up the opposition of the older members of the House and of the big-city press. In discussing the speech later he said:

After that experience, I went back in speechmaking to the method forced upon me when, as a young lawyer traveling a county circuit, I had to prepare my case in the saddle and fight with the catch as catch can plan. I considered the facts I had to deal with and used them if necessary, but did not make speeches to consume time or to cumber the record. More legislation is delayed and embarrassed by too much speaking by the defenders than by the opponents.[3]

Who Talks?

Because of the contribution that floor talking can make to legislative campaigns, the selection of those who speak for a given point of view is seldom left entirely to chance. A routine task of campaign leadership is to line up speakers. This is usually done behind the scenes and well in advance.

Occasionally the solicitation is openly visible on the floor itself. When the United Nations Charter came before the Senate, for example, the isolationist opposition had dwindled to an almost negligible fraction of what it had been many years earlier when participation in the League of Nations was before the Senate. Since little defense for the Charter was needed, few Senators planned to speak on its behalf and there was a genuine danger that an impression of disinterest would be created. As a last-minute measure, the chairman of the Foreign Relations Committee, Senator Connally of Texas, was seen walking around the Senate floor with a pad of paper in one hand and a pencil in the other, buttonholing one Senator after another and beseeching them to speak on behalf of the United Nations.

With many members pressing to be heard, the selection of those who are allowed to talk cannot often be left to chance. The free play of the personal desires of individual members would lead to chaos. Thus, methods have been developed for deciding who can speak and in what order.

In the early Congresses the presiding officers recognized the members who rose first and asked for the floor. With increasing membership and business, it became more and more usual for many members to rise at the same time.

[3] L. White Busbey, "Uncle Joe Cannon" (New York: Holt, 1927), pp. 134–135.

This necessarily concentrated a considerable degree of discretion and control in the hands of the presiding officers. In the House of Representatives, with its larger membership and stricter rules on the length of floor discussion, the power of recognition became—and still is—a powerful political weapon. For decades Speakers of the House have successfully rejected appeals against their refusals to grant recognition.

In both houses the presiding officers habitually keep an informal list of those who are to be recognized. When one member has finished talking, the next speaker will often be selected from the list rather than by the alacrity with which another member jumps to his feet or the shrillness of his shout for attention. "The right of recognition," declared Speaker Randall in 1881, "is just as absolute in the Chair as the judgment of the Supreme Court of the United States is absolute as to the interpretation of the law." [4] Randall's case for absolutism rests only on the ground that the Speakers of the House have succeeded in preventing appeals from their decisions. The decisions themselves are far from being the absolute whims of a czar.

By long-established custom, reinforced by the strategic power of their positions, committee chairmen and ranking minority members have first claims to recognition in both houses. These claims are modified only when other members of the same committee are officially handling a measure. Other committee members and party leaders have similar claims that must be honored by the Speaker and Vice-President. Often, these holders of high priorities themselves present the Presiding Officer with lists of members to be recognized.

To some extent, control of the floor is delegated to individual members other than the Presiding Officer. Under many special orders of the House and unanimous consent agreements of the Senate, a given amount of time is divided equally between the two committee members handling the pro and con of a bill. These members, in turn, subcontract their time by yielding the floor to others for so many minutes at a time. When the leading proponent and the leading opponent are both members of the majority party, problems arise about providing minority members with a chance to speak. Similar problems arise when, instead of two, there are three or more major points of view on a measure. With enough initiative and drive on the part of those who want to speak, these problems are usually resolved without creating much dissatisfaction.

The process of subcontracting extends still further. Under most conditions any individual member may yield to another. "Will the Senator yield?" and "Will the gentleman yield?" are questions heard repeatedly on the floor of the Senate and House. The member who has the floor may yield or not, as he chooses. He may give the petitioner free rein to make a speech of his own or may limit him to the asking of a question. Once a question has been asked,

[4] Asher C. Hinds, "House Precedents," Vol. II (U.S. Government Printing Office), p. 1425.

the talk often flows back and forth between the two members without any repeated requests for yielding. Some of the most skillful and dramatic interchanges of verbal blows take place through this method.

Style and Content

The first thing about talk on the floor that can be observed from the gallery or by reading the record is the stylized form of address.

"Mr. President," a Senator points out, "this bill would undermine all that Americans hold dear."

"Mr. Speaker," a Representative declares, "this amendment is necessary if we are to keep faith with the taxpayer."

Neither of the Presiding Officers may have any interest in what is being said to them. For that matter, they may not even be listening. Yet everything that is said is invariably directed to the man who holds the Chair. Only rarely does a member use such profane language as "you" in referring to a colleague. Rather, it is "the Senior Senator from Ohio" or "the gentleman from Maine." This aversion to personal pronouns even extends at times to the first person. In tones of great dignity members often refer to themselves in "Senator-from" or "gentleman-from" terms.

As a matter of course one member refers to another as "the able" or "the able and distinguished." If perchance he *really* means to convey the meaning customarily attached to these words, he then goes somewhat further—such as, "the able and distinguished gentleman whose learning we all admire and whose sterling capacities for leadership are everywhere appreciated." If he has nothing but contempt and distaste for the member in question, he is apt to go further still and speak as follows: "The gentleman from Virginia has a brilliant mind and a redoubtable command of logic. His well-reasoned arguments are always persuasive, and if not persuasive, at least entertaining, but in this case . . ."

Derogatory language is forbidden by the rules. If a member of the House impugns the motives of another member, his remarks may be expunged from the record. The guilty Senator may be forced to sit down and lose the floor. When passions are boiling in a member's breast, he may attempt an indirect manner of insult. "Mr. President," an excited Senator once asked, although he knew full well what the answer would be, "I wish to know if there is any under the parliamentary rules of the Senate whereby one member may refer to another as a wilful, malicious liar?" After being called out of order, he subsequently restated his views as follows: "The charges made by the Senator from Michigan, I will say, in parliamentary language, are as much without foundation as it is possible for any charges to be." [5]

[5] *Congressional Record*, 69th Cong., Special Sess., Mar. 14, 1925, p. 226. It is interesting

Sometimes an anecdote will be employed as the method of expressing one's sentiments. Senator Connally of Texas, chairman of the Foreign Relations Committee, was on one occasion considerably irritated by a series of questions asked of him by Senator Wherry of Nebraska. He expressed his opinion of Senator Wherry by the following story:

I feel very much like an old lawyer in my section of the country once did. He had as his legal antagonist a very loud and enthusiastic lawyer, who shouted and foamed at the mouth in addressing the jury, and when it came the turn of the other lawyer to answer him, he stood up and said, "If Your Honor please, Bow- wow- wow- wow."

Whereupon Senator Wherry proceeded to express *his* opinion of Senator Connally by replying: "Bow-wow-wow-wow-wow." [6]

The elaborate formality is pomp; at times, it is also horseplay. But it does have a deeper meaning. The stylized forms of address grew up and have been maintained to serve a purpose: the lubrication of relationships among people who have at one time interests in conflict and interests in common. Flattering words that serve to mask inner animosity between two members make it easier for them to work together on future occasions when they may be on the same side of the fence. They also help avoid the use of direct physical violence between hotly embattled members. Occasionally, it is true, members have assaulted each other with fists, knives, or canes. These are great rarities, however, in contrast to legislative bodies in many other countries where outbreaks of violence are recurrent manifestations of sharp conflicts elsewhere within the body politic.

Another obvious fact about floor talk is its frequent discontinuity. Discussion of a measure to expand the armed forces may be interrupted by a speech on the potato blight in Idaho. While there are rules against irrelevancy, they often lie unenforced, particularly in the Senate. Senators will often wander from one subject to another without any concern for orderly floor discussion. Many members will often talk on the same subject, but at tangents, without directing themselves to the arguments offered by others. This is one of the reasons why the term "debate" is inapplicable to floor talk.

Particularly disconcerting to gallery observers are the frequent quorum calls which completely halt proceedings for ten to fifteen minutes in the Senate or forty-five minutes or more in the House. Supposed to check on the volume of floor attendance or to bring more members to the floor, the motive behind

---

to note that parliamentary language is not required for personal references to individuals who are not members of Congress. In fact, under the constitutional provisions that "for any speech or debate in either House, they shall not be questioned in any other Place," members are secure against any libel suits. This has led to many dramatic instances of vehement personal attacks upon the integrity and loyalty of various individuals. These attacks, however, are usually quite apart from the legitimate legislative operations of Congress.

[6] *Congressional Record* (daily edition), Sept. 7, 1949, p. 12870.

the quorum call is often to end the talking so that various members can huddle together to develop new lines of tactic or strategy.

What one hears from the gallery is not the same as what one may read in the *Congressional Record* the next day. In both houses, members are given the privilege of revising their remarks. Under the rules this is supposed to be limited to the correction of transcription errors and minor grammatical editing. Despite recurrent protests, however, members always succeed in using this privilege as a method of changing the substance of their remarks. In addition, they are given the privilege of turning manuscript copy over to the floor reporters while they are talking and having large portions of their statement, sometimes the entire statement, printed as though they had actually delivered it. This is a convenient way of getting more space in the printed record than one has time to use on the floor itself. It is also a method of making statements that other members might challenge if they heard them on the floor but cannot challenge immediately if inserted in this manner.

Still further removed from public observation is the considerable amount of advance preparation that enters into the preparation of floor statements. When members read from manuscript, as is frequently done, it is obvious that their remarks are not merely spontaneous outpourings. Even when they talk without reference to a manuscript, they may have the guidance of fully prepared notes or of a recent briefing session. Given a set of notes to build upon, some members of Congress can develop splendid orations.

A prodigious amount of ghost writing goes into the preparation of floor statements and speech outlines. This is by no means a reflection upon the personal abilities of members of Congress. It is rather the result of the tremendous complexity of the legislative matters on which members must speak and the necessity for tapping the minds of experts. Many of the most fervent harangues appealing to members to preserve Congress from outside pressure are read verbatim from manuscripts prepared by employees of executive agencies or private organizations. Any self-respecting organization eager to have a member of Congress speak on its behalf must be prepared to provide speech materials. When a member uses such materials, such use makes it his own just as when he introduces a bill drafted by others or signs a letter written by his secretary. The fact that speeches in Congress today are on the whole more informative than they were in the early days of the Republic and that they in fact represent the largest bulk of informative talk done anywhere in the nation flows to a considerable extent from the wide use of specialized writing talent.

The Control of Debate in the House

Talk, once started in a legislative assembly, tends to keep on going. It provides an opportunity for continued self-expression. The longer one member speaks, the greater the chance he will touch on questions which others seek to answer and the more his colleagues may become aware of the impressiveness of a full record as contrasted with a skimpy one. If every member were allowed to speak as long as he chooses, Congress could meet sixteen hours a day every day in the year without keeping up with its business.

The intentional prolongation of talk is a useful weapon of obstruction. It not only can postpone action but under some circumstances can prevent action. Cato and other members of the Roman Senate used this weapon in their struggles against Caesar. It has been used in countless other legislative bodies. Its early use in the United States was so frequent that the colorful word filibuster, which originally referred to a small swift vessel and then to a lawless piratical adventure, was taken over to describe it.

Early in its history, members of the House were faced with the problems of aimless prolongation as well as intentional obstruction. Its membership was considerably larger than that of the Senate. It was the arena for the testing of outstanding political leaders and the resolution of the major political struggles. During the years preceding the War of 1812, for example, New England members who wanted to continue trade relations with England and France and opposed the emerging military conflict used prolonged debate as a major weapon. Their struggle with proponents of the nonintercourse legislation became a battle over whether or not the previous question would be used to conclude debate. In 1812 a filibuster was launched against the declaration of war itself. In order to get the floor and move the previous question, rather novel methods were used. A squad of members suddenly burst into the chamber and ran down the aisles using the spittoons as drums. Completely taken aback, the droning speaker sat down in fright. "A belligerent Democrat snatched the pause to move the 'previous question,' which was seconded, and the declaration of war against Great Britain was thus reached and carried in the House of Representatives of the Congress of the United States in June, 1812." [7]

It became evident over the following decades that the mere use of a motion to end debate—which is what the previous question amounts to—cannot sufficiently control the use of time in so large a body as the House. As a result, an extremely intricate system of additional time controls has been developed. One element in this system is the prohibition of all talk on certain questions. Cannon lists thirty *nondebatable* questions.[8] Included in this list are motions

[7] Henry A. Wise, "Seven Decades of the Union" (Philadelphia: Lippincott, 1872).
[8] Clarence Cannon, "Cannon's Procedure in the House of Representatives," pp. 143–144.

dealing with the previous question itself, adjournment, laying on the table, and certain appeals from the decision of the Chair.

Another is a set of barriers on the length of time that individual members may speak. Under what is called "general debate" a member can speak no more than an hour on any question and another hour on any amendment. The effort is usually made to avoid amendments under general debate and, in fact, general debate itself is forbidden when the House meets "in the House as in the Committee of the Whole."

A special system for amendments is provided in the "five-minute rule." Debate under this rule usually begins once general debate has ended. Any member is allowed to speak for five minutes on an amendment that he himself has offered. Then one opposition statement for five minutes is allowed. This process is frequently prolonged by the use of mock amendments, termed *pro forma* amendments. "Mr. Speaker," a member will state in all seriousness, "I move to strike out the last word." By inviolate custom, the Speaker will then allow him to speak for five minutes. Another member may then rise to say, "I move to strike out the last two words," and so on. Some of the most lively debate in the House occurs under this make-believe procedure.

Finally, various limits are set upon the total time that may be used in debate. On Calendar Wednesday and other special days there are restrictions to prevent debate from spilling over into other days. By unanimous consent, debate may be limited to a given number of hours or days. Special orders proposed by the Rules Committee usually provide a limitation on general debate or even, when the offering of amendments is prevented, upon debate under the five-minute rule as well.

The cumulative effect of all these devices is to give the majority of the House substantial protection against too much talk. The members may not be free to talk indefinitely but at least they are free from indefinitely prolonged discussion. Those who seek to stall action by the House can rarely do so by talking but rather must use other tactics—such as appeals, quorum calls, roll-call votes, amendments, and motions for adjournment or recess—to consume time.

Filibustering in the Senate

When water is dammed up at one spot, it seeks an outlet somewhere else. During the first half of the nineteenth century, at a time before the control of debate in the House had fully matured, filibustering in the Senate was but a mild foretaste of what was to come later. In the latter half of the century, even as floor talk in the House came under more rigid control, in the Senate it became a more frequent and effective legislative weapon. In the eighty-one years from 1865 to 1946, thirty-seven measures, exclusive of appropriation bills, were filibustered to death.[9] Probably four times as many appropriation bills were killed in the same fashion. Countless measures have been defeated, passed, or modified through the mere threat of a filibuster. Many Senators—such as Huey Long and Robert M. La Follette—have made or enhanced their reputations through their filibustering ability.

Who Filibusters? Southern Senators are probably better known than any others for their filibustering activities. The first major filibuster—and one of the most dramatic of all time—took place in 1890 when Southern Senators spoke for 29 days to kill the "Force bill," which would have meant Federal supervision of elections in the South. Southern political leaders have persistently used the filibuster in staving off legislation affecting the status of race relations in the South. Again and again, they have filibustered against antilynching, anti-poll tax, and fair-employment measures. As a result, the ability to talk for long periods has become a positive campaign asset in many areas of the South, and Southern Senators have been known to engage in jealous rivalries over the number of hours they are able to talk without stopping.

Yet the use of the filibuster extends far beyond racial issues and Southern Senators. One of the most notorious of all filibusters was leveled in 1917 against President Wilson's proposal for the arming of merchant ships. Filibustering was unsuccessfully attempted in 1919 against the Versailles Treaty and in 1926 against the World Court Protocol. It has been used in connection with legislation affecting banking, oil, mining, shipping, and power. It has been used by Senators from all sections of the country. It has been supported from time to time by a broad variety of groups who are unable to obtain what they want by a majority vote and feel strongly enough to resort to extreme methods. On this matter, for example, Senator George Norris, one of the greatest of liberal leaders, stood in company with many deep-dyed reactionaries. In his autobiography, Norris expressed his general aversion to filibustering but in frank language justified his leading role in the 1917 filibuster against President Wilson's proposal to arm merchant ships: "I felt the passage of the proposed bill . . . would automatically plunge the United States into the war. . . . Feeling so strongly, I felt the filibuster was justified in spite of my repugnance to the method." [10]

Methods. Talk and discussion are often classified as substitutes for physical force in the settlement of disputes. Filibustering steps over into the borderland between talk and force. In addition to the physical and emotional pain that may be inflicted on listeners, the filibuster itself is an exercise of unabashed

---

[9] George Galloway, "Limitation of Debate in the United States Senate," Public Affairs Bulletin, No. 64 (Washington, D.C.: Library of Congress, Legislative Reference Service), pp. 20–21.

[10] "Fighting Liberal, the Autobiography of George Norris" (New York: Macmillan, 1946), p. 176.

physical strength. Indispensable to success is the staying power of a Senator's larynx, knees (he can lose the floor if he sits down), and digestive system.

But stamina is not enough. There are many tricks of the trade that the filibuster wielders have developed to make their weapon stronger. The first lies in skillful timing. The most auspicious occasion for a filibuster is when preparations are being made for an early adjournment. Short of this, the best time is when the calendar is crowded with many other bills that are being strongly pressed by groups or agencies that cannot be ignored. A remarkably useful device, if consent is won for its use, is to have material read by the reading clerk. Quorum calls provide excellent rest periods. Appeals and dilatory motions provide useful diversions for talking on other subjects. Probably the most burdensome technique of all is to stick to the subject so that a pretense of meaningful debate may be kept up, public indignation prevented or appeased, and the bare possibility of being ruled out of order for irrelevancy eliminated. When a group of filibusterers are taking turns at speaking, care must be taken to see that the torch of debate is passed on when one member of the group stops. "I warned each member of the filibuster," writes Norris in relating the strategy used in the 1917 fight against the arming of merchant ships, "that he must be ready when the Senator who had the floor surrendered it, and that he must immediately address the presiding officer. If we permitted a moment to elapse, the presiding officer would put the question, and the conference report would be agreed to." [11]

Support from other Senators is also needed. Except for a brief space at the end of a session, a one-man filibuster is impossible. Even then, passive support is usually necessary. The extent of such passive support is usually much wider than is apparent from a mere reading of the *Congressional Record*. The filibustering record of the Senate has demonstrated the great power that can be wielded by a few Senators. Every Senator, therefore, has a potential stake in the preservation of this power. Many Senators who themselves have never filibustered are reluctant to take any steps that could, by way of precedent, interfere with their own use or threatened use of the weapon in the future.

Pressure and propaganda activities by private organizations also have a great bearing on the outcome of a filibuster. This was strikingly illustrated in September, 1950, when the Senate was about to conclude its work before the mid-term elections of that year. A small group of Senators initiated a prolonged series of speeches on behalf of President Truman's veto of an omnibus internal-security bill. One of them, Senator Langer of North Dakota, spoke until he collapsed and had to be carried off the floor on a stretcher. The pressure of business and veterans' organizations and other groups on behalf of the bill was so great that the majority forced continuous sessions of the Senate, wore the speakers down, and overrode the President's veto. In sharp contrast,

[11] *Ibid.*, p. 178.

approval of a conference-committee bill to limit the interstate shipment of slot machines was held up by an eleven-hour-and-ten-minute filibuster by Senator George Malone of Nevada, with only passive encouragement from other Senators. The difference lay in relative weakness of organized group opposition to gambling as contrasted with the strength of group opposition to communism and radicalism.

Restraints. There are a number of Senate rules designed to restrain floor talk. As in the House, many questions are *nondebatable*. These include motions to adjourn, to take a recess, to lay a matter on the table, and nineteen other motions.[12] When the calendar is being called and a bill is allowed to come up for consideration, no Senator may speak more than once or for more than five minutes. On all other bills no Senator is allowed to speak more than once on the same day. Although these restrictions are often suspended or winked at, they help to expedite part of the Senate's business, particularly in routine matters.

Quite frequently the Senate limits itself to a specific number of hours of talking or sets a specific hour at which talk shall cease and a vote be taken. But unlike the House, where this is accomplished by a majority vote on resolutions brought forth from the Rules Committee, the Senate does this by unanimous consent. Debate usually proceeds without limitation for a number of hours before such a step is taken. Meanwhile, the floor leaders canvass the Senators who are most directly concerned with the pending business and try to negotiate a satisfactory arrangement. Once a unanimous-consent agreement to limit debate has been made, it is almost ironclad, for it may later be amended not by a majority vote but only by another unanimous-consent action.

While any Senator's objection can in the first place prevent the limitation of debate through this method, it should also be borne in mind that any Senator who is not on the floor at the time a unanimous-consent agreement is offered may lose not only his right to filibuster but also his right to speak at all. Under Rule 12 of the Senate, a quorum call must be made before the Senate may consider a unanimous-consent request for the taking of a final vote on the passage of a bill or a joint resolution. This does not apply, however, to amendments or to Senate resolutions. Many Senators who have been off the floor for other business and who had been planning to talk on a pending matter have suddenly been surprised by being summoned to the floor to vote without getting any chance to talk.[13]

[12] A full list of the 22 questions that are nondebatable in the Senate may be found in Floyd M. Riddick, "The United States Congress: Organization and Procedure" (Washington, D.C.: National Capitol Publishers, 1949), p. 375.

[13] Sharp protests against the practice of submitting unanimous-consent agreements with prior quorum calls have been made repeatedly by Senator Morse of Oregon. See *Congressional Record,* 80th Cong., 1st Sess., Jan. 22, 1947, pp. 561–562, and May 16, 1947, pp. 5550–5552.

A minor step toward the control of filibustering was taken in the adoption in 1933 of the Twentieth Amendment to the Constitution. Prior to that time, the second session of every Congress, called the "lame-duck session," convened in December after the congressional elections and ended on the fourth day of the following year when the newly-elected President and members of Congress took office. With such a short span of life and such a firm date of adjournment, the closing days of lame-duck sessions offered an ideal filibuster season. The Twentieth Amendment, by providing for two sessions of every Congress beginning in January, removed some of the biennial congestion. As in the case of so many reform actions, however, its effect has proved less than its advocates promised. In addition, the idea of a fixed adjournment date, which provides an auspicious opportunity for filibusterers, was in part brought back by Sec. 132 of the Legislative Reorganization Act of 1946 providing for automatic adjournment, unless direct action is taken for an extension, by the last day in July.

The first frontal attack of consequence came in 1917 when President Wilson made his historic attack on the Senators who were filibustering against his proposal to arm merchant ships:

The Senate of the United States is the only legislative body in the world which cannot act when its majority is ready for action. A little group of wilful men, representing no opinion but their own, have rendered the great government of the United States helpless and contemptible. . . . The only remedy is that the rules of the Senate shall be so altered that it can act.[14]

Four days later, with only three dissenting votes, the Senate approved the famous "cloture rule." Under this rule, sixteen Senators may present to the Senate a signed petition to close debate. Two calendar days later the Presiding Officer must submit to the Senate the question: "Is it the sense of the Senate that the debate shall be brought to a close?" No debate is allowed on this question. In its original form, cloture would be invoked by a simple two-thirds majority of those present and voting. Once invoked, no Senator could speak more than one hour on anything that might arise concerning the pending measure, including any amendments and motions.[15]

The relative ineffectiveness of the cloture rule is shown by the record of its use during the thirty years from 1917 to 1946. Of nineteen cloture motions presented to the Senate during that period, fifteen failed to get a two-thirds majority. Debate was ordered closed on only four occasions, each of them during the first ten years of its operation.[16] By the end of its first thirty years, the

---

[14] *The Washington Post*, Mar. 5, 1917.
[15] For other details on the nature of the limitation, see Senate Rule XXII.
[16] Galloway, *op. cit.*, p. 22.

cloture rule broke down almost completely, suffering three devastating blows one after the other. During the 1946 filibuster on fair-employment legislation, the President pro tem of the Senate, Senator McKellar of Tennessee, ruled a cloture petition out of order on the ground that the cloture rule applied only to bills and not to *debate* on amendments to the Journal. In 1948, when the filibuster was in progress against a motion to call up the anti-poll-tax bill, the next President pro tem, Senator Vandenberg of Michigan, held that the cloture rule did not apply to motions to consider a *particular* piece of legislation.

Finally, in 1949, the cloture rule itself was substantially weakened. The Senate Rules Committee reported a resolution to make the existing rule applicable not only to a "pending measure" but also to any "measure, motion, or other matter pending before the Senate, or other unfinished business." In this form, the resolution would have strengthened the cloture rule. But when the motion was made to take up the resolution for consideration, Southern Senators, who regarded it as a prelude to civil-rights legislation, immediately started a filibuster. After long debate a cloture petition was filed to force a vote on the pending motion. An appeal was immediately made. The new Vice-President Alben Barkley reversed his predecessor by dramatically ruling that the cloture rule was applicable to the motion to consider the Rules Committee resolution. But by a narrow vote of 46 to 41, Barkley's ruling was overthrown. A large group of Senators then brought in a substitute for the Rules Committee resolution, one which the Southern Senators agreed to beforehand. Under this substitute, the cloture rule was slightly broadened so that it would cover motions to take up a measure. But a specific exception was made for motions to take up any changes in the rules (including, of course, the cloture rule itself). The voting provision was stiffened by requiring that cloture could be effected only by a vote of at least two-thirds of the Senate membership, irrespective of how many Senators were present and voting. Under this arrangement, with eighty Senators voting—and eighty is a large turnout—one-fifth plus one could prevent debate from being closed.

In a few carefully restricted areas, however, rigid cloture rules have been established. As far back as 1877, the time of the Tilden-Hayes electoral-vote controversy, a law was passed providing that, when an objection is raised to the counting of the electoral votes from any state, no Senator or Representative can speak more than five minutes and no debate can last more than two hours. Without this provision dilatory tactics could be used to prevent the election of President and Vice-President. Under recent executive reorganization acts, Presidential reorganization plans become effective unless disapproved by congressional resolution. To protect against the use of dilatory tactics to prevent congressional disapproval, the Executive Reorganization Act of 1949 provides that, on resolutions disapproving Presidential reorganization plans, debate in either house cannot exceed ten hours and that no motions to amend, recommit, or reconsider shall be in order.

THE VOTING

After a bill is called up, after the questions for decision are offered, after the talking is over—the time arrives for decision by vote.

If the vote is a roll call, electric bells ring throughout the Senate or House office buildings, and the members come streaming into the chambers from all directions. Roll call or not, the air becomes electric with tension. Even when the outcome is known by everyone, every member knows that what he does will be closely followed by his campaign opponents, his supporters, his rivals, and the many groups that seek his voting allegiance. The bills he introduces, his committee activities, the speeches he makes, the investigations he takes part in, the patronage he obtains, the motions he himself offers—all these have their place. In many cases, they represent a far bigger, though less tangible, impact on government than anything he can achieve by floor votes. But neither separately nor cumulatively can they displace his voting record as the central point of attention on the part of major contestants in the legislative struggle.

Day in and day out, moreover, the problem of how to vote on the floor is always in the back of his mind. His voting decisions comprise the overwhelming majority of all the decisions he must face as a participant in the legislative process. During any given two years his vote may be recorded 200 times and he may participate in an equal number of unrecorded votes. The questions upon which he must express himself cover the broadest conceivable gamut of public-policy issues and extend far beyond his fields of special competence. To a certain extent, the voting process is much the same as in the committees of Congress. Floor voting, however, is more public. It is a more formalized operation. It is subjected to more, and somewhat different, rules of procedure. To understand it, one must give special attention to the number of votes needed on the floor, the methods of recording floor votes and the ways in which floor-voting decisions may be made.

The Number of Votes Needed

In committee sessions, disputed questions are decided by a majority vote. On the floor, the mathematical requirements are more complex. Unanimous consent is required for the approval of bills taken from the Consent and Private Calendars in the House. In both houses, as already indicated, widespread use is also made of unanimous-consent requests to take up bills for consideration and to conduct various activities outside the rules.

Many questions call for a two-thirds vote of approval. A two-thirds vote is needed to override a Presidential veto. It is also needed to approve a resolution proposing a constitutional amendment, to expel a member, or to impeach. In the Senate are found two of the best-known requirements for a two-thirds vote. The first is in connection with treaties. One-third of the Senators voting plus one may reject a treaty, as has been done on several occasions.[17] It is important to note, however, that a treaty can be amended by a simple majority vote and that an executive agreement to accomplish the same objectives can be approved by a majority vote of both houses. The cloture rule is a second occasion calling for a two-thirds vote of the entire Senate. Aside from the provisions for counting a quorum, and for electing the President or Vice-President if a majority in the electoral college is not obtained, this is the only instance in which the full membership of either house of Congress is used as a basis for computing the number of votes.

There are also certain special instances, although less celebrated ones, in which the House of Representatives requires a two-thirds vote. Under the House rules, a two-thirds vote is needed for such action as dispensing with Calendar Wednesday or for the call of the Private Calendar, suspending the rules, or considering a report from the Rules Committee instead of waiting until the following day. In all other cases a simple majority vote is sufficient for approval of a pending question. This, of course, does not mean that a majority of either house—or anything approaching it—is needed. With a bare quorum present and voting, a motion on a bill or an amendment may be carried by one-quarter plus one of the full membership. On unrecorded votes, even a bare quorum is often not present. Moreover, in the Committee of the Whole in the House, where one hundred members constitute a quorum, major amendments can be approved when supported by only 51 votes—less than one-eighth of the total membership in the House.

Critics of the two-thirds needed for Senate approval of treaties are fond of pointing out that under this requirement a treaty may be rejected by a relatively small group of Senators, representing a small minority of the country's population. One might suppose that on questions that can be decided by a majority vote, the winning side has some relationship to a majority of the population. Yet in the Senate, by virtue of the fact that every state has two Senators regardless of population, even a full majority may represent constituencies totaling much less than a majority of the country's population.

In the House, of course, there is a closer relationship between national

[17] As of the close of the 82d Congress, a total of 15 treaties have been rejected in this fashion since the First Congress, as contrasted with 1,128 that have been approved. Another 146 received no final action, have been withdrawn, or remain pending action. See U.S. Department of State, *List of Treaties Submitted to the Senate, 1789–1934* (1935) and the later edition of this listing covering 1934 to 1944.

population and House membership. But this relationship is dissipated by the uneven distribution of those members who actually vote on any given question. Even in the House, the members who line up on the majority side in any individual test of strength may represent a minority of the population, while the minority side may represent a majority of the population.

The Recording of Votes

The question of whether or not a vote is recorded is an extremely important one in the operations of Congress and in the political fortunes of its members. A record vote means a roll call and a roll call consumes a considerable amount of time. A record vote also means that many members must publicly declare themselves on questions concerning which they had hitherto taken an equivocal position or maintained silence. Hence, on the side of avoiding a record vote can be found those concerned with expediting action and those interested in avoiding showdowns. On the side of forcing record votes are those interested in dilatory tactics and those concerned with clarifying the positions of various members.

The overwhelming weight would often be on the side of avoiding record votes if it were not for the constitutional requirement that "the Yeas and Nays of the Members of either House on any question shall, at the desire of one-fifth of those Present, be entered upon the Journal." [18] Under this provision any member may arise and, addressing the Chair, call out, "I demand the 'Yeas' and 'Nays.' "

It is interesting to note that at any typical sessions of Congress there are more roll-call votes in the Senate than in the House. During the Eightieth Congress for example, there were 162 roll-call votes in the House. The records for the Senate for the same period show 248 roll-call votes, more than 50 per cent above the House level. This disparity is largely a reflection of the fact that in the House most of the voting on amendments takes place in the Committee of the Whole and that in the Committee of the Whole the constitutional provision on the Yeas and Nays is evaded.

In both houses, there are two types of nonrecord votes: a voice vote and a division. A voice vote takes place when the Presiding Officer makes a judgment on the basis of the number of members whom he hears calling out "Yea" or "Nay." Many minor and noncontroversial measures are passed by voice vote. This includes a surprising number of conference-committee measures which, before the conference, were the center of major controversies. Under it there are often no objections voiced at all. However, if there is objection and if the vote seems to be close, any member may demand a division. The Chair will then ask those in favor of the pending question to rise and stand until

[18] Art. I, Sec. 5.

counted. The opponents will then be asked to do the same. The Chair will then announce the result of the count but no names will be recorded.

The House has still a third system of providing for a nonrecord vote, namely, the use of tellers. One-fifth of a quorum—44 in the House and 20 in the Committee of the Whole—may demand tellers. Under the teller system, the members leave their seats and gather in the well of the House. Those in favor of the pending question pass in single file up the center aisle and are counted. The opponents then walk down the aisle and are counted. This system has the advantage of providing an accurate vote and at the same time enabling members to have their individual votes go unrecorded. At the same time, it makes it possible for careful observers in the gallery to check off how individual members behave, something that cannot really be done on a voice vote or on a division. Senator Kefauver and Jack Levin tell an interesting story of a "gallery check" that was attempted when the House was voting on the famous "death-sentence" clause in the Public Utilities Holding Company Bill. The House Rules Committee had brought in a special order permitting only a teller vote on this provision. The Scripps-Howard editors, who were supporting the death-sentence clause, felt that a clear record was needed in order to deal with members of the House who, they believed, were dodging the issue.

On the Scripps-Howard staff at the time was a young reporter with an unusual memory for names and faces. While members, gathering in the well to pass by the tellers, either smiled encouragement or shook their fists at the press gallery, the reporter coolly called off 286 names to four other staffers who recorded the names and passed them to other reporters at telephones. The Scripps-Howard paper was on the streets in 40 minutes with a tally of names that subsequently proved to contain only one error.[19]

Calculations as to how members voted under one form of voting cannot be ascertained when a recount is taken under another form. As visibility regarding a legislator's conduct increases, some votes move from one side to the other or drop out completely.

The Range of Alternatives

In most cases, most members vote a clear "Yea" or "Nay." Yet these are by no means the only alternatives in registering a decision.

Delays and Switches. There are a number of variations in the manner in which a member can cast his vote. The voting process during a roll-call vote takes time. A member can refrain from answering when his name is called, keep a close tally of how the votes are lining up, and can then come in at the very end when the names of those who did not answer at first are being read

[19] Estes Kefauver and Jack Levin, "A Twentieth Century Congress" (New York: Duell, Sloan & Pearce, 1947), p. 63.

again. In this way he can either jump on the band wagon or else vote on the losing side to satisfy one set of interests and prepare himself to tell the interests on the other side that his voting for them would not have helped.

An illustration of this tactic is found in the history of Administration tactics in combating the silver bloc during the early days of the New Deal. Everest records the story as follows:

> Equally effective was the counsel that Administration advisers gave those Senators who sought help in escaping a dilemma. Some of them were not sure bimetallism was sound, but had the "folks back home" to think about, and disliked being recorded in opposition to any inflationary proposal. They were told to absent themselves until the end of the roll call, when they should vote against the bill if there were already thirty votes for free silver, and when they might safely vote for it if there were under thirty votes. Hence the Administration knew that at least ten Senators failed to help the amendment, although they favored inflation of some sort. Since that many additional votes would have secured passage, there was no longer doubt about the inflationary majority in the Senate.[20]

A member can also vote one way when his name is first called and then, after keeping a close tally on the votes and before the outcome is announced, obtain permission to switch to the other side. It was this tactic which succeeded in obtaining a majority vote in the House for the Kerr gas bill in 1950. The first call of the House showed that the bill was about to be defeated by a slim margin.

> However, just before the outcome could be announced, Congressmen from the Southwestern states swarmed into the well of the House, demanding to know how they had been recorded on the roll-call. This was a delaying tactic. . . . Speaker Rayburn, who was presiding, informed Halleck that two more votes were needed if the bill was to be saved from defeat. In other words, it was up to Halleck to produce two switch votes on the Republican side. How well he succeeded may be attested by the fact that not two but three Republicans, who had voted against the Kerr Bill, soon appeared in the House well and informed Rayburn that they would like to change their vote and be recorded for the Bill.[21]

Absence. A member may readily dodge an issue by being absent. Although no statistics on this subject could be compiled, it is obvious to any observer that many members conveniently absent themselves from Washington at the time when difficult questions are up for decision and when it appears safer to take no position at all. Absenteeism may be purposeful even when a member goes to the trouble of stating how he would have voted if present. Through this in-between method of recording one's views a member can express himself

---

[20] Allan Seymour Everest, "Morgenthau, the New Deal and Silver" (New York: King's Crown Press, Columbia University Press, 1950), pp. 24–25.

[21] Drew Pearson, "Washington Merry-Go-Round," *Washington Post*, Apr. 5, 1950.

for a certain proposition and at the same time go along with those groups who are anxious that he not vote at all rather than that he vote in favor of it.

Many absences, of course, are occasioned by sickness or by important business. On hotly contested measures intense pressure is put on absentees to return. There are many recorded instances of members making dramatic, last-minute airplane flights back to Washington, tottering onto the floor against doctors' orders, or even being brought in a wheel chair or on a stretcher. In 1940, for example, the fate of legislation extending the terms of service for national-guard and reserve officers and Selective-Service trainees hinged on the number of absent Senators who could be brought back to vote. A Senate-approved bill was passed in the House after many changes, by a vote of 203 to 202. It became evident that if the Senate sent the bill to conference, the measure might be killed. The sponsors of the measure then decided to seek Senate acceptance of the House version without alteration.

. . . This agreed upon, the Senate leaders made sure of an impressive majority, larger than legally necessary, by sending airplanes to bring back as many friendly Senators as possible, and, in the case of several who could not return to Washington, arranging to "pair" them with opposition Senators whose votes would thus be neutralized. On the day of the vote two friendly Senators (Harry S. Truman and Sherman Minton) held the floor and thus deferred the vote until given the assurance that a maximum majority was on hand.[22]

Not Voting. A member may refrain from voting even when present. On this matter one finds a fascinating tangle of conflicting rules and precedents. The rules, for example, indicate that every member must vote unless excused. Attempts during the nineteenth century to compel members to vote proved futile. As early as 1832 John Quincy Adams successfully defied the attempts of other House members to force him to vote. In 1893 when Senator du Bois refused to vote, the Senate, by a large vote, refused to excuse him. The Senator, nevertheless, maintained his silence. In sharp contrast to the written rules in both houses, therefore, there has grown up the unwritten rule of "the right to silence."

Another long-standing parliamentary tradition is that, to use the words of Sec. XVII of Jefferson's Manual, "where the private interests of a member are concerned in a bill or question, he is to withdraw." This principle also is clearly set forth in Rule VIII, Sec. 1, of the House, which provides that every member shall vote on each question put "unless he has a direct personal or pecuniary interest in the event of such question." On rare occasions in both houses members have asked to be excused because of their private financial interests in a pending measure. On equally rare occasions the Speaker of the House has

[22] Mark S. Watson, "Chief of Staff: Prewar Plans and Preparations" (Washington, D.C.: Government Printing Office, 1950), pp. 230–231.

ruled that because of his private interests a member should not be allowed to vote. But with these few exceptions both the ancient principle and the House rule are consistently violated. Members who have the most direct personal or private interests in pending legislation generally have no hesitation in taking part in the voting.

Pairs. A member may enter into a "pair" with another member. The avowed purpose of a pair is to redress the imbalance that is created when one member unavoidably is forced to be absent while a record vote is taken. One member, who would have voted on the other side, presumably enters into a gentleman's agreement with the absentee that neither of them will vote but that the one will be recorded as "paired for" and that the other as "paired against." Some members have "indefinite" or "general" pairs with each other. Under such cases when one party to this two-man agreement is absent, the other is regarded as obliged not to vote unless "released." In other cases, specific pairs are arranged for individual votes or for stated periods of time in both the House and the Senate. Secretaries and clerks are kept busy with the handling of these arrangements.

In actual practice, however, pairs often turn out to be a specialized method of avoiding a vote. "Members pair off, and do as they please," wrote Senator Benton, more than a century ago, ". . . either remain in the city and refuse to attend to any duty, or go off together to neighboring cities; or separate; one staying and one going; and the one that remains sometimes standing up in his place, and telling the Speaker of the House that he had paired off; and so refusing to vote." [23] Benton might have added that the pairing system often becomes a bitter and decisive part of the legislative struggle on the floor of both houses. In preparing for the showdown on any measure where the margin of victory or defeat may be narrow, each side endeavors to convince certain members who are leaning against them that they should "pair against" instead of voting "Nay." On hotly contested party issues, leaders of one party may "declare all pairs off" if they calculate that the other party has a greater number of members who are sick or unavoidably out of town. During the Eightieth Congress's conflict over tax reduction, Senator Lucas of Illinois, who was then minority Whip, charged that the Republican leaders violated "all rules of courtesy and decency" by refusing pairs. When the Democrats were in power, he said, they always arranged for pairs with the Republicans. "If enough Republicans to change the situation were too ill to be present," retorted Republican leader Taft, "we could not get a pair from the Democrats for love or money. They have never given us pairs under those circumstances, and they never will." [24]

[23] Thomas H. Benton, "Thirty Years' View" (New York: Appleton-Century-Crofts, 1856), Vol. II, p. 178.
[24] *The New York Times,* May 27, 1947.

In view of all these variations it is impossible to analyze the recorded votes in the House or in the Senate by merely listing the Yeas and Nays. It is also essential to list announcements by members on how they would have voted if present and to record their pairs. Information on members who neither voted nor paired can be obtained by polling them on how they would have voted if present, as is done regularly by *Congressional Quarterly*. In this manner, *Congressional Quarterly* provides as full an analysis of the voting in Congress as one can get without identifying individual action on voice, division, and teller votes and without going into the motives and pressures that lie behind the members' decisions.

The Pain of Decision

"When the committee hearings and the important books and articles on a proposal are heard; when the mail has been appraised; when the briefs and arguments have been weighed; when the wise men, living and dead, have been consulted, the Senator still faces the task of moving his own lips to say 'Yes' or 'No.' " [25]

The task is often painful. A simple Yes or No, no matter how qualified it may be in explanatory speech making, rarely covers an important issue. There is almost always something to be said on both sides of a question. No one can better appreciate this than a member of Congress subjected to pressure and propaganda from people who are doing the saying on both sides and will probably continue to speak their piece when he next comes up for reelection.

Most members of Congress will probably join with former Representative Voorhis in his rueful comment on the pain of voting: "It would be a great deal easier if only one could answer 'Fifty-five per cent aye,' or 'seventy per cent no,' or 'I vote aye but with the reservation that I do not like Section 3 of the bill,' or 'I vote no, but God have mercy on my soul if I am wrong, as I may very well be.' " [26]

A researcher into the mysteries of congressional voting, after trying to find out how members of the House made up their minds on the 1939 legislation to repeal the embargo provisions of the Neutrality Act, concluded his analysis with the following observation:

Considering the bewildering complexity of the questions involved, it is with no sense of superiority but profound sympathy and understanding that we close by recording the fact that one member made his decision when a newspaper reporter wrote out a 15-word statement that looked so well in print and offered such a peace-

[25] Paul H. Douglas, "A Senator's Voice: A Searching of the Soul," *The New York Times Magazine*, Apr. 30, 1950.

[26] Jerry Voorhis, "Confessions of a Congressman" (Garden City, N.Y.: Doubleday, 1947), p. 233.

ful refuge from the agonies of indecision that the Congressman adopted and maintained it as his own.[27]

There are few formulas on how to vote that are anything more than witticisms or rough-and-ready guides on unimportant matters. In the first category belongs the overgeneral motto "When in doubt, do right" and the cynical slogan "Vote for every appropriation and against every tax." Of the rough-and-ready type is the formula of voting against a bill when in doubt, presumably on the theory that there is too much legislation anyway. "I have tried to follow a rule," stated Senator Elmer Thomas of Oklahoma during one vote, "that when I do not know a thing about a matter before the Senate, I vote 'Nay.' . . ."[28] On the occasion which prompted this remark the Senator went on to explain that he had just learned more about the subject at hand and that he intended, if a motion to reconsider be offered, to change his vote.

Of somewhat more value as a guide is the action of leaders and blocs with which a member may be associated. On some questions party leadership is important.[29] On others, the example of ranking committee members and individuals whose judgment has been confirmed by experience may be extremely influential. The band-wagon theory also has a role; there is a certain safety in numbers.

On the other hand, these factors tell only part of the story. Leaders who are devoutly followed on some subjects may be respectfully ignored on others. There is also a band-wagon theory in reverse. When there is an overwhelming majority lined up on behalf of a bill, a member may then vote more confidently against it and be able to tell its supporters in all honesty that his negative vote could not have made a particle of difference.

At times it has been suggested that many Congressmen decide how to vote by watching the public-opinion polls. This has been regarded with horror by those who see in the polling operations themselves instruments of irresponsible political power and who believe that members of Congress should guide public opinion rather than follow it. Actually, however, the polls probably play only a very incidental role. This is borne out by the various attempts that have been made to find out from Congressmen themselves exactly what value they place upon public-opinion polls.[30] Public-opinion polls cannot enter very de-

---

[27] L. E. Gleeck, "96 Congressmen Make Up Their Minds," *Public Opinion Quarterly,* Vol. 4, March, 1940, p. 24.

[28] *Congressional Record,* 73d Cong., 2d Sess., May 22, 1934, p. 9244.

[29] For a detailed study of the role of party policy and other pressures on the roll-call votes of Representatives during four different sessions, see Julius Turner, "Party and Constituency: Pressures on Congress" (Baltimore: Johns Hopkins Press, 1951).

[30] Gleeck, *op. cit.,* pp. 8–9; George F. Lewis, Jr., "Congressmen Look at the Polls," *Public Opinion Quarterly,* Vol. 4, June, 1940, pp. 229–231; J. K. Javits, "How I Used a Poll in

cisively into the thinking of a member of Congress because they do not reflect and appraise the nature and intensities of opinions held by those people in their constituencies whose views, by virtue of the power they represent, count the most.

A member's voting decision is his own reconciliation of all the pressures and propaganda to which he has been subjected. How this reconciliation is made depends upon the legislation situation itself and each member's personal attributes. In situations where the weight of the pressures is all on one side, the decisions naturally tend to move in the same direction. Where members are dealing with more equally balanced conflicts and where their personal advancement depends upon bringing together the support of conflicting groups, the decisions are less predictable. It is on these occasions that a member must truly search his soul. Whether he is an introspective ponderer or whether he relies on a last-minute intuition, it is *his* decision and not that of someone who pulls the strings or gives the signals.

His hour of decision is not seen by the outer world. It can come in the dead of night, in periods of reverie in one's office, after the day's work is done, over the breakfast or dinner table with one's family, or in a taxicab ride to or from the Capitol. It is at these times, I believe, that the final decisions which affect the life of the nation are generally made. The tension of the roll-call merely expresses the decisions which ninety-six widely differing men, with different background, have already made in the quiet of their individual consciences.[31]

Campaigning for Congress," *ibid.*, Vol. 11, Summer, 1947, pp. 222–226. According to Martin Kriesberg, "What Congressmen and Administrators Think of the Polls" (*ibid.*, Vol. 9, Fall, 1945, pp. 333–337), members of Congress place less weight upon public-opinion polls than do administrators. The reason for this may well be that members of Congress are much more interested in the opinions of group leaders in *specific* constituencies, while administrators are more interested in *general* public opinion which might at some time shape itself into forces affecting their agency activities.

[31] Douglas, *op. cit.*

Chapter 19

THE PRESIDENT VOTES: APPROVAL OR VETO

ONCE A BILL has been successfully steered through the tortuous shoals of Congress, it undergoes a rather quick and routinized processing so that a certified product can be presented to the President.[1] It is checked by clerks of the two houses,[2] printed on parchment as an "enrolled bill," and signed by the Speaker of the House and the President of the Senate. A clerk of the house in which it was first passed takes it to the White House where it becomes another piece of paper to burden the most heavily burdened public official in the world.

At previous stages in the legislative history of the measure—from the decision on whether or not to have a bill to the floor action in Congress—the President may have been an active participant or may have had nothing whatsoever to do with it. Now he sits in the center of the picture. If there is no longer any dispute over the measure or if for any combination of reasons his action is a foregone conclusion, there will be little attempt to influence him. If there is still a conflict and any doubt about his decision, the White House now becomes the focal point of the legislative struggle and, for the time being at least, the key concern of other participants in the legislative struggle is the decision making of one man.[3]

[1] For background material on the President's role in the approval and disapproval of legislative measures see Edward S. Corwin, "The President: Office and Powers" (New York: New York University Press, 1948), Chap. 7; Richard E. Neustadt, "Presidential Clearance of Legislation" (unpublished doctoral dissertation, Harvard University, June, 1950); and Norman J. Small, "Some Presidential Interpretations of the Presidency" (Baltimore: Johns Hopkins Press, 1932); Edward C. Mason, "The Veto Power" (Boston: Ginn, 1891); and Charles J. Zinn, "The Veto Power of the President" (Washington, D.C.: Government Printing Office, 1951).

[2] If any errors are found, they may be corrected at this stage by a concurrent resolution. If errors are discovered after a bill has been delivered to the White House, it can be recalled and corrected by concurrent resolution. Once a bill has become law, a joint resolution or another act is required.

[3] There have been many learned debates as to whether the President has any part of the "legislative power." Strict constructionists pointed to the first section of the Constitution: "All legislative powers herein granted shall be vested in a Congress of the United States. . . ." Others have retorted that this section is modified by the provisions of Art. I, Sec. 7, which give the President his veto power. (See Howard L. McBain, "The Living Constitution."

On questions of how Presidents really function and how pressures operate upon them, there is probably greater public interest and less public knowledge than on any other phase of government. The interest arises from the glamour and high prestige of the Presidency. The lack of public knowledge results in part from the protective shroud of secrecy that necessarily surrounds a President during his period of tenure and from the unfortunate dearth of frank and detailed memoirs by former Presidents or reliable associates. Yet to understand this final stage in the legislative struggle, we must deal as directly as possible with the scope of Presidential choice, the process of Presidential choice, and the decisions themselves.

THE SCOPE OF PRESIDENTIAL CHOICE

The scope of Presidential choice is not unlimited. Constitutional requirements, informal usages, and strategic maneuvering combine to set the limits within which he operates. These limits may be discussed in terms of the measures sent to the White House, the necessity of a President's accepting or rejecting a bill *in toto,* and the time allowed for him to make a decision.

Measures Sent to the White House

When the veto function of the President was being considered in the Constitutional Convention, James Madison observed that "if the negative of the President was confined to *bills,* it would be evaded by acts under the form and name of resolution, votes, etc." [4] Shortly thereafter, Edmund Randolph proposed that the possibility of evasion be dealt with by an additional clause. This resulted in the provision in Article I, Section 7, that "every order, resolution, or vote, to which the concurrence of the Senate and the House of Representatives may be necessary (except on a question of adjournment), shall be presented to the President of the United States" and shall be handled in the same manner as a bill.

The great bulk of measures jointly acted upon by Congress has always been presented to the President. But there are two interesting exceptions to, or rather evasions of, this provision: constitutional amendments and concurrent resolutions.

Exactly two years after Madison, Randolph, and their colleagues had signed the proposed Constitution, the First Congress of the United States presented

(New York: Workers Education Bureau Press, 1927), p. 170. To this writer, at least, such debates about "legislative power" seem to be arid. There is no doubt that the Constitution provides for Presidential participation at many points in the legislative process and not merely at the signature or veto stage.

[4] Arthur Taylor Prescott, "Drafting the Federal Constitution" (Baton Rouge, La.: Louisiana State University Press, 1941), p. 612.

to the state legislatures the first ten amendments which comprised the famous Bill of Rights. These were acted upon by Congress in the form of joint resolutions "to which the concurrence of the Senate and the House of Representatives" was necessary. Yet they were not presented to President Washington. In 1798, almost a decade later, the Eleventh Amendment to the Constitution was ratified by the states after having been handled in the same manner. It was promptly challenged in the Supreme Court on the ground that "the amendment was never submitted to the President for his approbation." One of the arguments used in defense of the procedure that had been used was "that as two-thirds of both Houses are required to originate the proposition, it would be nugatory to return it with the President's negative, to be re-passed by the same number." This argument was countered by the assertion that "the reasons assigned for his disapprobation might be so satisfactory so as to reduce the majority below the Constitutional proportion." It was further stated: "The Concurrence of the President is required in matters of infinitely less importance and whether on subjects of ordinary legislation or of Constitutional amendments, the expression is the same, and equally applies to the act of both Houses of Congress."

On the day after the argument had been made, the judges unanimously threw the case out of Court on the ground that the amendment had been constitutionally adopted. Justice Chase added the following comment: "The negative of the President applies only to the ordinary cases of legislation. He has nothing to do with the proposition, or adoption of amendments to the Constitution." [5]

A more tortured misreading of the clear constitutional provision could scarcely be imagined. And yet if the judges had adhered to the obvious meaning of the Madison-Randolph proviso, they would by that very act of faithfulness to the Constitution have beclouded the validity of the entire Bill of Rights and shaken the foundation of the great compromises which brought the Republic into being. Since then, by the same type of reasoning, *Hollingsworth et al. v. Virginia* has been accepted as constitutional dogma and the whole structure of subsequent formal amendments to the Constitution and of Court decisions concerning these amendments has been based upon the procedural misreading contained in the 1798 decision. Only twice has a President signed a proposed constitutional amendment; Buchanan in 1861, and Lincoln in 1865. The joint resolution signed by Lincoln became the Thirteenth Amendment. It is interesting to note that in this case, after Lincoln notified Congress that he had signed the proposed amendment, the Senate immediately adopted a resolution declaring that Lincoln's signature to the amendment was unnecessary.

Concurrent resolutions represent a more frequent type of evasion of the

---

[5] *Hollingsworth et al. v. Virginia*, 3 Dall. 378.

requirement for *both* congressional and Presidential participation in lawmaking. During World War II, it was found that congressional opposition to various emergency measures could be circumvented to some degree by providing for the authorization of these measures either by Presidential proclamation or by joint action of the two houses alone through a concurrent resolution. It is deemed highly probable that if it had not been for a provision of this type, the Selective Service Act of 1941 would have been defeated. Similar provisions were also used in the Lend-Lease Act, the First War Powers Act, and the Emergency Price Control Act. In a somewhat different form, provisions have been made for the use of concurrent resolution as a "legislative veto" over action initiated by the President. The outstanding examples are the executive reorganization acts of 1932, 1937, and 1945, under which a reorganization plan promulgated by the President would become effective unless a concurrent resolution disapproving it were enacted within a specified period of time. In 1949 President Truman tried to obtain the same provision in a new Executive Reorganization Act. His intention was frustrated, however, by members of the Senate who were interested in protecting the Army Corps of Engineers and other agencies from being reorganized. They, therefore, succeeded in writing into the 1949 Reorganization Act a provision that a Presidential reorganization plan could be jettisoned by a simple resolution adopted in one house alone.

Questions have been raised as to how the Supreme Court might conceivably rule on provisions of this type. While they certainly seem to violate the prescription of the Constitution, they do so to a lesser degree than already sanctioned in the handling of constitutional amendments. It is easy to develop an impressive theory rationalizing this procedure on the ground that the President is not deprived of the privilege given him by the Constitution just so long as the original act providing for one or another form of legislative veto is handled strictly in accordance with constitutional procedures. Above all, so much legislation and so many decisions affecting the lives of people and agencies have already been handled on this basis that any adverse decision by the Court would be highly improbable.

All or None

Unlike the governors of most states, who have an "item-veto" power,[6] the President cannot approve part of a bill and reject another part. But there are

[6] As of 1947, 38 states provided for an Executive veto of items in appropriations bills. The item veto in the states "has been somewhat less drastically involved than formerly, but it retains a measure of popularity as a 'gun behind the door.'" Frank W. Prescott, "The Executive Veto in American States," *Western Political Quarterly*, Vol. 3, No. 1, March, 1950, p. 112.

three ways in which this procedural fact can be circumvented and in which the President may obtain a wider area of choice.

First, the President may veto an entire bill on the ground that it contains a few items that he disapproves. In the case of appropriation and revenue measures, where delayed action might impede the normal operations of government, such a course is obviously not an easy one. Nevertheless, it has been taken. Both President Hayes and President Wilson have vetoed major appropriation bills because of their objections to particular items. In many instances, the threat of a Presidential veto has served the purpose.

Second, the effect of a selective veto can be obtained by administrative policies. When a rider providing for a loan to Spain was added to the Omnibus Appropriation Act for fiscal year 1951, President Truman disposed of it by simply announcing that he would not proceed with the loan. This type of procedure is regarded as more legitimate on matters of expenditure than in any other fields. In fact, the Federal-budget system makes direct provision for the Presidential impounding of agency funds. The mores of government life, however, are different with respect to regulatory provisions. If President Truman had expressed the same disregard for any provision of the Taft-Hartley Act as he expressed toward the Spanish-loan provision in the 1951 Appropriation Act, the result would have been a public uproar of incalculable proportions. With respect to the labor measure, President Truman solemnly and sincerely assured the country that he would do his best to have every provision fairly administered in accordance with congressional intentions.

Third, a bill passed by Congress could give the President the authority to accept some provisions and disapprove others. This was proposed by President Franklin D. Roosevelt both in 1938 and in 1942. In both instances, however, Congress refused to include the provision of this type. In 1950, President Roosevelt's son, Representative Franklin D. Roosevelt, Jr., of New York, proposed a general budgetary reform measure which would have provided, among other things, a joint rule of Congress to the effect that every appropriation bill must include the specific authorization for the President to disapprove individual items. Under this proposal the President's disapproval could then be overridden by a simple majority vote in Congress, rather than a two-thirds vote. This method, it must be recognized, is more aspiration than possibility, for assent to a procedure of this type would require that powerful groups in Congress voluntarily yield an important part of their power, thereby placing the President in a more strategic position in the legislative struggle.

The Time Allowed

Instead of being given unlimited time in which to make his choice, the President must act in ten days. A number of questions naturally arise as to how the ten days are to be counted. The first is whether or not Sundays are included. This was answered in the Constitution itself, which specifically provided that Sundays are excepted. A second question is, when do the counted days begin. The Constitution gives the President ten days "after it shall have been presented to him." This has been uniformly interpreted as meaning that the first of the ten days is the day after a bill has been presented to the President.

A third question is how much time may elapse between the day that a bill is passed by Congress and the day that it is presented to the President. Here there is no rule, merely a presumption that the officers of Congress should act without undue delay. But since a bill must be printed and then signed by the Speaker of the House and the Presiding Officer of the Senate, a certain amount of delay will take place. This amount can be stretched into a considerable period whenever there is sufficient motive for doing so. When President Wilson went to Europe to negotiate the Versailles Treaty, he reached an agreement with the Speaker of the House and the Vice-President under which they would not sign the bills passed by Congress until he returned to the country, thus permitting him to exercise his power of choice.[7]

A fourth question is whether the President still has ten days if, before the ten days have elapsed, Congress either recesses or adjourns. Some decades ago there were confusion and controversy on this matter. In recent years the Supreme Court has settled this question by ruling that the President may effectively sign a bill at any time within ten calendar days of its presentation to him, whether or not Congress has adjourned or recessed.[8]

A final question is whether an incoming President can handle a bill that had been presented to his predecessor. The Court, viewing the office in terms of the person rather than the institution, has ruled that he cannot.[9]

THE PROCESS OF PRESIDENTIAL CHOICE

In a sense, Presidential handling of bills passed by Congress is one of the more institutionalized aspects of the Presidency. "Agency clearance," for example, has become a complicated procedural operation which is winning increasing attention of students of government. Yet it is also as important to understand how Presidential freedom of choice may be measured by previous commitments and how specialized forms of campaigning may be used at this stage by the various participants in the legislative struggle.

[7] *New York Tribune*, Nov. 21, 1918.
[8] *Edwards v. United States*, 286 U.S. 482 (1932).
[9] *Ibid.*, p. 493.

Previous Commitments

In a very major sense, the process of Presidential decision gets under way long before a bill arrives at the White House. The President is committed to specific legislative enactments by the affirmative programs he presents to Congress, by proposals presented by agency officials and congressional leaders, and even by campaign platforms. Affirmative statements of this type provide a series of commitments that serve as a general framework for Presidential decision after a bill has been passed by Congress.

But commitments of this type generally leave ample leeway. A Presidential recommendation for a national-science-research foundation does not commit a President to signing *any* bill that may set up a national-science-research foundation. Thus, a bill dealing with this subject was vetoed during the Eightieth Congress because of administrative arrangements which the President and his advisers on the subject regarded as unsatisfactory. It was not until the following Congress that the bill was passed in satisfactory form.

Even when the President himself may favor or strongly indorse a measure in a very specific form, there is no telling whether or not the bill might be redrafted completely and still meet with his approval. This happened in the case of the Employment Act of 1946: President Truman strongly indorsed the version which was passed by the Senate and criticized the version adopted by the House of Representatives. Yet he willingly signed an entirely different measure which was brought forth by the Conference Committee. In many cases, moreover, legislation moves through Congress without having been initiated by the Administration, and in these cases the proposals of the Administration are no guide for Presidential action.

"Will the President sign this bill or not?" This question is repeatedly asked during the course of the congressional consideration of a measure. It is asked of the President himself, of his closest advisers, of various executive officials, and of members in Congress who presumably are in a position to know. Sometimes the answers are uninformative or misleading. At the end of the Seventy-ninth Congress in 1946 one of the most important measures was the bill to extend price control. Before action on the Conference Committee compromise, reporters at one of his press conferences asked if he would veto the bill. Tris Coffin has recorded his answer: "The President replied primly, 'I never discuss legislation.' " [10] In this particular case Democratic leaders in Congress thought that the President would sign the bill. Yet the President took the position that the bill was unworkable and vetoed it. Coffin has recorded their reaction: "When Kenneth McKellar, the elderly presiding officer of the Senate, heard of the veto he swore a streak of emphatic and colorful profanity. Alben

[10] Tristram Coffin, "Missouri Compromise" (Boston: Little, Brown, 1947), p. 170.

Barkley was stunned. . . . In the House, Representative Spence sat bolt upright, folding and unfolding his fingers. . . ." [11]

In situations like this, it is obvious that if the President does not commit himself ahead of time, both supporters and opponents of a bill may claim that they have been nourished on false hopes or kept in the dark. Nevertheless, Presidents often refuse to predict whether they will sign or veto. "How can I say what I will do about a bill until it comes to my desk and I can see what is really in it?" is the question with which a President often retorts to those who seek a commitment on a pending measure. It is a wise question, for, in many cases, not until the last stage in the congressional phase of the legislative process is completed can anyone know what the words in a bill are really to be; and not for some days later, after careful study by experts, can one find out what these words mean or may be construed to mean.

Presidential action, however, follows no set formula. In some cases the President will state precisely what he will or will not sign. Wilson, for example, was often exceedingly specific, pointing out precisely what provisions must be included in a bill if he were to approve it. Despite his statement that he would never discuss pending legislation, Truman has done likewise. During the Eightieth Congress controversy over tax reduction, he announced that he would veto any bill that would reduce taxes. This immediately met with a blast from Senator Millikin of Colorado, who charged that "It is improper for Mr. Truman to tell Congress in advance what it can or can't do." [12] Millikin later told the Senate that this was the first time in history that a President had vetoed a bill before it had been sent to him.

Rather than make the final commitments in the name of his office ahead of time, the President will often have advance commitments made by members of his staff, heads of agencies, and members of Congress. This has the advantage of providing specific leadership during the course of the congressional process and at the same time of leaving the President free to modify his course, if necessary. A Presidential spokesman can be disowned without the President himself losing face. This was done by President Truman in the case of the basing-point legislation in 1950. Although a high White House official had stated in writing that the bill was in accordance with the President's program, and the Department of Justice had also indicated that it had Administration approval, the President felt that these statements provided no ironclad commitment and he vetoed the bill.

In some cases Administration officials speak for the President without authorization to do so. Members of Congress will do the same. Without authority to commit the President to the acceptance or rejection of a measure, they will

[11] *Ibid.*, p. 172.
[12] *The New York Times*, July 11, 1947.

hint broadly that they know which course the President will follow. There have been cases when both opponents and proponents of a controversial measure have been spreading the word around that the President would act as they wanted him to. When this happens, it is not unusual for the disappointed side to charge that the President has "broken faith."

Agency Clearance

The uninitiated probably think that a President looks at a bill that has been sent to him by Congress and makes up his mind himself after giving the matter whatever amount of thought is necessary. But it is not so simple. From the time of George Washington to the present, Presidents have requested the views of agency heads on whether they should approve or disapprove enrolled bills, particularly in really doubtful cases. It has also been customary for Presidents to ask that agencies recommending a veto submit to him a draft veto message, and that agencies recommending signature submit a draft of any statement that they might feel should be made at the time of signing the measure.

In recent years the task of obtaining agency views on enrolled bills has been handled by the Bureau of the Budget. Without even waiting for an enrolled bill formally to arrive at the White House, the Legislative Reference Division of the Bureau of the Budget obtains printed copies and sends them by special messenger to the various executive agency officials whose views it believes are needed. "In order that your views may be presented with the reports of the Bureau to the President," a typical communication will read, "please send to the Bureau, by messenger, within two working days, in accordance with Budget Circular No. A-9, your comments on this bill."

This enrolled-bill function of the Bureau has been the foundation for its other functions in clearing agency proposals for legislation and reports to Congress. Objections have often been voiced—loudly by some members of Congress, less loudly by some executive officials—to the Budget Bureau's work in policing agency proposals for legislation and agency reports to Congress on pending bills. Its work on enrolled bills, however, has generally escaped such attack; for it is hard to say that the President should not get staff help in discharging his clearly appointed constitutional function with respect to bills that have been passed by Congress.

In the entire process of handling legislation for the President, the Budget Bureau operates under the fiction that its job is merely to ascertain whether or not a bill conforms with the President's program. This fiction suggests that the Bureau is not wandering beyond the realm of budget making, and above all, is not engaged in advising the President on the formation of new policies.

In actual practice, however, the clearance process involves the Bureau of the Budget very heavily in the formation of the President's program—and particularly so at the stage of action upon enrolled bills. The Bureau summarizes the formal recommendations of the other agencies and invariably presents its own recommendations as well. On the great majority of measures this puts the Bureau in a position of tremendous influence. As Neustadt says, "On most of them—particularly the private bills—the Budget file was the 'works.' "[13] On many bills the Budget Bureau file goes right back to the birth of a measure and includes vital documents that were prepared at a time when the proposed measure was first being discussed. On still more measures the file covers the preparation of agency reports to congressional committees. Often it goes back to prior years of congressional handling of similar or identical measures. The information alone in files such as these is a tremendous source of influence.

Many Budget Bureau officials have also developed an uncanny skill to sense what the President wants them to recommend or to rationalize.

On private bills and similar sorts of issues, one of Bailey's greatest strengths was his ability to anticipate the President's instincts about the equities involved, and provide him with the ammunition to justify them. If, as a matter of budget policy or personal conviction, he could not see his way to recommending what he suspected the President would want, he could and did try to provide a loophole in his own proposals, which the President could use if he so desired. Bailey's record of acceptance for his recommendations was no accident. This was an art, which the Bureau lost somehow in 1948, when its recommendations were reversed on eleven private and five public bills—a low point for the decade. In 1949 the record clearly improved, with the proportion of reversals reduced by half. The artistry has apparently been recovered.[14]

Yet a President cannot always depend entirely upon agency advice or the assistance of the Bureau of the Budget in completely pulling agency views together. Agency recommendations tend to become specialized. Agency officials tend to see the problem in terms of their agency and their personal records rather than from the standpoint of the President. Budget Bureau officials often seem inclined to use technical criteria which are politically unreliable.

The President's problem is an old one. Consider the example of Andrew Jackson and the bill to recharter the Bank of the United States. When the bill was passed by Congress every member of the President's Cabinet, with the exception of the Attorney General, was opposed to Jackson's plan for a strong veto message. Many agency officials suggested an easy veto that would open the door for approval of a modified bill a little later. Sensing the lack of support among the Cabinet, Jackson declined offers of assistance in the preparation of a message and put his "Kitchen Cabinet" to work on a veto message.[15]

[13] Neustadt, *op. cit.*, p. 80.

[14] *Ibid.*, p. 214.

[15] For a useful capsule discussion of this veto message see Marquis James, "The Life of Andrew Jackson" (New York: Merrill, 1938), pp. 600–602.

Most Presidents have solved this problem by entrusting vital clearance matters to their closest associates and personal assistants. This practice has paralleled the growth of the Budget Bureau's clearance function. Franklin Roosevelt and Harry Truman designated specific staff assistants in the White House—although their titles often varied—to maintain general surveillance of the Budget Bureau's clearance work, particularly on the more important enrolled bills. In cases of extraordinary political delicacy a White House aide may take over from the Budget Bureau completely and himself handle the entire job of obtaining agency recommendations, analyzing them, and presenting pertinent views to the President.

Campaigning

One difference between legislative campaigns at earlier stages in the legislative struggle and those after a bill has been sent to the White House is that in the latter instance the campaigning centers more than ever upon the thoughts and actions of one man. At this stage any road that can lead to that one man is usually deemed a worth-while road to travel. Members of Congress and leaders of private organizations will often call upon a President personally or write him beseeching letters in an effort to obtain the decision they prefer. Heavy contributors to the President's election chest may be brought into the picture. In fact, any person who knows a person who knows a person who knows how to get the President's ear fits into this phase of the legislative battle. All the established techniques involved in the organization of group support, the application of pressure, and the dissemination of propaganda may again be called into use.

Behind the formalities of the clearance process, executive-agency officials often enter vigorously into the conflict, if there is one. A Cabinet member who feels strongly about a measure whose future is in doubt will dutifully send his views in writing to the Budget Bureau and, in addition, circumvent the Bureau in an appeal directly to the President. An interesting example is found in the successful efforts of Oscar Chapman, Secretary of the Interior, to have President Truman veto a bill that would have stripped the Federal Power Commission of authority over consumers' gas rates.

Truman had promised Speaker Sam Rayburn to sign the bill, and the promise was still very much in force three days after the measure reached the White House. Then Chapman swung into action. He drafted a lengthy memorandum showing the President in detail that he need not feel bound to his promise to the oil and gas crowd, for they had deceived him in declaring the bill would not raise consumers' gas rates "one red cent." Next, he persuaded Commerce Secretary Charlie Sawyer to write a memorandum counseling a veto because many industries would be adversely affected by an increase in gas rates. Then he collared pussyfooting Mon Wallgren, the odd man on the five-man Power Commission, who had made a hurry-up trip to California in order to escape the backstairs pulling and hauling on the bill. Chapman convinced Wallgren that he should vote for a veto. Wallgren capitulated, and thus the Federal Power Commission went officially on record against the bill by a 3 to 2 count. It was this lightning-fast triple play, with Chapman the man in the middle, that shut out the Kerr Bill.[16]

Budget Bureau officials and members of the White House staff also engage, with the circumspection that their position necessitates, in activities to influence the President's decisions. At times they will go so far as to actively promote agency reports that will embody their own views and thus help to "put the heat on" in support of those views.

The clearance process, of course, is much more than a façade behind which legislative campaigning takes place. It is often a direct vehicle for such campaigning, and, in some instances, the most important one. The essence of a campaign for or against an enrolled bill lies in presenting in specific form both the detailed reasoning behind a desired course of action and an explanation of such a course in terms suitable for public consideration. In many cases the ultimate decision of the President will depend in large part upon whether or not a case has been adequately organized, both in terms of the reasoning that might appeal to the President and in terms of the public position which is most tenable for him to take if he signs or vetoes the measure.

An interesting case of effective campaigning occurred in 1950 when an enrolled bill to amend the Hatch Act reached the White House. The basic provisions of this bill would have allowed the Civil Service Commission to punish violators of the Hatch Act prohibitions against political activities by Federal employees with something less than permanent exclusion from the Federal service. There was little opposition to these provisions. However, the bill contained a provision that had been prepared by old-line Democrats in Virginia for the purpose of helping their state organization to win back control of the governing body in Arlington County, which had been captured by a coalition of liberal Democrats, Republicans, and independent voters who wanted a "new deal." Although the measure had been passed by an overwhelming majority in both houses of Congress, the liberal Democrats in Arlington County led an active campaign for veto. Through many channels they succeeded in conveying the idea to the President that signature of the measure would serve to favor the anti-Truman Democrats in Virginia. At the same time they developed an extremely detailed and effective critique of the measure itself, with particular emphasis upon the points other than the anti-Truman implications of the

[16] Robert S. Allen and William V. Shannon, "The Truman Merry-Go-Round" (New York: Vanguard, 1950), pp. 97–98. Chapman's efforts, it should be noted, did not take place in a vacuum. A group of Senators and Representatives and a number of private organizations played a vital role in the entire campaign.

measure. This point of view was presented to officials in the Department of Justice. As a result, the Justice Department, through the medium of the clearance process, suggested a Presidential veto, preparing as well a draft veto message. The only other point of view urged through the clearance process was that of the Civil Service Commission, which recommended approval of the measure—mainly on the ground that the provisions giving it more discretion for punishing violators of the Hatch Act were sorely needed. The opponents of the bill countered with the argument that the bill as a whole should be vetoed and that immediate steps should be taken to obtain congressional action on the particular provisions so strongly desired by the Civil Service Commission.

If the opponents of the bill had had nothing to rely upon except the conflict between President Truman and the anti-Truman Democrats in Virginia, the bill would probably have been signed. However, the campaign included the following factors: personal appeals to the President, an expertly prepared Justice Department report together with a draft veto message, and a plan for action to obtain through a separate bill the provisions desired by the Civil Service Commission. The sum of these factors succeeded and the bill was vetoed. A few days later a new bill was introduced to handle the provisions desired by the Civil Service Commission, and with strong Administration support it soon became law.

During the course of a campaign for the signature or veto of a measure the President is not necessarily a mere passive recipient of the pressure and propaganda generated by others. The President is invariably fully aware of the swirling conflict around him, knowing that he could not stop or evade it if he wanted to. He will often plunge into the conflict himself. At times his intervention may merely be to encourage one or another group whose potentialities for broader support he wants to put to the test. At other times, he may intervene more directly by laying the basis for the course of action upon which he knows he will embark.

THE PRESIDENT'S APPROVAL

By the time a bill has surmounted all the obstacles it has faced from the time of introduction to approval by both houses of Congress, the odds are in its favor. In the great majority of cases, the President's decision is to interpose no additional obstacles. The choices that arise at the stage when assent is given are relatively minor, particularly in comparison with the problems involved in disapproval, as outlined in the subsequent section of this chapter. Attention need be paid only to the methods of assent and the use of statements concerning the legislation that has just come into being.

Signing and "Celebrating"

The regular method of assent is very simple. "If he approve," the Constitution provides, "he shall sign it." Most enrolled bills are handled in this manner. But what if he does not approve and yet does not want to disapprove? What if he merely wants to register reluctant acquiescence? It is testimony to the realism of the Founding Fathers that they provided a formula which facilitates the handling of such situations. If the President does not sign an enrolled bill and if at the end of ten days Congress is still in session, "the Same shall be a Law, in like Manner as if he had signed it. . . ."

Over the course of the decades other methods have arisen for registering the degree of Presidential approval or reluctance. One method is to develop the act of signature into a full-fledged ceremony. This can be done only in a limited number of instances, since the ceremonial functions of the President are so extensive entirely apart from the legislative process, and since there are so many bills that he must sign every year. It is usually done when the President wants to attract attention to a legislative victory or when members of Congress, executive officials, or important private organizations can convince him of the desirability of a "victory celebration." On such occasions the President's staff assistants must carefully prepare the list of invited guests, for accidental omissions can seriously wound the feelings of people who regard their own presence as essential. The newspapers will then carry pictures of Very Important People crowding around the President as he signs his name, and the most important of the Very Important People may even carry back with them, for mounting on a wall like a hunting trophy, one of the President's pens.

Statements of Clarification or Qualification

Another method of registering views at the time of signature is the issuance of a public statement. This can be done through the simple medium of a press release whether or not there is an accompanying formal ceremony.

A Presidential statement is an ideal way to underscore the importance of a bill. Sometimes this is needed to provide a bridge between the interest that was aroused during the course of the legislative struggle and the interest that will be needed in the future to support a successful administration of a measure. In the case of the Employment Act of 1946, the President's statement upon signature was designed to deal with those critics in both the "pro" and "anti" camps who had charged that the Act was meaningless because it was so different from the original Full Employment Bill. "In enacting this legislation, the Congress and the President were responding to an overwhelming demand of the people. The legislation gives expression to a deep-seated desire for a conscious and positive attack upon the ever-recurring problems of mass unemployment and ruinous depression." [17] Statements of this type can also serve to orient Administration policy. In the statement referred to above, President Truman described the Employment Act as "a commitment by the Government to the people—a commitment to take any and all of the measures necessary for a healthy economy, one that provides opportunity for those able, willing, and seeking to work." [18] This description of the Employment Act constituted a vigorous interpretation, one based upon a deliberate underplaying of the various limitations contained in the policy section of the Act upon the Government's "commitment to the people."

At times Presidents have used the occasion of signatures to voice much more controversial interpretations. When the Hobbs Anti-Racketeering Act was passed in 1946, President Truman sent a message to Congress which put a special interpretation of his own upon certain ambiguous provisions. Many of the sponsors of the Act had intended it to modify in various respects such labor legislation as the Railway Labor Act, the Norris–La Guardia Act, the Wagner Act, and the Clayton Act. However, the matter was left open for interpretation. The President's message to Congress dealt with this problem as follows:

> The Attorney General advises me that the present Bill does not in any way interfere with the rights of unions in carrying out their legitimate objectives. He bases this conclusion upon the language of the Bill, as a separate measure, and upon the legislative history.
>
> He makes reference, in particular, to Title II of the Bill. That title provides that nothing in the Bill should be construed to repeal, modify, or affect the Railway Labor Act, the Norris–La Guardia Act, the Wagner Act, and specified sections of the Clayton Act, *i.e.*, the great legislative safeguards which the Congress has established for the protection of labor in the exercise of its fundamental rights. The Attorney General also advises that the legislative history shows that the Bill is not intended to deprive labor of any of its recognized rights, including the right to strike and to picket, and to take other legitimate and peaceful concerted action.
>
> On this understanding, I am approving the Bill.[19]

This statement aroused a storm of protest from those who favored a more antilabor interpretation of the measure. A well-known columnist attacked the President's message on the ground that it would now become an essential part of the Legislative Record and enter into judicial consideration of the meaning of the Act.[20] A learned political scientist, however, has maintained that for a court to consider the President's views on matters of this type "would be to

[17] White House press release, Feb. 20, 1946.
[18] *Ibid.*
[19] White House press release, July 3, 1946.
[20] Arthur Krock, *The New York Times*, May 16, 1947.

attribute to the latter (the President) the power to foist upon the houses intentions which they never entertained." [21]

Presidential statements have also been used to voice direct objections to individual provisions, and by so doing help prepare the ground for future legislation that more adequately conforms with the President's standards. In 1910 President Taft signed an important rivers and harbors bill, and, at the same time, submitted to Congress a memorandum in which he pointed out what appeared to him to be some serious defects in the measure. The memorandum concluded with the following statement:

I do not think, therefore, the defects of the Bill which I have pointed out will justify the postponement of all this important work. But I do think that in preparation of the proposed future yearly bills Congress should adopt the reforms above suggested and that a failure to do so would justify withholding Executive approval, even though a river and harbor bill failed.[22]

One of the most controversial of such statements was presented to Congress in 1947 by President Truman, at the time when he signed a measure to extend the time of rent control. Truman's opposition in Congress had presented him with a difficult dilemma. On the one hand, the bill that was passed by Congress provided for inadequate rent control, and if he had simply accepted it, he might have clearly been held to blame by thousands of tenants when they saw sharp increases in their rent bills. On the other hand, if he vetoed the bill, there was no question but that the result would probably have been no rent control whatsoever. This also would have been a bitter pill for the Truman Administration. The President solved this problem by sending to Congress a message which started as follows:

I have today signed H.R. 3203, the Housing and Rent Act of 1947, despite the fact that its rent-control provisions are plainly inadequate and its housing provisions actually repeal parts of the Veterans' Emergency Housing Act which have been most helpful in meeting the housing needs of veterans.

Had I withheld my signature, national rent control would die tonight. It is clear that, insofar as the Congress is concerned, it is this bill or no rent control at all. I have chosen the lesser of two evils.

He then proceeded to outline the defects of the bill, called upon governors to help remedy these defects by doing what they could to protect tenants, and proposed a number of other measures to help relieve the housing shortage.

A number of anti-Administration Senators immediately objected. "As I understand the Constitution," said one of them, "the President has no right to file with Congress any memorandum or any document when he signs an act.

[21] Corwin, op. cit., p. 344.
[22] Message to Congress, June 25, 1910.

The only time when the President is permitted to file a memorandum or document is when he returns a bill unsigned, vetoed, and gives his reasons for doing so." [23] A number of Truman supporters in the Senate countered this argument by showing that President Taft had provided a precedent for the Truman message and that the President's constitutional authority to present his recommendations to Congress provided an ample basis for the action President Truman had taken.

Whether or not the President issues a statement upon signing a bill, other participants in the legislative struggle are apt to do so themselves. One group might issue a victory statement, another a blast. One group might use the occasion to point out the things they like and dislike about the measure, while another might call attention to the administrative problems that now must be faced.

THE PRESIDENT'S DISAPPROVAL

From the purely statistical viewpoint, Presidential disapproval of bills that have been approved by Congress is of little consequence. The total number of vetoes from 1789 to 1950 was only 2,002.[24] During the twenty-eight-year period from the beginning of the Sixty-seventh Congress in 1921 to the end of the Eightieth Congress in 1948, the total number of vetoed bills was only about two-tenths of one per cent of all bills enacted into law.

From the broader viewpoint of social combat, however, Presidential disapproval is of major consequence. It provides the most dramatic example of direct conflict between President and Congress. The role of the President in the legislative process cannot possibly be understood without an examination of the role of the Presidential veto, of postveto battles, and of the pocket veto.

The Role of the Veto

The development of the Presidential veto revives a striking example of the sharp contrast that often exists between the intention of the Founding Fathers and the subsequent realities. The men who drafted the Constitution saw in the President's veto power a means of protecting people of property and rank whose interests would presumably be better represented by the Presidency, and against assaults by the masses who might be expected to achieve more effective representation in Congress. With the extension of popular suffrage, however,

[23] Statement by Senator Ferguson of Michigan, *Congressional Record* (daily edition), July 1, 1947, p. 8160.

[24] Secretary of the Senate, "Veto Messages" (Washington, D.C.: Government Printing Office, 1948), p. iv. Daily Digest of *Congressional Record* for data on vetoes during 81st and 82d Cong., 1st Sess.

the "masses" more often than not were given more effective representation through the Presidency than through Congress.

By 1841 a Cabinet officer who served under both Jackson and Van Buren was able to say, with considerable justification, that "the veto power is the people's tribunative prerogative speaking again through their Executive." [25] Seventy or eighty years later there were enough examples of this "tribunative prerogative" to provide a real degree of justification for the following statement by Theodore Roosevelt: "as things now are, the Executive is or ought to be peculiarly representative of the people as a whole. As often as not the action of the Executive offers the only means by which the people can get the legislation they demand and ought to have." [26]

The original intent seems to have been that the President's veto would be used very rarely. Looking backward, our earliest government officials could well recall the attack in the Declaration of Independence against King George's abuse of the veto power: "He has refused his assent to laws most wholesome and necessary for the public good." They regarded the President's veto as something to be used very gingerly—mainly as a shield "against invasion by the legislature: (1) of the right of the Executive, (2) of the judiciary, (3) of the states and the state legislatures." [27] Another justification for the use of the veto was protection of the Constitution itself against legislation which in the President's judgment violated the Constitution. Rarely was the President expected to veto a bill merely because he felt that his judgment was better than that of Congress.

George Washington expressed his views this way: "From motives of respect to the Legislature (and I might add from my interpretation of the Constitution) I give my signature to many bills with which my judgment is at variance." [28] Faithful to this interpretation, Washington vetoed only two bills. In the case of one of these, a major consideration was to demonstrate that the veto power was something that would be used rather than be allowed to die. John Adams vetoed no bills whatsoever. Jefferson vetoed no bills. In fact, Jefferson's opinion was that, "unless the President's mind, on a view with everything which is urged for and against the bill, is tolerably clear that it is unauthorized by the Constitution—if the pro and con hangs so even as to balance his judgment—a just respect for the wisdom of the Legislature would naturally decide the balance in favor of their opinion." [29] With Madison and Monroe, the veto came more into use—with constitutional grounds being

[25] Levy Woodbury, quoted in Henry Jones Ford, "The Rise and Growth of American Politics" (New York: Macmillan, 1898), p. 187.

[26] Theodore Roosevelt, "Autobiography" (New York: Scribner, 1925), p. 282.

[27] Thomas Jefferson, "Writings," Ford ed., Vol. V, p. 289.

[28] Jared Sparks, "Writings of George Washington" (Auburn, N.Y.: Derby and Miller 1851), Vol. X, p. 371.

[29] Quoted in Mason, *op. cit.*, p. 186.

offered for justification on six out of seven measures vetoed by these two Presidents. John Quincy Adams vetoed nothing.

With Jackson the whole picture underwent a great change. Jackson's twelve vetoes, as one commentator has put it, "descended upon Congress like the blows of an iron flail." [30] From then on the veto was established as a major weapon in the social struggle in America. Although for a little while Presidents continued to garb their judgment in constitutional phrases, it soon became perfectly clear that vetoes were to be based upon the President's judgment of what was right and what was wrong.

This trend was accelerated by the increasing use of the veto after the Civil War as a major protection against private bills which represented personal raids upon the Treasury. Of Grant's 43 vetoes, 29 dealt with private bills. With Cleveland, the proportion rose even higher.

Cleveland vetoed more bills and resolutions from Congress than all the Presidents together before him. Most of his 250 messages of disapproval concerned private pension bills, which had become almost a racket. The President began reading these acts, sending for the case record, getting the facts and vetoing scores of them; John McBlair had died from epilepsy, not a war wound; Congress should not double Andrew Hill's present pension; another had been lamed as a boy, not in service; here was a man who had never served a day in the Army getting a gratuity . . . and so forth and so on. In June, 1886, he exposed the machinations behind this mass of pension bills giving public money to individuals who had no claim. There had been no real Congressional sanction for these gratuities. In fact, most of these bills had never come before a majority of either House, but passed at nominal sessions held for the express purpose of their consideration, and attended by a small minority of the members. The rebuke had some effect.[31]

A special analysis of Presidential vetoes has shown that since Cleveland's time private bills have remained a major target for Presidential vetoes, and, in fact, represent about 40 per cent of all bills that have been vetoed since 1789.[32]

In the field of public bills two types of measures were long considered safe from possibility of a Presidential veto: appropriation bills and tax bills. In more recent years these taboos have also been broken. Presidents Hayes, Wilson, and Truman have all vetoed appropriation bills. It remained for President Franklin Roosevelt to break the ice on tax measures. In February, 1944, he vetoed the proposed Revenue Act of 1944 on the ground that it would

[30] Ford, op. cit., p. 180.

[31] George Fort Milton, "The Use of Presidential Power" (Boston: Little, Brown, 1944), pp. 157–158.

[32] Clarence A. Berdahl, "The President's Veto of Private Bills," Political Science Quarterly, Vol. 52, 1937, p. 508.

provide tax relief "not for the needy, but for the greedy." [33] Following this example, Truman vetoed tax measures on three occasions during the Republican-controlled Eightieth Congress.

Franklin Roosevelt was merely summarizing the practice of a good number of Presidents who preceded him when he told his department heads to review enrolled bills very carefully. He said: "If the decision is close, I want to veto." [34] It had already become clear that a veto can be used as a positive, not merely a negative, weapon in the legislative process. It had also become clear that veto can have a value far beyond its effect upon a particular phase of the legislative struggle. Frequent use of the veto power can place members of Congress on notice that they must reckon with the President. It can build his personal strength with executive officials and private organizations. It can provide a dramatic method for appeals to the country at large, particularly when Presidential action is overridden in Congress. There is little doubt that President Truman's repeated vetoes of major measures during the Republican-controlled Eightieth Congress were a major factor in his successful campaign for election in 1948.[35]

But it must not be thought that the "strength" of a President can be gauged directly by the number of his vetoes. Jefferson, with no vetoes in his record, was one of the strongest of all Presidents. His success in getting Congress to do what he wanted it to do in the first place made veto action unnecessary. In the case of Johnson, who vetoed more bills than any President preceding him, the vetoes were in large part a by-product of Presidential weakness.

Postveto Battles

The term "veto" is misleading. In Latin it means "I forbid." The term is used accurately when applied to the ability of a permanent member of the Security Council of the United Nations, under the United Nations Charter, to prevent many types of action by a single dissenting vote. It is inaccurate when applied to the President's disapproval of a measure, for the simple reason that the President cannot forbid; his disapproval can be overruled by a two-thirds majority in both houses.

[33] White House press release, Feb. 22, 1944. It was on this historic occasion that Senator Barkley dramatically resigned as Majority Leader, only to be reelected unanimously by the Senate Democrats.

[34] Proceedings, Twenty-eighth meeting, National Emergency Council, Dec. 17, 1935, p. 17.

[35] Hindsight, of course, is very helpful in such a judgment. Before the election took place, David Lawrence, an able commentator relying on foresight alone, wrote that "from a Republican point of view, nothing could bring a better break politically than a series of Truman vetoes, for it would furnish the spark for the 1948 campaign which would then be designed to get rid of an obstructionist President." *Washington Star*, Mar. 25, 1947.

Under clear provisions in the Constitution every veto message is supposed to be put to the test. A disapproved bill is to be returned to the house in which it originated, "who shall enter the Objections at large on their Journal, and proceed to reconsider it." This constitutional requirement, conceived at a time when it was thought that veto messages would be few and far between, is followed only when there is a genuine attempt to override the President's veto, rather than as a matter of routine. If no fight is contemplated, the house to which the vetoed bill has been returned simply ignores the constitutional prescription. Rather, the vetoed bill is usually referred to a committee or laid on the table. When one house has overruled the President and sent the vetoed bill to the other house, the second house may likewise avoid reconsideration. In either house, moreover, reconsideration may be delayed for a considerable period of time. It has occasionally happened that a bill has been vetoed by the President at one session of a Congress and reconsidered at the next session of the same Congress.

Some of the most dramatic debates in Congress have taken place upon consideration of a resolution to override the President's veto. Here the conflicting forces reach the last possible stage in the legislative struggle over an individual bill and mobilize their forces of pressure and propaganda to the fullest.

On a postveto bill, voting participation is also unusually high. Under the Constitution the votes must be recorded. The largest of all record votes are usually found on these occasions.

The conflict at this particular point is on an all-or-none basis. Amendments may not be offered. Although a substitute bill may be brought in by a committee, it must be handled as a new bill. And those who attempt to handle it must reckon with the fact that it does not enjoy the same privileged status as a vetoed bill.

Vetoed bills, however, are not customarily passed over the President's disapproval. Of the 1,106 direct vetoes, as distinguished from the 804 pocket vetoes, from the first Administration of George Washington to the end of the Eightieth Congress, only 65 vetoes were overridden—far less than 1 per cent of the total. Even during the Eightieth Congress, when President Truman was opposed by a strongly hostile majority in Congress, only 6 of his 42 vetoes were overridden—or about 14 per cent.[36] It should be kept in mind, however, that a large number of vetoed bills are either private-relief bills or other minor bills on which it is almost impossible to muster a two-thirds vote. On bills of a truly major character, it has been harder for a President to make his veto stick.

Whether a veto is sustained or overridden, however, the legislative struggle usually continues on new measures. When a veto is sustained, the effort is often made to reenact it—sometimes in changed form. During the Eightieth Congress

[36] Secretary of the Senate, "Veto Messages," p. 4.

the Republican leaders who campaigned for tax reduction saw their measures successfully vetoed on two occasions before they were finally able to pass a somewhat liberalized tax-reduction bill over President Truman's third veto. If a veto is overridden, on the other hand, the likelihood is that the effort will once again be made to achieve the objectives sought by the President. After President Truman's unsuccessful veto of the Taft-Hartley Labor-Management Relations Act, for example, both the Truman Administration and organized labor tried repeatedly to effectuate repeal of the Act.

Pocket Veto

There is one form of veto—the pocket veto—in which the President has complete power. Under the Constitution if the President does not sign a bill within ten days, and if the Congress in the meantime adjourns, the bill "shall not be a law." The records of the Secretary of the Senate show that for every three regular vetoes, there have been, on the average, two pocket vetoes.[37]

The end of a session rush, therefore, puts the President in an unusually strong position. Any bill which is sent to the White House during the ten days before adjournment can be prevented from becoming a law by Presidential decision with no possibility of overriding action by Congress. This fact has a direct bearing on the character of legislative campaigning. Because of it, delay in timing strengthens the position of those groups who feel that the President is on their side. Early action puts the President and those allied with him in a somewhat weaker position. At the same time, a postponement of adjournment can be used as a device to prevent the exercise of the President's pocket-veto power. This was one of the major strategies used by President Andrew Johnson's opponents during the embattled reconstruction days.

Until 1934 it was customary for a President to make no public explanations when he used the pocket veto. By virtue of the very circumstances, naturally, no pocket-veto message can be sent to Congress. But in 1934, this tradition was reversed by Franklin D. Roosevelt. In that year he pocket-vetoed 53 bills and gave to the press a full statement of the reasons for not signing each. He explained his course as follows: "The President has desired to take a more affirmative position than this, feeling that in the case of most legislation reasons for definite disapproval should be given." [38] This example was followed studiously by President Truman and will probably be followed by subsequent Presidents.

[37] *Loc. cit.*
[38] *Congressional Record,* 73d Cong., 2d Sess., p. 12456.

Chapter 20

SIGNIFICANT AVENUES OF PROCEDURAL REFORM

THE PREVIOUS prescriptive chapters in Part I dealt with proposals extending considerably beyond the legislative process. This was unavoidable because the activities of private organizations, political parties, and the Federal government cannot be discussed very meaningfully by putting on blinkers and focusing entirely on their direct implications for the legislative process.[1] Similarly, many of the most important proposals for change in the legislative process are those relating to the broader aspects of government and society rather than to the minutiae of legislative operations. In this chapter the perspective is narrowed. Attention is given exclusively to proposals for change in specific legislative activities of members of Congress and executive officials and ideas for the improvement of congressional methods and in certain specialized aspects of lawmaking.

NEW RULES FOR CONGRESSIONAL AND EXECUTIVE CONTESTANTS

Members of Congress

Proposals dealing specifically with members of Congress can be divided into four groups: those dealing with committee activities, with floor action, with staff assistance, and with better methods—particularly television and radio—of obtaining more public attention for legislative activities in Congress.

[1] For background material on proposals relating specifically to the legislative process see: Committee on Congress of The American Political Science Association, "The Reorganization of Congress" (Washington, D.C.: Public Affairs Press, 1945); George Galloway, "Congress at the Crossroads" (New York: Crowell, 1946); "The Operation of the Legislative Reorganization Act of 1946," *American Political Science Review*, Vol. 45, No. 1, March, 1951; Joseph P. Harris, "The Reorganization of Congress," *Public Administration Review*, Vol. 6, Summer, 1946; Joint Committee on the Organization of Congress: Hearings, 79th Cong., 1st Sess., 1945, and Report, 79th Cong., 2d Sess., Mar. 4, 1946; Estes Kefauver and Jack Levin, "A Twentieth Century Congress" (New York: Duell, Sloan & Pearce, 1947); Senate Committee on Expenditures in the Executive Departments, Hearings on Evaluation of Legislative Reorganization Act of 1946, 80th Cong., 2d Sess., 1948; Hearings on Organization and Operation of Congress, 82d Cong., 1st Sess., 1951.

Congressional Committees. STRUCTURE. It is occasionally proposed that steps be taken to go beyond the consolidation of congressional committees which was effected under the Legislative Reorganization Act of 1946. "Sound administration," argue Kefauver and Levin, "requires that the same number of committees exist in both bodies and that they have identical functions. This would facilitate combined hearings and provide for an easy exchange of ideas and information." [2]

While it is doubtful that joint hearings and joint-staff collaboration can be effected through a change in the rules, the most concrete form of joint action is the creation of joint committees. Proposals for joint committees in various fields have abounded and are likely to receive growing support. It is a fairly safe prediction that during future years the same kind of pressures which in the past have resulted in the creation of more committees within each house will express themselves instead through the creation of new joint committees.

A major point of concentration has been to prevent the creation of special committees. The substantive argument against special committees is as follows: "The jurisdiction of the standing committees has been so comprehensively defined in the reformed rules as to govern every conceivable subject of legislation. Thus, to set up a special committee is to trespass upon the assigned jurisdiction of some standing committee." [3] The standing committees have investigatory powers, investigatory staffs, and the power to report legislation developed as a result of their investigations. Special committees, on the other hand, result in the multiplication of committee assignments, duplicating requests for testimony by executive officials, and sporadic, rather than continuous, hearings.

One of the few defenses of special committees as such has been made by Dewey Anderson. He argued that the special-committee approach allows for more flexibility and dynamism. He pointed out that the author of a resolution to set up a special committee usually becomes the chairman of the committee if and when it is established, and that this is an important means of side-stepping the seniority rule. He also argued that special committees "have shown repeatedly that they can command outstanding men for special important tasks. . . . Numerous younger men on the make professionally come to special committees to serve for the relatively brief period of their existence who would be less likely to be attracted by the more routine tasks of a standing committee." [4] It should also be recognized that a special committee is often the only way to give expression to interests and new ideas not sympathetically represented by the leadership of standing committees.

A number of proposals have also been made for dealing with jurisdictional problems. The "grand-reform" approach is to redistribute jurisdiction among

[2] Kefauver and Levin, *op. cit.,* p. 117.

[3] Hearings on Evaluation of Legislative Reorganization Act of 1946, pp. 147–148.

[4] Hearings before the Joint Committee on the Organization of Congress, pp. 626–640.

the various standing committees. It is impossible, however, to devise a classi-fication method that will not yield a considerable amount of overlapping. Once one system of classification is established, new problems will develop or new tactics will be devised which will make it useless. Nor is overlapping, kept within limits, necessarily undesirable. It provides a committee structure more responsive to the needs of a complex society and better protected against the preservation of tight monopolies by individual committees and the groups with which their key members are closely affiliated.

OPERATIONS. "Every committee of Congress could perfectly properly set aside a day in which the individual members of the House or Senate who had filed bills could come before the committee and give their reasons as to why they think their bills should have a hearing, and what witnesses, if any, they know would come before the committee. . . . The committee itself would then vote as to whether a bill should be given a hearing." [5] Occasionally a committee has developed a "docket-day" arrangement of this type. Extension of this prac-tice would unquestionably strengthen the position of bills supported by weaker groups. However, it would not assure action on any given bill, but merely an opportunity for its sponsor to present the case on behalf of action.

Another area of committee operational reform has to do with holding hear-ings in open session rather than behind closed doors. While closed sessions are certainly appropriate for marking up a bill and voting upon it, some re-straints could well be imposed upon the decision of a committee majority to close the doors on other occasions. Safeguards are needed also to help assure compliance with the present requirement for a majority decision. Progress would be made toward both of these objectives by adding a number of condi-tions to the present authorization for closed hearings when approved by a majority of committee members. One condition would be that the names of those voting for and against closed hearings be recorded and be made publicly available. Another would be that the reasons for closing the hearings be clearly stated and made publicly available.

One of the major problems in connection with congressional hearings is the extent to which an airing is given to various viewpoints. On the one hand, the hearing which develops a clear-cut partisan case is usually the best organized. On the other hand, the hearing which is allegedly an ob-jective and dispassionate dissection of a problem is inevitably colored by the prejudices and predilections of the staff and committee members responsible for the decisions on who testifies and when. Apart from action to prevent un-justified closed hearings, the only formal step that can be taken to deal with this problem is to assure adequate advance notice and opportunity to testify. The growing practice of announcing hearings in advance at the end of the

[5] Testimony of Rep. Herter of Mass., Hearings before the Joint Committee on the Organi-zation of Congress, 79th Cong., 1st Sess., p. 100.

Congressional Record is a long step in this direction. Approved scheduling to prevent conflicts between the hearings and floor operations will make more time available and thus facilitate presentation of views by witnesses. Moreover, committee funds should be allocated more liberally toward the payment of traveling expenses to bring witnesses and committees together. Many representatives of weaker organizations and individuals who have valuable statements to make (including impecunious experts from universities) could well be brought to Washington at committee expense. In some cases, moreover, field hearings by standing committees would go a long way toward providing local organizations and individuals with an opportunity to present their views to congressional committees. If properly planned, they would more than repay the committees for the extra effort expended.

A number of proposals have been made to improve the operations of conference committees. Among the most important is the proposal of the Joint Committee on the Organization of Congress that "Rules governing conferences be clarified and enforced so as to permit consideration only on sections or parts of a bill on which the Houses have, in fact, disagreed and to forbid conferees to change those parts of legislation agreed to by both Houses." [6] The provisions of the Legislative Reorganization Act, however, did not go as far as this recommendation. Particularly, the Act contains no specific prohibition against the deletion of matter agreed to by both houses. One student of congressional conference-committee operations, therefore, has concluded that either the language of the Act should be amended to clarify the situation or the same objective should be obtained through the development of a significant body of precedent under rulings by the Presiding Officer. [7]

Floor Action. CONTROL OF DILATORY ACTION. When one considers the problem of dilatory action other than the filibuster, there are no proposals for changing congressional rules that deal squarely with the issue. True, various minor proposals might slightly circumscribe the use of specific tactics. There would certainly be less use of quorum calls, for example, if it were made more difficult for an individual member to initiate a quorum call, or if the responsibility for counting a quorum were placed in the hands of the Presiding Officer. Similarly, electric voting would reduce the amount of time wasted through either quorum calls or roll calls. Year-long sessions would tend to reduce the number of situations in which, because of the imminence of adjournment, dilatory tactics are particularly effective. Nevertheless, short of a complete concentration of control over floor action in the hands of the Presiding Officer, no changes in rules can strip any group of members of all their opportunities to resort to dilatory tactics through one device or another. Floor

[6] Organization of Congress, 79th Cong., 2d Sess., Rept. 1011, p. 8.

[7] Gilbert Y. Steiner, "The Congressional Conference Committee, 70th to 80th Congresses" (Urbana, Ill.: The University of Illinois Press, 1951), pp. 173–174.

action is so intricate—and necessarily so—that it takes but a moderate degree of ingenuity to develop a new method of delaying action whenever the use of an older method is forestalled. The only effective control of dilatory tactics, therefore, is direct organized opposition by the opposing forces.

In the case of the filibuster, the theoretical possibilities of reform are quite different. It is entirely possible to formulate a set of rules that would allow members of the Senate reasonable opportunities to talk, but at the same time would enable talk to be stopped through a majority vote. One such proposal, for example, would authorize cloture on a two-thirds vote within forty-eight hours after the presentation of the pending question, with cloture by a majority vote possible after fifteen days of debate. Another variation would assign one or two hours of talking time to each individual member of the Senate. It is also easy to draft a rule which is applicable to all pending matters of any type, including resolutions to amend the rules.

In actual practice, however, the problem of filibuster control is one of how to organize an antifilibuster campaign. To an important extent this has always been the case. Under the present cloture rule, which is inapplicable to resolutions to provide for a tighter cloture, it is more so than ever before.

Essentially, the only way to beat the filibuster is to wear down the filibusterers. This can be done only if a majority group is determined to win and is strongly organized. This necessarily involves substantial support from private groups and government agencies. It also calls for skilled leadership. Filibusterers use every parliamentary trick of the trade. A counterfilibuster must proceed on the same basis. An illustration of the many tactics that are available is provided in a memorandum entitled, "How to Beat a Filibuster Without Cloture," which was prepared by Will Maslow of the American Jewish Congress on the basis of his experience with the 1946 filibuster against fair-employment-practices legislation. Because it so fully illustrates the inevitable intricacies of an antifilibuster struggle, it is here reproduced in full:

A resolute majority, determined to uphold democratic rule in the Senate, can beat down a filibuster if enough courage and determination are applied.

1. The bill should be brought to the floor as early in the session as possible, when no vital legislation or appropriation bills are pressing and no end-of-session log jam piles up.

1a. The motion to consider the bill should be made before 2 P.M., when by Senate Rule VIII it is not debatable.

2. At the close of debate on this first day, the Senate should *recess*, not *adjourn*. Thus the legislative day will continue and on the next *calendar* day the Senate will resume its unfinished business where it left off.

3. During the course of the filibuster, the Senate must continue to *recess* from day to day.

4. When the Senate reconvenes after such recess, reading of the Journal is in order and unanimous consent to read it should be denied.

5. If a Senator while speaking uses unparliamentary language or otherwise violates the rules, he should be required to take his seat (Rule XIX).

6. A Senator should not be allowed to yield to another except for a question, and particularly not for a time-consuming quorum call (Huey Long filibuster, June 13, 1935).

7. Permission to yield the floor to transact any business of importance to the filibusterers should be denied.

8. The Senator occupying the floor should not be allowed to make a second quorum call in the absence of intervening business. This prevents dilatory quorum calls.

9. Enforce the rule that a quorum call cannot be made by one Senator while another has the floor.

10. A Senator who makes a quorum call should not himself be allowed to leave the Senate chamber. If he does, the precedent declaring that he loses possession of the floor should be invoked and insisted upon (Huey Long filibuster, May 21, 1935).

11. A Senator should not be allowed to rest on his desk while speaking and the precedent "Keep your feet or take your seat" should be enforced (Reed-Smoot ship purchase filibuster, Jan. 29, 1915).

12. Permission to have the clerk read any material furnished by the filibusterer should be denied.

13. Rule XIV forbidding a Senator to speak more than twice upon any question during the same day (interpreted as *legislative, not calendar* day) should be rigorously enforced. In time therefore the filibusterers will have each spoken twice and thereafter be barred from further debate (O'Daniel OPA filibuster, June 27, 1946).

14. Evening sessions should be held particularly when the Senator holding the floor is unable to make a second quorum call. Such long hours will soon fray the strongest vocal cords.

15. Opponents of the filibuster should not be provoked to reply to the obstructionists, should not seek the floor, and should not interrupt for questions. A filibuster is not a debate; it is an endurance contest. The opposing point of view can be presented at press conferences.

How anyone reacts to antifilibuster efforts is inseparably connected with his general views on party responsibility and with his opinions concerning specific legislative measures. "With the American Executive holding office for a fixed term and never appearing before the legislature to account for his actions," writes Lindsay Rogers, "it is essential that there be some place in the congressional system where the party steam roller will meet an effective barrier. . . . Without the possibility of parliamentary obstruction—that is, filibustering—the party steam roller driven by a President, could move as ruthlessly on the Senate side as it does on the House side of the Capitol." In answer to the argument that a filibuster could hold up essential action in time of national emergency, Rogers suggests that under such circumstances a Presiding Officer could simply ignore the rules and close debate.[8]

[8] Lindsay Rogers, "The Senate and the Filibuster," *Survey,* May, 1949.

On the other side of this issue, the Committee on Political Parties took the position that the present cloture rule represented "a serious obstacle to responsible lawmaking." [9] Others have attacked the filibuster on the ground that it prevents control by any majority whatsoever and places an undue amount of power in the hands of tightly organized minorities. This point of view has been widely publicized by Senator Wayne Morse of Oregon, who has charged that "Under the filibuster, with all its insidious affrontery, the principle of rule by majority is denied the people in the determination of Congressional policy." [10]

Attitudes on this question, of course, are inescapably affected by the character of existing majorities. For example, when Vice-President Dawes launched a vehement but futile attack on filibustering in 1925, the leaders of the American Federation of Labor responded with a rousing attack on Dawes. A statement approved by its national convention in that year branded the Dawes proposal as one that "does not come from the people but emanates from the secret chambers of the predatory interests." The Senate itself was warmly described as "the only forum in the world where cloture does not exist and where members can prevent the passage of reactionary legislation." [11]

In subsequent years the bulk of liberal support was lined up behind measures that were endangered by filibusters and most labor organizations swung into opposition against filibustering. In 1947, when labor and liberal groups were organizing in another futile effort to control filibustering, the National Association of Manufacturers attacked the move as dangerous to the free-enterprise system. "The real reason for the continuous drive to change the rule," the N.A.M. charged, "is to make possible the enactment of socialistic and unsound fiscal legislation." [12]

By 1952 the filibuster question had become a major issue in the internal struggle within the Democratic party. Against the opposition of conservative Democrats, liberal Democrats pressed for a platform pledge to amend the rules. As a result of conciliatory attitudes by certain Southern Democrats, they succeeded in obtaining the following plank: "In order that the will of the American people may be expressed on all legislative proposals, we urge that action be taken at the beginning of the 83rd Congress to improve congressional procedures so that majority rule prevails and decisions can be made after reasonable debate without being blocked by a minority in either House." [12a] See "Additional Comments," pp. 445–446.

CONSTITUTIONAL PROVISIONS ON TREATY RATIFICATION. The proposal to

[9] "Toward a More Responsible Two-party System," *American Political Science Review*, Vol. 44, No. 3, Part II, Supplement, September, 1950, p. 65.

[10] Wayne Morse, "D-Day on Capitol Hill," *Collier's*, June 15, 1946.

[11] American Federation of Labor Information and Publicity Service, Oct. 17, 1925.

[12] *N.A.M. News*, Nov. 1, 1947.

[12a] "The Democratic Platform, 1952" (Washington, D.C.: Democratic National Committee, 1952), p. 43.

amend the constitutional requirement for a two-thirds vote on the ratification of treaties, along with those dealing with the Senate filibuster, the seniority system, and the powers of the House Rules Committee, rounds out the great quadrumvirate of perennial congressional reform measures.

The most eloquent case for amending the treaty provisions of the Constitution has been developed by Kenneth Colegrove, who argues that "the two-thirds rule, permitting the veto of treaties by a minority in the Senate, destroys international cooperation and constitutes a menace to the foreign policy of this country." [13] He recognizes that Executive agreements can achieve the same objectives as treaties and, when followed by legislative resolutions or statutes, have the full effect of law. But he maintains that an Executive agreement lacks the symbolic significance of a treaty and that "an agreement reached between executives, even when supported by joint resolutions of the legislatures, lacks, in the popular mind, that impression of solidarity of mutually accepted obligations, which comes from the solemn covenant negotiated by the Chief Executive and approved by the legislature in the very same form as signed by the minister's plenipotentiary." [14] He, therefore, recommends a constitutional amendment which would make treaty ratification no different from any other majority-vote part of the legislative process. Many Representatives have also emphasized the desirability of including the House of Representatives in the treaty-making process.[15]

Senators have often been hard put to justify their opposition to change in the treaty-ratification provisions of the Constitution. The obvious reason is that, when a treaty is presented to the Senate, the present constitutional provisions for ratification give every Senator at least one thirty-third of a treaty veto and considerably enhance his personal power.

The debate is reduced to relatively inconsequential proportions, however, when one recognizes that through seeking legislative ratification of Executive agreements the President of the United States can achieve Colegrove's objective without a constitutional amendment. Quincy Wright has put the case very bluntly:

The Senate's tradition and prestige . . . seemed to have obscured from Constitutional jurists the opinion, earlier held, that the treaty process was intended only as an alternative, and that Congress is free to exercise its delegated powers in supporting or authorizing agreements made by the President. The conclusion may be drawn that in the making of international agreements, particularly those concerned with the conclusion of peace and establishment of institutions for perpetuating it, the matter rests in a very real sense in the hands of the President and the people. The

[13] Kenneth Colegrove, "The American Senate and World Peace" (New York: Vanguard, 1944), p. 135.

[14] *Ibid.*, p. 106.

[15] House Judiciary Committee, 78th Cong., 2d Sess., H. Rept. 2061, Dec. 13, 1944, p. 7.

President has ample legal power to negotiate on these subjects, and ample political power if he can command that majority for a peace which the public clearly desires. Difficulties which have in the past been found in the two-thirds vote in the Senate appear to have risen from political timidity and Constitutional misapprehension.[16]

MISCELLANEOUS. Among the most important of the miscellaneous proposals that have been made with respect to floor operations are those dealing with riders, talking opportunities on the floor of the House of Representatives, voting, and the printing of pending bills and amendments.

On a number of these items, Kefauver and Levin have offered or reiterated suggestions. They criticize the practice of the House Rules Committee in bringing forth rules which, by waiving points of order, encourage the insertion of riders in appropriation bills.[17] Yet they suggest no specific prohibition. If it is difficult in many cases to distinguish between a legislative appropriation item and an illegitimate rider to an appropriation bill, it would be still more difficult to make a clear distinction between a germane and a nongermane amendment to an ordinary bill.

Other Kefauver-Levin proposals would allow members of the House more talking time than allowed them under the present one-minute rule or under the usual unanimous-consent arrangement. Electric voting is advocated in order to make more time available. A major obstacle to electric voting is the fact that it would eliminate the roll call as a useful dilatory tactic. Also, under this system members of Congress would have to relinquish their practice of wandering at will while a vote was being taken and would have to appear at their regularly assigned desks in order to insert their voting key into an electric plug.

It has often been suggested that provision should be made for having more record votes on amendments and on the final passage of measures. An electric voting system, of course, would do more than anything else to facilitate record votes. The same objective could be furthered by requiring record votes on certain types of measures or by allowing more record votes in the House of Representatives on bills reported from the Committee of the Whole.

One of the provisions of the Legislative Reorganization Act requires that "no general appropriation bill shall be considered in either house unless, prior to the consideration of such bill, printed committee hearings and reports on such bill have been available for at least 3 calendar days for the members of the house in which such bill is to be considered." (Sec. 139.) This is a procedure which also might well be adapted to all bills, and proposals toward this end have often been advanced by members of Congress who object to voting in the dark. With respect to amendments, it has been proposed that no amendment be

16 "The United States and International Agreements," *American Journal of International Law*, Vol. 38, No. 3, July, 1944.
17 Kefauver and Levin, *op. cit.*, p. 53.

considered unless it is read fully to the House. The difficulty in this approach is that the reading of an amendment by the clerk is scarcely an effective way of acquainting members of Congress with its provisions. In fact, the present practice of reading bills before action is a vestige of an old-fashioned method of telling members what is before the House. It is dispensed with on many occasions and might well be dispensed with completely. To require that amendments be printed, on the other hand, might result in undue delay. This dilemma could probably be escaped through the use of modern duplicating services to make written copies of pending amendments available to all members before a vote is taken.

Staff Assistance.[18] FALLACIES. Before discussing possible improvements, it might be well to touch upon certain fallacies concerning the utility of staff facilities in Congress.

The most shallow fallacy is the assumption that congressional staff facilities could meet the total need that members of Congress have for staff work. Staffs of executive agencies and private organizations have always been used by members of Congress and will always continue to be used. This is not only because the officials of these groups constantly offer staff assistance in order to enhance their own influence. In terms of quantity, members of Congress need far more staff help than could conceivably be placed on congressional pay rolls. In terms of quality, they need the expertise that can be obtained only from people who have been intimately engaged in the operations of executive agencies and private organizations. In many instances skilled congressional staff members are needed primarily to serve as organizers of staff work outside Congress, or as intermediaries through whom staff experts outside Congress can present their work to the members and committees of Congress.

A second fallacy is the idea that larger and more adequate congressional staffs will inevitably provide a counterweight to the influence of executive officials and private organizations. It must be recognized that staff aides often serve as vehicles for the conveyance of outside influences. In fact, it might be said that effective staff work in Congress by employees who are sympathetic with executive officials is essential for good executive-congressional relations. The same might be said for the relationships between any given group in Congress and any given private organizations.

A third fallacy is the thought that the primary need in Congress is for objective staff assistance. In the sense that the word "objective" is taken to mean a quality of mind that induces one to recognize his own biases, this con-

---

[18] On this increasingly important subject see Lindsay Rogers, "The Staffing of Congress," *Political Science Quarterly,* Vol. 56, March, 1941, pp. 3–20; Gladys M. Kammerer, "The Record of Congress in Committee Staffing," *American Political Science Review,* Vol. 45, December, 1951, pp. 1126–1136; and Kenneth Kofmehl, "Congressional Staffing, with Emphasis on the Professional Staff" (doctoral dissertation in preparation, Columbia University).

tention is undoubtedly valid. But the term is also used to imply that an objective expert is one who does not take sides on issues. In this sense, the need of members of Congress for objective staff assistance is a relatively minor one and can be supplied entirely by the compilations of fact and opinion provided through the Library of Congress. The important need is for qualified staff assistants who take sides on issues and competently assist in the development of legislative positions and legislative campaigning.

A final fallacy is the theory that a more adequate staff will materially lighten the burden of work of the members of Congress. Actually, the provision of staff facilities cannot lighten the burden of work at all. The most it can do is to enable members of Congress to do a better job. But it must be kept in mind that the man who tries to do a better job often turns out to be one who sees that the better job is really a bigger job. Moreover, imaginative staff aides often uncover new problems, new opportunities, and new challenges. They tend to create—or at least attract—heavier burdens.

IMPROVEMENTS. When the exaggerated claims are trimmed down, there still remains an unquestioned need for additional staffing in Congress. First of all, there is a real need for more staff in the offices of most members. Ideally, each member should be authorized to hire a well-paid legislative assistant and a well-paid administrative assistant. With respect to the committees of Congress, the provisions of the Legislative Reorganization Act limiting professional staff to four employees is unduly restrictive. While some committees have not chosen to use this many positions, other committees operate in more than four major areas. Galloway has very pertinently suggested, therefore, "that each standing committee should be authorized to employ at least one staff specialist in each major subject matter within its jurisdiction." [19]

More attention is needed toward providing staff along party lines. "There are situations in the legislative committees of Congress where no specialized staff need be assigned to the minority members of a committee. On the other hand, when the minority members feel that they need staff help under their direction, they should not be dependent upon the good will or charity of the majority members of a committee." [20] The present arrangements providing staff assistance to the majority and minority policy committees in the Senate should be extended to cover the House of Representatives as well.

Many proposals have often been made for some central pool of staff experts available to Congress, but directly controlled neither by individual members nor individual committees. Walter Lippmann's "intelligence bureaus" were designed to achieve this objective. A more recent writer has picked this idea

[19] Hearings on Evaluation of Legislative Reorganization Act of 1946, p. 150.

[20] John Phillips, "The Hadacol of the Budget Makers," *National Tax Journal*, Vol. 4, No. 3, September, 1951, pp. 265–266.

up and has come forth with a proposal for a "National Institute for Policy Analysis," which would "provide Congress with analyses of proposed public policies, examine alternative policies, estimate the probable consequences of each alternative, indicate the degree of consensus or disagreement among qualified experts on the public consequences, and so on." [21] George H. E. Smith has developed the same theme in his proposal for a Congressional Advisory Council on Federal Legislation.[22]

If such proposals are oriented toward providing genuine policy guidance for members and committees of Congress, it is difficult to find much merit in them. If they are aimed at providing members and committees of Congress with analyses of facts and opinions, it should be pointed out that this work is already being done through the admirable facilities of the Library of Congress, and that any improvements in this work could unquestionably be handled best through an expansion or sharpening of the Library's operations.

A number of administrative improvements are needed in order to grease the wheels that result in congressional staffing. A personnel office is needed to serve as an informational clearinghouse between applicants or potential applicants and the members and committees of Congress with positions to fill. Moreover, special attention should be paid to the provision of promotion, salary, vacation, and retirement standards comparable with those enjoyed by personnel in the executive agencies.

Public Attention. "I think the Congress has been badly represented to the people in the public press and the public platform," testified Representative John M. Coffee of Washington. "That is due, in my judgment, to the fact that we do not have a press relations department." [23] What is needed is not a congressional public-relations department, but a number of operations which help make the facts of congressional activity more available to those who are interested in them.

TELEVISION AND RADIO. There is growing interest in proposals to televise and broadcast the proceedings of Congress. Because of its novelty and impact upon both eye and ear, recent telecasting of congressional investigations has had a sensational response from the general public. In radio alone there has been an extensive experience with the broadcasting of legislative proceedings, revealing a rich variety of institutional and technical arrangements developed to overcome difficulties in doing so. The United Nations and the national legislatures of New Zealand and Australia have been on the airways regularly. Saskatchewan Province, New York City, Connecticut, and other states and

[21] Robert A. Dahl, "Congress and Foreign Policy" (New York: Harcourt, Brace, 1950), pp. 159–160.

[22] Hearings on Evaluation of Legislative Reorganization Act of 1946, p. 181.

[23] Hearings before the Joint Committee on the Organization of Congress, p. 320.

localities have put their lawmakers on radio. Nor is broadcasting a novelty for the members of Congress, most of whom have faced the microphone as campaigners, as guest speakers, and in the normal course of their legislative duties.

A new synthesis of legislative process and mass (communications) media is in the making and seems only to wait upon the appropriate catalyst, for the elements to be combined are many and the inertia to be overcome is great. . . . The American system of radio broadcasting is a complex commercial process, involving relationships among network, regional, and local broadcasters, advertisers, advertising agencies, the Federal Communications Commission, the manufacturers of radio sets, programming organizations, and trade, labor, professional, and audience groups. The United States Congress is an equally complex legislative process, involving relationships among its Members, political parties, pressure groups, constituents, and other branches of the National Government. . . . One thing, however, seems certain. The Congress of the United States should enjoy all the advantages and disadvantages of twentieth-century communications in the same way that the Presidency does. Furthermore, putting Congress on the air would demonstrate for all the world to hear how a democracy is able to create unity out of diversity.[24]

A memorandum, prepared by the New Zealand Legation, concluded that the broadcasting of parliamentary proceedings in New Zealand has assisted in

. . . maintaining and perhaps improving the conduct of parliamentary proceedings —the listening public having shown themselves to respond very quickly and very critically to conduct which does not conform to accepted ideas of Parliament as a dignified and very serious institution. As a principle it is not now doubted in any quarter that the innovation has created a better informed and more responsible electorate.[25]

There are technical problems, which, in the case of radio, seem easy to master. Electrical recording machines can readily be made available for use at all committee hearings and during all operations on the floors of both houses. In fact, this is the most efficient way of recording testimony or debate for subsequent publication in committee hearings or the *Congressional Record*. It is far more accurate than the use of court reporters or stenotypists; it is less expensive; it is quicker. However, a distinction should be made between recording and actual broadcasting. Radio and television recording can easily be done on a large scale and a nonselected basis. From the materials compiled, selections can be made for use on subsequent radio and television programs. Continuous broadcasting, however, is an entirely different matter. This would

[24] Ralph M. Goldman, "Congress on the Air," Hearings on Organization and Operation of Congress, 82d Cong., 1st Sess., 1952, reprinted from *Public Opinion Quarterly* (Winter, 1950–1951). This article admirably summarizes past experience and continuing obstacles in legislative broadcasting.

[25] Hearings before the Joint Committee on the Organization of Congress, 79th Cong., 1st Sess., p. 944.

require the complete use, during long hours of many days, of time available to two stations, one for the Senate and one for the House. Arrangements of this type would necessarily imply government-owned or government-subsidized facilities.

The big problems, however, are not technical. For one thing, the more extended use of either radio or television makes correction of the record more difficult for members of Congress who are accustomed to revise their remarks before they are printed. A more important result would be tighter control of debate. A Senator may have a right to speak as long as he wants to, but the right to project his voice and image on the air waves as long as he can hold out is something else, something that would unquestionably run into the resistance of colleagues who resented such a monopolization of the channels of personal publicity. Thus, lurking behind any inertia with respect to extending the use of radio and television to the floor of the Senate are the fears of those interested in preserving the filibuster as a major weapon of legislative struggle.

Finally, there is the danger that television of congressional hearings can be "a monster which can destroy innocent individuals, whole corporations, political parties, and entire administrations." Because of this danger, Senator Wiley proposed a study by the Senate Rules Committee to survey the various problems involved in using television, radio, or the motion pictures with respect to the proceedings of Congress and its committees.[26]

CONGRESSIONAL DOCUMENTS. There are a number of methods by which congressional documents can be rendered more useful to those interested in finding out what has taken place during the course of legislative operations.

First of all, much can be done to make printed committee hearings more useful and readable documents. A rare example of good editing is found in the 1945 hearings of the Joint Committee on the Organization of Congress. These hearings contain, in addition to the customary table of contents listing the names of the witnesses, a subject-matter index, a brief summary of each day's hearings, and a critical bibliography prepared by a Library of Congress technician on the entire question of congressional organization. Other hearing volumes have occasionally included subheads in the text to indicate each phase of the testimony or interrogation. Furthermore, it would be extremely helpful if each committee published more extensive reports both weekly and annually, indicating the status of all bills referred to it or reported from it and a summary of all committee reports that have been made, together with an indication of the members whose names are attached to each report. In addition, Kefauver and Levin advocate that "it should be mandatory that committees

[26] "Televising of Congress," Hearings on Organization and Operation of Congress, 82d Cong., 1st Sess., 1952, pp. 601–603.

publish all votes on pending legislation and amendments considered, including adverse votes." [27]

A number of proposals have been made concerning improvements in the *Congressional Record*. Kefauver and Levin have suggested that Congress "should dignify it and improve its design and give it a fixed selling price, regardless of size, that would cover manufacturing and distribution costs. It then could be put on sale at news stands all over the country." [28] They also ask that an effort be made to control the insertion of miscellaneous documents and the extension of remarks beyond what was actually said on the floor. Another proposal is for greater control over the corrections that a member is allowed to make in his floor remarks before they are printed in the *Congressional Record*.

It would also be useful to have the Library of Congress prepare a legislative history of every major statute, shortly after it is enacted. No matter how important a piece of legislation may be, the records concerning its development are invariably scattered through scores of separate documents, many of which soon become unobtainable. Within a year or so after the time a proposed bill becomes law, the full story of its legislative development usually is known by only a few persons who were close to the picture. The publication of legislative histories would make this valuable information public property.

The Executive Officials

Proposals concerning the legislative role of executive officials tend to be less abundant than those which relate to members of Congress. The idea that legislation is the job of Congress alone has misled many students of the subject. The more dramatic proposals dealing with the broad problems of congressional-executive relations are discussed in Chap. 6. Here attention will be given to the less sweeping reforms affecting executive proposals for legislation, the President's veto, and executive campaigning.

Executive Proposals for Legislation. Reform recommendations on this aspect of the legislative process are of two types: ideas concerning what the role of executive proposals should be, and ideas concerning the preparation and transmittal to Congress of executive proposals.

THEIR ROLE. There is a widely held conception that the officials of the executive branch—and the President in particular—should occupy a special role in the initiation of legislative proposals. For some, this is the only way to approximate under American conditions the much-admired ideal of Cabinet leadership as exercised under a parliamentary system. For others, it is more the natural consequence of our own political structure. Only the executive officials, it is

[27] Kefauver and Levin, *op. cit.*, p. 140.
[28] *Ibid.*, p. 204.

argued, have the specialized expertise and the familiarity with administrative operations necessary for the preparation of a sound legislative proposal. In these officials alone can one find the aloofness and objectivity needed to protect the public interest against the assaults of private groups. In the President alone can one find a national leader elected by the entire people and responsive to the interests of the entire people.

This point of view is more widely held than the occasions of its formal expressions would indicate. Moreover, when formally expressed, it is usually presented in abstract terms, unaccompanied by specifics.

One of the best expressions of this point of view has been voiced by Luther Gulick in the concluding paragraph of an important journal article:

In the world into which government is moving, the executive will be called upon to draft the master plan. Deliberative and advisory representative groups will be asked to consider and adopt the broad outline of various parts of this plan. The executive will then be given full power to work out the remainder and the inter-relations of the program and to carry it into effect, not only through the established agencies of government but also through new agencies of a quasi-private character. The legislature of the future will have two primary powers: first, the veto over major policy, and second, the right to audit and investigate. Behind the entire process will be the controlling hand of the mass of citizens in party and pressure groups. These are the bricks and straws from which the new theory of the division of powers must be constructed.[29]

In less general terms, the proposal has often been made that some form of special status be given to Executive-sponsored bills. Galloway, for example, has proposed a semimonopoly for executive officials in the initiation of legislative action.[30] Black has proposed that each house of Congress establish a "Committee on Presidential Bills" to which Presidential recommendations for legislation "could be sent openly and as a matter of usual and formal routine, and not by the devious hands of some unacknowledged agent." When reported, an executive bill would then enjoy a privileged place on the calendar.[31] Others have occasionally proposed a formal method of identifying executive bills, not as a method of bestowing honor, but more in order to place members of Congress on their guard against executive domination of the legislative process.

There is a compelling case, however, against the general approach toward executive leadership, which is exemplified by the Gulick, Galloway, and Black proposals. For one thing, executive officials have no monopoly of expertise and

[29] "Politics, Administration, and the New Deal," *The Annals*, Vol. 169, September, 1933, p. 66. This entire article bears careful reading by those interested in the development of modern thought on American government.

[30] Galloway, *op. cit.*, p. 308.

[31] Henry Campbell Black, "The Relation of the Executive Power to Legislation" (Princeton, N.J.: Princeton University Press, 1919), p. 185.

specialized experience in administrative operations. Many private organizations are far better equipped to initiate legislative action in certain matters than the employees of any government agency. The expertise and experience that exist within the executive branch is often completely disregarded by agency heads and Presidents, or is not made available to them. Various members of Congress often enjoy a better opportunity to harness executive-staff resources. When executive experts engage in informal or "bootleg" work for members of Congress, they are often able to free themselves from the wraps of hierarchical control and perform creative tasks that could never be equaled within the regular procedures of the executive branch.

Furthermore, it is sheer nonsense to regard executive officials, even Presidents, as people who somehow are free of the influence of group pressures and have the interests of the "whole people" at heart. Among many agency heads and their appointees there is as much localism and narrowness of perspective as there is in either house of the Congress. In contrast with a Senator or a Representative, for example, who must deal with many groups with divergent views, the executive official is often responsive only to a limited clientele interested in one objective. In so far as the President is concerned, one finds not freedom from pressures, but a somewhat different orientation toward group interests. A President must necessarily give particularly heavy weight to the interests and views of those who hold the balance of power in pivotal states. This often produces a noticeable leaning toward the views of important mass organizations in urbanized areas rather than the dominant views in Congress, where the formal pattern of representation accentuates the influence of prominent political groups in rural areas. The thought that Congress can develop its own legislative program is even more unrealistic than the idea that it can be developed for them by executive officials only. The point of view here expressed is that it is entirely legitimate for all contestants in the legislative process to have their own sets of legislative proposals, and that there is nothing either inherently desirable or at all practical in the idea that any given set of contestants be given a monopoly of the initiation of legislative proposals.

THEIR PREPARATION AND TRANSMISSION. How can a President best select those legislative proposals which shall be regarded as peculiarly his own, those which other executive officials might be allowed to present as their own, and those which should be killed or revised? Should a President attempt to reconcile all intra-Administration differences before a measure is presented to Congress? "Conflicts and differences between administrative departments concerning proposed legislation, whether on major policies or details," advised the President's Committee on Administrative Management, "should, so far as possible, be adjusted before such bills are presented to the Congress." [32] The

[32] Report of President's Committee on Administrative Management (U.S. Government Printing Office, 1937), p. 20.

merit of this point of view lies in the obvious fact that any President who allows too many policy controversies among his agency heads will seriously weaken his position before Congress and his standing before the country. On the other hand, the settling of all agency disputes before legislation is proposed to Congress seems hardly possible and, in some cases, undesirable. Often the only way to settle an intra-Administration quarrel is for the President to organize enough support in Congress to win over or sidetrack officials who have opposed him within the executive branch. In many cases, also, a constructive compromise can be worked out only after there have been public hearings before congressional committees and a certain amount of congressional debate.

Another aspect of the problem is the location of the legislative clearance function. The President's Committee on Administrative Management recommended a double approach: a legislative counsel on the White House staff to assist the President on major bills, and a legislative clearance function in the Bureau of the Budget to handle the clearance operation on other bills. Both these proposals have been carried out in practice. There is no reason whatsoever to question the utility of a legislative counsel in the White House, but a legitimate question can be raised on whether or not the Bureau of the Budget is the proper location for the remainder of the legislative clearance function.

It would probably be advisable to end the myth that the Budget Bureau's operation on bills is limited to ascertaining whether or not a proposed measure happens to conform to "the President's program." This myth serves to concentrate a considerable amount of policy-making power in the hands of Budget Bureau technicians who may have only limited understanding of the broad problems involved and even less familiarity with legislative and political strategy. Any President would be well advised to insist that Budget Bureau work in this field be openly recognized as dealing directly with the formation of Presidential policy.

Where and how should legislative drafting in the executive branch be done? Many agency officials have made the mistake of regarding legislative drafting as a matter to be handled by lawyers alone. This has often conferred undue policy-initiating power upon lawyers having an inadequate grasp of the total objectives to be sought. It has denied to many agencies the strength which comes from the cross-fertilization of ideas by personnel with varying skills and backgrounds. Moreover, many executive officials are accustomed to handling the drafting process without sufficient consultation with potential supporters in Congress and in private organizations. This attitude stems in part from an unrealistic emphasis upon the theoretical lines which divide the executive branch from Congress, and government from private groups. It is nourished by a psychological frame of mind which places greater value upon the self-expression achieved by writing one's views in a draft bill than upon the actual results to be obtained through the organization of support behind a legislative proposal.

Still another problem is whether executive proposals should be transmitted to Congress seriatim or in some sort of comprehensive listing. Both Woodrow Wilson and Franklin Roosevelt emphasized the former approach. Under Truman, however, much greater emphasis has been given to formal listing. The first major Truman message to Congress, in September, 1945, after the surrender of Japan, listed 21 points for legislative action. The same pattern was followed by Truman in subsequent years in his annual State of the Union Messages and the accompanying Economic Reports and Budget Messages. This approach should be continued. Also, the major executive agencies should follow suit and develop comprehensive legislative programs that can be presented *in toto* to the appropriate committees of Congress at the beginning of each session. This would assist in the elimination of many legislative conflicts among executive agencies and facilitate the planning of an orderly schedule by congressional leaders. Special requests during the course of the year can readily deal with individual matters in greater detail and with unforeseen legislative needs that are always bound to develop.

The President's Veto. The proposals of greatest consequence in this area are those which would in one way or another give the President the power to veto individual items in a measure that has been passed by Congress. In addition, there are a number of other proposals of lesser importance.

THE ITEM VETO. "An important feature of the fiscal procedure in the majority of our states is the authority given to the Executive to withhold approval of individual items in an appropriation bill and, while approving the remainder of the bill, to return such rejected items for the further consideration of the legislature. This grant of power has been considered a consistent corollary of the power of the legislature to withhold approval of items in the Budget of the Executive; and the system meets with general approval in the many states which have adopted it." [33]

In making this proposal, President Franklin Roosevelt echoed the views of Presidents Grant and Arthur and of many students of fiscal affairs. In supporting President Roosevelt's proposal, Senator Arthur Vandenberg of Michigan added an additional argument: "Now that we suddenly confront fabulous appropriation totals . . . it seems more than ever necessary that the Presidential veto should be afforded some degree of that same discretion and selectivity in respect to the component parts of an appropriation bill which the Congress itself enjoys when it formulates and passes these bills." [34] The argument has also been advanced that the Presidential item veto is essential if the President is to trim the pork-barrel appropriations and cope with riders on

[33] Budget Message for Fiscal Year 1939, transmitted to Congress, January, 1938.

[34] *Congressional Record,* 77th Cong., 2d Sess., Mar. 10, 1942, p. 2153.

appropriation bills. This theme is particularly pertinent if and when appropriation measures are merged into an omnibus bill, a position stated by Representative Franklin D. Roosevelt, Jr.[35]

Many arguments have been advanced against the item-veto proposal. Herring comments:

> If the President possessed the selective veto, this would mean an enormous additional increase in his responsibilities. Legislatures would be more prone to give in to the demands of particular interests and include items with the expectation that the President would veto these undesirable elements. Much of the pressure now exerted on Congress would be transferred to the Executive. . . . Congress would become a less responsible body both in its substantive law-making and in the ease with which it could find shelter from political difficulties behind the White House.[36]

In similar terms Young argues that, "It is better for Congress to assume full responsibility for the budget which it passes rather than play hide-and-seek with the President on particular items." [37] Members of Congress have repeatedly attacked the proposal on the ground that it would concentrate too much power in the hands of the President.

The best reasons against the item veto have usually been ignored. First, the President already enjoys the power of curtailing expenditures. To the extent that he exercises it, he is not subject to a congressional resolution overriding his action. Second, once one goes beyond the dropping of individual sums of money in appropriation bills, it is really impossible to contrive an item-veto system which can deal with either legislation in appropriation bills or riders in general. Provisions of this type can be written in such a manner as to make them well-nigh inseparable from the rest of a measure. In part, therefore, the item-veto power is in effect enjoyed by the President and in part it is the kind of power that could not be conferred upon him.

OTHER PROPOSALS. For decades individual members of Congress who have objected to specific Presidential vetoes have proposed that either the President's veto power be abolished or that Congress be given the power to override a Presidential veto by a majority instead of a two-thirds vote. Neither is very practical. A more effective means of undercutting the President's veto power is through the use of concurrent resolutions. The concurrent resolution has the advantage that provisions authorizing its use can be tucked away in a broader measure which has Presidential approval. A concurrent resolution terminating a statute or directing that specific actions be taken need not be transmitted to the White House for the President's approval.

A minor proposal to weaken the President's veto position would eliminate the pocket veto by authorizing a designated representative of either house of

[35] *Congressional Record,* 81st Cong., 2d Sess., Apr. 6, 1950, p. 4928.

[36] Pendleton Herring, "Presidential Leadership" (New York: Rinehart, 1940), pp. 76–77.

[37] Roland A. Young, "This Is Congress" (New York: Knopf, 1946), p. 235.

Congress to receive a vetoed bill during a recess or adjournment.[38] Since there is no limitation upon the number of days in which Congress must act in order to override a Presidential veto, the Clerk of the House or the Secretary of the Senate could then refer the vetoed bill to the House or the Senate for action upon the end of the recess or adjournment. This plan would be still more effective if Congress met in year-round sessions and abandoned the idea of an early adjournment.

A number of minor proposals have been made for strengthening the President's veto. Brogan has argued that a President should be able to combat a measure with which he is in disagreement by going over the heads of Congress and calling for a national referendum.[39] Yet despite the popularity of the referendum in state and local affairs, there has been singularly little interest in this approach toward national affairs. Both the practical problem of handling a referendum on a national scale and the tremendous number of conflicts which might be channelized in this direction if the national referendum were accepted as a method of legislation have tempered the ardor of referendum enthusiasts.[40]

A question that has been long neglected and that deserves more attention concerns the amendment of vetoed measures. It is customary for a President, upon vetoing a bill, to indicate the nature of the changes that would be required to enable him to reverse his position; at times Presidents have offered such amendments in detailed form. Yet under the rules of Congress, a vetoed bill cannot be amended. A new bill embodying the proposals that the President has submitted for a compromise between the President's proposals and the provisions of the vetoed bill must start at the beginning of the legislative process and run the gauntlet of two committees and action on the floor of both houses before it can be sent back to the White House. "The rule is wise," comments Luce, "not only because there must be an end to everything, but also because the work of engrossing ought not to have to be done twice." [41] Yet in effect the rule postpones an end to the consideration of a vetoed matter rather than facilitating a prompt ending; and the clerical work involved in engrossing is too minor a matter to affect the case one way or another. If it were possible for Congress to amend a vetoed bill promptly and then send it back to the White House, it would be possible to save a lot of lost motion and facilitate executive-congressional agreement.

[38] Testimony of Representative Hatton Sumners, Hearings before the Joint Committee on Organization of Congress, 79th Cong., 1st Sess., p. 180.

[39] D. W. Brogan, "Government of the People" (New York: Harper, 1943), p. 382.

[40] For another approach to the use of the referendum, and particularly a national advisory referendum, see Ralph M. Goldman, "The Advisory Referendum in America," *Public Opinion Quarterly*, Summer, 1950.

[41] Robert Luce, "Legislative Problems" (Boston: Houghton Mifflin, 1935), p. 170.

Executive Campaigning. CURTAILMENT. When the Select Committee on Lobbying Activities was set up in the House of Representatives during the Eighty-first Congress, Republican members of the House insisted that the Committee deal not only with lobbying by private groups, but also with "all activities of agencies of the Federal government intended to influence, encourage, promote or retard legislation." [42]

The majority members of the committee developed the point of view that executive officials have the responsibility of "speaking on those issues which transcend group lines or which have no other effective voice," and that executive participation in legislative campaigns is essential to prevent public policy from being "the product of willy-nilly submission to the demands of whatever group has the largest material resources at its disposal." [43] They pointed out that the Constitution gave the President responsibilities for participating in the legislative process, that many executive agencies are required by law to submit legislative proposals to Congress, and that committees and members of Congress continually seek the help of executive officials on legislative matters. At the same time, the majority of the committee stated "that there are limits beyond which executive participation in legislative policy-making may impinge on the authority of Congress and thus endanger our Constitutional system." [44]

When it comes to the question of what might actually be done to curtail executive campaigning the purely abstract or general approach once again breaks down. Unless one would curtail the President's powers under the Constitution, there seems to be no formal procedure for limiting executive influence upon the legislative process.

Should executive lobbyists be required to register under the Regulation of Lobbying Act? Dorothy Detzer thinks so:

> If the LaFollette-Monroney Act were amended to include the government lobbyists, this step, to be sure, would not be an absolute guarantee against misuse of office, any more than the Act now affords complete protection against the nefarious activities of private lobbyists. It would, however, provide an open record, and that record could reveal who lobbied, when, and on what. And with that record, as well as the one now required for private lobbyists, the public would possess a tool with which to secure a new and more effective measure of democratic control.[45]

This proposal was well answered in the testimony of Roger Jones, Director of the Division of Legislative Reference in the Bureau of the Budget, during the hearings of the House Select Committee on Lobbying Activities:

[42] H. Res. 298, 81st Cong., 1st Sess.
[43] Hearings before the Select Committee on Lobbying Activities of the House of Representatives, 81st Cong., 2d Sess., Oct. 20, 1950, General Interim Report, pp. 61–62.
[44] *Ibid.*, p. 62.
[45] *Ibid.*, p. 53.

In one sense [executive officials] are actually registered. If you will, I think the listing of Executive Branch officials that is contained in the Congressional Directory and in the Official Register of the United States is practically a public notice that anyone there listed may be given a specific job by the proper superior, on up the line to the President of the United States, which could probably be construed as an effort to influence legislation.[46]

Other methods of curtailing executive campaigning are listed in the General Interim Report of the House Select Committee on Lobbying Activities. One method is to use appropriation acts for the purpose of forbidding the expenditure of money for certain public-relations activities. Another is to investigate activities of officials whose actions have been offensive. Still another check is the possibility of having an executive underling fired or voting an administration out of office. Yet all of these techniques, it should be kept in mind, are methods of dealing with specific situations. In effect, they are instruments for countercampaigning rather than for providing a general curtailment in the legislative campaign functions of executive officials.

STRENGTHENING. Quite a number of the proposals already discussed are justified on the ground that they would strengthen the role of the President or other executive officials in the determination of final legislative decisions. Among the most important of these are the proposals for congressional-executive merger and congressional-executive cooperation which were discussed in Chap. 6 and those discussed in this chapter for strengthening the role of executive officials in initiating legislation and extending the President's veto power.

In addition, there are a number of other lines of thought that deserve consideration. The first is the thesis that the greatest potential strength of a President lies in his ability to appeal over the heads of Congress to the American people. In part, it has become a commonplace, when a President's legislative program faces trouble in Congress, for his supporters immediately to suggest that he "go on the air," "get on a train," or otherwise take his case to the people.

This thesis has much to commend it. The White House is an ideal springboard for propaganda activities. Every President is in a peculiarly strategic position to reach vast numbers of people with his message. His message is particularly important when it can appeal to the millions of individuals who are not represented by effective private organizations, but who, through the exigencies of Presidential political campaigns, may become a decisive force at the next Presidential election. In this sense the President's appeals to the people are a method of organizing the unorganized for practical political action.

[46] "The Role of Lobbying in Representative Self-government," Hearings before the Select Committee on Lobbying Activities of the House of Representatives, 81st Cong., 2d Sess., p. 142.

They are also a method of strengthening whatever support he may have among the big-city voters of the pivotal states.

Yet it is also important to recognize a number of major weaknesses in the "Presidential appeal" approach. In the first place, a Presidential appeal to public opinion cannot possibly have the same effect upon electoral behavior in all areas of the country, even if one assumes, for the sake of discussion, a national audience comprising a uniform percentage of the voting population. Furthermore, there is a very real limit—although it can never be precisely measured ahead of time—upon the number and type of legislative issues that the President can take to the public. The President is limited not only by the time available to him, but also by considerations of timing. Long writes:

> When the staff of the Office of War Mobilization and Reconversion advised a hard-pressed agency to go out and get itself some popular support so that the President could afford to support it, their action reflected the realities of power rather than political cynicism . . . the bureaucracy under the American political system has a large share of responsibility before the public promotion of policy. . . .[47]

Further, to emphasize the desirability of propagandizing the public as a means of putting pressure upon Congress may lead to a neglect of the need for directly persuading members of Congress. Many a legislative cause has been weakened in modern-day America because executive officials have used pressure tactics only and disdained to use the more difficult instruments of persuasion. More frequently, many congressional opponents of legislative proposals advocated by executive officials have been goaded into still more bitter opposition by efforts to build fires beneath them without attempting to convince them personally. Although persuasion by itself can scarcely serve as *the* decisive weapon in the legislative struggle, one of the best tests of executive statesmanship is the ability to blend persuasion and pressure in judicious proportions.[48]

Another major approach toward strengthening executive campaigning is found in the thesis that we need more effective political parties. In fact, many of the advocates of stronger parties find that "the best hope for the future of American politics and government lies in a fruitful union between Presi-

[47] Norton Long, "Power and Administration," *Public Administration Review*, Vol. 9, Autumn, 1949, pp. 258–259.

[48] "Fear is in almost all cases a wretched instrument of government, and ought in particular never to be employed against any order of men who have the smallest pretensions to independency. To attempt to terrify them, serves only to irritate their bad humor, and to confirm them in an opposition which more gentle usage perhaps might easily induce them, either to soften, or to lay aside altogether. . . . For though management and persuasion are always the easiest and safest instruments of government, as force and violence are the worst and the most dangerous, yet such, it seems, is the natural insolence of man, that he always disdains to use the good instrument, except when he cannot or dare not use the bad one." Adam Smith, "The Wealth of Nations" (Modern Library edition, New York: Random House, 1937), pp. 750–751.

dential power and party government," [49] or that the future of the American system lies in "strengthening the only two instruments in our political life, which have an inherent responsibility to the nation as nation: The President and the national political parties." [50] The logic here is that a stronger party organization will not only prevent a President from watching ill-considered legislative ventures, but also provide him with the organized support which is needed to make him a more effective legislative leader.

Anything which is done to strengthen the majority-party organization in Congress and the President's associations with it will obviously strengthen the hand of the President and other executive officials in legislative matters. But nothing effective along these lines can be done unless a combination of private nonparty organizations is brought together to provide the sources of party strength. With any conceivable augmentation in the strength of our national parties, it will still be necessary for both the President and other executive officials to organize support for many legislative measures entirely outside party channels.

IMPROVEMENTS OF CONGRESSIONAL TECHNIQUE IN LAWMAKING

Finally, attention should be directed to a number of proposals that deal with such legislative methods as the handling of appropriations, the improvement of drafting, the control of congestion, the length of sessions, and codification and revision.

Appropriation Methods

The sheer bulk of appropriation legislation enacted every year and its importance to so many groups and agencies throughout the country have inspired a large number of proposals for changing the manner in which money is appropriated. Among them are the item-veto proposal discussed earlier and the idea that executive proposals for legislative action should be acted upon by Congress through exception or rejection but without an opportunity for amendment.

At this point consideration will be given to the so-called "legislative budget," the omnibus appropriation bill, and a number of minor items.

The Legislative Budget. One of the most ambitious attempts to bring "order" into the handling of appropriation bills in Congress was the ill-fated legislative-budget section (Sec. 138) of the Legislative Reorganization Act of 1946. Under this provision the two committees on appropriations and the two committees on revenue were supposed to meet jointly at the beginning of each regular ses-

[49] James M. Burns, "Congress on Trial" (New York: Harper, 1949), p. 195.
[50] Stephen K. Bailey, "Congress Makes a Law" (New York: Columbia University Press, 1949), p. 239.

sion of the Congress, study the President's budget recommendations, and report to the Congress a concurrent resolution containing "a recommendation for the maximum amount to be appropriated for expenditure in such year, which shall include such an amount to be reserved for deficiencies as may be deemed necessary by such committees." This was supposed to confront Congress with the necessity of discussing and voting upon the total amount of funds to be appropriated for the ensuing fiscal year.

Despite the high hopes held for it, no concurrent budget resolution was adopted in 1947. In 1948, when one was adopted, it was completely disregarded by both houses of Congress as decisions were reached on individual appropriation bills. For a while it seemed to some members of Congress that the concurrent resolution would work out better if the date on which it was supposed to be reported to the two houses of Congress were changed from February 15 to May 1. This change was made in 1949, but from then on no attempt was made to report a concurrent resolution to Congress. The statutory provisions requiring that such a resolution be reported were in effect repealed by congressional inaction.

"The legislative budget went on the rocks," writes Representative John Phillips of California, "for the simple reason that the concurrent resolution setting a maximum amount of appropriations called for a premature commitment by the members of Congress. Moreover, it provided no means of focusing sustained attention upon the relationship between appropriations and revenues." Accordingly, he proposed the complete deletion of the provisions for a concurrent resolution. In its place he would substitute a written report to be presented to Congress every thirty to sixty days and to include "a continuing analysis of such basic information as to the level of the national debt, the conventional deficit or surplus, the cash budget or surplus, and committee and floor actions taken with respect to individual appropriation bills." [51]

Practically every proponent of a revised legislative budget has suggested the formal creation of a joint committee. Many types of joint committees have been proposed. At one extreme, it is suggested that a joint budget committee be given the job of actually preparing the budget; thus, to all intents and purposes, taking over the functions of the Bureau of the Budget.

Hardly less extreme are the proposals that Congress go back to the arrangements existing in the House of Representatives before 1865 and in the Senate before 1867, when both revenue and appropriation bills were handled by the same committees, or to streamline these arrangements by having the entire operation handled by a single joint committee. Roland Young's comment is pertinent:

There is no need to combine the Revenue and Appropriations Committees, as they were combined before 1865. Congressional practice has become too traditionalized for such change, and there would perhaps be difficulty preserving a committee with

[51] Phillips, *op. cit.*, p. 263.

such great power. Even now, the extensive power of the House Committee on appropriations is occasionally attacked, and one can imagine the reaction of the House if this power were doubled.[52]

Less impractical is the proposal that the two committees on appropriations and the two committees on revenue meet together to frame a general "fiscal policy." The fact remains, however, that the members of these four committees will remain overburdened with the specialized problems of appropriations or of revenue taxation. A strong case can be made that general leadership on fiscal problems can be provided, if at all, by the party-leadership committees in Congress or by the Joint Committee on the Economic Report.

This line of reasoning leads to the conception that any new joint committee in this field should be a joint committee on appropriations which would parallel the Joint Committee on Internal Revenue Taxation. Representative Phillips discusses the jurisdictional relationship between a joint committee of this type and the work of the two committees on expenditures in the executive departments. He suggests that the entire function of checking upon executive expenditures be transferred to the appropriations committees and to his proposed joint committee on appropriations. With this shift in jurisdiction the joint committee could become the recipient of the investigatory reports of the General Accounting Office. This brings his proposal closely in line with previous proposals, such as the one made by Lucius Wilmerding, for the creation of a joint committee on public accounts.[53]

The Omnibus Appropriation Bill. Another major proposal for changing appropriation methods is to consolidate all appropriation bills—with the exception of those deficiency and supplemental bills that cannot be avoided—into one omnibus measure, or "packaged budget." Roland Young believed that the "Budget Bill should be shorn of verbosity and confined to a few hundred, or less, appropriation items . . ." and that it "would contain but a dozen or so pages rather than the several hundred the bills now contained." [54] Both these points of view have been expressed in abstract form by the argument that the consolidated bill would make it easier for Congress to deal with appropriations in an "orderly" fashion.

In 1950, a one-year experiment was attempted.[55] However, it was a short-lived one. In January, 1951, the House Appropriations Committee voted to abandon the omnibus appropriation bill. An analysis of the one-year experiment

[52] Young, *op. cit.*, pp. 262–263.

[53] See Lucius Wilmerding, "The Spending Power" (New Haven, Conn.: Yale University Press, 1943), pp. 253–254, 286–288, 291–292.

[54] Young, *op. cit.*, pp. 260–261.

[55] For divergent congressional résumés of what was accomplished during this experiment, see statements by Representative Clarence Cannon of Missouri, in the *Congressional Record* (daily edition), Jan. 29, 1951, pp. 796–800, and Feb. 27, 1951, pp. 1665–1681. Also see Phillips, "The Hadacol of the Budget Makers."

indicates five interesting conclusions. First, it is difficult to see how the omnibus approach contributed toward the holding down of expenditures. As Representative Phillips has pointed out: "Changing conditions—including the invasion of the Republic of Korea—required the enactment of five deficiency and supplemental bills for fiscal year 1951." [56] Moreover, when the omnibus appropriation bill came before the Senate, the senatorial friends of the Franco regime in Spain succeeded in adding a provision calling for a substantial American loan to the Spanish government. Although President Truman subsequently evaded this requirement, the incident indicated how the omnibus appropriation bill can be a vehicle to which may be attached additional appropriation provisions of all sorts.

Second, the device never succeeded in centralizing additional powers in the hands of the managers of the bill. Although the procedure for the handling of the bill formally called for the creation of an executive committee of ten members in the House Appropriations Committee, the resistance to any "super-duper committee" was so great that the procedure broke down and all questions were referred to the individual subcommittees in the same way as though each portion of the bill were being handled separately. The final bill, of course, was written in the conference committee but the formal selection of nine members of the House Appropriations Committee to serve as House conferees obscured the actual fact that behind this formality each of the individual subcommittees performed the function of conferees with respect to their particular portions of the bill.

Third, the omnibus appropriation bill led to a situation where the President, instead of being weakened by his inability to contemplate the veto of such an important measure, was given an unusually great opportunity to strengthen his political power. Representative Phillips has explained this paradoxical situation as follows:

The package budget inevitably invites amendments directing the President to cut the total amount by a given sum or percentage. In fact, one of the greatest boasts of the package budget advocates is that the experiment on the fiscal year 1951 bill facilitated the amendment which directed the President to cut down the final total by an amount approximating 550 million dollars. From the viewpoint of high principle, this approach represents an abdication of Congressional responsibility over the power of the purse. From the viewpoint of practical politics, it confers upon the President the power to penalize his political opponents by eliminating expenditures in their home districts. Any President of the United States who wanted to achieve dictatorial control over Congress could hope for little more than the restoration of the package budget and the inevitable move to amend it every year by directing him to make a cut of a given size in any manner he chooses. . . . It is an ironic paradox that members of Congress who shudder at the thought of a constitutional amendment allowing a President to veto individual items in a bill have supported an extra-constitutional

[56] *Ibid.*, pp. 258–259.

device which in effect gives the President the same veto power but allows the Congress no opportunity to over-ride him.[57]

Fourth, the omnibus appropriation bill offered nothing to those who had hoped that it would lead to a reduction in detailed itemization. Rather than being a brief bill of only a dozen or so pages, it ended up as a law of 192 pages. Fifth, rather than contribute to a more "orderly procedure," it assured a more cursory procedure. The measure was so large and so complicated that it defied either careful examination or an approximation to understanding. Less time was spent on each major section in committee; fewer members of Congress had an opportunity to familiarize themselves with the issues in the floor debate. There was less opportunity than usual to obtain a record vote on the floor of the House of Representatives—since under the consolidated-bill procedure only a single motion to recommit was possible.[58]

Despite the countless recommendations relating to the details of the appropriations process, this function will probably continue to be the most complex, cumbersome, and central one confronting Congress. Reviewing a massive budget document within the short time of a few weeks and at the same time equating broad social purposes with dollar units will continue to push legislators from one difficult choice to the next. No number of procedural changes will ever take the place of consensus on broad social purposes as the lubricant of mutual confidence between the askers and the givers of Federal funds. No number of "safeguards" can suffice if demands for "economy" and protestations that "the fat" is out of a budget request evolve into a ritual designed primarily to help avoid the difficult decisions of modern public finance.

The Improvement of Drafting

There are limits on the extent to which either precision or simplicity can be achieved in legislative drafting. Nevertheless, better drafting can help avoid needless conflicts and contribute to understanding of the final product.

First, provisions might well be made for a technical review of every bill that is reported from a congressional committee. In some state legislatures this has been attempted through the use of committees on revision. To saddle members of Congress with a function of this type would hardly be practical. It could be assigned much more satisfactorily to the Office of the Legislative Counsel.

---

[57] *Ibid.*, p. 261.

[58] For a lucid review of other proposals in this field, see George B. Galloway, "Reform of the Federal Budget," Public Affairs Bulletin, No. 80 (Washington, D.C.: Library of Congress, Legislative Reference Service, April, 1950). These proposals for the most part deal with the President's budget presentation to Congress, the general character of appropriations legislation, the committee and floor procedures in dealing with appropriations bills, and the review or audit of executive expenditures.

Second, steps should be taken toward the preparation of a comprehensive drafting manual. Just as the Government Printing Office issues a manual on the style in which government documents are to be written and printed, the Office of the Legislative Counsel should develop a manual which will deal in comprehensive terms with such matters as the division of a measure into title, parts, sections, and paragraphs, references to existing statutes, abbreviations, amendments, standard clauses and sections, and kindred matters. A manual of this type will promote skillful draftsmanship and make the review process at the committee stage much easier.[59]

Finally, if significant progress is made in the development of a legislative style manual, it might prove desirable to enact a number of style requirements into law. In any such endeavor, however, great care must be taken that requirements of this type not become too complex. The experience of style requirements in state constitutions, as Luce points out, is that in many cases "they have led to a distressing amount of litigation and have brought about the nullification of what might have been useful statutes." [60]

The Control of Congestion

"Congress should jealously guard its time for ample debate and consideration of matters of national and international importance," stated the Joint Committee on the Organization of Congress. "It seems hardly consistent to hear the excuse that Congressional calendars are too crowded to take up and discuss issues of great national interest when so much time is devoted to these minor matters." [61]

Although there is much to commend this logic, it should be pointed out that it also conceals two false assumptions often made regarding the problem of reducing legislative congestion. First, it is often assumed that the time which would be saved by trimming down a portion of the legislative burden would be put to good use. Yet there is little reason for anyone to believe that additional time thus made available would be used in a uniform fashion. Some members of Congress may use it to work on major bills, some to handle their own private affairs, some to give more attention to constituents. Second, it is often forgotten that the volume of legislative business which cannot possibly be reduced is growing so rapidly as to counterbalance any reductions of the legislative burden that could be effected in specific areas. Both American society and American government are becoming increasingly complex. This gives birth to growing pressures for new laws and changes in existing laws. Almost every law which is

[59] An interesting example of a document of this type is "Legislative Procedure in Kansas," published in 1946 by the Bureau of Government Research of the University of Kansas.

[60] Luce, *op. cit.*, p. 558.

[61] Report of the Joint Committee on the Organization of Congress, p. 24.

enacted is a compromise which in turn gives rise to the need for new adjustments and new compromises. Both quantitatively and qualitatively the outlook is clearly one of a major increase in the total legislative burden over the decades that lie ahead.

For those who aim at the elimination of minor bills and the concentration of legislative attention upon major issues only, the easy remedy appears to be a sweeping prohibition against the introduction of broad categories of legislative proposals. "Why not prohibit the introduction of all bills dealing with individual localities?" it is often asked. "Why not confine the introduction of bills to a given number of weeks or months?" Such sweeping proposals are as impractical as the suggestion that legislative initiative be monopolized by executive officials and congressional committees and denied to individual members of Congress. A more discriminating approach is essential.

The Legislative Reorganization Act of 1946 has already banned all bills for the construction of bridges across navigable streams, the correction of military or naval records, the payment of pensions, and tort claims under $1,000. This ban could well be expanded to include tort claims up to $10,000. The adjustment of immigration and deportation cases could be delegated to the Immigration and Naturalization Service and the issuance of land patents to one of the bureaus of the Department of the Interior. The major obstacle to this kind of reform probably lies in the fact that minor bills of this type provide opportunities for members of Congress to perform various favors for constituents and that many members of Congress are probably more interested in continuing to enjoy these opportunities than they are in any program to reduce the legislative burden. It should also be kept in mind that in many cases the prohibition of a certain type of legislation may merely transform a legislative burden into an administrative burden, with the offices of members of Congress being kept busy in arranging negotiations with executive officials to handle the same problems previously dealt with through private legislation.

On the other hand, anything which would take away from the Congress the responsibility of serving as a city council for the nation's capital would make a real contribution toward reducing the number of bills introduced and acted upon at every session. The majority of the proposals that have been presented on this subject aim at the delegation of legislative authority in one method or another to an elected city council. They usually provide that local ordinances enacted by the locally-elected city council will have the force of Federal law unless overthrown by a concurrent resolution of Congress or when ratified by a concurrent resolution of Congress. The most that can be said for proposals of this type is that they represent an important step toward home rule. They would not lift the burden of District legislation from the shoulders of Congress but merely lighten it. Under any arrangements of this type it is inevitable that those who are displeased with actions of the locally-elected council will appeal to members of Congress for the introduction of resolutions or bills which would redress their grievances.

The most direct way to relieve Congress of the burden of legislating for the nation's capital would be to cede the entire District of Columbia—with the possible exception of the Capitol Building, the White House, and the land in between—back to the State of Maryland.[62] Under this plan the city of Washington would govern itself in the same way as the city of Baltimore; and of course, it would no longer be Washington, District of Columbia, but Washington, Maryland. The only legislative matters relating to the District which would come before Congress would be those dealing with the construction or protection of Federal buildings in the city of Washington. The residents of Washington would be able to handle their local affairs for themselves as do the residents of any other city and would be able to have voting representatives in Congress and take part in Presidential elections.

Apart from the problem of the District of Columbia, there is little opportunity for other types of action to reduce the volume of local legislation. Not only are local pressures or local projects extremely strong, but they are in many cases inseparable from national problems. In fact, many of the most important national bills will prove, upon close examination, to be little more than instruments for dealing in some uniform manner with a large number of local projects.

The Length of Sessions

The Legislative Reorganization Act of 1946 provided that Congress should adjourn each year on July 31, unless a decision were made to postpone the date. The major argument offered in defense of early adjournment was that otherwise members would have insufficient time to keep in touch with their constituencies. Under present-day conditions, however, it is becoming increasingly clear that an early adjournment inevitably deprives members of Congress of the time needed to take care of their legislative duties and other congressional burdens. The volume of congressional business is so great that only continuous sessions can provide sufficient time. Year-round sessions would also help eliminate the congestion of bills that usually takes place at the end of the session, reduce the opportunities for success of filibusters, and in most cases do away with pocket vetoes. Nor would they in this day of modern transportation and communication prevent members of Congress from maintaining close contact with their constituents. Year-round sessions could easily be interspersed with a

[62] The seed for such a proposal can be found in the writings of Thomas Jefferson, who proposed that the Federal District be limited to a three-mile-square piece of territory rather than the ten-mile square authorized under the Constitution.

number of recesses to provide opportunities for relaxation, mending fences back home, campaigning, and the increasingly popular business of traveling throughout America and the world.

Codification and Revision

There have been many times in the historical development of various countries when the codification and revision of a country's laws have been acts of major political significance. The Corpus Juris Civitis of Justinian, the French *Code Napoléon,* and similar legal compilations have resulted from interest in unifying a nation or an empire, achieving a transition from judge-made law to statutory law, attaining a greater measure of legal stability, or enhancing the prestige of the code's sponsor.[63]

Today, codification and revision are more prosaic enterprises. Codification is of utility to the legislative draftsmen because it brings together past statutes in an orderly arrangement. Revisions serve to eliminate obsolete provisions, simplify language, resolve conflicts, or even fill minor gaps. Both are of use not only in the drafting of new laws, but also in the administrative and judicial processes connected with old laws.

The present United States Code, which consists of 50 titles enacted in 1926, is not an entirely formalized restatement of previous law. It was enacted as "prima-facie evidence" of the law rather than as the law itself, which can be found only in the Statutes at Large.[64]

It is often proposed, therefore, that the United States Code be enacted into positive law, thus making it unnecessary to refer back to individual statutes. However, a formal ratification of the Code would hardly be worth the effort unless a revision were accomplished at the same time. Accordingly the House Judiciary Committee (and its predecessor the House Committee on the Revision of the Laws) has attempted to prepare revisions of individual titles of the United States Code and to have them enacted one by one. As of 1951 eight titles were enacted into law.

The complexity of this has often led to the suggestion that the program be expedited by provision for additional staff facilities. For example, Representative Keogh testified before the Joint Committee on the Organization of Congress in support of a bill which would establish a special office of law-revision counsel in the House of Representatives. As a service to the appropriate

---

[63] For a trenchant critique of such codes see "The Age of Codification," in William Seagle, "The History of Law" (New York: Tudor, 1946), pp. 277–298.

[64] The United States Code is published by the West Publishing Co. and the Edward B. Thompson Co. and sold commercially. Every year since 1926 an annual cumulative supplement has been prepared which brings each of the volumes up to date. An annotated edition provides references to the relevant judicial decisions on each section.

committees of Congress, the function of the office of the law-revision counsel would be as follows:

(a) Examine all the public acts of Congress and submit recommendation to such committee for the repeal of obsolete, superfluous, and superseded provision of law contained therein; (b) prepare and submit to such committee a complete compilation, restatement, and revision of the general and permanent laws of the United States, one title at a time, which will conform to the understood policy, intent, and purpose of Congress in the original enactments with such amendments and corrections as will remove ambiguities, contradictions, and other imperfections both of substance and of form with the view of the enactment of each title as positive law. . . .[65]

The Joint Committee, however, felt that this function could be handled by the Office of the Legislative Counsel and recommended additional funds for this office.[66]

Nevertheless, the Office of the Legislative Counsel has been too busy with its regular duties to attempt any sustained work on problems of codification and revision, and it seems obvious that specialized staff resources are needed. Such resources should be provided for on a permanent basis, inasmuch as no revised code can ever be final.

However, staff facilities are not sufficient of themselves. When revisions are made, there is always the possibility that certain changes may be written into the law which unduly strengthen the position of some groups and weaken the position of other groups. It is for this reason that any revisions which attempted to go beyond the technical level and resolve major ambiguities and contradictions would be doomed to failure in advance. The reason that the United States Code of 1926 was not enacted into positive law was that many members of Congress were fearful lest they might find out some years later that unwittingly they had approved of changes which impaired the interests of important groups. This fear could be set to rest by extensive consultation with administrative agencies and private organizations, perhaps through a broadly representative commission for sponsoring revision measures.

Additional Comments

Although the Democrats lost the 1952 election, a number of liberal Democrats—with a bare handful of Republican supporters—decided to pay tribute to their party's pledge by trying to amend the cloture rule at the beginning of the Eighty-third Congress. On January 3, 1953, Senator Anderson of New Mexico submitted a motion "that this body take up for immediate consideration the

[65] Hearings before the Joint Committee on the Organization of Congress, p. 131.
[66] Report of the Joint Committee on the Organization of Congress, p. 12.

adoption of rules for the Senate of the Eighty-third Congress." [67] In defense of this motion Senator Anderson argued that the Senate is not—and should not be —a continuing body and that like the House of Representatives it should adopt new rules every two years. The purpose of the motion was to sweep aside the old rules, particularly the existing cloture rule, so that the Senate could then operate under general parliamentary procedure. It would then be possible to use the previous question (which is decided by majority vote) to curtail debate on the new rules, thus facilitating adoption of a tighter cloture rule.

The supporters of the motion had hoped that a point of order would be raised at once. Vice-President Barkley, who still had about two weeks to remain in office, might then rule the motion in order. The Vice-President, however, was never put to the test. After insisting that the Senate is a continuous body with a continuing set of rules, the new majority leader, Senator Taft, moved to lay Senator Anderson's motion on the table. The motion to table was carried by a resounding vote of 70 to 21.[68]

[67] *Congressional Record*, Jan. 3, 1953, p. 9.

[68] For a detailed presentation of the conflicting viewpoints on this question, see the brief prepared under the auspices of the 1952 Leadership Conference on Civil Rights, *Congressional Record*, Jan. 7, 1953, pp. 182–201, and the brief prepared by the Senate Republican Policy Committee, "Senate Rules and the Senate as a Continuing Body," *Congressional Record*, Jan. 7, 1953, pp. 165–178 (also printed as Sen. Doc. 4, 83d Cong., 1st Sess.).

PART III

CONCLUSION

Chapter 21

THE FUTURE OF THE LEGISLATIVE PROCESS

IN THE concluding chapter of a book dealing with government in America, there are a number of attractive opportunities confronting the author.

On the one hand, he can close with an eloquent peroration which summarizes the proposals for improvement which he himself advocates and in guarded terms suggest that the entire future of American democracy depends upon the fate of these proposals.

On the other hand, in more academic and less personal terms, he can summarize the pros and cons of the most important proposals that have been discussed and assign to the future the challenging task of deciding what shall be done.

But the first of these approaches would be more appropriate to a propaganda document, which this book could scarcely attempt to be. The second would run the risk of becoming pseudoobjective and overstatic.

Both, therefore, will be rejected. Instead, I shall close with a brief attempt to evaluate the dynamics of change in the processes of government, to appraise the special problems involved in campaigns for change in the legislative process, and to discuss the contributions of social scientists to the future of the legislative process.

THE DYNAMICS OF CHANGE

Prediction of the course of future change in the legislative process is necessarily a precarious and pretentious enterprise. However, some basic variables which will probably affect the future of the legislative process can be indicated: the broad sweep of change throughout all of American society, the production of specific proposals for change, and the social power behind such proposals.

The Broad Sweep of Social Change

If the history of the first decades of the twentieth century can be used as a partial guide, a number of probabilities and possibilities can be suggested concerning both short-range swings of the pendulum and underlying long-range trends.

On the international side, we can expect successive periods of international crisis and relapse—with the ever-present possibility of a new World War. On the domestic front, we can expect recurring ups and downs in economic activity —with the possibility that increasing armaments and foreign aid may use so much of our resources as to abolish the specter of large-scale unemployment and intensify the prospect of recurring shortages and inflation. The signs suggest that accelerated advances in technology will make the Industrial Revolution of the nineteenth century look like a mere dash of surf preceding a massive wave. This, in turn, should accelerate the industrialization of the relatively underdeveloped regions, the mechanization of farms, and the urbanization of rural areas.

Another long-range trend holds forth the double promise of new heights in the level of education, with illiteracy abolished, a growing percentage of the population obtaining a college education, and new achievements realized in mass communication through television, radio, motion pictures, the press, and transport.

A number of observations can also be made concerning the major contestants in the legislative struggle. The probability is that private organizations will extend their scope and that increasing power will be concentrated in the hands of dominant groups. For industrial and white-collar labor, this means the further extension of unions. For business and industrial enterprise, it means further growth in mergers, monopolies, monopolistic arrangements, trade associations, and farm associations. There is no reason to assume that any will fail to intensify efforts to use government as an instrument for obtaining their objectives. The extension of industrialization, unionization, and education will also create opportunities for the development of more two-party rivalry in the South and other one-party areas in the United States. Rivalry between business and labor organizations may create situations in which sharper socioeconomic distinctions will be drawn between the coalitions comprising the two major parties.

In government, the long-range outlook seems to favor continued expansion of executive agencies and stronger Federal government as compared with state and local governments on the one hand and the realm of private action on the other. The dominant role in the Federal government's handling of various issues will continue to shift back and forth between executive officials and members of Congress, with the Justices of the Supreme Court, on occasion, adjusting the driver's seat. We can look forward to periods of reform in the social structure and to periods of conservatism.

With the United States playing a larger part in world affairs, an ever-increasing number of issues will arise that can be settled only at the international level. Whether these settlements are made through *ad hoc* diplomatic negotiations, through a loose consultative body like the United Nations, or through a stronger world organization, they will tend to influence the character of policy decisions taken at the national level and to convert national policy making into a subordinate process. Developments of this type will tend to set certain limits within which changes in the processes of government will take place, or, to put it in other terms, they will provide basic materials from which changes in the legislative process will be molded.

The Production of Proposals for Change

There is an important distinction between normative judgments and proposals for change. Every proposal implies a judgment that the *status quo* is not good enough. But every judgment that things might be better does not result in proposals for making them better. In some areas one can find a plentiful supply of suggested remedies, in others a shortage of remedies, and everywhere an abundance of descriptive analyses and of diagnoses.

Negative Approaches. One can be a good music critic without knowing how to write a sonata. In the same way, one can be skilled at describing or finding fault with the legislative process without having either the inclination or the talent to produce proposals for change. In his "Process of Government," for example, Bentley produced an invaluable description of the legislative process. But he limited himself to an explanation and did not attempt a critique. In "Congressional Government," Woodrow Wilson produced a brilliant attack upon congressional operations as he saw them. But, after tilting with the constitutional separation between Congress and the executive branch and pointing out that "the Constitution is not honored by blind worship," he stopped short, barely wetting his toes in the waters of constitutional reconstruction and leaving it for others to jump in to make the proposals for which his own writing prepared a foundation.

Although the negative approach is in part a matter of temperament, the roots of negativism and neutralism go deeper. They are nourished by unsureness. The reflective analyst is often so aware of the difficulties to be surmounted and so doubtful as to the adequacy of what he might propose that he stops short at description and critique. They feed upon cynicism, which itself is often a reflex resulting from an excess of idealism. The idealist, finding out what some aspects of group life can be like, may come to the conclusion that all reform should be left to others who are more innocent about the stubborn realities. He may then confine himself to the task of wielding a scathing analytical scalpel and leaving the body politic exposed to the view of the shocked student and the occasional reader.

Finally, a negative approach may be expected from those whose standards lead them to endorse the *status quo* or accept it without challenge. In times of social quiescence or in times of national emergency when the ordinary pressures of life compel the postponement of thoughts of change, negativism is usually in the ascendancy.

Positive Approaches. Personal temperament is clearly an important factor in the production of proposals for change. For some minds, the development of such proposals offers a fascinating intellectual exercise, like playing chess. It is an exercise that can give one a tremendous sense of power; for, on paper at least, one can build and rebuild the world at pleasure. It can also provide a form of escapism, particularly for those who specialize in the intricacies of institutional gadgetry. It can be a means of talking and acting constructively without direct involvement in conflicts that wound. It is a method of participating in social combat without letting down one's guard. Being for "good government" is as safe as being against sin.

In times of intense national stress, when great shifts of power are imminent or taking place, formal relationships inside and outside government must also be readjusted. Proposals for institutional reform not only provide rational patterns for readjustment but also serve as rallying points around which the major contestants in the social combat can organize their forces. At such times there is always a market for the ideas or services of men and women who can produce the ideas and techniques that meet the needs of particular groups and individual leaders.

The Power behind Specific Proposals

The power of ideas for change in the processes of government should not be minimized. "One person with a belief in a social power is equal to ninety-nine who have only interests," observed John Stuart Mill. "They who can succeed in creating a general persuasion that a certain form of government, or social fact of any kind, deserves to be preferred, have made nearly the most important step which can possibly be taken towards ranging the powers of society on its side." [1]

Many ideas, of course, have no impact at all. The difference between the powerful idea and the weak idea is that the former is one having greater appeal to various interests and is thus more closely bound up with the processes of organizing group support. To enlarge upon Mill's formula, one person with a belief, when supported by ninety-nine with interests to whom this particular belief appeals, can develop social power equal to a thousand separate individuals who have distinct beliefs or interests.

In short, proposals for change in the legislative process are much like

[1] John Stuart Mill, "Considerations on Representative Government" (New York: Macmillan, 1947), p. 117.

legislative bills in that their chances of success depend upon the campaigns waged for and against them. No idea for improvement in the legislative process can have any effect unless it seems attractive enough to have a campaign built around it and unless there are people who develop this campaign.

Sometimes a new twist to an old idea is all that is needed to tap new sources of support and harness new sources of energy behind a campaign effort. Sometimes when new twists or totally new ideas are launched, what is really needed is a new and better approach to sources of support. For instance, efforts to prevent the automatic selection of committee chairmen in accordance with seniority do not need some dramatic new substitute for the seniority principle but rather the organization of sufficient support to force departures of one sort or another from the seniority principle. At some point this necessarily entails a choice between alternative "departures." But an effective choice cannot be made in abstract terms. It must fit into the strategy and tactics of a given campaign.

CAMPAIGNS FOR CHANGE

A variety of motivations is needed for the development of a meaningful campaign for changes in governmental processes. This diversity is usually blended in varying proportions in the minds of campaign leaders. The campaigns themselves follow closely along the lines of any campaign for enactment of a legislative measure. However, such aspects as the choice of objectives, the development of support, and the character of defeats and victories merit special attention.

Objectives

There is hardly a limit to the number of variations and combinations of proposals for change in the legislative process. But there are very substantial limits to the number of objectives behind which any given campaign can be organized. None can cover too much territory. Available resources must be used sparingly, not scattered profusely in the effort to obtain action on a relatively coherent program. A truly comprehensive program can be little more than a stock pile of ideas from which campaign objectives can be drawn from time to time. The more fully and ably developed these ideas are, the more opportunely and successfully can they be selected for use.

As with the drafting of a bill, there is always the problem of how high to set one's sights. To set an objective which requires too great a change from present reality may be to indulge in daydreaming and to mislead supporters into needless activities. On the other hand, too much "realism" can lead to cynicism or smugness. The motto "Make no small plans" often has practical justification.

A high or difficult objective may be useful in evoking support. It may leave
more leeway for bargaining and compromise. Moreover, feasibilities cannot be
judged in a routine, mechanical manner. A shift in circumstances and the improbable may suddenly be converted into the possible. With the passage of
time, the wild-eyed dream may become a highly practical, and indeed moderate, reform.

At times, a paradoxical situation occurs in that, on the one hand, a proposal
for change may be impossible to put into effect unless and until there is a marked
shift in power between contending forces. On the other hand, if the needed
shift in power were to take place, there might no longer be any interest in acting upon the proposed change. This is another way of saying that, when substantive objectives are attained, the support for procedural or organizational
reforms that would have contributed to their attainment may no longer be
pressed with the same enthusiasm. Yet in some cases the proposed procedural
changes will continue to be supported, as a method of consolidating advantages
already won.

Another problem is how concretely or specifically an objective should be
stated. An abstract principle is hard for many people to understand. A new
"gadget," on the other hand, may have great symbolic value. The fact that it is
specific may make it easier to understand. If elaborated upon, people may
more readily visualize how it will operate. If the details provoke controversy,
that also may be an advantage because it brings it to the attention of more
people and makes potential supporters out of those critics whose views are
accepted. On the other hand, the details of a specific proposal will often be
subject to considerable evolution. As a guide to the shifts in detail, therefore,
it is always helpful to accompany a specific device with a full statement of the
purposes it is supposed to achieve.

Support

The marketing of an idea for changes in governmental processes is fraught
with difficulties. Hope for awakening interest in governmental improvement
is often pinned on "the responsible, the alert, the active, the informed, and
the confident men and women in the street." [2] Yet these citizens often may
be puzzled, confused, misinformed, ignorant, disinterested, or groggy from
the multiplicity of problems impinging upon them. Or they may be interested
in other matters. "Opinion is in most countries too much absorbed with the
economic and social aims to which legislation should be directed," wrote
Bryce a number of decades ago, "to give due attention to legislative methods." [3]

[2] Barbara Wootton, "Freedom under Planning" (Chapel Hill, N.C.: University of North
Carolina Press, 1945), p. 180.
[3] James Bryce, "Modern Democracies" (New York: Macmillan, 1921), Vol. II, p. 356.

Many practical men and women who play leading roles in public affairs are so preoccupied with the specifics of substantive action that discussion of change in governmental processes brings them into a realm where they feel out of place and unprepared to judge. Moreover, a good measure of wariness enters the picture because "No man can be sure that he may not be the victim tomorrow of that by which he may be a gainer today." [4] Nor can he be sure that he may not be the immediate victim of that which has been proposed as causing loss to none.

These difficulties can rarely be overcome without direct, though not necessarily public, appeals to various groups on the hard ground of self-interest. It is for this reason that Burns concludes that if significant congressional reform can ever come "it will doubtless be part of a great popular movement to achieve certain social ends, rather than an isolated effort to improve Congress." [5] This was certainly the case with the 1910 revolt against the powers of the Speaker of the House; the motive power for the anti-Cannon campaign came from the rising forces of social and economic liberalism. Such appeals to various groups can sometimes, particularly with more modest proposals, bring together interests that are usually opposed. When the impact of a proposal is blurred by its very nature or by what is said about it, there is more opportunity to unite divergent groups. Support for the Legislative Reorganization Act of 1946, for example, in addition to being forthcoming from political scientists and publicists interested mainly in abstract principles, was obtained from both conservative and liberal members of Congress, from liberal-reform organizations, and from a number of conservative organizations, the latter particularly appreciative of the economizing potentialities in the legislative budget and favoring a stronger Congress as a means of combating certain liberal tendencies in the executive branch.

Defeats and Victories

As with campaigns on behalf of legislative proposals, efforts to win changes in the legislative process can rarely end in a complete victory. This is inherent in the bargaining nature of the process of change. It also stems from the fact that propaganda to create enthusiastic support invariably gives rise to exaggerated expectations sure to be frustrated if "victory" ever comes.

Moreover, organizational and procedural changes are tools that can be used for a variety of purposes. When they are put to unsuspected uses, those who fought to bring them into existence may conclude that they had created a Frankenstein. Or, such changes, once put into action, may prove to have a blunt cutting edge and to be of little consequence. "It is those who magnify

---

[4] Federalist Papers.

[5] James M. Burns, "Congress on Trial" (New York: Harper, 1949), p. 140.

gadgets," writes T. V. Smith, "and seek to cure the grudges that attend their malfunctioning who will be disappointed at any and every reorganization of Congress." [6]

The degree to which the outcome of a campaign is regarded as victory or defeat will depend on many factors. One's interest in future combat may lead to exaggeration of the progress already made in order to prevent a sense of defeatism among supporters or to exaggeration of defeats sustained in order to arouse antagonism toward opponents. More broadly, the judgment of defeat or victory will depend upon one's historical perspective and upon the links in the chain of events which one regards as the main objective. Bolles, for example, describes the 1910–1911 curbing of Speaker Cannon's powers as a revolution which freed "the house, the President, the party, and the country from the control of a despot." [7] In reviewing Bolles's book, V. O. Key takes issue with this judgment on the ground that in effect these curbs destroyed an instrument of party leadership.

Norris and his insurgents could join with the Democrats to deflate the Speaker, but they could not manage the House. Uncle Joe dared the new "majority" to elect a Speaker and to assume responsibility for legislative leadership. They could not do it; and by the "revolution" they destroyed the machinery they might use if and when they became a genuine majority.[8]

But from the perspective of substantive political action, Key's verdict— sound though it may be in the abstract context of governmental forms—seems somewhat narrow. After all, the objectives of the anti-Cannon alliance included, in addition to changes in the House rules, reform of the tariff laws, enactment of a constitutional amendment authorizing income taxes, and other liberal measures. The curbing of Cannonism contributed to the attaining of these objectives and was also a factor in the Democratic march to victory at the polls in 1912 and the oncoming of Wilson's new era. From this viewpoint, it was an operation aimed at removing an obstacle to substantive objectives and was unquestionably a victory.

Sometimes, as a result of untiring efforts, a series of repeated defeats can end in victory. In 1790, for example, a group of Southern Senators started a campaign to require the Senate to open its sessions to the public. The House had set up spectator galleries at its first session in 1789. But the Senate, probably on the ground that its dignity and protection from popular pressure would be enhanced thereby, kept its proceedings secret. Even members of the House were excluded from the Senate's sessions. The Southerners found that in the

[6] T. V. Smith, Review of "Congress at the Crossroads," *Saturday Review of Literature,* Vol. 29, 1946, p. 12.

[7] Blair Bolles, "Tyrant from Illinois: Uncle Joe Cannon's Experiment with Personal Power" (New York: Norton, 1951), p. 224.

[8] *New Republic,* June 4, 1951, p. 18.

secrecy of the Senate, the Federalists would be better able to put across Hamiltonian measures. They believed that with open sessions it would be easier for them to organize a more vigorous opposition to the Federalists. The struggle started in April, 1790, when the two Senators from Virginia moved that the doors of the Senate be opened to the public. When the question was put, only three Senators voted for the resolution. In 1791 the effort was made again, with the leadership this time in the hands of Senator James Monroe of Virginia. Again, the result was failure—but this time nine Senators voted for open sessions, with seventeen supporting secrecy. In 1792 Monroe tried again and failed again, with the opposition at seventeen and the proponents dwindling to eight. By 1793 the issue of open Senate sessions had become still more popular in the South. But increased Southern support led to a decrease in the support that had previously been obtained from Northern Senators. In 1794 another resolution was introduced. In the meantime the Senate agreed to open its doors during the debate on the question of the seating of Albert Gallatin. When the experiment was concluded and it became evident that public sessions were not as fearsome as they had been described by some, the Senate then decided by a vote of 19 to 8 to have public galleries built and to admit spectators at the next session.

The first public sessions were held in 1795. Yet the Senate refused to provide suitable accommodations for reporters. A new struggle ensued and it was not until 1802, twelve years after the original campaign had started, that adequate provision was made for allowing the public to be informed about action on the Senate floor.[9]

In contrast with this memorable example of the fruits of persistence, the passage of time invariably deprives victory of its savor. Any "final" reform is out of the question. John Dewey writes:

No matter what the present success in straightening out difficulties and harmonizing conflicts, it is certain that problems will recur in the future in a new form or on a different plane. Indeed, every genuine accomplishment, instead of winding up an affair and enclosing it as a jewel in a casket for future contemplation, complicates the practical situation. . . . There is something pitifully juvenile in the idea that "evolution," "progress," means a definite sum of accomplishment which will forever stay done, and which by an exact amount lessens the amount still to be done, disposing once and for all of just so many perplexities and advancing us just so far on our road to a final stable and unperplexed goal. . . .[10]

[9] This account is based on a fascinating article by Elizabeth G. McPherson, "The Southern States and the Reporting of Senate Debates, 1789–1802," *Journal of Southern History,* Vol. 12, No. 2, May, 1946. This action, however, did not apply to executive sessions for the consideration of Presidential nominations. It was not until 1929, after many decades of controversy, that these sessions were also opened to the public.

[10] John Dewey, "Human Nature and Conduct" (New York: Holt, 1944), pp. 284–285.

SOCIAL SCIENTISTS AND SOCIAL CHANGE

In previous chapters this writer has tried to deflate pretentious conceptions of the role of social scientists in the process of social change. He has criticized the idea that there can be absolute standards by which governmental forms may be evaluated and has shown that skilled observers may disagree in their judgments of what is good or bad and in their prescriptions for improvement. He has also taken issue with the theory that experts of one variety or another can displace social conflict by some mystic application of science and intelligence, for the resources mobilized behind specific ideas for change depend upon the interests to which these ideas appeal and the amount of support which they are given.

Despite these limitations upon the effectiveness of their work, social scientists should be urged to give more intensive and sustained attention to proposals for change. A review of the proposals discussed in this volume indicates more variety than quality. Many are little more than off-the-cuff suggestions for future thought. Many have never been developed in sufficient detail to be actionable. Few have been carefully analyzed on the basis of a study of the most relevant facts concerning the *status quo* or tested in terms of their probable impact upon the distribution of power. Few efforts have been made to bring separate proposals together into a systematic framework. This is partly the result of a casual, dilettante attitude toward social change and a gnawing cynicism that stifles imagination and undermines sustained creative effort.

Is it an exaggerated conception of the role of social scientists to ask that they give more vigorous and sustained efforts to the production and analyses of proposals for change? The well-adjusted social scientists need not be chagrined at the idea that their conclusions may be something less than apocalyptic revelations, that they cannot themselves bring order out of conflict, and that their power lies in the support they receive. Some can function creatively only when they see themselves at the center of the universe. Perhaps it is better to permit such personalities the luxury of their delusions. It is a simple truism that one man with a mission can contribute more to the march of human thought than a score of cynics who "know" how little a single mind can accomplish and are resolved to prove the accuracy of their knowledge by their collective inertia. That nation which protects and develops its "men with missions," is likely to enjoy the most abundant fruits of human initiative and creativity.

A more wholehearted entry by social scientists into the field of remedial action could have many effects. First, it could serve to enrich the study of "what is." Only when people have reason to believe that their inquiries may serve some purpose can they amass the time and energy needed for intensive descriptive studies. Little stock is to be placed in the notion that facts need or can be gathered in the name of fact gathering alone. Second, it would inevitably lead more and more toward taking sides in the great social issues of the day. This is all to the good. Meaningful research and effective teaching can be handled best by men and women who are in touch with the currents that energize American society. Great theories can be born only from participation in great social developments. To rewrite a phrase of Karl Mannheim, the socially-attached intelligentsia can "play the part of watchmen in what otherwise would be a pitch-black night." [11]

Finally, such participation by social scientists may encourage a move away from overspecialization. No problem in social change is something that can be neatly classified as a problem in political science, jurisprudence, social psychology, public administration, economics, or sociology. These terms refer to specialized tools, many of which are needed to deal effectively with any problem of social change. To argue that any one set of tools may suffice to handle the complexities of social conflict is to prepare the way for stultification.[12] It has become standard practice to seek a bridge for the chasm between overspecialized disciplines by bringing assorted specialists together in joint teaching and research ventures. This has undoubted merit, just as a growth in the tourist trade might contribute to better international understanding. But it is only a fragmentary approach. Joint action by specialists can never be very fruitful without a merger or synthesis of the social-sciences disciplines at the level of general theories of social action. Only through the development of comprehensive and competing theories of social action can all the available tools of analysis, measurement, and judgment be brought to bear upon problems of social change.

This emphasis on theory does not suggest the abandonment of a practical approach. In fact, the more adequate the theory one has, the more satisfactory the analysis of practicalities. The social sciences attain their highest performance at the point where theory and practice merge and realism and idealism can be fused into a meaningful guide to action.

[11] Karl Mannheim, "Ideology and Utopia" (New York: Oxford, 1936), p. 143. Mannheim assigns this part to the socially "unattached." But these are the modern Cassandras; unattached they are also unnoticed. "Guardianship," as stated at the end of Chap. 2, "comes from the affiliations of the guardians—and from the process of social combat itself."

[12] The result of overspecialization may be even worse: "By way of introducing the specialist as a psychological problem, I should like to refer to an accident that occurred several years ago in a system of caves in one of our Southern states. A professional geologist, who had set out to explore the formation of rocks and their enclosures was found dead near the entrance to which he had been unable to make his way back. Traces of his footsteps told of endless, circular, and repetitive wanderings which at many points had come close to the sunlight, never to reach it. The circle this particular specialist described proved fatal to himself, which was strange in view of the fact that he had been a cave explorer for years and was not unfamiliar with the area where death overtook him. He had concentrated on the composition, the texture, and the stratification of rocks as keys to their genesis: he had paid little attention, it appeared, to their topology. . . ." Ulrich Sonneman, "The Specialist as a Psychological Problem," *Social Research*, March, 1951.

INDEX

A

Absenteeism in voting, 384–385
Acheson, Dean, 293
Adams, John, 98, 362, 407
Adams, John Quincy, 385, 408
Adamson Eight-Hour Law, 258
Administrative process, congressional par-
  ticipation in, 135–141
  and legislative process, 131–141, 154–161
  scope of, 131–135
Aeronautical Chamber of Commerce, 186
Agar, Herbert, 73–74
Agricultural Adjustment Act of 1933, 164,
  291, 322, 326, 354
Agriculture, Department of, 155, 168, 233
Aiken, Senator, 277
Albright, Robert C., 332n.
Aldrich, Senator, 313, 315
Aleksandrov, G. F., 70–71
Alexander, De Alva S., 322n., 338n.
Allen, Robert S., 258n., 261n., 401n.
Allport, Floyd Henry, 17n.
Amendments, 218–222, 352–356
American Arbitration Association, 186
American Association of State Highway Of-
  ficials, 108
American Bankers' Association, 236
American Bar Association, 21
American Farm Bureau Federation, 236,
  254
American Federation of Labor (A.F.L.), 24,
  147, 238, 263, 276, 418
American Jewish Congress, 341, 416
American Legion, 253
American Medical Association (A.M.A.), 21,
  47, 228–229, 233, 287
American Petroleum Institute, 301
American Political Science Association, 21
  (See also Committee, on Congress, on
  Political Parties, on Reapportionment
  of Congress)
American Trucking Association, Inc., 292
Americans for Democratic Action, 21
Anderson, Dewey, 413

Appropriation bills, difference in, from other
  bills, 106
  proposals concerning, 436–440
Arlington County, 307, 401
Army Corps of Engineers, 104, 238, 393
Arnold, Thurman, 57n., 365n.
Arthur, President, 430
Atlantic Charter, 157, 207
Atomic-energy legislation, 8, 183, 203, 249n.,
  264, 280–281, 288, 304, 310, 317, 318

B

Bagehot, Walter, 121, 124
Bailey, Stephen K., 13, 182, 185n., 187, 234n.,
  243, 272n., 294n., 302, 436n.
Bailey, Thomas A., 134n.
Ball, Senator, 311
Ball-Burton-Hatch-Hill Resolution, 184
Bank of the United States, 399
Banking Act of 1935, 236
Barkley, Alben, 162, 168, 328, 397, 409n.
Barnard, Chester, 146n.
Baruch, Bernard, 250
Beaman, Middleton, 187, 188, 214–215
Beard, Charles A., 64n., 130, 158n.
Bentham, Jeremy, 191, 214, 218
Bentley, Arthur F., 4, 5, 7, 13, 100, 103, 150,
  177–178, 451
Benton, Senator Thomas, 386
Benton, Senator William, 45
Berdahl, Clarence A., 408n.
Bierstadt, Robert, 142n., 143n.
Binkley, Wilfred, 59n., 103
Black, Henry Campbell, 427
Black, Senator, 24, 262
Blaisdell, Donald, 33
Blough, Roy, 190, 202n., 246–247, 310n.,
  312n., 355
Boileau, Representative, 326
Bolles, Blair, 456
Bone, Senator, 130
Bonus March, 260
Borah, Senator, 219
Bowles, Chester, 219

461

MUNICIPAL ADMINISTRATION
IN THE ROMAN EMPIRE

MUNICIPAL ADMINISTRATION
IN THE ROMAN EMPIRE

BY

FRANK FROST ABBOTT
Late Kennedy Professor of Latin, Princeton University

AND

ALLAN CHESTER JOHNSON
Professor of Classics, Princeton University

NEW YORK / RUSSELL & RUSSELL

FIRST PUBLISHED IN 1926 BY PRINCETON UNIVERSITY PRESS
REISSUED, 1968, BY RUSSELL & RUSSELL
A DIVISION OF ATHENEUM PUBLISHERS, INC.
BY ARRANGEMENT WITH PRINCETON UNIVERSITY PRESS
L. C. CATALOG CARD NO: 68-25670
PRINTED IN THE UNITED STATES OF AMERICA

The studies set forth in this volume were first planned by Professor Frank Frost Abbott in 1914. In collaboration with the present writer the work was carried on with many interruptions under the general editorship of Professor Abbott until his death, July 23, 1924. For his kindly criticisms and generous help I shall always remain profoundly grateful.

The municipal institutions of the Roman Empire contain in large measure the secret of the vitality and the decay of that ancient civilization which controlled the destinies of the world for a longer span than any imperial power whose history has yet been recorded. For this reason it has been our aim to trace the history of the relations of these municipalities to Rome, their differing status, the development of Roman policy towards them, and the circumstances attending their decline, and therefore the decline of the empire. These matters and certain others clearly relating to them are set forth systematically in the Introduction. In this portion of the book we have made a study of the juridical and fiscal relations to Rome of communities of various classes, of the political organization and financial systems of these communities, of the attempts which were made to combine them into larger political entities through the provincial assemblies, of the development of the municipal policy of Rome, and the decline of the municipality.

The last chapter, on municipal documents, may serve as a technical introduction to Part ɪɪ of the book, in which are brought together inscriptions and papyri that throw light on the relations which the municipalities bore to Rome. These documents have hitherto been so widely scattered that it was thought advisable to gather them together in order that those interested in municipal institutions might be able to gain a first-hand comprehensive survey of the problems involved in their study. No collection of this kind exists and the information which such a corpus provides is definite and accurate. The lower limit of time for this collection has been set at the end of the third century, for the reason that most constitutions antedate the fourth century and the influences which determined the course of events are clearly discernible in the earlier period. Moreover, it would be impossible to deal fully with the Byzantine period without doubling the compass of the book.

It has been the aim of the editors to include all inscriptions which furnish information of importance bearing upon the relations of Rome to her municipalities. Very fragmentary inscriptions and those which gave no information, known from documents already included, have been omitted. In the case of the documents from Egypt our choice has been limited more especially to the more important and representative papyri dealing with the towns and villages from the Roman occupation to the beginning of the Byzantine period.

In general it should be stated for the purpose of defining the work of the two collaborators, that Mr Abbott directed his attention to conditions in the West, and the present writer to those in the East. This means, practically, that the former is primarily responsible for the Latin inscriptions and for the commentaries on them, and the latter for the Greek and bilingual inscriptions, the papyri, and the commentaries on the documents of these three classes. The authorship of each chapter in the Introduction is indicated in the Table of Contents. The manuscript of Mr Abbott's portion was fortunately in final form, and is here published with slight editorial revision.

In view of the cost of printing, critical notes have been reduced to a minimum, typographical devices in the texts

have been used as sparingly as possible, and in the Latin
inscriptions in particular deviations from the text of a stone
or tablet have been indicated simply by the use of italic
letters. In the text of the papyri indications of obscure or
doubtful letters by the customary convention have been
omitted, but in all cases where the interpretation of a
document depends upon the reading, the fact has been
indicated in the commentary.

In conclusion, thanks are due to Professor John W.
Basore for reading the manuscript; to Professor Paul R.
Coleman-Norton for undertaking the arduous task of
verifying references and reading proof; to Professor D. M.
Robinson for furnishing in advance of publication his text
and commentary on the inscription discovered by him at
Antioch; to Professor Edward Capps for his generous
and helpful interest in these studies; and finally, to the
Secretary and staff of the Cambridge University Press for
their unfailing courtesy and care.

ALLAN CHESTER JOHNSON

PRINCETON
March 20, 1926

CONTENTS

PART I

PART II

PART I

INTRODUCTION

CHAPTER I

COLONIAE AND MUNICIPIA[1]

LONG before the republic came to an end Rome had placed the different communities which had been brought under her control in five or six well defined categories, according to their political status. But these distinctions do not hold for the earliest settlements or acquisitions of territory outside the physical limits of the city. The little market-towns which sprang up in early days on Roman territory had no separate political existence, and those who lived in them enjoyed no political rights or privileges because of their residence in them. Even Ostia had no local magistrates at the outset[2]. It was a part of the city-state of Rome. In other words Rome did not recognize the possibility of local self-government in any community dependent upon her or under her suzerainty.

This policy was violated when Rome took certain communities under her control, but allowed them to retain some part of their previous sovereignty. She adopted the new practice for the first time, according to tradition, in the case of Antium, whose people were made up partly of Roman colonists and partly of earlier settlers[3]. Livy tells

[1] The early chapters of this Introduction are intended to present in outline the characteristic features of the different classes of municipalities under the Roman government, and to observe the changes in the political status of these towns or in the method of founding them which we notice in passing from one period to another, or from one part of the Roman world to another. It should be observed, however, that no description can be given which will be applicable to all the members of a class, because they did not all enjoy identical rights and privileges. Some of the differences between towns of the same class in the matter of autonomy will be discussed in the commentaries on the several inscriptions.

[2] Cf. Mommsen, St. R. 3, 775.

[3] Mommsen, St. R. 3, 778; Kornemann, R.E. 4, 585.

[3]

us: Antiatibus quoque, qui se sine legibus certis, sine magistratibus agere querebantur, dati ab senatu ad iura statuenda ipsius coloniae patroni. Communities of this sort had their own charters, and elected magistrates took the place of the prefects heretofore sent out by Rome. Local pride probably played a part in bringing about this change, and a desire to retain as much as possible of the old institutions and customs of the place, and the feeling that residents could administer the affairs of a village better than nonresidents. Whether Rome thought it a wise policy to yield to these pleas for self-government, or whether she followed the line of least resistance, it is hard to say.

At all events the way was open for the incorporation into the Roman state of communities possessing some measure of local autonomy. Such a political unit was called a *civitas*, whether it took the form of a city or not, whereas the term *oppidum* was used only of a city. The free use of the word *civitas* for Roman as well as for non-Roman communities begins in the second century of our era[1]. Before that time it was usually applied to native communities only, while those of Roman origin were styled *coloniae* or *municipia*. It is convenient for us to make this early distinction in the present discussion.

Colonies were cities or villages made up of settlers sent out by Rome[2]. They fell into two classes, *coloniae civium Romanorum* and *coloniae Latinorum*, according to the political rights of the settlers and the status of the colony. The founding of a colony was a sovereign act, and, therefore, under the early republic it was effected by a *lex*, while under the empire it was the prerogative of the emperor. Before the period of the revolution the establish-

[1] Kornemann, *R.E. Suppl. Erstes Heft*, 302 *f.*
[2] Much use has been made in this discussion of colonies of Kornemann's excellent article *colonia* in *R.E.* 4, 511 *ff.* Other important articles are de Ruggiero, *Diz. Ep.* 2, 415 *ff.*; Lenormant, *Dict. Dar.* 1. 1303 *ff.*; Mommsen, *St. R.* 3 *passim*; Marquardt, *St. Verw.* 1 *passim*; Abbott, *Class. Phil.* 10 (1915), 365 *ff.*

[4]

ment of a colony called for the enactment of a special law
by the popular assembly. This law specified the location
of the colony, and the amount of state-land to be assigned,
fixed the number of commissioners entrusted with the duty
of making the settlement, and determined their duties. A
typical instance of the method of founding a colony is the
case of Antium[1]. In the period of transition, Sulla, Caesar,
and the triumvirs did not trouble themselves to secure the
passage of a special law, but acted by virtue of the general
powers given to them. Thus Urso is styled a *colonia iussu
C. Caesaris dictatoris deducta*[2]. Octavius, Antony, and
Lepidus based their right to found colonies on the *lex
Titia*, which established the triumvirate. When this
transfer of authority had come about, of course the new
sovereign named the commissioners, as the people had
done in earlier days. It was the duty of the commissioners
to lead the colonists out, settle them upon the land, establish the form of government, and nominate the first
incumbents of office. The colonists were given conquered
land set aside for the purpose.

The settlers in a Roman colony were Roman citizens,
with an occasional admixture of *socii*, and in Italy they had
full right of ownership in their land (*ex iure Quiritium*), and
the Roman settlers enjoyed all the other public and private
rights of Roman citizens, except in the matter of holding
Roman magistracies. In the enjoyment of this privilege
they were for a time restricted[3]. When Roman colonies
in the later period were established in the provinces, the
land was usually left subject to the burdens of other provincial land.

The Latin differed from the Roman colonies in size,
composition, and political status. Three hundred was the
normal number sent out to a Roman colony[4], rarely as
many as 2000 or 3000[5], while Latin colonies usually

[1] Livy, 3. 1. 5–7.   [2] *Cf.* no. 26, chap. 106.
[3] *Cf.* no. 11.   [4] *Cf. e.g.* Livy, 8. 21. 11.
[5] *Cf.* Livy, 39. 55; 41. 13.

[5]

numbered several thousand[1]. The majority of those who were sent out to a Latin colony were Latins or Italian allies, but Romans who were willing to accept Latin in place of their Roman citizenship were also enrolled. The Latin colonies of the early period bore the same relation to Rome that the members of the Latin League had held. They were free from the payment of tribute. They had the right of coinage. They had their own magistrates and laws, and they enjoyed the same private rights as Roman citizens[2]. On the other hand, while the settlers in the early Roman colonies were excused from regular military service, each Latin colony was required to furnish a military contingent to serve in the *alae* or *cohortes*. However, the twelve Latin colonies which were founded after 268 B.C. suffered a diminution in their privileges. They lost the right of coinage and the *ius conubii*, and they found it more difficult to obtain Roman citizenship[3]. Still another change in the situation came about in 89 B.C., for by virtue of the grant of Roman citizenship to the Italians in this year, all Latin colonies south of the Po were transformed into Roman *municipia*. In the same year the cities in Transpadane Gaul were given the rights of Latin citizenship, to be transformed in 49 B.C. into those of Roman citizenship. Consequently Latin colonies henceforth disappear from the peninsula.

In Italy and the provinces the Latin colonies numbered about sixty-one, and the Roman colonies, about three hundred and eighty-one[4]. The earliest colonies were established as military outposts to hold and Romanize newly acquired territory. The most characteristic feature of the Roman colonies was the fact that they were established on the coast. This practice was followed without exception until 183 B.C., when the rule was broken by sending

---

[1] *Cf.* Livy, 10. 1. 1–2.
[2] Mommsen, *St. R.* 3, 627 *ff.*
[3] Kornemann, *R.E.* 4, 518; *cf.*, however, Steinwenter, *R.E.* 10, 1267 *f.*
[4] Kornemann, *R.E.* 4, 514 *ff.*; v. Premerstein, *R.E.* 10, 1240.

Roman colonies to Mutina, Parma, and Saturnia. A change in the motives which led to the founding of colonies appears under the Gracchi, who used colonization for the purpose of relieving the needy population of Rome, of promoting the prosperity of the country districts, and of stimulating trade. The admission of the proletariat to the army by Marius naturally led him to found colonies for needy veterans. A step which looked to this change in policy had been taken as early as 171 B.C. in the case of Carteia in Spain, which was settled by the sons born of Roman soldiers and Spanish women. The precedent thus set at Carteia, and taken up by Marius, of providing for veterans in colonies, was freely followed by the triumvirs and under the empire.

Narbo Martius, established in Gallia Narbonensis in 118 B.C., is the first clear instance of a colony outside the peninsula of Italy, a precedent which was not fully accepted until we come to the time of Caesar and the triumvirs, under whom between forty and fifty such settlements were made in the provinces[1]. Under the empire this policy was gradually discontinued. From the time of Hadrian almost all the new colonies in the provinces were not newly established settlements, but existing *municipia* or native *civitates* to which the title and rights of a colony were given by the emperor. This change in status was usually in the provinces the first step towards the acquisition of Latin rights and of immunity from the payment of tribute[2].

The change which the republican system of nomenclature underwent under the dictators of the first century B.C. is significant of a change in the seat of power. The earliest instance of the new practice of naming a colony in honor of its autocratic founder is probably that of the colonia Mariana. The practice became the accepted one under the

---

[1] Abbott, *Class. Phil.* 10 (1915), 372 *ff.*
[2] Kornemann, *R.E.* 4, 566.

empire, and is helpful in determining the foundation-date of a colony[1].

A *municipium* was not a new settlement, as a colony was, but resulted from the incorporation of a conquered town into the Roman state[2]. The functions of its local magistrates and the limitations put upon their powers were determined in each case by the charter granted to it. Some interesting specimens of charters granted to colonies and *municipia* have come down to us from the time of the late republic, for Tarentum in Italy[3] and for the colony of Urso in Spain[4], and from the time of the empire, for the *municipia* of Salpensa and Malaca in Spain[5]. The inhabitants of a *municipium* received complete Roman citizenship, as in Lanuvium and Aricia[6], or received it in a restricted form, *sine suffragio*, as in Fundi and Formiae, or with such limitations as the provincial *municipia* of Salpensa and Malaca had at a later date[7]. As we have already noticed, all the *civitates sine suffragio* south of the Po were given Roman citizenship by the *leges Iulia et Plautia Papiria* of 90–89 B.C. Like Roman colonists the citizens in *municipia* were liable to service in the legions, and were subject to all the *munera* to which Roman citizens were subject. Indeed the ancients believed that the word *municipium* was derived from *munus* and *capere*. In their juridical position the *municipia* differed from the colonies in the fact that they could retain their traditional procedure in cases heard by their local magistrates, whereas the colonies

---

[1] For a list of the imperial appellatives used, *cf.* de Ruggiero, *Le Colonie dei Romani*, 96.

[2] Recent literature: Comparette, *A. J. Ph.* 27 (1906), 166 *ff.*; Declareuil, *Quelques problèmes d'histoire des institutions municipales au temps de l'Empire romain*; Heisterbergk in *Philol.* 50 (1891), 639 *ff.*; Jouguet, *Vie munic.*; Jung, *Hist. Zeitschr.* 67 (1891), 1 *ff.*; Levy, *Rev. d. ét. grecq.* 8 (1895), 203 *ff.*; 12 (1899), 255 *ff.*; 14 (1899), 350 *ff.*; Liebenam, *St. Verw.*; Mommsen, *Ges. Schr.* 1, 293 *ff.*; Toutain, *Dict. Dar. s.v. municipium*; Toutain, *Les cités romaines de la Tunisie*.

[3] No. 20. [4] No. 26. [5] Nos. 64 and 65.
[6] Livy, 8. 14. 2–3. [7] Livy, 8. 14. 10; no. 64.

followed Roman law. If a *municipium* in Italy adopted Roman law, it was known as a *municipium fundanum*[1].

In the provinces we find two main classes of *municipia*, those whose citizens had Roman, and those whose citizens were restricted to Latin citizenship[2]. Some cities of the second class had the *maius Latium*, others only the *minus Latium*. Citizens in communities having the *maius Latium* gained Roman citizenship when admitted to the local senate. In towns having minor Latin rights only election to a local magistracy could win this privilege for them[3]. Provincial *municipia*, like colonies and peregrine *civitates*, were subject to tribute, and did not enjoy full ownership of land, although perhaps the *ius Italicum* was granted to favored *municipia*. This right by a legal fiction made their land part of Italy, and therefore conferred full ownership, or *dominium*, on the holders, as well as freedom from the payment of tribute[4]. So far as local administration was concerned, most *municipia* were more or less under the control of the governor of their province, whereas the colonies were strictly autonomous in the matter of local affairs[5]. This difference explains in part why so many provincial *municipia* begged the emperors to make them colonies.

[1] *Cf.* Elmore, *Trans. Am. Phil. Assoc.* 47, 35 *ff.*
[2] Toutain, *Dict. Dar. s.v. municipium*, 2030 *f.*
[3] Gaius, 1. 95–96; no. 64.
[4] *Cf.* v. Premerstein, *R.E.* 10, 1242 *ff.*
[5] On the possession of *libertas* by Roman colonies, *cf.* Toutain, *Mél. d. arch.* 18 (1898), 141 *ff.*; v. Premerstein, *op. cit.* 1248.

PRAEFECTURAE, FORA, VICI, CASTELLA, CONCILIABULA, CANABAE, PAGI, GENTES, ⊃ALTUS[1]

THE writer of the *lex de Gallia Cisalpina*, in designating the communities in Cisalpine Gaul to which a certain provision is to apply, mentions *oppidum municipium colonia praefectura forum vicus conciliabulum castellum territorium*[2]. *Oppidum* is a generic word for an autonomous community, and *territorium* is used of the country district outside the limits of a settlement, but belonging to it. The other words in the list have more or less definite technical meaning, and if to them we add the terms *pagus, gens, canabae*, and *saltus*, we shall probably have a complete catalogue of the names given in the West to the smaller administrative units. The first three of these terms, *municipium, colonia*, and *praefectura*, stand apart from the rest to indicate communities of a clearly marked, general type, and again the *praefectura*, which did not enjoy all the rights of self-government in local affairs, stands opposed to the more fortunate *municipium* and *colonia*. *Praefectura*, in fact, may be thought of as a generic term applicable to any community which lacked the full right of self-government. In this sense, as we shall see,

[1] Outside of the discussions in the standard treatises of Mommsen (*St. R.* 3, 765 *ff.*), Marquardt (*St. Verw.* 1, 34 *ff.*), Willems (*Droit public rom.* 357 *f.*) and Madvig (*Verf. u. Verw.* 1, 44, 49), some of the most recent literature on the communities treated in this chapter are papers by Schulten in *Philol.* 53 (1894), 629–686; *Hermes*, 29 (1894), 481–516; and *Rh. Mus.* 50 (1895), 489–557; Hardy, *Six Roman Laws*, 143 *ff.* and articles under the pertinent headings in *Dict. Dar., R.E.* and the *Diz. Ep.* For a convenient list of the *praefecturae, fora, vici, castella, pagi*, and *saltus* mentioned in Dessau's collection of inscriptions, *cf.* Dessau, 3, pp. 619, 660–664, 669.

[2] No. 27, c. 21, ll. 2 *f.*

it comprehends all the terms, except *territorium*, which follow it in the list given above.

The title *praefectus* was given to an official to whom some higher authority had delegated the power to perform certain functions. So far as the villages and cities of the empire were concerned, the source of authority might be the central government at Rome or some one of the *civitates*. The officials of the first sort were the *praefecti iure dicundo* sent out by the urban praetor to administer justice in the settlements founded by Rome or annexed by her, as well as the special *praefecti iure dicundo Capuae Cumis* who were elected in the *comitia* on the nomination of the praetor. The term prefecture could also be applied to the small communities which did not have an independent status, but were attached to a neighboring *civitas*. In this case the authority of the prefect came, not from Rome, but from the *civitas*. The residents in Italian prefectures connected with Rome lacked in the early period some of the qualities of citizenship, but later these communities either attained the position of *municipia*, or while retaining the name of *praefecturae*, differed from *municipia* only in the fact that they did not have *II viri* or *IV viri*[1]. As for the other class of prefectures, they maintained their existence down to a late date. *Civitates* usually had *territoria* dependent upon them. In these *territoria* hamlets were scattered here and there, and in the villages at a distance from the governing city justice was administered and certain other powers were exercised by a prefect sent out for that purpose by the municipal authorities. To such an official, for instance, reference seems to be made in *CIL*. x, 6104, an inscription of the Augustan age: Carthagine aedilis, praefectus iure dicundo vectigalibusque quinquennalibus locandis in castellis LXXXIII. Similarly the magistrates of the Genuenses exercised jurisdiction over the residents of the castellum

---

[1] Cagnat, *Dict. Dar. s.v. praefectura.*

Vituriorum[1]. In one case we hear of the duovir of a colony acting as prefect of a *castellum*[2]. It is impossible to draw an exact line of distinction between the several minor communities, but for purposes of convenience in discussion the *fora, conciliabula, vici,* and *castella* may be put together. These in turn fall into two groups, the *fora* and *conciliabula* on the one hand, and the *vici* and *castella* on the other. Settlements of the first two classes were always authorized by the central government and thus bore a certain resemblance to colonies[3]. Indeed it is quite possible that in the earliest period Roman colonies held the same legal relation to Rome as the *fora* and *conciliabula* did in later times[4]. This official relation for the *fora* is indicated by such typical names as Forum Popili and Forum Livi. Most of them were founded by Roman magistrates charged with the construction of a highway, and the name is found most frequently in northern Italy[5], and for settlements made under the republic. In the last century of the republic most of the *fora* and *conciliabula* were erected into communities with full rights of local self-government.

On a somewhat lower plane stood the *vici* and *castella.* Of them Isidore remarks[6]: vici et castella et pagi sunt, quae nulla dignitate civitatis ornantur, sed vulgari hominum conventu incoluntur et propter parvitatem sui maioribus civitatibus attribuuntur. The *vici,* at least, were usually private settlements, and the *castella* may be regarded as fortified *vici,* although in the founding of a *castellum* probably the initiative would ordinarily be taken by a military authority, and the commandant may well have acted at the outset as the local magistrate[7]. Most of

---

[1] No. 10, ll. 43–44. For a specific illustration of the relations between a *civitas* and its *attributi*, see commentary on no. 49 on the question at issue between the *municipium* of Tridentum and the Anauni.

[2] *CIL.* VIII, 15726.   [3] Schulten, *R.E.* 4, 799 *f.*

[4] Mommsen, *St. R.* 3, 775 *ff.*   [5] Schulten, *R.E.* 7, 62.

[6] *Orig.* 15. 2. 11.   [7] Mommsen, *Hermes,* 24 (1889), 200.

the *castella* were naturally on the frontiers[1]. Some of the *vici* and *castella* were in time made independent communities. This happened, for instance, in the case of Sufes[2], and occasionally a *civitas* was reduced to the position of a dependent *vicus*. An interesting instance of this sort is furnished by the petition of the people of Orcistus[3]. In a few cases we find the name *vicus canabarum*[4] applied to a community, but settlements of this sort do not seem to have differed from *canabae*, which come next in the order of discussion.

This word in its general sense was applied to the temporary shops and booths put up by merchants. It was natural to use it also of the settlements of merchants and camp-followers which sprang up about the camps. They were usually located so as to leave a free space between the fortifications of the camp and the hamlet in question. The organization was based on the resident Roman citizens, and, with its *magistri* or *curatores*[5], probably bore a close resemblance to the *conventus civium Romanorum*, of which we have a reasonably complete record[6]. Probably the native women by whom the soldiers in the camp had children lived in these nearby villages, so that it was natural for the veterans on receiving their discharge and the legalization of their marriages to settle in the *canabae* with their wives and children. To them we have reference in an inscription from Aquincum[7] and elsewhere. In the history of the Roman municipality the *canabae* have a special interest for us, because we can,

---

[1] For a list, not absolutely complete, *cf. Diz. Ep.* 2, 130 f. The castellum Carcassonne has preserved its external features up to the present day.
[2] *CIL.* VIII, 11427; Kubitschek, *R.E.* 3, 1757.
[3] No. 154.   [4] Schulten, *Philol.* 53 (1894), 671 f.
[5] *CIL.* III, 6166; V, 5747; and the phrase civibus Romanis consistentibus ad canabas leg. V (*An. ép.* 1920, no. 54).
[6] See Kornemann, *s.v. conventus*, *R.E.* 4, 1182–1200. Mommsen's theory (*Hermes*, 7 (1873), 299 ff.) that the *canabae* had a military organization is no longer held; *cf.* Schulten, *R.E.* 3, 1452; *Hermes* 29 (1894), 507.
[7] *CIL.* III, 3505.

in some instances, trace their growth from the earliest settlement by Roman citizens up to the granting of a municipal charter. This is true, for example, of Apulum[1], Aquincum[2], Carnuntum[3], and notably of Lambaesis[4]. Some of these settlements, like Carnuntum, even attained the dignity of a colony[5].

The *pagus*[6] differed essentially from all the communities which have been mentioned thus far. The meaning of the term varied somewhat from one period to another and from one part of the Roman world to another, but the canton was always thought of as a rural administrative unit, and was opposed in sense to *civitas*, *urbs*, or *oppidum*. The Romans found these rural subdivisions in their conquest of Italy and of other parts of the western world, and they were frequently preserved intact, but were usually given a Roman name. Caesar uses the term to indicate part of a native tribe[7], but under the empire it came to designate very definitely a territorial unit.

The inhabitants of a canton might live dispersed or in hamlets (*vici*). They formed a commune for such religious purposes as the celebration of festivals and the maintenance of the local cult, and for such administrative purposes as the repairing of roads and the apportionment of the water supply. The religious side of the community life is indicated by such names as *pagus Martius* and *pagus Apollinaris*, although other cantons bore a local name, e.g. *pagus Veronensis*, or even a gentile name, as was the case, for instance, with the *pagus Valerius*. The cantons enjoyed a certain degree of autonomy. We read in the inscriptions

---

[1] Tomaschek, *R.E.* 2, 290 *f.*
[2] Tomaschek, *R.E.* 2, 333.   [3] Kubitschek, *R.E.* 3, 1601 *f.*
[4] Wilmanns, *Comm. Mommsen*, 190 *ff.*; Cagnat, *L'armée romaine d'Afrique, passim.*
[5] *CIL.* III, 4236.
[6] An extended discussion of the subject is given by A. Schulten, *Die Landgemeinden in röm. Reich, Philol.* 53 (1894), 629–655. For recent literature, see Toutain in *Dict. Dar.* and Lübker, *Reallexikon, s.v. pagus.*
[7] *B.G.* I. 12.

of their *magistri* and their decrees. In most cases probably the decrees were passed in popular assemblies, but in one case at least, we hear of the decurions of a canton[1]. In later days the *pagi* must have lost largely their rights of self-government, because after Diocletian's time we hear frequently of the *praefecti* or *praepositi pagorum*[2].

A larger rural unit than the *pagus* was the *gens* or *populus*. In Spain and Gaul, for instance, the Romans found it convenient to deal with the tribal organizations, and to accept the division of these tribes into the traditionally accepted smaller cantons. The Helvetii, for example, were divided into four cantons in Caesar's time[3]. A judicial prefect was put in charge of a tribe or group of cantons. Thus we hear of a *praef. gentis Cinithiorum*[4] and a *praefectus civitatium in Alpibus Maritumis*[5]. In these cases Rome dealt with a whole people, not with single cities. Each tribe, however, had one or more villages, which were made centres of administration. If these grew in importance, they might develop into autonomous cities, and receive Latin or Roman rights as the principal village of the Vocontii did[6].

At the bottom of the scale, so far as the enjoyment of self-government was concerned, were the *coloni* on large private and imperial estates. Our information about the political and economic organization of these estates in the West comes almost entirely from inscriptions found during the last forty years[7]. All but one of these docu-

---

[1] *CIL.* VIII, 1548.

[2] The *conventus civium Romanorum* scarcely belong among the communities under discussion here.

[3] *B.G.* I. 12.   [4] *CIL.* VIII, 10500.   [5] *CIL.* v, 1838.

[6] *Cf.* Kornemann, *R.E.* 4, 545 and Schulten, *Rh. Mus.* 50 (1895), 521.

[7] These inscriptions are the *Epistula data a Licinio Maximo et Feliciore Augusti liberto procuratoribus ad exemplum legis Mancianae* (no. 74) found in 1896 at Henchir-Mettich, the *Ara legis Hadrianae* (Bruns, 115) found in 1892 at Aïn-Ouassel, the *Sermo et epistulae procuratorum de terris vacuis excolendis* (no. 93) found in 1906 at Aïn-el-Djemala, the *Rescriptum Commodi de saltu Burunitano* (no. 111) found in 1879 at Souk-el-Khmis, and

ments come from Africa, so that a description of the organization of the *saltus* based on them applies strictly to that region, although the same system in its general outlines probably prevailed in other parts of the empire. The growth of great estates is closely connected with the policy which Rome adopted in dealing with the *ager publicus*. The land of a conquered people passed automatically under Roman ownership. Some of the cultivated land might be used as the site of a colony, some turned back to the natives in return for a rental. As for the uncultivated land, capital was needed for its development, and it was occupied to a great extent by rich Roman landlords. Under this system immense estates came under the control of private owners both in Italy and the provinces. This was particularly true of Africa, of which Pliny tells us that in Nero's time *sex domini semissem Africae possidebant, cum interfecit eos Nero princeps*[1]. The early emperors, as one may infer from Pliny's remark, saw clearly the political and economic danger with which this situation threatened the government and society, and set themselves to work to remove it[2]. The land must belong to the state. This change in ownership was accomplished partly by way of legacies, but in larger measure through confiscation. The land became again public land, to be administered henceforth by the emperor, and by the time of the Flavians most of the great estates had become crown-lands[3]. They were too large to be made the *territoria* of neighboring cities. They were therefore organized on an independent basis, and with the formation of the *saltus* a new and far-reaching principle was introduced into the imperial system. Hitherto Rome had made

the *Rescriptum Philipporum ad colonos vici cuiusdam Phrygiae*, found in 1897 in Phrygia (no. 141). *Cf.* also nos. 122 and 142. Information concerning the system followed on each of these imperial domains may be found in the commentaries on the inscriptions mentioned.

[1] *N.H.* 18. 6. 35.
[2] *Cf.* Rostowzew, *Gesch. d. röm. Kol.* 378.
[3] Rostowzew, *op. cit.* 379.

the *civitas* the political and social unit. It had dealt administratively with the individual through the magistrates or decurions of his community. The *coloni* on an imperial estate had no political organization, or at most only a rudimentary one. They were, therefore, brought into direct relations with the emperor or his personal representative. In carrying out this plan of government for the domains located in a given region, a method was adopted not unlike that which had been followed in the case of a newly acquired province. Just as a senatorial commission under the republic had drawn up a *lex provinciae* to fix the relations of the *civitates* to the central government and the form of government for the province within which they lay, or just as emperors granted charters to municipalities, so representatives of the emperor drew up a statute for the domains of a given district. The earliest of these statutes to which we have any reference is the *lex Manciana*[1], which was probably not a system of regulations drawn up by the owner of a private estate, as is commonly supposed[2], but was rather the work of an imperial legate, perhaps of the Emperor Vespasian[3]. The *lex Manciana* continued in force in Africa until it was supplanted by the *lex Hadriana*, to which reference is made in a document of the time of Commodus[4] and in another of a later date[5]. From a study of these documents, supplemented by information to be had from other inscriptions, it is possible to determine the administrative system which was introduced into the imperial domains. Each estate, or *saltus*, was in charge of a *procurator saltus*, who was usually a freedman, and all the procurators of a given region were under a *procurator tractus*, of equestrian

---

[1] No. 74, l. 6.
[2] Hirschfeld, 123, n. 3; Seeck, *R.E.* 4, 484; Toutain, *Nouv. rev. hist. de droit fr. et étr.* 21 (1897), 393 *ff.*; 23 (1899), 141 *ff.*
[3] Rostowzew, *op. cit.* 329.   [4] No. 111, ll. 5, 26.
[5] Bruns, 115, l. 7.

rank[1]. Sometimes between these two officials was a *procurator regionis*. The procurators were not under the control of the proconsul, but were directly responsible to the emperor[2]. The business affairs of an estate were in charge of a *conductor*, who was a freeman or a freedman and was responsible for the management of the entire estate. Most of the land was rented to tenants under five-year contracts, and each tenant was personally responsible for the payment of the rental to the imperial collector. In case of non-payment the *conductor* proceeded against him[3]. Part of the land in an estate could be leased by the *conductor* and worked directly by him or leased to tenants[4]. For the purpose of working this land he could require a certain number of days' labor annually from each tenant.

With this sketch in mind of the administrative arrangements on an estate, let us fill in some of the details of the plan. No specimen of the fundamental law for an estate has come down to us in its entirety, but the articles of the *lex Manciana* and *lex Hadriana* which are extant prove that it provided in the minutest detail for the regulation of the affairs of the imperial domains. It established a system of administration; it specified the powers and duties of the *procurator*, the *conductor*, and their assistants; it determined the rights and duties of the *colonus*, fixed his rental, and provided for him a method of appeal. Such a law was drawn up for a large region. Consequently it might violate the usage of a particular locality. There were two points especially in which this seems to have happened, viz. in determining the amount of corn, wine, or other

---

[1] For a list of the *tractus* in Africa, *cf.* Schulten, *Die römischen Grundherrschaften*, 62 *ff.* For a list of the imperial domains in other parts of the Roman world, *cf.* Hirschfeld, *Der Grundbesitz d. röm. Kaiser in d. ersten drei Jahrhunderten*, *Klio*, 2 (1902), 45–72; 284–315.

[2] Hirschfeld, *Klio*, 2 (1902), 295.

[3] Rostowzew, *Geschichte d. Staatspacht*, 443.

[4] Rostowzew, *op. cit.* 443–4.

produce which the tenant should pay as rental[1], and in fixing the number of days' labor which the *conductor* might require of the tenant. In case of dispute on such points the matter was referred to the *procurator saltus,* or was carried up to the emperor or his deputy, the *procurator tractus.* The same method of appeal was followed if the fundamental law was violated. Thus the tenants on the *saltus Burunitanus* complain that they are required to give more than six days' labor each year to the *conductor*[2], that the *conductor* is very wealthy and has secured the support of the procurator of the estate[3], and that they have been flogged and maltreated by soldiers, although some of them are Roman citizens[4]. In the case of such petitions as this the emperor caused his decision to be engraved on a tablet and to be placed where it could be seen by all the tenants.

Within the limitations of, and in accordance with, the forms imposed by the statute and by subsequent decisions of the emperor, the procurator was the administrative and judicial officer of the domain. It is his duty to maintain order, and he may even employ soldiers for this purpose[5]. The tenants on the *saltus Burunitanus* recognize their lowly condition in their petition to the emperor by speaking of themselves as *rustici tui vernulae et alumni saltuum tuorum*[6]. Inasmuch as they had the right to petition the emperor and had a *magister*, they evidently had a rudimentary political organization, but they had no form of local government[7]. They did not even have the political rights which *attributi* enjoyed, because they were attached to no *civitas.* The fact that the domains were extra-municipal carried with it certain advantages as well as

---

[1] Hyginus, *Gromatici veteres* (Lachmann), 205.
[2] *Cf.* no. 111, Col. iii, ll. 12–13.
[3] *Ibid.* Col. iii, ll. 1–12. [4] *Ibid.* Col. ii, ll. 11–16.
[5] *Ibid.* Col. ii, l. 11. [6] *Ibid.* Col. iii, ll. 28–29.
[7] *Ibid.* Col. iv, l. 27; *cf.* also Lécrivain, *Dict. Dar.* 3, 963 *f.*

[19]

disadvantages[1]. The *coloni* were thereby relieved from all the municipal charges which in the later period weighed so heavily on the *civitates*. The evil side of their political situation lay in the fact that they formed a special social class, in a territory of well marked limits, under officials with large powers whose sympathies lay with their masters, the *conductores*. Their only recourse was to the emperor, and appeal to him was difficult and dangerous. As the control of the central government over the outlying regions became weaker, the *coloni* were more and more at the mercy of the *conductores*[2].

As we have noticed in another connection[3], the debasement of the coinage and the pressing need of food for the Roman rabble and for the armies, forced Diocletian to make contributions in kind a fixed part of the tribute from the provinces. This heavy demand, coming as it did at a time when the amount of cultivated land was decreasing, and the productivity of the soil declining, called for higher rentals than tenants were willing to pay. Their only recourse was to abandon their holdings, but this would have made matters still worse. It must be prevented at all hazards, and Constantine made it illegal for tenants to leave their farms. But probably his edict only gave legal recognition to a situation which already existed. In earlier times tenants had been inclined to retain their holdings, the renewal of leases was probably taken for granted, and tenancies descended from father to son. As for the *conductor* also, some time after the third century, he ceased to take a *saltus* for a fixed period, but settled on it for life, became its practical owner, and bequeathed it to his heir[4]. It was ruinous for him to have frequent changes in his tenants, or to have his land pass out of cultivation, and this he prevented. When this point had been reached, the *colonus* had become a serf.

[1] For the history of extra-territoriality, which seems to be of eastern origin, *cf.* Rostowzew, *Gesch. d. röm. Kol.* 375 *ff.*
[2] For a few instances of the development of *vici* of tenants into *civitates,* *cf.* Pelham, *Essays,* 298.   [3] *Cf.* pp. 129 *ff.*
[4] Rostowzew, *op. cit.* 396 *ff.*

CHAPTER III

VILLAGES IN THE ORIENT

IN the early history of Greece the union of villages and cities (συνοικισμός) had led to the grouping of a large number of tribes (ἔθνη) in city-states. These became the political centres of the groups, although a large part of the population remained in the original villages and retained some form of administration in the management of local affairs, such as games and religious festivals[1]. Occasionally we find some political legislation, as, for example, in the Mesogaea of Attica where, in the third century, certain demes united to protect their lands against raids[2]. When Demetrius founded Demetrias by the union of neighboring cities and villages, the former of these, as demes of the new town, still retained a local assembly and local magistrates, although the sovereignty which they possessed must have been limited[3]. In some of the more backward districts of Greece, such as Aetolia, Arcadia, and Epirus, villages existed with an independent organization, and were not attached to any city. The records of such communities, however, have not been preserved[4]. In Thrace the tribal organization was governed by a phylarch. The people lived in villages, several of which sometimes united in a κοινόν, whose chief magistrates were called comarchs[5]. In this province we also find toparchies, which seem to have had a central government modelled on that of the Greek city[6].

[1] Dict. Dar. s.v. κώμη; Kuhn, Die Entstehung der Stadt, 188 f.; R.E. s.v. κατοικία, κώμη.
[2] Ferguson, Hellenistic Athens, 207.
[3] Ath. Mitt. 14 (1889), 196 ff.
[4] Dict. Dar. s.v. κώμη; Kuhn, op. cit. 24 ff., 79 ff.
[5] Cagnat, IGRR. 1, 721, 728.   [6] No. 131.

Villages sometimes developed independently into cities, or were detached by force from the municipality, and constituted as independent communities. A case like the dispersion of Mantinea by Agesilaus was rare[1]. Mantinea and Corinth were, for a time, made villages of Argos as a result of war[2], but, in general, the loss of civic status by a municipality was due to economic weakness, especially in Hellenistic and Roman times.

In Asia Greek culture had not penetrated beyond the maritime regions before the conquests of Alexander, and the interior of the Persian kingdom was almost entirely composed of village-communities. Under Roman rule we find these organizations still existing in various forms. Such names as δῆμος, κώμη, κωμόπολις, μητροκωμία, πόλισμα, περιοικίς, πολίχνη, πολίχνιον, κατοικία, κτοινά, τόπος, χώρα, χωρίον, ἐμπόριον, ἔρυμα, φρούριον, πύργος, and τεῖχος are common[3]. To these might be added *stationes*, *regiones*, and *mansiones* which came in under Roman administration[4]. In inscriptions δῆμος, κώμη, and κατοικία are the terms usually applied to villages[5].

Under Roman rule village-communities which were not under the control of a municipality might be found on private or imperial estates, or under the control of priests in a temple-state, or grouped in a sort of commonwealth (κοινόν or ἐπαρχία) whose administrative centre was a μητροκωμία. Since the Romans followed the Greek policy of extending the municipal organization wherever possible,

---

[1] Xenophon, *Hellenica*, 5. 2. 7. For the dispersion of Phocian towns by the Amphictyonic Council in 346, see Diodorus, 16. 60. 2.

[2] Plutarch, *Aratus*, 45; Xenophon, *op. cit.* 4. 4. 6.

[3] These terms are found constantly in Strabo.

[4] Kuhn, *Die städt. u. bürgerl. Verfassung d. röm. Reichs*, 2, 238, 317 n. The development of military *canabae* into municipalities is not common in the Orient. Leğğûn in Syria probably took its name from the military camp established in the town Caparcotna (*Rh. Mus.* 58 (1903), 633). *Cf.* Brünnow, *Prov. Arab.* 2. 24 ff.

[5] For the distinction between κώμη and κατοικία, cf. Chapot, *La prov. rom. proc. d'Asie*, 97 f. *R.E. s.v.* κατοικία.

many of these villages were transformed into cities. The
μητροκωμία usually became the metropolis and the dependent districts formed the *territorium* of the new city.
In founding Zela, Pompey added to its territory several
eparchies[1]. The temple-states, which were a characteristic
organization in Asia, were composed of groups of villages
under the administration of the priests attached to the
temple. Although the residents in these communities
were usually *hieroi* or *hierodouloi*, whose status was virtually serfdom, some form of political organization was
probably permitted[2]. The temple-states were deprived
of their power either by the Greek kings or by the Roman
rulers, and the seat of the temple usually became the civic
centre, while the estate was converted into the *territorium*
of the city. The worship of the god became the civic cult.
Some of these temple-states were added to the estates of
the emperors[3]. In Judea the destruction of Jerusalem
brought an end to the power of the temple as an administrative factor in the control of the Jewish villages.

On the imperial estates the agent of the emperor was
probably the administrator of the smaller communities,
where the tenants were chiefly serfs. In the larger villages
there was a quasi-municipal organization which probably
developed as a result of the settlement of free tenants who
formed the nucleus of a *curia*, or it arose from a *collegium*
of residents formed for social or religious purposes. The
development of political institutions seems to have been
encouraged, for many of the imperial estates were incorporated as municipal *territoria*. A good example of this
may be seen in the inscription from Pogla which shows the
two stages of its development[4].

Since the Romans were eager to extend the municipal
system over the provinces as soon as possible, many of the

[1] Strabo, 12. 37. 1.
[2] Ramsay, *Cities and Bishoprics*, 1, 102; Strabo, 12. 3. 1; 12. 34–37.
[3] Rostowzew, *Gesch. d. röm. Kol.* 276 *ff.*
[4] No. 122; *cf.* p. 32.

[23]

new cities founded by them were given territory of vast extent. In the course of time many of the larger villages within the *territorium* were given municipal charters of their own. Tymanda may be cited as an example of this development, and Orcistus, which had once been a city before it was reduced to the status of a village under the jurisdiction of Nacoleia, was restored to its former status in the fourth century[1]. The process of development and decay may be traced in different parts of the empire at all periods. Ilium had degenerated into a sort of village-town ($\kappa\omega\mu\acute{o}\pi o\lambda\iota s$) before it was restored by the emperors[2]. Strabo describes Chrysopolis as a village in his day[3]. Byzantium and Antioch were penalized by the emperors for political reasons and were deprived of civic rights for a time by being made villages of neighboring cities[4]. The large number of cities named Hierapolis shows how the temple-states were transformed into municipalities, and among the seats of Christian bishoprics such names as Chorio Myliadica, Agathe Come, Demulycaon, Panemo-teichus, Regepodandus, Chora Patrimonia, Ktema Maxi-mianopoleos, and Salton Toxus may serve to illustrate the development of cities out of villages, of which some were originally part of an imperial estate[5]. Constantine is credited with great activity in transforming villages into cities, and all emperors encouraged this policy in order to create a body of *curiales* who would be responsible for the collection of imperial taxes[6].

In distinguishing between a village and a city, ancient writers imply that the former possessed no political sovereignty, but it is evident that most villages had some form of organization whereby the members could legislate

---

[1] Nos. 151, 154.   [2] Strabo, 13. 27. 1.
[3] Strabo, 12. 42. 2; Cicero, *ad fam.* 4. 5. 4.
[4] Herodian, 3. 6. 9.
[5] Ramsay, *op. cit.* 1. 84 *ff.*; Kuhn, *op. cit.* 238–9, 289, 299, 301, 304, 368; no. 122.
[6] Socrates, *Hist. Eccl.* 1. 18; *cf.* nos. 151, 154.

in social, religious, and administrative matters, however much their freedom in initiative and performance may have been restricted. Many communities copied their metropolis by adopting civic institutions, such as the *ecclesia* and *gerousia*. Sometimes a group of villages united in a κοινόν for the celebration of festivals and games[1]. We find frequent records of honorary decrees passed by village-assemblies, and of public works undertaken at their expense[2]. They had revenues under their control, some of which came from lands which they owned and could dispose of by sale[3]. They had advocates (ἔκδικοι) to defend their interests, and judges to administer the law[4]. Officials such as comarch, demarch, *brabeutae*, *logistae*, *prytaneis*, recorders (ἀναγραφεῖς), agoranomi, secretary, and οἱ βασιλεύοντες are found, and even the *summa honoraria* is sometimes exacted[5]. In Syrian villages mention is made of σύνδικοι, πίστοι, διοικηταί, προνοηταί, στρατηγοί, and ἐπιμεληταί[6]. We cannot tell whether the officials in the villages were elected locally or were appointed by the municipal government. According to the Codes the government of villages and *mansiones* in the fourth century was entrusted to citizens as a municipal liturgy[7]. It is doubtful if this system was universal, since Syrian inscriptions and the statements of Libanius imply that the village-officials were independent of the municipal govern-

---

[1] *Dict. Dar. s.v.* κώμη.

[2] Cagnat, *IGRR*. 3, 692, 1397; 4, 756, 1367; Ramsay, *op. cit.* no. 498. Juristic personality recognized by law, *cf. Dig.* 3. 4. 1; 30. 1. 73; 47. 22. 4; *Cod. J.* 2. 59. 2.

[3] Cagnat, *IGRR*. 4, 1387, 1607; Lebas-Waddington, 2556; Ditt. *Or. Gr.* 488.   [4] No. 113.

[5] *Cf.* indices to Lebas-Waddington, Cagnat, *IGRR*, and *IG*. The *comogrammateus* of Judaean villages shows the persistence of Ptolemaic influence. In Cagnat, *IGRR*. 4, 1371 οἱ βασιλεύοντες imply the priest-kings of a temple-state. For the *summa honoraria*, *cf.* no. 150 and *Journ. Rom. Studies*, 8 (1918), 26 *ff.*

[6] Lebas-Waddington, 2127, 2130, 2240, 2399, 2547, 2556; Prentice, *Trans. Am. Phil. Assoc.* 43 (1912), 113 *ff.*

[7] *Cod. Th.* 12. 1. 21 (335); *Cod. J.* 10. 72. 2.

ment[1]. It is evident that, in the disorder which prevailed
during the third and fourth centuries, villages distant
from the metropolis and unprotected by it had either
fortified themselves and become semi-independent, or had
placed themselves under the protection of some powerful
noble, to whom they gave their full allegiance. The
development of this type of patronage was an important
cause of the decline of municipal institutions, since great
stretches of territory passed out of the control of the cities,
especially when brigandage and war were factors of everyday life. In the Byzantine empire the spread of independent village-communities was a characteristic feature of
the revival of oriental influences and the decay of Hellenism, although their development was also due in large
measure to the peculiar political and economic conditions
of the age[2].

The relation of the village to the metropolis in financial
matters cannot be traced in detail, since few documents
throw light on the subject. The revenues of the city were
chiefly derived from the *territorium*, and the villagers were,
in effect, regarded as lessees in perpetuity of the lands
which they worked. The rental which they paid not only
contributed to the support of the municipality, but also
helped to make up the quota of imperial tribute. Other
requisitions, such as the head and house tax, were levied[3].
Villagers, drafted for the settlement of the *emporium* at
Pizus, were granted exemption from the quota of grain
usually demanded from the villages, from the tax for the
support of the *burgarii* or border police, and from garrison
duty. No levies could be imposed upon them for beasts
of burden required for the public post[4]. The recruiting
tax (*aurum tironicum*) was levied on villages as well as on
towns in the third century, but we cannot determine

[1] Libanius, *De patrociniis.*
[2] Ramsay, *Tekmorian Guest Friends,* 306 *ff.*
[3] Cicero, *ad fam.* 3., 8. 5; *Cod. Th.* 11. 24. 6.
[4] No. 131.

whether the municipality collected it, or whether imperial agents enforced the payment[1]. Valens imposed the tax directly on the villages[2]. In Hierapolis the municipal police (παραφύλακες), who were assigned to guard-duty in the country districts, were not allowed to make requisitions upon the villagers except for certain specified requirements[3]. It would seem that every imperial tax and liturgy imposed upon the municipality was passed on to the dependent communities, while a few more were added by the civic authorities as a special act of grace. The plaint that every *curialis* was a tyrant was probably not unjustified. Above all, the imperial requisitions for service in the public post were applied directly to the villages. The drafting of their cattle for angary was particularly burdensome on farmers. Frequent complaints from villages on imperial estates happen to be preserved, since they presented their wrongs to the emperor direct and were able to secure some relief, but the municipal *territoria* must have suffered far more from the exactions of troops and imperial officials[4]. Since the cities were unable to protect the country districts, the villagers were forced to turn for help to the powerful proprietors in their vicinity, and where this protection could not be secured, their impoverishment was only a question of time.

In Egypt the Ptolemaic system was perpetuated for the first two centuries of Roman rule. The country was organized in nomes composed of village-communities, each with a metropolis which, by courtesy, was often called a πόλις. The village is usually styled κώμη, but such terms as ἐποικία, ἐποικίον, χωρίον, and τόπος are also found[5]. The chief official (κωμογραμματεύς) was an agent of the

---

[1] No. 150; *Journ. Rom. Studies*, 8 (1918), 26 ff.
[2] Socrates, *Hist. Eccl.* 4. 34.   [3] No. 117.
[4] Nos. 113, 139, 141–144, 152.
[5] *Musée Belge*, 10 (1906), 38 ff., 160 ff.; Engers, *De Aegyptiarum κωμῶν administratione qualis fuerit aetate Lagidarum*; Wilcken, *Grundzüge*, c. 1; Jouguet, *Vie munic.* 202 ff.

imperial government, and sometimes combined two or more villages under his jurisdiction[1]. Police duties were under the supervision of the *archephodus* and *phylaces* of various kinds[2]. The office of *epistates* seems to have disappeared soon after the Roman occupation[3]. The board or council of elders (πρεσβύτεροι) acted with the secretary as the governing body. In this capacity the councillors had no initiative of their own, but served merely as agents of the imperial government. Their responsibility was fixed by law, and the proper performance of their duties was guaranteed by sureties[4]. Each member of the board had to possess a certain standard of wealth which varied according to the importance of the village[5]. Nominations to office were made by the secretary and elders, sometimes jointly, sometimes separately. The appointments were made by the *epistrategus*[6]. The larger villages were sometimes divided into wards, each of which had officials of its own.

The religious and administrative centre of each nome was called a metropolis, and its organization differed from the villages but slightly. The council of elders was replaced by a council of magistrates (κοινὸν τῶν ἀρχόντων) as a concession to the Greek element which had settled in the community. The magistracies have been classified in three grades as follows: (1) gymnasiarch, (2) exegete, cosmete, eutheniarch, (3) archiereus, agoranomus[7]. The *hypomnematographus* rarely appears in the records, and his official rank is a matter of dispute[8]. Some of these offices were shared by several persons. There were at least six, and probably twelve, gymnasiarchs, but the variation in

[1] *BGU.* 91, 163; *P. Fay.* 40; *P. Fi.* 8; Jouguet, *op. cit.* 269 *ff.*
[2] Jouguet, *op. cit.* 261 *ff.*
[3] Oertel, *Die Liturgie*, 385; Jouguet, *op. cit.* 259.
[4] Jouguet, *op. cit.* 231; nos. 172, 182, 187, 196.
[5] Jouguet, *op. cit.* 219 *f.*; Wilcken, *Gr. Ostraka*, 506 *ff.*; *P. Giess.* 58.
[6] Jouguet, *op. cit.* 222 *ff.*
[7] Preisigke, *Städtisches Beamtenwesen im römischen Ägypten*, 30 *ff.*; Jouguet, *op. cit.* 292 *ff.*   [8] *P. Oxy.* 1412.

numbers was regulated by the size of the community and
its prosperity at different periods. There were two annual
secretaries who acted as imperial agents[1]. They drew up
the list of candidates for the manifold liturgies, probably
in consultation with the board of magistrates. They also
nominated their successors in office. The method of appointment to magistracies cannot be definitely determined
for all periods. As a general rule, however, the outgoing
officials nominated their successors[2].

At the beginning of the third century Severus introduced several reforms in the administration of Egypt. A
senate was constituted in each metropolis of the nomes. In
form each of these towns became a municipality, and its
later history need not concern us in this study. The
villages of the nome, however, were not included in the
territorium of the city at first. They continued to be administered by the state, although the nomarch was
appointed by the municipal senate which acted merely
as an agent of the imperial government in the nome[3].
The villages were also placed under a different administration, for the *comogrammateus* and the elders disappear
from the records before the middle of the century[4]. They
were replaced by comarchs who seem to have been
associated with other officials in a council[5]. The comarchs
nominated the *sitologi*, *ephorus*, *quadrarius*, and other local
officials, and were responsible for the proper discharge
of the duties to which the nominees were assigned. In
the fourth century the nome was divided into *pagi*, which
were now included in the territory of the city and under its
jurisdiction[6].

The Egyptian village was originally a part of the estate

[1] Jouguet, *op. cit.* 291.   [2] No. 181.
[3] Wilcken, *Gr. Ostraka*, 625; Jouguet, *op. cit.* 387, 390; *cf.* however,
no. 200.
[4] Jouguet, *op. cit.* 214 f.   [5] *Ibid.* 393.
[6] Gelzer, *Studien zur byzantinischen Verwaltung Ägyptens*, 57 ff.;
cf. however, Jouguet, *op. cit.* 397.

of the emperor, and it was organized and exploited solely in the interest of the *fiscus*. Here the liturgy was developed in its most oppressive form[1], and here the peasant was first bound to the soil. The development of municipal government in the third century, which we have described elsewhere, was powerfully influenced by the methods of administration which prevailed in the village-communities in Egypt.

[1] We have omitted a discussion of the Egyptian liturgy here. *Cf.* pp. 99 *ff.* and especially the comprehensive work by Oertel, *Die Liturgie*.

CHAPTER IV

THE SALTUS IN ASIA AND EGYPT

THE Greek cities in Asia, under the Diadochi, were allowed the right of ownership of land within their own *territoria*, but, unless especially exempted, they were required to pay to the king a tax on property under their jurisdiction[1]. The remainder of the royal dominions consisted of crown-lands, which could either be leased or worked by royal agents with slave or free labor, or by tenants who paid a tithe of their produce to the king. These tenants held their leaseholds in hereditary succession, and, in case the land was sold, they passed with the property into the possession of the new owner. They were grouped in villages (κατοικίαι, κῶμαι, or χωρία), where they enjoyed a limited measure of political activity. The royal estates were frequently reduced in extent by the foundation of military colonies, by the grant of civic status to villages, by sale, or by gift[2]. When the king transferred his right of possession to another, the land was usually included within the territory of the city in which the new owner resided. Hereditary tenants, therefore, were not peculiar to the royal possessions, but were often found on the lands belonging to the cities, or on private estates within their bounds. Such was the system of land tenure which the Romans found in Asia, and it is apparent that they adopted it with slight change. The crown-lands became the *ager publicus* of Rome and the cities retained possession of their territory, for which they paid rental in the form of an annual tribute to Rome. The Roman

[1] The history of land tenure on the royal and imperial estates of Asia is summed up by Rostowzew, *Gesch. d. röm. Kol.* 229 ff. Cf. *R.E. s.v. Domänen.*

[2] Rostowzew, *op. cit.* 248 ff. Cf. Buckler and Robinson, *AJA.* 16 (1912), 11 ff.

governors followed the policy of the Hellenistic kings in extending the municipal system at the expense of the public lands as well as of the temple-states. This movement was doubtless favored by the *publicani* since it simplified the problem of tax-gathering and facilitated the collection of loans[1].

Under the empire, the private estates of the emperor and the *ager publicus* came ultimately under the same administration. The imperial possessions were augmented by confiscation, fines, and bequests. As the kingdoms of client princes came into the empire, many of the royal estates were added to those of the emperor, while others were devoted to the foundation of cities. Fortunately, the tendency to over-expansion in the imperial estates was counterbalanced by the policy of extending the municipal system as widely as possible. The inscription from Pogla shows the transition from a village on one of the estates to municipal rank, and the names of the early Christian bishoprics indicate that many of them had once been imperial property[2].

Little is known of the actual methods of administration of the Asiatic imperial estates. We have, however, traced elsewhere the details of the western organization, and, since the latter was probably borrowed from the East, we refer the reader to the description of the western *saltus*[3]. The tenants were largely of the class of hereditary serfs, although we also find records of citizens from the municipalities who held imperial leaseholds[4]. The position of imperial tenants was probably more favorable than that of landowners in the towns since the former were assured of imperial protection, and were free from the oppressive municipal liturgies. With the development of imperial liturgies, however, the inhabitants of the villages on the

---

[1] Rostowzew, *op. cit.* 277 *ff.*; *cf.* no. 14.
[2] No. 122; *cf.* p. 23.   [3] *Cf.* pp. 15 *ff.*
[4] Ramsay, *The Tekmorian Guest Friends*, 361 *ff.* *Cf.* no. 142.

estates of the emperor were subjected to these charges, and in the third century we have several records of their complaints against the exactions of soldiers and officials[1]. When a municipal charter was granted to a village on an imperial estate, some change must have been made in the status of the residents. The free tenants would naturally form the nucleus of the senate, and the imperial agents may have become the first magistrates of the new town. Of the hereditary tenants, some continued to hold the position of serfs on the public lands of the city, but the more wealthy were undoubtedly raised to the rank of free citizens in order to create a sufficient number of *curiales* who would be responsible for the various obligations of the municipality. Unfortunately, no evidence has been preserved which enables us to determine definitely these points, but inscriptions from Asiatic towns sometimes reveal that the population was divided into classes of different status[2]. The lower grades may represent the original stock or the class of hereditary serfs.

In order to understand fully the Roman administration of Egypt, it is necessary to describe briefly the system of land tenure under the Ptolemies[3]. With the exception of the few cities which were founded by them, the Nile valley was the personal property of the sovereign. The crown lands (γῆ βασιλική) were under the direct administration of the royal bureaus. The remainder was called γῆ ἐν ἀφέσει or "surrendered" land.

The "surrendered" land may be subdivided as sacred (ἱερά), military (κληρουχική), and private (ἰδιόκτητος). Royal agents administered the sacred assignments in the interests of the temples[4]. The cleruchic land was assigned to the soldiers and to certain members of the bureaucracy.

---

[1] Nos. 139, 141–144.
[2] Liebenam, *St. Verw.* 216 *ff.*; no. 122.
[3] *Cf.* Rostowzew, *op. cit.* 1 *ff.*; Wilcken, *Grundzüge*, 270 *ff.*; Bell, *Journal of Egyptian Archaeology*, 4 (1917), 86 *ff.*
[4] Wilcken, *op. cit.* 278 *ff.*

The lessees, who were usually Greeks, were under obligation to render military service when called upon, and to pay a small ground rent. In making these grants the Ptolemies had a double purpose in view. The Greek soldiers were given a stake in their new home, and the cultivated area of the Nile valley was extended, for the military leases usually covered lands technically classified as sterile (ὑπόλογον, χέρσος), and the lessee was under obligation to cultivate his holdings. The lease could be cancelled at the will of the king, but the lessee had the right to sublet his property, and it could pass to his heirs as a virtual inheritance[1]. Land "surrendered" to private individuals (γῆ ἰδιόκτητος) consisted of two main classes: (1) Vineyards and orchards called κτήματα. These holdings are generally supposed to represent property privately owned in Persian times, or new land brought under cultivation by the owner. (2) Lands held on hereditary leasehold which could be bought, sold, mortgaged, or bequeathed with the same freedom as if held in full private ownership. The "surrendered" land was taxed with an annual rental to the crown, and if the tenant fell into arrears in his rental, his lease was liable to confiscation[2]. There was also another class which might properly be included under private ownership: favorites of the king were often given grants (γῆ ἐν δωρεᾷ), on which no rental was imposed.

The greater part of Egypt and the most fertile soil was crown land (γῆ βασιλική), which was worked by royal tenants (γεωργοὶ βασιλικοί). The leases ran for a term of years (usually five), and were granted to the highest bidder at public auction. The lessees were under oath not to leave their holdings between seed-time and harvest. In this arrangement we may find the beginning of the system which was later to bind the tenants to the soil as were the royal serfs of Asia. While the interests of his tenants were

---

[1] Wilcken, *op. cit.* 280 *ff.*   [2] *Op. cit.* 284 *ff.*

safeguarded by the king, they were subjected to unusual burdens in times of economic stress, and were often compelled to take over leases against their will. In some cases they even resorted to flight to escape their obligations[1].

Under Roman rule the "surrendered" land disappeared as a separate class, and in its place we find land which was held in complete private possession (γῆ ἰδιωτική, γῆ κατοικική, γῆ κληρουχική, and οὐσίαι). The public lands fell into two great categories: the λόγος διοικήσεως (including the γῆ βασιλική, γῆ δημοσία, γῆ ἱερά, and probably the γῆ προσόδου), and the λόγος οὐσιακός. The royal lands were leased under the same conditions as before. The "public" lands (γῆ δημοσία) cannot be distinguished from the royal lands except in details of administration[2]. The term δημόσιοι γεωργοί came to be applied to tenants on both crown and public lands. The sacred lands were very materially diminished by the Romans[3]. The confiscated properties were added to the imperial possessions, while the remainder was administered by imperial agents in the interest of the temples. In the third century the temples seem to have been brought under the control of the local senate in each metropolis, and the sacred lands gradually passed into the municipal *territorium*. The "revenue" lands (γῆ προσόδου) appear as a new class under Roman rule, and their characteristics cannot be clearly determined. Rostowzew believes that they represent sequestered property which remained in the hands of the original owner until the obligations to the state were discharged[4]. Meanwhile the land formed a special class, and the revenue went to a special division of the imperial bureaus.

The γῆ οὐσιακή consisted largely of estates which had once been held by members of the imperial family, favorites, or friends in the senatorial and equestrian order,

---

[1] Wilcken, *op. cit.* 272 *ff.*   [2] *Op. cit.* 288 *ff.*   [3] *Op. cit.* 300 *ff.*
[4] Rostowzew, *op. cit.* 135 *ff.* Cf. Wilcken, *op. cit.* 296 *ff.*

and had probably been free of any tax or rental. In the course of the first century these estates came into the possession of the emperors, and constituted a curious sort of imperial patrimony within Egypt, which as a whole was regarded as a personal possession of the crown[1]. While the γῆ οὐσιακή was under the administration of a separate bureau (λόγος οὐσιακός), the tenants, known as γεωργοὶ οὐσιακοί, seem to have received the same treatment as those on public property. The μισθωταὶ οὐσιακοί are also found as tenants, apparently with the same status as the γεωργοί, although it is believed that their leases were for fixed periods and were assigned to the less valuable land. Such leaseholds could be sublet, but the sublessees were directly responsible to the imperial agents from whom also they received the right of taking over the lease.

The administration of Egypt as an imperial domain was under the control of a prefect assisted by an elaborate bureaucracy[2]. Apart from the Greek cities, the whole Nile valley was divided into three administrative districts over each of which an *epistrategus* exercised authority as the deputy of the prefect. These districts were again divided into nomes under the supervision of a *strategus*. The nomes were divided into toparchies in which were the villages. The administrative centre of each nome was the metropolis. The organization of the village-communities and the metropolis has been described elsewhere[3]. Here we need only recall the fact that the officials of the villages acted as agents of the bureaucracy rather than as servants of the community. Corporate liability was early recognized and enforced[4]. The community as a whole was liable for the default of any of its members, and in some cases the village was compelled to take over leaseholds which had been vacated, or for which no tenant had bidden at the official auctions.

[1] Rostowzew, *op. cit.* 119 *ff.*   [2] Wilcken, *op. cit.* 28 *ff.*
[3] *Cf.* pp. 27 *ff.*   [4] Wilcken, *Chrestomathie*, 345

[36]

THE SALTUS IN ASIA AND EGYPT

One of the most noteworthy features of the Roman administration of Egypt was the growth of private ownership of land. The descendants of the soldiers of the Ptolemies were no longer subject to military service and the cleruchic land, in so far as it had not been confiscated by Augustus, passed into the private possession of the former occupants[1]. The catoecic lands were also treated in the same way. Both paid an annual tax to the bureaus. Thus there was created a large class of landowners with small holdings. The development of the liturgical system probably had decisive influence in the new policy. Liturgies could not be imposed upon a citizen unless he owned property which could be held as surety for the proper discharge of his obligations, and the Romans doubtless found that tenants could evade their responsibilities more easily than owners. Private ownership must have been common when the municipal organization was extended to the metropolis of each nome in A.D. 202. In the fourth century the γῆ βασιλική and the γῆ δημοσία disappear from the records. These lands either became the property of private individuals who were given possession under an obligation to cultivate them, or they had been incorporated in the territory of the municipalities.

As the economic pressure increased in Egypt, it became more and more difficult to find tenants for the imperial lands. Two solutions of the problem were attempted. Compulsory tenantry was adopted, which led to the development of serfdom. In some cases tenants were arbitrarily transferred to abandoned districts from profitable holdings, in the hope that successful farmers might be able to reclaim the exhausted land[2]. The second device was the principle of *adiectio* (ἐπιβολή). This was a form of compulsory leasehold, whereby lands, for which no tenants had applied, were arbitrarily assigned to private owners, or to tenants on the imperial estates, or even to the villages

---

[1] Bell, *loc. cit.* 89 *ff.*   [2] Wilcken, *Grundzüge*, 293 *f.*

as corporate communities[1]. As a rental was imposed, the unwilling lessee was obliged to cultivate the land in some fashion. In a few cases we find records of leases which specified "that the land was free from the obligation to cultivate royal or public lands," and where this clause does not appear it is probable that the liability to *adiectio* was implied[2].

In a narrow sense, the history of Egypt under Roman rule may be viewed as a struggle for supremacy between two systems of administration; the bureaucratic imperial estate *versus* the municipal organization. The victory rested, though only in name, with the latter, since the imperial estates were gradually merged in the municipal *territorium*, but in fact the city became a mere instrument in the hands of the bureaucracy and functioned solely as an agent of the imperial government. This development and its influence on the cities in other parts of the empire are subjects treated elsewhere[3]. The failure of the Romans to carry out the system of the Ptolemies is due to a variety of causes. Egypt was too remote from the capital, and the natives were exploited by the official class. The tribute imposed upon the country exhausted its resources. Depopulation and abandonment of the less fertile areas followed. Finally, the exaction of imperial requisitions and the development of the liturgical system resulted in the restraint of personal liberty and reduced the population to political and economic serfdom[4].

[1] Wilcken, *op. cit.* 292; Zulueta, *de patrociniis vicorum*, 43.
[2] Wilcken, *Chrestomathie*, 355–359.
[3] *Cf.* pp. 194 *ff.*
[4] For the development of the principle of *origo* in Egypt, *cf.* nos. 168, 175, 192, 193 and pp. 194, 217 *ff.*

CHAPTER V

CIVITATES LIBERAE ET IMMUNES AND CIVITATES STIPENDIARIAE

W E have tried to classify communities in the Roman empire according to their origin, character, and juridical relation to Rome or to other cities. It is convenient to group them also on the basis of their freedom from the payment of tribute, or their obligation to pay it. From 89 B.C. to the time of Diocletian Italy was free from this charge[1], but from land outside Italy a rental in kind (*decumae*), or a fixed sum of money (*stipendium* or *tributum*) was expected. Exemption from this payment could be had only as a privilege. We find, therefore, in the provinces two classes of communities, *civitates stipendiariae* and *civitates immunes*, or, to use for the second class the term more commonly employed in antiquity, *civitates liberae et immunes*. The circumstances which often led Rome to grant freedom or exemption from taxation to a city are illustrated in the case of Utica which assisted Rome in the third Punic war[2]. For a similar reason Antony made Laodicea a *civitas libera et immunis*, because of the sturdy resistance which it had offered to Cassius in 43 B.C.[3] Sometimes the fortunate city owed its privileges to the generosity of the Roman people, as Delphi did[4], or to the favor of a Roman general, as in the case of Aphrodisias[5].

[1] Marquardt, *St. Verw.* 2, 177 *ff.*
[2] Appian, *Pun.* 75, 135; *cf. CIL.* 1, 200, l. 75.
[3] Appian, *B.C.* 4. 62; 5. 7.
[4] *Cf.* Henze, *De civitatibus liberis*, 34.
[5] *Cf.* Henze, *op. cit.* 52 *f.*

[39]

CIVITATES LIBERAE ET IMMUNES

The recognition of a community as a free city[1] usually carried along with it exemption from the payment of tribute, but under the republic the free cities were not always safe from the imposition of taxes at the hands of greedy governors or needy generals[2], and under the early empire cities made "free" did not necessarily have even a technical claim to immunity from taxation[3]. However, in the great majority of cases in both periods it is probable that cities of this class enjoyed the privilege mentioned[4], so that in a particular instance, when evidence to the contrary is not available, it is wise to take it for granted that a free city was *immunis*.

Freedom might be granted to a city by a treaty, in which case the city bore the title of a *civitas foederata*[5], or in the second place it might come through a law, or through a decree of the senate. Cities of the latter sort were called *civitates sine foedere liberae et immunes*. The rights of these two classes of communities

---

[1] It is important to notice that cities which are styled free by the ancient historians are sometimes not technically *civitates liberae*. Thus, for instance, Flamininus in 196 B.C. declared (*cf.* Livy, 33. 32. 5–6) the Corinthians and certain other peoples free, because they were released from the domination of Philip, but this action did not make them *civitates liberae* (*cf.* Henze, *op. cit.* 2). The term αὐτονομία, used in the East, must also be distinguished from *libertas*. It indicates the granting to a city of the privilege *suis legibus uti* (*cf.* Mommsen, *St. R.* 3, 724), but these laws may be administered under the supervision of Roman magistrates.

[2] *Cf.* Marquardt, *St. Verw.* 1, 72, n. 1; Henze, *op. cit.* 4.

[3] This seems to have been true, for instance, of Magnesia and Sipylum, Chios and Apollonidea (*cf.* Mommsen, *St. R.* 3, 683, n. 4; 682, n. 3).

[4] The fact that Pliny in his lists characterizes only a few free cities as *civitates immunes* does not prove that many others were not free from the payment of tribute (*cf.* Mommsen, *St. R.* 3, 683, n. 4).

[5] This term is used in its technical sense only once in the Latin inscriptions, but it is frequent in literature; *cf. Diz. Ep.* 2, 255 *f.* To the list of *civitates foederatae* given by Marquardt (*St. Verw.* 1, 75 *f.*) Kabbadias has recently added Troezen (*cf. IG.* iv, 791), Thurreium of Acarnania (*cf. IG.* ix, 483), and Epidaurus (*cf.* 'Εφ. 'Αρχ. 1918, 166 *ff.*). The term *socii* was a purely honorary title, and did not imply a treaty nor the possession of special rights; *cf.* Henze, *op. cit.* 6.

were essentially the same, but the privileges of a federated city were based upon a treaty, and, therefore, irrevocable[1], whereas a law or a decree of the senate, upon which the claims of cities of the second class were based, could be repealed at the will of the Roman people or senate[2]. Reference is frequently made to the treaties into which Rome had entered with other cities, but none of the treaties has been preserved in its entirety[3]. Almost all of them, so far as we can determine their dates, belong to the period of the republic[4]. Evidently, as time went on, Rome became less generous than she had been in earlier days in granting rights in perpetuity. Her early acts of generosity had come out of a grateful recognition of services rendered in times of great peril. Then too these favors granted to her supporters and her stern treatment of hostile cities would serve to show in future wars what friend and foe

---

[1] Occasionally the Romans did not observe the sanctity of these treaties. Suetonius writes (*Aug.* 47): urbium quasdam, foederatas sed ad exitium licentia praecipites, libertate privavit. From Cassius Dio, 54. 7. 6, Cyzicus, Tyre, and Sidon would seem to be the cities concerned. Rhodes and Malaca were at one time federated cities. Later they lost this status. Perhaps they were thought to have denounced the treaty with Rome, when they took sides against her.

[2] An interesting commentary on the uncertain position of the *civitates sine foedere* seems to be furnished by the statement of Suetonius concerning the exceptional good fortune of the people of Ilium. Of them he says: Iliensibus quasi Romanae gentis auctoribus, tributa *in perpetuum* remisit (*Claud.* 25).

[3] Such references may be seen in Livy, 38. 8. 10 and Tac. *Ann.* 2. 53. For fragments of the treaty with Astypalaea, *cf.* Viereck, *Sermo Graecus*, p. 42, no. 21 and *Rhein. Mus.* 44 (1889), 446.

[4] *E.g.* the treaty with Massilia is perhaps as early as 389 b.c. (*cf.* Justin, 43. 5. 10); that with the Vocontii is known in the first century b.c. (*CIL.* xii, p. 160); the treaties with Tauromenium and Neaetum are mentioned by Cicero (*in Verr.* 2. 160; 3. 13 and *ibid.* 5. 56; 5. 133); the treaty with Rhodes grew out of the war with Perseus (Livy, 45. 25. 7), and the treaty with Astypalaea belongs to the year 104 b.c. The treaty with Aphrodisias (*cf.* no. 29) is also of the republican period. Perhaps an example of a treaty, made under the empire, conferring the rights of a free city, exists in the case of Tyrus (Henze, *op. cit.* 76).

might expect from her. With the world at her feet, she had no more crises to face.

The *lex Antonia de Termessibus* of 71 B.C. gives us a typical specimen of a plebiscite establishing a free city, and there is a decree of the senate with the same object in view in the case of Stratonicea[1]. The initiative in granting this privilege was frequently taken by some successful general or by the emperor[2].

The rights of free cities, whether guaranteed by a treaty with Rome or granted in a law or in a decree of the senate, were liable to cancellation or abridgment on the ground that the cities had broken faith with Rome or had not been loyal to her. On the other hand, a city sometimes regained its lost rights, or the privileges of a free city were conferred on a community which previously had lacked them. Thus Tyre was free under the republic, lost its freedom under Augustus[3], but regained it later[4]. Mitylene had the right of receiving exiles in Cicero's time[5] and was, therefore, probably free, lost its privileges, apparently in the first Mithradatic war[6], but received them later again at the hands of Pompey[7]. The people of Locri Ozolae seem to have been *immunes* at the beginning of the reign of Augustus, but to have been reduced to the position of *attributi* of Patrae before the close of it[8]. Altogether in the Roman world there were two hundred or more cities which permanently or temporarily bore the title of "free cities[9]." Of these, Africa and Asia, with approximately

---

[1] The *Lex Antonia* is no. 19 in this book. The decree in the case of Stratonicea is no. 17. An inscription found in the ruins of Tabae (no. 16) is a *senatus consultum*, apparently conferring the rights of *civitates liberae* on a group of cities; cf. Chapot, *La prov. rom. proc. d'Asie*, 38 *ff.*

[2] Cf. Tac. *Ann.* 12. 61 and Kuhn, *Die städt. u. bürgerl. Verfassung d. röm. Reichs*, 2, 20 *f.*

[3] Cf. Marquardt, *St. Verw.* 1, 395, n. 2.

[4] Cf. *Dig.* 50. 15. 1.

[5] Cf. Cic. *Brut.* 250; *ad Att.* 5. 11. 6.

[6] Cf. Suet. *Iul.* 2.   [7] Cf. Vell. 2. 18.

[8] Cf. Henze, *op. cit.* 34.   [9] Cf. Henze, *op. cit.*

thirty-nine and thirty-five respectively, could boast the largest number[1].

The nature of the rights and privileges which a free city enjoyed may be best inferred from the *lex Antonia de Termessibus*. The first privilege mentioned in this document is the right *uti suis legibus*[2]. It gave Termessus the right to govern under its own laws, to repeal and amend them, and to pass new ones, subject only to the limitation, *quod advorsus hanc legem non fiat*[3]. It implied also the administration of justice by local courts. Next in order in the law is the right to hold land free from the land tax[4]. This freedom from taxation is set forth more fully in the case of certain free cities in Africa[5]. Inasmuch as the people of Termessus are made masters of their own territory by this concession, the Roman governor may not exercise authority in it, and it is thought of as lying outside of his province[6]. He may not even enter the city in his official capacity[7]. The two rights which have just been mentioned are the most fundamental ones, and the autonomy of the free city was based primarily on them.

The third right guaranteed in the *lex Antonia* is freedom

---

[1] For the free cities of Asia, *cf.* Brandis, *R.E.* 2, 1540–1543.

[2] *Cf.* no. 19, Col. I, ll. 8–9. For similar expressions, *cf.* Livy's statement (38. 39. 12) concerning the Phocaeans: ut legibus antiquis uterentur permissum, and Trajan's remark concerning Amisus (Plin. *Epp. ad Trai.* 92): Amisenorum civitas libera et foederata beneficio indulgentiae tuae legibus suis utitur.

[3] No. 19, Col. I, ll. 10–11.   [4] *Ibid.* Col. I, ll. 12–35.

[5] *Cf. lex agraria* (= *CIL.* I, 200), ll. 85 *ff.*

[6] This is the significance of the account which Suetonius gives (*Iul.* 25) of Caesar's arrangements in Gaul: omnem Galliam,...praeter socias ac bene meritas civitates, in provinciae formam redegit eique ⌈cccc⌉ in singulos annos stipendii nomine imposuit; *cf.* Suet. *Vesp.* 8: Achaiam, Lyciam, Rhodum, Byzantium, Samum libertate adempta...in provinciarum formam redegit.

[7] *Cf.* Mommsen, *St. R.* 1, 378, n. 1; 3, 689. When we find Roman governors holding court in certain free cities in later times (*cf. op. cit.* 3, 689, n. 4) we may surmise that permission had been granted by the cities themselves, whose trade would profit by the influx of litigants, witnesses, and officials; *cf.* the case of Apamea in Dio Chrys. 35. 14.

from the establishment of winter quarters for Roman troops in Termessus[1]. This provision does not prevent Roman soldiers from passing through the city or being billeted temporarily in it, and by special authorization of the Roman senate troops may be quartered in Termessus[2]. In the same paragraph the right of Roman officials to requisition supplies in accordance with the limitations of the unknown Porcian law is recognized[3].

The next paragraph in the law seems to reestablish certain preexisting rights of the people of Termessus in their relations with the Romans[4]. The local courts could take cognizance even of cases where Roman citizens were concerned, but probably in such cases certain restrictions were put on the exercise of authority by the local magistrate[5].

The last article recognizes the right of Termessus to levy inland and maritime customs dues[6]. This privilege was not restricted to *civitates liberae*. Indeed the one extant specimen of a table setting forth port dues or *octroi* is from Palmyra, a city which was not free[7]. In the matter of allowing the imposition of customs dues by local authorities the policy of the central government changed from one period to another. Under later emperors, like Alexander Severus and Julian, Rome was more liberal than she had been under Tiberius[8]. This change in policy

---

[1] No. 19, Col. ii, ll. 6–13.   [2] *Ibid.* Col. ii, ll. 11–13.
[3] *Cf.* G. Rotondi, *Leges publicae populi Romani*, 269.
[4] No. 19, Col. ii, ll. 18–30.
[5] *Cf.* Mommsen, *St. R.* 3, 701–706.
[6] No. 19, Col. ii, ll. 31–37.
[7] *Cf.* Dessau in *Hermes*, 19 (1884), 486–533. The Palmyra tariff is clearly municipal; cf. *ibid.* 527 *ff.*; Rostowzew, *Geschichte d. Staatspacht*, 405; Hirschfeld, 81, n. 1; *cf.* also commentary on no. 61 and p. 140, n. 2. The dues collected at Zarai (*cf. CIL.* viii, 4508) were probably imperial; *cf.* Cagnat, *Les impôts indirects chez les Romains*, 116; Rostowzew, *op. cit.* 403. For the case of Koptos in Egypt, *cf.* Dittenberger, *Or. Gr.* 674; *Rom. Mitth.* 1897, 75 *ff.*; Wilcken, *Ostraka*, 1, 347 *ff.*
[8] Liebenam, *St. Verw.* 22 *f.*

may be due to the general demoralization of civic finance. In Termessus the produce belonging to Roman tax farmers was exempt from the payment of duty[1]. In other cases Roman citizens and even Latins were not required to pay local *portoria*[2]. Three considerations probably influenced the central government to limit and, in some cases, to cancel the local right to levy customs duties: (1) the desire to give preferential treatment to Roman citizens, and to bring the trade of the world into the hands of Rome; (2) the importance of lowering the cost of merchandise brought to Italy, and (3) the establishment of an imperial tariff for revenue[3].

Two privileges which were frequently enjoyed by free cities are not mentioned in the *lex Antonia*, viz. the right of receiving exiles and the right of coinage, although it may be noted in passing that the right of a city in the Orient to coin money is not evidence that it was a free city. Up to the time of the first Punic war the federated cities retained their unrestricted right of coinage, although their coins were not legal tender in Rome[4]. However, by the close of the republican period, or in the early empire, with few exceptions, these cities were allowed to issue small coins only, and even the exercise of this privilege was subject to the consent and the control of the central government[5]. By these means Roman coins were made the medium of circulation throughout the world, trade was fostered, and a long step was taken toward making Rome

---

[1] No. 19, Col. II, ll. 34–37.
[2] *Cf.* Livy's statement (38. 44) of the concession to the people of Ambracia: portoria, quae vellent, terra marique caperent, dum eorum immunes Romani ac socii nominis Latini essent.
[3] The way in which the Roman world was divided into tariff districts with stations for the collection of imperial customs in each may be seen in Cagnat, *op. cit.* 19–82. By the side of this imperial system non-imperial tariff arrangements could not be expected to survive in many cases.
[4] *Cf.* Mommsen, *St. R.* 3, 710.
[5] Mommsen, *St. R.* 3, 713, n. 1, notes on a coin of the free city of Cercina in Africa the phrase *permissu L. Volusi procos.*

the banking and commercial centre of the world. Incidentally nothing illustrates better than the history of local coinage Rome's policy, as time went on, of restricting more and more the traditional rights of the free cities.

The foreign relations of a free city were determined by Rome. Even the federated cities suffered this limitation of complete sovereignty. The treaty with them was a *foedus iniquum*. Perhaps the nearest approach to the exercise of international rights which they had, lay in the privilege of receiving exiles—a privilege of doubtful value to them. This right was enjoyed by free cities of both classes[1].

While the privileges mentioned above were those commonly granted to free cities, the fact should be borne in mind that Rome's policy changed from period to period, that she was more generous to one city than to another, and that in the case of some cities *libertas* may have been little more than an honorary distinction.

The system of taxation which the Romans followed in their provinces was first adopted in Sicily, and it is clearly set forth by Cicero in one of his Verrine orations[2]. In this passage he remarks:

Between Sicily and the other provinces there is this difference in the matter of the land tax, that on the others a fixed contribution, called a *stipendium*, is levied, representing the fruits of victory or a punishment for engaging in war with us. This plan is followed in the Spains and with many districts of the Carthaginians. Or the contract system under the censors has been adopted, as it was in Asia under the Sempronian law. As for the cities of Sicily we accepted jurisdiction over them with the proviso that they should retain the same legal status (*eodem iure*) which they had before, and should submit to the Roman people on the terms (*eadem con-*

---

[1] There is no evidence that Smyrna, whither Q. Caepio went into exile (*cf.* Cic. *pro Balbo*, 28), or Patrae, where the exile C. Maenius Gemellus stayed (*cf.* Cic. *ad fam.* 13. 19. 2), were federated cities.
[2] 3. 12–14.

dicione) on which they had submitted to their own rulers. A very few of these cities were brought under our rule by our ancestors by force of arms, and, although their territory was made *ager publicus populi Romani*, still it has been given back to them. There are two federated (*foederatae*) cities, viz. Messana and Tauromenium[1], where it is not our practice to collect tithes. Then there are five cities *sine foedere immunes ac liberae*, Centuripae, Halaesa, Segesta, Halicyae, and Panormus. Outside of these, all the land of the cities of Sicily is subject to tithes, and was so before the Roman people ruled it, in accordance with the wish and under the institutions of the Sicilians themselves.

In this statement Cicero tells us plainly that when the Romans acquired Sicily they took over the system of taxation which the Syracusans and Carthaginians had employed before them, the *lex Hieronica*, as he calls it elsewhere[2]. The system may be traced back to Persia through the monarchies of the East and the arrangements of Alexander[3]. The territory of Sicily falls into three main categories. Certain districts which had made a determined resistance were converted into imperial domains[4], a few were exempted from taxation, and all the rest of the island was subject to the payment of tribute. The tax-free cities are of two kinds, as we have already noticed, those whose privileges were guaranteed by a treaty, and those whose rights were granted in some other way. The third class of communities were the *civitates stipendiariae*. In Sicily there were sixty-five *civitates*[5]. Now eight of these were exempt from taxation, because to the two allied cities mentioned here Cicero elsewhere adds a third, Netum[6]. The land of very few (*perpaucae*), perhaps of six cities, styled *civitates censoriae*, was declared *ager publicus*.

---

[1] In 5. 56 a third city, Netum, is added.   [2] *in Verr*. 2. 32.

[3] *Cf*. Rostowzew, *Gesch. d. röm. Kol*. 229–240, and the illuminating treatment by Frank, *Roman Imperialism*, 93–99, 108, n. 17.

[4] *Cf*. pp. 15 *ff*.   [5] *Cf*. Cic. *in Verr*. 2. 133 and 137.

[6] *in Verr*. 5. 56.

Consequently, the rest of the cities, about fifty-one in number, were *civitates stipendiariae*. Exact figures for the other provinces are difficult to obtain, but in all of them the taxed communities far outnumbered those which were free from taxation by the central government. Thus, in the time of Pliny the Elder, in Baetica one hundred and twenty out of one hundred and seventy-five cities were tributary cities, in Tarraconensis, one hundred and thirty-five out of one hundred and seventy-nine, in Lusitania, thirty-five out of forty-six[1]. We do not find evidence that in all Asia more than thirty or thirty-five cities out of a total of about five hundred were free at any time[2].

It was the payment by these communities of taxes[3], in Sicily in the form of tithes, which constituted the chief mark of difference between them and the free cities. The other essential feature in their status which distinguished them from the free cities was the fact that each of them belonged to the province, and its internal affairs were subject to the supervision and control of the governor of the province.

Such rights as these cities had they received in the first instance through a *lex provinciae*, drawn up usually by the general who brought the district into subjection or by a senatorial commission[4]. Their status in certain matters was still further defined by the successive edicts of emperors and provincial governors and by occasional decrees of the senate concerning a particular city[5]. Under the

[1] *Cf.* Schulten, *R.E.* 8, 2037–8.

[2] *Cf.* Brandis, *R.E.* 2, 1540–3; Chapot, *La prov. rom. proc. d'Asie*, 114–121; Kuhn, *Die städt. u. bürgerl. Verfassung d. röm. Reichs*, 2, 6.

[3] For a discussion of taxation in the provinces, see pp. 117 *ff*.

[4] For senatorial commissions in the second and first centuries B.C., *cf.* Willems, *Le sénat de la république rom.* 2, 507, n. 2.

[5] The large number of special measures in existence in the first century of our era, conferring certain privileges on provincial cities, is attested by Suetonius (*Vesp.* 8): aerearumque tabularum tria milia quae simul conflagraverant restituenda suscepit...instrumentum imperii pulcherrimum ac vetustissimum, quo continebantur...senatus consulta, plebiscita de societate et foedere ac privilegio...concessis.

[48]

republic the power to organize a newly acquired territory into a province rested with the senate, and it was necessary for this body to draw up the fundamental statutes of the province or to ratify the arrangements made by a Roman general[1]. None of the *leges provinciarum* has come down to us, but we have frequent references to them in ancient literature[2], and from these references we can get a conception of the contents of the constitutions drawn up for provincial cities. Thus, under the *lex Rupilia*, the citizens of a given Sicilian community in dealing with one another enjoy the privilege of being subject to their own laws. In an action brought by a citizen of one Sicilian town against another, the Roman praetor chooses the jurors. In an action brought by a Roman against a Sicilian, the judge must be a Sicilian; in the reverse situation, the judge is a Roman[3]. The *lex Pompeia*, among other matters, fixed certain conditions of eligibility to the local magistracies and senates in Pontus and Bithynia, and regulates admission to local citizenship[4]. Outside the *leges provinciarum*, the leader or the commission which organized a province often drew up a special charter for a particular city. Rupilius, for instance, in 132 B.C. gave Heracleia in Sicily a charter, one of whose articles prescribed the method of choosing the members of the local senate[5], and the charters granted to various cities in Bithynia and Pontus, perhaps by Pompey, seem to have differed from one another in some particulars[6]. Probably each city was

---

[1] *Cf.* Willems, *op. cit.* 2, 703–717.

[2] For the *lex Rupilia* which P. Rupilius drew up for Sicily in 132 B.C., after the Slave war, *cf.* Cic. *in Verr.* 2. 32; 2. 38–40; 2. 90; 2. 125; 3. 40. For the *lex Pompeia* in Bithynia, *cf.* Plin. *Epp. ad Trai.* 79, 80, 112, 114, 115; Strabo, 12. 3. 1; Cass. Dio, 37. 20. 2; Livy, *Ep.* 102. For the *lex Metelli* in Crete, *cf.* Livy, *Ep.* 100, and for the *lex Aemilia* in Macedonia, Livy, 45. 32. For Pompey's general arrangements in the East, *cf.* Drumann-Groebe, *Geschichte Roms*, 4, 477 ff.

[3] *Cf.* Cic. *in Verr.* 2. 32.   [4] *Cf.* Plin. *Epp. ad Trai.* 79, 112.

[5] *Cf.* Cic. *in Verr.* 2. 125.

[6] *Cf.* Plin. *Epp. ad Trai.* 109: quo iure uti debeant Bithyniae vel

allowed to preserve in large measure its traditional usages. These original grants were reaffirmed, extended, restricted, or cancelled in subsequent periods by the Roman senate, or by the emperor, and defined in the successive edicts of provincial governors. Two specimens of *senatus consulta*, regulating in some respects the affairs of Teos[1] and Thisbe[2], are extant, but these decrees were adopted in 193 and 170 B.C. respectively, before Teos and Thisbe became parts of a Roman province.

We may form a general conception of the part which the edict of the governor of a province played in building up the law of the land by looking at the summary which Cicero gives his friend Atticus of his Cilician edict[3]. This edict is an *edictum tralaticium*, inasmuch as Cicero has taken over in large measure the edict of his predecessor[4]. He has, however, introduced some provisions from the "Asiatic edict" of Q. Mucius Scaevola. In the same way the *edictum Siciliense* for a given year was modelled on

Ponticae civitates in iis pecuniis quae ex quaque causa rei publicae debebuntur ex lege cuiusque animadvertendum est.

[1] *CIG.* 3045 = Viereck, *op. eit.* p. 2, no. 2.

[2] *Cf.* no. 5.

[3] *Cf.* Cic. *ad Att.* 6. 1. 15: De Bibuli edicto nihil novi praeter illam exceptionem, de qua tu ad me scripseras, "nimis gravi praeiudicio in ordinem nostrum." Ego tamen habeo ἰσοδυναμοῦσαν sed tectiorem, ex Q. Mucii P. F. edicto Asiatico, "extra quam si ita negotium gestum est, ut eo stari non oporteat ex fide bona," multaque sum secutus Scaevolae, in iis illud, in quo sibi libertatem censent Graeci datam, ut Graeci inter se disceptent suis legibus. Breve autem edictum est propter hanc meam διαίρεσιν quod duobus generibus edicendum putavi; quorum unum est provinciale, in quo est de rationibus civitatum, de aere alieno, de usura, de syngraphis, in eodem omnia de publicanis; alterum, quod sine edicto satis commode transigi non potest, de hereditatum possessionibus, de bonis possidendis, vendendis, magistris faciendis, quae ex edicto et postulari et fieri solent, tertium de reliquo iure dicundo ἄγραφον reliqui. Dixi me de eo genere mea decreta ad edicta urbana accommodaturum, itaque curo et satis facio adhuc omnibus. Graeci vero exsultant, quod peregrinis iudicibus utuntur. Nugatoribus quidem, inquies. Quid refert? Tamen se a᾽τονομίαν adeptos putant. *Cf.* also Cic. *ad fam.* 3. 8. 4; *ad Att.* 5. 21. 11.

[4] *Cf.* Cic. *ad Att.* 5. 21. 11; 6. 1. 15; *ad fam.* 3. 8. 4.

that of the preceding year[1]. Cicero tells us that his edict was in three sections. The second part dealt with such matters as the granting of *bonorum possessiones* and *missiones in bona*, and the third section, which was modelled on the edict of the urban praetor, treated *de reliquo iure dicundo*. It is the first section, the part which Cicero characterizes as *provinciale*, which is of special interest to us. This portion of the edict described the policy which Cicero would follow and the rules which he would adopt in handling the accounts of cities, and in dealing with questions involving debt, the taking of usury, transactions in bonds, and the business of the tax farmers. Arrangements were made to relieve many cities of their debts[2], to force dishonest local magistrates to return their ill-gotten gains[3], to keep down the expenses of the Cilician cities[4], to prevent usurers from exacting more than the legal rate of 12 per cent.[5], to save the cities from exorbitant requisitions[6], and to secure their rights alike to the provincials and the tax farmers[7]. These were some of the practical applications of the principles laid down in the first section of Cicero's edict. Governors of provinces, even under the empire, retained the *ius edicendi* which Cicero exercised, but after the codification of the provincial edict under Hadrian, and its legalization by a decree of the senate[8], this right had little practical meaning[9]. Under the empire changes in the status of cities in imperial provinces

---

[1] *Cf.* Cic. *in Verr.* 2. 90; 5. 3.   [2] *Cf.* Cic. *ad Att.* 6. 2. 4.
[3] *Cf.* Cic. *ad Att.* 6. 2. 5.   [4] *Cf.* Cic. *ad fam.* 3. 8. 5.
[5] *Cf.* Cic. *ad Att.* 5. 21. 11.   [6] *Cf.* Cic. *ad Att.* 5. 16. 3.
[7] *Cf.* Cic. *ad Att.* 6. 2. 5.

[8] It is still a disputed question whether after the reforms of Salvius Julianus there was an *edictum perpetuum* for each province or a uniform edict for all the provinces; *cf.* Karlowa, 631 *f.* and Girard, *Manuel élém. de droit rom.* 52 *ff.*

[9] In this connection it is interesting to notice that Anicius Maximus, a governor of Bithynia under Trajan, ruled that in certain cities of his province men chosen to the local senates by the censors should pay an initiation fee (*cf.* Plin. *Epp. ad Trai.* 112).

CIVITATES LIBERAE ET IMMUNES

at least were made under direct instructions from the emperor[1]. Legally these changes held good only during the reign of the emperor who made them, but after the middle of the first century of our era it was customary for an emperor to ratify the acts of his predecessor[2].

To sum up our conclusions then, the working constitution and the laws of the city of Apamea, for instance, in the second century of our era would be based on the *lex provinciae* of Cilicia, as modified by special concessions, restrictions, or changes made by the senatorial commission or the general who organized the province, and as subsequently changed by decrees of the senate, by edicts or rulings of the governors of Cilicia, or by imperial constitutions or *mandata*. It is impossible, therefore, to give a list of the rights enjoyed by provincial cities of a certain class which will hold for all the cities of that class. This statement is true in particular of the *civitates stipendiariae*. We can, however, specify the privileges which were frequently granted to cities of this sort. The privilege most highly prized by the people of these cities was the retention of their local codes[3] and the right of having their actions at law decided by their fellow-citizens. They retained also their local organs of government—magistracies,

---

[1] See pp. 233 *ff*. For literary specimens of these imperial communications, see the two epistles of Domitian and an edict and epistle of Nerva in Plin. *Ep. ad Trai*. 58. In the seventy-ninth letter an edict of Augustus fixing the minimum age for incumbency of the local magistracies in Bithynia is mentioned by Pliny; in the sixty-fifth letter he speaks of various imperial edicts concerning Asia, Sparta, and Achaea.

[2] *Cf.* Suet. *Tit.* 8.

[3] *Cf.* Cicero's remark in a letter from Cilicia (*ad Att.* 6. 1. 15): multaque sum secutus Scaevolae, in iis illud, in quo sibi libertatem censent Graeci datam, ut Graeci inter se disceptent suis legibus, and, in speaking of the court which he held at Laodicea, he says (*ad Att.* 6. 2. 4): omnes (civitates) suis legibus et iudiciis usae, αὐτονομίαν adeptae, revixerunt. *Cf.* also Cic. *in Verr.* 2. 32. Scaevola had been governor of Asia, so that the same principle must have held in that province also. For the method of choosing jurors in Sicily when Romans or Sicilians of different towns were involved, *cf.* p. 49.

senates, and popular assemblies—as we can see clearly from Pliny's letters to Trajan, and communities on the frontier probably had the privilege of raising an armed force in an emergency for self-defence. Cities of this class, with the approval of the emperor or governor, also had the right to lay taxes on their citizens[1], and in some cases to issue copper coins, although the minting of other coins was in the hands of the central government[2].

The rights of the tributary cities do not at the first glance seem to differ materially from those of the free cities. Communities of both classes retained their local codes, had their own senates, assemblies, and courts, and had the right to lay taxes and make contracts. But, as we noticed above, the stipendiary cities were subject to the payment of tribute and to all the abuses attendant upon it; they were liable to the constant interference of the governor of the province in their internal affairs, as we can infer from the letters of Pliny, and they had to submit to the billeting of troops and to the requisitions and exactions of Roman officials and soldiers[3]. The two classes of cities discussed in this chapter shared with the *municipia* the privilege of retaining their traditional procedure[4]. Only colonies were required to adopt Roman law. In other words all provincial cities of native origin, except those which were raised to the status of a colony, had the common characteristic of being governed by their own local codes of laws. The edict of Caracalla went far toward raising the stipendiary cities to a level with the other cities of the empire. Up to A.D. 212 the Romans residing in these cities enjoyed a general immunity from local liturgies. Their exemption

---

[1] See the permission to levy *vectigalia* granted by Augustus to the Saborenses and confirmed by Vespasian, no. 61.

[2] *Cf.* Mommsen, *St. R.* 3, 762.

[3] How vexatious were the requisitions of the soldiers and imperial freedmen is brought out in the appeals for relief made to the emperor in the third century by the Aragueni (no. 141) and the people of Scaptoparene (no. 139).

[4] *Cf.* p. 9.

made the financial burdens of their less fortunate fellow-citizens very heavy. Consequently the granting of Roman citizenship to the natives of tribute-paying cities by Caracalla[1] put all the residents of these cities on an equality, and removed the financial disabilities from which the non-Roman element had suffered.

This chapter brings to an end our study of the various political units which the Romans used in the administration of the empire, and we may stop for a moment to survey the growth of the policy which Rome adopted in her relations with the rest of the world. As Schulten has well said[2], the history of Rome illustrates the steady development of the imperial idea. At the outset the city of Rome stands alone. In time she gains hegemony over the members of the Latin League. Through the conquest of Italy comes her supremacy over the whole peninsula, with the forced concession of liberal rights to Italian communities as a result of the Social war. The acquisition of the provinces brought her into relations not only with cities, which were granted autonomy under treaty rights, but also with subject towns and tribes, and finally the theory, not that Rome, but that the emperor was master of the world developed, and the city of Rome sank to the level of the other cities of the empire.

[1] See especially the commentary on no. 192.
[2] *Rh. Mus.* 50 (1895), 556.

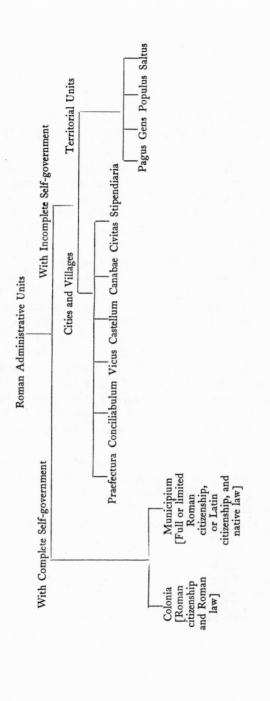

Roman Administrative Units

With Complete Self-government

With Incomplete Self-government

Territorial Units

Cities and Villages

Colonia [Roman citizenship and Roman law]

Municipium [Full or limited Roman citizenship, or Latin citizenship, and native law]

Praefectura Conciliabulum Vicus Castellum Canabae Civitas Stipendiaria

Pagus Gens Populus Saltus

CHAPTER VI

THE MUNICIPAL SYSTEM OF THE REPUBLIC
AND EARLY EMPIRE IN THE WEST

THE Romans found in the cities which were brought under their control forms of government which differed from one another in many particulars. They differed in respect to the numbers, titles, and functions of the city magistrates, and in the share which the people or the aristocracy had in the control of affairs. The chief magistrate, for instance, in many of the old Italian cities was called praetor[1], or dictator[2], or interrex[3], or consul[4]. In Africa he was usually styled sufes[5], while in Greek lands the commonest titles were ἄρχων and στρατηγός. Usually the college of chief magistrates was composed of two members, but we occasionally find *III viri* and even *X viri* mentioned in the inscriptions[6]. In the East the local senate was, nominally at least, more quickly responsive to the popular will than it was in the West, because its members in Greek cities were frequently chosen by a direct vote of the people and held their positions for a year only, whereas in the West senates were largely made up of ex-magistrates who served for life. In the West a large measure of uniformity was introduced into the municipal system before the close of the republican period. This change was largely due to the fact that the cities in the western provinces rarely had long political traditions behind them, so that they found no great

---

[1] *E.g.* at Anagnia, Auximum, Beneventum. *Cf.* Dessau, 3, p. 694.
[2] *E.g.* at Aricia, Caere, Lanuvium. *Cf. op. cit.* p. 686.
[3] *E.g.* at Formiae and Fundi. *Cf. op. cit.* p. 690.
[4] *E.g.* at Ariminum. *Cf. op. cit.* p. 684.
[5] *E.g.* at Thugga and Avitta Bibba. *Cf. op. cit.* p. 698.
[6] *Cf. op. cit.* pp. 686, 698.

difficulty in accepting a ready-made system. In fact in this quarter of the world Roman institutions and the Latin language made rapid headway, and partly by voluntary imitation, partly by legislation, the system which had developed in the city of Rome prevailed. In the East, however, Greek culture and the Greek language stood in the way of the ready adoption of Latin institutions, and titles and practices which had existed for generations could not be easily changed. But it is true that, while old titles and forms were tenaciously held, magisterial functions and essential governmental methods were brought into greater conformity with western practice, and after the promulgation of Caracalla's constitution the tendency toward uniformity was very marked. It will be convenient therefore to take up separately the municipal systems of the West and the East, while recognizing the fact that even in the West[1] no description in all its details will be applicable to every city.

Municipalities all over the Roman world enjoyed complete or limited self-government. They chose their own magistrates and passed their own ordinances. The governing powers in them were the local magistrates, the local senate, and the popular assembly. In the West the titles and functions of these three organs of government were made reasonably uniform toward the end of the republic. Whether the natural tendency toward uniformity was stimulated by drawing up model municipal charters or not is a matter of much doubt[2].

The *populus* or *plebs urbana* was made up of citizens

[1] Our principal sources of information concerning the municipal system are the inscriptions, and in particular eleven municipal laws and charters, of which seven are given in this book (*cf.* nos. 20, 24, 26, 27, 28, 64 and 65). The others, which are very fragmentary and add little, if anything, to our knowledge of the subject, are Bruns, 31, 32, 33 and 33 *a*. All these legal documents come from the West and four of them belong to Caesar's time.

[2] Many scholars have supposed that the *lex Iulia municipalis* was intended as a model, but *cf.* commentary on no. 24.

THE MUNICIPAL SYSTEM OF THE REPUBLIC

(*coloni, municipes, cives*) and of resident aliens (*incolae*). Both classes were subject to the *munera*, and both had the right to vote, but resident aliens were not allowed to hold office until a later period in the empire. Resident aliens were also subject to the court processes and to the *munera* of their native city. Local citizenship was gained, as at Rome, by birth or adoption, by manumission[1], or through the gift of the emperor or the local senate. For voting purposes citizens were grouped in *curiae*, tribes, or centuries. In Malaca resident aliens, who were Roman or Latin citizens, were assigned by lot to one of the *curiae* in the popular assembly[2], and a similar practice was probably followed in other municipalities. We are particularly concerned with the relations of the central government to the municipalities, and in connection with resident aliens there is an exercise of imperial power in the municipalities which is of interest to us[3]. An instance in point is the transfer of the citizenship of a certain C. Valerius Avitus by Pius from the municipium Augustum to the colonia Tarraconensis[4]. Another interesting case is the *adlectio* by Hadrian of a certain Valerius into the colonia Caesaraugustana[5]. Under the republic the people seem to have exercised freely their power to legislate on many matters[6], but under the empire the principal function of the popular assembly was the election of magistrates or priests for which elaborate provisions are made in chapters 52–60 of the *lex municipalis Malacitana* of Domitian's time. Many municipal inscriptions record the fact that a statue has been set up in honor of a certain individual *postulante populo* or *ex consensu et postulatione populi*, but the formal

[1] *Dig.* 50. 1. 1; *Cod. J.* 10. 40. 7.
[2] *Cf.* no. 65, chap. 53. This is the custom followed in the case of resident Latins at Rome in early days; *cf.* Livy, 25. 3.
[3] Mommsen, *St. R.* 2, 883 *ff.*; 1081, nn. 2 and 4.
[4] *CIL.* ii, 4277.
[5] *CIL.* ii, 4249; *cf.* also Schmidt, *R.E.* 1, 369 and *Diz. Ep.* 1, 414 *ff.*
[6] Cic. *de leg.* 3. 16. 36: et avus quidem noster singulari virtute in hoc municipio, quoad vixit, restitit M. Gratidio...ferenti legem tabellariam.

action in such cases was taken by the local senate, and popular approval was probably indicated in some informal way.

The chief magistrates in western municipalities were usually styled *duoviri iure dicundo*. Below them were the *duoviri aediles*. Sometimes these two boards formed a single college and the members of it were known as *quattuorviri iure dicundo* and *quattuorviri aediles*. Usually the magistrates in colonies were called duovirs, and in *municipia*, quattuorvirs[1]. Every fifth year the chief magistrates took the census and then received the title *quinquennales*. In the absence of the duovirs their place was taken by a prefect. The treasury was managed by quaestors, usually two in number.

The conditions of eligibility to the duovirate are laid down with great precision in the *tabula Heracleensis*[2] and in the *lex municipalis Malacitana*[3], and in the *lex coloniae Genetivae Iuliae*[4] it is provided that no one shall be eligible to a magistracy who may not be made a decurion. In the *tabula Heracleensis* of Caesar's time the age requirement is thirty years[5], but toward the close of the first century of our era it has been reduced to twenty-five at least. Perhaps this change was made by Augustus[6]. A candidate must of course be a free-born citizen, solvent, never convicted in the courts or brought into disrepute by following an ignoble trade, and he must follow the *cursus honorum* through the quaestorship and aedileship. Nomination and election proceeded as at Rome. The *lex municipalis Malacitana*, however, has a significant provision[7] to the effect that, if an insufficient number of candidates offer themselves, the official who is to preside may make the necessary nominations, but the men thus

---

[1] Liebenam in *R.E.* 5, 1804.
[2] No. 24, ll. 89 *ff.*
[3] No. 65, chap. 54.
[4] No. 26, chap. 101; *cf.* also no. 24, ll. 135 *ff.*
[5] No. 65, chap. 54.
[6] Pliny, *Epp. ad Trai.* 79. 2.
[7] No. 65, chap. 51.

nominated by him may propose the names of other people in place of their own.

As chief magistrate one of the duovirs presided at meetings of the popular assembly and senate, and carried out measures passed by either of these bodies. A good illustration of his functions in such matters is furnished by the famous inscription of 105 B.C. from Puteoli[1]. He had general charge, not only of public works and buildings, but also of public funds. He managed public festivals and games, and every five years took the census. Reference seems clearly to be made to the criminal and civil juris-diction of the municipal magistrate in the *tabula Heracleensis*[2], in the *lex Iulia agraria*[3], and in the *lex de Gallia Cisalpina*[4], while in the *lex col. Gen. Iul.*[5] we read: ne quis in hac colonia ius dicito neve cuius in ea colonia iuris dictio esto nisi II viri aut quem II vir praefectum reliquerit aut aedilis uti hac lege oportebit, neve quis pro eo imperio potestateve facito, quo quis in ea colonia ius dicat, nisi quem ex hac lege dicere oportebit. The criminal juris-diction which the duovir exercised in Italy under the republic was transferred under the early empire to the praetorian prefect and the city prefect. In the provinces the governor absorbed the judicial powers of the local magistrate. This encroachment of the imperial govern-ment on the functions of the municipal magistrate came about gradually, and it is important for our purpose to trace briefly the development of the process. To the office of *praefectus praetorio*, as established by Augustus, only military functions were assigned[6]. The appointment of Sejanus to the post and the long absence of Tiberius from Rome gave it a political significance. Later Burrus, as one of the chief councillors of Nero, held the position, and

---

[1] *CIL.* I, 577 = x, 1781 = Dessau, 5317 = Wilmanns, 697. *Cf.* also Wiegand, *Jahr. f. class. Phil. suppl.* 20 (1894), 661 *ff.*
[2] No. 24, l. 119.   [3] Bruns, 15, chap. 3.
[4] No. 27, chap. 20, ll. 5–15, 23, 31; chap. 23, l. 54.
[5] No. 26, chap. 94.   [6] Herzog, 2, 203 *ff.*

under Commodus the praetorian prefect Perennis became practically prime minister[1]. From this time on the civil functions of the office predominated, and that its judicial importance increased is clearly proved by the appointment to it of such eminent jurists as Papinian, Paulus, and Ulpian[2]. Like the office of praetorian prefect that of city prefect gained greatly in importance during the absence of Tiberius from Rome. It was the duty of the *praefectus urbi* to maintain order, and naturally the power was given him to try and to inflict punishment on those guilty of crimes. In this way his court soon crowded out the *quaestiones* in Rome and put an end to the criminal jurisdiction of municipal magistrates in villages up to one hundred miles from Rome. Criminal jurisdiction in the rest of Italy beyond that point was under the control of the praetorian prefect[3], while in the provinces it was administered by the governor. By this transfer of power municipal magistrates lost an important part of their functions, and their dignity was correspondingly lessened. In the middle of the first century b.c., in civil actions the duovirs or quattuorvirs were competent to hear cases involving as much as ten thousand or fifteen thousand sesterces[4], and in certain cases they had jurisdiction irrespective of the amount involved. In Latin *municipia* they could also legalize manumission, emancipation from the *patria potestas* and adoption[5], and could impose penalties for the violation of local ordinances[6]. These various

---

[1] *Hist. Aug. Com.* 5.

[2] *Hist. Aug. Pesc. Nig.* 7; *Alex. Sev.* 26. *Cf.* also *ibid. Ant. Phil.* 11; *Sept. Sev.* 4.

[3] See the passage quoted by Mommsen, *St. R.* 2, 969, n. 2 from Ulpianus, *lib.* 9 *de officio proconsulis* (written under Caracalla; *Coll. Mos. Rom. Leg.* 14. 3. 2): iam eo perventum est constitutionibus, ut Romae quidem praefectus urbis solus super ea re cognoscat, si intra miliarium centesimum sit in via commissa. Enimvero si ultra centesimum, praefectorum praetorio erit cognitio, in provincia (vero) praesidum provinciarum.

[4] *Cf.* commentary on nos. 27 and 28.

[5] Liebenam, *R.E.* 5, 1834.   [6] *Op. cit.* 5, 1835.

powers were much curtailed in the later period as we shall have occasion to notice in another connection[1].

The same principle of collegiality held good for the duovirs as was observed by the consuls in Rome. In Salpensa and Malaca each could veto the action of the other within certain limits[2]. In matters where only one duovir could officiate, preference was given to the older one in Malaca[3]. Municipal aediles were colleagues of the duovirs, just as praetors at Rome were colleagues of the consuls, but like the praetors they were *collegae minores*, and could not oppose the action of the duovirs.

In many cities a magistrate on taking office was required to pay an initiation fee[4], and during his term to contribute to the public games[5], and he was expected to give large sums for the improvement of his native city, or for the entertainment of his fellow-townsmen. While in office he was served by attendants, had a special seat in the theatre, and enjoyed certain other marks of distinction[6].

It is interesting to notice that the emperor was not infrequently chosen duovir, and provision was made for this purpose in the charter of Salpensa[7]. The usage in this matter becomes more sharply defined as we advance into the empire. Three early instances of an honorary duovirate occur in the case of T. Statilius Taurus[8], a prominent political leader under Augustus[9], and M. Barbatius[10], another supporter of Augustus, and Ti. Statilius Severus[11].

[1] See pp. 200 f.
[2] No. 64, chap. 27; no. 65, chap. 58.
[3] No. 65, chap. 52.
[4] Liebenam, *St. Verw.* 54 ff.
[5] No. 26, chap. 70.
[6] Liebenam, *R.E.* 5, 1815 f.
[7] No. 64, chap. 24.
[8] See the inscription from Dyrrhachium (*CIL*, III, 605) *praefectus quinq. T. Statili Tauri.*
[9] *Prosop.* 3, 263, no. 615. Taurus held the consulship for the first time in 37 B.C. and was consul again in 26 B.C. In the year 16 B.C. (*cf.* Tac. *Ann.* 6. 11) he was very advanced in age, so that he must have been honorary duovir at Dyrrhachium early in the reign of Augustus.
[10] Mommsen, *St. R.* 2, 828, n. 5. He was quaestor in 41 B.C.; *cf.* Klebs, *R.E.* 3, 2.
[11] *CIL.* x, 3910.

These are the only known cases in which the honor was granted to anyone not connected with the imperial family[1]. Under Augustus, and for a time under Tiberius, it might be conferred on any member of the imperial family[2], but from the closing years of Tiberius' reign no other representative of the ruling house than the emperor or his destined successor could hold it[3]. When a private citizen or a prince held the office he had a colleague, but apparently from the last years of Tiberius' reign it was provided that the emperor should have no colleague in the office[4]. When an honorary duovir was appointed, the actual duties of the office were performed by a prefect[5]. In other words an imperial appointee became chief magistrate in a city in such a case. The number of imperial prefects of whom we have a record is not large enough to make this official an important factor in bringing the cities under the control of the central government, but the importance of the office lies in the fact that we have here the earliest instance of the appointment of an imperial official to take charge of the affairs of a city. The *praefectus imperatoris* is the progenitor of the *curator rei publicae* who played so important a rôle in robbing local magistrates of their authority[6] and in bringing local affairs under the control of Rome. It may, in fact, be significant that the imperial prefect disappears at about the time when the curatorship was established[7].

The functions of the municipal aedile were identical with those of his counterpart in Rome, and, therefore,

---

[1] Cn. Domitius Ahenobarbus, who was honorary duovir in Pisidian Antioch (*cf. CIL.* iii, *S.* 6809), was the father of Nero.

[2] *Cf. e.g. CIL.* ii, 1534, *S.* 5617; iii, *S.* 6843; v, 7567; x, 901, 902, 904, 6101.

[3] Mommsen, *Stadtrechte von Salpensa u. Malaca*, 415.

[4] *Op. cit.* 431.

[5] This procedure involved the exercise within well defined limits of an autocratic power granted to Caesar in the *lex col. Gen. Iul.* no. 26, chap. 125.

[6] *Cf.* pp. 90 *ff.*

[7] Kornemann, *R.E.* 4, 1806 *f.*; *Hist. Aug. Had.* 19.

need not be described here. In fact it is reasonably certain that the office did not develop independently in the various Italian cities, but that it was directly introduced into their municipal systems by Rome[1]. In a very small number of Italian cities, where there had been in early times a *praefectus iure dicundo*, on the removal of this official, the aedile became the chief magistrate and even held the census[2].

Most municipalities had quaestors whose powers were similar to those of the quaestor in Rome. Where the office of quaestor was lacking, its duties were taken over by a third aedile chosen for the purpose or by one of the duovirs[3].

In connection with the magistrates we should also notice the local priests, the pontiffs, augurs, *sacerdotes*, and, under the empire, the flamens[4]. Provision is made in the *lex col. Gen. Iul.*[5] for the election of certain of these priests in the local *comitia*. Of these priests the flamens who were attached to the cult of the emperor and of the imperial house are of the most interest to us, because they played an important part in developing loyalty to the emperor and in giving unity to the empire; through the imperial cult which they fostered, the *concilia* of the provinces developed, which exerted considerable influence in bringing the cities, the provinces, and the imperial government into closer relations[6].

In the cities of Italy the municipal senate was often called *senatus*[7], but it was repugnant to Roman sentiment to allow Roman official titles to be used by magistrates or

---

[1] Kubitschek, *R.E.* 1, 459.
[2] Kubitschek, *op. cit.* 1, 461.
[3] Marquardt, *St. Verw.* 1, 167.
[4] For the various priestly offices, *cf.* Dessau, 3, 568–584.
[5] No. 26, chap. 66.
[6] For a list of imperial flamens in the municipalities, see Dessau, 3, 571–574.
[7] Kübler, *R.E.* 4, 2319 *ff.* Constant use has been made of Kübler's excellent article in the rest of this chapter.

organizations outside Rome, and in new colonies senators were commonly called *decuriones* and the body to which they belonged, *ordo decurionum*. In all the different classes of cities or villages described in chapters I and II, except the *vici*, *castella*, and *canabae*, there was a local senate. Usually this body had one hundred members. This is the case, for instance, at Canusium[1], Cures, and Veii[2]. Smaller numbers are occasionally found, however[3]. The rolls of the *ordo* were prepared at intervals of five years by the *quinquennales* from the list of ex-magistrates, with such additions as were needed to make up the normal number. In some Greek cities, however, we find the method of popular election or of cooptation followed[4]. Under the republic venal or autocratic governors interfered with the free choice of local senators[5]. Under the empire governors acted within the law, but, if we may draw an inference from Pliny's experience in Bithynia[6], questions of eligibility and conditions of admission to local senates were settled by the governor. Occasionally the emperor directly nominated a senator[7]. The senatorial lists from Canusium[8] and Thamugadi[9] show us the composition of senates in the third and fourth centuries respectively. In the senate of Canusium there were sixty-eight ex-magistrates and thirty-two members who had held no office. In addition to this list of one hundred active members there stand in the album the names of thirty-nine *patroni*, who were honorary members, and of twenty-five *praetextati*, or sons of senators, who of course did not have the right to speak or vote. Inasmuch as most senators were ex-magistrates,

---

[1] *Cf.* commentary on no. 136.   [2] Mommsen, *St. R.* 3, 845, n. 1.
[3] *Cf.* commentary on no. 151.   [4] Kübler, *op. cit.* 4, 2324 *f.*
[5] Cic. *in Verr.* 2. 120: quorum ex testimoniis cognoscere potuistis tota Sicilia per triennium neminem ulla in civitate senatorem factum esse gratis, neminem, ut leges eorum sunt, suffragiis, neminem nisi istius imperio aut litteris.
[6] Plin. *Epp. ad Trai.* 79, 80, 112, 113.
[7] *CIL.* x, 1271 = Dessau, 6343.
[8] No. 136.   [9] *CIL.* VIII, 2403 = Dessau, 6122.

THE MUNICIPAL SYSTEM OF THE REPUBLIC

conditions of eligibility for a magistracy were applicable
to membership in the *ordo*[1]. In almost every municipality
free birth was a prerequisite to membership, but in certain
ultramarine colonies, like Urso, Corinth, and Carthage,
to which Caesar probably took out many freedmen, the
requirement of free birth was relaxed for a time[2]. Although
local citizenship was a condition of eligibility, we occasionally find a resident alien admitted to the senate[3], and in
other cases citizens of one community were also granted
the right of citizenship in another municipality, and in
this way could hold office in both places[4]. The minimum
age requirement in the early period for a magistracy, and
consequently for the senate, was thirty years[5]. Later it
was reduced to twenty-five years[6], and an edict of Augustus
perhaps set it at twenty-two[7], but Trajan interpreted the
edict as requiring a minimum of thirty years from those
who had not held a magistracy. The property qualification
was usually one hundred thousand sesterces[8]. The initiation fee varied in amount from one city to another[9]. In
Rusicade it reached the exceptional sum of twenty thousand sesterces[10]. Decurions wore a characteristic dress,
had special seats at the plays and games, were exempt
from certain forms of punishment, and could appeal to the
emperor when under a capital charge[11].

[1] *Cf.* pp. 59 *f.*
[2] Hardy, *Three Spanish Charters*, 49, n. 116.
[3] Dessau, 6916: *ex incolatu decurio*; *cf.* also 6992.
[4] Dessau, 6624: C. Alfius C. f. Lem. Ruf. II vir quinq. col. Iul. Hispelli
et II vir quinq. in municipio suo Casini; 7005: omnibus honoribus in
colonia Equestr. et in col. Viennensium functus. The case of a certain M.
Valerius is interesting (*cf.* Dessau, 6933). He was a citizen of the res
publica Damanitanorum, adlectus in coloniam Caesaraugustanam ex bene-
fic. divi Hadriani, and then is spoken of as omnib. honorib. in utraq. re p.
funct.
[5] No. 24, ll. 89 *f.*   [6] No. 65, chap. 54.
[7] *Cf. supra*, p. 59, n. 6.
[8] Plin. *Epp.* 1. 19. 2; Petronius, 44.
[9] Kübler, *R.E.* 4, 2329.   [10] *CIL.* VIII, 7983.
[11] Kübler, *R.E.* 4, 2331–2.

The procedure in a local senate was modelled on that of the Roman senate. Indeed many probable conclusions concerning the method of transacting business in the Roman senate may be drawn from a study of the municipal charters and from pertinent inscriptions. Not only do the articles found in the charters providing for the presence of a fixed number of senators when certain matters are being settled remind one of the practices of the Roman senate, but they also indicate the items of business which were considered of the most importance. Two-thirds of the members of the *ordo* of the colonia Genetiva Iulia must be present to authorize the building of new aqueducts[1], or the choosing of festival days[2], and under the *lex municipalis Malacitana* the same number must be present to audit accounts[3], or to settle the question of bondsmen[4]. Fifty members constituted a quorum in the colonia Genetiva Iulia in authorizing the sending of embassies[5], the demolition of buildings[6], in legislating concerning public funds, public buildings, public squares[7], and roads[8], in assigning places for the people at the public games[9], and in choosing patrons[10], except that, if a Roman senator or the son of a Roman senator were proposed as patron, the presence of three-fourths of the decurions was required[11]. Favorable action could be taken in the colonia Genetiva Iulia to grant citizens the right to use waste water from the reservoirs, if forty senators were present[12], and an act could be passed empowering the duovirs to pay the contractors who had provided sacrifices, if twenty

---

[1] No. 26, chap. 99.
[2] *Ibid*. chap. 64.
[3] No. 65, chap. 67.
[4] *Ibid*. chap. 64.
[5] No. 26, chap. 92.
[6] *Ibid*. chap. 75; *cf*. also no. 65, chap. 62.
[7] No. 26, chap. 96.
[8] *Ibid*. chap. 98.
[9] *Ibid*. chapp. 125, 126.
[10] *Ibid*. chap. 97.
[11] *Ibid*. chap. 130. In Malaca a quorum of two-thirds of the members was required when patrons were chosen; *cf*. no. 65, chap. 61.
[12] No. 26, chap. 100, and commentary on no. 33.

members were present[1]. The calling out of the militia, which did not permit of delay, could be authorized without the presence of any specified number[2]. These items of business illustrate the wide range of powers which the decurions enjoyed. It is clear that, in the first century, they, and not the magistrates, were the directing power in the municipality. It is rather surprising that Caesar, in founding the colonia Genetiva Iulia after his hard struggle with the Roman senate, did not magnify the power of the magistrates or the popular assembly at the expense of the *ordo*, but he adopted the pure Roman tradition for the three branches of the government. The municipal assembly, as we have already noticed, exercised practically no legislative powers. In view of the fact that the senate's power predominated in the municipality, it is not strange that in the later period, when the central government found it difficult to collect taxes, it should put the responsibility for them on the decurions. We shall see later that the *curator rei publicae* exercised at times the power of annulling *decreta decurionum*.

The encroachment of the imperial power on the legislative rights of municipal senates is noticeable as early as the beginning of the second century. Pliny writes[3] to ask Trajan what shall be done about the aqueduct at Nicomedeia, the theatre at Nicaea, and whether he shall audit the accounts of Apamea. In Byzantium he cuts off the appropriation for a legate. All of these matters, as we have noticed, were within the jurisdiction of the local senate. These are indications of an overshadowing of the local senate by the imperial government and of a decline in its importance, but, in the main, membership in it seems to have been prized up to the close of the second century of our era.

---

[1] No. 26, chap. 69.   [2] *Ibid.* chap. 103.   [3] *Cf.* pp. 143 *ff.*

CHAPTER VII

THE MUNICIPAL SYSTEM OF THE REPUBLIC AND EARLY EMPIRE IN THE EAST[1]

WHEN the Romans first entered Greece, the era of the independent city-state had already passed. Some of these had come, directly or indirectly, under the control of the Macedonian monarchy. Others had already joined a federation wherein they preserved their autonomy in local affairs, while the control of their armies and the conduct of their foreign relations were under the direction of a federal council. Membership in the Achaean League seems to have been voluntary, if we except the case of Sparta. On the other hand, the Aetolian League seems to have brought some of its members into the federation by force, and in such cases the local government must have been controlled by a pro-league party, or by force of arms. The development of these great Leagues was an important factor in restraining the Macedonian kings from exercising despotic sway over the Greek cities under their hegemony. While many states retained their traditional forms, the local government was controlled by a system of tyrannies, or by royal agents who effectively checked any expression of the ancient political freedom.

When the freedom of the Greek cities had been proclaimed by Flamininus, the Roman senate became involved as arbiter in all the disputes which broke out as

---

[1] This subject is treated in the following works: Kuhn, *Die städt. u. bürgerl. Verfassung d. röm. Reichs*, 2. 144 *ff.*; Marquardt, *St. Verw.* 1. 316 *ff.*; Mommsen, *The Provinces of the Roman Empire*, 1. 252 *ff.*; Levy, *La vie municipale de l'Asie Mineure, Rev. d. ét. grec.* 8 (1895), 203 *ff.*, 12 (1899), 255 *ff.*, 14 (1901), 350 *ff.*; Chapot, *La prov. rom. proc. d'Asie*; Ramsay, *The Cities and Bishoprics of Phrygia*; Reid, *The Municipalities of the Roman Empire*; Jouguet, *La vie municipale dans l'Égypte romaine*.

soon as the Roman forces were withdrawn. The commissions sent out to settle the local quarrels of the various cities usually threw their influence on the side of oligarchy; and, since the Roman senate preferred to treat with the aristocratic party represented by the magistrates and local senate rather than with the fickle popular assembly, the democratic institutions steadily declined in political importance[1].

When the kingdom of Perseus was finally overthrown by the Romans, Paullus established four republics on the ruins of the Macedonian Empire. It is unfortunate that we have no evidence as to the form of government established in the individual cities, or their relation to the federal administration. We may safely assume, however, that the municipalities were controlled by an oligarchy friendly to Rome. When Macedonia was finally organized as a Roman province, the republics were abolished, but traces of their existence may be discerned in later times[2].

After the destruction of Corinth Mummius modelled the constitutions of Peloponnesian cities on oligarchical lines, and revolutionary tendencies on the part of democratic factions were rigorously checked[3]. In other parts of Greece the aristocratic party, emboldened by the support of Rome, usurped the powers of the popular assemblies. This movement was fostered, directly or indirectly, by Roman magistrates and commissioners.

In Greece the Romans had found the country wholly organized in civic communities, but in Asia conditions were very different. Here the Persians, in their advance to the shores of the Mediterranean, had found tribal organizations, villages grouped in principalities or kingdoms, temple-states of various oriental cults, and Greek commonwealths in various stages of development between

[1] Colin, *Rome et la Grèce*, 652.
[2] Frank, *Class. Phil.* 9 (1914), 49 *ff.*
[3] Pausanias, 7. 16. 9; no. 9.

tyranny and democracy. The conquerors made no attempt to found new cities. Those already established they governed through a system of tyrants, which was ended by Alexander. His biographers claim for him the credit of restoring democracy, but it may be doubted whether he was more liberal in Asia than he had been in Greece. The system of Persian satrapies was continued by the appointment of governors in the various provinces. The cities were given a measure of independence in local affairs, and their administration was vested in the hands of the Greeks, who thus constituted a ruling oligarchy. Some features of the oriental bureaucracy must have been retained for the administration of the royal estates. Very little is known of the constitutions granted to the cities founded by Alexander. Apparently Alexandria had a senate and a popular assembly, at least for a time[1]. The Diadochi posed as patrons of Hellenism, and this attitude found expression in the foundation of new cities. The extension of this policy was made possible by the great influx of Greek soldiers, merchants, and farmers who settled in every part of Asia. Cities sprang up along the great trade-routes, around military stations, and at other strategic centers. Above all, the city served as a useful unit in governing the country and in securing its loyalty. Many of the towns became very wealthy and powerful, and in time of war, or when the royal exchequer was low, they were able to secure concessions which gave them greater liberty in self-government.

When the Romans extended their sway over Asia Minor, they adopted the same policy which they had pursued in Sicily. A few cities were allied to Rome; others were given their freedom with the right to use their own laws and institutions, and these cities probably enjoyed immunity from tribute; the majority, however, became *civitates stipendiariae*, and paid tithes to Rome. The honorary

[1] Plaumann, *Klio*, 13 (1913), 485 *ff.*

title of *colonia*, with or without the *ius Italicum*, was conferred by Caesar and later emperors on cities already established. After the age of Augustus new colonies were seldom founded in the eastern provinces[1].

The Roman senate appointed a commission to draw up a *lex provinciae* and to organize each province as it was admitted, although some commanders, as Pompey and Sulla, formulated laws for the provincials without the aid of a senatorial committee. The acts of military commanders, however, had to be ratified by the senate. We cannot tell how far the commissions interfered with the problems of local administration, but it is evident that no attempt was made to secure uniformity in municipal government[2]. The *lex Cornelia* regulated the amount which might be spent on embassies, and required the cities to elect their magistrates fifty days before the end of the year[3]. The *lex Pompeia* determined the age at which a candidate should stand for office, and provided that ex-magistrates should be enrolled as members of the local senate. The law also specified the reasons for which the censor might remove a senator from his seat[4]. These laws could be modified by edicts of the emperor or of the provincial governor, and some of the provisions were disregarded by the municipalities themselves[5]. Gabinius is said to have revised the constitutional forms of Syrian cities in favor of oligarchy, and it is probable that this was the general tendency of Roman governors[6].

The Romans followed the Greek policy by founding new cities. Pompey alone is said to have founded thirty-nine[7]. Since he was a representative of the equestrian order, we may suppose that his purpose was to simplify

---

[1] *R.E. s.v. colonia*; *cf.* pp. 3 *ff.*

[2] Marquardt is of the opinion that laws were devised for each autonomous city, *op. cit.* 1. 65, 78.   [3] No. 34.

[4] Pliny, *Epp. ad Trai.* 79, 80, 112, 113, 114, 115.

[5] *Ibid.* 55, 65, 72, 79, 84, 108, 109, 111, 112.

[6] Josephus, *Ant. Iud.* 14. 5. 4.   [7] Plutarch, *Pompeius*, 45.

the collection of taxes. The creation of a municipal organization, whose members would be responsible for the payment of the tribute from their district, not only made it easier to collect taxes, but also gave the *publicani* greater opportunity for making loans and greater security for their repayment. It is not necessary to dwell upon the terrible exploitation of the Asiatic cities by tax-gatherers and Roman officials, as well as by the leaders of the various factions, who supported their armies by forced levies during the civil wars[1]. There is no evidence that the economic pressure resulted in any constitutional changes in the municipalities, but we may suppose that those interested in the collection of tribute would favor the election of the wealthier members of the community to office, while the constant arrears in the annual quota would give the governor unlimited opportunities to interfere in the problems of local administration. This state of affairs may explain the statement of Strabo that the ancient institutions of Cretan cities had fallen into abeyance, because the towns of Crete, as well as those of other provinces, were governed by the edicts of Roman rulers[2].

In their long experience in provincial government the Romans had found that the city, with its dependent *territorium*, was the unit through which the province could be best administered and the taxes most easily collected. For this reason the emperors devoted their attention to the spread of the municipal organization in every province. As the client kingdoms were incorporated in the empire, their territory was divided among cities or added to imperial estates. The tribal units of Galatia and the prefectureships of Cappadocia were replaced by towns[3]. The *territoria* granted to many of the new foundations were often necessarily of vast extent. The larger village-communities, therefore, had an opportunity to develop

---

[1] Chapot, *op. cit.* 18 *ff*.   [2] Strabo, 10. 4. 22.
[3] Kuhn, *op. cit.* 2. 231; Perrot, *de Galatia provincia Romana*, 83.

along independent lines, and many of them ultimately attained the rank of cities. By the beginning of the fourth century of the Christian era municipal institutions had spread throughout the Orient as the chief instrument of imperial administration.

It would be impossible to outline, even in brief, the manifold forms of government found in the Greek cities. The ancient states had developed along individual lines, and all of them cherished their traditional customs with peculiar reverence. The Romans also had great respect for *longa consuetudo*, and since it was their policy to accept existing institutions as they found them, they contented themselves with modifying the powers exercised by the different branches of local administration. The *lex Pompeia*, which was followed in the cities of Pontus and Bithynia, determined the qualifications of senators and magistrates and the method of their appointment, but, apparently, abolished none of the traditional offices. For this reason a great variety of titles survived until late in the empire in the older towns, and especially in the free cities. Unfortunately we know nothing of the charters granted to eastern cities, if we except the fragmentary letter of an unknown emperor to the citizens of Tymanda. While the constitution given to new foundations may have varied according to local conditions, yet precedent was powerful in Roman law and custom, and it is equally possible that imperial charters followed some model, such as the *lex Iulia municipalis*. Special commissioners (*correctores*) were sometimes sent out to regulate the affairs of provincial cities, but we do not know whether they made any attempt to revise the constitutions of the towns under their jurisdiction. The emperors in their travels occasionally devoted their attention to municipal problems, but the nature of their reforms cannot be determined[1]. Caesar is said to have made some changes in the administration

---

[1] *Hist. Aug. Hadr.* 19, 21; Herodian, 4. 8. 3; Tarsus was given laws by Augustus, Dio Chrys. 34. 8.

of Athens[1], and in later times Hadrian attempted to revive the laws of Solon for the Athenians[2]; but, for the most part, it is probable that the emperors contented themselves with financial and legal problems, and that in return for such benefits as were conferred the Greeks called them the benefactors and founders of their cities[3].

The popular assembly declined steadily as a political influence in the Greek cities under Roman rule. In the republican period the *ecclesia* in a few cities retained a certain amount of initiative and took some share in the work of local administration. Under the empire the evidence shows that the popular assembly was called together largely for the purpose of ratifying honorary decrees and such proposals as the magistrates chose to present to the people. The right of debate or amendment does not seem to have been exercised at any of these meetings[4]. In a few cities, however, exceptions may be found. The Athenian assembly retained some power as late as the third century[5]. At Tarsus Dio rebuked the citizens because the council of elders, the senate, and the people each strove for its own interest, and failed to cooperate for the common good[6]. The same orator also urged the citizens of Prusa, who had recently recovered the right to meet in assembly (ἐκκλησιάζειν), to exercise their powers with discretion so that they might not again lose their privileges[7]. In some of the eastern cities we find a distinction drawn between members of the *ecclesia* (ἐκκλησιασταί), citizens, and other residents of the community[8]. This does not necessarily imply that there was an active popular assembly

[1] Swoboda, *Gr. Volksbeschl.* 192.   [2] *Cf.* no. 90, commentary.
[3] The title κτίστης is frequently applied in Greek inscriptions to the emperor, governor, and even to private citizens. *Cf.* Anderson, *Journ. Hell. Studies*, 17 (1897), 402; *B.C.H.* 17 (1893), 247; Ditt. *Or. Gr.* 471.
[4] Swoboda, *op. cit.* 176 ff.; but *cf. R.E. s.v.* ἐκκλησία, p. 2199.
[5] Swoboda, *op. cit.* 190 ff.   [6] Dio Chrys. 34. 16.
[7] *Ibid.* 48. 1 ff.
[8] Lanckoronski, *Städte Pamphyliens und Pisidiens*, 58 ff.; Liebenam, *St. Verw.* 216 ff.; no. 122.

[75]

in such cities, while it is true that, if the membership was limited in some way, the *ecclesia* naturally gained greater prestige and had a longer lease of life in the affairs of government. The edict of Caracalla, however, swept away the distinctions between the various classes in the community, and after the beginning of the third century the assembly disappeared as a legislative body.

By the *lex Pompeia* the membership of the senate in Bithynian towns seems to have been limited to a prescribed number. The senators held office for life; magistrates were admitted to the order on the completion of their term of office; the revision of the rolls was entrusted to a censor; honorary members could be appointed with the consent of the emperor and on the payment of a fee; it was illegal to enroll citizens from other cities in the province[1]. These provisions show that Pompey took the Roman senate as his model in framing the law, and senates of this type are sometimes called "western" in contrast to those of the Greek cities which retained their former regulations. As a matter of fact, however, we know practically nothing of the method of appointing senators in eastern cities under Roman rule[2]. Censors are found in cities outside the province of Bithynia, but we do not know whether they had any duties in connection with the enrolment of senators. It is probable that selection by lot had been abandoned in the republican period, since it was necessary that men of wealth should be enrolled. Hadrian wrote to the magistrates and senate of Ephesus, requesting that his friend Erastus be admitted to the senate. He agreed to pay the *summa honoraria* required from new members if the official scrutiny of the candidate proved satisfactory[3]. It would seem as if appointments were made at the time when the senate (?) was called together to elect the magistrates for the coming year. Distinguished actors and athletes were often re-

1 Pliny, *Epp. ad Trai.* 79, 80, 114, 115.
2 Chapot, *op. cit.* 195 *ff.*   3 No. 85.

warded by being admitted as honorary senators. In the golden age of Greek democracy a senator held office for a year only, but with the development of oligarchy, it is probable that longer terms became the rule. Life-membership may have been introduced soon after, if not before, the cities came under Roman rule. In the later empire membership in the senate became hereditary.

In a number of cities we find other organizations acting with the senate and assembly, especially in adopting honorary decrees. At Athens the council of the Areopagus was revived and attained great influence. In the Asiatic cities the *gerusia*, the νέοι, the *conventus* of Roman citizens, the trade-guilds, and even villages united with the city to do honor to benefactors. The nature of the *gerusiae* is disputed. Their functions were not always political, and in some cities they appear to have been purely social or religious organizations[1]. The Roman citizens resident in Greek cities usually united in a guild and held themselves aloof from local affairs[2]. They were probably exempt from magistracies and liturgies and rarely held such offices. They were usually free from the jurisdiction of the local courts. Their privileged position, however, was destroyed by Caracalla, who gave Roman citizenship to the provincials. The guilds of the various trades were not encouraged by the earlier emperors. Trajan had forbidden all associations of this kind fearing that they might become centres of political agitation and disaffection[3]. In the second and third centuries, however, these organizations were widely established.

An extraordinary variety of titles may be found in the magistracies of the Greek cities, and no uniformity was attained or desired by the imperial government[4]. Many

[1] Chapot, *op. cit.* 216 *ff.*   [2] *Ibid.* 186 *ff. Ath. Mitth.* 16, 144 *ff.*
[3] Pliny, *Epp. ad Trai.* 34, 96.
[4] Owing to the difficulty of distinguishing between magistracies and liturgies we have not attempted to classify the different offices in the Greek cities; *cf.* indices to *IG.*; Cagnat, *IGRR.*; Liebenam, *op. cit.* 539 *ff.*

of the offices, however, were modified under Roman rule. For example, the *strategus* became an important official although he had long since lost all trace of military power, and with the increasing importance of the senate the secretaryship of this body rose into prominence. In many eastern cities a board of magistrates (κοινὸν τῶν ἀρχόντων) is found[1]. This usually consisted of the generals (who are sometimes identified with the archons), the archons, and the secretary. These annual officials were dominated by the senate, and their powers were limited by the supervision of the provincial governors and of imperial agents, especially the *curator rei publicae* and the *defensor*. We have traced elsewhere the decline of the local magistracies under the pressure of the imperial bureaucracy. In the late empire the *curator rei publicae* was replaced by the πατὴρ τῆς πόλεως[2]. In the fourth and fifth centuries the office of *defensor* (ἔκδικος) attained great importance in municipal government. By this time the traditional magistracies had either disappeared or had become mere liturgies.

Election by lot or by popular vote had probably ceased soon after the Roman occupation, if not before[3]. For the most part officials seem to have been elected by the senate[4]. There is no evidence that the *cursus honorum*, required in the West, was followed in the East, and the law, enunciated by Paulus, that decurions only should be elected to public office, does not seem to have been applied to Greek

---

[1] Levy, *Rev. d. ét. grec.* 12 (1899), 264, 268 ff.

[2] Declareuil, *Quelques problèmes d'histoire des institutions municipales au temps de l'Empire romain*, 269 ff.

[3] For a late example of the lot, *cf.* Cagnat, *IGRR.* 4, 259. For a priesthood, *cf.* Ditt. *Or. Gr.* 494.

[4] *Cod. Th.* 12. 5. 1 (326). Election to office seems to have been regulated by the provincial edict and the *lex provinciae*; *cf.* no. 34; Cicero, *ad Att.* 6. 1. 15; Pliny, *Epp. ad Trai.* 79. For the ἀρχαιρεσία of the senate, *cf.* no. 117; of the *ecclesia*, *cf. Journ. Hell. Studies*, 15 (1895), 118; 17 (1897), 411; *B.C.H.* 12 (1888), 17; Cagnat, *IGRR.* 3, 649.

cities[1]. Women were not infrequently named for office. In such cases it is unlikely that they exercised the duties of the magistracy, but were content with making a generous contribution towards the expenses attached to the position. The *summa honoraria* was usually exacted from magistrates on entering upon the duties of their office[2].

In the cities of the Orient the system of liturgies was one of their most characteristic features, and here it was developed to its fullest extent as a regular part of the civic administration. In his discussion of magistracies and liturgies Aristotle observed the varying practice of different cities, and regarded the distinction between the two kinds of public service as largely an academic matter[3]. This is especially true in the case of the more important liturgies, such as the priesthoods, the *choregia*, and the gymnasiarchy. In many cases the liturgies and the magistracies cannot be distinguished. Aristotle called the humbler duties ἐπιμέλειαι or διακονίαι. These terms do not appear in the inscriptions, but they correspond in general to the Latin *curae*, and are described in the Codes and Digest as *munera*. In one case we find liturgies classified as βουλευτικαί and δημοτικαί[4]. These terms are not defined, and it is possible that the former refer to magistracies. Under Rōman administration the appointment to liturgies was probably made in the local senates[5]. In a few cases liturgies were undertaken voluntarily, and sometimes endowments were provided by wealthy citizens to meet the expenses of a particular service. The priesthoods, in a few instances, were sold to the highest bidder[6]. As new liturgies were devised from time to time, especially in the imperial service, uniform regulations were applied

---

[1] *Dig.* 50. 2. 7; 50. 4. 11.   [2] Chapot, *op. cit.* 158 *ff.*
[3] Aristotle, *Politics*, 6. 12. 2.   [4] Cagnat, *IGRR.* 3, 623.
[5] This, at least, was the rule in the third century; *cf. Cod. J.* 10. 32. 2.
[6] Bischoff, *Kauf und Verkauf von Priestertümern bei den Griechen*, *Rh. Mus.* 54 (1899), 9 *ff.*; *cf.* Otto, *Hermes*, 44 (1909), 594 *ff.*

to them throughout the empire. Ultimately the older municipal liturgies and the magistracies, which had virtually become liturgies, came under imperial regulation, and all were governed by uniform principles.

The right of coining gold was forbidden, but in a few instances silver coins were struck under imperial supervision. Permission to issue bronze or token-money was freely granted in the East. The exchange of the local coins for foreign money was a municipal monopoly, and some revenue was derived therefrom[1]. When the local mints were abolished by Aurelian, this source of income ceased.

The relation of the provincial governors to the municipal administration cannot be definitely determined. The statement of Strabo that most provincial cities were governed by edict is doubtless exaggerated, but it is evident that the governor had the right to interfere in the administration of the *civitates stipendiariae* at any time, and that the privileges of free states were not always regarded by unscrupulous officials[2]. Cicero, who was fairly conscientious in his administration of Cilicia, devoted himself to lessening the expenses of the municipalities, to correcting the license of civic officials, and to the administration of justice. He delighted the cities by restoring to them their *autonomia*, which former governors had apparently taken away. He incurred the ill-will of Appius by restricting the embassies which the provincials sent to Rome with decrees in honor of their departing governor. Under the republic most questions concerning the internal administration of the province were decided by the governor without consulting Rome. Under the empire, as is shown by the correspondence of Pliny, paternalism had developed. While minor problems were referred to the emperor for decision, it is evident that the provincial governor still retained considerable power. All appeals were submitted to him before they were allowed to go to Rome. Not

[1] Nos. 81, 133, 199.
[2] Marquardt, *op. cit.* 1. 85 f.; Chapot, *op. cit.* 126 ff.

infrequently decrees of the municipalities were presented for approval or for veto, and it is probable that no city could engage in any important outlay of public money without securing the approval of the governor[1]. In the third and fourth centuries the duties of the imperial legates were probably closely defined in the writings of the jurists, but of these only fragments are now extant.

The civic rivalries, peculiar to Asiatic towns, may have served to divert the attention of the provincials from the loss of political freedom. The honor of preeminence in rank and the privilege of the neocorate were eagerly sought[2]. While the imperial government permitted this rivalry, it was costly to the cities, because local pride led them to indulge in extravagant expenditures upon public buildings, games, and festivals in their efforts to outdo their neighbors. When this extravagance was combined with an inefficient and corrupt oligarchical government, many cities were reduced to serious financial straits. As a result the appointment of special commissioners, such as the *curator* and the *corrector*, to regulate the administration of provincial cities became a common practice in the second century. The influence of these officials in the history of the municipalities has been traced elsewhere[3].

Although the Romans found in the East a fully developed legal system which had a profound influence in modifying their own jurisprudence, yet the use of Roman law gradually prevailed. This was due to the influence of the provincial edict and of the provincial assizes, at which the governor presided and dispensed justice in accordance with Roman juristic principles. The extension of Roman citizenship, especially by Caracalla, must have increased the use of Roman law, but the Greek elements in the Syrian Code of the fifth century and in the Egyptian papyri of the Byzantine age show that the native law never

---

[1] Nos. 69, 71, 80, 98, 99, 114.   [2] Chapot, *op. cit.* 136 *ff.*
[3] *Cf.* pp. 90 *ff.*

wholly disappeared[1]. The supremacy of Roman law may be due, in part, to the fact that advancement in the legal profession depended upon a knowledge of Roman jurisprudence, and for this reason the scientific study of Greek law received little attention in the schools.

The evidence for the administration of law in the eastern cities is scanty. A few cities had the right to try cases which arose between Romans and civilians, but there is no evidence that they retained this privilege beyond the age of Augustus[2]. The courts instituted by the governor were held according to a fixed circuit, and were open to provincials as well as to Romans. Plutarch rebuked the Greeks for abandoning their local courts in favor of those held by the praetor[3]. The governor's court, however, could only take cognizance of a small proportion of the cases arising in a large and busy province, and the local courts must have retained jurisdiction over minor cases until late in the empire. The right of cities to use their native law was probably determined by the *lex provinciae*, but the privilege could be withheld or restored by the governor, or the senate, or the emperor. For example, Cicero restored *autonomia* to the Cilician cities, and Chios was granted the right to use her own laws and courts by the senate[4]. The question as to the administration of law in those cities which did not possess autonomy cannot be definitely decided[5]. Probably all cases involving sums of money in excess of a certain minimum were referred to the governor's court; regulations of this kind are found in western charters. The powers of the local courts were weakened by the appointment of the *curator rei publicae*, who exercised judicial authority. The subdivision of the provinces under Diocletian and the separation of the civil

---

1 Mitteis, *Reichsrecht und Volksrecht*, 313 *ff.*; *Grundzüge* (*Juristischer Teil*), I. Introduction.
2 No. 40.   3 Plutarch, *reip. ger. praec.* 19.
4 *ad Att.* 6. 1. 15; no. 40.
5 Marquardt, *op. cit.* 1. 78; Chapot, *op. cit.* 103 *ff.*

and military powers gave the governor greater opportunity to supervise the administration of justice. This is indicated by the fact that he is usually styled *praeses* or *iudex* in the juristic literature of the period. His power to appoint *iudices pedanei* to deal with minor offences implies that the municipal courts were no longer of any importance[1].

Since we have described the liturgies and magistracies of Egyptian cities in another chapter[2], we need only outline the development of their municipal system at this point. In the Ptolemaic period there were only three Greek cities, Alexandria, Naucratis, and Ptolemais, and of their organization little is known. The remainder of Egypt was divided into administrative districts called nomes, the units of which were village-communities. The Romans adopted the Ptolemaic system in its main outlines. Hadrian was the first emperor to found a city in this part of the empire, and he thus set a precedent for future emperors in recognizing the fact that the Egyptians were capable of self-government. Early in the third century Septimius Severus gave to the capital of each nome a senate whose members not only bore the responsibility of administration, but also assumed the liabilities for the collection of the tribute. The senate thus created consisted of members who held office for life. The magistracies differed from those in the western cities in that the incumbents, apparently, did not have to be chosen from the senate. At first the nome was not regarded as the territory of the city, but in the course of time the responsibility of governing it and collecting the revenues therefrom was transferred to the city. By the beginning of the fourth century the Egyptian municipalities were brought into conformity with the system which prevailed in other parts of the empire.

---

[1] *Cod. J.* 3. 3. 2.   [2] *Cf.* pp. 99 *ff.*

CHAPTER VIII

HONORES AND MUNERA[1]

IN the regal period of Roman history the king exercised legislative, judicial, and religious powers. When the republican form of government was created, these functions were transferred to several magistrates whose offices were appropriately called *honores*. As for the citizen, the most important duty which he owed to the community was the defense of its lands and flocks. This was a *munus* in the true sense of the word, and it is not strange that the same term should have been applied to any service rendered to the community, when the needs of society became more numerous[2].

While the development of Greek and Roman cities followed the same general lines, there was great diversity in matters of detail, and it would be difficult to discover a definition of *honores* and *munera* applicable to all periods or to all cities of the Roman empire. Callistratus, the Roman jurist, defined a municipal magistracy as an administrative office in the *cursus honorum* which might or might not involve the incumbent in personal expense. The liturgy differed only in the fact that it carried with it the right to spend money without receiving the distinction of an official title[3]. Callistratus probably lived in the third or early fourth century, when it was evident that the distinction between magistracy and liturgy rested largely on ancient tradition. In fact, many liturgies in Greek cities carried the title of ἀρχή although they were in no sense regarded as magistracies.

[1] The best treatment of this subject is found in Kuhn, *Die städt. u. bürgerl. Verfassung d. röm. Reichs*, 7 *ff.*; cf. Houdoy, *Le droit municipal*, 441 *ff.*
[2] The Greek term corresponding to *honor* is ἀρχή. *Munera* is represented by λειτουργία or ἐπιμέλεια.   [3] *Dig.* 50. 4. 14.

In Rome the *cursus honorum* was fixed by law, and municipal charters in the West followed the Roman system in general outline with minor variations in detail. The Greek cities inherited a varied and complicated administrative machinery from the past, and the Romans made few changes in outward form. The system of popular election gave way to a more oligarchic method in Roman times, and some of the magistracies were gradually modified[1]. Even the oriental cities founded by Roman generals or governors followed Greek patterns in regard to magistracies, except in the case of a few early colonial settlements.

Under the earlier western charters municipal magistrates were chosen by the residents voting in *comitia* or tribes[2]. If candidates did not present themselves in sufficient numbers, nominations were made by the magistrate who presided over the election. Such nominees had each the right of nominating another. In later times, when public office became undesirable because of the heavy expense attached to it, the outgoing magistrate nominated his successor, or, if he failed to do so, the provincial governor presented a name to the *curia* which then made the election by formal vote[3]. It is not clear when the election was transferred from the people to the *curia*. In the fourth century only a few African towns elected their magistrates by popular vote[4]. As oligarchical tendencies developed, plebeians were barred from honors, and at the beginning of the third century only decurions were eligible for public office[5]. It is probable that the method of popular election was discontinued when this qualification was introduced, or soon thereafter. Apparently some

[1] For example the στρατηγός became an important magistrate in some Greek cities under Roman rule, although the office no longer carried military power.

[2] No. 65, chapp. 51–54.   [3] *Dig.* 49. 4. 1, 3.

[4] *Cod. Th.* 12. 5. 1.

[5] *Dig.* 50. 2. 7. There are a few exceptions, *e.g. Cod. J.* 10. 44. 2 provides for a citizen holding office without being a decurion.

system of rotation was now followed, and nominations were made in order of seniority with due regard to the financial standing of the members of the *curia*[1]. Magistrates entrusted with the administration of public funds were required to furnish bondsmen, whom the municipality held responsible for their candidate. The sureties were examined by a third party, who also shared the liability of the bondsmen if he approved their securities[2]. In magistracies shared by two or more there was always joint responsibility, unless the contrary was stipulated in the nomination[3]. When a candidate refused to discharge the duties of the office to which he was elected, his bondsmen and nominators were liable for his obligations. The governor, however, had the power to compel a magistrate to fulfil his duties[4]. If he sought to escape office by flight, his property was surrendered to his successor; and if the fugitive was brought back, he was punished by being compelled to serve two years instead of one[5]. Any nominee had the right of appeal to the governor. Until a decision was rendered, his colleague held office alone. If both appealed, an interim appointment was made, but if the city suffered any loss, the candidate who appealed without just cause was held responsible[6].

The qualifications of candidates varied in different localities and in different periods. The Julian law fixed the minimum age for magistrates in Italian cities at thirty, although concessions were made to those who had served a certain term in the army[7]. Pompey had previously established the same minimum in Bithynian cities, but his law was modified by Augustus, who permitted candidates to enter the minor offices at twenty-five, and this

---

[1] This seems to be implied in *Dig.* 50. 2. 7; 50. 4. 6, 14.
[2] No. 65, chap. 59; *Dig.* 50. 1. 15; *Cod. J.* 11. 34. 1, 2; 11. 35. 1; 11. 36. 1.
[3] *Dig.* 50. 1. 11.   [4] *Ibid.* 50. 4. 9.
[5] *Cod. Th.* 12. 1. 16 (329).   [6] *Dig.* 49. 1. 21.
[7] No. 24.

appears to have become the universal practice in the third century[1]. In a few cases minors were elected to magistracies, for the proper conduct of which their parents were held responsible. No candidate could secure exemption on the plea of old age[2]. The amount of property which he must possess was undoubtedly determined by local conditions, since it would be impossible to frame a uniform law applicable to every city within the empire. No magistrate received a salary, and the expenses of his office were heavy, When honors were eagerly sought, it was not illegal nor unusual for candidates to promise money for public works, games, banquets, or other entertainments, but it was forbidden to canvass for office by gifts or dinners to private individuals[3]. It was also customary for a magistrate on entering office to contribute a sum of money to the municipal treasury. This *summa honoraria* seems to have originated as a freewill offering, but it later became obligatory unless waived by special enactment[4]. During his term of office the magistrate was also compelled by law to contribute to various forms of municipal welfare[5].

The Julian law specified that no auctioneer, beadle, or undertaker should hold office; and all those who were barred from membership in the local senate by virtue of their profession or because of legal disabilities were forbidden to stand for a magistracy[6]. Freedmen were disqualified except in colonies composed of citizens of this class[7]. Appointments of women to magistracies were purely honorary, and seem to have been made chiefly in the East[8].

---

[1] Pliny, *Epp. ad Trai.* 79, 80: *Dig.* 50. 4. 8; 50. 5. 2.
[2] *Dig.* 50. 5. 2, 1.   [3] No. 26.
[4] Liebenam, *St. Verw.* 54 *ff.*; *Cod. Th.* 12. 1. 169 (409).   [5] No. 26.
[6] No. 24. Other reasons for disqualification are added in *Dig.* 50. 1. 17, 20; 50. 2. 7, 9, 12; 50. 4. 6, 7, 12, 16. For professions exempt, *cf. Dig.* 50. 4. 18; 50. 5. 10.
[7] No. 24.
[8] Chapot, *La prov. rom. proc. d'Asie*, 158 *ff.*; Paris, *Quatenus feminae res publicas in Asia minore, Romanis imperantibus, attigerint*; *Cod. J.* 10. 64. 1.

Ordinarily a magistrate was exempt from holding the same office twice. If, however, there was a lack of eligible candidates, he could be compelled to serve a second time, but not until five years had elapsed. In case of voluntary service an interval of a year was prescribed. Between magistracies of different rank the legal interval was three years[1]. If a citizen had served as an ambassador of his city, he could not be nominated to another office for two years, but Diocletian limited the application of this law to those who had undertaken an embassy to Rome[2]. Magistrates could not hold office in two cities at the same time. In the case of such elections the birthplace of the candidate determined priority[3].

Magistrates wore the *toga praetexta*, possessed the privilege of the *fasces* within their own territory, and were entitled to special seats in the theatre. In cities possessing Latin rights magistrates were granted Roman citizenship on completing their term of office. Not more than six could receive this gift in one year, but in each case, apparently, their parents, wives, children, and grandchildren in the male line were included[4]. During his term of office no liturgies could be imposed upon him, and as ex-magistrate he was free from the imposition of burdens of inferior rank[5].

There is a bewildering variety of municipal offices in every province, and it is difficult in many instances to distinguish between honors and liturgies[6]. The Codes use the general title *magistratus municipales* for the whole

---

[1] *Dig.* 50. 1. 18; 50. 4. 14; *Cod. J.* 10. 41. 2.
[2] *Dig.* 50. 7. 9; *Cod. J.* 10. 41. 2; 10. 65. 3.
[3] *Dig.* 50. 1. 17, 4.
[4] No. 64; *R.E. s.v. Jus Latii.*
[5] *Dig.* 50. 4. 10; *Cod. J.* 10. 43. 2.
[6] Chapot, *op. cit.* 231 *ff.*; Preisigke, *Städtische Beamtenwesen im römischen Aegypten*, 11; for different titles of municipal magistrates, see indices to the *corpora* of Greek and Latin inscriptions, Dessau, and Cagnat, *IGRR. s.v. magistratus municipales. Cf.* Liebenam, *St. Verw.* 279 *ff.*; Prentice, *Trans. Am. Phil. Assoc.* 43, 113 *ff.*

empire and never specify the offices in detail. In the common type of western municipality we find duumvirs, aediles, and quaestors ranking in the order named. The principle of collegiality was followed in most magistracies, but when the emperor was elected to any municipal office, he appointed a prefect who, as an imperial agent, divided his authority with no one[1]. In case of an interregnum the local senate could appoint a prefect who had dictatorial power[2]. In the third century the quaestor and aedile are seldom found, and the latter office was regarded as a liturgy in many cities[3].

In Egypt the municipal form of government did not develop until the third century, and in this period the liturgies can be distinguished from magistracies only with great difficulty. Municipal offices were divided into three classes, and a citizen might hold the different offices in each class without observing any rule of seniority[4]. Appointments to municipal magistracies were apparently made in the local senate in conjunction with the *prytanis*. At the end of the third century we find nominations made by outgoing magistrates or by the senate as a body[5]. Peculiar to Egypt is the plan of appointing supervisors for the newly elected magistrate, apparently to prevent his escape by flight from the burdens of his office[6]. A nominee might avoid office by offering to surrender his property to his nominators. In such cases the nominee transmitted his offer to the prefect, who, if he gave his approval, instructed the *strategus* to see that the appellant suffered no hurt nor loss of status during the period while his property was being administered by the nominators.

---

[1] *Cf.* pp. 62 *ff.*

[2] Hardy, *Three Spanish Charters*, p. 88. A magistrate absent from office more than a day nominated a prefect in his place.

[3] *Dig.* 50. 4. 18.

[4] Preisigke, *op. cit.*; Jouguet, *Vie munic.* 292 *ff.*; no. 181.

[5] No. 203.

[6] No. 203. This is probably a substitute for the *cautio* usually required.

Apparently the law permitted them to devote not more than two-thirds of the revenue to defray the expense of the magistracy and the remainder was returned to the owner. Even after the prefect had given his consent to the surrender of the property, the local senate apparently had the privilege of rejecting the offer and compelling the nominee to accept office[1]. In other respects also the procedure in Egypt seems to have differed from that in the provinces. For example, citizens who were not members of the senate were eligible for office much later than was customary in the rest of the empire.

In the eastern provinces magistrates were usually appointed by the local senate at a meeting specially devoted to that purpose[2]. Little is known about methods of nomination or qualifications, but it is probable that old customs survived, for we find many of the ancient magistracies still existing in the Greek cities until late in the Christian era[3]. There was, however, a tendency towards uniformity in all parts of the empire especially after Roman citizenship had been extended to all free subjects by Caracalla. No distinction is made between the East and the West in the laws recorded in the Digest and Codes, but the jurists were not concerned with local peculiarities and customs, and it would be unsafe to assume that local privileges and customs did not persist.

The *curator rei publicae* and the *defensor civitatis* held offices which were not regarded as municipal *honores*, but as *curae*. Their importance in civic government is such that they should be mentioned here. The *curator* was first

---

[1] No. 198. For the procedure in a metropolis before the introduction of the municipal system, cf. no. 181 and pp. 28 ff.

[2] No. 34.

[3] There is no evidence that the Greek cities were subject to the law of Antoninus which required that magistracies should be held according to a fixed *cursus* (*Dig.* 50. 4. 11). The inscriptions from eastern cities record honors and liturgies indiscriminately, and the classification of the various kinds of public duties varied from city to city (*cf.* Aristotle, *Politics*, 4. 14 ff.).

appointed in the reign of Trajan as an imperial agent whose chief duty was the supervision of the financial administration of the municipality to which he was attached[1]. In some cases his jurisdiction extended over several towns. At first he was chosen from the senatorial or equestrian ranks, although men of humbler position sometimes filled the office. In the third century he was chosen from the members of the *curia* by the votes of his fellow-senators, and his election was ratified by the emperor. Constantine permitted no one to be a candidate until he had performed all his civic liturgies, and he cancelled all appointments gained by corrupt practices. In the Greek cities the *curator* was known as λογιστής and in the fourth century his duties were taken over by the πατὴρ τῆς πόλεως. The latter official was elected by the bishop, the *primates*, and the *possessores* in the reign of Justinian. The bishop and five *primates* had the power to depose their candidate if, in their annual survey, they found his administration unsatisfactory[2].

Since the *curator* was an imperial appointment, the principle of collegiality was never applied to the office, even when it became in form a municipal magistracy. Nothing can be determined about the length of appointment except that it was not limited to one year and reappointments were not forbidden[3]. In some cases the office was combined with other imperial duties. While it is probable that many cities came under the jurisdiction of the *curator*, the record of the office on stone is comparatively rare, and in very few cities do we find the name of more than one, although there must have been a

[1] Liebenam, *Philol.* 56 (1897), 290 ff., gives a full treatment of this office. Cf. *R.E. s.v. curator.*

[2] Justinian, *Novellae*, 128. 16; Declareuil, *Quelques problèmes d'histoire des institutions municipales au temps de l'Empire romain*, 276 ff.

[3] At Timgad three *curatores rei publicae* are recorded between 360 and 367 (*CIL.* VIII, 2387, 2388, 2403), and their term could not have been longer than five years in any case. An inscription published in *B.C.H.* 17 (1893), 98, records a term of ten years.

succession of *curatores* when once a city had come under their control[1].

Since the *curator* controlled the municipal revenues, and had the power to veto municipal legislation, his appointment dealt a serious blow to the development of the principle of local self-government[2]. When the emperors transferred the election to the *curiae*, the power of the landed proprietors who constituted the senates was greatly increased, as they were able to choose a candidate favorable to their own interests. The corrupt administration of the *curatores* led to such abuses that the imperial government was led to create a new office to care for the interests of the common people.

The *defensor civitatis* (ἔκδικος) is found in Egypt in the first half of the fourth century. Apparently the office was not established in other parts of the empire before 364 when it appears in Illyria[3]. At this time the appointments were made by the pretorian prefect and confirmed by the emperor. In 387 the nominations were made by the local *curiae* subject to the emperor's approval[4]. Under Honorius the bishop, clergy, *honorati*, *possessores*, and *curiales* chose the *defensor*[5]. Majorian gave the plebeians a voice in the election, and Justinian made the office a municipal liturgy imposed for a term of two years in rotation from an *album* of suitable candidates[6].

While the duties of the *defensor* were ill-defined at first, the office soon acquired great prestige, and overshadowed that of the *curator* and other magistrates. It was apparently conceived as an imperial *patrocinium* to offset the growth of private patronage, which was undermining state and civic authority and imposing serious hardships

---

[1] de Ruggiero, *Diz. Ep. s.v. curator.*

[2] *Dig.* 39. 2. 46; 50. 8. 2, 5, 11; 50. 9. 4. His judicial powers were limited (*Cod. J.* 1. 54. 3 (239)).

[3] *P. Oxy.* 901; *Cod. Th.* 1. 29. 1 (364). Cf. *ibid.* 12. 1. 20 (381).

[4] *Cod. Th.* 1. 29. 1 (364), 3 (368), 6 (387).

[5] *Cod. J.* 1. 55. 8 (409).

[6] Majorian, *Novellae*, 3. 1; Justinian, *Novellae*, 15.

on citizens who had no other means of protecting themselves against the evils of the age. The *defensor* was
especially charged with the protection of the lower orders
against illegal exactions and other abuses. He supervised
the revision of the tax lists and the collection of taxes from
the smaller landowners. Municipal property was under
his jurisdiction and he kept the public records (*acta*). At
first he exercised no police or judiciary power except in
minor cases, but his authority was extended by various
rescripts until he had jurisdiction in civil cases up to 300
solidi. These functions brought the *defensor* into all branches
of municipal administration and the other magistracies
declined greatly in importance. In the fifth century he
appears to have exercised sole power in many cities. Unfortunately the development of the office of *defensor*
followed the same lines as that of the *curator* and instead
of defending the interests of the common people, he became
their oppressor[1].

As the magistrates administered civil affairs, so the
religious life of the community was in the charge of priests
of the local and imperial cults, and these priesthoods were
sometimes regarded as liturgies, sometimes as *honores*[2].
Usually those citizens were elected to priesthoods who
had already discharged their municipal obligations, and
they were thus exempt from liturgies of a personal
character, but their patrimony remained liable to the
customary charges. While priests were usually chosen by
election or cooptation, the honor was in some cases
hereditary, in others it was sold to the highest bidder.
The term of service was annual, or for a prescribed period,
or for life[3]. After Christianity was officially recognized,
the pagan cults began to fall into disrepute, and their
priesthoods were finally abolished.

---

[1] *R.E. s.v. defensor.*

[2] The codes vary in their classification of priesthoods. *Cf. Cod. Th.* 12. 1.
75 (371), 77 (372), 103 (383).

[3] Liebenam, *St. Verw.* 342 *ff.*

HONORES AND MUNERA

In the fourth century the Codes give to the *principales* (*primarii, primates, summates*), or leading men of the local *curiae*, a position which seems to have been regarded as a virtual *honor*[1]. As the magistracies weakened or disappeared, the *principales* acquired administrative power, and they are grouped sometimes with the decurions, sometimes with the *defensor*, in municipal duties. The title was conferred in some cases by a vote of the senate, and was even granted to minors, although it was usually reserved for those who had satisfied all their municipal obligations. The προπολιτευόμενοι of Egypt are probably the eastern equivalent of the *principales*. The *primus curiae* or the chief member of the senate received special honors and privileges, and on the fulfilment of certain conditions was eligible for the imperial rank of *comes primi ordinis*.

Next to the municipal magistracies, the liturgies or *munera* were the most important factor in carrying on the civic organization. The imposition of a direct tax on the commonwealth had never been popular in democratic states and the liturgy was resorted to in supplementing municipal revenues. The extension and development of this method of administration is one of the most important features of municipal history in the Roman empire.

Liturgies (*munera publica*) were classified as *munera personalia* and *munera patrimoniorum*. Under the latter might be placed those called *munera locorum*[2]. The former did not require the expenditure of money, while the patrimonial liturgies were virtually a form of taxation on the estate of the incumbent. Certain liturgies were called *munera mixta*[3]. The oriental *decaprotia* is an example of this class, for those who undertook the office were responsible for the payment of the imperial tribute from their municipality. If the full assessment was paid by the citizens, the liturgy involved no expense, but if the *decaproti* had to make up the deficit, the liturgy became a

[1] Declareuil, *op. cit.* 164 *ff.*   [2] *Dig.* 50. 4. 6, 14.
[3] *Dig.* 50. 4. 18.

munus patrimoniorum. Extraordinary liturgies (*munera extraordinaria*) were devised to meet special needs, particularly in the imperial service, and ultimately many of this class were incorporated in the regular burdens of the municipality as *munera personalia* or *patrimoniorum.* In the Greek cities we sometimes find liturgies described as δημοτικαί and βουλευτικαί, which may imply that members of the senate were not called upon to undertake liturgies beneath their station, or those which called for the performance of menial labor[1].

The classification of liturgies varied naturally in different cities and in different periods. When there was plenty of money in the municipal treasury, the expense of most liturgies could be met from public funds, but in times of economic depression there was a tendency to transfer personal liturgies to charges on estates. The provincial governor or emperor often made such changes in the classification if the municipality refused to act[2]. In the third century the laws governing *munera* were framed by the imperial bureaus, and in the case of liturgies in the imperial service the regulations were applied uniformly throughout the empire. It is probable that municipal liturgies of all kinds were ultimately regulated by universal laws.

Personal liturgies are described in the Codes and Digest as *munera personalia, corporalia,* or *sordida.* It is probable that the last-mentioned liturgies required manual labor, since women and decurions were excused therefrom[3]. The charter of Urso provided that not more than five days' labor could be required from any property-holder within the bounds of the colony[4]. A similar law is found in Egypt regulating the amount of labor to be given annually by the peasant to ditches and dykes[5]. In the fourth century no distinction seems to be drawn between *munera personalia*

---

[1] Cagnat, *IGRR.* 3, 623.   [2] *Cod. J.* 10. 42. 4.
[3] *Dig.* 50. 1. 17; 50. 1. 22, 37, 38; 50. 4. 3, 3.
[4] No. 26.   [5] Oertel, *Die Liturgie,* 64 *ff.*

and *sordida*. In his treatise on liturgies Arcadius Charisius included under *munera personalia* such duties as the care of aqueducts, temples, archives, and public buildings, the heating of public baths, the purchase of grain and oil, the management of civic revenues, the collection of the *annona*, and the convoying of recruits, horses, and other beasts of burden for the imperial service. Irenarchs (police officials), limenarchs (harbor masters), public advocates, local judges, ambassadors, scribes, and other minor officials discharged liturgies of this class[1]. Other duties, which, in different cities, had been recognized by custom as personal charges, may be added to this list.

Charges on estates (*munera patrimoniorum* or *pecuniaria*) included such liturgies as the holding of the gymnasiarchy, or of priesthoods, the provision of transport for the imperial service, the sheltering of troops, and the performance of any public duty for which the incumbent had to provide funds from his private means[2].

Certain liturgies were classified and apparently held according to a fixed *cursus*. When the series was once completed, a citizen could not be compelled to discharge further obligations in that series unless there was a lack of other candidates[3]. Laws were also devised determining the intervals which should elapse between the different liturgies, but in times of stress evasions are known to have been frequent[4].

Every resident of the municipality could be required to undertake his share of the liturgies unless he was excused by law. Aliens were also subject to the liturgies of their

---

[1] *Dig.* 50. 4. 18.

[2] These *munera* were also classified according as the owner of an estate was a citizen of the municipality or an alien. In the latter case the *munus* was called an *intributio* (*Dig.* 50. 4. 6), and was apparently a direct tax levied on the owner (*Dig.* 50. 4. 18, 25).

[3] *Dig.* 50. 4. 3, 15; *Cod. J.* 10. 42. 1; 10. 43. 3. While the usual term was annual, shorter periods are known; *cf. Athen. Mitth.* 8, 318, for four-month terms at Tralles.

[4] *Cod. J.* 10. 41. 1; Oertel, *op. cit.* 388 *ff.*; nos. 180, 194, 203.

native city in addition to those of the city in which they resided. If, however, they lived outside the town limits, they were exempt from regular *munera*, but their property was subjected to a special tax called *intributio*[1]. It is probable that the laws regulating the liturgies of aliens were devised to prevent the migration of wealthy citizens from communities where such burdens were heavy to more favored municipalities such as Roman colonies, or federated states which enjoyed special privileges or were subject to lighter taxation. Citizenship in such cities would be eagerly sought after and the right of conferring it must have been closely guarded. In Tyra decrees of naturalization were required to be submitted to the governor for approval and we may infer that this city enjoyed certain privileges which made citizenship in it desirable[2]. In later times the rigid application of the laws regarding alien residents made it practically impossible for anyone to reside elsewhere than in his place of birth. The law, however, might be evaded by adoption. To prevent this practice an adopted son was required to perform the liturgies of his native city as well as of his new home, and on being emancipated he ceased to be a citizen of his adopted city[3]. On the other hand, when a woman married a citizen of another city, she became a resident of that city, and was under no obligation to perform the *munera patrimoniorum* to which her estate might be subjected in her native place, nor could her dowry be reckoned as part of her husband's property[4]. In the fourth century this law was modified in the case of heiresses of curial estates[5].

When public funds were appropriated for the discharge of municipal liturgies, the appointee was required to pro-

---

[1] *Dig.* 50. 1. 29, 35; 50. 4. 6; *cf.* 50. 4. 18, 21 *ff.*
[2] No. 130. *Cf.* Cass. Dio, 54. 7, where Augustus is said to have deprived the Athenians of the right of granting citizenship because of the abuse of the privilege.
[3] *Dig.* 50. 1. 15, 16.   [4] *Dig.* 50. 1. 21. 37, 38.
[5] *Cod. Th.* 12. 1. 124 (392).

vide bondsmen as sureties for the proper fulfilment of his duties[1]. If he died before the end of his term, the obligation fell on his heirs[2]. In cases of mal-administration the nominator and bondsmen were liable for the obligations of the defaulter[3]. Sometimes, especially in the case of imperial liturgies, the whole *curia* was held responsible[4]. It may be doubted whether the *curia* was responsible as a corporate body for all candidates nominated by it in regular session, but where a large number of liturgies were imposed, it is probable that every member was involved either as a candidate, or as nominator, or as surety. In those cases where the liturgy was shared by two or more, the principle of solidary liability was enforced unless it was stipulated otherwise in the appointment[5].

Outside Egypt we find various methods of appointment to liturgies. Sometimes the emperor or the provincial governor sent nominations to the *curia*, or made the appointment directly[6]. The *curator rei publicae* had power to act in certain cases[7]. Usually appointments were made by the magistrates and decurions at a regular meeting of the *curia*, at which a quorum of two-thirds of the members was required by law[8]. We may suppose that, when the principle of liability had developed to such an extent that members of the senate were heavily burdened, they preferred to escape the obligations of nomination and surety by allowing the appointments to pass into the hands of imperial officials. The financial gain, however, was far outweighed by the loss of independence which was entailed thereby. In the fifth century it is probable that the decurions drew up lists of citizens for each liturgy and

1 *Dig.* 50. 8. 11; *Cod. J.* 10. 70. 1.   2 *Dig.* 50. 8. 12.
3 *Cod. J.* 11. 36. 1, 2; 11. 37. 1; *Cod. Th.* 12. 6. 1. 8, 9; *Dig.* 50. 8. 4.
4 *Cod. Th.* 12. 6. 9 (365?).
5 *Cod. J.* 10. 43. 1; 11. 36. 2; 11. 38. 1; *Dig.* 50. 8. 3, 12.
6 Julian, *Misopogon*, 370–371; *Dig.* 49. 4. 1, 3; 50. 5. 2, 7; *Cod. Th.* 11. 16. 4 (328); *Cod. J.* 10. 77. 1 (409).
7 *Cod. J.* 11. 37. 1.
8 *Cod. J.* 10. 32. 2; 10. 72. 8; *Dig.* 50. 1. 21; 50. 9. 3. *Cf.* no. 34.

forwarded them to the provincial governor who made the appointments. This at least was the method of appointing the irenarch according to a law of Honorius[1]. Extraordinary liturgies were assigned by the magistrates at first; in the fourth century by the *principales*, and later by the governor[2]. The latter also decided appeals, although they were frequently carried to the emperor, and after 313 the imperial court decided all such questions[3]. Those who made illegal nominations were compelled to defray the expenses of the appeal[4].

The liturgical system in Egypt was governed by special laws owing to the peculiar organization of this region[5]. Very little is known of the system which prevailed in the three Ptolemaic cities, although it is probable that they did not differ from other Greek cities in their forms of administration, if they possessed public lands from which they derived revenues. In the rest of Egypt the Ptolemies forbade private ownership of land, and *munera patrimoniorum* were consequently impossible. The Romans created a land-owning class and replaced the voluntary Greek bureaucracy with a liturgical system which was gradually extended throughout Egypt to apply to all but a few of the highest positions in the administration. The precise date of the introduction of the liturgical system cannot be determined, but it was already in existence in A.D. 91, and in the following century there is abundant evidence that liturgies were compulsory and extremely burdensome[6].

The Egyptian liturgies are usually classified as χωρικαί and πολιτικαί. The former probably denote those peculiar

---

[1] *Cod. J.* 10. 77. 1.   [2] *Cod. J.* 10. 46. 1; *Cod. Th.* 11. 16. 4 (328).
[3] *Dig.* 50. 4. 4; 50. 5. 2, 7; *Cod. J.* 10. 32. 2; 10. 50. 3; 10. 51. 3; *Cod. Th.* 12. 1. 1 (313).   [4] *Cod. J.* 10. 32. 2.
[5] Jouguet, *op. cit.* 227 ff.; Wilcken, *Grundzüge*, 347 ff.; Oertel, *Die Liturgie*.
[6] Bell, *Journal of Egyptian Archaeology*, 4 (1917), 86 ff.; nos. 180, 181, 187, 189, 194.

to the administration of the nome and the village; the latter belong to the municipal administration of the cities and the metropolis. It is often difficult to distinguish between the imperial and municipal liturgies and the variations in the methods of appointment and appeal in the villages and in the metropolis at different periods make the study of the liturgical system in Egypt particularly difficult[1].

In the villages the nominations were made by the elders or, more commonly, by the secretary. The latter forwarded the list of nominees to the *strategus*, from whose office it went to the *epistrategus* who, if there were sufficient candidates, chose by lot and made the appointments. In some cases the prefect made appointments[2]. The sureties of the nominee were responsible for the proper discharge of the liturgy, but in case of their failure the obligation fell upon the entire village[3]. After the introduction of the municipal system the evidence for the methods of nomination in the villages is scanty. In some cases outgoing officials named their successors, in others the candidates were designated by the comarch who sent the list to the *strategus* for appointment.

In the metropolis of the nome the scribe drew up the list of eligible candidates in consultation with the Council of Archons. The list was probably transmitted to the *epistrategus* through the office of the *strategus*. After 202 the nominations were probably made in the senate. A system of tribal rotation was followed, but if the tribal representatives in the senate failed to make sufficient or proper nominations, the duty fell upon the senate as a whole[4]. For extraordinary liturgies the *prytanis* might make appointments, but confirmation by the senate was required[5].

---

[1] Jouguet, *op. cit.* 98; Oertel, *op. cit.* In an unpublished papyrus in the Princeton collection the distinction is made between βουλευτικαὶ λειτουργίαι and δημοτικαὶ ὑπηρεσίαι.

[2] Nos. 181, 185, 198, 200; *cf.* pp. 89 *ff.*   [3] No. 203.

[4] No. 203.   [5] *Cf.* Wilcken, *op. cit.* 399 *ff.*

The senate seems to have had authority to make the final appointment for purely local liturgies. In the case of imperial or state liturgies the appointments seem to have been made from the lists forwarded from the senate to the *epistrategus*, and in some cases to the prefect[1]. Certain liturgies could be transferred by the incumbent to others by mutual agreement. In other cases any transfer or commutation by a money payment was strictly forbidden[2].

Appeals were directed to the prefect, or, more commonly, to the *epistrategus*. In some cases they were forwarded to the *strategus*, but probably he was only a medium of communication with the *epistrategus*[3]. A nominee had the right to surrender his property to his nominator if the latter was better able to perform the liturgy, and if the nominee claimed that his own resources were insufficient. Apparently the entire revenue was surrendered for the discharge of liturgies, whereas in magistracies only two-thirds of the revenue could be taken for the expenses of the office[4].

As the liturgies in the empire increased in number and severity, the privilege of exemption became especially desirable. Antoninus withdrew the right of cities to confer immunity (ἀτέλεια), except in the case of physicians, teachers, and philosophers, and the number of exemptions which a city could grant was strictly limited according to its rank[5]. The provincial governors exercised some authority in this matter until Constantine transferred all questions of exemption to the imperial bureaus[6]. The Codes contain a vast number of laws on the subject, regulating the grants of immunity in minute detail. It would be

[1] Jouguet, *op. cit.* 410 *ff.*; nos. 172, 180, 181, 182, 187, 200.
[2] No. 181; *P. Fior.* 3–9, 382; *BGU.* 1073; *P. Gen.* 73.
[3] *P. Fior.* 57; Wilcken, *Chrestomathie*, 263; *Cod. J.* 10. 48. 9.
[4] Nos. 185, 198.
[5] *Dig.* 27. 1. 6; *Cod. J.* 10. 47. 1. It should be noted that the rescript of Antoninus was addressed to Asia only, but it is probable that it came to be applied to other provinces as well.
[6] *Cod. Th.* 12. 1. 1 (313).

impossible, within the limits of this study, to record the legislation in its entirety, and we shall attempt to give only the main outlines[1].

Individual citizens received the grant of immunity from liturgies by imperial decree. In the case of personal liturgies the grant was not heritable, while immunity from *munera patrimoniorum* passed to descendants in the male line. Any grant was revocable when the safety of the state was endangered[2].

Personal liturgies were not imposed on those suffering from physical disability, on minors, on those over seventy years of age, on women, or on parents of five or more living children[3].

Owners of estates subject to liturgies could not escape their obligations on any claim based on age, sickness, number of children, or sex. It was forbidden to commute the personal service required in *munera patrimoniorum* by a money payment or by providing a substitute[4]. The latter provision seems to have been disregarded in Egypt and the Orient[5].

[1] Bks. 6, 7, 8, 11, 12, 13, 16 in the Theodosian Code; 10–12 in the Justinian Code; 50 in the Digest, *passim*.

[2] *Dig.* 50. 6. 1; *Cod. J.* 10. 48. 13 (385); *Cod. Th.* 10. 49. 1–3; 11. 16. 16 (385); Bruns, 41.

[3] *Dig.* 50. 2. 6, 7; 50. 4. 3; 50. 5. 2, 13, 14; *Cod. J.* 10. 42. 7, 9; 10. 50. 2, 3; 10. 51. 1–4; 10. 52. 2, 3; *Cod. Th.* 12. 1. 7 (320), 19 (331), 35 (343); 12. 17. 1 (324). From these laws it may be seen that the age limit was reduced from 25 to 16. Oertel thinks that 14 was the lower limit in Egypt (*op. cit.* 374). Parents often undertook liturgies in the name of a son who was a minor, and sometimes minors were nominated without the consent of the parent. In the latter case the estate of the parent could not be held responsible for any obligations which might be incurred by the son (*Dig.* 50. 2. 6). In Rome the father of three children, in Italy the father of four, and in the provinces the father of five children was excused from liturgies (Justinian, *Inst.* 1. 25). Special grants were sometimes made personally to fathers of large families (*Dig.* 50. 6. 6; *Cod. Th.* 12. 1. 55 (363); *Cod. J.* 10. 52. 1).

[4] *Dig.* 50. 4. 16.

[5] Wilcken, *Chrestomathie*, 350; *P. Fior.* 57. In the fourth century members of the local senates who had received appointments in the im-

The following classes of citizens were excused from liturgies: members of the imperial nobility, officials in the state bureaus, soldiers and officers in the army, veterans, members of guilds in the imperial service and of certain local guilds in the service of the municipality, or engaged in trades under imperial charter, teachers, physicians, actors, athletes, priests of pagan cults and of the Christian church after its recognition by Constantine, tenants on imperial estates (provided that their leasehold covered twenty-five *iugera*), Roman citizens resident in non-Roman towns previous to the edict of Caracalla[1], and citizens of Alexandria and Antinoopolis resident in other towns and villages in Egypt. As the property of *conductores* of the imperial taxes was pledged to the *fiscus* as security, they were also exempted. Tenants of waste land who brought it back into cultivation were released from all extraordinary liturgies as also were farmers at seed-time and harvest.

The *clarissimi* or members of the imperial nobility were the most important class of citizens who enjoyed exemption

---

perial body were required to provide substitutes for the discharge of municipal liturgies (*Cod. Th.* 12. 1. 69 (369?), 91 (382), 98 (382), 111 (386), 312 (391) *inter alia*).

[1] Ulpian says (*Dig.* 50. 4. 3) that a citizen of Rome ought also to perform the liturgies of his *domicilium*. This is probably later than the Edict of Caracalla as the compilers of the Digest would probably not include regulations prior to that period. There are very few inscriptions which record liturgies of Roman citizens in non-Roman towns and these cases may be explained as an act of voluntary generosity, or because the liturgy was held before the grant of citizenship was conferred. In the *diplomata* issued to veterans on their discharge, immunity was conferred upon them and their children, and in the single decree of the Senate which we possess conferring citizenship upon an alien (Bruns, 41), he was granted immunity from taxation and all duties, and the gift was transmitted to his heirs, who would also be Roman citizens. In Egypt citizens of Alexandria were exempt from liturgies outside their native place, and since an Egyptian could not become a Roman citizen without being made a citizen of Alexandria first (Pliny, *Epp. ad Trai.* 5, 6), it follows that Romans enjoyed immunity in Egypt. The same rule undoubtedly applied in all Roman provinces, and the guilds of Roman citizens which are found prior to the Edict of Caracalla were probably formed of members of this privileged class.

from municipal obligations since they controlled most of the wealth of the community. Membership in the order was hereditary and, while the title was legally secured through imperial favor, it was often purchased fraudulently through the connivance of palace officials, and in some cases it was assumed by powerful citizens without any warrant whatsoever. Since every accession to the order weakened the municipality by depriving it of citizens or estates subject to liturgies, the emperors were ultimately compelled to restrict grants of this class. In the fourth and fifth centuries elaborate legislation was devised regulating the elevation of decurions or members of the curial order to the rank of imperial nobility. In 340 the fulfilment of all municipal obligations was required before any senatorial honors were conferred[1]. Two years earlier a decree had been issued compelling those who had no legal claim to imperial honors to return to the curial order[2]. Twenty years later the situation in the municipalities again became serious, and all decurions who had obtained the rank of imperial senator were compelled to resign this title. A few exceptions were made, but even in these cases those who held the rank in question were required to fulfil the *munera patrimoniorum* upon their estates within the municipality or to resign the property to the *curia*[3]. The next step in imperial legislation was to attack the principle of hereditary succession. Hitherto the senatorial rank had been transmitted to a senator's children with all the privileges which it entailed. After 364 the newly elected senator (*clarissimus*) was required to leave one son in the curial order to discharge the obligations of the estate towards the municipality[4]. After 390 senatorial appointments no longer carried the hereditary privilege[5].

[1] *Cod. Th.* 12. 1. 29 (340). [2] *Cod. Th.* 12. 1. 25 (338).
[3] *Cod. Th.* 12. 1. 48 (361), 58 (364), 69 (365), 74 (371), 111 (386), 118 (387).
[4] *Cod. Th.* 12. 1. 57 (364), 90 (382).
[5] *Cod. Th.* 12. 1. 130 (393), 160 (398).

This law was later amended, permitting sons born after the appointment to inherit their father's title and privileges, while in the case of the highest class, the *illustres*, all the sons enjoyed the right of hereditary succession[1]. At the same time permission was given senators to provide substitutes to discharge municipal liturgies. In 436 members of the *curia* elevated to the rank of *spectabiles* were compelled to undertake the municipal liturgies in addition to those imposed upon the imperial order, while those appointed to the higher rank of *illustres* were ordered to provide substitutes to discharge the *munera patrimoniorum*. The sons of *spectabiles* and *illustres* of curial origin remained in the order to which they were born[2]. This law must have made it impossible for residents in the municipality to hold municipal and imperial honors at the same time, but it is probable that members of the senatorial order found means of escaping their municipal obligations. Accordingly Theodosius closed the senatorial order to all *curiales* and this method of securing immunity from liturgies ceased[3].

Exemption from municipal duties was one of the privileges granted to those who held the title of *perfectissimi* or *egregii*, if this honor was conferred in recognition of public service or after all liturgies had been duly performed. Constantine ordained that this honor should no longer be conferred on citizens who were eligible for membership in their local *curia*[4].

Those engaged in imperial service abroad (*absentes rei publicae causa*) were exempt from municipal obligations[5]. This class of persons included the retinue of the provincial governors, members of the imperial bureaucracy,

---

[1] *Cod. Th.* 12. 1. 155 (397).   [2] *Cod. Th.* 12. 1. 187 (436).

[3] Theodosius, *Novellae*, 15. 1 (439), 2 (441). Zeno and Justinian gave immunity to *curiales* only after reaching the highest offices in the imperial service (*Cod. J.* 10. 32. 64, 67).

[4] *Cod. Th.* 12. 1. 5 (317); *cf. ibid.* 12. 1. 15 (327), 26 (338), 42 (354), 44 (358); *Cod. J.* 12. 32. 1.

[5] *Dig.* 4. 6. 35*ff.*; 50. 5. 4. *Cf. Cod. J.* 10. 48. 1, 5.

ambassadors to Rome or neighboring cities, and soldiers or officers in the army. Similar privileges were naturally extended to members of the palace bureaus who were ultimately organized on military lines[1]. The *curiales* sought to escape from their local obligations by securing positions in one or other of the great bureaus, and in the fourth century there was a constant succession of enactments forbidding their employment. The frequent adoption of such measures shows that the laws were constantly evaded. Occasionally attempts were made to seek out all *curiales* in these positions and to compel them to return to their cities, but evasions were always possible and provision was usually made whereby those who had served for some time or had attained a certain rank were allowed to remain at their posts[2]. It is, however, probable that the members of the bureaucracy did not always secure complete exemption from their municipal obligations, especially as the higher officials of curial origin were not exempt from all *munera patrimoniorum*[3]. In a few departments the privilege of exemption was hereditary for a time in the case of officers of higher rank[4]. The liberality of emperors varied. Sometimes officials enjoyed exemption from certain specified liturgies, sometimes from all of them, and in times of stress all privileges might be suspended[5]. The laws of Zeno and Justinian gave exemption from municipal obligations only to those *curiales* who had attained positions of very high rank in the palace[6].

The laws governing the exemption of soldiers and

---

[1] *Cf.* bks 6–8 in the Theodosian Code, and bk 12 in the Justinian Code, *passim*.

[2] *Cod. Th.* 12. 1. 26 (338), 31 (341), 36 (343), 44 (358), 78 (372); 1. 12. 4 (393), 6 (398); 6. 35 *passim*.

[3] *Cod. Th.* 6. 35. 1 (314), 3 (319).

[4] *Cod. Th.* 12. 1. 14 (326); *cf.* pp. 205 *ff*.

[5] *Cod. Th.* 6. 35. 1 (314), 3 (319); 11. 16. 18 (390); 6. 26. 14 (407); *Cod. J.* 12. 23. 1; 12. 26. 1–4; 10. 48. 11–12; 12. 19. 4; 10. 49. 1 (408), 2 (445), 3 (472).

[6] *Cod. J.* 10. 32. 64, 67.

veterans are of interest. While soldiers were excused from most municipal obligations, they were liable to certain charges upon their estates[1]. A soldier home on furlough was technically liable for any liturgies which might be imposed[2]. When military service became hereditary, sons of soldiers, who did not enter the army, were compelled to join the curial order[3]. Veterans were given special privileges[4]. In the second century the Egyptian veteran enjoyed immunity from liturgies (on estates?) for five years after his discharge[5]. In other parts of the empire no term is ever specified, and it is usually assumed that exemption was for life. It may be questioned, however, whether the law applying to Egypt did not extend over the whole empire. If a veteran entered the *curia* of his own accord, he was liable for all the liturgies of the order unless he had especially reserved his privilege of exemption[6]. In the third century the veterans were obliged to do road-work and to pay certain *vectigalia* and *intributiones*[7]. Apparently their privileges were steadily encroached upon, since Constantine was compelled to confirm them by special laws[8].

Members of guilds engaged in the imperial service—especially in the alimentation of the capital and in supplying the armies—enjoyed special privileges and were exempt from all municipal obligations; in fact, shipowners were forbidden to take up the duties of a decurion in their

---

[1] *Dig.* 50. 4. 18; 50. 5. 7, 11; 49. 18. 2–4.

[2] *Dig.* 4. 6. 34–35.

[3] *Hist. Aug. Alex. Sev.* 58; *Cod. Th.* 7. 22. 1 (319), 4 (326); 7. 1. 5 (364); 12. 1. 18 (329), 35 (343), 79 (379); *Cod. J.* 12. 33. 2–4.

[4] *BGU.* 628.   [5] No. 177.

[6] *Cod. J.* 10. 44. 1; *Dig.* 49. 18. 2. Loss of privilege through misconduct: *Cod. Th.* 7. 20. 7 (353).

[7] The testimony of Arcadius Charisius, Ulpian, and Hermogenianus varies, *cf. Dig.* 49. 18. 4; 50. 4. 18; 50. 5. 11.

[8] *Cod. Th.* 7. 20. 2 (320), 3 (320), 6 (342), 9 (362). Apparently the first promises of Constantine were made under compulsion, and the veterans later found that there was a tendency to ignore them.

native cities[1]. Membership in this guild was not only hereditary, but also obligatory in the fourth century[2]. The estate of a *navicularius* was bound to the service of his order, and if he bequeathed it to anyone not a member of the guild, the legatee was required to assume the obligations of the estate towards the guild by becoming a member[3]. On the other hand, a member of the *curia* was strictly forbidden to attempt the avoidance of his municipal duties by entering the guild of *navicularii*[4]. There was a large number of other guilds devoted to the imperial service, and it is probable that the rules for membership in these societies were ultimately brought into conformity with those governing the shipowners[5]. Besides the imperial guilds there were local corporations in each municipality formed for the special needs of the community, whose members were excused from other liturgies as a recompense. These guilds were under the control of the municipal authorities by whom their duties were designated. The earlier emperors discouraged the formation of these local societies for political reasons, but the ban was later removed[6], and numerous records show that these organizations were widespread throughout the empire. A law of Honorius at the end of the fourth century even went so far as to order all citizens to enroll themselves either in the curial order or in some guild[7]. Constantine granted exemption from personal liturgies to artisans in a large number of professions, and it is prob-

---

[1] At first the period of immunity was five years (*Dig.* 50. 4. 5), but later immunity was conferred as long as one remained a member of his guild (*Dig.* 50. 5. 3; 50. 6. 6).

[2] *Cod. Th.* 13. 5. 2 (315), 3 (319), 11 (365), 14 (369), 19 (390), 20 (392), 21 (392), 35 (412); Valentinian, *Novellae*, 29.

[3] *Cod. Th.* 13. 5. 19 (390).   [4] *Cod. Th.* 12. 1. 149 (395).

[5] Waltzing, *Les corporations professionnelles chez les Romains*; *R.E. s.v. collegium*; *Dig.* 50. 6. 7.

[6] Many of these were organized by Alexander Severus (*Hist. Aug. Alex. Sev.* 33). For legislation in regard to immunity, *cf. Dig.* 50. 6. 6.

[7] *Cod. Th.* 12. 1. 179 (415); *cf.* 7. 21. 3 (396).

able that they were grouped in guilds at that time[1]. Wealthier members of the guilds were sometimes drafted into the *curiae*, but it is probable that in the fourth century membership in these societies was hereditary and could not be resigned at will[2].

Physicians, teachers, and professors of philosophy were excused from all personal liturgies and from providing billets as early as the reign of Vespasian[3]. Antoninus divided the cities of Asia into grades, and limited the number in each of these professions which might be granted immunity by the municipal authorities according to the rank of the city[4]. Elementary teachers were excluded from these privileges[5]. Instructors in civil law enjoyed immunity in Rome but not in the provinces, a law which must have had considerable importance in the spread of Roman jurisprudence[6]. Constantine granted physicians and teachers exemption from all charges, and this privilege was later extended to their wives and children[7]. Architects and members of allied professions were also excused from personal liturgies. Constantine sought to revive the architectural profession by conferring immunity on the parent as well as the student[8].

Priests of local and imperial cults were free from personal liturgies, but were not excused from charges imposed upon estates[9]. Their children also enjoyed the same privileges. In Egypt the number of exemptions granted

---

[1] *Cod. Th.* 13. 4. 2 (337); *Cod. J.* 10. 66. 1.

[2] *Cod. Th.* 12. 1. 96 (383); Julian, *Misopogon*, 368.

[3] *Dig.* 27. 1. 6; 50. 4. 18; 50. 5. 10; *cf. ibid.* 50. 5. 8, where the lawgiver ironically remarks that philosophers, since they despise wealth, should not be exempt from *munera patrimoniorum*, or, if they desire exemption, they are not true philosophers.

[4] *Dig.* 27. 1. 6; 50. 5. 8; *Cod. J.* 10. 47. 1; 10. 53. 5.

[5] *Dig.* 50. 4. 11.   [6] *Dig.* 27. 1. 6, 12.

[7] *Cod. Th.* 13. 3. 1 (321), 2 (324), 3 (344), 4 (362), 15 (393), 16 (414), 17 (414).

[8] *Cod. Th.* 13. 4. 1 (334), 3 (344), 4 (374); *cf. Dig.* 50. 6. 7.

[9] Nos. 164, 178; *Dig.* 50. 4. 18; *Cod. Th.* 12. 1. 21 (335); 12. 5. 2 (337).

to the priesthood in each district appears to have been limited under Roman rule[1]. A provincial priesthood could not be held until all local liturgies were discharged by the candidate, but this high office carried with it the honorary title of *comes* and conferred immunity from all other charges[2].

Since magistracies were open to members of the Jewish faith, it may be assumed that Jews were also required to perform municipal liturgies, although those in the Orient claimed exemption[3]. Constantine required the Jews to be enrolled as *curiales*, granting exemption to a few—presumably the priests—in each community. By later laws those who devoted their time to the synagogue were excused from personal and civil obligations[4]. In 383 and again in 398 the immunity of all sects, and particularly of the Jews, was revoked[5]. The emperor Theodosius again withdrew all privileges in regard to exemption from liturgies which the Jews may have enjoyed at that time and forbade them to be appointed to administrative posts or to imperial honors[6].

Christians were not distinguished from Jews at first, but when the political significance of the new religion was realized the government granted them no favors. While their religious beliefs may have prevented Christians from participating voluntarily in municipal duties which involved the performance of pagan ritual, it is evident from the proceedings of the Council of Iliberris that Christians held magistracies and even pagan priesthoods[7]. Imperial legislation dealing with Christians who avoided their civic duties began with Constantine who, in 313, granted

---

[1] Otto, *Priester und Tempel*, 2. 250; Oertel, *op. cit.* 392; no. 178.
[2] *Cod. Th.* 12. 1. 75 (371), 77 (372).
[3] *Cod. Th.* 12. 1. 158 (398); 16. 8. 24 (418); *Dig.* 50. 2. 3.
[4] *Cod. Th.* 16. 8. 2 (320), 3 (321), 4 (331), 13 (397).
[5] *Cod. Th.* 12. 1. 99 (383), 158 (398); *Cod. J.* 1. 9. 5, 10.
[6] *Cod. J.* 1. 9. 18; Theodosius, *Novellae*, 3; Justinian, *Novellae*, 45.
[7] Declareuil, *op. cit.* 97 *ff.*

clerici exemption from all municipal charges[1]. Evidently the suffering *curiales* found in this law an easy way of escape from taxation, and shortly afterwards the emperor was forced to issue an edict by which members of the *curiae* or wealthy plebeians were forbidden to enter holy orders[2]. The frequent re-enactment of this law in later times shows that it was persistently violated, and the general trend of the legislation of the fourth and fifth centuries followed the principle applied to *curiales* who aspired to membership in the imperial nobility. The Church as a career or as means of escape from liturgies was closed to members of the curial order as far as possible. If they sought to enter the priesthood, their convictions were put to a severe test by laws requiring that their property must be surrendered to the *curia* in whole or in part, and by the provision of substitutes to perform their curial liturgies[3]. Valentinian cancelled all exemptions from tribute and from *munera patrimoniorum*[4]. Majorian ordered all *curiales* in the lower offices of the Church to return to their former station in life, while deacons, presbyters, and bishops were compelled to fulfil all their liturgies as citizens[5]. According to a law of Justinian, *curiales* were forbidden to enter the priesthood except in early life, and on condition of surrendering a fourth of their estate to the municipality[6].

Tenants on imperial estates were excused from municipal charges unless they owned other property privately. Even these tenants were exempted by a law of Constantine if their lease of crown lands covered twenty-five *iugera* or more[7]. Since the emperors wished to increase the area of land under cultivation, special immunity was

---

[1] *Cod. Th.* 16. 2. 1 (313); *cf. ibid.* 16. 2. 2 (319), 7 (330), 24 (377).
[2] *Cod. Th.* 16. 2. 3 (320).
[3] *Cod. Th.* 12. 1. 49 (361), 59 (364), 99 (383), 104 (383), 163 (399); 16. 2. 19 (370), 21 (371).
[4] Valentinian, *Novellae*, 10.   [5] Majorian, *Novellae*, 7, 7 (458).
[6] Justinian, *Novellae*, 6, 1 (535).   [7] *Cod. Th.* 12. 1. 33 (342).

granted to those who brought waste land under tillage, and full ownership was given to the occupants[1].

In studying the numerous documents dealing with *honores* and *munera* we may easily discern certain tendencies which have an important bearing on the history of the municipalities. The magistracies were coveted in the earlier period of the empire, when economic conditions were favorable and civic life was distinguished for its splendor. Even then indications are not lacking that decay had already set in. The charter of Malaca provided for a possible lack of candidates for civic positions, and we may infer that some municipalities had already been confronted with this difficulty. Doubtless many weaker communities had already been impoverished because of the loss of citizens through various economic changes. In the third century when famine, plague, civil war, and social disorders were widespread, the magistracies became serious burdens on the incumbents, and willing candidates ceased to present themselves for office, except possibly in a few cities which enjoyed unusual economic advantages. The Codes now lay more stress on the burdens attached to magistracies than upon the distinction which they conferred, and while some traces of the former privileges still remained, the *honores* differed but little from liturgies. In Egypt it is difficult to distinguish between the classes of public service, and the charges attached to certain magistracies were so ruinous that they involved not only the annual income of the incumbent, but trenched upon his capital resources. The laws reveal the fact that citizens designated for office often preferred to abandon their property rather than to accept a magistracy, and that many sought to escape their obligations by flight. While the decay of the traditional offices may be ascribed in part to the development of their liturgical character, the creation of the imperial *curatores* and *defensores* contributed greatly in diminishing the

---

[1] *Cod. Th.* 15. 3. 1 (319); *cf.* pp. 211 *ff.*

powers and prerogatives of the local magistrates. Officials
designated by the emperor naturally usurped authority
because of their greater prestige, and it is not surprising
to find that the ordinary magistracies disappeared in
many towns to which a *curator* had been assigned.

In the development of liturgies the decurionate fell
into greater disrepute than the magistracies. Membership
in the *curia* became hereditary, probably about the beginning of the third century, and in the fourth we find an
order of *curiales* which apparently included all citizens who
were landowners and eligible for membership in the local
senate. Their rank was not only hereditary but also compulsory. The history of imperial legislation concerning
curiales may be briefly traced. When the collection of
taxes was transferred from the publicans to the municipality, the duty was assigned to a committee of ten chosen
from the senate (*decemprimi*) or, as in the East, from
wealthy citizens (δεκάπρωτοι), who were not necessarily
members of the order. It is probable that many cities
farmed their own taxes and the senate as a whole was
responsible for their payment. When Septimius Severus
granted a municipal senate to the metropolis of each nome
in Egypt, he made the members of this body responsible
for the collection of the taxes from their nome. The
Egyptian system was soon extended to other municipalities throughout the empire. At least, in the reign of
Aurelian, the *curiales* were responsible for the taxes on
abandoned property, and there is no reason to doubt that
other deficiencies were made up by them. When they
attempted to shift this burden to others, the villagers
were oppressed and the charge was made that every
curialis was a tyrant. As liturgies and taxes grew in
severity, as great landed estates arose owned by proprietors who enjoyed immunity from municipal obligations
either by virtue of their patents of imperial nobility or by
their ability to defy the municipal authorities, and as a
system of patronage developed whereby many of the rural

[113]

population escaped their share of taxation by placing themselves under the protection of some wealthy and powerful landowner, the *curiales* themselves had to bear alone the increasing burdens placed upon their order. Their unhappy lot was further aggravated by the loss of revenues from the public lands, which were frequently confiscated by the emperors or forcibly occupied by wealthy citizens. In order to preserve the municipal institutions from the danger of disintegration, since many *curiales* were abandoning their property rather than facing the burdens placed upon them, the emperors devised stringent legislation to control citizens who were members of the order. Not only were severe penalties imposed upon those who attempted to evade their obligations, but every avenue of escape was closed. The *curiales* became a guild in which membership was hereditary and compulsory. In the fourth century the laws regarded the estate as more important than the citizen in the imposition of taxes and liturgies, and the owner was virtually reduced to the position of an imperial serf.

While the unfortunate position in which the *curiales* found themselves in the later empire was due to a variety of causes, the most important factor was the development of the liturgical system. When a volume of tribute flowed into the treasury at Rome sufficient to relieve her citizens of all taxes, an elaborate system of liturgies was unnecessary. In western municipalities our records are unfortunately incomplete, and the clauses of the charters pertaining to liturgies are lacking, but it is probable that sufficient revenue was derived from the public lands in each city to defray the ordinary administrative expenses. The citizens could be called upon to give their labour to an amount not exceeding five days in public service, and the magistrates were expected to supplement the revenues by contributions towards public amusements or in other ways, such as by the *summa honoraria*. In the Greek cities, however, the Romans found a fully developed system of liturgies. This they adopted and in the course of time they extended it over the empire. An important factor in the extension and development of this system as a form of imperial taxation was the depreciation of the coinage by successive emperors. By reducing the gold and silver content in the various issues, embarrassing financial difficulties could be avoided, and the consequent rise in prices produced an appearance of prosperity, at least among the agricultural classes. When the taxes returned to the *fiscus* in the depreciated coinage, there was trouble. It was found that the revenues were no longer sufficient to meet the increased cost of administration. Since it would be extremely unpopular and possibly dangerous to increase the rate of taxation, the rulers were left with the alternative of further depreciation or of extending the municipal system of liturgies to cover various forms of the imperial service. As a matter of fact both methods were resorted to, until the emperors refused to accept their own coinage and demanded the taxes paid in kind. In collecting these and transporting them to the public storehouses, an additional burden was placed upon the municipality. The liturgies, which we may call imperial, were distributed throughout the provincial cities and were regulated by laws applied uniformly to the whole empire. In the course of time the local liturgies came under similar provisions and tended to become universally applied. Of the imperial liturgies the most exacting were those in connection with the imperial post and the billeting of troops or public servants. The severity of these liturgies was increased by the venality and extortion practiced by the officials, and although the emperors frequently sought to correct abuses they were powerless to cope with the widespread corruption which permeated the bureaucracy. In addition to the imperial liturgies, the local *munera* grew more burdensome. This was due to economic causes. The decline in the fertility of the soil, the alienation of municipal lands by confiscation or otherwise, and the appropriation of a large part of the municipal revenues by Valentinian and his successors were instrumental in impoverishing the municipal treasury and causing the transfer of many *munera personalia* to the class of *munera patrimoniorum*. In this way another burden was imposed on the citizens already struggling to meet the increasing cost of the administration and the defense of the empire. For these reasons it was necessary that the right of immunity from liturgies should be carefully restricted. The earliest legislation on this question dates from the reign of Antoninus, who limited the power of the municipalities to confer this privilege. We believe that the edict of Caracalla was actuated by similar motives. By granting citizenship to all free subjects in the provinces, the privilege of immunity which Romans had hitherto enjoyed was taken away, and the liturgies were more equitably distributed. In the fourth and fifth centuries there is a constant succession of laws which steadily narrowed the right of persons holding property in the municipalities to avoid the charges which such possession entailed. In the age of Zeno and Justinian no citizen of curial origin could escape his municipal obligations except by appointment to the highest positions in the imperial bureaucracy. Unfortunately the general trend of this legislation aggravated rather than mitigated the lot of the *curiales*. In fact the study of the laws governing the magistracies, the liturgies, and immunities reveals to the modern student the most significant phases in the decline of municipal life in the Roman Empire.

CHAPTER IX

IMPERIAL TAXES AND REQUISITIONS
IN THE PROVINCES

NO adequate conception may be had of the relations which the municipalities bore to the central government, nor of certain important influences which affected the welfare of the cities, unless one knows something of the imperial taxes which were levied in the provinces, of the methods employed in collecting them, and of the requisitions made by imperial officials[1].

The principal tax in the provinces was on land, and in Sicily, the first district acquired outside of Italy, it took the form of tithes. The Romans simply took over the system of taxation there which their predecessors had followed[2]. Had they not found taxes already being collected there by the central government which they dispossessed, it is not impossible that the municipalities in Sicily and elsewhere might have gone untaxed, and might have been incorporated into the Roman state as the *civitates* in Italy had been. In that case the organization of the Roman empire would have taken an entirely different course, and the provincial cities would have had a very different history from that which they did have. But finding a careful system of taxation worked out in Sicily, and finding machinery in operation which would pour a large revenue into the treasury, the Romans continued the system. In a similar way, on acquiring Macedonia, they took over the method of collecting taxes there which their predecessors had followed, as we shall see later. Two centuries after the conquest of Sicily Cicero

---

[1] The *munera* are treated in another chapter. The Roman financial system and its administration have been left out of account in this chapter, as not pertinent to our purpose.

[2] *Cf.* pp. 47 *ff.*

thought of the provincial contribution to the treasury as "representing the fruits of victory, or as a punishment for engaging in war with the Romans[1]." And this may well have been the conception which the Romans held, down to the close of the second century B.C. But in the *lex agraria* of 111 B.C.[2] the theory is taking shape that the Roman state owned all conquered territory outside Italy[3]. By the early empire the new theory, which came perhaps from Egypt, was generally accepted by Roman lawyers. From this time forth the essential part of the tribute paid by the provinces is thought of as rent. This rent may be paid in the form of a quota, usually a tenth of the produce (*decuma*), or as a fixed contribution (*stipendium*). Sicily, as we have noticed, paid tithes, and it seems probable that the next important province to be acquired, Spain, made her contribution to the imperial treasury in a similar way at the outset[4]. In course of time the Spanish assessment was commuted to a fixed money payment[5]. The first sure instance of the imposition of a *stipendium* on subduing a new territory occurs in the case of Macedonia. Here again, as in Sicily, the Romans took over the system of taxation which they found in existence in the newly conquered region[6]. By 168 B.C., then, two different

[1] *Cf.* the quotation from Cic. *in Verr.* 3. 12–14, given on p. 46.

[2] *CIL.* 1, 200.

[3] Mommsen (*St. R.* 3, 731) thinks that this theory was recognized in the Sempronian law of 123 B.C. under which Asia was organized, but *cf.* Lécrivain, *Dict. Dar. s.v. tributum*, p. 431, col. 2.

[4] Livy (43. 2. 12) speaks of the demand of the Roman magistrate in 171 B.C.: ne cogeret vicesimas vendere Hispanos nisi quanti ipse vellet. From this remark it looks as if the Spaniards originally contributed one-twentieth of their grain. For a different explanation of this passage, *cf.* Marquardt, *St. Verw.* 2, 197. See also Rostowzew, *R.E.* 7, 154. The earliest arrangements in Sardinia cannot be made out with certainty; *cf.* Lécrivain, *Dict. Dar. s.v. tributum*, p. 432, n. 2. At all events a *decuma* was exacted of the people in the island.   [5] *Cf.* Cic. *in Verr.* 3. 12.

[6] Frank (*Roman Imperialism*, 209 f.) makes the interesting suggestion that this fixed annual payment was in lieu of a war indemnity. Thus Carthage at the end of the first Punic war was required to pay an indemnity of 3200 talents, and at the close of the second, 10,000. Macedonia, how-

methods of levying tribute in the provinces had been adopted. In some provinces one of these systems prevailed to the exclusion of the other. In others the two methods were combined, and in still other cases part of a province paid tithes, and the other part a fixed sum of money. Thus Sicily and Asia for many years paid tithes only, Gaul always paid a *stipendium*, one part of Africa contributed money, another part, a quota of its produce, while Sardinia for some time apparently contributed both. It was clearly the general policy of Rome to substitute a money payment for a payment in kind. This change was made probably in Spain and Sardinia, and certainly in Asia, Judaea, and Africa. Undoubtedly it lightened the burdens of the provincial cities, because a system of tithes always bears heavily on the farmer. So far as the rate of taxation goes, assuming that it was 10 per cent. on the average, it was not exorbitant. While the land-tax was the commonest and most important tax outside Italy, it was not the only impost peculiar to the provinces in the time of the republic. In the regions conquered by them the Romans found not only a *tributum soli* but also a *tributum capitis*. The latter tax was levied in Judaea, Africa, Cilicia, Asia, and Britain, and in some of these districts at least Rome continued to levy it regularly or occasionally[1]. This impost seems to have taken a variety of forms, according to the usages and economic conditions of a province. In some cases it was a simple poll tax, in others, a license paid by pedlars, shopkeepers, and men engaged in other trades, and in still others, an income or property tax[2]. Probably the *tributum capitis*, however, was thought of under the

ever, after the victory of Paullus was not in a position to pay down an adequate amount. The annual payment, therefore, required of her may have been thought of as interest upon such a sum. It is more natural to suppose, however, that Rome simply continued the Macedonian system of a fixed payment of money each year. This conclusion seems to harmonize with the fact that the amount which the Romans exacted each year was exactly half that required by the kings.

[1] *Cf.* Marquardt, *St. Verw.* 2. 198 and nn.   [2] *Op. cit.* 200.

republic as a tax intended to supplement or fill out the contribution required under the *tributum soli*[1]. But as the policy of substituting payment in money for payment in kind developed, it was natural that this tax should become more important. The census which Augustus began in 27 B.C. in the provinces would furnish a sound basis not only for a just valuation of property[2], but for the imposition of a tax on all kinds of property, and the *tributum soli* took into account, not only the acreage and the character of land, but also the number of slaves employed and the equipment owned, while the *tributum capitis* was extended to cover other kinds of property[3].

In this connection a word may be said about the *scriptura*, or payment made by those who pastured their flocks and herds on state-land. Under the republic the right to collect the fees due for pasturage was let out to companies, but in imperial times the privilege of using public pasture-land was let out to the owners of large herds, or the lands were occupied by herds belonging to the emperor[4].

We have had occasion to notice in a preceding chapter that in the provinces the unit with which Rome dealt was rather the community than the individual[5]. In accordance with this principle the tribute was ordinarily paid, not by the *homo stipendiarius*, but by the *civitas stipendiaria*[6]. The

---

[1] Marquardt, *op. cit.* 203.

[2] Humbert, *Dict. Dar. s.v. census*, p. 1007, col. 1 and Kubitschek, *R.E.* 3, 1918 *f.*

[3] Chapot, *La prov. rom. proc. d'Asie*, 331. The house tax exacted in Cilicia (Cic. *ad fam.* 3. 8. 5) was an old Jewish tax (Josephus, *Ant. Iud.* 19. 6. 3) and was also levied in Egypt. This tax may explain the law against removing or tearing down houses in some municipalities.

[4] *Cf.* Humbert, *Dict. Dar. s.v. scriptura*; Rostowzew, *Gesch. d. Staatspacht*, 410 (62). [5] *Cf.* p. 17.

[6] *Cf.* Marquardt, *St. Verw.* 2, 185, n. 7; Hirschfeld, 74, n. 6. This is clearly shown, for instance, by the statement of Apuleius (*Apol.* 101) that the *tributum soli* of Pudentilla was paid in for her to the quaestor of the village of Oea: Pudentillae nomine pro eo agello tributum dependi; praesens est quaestor publicus, cui depensum est, Corvinius.

provincial municipality therefore was made responsible for the payment of a certain amount, and this fact proved to be of tremendous significance in the subsequent history of Roman municipalities. When a government lays an obligation on a corporation, it must look to the officials of that corporation to satisfy it. If the obligation is a financial one, and if the corporation cannot or will not meet it in full, the officials must make up the deficit. This was the situation to which a municipality in the provinces was brought in the course of time by Rome's method of imposing a tax upon it and not on the individual subject.

Just as the Romans had taken over Hiero's system of taxation in Sicily, so they adopted his method of collecting taxes. Instead of collecting the tribute by means of government officials, they divided Sicily[1], and later the other provinces, into districts, and farmed out the privilege of gathering the taxes in each district to the highest bidder[2]. The difference between the amount bid by a *redemptor* and the sum which he was able to squeeze out of the taxpayers represented his profits under the contract, and Livy, Cicero's Verrine orations, and his letters from Cilicia set forth clearly the sufferings of the municipalities in the republican period under this iniquitous practice. Julius Caesar introduced a measure of reform into this system in Asia[3]. Augustus probably took the collection of the tribute away from the publicans in the imperial provinces[4], and by the time of Nero their activities were confined to the collection of the *vectigalia*[5]. It would be

---

[1] *Cf.* Cic. *in Verr.* 3. 67, 75, 84, 86, 99.

[2] For the organization of the *societates publicanorum*, the technical terms applied to the officials in these organizations, and the method of collecting taxes, *cf.* Marquardt, *St. Verw.* 2, 184 *ff.*, 298 *ff.*; Rostowzew, *Gesch. d. Staatspacht*, 374 *ff.*; Hirschfeld, 68 *ff.*; Chapot, *La prov. rom. proc. d'Asie*, 324 *ff.*; Arnold, *Roman Provincial Administration*, 201 *ff.*

[3] *Cf.* Chapot, *op. cit.* 328.

[4] *Cf.* Lécrivain, *Dict. Dar. s.v. tributum*, 433, col. 2.

[5] *Cf.* Rostowzew, *op. cit.* 379; Mommsen, *St. R.* 2, 1017 *f.* and n. 1 end.

hard to imagine a more vicious method of collecting taxes than that which had grown up in the Roman world during the last century of the republic. Hiero's system in Sicily of farming the taxes out to local contractors made the tax-farmers amenable in some measure to local public sentiment. But when the Sempronian Law in 123 B.C. provided for the letting of the Asiatic tax-contracts to companies in Rome, it removed this salutary restraint on the greed of the tax-gatherer, and, what was worse, it led to the growth of financial organizations in Rome, which were strong enough to bend governors to their purpose and influence the senate and the courts. It was the irony of fate that this vicious system which bore so heavily on the subject peoples of Rome should have gained its strength from a law fathered by the great democratic leader, Gaius Gracchus. The empire not only did away with this method of collecting tribute, but it introduced other important reforms in provincial taxation. It substituted a money payment in most cases for the more harassing payment in kind. Provincial governors were kept under a stricter and more constant supervision. Their terms were long enough to enable them to inform themselves of conditions in their provinces and to remedy abuses. The taking of a careful census furnished a more equitable basis for taxation than had existed under the republic, and cities had the right of appealing to Rome from unjust decisions on matters of taxation.

Up to this point we have been discussing the principal imperial tax paid by the provincial *civitates*. But in addition to the *tributum* the central government levied *portoria*, the *vicesima libertatis*, the *vicesima hereditatium*, the *centesima rerum venalium*, the *vicesima quinta venalium mancipiorum*, the *capitulum lenocinii*, a tax on gladiatorial shows[1], and, in the later period, the *annona*, the *collatio lustralis*, the *capitatio plebeia*, not to mention certain *vecti-*

[1] *Cf.* no. 110.

galia of a temporary character[1]. The first of these imposts were laid under the republic. The *portoria* go back to the beginning of the republic[2], while Livy refers the *vicesima libertatis* to the fourth century[3].

The Romans applied the term *portorium* to a duty levied on merchandise in transit at a frontier, or when brought into a harbor or a city, or when transported over a bridge or along a road[4]. The establishment of an imperial customs duty was the result of natural development. At a very early period the Romans collected a duty on goods brought into their city. In the territory which they conquered they found states collecting such a tax on their frontiers or at the gates of cities. The victors took over from these subject communities the right to the duties, and developed in course of time a tariff system for the whole Roman world[5]. In other words they adopted the *portorium* from the conquered cities just as they had taken over the tribute from Hiero in Sicily[6]. Of the tariff districts in the West we can clearly make out four, viz. Spain, the Gauls, Illyricum, and the four divisions of Africa[7]. At the frontiers of these districts and also within the districts themselves, at river crossings or on the main highways, posts were established for the collection of customs[8]. The tariff was a flat *ad valorem* duty, levied for revenue only, and varied somewhat from district to district and from one period to another. Under the early empire it was $2\frac{1}{2}$ per cent. in Gaul and Asia, and probably 5 per

---

[1] *Cf.* Hirschfeld, 92, nn. 2, 3. A salt tax is recorded in Priene, *Inschr. von Priene*, 111; *cf.* Rostowzew, *op. cit.* 411 *ff.*; *Cod. J.* 4. 61. 11.

[2] *Cf.* Cagnat, *Les impôts indirects chez les Romains*, 6 *f.*

[3] *Cf. Hist.* 7. 16.

[4] *Cf.* Rostowzew, *op. cit.* 390, n. 115 and Lübker, *Reallexikon*, 373, col. 1.

[5] *Cf.* Cagnat, *op. cit.* 17 *f.*   [6] *Cf.* pp. 47 *ff.*

[7] *Cf.* Hirschfeld, 78; Rostowzew, *op. cit.* 391. Cagnat (*op. cit.* 17) gives seven districts in the West. Hirschfeld and Rostowzew omit Spain.

[8] For the Gallic region, *cf.* Cagnat, *op. cit.* 47–69; *cf.* also *An. ép.* 1919, no. 10, ll. 65–70.

cent. in Africa and Illyricum[1]. Shortly after the time of Theodosius it seems to have been raised to $12\frac{1}{2}$ per cent.[2] All articles intended for sale were subject to this duty, and it was exacted of all persons except those officially connected with the central government and excepting the members of certain privileged classes, like the veterans and the *navicularii*[3]. This tax and the method of collecting it were open to two serious objections. In the first place it interfered grievously with the freedom of trade, and enhanced the prices of raw material and manufactured wares. The trade of the empire suffered in the same way from the multiplicity of tariff districts as did that of France in the eighteenth century. It is only necessary to glance at a map of the Roman world to appreciate the delays and the expense to which a merchant would be subject, for instance, in importing wares into Italy from the East. The situation was made worse by the extortionate practices and the high-handed methods which the publicans adopted[4]. Literature is full of complaints of their conduct, and certain emperors went so far as to propose the abolition of the tax altogether[5]. But it was such a fruitful source of revenue that it lasted into the later empire.

The *vicesima libertatis* or *manumissionum* continued into the empire, but was probably abolished by Diocletian[6]. We may infer from the large number of freedmen of whom we hear in the late republic and the early empire that this tax brought a large sum into the treasury[7]. The master would naturally pay it when he rewarded a slave by granting him his freedom, the slave, when the enfranchisement was bought from the master. It was

[1] *Cf.* Hirschfeld, 79 *ff.*   [2] *Cf.* Cagnat, *op. cit.* 15 *ff.*
[3] *Cf.* Cagnat, *op. cit.* 119–125. Now and then people of a favored city were exempted from the payment of the *portorium*; *cf. ibid.* 125.
[4] *Cf.* Cagnat, *op. cit.* 88 *f.*   [5] *Cf.* Cagnat, *op. cit.* 9 *ff.*
[6] *Cf.* Hirschfeld, 109.
[7] For an attempt to calculate the amount in an early period, *cf.* Cagnat, *op. cit.* 173.

collected by publicans under the republic and the early empire[1]. It is interesting to notice that in some cases this tax went into the treasuries of the municipalities[2]. Augustus introduced the *centesima rerum venalium*, the *vicesima quinta venalium mancipiorum*, and the *vicesima hereditatium*. The first-mentioned tax was levied on goods sold at auction, and must have been regarded as oppressive, because several attempts were made to abolish or reduce it[3]. It continued however into the later empire. The 4 per cent. impost on the sale of slaves involved only an increase in the rate of the *centesima* when applied to a particular kind of property.

In this chapter we are not making a survey of Roman finances nor even of the Roman system of taxation. We are only concerned with the bearing of that system on the municipalities of the empire. We are interested therefore, primarily, in the imperial taxes which the provincials were required to pay. Now the inheritance tax was levied on citizens only, and, so far as the provinces were directly concerned, would affect merely the Roman citizens resident in them[4]. However, after the publication of Caracalla's edicts of A.D. 212 and 213, this tax was payable by all freemen throughout the Roman world, and from this time on the burden of it fell as heavily on provincial municipalities as in the earlier period it had fallen on Italian cities[5]. The tax was levied on estates above 100,000 sesterces bequeathed to heirs other than blood-relations[6]. The collection of it was farmed out up to the time of Hadrian. Thenceforth it was collected directly by the

---

[1] *Cf.* Hirschfeld, 106 *f.*; Rostowzew, *op. cit.* 380.
[2] *Cf.* p. 140, n. 6.   [3] *Cf.* Hirschfeld, 93.
[4] *Cf.* Pliny, *Panegyricus*, 37–39.
[5] For certain probable limitations on the extension of Roman citizenship, *cf.* Girard, *Textes*, 203–204, and the literature there cited.
[6] Outside of the fact that Augustus established it primarily as a source of revenue, he may well have thought that its provisions would help check race suicide. On this point *cf.* Hirschfeld, 98, n. 1.

central government[1]. In the time of Justinian we hear no more of it[2]. One important point in the incidence of this tax in the provinces is not clear to us. Did it apply to land owned and bequeathed by Roman citizens? If it did, such land must have been subject to a double tax, since a *tributum* was also levied upon it[3]. Possibly in the provinces only movable property was liable to this impost. The history of this tax illustrates at the same time the gradual leveling of Italy and the provinces and the influence of an economic factor in bringing about a political change. When Augustus proposed an inheritance tax, to fall on Roman citizens, Italy had been free from the payment of the *tributum* for many years. The proposed tax, while not a *tributum*, was viewed in the light of a tribute[4]. It was a step toward removing Italy from the favored position which she had hitherto held when compared with the provinces, and Augustus carried out his purpose against the strong opposition of the senate only by threatening to impose the tribute on Italy. The extension of Roman citizenship by Caracalla to all freemen in the provinces is the last important step in the process of equalizing the political rights of provincials and Italians. The result of his action was to bring the provincials under the operation of the inheritance law[5]. Consequently the history of this tax, from Augustus to Caracalla, is synchronous with the process of reducing Italy to the political and social level of the provinces, and is intimately connected with it. The

[1] *Cf.* Rostowzew, *op. cit.* 385.

[2] *Cf.* Marquardt, *St. Verw.* 2, 269.

[3] Hyginus (Lachmann, *Gromatici veteres*, 197) says: Excepti sunt fundi bene meritorum, ut in totum privati iuris essent, nec ullam coloniae munificentiam deberent, et essent in solo populi Romani. This raises the point whether Roman citizens living in non-Roman communities owned their property by Quiritary law. If so, their real estate would be virtually Roman soil. The statement of Hyginus would imply that the possessions of favored individuals were so regarded. We cannot tell whether Hyginus includes Romans under the class of *bene meriti*.

[4] *Cf.* Hirschfeld, 98, n. 2.

[5] For Caracalla's purpose, *cf.* no. 192 and pp. 191 *ff.*

last step in this movement was taken by Diocletian. The *vectigal lenocinii* or *capitulum lenocinii* was at first farmed out, but later collected by agents of the government[1].

In the later empire four important changes were made in the imperial system of taxation. For the first time, under Diocletian, a property tax was imposed on all the free cities in the provinces and on the cities of Italy. By this action the free cities lost in large measure their exceptional position, and Italy, in the matter of taxation, was reduced to the level of the provinces. A systematic contribution of food, in the form of the *annona*, was required throughout the empire. In the third place assessments were based on certain fixed fiscal units, and finally comprehensive changes were made in the method of collecting taxes.

To take up the second change, as we have already noticed, when the Romans acquired Sicily they took over the system of taxation which they found in existence there[2]. They exacted from the Sicilian cities the payment of a tenth part of their produce. Part of this contribution was used for the army of occupation, part of it for the city of Rome. As the population of the capital grew and agriculture in Italy declined, the quantity of grain which the Romans needed from the island increased correspondingly. Consequently, in addition to the regular *decumae*, which constituted the *tributum* of the island, *alterae decumae* were called for in times of need under a special law or decree of the senate. For this contribution a fixed price was paid[3]. Not infrequently a third contribution, the *frumentum imperatum*, was required. For this also payment was made. Rome paid too for the supplies delivered to the governor, the *frumentum in cellam*, or *frumentum emptum*, or

---

[1] *Cf.* no. 112.   [2] *Cf.* p. 47.

[3] *Cf.* Cic. *in Verr.* 3. 42: senatus cum temporibus rei publicae cogitur ut decernat ut alterae decumae exigantur, ita decernit, ut pro his decumis pecunia solvatur aratoribus; ut, quo plus sumitur quam debetur, id emi non auferri putetur. *Cf. loc. cit.* 3. 163, 172.

annona, as it was called[1]. It is significant of the future that even the *civitates immunes* were required to join in furnishing these extra supplies. Payment in kind, as in the case of Sicily, either in the form of a quota of the produce or a fixed number of measures of grain, was required in certain other provinces[2]. On the other hand, from Macedonia and some other provinces a tribute in money was exacted. In the arrangements which were made in the early period we find all the elements out of which the system of Diocletian developed. Tribute was required from the *civitates* of the provinces in kind or in the form of money payments. Food was provided for the city of Rome and for the armies of occupation from the supplies which were levied as tribute and from those which were requisitioned, and the free cities, of Sicily at least, had to submit to requisitions. The development of the earlier system into that of Diocletian can be followed with some confidence. In the early days subject cities fell into classes. Those of the first class were called upon each year for a fixed sum of money. Residents in the other cities were required to contribute a quota of their produce, or a poll tax, or both. Gradually the exaction of a quota from the second class of cities gave way to the contribution of a fixed annual amount in kind, and still later for the contribution in kind a fixed money payment was established for most of the provinces. The first change made it possible to do away with the tax-farmers; the second one relieved the state from the trouble and expense attendant on storage and carriage. Two circumstances,

---

[1] *Cf.* Rostowzew, *R.E.* 7, 165; Liebenam, *R.E.* 4, 2310; Marquardt, *St. Verw.* 2, 113.

[2] Hyginus (Lachmann, *Gromatici veteres*, 205) says: Agri vectigales multas habent constitutiones; in quibusdam provinciis fructus partem praestant certam, alii quintas, alii septimas, alii pecuniam, et hoc per soli aestimationem. Certa pretia agris constituta sunt, ut in Pannonia arvi primi, arvi secundi, prati, silvae vulgaris, pascuae. His omnibus agris vectigal est ad modum ubertatis per singula iugera constitutum. The taxes on public lands varied as the provincial tribute seems to have varied.

however, in the later situation brought about a reversion to the earlier practices. The first of these two factors was the debasement of the currency, which began under Nero and had reached such a point under Gallienus that silver coins contained but 4 per cent. of silver[1]. The tax receipts in this depreciated currency left the treasury in great straits, and this situation in itself would have been sufficient to force a return to the practice of requiring payment in kind, but it was reinforced by the increasing demands for food of the city of Rome and of the armies. We are not surprised, therefore, to find Diocletian making a contribution of grain a fixed part of the tribute levied on all the provinces, and, since this contribution was intended primarily for the annual supply of Rome, it was naturally called the *annona*[2]. The decision of the government to collect a large part of the taxes in kind put a tremendous strain on the imperial post, which was charged with the transportation of this produce, and we may thus understand the bitter protests against the post made by the agricultural classes, for the burden of its maintenance fell largely on them[3]. Grain could be had only from farm land, and consequently this tax was laid only on the owners of such land. The objects of it were land, men, and animals. After A.D. 289 the rate of taxation and other pertinent matters were set forth each year in the *indictio* of the emperor[4]. The owners of other property than farm-land continued to pay the tribute. Subject cities were called on for both the *annona* and the tribute, while *civitates immunes* probably contributed only the *annona*[5].

[1] *Cf.* Seeck, *R.E.* 3, 1515. Probably the mines of the empire did not produce a quantity of gold and silver sufficient for trade, and large amounts of the precious metals were exported to Arabia, India, and China; *cf.* Pliny, *N.H.* 12. 18, 82–84.

[2] Egypt and Africa, upon which Rome depended for supplies, had always continued to pay their tribute in kind. Consequently when the contributions of the other provinces, hitherto paid in depreciated currency, were converted into payments in kind, these two provinces were much less heavily taxed than the others; *cf.* Seeck, *R.E.* 3, 1516.

[3] *Cf.* nos. 51, 156.   [4] *Cf.* Seeck, *R.E.* 3, 1516.   [5] *Ibid.*

Diocletian based the assessment of taxes on a fiscal unit called the *caput* or *iugum*. A uniform tax was collected on all *capita* and *iuga*. A *caput* was the working power of a man in good health[1]. In the West this was the term commonly used of the fiscal unit. Less frequently the terms *millena* and *centuria* were employed. Two women, a certain number of animals, or a fixed amount of land of a specified sort also constituted a *caput*. In the East the unit, when made up of men, women, or animals, was called a *caput*, when composed of land, a *iugum*. Thus in the Diocese of the Orient a vineyard of five *iugera*, cultivated land of twenty *iugera*, or a certain number of olive trees made up a *iugum*[2]. The amount due on each *iugum* or *caput* was fixed by an imperial edict, and the taxes thus assessed were levied under the general supervision of the praetorian prefects, the *vicarii*, and the governors of provinces. When the amount to be paid by a province had been determined, the governor apportioned it among the several cities within the province according to the number of taxable *capita* or *iuga*[3].

Diocletian's system was devised to bring within its sweep all the property in the empire, and for convenience

---

[1] *Cf.* Seeck, *R.E.* 3, 1517, 1564 and the passage from the *Cod. Th.* 13.11.2 there quoted: cum antea per singulos viros, per binas vero mulieres capitis norma sit censa. See also in general Seeck, *R.E.* 3, 1513 *ff.*; Lécrivain, *Dict. Dar. s.v. tributum*, 434 *ff.* and Marquardt, *St. Verw.* 2, 224 *ff.* The value of the *caput* was somewhat changed by Theodosius the Great in A.D. 386. He rated five men or eight women as two *capita*; *cf.* Seeck, *R.E.* 3, 1517 and *Cod. Th.* 13.11.2.

[2] *Cf.* Seeck, *R.E.* 3, 1519; Marquardt, *St. Verw.* 2, 221 *ff.* See also the description of the *iugum* in a passage cited by Mommsen (*Hermes*, 3 (1869), 430) from a Syriac collection of laws of A.D. 501 and *CIL.* x, 407 and *IG.* xi, 3, 180, 182, 343–9.

[3] The inscription of the year 323 from Vulceii in Lucania (*CIL.* x, 407) cited by Marquardt, *St. Verw.* 2, 229, is very illuminating in this connection. It specifies the sum to be paid by the entire commune, and gives a list of the *possessores*, arranged according to *pagi*, with the amount to be paid by each taxpayer. Inscriptions from Thera and Astypalaea (*IG.* xi, 3, 180, 182, 343–9) and fragments of inscriptions from Lesbos and Tralles (*B.C.H.* 4 (1880), 336, 417 *ff.*) contain other pertinent information.

[130]

in discussion the people may be thought of as falling into three great classes, the *possessores*, the *negotiatores*, and the *coloni*. The *possessores*, or owners of land or of other property, paid the *annona* or the tribute. The tax on the *coloni* or *plebs rusticana extra muros*, who presumably had no property, was the *capitatio plebeia* or *humana*. Perhaps this impost may be thought of as the lineal descendant of the *tributum capitis* of the earlier period, but limited in its incidence to the lowest class of freemen, and amounting essentially to a poll tax. The merchants, or *negotiatores*, were subject to an impost called the *collatio lustralis* or, more fully, the *lustralis auri argentive collatio*. We find it first mentioned as *aurum negotiatorium* in the reign of Alexander Severus[1]. With few exceptions it fell upon all those who sold articles of any sort, and it was levied on the basis of the capital invested in the business[2]. As the name of the tax indicates, it was properly collected every five years or every four years, but evidently it was also frequently collected when a new emperor ascended the throne. Each new emperor found it very important to win the support of the troops by giving them largesses, and these gratuities had to be given in money. Thus, for instance, Julian on being made Augustus in the fourth century gave to each soldier five *solidi* and a pound of silver[3]. Each city was required to contribute a specified sum. Similar in character was the *aurum oblaticium*, theoretically a voluntary gift of money made by the Roman senate on the accession of an emperor and on certain other occasions.

The officials directly responsible for the collection of the taxes were the annually chosen *exactores*, who based the collection on the lists drawn up by the municipal *tabularii*, and gathered the taxes with the help of groups of *susceptores*, each group being chosen to take charge of

---

[1] *Cf. Hist. Aug. Alex.* 32. 5.   [2] *Cf.* Seeck, *R.E.* 4, 370.
[3] *Cf.* Ammianus, 20. 4. 18 and Seeck, *op. cit.* 4, 374 *ff.*

a particular kind of impost[1]. Decurions were generally selected as *susceptores*, and the *exactores* also were usually *curiales*. Even in Egypt, where the civic and fiscal arrangements at first differed in many respects from those which had been adopted elsewhere in the Roman world, the tax system under the later empire resembled in many ways that which has just been described[2]. The fact that a fixed amount was expected of each city and that the decurions of the city were called upon to collect this sum dealt a fatal blow to municipal government when the prosperity of the empire declined. Diocletian's system presupposed periodical revisions of the census. If these had been made regularly and systematically, and if the taxes of a city had been reduced as its property declined in value, the cities could have borne their burden, but frequent and thoroughgoing revisions were not made, land was abandoned, and tax-payers became insolvent[3]. In point of fact the imperial government could not see its way clear to reduce the running expenses of the civil and military establishments, and the situation was made worse by civil and foreign wars. When land was abandoned, some efforts were made to collect the lost taxes from adjacent owners[4], to bring lands into cultivation again by settling *coloni* upon them[5], but in the end the responsibility of paying over the taxes to the government rested on the shoulders of the *curiales*[6]; their lands were made inalienable, they were forbidden to leave their *civitas*, or to escape their responsibility by entering the army, the civil administration, or even a cloister[7].

The Egyptian tax system differed in some respects

---

[1] *Cf.* Lécrivain, *Dict. Dar. s.v. tributum*, 436, col. 2.
[2] *Cf.* pp. 133 *f. infra* and Wilcken, *Grundzüge*, 356 *ff.*
[3] *Cf.* Lécrivain, *op. cit.* 434, col. 2.
[4] *Cf.* Lécrivain, *op. cit.* 437, col. 1.
[5] *Cf.* Humbert, *Dict. Dar. s.v. deserti agri*, 107, col. 2.
[6] *Cf.* Humbert, *op. cit.* 108, col. 1 and the references there given to *Cod. Th.* 12. 1. 54; *Cod. J.* 10. 72 (70). 2, and other sources.
[7] *Cf.* pp. 103 *ff.*, 206 *ff.*

from the system in vogue elsewhere in the Roman world and requires a few words of explanation. The revenues of the Ptolemies came chiefly from the rent of the land, for all the land in Egypt was owned by the crown. Certain monopolies also were controlled by the state and must have yielded a good profit. Taxes were levied on buildings, stock, and slaves, and a head tax was imposed from which Greeks and Macedonians were exempt. Artisans and traders paid a license fee. Export and import duties were levied. In addition to these taxes liturgies were imposed for such public purposes as surveying, the construction of irrigation works, the maintenance of the police, the entertainment of the court or of public officials on their journeys, and the billeting of troops[1].

The Romans made very few changes in the Ptolemaic system, and in respect to taxation the period from Alexander the Great to Diocletian may be regarded as a unit[2]. Two important changes were made, however, which were destined to affect the economic life of Egypt profoundly. The court at Alexandria to which tribute had hitherto gone was abolished by Augustus, and a tax of twenty million Roman bushels of wheat was demanded annually for the provisioning of Rome. The tribute paid to the Ptolemies had for the most part remained within the country, but there was no economic return for the wheat sent to the capital. In the second place certain changes were introduced in regard to the ownership of land by which private tenure was recognized. With the consequent growth of a propertied class, the introduction of such a liturgical system as prevailed in other parts of the Orient was made possible. The Ptolemaic administration had been carried on by a highly organized bureaucracy, in which service was voluntary and requited by the

[1] The subject of taxes in Roman Egypt is treated by Wilcken, *Gr. Ostraka*, 422 *ff.*; *Grundzüge*, 169 *ff.*; Jouguet, *Vie munic.* 234 *ff.*; 385 *ff.*; 415 *ff.*

[2] Wilcken, *Grundzüge*, 186.

government. With the development of liturgies by the Romans, the Egyptians were forced to give their services to the state, and their property was liable to distraint in case of default or losses incurred in the discharge of their duty[1].

The Romans introduced a few new levies such as the tax on Jews, on manumissions, and on inheritances. The poll tax, which is mentioned only once in the Ptolemaic period, was applied more generally than had been the case in the previous period. The fixed price for the purchase of military supplies, in so far as it was below current market quotations, virtually constituted a tax on the producer[2].

The metropolis of each nome acted merely as an agent of the state in collecting the taxes. Apparently the city had no public revenue of its own, but in cases where expenses were incurred, the officials of the metropolis could draw upon the reserves of the state funds still on deposit in the local treasury, possibly under the supervision of the *strategus* of the nome[3].

When Septimius Severus gave a senate to the capitals of the nomes, it is probable that there was some reorganization of the financial status of the new cities, but the evidence bearing on the question is so slight that no clear picture of conditions can be presented. The chief revenues of cities in other parts of the empire came from lands in their *territoria*. There is no evidence that Severus transferred any of the crown lands to the new cities, but since, in creating a senate, it was his evident purpose to provide greater security for the proper discharge of liturgical duties, the new order may have had a greater measure of control of the imperial treasury in the metropolis which virtually guarded the revenues of the nome. Jouguet points out that the powers of the στρατηγός steadily

---

[1] Bell, *Journal of Egyptian Archaeology*, 4 (1917), 86 *ff.*
[2] Wilcken, *Grundzüge*, 187, 356 *ff.*, 374 *ff.*
[3] Jouguet, *op. cit.* 309 *ff.*

diminished in the third century until the office finally disappeared[1]. Its decadence may indicate that the state recognized in a passive way that the nome was municipal territory. Temple property ($\iota\epsilon\rho\grave{\alpha}$ $\gamma\hat{\eta}$) seems to have come under control of the local senates to a certain extent, and the state often assigned lands to communal organizations for forced cultivation[2]. By gifts, confiscation, and by the surrender of land which had been abandoned by owners for various reasons, the city acquired a certain amount of revenue and became the owner of new territory, although in the case of abandoned estates the city experienced an increase in burdens rather than in revenues[3]. We hear also of water rates, rents of stands in the public market, and taxes on buildings[4]. It is possible that monopolies of mines and of oil were in some cases taken over from the state by the city and exploited in the latter's interest[5]. It is probable, however, that the local administration was largely supported by the personal charges of the magistrates and of incumbents of liturgical offices. Legislation was enacted to restrain the extravagance of ambitious office-holders, who had raised the standard of outlay so high that it was often difficult to find candidates for office[6]. In some cases endowments were provided to relieve the expenses attached to liturgies[7]. Under the reorganization of the fourth century the system of taxation in the Egyptian municipality conformed to that in the rest of the empire[8].

To return now to another phase of general financial conditions in the empire, nothing need be said of the imperial taxes levied for a short period, but no clear idea can be had of the financial demands made on the

[1] *Ibid.* 386. [2] Wilcken, *Grundzüge*, 126.
[3] Jouguet, *op. cit.* 418. [4] *Ibid.* 426.
[5] *Ibid.* 428; *cf.* no. 204, where the municipality exercises a certain amount of control over the guild of weavers. Ll. 1 *ff.* bear on the relation of the nome to the municipality in financial matters.
[6] No. 169. [7] No. 189. [8] Bell, *loc. cit.*

provincials by the central government, unless one takes into consideration also the requisitions and other exactions to which the people in the provinces were subject especially under the republic. The Verrine orations of Cicero, his letters from Cilicia, the *Annals* of Tacitus, and the letters of Pliny give us abundant information on this point. Rich provincials, like Heraclius[1], suffered the confiscation of their property on some legal pretext. Country districts were required to furnish wild animals for games to be given in Rome by some friend of a governor[2]. Extortion was practiced in securing the grain needed for the governor's household[3], and cities paid large sums for altars, statues, and festivals in honor of the governor[4], for honorary deputations to Rome[5], and for the privilege of being relieved from the billeting of soldiers[6]. The disastrous effect on the provinces of such practices as these is clearly shown in Cicero's account of the condition of Cilicia when he took over this province from his predecessor, Appius[7]. With the establishment of the empire these abuses diminished. Provincial governors received an adequate salary, so that the temptation to fill their pockets by irregular means decreased. They held their offices for a longer term than republican governors had, and therefore came to know better the needs and difficulties of the provincials. The building of roads, the introduction of a postal system, and the establishment of provincial bureaus at Rome kept them constantly under the supervision of the emperor, and the favor which the early emperors showed for the provincial assemblies gave the provinces an opportunity to lodge formal complaints against extortionate governors. Tacitus records eight

[1] Cic. *in Verr.* 2. 35–42.   [2] Cic. *ad fam.* 2. 11. 2.
[3] Cic. *in Verr.* 2. 169–173.   [4] Cic. *op. cit.* 2. 144 *ff.*
[5] Cic. *ad fam.* 3. 8. 2 *ff.*   [6] Cic. *ad Att.* 5. 21. 7.
[7] Cic. *ad Att.* 5. 16. 2: Audivimus nihil aliud nisi imperata ἐπικεφάλια solvere non posse, ὠνὰς omnium venditas; civitatum gemitus, ploratus: monstra quaedam non hominis, sed ferae nescio cuius immanis. Quid quaeris? taedet omnino eos vitae.

cases of provincial governors tried by the senate under Tiberius, two under Claudius, and eleven under Nero, and in most of these cases the accused governor was convicted and punished. The bad practice of making contributions to the emperor, which were ostensibly voluntary, still continued, and in the later period these contributions, as we have seen, were converted into required money payments[1]. One new form of exaction under the empire, that connected with the *cursus publicus*, gave rise to endless complaints on the part of the provincials[2]. In this connection the restriction placed on private enterprise in the provinces by the government ownership of mines and quarries, by the state monopoly in salt, and by the refusal to allow wine and oil to be produced in certain districts may be mentioned[3], but does not call for extended comment.

[1] *Cf. supra*, pp. 131 *f*.; Seeck, *R.E.* 3, 1543 *f*.
[2] Nos. 51, 156.   [3] Frank, *Roman Imperialism*, 210, 280 *f*.

CHAPTER X

MUNICIPAL FINANCES[1]

THE residents of a *civitas* were practically exempt from the payment of municipal taxes. Local taxation could not be introduced, because the tax was a sign of servitude. Rome could exact tribute, because she was mistress of the world, but for citizens of a municipality to pay taxes to a government which they themselves had established was out of harmony with their way of thinking. At the most, municipal charges could be made for the enjoyment of certain privileges. A city's revenues came largely from the *territorium* owned by it. The cities conquered by Rome usually owned land adjacent to their walls, and Rome commonly allowed them to retain at least a part of it. To the colonies an outlying district was assigned when they were founded[2]. Generals under the republic and emperors not infrequently gave large districts to a friendly or favored city. Thus S. Calvinus made large additions to the territory of Massilia, and the mother city, Ilium, received similar favors at the hands of emperors. Occasionally a city received gifts of land from private persons[3]. Many of these dependent districts were of great extent. Nemausus had twenty-four *oppida attributa*, and Centuripae owned lands in many parts of Sicily[4]. Sometimes a *territorium* was far away. Arpinum, for instance, drew most of its revenue from land in Cisalpine Gaul[5]. For the use of such land dependent communities

---

[1] In this chapter, in discussing municipal revenues and expenditure, frequent use has been made of the large amount of material collected by Liebenam, *St. Verw. Cf.* also Laum, *Stiftungen in der gr. u. röm. Antike*, for endowments in ancient cities.

[2] Kornemann, *R.E.* 4, 573 *ff.*   [3] Liebenam, *op. cit.* 10 *f.*

[4] Pliny, *N.H.* 3. 4. 37; Cic. *in Verr.* 3. 108.

[5] Cic. *ad fam.* 13. 11. 1; *CIL.* v, 7749, l. 25.

paid a fixed sum to the city treasury each year, as we can see from the famous award made to Genua in its action against the Langenses in 117 B.C.[1] Monopolies formed a source of municipal revenue in some cases. The banking privilege was controlled by eastern cities where they still preserved the right to issue a local coinage. The exchange of the native money for foreign currency was usually regulated by the municipality under imperial supervision and leased to private corporations[2]. The problem of industrial monopolies is obscure and little evidence can be found. Ferries seem to have been controlled by some seaport towns[3]. At Urso the charter threatens confiscation if anyone owns a tile or pottery factory above a limited capacity[4]. This clause may have been inserted because the industry was a municipal monopoly. In Egypt the towns took over certain industries from the state in later times[5]. A source of revenue came from the sale of the privilege of citizenship in more favored communities[6]. Some cities owned the fishing privileges in adjacent lakes or rivers[7], and these privileges were farmed out[8]. The municipal charges which came nearest to being taxes were the *portoria*, the octroi, and the water rates. Probably in the early period many towns were allowed to cover port duties into the municipal treasury. Athens, for instance, enjoyed this privilege at one time[9], and, as late as the fifth century, the Carian city of Mylasa recovered this right,

[1] No. 10. [2] Nos. 81, 133, 199; *I.B.M.* 1000.
[3] Nos. 70, 128; *cf. P. Oxy.* 1454 for municipal bakers, and no. 124 for a strike at Ephesus.
[4] No. 26, chap. 76. [5] No. 204.
[6] No. 130; at Tarsus a fee of 500 drachmae was exacted for the grant of citizenship (Dio Chrys. 34. 23). Augustus forbade the Athenians the right of conferring such decrees for a price (Cassius Dio, 54. 7).
[7] No. 68. In this case the fisheries seem to be the sole source of municipal income. *Cf.* Strabo, 12. 8, p. 576.
[8] *Dig.* 43. 14. 1, 7.
[9] Liebenam, *op. cit.* 24. In no. 96 the senate grants permission to establish a market (*cf.* nos. 147, 148). Was this permission required because of a state or municipal tax which was involved in the concession?

which it had enjoyed under the republic, for its harbor of Passala[1]. But gradually Rome took over in most cases the right to fix and receive port duties. An interesting list of duties imposed for the benefit of a municipality is furnished by the tariff of A.D. 137 of the inland city of Palmyra[2]. The dutiable articles include among other things slaves, cattle, salt fish, olive oil, and cloth. From an edict of Augustus found at Venafrum[3], from the Palmyra list[4], and from references in literature[5], it seems clear that many municipalities laid an annual charge at least upon the proprietors of industrial establishments and private baths, upon the owners of large houses and villas, and upon others who drew a large quantity of water from the public supply. Some inscriptions, coming from Thessalian towns, show that in certain municipalities manumitted freedmen paid the fee for manumission into the municipal treasury. It is possible that these municipalities acted as receivers for the imperial government, but it is more probable that the fee in these cases constituted a municipal charge and not an imperial tax[6]. In some oriental cities also priesthoods were sold to the highest bidders[7].

[1] *CIL.* III, *S.* 7151; Dessau, *Hermes,* 19 (1884), 531. Possibly Vespasian's edict made a similar concession to Sabora in Baetica, *cf.* no. 61.

[2] This list was published in Aramaic and Greek. For the Aramaic version, *cf.* de Vogüé, *Journal asiatique,* 8 (1883), série 1, 231 *ff.*; II, 149 *ff.*; Schroeder, *Sitzungsber. d. Berl. Akad.* 1884, 417 *ff.* For the preface to the Greek version, *cf.* no. 89. The tariff at Zaraï (*CIL.* VIII, 4508) was imperial, not municipal, although the dutiable articles are similar to those mentioned at Palmyra. The tariff at Koptos (Ditt. *Or. Gr.* 674) was imperial.

[3] No. 33.   [4] Dessau, *Hermes,* 19 (1884), 522.

[5] *E.g.* Cic. *de lege agr.* 3. 9.

[6] The fee for manumissions was usually taken by the imperial government (*cf.* pp. 124 *ff.*). That the payment was made to the municipal treasury in the case of the towns mentioned, *cf.* the inscriptions published in Ἐφ. Ἀρχ. 1915, 8 *ff.*, 1916, 28 *ff.*, 73 *ff.*, 1917, 7 *ff.*, 111 *ff.* in which the fact is recorded that certain manumitted freedmen paid the fee to the municipality according to law (κατὰ τὸν νόμον).

[7] *Cf.* p. 79 and n. 6.

Fines imposed for the violation of local ordinances or of the fundamental law of a city of course came into the municipal treasury, so long as the local magistrates exercised judicial functions. Offenses of the first sort included infringement of traffic ordinances, displacement of *termini*, injuring public property, defiling sacred or public places, burying the dead within certain proscribed limits, and maltreatment of a tomb or place of burial. Hundreds of epitaphs have been found, especially in Italy and the Greek East, which threaten with heavy fines anyone who violates the sanctity of the tombs on which the inscriptions are engraved[1]. Sometimes payment is to be made to the imperial fisc[2], sometimes to a priesthood[3], but commonly to the municipal treasury[4]. The fine threatened amounts in some cases to as much as 100,000 sesterces[5]. Under what authority such fines could be imposed is a matter of great dispute[6]. Was action taken under local ordinances, and did these ordinances fix the penalty or leave it to be determined by the builder of the tomb? These are difficult questions, which admit of no satisfactory answer as yet[7]. It would seem highly improbable, however, that so many epitaphs should threaten the imposition of a fine, if it could not be collected by legal action. Perhaps the difficulty is explained by the fact that municipalities and imperial estates often laid out cemeteries on their land and sold burial lots. In that case there would have been legal authority for the imposition of these fines. From this source therefore, in certain parts of the Roman world, some revenue would come into the

---

[1] Liebenam, *op. cit.* 43–53.

[2] *CIL.* iii, 168. [3] Wilmans, 291.

[4] A typical case is *CIL.* iii, 2098: veto autem in hac arca alium corpus inferri aut ossua poni; si quis autem intulerit, dabit rei publicae Salonitarum nummum x milia. [5] *E.g. CIL.* x, 2015.

[6] Liebenam, *op. cit.* 37 *ff.* and the literature cited by him, p. 37, n. 4.

[7] Some references to local ordinances have been found (Liebenam, *op. cit.* 42, n. 4) and sometimes the statements on tombstones specifying the fine are couched in legal form.

municipal treasury. The penalties for malfeasance in office or for corrupt practices in the elections were very severe. A duovir, for instance, convicted of receiving a gift from a contractor was subject to a fine of 20,000 sesterces in the colonia Genetiva Julia[1], and in the same city any person making a gift with a view to his candidature for office was required to pay 5000 sesterces[2].

A surer and larger revenue, however, came into the city treasury from the voluntary or required gifts made by magistrates or priests on their accession to office. The charter of the colonia Genetiva Julia required each duovir and aedile to contribute out of his own pocket at least 2000 sesterces toward the cost of the public games[3]. The initiation fees in this case were unusually small, because the colonists were drawn from the Roman proletariat, and the sum mentioned in the charter is the minimum amount required, the *summa legitima*, to which officials often made large additions[4]. Inscriptions record the payment into the city treasury by magistrates and priests of sums ranging from 3000 to 35,000 sesterces. In one instance, at Calama in Africa, a newly elected pontifex contributed 600,000 sesterces[5]. Mention of these initiation fees is made more commonly in the West than in the East. Their place was taken in the Greek Orient by the liturgy which was imposed there on the richer people in a city without regard to their incumbency of office. In fact the practice of requiring or expecting contributions from newly elected officials in the West may well have been suggested by the eastern liturgy. In addition to the required or voluntary contributions made by officials large gifts were made by private citizens for public purposes. The spirit of rivalry between the towns of a province made each one anxious to surpass its neighbors in the

---

[1] No. 26, chap. 93.   [2] *Ibid.* chap. 132.   [3] *Ibid.* chaps. 70, 71.
[4] *CIL.* viii, 8300: statuam quam ob honorem aed. super legitimam ex sestertium iiii mil. mun. pollicitus ampliata pec. anno suo posuit. *Cf.* also viii, 4594.   [5] *CIL.* viii, 5295.

beauty and magnificence of its buildings and streets, and the local pride which this sentiment developed laid an obligation on the wealthy to contribute generously to the construction and maintenance of temples, markets, and baths, the laying of pavements and sewers, and to the cost of public games and festivals[1]. During the early centuries of our era, while the empire was prosperous, gifts of this sort must have formed an important part of municipal revenues.

Let us turn now to the expense side of an ancient municipal budget. One of the items which bulks largest in its modern counterpart, the outgo for salaries, found no place in it. As we have just noticed, magistrates, instead of receiving salaries, helped to pay for the public improvements and running expenses of the city, and menial labor was performed by slaves which the city owned, so that only a few minor officials received pay. The public slaves cleaned the streets, took care of the public buildings, and performed other similar duties. We have left then to consider the construction and repair of public works, the prevention of fires, the policing and lighting of the streets, and provision for amusement, education, charity, the preservation of health, and the maintenance of religion. Of these items the expenditure for public works and for the amusement of the people made the heaviest drain on the city treasury.

Those who visit today the sites of ancient cities like Pompeii or Timgad are surprised at the number and size of the basilicas, colonnades, baths, theatres, market halls, arches, and aqueducts which they find. Immense sums of money were spent on public works of these kinds, and thereby the financial condition of many cities was imperilled. One may recall in this connection the expenditure at Nicomedeia of 3,000,000 sesterces on an aqueduct which had to be given up[2], and the appropriation

---

[1] Abbott, *The Common People of Ancient Rome*, 179 *ff*.
[2] Plin. *Epp. ad Trai.* 37. 1.

of 10,000,000 sesterces at Nicaea for a theatre which was found to be structurally defective before it was completed[1]. As we learn from the inscriptions, municipal funds for the construction of public buildings were lavishly supplemented by private gifts, and sometimes legacies were left for the maintenance of the buildings, but many cities must have found themselves the proud possessors of theatres, colonnades, and market halls, whose repair and maintenance made an intolerable drain on the public treasury when prosperity declined. Baths in particular were a source of great expense. Not only did they have to be repaired, but the cost of heating them and of furnishing oil to the bathers was heavy. The small city of Pompeii had three large public baths, and it would seem as if no town in the empire was small enough to get on without them. In 387 the emperor could find no more severe way to punish the people of Antioch for an uprising than to close the public baths of that city. An ancient item which is not to be found in a modern municipal budget was the cost of building and repairing the city-walls. This expense naturally varied from one period to another and was different for the different parts of the Roman world. For many generations after the position of Italy had been made secure, walls were allowed to fall into decay, but the pressure of the northern barbarians spurred the Italians on to improve their defenses. City-walls in the provinces, especially near the frontier, were always kept in better repair than those of Italy, and in the later period, when the empire was threatened on all sides, a large part of a city's revenues had to be devoted to this object[2]. The paving of the streets and the nearby roads was of course a charge on the municipal budget, and must have been heavy because of the costly nature of the ancient system of paving. In the early empire the state assumed the cost of building and maintaining the main highways, but from the third century on this burden fell mainly on the

[1] Plin. *Epp. ad Trai.* 39. 1.   [2] *Cod. Th.* 5. 14. 35.

municipalities. The cost of constructing and maintaining the water and drainage systems in an ancient city must have been an important item in the municipal budget. The treatise of Frontinus for the city of Rome, the remains of aqueducts elsewhere, the large number of public and private baths, and the elaborate drainage system brought to light in Pompeii all testify to this fact[1].

Next in size to the outlay for public works, as we noticed above, came the expenditure for amusement, especially in the form of public games and festivals. The public *ludi circenses, ludi scaenici, munera gladiatoria*, and *venationes* were given in connection with some religious festival or were in commemoration of some important public event, and rapidly increased in number under the empire[2], until under Constantius II there were one hundred and seventy-six festivals each year in Rome[3]. Numerous inscriptions referring to local public games, found in all parts of the empire, show that this form of amusement was as popular outside of Rome as it was in the capital. The cost of these games, except in so far as it was met by the contributions required of magistrates and by private gift, was defrayed by the municipality. The central government made earnest efforts to check this form of local extravagance, but probably without much success[4]. While the celebration of religious festivals constituted a heavy charge on the local treasury, a city was required to pay very little for the maintenance of religious cults, because most temples had endowments of their own[5]. The cost of policing and lighting the streets, and of protecting a city from fire, must have been very small, because little attention was paid to these matters[6]. Except in rare cases,

[1] Puchstein, *R.E.* 4, 58 *f.* and literature there cited.
[2] For a history of this development, see Wissowa, *Religion u. Kultus d. Römer*, 365–399.
[3] *CIL.* 1, 293 *f.* and Wissowa, *op. cit.* 492–515.
[4] No. 110. The imperial tax upon the gladiators virtually fell upon the municipality or those who gave the shows.
[5] Liebenam, *op. cit.* 69 *ff.*   [6] *Ibid.* 153, 357 *ff.*, 408, n. 2.

municipalities paid out little money for education[1], for
public libraries[2], or for charity[3]. In one respect only did
the cities make a systematic effort to relieve the poor.
Many of them imitated the capital in supplying grain to
the needy at a low price[4]. This form of charity, if it deserves to have that word applied to it, must be distinguished of course from the *alimenta*. Italian municipalities
had some control over the *alimenta*[5], but they did not
supply the funds for the purpose[6], and therefore a
consideration of this subject does not come within the
scope of this chapter.

We are especially concerned with the attitude which
the central government took toward the municipalities
in the matter of their finances. In general it adopted the
policy of rewarding those who were friendly and of
punishing those who were hostile. For the firm stand
which it took in favor of Rome in the Mithradatic war
Sulla made several neighboring villages dependent on
Stratonicea in Caria[7]. Amisus in Pontus won the favor
of Lucullus and received an addition of one hundred
and twenty stadia to its *territorium*[8]. On the other hand
Caesar deprived Massilia of most of its *territorium* because
of its opposition to him in 48 B.C.[9] Other instances of a
similar kind occur in the later period.

So far as the *portoria* were concerned, we have already

---

[1] Barbagallo, *Lo stato e l'istruzione pubbl. nell' Imp. rom.*
[2] For the city of Rome, *cf.* Boyd, *Public Libraries and Literary Culture in Ancient Rome*; for other cities, *cf.* Lübker's *Reallexikon*, 169 f. and the literature there cited, and Cagnat, *Les bibliothèques municipales dans l'empire romaine.*
[3] Liebenam, *op. cit.* 98 ff.
[4] *Ibid.* 109 ff. The compulsion to sell supplies at a fixed price, in so far as this was below the current quotations, virtually formed a tax upon the producers. *Cf.* no. 90.
[5] Hirschfeld, 215 ff.   [6] Kubitschek, *R.E.* I, 1484 ff.
[7] *B.C.H.* 9 (1885), 437–474 and Chapot, *La prov. rom. proc. d'Asie,* 26 f., 37, 38, 81; no. 17.
[8] Appian, *Mithr.* 83; Plutarch, *Luc.* 19.
[9] Cassius Dio, 41. 25; Florus, 2. 13; Oros. 6. 15. 7.

noticed that Rome followed the general policy of taking these over for her own use[1]. She probably adopted this policy not only for the sake of the revenue which the customs duties brought her, but, if she had left the right of imposing them to the municipalities, some coast towns might have abolished their tariffs altogether, and diverted all the seagoing trade from their rivals. Perhaps reference is made to the assumption by the central government of the right of collecting the *portoria* in the brief account which Suetonius gives of the policy of Tiberius in this matter[2]. Certain of the later emperors, for instance, Hadrian, Alexander Severus, and Julian, reversed this policy and allowed the *vectigalia* to be paid into the municipal treasury[3]. In Hadrian's case this act of generosity may have been due to his interest in the provinces. Alexander Severus and Julian may well have made their concessions because of the financial needs of the municipalities concerned.

With the establishment of the empire came a better acquaintance with provincial conditions and greater sympathy with provincial needs. It is an interesting thing to notice that the last paragraph of the *Res Gestae Divi Augusti* records the generosity of Augustus toward cities destroyed by fire or earthquake[4]. The statement does not come from the pen of Augustus. It stands in a supplement which was added, probably, under the instructions of a local magistrate of Ancyra. The rest of the appendix simply summarizes the document proper. The item in question, however, is not mentioned in the main body of the text. It seems therefore to be a tribute to Augustus, spontaneous or official, from the point of view of a

---

[1] *Cf.* pp. 123 *ff.*

[2] Plurimis etiam civitatibus et privatis veteres immunitates et ius metallorum ac vectigalium adempta, Suet. *Tib.* 49.

[3] For Hadrian's action in the case of Stratonicea, *cf.* no. 83. Alexander Severus (*Hist. Aug. Alex. Sev.* 21) "vectigalia civitatibus ad proprias fabricas deputavit." *Cf.* Ammianus (25. 4. 15) who says of Julian, vectigalia civitatibus restituta cum fundis. [4] No. 38.

provincial living in a part of the world where the generosity
of the emperor had been especially shown, and it may not
be unnatural to think that the writer of it felt that the
generous efforts of Augustus in behalf of cities in distress
marked a new era in the relations between Rome and the
municipalities. Both Suetonius[1] and Cassius Dio[2] speak
of the help which Augustus gave to many cities injured
by earthquakes, and we hear specifically of assistance
rendered to Neapolis[3] and Paphos[4]. Tiberius followed
this policy[5], notably in the case of the fourteen cities of
Asia which were destroyed by an earthquake[6], and similar
acts of generosity are set down to the credit of Claudius,
Nero, Vespasian, Titus, and of emperors of the second
century[7]. The personal interest of Trajan and Hadrian
in the provincial cities went still farther. Trajan built
roads and bridges and dug canals in the Danubian region,
in Spain and Egypt[8], and the tribute of Hadrian's bio-
grapher that *in omnibus paene urbibus aliquid aedificavit*[9] is
abundantly confirmed by the records[10]. The emperors were
especially generous in helping cities to construct their
aqueducts, and we have many inscriptions commemo-
rating the assistance which they rendered for this purpose[11].
We have already had occasion to notice that as the danger
from the barbarians increased it was necessary to rebuild
and strengthen the walls of many cities[12]. This measure
was so vital to the safety of the empire that the central
government sometimes devoted a part of the imperial
revenue to this purpose and sometimes compelled a city
to apply to it a fixed portion of its receipts. Alexander
Severus helped cities to restore their walls, and Liebenam
recalls the fact that Constantius in the year 358 turned

[1] No. 38 and *cf.* Suet. *Aug.* 47.   [2] Cass. Dio, 54. 23 and 30.
[3] *Ibid.* 55. 10.   [4] *Ibid.* 54. 23.   [5] Suet. *Tib.* 8.
[6] *CIL.* x, 4842; Tac. *Ann.* 2. 47; 4. 13.
[7] Liebenam, *op. cit.* 172 *f.*
[8] Schiller, *Gesch. d. röm. Kaiserzeit*, I, 567 *f.*
[9] *Hist. Aug. Hadr.* 19. 2.   [10] v. Rohden, *R.E.* I, 516 *f.*
[11] *E.g.* Liebenam, *op. cit.* 158, n. 1.   [12] *Cf. supra*, p. 144.

over one-fourth of the revenue from the *vectigalia* to be used in building the walls of the cities of Africa, and Diocletian recommended the diversion to a similar purpose of municipal funds collected for public games[1]. On the other hand, there was a growing tendency to put imperial charges on the treasuries of the municipalities. Cases in point are the building and mending of the roads and the maintenance of the *cursus publicus*[2].

We shall have occasion in another connection to see how the cities lost control in large measure of their own funds[3], but it may not be inappropriate here to notice the way in which the imperial government was led to undertake the supervision of municipal finances. In his Verrine orations and in his letters from Cilicia Cicero describes the desperate condition in which the cities of Sicily and Cilicia found themselves in his day in consequence of the taxes and requisitions imposed upon them and the exactions of money lenders[4]. Many of these evils grew less under the empire, but the unwise and extravagant expenditure of money, in the eastern cities especially, frequently got them into serious difficulties. It was this situation which led the central government to interfere in their financial affairs. Perhaps a way was paved for such intervention by the establishment of imperial commissions to superintend the spending of money appropriated from the imperial treasury for the rebuilding of cities destroyed by earthquakes or fire[5]. If the central government was to bring relief and assume a certain measure of control of local finances when the property of a city had been lost in a fire or destroyed by an earthquake, why should it not take some responsibility for the finances of a city which

[1] *Cf.* an inscription of A.D. 227 (*An. ép.* 1917–8, no. 68): Infatigabile indulgentia domini Severi Alexandri Pii Felicis Aug. auctis viribus et moenibus suis castellan(i) cito Factenses muros extruxerunt curante Licinio Hieroclete procuratore Aug(usti) praeside provinciae a(nno) p(rovinciae) CLXXXVIII; *cf.* also Liebenam, *op. cit.* 144, n. 1 and commentary on no. 157.
[2] Nos. 51, 156 and *supra*, p. 137. [3] *Cf.* pp. 200 *ff.*
[4] *Cf.* pp. 121 *ff.* [5] Tac. *Ann.* 2, 47 and *supra*, p. 147.

was wasting its funds in elaborate stadia or theatres? To Pliny there seemed to be only one answer to this question for the cities under his jurisdiction, and when he found that the people of Nicaea had almost completed a theatre, which was structurally defective, at a cost of 10,000,000 sesterces, and a gymnasium which was badly built, he at once intervened and turned to Trajan for advice[1]. In like manner, Claudiopolis was constructing a bathhouse on a badly chosen site[2], and Nicomedeia had spent 3,000,000 sesterces for an aqueduct which had to be abandoned[3], and again Pliny asks Trajan what steps he shall take in the matter. Prusa petitions the emperor for permission to build a bathhouse[4], and Amastris to cover a sewer[5]. Even for the free city of Sinope Pliny asks of Trajan the right to construct an aqueduct[6]. He takes cognizance of many other matters connected with the finances of the municipalities. Annual allowances made by Byzantium for the expenses of one legate to Rome and another to the governor of Moesia are cut off[7]. The extravagance attendant on weddings and festivals is limited[8]. The propriety of requiring an initiation fee from men whose names are put on the rolls of the municipal senates is referred to Trajan[9]. To him is referred the claim of Nicaea to the property of citizens who die intestate[10], and the right of the cities of Bithynia and Pontus to be preferred creditors[11]. In one of his letters Pliny submits to Trajan a question that is one of the earliest indications which we have of the coming of the later ruinous policy of holding the decurions of a city personally responsible for its financial obligations[12]. Some of the towns in Pliny's province find it hard to loan their public funds at 12 per cent., and Pliny asks Trajan if he may force the decurions to borrow the money at this rate. The empire was not yet ready for this step, and Trajan did not approve the pro-

[1] Plin. *Epp. ad Trai.* 39. 1, 4.   [2] *Ibid.* 39. 5, 6.   [3] *Ibid.* 37.
[4] *Ibid.* 23.   [5] *Ibid.* 98.   [6] *Ibid.* 90.   [7] *Ibid.* 43.
[8] *Ibid.* 116, 117.   [9] *Ibid.* 112.   [10] *Ibid.* 84.   [11] *Ibid.* 108.   [12] *Ibid.* 54.

posal. The most far-reaching question in the correspondence, connected with the imperial control of municipal finances, concerns the right of the governor to inspect municipal accounts. Pliny examined the accounts of Prusa without hesitation[1], but when he proposed to look into those of Apamea, the people, while expressing a willingness in this particular case to submit to the scrutiny, stated that (rationes coloniae) numquam tamen esse lectas ab ullo proconsulum, habuisse privilegium et vetustissimum morem arbitrio suo rem publicam administrare[2]. Trajan, in his reply, advises Pliny to proceed with the examination, with the understanding that it will not prejudice their existing privileges. We can readily see, however, that this procedure in the case of a Roman colony set a dangerous precedent. We have followed the policy of Pliny in these matters in some detail, because it illustrates the paternal motives which actuated the imperial government in exercising a close oversight over the finances of provincial cities. Under the republic such supervision was impossible, but in the time of Trajan, with a governor well supplied with subordinates, and holding office long enough to be thoroughly familiar with local conditions, and with bureaus in Rome ready to answer promptly all sorts of provincial inquiries, it was possible to supervise carefully the finances of every city of the empire, and it does not surprise us to find the practices which Pliny followed in controlling municipal expenditures given a systematic form by his imperial master through the establishment of the new imperial office of *curator rei publicae*[3].

No discussion of the finances of the municipalities would be complete without some reference to the method followed in the adjustment of financial controversies between neighboring cities, but the way in which these and other disputes were settled will be discussed in another connection[4].

[1] *Ibid.* 17.   [2] *Ibid.* 47.   [3] See pp. 90 *ff.*   [4] See pp. 152 *ff.*

CHAPTER XI

ARBITRATION AND TREATIES

THE principle of arbitral settlement of international disputes was familiar in the ancient oriental kingdoms almost from the beginning of recorded history, but in the growth of great empires that equality between independent powers which is essential for the proper development of arbitration was destroyed[1]. In Greece the rise of a large number of small independent city-states produced ideal conditions for fostering this system of settling disputes, since war was uncertain in its results, and the loss of power and resources, even in a successful campaign, was not always compensated by gaining the point at issue. For this reason the disputants often preferred to refer their quarrel to the decision of some neutral and impartial judge, or some friendly state might intervene with an offer of mediation or arbitration. Whether the Greeks borrowed this idea from the Orient or discovered it for themselves cannot be determined, but we owe to them the introduction of arbitration into Europe[2]. There are well authenticated examples of arbitral settlements in the seventh century, and as early as the fifth the Greeks had developed the principle so far that treaties were made containing a clause whereby the contracting parties agreed to settle in this way disputes which might arise in the future. Unfortunately the Greek states were

[1] The best treatment of the subject of arbitration in Roman history is found in De Ruggiero, *L'arbitrato pubblico presso i Romani*. His classification of the different examples in Roman history has been followed in this chapter. Tod (*International Arbitration amongst the Greeks*) and Raeder (*L'arbitrage international chez les Hellènes*) have recently discussed briefly those cases of arbitration wherein Rome was called upon to decide disputes arising between Greek cities. *Cf.* Boak, *Am. Journal of International Law*, 15 (1921), 375 *ff.*

[2] Westermann, *C.J.* 2 (1906), 198; Tod, *op. cit.* 169 *ff.*

no better than modern nations in observing treaty obligations, and this provision was not always kept. A notable instance is the refusal of the Spartans to submit their dispute with Athens to arbitration before the outbreak of the Peloponnesian war.

In the third century examples of international arbitration among the Greeks are frequently recorded. Under this head we may include the disputes which arose between members of the great federal leagues that were usually settled by the central government, which also enforced the decision under the necessity of preserving internal peace and concord. In most cases of arbitration in this period we may note a tendency to appeal to some power or state whose prestige was great enough to make the decision respected. Thus the kings of Macedon were frequently requested to act as arbiters. After the conquest of Macedon, when Rome became a factor in eastern politics, the Greek cities frequently referred their disputes to the senate, and, in so doing, introduced the principle of arbitration into Roman political life.

The history of Rome's part in international arbitration is somewhat complicated by the relations existing between Rome and Greece after the issuance of the edict of Flamininus. While the Greek states remained virtually independent, Rome exercised a modified form of protectorate, and did not hesitate to interfere in the settlement of internal or inter-state quarrels. But so long as a city was nominally free and not incorporated in a Roman province, the settlement of its disputes with a neighbor by an appeal to Roman magistrates or to the senate may be considered as a true case of international arbitration. Since all such appeals came from Greek cities, the history of international arbitration in Rome began with her first contact with the East and ended when she became mistress of the Orient. Since the senate controlled the conduct of foreign relations, all these disputes were referred to this body or to her agents who transmitted the appeal to Rome. The only recorded exception is the settlement of the dispute between Cnossus and Gortyna, which was decided by Appius Claudius and his fellow-commissioners[1]. In this case, however, the commission probably had plenipotentiary powers to examine the condition of Greek cities and to settle disputes.

While the senate decided some of the disputes referred to it, certain questions such as the determination of boundaries could not be settled at a distance, and these were delegated to a special commission or to another state. The delegation of powers was made in a *senatus consultum*, and the question to be decided by the arbitrator was often very narrowly defined. Thus in the dispute between Athens and Oropus, Sicyon was asked merely to determine the penalty to be inflicted on Athens[2]. Magnesia on the Maeander was asked by Rome to arbitrate between Hierapytna and Itanus, but in so doing the only point to be determined was which state occupied the disputed territory at a certain date[3]. The dispute between Magnesia and Priene was delegated to Mylasa under the same conditions[4].

In the instructions given by the senate we find that there is often a desire on the part of Rome not so much to render a judicial decision on the point at issue, as to preserve the status which the disputants had held when they came into political relations with Rome. This policy may have been adopted for the purpose of cementing treaty relations, but it is not altogether in accord with the principles of strict justice. Rome cannot justly be accused, however, of using the arbitral awards as a means of extending her power over the eastern cities. She did not use her extraordinary power either in enforcing the decisions which she or her delegates had pronounced, or in guaranteeing

---

[1] Polybius, 33. 15. We may assume that Roman agents settled many other similar disputes in Greece.

[2] Pausanias, 7. 11. 4–8. [3] *Inschriften von Magnesia*, 105.

[4] *Inschriften von Priene*, 531; *Inschriften von Magnesia*, 93.

the terms of settlement. Athens not only appealed from the decision of Sicyon against her in the quarrel with Oropus, but even evaded the reduced penalty which the senate imposed by making a private settlement with Oropus[1]. In the dispute between Samos and Priene the senate confirmed a previous award made by Rhodes. In 136 the case was again referred to Rome, but no change was made in the decision. Even after both cities had become incorporated in the province of Asia, the quarrel broke out afresh, and this time Mylasa was deputed to review the case[2]. Likewise the dispute over temple-lands at Delphi was reopened at least twice after Greece had become a Roman province[3]. In arbitrating the dispute between the Achaean League and Sparta the Romans exceeded their function in violating the sovereign power of both disputants. Sparta was required to remain a member of the League, but the latter was compelled to resign her judicial authority over Spartan citizens[4].

Where states were quasi-independent, possessing jurisdiction over their internal affairs, but acknowledging the hegemony of Rome in foreign relations, inter-state disputes could only be adjudicated by a direct appeal to Rome, since the reference of the question to any other state would have been regarded as an offense to the sovereign power. In these cases the arbitration was not always purely voluntary, for if one side appealed to Rome, the other was virtually compelled to present its case unless it chose to let the judgment go by default. This class of arbitration is known as federal, since one or both of the parties to the dispute were bound to Rome by treaties of alliance.

In the earliest recorded case of federal arbitration, if the traditional account in Livy is to be believed, two members of the Latin League quarreled over a piece of land, and when the dispute was referred to Rome, the *comitia tributa*

[1] Pausanias, 7. 11. 4–8.   [2] Tod, *op. cit.* nos. 61–65.
[3] *Ibid.* no. 26.   [4] de Ruggiero, *op. cit.* 240 *ff.*

took the matter out of the hands of the senate and voted that the land in question should belong to Rome[1]. There is much about this story which renders it unlikely, but if it is true, we can well understand why arbitration did not become popular amongst Rome's allies in Italy.

The dispute between Sparta and Messene over the possession of the *ager Dentheliates* forms one of the most interesting cases which come within the scope of federal arbitration. Philip of Macedon in 338 and Antigonus in 221 had acted as arbiters in this long-standing dispute. Then Mummius in 146–5, if we may believe the account in Tacitus, pronounced a decision, but from the wording of the decree of the Milesians, it would appear that he merely recognized the *status quo*. Between 146 and 137 the dispute was again brought before the senate, which referred the question to Miletus, at that time an independent state. The Milesians were instructed to determine only which of the two parties occupied the disputed territory when Mummius was consul or proconsul. The Milesians chose by lot a court of 600, and when the evidence was heard the court voted 584 to 16 in favor of Messene[2]. It may be noted that no attempt was made to determine the legality of the claim of either party, but that Rome was concerned solely in determining the status of the territory when one or other of the two states became politically related to Rome. This solution of the problem was manifestly unjust, and showed undue favor to Rome's allies. So Caesar, in his interview with Ariovistus, states it as an axiom of Rome's foreign policy that her allies should suffer no loss, but rather should be increased in influence, dignity, and honor[3]. In this respect, then, Rome's arbitral judgments were dictated by the desire to extend her influence and to bind her allies to her by shaping the arbitral awards in their favor.

A somewhat similar situation is found in the dispute between Carthage and Masinissa, which seems to have

[1] de Ruggiero, *op. cit.* 268 *ff.*   [2] *Ibid.* 283 *ff.*   [3] Caesar, *B.G.* 1. 43.

been deliberately prolonged by the senate in order to weaken the power of her former enemy, now, however, formally regarded as an ally. In 193 the senate appointed a commission which made no decision, probably in obedience to secret instructions from the home authorities. Masinissa was thus encouraged in his acts of aggression and occupied other territory which, when Carthage appealed to Rome, was apparently granted to Masinissa. In 160 the injustice of Rome was still more flagrant in her award to the Numidian king, for Carthage was compelled to cede the town of Emporia in addition to the land which he had already occupied and to pay an indemnity of 500 talents. When Masinissa seized further territory some three years later and Carthage appealed to Rome, the Carthaginians refused to entrust their cause to the arbitrators whom Rome sent out, and, apparently, the Numidian was allowed to remain in possession[1]. In Rome's conduct of arbitral relations in these disputes we find one of the darkest chapters in her judicial history. No doubt the bitter prejudice against Carthage and high imperial policy dictated her decisions, but these considerations furnish no excuse for the violation of the principles of justice, and her guilt is the greater in that Carthage was bound to her by a treaty of friendship and alliance. In later federal arbitration Rome recovered her judicial sanity, since her position as a dominant power in the Mediterranean was secure. In the few cases of this class which belong to later times none gives any indication of favoritism on the part of Rome. As a matter of fact, the extension of Roman power in the last century of the republic had brought most of the ancient city-states under the Roman provincial system, and cases of international and federal arbitration could no longer occur.

While it is true that many of the cities still retained the nominal title of "free" or "allied" states, there are no records of disputes which arose involving them, and

---

[1] de Ruggiero, *op. cit.* 270 *ff*.

apparently when once they had become incorporated in provinces, their disputes were settled by the central authority on the same basis as the disputes of other states under Roman dominion. This method of settling disputes is called administrative arbitration, and of this class we possess a large number of records, ranging from the beginning of provincial government up to the end of the third century of the Christian era, and found in every part of the empire. Most questions of administrative arbitration concern boundary disputes arising between adjacent municipalities, or between municipalities and state or imperial domains. Some of these quarrels were inherited from pre-Roman times, but others developed under Roman administration in cases where boundaries had not been definitely determined in the settlement of a province, or where the creation of new municipal organizations gave rise to litigation in the delimitation of territorial possessions. Disputes also arose over water rights in connection with rivers, or over roads, or took the form of quarrels like that between Pompeii and Nuceria. In these cases the local authorities were without jurisdiction, and the sovereign power was called upon to settle the dispute. It was impossible for cities in such cases to have recourse to war or to choose some foreign state as arbiter, since either procedure would have been offensive to the sovereign power of Rome. While the *lex Rupilia* allowed Sicilian towns to call upon another city to decide disputes arising between them and their citizens, there is no evidence that similar latitude was allowed in boundary settlements, although Mucius Scaevola invited Sardis and Ephesus to settle their differences by arbitration and to call in any city which they chose as arbiter[1]. Not infrequently a third state was appointed as arbiter in disputes which arose between Greek cities, but more commonly the senate, or emperor, named a special commission or some official to act. In such cases the delegated power

[1] Cicero, *in Verr.* 2. 12. 13; *Inschriften von Pergamum*, 268.

was plenipotentiary, and the decision was not subject to review by the central authority.

When the local authorities were not able to control internal factions, and the magistrates appealed to the central government, or, as in one case, to the patron of the city, the settlement of the dispute was sometimes arranged by arbitration, which may be classed as administrative. Sulla was delegated by the senate to settle a quarrel among the citizens of Puteoli, and to frame a new constitution for the city[1]. In imperial times the senate appointed two of its members to settle a similar dispute in this city. In Pompeii the patron of the town was accepted by both factions as arbiter apparently without any reference of the quarrel to the senate[2]. Doubtless the numerous commissions and special agents sent out from Rome to the provinces acted as arbiters in settling the disputes of party factions, and in so doing they favored the aristocratic class. Although the local authorities were empowered to settle all questions concerning internal affairs, the sovereign power exercised by the senate or by the emperors gave them authority to interfere in the local affairs of all provincial cities. By virtue of this authority Trajan and his successors appointed the *curatores rei publicae* and *correctores*, by whom local disputes were settled by administrative processes without recourse to arbitration.

A third class of cases of arbitration may be distinguished in the disputes which arose between cities and private individuals, whether alien or resident citizens[3]. As we have already indicated, the *lex Rupilia* allowed Sicilian cities to call upon the services of another city in arbitrating such disputes, and this arrangement was probably allowed in other provinces. But where the local authorities possessed jurisdiction, cases of appeal to arbitration are comparatively rare, nor was the appeal necessarily made to Rome, or to the governor, but could be made to another

[1] Plutarch, *Sulla*, 37.   [2] Cicero, *pro P. Sulla*, 21, 60, 61.
[3] de Ruggiero, *op. cit.* 96 ff.

city in the province or to a private citizen. In most cities, however, the local magistrates did not have jurisdiction over Roman citizens, and in disputes arising between a city and Romans the case must of necessity be referred to the governor, who, however, had the right to appoint arbiters if he so desired.

Finally, there is a series of disputes which arose between the cities and the Roman state, or rather its representatives —the publicans[1]. We may also include here the boundary disputes arising over the municipal lands and those of the state or of the emperor. In such cases the state might settle the dispute by regular administrative methods, but in some instances the question was referred to the decision of an arbiter appointed by the senate or by the emperor.

Arbitral procedure was foreign to Roman policy and was introduced only through contact with, and under the influence of, Greek culture. Its continuance in imperial times was apparently determined by a desire on the part of the central government to flatter the vanity of the city-states which had been incorporated in the empire. In the third century the military autocracy was no longer influenced by these motives, and records of arbitral judgments disappear. Henceforth the settlement of all disputes passed to the regular provincial courts or became a matter of ordinary administrative routine.

The special relation which *civitates foederatae* bore to Rome ceased to exist in Italy after the towns received Roman citizenship. In other parts of the empire very few states enjoyed the privilege of *foedus aequum* with Rome. Some of these jealously maintained their rights, as, for example, when the Amiseni appealed to Rome in regard to the law forbidding the organization of clubs in Bithynia[2]. Trajan replied that if the laws of the city permitted such associations, the imperial authorities could not forbid them provided the clubs were not devoted to seditious or illegal gatherings. There is an undertone in Trajan's letter which

[1] de Ruggiero, *op. cit.* 99 *ff.*; nos. 12, 18.   [2] Pliny, *Epp. ad Trai.* 92, 93.

implies that treaties would be respected only if they did not contravene the best interests of Rome. In 210 the Camerinians thanked Septimius Severus for confirming the right of *foedus aequum*, and in Astypalaea the treaty with Rome was maintained as late as the reign of Gordian[1]. The *lex de imperio Vespasiani* placed the power of making treaties in the hands of the emperor, confirming the privilege which Augustus had held. The economic pressure which began to be severe in the second century probably led many cities to surrender their special privileges. Thus we find an imperial *corrector* in Athens under Hadrian[2]. The edict of Caracalla probably swept away other treaties when the cities accepted Roman citizenship, although it is evident that Astypalaea preserved her status as a *civitas foederata* for some time longer.

In the eastern empire coins were frequently struck celebrating the ὁμόνοια of various states[3]. It is impossible to determine exactly what is meant by this term under Roman rule, but it seems to indicate that the Romans permitted these states to conclude some form of treaty which flattered their vanity and infringed in no way on Roman sovereignty. With the development of the bureaucracy and the military autocracy the fiction of sovereignty which the Romans had permitted as a matter of policy soon disappeared.

[1] *CIL.* xi, 5631.   [2] *CIL.* viii, 7059.
[3] Head, *Historia Nummorum, s.v.* ὁμόνοια.

CHAPTER XII

PROVINCIAL ASSEMBLIES

IN the organization of a conquered province the senate treated with each city and each tribe as an individual unit. Under the republic the governor, who was sent out with the *imperium*, had no tribune to interpose a veto on his acts, and the provincial subjects had no means to check illegal action or extortion except through indirect pressure applied by their patron in Rome. After the governor laid down his command, he might be prosecuted before a jury made up of members of the senate, but it was difficult and practically impossible to secure a conviction before a court of his peers. Later, when the juries were composed of members of the equestrian order and party feeling had become intensified, convictions were easier to obtain, although the court was not so much prompted by a desire to secure justice for the provincials as it was concerned in furthering the interests of the *equites*. In appearing before the court the provincials had no other bond than their common interests, and each city acted singly, or their delegates represented municipalities which had united to present their complaints before the senate. Since it was the policy of the Romans to discourage combinations of the different communities in each province, it is very unlikely that the *lex provinciae* provided any machinery for common action, but in the informal meeting of representatives of two or more towns for the discussion of matters of mutual interest we may discern the beginnings of a provincial assembly[1].

---

[1] Marquardt, *de Romanarum provinciarum conciliis et sacerdotibus*; Guiraud, *Les assemblées prov.*; Carette, *Les assemblées prov. de la Gaule rom.*; Fougères, *de communi Lyciorum*; Monceaux, *de communi provinciae Asiae*; Dict. Dar. *s.v.* κοινόν; Kornemann, *R.E. s.v. concilium,* κοινόν;

PROVINCIAL ASSEMBLIES

In the East the Romans found a large number of κοινά already existing, of which some were religious organizations, and others political federations. In Greece Flamininus encouraged those which might serve to check the power of Macedon. After the sack of Corinth by Mummius political unions were suppressed in the fear that they might form centres for the revival of a national consciousness[1]. Later the ban was removed and the assemblies were permitted to meet for religious purposes. Similar organizations existed in Asia, and shortly after the province was established we find games instituted by the cities in honor of the governor, Mucius Scaevola, who held the office about 98 B.C.[2] Antony addressed a letter to the κοινόν of Asia granting certain privileges to the guilds taking part in the provincial games[3]. This action must have been taken in response to a request from the assembly and, although no political issue was involved, it is apparent that the delegates from the cities of Asia were developing an organization in which questions of common interest might come up for discussion.

In 29 B.C. the cities of Asia in their provincial organization requested that they be allowed to establish the cult of Roma and Augustus at Pergamum[4]. In granting their request the emperor established a precedent which was soon followed by the other provinces. In some cases we find two distinct provincial assemblies, as in Bithynia-Pontus, Galatia, Lycia-Pamphylia, and Syria. In Achaea the local κοινά of Central Greece united their assemblies in a joint federation which seems to have represented the province[5]. Thessaly preserved the independence of its

Krascheninnikoff, *Philol.* 53 (1894), 147 *ff*.; Ramsay, *Journ. Rom. St.* 12 (1922), 154 *ff*.

[1] Pausanias, 7. 16. 9.   [2] Ditt. *Or. Gr.* 438; Ditt. *Syll.*[3] 760.
[3] Brandis thinks that Antony established the provincial *concilium* in Asia about 33–32 (*Hermes*, 32 (1897), 512 *ff*.).
[4] Tac. *Ann.* 4. 37; Cass. Dio, 51. 20.
[5] We find this prescript: τὸ κοινὸν τῶν Ἀχαιῶν καὶ Βοιωτῶν καὶ Λοκρῶν καὶ Εὐβοέων καὶ Φωκέων, IG. VII, 2711.

assembly, since this district was separated for administrative purposes from the rest of Greece and placed under
the control of the governor of Macedon in the imperial
period. While the meeting-place of the provincial κοινόν
was usually fixed in some convenient centre, the leading
cities of Asia, Lycia, and Lycaonia shared the honor in
rotation.

In the West the provincial assemblies were slower in
developing than in the East. Municipal institutions replaced the tribal units slowly and the majority of the
provinces lacked the political traditions of the Orient
which might have given them a feeling of unity. Outside
Gaul there was no common cult such as had united many
Greek cities in their κοινά. Moreover, the religious
mentality of the western peoples differed widely from that
of the Orient, and was less facile in adopting new cults,
especially in accepting a cult which deified a reigning
emperor. We have already seen that even under the
republic the western provinces had informal organizations
in which the cities could unite in conducting prosecutions
of officials and in sending embassies to Rome. An edict
of Augustus forbade the provincials to take any action
in praising a governor until sixty days after he left his
province[1], but it is not necessary to infer that provincial
assemblies existed generally at this period (2 B.C.). The
first formal organization of such an assembly may be
found in Tres Galliae when Drusus called representatives
of the various *civitates* to Lugudunum in 12 B.C. The
worship of the imperial cult was founded at that time[2].
This gathering formed the nucleus of a provincial assembly
which met annually thereafter at the same place. In A.D. 15
the cities of Hispania Tarraconensis requested the privilege of founding a temple of Augustus in Tarraco, and
Tacitus observes that the granting of this petition formed
a precedent for other provinces[3]. This would imply that

[1] Cass. Dio, 56. 25.   [2] Kornemann, *op. cit.* 809 *f.*
[3] Tac. *Ann.* 1. 78.

the initiative was taken by the provincial cities and not by the central government, although the theory has been advanced that the assemblies were founded by the emperors in some cases in order to hasten the Romanization of the province[1]. We might infer from the remark of Tacitus that the example of Spain was soon followed by other provinces, but there is no evidence which enables us to date the foundation of the other assemblies, nor can we determine whether they were created in all the provinces of the empire. In the fourth century these organizations were made obligatory by imperial mandate.

Primarily, the provincial assemblies were charged with the annual services of the imperial cult, the care of the temple, and the celebration of games in honor of the deified emperor. However, when the delegates met to transact their official business, they discussed also matters of general interest, and the administration of the governor and his subordinates came under review for praise or blame. For the first time, therefore, the provincial cities had an official organization in which they could voice their opinion collectively in regard to the administration of their governor, and since his future career in public service might be largely determined by the action of the assembly, it was a powerful influence in securing better government in the province. In the case of dishonest and corrupt officials, the assembly under the empire took upon itself the duty of prosecuting the offender at Rome before the senate or the praetorian prefect. The earlier emperors doubtless encouraged this phase of the assembly's activity in order to keep a closer check on governors, especially in senatorial provinces. At any rate a large number of accusations were lodged in Rome against provincial officials during the first century[2]. Later, when the imperial bureaucracy had developed more fully and agents of the emperor were sent out to the provinces and to individual municipalities, the number of prosecutions

---

[1] Krascheninnikoff, *op. cit.* 168 *ff.*   [2] Guiraud, *op. cit.* 172 *ff.*

steadily diminished, and the influence of the assemblies was apparently weakened.

The relation of the provincial assemblies to the municipalities is obscure. Each municipality, or each tribal unit, sent a certain number of delegates to the assembly, and in Achaea it is possible that the smaller κοινά were represented in the provincial organization, either by delegates or, though less probably, in a body. The chief priest was elected annually by the assembly from candidates nominated by the municipalities. He presided over the meetings of the assembly, and defrayed the expenses of the sacrifices and games as a form of liturgy[1]. In the ancient κοινόν of Lycia the delegates were appointed according to a system of proportionate representation, the cities being graded in three classes, of which the first sent three delegates, the second two, and the third one each[2]. In the age of the Antonines the cities of Asia, and presumably those of the other provinces, were graded in a similar way for the distribution of the gift of immunity to teachers and physicians[3]. It is therefore possible that the Lycian system of representation was universally adopted in imperial times, but there is no evidence on the subject beyond the fact that some cities sent more than one delegate, and that there were at least 150 members of the κοινόν of Asia[4]. In Bithynia the members were sometimes appointed for life, although this distinction may have been purely honorary, as was true in the case of the life-appointment of the provincial priest, and of other liturgies which had been discharged with special merit[5].

In the proceedings of the assembly there is no evidence that mandatory instructions were given to its delegates by the civic government, but they were undoubtedly aware of

[1] Guiraud, *op. cit.* 82 *ff.*   [2] Strabo, 14. 3, p. 664.   [3] *Dig.* 27. 1. 6.
[4] Buckler and Robinson, *AJA.* 18 (1914), 356. In Aristides (p. 767 Dind.) 407 votes are recorded as cast in a meeting of the assembly.
[5] Cagnat, *IGRR.* 3, 7. Brandis, however, believes that the title does not refer to membership in the provincial assembly.

public opinion and were guided accordingly. In the inscription from Thorigny it is recorded that the delegates gave up their attempt to attack Paulinus on the protest of Sollemnis[1]. Had they received a mandate from their respective cities, they would hardly have desisted on the protest of a single delegate from one state. Timarchus of Crete is said to have boasted that the power of granting an honorary decree to the retiring governor rested in his hands[2]. In later times the governor undoubtedly found means to control the election of deputies through the power which he exercised in municipal affairs, and this fact may account in part for the decreasing importance of the assembly in the second and third centuries in indicting provincial governors.

Since the assemblies met but once a year, administrative matters of local interest were probably referred directly to the governor, or a delegation was sent to the emperor by individual cities who were eager to bring themselves to imperial notice. Occasionally, however, joint action was taken. Thus Asia honored T. Claudius Amphimachus for an embassy by which he undertook to secure a remission of the inheritance tax ($\epsilon i \kappa o \sigma \tau \acute{\eta}$)[3]. When Domitian forbade the cultivation of the vine in Asia, the provincial assembly sent Scopelianus to Rome, and he succeeded in having the decree revoked[4]. The same assembly asked Caracalla to fix Ephesus as the port where the new governor should land in coming to his province[5]. While an advocate ($\H{\epsilon}\kappa\delta\iota\kappa o\varsigma$) is mentioned in the case of the provincial assembly in Asia only[6], it is probable that this official was attached to other assemblies as well, and, although his duties are nowhere defined, we may assume that he bore the same relation to the assembly as the municipal

---

[1] No. 140.   [2] Tac. *Ann.* 15. 20.

[3] Cagnat, *IGRR.* 4, 1236; Keil and Premerstein, *Denkschriften der Wiener Akademie,* 54 (1911), no. 53.

[4] Philostratus, *Vit. Soph.* 1. 21. 12.

[5] *Dig.* 1. 16. 4, 5.   [6] *AJA.* 18 (1914), 350.

advocate to the city, and that one of his most important duties was in connection with the prosecution of provincial officials.

The only example of a provincial decree which was mandatory in the cities is found in Asia, where the assembly, at the request of the governor, adopted the Julian calendar throughout the province[1]. This business was apparently entrusted to the assembly because of the importance of the matter in connection with religious observances—especially with those relating to the imperial cult. Titus wrote to the Achaeans, probably to the assembly, about the exposure of infants, although Domitian and Trajan communicated with the provincial governors on this subject[2]. Antoninus wrote to the province of Asia forbidding the unrestricted grant of immunity from liturgies by the municipalities, and regulating the number of such grants which could be made in each city[3]. It is probable that this letter was addressed to the provincial assembly. It would seem that the assemblies had no administrative power over the cities of the province except in matters pertaining to the imperial cult, the games in honor of the emperor, and in cases where they received a mandate from the governor or emperor. The governor had the right of taking part in the regular proceedings of the assembly, and even in the case of honorary decrees could exercise the right of veto. The assembly could, however, appeal to Rome over the governor's veto, and in one case the emperor reversed the action of the governor, whereupon the decree became law[4].

The ancient κοινόν of Thessaly had the privilege of granting citizenship and the right of owning property in any city of the federation[5]. Under Roman rule similar

---

[1] No. 34; Ditt. *Or. Gr.* 458; Keil and Premerstein, *op. cit.* no. 166.
[2] Pliny, *Ep. ad Trai.* 65.   [3] *Dig.* 27. 1. 6.
[4] Cagnat, *IGRR.* 3, 739, chaps. 24, 26, 28. Whether the governor called together the provincial assembly may be doubted, *cf.* Ditt. *Or. Gr.* 494, n.   [5] *IG.* ix, 2, 507, 508.

privileges were apparently enjoyed by a few provincial assemblies. In Lycia officers of the assembly were sometimes recorded as citizens of one or more towns, and the additional qualification is added πολιτευόμενος δὲ καὶ ἐν ταῖς κατὰ Λυκίαν πόλεσι πάσαις. This phrase seems to imply that the official named exercised the rights of citizenship in all Lycian cities[1]. The citizenship in specified municipalities is contrasted with that in all the cities, and it may be possible that a form of honorary citizenship was conferred by the assembly. The κοινόν of Asia conferred the title of Ἀσιανός on Isidorus, the son of Menogenes, who was provincial advocate[2]. It is probable that this title implies a kind of honorary provincial citizenship. The tragic actor C. Julius Julianus was a citizen of Smyrna and enjoyed the rights of citizenship in all Hellas, Macedonia, and Thessaly (πολιτευθεὶς δὲ ἐν ὅλῃ τῇ Ἑλλάδι καὶ Μακεδονίᾳ καὶ Θεσσαλίᾳ). This claim may be an idle boast, but more probably his services at provincial festivals won him the grant of honorary citizenship[3].

The various municipalities which were members of the assembly contributed to the expenses of the organization, such as those required for the games, the religious ceremonies, buildings, repairs, maintenance of staff, embassies. They also met the charges in connection with the prosecution of officials and the erection of statues[4]. There is a record of an endowment fund for the games in Asia, but the games were usually regarded as a liturgy pertaining to the priesthood. An African inscription dated A.D. 366 shows that this liturgy had become so burdensome to the candidates that the governor intervened by reducing the scale of extravagance which had hitherto prevailed[5]. Not

---

[1] Cagnat, *IGRR.* 3, 527, 539, 603, 628, 704, 739, chap. 5. In some cases, however, the phrase seems to imply the discharge of municipal liturgies, *cf.* Cagnat, *op. cit.* 563, 584, 680.

[2] *AJA.* 18 (1914), 321 *ff.*

[3] *IG.* v, 1, 662.

[4] Guiraud, *op. cit.* 128 *ff.*

[5] No. 110; *cf.* Dessau, 1256.

infrequently the cost of buildings or of statues was defrayed by the emperor; embassies were undertaken by private citizens at their own expense; and statues were often erected by the individual on whom the honor had been conferred.

If we except the "Altar" series of Lugudunum issued by the authority of the emperor, western assemblies possessed no right to coin money[1]. In the East silver coins were issued by towns and provinces, usually with imperial sanction and control. In Crete the provincial issue replaced that of the individual towns[2]. Bronze or token money seems to have been issued by any organized city-community that chose to exercise the right, and the provincial κοινά not infrequently issued communal bronze coinage[3]. There is no evidence that the provincial assembly exercised any control over the coinage of the cities. Since the imperial government probably determined the rate of exchange between the various currencies, it is probable that the revenue derived from the mint was slight, if any.

Officials of the provincial assemblies sometimes held other positions. In Gaul the chief priest was appointed to some duty in connection with the census, and another official was patron of a guild of boatmen, but it would be unwise to infer from these examples that the assembly exercised any control over taxation or trade[4]. Opramoas, archiphylax of Lycia, made arrangements for securing order (εἰρήνη) and supplying provisions (εὐθηνία) at an annual meeting of the assembly[5]. He also advanced money as a loan to those provincial cities which had been unable to make up their annual quota of imperial tribute. Rostowzew thought that the assembly, through its officials, controlled the municipal irenarchs, sitonae, and decaproti, but this interpretation of the activities of Opramoas is hardly

---

[1] *Coins of the Roman Empire in the British Museum*, I, xvii *ff*.
[2] *Ibid*. I, xxv; *R.E. s.v. κοινόν*.   [3] *Ibid*. I, xxvii.
[4] Kornemann, *op. cit.* 815 *ff*.   [5] Cagnat, *IGRR*. 3, 739, chap. 5.

justified[1]. There must have been some coöperation between local and provincial officials at every meeting of the assembly, but it is unlikely that the local government surrendered its autonomy in any respect. The loan made by Opramoas to the cities was a political investment against the time when he should be a candidate for higher office in the assembly. Other Lycian inscriptions show that provincial officials sometimes contributed to the taxes, erection of public buildings, or cost of games[2]. These payments were not a regular liturgy attached to their post in the assembly, but were undoubtedly voluntary obligations undertaken from the same motive which influenced Opramoas. It is also recorded that the chief priest of the Macedonian assembly paid the head tax for the province and provided grain at reduced prices during a famine which occurred in his year of office[3]. The assumption of these voluntary obligations was a dangerous precedent, which might easily have developed into a regular liturgy attached to officials in the provincial assemblies, especially if the pressure for the payment of imperial taxes had become severe at the time the gifts were made.

Apart from the prosecution of government officials, the provincial assemblies seldom, if ever, took the initiative in political matters. One doubtful instance may be mentioned here. In A.D. 70 the Treveri sided with Sabinus in his revolution. The Remi summoned a provincial *concilium* which asked the Treveri to lay down their arms[4]. The appeal was not heeded and the assembly—whether regularly constituted or not, it is difficult to determine—had no power to enforce its request.

When the city of Sidyma established a *gerusia*, the governor of the province was notified of the fact by the Lyciarch. The latter, however, was a citizen of Sidyma

---

[1] Rostowzew, *Gesch. d. Staatspacht*, 418 ff.
[2] Cagnat, *IGRR.* 3, 704; 739, p. 298.
[3] Ἀρχ. Δελτ. 1916, 148.   [4] Tac. *Hist.* 4. 67, 69 ff.

and it is probable that he acted in his private capacity as a resident of the city, rather than as an official of the provincial assembly[1].

The assemblies frequently appealed to Rome for decisions on points of law and procedure, as we may infer from the frequent communications of the emperors to the provincials recorded in the Digest and Codes[2]. Only in Lycia, however, do we find any evidence of a provincial court under the control of the assembly[3]. The records of the κοινόν of this province refer to specially summoned courts which were apparently under the control of the assembly. Unfortunately we have no other information which would help us to determine the relation of these courts to those of the Romans or of the municipalities. It is probable that they were constituted by the κοινόν to settle disputes between municipalities which preferred the native to the Roman law, or they may have been called together to decide violations of the law in connection with the annual games and ceremonies of the assembly. Opramoas, as archiphylax of Lycia, was entrusted with judicial power by the governor, although it is doubtful whether he received his commission as an official of the assembly or as a citizen of Rhodiapolis, and we cannot determine whether he had any connection with the special court of the assembly[4]. One of the officials of the Lycian κοινόν was called the recorder (νομογραφεύς), and the title implies that laws were enacted by the assembly[5]. The κοινόν of Thessaly was asked by the governor to act as arbiter in a boundary dispute between Cierium and Metropolis[6]. The decision was rendered by a secret vote— probably because of the necessity of preserving harmony

[1] No. 114. Note that the ratification of this act by the provincial governor seems to be required.

[2] Kornemann, *op. cit.* 820 *f.*

[3] Cagnat, *IGRR.* 3, 563, 680, 736, 739, chap. 12. These may refer to settlements of disputes between members of the *concilium*; *cf.* no. 46.

[4] Cagnat, *IGRR.* 3, 739, chap. 12.

[5] Cagnat, *IGRR.* 3, 680.   [6] No. 46.

within the assembly. It would be interesting to know whether the cities concerned took part as advocates as well as judges.

The growth of Christianity and the abolition of the imperial cult turned the provincial assemblies into purely secular organizations in the fourth century. Their prestige had already been lowered by the redistribution of the provinces of Diocletian, and the creation of diocesan assemblies must have affected the smaller provincial organizations materially[1]. In the late empire our chief evidence for the history of the assemblies comes from the Theodosian Code. The rescripts which this Code contains, addressed directly to *concilia*, deal with points of law, the right of appeal, and the immunity of provincial priests and civic magistrates from certain liturgies. Other rescripts addressed to provincials are usually interpreted as directed to the assemblies[2]. If this is the case, the *concilia* discussed taxation, the regulation of *curiales*, the public post, extortion by imperial officials, and similar matters. In all these cases the assembly had no powers beyond that of bringing the questions to the notice of the emperor in appeals or complaints against the injustice and corruption of imperial agents in the province. Various rescripts addressed by the emperor to the praetorian prefect safeguard the right of assembly in ordinary and special meetings, as well as the freedom of discussion and appeal[3]. In all of these there is an implication that these privileges were often disregarded, and that the provincial assembly, where it existed, was brought under the control of governors to serve their personal interests. Ammianus tells us that Iphicles brought to the praetorian prefect the honorary decree conferred upon the governor by the Epirotes. On seeing the emperor afterwards and being questioned as to the sincerity of this expression of praise, Iphicles replied that his fellow-citizens passed the decree

[1] Guiraud, *op. cit.* 228 *ff.*   [2] Kornemann, *op. cit.* 825 *ff.*
[3] *Cod. Th.* 12. 12. 1 (355), 12 (392).

with groans and in spite of themselves[1]. Some of the emperors made an honest attempt to re-establish the councils on their former independent basis as a means of checking the corruption of provincial officials, but the forces of venality and extortion combined with bureaucracy to nullify their efforts. When the Justinian Code was compiled, the assemblies had ceased to exist as a political force, and their organization survived only in the institutions of the Christian church.

It has been said that the provincial assemblies contained the germ of representative government. It is true that they were representative, and elected organizations, but they never acquired any legislative, administrative, or judicial power, save in the rare cases when they acted on the direct authority of the emperor or governor in promulgating their edicts or publishing their decisions. The assemblies commanded no armies, and had control of no revenues beyond the contributions made by the municipalities for minor expenses and the funds from minor endowments. The money expended in the imperial worship and games was provided by the generosity of the officials appointed to the several liturgies. The primary function of the assemblies was religious, and through the grandeur of their display they undoubtedly acquired considerable prestige. In their secondary capacity as a board of review of the governor's policies, they were, we believe, encouraged by the emperors who desired to keep a close check on provincial administration, especially in the senatorial provinces. Most of the accusations lodged against corrupt officials came from provinces governed by the senate, and it must have been especially galling for this body to try its own agents. When the provinces all came under imperial control, the activities of the assemblies ceased. At least the records of impeachments disappear. In the late empire the imperial government sought to

---

[1] Ammianus, 30. 5. 8.

revive this function of the assemblies, but we have already seen that the attempt failed.

The assemblies were seriously handicapped by meeting, usually, but once a year, and with a membership which was constantly changing, no continuous political traditions could be established. The appointment of the *curator* as an imperial agent, and the closer supervision of municipal affairs by the governors were important elements in checking the development of the provincial organizations. Moreover, the ingrained individualism of ancient states persisted long after they became municipalities of the empire and prevented concerted action for a common cause. Most of these cities, through their inordinate vanity, preferred to bring their difficulties directly to Rome by means of expensive embassies which might commend them to imperial notice. As a result of this practice, bureaus were created to deal with all phases of municipal administration, and in the development of imperial bureaucracy we have perhaps the most potent factor in preventing the political growth of the *concilia*, for legislative, administrative, and judicial powers were gradually concentrated in the hands of the palace officials. For these reasons we believe that it is not altogether accidental that scarcely any records of the assemblies are preserved in the third century, and while the emperors sought to revive the assemblies in the fourth century in order to correct abuses in provincial government, they were powerless against the forces of the corrupt bureaucracy.

Although this sketch of the provincial assemblies in their relation to municipal institutions shows that the assemblies were relatively unimportant politically, we must not disregard them as wholly negligible. It is possible that the Councils of the early Church based their organization on that of the provincial assemblies, for the bishops were virtually the delegates of their municipal dioceses, and although the Councils were not always provincial in scope, the representative principle may well have been borrowed from this pagan source. The modern parliament also resembles the provincial assembly in form, but it would be unsafe to trace its development in a direct line through the medium of the Church Councils, although the latter may have transmitted the representative idea to the modern world. But the provincial assemblies served a more immediate purpose. They bound the whole empire together in a common cult, and, in the universal worship of Rome and the emperors, the subject states acknowledged the temporal and spiritual sovereignty of Rome. One may question whether the annual provincial rites, though celebrated with great pomp and splendor, were really as important, politically, as the local municipal cults, for only a small proportion of the population could attend the annual ceremonies. But the assemblies served their most useful purpose in safeguarding the interests of the municipalities against the excesses of imperial officials, and, in the common bond of mutual protection, they contributed in no slight measure to the breaking up of the old individualistic spirit, especially in the Greek states, and, by uniting all the municipalities in a province in a common interest, they gave birth to the spirit of nationalism; and though the importance of the assemblies had greatly diminished before the empire disintegrated, and though the separatist movement did not always follow the lines of the provincial organization, nevertheless the development of nationalism may be traced in no small measure to the influence of the provincial assemblies.

CHAPTER XIII

THE DEVELOPMENT OF MUNICIPAL POLICY

UNTIL the middle of the fourth century Rome incorporated the peoples of conquered territory in her own state or permitted them to unite with the various members of the Latin League[1]. The ancient conception of the city-state did not allow an unlimited extension of this policy, and the principle of founding Latin colonies was already formulated in 384 B.C. At the close of the war with the Latins in 338 B.C. Rome was for the first time faced with the problem of imperialism. In dealing with her former allies she was fortunately guided by the statesmanship of wise and generous leaders, who repudiated the oriental idea that the sovereign state was entitled to be supported at the expense of the subject peoples. Some of the Latin states, hereafter to be known as *municipia*, were given full Roman citizenship, retaining their own territories and apparently also their own local governments. Others, the *civitates sine suffragio*, were not admitted to full citizenship, but enjoyed the privileges conferred thereby, except the right to vote or to hold office in Rome. These states, also, were left with complete jurisdiction over their local institutions. At the seaport of Antium a Roman colony was founded to which three hundred Roman citizens were assigned. The relation of the colonists to the native population is obscure, but ultimately the two groups were united politically and all enjoyed the privileges of Roman citizenship. Other Latin cities retained their former status and government, but as allied states (*civitates foederatae*) their treaties with

[1] Marquardt, *St. Verw.* I, 21 ff.

[177]

Rome either tacitly or explicitly recognized her supremacy[1]. The Latin colonies, whether founded before or after 338, were bound to Rome in the same relationship which they had formerly had with the Latin League. In all cases Rome controlled their foreign relations, and in the event of war military contingents had to be furnished by every member of the federation to defend the common cause. By this system of graduated relationship and by binding the various states of Latium to herself individually, Rome was able to maintain her supremacy in the federation without difficulty and, as a result of her fair treatment, the various members remained uniformly loyal, and many non-Latin cities voluntarily sought treaties of alliance with the state whose power was so rapidly expanding on the banks of the Tiber.

The treatment of her Latin allies presents in miniature Rome's policy towards the Italian cities and tribes in extending her dominion over the peninsula. Roman and Latin colonies were planted throughout Italy. By friendly negotiations or by war Rome brought every tribe and state from the Apennines to the Sicilian Straits within the sphere of her influence, and by the beginning of the first Punic war Italy formed a federation, under the hegemony of Rome, which was composed of Roman and Latin colonies, *municipia*, *civitates sine suffragio*, and *civitates foederatae*. We hear also of organizations, such as *praefecturae*, *fora*, and *conciliabula*, whose status was beneath that of the more fully developed civic communities. For the most part people living under the tribal form of government were encouraged to settle in municipalities, since the Roman senate preferred to deal with a more stable form of government than was usually found amongst the primitive mountain tribes of Italy. The policy of differentiating the status of the various members of the federation was probably devised as a means of rewarding or punishing those

---

[1] Reid, *Municipalities of the Roman Empire*, 51 *ff.*; Frank, *Roman Imperialism*, 33 *ff.*

communities which had entered the federation willingly or by compulsion, but it also served to prevent disloyal combinations amongst the various states against the supremacy of Rome.

Rome continued her policy of liberalism towards the members of her Italian federation until the close of the third century. The right of Roman citizenship was generously granted to the more favored communities. Common service in the army spread the knowledge of the Roman language and institutions over Italy, and the colonial foundations helped the prefects and praetors in introducing the principles of Roman law throughout the peninsula.

The second Punic war marks a turning-point in the policy of Rome towards the federation. This was due in part to the disintegration of political ideals as a result of the exhausting struggle, and partly to the influence of imperialistic principles acquired from her experiences in provincial government. Members of the federation who had joined Hannibal were punished with the utmost severity. In the century following the close of the war Rome began to regard the federated states as subjects. Roman citizenship was seldom granted to the Latin or Italian cities, and the Latins were no longer invited to share in the colonial foundations of Rome. In many ways the rights of the allies were violated. Fields which had been laid waste or abandoned during the war with Hannibal were apparently regarded as *ager publicus* of Rome, and the allies were deprived of their jurisdiction over them. In 193 the courts were authorized to apply only Roman law to cases of usury[1]. In the Bacchanalian conspiracy (186 B.C.) the senate assumed criminal jurisdiction over Romans, Latins, and allies, condemning all classes with fine impartiality[2]. Other infringements of local rights by Roman magistrates were cited by Gracchus in pleading the cause of the Italians. On the other hand,

[1] Livy, 35. 7.   [2] Livy, 39. 14 *ff*. *Cf.* Bruns, 36.

Roman law was being adopted more and more throughout Italy, and many cities had the privilege of incorporating in their statutes the laws of the Roman senate or assemblies. Rome does not appear to have exerted any influence on the constitutional forms of the allied states, but allowed them to preserve their traditional institutions unchanged. It is possible that Roman commissioners or officials devised charters for some of the cities, but in most cases the changes were made at the request of the municipality itself and were not imposed by Rome. A case in point is the charter devised for Puteoli by Sulla. When colonies were founded, a commission was appointed to draw up their laws. These charters were not necessarily uniform, and doubtless varied in different localities and in different periods, but, in general, the commissioners must have followed the models framed by their predecessors.

The Social war brought the gift of Roman citizenship to all Italians, but it is probable that no immediate changes were made in the forms of municipal government, since the troubled times which followed were not suitable for the settlement of constitutional problems. During the revolutionary period the Italian cities suffered from the tyrannical acts of both senatorial and popular factions. Sulla and his successors freely confiscated the territory of cities unfriendly to their cause, and colonies of veterans were often settled on these lands, where they enjoyed a quasi-municipal organization of their own, independent of the local government. Such a situation was intolerable, and could only be remedied by the fusion of the two classes of citizens. In the cities where the two groups combined, some changes would have to be made in constitutional forms. Probably the *lex Iulia municipalis* was devised to bring some uniformity out of the chaos which had developed in Italy when Italian towns were transformed into Roman municipalities, and in the confusion incident to the civil wars. The Julian law marks the first attempt at uniformity in civic government. The law, however, was limited in scope, and affected only certain details of administration, such as the election and qualifications of officials and decurions and the administration of law. In other respects the municipalities preserved their traditional forms and customs, although it is probable that the tendency to ape Roman institutions had long been active[1], and that, in the course of time, the cities conformed more and more to a uniform pattern.

Rome acquired her first province at the close of the first Punic war, and in Sicily she came into contact with the oriental conception of imperialism, according to which the conquered races paid tribute to the conqueror. Three cities in Sicily were admitted as allies of Rome and five were given the status of *civitates liberae*. The latter were regarded as independent communities, but their right to conduct negotiations with other states was circumscribed, and in actual practice they probably differed but little from the federated states of Italy. The territory of certain cities which had shown bitter hostility to Rome was confiscated and became *ager publicus* of Rome. These cities were called *civitates censoriae*, because the leasing of their land was under the control of the Roman censor. The remainder of Sicily was divided among the *civitates stipendiariae*, which paid an annual tithe of their produce to the sovereign state[2]. In organizing the province a commission was sent out to draw up a *lex provinciae*, which determined the rights and privileges of the various cities in the district. It is uncertain how far the constitutions of the various cities were modified by this law, but it is probable that traditional forms were preserved as far as possible, while the control of the municipal government was placed in the hands of an oligarchy friendly to the conquerors. No attempt was made to

[1] For the *municipia fundana* which had the right in republican times to copy Roman statutes, *cf.* Elmore, *Trans. Am. Phil. Assoc.* 47 (1916), 35 *ff.*
[2] *Cf.* pp. 47 *ff.* On the various theories concerning the *lex Iulia*, *cf.* no. 24.

provide uniform charters for the provincial cities, although the system of collecting the tribute and of administering the law may have tended to standardize the legal and financial administration in the towns within the bounds of each province.

In adding new provinces to their dominion the Romans were guided in some measure by the results of their experience in dealing with older acquisitions. In general the principle of exacting tribute was followed. We also find that some cities were given more liberal privileges than others, probably with the idea of lessening the danger of disloyal combinations in alien lands. In Africa and in the eastern provinces which were thoroughly Hellenized, the Romans found the municipal system generally established, and no changes were made in it, except to modify the government of the more democratic cities by strengthening the oligarchy. It is probable that most of the Greek cities had already become timocratic under the rule of the Macedonian and Seleucid princes[1]. Wherever the civic commonwealths had not fully developed, the Romans set themselves the task of organizing them as soon as possible. New cities were founded or the territory of older ones was extended. In some cases the *territorium* assigned to cities was very extensive, and as the villages developed in importance, new cities were created within the territory of the old. No uniform laws were prescribed for the new foundations so far as we can discover, although Bithynian cities were given senates formed on western models, and the charters of other cities, established by later governors, probably followed similar lines. Great flexibility was permitted, since the political development of the inhabitants and other local conditions were undoubtedly taken into account.

While little effort was made to secure uniformity in municipal government, the legislation of the Gracchi took an important, if ill-advised, step in this direction when

[1] *Cf.* no. 9; Colin, *Rome et la Grèce*, 651 *ff.*

provision was made that the contracts for the collection of the tribute from Asia should be let in the city of Rome. By this law tax-gathering became the special prerogative of the *equites*. They and their agents were absolutely unscrupulous in carrying out their contracts. In raising the quota from each city they held the magistrates and senators responsible for all deficiencies, as well as for loans contracted by the city to meet the obligations to the state. This is well illustrated by the story of the agents of Brutus, who enforced the payment of a loan by shutting up the senators of Cypriote Salamis in the town hall until some of them perished from starvation[1]. The theory of collective liability was probably borrowed from the practice of the old Hellenistic bureaucracy, or it may have developed from the Sicilian custom, where the municipalities often availed themselves of the privilege of farming their own quota of taxes in order to save collectors' profits. The Gracchan legislation applied, in the first instance, to Asia, but the system was soon extended to other provinces. Under these conditions cities suffering from the burden of taxation would insensibly abandon their more democratic institutions by choosing their official class from the wealthier members of the community—a tendency which was, no doubt, fostered by the Romans, whose chief interest was the collection of revenue.

In the administration of law the rights of individual cities were usually defined by the *lex provinciae*. The cities were usually permitted to use their own laws, at all events in certain cases, and the republican senate brought no pressure upon them to adopt the laws of Rome. The governor, however, had large judicial powers, and in issuing his edict he not only followed the provisions of the *lex provinciae*, but also copied extensively from the praetor's edict[2]. In his circuit, therefore, the principles of Roman law were made familiar to the various cities, and just as their law influenced the development of Roman

[1] Cicero, *ad Att.* 6. 2.   [2] Cicero, *ad fam.* 3. 8. 4; *ad Att.* 6. 1. 15.

jurisprudence, so it is probable that many cities, in turn, adopted the better features of Roman law[1].

The colonial policy of the Romans was at first dictated by military requirements, although it served the secondary purpose of providing lands for the indigent populace[2]. Colonial foundations of the Latin type ceased after 181 B.C., and Rome thereafter shared none of the privileges of the new settlements with her Latin allies. In 172 B.C., however, Carteia in Spain was given Latin rights by the *comitia*. An important precedent was thus established by which the provincial lands could be recognized as Italian soil. The foundation of transmarine colonies was not popular at Rome, and Gracchus met with bitter opposition when he attempted to carry his proposal to found a Roman colony on the site of Carthage. After his death the portion of the Rubrian law providing for the settlement of Carthage was repealed. The motives which led the senate to reverse its policy by the foundation of Narbo Martius in 118 B.C. cannot be determined. Thereafter the senatorial party was opposed to colonial foundations beyond the bounds of Italy and bitterly fought the proposals of those democrats who sought to establish colonies in various provinces, and who succeeded in conferring Latin rights on the trans-Padane cities of Northern Italy. Marius initiated the policy of settling his soldiers in colonies of veterans, and later military leaders followed his example. Sulla and Caesar established their veterans, for the most part, on Italian farms confiscated from those opposed to them in the wars. Augustus and later emperors purchased lands for the purpose.

Caesar was the first Roman statesman to comprehend fully the fact that the safety of Rome as the capital of the empire could be secured only by fair and equitable government of the provinces, which now constituted the real source of imperial revenue and power. He and his

[1] Mommsen, *Römisches Strafrecht*, 113 *ff.*
[2] Abbott, *Class. Phil.* 10 (1915), 365 *ff.*

successors devoted their best efforts to administrative problems, and they eliminated most of the abuses which had grown up during republican times. The equestrian order was deprived of its privilege of farming the provincial taxes, and in placing the collection of the imperial revenues as a charge upon the municipalities themselves, the emperors returned to a policy of decentralization. The convenience of this system led to important results in the extension of the municipal organization. Where a district was not sufficiently advanced for self-governing municipal institutions, various devices were adopted. For example, client princes were placed over certain kingdoms in Asia; Egypt was governed through a prefect; Cappadocia was divided into στρατηγίαι; in Thrace we find toparchies; and in Illyria *regiones* were established[1]. In all parts of the empire, however, the rulers fostered the development of municipal life, and by the beginning of the fourth century the whole empire might be considered as a group of administrative units made up of municipalities and imperial estates. Caesar also set an imperial precedent for the practice of regarding the provinces as Roman soil by founding transmarine colonies of Roman citizens, and he thus prepared the way for the grant of citizenship to provincial cities. The *lex Iulia municipalis* played an important rôle in developing the idea that municipal institutions in a particular district or province should be regulated by uniform laws; the reorganization of Gaul by Augustus, and of Spain by Vespasian was undoubtedly governed by this principle.

In the first century of the empire the municipalities were left with a great amount of freedom and independence. Universal peace brought general prosperity. The borders of the empire were for the most part undisturbed, and there were no costly wars to lay any undue burden

[1] For the organization of the provinces, *cf.* Marquardt, *op. cit.* 1, 241 *ff.*; Kuhn, *Die städt. u. bürgerl. Verfassung d. röm. Reichs*, 2, 41 *ff.*; Mommsen, *Roman Provinces, passim.*

upon the imperial treasury. Until the principate was secure, provincial governors were under close scrutiny, since the danger to the succession lay in that quarter. As a result there was a tendency to encourage the independence of the municipalities in their relations to the governor. This may be seen in the revival and extension of the provincial assemblies which served as an important check on the governors, especially in the senatorial provinces, and in the encouragement afforded to embassies which came from the provincial cities direct to Rome. The emperor was universally regarded as the great benefactor who had released the provinces from the iniquities of senatorial government and from the miseries which had befallen them in the last century of the republic. The worship of the imperial godhead, established in every province and in every city, was not inspired by senseless flattery, but by a real sense of obligation. To the emperor, accordingly, the cities were eager to appeal on every conceivable question which affected their interests, although many embassies, from a desire to bring themselves to the imperial notice, were inspired by motives of vanity. It was inevitable that bureaus should be created to handle the great variety of business which was referred to Rome. Thus the paternal benevolence of the central administration and the servility of the local oligarchies reacted constantly on each other, until the central bureaus absorbed local legislative and administrative functions, while the municipal governments gradually lost their political initiative and power.

Under the imperial administration the decline of democracy in the provincial cities continued. In the West the popular assembly had never been important. The people expressed their will largely through their power of election, and this privilege seems to have been transferred to the senate before the beginning of the third century except in the case of a few cities in Africa[1]. The local senate was the chief organ of administration; and

[1] *Cod. Th.* 12. 5. 1 (326).

since its members held office for life, they controlled the
annual magistrates as thoroughly as the Roman senate
had once controlled the consuls. In the East democratic
forms were cherished as a heritage of the past, but it is
doubtful if the popular assemblies had exerted any real
influence on the local administration even during the last
century of the republic[1]. The loss of political instincts in
the mass of the population was fatal to the best interests
of municipal government. During the first century of the
Christian era the administration came more and more
under the control of vested interests which were no longer
held in restraint by the scrutiny of a popular assembly.
In spite of the outward brilliance of municipal life at this
period and the intense rivalry of cities in building public
works and in celebrating magnificent games and spec-
tacles, it is undoubtedly true that corruption and mis-
government flourished. The eagerness with which wealthy
citizens sought high office and undertook expensive
liturgies was not always due to patriotic motives and to
civic pride, but was more often inspired by a desire to
enrich themselves at the expense of the municipality.
Cicero had observed this tendency in Cilicia[2], and Germanicus was called upon to correct the abuses of local
magistrates in the East[3]. Tacitus records the incident of
Atilius of Fidena, who gave a gladiatorial show from
motives of sordid gain, when, by the collapse of the flimsy
stands which he erected, fifty thousand people were
killed or injured[4]. Had we the full records of municipal
history from the standpoint of the common people, we
should undoubtedly find that many a record of brilliant
service carved on enduring marble was amply repaid by
the emoluments of office. Proof of this statement is not
absolutely lacking, for the appointment of imperial agents

[1] *Cf.* pp. 69 *ff.* The Athenian assembly exercised important powers in
the reign of Hadrian; *cf.* no. 90, Chapot, *La prov. rom. proc. d'Asie*, 205 *ff.*
[2] Cicero, *ad Att.* 5. 16. 62.　　[3] Tac. *Ann.* 2. 54.
[4] Tac. *Ann.* 4. 62.

and commissioners was not unknown in the first century; moreover, early in the second century, the *curator rei publicae* was created as a regular official for managing those communities whose internal affairs had become so entangled that the local authorities were incapable of solving their problems[1].

In the first two centuries of the Christian era the great achievement of the empire was the Romanization of the West. The early emperors may have dreamed of accomplishing the same task in the East, but the forces of Greek tradition were too strong to be successfully overcome. The extension of the municipal system in the western provinces was an important factor in this movement, and, as the native population was for the most part unhampered by any cultural traditions, greater uniformity was attainable in the West than was possible in those provinces where Rome came into contact with older civilizations. For the empire as a whole uniformity was impossible; the effective obstacles were the fundamental differences between East and West, the division of administration between the senate and the emperor, and the inequalities of status in the various provincial cities, which continued from republican to imperial times. While few new colonies were founded after the age of Hadrian, the honorary title *colonia* was often conferred upon older cities, although the honor did not, necessarily, involve any change in constitutional forms[2]. Roman citizenship, however, was conferred with great liberality upon individuals and entire communities. Similarly, the *ius Italicum* and *ius Latii* were freely granted to provincial cities[3]. Since provinces were composed of federated, free, and stipendiary communities, and of Roman, Latin, and provincial citizens, uniformity in legislation was difficult. However, the knowledge and use of Roman law, as it was extended over the Roman world, carried the idea of universal legislation.

---

[1] *Cf.* pp. 90 *ff.*; no. 65 *a.*   [2] *Cf.* pp. 71 *ff.*
[3] *R.E. s.v. ius Italicum, ius Latii.*

The regulations in regard to the *fiscus* and the imperial liturgies were undoubtedly universal in their application. In the course of time it is probable that the imperial regulations were adopted by the municipalities to apply to purely local liturgies. Furthermore, the imperial will was supreme in every province, and while it is evident that the earlier emperors legislated for each city individually, yet it is probable that the tendency to frame universal regulations for all parts of the empire steadily developed. An edict of Augustus, lowering the age limit of municipal magistrates, and one of Trajan, forbidding the formation of clubs, were effective in the senatorial province of Bithynia[1]. Finally, the development of bureaucracy implies that the details of administration passed more and more into the hands of the civil service, and it was inevitable that uniform laws should become the prevailing practice in these departments.

The appointment of the *curator rei publicae*, to whose office we have already referred, shows the trend of paternalistic legislation under Trajan[2]. The evidence implies that the office soon became widespread, and if this was the case, inefficiency and corruption in the local municipal administration must have been general. As the personal representative of the emperor, the *curator* played an important part in undermining the power of the local authorities, and in later times he seems to have supplanted them in many cities. The office became so important that Ulpian devoted a special treatise to its duties. The correspondence between Trajan and Pliny shows the attitude of a benevolent and painstakingly conscientious emperor, and reveals the unhappy state into which the cities of Bithynia had fallen, when, for example, one of them could not decide on its own initiative whether a sewer should be covered. Hadrian devoted particular attention to the problems of municipal government in his travels. He also reorganized the civil service and placed it upon a more

[1] Pliny, *Epp. ad Trai.* 34, 79, 92, 93, 96; *cf.* 65.   [2] *Cf.* pp. 90 *ff.*

efficient basis. To him, also, is probably to be ascribed the codification of the provincial edict. By this act the administration of justice by the governor was placed on a uniform basis in the provincial courts.

During the first two centuries of the Christian era the imperial policy in respect to municipal government, in so far as a policy can be discovered, was consistent and uniform. In the third century the attitude of the central government towards the provinces changed. The new policy was due, in part, to the character of the government. The senate was now reduced to a very minor part in the administration, and all the provinces were under the control of the emperor. The army was all-powerful. The emperors, who were usually chosen by it, were not selected from the Roman nobility, but were successful or popular military leaders, unfamiliar with Roman traditions and unacquainted with the problems of civil administration. The government thus became a military autocracy, whose chief concern was the collection of sufficient revenue to secure the loyalty of the legions, and this consideration determined its attitude in framing the imperial policy towards the municipalities in the third century and the later empire.

Professor Rostovtseff has recently advocated the theory that the imperial policy of the third century was dictated by the hostility which existed between the army and the cities[1]. He believes that, since the legions were made up of conscripts drawn from the villages, where they had been exploited by the civic authorities, the peasant soldiers forced the emperors, chosen by them, to avenge past injuries by oppressing the cities. The military autocracy sought to bring about a levelling, politically, socially, and economically, of the wealthy governing class in the cities. Rostovtseff believes, somewhat inconsistently, that the emperors sought to strengthen the municipalities by

[1] Rostovtseff (formerly Rostowzew), *Mus. Belge*, 27 (1923), 233*ff*. *Cf.* nos. 139, 192.

creating a strong peasantry. Here, however, they only succeeded in intensifying the antagonism between town and country. The peasant began to be conscious of his power and looked to the emperor as his protector against the city. We have discussed this theory more fully elsewhere[1]. The chief objection to it is the fact that the majority of the complaints lodged by the villagers in the third century are directed against the soldiers and imperial officials who were supposed to protect them.

Early in the third century the edict of Caracalla, extending the Roman franchise to all provincials, is one of the most important acts of the imperial government in the history of Roman municipal legislation. The motive of the emperor in issuing this edict has been variously interpreted. Cassius Dio, the only ancient historian who refers to it, states that the purpose was to collect more revenue[2]. This might have been done, however, by extending the inheritance tax, hitherto levied only on Romans, to all provincials[3]. Rostovtseff advances the theory that Caracalla, being of non-Roman origin, took delight in reducing the Romans to the same level as the provincials[4]. From the standpoint of municipal history, we believe that the edict served a different purpose, and we venture the following interpretation. Heavy taxation and burdensome liturgies had already begun to press with great severity on the governing bodies of the municipalities, especially since the resources of the empire were dwindling and the cost of administration and defense was increasing. The necessary revenue could not be raised unless the municipal organization continued unimpaired. But, as we have pointed out in our discussion of liturgies, it was more and more difficult to find suitable candidates for public office[5]. Before adopting compulsory legislation, the government had resorted to various devices in order to secure eligible candidates for the local senate and magistracies, chief of

[1] No. 139.   [2] Cf. no. 192.   [3] Hirschfeld, 97.
[4] Cf. p. 190, n. 1.   [5] Cf. pp. 112 ff.

which was the grant of *Latium maius* or *minus*, whereby members of the *curia* or magistrates, respectively, earned the right of Roman citizenship. For a time this legislation may have succeeded in inducing candidates to stand for office, but ultimately it defeated its purpose, since no one who became a Roman citizen could be required to hold office or to perform liturgies in any other city unless he chose to do so voluntarily[1]. Since those chosen for this honor were usually the wealthier citizens, and since the number of Romans steadily increased in each community, the local government became proportionately weaker. It is probable, therefore, that the edict of Caracalla was devised as a means of reviving the municipal administration in non-Roman communities. The *conventus civium Romanorum* disappeared, and all members of the community were placed upon the same footing in regard to municipal obligations. In this way the collection of the imperial revenues was better secured. Furthermore, the edict must have swept away the inequalities in the status of provincial cities. It has been noted that the title *civitas* began to supplant *municipium* and *colonia* about this time, and the distinction between free, federated, and tributary states must have been largely eliminated, although it is probable that the privileges of some cities were renewed or confirmed by special grant. For example, the *ius Italicum* was cherished by a few cities until later times, and Antinoöpolis in Egypt seems to have retained the privileges granted by Hadrian as late as the end of the third century[2]. Unfortunately, the amelioration of conditions in the cities, which was accomplished by the edict, was more than nullified by the famines, plagues, civil wars, and the complete demoralization of economic life in the century which followed. Moreover, the wealthier class was still able to secure exemption from municipal obligations by obtaining the rank of imperial senator.

[1] *Cf.* p. 103, n. 1.
[2] Wilcken, *Chrestomathie*, 397; *cf.* nos. 137, 170, 183, 184.

The social effects of the edict may be seen more clearly in the oriental cities. Here the administration had been controlled by a Greco-Roman oligarchy which was very much in the minority. When all citizens obtained Roman rights, the ruling aristocracy was submerged in a rising tide of orientalism, and as the central government became weaker, the spirit of nationalism began to manifest itself in various provinces. Native law, however, was supplanted by Roman jurisprudence much more rapidly under the new conditions, and it is probable that the municipal courts declined rapidly in the following century. Moreover, since the status of all cities was now the same, and since the military emperors cared little for local traditions, a policy of uniform legislation for the whole empire developed more rapidly. It must not be understood from this that the internal constitutions of all cities were brought into conformity. The imperial government cared little for such details so long as tribute continued to be paid. There is, however, some evidence that local charters were overridden, as for example, in the law which required that magistrates should be elected from among the decurions[1]. Ulpian defined the duties of the *curator rei publicae* in a special treatise, and Arcadius Charisius wrote a book on municipal *munera*. The Digest contains numerous extracts from the jurists dealing with municipal administration. Paulus, Ulpian, Hermogenianus, and others dealt with the office of governor, and his relations with the municipalities were closely defined. The power of veto, the right of making nominations for magistracies and liturgies, the oversight of public works, the formation of the *album*, the administration of justice, the enforcement of laws regarding honors and liturgies, and other details of municipal administration were vested in the governor or *curator*.

[1] The laws in regard to the privileges, responsibilities and status of decurions seem to have been enacted before the time of Ulpian. *Cf. Dig.* 50. 2 *passim.*

The preservation of the municipality as a medium for the collection of revenues offers the best explanation of the imperial policy of the third century. This was undoubtedly the reason why Severus extended the municipal system to Egypt in A.D. 202. The formation of local guilds of workmen in various trades was also dictated by a desire to create a new class that would be responsible for a portion of the liturgies which were pressing so heavily upon the municipalities. We cannot determine at what period the principle of *origo* was extended from the Orient to other parts of the empire. The emperors early recognized that a citizen's birthplace had priority in claiming his services for magistracies and liturgies[1]. According to a law recorded by Ulpian, the provincial governor had the power to compel decurions, who had left their native city, to return and fulfil their obligations in the *curia*[2]. This is the beginning of a long line of legislation dealing with the *curiales*, the purport of which was to bind them to their birthplace and to reduce them to virtual serfdom. This development was slow, but it was accelerated by the legislation of Diocletian, who by separating the civil and military power in the provincial administration and by his subdivision of the empire and the provinces greatly increased the cost of administration. To meet the additional outlay a new system of taxation was devised which not only placed a heavier burden upon the subject peoples, but also forced them to exploit their lands to the point of exhaustion.

The imperial policies of the fourth and fifth centuries do not differ from those of the third, except that the emperors resorted to more desperate expedients in order to preserve the civic organization. The *curiales* and members of guilds were bound to their order and their place of

---

[1] This principle seems to be indicated in the *lex provinciae* of Bithynia when Pompey forbade the cities to grant rights of citizenship to anyone who was already citizen of another town within the bounds of the province, Pliny, *Epp. ad Trai.* 114.   [2] *Dig.* 50. 2. 1.

origin, and all citizens transmitted their rank and their profession in hereditary succession to their descendants. The misery of the civilian population was aggravated by the oppression of the bureaucracy, whose members exploited the provincials in every conceivable way. The last great act of imperial charity was the creation of the office of *defensor plebis*, whose duty it was to protect the common people and to safeguard their interests. How far he succeeded it is impossible to say. In the later empire he seems to have joined with the wealthy proprietors in their work of spoliation. He also contributed to the weakening of the powers of the local municipal magistrates, especially in legal and in administrative functions[1].

We have traced elsewhere the results of Rome's failure to develop a sound social, political, and economic policy in municipal administration[2]. Her statesmen were usually opportunists, and few clearly defined policies which were steadily or consciously pursued can be discovered. The greatest achievement of Rome was the extension of the municipal system over the greater part of her empire, thereby preparing the way for the more rapid infiltration of the cultural ideas of the age. One of the gravest defects in her policy was the preservation of the particularism of the ancient city-state. Had the provincial councils been allowed to develop, they might have created an organization along modern lines where there would have been cooperation for the common good, and where a national consciousness might have arisen which would have united and strengthened the empire. As it was, each city was encouraged to preserve its individuality as an isolated unit. More fatal still was the elimination of the democracy as a factor in local government. Thus the mass of the people was deprived of the power of exercising its political instincts. An irresponsible oligarchy gained control of the municipal administration, and the way was opened for widespread corruption and inefficiency. Finally the central

---

[1] *Cf.* pp. 92 *ff.*   [2] *Cf.* pp. 197 *ff.*

government was compelled to come to the rescue, but the statesmen of that age could discover no other remedy for the situation than by the creation of new bureaus and by the multiplication of officials. When the imperial power became a military autocracy, the city was regarded chiefly as a convenient agent for the collection of taxes to support the army and the bureaucracy, and thereafter the preservation of this instrument was the motive of all legislation dealing with municipal institutions.

CHAPTER XIV

THE DECLINE OF ROMAN MUNICIPALITIES

"THE world," wrote Tertullian[1], "is every day better known, better cultivated, and more civilized than before. Everywhere roads are traced, every district is known, every country opened to commerce. Smiling fields have invaded the forests; flocks and herds have routed the wild beasts; the very sands are sown; the rocks are broken up; the marshes drained. There are now as many cities as there were formerly cottages. Reefs and shoals have lost their terrors. Wherever there is a trace of life there are houses, human habitations, and well ordered governments." While the rhetorical exaggeration of this panegyric of the Roman world under Aurelius may be readily discounted, and exceptions to the general happiness and content may be granted, the prosperity of the empire in the first and second centuries of its history is everywhere apparent. In the long era of peace trade and commerce developed unhindered, and agricultural or industrial communities were free from the wastage of foreign wars and internal strife. Municipal institutions spread far and wide until the empire became in great part an aggregate of city-states. In each of these the citizens displayed an intense pride in public welfare, and endowed their native town with splendid monuments, buildings, and gifts for special purposes, such as libraries and schools. Offices and honors were eagerly sought, and lavish contributions were made in attaining them. Public spirited citizens, civic pride, and keen urban rivalries combined to produce a brilliant municipal life throughout the empire.

[1] Tertullian, *de anima*, 30 (Ferrero's translation).

THE DECLINE OF ROMAN MUNICIPALITIES

In bitter contrast to the prosperity of the early days of the empire, the records of the fourth century present a far different picture. The citizens now sought every possible means of avoiding public service. Oppressed by heavy burdens of taxation and liturgies, they often preferred to abandon their property and take refuge in flight rather than discharge their obligations. Local senates no longer had members sufficient in numbers to preserve the municipal organization, and many cities had degenerated into villages, or had been completely abandoned. The law codes are filled with references to deserted *curiae* and fugitive citizens[1]. Desperate remedies were applied to restore civic life, but so severe was their nature that the process of decline was aggravated. It is everywhere apparent that the ancient city-state had become bankrupt in its social, political, and economic life, and had passed into the hands of an imperial receivership administered by an autocratic bureaucracy.

The problem of the decay of municipal institutions has not received the same attention as the decline of the empire, but the factors which determined the fate of each were essentially the same, for the vitality of a nation depends on the strength of its component parts. Many theories have been set forth to account for the disintegration of Roman power, of which none can be accepted as the sole explanation[2]. Many factors played a part, and the most difficult problem, after the lapse of centuries, is to determine their relative importance. In some cases purely local conditions, such as the shifting of trade-routes, or

[1] *Cod. Th.* 12. 1. 6 (319), 11 (325), 13 (326), 22 (336), 24 (338), 25 (338), 40 (353), 43 (355), 49 (361), 63 (370), *et alia*.
[2] There is a good summary and critique of theories advanced by earlier scholars in *Am. Hist. Rev.* 20 (1915), 724 *ff*. *Cf.* Declareuil, *Quelques problèmes d'histoire des institutions municipales au temps de l'Empire romain*; Hadley, *Rome and the World Today*; Heitland, *The Roman Fate*; Ferrero, *The Ruin of Ancient Civilization*; Seeck, *Geschichte des Untergangs der antiken Welt*; Simkhovitch, "Rome's Fall Reconsidered," one of the essays in *Towards a Better Understanding of Jesus*; Heitland, *Iterum*.

the exhaustion of mines, clay deposits, or forests, affected the prosperity of communities depending upon them. It is our purpose, however, to outline briefly the history of the political, social, and economic developments in municipal life under the empire, and to determine if possible what factors were universally operative in reducing municipal institutions to their unhappy plight in the fourth century.

The most important problem of statecraft in the Roman Empire was the adjustment of the political relations between the central government and the municipalities. The civic organization had been retained wherever the Romans found it existing, as a convenient unit of administration; and where the native population lived under a more primitive social organization, municipal government was introduced as soon as it was found practicable to do so. The cities already established in conquered territory were deprived of their military authority, and usually lost, or were seriously limited in, the power of conducting negotiations with other states. The privilege of using their own laws in their courts was highly prized by them, and the right was sometimes accorded, but in most cases the law was administered by the governor in accordance with the provisions of his own edict[1]. The Romans seldom concerned themselves with constitutional changes in subject cities, but since they preferred to deal with a stable oligarchy rather than with a fickle democracy, the popular assemblies gradually ceased to exercise any power, and the senate became the chief organ of municipal government[2]. Theoretically, each municipality was responsible for the administration of its own territory, but governors often found excuses, legitimate or otherwise, for interference. The system of farming out the collection of taxes to *publicani* was especially fruitful in involving the cities in financial troubles; and in the regulation of these and other matters the decision of the governor was final.

[1] *Cf.* pp. 48 *ff.*   [2] *Cf.* pp. 186 *ff.*

THE DECLINE OF ROMAN MUNICIPALITIES

With the establishment of the empire the position of the subject races improved immeasurably. The paternalistic administration relieved the provincials from the countless exactions of the old *régime*, and the emperor was always willing to hear complaints and to remedy them. It is little wonder that the cities regarded the head of the state as an all-wise, all-powerful, and beneficent prince, and we may well believe that their decrees of adulation were thoroughly sincere. Partly from gratitude, partly from servility, they constantly referred their difficulties to the emperor, and the roads to Rome were thronged with embassies from senatorial and imperial provinces alike. This practice led to the creation of bureaucratic offices which, once inaugurated, tended to perpetuate themselves. Since a great number of problems were decided by the central administration, precedents and rules of procedure were established which were ultimately incorporated in laws and applied to the whole empire without regard to local charters or privileges. The bureaus thus played an extremely important part in transferring the legislative functions of the municipal governments to Rome, and in clearly defining the relations of the provincial governors to the cities by formulating universal laws in regard to the magistracies, the *curator*, the *defensor*, the decurions, the liturgies, and other details of civic life[1].

While the legislative functions of municipal governments had largely passed into the hands of the central authorities by the beginning of the third century, the usurpation of administrative powers was a matter of slow growth. The sporadic practice of sending out imperial commissions, vice-imperial prefects, and special agents (*curatores*) who controlled the expenditure of money from the imperial treasury, gave way to a more systematic control of municipal affairs under Trajan. In his reign many cities had become involved in serious difficulties either through mismanagement of their funds, or decline

[1] *Cf.* pp. 84 *ff.*

in their revenues, and special officers were appointed by the imperial government to examine and regulate methods of civic administration. There were two classes of these, the *curator rei publicae* (λογιστής) and the *legatus Augusti ad corrigendum statum liberarum civitatum*, more commonly known as *corrector* (διορθωτής or ἐπανορθωτής). In a few instances in the East the titles were combined.

The *curator rei publicae*[1] was found in all parts of the empire, and apparently very few cities escaped his supervision. Although he was elected in later times by the local senate, he probably retained the dignity of an imperial agent, outranking the other magistrates and gradually usurping their functions. As controller of the revenues and public lands, and possessing the right of veto, the *curator* played an important rôle in undermining the institutions, and in paralyzing the political initiative and independence of the municipalities with which he came in contact. The *corrector* exercised functions somewhat similar to those of the *curator*, but his powers were greater[2]. This official was usually appointed in senatorial provinces, in free cities (*liberae civitates*), and in Italy and Sicily, and was a powerful factor in bringing those municipalities enjoying special privileges to the same footing as other towns in the empire. He also paved the way for the transfer of senatorial provinces to imperial jurisdiction.

In the latter half of the fourth century the office of *defensor civitatis* (*plebis*) was created, primarily, to safeguard the interests of the common people[3]. While his duties were ill-defined at first, his high rank, long tenure of office, and the privilege of easy access to the governor or his superiors soon gave the *defensor* such prestige that the other municipal authorities were completely overshadowed, and by the beginning of the fifth century he was the sole magistrate in many towns. There is ample evidence that he sometimes allied himself with the land-holders and

---

[1] Liebenam, *Philol.* 56 (1897), 290 *ff.*; *R.E. s.v. curator*; *cf.* pp. 90 *ff.*
[2] *R.E. s.v. corrector.*   [3] *R.E. s.v. defensor; cf.* pp. 92 *ff.*

cruelly oppressed the people whom he was supposed to protect. The office thus fell into disrepute, and in the reorganization effected by Justinian it became a liturgy imposed upon the leading citizens in rotation.

The provincial governor in the republican period was supreme in the territory over which he exercised jurisdiction. His powers were limited only by the *lex provinciae*, his own conscience, and the force of public opinion at Rome. Verres in Sicily and Cicero in Cilicia busied themselves with the details of municipal administration, and the former had little regard for the interests or privileges of the cities under his authority[1]. In the early empire the rights of the towns were more jealously guarded, especially in senatorial provinces, and many cities, disregarding the governor, appealed directly to Rome. The correspondence of Pliny reveals how far he was restricted in initiative even in matters of trifling detail[2]. In the latter part of the second century the governor exercised more extensive powers. He had the privilege—frequently exercised—of taking part in the deliberations of the local senates, and of making nominations for magistracies and liturgies[3]. Since civilians were usually responsible as sureties for the candidates whom they nominated, the governor was called upon to exercise this duty more and more frequently as the burdens of office and public service became more oppressive[4]. If any candidate refused to hold office or to discharge a liturgy, the governor had the power to compel him to do so. Many other matters of municipal administration came under his jurisdiction, such as the formation of the *album*, the construction of public works, the sending of embassies, and the enforcement of the laws regarding *curiales* and guilds[5]. In the reorganization of the empire effected by Diocletian, the limitation of the size of the provinces

[1] Cicero, *in Verr.* 2. 15, 22, 24, 25, 40; Cowles, *Gaius Verres*, 27 *ff*.
[2] *Cf.* pp. 149 *ff*.   [3] *Dig.* 49. 4. 1, 3, 4; *cf.* pp. 85 *ff.*, 98 *ff*.
[4] *Cf.* pp. 97 *ff*.
[5] *Dig.* 1. 16. 18; 50. 3. 1, 2; 50. 4. 3, 8, 9; 50. 10. 2, 3, 5; *cf.* pp. 193 *ff*.

greatly increased the powers of the governor by enabling him to exercise a closer supervision of the municipalities within his district.

While the growth of vast imperial and private estates checked the spread of municipal institutions, it is difficult to determine how far the presence of such estates in municipal territories limited the administrative powers of the local authorities. In the civil wars of the third century and in the late empire when the central government was powerless to check the oppressive exactions of the bureaucratic officials or the ravages of lawless troops and local brigands, individual citizens, and sometimes entire villages, placed themselves under the protection of some wealthy landlord[1]. As a result their properties passed from municipal control, although the local senate was still liable for the taxes on such lands. The emperors sought in vain to check the growth of private patronage. The owners of the great estates were able to defy the tax-collectors; and since any deficiency in the quota of taxes assessed upon the municipality had to be made up by the *curiales*, many of them were impoverished by the increase of *latifundia*, and the municipal organization was so seriously weakened that it ceased to fulfil its functions in many cities[2]. The same effect was produced by the development of great imperial estates which rapidly increased in all parts of the empire through bequests, fines, and confiscations[3]. Not only were these lands withdrawn as a source of municipal revenue, but tenants of the emperor were exempted from municipal charges. In 342 a law was passed by which *curiales* who leased less than twenty-five *iugera* were required to discharge their curial obligations, but in view of the increasing difficulty of finding

---

[1] Zulueta, *de patrociniis vicorum*; Libanius, *de patrociniis*, 4 *ff*.
[2] Libanius, *loc. cit.*; *cf.* no. 190.
[3] Mommsen, *Strafrecht*, 1005 *ff*.; *Cod .J.* 10. 38. 1 (396); nos. 90, 157.

suitable tenants, it is doubtful if the law was ever rigidly enforced[1].

The extant municipal charters show that the local magistrates had jurisdiction over civil and criminal cases within certain limits[2]. The *lex provinciae* probably defined the right of individual cities in the administration of justice. In cases where local jurisdiction was not permitted, the law was administered by the governor or by his agents delegated for the purpose[3]. The governor's edict, according to which he dispensed justice in his circuit, was based on that of the Roman praetor, and was instrumental in spreading familiarity with Roman jurisprudence among the provincials. In Spain and Gaul the native law was primitive and had little importance under Roman rule. Under the republic the Greek cities clung jealously to their own legal system, and valued the right to use their own laws as an evidence of fancied autonomy. While the influence of Greek jurisprudence may be traced in the Byzantine age, the existence of local courts is rarely proved after the third century[4]. In the imperial period the Roman law and the Roman courts seem to have grown steadily in favor. Various causes may have influenced this development. The dominance of the state and of imperial legislation, the partiality and corruption of a local judiciary in an oligarchical government, the appointment of *iuridici* in Spain and Italy and of *curatores rei publicae* in provincial cities, the right of appeal, and the extension of Roman citizenship all tended to weaken the local courts and extend the use of Roman law. The reorganization of the provinces by Diocletian gave the civil governor (now usually styled *iudex*) greater opportunity to supervise the administration of justice. Legislation enabling the governor to decide cases summarily without the assistance of a

1 *Cod. Th.* 12. 1. 33 (342); no. 142.
2 Nos. 27, 64, 65; *cf.* pp. 60 *ff.*
3 Chapot, *La prov. rom. proc. d'Asie*, 352 and note.
4 *Cf.* no. 133 and *CIL.* III, 412 for late examples of municipal courts.

THE DECLINE OF ROMAN MUNICIPALITIES

bench of *iudices*[1], and to appoint judges (*iudices pedanei*) for petty cases must have weakened the power of local magistrates very considerably[2]. The Codes of Theodosius and Justinian scarcely mention them in a judicial capacity[3]. In the fourth century the *defensor plebis* and the Christian bishops probably absorbed whatever judicial power still remained in the hands of the local magistrates. While resort to the ecclesiastical courts was purely voluntary, their simplified procedure and the moral weight of their decisions made them so popular that they attracted cases even from the courts presided over by the governor[4].

As the political institutions of the municipalities were decaying, the structure of their social life was being slowly transformed. The citizens might be divided into two great classes, those who were under obligation to discharge municipal liturgies, and those who were exempt from such burdens. The privilege of exemption was enjoyed by priests of the local and provincial cults, soldiers and veterans, members of the imperial bureaucracy, a limited number of physicians and teachers in each community, and, after the beginning of the fourth century, by officers of the Jewish and Christian churches. But the most important group was composed of those who held patents of imperial nobility, for in their hands was concentrated the wealth of the municipality. The passion for imperial honors almost became a mania amongst provincials, and the emperors bestowed the grant freely, either as a means of purchasing the loyalty of the provinces, or as a source of revenue, or as a reward for public service. The privileges of the senatorial order were hereditary, and in the fourth century, when municipal duties became a burden to

---

[1] Arnold, *Roman Provincial Administration*, 189.
[2] *Cod. Th.* 1. 16. 8 (362). The office of *iudex* as a municipal liturgy is referred to in *Dig.* 50. 4. 18, 14. *Cf.* Mitteis, *Reichsrecht und Volksrecht* and *Grundzüge zur Papyruskunde*.
[3] *Cod. Th.* 8. 5. 1 (315); 11. 31. 3 (368).
[4] Vinogradoff, *Cam. Med. Hist.* 1, 565 *f.*

citizens, the titles of nobility were illegally purchased or fraudulently assumed by wealthy families in order that they might escape their local obligations. This evil became so serious that the order of *curiales* was in danger of disappearing in many cities, and the emperors sought to remedy conditions by cancelling all honors illegally secured, and by raising the standard of requirements for future grants. In 390 the hereditary privileges were withdrawn, except in the case of the highest rank (*illustres*), and three years later it was decreed that the property of those receiving senatorial honors should remain subject to its former liturgies. Theodosius II finally closed the ranks of the nobility to those of curial origin.

In the fourth century the *curiales* constituted the great middle class in the municipalities, and they were grouped by the laws into a distinct order composed of all citizens eligible for public office, or capable of discharging the liturgies imposed for the maintenance of civic and imperial administration[1]. In consequence of their oppressive burdens members of this class attempted in every possible way to escape from their order, and the emperors were continually devising legislation to hold them to their obligations. Membership became hereditary, and no one could leave his native place except on pain of discharging the liturgies of his former as well as of his new home. He was even forbidden to take up his residence on his country estate to escape the liturgies of the city. No one of curial birth could enter the army, the clerical orders, the monastic life, the imperial service, the guilds, or the service of a wealthy proprietor as a steward or a *colonus*. The goal of imperial honors was only possible under conditions which were made increasingly difficult, and was finally denied to *curiales* altogether. Those who sought to enter any order or profession which carried the privilege of exemption from liturgies, were compelled to return to their former station. The emperors finally found a simple

---

[1] *Cf.* pp. 112*ff.*

remedy to prevent defection from the order by attaching the liturgies to the estate instead of to the individual. Property of *curiales* could not be sold without the consent of the governor or of the *curia*. The purchaser of such an estate assumed the civic liabilities attached to it. Bequests to non-members of the order were penalized by partial confiscation, and special legislation was devised in regard to the property of heiresses who married outside of their order or of their city. In spite of the laws, the *curiales* steadily diminished in number, although they were recruited in various ways. Sons of veterans who did not enter the army were regularly enrolled, although it is difficult to see what strength they could have given to the order. On occasion, plebeians and members of guilds who had acquired a certain amount of wealth were compelled to join[1]. Provincial governors even condemned criminals to the order as a punishment, although it is probable that such cases were limited to those of curial origin, or to those who were avoiding military service[2].

Members of guilds of various trades were granted partial immunity from liturgies in return for some specific duty which they undertook for the common weal[3]. Most of these guilds were in the imperial service, such as the alimentation of Rome, the mint, the mines, the factories for textiles and arms, and the like. A few were under the control of the municipal authorities and their members were required to act as firemen, to provide for public baths, to furnish entertainment in the theatres, or to discharge other duties. While we are fully informed about the imperial guilds, the Codes give little attention to the municipal corporations, but it is probable that the legislation governing the former applied to the latter as well.

---

[1] The fullest treatment of the subject of guilds may be found in Waltzing, *Études historiques sur les corporations professionnelles chez les Romains*; cf. *R.E. s.v. collegium*; Abbott, *The Common People of Ancient Rome*, 205 ff.; Declareuil, *op. cit.* 153 ff., 185 ff.

[2] Declareuil, *op. cit.* 192 f.   [3] Cf. pp. 107 ff.

THE DECLINE OF ROMAN MUNICIPALITIES

In 337 Constantine granted complete exemption to a large number of trades in the municipalities, without specifying that they should be united in corporations for any special duty, but the evidence from inscriptions would lead us to believe that the guilds had become universal, at least throughout the western provinces, by that time. Early in the fifth century all citizens of towns were required to enroll themselves either in the order of *curiales* or in one of the guilds[1].

Under the early empire the service rendered to the state by the guild was not compulsory, and partly by grants of immunity, partly by pay, the government was willingly served. But in time the burdens became intolerable. Membership became hereditary, and the choice of a profession was no longer a matter of personal preference but of birth[2]. Once enrolled in a guild, no member could escape, and he was confined for life to his profession and his place of origin[3]. One suspects that this legislation was devised in favor of vested interests as a means of controlling the supply of labor, but it is also possible that it was demanded by the guilds themselves to protect their own organization when the duties imposed upon them became so heavy that it was difficult to retain their membership. Be that as it may, the most important source for recruiting new *curiales* was closed, and the development of trades and industries in new places was checked because the free movement of skilled labor ceased.

The only class in the municipalities not affected by imperial legislation was the proletariat or *ima plebs*. The practice of Rome in maintaining this parasitic element by public charity was unfortunately widely copied, and

---

[1] *Cod. Th.* 12. 1. 179 (415). This law does not reappear in the Justinian code and may not have been long enforced.

[2] *R.E. s.v. collegium.*

[3] In 371 Valentinian ordered that *navicularii* should be *perpetuo obnoxii functioni* (*Cod. Th.* 13. 5. 14). Other guilds were soon brought under the same regulations (Declareuil, *op. cit.* 186).

imposed a serious charge on the civic budget. Not only that, but the glamour of ancient urban life attracted labor from farms and other industries where a bare livelihood was gained by arduous toil. In the city one could be fed and amused at the expense of the state, and when the *capitatio plebeia* was removed from the residents of the towns, we cannot wonder that the urban movement went on apace.

This survey of the social organization in the fourth century reveals the deplorable plight into which the citizens of the municipalities had fallen. While it is doubtless true that the heavy taxes and the oppressive liturgies contributed a great deal to the distress of the *curiales* and guilds, these burdens could have been borne if they had been imposed while the municipalities were enjoying uninterrupted prosperity. But it is clear that the favorable economic conditions which prevailed in the first century had given way to widespread and long continued depression. The population was decreasing in numbers, and the revenues of the towns as well as the wealth of the citizens were diminishing. There was grave danger that the municipal organization, which was still of the highest importance, especially as an instrument of tax-gathering, might disappear. This was the compelling reason which led the central government to interfere in municipal administration, to build up elaborate bureaucratic machinery, and to devise stringent legislation controlling the private life of the individual citizen.

In studying the economic conditions of municipal life in the ancient world we must bear in mind that the industrial city of the modern type was unknown. Labor costs were practically uniform throughout the empire, and inland towns could not build up a foreign trade because of the difficulties and costs of transportation. Only in cases where there was a monopoly of some natural product, such as papyrus, dyes, metals, special clays, or finer grades of wool, could industries develop and compete successfully in distant markets. Cities favored by

[209]

exceptional facilities for transportation, either on some great trade-route or with easy access to the sea, often developed important industries, but manufacturers usually depended on the local market within the bounds of their own *territorium*[1]. In the vast majority of cases the wealth of the city and the prosperity of its industries depended upon the economic welfare of its agricultural class. In the modern world all industrial activities are powerfully affected in normal times by rich harvests or by the failure of crops; and in the ancient world industry and agriculture were even more closely related. Besides, the revenues of the cities were largely derived from public lands, and the majority of wealthy citizens were owners of great estates. It is, therefore, apparent that the most powerful factors affecting both public and private economic life must be sought in an investigation of agricultural conditions throughout the empire.

There is ample ,vidence that the soil was being gradually exhausteu in the older provinces even under the republic[2]. The early colonial assignments were seven *iugera*. These were increased to thirty by Gracchus and to sixty-six by Caesar[3]. While it might be unsafe to draw the inference that land which once supported nine persons hardly sufficed for one at the beginning of the empire, yet the increased area of the later assignments is significant of a progressive decline in fertility. Columella, writing about A.D. 60, states that a fourfold return in grain was unknown on Italian farms at that time[4]. The soil of Sicily, Sardinia, Spain, Gaul, and Africa was exhausted in turn. The eastern empire undoubtedly gained its longer lease of life from the bounty of the Nile and the rich lands bordering on the Black Sea. As the soil grew sterile,

[1] Westermann, *Am. Hist. Rev.* 20 (1915), 724 *ff.*; Meyer, *Kleine Schriften*, 79 *ff.*; *R.E. s.v. Industrie.*

[2] Weber, *Handwörterbuch der Staatswissenschaft, s.v. Agrärgeschichte*; Simkhovitch, *Political Science Quarterly*, 31 (1916), 201 *ff.*; Heitland, *Agricola.*

[3] Mommsen, *Ges. Schr.* 2. 87 *ff.*   [4] Columella, 3. 3.

agriculture became unprofitable and farms were abandoned. Under such conditions there would naturally be a shift of the agricultural population to more fertile areas, but the law of *origo*, which forbade the free movement of settlers from one municipal territory to another, was fatal to the best interests of agricultural development. The poorer farmers had the choice of two alternatives, either to join the urban movement, or to attach themselves to some patron as his *coloni*. The problem of resettling the waste fields was attacked by all the emperors. Augustus and his successors founded colonies. Tiberius forced capitalists to invest in lands[1]. Nerva spent sixty million sesterces in purchasing estates to be distributed among farmers[2]. Generous alimentary laws were enacted for the support of the agricultural classes. Veterans were given free allotments. Pertinax allowed squatters to occupy uncultivated fields, even on imperial estates, and if they brought their land under cultivation, full title of ownership was granted[3]. Three years' exemption from taxes was also allowed. Later more drastic legislation was attempted. Owners of fertile fields were required to take over deserted plots, and taxes were imposed in order to compel them to cultivate these lands. This system, called *adiectio*[4], was oppressive and naturally unpopular, and was finally abandoned in 412. Restrictive laws were also drafted. An owner who found his estate unprofitable was forbidden to sell his farm slaves without a proportionate amount of his land[5]. The slaves were thus bound to the soil; and the same law was ultimately applied to the tenants or *coloni*[6].

---

[1] Tac. *Ann.* 6. 16, 17; Suet. *Tib.* 48. Trajan required provincials who were candidates for office in Rome to invest a third of their wealth in Italian real estate (Pliny, *Epp.* 6. 1. 9).

[2] Heitland, *Agricola*, 272.   [3] Herodian, 2. 4, 6.

[4] *Cod. J.* 11. 58. 1; 11. 59. 5 (364–375), 9 (394), 11 (400), 14 (415), 16 (419).

[5] *Cod. J.* 11. 48. 2 (357), 6 (366), 7, 8.

[6] The *coloni* were virtually bound to the soil by the legislation of Constantine (Heitland, *op. cit.* 393 *ff.*).

It was also forbidden to sell a fertile part of an estate without a proportionate amount of sterile land[1]. That all these measures failed in their purpose may be seen from the fact that in 395 there were over half a million *iugera* of deserted farms in the single district of Campania[2].

The exhaustion of the soil was due in large measure to the primitive methods of agriculture which had been inherited from prehistoric times[3]. Such antiquated tools were used that two or even three plowings were necessary before the ground was ready for seeding. Shallow cultivation was the rule, and the resources of the subsoil were never tapped. Under these conditions the surface soil soon lost its accumulated store of humus. The supply of natural fertilizer was insufficient to restore the necessary elements to the land when it had become impoverished by frequent cropping. Artificial fertilizers were not available, and the modern practice of restoring nitrogenous elements by sowing clover was unknown. While the theory of rotation of crops was familiar to writers on agriculture, the majority of the farmers preferred to allow the land to lie fallow in alternate years[4]. It cannot be determined whether the general desiccation, which spread over central Asia about the beginning of the Christian era, extended also over the Mediterranean basin and affected the fertility of the soil; but it is probable that cities of Syria and northern Africa developed under conditions of greater humidity than now prevail in those regions.

Deforestation played a large part in destroying agricultural lands. As cities developed, the hills were stripped of forests to supply building material. As a result the moisture was not conserved in the ground, and the rain, flowing in torrential streams down the mountain-sides, not only left them bare of soil, as they are at the present

---

1 Simkhovitch, *op. cit.* 237; *Cod. J.* 11. 59. 10 (398).
2 *Cod. Th.* 11. 28. 2 (395).
3 Simkhovitch, *Political Science Quarterly*, 28 (1913), 383 ff.
4 Heitland, *op. cit.* 291.

day, but also filled up the water-courses in the plains below, creating malarial swamps where rich fields had once supported a large population. In Syria ruins of numberless towns are found in a region where wastes of barren rock now render the country absolutely impossible for human habitation. Yet this district once supported a great population enriched by the culture of the vine and olive. Recent investigation has shown that lumber was once plentiful in this region, and that the reckless stripping of the forests on the hillsides was the chief cause of the desolation which exists today[1]. In Greece, Italy, and in fact in every part of the Mediterranean basin where forests could be exploited for their lumber, the same process may be traced[2].

Not only was the fertility of the soil declining, but other adverse economic conditions faced the agricultural class. Those settled in the older provinces were brought into competition with farmers exploiting the virgin soil of each new addition to the empire. In particular, Egypt was not only endowed with a marvellous system of transportation, but also renewed its rich fertility annually. Although Egypt as a granary was a source of strength to the empire, its possession dealt a serious blow to agriculture in other provinces where the yield per acre and per unit of labor was immeasurably less. Moreover, the great estates which rapidly developed in every province could be worked more economically than the small farm[3]. The owner of small holdings was compelled either to exploit his land and exhaust it more rapidly, or to bring larger areas under cultivation, although the latter alternative was almost impossible because of the difficulty of securing labor. In

[1] Butler, *Geographical Review*, 9 (1920), 78 ff.

[2] *Cf.* no. 118. The effects of deforestation in Greece and Italy are well known, but no study of the ancient problem has yet been made.

[3] On the great estates there was greater opportunity for diversity of crops, and probably more scientific methods were followed there than on the small farms. The wealthier landowner could tide over a succession of bad years in certain crops where his poorer rival must succumb.

the era of peace which followed the establishment of the empire, cheap slaves disappeared from the market, and the constant demand for recruits for the army drained the country districts of their vigorous manhood[1]. The poorer farmers were unable to meet the new conditions and many became involved in debt to the wealthy proprietors in their neighborhood. In the course of time they were obliged to surrender their property in payment of debts, and many were compelled to work out their obligations by remaining on their farms as tenants, and thus the way was prepared for the introduction of the colonate. Others abandoned their farms and flocked to the cities to be supported by municipal charities[2].

The lack of a cheap and adequate system of transportation was a most serious handicap to farmers living in inland districts. Grain is a difficult commodity to transport by land, and only those living within easy access to waterroutes could hope to compete in distant markets. In the fourth century even the sea became practically closed to free commerce, partly because of the rigorous control of shipping by the government and partly because of civil wars. In the case of those farmers who were compelled to seek a market within the limits of their own township, prices were often controlled by the system of municipal charities whereby grain was purchased at a fixed price and distributed to the proletariat as a free gift, or at a nominal charge. Where transportation was difficult, the burden on the agricultural class was further increased by the heavy cost in time and labor of the liturgies imposed for convoying supplies for the army, or for the taxes paid in kind. The charges for the imperial post were particularly severe, especially in the later empire.

Municipalities not only suffered a loss in revenues from the decline in value of their public lands, but also lost

[1] The *aurum tironicum* was later substituted, *cf. Journ. Rom. Stud.* 8 (1918), 26 *ff.*
[2] Heitland, *op. cit.* 336 to end, *passim.*

large portions of their territory, either through enforced sales to discharge public indebtedness, or by confiscation. Some of the emperors regarded municipal ownership lightly, and rounded out their own estates or gave generous gifts to friends from this source[1]. Prosperous villages often gained municipal status, and were assigned a part of the territory of their mother city. Similar losses were incurred in the anarchy which prevailed during long periods of wars, when fortified villages usually became isolated and independent communities (*castra, oppida*). Some of these villages adopted the magistracies and forms of municipal administration, but the majority were governed by an imperial or municipal official such as a *curator, defensor,* or *magister vici*[2]. In consequence of the development of private patronage, as we have already seen, village-communities and private property passed out of the control of the municipalities. On the other hand, gifts and endowments in the early empire were often made by transferring landed estates to a commonwealth. The problem of making an endowment perpetual was a matter of genuine concern in the ancient world, and the method devised by Pliny, though expensive, probably represented the best policy which the jurists could devise in that age[3]. He also confesses the defect in the system which must have applied to all public leases, especially to those of short terms, namely, that the lessee was prone to exploit the land during the tenure of his contract, and to surrender the property at the expiration of the lease with its value seriously depreciated. A certain amount of territory was acquired through fines, but this source disappeared as the local magistrates lost judicial power. The estates abandoned by *curiales* could be added to the territorial possessions after three years, but it is doubtful if such additions were any gain[4]. If property could not be successfully managed

---

[1] Nos. 90, 157.   [2] Declareuil, *op. cit.* 310 *ff.*   [3] Pliny, *Ep.* 7. 18.
[4] *Cod. J.* 10. 59. 1. The property of decurions who died intestate went to the curia in later times (*Cod. Th.* 5. 2. 1).

under private ownership, it was likely to be still less profitable under public administration.

Shortly before the second Punic war a law was passed forbidding Roman senators to engage in foreign trade[1]. This legislation was destined to play an important part in the history of Roman agriculture, for the senatorial class was forced to invest in land. The possession of great estates soon became desirable in acquiring social prestige, and the growth of *latifundia* began. But the prosperity of an agricultural state rests on the welfare of the small independent farmers in the community. This class, as we have seen, gradually disappeared as a few acquired wealth and gained senatorial honors, while the vast majority, unable to meet the competition of great estates or foreign producers, either joined the urban movement, or became tenants. As land became concentrated in the hands of a few, who were usually exempt from municipal obligations by virtue of their title of imperial nobility, the burdens of taxation and liturgies for the remaining citizens were greatly increased. Since the *curiales* were usually land-owners, their increasing charges became intolerable as their property steadily depreciated. In order to meet these charges, they were forced to exploit the land still more, and the process of deterioration was thus accelerated. Finally, many of them abandoned their property and fled[2]. Others sought to enter some vocation which would give them exemption from municipal charges. The emperors strove to check this movement by binding the *curiales* to their place of origin, and by forbidding them to enter any of the privileged professions. Since these measures were ineffectual, laws were passed requiring that the property of anyone who gained exemption should remain under the jurisdiction of the *curia*. The sole recourse left to the distressed curial, short of abandonment of his property and flight, was the right of disposing of his property by sale. This privilege was virtually withdrawn when it was

[1] Livy, 21. 63.   [2] *Cf.* pp. 113*ff.*

decreed that the consent of the governor or the *curia* was necessary before any legal transfer could be made. Violations of the civil code were frequently punished by confiscation of property, which was added to the imperial estates. The municipalities accordingly suffered serious losses not only in the growth of private *latifundia*, but also in the development of imperial holdings. In the fourth and fifth centuries the Church also gained control of great estates by gifts and bequests. These estates were all exempt from municipal obligations, until Leo and Anthemius decreed that all curial property should remain under the jurisdiction of the *curia*, even if it passed out of the hands of the *curiales*[1].

The legislation pertaining to the *coloni* may be traced in part to the scarcity of labor as the supply of slaves decreased, but the depreciation of the soil was also an important factor[2]. In early Roman husbandry voluntary tenancy was a familiar practice, but when Rome acquired her eastern provinces, she found a system of compulsory tenancy developed which differed little from medieval serfdom. The latter institution gradually spread over the whole empire, probably from the example set by the imperial estates. As we have already seen, the decline in the fertility of the soil led large numbers of farmers to incur indebtedness, which could only be discharged by working out their obligations in an involuntary tenancy from which they or their children could not escape. The spread of private patronage also fostered the development of the colonate, as farmers placed themselves under the protection of some neighboring land-baron, and, in return for the security of life and property granted them, entered his service in a relationship which ultimately became that of a *colonus*[3]. The emperors were forced to hold these

---

[1] *Cod. J.* 10. 19. 8 (468).
[2] For the history of the colonate, *cf.* especially Rostowzew, *Gesch. d. röm. Kol.* and Heitland, *Agricola*.
[3] Zulueta, *de patrociniis vicorum*.

tenants in a form of perpetual leasehold in the effort to check the urban movement, and to secure an adequate supply of trained agricultural workers on imperial and private estates. By the beginning of the fourth century the *coloni* were bound to the soil in all parts of the empire, and in 357 it was further enacted that no land could be sold without the tenants attached to it[1]. A powerful instrument of oppression was put in the hands of the proprietors when they were held for the taxes of their tenants, and were authorized to collect them[2]. They were thus enabled to pass on the increasing weight of taxation to their *coloni*, who were thus reduced to greater poverty. While the laws provided means of redress in cases of over-exactions, it is doubtful if any tenant ever dared to enter an action against his landlord[3]. In the fourth century the *coloni* were reduced almost to the level of agricultural slaves.

Keen civic rivalries led to the construction of great public works to vie with those of neighboring towns without regard to economic advantages or necessities, and in this way the civic treasuries were so often exhausted that the emperors forbade such undertakings without the approval of the provincial governor. Wealthy citizens were usually not averse to providing temples, baths, or other public works as a memorial for themselves, or as a means of securing civic honors, but there was no glory in providing an endowment for maintenance, and this charge usually fell on the municipality. From the modern point of view the ancient city spent a disproportionate part of its revenues on the amenities of life, for example, games, theatres, baths, banquets, religious ceremonies, and the like, while little was used for the development of economic resources. The widespread system of municipal charities, whereby the urban poor were fed and amused, was also based upon a vicious policy,

[1] *Cod. J.* 11. 48. 2 (357).   [2] *Cod. Th.* 11. 1. 14 (366).
[3] *Cf.* nos. 175, 180, 186, 190, 192.

for it placed a premium on idleness, and fostered the movement from country districts to the towns. Moreover, the system of financial administration did not provide reserve funds from prosperous years against seasons of adversity. When hard times came, deficits were inevitable, and loans had to be made at ruinous rates of interest; and when a city once became involved in debt, escape was difficult.

The cost of defending and governing the Roman empire steadily increased, while its resources in men and in wealth were steadily diminishing. The long series of defensive wars, and the struggles for the imperial power in the third century drained the resources of the citizens. When the power of choosing the emperor passed into the hands of the soldiers, they were quick to take advantage of their privilege, and increases in pay were often demanded and granted[1]. Besides, the donatives were liberal and all too frequent in the quick succession of imperial rulers. Fresh levies of recruits were constantly required because of the steady and severe fighting, and the virile man-power was heavily drawn on, or if levies were not provided, an equivalent in money was exacted. A serious burden was imposed by the billeting of troops in towns and villages. The unfortunate residents suffered from their greed and licentiousness, and frequent appeals were directed to the emperor, but although stringent legislation was enacted to check the evil, the laws were not backed by any power which could enforce them, and the evil appears to have continued unabated[2].

In the gradual concentration of power in the hands of the central government, the number of bureaus was

[1] The notorious case of the auction of the imperial throne by the praetorian guard may be cited (Herodian, 2. 6. 6).

[2] It is recorded as one of the merits of Pescennius Niger that he restrained the exactions of the soldiery (*Hist. Aug. Pescennius*, 3). Cf. nos. 113, 139, 141, 142, 143, 144, 152, 162, 163; Rostovtseff, *Mus. Belge*, 27 (1923), 233 ff.

steadily increasing. The reorganization of Diocletian, by which the empire was divided into prefectures, dioceses, and small provincial units, while at the same time civil and military commands were separated, saved the empire from civil war and lessened the political power of militarism; but the number of officials was vastly increased, and the expense of administration was more than doubled with, unfortunately, no corresponding increase in efficiency[1]. There was no effective method of controlling the various departments, and the elaborate system of espionage, created partly through a genuine desire on the part of the emperors to control abuses, and partly as a result of the natural suspiciousness of an autocratic government, only served to create new methods of oppression and corruption.   An edict of Constantine in 331 reveals the deplorable inefficiency of the central government in controlling abuses, and the widespread corruption of officials of all classes, not even excepting the provincial governors themselves[2]. The complaint that there were more people living upon taxes than paying them was undoubtedly an exaggeration, but there was a sufficient basis in fact to justify the statement[3].   In the fourth century the proportion of consumers and producers had become too nearly equalized for an agricultural commonwealth whose resources were declining, and which could not exchange its manufactured goods for food and raw materials from other nations in any appreciable quantity.

The depreciation of the currency which had begun under Nero was continued by successive emperors, ignorant of fundamental economic principles, as a means of replenishing their exhausted treasuries and of meeting the mounting expenses of bureaucratic administration. By the time of Aurelian gold had disappeared from circulation. The coins purporting to be silver contained about 5 per cent. of that metal. Where the tribute or dues were

---

[1] *Cam. Med. Hist.* 1. 24 *ff.*   [2] *Cod. Th.* 1. 16. 7 (331).
[3] Lactantius, *de mort. persec.* 7. 3.

fixed, the depreciated currency meant a lightening of taxation, but when Aurelian made payments in debased coin and demanded taxes in another standard, he virtually multiplied the rates by eight. Diocletian devised a new system of taxation which applied to all provinces alike, and he abolished the tributes, which had been very unequally apportioned. Under the new arrangement the privileges of immunity, which free cities and Italian towns enjoyed hitherto, were revoked[1]. The taxes were laid on land, which was classified according to its use for growing grain, or producing oil or wine. The various units were called *iuga*, each of which represented the number of acres which one man could work, and in the case of vineyards or olive orchards were often rated by the number of vines or trees. Pasture lands were assessed according to the number of cattle. A head-tax was also imposed upon the agricultural laborers, men, women, and slaves. These taxes were levied in addition to those which had long been customary, the inheritance tax, customs dues, the *aurum coronarium*, the *aurum oblaticium*, and the *tironicum*. The taxes instituted by Diocletian were reckoned in the produce of the soil and not in coin. He thus extended the system which had already begun under Alexander Severus when salaries were paid in kind. While Diocletian's system of taxation was uniform in its application throughout the empire, and undoubtedly secured greater revenues, its injustice is apparent in that no discrimination was made between rich and poor *iuga*[2]. The assessment thus fell with undue severity upon the owner of unproductive farm land while his richer neighbor would escape with a comparatively light tax. The fact that the law-givers of the empire failed to devise an equitable system of taxation based on sound economic principles must be considered as a very important factor in the decline of the middle and lower classes of land-

[1] *Cf.* pp. 127 *ff.*
[2] Seligman, *Essays on Taxation, s.v. Regressive Taxation.*

owners, on whom the assessments fell with disproportionate severity.

The collection of taxes had been placed in the hands of local authorities ever since the system of farming out the revenues to the *publicani* had been generally abolished. The *decemprimi* and *decaproti* were responsible for the collection[1], and any deficiencies were made up by them, but there is no evidence that this system was continued after Diocletian. A rescript of Aurelian made the whole order of *curiales* responsible, after the third year, for the taxes on estates abandoned by their fellow-members. In case they were unable to bear the burden, the land was to be distributed among the various local villages and estates[2]. Constantine issued an edict forbidding decurions to be held for the taxes of others[3], but he later revived the law of Aurelian. Special imperial agents, called *exactores*, were deputed to assist in collecting arrears, but the principle of collective liability of the *curiales* seems to have been the rule. Not only were the *curiales* responsible for the taxes on their own lands, but also, at least in certain periods, for those on senatorial estates. This burden was particularly heavy, because powerful land-owners could not be compelled to pay taxes. An interesting illustration of this is found in a law of 396 which separated senatorial and curial property, but when in the following year it was found that the revenue from the former had decreased by half, the old custom was revived whereby the *curiales* were responsible for both[4].

In addition to the taxes on land and on the agricultural classes, whether free, serf, or slave, the liturgies, both municipal and imperial, were imposed upon *curiales* with increasing severity. The maintenance of the imperial post was most oppressive; and the confiscation of municipal revenues caused the transfer of many liturgies, which had hitherto involved only personal service, to charges on

[1] *Dig.* 50. 4. 1, 18, 26.   [2] *Cod. J.* 11. 59. 1.
[3] *Cod. Th.* 11. 7. 2 (319).   [4] *Cod. Th.* 6. 3. 3 (396), 4 (397).

THE DECLINE OF ROMAN MUNICIPALITIES

property[1]. All these burdens fell on the land-owners, and were fatal to the development of agriculture. The imposition of the plebeian head-tax on the farmer and his help, while the city proletariat was exempt, gave, as a direct result, great impetus to the urban movement. Normally, the shifting of the population from the country to the town would inevitably adjust itself by bringing grain to a price which would encourage the revival of farming, but other factors prevented it. The population of the whole empire was decreasing as the result of plagues and famine, of the wastage of civil and foreign wars, and of religious persecutions[2]. The birth-rate also was steadily declining, although the emperors sought to encourage large families by elaborate alimentary laws and by grants of special privilege to families of three or more children. The maintenance of a large standing army where soldiers served long terms, although marriage was permitted them by Severus, the rapid rise of Christianity with the consequent increase in the number of men entering religious orders, and the development of monasticism increased the number of people who lived in celibacy. Towns dwindled to villages and finally disappeared. Only the few favored by exceptional environment, or protected by secure walls of defence, survived the general decay.

The growth of great estates and the disappearance of the small farmer deprived the local industries of their chief market[3]. Most of the estates had their own workshops where the simple tools and equipment were made, and much, if not all, of the food and clothing of the tenants was produced on the estate. There was little trade with the city, and this was carried on by primitive barter, since the depreciated coinage had no value as a medium of exchange. Foreign trade also declined as the local markets

[1] Cf. pp. 95 ff.
[2] Seeck, *Geschichte des Untergangs der antiken Welt*, 1, 296 ff.
[3] Westermann, *op. cit.* 723 ff.

weakened. The division of the empire served to break trade-connections between the East and West, while the creation of the new capital at Constantinople put an end to many of the old trade-routes, and seriously affected the cities depending on them. The frontiers were frequently closed by wars, and trade with peoples outside the empire was broken off for long periods. The heavy burdens imposed upon ship-owners for the alimentation of the capitals strained the transportation system to the utmost. The cost of the government service was charged to the freight carried for private interests, and this practice served to discourage trade by sea. In the fourth century the feeling of imperial unity disappeared, and each province began to develop its own independent life as intercourse with other provinces ceased, and most of them became self-supporting and self-sufficient by necessity.

Methods of manufacture were never improved in the ancient world, either because an adequate supply of slaves removed any incentive to develop mechanical devices so long as labor was cheap, or because inventive genius was lacking, or because traditional methods could not be varied by conservative people[1]. The restrictions imposed upon guild members controlled the supply of workmen, but were fatal to the establishment of new industries and to intellectual or material progress on the part of the skilled worker. The influence of state and municipal monopolies and the imperial workshops for munitions, clothes, and other articles may have played some part in the economic life of the municipalities in which they were located, but it is doubtful if they were important factors.

While the worship of local deities undoubtedly contributed to the development of patriotism in the ancient city-state, the growth of scepticism and the influence of various philosophic systems had impaired the vitality of local cults long before the founding of the empire. The worship of the emperor was universal, and in this way may

[1] Meyer, *Kleine Schriften*, 79 *ff.*; *R.E. s.v. Industrie.*

be said to have prepared the way for the adoption of Christianity, but it may be doubted if either of these cults had any real importance in municipal history in the imperial period. The religious observances of pagan magistracies may have deterred Christians from seeking positions in the local government, but the early Church drew its members largely from a class which was ineligible for office. In the later period, when the Church began to attract members of the wealthier class, there is ample evidence that Christians took their part in municipal government[1]. After the recognition of Christianity as an official religion of the state every member of the community stood on equal footing in regard to civic duties. When Julian sought to re-establish paganism, Christians "struck" in protest, but this is the only evidence of their unwillingness to take part in local affairs after Constantine[2].

The legislation dealing with the relations of Christians to the local *curiae* begins with Constantine. When he exempted officers of the Church from municipal liturgies, the *curiales* at once sought to enter holy orders, more from a desire to escape civil obligations than from any sincere religious conviction. There must have been a large number of Christians in the curial order, for Constantine was soon obliged to issue an edict forbidding them to enter the service of the Church. Similar laws were frequently issued by later emperors, but the very frequency of such legislation shows that the laws were continually violated[3]. In this way the municipality suffered a loss of curial members, but a remedy was found, as we have already seen, by subjecting the property of *curiales* to the *curiae* when any member of the order took up a profession which gave him exemption from local obligations. Church estates also developed at the expense of the municipalities, and the burdens on the laity increased proportionately.

[1] Declareuil, *op. cit.* 97 *ff.*   [2] *Cod. Th.* 12. 1. 50 (362).
[3] *Cod. Th.* 12. 1 *passim*; 16. 2 *passim*; *cf.* pp. 110 *ff.*

On the other hand, where the revenues of Church properties were distributed in local charities, there was no economic loss to the community.

While it may be true that Christianity turned the attention of its votaries to the future life rather than to the problems of the world about them, yet the identification of the municipality with the bishopric gave the Church a real interest in the preservation of the civic commonwealth. The development of the power of the bishop in judicial and administrative matters detracted from the influence of local magistrates, but the decline of municipal institutions began long before Christianity had become an important factor in the Roman empire.

The biological theory of the decline of nations has received considerable attention in recent years. The problem of race-mixture in the municipalities of the ancient world is a difficult study not only because of the lapse of so many centuries, but also because of the conflicting nature of the evidence. It is probable that most Italic and Greek stocks were themselves a mixture of different races. There is, however, little doubt that races of the Italic peninsula in the era of republican Rome were, in the course of time, replaced by other nationalities. Few of the old Roman families can be traced far down in the imperial period, and recent investigation has shown that the population of Rome in the imperial period was largely of foreign origin[1]. Many of the Italians went out to the provinces where they were ultimately submerged in the native population. Italy became peopled by provincials and aliens, many of whom had risen from slavery. In all provincial cities the liberal attitude of slave-owners led to the development of a large class of freedmen whose descendants were politically indistinguishable from the original members of the community. The development of the doctrine of *origo* in the imperial period tended to keep each city a self-contained unit as far as race-mixture

[1] Frank, *Am. Hist. Rev.* 21 (1916), 689 *ff.*

is concerned. Thus when the older members of the curial stock died out, their places would usually be taken by more progressive members of freedman origin. From the economic point of view, such replacements could hardly be considered as a loss to the community. The large influx of Nordic races in the later empire was far from being a source of strength to the community from the admixture of a purer and more virile stock. We are inclined to believe that the blending of races had less importance than the economic factors which we have already described in the decline of municipal life. Not less important is the fact that in the ancient city-state intellectual progress was closely related to political freedom and independence. Under the empire the government of each municipality came into the hands of a narrow oligarchy, which in turn was closely supervised by a paternalistic state. In the general atrophy of political institutions, even when the municipalities were enjoying great material prosperity, we must find the explanation of the loss of intellectual vigor, and the decline of literature, art, science, and philosophy. The influence of a court based upon military power and inspired by military traditions was also unfavorable to the development of any of the arts. Christianity turned its back on pagan culture, and when the new religion was adopted by the wealthier classes, the system of education which was devised for Christian youths led to a general disregard for the heritage of the past.

In the later empire, when Hellenic culture had spent its force, the revival of Orientalism seems to have contributed to the return to the ancient village-communities which are characteristic of the Byzantine empire[1]. In the West the barbarian invasions caused the submergence of many municipalities and a form of tribal government appeared in many districts. Here also the village-community was established and extended until it became a most important factor in the medieval period. It is,

[1] Ramsay, *The Tekmorian Guest Friends*, pp. 357–8.

however, beyond the scope of this investigation to study the conflict of municipality, tribe, and village in the Middle Ages.

To sum up briefly the principal causes which contributed to the decline of municipal life, economic decay was due primarily to widespread depreciation of the agricultural resources of the *territoria* through unscientific methods of farming and the exhaustion of the soil. The independent farmers who owned small estates constituted the most important class in the community, and they went down in the struggle for existence under unfavorable conditions of production and competition. Their farms were swallowed up in the *latifundia*, or great estates in private or imperial hands, or they were abandoned and became waste. Rural desolation was aggravated by the urban movement, and as wide areas lay uncultivated, malaria, famine, and plagues followed, each taking its toll of vital energy and of the productive power of the empire. Trades and industries in the towns depended largely on the purchasing power of the local markets, and as these declined factories became idle and trade with other provincial cities fell off. While the resources of the municipalities and of their citizens were steadily declining, financial burdens were steadily increasing. The necessity of supporting a highly organized bureaucracy and of maintaining a huge standing army, almost constantly engaged in costly defensive wars, proved too great a task for a nation whose resources were largely agricultural and were in process of exhaustion. An attempt was made to meet financial difficulties by successive depreciations of the gold and silver content in the currency, but finally the imperial coinage ceased to have any value, and trade was carried on by barter, while taxes were collected in kind. Finally, Diocletian attempted a reform in the currency and in the system of taxation. The latter, although it swept away certain inequalities of the old levy, fell with especial severity on the agricultural classes, and was economically unsound in its discrimination against the owners of less fertile land. The farmers were forced to exploit their lands for immediate returns, and the process of exhaustion was accelerated. In addition to the heavy taxes, the liturgies imposed for municipal and imperial service became more and more burdensome as the number of citizens liable to such duties not only decreased, but also found their capital resources declining. When the fixed charges approximated to or surpassed the income of *curiales*, many of them abandoned their estates, or sought some way of escape from their obligations. Thus it is that we hear of deserted *curiae*, abandoned towns, and the rapid decline of municipal institutions.

We have already traced the history of the transfer of judicial and administrative power from the municipalities to the central bureaucracy. To some extent this was due to economic causes, but imperial autocracy and local inefficiency played an important part. The whole tendency of Roman administration was to discourage democratic government in the cities, and to place all power in the hands of an oligarchy. Thus the vast mass of the people lost the political instincts which they had developed in their ancient city-states, which had played so important a part in the growth of intellectual vigor. Under the empire the local senatorial oligarchy, usually limited to a hundred men in each city, became an hereditary organization, and as its members were secured from all danger of overthrow by internal revolution, we must believe that they ultimately became dominated by personal interests. The wealthy senators gradually withdrew from the local organization as they became members of the imperial nobility. The remainder, secure in their hereditary privileges, squandered the resources of the city and oppressed the people. For this reason imperial appointments of *curatores* and *defensores* were made, and the transfer of legislative, judicial and administrative power to provincial governors and bureaucratic officials began and speedily developed. A vicious circle was established as the atrophy of municipal institutions led to increased imperial supervision, and bureaucratic control stifled political independence and initiative. Finally, the *curiales*, facing economic ruin, were reduced to the position of an imperial guild, whose sole purpose seems to have been the collection of taxes and the performance of liturgies. As the municipal governments lost political responsibility, political ideas, and political instincts, the vital spark of ancient civic life perished, and this factor, no less than the economic forces, had a powerful influence on the decline of municipal institutions, and reacted with deadly effect on the political vigor of the whole empire.

The paralysis of social institutions, manifested in the creation of a rigid caste-system, binding the *curiales*, members of guilds, and agricultural workers to their place of origin and to the station of life in which they were born, was due in large measure to economic and political factors. The emperors owning vast landed estates, and controlling industrial monopolies, favored legislation which bound the laborer to the farm or factory. While this policy provided a temporary solution of the labor problem, and served vested interests, the result was not only fatal, economically, to the development of new industries, but by depriving the individual of all power of initiative or free choice in his vocation, and of all incentive to material and intellectual progress, his powers of production were lessened; and the reduction of the bulk of the population to a condition of serfdom affected the cultural standards of the empire far more than did the barbarian inroads. In the effort to preserve the municipal organization, the *curiales* were bound by legislation similar to that governing the guilds and *coloni*. When the citizen became less important to the state than his property, the "sinews of the commonwealth," as the *curiales* were styled in some of the Codes, were also paralyzed.

It is futile to attempt to date the beginning of municipal

decline. Many of the forces which combined to destroy civic prosperity and political vigor were already operative in the days of the republic. Their development was somewhat arrested and obscured by the expansion of the empire, and by the prosperity which followed the restoration of peace and security. But the newer provinces soon came under the influence of the forces of decay, and the weakness of the municipal units quickly reacted on the empire as a whole. This was clearly revealed in the civil wars and barbarian invasions of the age preceding Diocletian. Thereafter the history of municipal institutions as a vital element in the Roman empire draws rapidly to a close. The outward forms survived, but the breath of political life had departed.

CHAPTER XV

MUNICIPAL DOCUMENTS AND THEIR PREPARATION

FOR the purpose of interpreting correctly the documents on which our knowledge of the relations of the municipalities to the central government rests, it is important for us to have in mind the different forms which documents affecting the cities took, to know the procedure which was followed in receiving petitions from the municipalities or from citizens of municipalities, or inquiries from the governors of provinces, and to be familiar with the method of reaching decisions on the points involved, and of transmitting them to the persons or communities concerned. In such an inquiry it is convenient to consider the republic and empire separately, because the attitude taken by the government at Rome toward provincial communities and its method of dealing with them changed from the one period to the other. We shall limit our discussion to the period preceding the accession of Diocletian, because almost all our documents antedate his assumption of the imperial purple.

The documents under the republic with which we are concerned fall into three classes: *leges*, *senatus consulta*, and *edicta*. *Leges*, including under this head *plebis scita*, were enactments of the popular assembly under the chairmanship of a Roman official. Measures whose precise terms were specified in the bill submitted to the assembly, and which the people were asked (*rogatus*) to adopt, were styled *leges rogatae*[1]. When the people delegated to a magistrate or to several officials the right to draw up a measure, the

---

[1] Specimens of these laws preserved to us on tablets are the *lex Antonia de Termessibus* (no. 19) of 71 B.C. which is a plebiscite, and the *lex de Gallia Cisalpina* (no. 27) enacted between 49 and 42 B.C. For a full list of known *leges rogatae*, *cf.* Rotondi, *Leges publicae populi Romani*, 189–486.

enactment was called a *lex data*. Among the earliest of these measures were the *leges provinciarum*[1], which were prepared by commissions of ten senators. Municipal charters are commonly *leges datae*[2], and in one of them reference is made to the appointment of a commissioner to draw up the measure[3]. Less important matters affecting municipalities sometimes came before the senate[4], and not infrequently the decision of the senate was communicated to the community in question in the form of a letter from a magistrate[5].

Of the edicts which magistrates of a certain rank were empowered to issue, we are concerned primarily with the edicts of the governors of provinces, which have been described in another connection[6]. The originals of the *leges* or *senatus consulta* were kept in the *aerarium* at Rome in the care of the quaestors[7], and copies were sent to the communities concerned. The edicts of governors were also of course published in the provinces.

Under the empire we find the two classes of *leges* mentioned above, *senatus consulta*, and edicts, as well as the *constitutiones principum*. During the principate of Augustus and in the first half of that of Tiberius we find some *leges rogatae*[8], but before the close of Tiberius' reign the popular assembly ceased to play an important part in legislation[9]. It was summoned, however, to confer the

---

[1] *Cf.* pp. 48 *ff.*

[2] Good specimens for the republican period are the *tabula Heracleensis* (no. 24) of 45 B.C. and the *lex coloniae Genetivae Iuliae* (no. 26) of 44 B.C. For a list of known *leges datae*, see Rotondi, *op. cit.* 487–507.

[3] *Cf.* no. 26, l. 159.   [4] *Cf.* nos. 5, 7, 10, and Bruns, 41.

[5] The *S.C. de Tiburtibus* (no. 7) takes the form of a letter from the praetor who presided over the senate. The *S.C. de Oropiis* (no. 18) of 79 B.C. is a letter of the consuls embodying the decree of the senate.

[6] *Cf.* pp. 50 *ff.*; no. 2.

[7] *Cf.* Servius on *Aen.* 8. 322; Livy, 39. 4. 8; Cic. *Phil.* 5. 4. 12.

[8] *Cf.* Rotondi, *op. cit.* 441 *ff.*

[9] Sporadic instances of the calling of the *comitia* for legislative purposes occur under Claudius (Tac. *Ann.* 11. 14) and Nerva (*Dig.* 47. 21. 3, 1). *Cf.* Liebenam, *R.E. s.v. comitia*, 711.

tribunician power on the *princeps* and to define the functions of that office[1], and probably in this measure he was empowered to found colonies[2], to change the status of a colony or a *municipium*, to grant Latin rights to provincial communities, to give Latin communities Roman rights, and to grant municipal charters. One may say therefore that all the *leges* of the imperial period, with which we are concerned, were *leges datae*[3].

With the disappearance of the popular assembly, the importance of the senate as a legislative body increased for a time. This was a very natural result, and the prince may not have been unwilling to see the change come about, because the time was not yet ripe for him to make himself the sole law-making power in the state. A survey of the known decrees of the senate of the early empire confirms from the negative side the conclusion which we have just reached from the positive point of view in discussing the *leges datae*, for although we have a long list of senatorial decrees of this period of a legislative character[4], none of them, except the "discourses of the prince," deals with the relations of the imperial government to the *civitates*. It is clear therefore that measures affecting the cities emanated directly from the emperor, and that the *oratio principis in senatu habita* is important for our discussion. In the year 23 B.C. Augustus received the privilege of bringing up any matter in the senate which he chose to submit[5]. This right was later extended, so that the prince could make as many as five proposals, all of them to take precedence of motions made by other members of the senate[6]. In the absence of the emperor these messages, or "discourses of the prince," were read by a quaestor and adopted as decrees of the senate without

---

[1] *Cf.* Mommsen, *St. R.* 3, 346, 349, n. 4.   [2] *Op. cit.* 2, 888 *ff.*
[3] *Cf.* the *leges Salpensana et Malacitana* (nos. 64 and 65) of A.D. 81–84.
[4] *Cf.* Karlowa, 1, 644–646 and Rudorff, *Röm. Rechtsgeschichte*, 1, 106–129.
[5] *Cf.* Cassius Dio, 53. 32.   [6] *Cf.* Herzog, 2, 691, n. 2.

change. Perhaps from the time of Hadrian no one but the emperor proposed a measure in the senate. From the close of the second century the jurists cite decrees of the senate as *orationes* rather than *senatus consulta*, and the language of command takes the place of conventional parliamentary forms[1]. Several of these "discourses" concern the municipalities[2]. The most noteworthy is the *oratio Claudii de iure honorem Gallis dando*[3]. Historically the "discourses of the prince" were related in their origin to the decrees of the senate, but later took legally the character of *constitutiones imperatorum*. The part which the senate played in the trial of provincial governors has been discussed elsewhere[4].

If we turn to the *edicta*, in addition to the edicts of the emperor, which will be discussed later, we find *decreta* concerning provincial communities[5], especially to settle matters in dispute between them[6].

Along with the *leges datae* the most important measures affecting the cities were the imperial constitutions. Of the constitutions we read in the *Institutes*: quodcumque igitur imperator per epistulam constituit vel cognoscens decrevit vel edicto praecepit, legem esse constat: haec sunt, quae constitutiones appellantur[7]. This is essentially the definition of Ulpian, quoted later in the *Institutiones*[8]: Quod principi placuit, legis habet vigorem;...quodcumque igitur imperator per epistulam et subscriptionem statuit vel cognoscens decrevit vel de plano interlocutus est vel edicto praecepit, legem esse constat. Haec sunt quas vulgo constitutiones appellamus. These two lists

---

1 *Cf.* Girard, *Manuel élém. de droit rom.*[5] 57.
2 For a list of the principal *orationes*, *cf.* Cuq, "Mémoire sur le consilium principis d'Auguste à Dioclétien" in *Mém. prés. par div. sav.* 9, 2, 424–426. See especially no. 11.
3 *Cf.* no. 50 and Tac. *Ann.* 11. 24. 4 *Cf.* pp. 135 ff., 165 ff.
5 *Cf.* nos. 58, 109, 165 and *CIG.* 11, 2222. 6 *Cf.* pp. 152 ff.
7 *Cf.* Justinian, *Inst.* 1. 2. 6.
8 *Cf. Dig.* 1. 4. 1. 1. Gaius (*Inst.* 1. 5) writes "constitutio principis est, quod imperator decreto vel edicto vel epistula constituit."

agree in their inclusion of the *epistula*, *decretum*, and *edictum*. They differ only in the fact that Ulpian adds the *subscriptio*, a special form of the letter, and mentions the interlocutory decree along with the *decretum*. To these three classes of constitutions most scholars add the *mandatum*, and the term *rescriptum*, rather than *epistula*, is a more exact general term for a public letter of the emperor[1].

Imperial edicts were similar in form to those issued by republican magistrates, but the right to issue them seems to have been conferred on Augustus by a special act about 19 B.C.[2] They were written in black letters on a white background[3], and displayed in Rome and in the provinces, in both Latin and Greek, when necessary. Sometimes it was provided that the edict should be engraved on a bronze[4] or marble tablet[5]. They were sometimes addressed to a community. In this case they were published unchanged[6]. At other times they were addressed to an imperial official or the governor of a province. Such edicts the official incorporated in a proclamation of his own[7]. A fair number of *edicta principum* are extant[8], and some of

---

[1] For discussions of the different classes of *constitutiones* and their nature, *cf.* Cuq, *op. cit.* 424–461; Mommsen, *St. R.* 2, 905 *ff.*; Karlowa, 1, 646–654; Krueger, *Gesch. d. Quellen u. Litt. d. röm. Rechts*, 92–100; Bruns-Pernice in Holtzendorff's *Encyclopädie d. Rechtswissenschaft*, 1, 143; Girard, *op. cit.* 58–61; Wilcken, *Hermes*, 55 (1920), 2 *ff.*; Haberleitner, *Philol.* 68 (1909), 283 *ff.* Haberleitner adopts the following classification: I (*a*) *edicta*, (*b*) *orationes*, (*c*) *adlocutiones*; II (*a*) *epistulae*, (*b*) *rescripta*, (*c*) *subscriptiones*; III (*a*) *decreta*, (*b*) *interlocutiones*. Faass, *Archiv für Urkundenforschung*, 1 (1908), 221 *f.*, finds one hundred and sixty-four imperial constitutions extant in epigraphical form. Of these one hundred and twenty-one are in Greek and forty-three in Latin. The most prolific emperors are Pius, Hadrian and Severus, with thirty-two, twenty-six, and sixteen respectively to their credit. Of the one hundred and forty epigraphical constitutions which can be dated, one hundred and twenty-three antedate Diocletian.

[2] *Cf.* Herzog, 2, 151, n. 1. [3] *Cf.* Livy, 1. 32. 2; 9. 46. 5.
[4] *Cf. Cod. Th.* 2. 27. 1, 6; 14. 4. 4; no. 49. [5] *Cf.* no. 51.
[6] *Cf.* no. 49. [7] *Cf.* no. 165.
[8] Rudorff, *op. cit.* 1, 132–136; Cuq, *op. cit.* 456–459.

AND THEIR PREPARATION

them concern the cities[1]. Technically edicts held good only during the reign of the emperor who issued them, but frequently by formal act or tacit observance they continued in force after his death[2]. The subject-matter of an imperial edict was introduced by the characteristic formula: *Imperator...dicit* or Αὐτοκράτωρ...λέγει[3]. After this phrase the first person is used. The date and place of composition are indicated, usually at the beginning, sometimes at the end of the document[4]. The *edicta*, which have been discussed above, like the *orationes*, and the *adlocutiones*[5], with which we are not concerned here, were addressed to the public. The other constitutions, viz. the rescript, the *decretum*, and the *mandatum*, were not necessarily intended for publication.

Rescripts were sent in reply to the inquiries (*relationes*, *consultationes*) of provincial governors or other officials or in answer to the petitions (*preces*, *libelli*) of individuals or communities. Replies to officials usually took the form of independent letters (*epistulae*). In answering private persons or communities the emperor either appended his answer to the request or made notes upon it. His reply in the first case was called a *subscriptio*, in the second, *adnotationes*. The letters which passed between Pliny and Trajan furnish us with the best specimens to be found in literature of the inquiries of an official and the replies of the emperor. There are extant several important

---

[1] *Cf.* nos. 33, 49, 51; Gaius, *Inst.* 1. 33, an edict of Nero conferring the right of Roman citizenship upon any Latin, who, having a fortune of 200,000 sesterces, devotes half of it to the construction of a house in Rome; *Dig.* 50. 7. 5, 6, an edict of Vespasian forbidding cities to send a deputation of more than three members to Rome; Pliny, *N.H.* 3. 3. 30, an edict of Vespasian conferring the *ius Latii* on Spain; Gaius, *Inst.* 1. 93, defining the rights of *peregrini* admitted to citizenship; *Dig.* 50. 4. 11, an edict of Pius prescribing the *cursus honorum* for cities; *Dig.* 1. 5. 17, Caracalla's edict of A.D. 212 (*cf.* no. 192). [2] *Cf.* no. 33.
[3] *Cf.* no. 49 and Bruns, 68, 69; *Cod. J.* 3. 3. 2; 3. 11. 1; 7. 62. 6.
[4] *Cf.* no. 49 and Bruns, 94; *Cod. J.* 10. 61. 1.
[5] *Cf.* for instance, *Hadriani adlocutiones ad exercitum Africanum*, *CIL.* VIII, 2532 = Dessau, 2487.

[237]

MUNICIPAL DOCUMENTS

epigraphical rescripts dealing with municipal affairs[1]. Many imperial letters are of course to be found in the Justinian Code[2].

An *epistula* opened with the name and titles of the emperor in the nominative and the name of the addressee in the dative, sometimes with *salutem* or *salutem dicit* added[3]. This part of the letter is called the *inscriptio*. At the end of the letter there is usually a word of greeting, and an indication of the date and place of composition[4]. *Rescripsi* or *scripsi* found in *subscriptiones* is in the hand of the emperor[5], and *recognovi*, which appears at the end of them[6], is probably the counter-signature of the official in charge of the bureau and certifies that the document correctly represents the decision reached in the case[7]. *Proposita*, which is common at the end of certain rescripts up to A.D. 291[8] and rare thereafter, indicates the date and

---

[1] *Cf.* nos. 61, 63, 151. The most complete specimens of *subscriptiones* on municipal matters are nos. 111, 139, Bruns, 84, and *CIL.* VI, 3770. No. 139, after certain introductory formulae, contains the *preces* of the Scaptopareni, followed by the decision of the emperor. For an analysis of no. 154, see the commentary on that inscription. For the character of the subjects covered in an *adnotatio, cf.* Seeck, *R.E.* 1. 382 *f.*

[2] On *relationes* and *consultationes, cf.* especially *Cod. J.* 7. 61 and 62. For references to *subscriptiones, cf. Cod. J.* 7. 43. 1; *Dig.* 4. 8. 32, 14.

[3] *Cf.* nos. 61, 63.   [4] *Cf.* no. 61.

[5] *Cf.* no. 111, col. IV, l. 8; no. 139; Bruns, 84.

[6] *E.g.* nos. 111, 139, and Bruns, 84.

[7] *Cf.* Preisigke, *Die Inschr. v. Skaptoparene*, especially p. 63. The term *recognovi* has given rise to much discussion. Mommsen holds (*Ges. Schr.* 1, 479; 2, 179 *ff.*) that the memorandum, as prepared by the official, and the final document, were laid before the emperor. Upon the former he wrote *rescripsi*, on the latter *recognovi*. Karlowa (*Neue Heidelberger Jahrb.* 6, 214 and *Röm. Rechtsgesch.* 1, 652, n. 1) thinks that the words attest the correctness of the document, when compared with the official copy kept in the archives. *Cf.* Brassloff, *R.E.* 6, 207 *f.*, Krüger, *Gesch. d. Quellen u. Litt. d. röm. Rechts*, 96, Preisigke, *op. cit.* 4–12, and Wilcken, *Hermes*, 55 (1920), 55, 56, n. 3.

[8] *Cf.* for instance Bruns, 87, 88 and Krüger, *op. cit.* 96, n. 43. Wilcken (*op. cit.* 14 *ff.*) thinks that the *propositio* applied to *subscriptiones*, but that *epistulae* were only published on order of the emperor, or the magistrate receiving them.

place of publication[1]. Latin was the language regularly employed in rescripts, but some of those sent to Greek lands were in Greek[2]. Rescripts might confer a privilege or immunity on an individual or community, or decide an administrative matter, or they might settle a legal question. The influence of a letter of the former kind did not usually extend beyond the person or corporation concerned. Letters of the second sort furnished precedents or legal principles for the future. Judicial *epistulae* increase in number with Hadrian. The increase may well be due to the issuance of the *edictum perpetuum* by Hadrian, and the consequent necessity of consulting the emperor on doubtful points[3].

As we noticed above, the jurists speak of three classes of constitutions, viz. edicts, rescripts, and *decreta*. In the early period, however, the expression *decretum principis* was applied to any announcement of the emperor's will[4]. In this early wide sense, therefore, it included all classes of imperial constitutions. In the narrower meaning which it commonly took in the later period, it is applied to the emperor's decision on judicial questions submitted to him in the first instance or on appeal. To the list of constitutions given by the ancient jurists, modern scholars commonly add the *mandata* or individual instructions given to governors and other officials, by which they were to be guided in the administration of their offices. Naturally in course of time a somewhat fixed set of principles or methods of government in the provinces had developed, so that a large part of the mandates given to one governor was identical with that of another governor. The practice of sending out the governor of a province with instructions goes back to the republican period[5]. The mandates were

[1] *Cf.* Karlowa, 1, 651; Brassloff, *R.E.* 6, 208; Preisigke, *op. cit.* 65.

[2] *Cf. e.g. Dig.* 5. 1. 37; 5. 1. 48; 48. 3. 3; 50. 6. 6, 2.

[3] *Cf.* Girard, *Manuel élém. de droit rom.* 59.

[4] *Cf.* Hesky, *R.E.* 4, 2289. A document which some scholars style a *decretum* is called by others a *rescriptum*.

[5] *Cf.* Krüger, *op. cit.* 99, n. 59.

of great importance to the municipalities, because they dealt especially with police regulations, criminal law, and the competence of a governor[1]. Mandates, for instance, forbade cities to make grants of money[2], instructed governors to apprehend and punish culprits wrongfully released by municipal magistrates[3], and ordered them to send to the emperor for trial a decurion when charged with an offense which was punishable by exile or death[4].

If we turn now from a consideration of the documents themselves to their preparation, we notice that for a long time under the republic the senate directed the foreign policy of the Roman state. It appointed a commission of senators to draw up the *lex provinciae*[5]; it received requests from cities for charters[6], for a recognition of their independence[7], for the granting of privileges[8], and the redress of grievances[9]. With the coming of the new *régime*, the *princeps* took over the provinces in which an army was needed, appointed his own financial representative in senatorial provinces, and exerted a great moral influence over all the provinces. The growing importance of the "discourses of the prince" must also have lessened the authority of the senate in foreign affairs. Naturally, therefore, inquiries and petitions from abroad came to be addressed more and more frequently to the emperor. In making his replies he needed helpers and advisers. As foreign questions grew in importance and numbers, the business was systematized, bureaus were established, and a board of imperial counsellors was organized. These bureaus were known as the *officia* or *scrinia a rationibus, ab epistulis, a libellis, a memoria, a studiis*, and *a cognitionibus*[10]. The officials *a rationibus* had charge of imperial finances,

---

[1] For a list of items from certain *mandata*, cf. Cuq, *op. cit.* 460 f.
[2] *Cf.* Plin. *Epp. ad Trai.* 111.   [3] *Dig.* 48. 3. 10.
[4] *Dig.* 48. 19. 27, 1, 2.   [5] *Cf.* pp. 48 ff.   [6] Cic. *in Verr.* 2. 122.
[7] *Cf.* no. 5.   [8] Ditt. *Syll.*[3] 601.   [9] *Cf. Bell. Afr.* 97.
[10] For the development of these bureaus, cf. Hirschfeld, 29 ff., 318 ff.; Cuq, *op. cit.* 363 ff.; Karlowa, 1, 544 ff.; Rostowzew, *R.E.* 6, 210 ff.; von Premerstein, *R.E.* 4, 220 ff.

supervised, for instance, the collection of taxes, appropriations for the army, for *frumentationes*, and for the construction of public works. The officials *ab epistulis* prepared and despatched imperial replies to the letters of governors and generals, and drew up instructions for imperial officials. The bureau *a libellis* had charge of the petitions addressed to the emperor by private persons or by communities, and concerned itself primarily with legal questions arising between subjects, or subject communities, and between them and the state. The bureau *a memoria*, which is not mentioned until rather late, assisted the emperor in cases requiring immediate action. It probably set down in writing the official speeches and oral decisions of the emperor and *adnotationes*. The department *a studiis* grew out of the bureau *a libellis* and perhaps investigated questions outside of administration and law, such as those of religion. The officials *a cognitionibus* took up minor judicial questions, perhaps in civil cases only, which were not laid before the *consilium*.

Matters which were too important to be submitted to a bureau came before the *consilium principis*, which owed its definite organization to Hadrian[1]. It was made up of certain trained jurists, receiving salaries, and known as *consiliarii Augusti* and *adsumpti in consilium*, and the *amici* and *comites* of the emperor who had no fixed salary[2]. The emperor presided and rendered the decisions. A vote was taken, usually by ballot, but the emperor was not bound by the opinion of the majority.

It remains for us to consider briefly the method of preparing, publishing, and preserving state documents. An edict was of course drawn up by the magistrate issuing it. *Senatus consulta* under the republic were put into their final form by a committee of senators[3], and the method

[1] *Hist. Aug. Hadr.* 18. 1.

[2] On the *consilium principis*, cf. Cuq, *op. cit.* 328 *ff.*; Hirschfeld, 339 *ff.*; Mommsen, *St. R.* 2, 989 *ff.*; Seeck, *R.E.* 4, 926 *ff.*; Herzog, 2, 756 *ff.*

[3] *Cf.* the *S.C. de Bacchanalibus* (Bruns, 36) and *S.CC. de ludis saecularibus* of 17 B.C. (Bruns, 46).

of bringing bills before the popular assembly is so well known as to need no comment here. Important measures of any one of these three classes were engraved on wood, stone, copper, or bronze, displayed where they would be seen by people concerned, and copies of them kept in the temple of Saturn or in some other depository in Rome[1]. With the centralization of foreign affairs in the hands of the emperor, a large number of departments was organized, as we have already noticed. We can see in some detail the course which would be followed by a petition or an inquiry from a provincial community or a private person[2]. The request might come through the governor of a province[3], or it might be delivered at Rome in person or by a messenger[4]. On arrival at Rome it went to the proper department, and from there, if an important document, to the *consilium*. The emperor in the *consilium* gave his decision in general terms; and the appropriate department put the reply in proper form. The head of the department wrote *recognovi* upon it to indicate that it conformed to the emperor's decision and met the requirements in the case, and to attest its authenticity the emperor set down on it the word *rescripsi* or *scripsi*.

In cases of minor importance the facts and precedents were collected, and a tentative answer for the approval of the emperor was drawn up in a department. The answer might take the form of an *epistula*, or independent letter, sent alone[5], or accompanied by the *libellus*[6], or the form of a *subscriptio*[7] or of *adnotationes*. It might be sent directly to the inquirer[8], or to him through an imperial official[9] or some representative of the supplicant[10]. Sometimes it

[1] *Cf.* Dziatzko, *R.E.* 2, 561 *f.*; Mommsen, *St. R.* 3, 418 *f.*; Kubitschek, *R.E.* 1, 287 *ff.*

[2] *Cf.* Preisigke, *op. cit.* 44 *ff.*; Wilcken, *Hermes*, 55 (1920), 38 *ff.*

[3] Pliny, *Epp. ad Trai.* 58, 59.

[4] The protest from the Scaptopareni (no. 139) was delivered by a certain Aurelius Pyrrhus, acting as an intermediary.

[5] *Cf.* no. 61.   [6] Pliny, *Epp. ad Trai.* 59.   [7] *Cf.* no. 139.

[8] *Cf.* nos. 59, 61, 63.   [9] Pliny, *Epp. ad Trai.* 59.   [10] *Cf.* no. 111.

reached the petitioner in the form of a copy made at Rome by such a representative[1]. A brief analysis of one of the documents in which the last method of procedure was followed may illustrate many of the processes outlined above[2]. In Gordian's rescript we have at the beginning the words *Bona fortuna* prefixed by the Scaptopareni when the rescript was engraved. Then come the date and place at which the copy of the original in the archives was made: *Fulvio . . . scripta sunt*. It is made at the instance of Aurelius Pyrrhus, the representative of the Scaptopareni, whose name and position are given. Immediately thereafter stand the *preces* of the Scaptopareni, followed by the decision of the emperor (*Imp . . . debeas*). The emperor has written *rescripsi* and the director of the department, *recognovi*. In place of the names of the witnesses to the copy the Scaptopareni have had the word *signa* engraved. The original document in the archives, therefore, began with the *preces* and closed with *recognovi*.

Interesting facts concerning a particular inscription may often be learned from an examination of it. An imperial letter sent directly to a community was usually addressed to the magistrates, senate, and people[3], but sometimes to the magistrates and decurions only[4]. Occasionally reference is made to the deputies who brought the petition[5], or to the intermediary at Rome who presented it[6], or the deputy records the fact that he has delivered the emperor's reply to the local magistrate[7]. In one letter we are informed that it was written in Latin and translated into Greek[8]. This letter, intended for certain troops, was published in their winter quarters[9], and still another the *duoviri* had cut on stone[10]. In those

---

[1] *Cf.* no. 139.
[2] This analysis of no. 139 is based on Preisigke, *op. cit.* 74, 76, 78–79 and Wilcken, *op. cit.* 38 *ff.* See also the literature cited in note 7, p. 238.
[3] *Cf.* no. 130.   [4] *Cf.* no. 61.   [5] *Cf.* no. 61.
[6] In no. 111 a certain Lurius Lucullus.   [7] *Cf.* no. 83.
[8] *Cf.* Riccobono, no. 66.   [9] *Ibid.*   [10] *Cf.* no. 61.

which have been copied from the originals in the archives, the copyist sometimes notes the change from one handwriting to another in the original[1].

All *subscriptiones* were publicly displayed, as well as those *epistulae* whose publication the emperor or the magistrate receiving them should order. Those concerning provincial communities were displayed both in Rome and in the community concerned[2]. They were also preserved in the *Commentarii principum*[3], being assigned to different sections according to their contents. Inside these sections they were probably grouped under the several provinces, with subsections for each year[4]. Perhaps *undevicensimus* in the rescript of Pius to the Smyrnaei[5] indicates that this document is No. 19 in the roll for a certain quarter of the year[6]. With certain comparatively unimportant changes made in the organization and management of the archives in the period after Diocletian[7] we are not concerned here[8].

In Egypt the imperial will is expressed by means of the *oratio*[9], *edictum*[10], *rescriptum*[11], and *epistula*[12]. The language employed in these documents is usually Greek, but Latin is also found. Edicts were commonly promulgated from Alexandria, but were also issued from other cities[13]. Im-

---

[1] *Cf.* no. 111, col. iv, l. 9.
[2] *Cf.* Preisigke, *op. cit.* 64 *ff.*; Wilcken, *Hermes*, 55 (1920), 1–42.
[3] von Premerstein, *R.E.* 4, 737 *ff.*   [4] *Cf.* Preisigke, *op. cit.* 72.
[5] *Cf.* Bruns, 84.   [6] *Cf.* Wilcken, *op. cit.* 40.
[7] For these changes *cf.* Lécrivain, *Dict. Dar.* 4, 845 *f.*
[8] There is little definite information to be had about the archives, or *commentarii*, of the western municipalities except that which is to be found in two or three inscriptions (*e.g. CIL.* viii, *S.* 15497; xi, 3614). *Cf.* Kubitschek, *R.E.* 1, 298 *f.* For the Greek cities *cf. Jahreshefte d. öst. archäol. Inst.* 7, *Beiblatt*, 44; 16, 17 *ff.*, 270, and especially, Wilhelm, *Beiträge zur gr. Inschr.* 258 *ff.* By the time of Justinian town records were no longer kept with any care, *cf. Novellae*, xv, *praef.* "cum (defensores) nullum habeant archivum, in quo gesta apud se reponant, deperit quod conficitur."
[9] Mitteis, *Chrestomathie*, 370.
[10] Mitteis, *op. cit.* 372, 377; Ditt. *Or. Gr.* 664, 665.
[11] Mitteis, *op. cit.* 375, 376; Wilcken, *Hermes*, 55 (1920), 1 *ff.*; Bruns, 91.
[12] Wilcken, *Chrestomathie*, 153, 158; no. 189.   [13] No. 195.

perial rescripts, as a general rule, were forwarded to the prefect and published in Alexandria. In a few cases they were sent direct to a local magistrate, although it is probable that a copy was also sent to the prefect. Imperial *epistulae* were sent to private citizens of Greek or Roman birth. Copies of these documents are comparatively rare. The prefect also issued edicts in Greek. They were published in Alexandria and usually forwarded with an *epistula* to the *strategi* with instructions to post them in an appropriate public place[1]. In one instance local magistrates append their signatures to indicate their cognizance of the document, which seems to have been circulated for this purpose[2]. In another case the magistrate takes oath that the document had been published by him as directed[3]. It is evident that edicts of the emperor and of the prefects and their rescripts were widely known to the public, since copies are found throughout Egyptian nomes and they are frequently cited by the natives. The minor officials of the bureaucracy also issued their instructions in writing, usually in the form of *epistulae* or ἐπιστάλματα.

Since the bureaucracy in Egypt was highly developed and the number of secretaries very large, the task of caring for the official records must have been very serious. That the archives were not always properly housed is evident[4], and very little can be learned about the method of providing for the municipal or village records. None of the numerous buildings or offices recorded in the papyri can with certainty be ascribed to purely municipal purposes[5]. Possibly, since the relation of state and municipality was so close, the records of both may have been combined.

[1] Nos. 162–165.   [2] Wilcken, *Chrestomathie*, 13.
[3] *P. Fay.* 24.   [4] *Archiv für Papyrusforschung*, 6, 100 ff.
[5] The more important buildings for preserving records in Egypt are the following: γραφεῖον, ἀγορανομεῖον, μνημεῖον, ἀρχεῖον, γραμματοφυλάκιον, χωρικὴ βιβλιοθήκη ἐν τῶι πρυτανείωι, δημοσία βιβλιοθήκη and βιβλιοθήκη ἐγκτήσεων. Cf. Mitteis, *Chrestomathie*, 188; *Grundzüge*, 78 ff.

PART II

I. MUNICIPAL DOCUMENTS IN GREEK & LATIN FROM ITALY AND THE PROVINCES

SIGLA

LATIN INSCRIPTIONS:

Italics indicate the restoration of a lacuna, or minor corrections in the text.

⟨ ⟩ indicate ancient interpolations in the text.

( ) indicate the expansion of an abbreviation.

GREEK INSCRIPTIONS:

[ ] indicate the restoration of a lacuna.

⟨ ⟩ indicate an erasure by the editor.

( ) indicate the expansion of an abbreviation or an addition by the editor.

GREEK PAPYRI:

[ ] indicate the restoration of a lacuna.

[[ ]] indicate an erasure by the scribe.

≪ ≫ indicate an erasure by the editor.

⟨ ⟩ indicate additions by the editor.

( ) indicate the expansion of an abbreviation.

I. MUNICIPAL DOCUMENTS IN GREEK AND LATIN FROM ITALY AND THE PROVINCES

1. EPISTULA FLAMININI AD CHYRETIENSES
(196–194 a. Chr.)

Viereck, *Sermo Graecus*, 1; *IG.* IX, 2, 338; Ditt. *Syll.*³ 593; *CIG.* 1770.

Τίτος Κοίνκτιος, στρατηγὸς ὕπατος Ῥωμαίων, Χυρετιέων | τοῖς
ταγοῖς καὶ τῆι πόλει χαίρειν. Ἐπεὶ καὶ ἐν τοῖς λοιποῖς πᾶσιν |
φανερὰν πεποήκαμεν τήν τε ἰδίαν καὶ τοῦ δήμου τοῦ Ῥωμαίων |
προαίρεσιν ἣν ἔχομεν εἰς ὑμᾶς ὁλοσχερῶς, βεβουλήμεθα καὶ || ἐν 5
τοῖς ἑξῆς ἐπιδεῖξαι κατὰ πᾶν μέρος προεστηκότες | τοῦ ἐνδόξου,
ἵνα μηδ' ἐν τούτοις ἔχωσιν ἡμᾶς κατα|λαλεῖν οἱ οὐκ ἀπὸ τοῦ
βελτίστου εἰωθότες ἀνα|στρέφεσθαι. Ὅσαι γάρ ποτε ἀπολεί-
πονται κτήσεις | ἔγγειοι καὶ οἰκίαι τῶν καθηκουσῶν εἰς τὸ
δημόσιον || τὸ Ῥωμαίων, πάσας δίδομεν τῆι ὑμετέραι πόλει, | 10
ὅπως καὶ ἐν τούτοις μάθητε τὴν καλοκαγαθίαν ἡμῶν | καὶ ὅτι
τελέως ἐν οὐθενὶ φιλαργυρῆσ[α]ι βεβουλήμεθα, | περὶ πλείστου
ποιούμενοι χάριτα καὶ φιλοδοξίαν. Ὅσοι μέν|τοι μὴ κεκομισμένοι
εἰσὶν τῶν ἐπιβαλλόντων αὐτοῖς, || ἐὰν ὑμᾶς διδάξωσιν καὶ 15
φαίνωνται εὐγνώμονα λέ|γοντες, στοχαζομένων ὑμῶν ἐκ τῶν
ὑπ' ἐμοῦ γεγραμ|μένων ἐγκρίσεων, κρίνω δίκαιον εἶναι ἀποκαθ-
ίστασ|θαι αὐτοῖς. | Ἔρρωσθε.

From Chyretiae. This is the earliest document from inscriptional
sources which deals with the relations of Rome and the Greek states.
For this reason we have included it here, although Greece was not
subject to Rome at this time. The Aetolians as allies of Rome had
captured and sacked the city of Chyretiae in 200 B.C. (Livy, 31. 41. 5).
The property of the partisans of Philip in the city after the battle
of Cynoscephalae was confiscated, and became part of the public
property of Rome. When war with Antiochus threatened, Flamininus instituted a milder policy towards the Greek cities. Accordingly
he restored to the Chyretiaeans all lands confiscated from their

citizens still held by the Roman state. The restoration was made to the city with the right of reinstating the former owners if they satisfied the magistrates of the justice of their claim. While the tone of the letter is that of one desirous of securing the goodwill of the Greeks, the terms laid down for the restoration of the land to the former owners indicate the attitude of a master towards a subject people. It is also evident that, in settling the affairs of Chyretiae after the war with Philip, Flamininus favored the pro-Roman parties in the state (*cf.* pp. 69 *f.*; Rostowzew, *Gesch. d. röm. Kol.* 286).

2. DECRETUM PROCONSULIS HISPANIAE ULTERIORIS
(189 a. Chr.)

CIL. ii, 5041; Dessau, 15; Bruns, 70; Riccobono, p. 248.

L. Aimilius L. f. inpeirator decreivit, | utei quei Hastensium servei | in turri Lascutana habitarent, | leiberei essent; agrum
5 oppidumqu., || quod ea tempestate posedisent, | item possidere habereque | iousit, dum poplus senatusque | Romanus vellet. Act. in castreis | a. d. xii k. Febr.

A bronze tablet found in 1866 on the probable site of Lascuta in Spain, now in the Louvre. Paullus probably received the title of imperator, which he bears in this inscription, in consequence of his victory over the Lusitani in 190 B.C. (*cf.* Livy, 37. 57. 5). Since he probably left Spain in the autumn of 189 B.C., and since this decree is dated Jan. 19, the date of the inscription is probably 189 B.C. The people of the turris Lascutana were made free in the sense that they were taken from under the control of the Hastenses. Control of them was now transferred to the Romans. There are no cases known of *attributi* attached to communities which were not autonomous; *cf.* Mommsen, *St. R.* 3, 766. The Lascutani do not acquire full right of ownership to their land, but hold it at the pleasure of the Roman people and senate; *cf.* Mommsen, *St. R.* 3, xvii, n. 1; Karlowa, 1, 447. The order of the words *poplus senatusque*, as opposed to the imperial order, *senatus populusque*, is significant.

FROM ITALY AND THE PROVINCES

3. EPISTULA SPURI POSTUMI, PRAETORIS,
AD DELPHOS

(189 a. Chr.)

Ditt. *Syll.*³ 612; Viereck, *Sermo Graecus*, 10.

...... ους καὶ ... | ... [περὶ τῆς πόλεως ἐλευθερί]ας καὶ τοῦ
ἱερο[ῦ ἀσυλίας ...]
(*vacant versus duo*)
Σπόριος Ποστόμιος Λευκίου υἱός, στρατηγὸς 'Ρωμαίων, τῶι
κοι[νῶι τῶν Δελφῶν χαίρειν. Οἱ παρ' ὑμῶν ἀποσταλέντες
πρεσβευ]|ταὶ Βούλων, Θρασυκλῆς, 'Ορέστας περὶ τῆς ἀσυλίας
τοῦ ἱεροῦ κα[ὶ τῆς πόλεως διελέγησαν φιλοτιμίας οὐθὲν ἐλλεί-
ποντες] | καὶ περὶ τῆς ἐλευθερίας καὶ ἀνεισφορίας ἠξίουν, ὅπως
α[ὐτόνομοι καὶ ἀτελεῖς ὦσιν ἥ τε πόλις καὶ ἡ χώρα τῶν Δελφῶν]. |
Γινώσκετε οὖν δεδογμένον τῆι συγκλήτωι, τό τε ἱερὸν το[ῦ 'Απόλ-
λωνος καὶ τὴν πόλιν ἄσυλον εἶναι, ἀνεισφόρητον δὲ καὶ] ‖ τὴν 5
πόλιν τῶν Δελφῶν καὶ τὴν χώραν, καὶ δ[ιὰ παντ]ὸς αὐτονό[μους
εἶναι τοὺς πολίτας .... ἐλευθέρους ὄν]|τας καὶ πολι-
τεύοντας αὐτοὺς καθ' αὑτ[οὺς .. καὶ] κυριεύο[ντας .... τό τε ἱερὸν
καὶ τὸ τέ]‖μενος, καθὼς πάτριον αὐτοῖς ἐξ ἀρχῆς [ὑπῆρχεν· ἵνα]
οὖν εἰδ[ῆτε, στέλλομεν ὑμῖν ἀντίγραφον].
(*vacant versus duo*)
Πρὸ ἡμερῶν τεσσάρων νωνῶν Μαΐ[ων Σπόριος Ποστόμιος
Λευκίου υἱός, στρατηγὸς ἐν κομετίωι(?) συνε]‖βουλεύσατο τῆι
συγκλήτωι· γραφ[ομένωι παρῆσαν ὁ δεῖνα τοῦ δεῖνος ..., ὁ δεῖνα
τοῦ δεῖνος ...], | Γάϊος 'Ατίνιος Γαΐου, Τεβέριο[ς Κλαύδιος ......
περὶ ὧν Δελφοὶ λόγους ἐποιήσαντο, περὶ ἱεροῦ] | ἀσύλου, πόλεως
ἐλευθερί[ας, χώρας ἀνεισφορήτου καὶ αὐτονόμου, περὶ τούτου
τοῦ πράγματος οὕτως] ‖ ἔδοξεν· καθὼς πρότερο[ν Δελφοῖς ταῦτα 5
ὑπῆρχεν καὶ Μανίωι 'Ακιλίωι ἔδοξε, τούτωι τῶι κρίματι
ἐμμέ]‖νειν ἔδοξεν.
(*vacant versus duo*)
[Λ]εύκιος Φούριος Λ[ευκίου υἱός, στρατηγὸς ....]
[Δε]λφῶν ἐ[λευθερίας ....?]

From Delphi. After the Aetolian domination was ended the
Romans displayed great kindness to the Delphians. We publish one

[251]

MUNICIPAL DOCUMENTS IN GREEK AND LATIN

of a series of documents which bear upon the relations of Rome and Delphi (Ditt. *Syll.*[3] 607–615, 821, 822, 825–827).

In settling the affairs of Delphi Manius Acilius defined the limits of the *territorium*, a settlement which was later a subject of dispute (Tod, *International Arbitration*, nos. 23, 26). He also confiscated the lands of Aetolians and Locrians resident in this area and gave them to the city and to the temple (Ditt. *Syll.*[3] 610). The Delphians had difficulty in dispossessing the owners and appealed to Rome. The ambassadors were slain on their return journey, and a new embassy was sent to complain of the outrage and to secure a copy of the senatorial action on their former request. The answer of the senate is given in the letter of the consul (Ditt. *Syll.*[3] 611). The Delphians are permitted to expel those aliens whom they choose, and may allow others to remain who are amenable to the laws. It is evident that the Delphians were afraid of the vengeance of the Aetolians for the expulsion of their fellow-citizens, and desired the support of Rome before taking action. When the war was ended the Delphians sent another embassy to Rome to secure the confirmation of the acts of Manius. The document which is published above contains the record of the proceedings. At least four inscriptions were recorded on the stone. Of the first, only the last two lines are preserved, but it probably contained the plea of the ambassadors. The second is a letter of the praetor to the Delphians giving a summary of the decree of the senate and enclosing a copy which is recorded in the third document. The right of asylum is acknowledged; the city is granted freedom and immunity from tribute; the citizens are to be autonomous for all time and left in the enjoyment of their own laws. The subject of the fourth document is unknown. Compare the letter of the praetor Valerius to the Teians (Ditt. *Syll.*[3] 601), where the Romans promise immunity from taxation although there is as yet no question of Teos being subject to Rome.

FROM ITALY AND THE PROVINCES

4. EPISTULA CONSULIS AD HERACLEOTAS
(ca. 189–188 a. Chr.)

CIG. 3800; Viereck, *Sermo Graecus*, 3; Ditt. *Syll.*³ 618; *Rev. ét. an.* 19 (1917), 237 ff.

[. . . . .]στρατηγὸς ὕπατος Ῥωμαίων | [καὶ
δήμαρχοι καὶ ἡ σύγκλητ]ος Ἡρακλεωτῶν τῆι βουλῆι καὶ τῶι
δή|[μωι χαίρειν]. Ἐνέ[τυχον] ἡμῖν οἱ παρ' ὑμῶν πρέσβεις Διᾶς,
Διῆς, Διονύ|[σιος, ...]μ[αν]δρος, [Εὔ]δημος, Μόσχος, Ἀριστεί-
δης, Μένης, ἄνδρες κα‖[λοὶ κἀγαθοί], οἳ τό τε [ψήφ]ισμα   5
ἀπέδωκαν καὶ αὐτοὶ διελέγησαν ἀκολού|[θως τοῖ]ς ἐν τῶ[ι
ψη]φίσματι κατακεχωρισμένοις οὐδὲν ἐλλείποντες | [φιλοτι]μίας·
ἡμ[εῖ]ς δὲ πρὸς πάντας τοὺς Ἕλληνας εὐνόως διακείμεν[οι |
τυγχά]νομεγ καὶ πειρασόμεθα, παραγεγονότων ὑμῶν εἰς τὴν
ἡμετέρα[μ | πίστι]μ, πρόνοιαν ποιεῖσθαι τὴν ἐνδεχομένην, ἀεί
τινος ἀγαθοῦ παρα[ί‖|τιοι γεν]όμενοι· συγχωροῦμεν δὲ ὑμῖν τήν   10
τε ἐλευθερίαγ καθότι καὶ | [ταῖς ἄ]λλαις πόλεσιν, ὅσαι ἡμῖν τὴν
ἐπιτροπὴν ἔδωκαν, ἔχουσιν ὑ[φ' | αὑτοὺς πά]ντα τὰ αὑτῶμ
πολιτεύεσθαι κατὰ τοὺς ὑμετέρους νόμους, | [καὶ ἐν τ]οῖς ἄλλοις
πειρασόμεθα εὐχρηστοῦντες ὑμῖν ἀεί τινος ἀγαθοῦ | [παραίτ]ιοι
γίνεσθαι· ἀποδεχόμεθα δὲ καὶ τὰ παρ' ὑμῶμ φιλάνθρωπα καὶ
τὰς ‖ [πίστεις, κ]αὶ αὐτοὶ δὲ πειρασόμεθα μηδενὸς λείπεσθαι ἐγ   15
χάριτος ἀποδόσει· | [ἀπεστά]λκαμεν δὲ πρὸς ὑμᾶς Λεύκιον
Ὄρβιον τὸν ἐπιμελησόμενον τῆς | [πόλεως κ]α[ὶ] τῆς χώρας
ὅπως μηδεὶς ὑμᾶς παρενοχλῆι. Ἔρρωσθε.

From Heraclea at Latmus. We have adopted the readings of
Holleaux (*Rev. ét. an.* 19 (1917), 237 ff.). The period is evidently
the first invasion of Asia Minor by the Romans in the war against
Antiochus. The Heracleans hastened to join the Romans and
apparently sent an embassy to Rome to secure the ratification of the
promises made by the commander of the Roman forces in the field.
The consul at Rome promises the embassy that their state shall have
its freedom and the right to use its own laws. Henzen (*Ann. Inst.*
1852, 138) restored the name of Gnaeus Manlius Volso in the
first line and assumed that this was a letter issued by him as proconsul
in 188 B.C., when he had been sent out at the head of a commission
of ten to settle the affairs of Asia. Holleaux shows conclusively that
this restoration and interpretation is incorrect.

[253]

MUNICIPAL DOCUMENTS IN GREEK AND LATIN

5. SENATUS CONSULTA DE THISBENSIBUS
(170 a. Chr.)

Viereck, *Sermo Graecus*, 11; Bruns, 37; *IG.* VII, 2225; Ditt.
*Syll.*³ 646; Riccobono, p. 199.

Κόϊντος Μαίνιος Τίτου υἱὸς στρατηγὸς τῆι συνκλή|τωι συνε-
βουλεύσατο ἐν κομετίωι πρὸ ἡμερ|[ῶ]ν ἑπτὰ εἰδυῶν Ὀκτωμβρίων.
5 Γραφομένωι | παρῆσαν Μάνιος Ἀκίλιος Μανίου υἱὸς Ὀλτε[ι‖νί]α,
Τίτος Νομίσιος Τίτου υἱός. Περὶ ὧν Θισ|[β]εῖς λόγους ἐποιή-
σαντο περὶ τῶν καθ' αὑ|[τ]οὺς πραγμάτων, οἵτινες ἐν τῆι φιλίαι
τῆι | ἡμετέραι ἐνέμειναν, ὅπως αὐτοῖς δοθῶσιν, | [ο]ῖς τὰ καθ'
10 αὐτοὺς πράγματα ἐξηγήσωνται· περὶ τού‖του τοῦ πράγματος
οὕτως ἔδοξεν· ὅπως Κόϊντος | Μαίνιος στρατηγὸς τῶν ἐκ τῆς
συνκλήτου | [π]έντε ἀποτάξηι, οἳ ἂν αὐτῶι ἐκ τῶν δημοσίων
πρα|[γμ]άτων καὶ τῆς ἰδίας πίστεως φαίνωνται ἔδοξε. | Προτέραι
15 εἰδυῶν Ὀκτωμβρίων· γραφομένωι παρῆ‖σαν Πόπλιος Μούκιος
Κοΐντου υἱός, Μάαρκος Κλαύ|διος Μαάρκου υἱός, Μάνιος Σέργιος
Μανίου υἱός. | Ὡσαύτως περὶ ὧν οἱ αὐτοὶ λόγους ἐποιήσαντο
περὶ χώρας | [κ]αὶ περὶ λιμένων καὶ προσόδων καὶ περὶ ὀρέων·
ἃ αὐτῶν ἐγε‖[γ]όνεισαν, ταῦτα ἡμῶν μ[ὲ]ν ἕνεκεν ἔχειν ἐξεῖναι
20 ἔδο‖ξεν.—Περὶ ἀρχῶν καὶ περὶ ἱερῶν καὶ προσόδων ὅπως αὐτοὶ |
[κ]υριεύωσι, περὶ τούτου τοῦ πράγματος οὕτως ἔδοξεν· | οἵτινες
εἰς τὴν φιλίαν τὴν ἡμετέραν πρὸ τοῦ ἢ Γάϊος Λοκρέ|τιος τὸ
στρατόπεδον πρὸς τὴν πόλιν Θίσβας προσήγα|γεν, ὅπως οὗτοι
25 ἔτη δέκα τ[ὰ] ἔγγιστα κυριεύωσιν. Ἔδοξ[εν]. ‖ Περὶ χώρας,
οἰκιῶν καὶ τῶν ὑπαρχόντων αὐτοῖς· οὗ ποτέ | τι αὐτῶν γέγονεν,
ὅπως [τὰ] ἑαυτῶν αὐτοῖς ἔχειν ἐξῆι | ἔδοξεν. Ὡσαύτως περὶ ὧν
οἱ αὐτοὶ λόγους ἐποιήσαντο, ὅπω[ς] | οἱ αὐτόμολοι οἱ ἴδιοι ἐκεῖ
φυγάδες ὄντες, τὴν ἄκραν αὐτοῖς ὅπως | τειχίσαι ἐξῆι καὶ ἐκεῖ
30 κατοικῶσιν οὗτοι, καθότι ἐνεφάνισαν, οὕ‖τως ἔδοξεν· ὅπως ἐκεῖ
κατοικῶσιν καὶ τοῦτο τειχίσωσιν. Ἔδο|ξεν.—Τὴν πόλιν τειχίσαι
οὐκ ἔδοξεν. Ὡσαύτως περὶ ὧν οἱ αὐτοὶ | λόγους ἐποιήσαντο,
χρυσίον, ὃ συνήνεγκαν εἰς στέφανον, ὅ|πως εἰς τὸ Καπετώλιον
στέφανον κατασκευάσωσιν, τούτοις, καθ|[ότι] ἐνεφάνισαν, ὅπως
35 αὐτοῖς ἀποδοθῆ, ὅ[πω]ς τοῦτον τὸν στέφανον εἰς ‖ [τὸ] Καπετώ-
λιον κατασκευάσωσιν· οὕτως ἀποδοῦναι ἔδοξεν. Ὡσαύ|[τ]ως
περὶ ὧν οἱ αὐτοὶ λόγους ἐποιήσαντο, ἀνθρώπους, οἵτινες ὑπε-

[254]

FROM ITALY AND THE PROVINCES

να[ν|τί]α τοῖς δημοσίοις πράγμασι τοῖς ἡμετέροις καὶ τοῖς ἑαυτῶν
εἰσιν, | [ὅπ]ως οὗτοι κατέχωνται· περὶ τούτου τοῦ πράγματος,
καθὼς ἂν Κοίν|[τω]ι Μαινίωι στρατηγῶι ἐκ τῶν δημοσίων
πραγμάτων καὶ τῆς ἰδίας πί|[[σ]τεως δοκῇ, οὕτως ποιεῖν ἔδοξεν. 40
—Οἵτινες εἰς ἄλλας πόλεις ἀ|πήλθοσαν καὶ οὐχὶ πρὸς τὸν παρ'
ἡμῶν στρατηγὸν παρεγένοντο, ὅπως | μὴ εἰς τάξιν καταπορεύων-
ται· περὶ τούτου τοῦ πράγματος πρὸς Αὗλον | ['Ο]στιλιον
ὕπατον γράμματα ἀποστεῖλαι ἔδοξεν, ὅπως περὶ τούτου τῆι
δι|[αν]οίαι προσέχηι, καθὼς ἂν αὐτῶι ἐκ τῶν δημοσίων πραγ-
μάτων καὶ || [τ]ῆς ἰδίας πίστεως φαίνηται. ῎Εδοξεν. | Ὡσαύτως 45
περὶ ὧν οἱ αὐτοὶ λόγους ἐποιήσαντο περ[ὶ | τ]ῶν δικῶν Ξενοπι-
θίδος καὶ Μνασίδος, ὅπως ἐκ Χαλκίδος ἀφεθῶσι, | καὶ Δαμοκρίτα
Διονυσίου ἐχ Θηβῶν· ταύτας ἐκ τούτων τῶν πόλε|ων ἀφεῖναι
ἔδοξεν, καὶ ὅπως εἰς Θίσβας μὴ κατέλθωσιν. ῎Εδοξεν. ||['Ω]σαύτως 50
περὶ οὗ ταύτας τὰς γυναῖκας ὑδρίας σὺν ἀργυρίω[ι | εἰ]ς τὸν
στρατηγὸν ἐνενκεῖν εἴπασαν· περὶ τούτου τοῦ πράγ[μα|το]ς
ὕστερον ἔναντι Γαίου Λοκρετίου βουλεύσασθαι ἔδοξεν. |
—Ὡσαύτως περὶ ὧν οἱ αὐτοὶ Θισβεῖς ἐνεφάνισαν περὶ σίτου καὶ
ἐλ[αί]||ου ἑαυτοῖς κοινωνίαν πρὸς Γναῖον Πανδοσῖνον γεγονέναι·
περὶ τού||[τ]ου τοῦ πράγματος κἂν κριτὰς λαβεῖν βούλωνται, 55
τούτοις κριτὰς δο[ῦ]|ναι ἔδοξεν.—Ὡσαύτως περὶ ὧν οἱ αὐτοὶ
λόγους ἐποιήσαντο περὶ τοῦ | γράμματα δοῦναι Θισβεῦσιν εἰς
Αἰτωλίαν καὶ Φωκίδα· περὶ τούτου | τοῦ πράγματος Θισβεῦσι
καὶ Κορωνεῦσιν εἰς Αἰτωλίαν καὶ Φωκί|δα καὶ ἐάν που εἰς ἄλλας
πόλεις βούλωνται, γράμματα φιλάν||θρωπα δοῦναι ἔδοξεν. 60

From Thisbe. In the Macedonian war Thisbe, Haliartus, and
Coronea remained loyal to Perseus, driving out the Roman party
in their cities. When C. Lucretius advanced against Thisbe, it surrendered without a contest. The Roman praetor restored the city
to the partisans of Rome, who were recalled from exile, and the
Macedonian supporters remaining in the city when it surrendered
were sold into slavery (Livy, 42. 46, 63, where Mommsen reads
Thisbas instead of *Thebas* in both chapters). The pro-Roman party
in control of the city sent an embassy to Rome for the settlement
of problems which had not been adjusted by the praetor. The
public lands, revenues, harbor, and mountains, which had apparently been confiscated, were restored to the city. For the next ten

MUNICIPAL DOCUMENTS IN GREEK AND LATIN

years, only those citizens who had been friendly to Rome before Lucretius captured the city were eligible for magistracies, or priesthoods, or as treasurers of the public revenues. In view of the fact that there was danger of the anti-Roman party returning and driving out the supporters of Rome, the latter asked permission to fortify the citadel and dwell there. This request was granted, but the Romans refused permission to rebuild the walls of the city, probably with an eye to possible future complications. The Roman party was small and weak, and there was danger of their being driven out. The senate instructed Quintus Manius to take necessary steps to prevent an uprising on the part of residents of Thisbe whose loyalty was suspected. The direct request of the ambassadors to imprison these men was refused. The consul, Aulus Hostilius, then in Macedonia, was ordered to take such action as he deemed advisable about the return of the exiles. The senate probably left these questions in abeyance intentionally in order to have a reasonable ground for interference in the affairs of Thisbe at any time. The senate thereby definitely abandoned the policies of Flamininus in his first settlement of the affairs of Greece. It is interesting to note that the Italian trader had soon penetrated Greece after the first invasion by Roman troops. Gnaeus Pandosinus, a native of Pandosia in southern Italy, had leased a part of the public lands of Thisbe, paying a certain percentage of the yield in grain and oil to the municipal treasury as rental. There arose some dispute in connection with this contract, which the senate referred to arbiters.

6. SENATUS CONSULTUM DE DELO
(164 a. Chr.)

Ditt. *Syll.*³ 664.

Οἱ στρατηγοὶ Χαρμίδει ἐπιμελη|τεῖ Δήλου χαίρειν. Γενομένων|
πλειόνων λόγων ἐν τεῖ βουλεῖ | περὶ τοῦ δόγματος οὗ ἤνεγκεν ‖
5 ἐκ Ῥώμης Δημήτριος Ῥηναι|εὺς ὑπὲρ τῶν κατὰ τὸ Σαραπι|εῖον·
ἔδοξεν μὴ κωλύειν αὐ|τὸν ἀνοίγειν καὶ θεραπεύειν | τὸ ἱερὸν
10 καθάπερ καὶ πρότε‖ρον, γράψαι δὲ καὶ πρός σε πε|ρὶ τούτων
ἵνα εἰδῇς· ὑποτε|τάχαμεν δέ σοι καὶ τοῦ ἐνε|χθέντος ὑπ᾽ αὐτοῦ
δόγματος | τὸ ἀντίγραφον.‖
15 Κόϊντος Μινύκιος Κοΐντου | υἱὸς στρατηγὸς τεῖ συγκλή|τωι

[256]

συνεβουλεύσατο ἐν κο|μετίωι εἰδυιοῖς ἐντερκ(α)λα|[ρ]ίοις· γρα-
φομένου παρῆσαν || Πόπλιος Πόρκιος Ποπλίου, Τε|βέριος 20
Κλαύδιος Τεβερίου | Κρυστομίνας, Μάνιος Φοντή|ιος Γαΐου·
περὶ ὧν Δημήτριος | ῾Ρηναῖος λόγους ἐποιήσατο, || ὅπως τὸ ἐν 25
Δήλωι ἱερὸν Σαρά|πιδος αὐτῶι θεραπεύειν ἐ|ξεῖ, Δηλίους δὲ κω-
λύειν καὶ | τὸν ἐξ Ἀθηνῶν ἔπαρχον | παραγινόμενον ὧι ἔλασ||σον 30
θεραπεύει· περὶ τούτου | τοῦ πράγματος οὕτως ἔδο|ξεν· καθὼς
τὸ πρότερον ἐ|θεράπευεν, ἕνεκεν ἡμῶν | θεραπεύειν ἔξεστιν τοῦ || 35
μή τι ὑπεναντίον τῶι τῆς | συγκλήτου δόγματι γίνηται. | ῎Εδοξεν.

From Delos. Although Delos at this time was under the administration of Athens, and the latter was a free city allied with
Rome, the senate did not hesitate to interfere in the internal
government of the island. Demetrius appealed to Rome to permit
the opening of the Serapeum on Delos and the renewal of the cult
which the Athenians had forbidden. He secured a decree of the
senate in his favor, and, armed with this, he came to Athens and
presented it to the senate. It is apparent from the wording of the
letter which the Athenians sent to the governor of Delos that
considerable opposition had arisen in Athens over this decree which
is extremely brusque and softened by no diplomatic amenities. It
is not even addressed to the Athenians nor is any request made to
them to respect the wishes of Rome. Contrast with this the letter
of Flamininus (no. 1). For the date of this document *cf.* note by
Hiller, Ditt. *Syll.*³ 664.

7. SENATUS CONSULTUM DE TIBURTIBUS
(ca. 159 a. Chr.)

CIL. I, 201 = XIV, 3584; Dessau, 19; Bruns, 39; Riccobono,
p. 204.

Cornelius Cn. f. pr(aetor) sen(atum) cons(uluit) a. d. III nonas
Maias sub aede Kastorus. | Scr. adf. A. Manlius A. f., Sex. Iulius
..., L. Postumius S. f. |

Quod Teiburtes v(erba) f(ecistis) quibusque de rebus vos pur-
gavistis, ea senatus | animum advortit ita utei aequom fuit—nosque
ea ita audiveramus, || ut vos deixsistis vobeis nontiata esse—: ea nos 5
animum nostrum | non indoucebamus ita facta esse, propterea quod

MUNICIPAL DOCUMENTS IN GREEK AND LATIN

scibamus, | ea vos merito nostro facere non potuisse, neque vos
dignos esse | quei ea faceretis, neque id vobeis neque rei poplicae
vostrae | oitile esse facere; et postquam vostra verba senatus audivit, ||
10 tanto magis animum nostrum indoucimus, ita utei ante | arbitra-
bamur, de eieis rebus af vobeis peccatum non esse. | Quonque de
eieis rebus senatuei purgati estis, credimus vosque | animum vos-
trum indoucere oportet, item vos populo | Romano purgatos fore.

Bronze tablet found at Tibur in the sixteenth century, now lost.
The use of the second person in the verbs shows that this document
is a letter from the praetor, containing the substance of a *senatus
consultum*. It is in the form of a statement first made to the Tiburtine
deputies in the senate. For the conventional form of a *S.C.*, *cf.*
Abbott, 230, 413 *ff.* The date is fixed by the fact that L. Cornelius
Lentulus Lupus, who was consul in 156 B.C., held the praetorship
in 160 or 159 B.C. (*cf.* Münzer, *R.E.* 4, 1386 *f.*). For confirmation
of this date, *cf.* also Willems, *Le sénat de la république rom.* 1, 250 *f.*
Tibur had belonged to the old Latin League. It was at this time
a *civitas foederata*, being one of the *socii Latini nominis*. Whether or
not it was under the *aequum foedus* of Sp. Cassius is not clear (*cf.*
Marquardt, *St. Verw.* 1, 47, n. 3). It became a *municipium* by the
legislation of 90 B.C. A not uncommon cause of complaint against
Italian cities was their failure to furnish the required contingent
of troops (*cf.* Willems, *op. cit.* 2, 692). What the question at issue
in this case was we do not know, but the point of interest in the
document is that Tibur's explanation of the incident is laid before
the senate, probably by a legation (*cf. quod Teiburtes verba fecistis*),
and that the senate speaks for the Roman people and communicates
its decision through its presiding officer.

8. SENATUS CONSULTUM DE NARTHACIENSIBUS
ET MELITAEENSIBUS
(159–147 a. Chr.)

IG. IX, 2, 89; Ditt. *Syll.*[3] 674; de Ruggiero, *L'arbitrato pubblico*, 8; Tod, XXXIV; Viereck, *Sermo Graecus*, 12.

[Στρατ]αγέοντος τῶν Θεσσαλῶν Λέοντο[ς | τοῦ ῾Αγ]ησίππου
Λαρισαίου, ἐν δὲ Ναρθακίω[ι | ἀρχόντ]ων Κρίτωνος τοῦ ᾿Αμεινία,
Πολυκλέος | [τοῦ Φει]δίππου, Γλαυκέτα τοῦ ᾿Αγελάου, ἀν[ε||-

γράφη τὸ] δόγμα τὸ γενόμενον ὑπὸ συγκ[λή|του ἐπὶ σ]τρατηγοῦ 5
τῶν Θεσσαλῶν Θεσσα|[λοῦ τοῦ] Θρασυμήδεος Φεραίου. | [Γάϊος
Ὁσ]τίλιος Αὔλου υἱὸς Μαγκῖνος στρα|[τηγὸς τ]ῆι συγκλήτωι
συνεβουλεύσατο πρὸ||[. . . . νω]νῶν Κοϊντιλίων ἐγ κομετίωι· 10
γραφο|[μένωι π]αρῆσαν Κόϊντος (Σ)τατιλιηνὸς Κοΐντου | [υἱὸς
Κορ]νηλία, Γναῖος Λοτάτιος Γναίου υἱὸ[ς | Ἀ. . . . ήν]ση, Αὖλος
Σεμπρώνιος Αὔλου υἱὸς Φα|[λέρνα]. Περὶ ὧν Θεσσαλοὶ Μελι-
ταιεῖς Ἁρμό||[ξενος Λυ]σάνδρου, Λαμπρόμαχος Πολίτα | [πρε- 15
σβευ]ταὶ λόγους ἐποιήσαντο, ἄνδρες κα|[λοὶ κἀγα]θοὶ καὶ φίλοι
παρὰ δήμου καλοῦ | [κἀγαθο]ῦ καὶ φίλου συμμάχου (τε),
χάριτα | [φιλίαν σ]υμμαχίαν τε ἀνενεώσαντο, πε||[ρὶ χώρας] 20
δημοσίας καὶ περὶ χωρίου ἐρήμου | [εἴπασαν], μεθ᾿ ἧς χώρας
εἰς τὴμ φιλίαν τοῦ | [δήμου τ]οῦ Ῥωμαίων παρεγένοντο, ἣγ
χώ|[ραν Ναρθα]κιεῖς μετὰ ταῦτα ἑαυτῶν ἀδίκως | [ἐποιήσαντ]ο,
περὶ τούτου τοῦ πράγματος ὅπως || [τὴν διάνοι]αν πρόσ(σ)χωσιν, 25
ὅπως τοῦτο τὸ πρᾶ|[γμα ἀκέρα]ιον αὐτοῖς ἀποκατασταθῇ οὕτω |
[καθὼς πρότερο]ν ἐπὶ Μηδείωι καὶ ἐπὶ Θεσσαλῶν |. . . . .
καὶ ἐπὶ τῶν περὶ Πύλλον Μακε|[δόνων κεκρι]μένον αὐτοῖς ἦν,
ταῦτά τε τὰ κ[ρί||ματα κύρια αὐτοῖ]ς ῇ· περὶ τούτου τοῦ πρά- 30
γμα|[τος συνευδόκ]ησεν ἡμῖν καὶ Ναρθακιεῦσιν | [ὅπως τὸν
ἀγῶν]α τὸν παρόντα κρίνῃ ἐμ Μ[ελι|τείαι. . . . . . ἐ]ν ταύτηι τῆι
χώρα[ι. . . . . |. . ἀμφοτέρων] τῶν δήμων ἐ[πιτρεπόντων] || . . 35
ἐστὶν ὧι φα. .| . . ιη. . νη[. καὶ περὶ ὧν Θεσσαλοὶ | Ναρθακιεῖς
Ν]ικάτας Τα[. .|. . . . .,πρεσβε]υταὶ λόγο[υς] ἐπ[οιήσαντο κατὰ|
πρόσωπον ἐν τῆι] συγκλήτ[ωι. .ἄνδρες καλοὶ || κἀγα]θοὶ καὶ 40
φίλοι παρὰ δήμου κα[λοῦ κἀ|γαθοῦ κα]ὶ φίλ[ου συμμάχου τε
ἡμετέρου, χά|ριτα φιλ]ίαν συ[μ]μα[χίαν τε ἀνενεώσαντο καὶ |
περὶ τῶν πραγ]μάτω[ν τῶν καθ᾿ αὑτοὺς διελέ|γ]ησα[ν] περὶ
χώρας [καὶ] ἱ[ε]ρ[ῶν περὶ τῆ]ς τε || ἀφ[η]ρη[μένης] τ[ῆς κατὰ 45
Μελιτ]α[ι]έας ἀρχῆς [Να]ρ[θακιέ[ω]ν [τῶν] ἐν τ[ῆ Ἀχαι]ία[ι·
καὶ γὰρ] μετὰ τα[ύτης] | τ[ῆ]ς χώρας εἰς τὴ[ν φ]ιλία[ν] τ[οῦ
δή]μου [τοῦ Ῥω|μ]αίω[ν] Ναρθακιεῖς παραγ[εγονέν]αι, [κ]αὶ
[π]ερὶ | τῆς χώρας καὶ [τῶν] ἱερῶν κριτηρίοις [νεν]ικηκ[έ]||ναι 50
κατὰ νόμους τοὺς Θεσσα[λῶ]ν, οἷς [νό]|μοις ἕως τα[ν]ῦν χρῶν-
[τ]αι, οὓς νόμους Τίτος | Κόϊγκτιος ὕπατος ἀπὸ τῆς τῶν δέκα
πρεσ|βευτῶν γνώμης ἔδωκεν, καὶ κατὰ δόγμα | συγκλήτου, περί
τε τούτων τῶν π[ρ]αγμά||[τω]ν ἔτει ἀνώτερον τρίτῳ ἐπὶ τριῶν 55

MUNICIPAL DOCUMENTS IN GREEK AND LATIN

δικασ‖[τη]ρίων νενικηκέναι, ἐπὶ Σαμίων, Κολο[φ]ων[ί|ων,]
Μαγνήτων, κεκ[ρι]μένα εἶναι κατὰ νόμου[ς], | ὅπως ταῦτα κύρια
ᾖ οὕτως καθὼς καὶ ἄλλοις | γεγονός ἐστιν· περὶ τούτου τοῦ
60 πράγματος ‖ οὕτως ἔδοξεν· χάριτα φιλίαν συμμαχίαν | [ἀ]να-
νεώσασθαι τούτοις τε φιλανθρώπως ἀ|ποκριθῆναι, ἄνδρας καλοὺς
κἀγαθοὺς προσ|αγορεῦσαι, ὅσα κεκριμένα ἐστὶν κατὰ νόμους |
65 οὓς Τίτος Κοΐγκτιος ὕπατος ἔδωκεν, ταῦτα κα‖θὼς κεκριμένα
ἐστὶν οὕτω δοκεῖ κύρια εἶναι δεῖν· | τοῦτό τε μὴ εὐχερὲς εἶναι,
ὅσα κατὰ νόμους κε|κριμένα ἐστὶν ἄκυρα ποιεῖν. Ξένιά τε
ἑκατέροις Γάϊ|ος Ὀστίλιος στρατηγὸς τὸν ταμίαν δοῦναι
70 κε|[λ]εύσῃ ἀπὸ σηστερτίων νόμων ἑκατὸν εἴκοσι ‖ [πέ]ντε εἰς
ἑκάστην πρεσβείαν, οὕτω καθὼς ἂν | [αὐτῶι ἐκ] τῶν δημοσίων
πραγμάτων πίστε|[ώς τε τῆς] ἰδίας φαίνηται. Ἔδοξεν.

This inscription is engraved on two sides of a stone found at
Narthacium in Thessaly. It is probably earlier than 146 B.C., since
no reference is found in it to the provincial organization of Achaea
by Mummius and his commission of ten in that year (*cf.* Willems,
Le sénat de la république rom. 2, 705, n. 3; de Ruggiero, *op. cit.* 254),
and because the two peoples in the controversy are spoken of as
friends and allies of the Roman people—terms which would hardly
be applied to provincial cities. On the other hand the fact that
Hostilius, the praetor who presided over the senate, was not consul
until 137 B.C. prevents us from dating the inscription much earlier
than 150 B.C.

The inscription records the settlement of a dispute between the
cities of Melitaea and Narthacium by the Roman senate. The
Melitaeans claimed that they owned the territory in question when
they were admitted into the friendship of Rome and that the land
had been awarded to them by arbitration in previous decisions. The
ambassadors of Narthacium claimed that the land had been awarded
to them by Titus Quinctius and that his action had been ratified
by a decree of the senate. Furthermore, the dispute had been
arbitrated recently by a mixed tribunal from Samos, Colophon, and
Magnesia, which had given a decision in their favor. The senate
decided in favor of Narthacium, thus confirming the arrangement
of Flamininus. In the same way, in deciding a similar question at
issue between Priene and Samos, the senate upheld the arrangements

FROM ITALY AND THE PROVINCES

made by Manlius and the senatorial commission (Ditt. *Syll.*³ 688), which had been confirmed by a judicial decision rendered by the Rhodians acting as arbiters. *Cf.* pp. 153 *ff.*

9. EPISTULA Q. FABI MAXIMI AD DYMAEOS
(ca. 139 a. Chr.)

Viereck, *Sermo Graecus,* 4; *CIG.* 1543; Ditt. *Syll.*³ 684.

Ἐπὶ θεοκόλου Λέωνος, γραμματέ|ος τοῦ συνεδρίου Στρατο-
κλέος. | Κόϊντος Φάβιος Κοΐντου Μάξιμος, ἀνθύπατος Ῥωμαίων,
Δυμαί|ων τοῖς ἄρχουσι καὶ συνέδροις καὶ τῆι πόλει χαίρειν.
Τῶν περὶ ‖ Κυλλάνιον συνέδρων ἐμφανισάντων μοι περὶ τῶν   5
συντελε|σθέντων παρ᾽ ὑμῖν ἀδικημάτων, λέγω δὲ ὑπὲρ τῆς
ἐμπρήσε|ως καὶ φθορᾶς τῶν ἀρχ(εί)ων καὶ τῶν δημοσίων γραμ-
μάτων, ὧν ἐγε|γόνει ἀρχηγὸς τῆς ὅλης συγχύσεως Σῶσος
Ταυρομένεος ὁ | καὶ τοὺς νόμους γράψας ὑπεναντίους τῆι
ἀποδοθείσηι τοῖς ‖ [᾽Α]χαιοῖς ὑπὸ Ῥωμαίων πολιτ[εία]ι, περὶ   10
ὧν τὰ κατὰ μέρος διή[λ]θ[ο]μεν ἐν Πά]τραις μετὰ τοῦ πα[ρ]όν-
[το]ς συμβουλίου· ἐπεὶ οὖν οἱ διαπρα|[ξά]μενοι ταῦτα ἐφαίνοντό
μοι τῆς χειρίστης κα[τασ]τάσεως | [κα]ὶ ταραχῆς κα[τασκευὴν]
ποιούμενο[ι τοῖς ῞Ελλησι πᾶσ]ιν· οὐ μό|[νον γὰρ] τῆς πρ[ὸς
ἀ]λλήλου[ς] ἀσυναλλ[α]ξ[ίας] καὶ χρε[ωκοπίας οἰ‖κεῖα], ἀλλὰ   15
καὶ [τ]ῆς ἀποδεδομένης κατὰ [κ]οινὸν τοῖς ῞Ελλ[ησιν ἐ]‖λευθερίας
ἀλλότρια καὶ τῆ[ς] ἡμετέ[ρα]ς προαιρέσεως, ἐγ[ώ, πα]‖ρασχο-
μένων τῶν κατηγόρων ἀληθινὰς ἀποδείξεις, Σῶ|σον μέν, τὸν
γεγονότα ἀρχηγὸν [τ]ῶν πραχθέντων καὶ νο|μογραφήσαντα ἐπὶ
καταλύσει τῆς ἀποδοθείσης πολιτεί‖[α]ς, κρίνας ἔνοχον εἶναι   20
θανάτωι παρεχώρισα, ὁμοίως δὲ καὶ | [Φορ]μίσκον Ἐχεσθένεος
τῶν δαμιοργῶν τὸν συμπράξαντα | [τοῖς] ἐμπρήσασι τὰ ἀρχεῖα
καὶ τὰ δημόσια γράμματα, ἐπεὶ καὶ | [αὐτὸς] ὡμολόγησεν·
Τιμόθεον δὲ Νικία τὸμ μετὰ τοῦ Σώσου | [γεγονό]τα νομογράφον,
ἐπεὶ ἔλασσον ἐφαίνετο ἠδικηκώς, ἐ‖[κέλευσα] προάγειν εἰς Ῥώμην,   25
ὀρκίσας ἐφ᾽ [ᾧ]ι τῆι νουμηνίαι τοῦ ἐν[ίάτου μηνὸ]ς ἔστα[ι] ἐκεῖ,
καὶ ἐμφανίσας τ[ῶι ἐπ]ὶ τῶν ξένων στρατη‖[γῶι, ὅπω]ς ἂν [μὴ
π]ρότερον ἐπά[ν]εισ[ιν εἰ]ς οἶκον, ἐὰ[ν μ]ὴ αὐ..

From Dymae. Shortly after the destruction of Corinth by Mummius the Romans restored to the Greek cities their ancient

[261]

assemblies (Pausanias, 7. 16. 10), but apparently with a constitution modelled on oligarchical lines (ll. 9 ff.). In Dymae there was a party led by Sosus which attempted a revolution. The public records were destroyed by fire, and the revolutionary party enacted laws contrary to the spirit of the constitution proposed by Rome. The pro-Roman party appealed to Fabius who restored them to power and condemned Sosus to death together with Phormiscus who was one of the magistrates associated with the conspirators. Timotheus, another conspirator, was banished to Rome. This document is important evidence for the influence of Rome in shaping the constitutions of the Greek cities along oligarchical lines.

10. SENTENTIA Q. M. MINUCIORUM INTER GENUATES ET VITURIOS
(117 a. Chr.)

CIL. i¹, 199 = v, 7749; Dessau, 5946; Bruns, 184.

Q. M. Minucieis Q. f. Rufeis de controvorsieis inter | Genuateis et Veiturios in re praesente cognoverunt, et coram inter eos controvosias composeiverunt, | et qua lege agrum possiderent et qua fineis fierent dixserunt. Eos fineis facere terminosque statui iuserunt; | ubei ea facta essent, Romam coram venire iouserunt. Romae
5 coram sententiam ex senati consulto dixerunt eidib. || Decemb. L. Caecilio Q. f. Q. Muucio Q. f. cos.—Qua ager privatus casteli Vituriorum est, quem agrum eos vendere heredemque | sequi licet, is ager vectigal. nei siet.—Langatium fineis agri privati. Ab rivo infimo, qui oritur ab fontei in Mannicelo ad flovium | Edem; ibi terminus stat. Inde flovio suso vorsum in flovium Lemurim. Inde flovio Lemuri susum usque ad rivom Comberane........Agri poplici quod Langenses posident, hisce finis videntur esse. Ubi comfluont | Edus et Procobera, ibei terminus stat. Inde Ede flovio
15 sursuorsum in montem Lemurino infumo; ibei terminus || stat. Inde sursumvorsum iugo recto monte Lemurino; ibei termin*us* stat......Quem agrum poplicum | iudicamus esse, eum agrum castelanos Langenses Veiturios po*s*idere fruique videtur oportere.
25 Pro eo agro vectigal Langenses || Veituris in poplicum Genuam dent in anos singulos vic(toriatos) n(ummos) cccc. Sei Langenses

eam pequniam non dabunt neque satis | facient arbitratuu Genua-
tium, quod per Genuenses mora non fiat, quo setius eam pequniam
acipiant: tum quod in eo agro | natum erit frumenti partem vicen-
sumam, vini partem sextam Langenses in poplicum Genuam dare
debento | in annos singolos.—Quei intra eos fineis agrum posedet
Genuas aut Viturius, quei eorum posedeit k. Sextil. L. Caicilio |
Q. Muucio cos., eos ita posidere colereque liceat. Eis, quei poside-
bunt, vectigal Langensibus pro portione dent ita uti ceteri || Lan- 30
genses, qui eorum in eo agro agrum posidebunt fruenturque. Praeter
ea in eo agro niquis posideto nisi de maiore parte | Langensium
Veituriorum sententia, dum ne alium intro mitat nisi Genuatem
aut Veiturium colendi causa. Quei eorum | de maiore parte Langen-
sium Veiturium sententia ita non parebit, is eum agrum nei habeto
nive fruimino.—Quei | ager compascuos erit, in eo agro quo minus
pecus pascere Genuates Veituriosque liceat ita utei in cetero agro |
Genuati compascuo, niquis prohibeto, nive quis vim facito, neive
prohibeto quo minus ex eo agro ligna materiamque || sumant 35
utanturque.—Vectigal anni primi k. Ianuaris secundis Veturis
Langenses in poplicum Genuam dare | debento. Quod ante k.
Ianuar. primas Langenses fructi sunt eruntque, vectigal invitei dare
nei debento.— | Prata quae fuerunt proxuma faenisicei L. Caecilio
Q. Muucio cos. in agro poplico, quem Vituries Langenses | posident
et quem Odiates et quem Dectunines et quem Cavaturineis et quem
Mentovines posident, ea prata, | invitis Langensibus et Odiatibus
et Dectuninebus et Cavaturines et Mentovines, quem quisque eorum
agrum || posidebit, inviteis eis niquis sicet nive pascat nive fruatur. 40
Sei Langueses aut Odiates aut Dectunines aut Cavaturines | aut
Mentovines malent in eo agro alia prata inmittere defendere sicare,
id uti facere liceat, dum ne ampliorem | modum pratorum habeant,
quam proxuma aestate habuerunt fructique sunt.—Vituries quei
controvorsias | Genuensium ob iniourias iudicati aut damnati sunt,
sei quis in vinculeis ob eas res est, eos omneis | solvei mittei lei-
berareique a Genuensibus videtur oportere ante eidus Sextilis
primas.—Seiquoi de ea re || iniquom videbitur esse, ad nos adeant 45
primo quoque die et ab omnibus controversis et hono publ. li. | Leg
Moco Meticanio Meticoni f., Plaucus Peliani. Pelioni f.

l. 45. et hono publ. li; *something like* abstineant *required.*

MUNICIPAL DOCUMENTS IN GREEK AND LATIN

Bronze tablet found in 1506, near Genua, now in Genoa. Most of those parts of the inscription which describe the boundaries of the *ager privatus* (ll. 8–12) and the *ager publicus* (ll. 14–23) of the Langenses are omitted here. The document is dated in l. 5. It contains the settlement of a controversy between the *civitas foederata* of Genua and the neighboring tribe of the Viturii or Langenses and certain other tribes (l. 38). So far as the relations of the municipalities to the central government are concerned, its interest for us lies in the fact that it gives us the fullest account which we have in the republican period of the part which Rome played as arbitrator between dependent communities, and that it discloses the control which a *civitas* had over its *attributi*. The Viturii and the other tribes mentioned in l. 38 were *attributi* of Genua (*cf.* Mommsen, *St. R.* 3, 765 *ff.*; *cf.* pp. 138 *f.*, and commentary on no. 49). It is clear that the Viturii had some form of local government, because they were able to receive rental from those who occupied certain lands (ll. 29–30), and to decide certain questions *de maiore parte L. V. sententia* (ll. 30–31, 32). They were, however, not autonomous. The questions at issue between them and Genua have been heard by the local magistrates of Genua (ll. 43–44). So far as private rights go, the citizens may own land (*cf.* ll. 5–6), but, if they occupy any of the *ager publicus* of Genua, they must pay an annual tax to Genua in money or in kind (ll. 24–28).

The magistrates of Genua had proceeded to hear the cases which had arisen (ll. 43–44), but the Viturii appealed to the Roman senate. Such an appeal was quite in accordance with the Roman theory of her relation to all *civitates* in her confines. They were under her hegemony, and consequently their dealings with one another and with independent states, and their relations to communities subordinate to them, were regulated by her. As she expressed it in certain treaties (*cf.* Cic. *pro Balbo*, 35–37), the allied cities were required *maiestatem populi Romani comiter conservare*.

The senate in this case appointed two of its members, the Minucii, as arbitrators. They were descendants of Q. Minucius Rufus, who conquered the Ligurians in 197 B.C. (*cf.* Livy, 32. 27–31; Cic. *Brut.* 73), and were probably patrons of Genua. They proceeded to the locality concerned (*cf.* l. 2), investigated the matter, made

[264]

certain rulings, set up boundary stones, ordered local deputies to come to Rome (*cf.* ll. 4, 46), and reported to the senate. Their decision is: (1) that the Viturii may own certain *ager privatus* which shall be free from taxes (ll. 5–6); (2) that for the *ager publicus* of Genua which they occupy, they shall pay an annual *vectigal* to Genua (ll. 24–32); (3) that the common pasture land may be used by any Genuan or Viturian (ll. 33–34); (4) that the meadows in this public land are reserved for the Viturii (ll. 37–42); (5) that the Viturii who have been imprisoned by the Genuan magistrates shall be set free (ll. 43–44), and (6) that later grievances are to be referred to Rome (l. 45). For arbitration under Rome, *cf.* pp. 152 *ff.*, and nos. 8, 57, 90, etc.

11 LEX OSCA TABULAE BANTINAE
(150–100 a. Chr.)

Bruns, 8; Girard, p. 26; Riccobono, p. 130; Buck, *Oscan and Umbrian Grammar*, p. 230; v. Planta, *Gramm. d. osk.-umbr. Dial.* 2, 599; Conway, *Exempla Selecta*, 2.

Chap. 1. ...... is .... si ... quaestor multam *proposuerit* ....iurabit maximae partis senatus sententia *dummodo non minus* XL adsint, cum ea res consulta erit. Siquis peremerit, prius quam *peremerit,* iurato sciens in comitio sine dolo malo, se ea comitia magis rei publicae causa quam cuiuspiam gratiae aut inimicitiae causa, idque se de senatus sententia maximae partis perimere. Cui sic comitia perimet *quisquam,* is eo die comitia ne habuerit.

Chap. 2. Quis quandoque post hac comitia, habebit magistratus de *capite* vel in pecunias, facito ut populus iurati sententiam dicant, se de iis id sententiae dicere, quod optimum publicum censeat esse, neve fecerit quo quis de ea re minus iuret dolo malo. Siquis contra hoc fecerit aut comitia habuerit, multa tanta esto: n. MM. Et siquis eum potius magistratus multare volet, dumtaxat minoris partis pecuniae multae multare liceto.

Chap. 3. Siquis pro magistratu alteri *capitis* aut pecuniae diem dixerit, is comitia ne habuerit nisi cum apud populum quater oraverit sciens sine dolo malo et *quartum* diem populus perceperit. Quater, neque plus quinquiens, cum reo agito prius quam iudica-tionem dabit, et cum postremum cum reo oraverit, ab eo die in diebus xxx proximis comitia ne habuerit. Siquis contra hoc fecerit, eum siquis volet magistratus multare, liceto, dumtaxat minoris partis pecuniae liceto.

Chap. 4. Cum censores Bantiae populum censebunt, qui civis Bantinus erit, censetor ipse et pecuniam qua lege ii censores censere proposuerint. At siquis in censum non venerit dolo malo, et eius convincitur, ipse in comitio *caedatur* praetoris magistratu, populo praesente sine dolo malo, et immercato cetera familia et pecunia omnino quae eius erit, quae incensa erit, publica esto.

Chap. 5. Praetor, sive praefectus post hac Bantiae erit, siquis apud eos cum altero lege agere volet, aut pro iudicato manum adserere de eis rebus quae hisce in legibus scriptae sunt, ne quem prohibuerit plus diebus x proximis. Siquis contra hoc prohibuerit, multa tanta esto: n.M. Et siquis eum magistratus multare volet, liceto, *dumtaxat* minoris partis pecuniae multae multare liceto.

Chap. 6. Praetor censor Bantiae *ne quis* fuerit, nisi quaestor fuerit, neve censor fuerit nisi praetor fuerit. Et siquis praetor et si*quis censor* . . . . q . . . . virum fuerit, is post ea tr. pl. ne fuerit. Siquis *contra hoc tr. pl. factus* erit, is improbe factus esto. Id magisterium eo . . . . . *quandoque Bantiae* . . . . magisterium *annorum* VI proximorum . . . . quod . . . . magisterium.

A bronze tablet, about 15 by 10 inches, found in 1790 at Bantia, near the borders of Lucania and Apulia, now in the museum at Naples. On one side it has an Oscan inscription, written in Latin letters, and reproduced here in the Latin translation made by Buecheler, as modified by Buck. On the other side is a Latin inscription, of a somewhat later date, with which we are not concerned here. The Oscan inscription was in two columns, of which the right-hand column has been lost. Of the extant left-hand column, the upper and lower parts are broken. Six chapters, which represent about one-sixth of the original law, are preserved. The inscription contains a series of municipal regulations for the federated town of Bantia. This municipal charter was either granted to Bantia by Roman commissioners, and is, therefore, a *lex data*, or more probably, as Mommsen (*St. R.* 3, 701) and Girard think, was adopted by the local assembly. Its primary interest for us lies in

[266]

the fact that it is a fragment of the earliest extant municipal charter. It is also important, because it illustrates the policy of Rome in the second century B.C. of entering into relations with individual cities, rather than with tribes or large sections of country. It is also important as illustrating for the early period the blending of Roman institutions with local autonomy and traditional titles and practices.

The law prescribes the presence of a quorum in the local senate when certain action is taken. It defines the functions and procedure of the local assembly in hearing criminal cases. It lays down certain provisions concerning the census, describes the jurisdiction of the praetor, and establishes a *cursus honorum*. The characteristics of autonomy which we notice in this law are the regularly ordered magistracies, senate, and popular assembly, the taking of the census by the local authorities, the holding of court and the imposition of fines by the praetor of Bantia, and the exercise of criminal jurisdiction by the popular assembly. No mention is made of the exemption, even of Romans or Italians, from the jurisdiction of this popular court, although in most treaties probably Rome stipulated that they should not be tried by the local court (*cf.* Mommsen, *St. R.* 3, 702). The specification of a senatorial quorum for the transaction of certain business is characteristic of Roman practice and is found in later municipal charters. The right of *intercessio* is exercised at Bantia, as well as at Rome, but in the former city it may be used to prevent a meeting of the assembly only on the approval of the senate, and on the taking of an oath by the official exercising it; *cf.* the oath taken by Ti. Gracchus (Aul. Gell. 6. 19). The procedure of the assembly when sitting as a high court was, except for small details, identical with that at Rome (*cf.* Cic. *de domo sua*, 45; Livy, 26. 3). The census followed the same course at Bantia as at Rome, except that in Bantia the penalty for non-appearance was lighter. A still more striking instance of the adoption of a Roman institution occurs in the last paragraph which fixes legally the *cursus honorum*. In this matter the people of Bantia have outdone the Romans who had arrived indirectly at the same end by prescribing in the *lex Villia annalis* the minimum ages at which the several offices should be held (Livy, 40. 44. 1). Incidentally this fact shows that our law is later than 180 B.C. It is

MUNICIPAL DOCUMENTS IN GREEK AND LATIN

surprising to find that one of the municipal magistrates is a tribune (*cf.* last paragraph), but parallels are found at Nuceria (Dessau, 6445 *e*), and Teanum Sidicinum (*ibid.* 6298). For recent literature on this law, see Bruns and Girard.

12. SENATUS CONSULTUM DE CONTROVERSIA
INTER PUBLICANOS ET PERGAMENOS
(in. saec. I a. Chr.)

E.E. 4, 213 *ff.*; Viereck, *Sermo Graecus*, 15.

.... [στρ]ατ[ηγ]ὸν | [πρὸ ἡμερῶν τρι]ῶν καλανδῶν | [Φεβροα-
5 ρίων (?) ἐν] κομετίω μετὰ | [συμβουλίου ἐ]πεγνωκότα δό||[γματι
συγκλή]του περὶ χώρας, ἤ|[τις ἐν ἀντι]λογία ἐστὶν δημοσιώ-|
[ναις πρὸς] Περγαμηνούς· ἐν τῶι | [συμβουλ]ίω παρῆσαν—
(*sequuntur nomina*).

The date of this decree of the senate cannot be determined with accuracy. Willems (*Le sénat de la république rom.* 1, 693 *ff.*) has dated it ca. 98–94 B.C. The dispute between the *publicani* and the city of Pergamum was referred to the senate. Nothing is known about the nature of the dispute, but it is probable that the tax-collectors attempted to bring the temple-lands under their jurisdiction as at Ilium and Oropus (nos. 14, 18). If, however, Pergamum still enjoyed the privileges which were conferred upon it by the testament of Attalus, the dispute may be over lands claimed by the city and therefore exempt from tribute.

13. DECRETUM CN. POMPEI STRABONIS
(90 a. Chr.)

CIL. 1², 709; *Bull. arch. com.* 38 (1910), 275; *An. ép.* 1911, no. 126; Girard, p. 61; Dessau, 8888.

Cn. Pompeius Sex. *f. imperator* virtutis caussa | equites Hispanos ceives *Romanos fecit in castre*is apud Asculum a. d. xiv k. Dec. | ex lege Iulia. In consilio *fuerunt*: |

L. Gellius L. f. Tro. Cn. Octavius Q. f.

(*et alia nomina quinquaginta septem*)
TURMA SALLVITANA
Sanibelser Adingibas f.
(*et alia nomina viginti novem*)

[268]

FROM ITALY AND THE PROVINCES

Cn. Pompeius Sex. f. imperator | virtutis caussa turmam | Salluitanam donavit in | castreis apud Asculum | cornuculo et patella, torque, | armilla, palereis; et frumen*t*um | duplex.

A bronze plate, which, with some fragments missing, was first published in the *Bull. arch. com.* 36 (1908), 169 *ff.* Later a small but important fragment was found, and the inscription was brought out in its present form in the *Bull. arch. com.* 38 (1910), 273–280. The decree was issued in the camp at Asculum, but this copy of it was kept on the Capitol in Rome. It has been much discussed, both before and after the discovery of the new fragment; *cf. e.g., An. ép.* 1909, no. 30; 1910, pp. 30, 38, 41, 55; 1911, pp. 29–30; Pais, *Studi storici,* 2, 113–162; *Rendiconti della r. accad. dei Lincei,* Ser. v, 19 (1910), 72–87; de Sanctis, *Atti della r. accad. delle scienze di Torino,* 45 (1910), 144 *ff.;* V. Costa, *Rend. della r. accad. delle scienze dell' instit. di Bologna,* 2 (1908–1909), 37–40; *ibid.* 4 (1910–1911), 44–49; Girard, *op. cit.*; Stevenson, *Journ. Rom. Studies,* 9 (1919), 95–101. It confers Roman citizenship and other rewards, mentioned in the last paragraph, on certain persons. The first grant, that of Roman citizenship, is made with the approval of the *consilium,* which was composed ordinarily of the military tribunes and the chief centurion of each legion. The names of the members of the *consilium,* sixty in all, are given in the early part of the inscription. L. Caesar, after his great victory over the Samnites and Lucanians, and sometime in 90 B.C., secured the passage of a law which granted citizenship to the allies and Latins; *cf.* Rotondi, *Leges publicae populi Romani,* 339. Probably the same law also authorized the grant of citizenship to provincial auxiliaries of federated and stipendiary cities, who had contributed by their valor to Roman success. The grant of these rights to provincials at such an early date is surprising. It seems to indicate an unusually liberal attitude on the part of Strabo. The award in this case was made by him after the battle near Firmum (*cf.* Appian, *B.C.* 1. 6. 47; Livy, *Ep.* 74, 76). The decree was drawn up *in castreis apud Asculum,* and no mention is made in it of the consulship which Strabo held in 89 B.C. It belongs therefore to 90 B.C., and it bears the date of Nov. 17. For the arguments in favor of the date 89 B.C., *cf.* Dessau, *loc. cit.* and Stevenson, *loc. cit.* Perhaps similar rewards were given

MUNICIPAL DOCUMENTS IN GREEK AND LATIN

to other Spanish squadrons and to auxiliary troops from other provinces and recorded elsewhere, but no other tablets of this sort have yet been found. It is the first example of a *lex data* issued by a general, based on a *lex rogata*, *cf.* pp. 232 *ff.*, and Girard, *op. cit.* At a later date Pompey the Great was authorized to confer Roman citizenship *de consilii sententia singillatim* (Cic. *pro Balbo*, 8. 19), and under the empire the award was frequently made in military diplomas (*cf.* also no. 42). An interesting supplement and a parallel to Strabo's decree is furnished by a *S.C.* of 78 B.C. (Bruns, 41), which declared three Greek ship captains as *amici populi Romani*, and granted them immunity and other privileges for the services which they had rendered to Rome in time of war.

14. ILIENSES HONORANT LUCIUM IULIUM CAESAREM
(89 a. Chr.)

Ditt. *Or. Gr.* 440.

Ὁ δῆμος | Λεύκιον Ἰούλιον | Λευκίου υἱὸν Καίσαρα, | τιμητὴν
5 γενόμενον ‖ καὶ ἀποκαταστή|σαντα τὴν ἱερὰν | χώραν τῆι
Ἀθηνᾶι | τῆι Ἰλιάδι καὶ ἐξελόμενον | αὐτὴν ἐκ τῆς δημοσιωνίας.

From Troy. Lucius Julius Caesar, as censor, restored the sacred lands of the city to the goddess Ilian Athena, and thus exempted them from the tribute collected by the *publicani* (*cf.* Strabo, p. 642). The city of Priene appealed to Rome ca. 100 B.C. for a remission of the tax on salt and of the δημοσιῶναι (*Inschriften von Priene*, 111). *Cf.* nos. 12, 18, and Rostowzew, *Gesch. d. röm. Kol.* 284 *f.*

15. TABULAE AD MEMORIAM LIBERTATIS
RESTITUTAE SERVANDAM APTAE
(81 a. Chr.)

CIL. 1, 587, 588, 589.

(a)

...Populus Laodicensis af Lyco | populum Romanum quei sibei |
5 ...salutei fuit; benifici ergo quae sibei | benigne fecit ‖ ὁ δῆμος ὁ
...Λαοδικέων τῶν πρὸς | τῶι Λύκωι τὸν δῆμον τὸν | Ῥωμαίων
...γεγονότα ἑαυτῶι | σωτῆρα καὶ εὐεργέτην | ἀρετῆς ἕνεκεν καὶ
10 ...εὐνοίας ‖ τῆς εἰς ἑαυτόν.

The dots at the left in (a) mark a break in the stone.

[270]

FROM ITALY AND THE PROVINCES

(b)

Populus Ephesius *populum Romanum* | salutis ergo quod *optinuit maiorum* | sovom leibertatem i... | legatei Heraclitus H... *filius* ||
Hermocrates Dem*etri filius*   5

(c)

Communi restituto in maiorum leiber*tatem* | Roma Iovei Capitolino et poplo Romano *virtutis* | benivolentiae benificique caussa erga Lucios ab commun*i* | Λυκίων τὸ κοινὸν κομισάμενον τὴν πάτριον δη‖μοκρατίαν τὴν ʿΡώμην Διʾ Καπετωλίωι καὶ τῶι | 5
δήμωι τῶ[ι] ʿΡωμαίων ἀρετῆς ἕνεκεν καὶ εὐνοίας | καὶ εὐεργεσίας τῆς εἰς τὸ κοινὸν τὸ Λυκίων.

Three stone tablets found in Rome. Ephesus and the Commune Lyciae express their thanks to the Roman people for the gift of *libertas*, and Laodicea likewise shows its gratitude. The inscriptions probably belong to the year 81 B.C., when Sulla and Murena settled the affairs of Lycia (*cf.* Appian, *Mithr.* 61; Tac. *Ann.* 3. 62). It is probable, though not certain, that Rome recognized these cities as *civitates liberae* (*cf.* Henze, *De civitatibus liberis*, 70–71; Mommsen, *St. R.* 3, 670, n. 3; Marquardt, *St. Verw.* 1, 337, n. 9). An inscription found at Tabae (no. 16), as interpreted by Mommsen (*Hermes*, 26 (1891), 145–148 = *Ges. Schr.* 5, 514), throws a little light on some of Sulla's arrangements in Asia Minor (*cf.* nos. 17, 19). For a summary of them, *cf.* Chapot, *La prov. rom. proc. d'Asie*, 39. For Ephesus, *cf. ibid.* 116. The Commune Lyciae was one of the oldest leagues in the empire and in Strabo's time numbered twenty-three cities with the right of voting in the κοινόν (*cf.* Marquardt, *St. Verw.* 1, 376 *f.*; Reid, *Municipalities of the Roman Empire*, 363 *f.*; Guiraud, *Les assemblées prov.* 41).

16. SENATUS CONSULTUM DE TABENIS
(82 a. Chr.)
Ditt. *Or. Gr.* 442.

[......τοῖς τε βασιλέως ἡγεμόσιν | δυνάμεσίν] τε ἐπανδρότα[τα ὑπὲρ τῶν πόλεων τῆς Ἀσίας | καὶ τ]ῆς Ἑλλάδος ἀντιτετάχ[θαι· ἀρέσκειν ὁμοίως τῆι | συγ]κλήτωι καὶ τῶι δήμωι [τῶν ʿΡωμαίων ταῦτα πάντα κατὰ τὰ] || ἄριστα εἶναι ἔσεσθαί τε, 5

[271]

MUNICIPAL DOCUMENTS IN GREEK AND LATIN

[τήν τε πίστιν πρὸς τὴν σύν|κλη]τον καὶ τὸν δῆμον τῶν
'Ρωμα[ίων τετηρημένην ἀεὶ | διὰ μ]νήμης ἔχειν ἔξειν τε· ὅσ[ας
τέ τινας τῆς | τού]των ἀρετῆς καὶ καταλογῆς ἔ[νεκεν αὐτοῖς |
10 ἀπὸ] συνβουλίου γνώμης Λεύκιος [Κορνήλιος ‖ Σύλλ]ας αὐτο-
κράτωρ συνεχώρησεν [π]όλ[εις ὅπως | ἰδί]οις τοῖς νόμοις
αἱρέσεσίν τε ὦσιν· | [ὅπω]ς τε χωρίον Θυησσόν, ὅ ἐστιν ἐντὸς
τῶν [ὁ|ρίω]ν αὐτῶν, ἐὰν βούλωνται, ὀχυρώσωσιν· [τήν | τε σύ]ν-
15 κλητον τόν τε δῆμον τὸν 'Ρωμαίων [δι‖αλα]νβάνειν ταῦτα αὐτοῖς
καλῶς καὶ [προση|κόντ]ως καὶ ἀξίως αὐτῶν δεδόσθαι τε....

From Tabae. This city had remained loyal to the Romans during
the invasion of Asia by Mithradates, and was rewarded by Sulla
in a fashion similar to Stratonicea (cf. no. 17). It was given the
revenues of certain towns and, as an ally of Rome, was permitted
to use its own laws. Permission to fortify part of their territory
was also granted (cf. no. 5; Viereck, *Hermes*, 25 (1890), 624 ff.,
Mommsen, *Ges. Schr.* 5. 514 ff.).

17. SENATUS CONSULTUM DE STRATONICENSIBUS
(ca. 81 a. Chr.)

Ditt. *Or. Gr.* 441, ll. 1–129; Viereck, *Sermo Graecus*, 16.

[Λεύκιος Κορνήλιος Λ]ευκίου [υἱὸς] Σύλλας 'Επαφρόδιτος |
[δικτάτωρ Στρατονι]κέων ἄρ[χο]υσι βουλῆι δήμωι χαίρειν. |
[Οὐκ ἀγνοοῦμεν ὑμᾶς] διὰ προ[γ]όνων πάντα τὰ δίκαια | [πρὸς
5 τὴν ἡμετέρα]ν ἡγεμ[ον]ίαν πεποιηκότας καὶ ἐν ‖ [πάντι καιρῶι
τὴν πρὸς ἡ]μᾶς πί[στ]ιν εἰλικρινῶς τετηρηκότας | [ἔν τε τῶι
πρὸς Μιθραδά]την π[ο]λέμωι πρώτους τῶν ἐν τῆι | ['Ασίαι
ἀντιτεταγμένους κα]ὶ διὰ ταῦτα κινδύνους πολλούς | [τε καὶ
παντοδαποὺς] ὑπὲρ τῶν ἡμετέρων δημοσίων | [πραγμάτων
10 προθυμό]τατα ἀ[ν]αδεδεγμένους ‖ .... καὶ
τ[οὺς κοινοὺς] καὶ τοὺς ἰδιωτικοὺς | [φιλίας ἔ]νε[κεν π]ρὸς
ἡμᾶς εὐνοίας τε | [καὶ χάριτος, καὶ ἐν τῶι τοῦ πολ]έμου καιρῶι
πρός τε | [τὰς ἄλλας τῆς 'Ασίας πόλεις πεπρ]εσβευκότας
καὶ πρ[ὸ]ς | [τὰς τῆς 'Ελλάδος..........]Λεύκιος Κορ[νήλιος
15 Σύλλας 'Επαφρόδιτος δικτ]άτωρ ‖ Στρατο[νικέων ἄρχουσι
βουλῆι δήμωι χαίρειν.] | Πρεσβευταῖς ὑμ[ετέροις τὸ γενόμενον
ὑπὸ συγκλήτ]ου δόγμα | τοῦτο [παρέδωκα]. |
Λεύκιος Κορνήλι[ος Λευκίου υἱὸς Σύλλας 'Επαφρόδιτος

[272]

δικτ]άτωρ | συγκλήτωι συ[νεβουλεύσατο πρὸ ἡμερῶν ἐξ
κα]λανδῶν ‖ Ἀπριλίων ἐν τῶ[ι κομετίωι· γραφομένωι παρῆσαν 20
Γ]άιος | Φάννιος Γαΐου [υἱὸς..........., Γ]άιος | Φονδάνιος
Γαΐ[ου υἱὸς........· περὶ ὧν Στρατονικε]ῖς ἐκ Χρυ|σαο[ρέων] |
Παιώνιος Ἱερ[οκλέους,.............,..........
...], ‖ Ἑκαταῖος Πα......,................., | 25
Διονύσιος Ἑ[.......πρεσβευταὶ λόγους ἐποιή]σαντο | συμ[φώ-
νως καὶ ἀκολούθως τῶι Στρατονικέων ψηφίσματι | ἀξιοῦντες
συνήδεσθαι ἐπὶ τῶι τ]ὰ δημόσια πράγ[ματα τ]οῦ δήμου | [τοῦ
Ῥωμαίων ἐν βελτίονι κα]ταστάσει εἶναι· ‖ [ὅπως χρυσοῦν 30
στέφανον παρὰ τῆς ἰ]δίας πόλεως τῆι συγκλήτωι | [ἀναθεῖναι
ἐξῆι ἀπὸ ταλάντων δ]ιακοσίων, | [θυσίαν τε ἐν τῶι Καπετωλίωι
ὅπως] ποιῆσαι ἐξῆι ὑπὲρ τῆς ν[ίκ]ης | [καὶ τῆς ἡγεμονίας τοῦ
δήμου τοῦ] Ῥωμαίων, | [ὅπως τε τὸ λοιπὸν Λευκίωι Κορνηλίωι
Λ]ευκίου υἱῶι Σύλλαι Ἐπαφροδίτωι ‖ [δικτάτορι φαίνηται 35
Στρατονικέων] δήμωι φιλανθρώπως κεχρῆσ[θ]αι· | [ἐπεί τε ὁ
δῆμος ἐν τῶι καιρῶι τῆς εἰρήν]ης συνετήρησεν τὴν ἰδίαν | [εὔνοιάν
τε καὶ πίστιν καὶ φιλίαν] πρὸς τὸν δῆμον τὸν Ῥωμαίων | [καὶ
πρῶτος τῶν ἐν τῆι Ἀσίαι, ὅτε Μιθρ]αδάτης ἐν αὐτ[ῆι | δεινότατα
ἐτυράννευεν, προείλετο ἀν]τιτετάχθαι· ‖ [ἐπεὶ δὲ ὁ βασιλεὺς ἐπὶ 40
τὴν πόλιν ἐπῆλθεν], ἑλὼν δ' ἐκράτησ[ε]ν ....
[Λευκίωι Κορνηλίωι Λευκίου υἱῶι Σύλλαι] | δικτάτορι ἐπι[τά-
ξαντι............................| κ]αὶ ἐπεὶ ὁ δῆμος [συν-
ετήρησεν ἀεὶ τὴν ὑπάρχουσαν αὐτῶι] | εὔνοιαν καὶ πί[στιν] καὶ
συμμαχί[αν πρὸς τὸν δῆμον τὸν Ῥωμαίων, τὰ ἴ]|δια πράγματα
κ[ατὰ τ]ὴν προαίρεσιν [τὴν ἐκείνων διοικήσας, καὶ Μιθραδάτηι] ‖
πόλεμον ἐπο[ίησε, κα]ὶ τὸν ἴδιον δη[λώσας θυμὸν προθυμότατα 45
ἀντετάχθη] | τῆι βασιλικῆι β[ουλῆ]ι καὶ δυνάμει[..........
....
.... | δικαίοις τε κ]αὶ νόμοις καὶ ἐθισμ[οῖς τοῖς
ἰδίοις, οἷς ἐχρῶν|το ἐπάν]ω, ὅπως χρῶνται, ὅσα τε [ψηφίσματα
ἐποίησαν τού|του τοῦ πο]λέμου ἕνεκεν, ὃν πρὸς βασ[ιλέα
Μιθραδάτην ἀνέδειξαν, ‖ ὅπως τ]αῦτα πάντα κύρια ὦσιν· | 50
[Πήδασόν τε], Θεμησσόν, Κέραμον, χωρία [κώμας λιμένας
προσό|δους τε τῶν] πόλεων, ὧν Λεύκιος Κορν[ήλιος Σύλλας
αὐτοκράτωρ | τῆς τούτων] ἀρετῆς καταλογῆς τε ἕ[νεκεν προσ-
ώρισεν συνεχώρη|σεν, ὅπως τ]αῦτα αὐτοῖς ἔχειν ἐξ[ῆι· ‖ τὸ 55

ἱερὸν τῆς] Ἑκάτης, ἐπιφανεστά[της καὶ μεγίστης θεᾶς, ἐκ
πολ|λοῦ τε τι]μώμενον καὶ πολλα [. . . . .|
τό τε τέμεν]ος, ὅπως τοῦτο ἄσυ[λον ὑπάρχηι, | περί τε τῶν
ἀ]π[ολωλ]ότ[ων αὐτοῖς ἐν τῶι πολέμωι, ὅπως] | ἡ σ[ύγ]κλ[ητος
60 τῶι ἄρ]χοντ[ι τ]ῶι εἰς Ἀσίαν πορευομένωι ἐντολὰς || δῶι, ἵνα
φρο[ντίσ]ηι καὶ ἐπιστροφὴν ποιήσηται, ὅπως τὰ ἐμφανῆ | αὐτοῖς
ἀποδοθῆναι φροντίσηι, τούς τε αἰχμαλώτους | κομίσωνται περί
τε τῶν [λ]οιπῶν ἵνα τύχωσι τῶν δικαίων· | ὅπως τε πρεσβευ-
ταῖς τοῖς παρὰ Στρατονικέων εἰς Ῥώμην | παρεσομένοις ἐκτὸς
65 τοῦ στίχου οἱ ἄρχοντες σύγκλητον διδῶσ[ιν·] || περὶ τούτου τοῦ
πράγματος οὕτως ἔδοξεν· πρεσβευταῖς | Στρατονικέων κατὰ
πρόσωπον ἐν τῆι συγκλήτωι φιλανθρώ|πως ἀποκριθῆναι, χάριτα
φιλίαν συμμαχίαν ἀνανεώσασθαι, | τοὺς πρεσβευτὰς ἄν[δρα]ς
καλοὺς καὶ ἀγαθοὺς καὶ φίλους | συμμάχους τε ἡμε[τέρο]υς
70 παρὰ δήμου καλοῦ καὶ ἀγαθοῦ || καὶ φίλου συμμάχου [τε ἡμ]ετέ-
ρου προσαγορεῦσαι ἔδοξεν. | Περί τε ὧν οὗτοι οἱ [πρεσβευ]ταὶ
λόγους ἐποιήσαντο καὶ περ[ὶ ὧν] | Λεύκιος Κορνήλι[ος Σύλλα]ς
Ἐπαφρόδιτος δικτάτωρ λόγο[υς | ἐποιήσατο, γνωστὸν εἶναι
Ῥωμ]αίοις [κατὰ τὰς ἀποσταλείσας | παρ]ὰ τῶν Ἀσίαν τήν τε
75 Ἑλλάδα [διακατασχόντων τῶν τε ἐν || ταῦτα]ις ταῖς ἐπαρχείαις
πρεσβευ[τῶν γεγενημένων ἐπιστολὰς | τοὺς] Στρατονικεῖς τήν
τε φιλίαν κ[αὶ πίστιν καὶ εὔνοιαν πρὸς τὸν | δῆ]μον τὸν Ῥωμαίων
διὰ τέλους [ἐν καιρῶι εἰρήνης πολέμου | τε] (ἀ)εὶ συντετηρηκέναι
στρατιώ[ταις τε καὶ σίτωι καὶ μεγάλαις | δαπάν]αις τὰ δημόσια
80 πράγματα [τοῦ δήμου τοῦ Ῥωμαίων || προ]θυμότατα ὑπηρεσπι-
κέναι π. . . . .|. .υς ὑπὲρ τῆς μεγαλοφρο-
σύνη[ς τῆς ἑαυτῶν αὐτοῖς συμπε|πολ]εμηκέναι τοῖς τε βασιλέω[ς
Μιθραδάτου ἡγεμόσιν | δυν]άμεσίν τε ἐπανδρότατα πε[ρὶ τῶν
85 πόλεων τῆς Ἀσίας καὶ | τῆς] Ἑλλάδος ἀ[ν]τιτετάχθαι· || [περὶ
τούτων τῶν πραγμάτων οὕτως ἔδοξεν· ἀρέσκειν τῆι συγ|κλήτωι
ἀνδρῶν ἀγαθῶν] δικαίων [τε ἀπο]μνημ[ονεύειν καὶ προ|νοεῖν
ὅπως Λεύκι]ος Κορνήλιος Σύλλας Ἐπαφρόδιτ[ος | δικτάτωρ
τὸν ἀν]τιταμίαν ξένια αὐτοῖς κατὰ τὸ διάτα[γμα δοῦ|ναι κελεύσηι,
90 οἷς] τε νόμοις ἐθισμοῖς τε ἰδίοις πρότερον || [ἐχρῶντο, τούτοις]
χράσθωσαν· | [ὅσους τε νόμους αὐτο]ὶ ψηφίσματά τε ἐποίησαν
τούτου τοῦ [πολέ|μου] ἕνεκεν τοῦ πρ]ὸς Μιθραδάτην γενομένου,
ἵνα τούτο[ις ταῦτα | πάντα κύρια ὑπάρ]χωσιν· ἅς τέ τινας τῆς

τούτων ἀρετῆ[ς καταλο|γῆς τε ἕνεκεν μετ]ὰ συμβουλίου γνώμης
Λεύκιος Σύλ[λας αὐ‖τοκράτωρ τοῖς αὐ]τοῖς προσώρισεν συν- 95
εχώρησεν [πολιτεί|ας προσόδους χω]ρία κώμας λιμένας τε
τοῦτο[ις, ἵνα ταῦτα | αὐτοῖς ἔχειν ἐξῆι· τό]ν τε δῆμον τὸν Ῥω-
μαίων [...............|............... προση]κόντως ἀξίως
τε αὐτ[οῦ............................|......] τά τε Στρα-
τονικεῦσιν   [ἐψηφισμένα.....................‖.......] 100
ἀποδεκ[τὰ ὑπάρχει]ν δεῖν· | [ὅπω]ς τε Λεύκιος Κορνήλι[ος
Σύλ]λας Ἐπαφρόδιτος δικτάτ[ωρ, ἐὰν αὐτῶι | φα]ίνηται, ἃς αὐτὸς
αὐτοκράτωρ Στρατονικεῦσιν   πολι[τείας | κ]ώμας χώρας
λιμένας τε προσώρισεν, ἐπιγνῶι διατάξη[ι ὅσας ἑκάστη] | προσ-
όδους Στρατονικεῦσιν τελῆι· ‖ [ἐά]ν τε διατάξηι, πρὸς ταύτας 105
τὰς πολιτείας, ἃς Στρ[ατονικεῦσιν] | προσώρισεν, γράμματα
ἀποστείληι, ἵνα τοσοῦτον τ[έλος] | Στρατονικεῦσιν τελῶσιν· |
[τ]οῦτό τε, οἵτινες ἄν ποτε ἀεὶ Ἀσίαν τήν τε Ἑλλάδα ἐ[παρχείας |
δια]κατέχωσιν, φροντίζωσιν διδῶσίν τε ἐργασίαν, ἵν[α ταῦτα]‖
οὕτως γίν[ω]νται. | Τὸ [ἱερ]ὸν τῆς Ἑ[κάτης] ὅπως ἦ[ι ἄσυλον·] | 110
ἀνθύπατος ὅστις ἂν ἀεὶ Ἀσίαν ἐπ[αρχείαν] | διακατέχηι, ἐπι-
γνώτω ἅτινα αὐτοῖς ἄ[πε]στιν | οἵ τέ τινες ταῦτα διήρπασαν οἵ
τέ τινε[ς δ]ιακατέ‖χουσιν αὐτά, ἵνα παρ' αὐτῶν ἀποδοθῆναι 115
ἀποκατα|σταθῆναι φροντίσηι· ἵνα τε τοὺς αἰχμαλώτους | ἀνα-
κομίσασθαι δύνωνται ὑπέρ τε τῶν λ[ο]ιπῶν | πραγμάτων τῶν
δικαίων τύχωσιν ο[ὕ]τ[ω κα]θὼς ἂν | αὐτοῖς ἐκ τῶν δημοσίων
πραγμάτ[ων πίσ]τεώς ‖ τε τῆς ἰδίας φαίνηται· ἔδοξεν. | 120
Στέφανόν τε τὸν παρὰ τοῦ δήμου | [τῆι συγκλήτωι] ἀπεσταλ-
μένον, οὗ ἂν Λεύκιος [Κορνήλ]ιος | Σύλλας Ἐπαφρόδιτος
δικτάτ[ωρ | ἡγ]ῆται [ἀγαθὸν ὅπως ἀναθεῖναι αὐτοῖς ‖ ἐξῆι, 125
θυσίαν τε ἐν τῶι Καπετωλίωι ἂν θέ|λωσιν ὅπως αὐτοῖς ποιῆσαι
ἐξῆι. | Τοῖς τε πρεσβευταῖς παρὰ Στρατονικέων εἰς | Ῥώμην
παρεσομένοις ἔδοξε σ]ύγκλητον | [ὑπὸ τῶν ἀρχόντων ἐκτὸς τοῦ
στίχου δίδ]οσθαι. Ἔδοξεν.

From Lagina. The city of Stratonicea had remained loyal to
the Romans in the struggle with Mithradates. This decree of the
senate confirms the action taken by the dictator Sulla in regard to
the city. The alliance with Rome is renewed. The citizens are
allowed to keep their own laws and customs. Their legislation
during the invasion of Mithradates is confirmed. Sulla is authorized

MUNICIPAL DOCUMENTS IN GREEK AND LATIN

to determine the amount of tribute which should be paid to the
city by the towns and villages which he has assigned to Stratonicea.
The shrine of Hecate is granted the privilege of asylum (Tac.
Ann. 3. 62). *Cf.* nos. 15, 16, 67.

18. SENATUS CONSULTUM DE AMPHIARAI
OROPI AGRIS
(73 a. Chr.)

Viereck, *Sermo Graecus*, 18; *IG.* vii, 413; de Ruggiero, *L'arbitrato pubblico*, 25; Bruns, 42; Ditt. *Syll.*³ 747; Riccobono, p. 209.

Μ[άαρκ]ος Τερέντιος Μαάρκου υἱὸς Οὐάρρων Λεύκολλος,
Γάϊος Κάσιος Λευκί[ου υἱὸς | Λογ]γῖνος ὕπατοι Ὠρωπίων
ἄρχουσιν βουλῇ δήμωι χαίρειν. Εἰ ἔρρωσθε, εὖ ἂν ἔχ[οι].
|Ὑμᾶς εἰδέναι βουλόμεθα, ἡμᾶς κατὰ τὸ τῆς συνκλήτου δόγμα
τὸ γενόμενον ἐ[πὶ Λευκί]|ου Λικινίου Μαάρκου Αὐρηλίου
5 ὑπάτων ἐπεγνωκέναι περὶ ἀντιλογιῶν τῶν ἀνάμ[εσον] ‖ θεῶι
Ἀμφιαράωι καὶ τῶν δημοσιωνῶν γεγονότων ⟨ἐπεγνωκέναι⟩.

Πρὸ μιᾶς εἰ[δυῶν] | Ὀκτωμβρίων ἐμ βασιλικῇ Πορκίᾳ ἐν
συμβουλίωι παρῆσαν Μάαρκος Κλαύδιος Μααρκ[ου] | υἱὸς
Ἀρνήσσης Μαάρκελλος, Γάϊος Κλαύδιος Γαΐου υἱὸς Ἀρνήσσης
Γλάβερ, | Μάαρκος Κάσιος Μαάρκου υἱὸς Πωμεντίνα, Γάϊος
Λικίνιος Γαΐου υἱὸς | Πωμεντίνα, Γάϊος Λικίνιος Γαΐου υἱὸς
10 Στηλατίνα⟨ς⟩ Σακέρδως, ‖ Λεύκιος Οὐολύσκιος Λευκίου υἱὸς
Ἀρνιήσσης, Λεύκιος Λάρτιος Λευκίου υἱὸς | Πηπιρία, Γάϊος
Ἀνναῖος Γαΐου υἱὸς Κλυτομίνα, Μάαρκος Τύλλιος Μαάρκου
υἱὸς | Κορνηλία Κικέρων, Κόϊντος Ἄξιος Μαάρκου υἱὸς Κυρίνα,
Κόϊντος Πομπήϊος Κοΐν|του υἱὸς Ἀρ[νιή]σσης Ῥοῦφος, Αὖλος
Κασκέλλιος Αὔλου υἱὸς ὁ υἱὸς Ῥωμιλία, | Κόϊντος Μυννύκιος
15 Κοΐντου υἱὸς Τηρηντίνα Θέρμος, Μάαρκος Ποπλίκιος ‖ Μαάρκου
υἱὸς Ὁρατία Σκαιούας, Τίτος Μαίνιος Τίτου υἱὸς Λεμωνία,
Λεύκιος | Κλαύδιος Λευκίου υἱὸς Λεμωνία.

Περὶ ὧν Ἑρμόδωρος Ὀλυνπίχου υἱός, ἱερεὺς | Ἀνφιαράου,
ὅστις πρότερον ὑπὸ τῆς συνκλήτου σύνμαχος προσηγορευμέ|νος
ἐστίν, καὶ Ἀλεξίδημος Θεοδώρου υἱός, Δημαίνετος Θεοτέλου
υἱός, πρεσβευ|ταὶ Ὠρωπίων, λόγους ἐποιήσαντο
20 ἐπ(ε)ὶ ἐν τῷ τῆς μισθώσεως νόμῳ αὗται αἱ ‖ χῶραι ὑπεξ-
ειρημέναι εἰσίν, ἃς Λεύκιος Σύλλας θεῶν ἀθανάτων ἱερῶν

[276]

τεμενῶν | φυλακῆς ἕνεκεν συνεχώρησεν ⟨ὑπεξειρημέναι
εἰσίν⟩, ταύτας τε τὰς προσ|όδους, περὶ ὧν ἄγεται τὸ πρᾶγμα,
Λεύκιος Σύλλας τῶι θεῶι Ἀμφιαράωι πρ(ο)σώιρι|σεν(!),
ὅπως ὑπὲρ τούτων τῶν χωρῶν πρόσοδον τῶι δημοσιώνῃ
μὴ τελῶσιν· |
καὶ περὶ ὧν Λεύκιος Δομέτιος Αἰνόβαλβος ὑπὲρ δημοσιωνῶν
εἶπεν ‖

ἐπεὶ ἐν τῶι τῆς μισθώσεως νόμωι αὗται αἱ χῶραι ὑπεξειρη-   25
μέναι εἰσίν, | ἃς Λεύκιος Σύλλας θεῶν ἀθανάτων ἱερῶν
τεμενῶν φυλακῆς ἕνεκεν | συνεχώρησεν, οὔτε ὁ Ἀμφιάραος,
ὧι αὗται αἱ χῶραι συνκεχωρημέναι | λέγονται, θεός ἐστιν,
ὅπως ταύτας τὰς χώρας καρπίσζεσθαι ἐξῇ | τοὺς δημοσιώνας·
ἀπὸ συνβουλίου γνώμης γνώμην ἀπεφηνά‖μεθα· ὃ ἐπέγνωμεν   30
τῆι συνκλήτωι προσανοίσομεν, τοῦτο ὃ καὶ | εἰς τὴν τῶν
ὑπομνημάτων δέλτον κατεχωρίσαμεν·
περὶ χώρας | Ὠρωπίας, περὶ ἧς ἀντιλογία ἦν πρὸς τοὺς
δημοσιώνας, κατὰ τὸν τῆς | μισθώσεως νόμον αὕτη ὑπεξει-
ρημένη ἐστίν, ἵνα μὴ ὁ δημοσιώ|νης αὐτὴν καρπίζηται·
κατὰ τὸ τῆς συνκλήτου δόγμα ἐπέγνωμεν. ‖
Ἐν τῷ τῆς μισθώσεως νόμῳ ὑπεξειρημένην δοκεῖ εἶναι   A 35
οὕτως· | ἐκτός τε τούτων ἢ εἴ τι δόγμα συνκλήτου, αὐτο-
κράτωρ αὐτοκράτορές τ[ε] | ἡμέτεροι καταλογῆς θεῶν ἀθα-
νάτων ἱερῶν τεμενῶν τε φυλακῆς | καρπίζεσθαι ἔδωκαν
κατέλιπον, ἐκτός τε τούτων, ἃ Λεύκιος | Κορνήλιος Σύλλας
αὐτοκράτωρ ἀπὸ συνβουλίου γνώμης θεῶν ‖ ἀθανάτων   40
ἱερῶν τεμενῶν τε φυλακῆς ἕνεκεν καρπίζεσθαι ἔδωκεν, | ὃ
τὸ αὐτὸ ἡ σύνκλητος ἐπεκύρωσεν οὔτε μετὰ ταῦτα δόγματι |
συνκλήτου ἄκυρον ἐγενήθη.
Λεύκιος Κορνήλιος Σύλλας ἀπὸ συν|βουλίου γνώμης γνώμην
εἰρηκέναι δοκεῖ·
τῆς εὐχῆς ἀποδόσεως | ἕνεκεν τῶι ἱερῶ Ἀμφιαράου χώραν
προστίθημι πάντῃ πάντοθεν πόδας ‖ χιλίους, ἵνα καὶ αὕτη   45
ἡ χώρα ὑπάρχῃ ἄσυλος
ὡσαύτως τῶι θεῷ Ἀμφιαράωι | καθιερωκέναι
τῆς πόλεως καὶ τῆς χώρας λιμένων τε τῶν Ὠρωπίων | τὰς
προσόδους ἁπάσας εἰς τοὺς ἀγῶνας καὶ τὰς θυσίας, ἃς
Ὠρώπιοι | συντελοῦσιν θεῷ Ἀμφιαράωι, ὁμοίως δὲ καὶ ἃς

50

55

60

65

ἂν μετὰ ταῦτα ὑπὲρ τῆς | νίκης καὶ τῆς ἡγεμονίας τοῦ
δήμου τοῦ ῾Ρωμαίων συντελέσουσιν, ‖ ἐκτὸς ἀγρῶν τῶν
῾Ερμοδώρου᾽Ολυνπίχου υἱοῦ, ἱερέως ᾽Αμφιαράου, τοῦ | διὰ
τέλους ἐν τῇ φιλίᾳ τοῦ δήμου τοῦ ῾Ρωμαίων μεμενηκότος.

Περὶ τού|του τοῦ πράγματος δόγμα συνκλήτου ἐπὶ Λευκίου
Σύλλα ᾽Επαφροδίτου, | Κοΐντου Μετέλλου Εὐσεβοῦς ὑπάτων
ἐπικεκυρωμένον δοκεῖ εἶναι, | ὅπερ ἡ σύνκλητος ἐδογμάτισεν εἰς
τούτους τοὺς λόγους·

ὅσα τε θεῶι ‖ ᾽Αμφιαράωι καὶ τῶι ἱερῷ αὐτοῦ Λεύκιος
Κορνήλιος Σύλλας ἀπὸ συ(μ)βουλίου | γνώμης προσώρισεν
συνεχώρησεν, τὰ αὐτὰ ἡ σύνκλητος τούτωι τῶι θεῶι | δοθῆναι
συνχωρηθῆναι ἡγήσατο.

᾽Εν τῶι συμβουλίωι παρῆσαν | οἱ αὐτοὶ οἳ ἐμ πραγμάτων
συμβεβουλευμένων δέλτωι πρώτηι, | κηρώματι τεσσαρεσκαι-
δεκάτωι.

Δόγμα συνκλήτου τοῦτο γενόμενόν ‖ ἐστιν· πρὸ ἡμερῶν
δεκαεπτὰ καλανδῶν Νοενβρίων ἐν κομετίωι· | γραφομένου
παρῆσαν Τίτος Μαίνιος Τίτου υἱὸς Λεμωνία, | Κόϊντος ῾Ράγκιος
Κοΐντου υἱὸς Κλαυδία, Γάϊος Οὐσέλλιος Γαΐου | υἱὸς Κυρίνα
Οὐάρρων· περὶ ὧν Μάαρκος Λεύκολλος, Γάϊος Κάσιος | ὕπατοι
ἐπιγνόντες ἀπήνγειλαν περὶ ᾽Ωρωπίας χώρας καὶ τῶν ‖ δημο-
σιωνῶν ἑαυτοὺς ἐπεγνωκέναι, ὡσαύτως τὴν ᾽Ωρωπίων | χώραν
ὑπεξειρημένην δοκεῖν εἶναι κατὰ τὸν τῆς μισθώσεως νόμον, | μὴ
δοκεῖν τοὺς δημοσιώνας ταῦτα καρπίζεσθαι· οὕτως, | καθὼς ἂν
αὐτοῖς ἐκ τῶν δημοσίων πραγμάτων πίστεώς τε τῆς | ἰδίας
ἐφαίνετο, ἔδοξεν.

From Oropus. We have included in this collection only a few
of the examples of arbitration in the cities under the jurisdiction
of Rome (cf. no. 8). The citizens of Oropus had received from Sulla
certain revenues from lands and customs to be devoted to the worship
of the god Amphiaraus. The sources of this income could not be
taxed by the *publicani* in collecting the tithes from the province.
After the death of Sulla the *publicani* sought to collect the former
tax from the Oropians, claiming that Amphiaraus was not a god,
since he had once been a mortal (Cic. *de deor. nat.* 3. 49). Oropus
protested their claim, sending an embassy to Rome. The senate
referred the matter to the consuls for arbitration. They chose a

committee of fifteen senators who reviewed the evidence and decided in favor of Oropus. The document contains the letter of the consuls to the Oropians, the decision of the committee appointed to arbitrate the case, the record of Sulla's action, and the decree of the senate confirming it, and, finally, the decree of the senate confirming the decision of the court of arbitration. *Cf.* nos. 8, 46, 57, 104.

19. LEX ANTONIA DE TERMESSIBUS
(ca. 71 a. Chr.)

CIL. 1, 204; Bruns, 14; Dessau, 38; Girard, pp. 68–70; Riccobono, pp. 105–107.

C. Antonius M. f., Cn. Corne*lius*. *.f., Q. Marcius. .f.,* L. *Hostilius. .f.,* C. *Popilius. .f., M. Valerius. .f.,* C. *Antius. .f., Q. Caecilius. .f.,* L. *V......f.,* | C. Fundanius C. f. tr. pl. de s. s. plebem *ioure rogaverunt............*| preimus scivit. |

Quei Thermeses maiores Peisidae fuerunt, queique | eorum Col. 1 legibus Thermesium maior*um* Pisidarum | ante k. April., quae fuerunt L. Gellio Cn. Lentulo cos., | Thermeses maiores Pisidae factei sunt, queique ‖ ab ieis prognati sunt erunt, iei omnes | posterei- 5 que eorum Thermeses maiores Peisidae | leiberei amicei socieique populi Romani sunto, | eique legibus sueis ita utunto, itaque ieis | omnibus sueis legibus Thermensis maioribus ‖ Pisideis utei liceto, 10 quod advorsus hanc legem | non fiat. |

Quei agrei quae loco aedificia publica preivatave | Thermensium maiorum Pisidarum intra fineis | eorum sunt fueruntve L. Marcio Sex. Iulio cos., ‖ quaeque insulae eorum sunt fueruntve ieis | con- 15 solibus, quei supra scriptei sunt, quodque | earum rerum ieis consulibus iei habuerunt | possederunt us*ei fructeique* sunt, quae de ieis rebus | locata non s*unt, utei antea habeant possideant;* quaeque ‖ de 20 ieis rebus *agreis loceis aedificieis locata* sunt, ac ne | locentur *sancitum est sanctione,* quae facta | est e*x lege rogata* L. Gellio Cn. Lentulo cos., ea omnia | Therm*eses maiores Pisidae habean*t possideant, | ieisque *rebus loceis agreis aedificieis utantur f*ruantur ‖ ita, utei ant*e* 25 *Mitridatis bellum, quod* preimum | fuit, habueru*nt possederunt usei fruct*eique sunt. |

Quae Thermensorum m*aiorum* Pisidarum publica | preivatave

praeter loca*ta* agros aedificia sunt | fueruntve ante bellum Mitri-
30 datis, quod preimum || factum est, quodque earum rerum iei antea |
habuerunt possederunt usei fructeive sunt, | quod eius ipsei sua
voluntate ab se non abalienarunt, | ea omnia Termensium maiorum
Pisidarum, utei sunt | fuerunt, ita sunto, itemque ieis ea omnia ||
35 habere possidere uutei frueique liceto. |

Col. II   Quos Thermenses maiores Pisidae leiberos servosve | bello
Mitridatis ameiserunt, magistratus pr*ove* | magistratu, quoia de ea
re iuris dictio erit, qu*oque* | de ea re in ious aditum erit, ita de ea re
5 ious || deicunto iudicia recuperationes danto, utei ie*i* eos recuperare
possint. |

Nei quis magistratus prove magistratu legatus ne*ive* | quis alius
meilites in oppidum Thermesum maiorum | Pisidarum agrumve
Thermensium maiorum | Pisidarum hiemandi caussa introducito,
10 neive || facito, quo quis eo meilites introducat quove ibei | meilites
hiement, nisei senatus nominatim, utei Thermesum | maiorum
Pisidarum in hibernacula meilites | deducantur, decreverit; neive
quis magistratus | prove magistratu legatus neive quis alius facito ||
15 neive inperato, quo quid magis iei dent praebeant | ab ieisve aufe-
ratur, nisei quod e*os* ex lege Porcia | dare praebere oportet oportebit. |

Quae leges quodque ious quaeque consuetudo L. Marcio | Sex.
20 Iulio cos. inter civeis Romanos et Termenses || maiores Pisidas
fuit, eaedem leges eidemque ious | eademque consuetudo inter ceives
Romanos et | Termenses maiores Pisidas esto; quodque quibusque |
in rebus loceis agreis aedificieis oppideis iouris | Termensium maiorum
25 Pisidarum ieis consulibus, || quei supra scriptei sunt, fuit, quod eius
praeter | loca*ta* agros aedificia ipsei sua voluntate ab se non | ab-
alienarunt, idem in eisdem rebus loceis agreis | aedificieis oppideis
Termensium maiorum Pisidarum | ious esto; et quo minus ea, quae
30 in hoc capite scripta || sunt, ita sint fiant, eius hac lege nihilum
rogatur. |

Quam legem portorieis terrestribus maritumeisque | Termenses
maiores Phisidae capiundeis intra suos | fineis deixserint, ea lex ieis
portorieis capiundeis | esto, dum nei quid portori ab ieis capiatur,
35 quei publica || populi Romani vectigalia redempta habebunt. Quos |
per eorum fineis publicani ex eo vectigali transportabunt | . . . .
(*continuabatur in tabula deperdita*).

[280]

FROM ITALY AND THE PROVINCES

Bronze tablet found in Rome in the sixteenth century, now in the museum at Naples. The inscription is engraved in two columns. The second column begins with the words *Quos Thermenses*. The heading, *I de Termesi. Pisid. mai.*, shows that this is the first of several tablets which made up the original law. The Ambrosian Library at Milan has a copy of the first tablet, which purports to have been made by Mariangelus Accursius shortly after the discovery of the tablet. From this copy certain missing words have been supplied in the *CIL.*; but Bormann (*Festschrift Hirschfeld*, 434 *ff.*) has given reasons for believing that the tablet was defective when found, and that the added words are conjectures of Accursius. They are here printed in italics (col. 1, ll. 18 *ff.*). *Thermeses maiores Peisidae* (or Τερμησσεῖς οἱ μείζονες) distinguishes this town from Τερμησσεῖς οἱ πρὸς Οἰνοάνδοις. Many other inscriptions have been found on its site; cf. *Jahreshefte d. öst. archäol. Inst.* 3 (1900), 196 *ff.*; *B.C.H.* 23 (1899), 165 *ff.*, 280 *ff.*; 24 (1900), 334 *ff.*

The *praescriptio* shows that the law is a plebiscite, submitted by C. Antonius, Cicero's colleague in 63 B.C., and certain other tribunes. The names of the other tribunes have been supplied from the list of the colleagues of Antonius given in *CIL.* 1, 593. The presence of the phrase *de senatus sententia* in the *praescriptio* seems to fix the date of the plebiscite before 70 B.C., because the legislation of Sulla forbidding the tribunes to submit a measure to the popular assembly until the senate has taken action on it is apparently still in force. The document is subsequent to 72 B.C., the year of the consulship of Gellius and Lentulus, and probably falls in 71 B.C. Probably these privileges were granted to Termessus because of her loyalty in the Mithradatic wars. For other cities whose loyalty was rewarded in a similar way, cf. nos. 15, 16, 17, and 21. By virtue of this law Termessus became a *civitas sine foedere immunis et libera*. For an analysis of the rights of such a city, cf. pp. 42 *ff.* and Mommsen, *St. R.* 3, 686 *ff.*

The people of Termessus are styled *leiberei amicei socieique populi Romani*. They are given the right *legibus sueis uti*, the possession of their land without the payment of a *stipendium*, freedom from the billeting of troops, and payment for necessary requisitions made upon them. Their rights over against Roman citizens are guaranteed, and they may collect *portoria terrestria maritumaque*. Their right *legibus sueis uti* (*cf*. no. 40) is however limited by the proviso, *quod advorsus hanc legem non fiat*, and the billeting of troops may be authorized by a special vote of the Roman senate. No mention is made of the rights of coinage or of receiving exiles. With regard to the property rights granted to the people of Termessus in ll. 27–35, *cf*. Bormann, *op. cit.* 439.

20. LEX MUNICIPI TARENTINI
(88–62 a. Chr.?)

Dessau, 6086; Bruns, 27; Riccobono, p. 132; Girard, p. 61.

..ne esse liceat neive qu*is* quod eius municipi pequniae publicae sacrae | religios⟨s⟩ae est erit fra*u*dato neive av*o*rtito neive facito quo eorum | quid fiat, neive per li*tt*eras publicas fraudemve publicum peius | facito d(olo) m(alo). Quei faxit, quan*ti* ea res erit quadruplum
5 multae esto, ‖ eamque pequniam mu*n*icipio dare damnas esto eiusque pequniae | magistratus quei quomque in municipio erit petitio exactioque esto. |

IIIIvir(ei) aedilesque quei h. l. primei erunt quei eorum Tarentum venerit, | is in diebus xx proxumeis quibus post h. l. datam primum Tarentum venerit | facito quei pro se praes stat praedes praediaque
10 ad IIIIvir(os) det quod satis ‖ sit, quae pequnia public*a sa*cra religiosa eius municipi ad se in suo magistratu | pervenerit, eam pequni*a*m municipio Tarentino salvam recte esse futur*a*m, | eiusque rei rationem re*d*diturum ita utei senatus censuerit. Isque IIIIvir, | quoi ita praes dabitur, ac*c*ipito idque in tabu*l*eis *p*ubliceis scriptum sit | facito. Quique quomqu*e* comitia duovireis ae*d*ilibusve rogan-
15 deis ‖ habebit, is antequam maior pars curiarum quemque eorum quei | magistratum eis comitieis petent renuntiabit, ab eis quei petent praedes | quod satis sit accipito, *q*uae pequnia publica sacra religiosa eius municipi | *ad* quemque eorum in eo magistratu pervenerit, eam pequniam municipio | Tarentino salvam rec*te* ess*e futuram, ei*usque
20 rei ration*e*m redditurum ‖ ita utei senatus ce*n*s*u*erit, *i*dque in *tabul*eis publiceis scriptum sit facito, | quodque *quoi*que neg*oti pub*lice in m*unicip*io de s(enatus) s(ententia) datum erit negotive | publicei

gesserit pequniamque publicam *deder*it exegerit, is quoi ita negotium |
datum erit negotive quid publice gesser*it* pequniamve publicam
dederit | exegerit, eius rei rationem senatui reddito refertoque in
di*e*bus x proxume*is* || quibus senatus eius municipi censuer*it* sine 25
d(olo) m(alo). |

Quei decurio municipi Tarentiei est erit queive in municipio
Tarenti*no in* | senatu sententiam deixerit, is in o*pp*ido Tarentei
aut intra eius mun*icipi* | fineis aedificium quod non minu*s* MD tegu-
larum tectum sit habeto *sine* | d(olo) m(alo). Quei eorum ita aedi-
ficium suom non habebit seive quis eorum || aedificium emerit 30
mancupiove acceperit quo hoic legi fraudem *faxit*, | is in annos
singulos HS n. ID municipio Tarentino dare damnas esto. |

Nei quis in oppido quod eius municipi e*r*it aedificium detegito
neive dem*olito* | neive disturbato nisei quod non deterius restituturus
erit nisei d*e* s(enatus) s(ententia). | Sei quis adversus ea faxit, quant*i*
id aedificium f*u*erit, tantam pequni*am* || municipio dare damnas esto 35
eiusque pequniae *quei* vol*et* petiti*o* est. | Magi(stratus) quei exegerit
dimidium in *p*ublicum referto dimidium in l*u*deis quos | publice
in eo magistratu facie*t* consumito, seive ad monumentum suom | in
publico consumere volet l*iceto*, idque ei s(ine) f(raude) s(ua) facere
liceto. |

Sei quas vias fossas cloacas IIIIvir IIvir aedilisve eius municipi
caussa || publice facere immittere commutare aedificare munire 40
volet, intra | eos fineis quei eius municipi erun*t*, quod eius sine
iniuria fiat, id ei facere | liceto. |

Quei pequniam municipio Tarentin*o* non debebit sei quis eorum
quei | municeps erit neque eo sexennio *p*roxumo, quo exeire volet, |
duovirum.

(reliqui versus, maxime mutili, omissi sunt)

The charter of Tarentum was engraved on a brass tablet. Of the
original, only a fragment of the ninth table, found in an ancient
well, is now preserved in the museum of Naples.

Tarentum was founded as a Roman colony by Gracchus in
123 B.C. To this settlement the name Neptunia was given. After
the Social war Tarentum obtained the *civitas Romana* and became
a *municipium*. The date of this charter, which was a *lex data*, cannot
be determined with exactness. It is not earlier than 89 B.C. and

possibly should not be dated later than 62 B.C., when Cicero refers to Tarentum as a *municipium* (*pro Archia*, 5. 10). Yet Tarentum could be called a municipality at any time after the Social war, and the date of the speech for Archias is not necessarily a *post quod non* (*cf.* Hardy, *Six Roman Laws*, 104). It is possible that the charter was given as a result of Pompey's act in establishing some of the eastern pirates on the site of the old Roman colony (*cf.* Mommsen, *Ges. Schr.* 1, 151, n. 18). In this case the *lex* would date from the year 59 when Pompey's acts were finally ratified.

The extant portion of the charter deals with the peculation of public, sacred, and religious funds (ll. 1–6). In ll. 7–25 the charter provides for the *cautio* of magistrates (*cf.* no. 65, chap. 70). Since the first magistrates could not furnish securities to their predecessors, they were required to give them to quattuorvirs, who may have been the commissioners sent out from Rome (Mommsen, *op. cit.* 1, 156), or the clause may mean that the first magistrates gave a *cautio* to their colleagues in turn (Hardy, *op. cit.* 106, n. 2).

The members of the local curia are required to own a house within the territory of the municipality, and this dwelling must have not less than 1500 tiles on the roof. For this method of estimating property, *cf.* the tax paid by Roman senators in 43 B.C. of 4 obols for each tile (Cass. Dio, 46. 31). The law regarding the demolition of houses (ll. 32–38), and that regarding the right of officials to do paving or to dig drains (ll. 39–42) may be found with slight changes in the charter of Urso (no. 26, chapp. 75, 77). The clause contained in ll. 43 *ff.* was designed to check ex-officials from leaving the city before they had discharged all the liabilities which might have been incurred in the performance of their office.

21. LEX GABINIA CALPURNIA DE DELIIS
(58 a. Chr.)

Durrbach, *Choix d'inscr. Délos*, 163; *Suppl. Ep. Gr.* 1, 335.

A. Gabinius A. f. Capito cos., L. Calpurnius L. f. Piso cos. de s(*enatus*) s(*ententia*) populum iuure rogavere populusque iuure scivit.. pro aede Castor(is) a(nte) d(iem) VI kal(endas) (mensis). Tribus.. principium fuit, A. Gabinius A. f. Capito pro tribu primus scivit: ‖
5 Velitis iubeatis. Quom res publica pot...divinis..bus ac consilieis

sit aucta q*uomque*....*cl*arissumae ceivitatis sit confirma*ta*....
decorata, in quo numero fanum A*pollinis*....*antiquissum*um ac
religiosissumum sit constitutu*m*..‖..em et sanctitatem caerimoni- 10
asq(ue) pr....*Delum* insulam, in qua insula Apollinem et Dianam
natos esse arbitrantur?, vecteigalibus leiberari, quae insula post
hominum me*moriam semper fuit*? regum ceivitatium nationumque
imperieis sacra leib*era immunis*? *q*uomque praedones, quei orbem
terrarum complureis *annos vexarint*? ‖ *fana* delubra simu*l*acra 15
deorum immortalium loca religio*sissuma deva*starint, lege Ga*b*inia
superatei ac deletei s*i*nt, et omneis rel*iqua* praeter insu*l*am Delum
sedes Apollinis ac Dianae in antei*quom splendor*em sit resti*t*uta popu-
leique Romani dign*i*tatis maiestatis*que causa*? *pulcher*rume adminis-
trata, imperio am*pl*ificato *p*ace per orbe*m terrarum* ‖ *il*lam insul*am* 20
nobilissum*am* ac s*a*nctissum*a*m deis immor*talibus restitui*? *et in-*
sulam l*ei*berari. Neve.....sit...quom vectigal eius..*adiudic*atione
quam I. C. A...sup. (?) Delei fece*runt*..., neve quid aliud vec-
teigal neve pro c*ustodia publicei f*rumenti *nev*e quis post*ea* insulas
*illas vicin*as *qu*ae circum D*elum iacent* ‖ Artemeitam C. Iadeam.... 25
as locet neve...et eas insulas *f*aciat..*quei* (?) Delum inc*olunt*
queique postea incolent vect*eigal*...iure insul*as*?....verunt, fuerunt...Mitridates in...m iure insula Delus *queique eam in*colent
sint c..‖.udemve quam int...D*e*lumque ad...Delum queique 30
eam in*colent insulas*ve quae s(upra) s(criptae) s(unt)...*s*ei eius
familia pe*cuniav*e *plus* minus dim*inut*a sit...ere populei pleb*isv*e.
it magistr*atus prove magistratu*. ua iudicatioque...interced...
quominu‖s setiusve d(e) e(a) r(e) iu*dicetur sive* iudicium *fiat liceto.* 35
S(i) s(acrum) s(anctum) e(st) q(uod) *n*(*on*) *i*(*ure*) *s*(*it*) *r*(*ogatum*),
e(*ius*) *h*(*ac*) *l*(*ege*) n(ihil) r(ogatur).

[Αὖλος Γ]αβείνιος Αὔλου υ[ἰὸς Καπίτων] ὕπ[ατος καὶ Λεύκιος
Καλπούρνιος Λευκί|ου..υἰὸ]ς Πείσων ὕπατο[ς..... | δικαί]ως
ἐκύρω[σε....‖...πρὸ ἡμερ]ῶν ἐξ καλ[ανδῶν...... 40

From Delos. The date of the document is fixed by the names of
the consuls at the head of the Greek text. The law was passed by
the senate and confirmed by the *comitia tributa* (Cuq, *B.C.H.*
46 (1922), 201 *ff*.). Delos had suffered severely under Mithradates
and from the raids of the pirates until Pompey cleared the latter
from the seas. The Delians were granted immunity from certain

MUNICIPAL DOCUMENTS IN GREEK AND LATIN

taxes—probably the tithes,—and from the accessory expense of convoying or transporting grain to Rome. The island was also made free although it was still under the control of Athens (Cuq, *loc. cit.* 209 *ff.*). The implications of this law are interesting. Delos, although under Athenian jurisdiction, seems to have paid tribute to Rome before the passage of the Gabinian law; otherwise the gift of immunity is meaningless. Similarly the Caunians paid tribute to Rome and Rhodes; *cf.* Dio Chrys. 31. 125; see also Livy, 41. 6; and Cic. *ad fam.* 13. 56.

The interpretation of ll. 30 *ff.* is uncertain. Apparently those who had suffered in the late wars and raids were given the right to appeal to Roman magistrates in preference to local or Athenian judges for the settlement of claims (*cf.* no. 19, col. II, ll. 1 *ff.*). Cuq points out (*loc. cit.* 210 *ff.*) that this provision indicates the policy of the Roman senate in binding cities to Rome, even though they enjoyed the status of *civitates liberae*, by giving them the advantages of appealing to Roman law and of being protected by Roman magistrates.

22. EPISTULA PROCONSULIS ASIAE AD PROVINCIALES
(ca. 56–50 a. Chr.)

Knackfuss, *Das Rathaus von Milet*, p. 101, ll. 38 *ff.*

```
   ...ρας.....ἐπ᾽ ἀκυρώσει ὧ[ν] ἀνείλ[ηφε καὶ Μάρ|κωι]
40 Κικέρ[ων]ι συντυχὼν εὐχαρίστησε [τὰ ταχ]‖θέντα ἐπ[ιμ]ελῶς
   συντηρῶν τὰ ἐπ᾽ ἐμ[οὶ μὴ δια(?)]‖λύειν. "Οθεν πῶς ὑμεῖς τήν
   τινων περὶ [ταῦτα ἀ]|ναίδειαν ἀνέσχησθε, τεθαύμακα· δι᾽ ἃς
   [αἰτίας] | πρός τε τὸ κοινὸν τῶν Ἑλλήνων γέγραφα, [πρὸς |
45 ὑ]μᾶς, Ἐφεσίους, Τραλλιανούς, Ἀλαβανδεῖς, Μ[υ‖λ]ασεῖς,
   Σμυρναίους, Περγαμηνούς, Σαρδιανο[ύς], | Ἀδραμυτηνούς, ἵνα
   τε ὑμεῖς πρὸς τὰς ἐν τῆι δ[ιοι|κ]ήσει τῆι ἰδίαι πόλεις διαπο-
   στείλησθε ἔν τε τῶι ἐπ[ι]|φανεστάτωι τόπωι ἐν στυλοπαραστάδι
50 ἐπὶ | λίθου λευκοῦ ἐνχαραχθῆναι φροντίσητε τ[αῦ]‖τα τὰ
   γράμματα, ἵνα κοινῶς πάσηι τῆι ἐπαρχεία[ι τὸ] | δίκαιον
   ἐσταμένον ἦι εἰς τὸν ἀεὶ χρόνον, αἵ τε ἄλ|λαι πᾶσαι πόλεις καὶ
   δῆμοι τὸ αὐτὸν παρ᾽ αὐτοῖς | ποιήσωσιν, εἴς τε τὰ δημόσια
   ἀποθῶνται νομο[φυλά]‖κια καὶ χρηματιστήρια. Τὴν δὲ αἰτίαν
55 δι᾽ ἣν Ἑλλη[νι]‖κοῖς ἔγραψα, μὴ ἐπιζητήσητε· κατὰ νοῦν γὰρ
```

FROM ITALY AND THE PROVINCES

[ἔσ]|χον, μή τι παρὰ τὴν ἑρμηνείαν ἔλασσον τὰ [γεγραμ|μ]ένα
νοῆσαι δύνησθε· τὴν δὲ ἐπιστολὴ[ν ἔδωκα | Τι]μοκλῆι 'Αναξα-
γόρου καὶ Σωσικράτηι Πυ[θίωνος | πρ]εσβευταῖς Μαγνήτων
τῶν πρὸς τ[ῶι Μαιάν||δρ]ωι. Ἔρρωσθε.   60

This inscription comes from Miletus. A fragment of the same
letter is published in *Inschriften von Priene*, 106. Unfortunately
both inscriptions are so fragmentary that the purpose of the letter
cannot be determined. It is evident, however, that it was directed
to the κοινόν of Greeks throughout the province, and probably
contained regulations to be enforced uniformly throughout the
district. In ll. 46 f. we have a reference to the *regiones* into which
the province was divided by Sulla for administrative purposes
(Marquardt, *St. Verw.* 1, 339). It is interesting to note that the
writer explains his motive in publishing his edict in Greek instead
of Latin (ll. 54 ff.). This might imply that letters and edicts issued
by the Romans in the Greek provinces had hitherto been published
in Latin, but, if so, they had been translated into Greek before they
were recorded on stone in most cases where such records are found
(*cf.* no. 65a). The governor also requires that copies of his letter
be preserved in the proper archives in cities where copies were not
engraved on stone.

23. PERGAMENI HONORANT PUBLIUM SERVILIUM ISAURICUM

(ca. 46 a. Chr.)

Ditt. *Or. Gr.* 449; Fraenkel, *Alterthümer von Pergamon*, 413.

Ὁ δῆμος ἐτίμησεν | Πόπλιον Σεροΐλιον Ποπλίου υἱὸν
'Ισαυρι|κὸν, τὸν ἀνθύπατον, γεγονότα σωτῆρα καὶ | εὐεργέτην
τῆς πόλεως καὶ ἀποδεδωκότα τῆι || πόλει τοὺς πατρίους νόμους 5
καὶ τὴν δημοκρα|τίαν ἀδούλωτον.

From Pergamum. The reforms in provincial government introduced by Caesar brought great relief to the provinces suffering from
the exactions of the *publicani*. When Pergamum lost the right to
use her own laws is unknown. Other inscriptions from Asia indicate the gratitude of the cities and the relief which they experienced
under the new régime (*cf. Inschriften von Magnesia*, 142; Ditt. *Or.
Gr.* 450).

[287]

24. TABULA HERACLEENSIS, VULGO
LEX IULIA MUNICIPALIS
(45 a. Chr.)

CIL. 1, 206; Bruns, 18; Dessau, 6085; Girard, p. 80; Riccobono, p. 109.

. . . . . Quem h(ac) l(ege) ad co(n)s(ulem) profiterei oportebit, sei is, quom eum profiterei oportebit, Romae non erit, tum quei eius | negotia curabit, is e*a*dem omnia, quae eum, quoius negotia curabit, sei Romae esset, h. l. profiterei | oporter*et*, item isdemque diebus ad cos. profitemino. |

Quem h. l. ad cos. profiterei oportebit, sei is pup(illus) seive ea pu(pilla) erit, tum quei eius pup(illi) pu(pillae)ve tutor erit, item 5 eadem‖que omnia in iisdem diebus ad cos. profitemino, ita utei e*t* quae quibusque diebus eum eamve, sei pup(illus) pu(pilla)ve non | es*s*et, h. l. profiterei oporteret. |

Sei cos., a*d* que*m* h. l. professiones fierei oportebit, Romae non erit, tum is, quem profiterei oportebit, quod eum profiterei | oportebit, ad pr(aetorem) ur(banum) aut, sei is Romae non erit, ad eum pr(aetorem), quei inter peregrinos ius deicet, profitem*i*no, ita utei | eum ad cos., sei tum Romae esset, h. l. profiterei oporteret. ‖

10 Sei ex eis cos. et pr(aetoribus), ad quos h. l. professiones fierei oportebit, nemo eorum Romae erit, tum is, quem profiterei oportebit, | quod eum profiterei oportebit, ad tr(ibunum) pl(ebei) profitemino, ita ute*i* eum ad cos. pr(aetorem)*que* urb(anum) eumque quei inter peregri|nos ius deicet, sei tum Romae esset, h. l. profiterei oporteret. |

Quod quemquem h. l. profiterei oportebit, is, apud quem ea professio fiet, eius que*i* profitebitur nomen, et ea quae pro|fessus erit, et quo die professus sit, in tabulas publicas referunda curato, 15 eademque omnia, quae uteique in tabulas ‖ rettulerit, *i*ta in tabulam in album referunda | *curato*, idque aput *f*orum, et quom frumentum populo dabitur, ibei ubei frumen|tum populo dabitur, cottidie maiorem partem diei propositum habeto, u(nde) d(e) p(lano) r(ecte) l(egi) p(ossit). |

Queiquomque frumentum populo dab*i*t damdumve curabit, nei qu*oi* eorum, quorum nomina h. l. ad cos. pr(aetorem) tr(ibunum) pl(ebei) in ta|bula in albo proposita erunt, frumentum dato neve dare iubeto neve sinito. Quei adversus ea eorum quoi frumentum | dederit, is in tr(itici) m(odios) I HS IƆƆ populo dare damnas esto, eiusque pecuniae quei volet petitio esto. ||

Quae viae in urbe Rom(a) propiusve u(rbem) R(omam) p(assus) 20 M, ubei continente habitabitur, sunt erunt, quoius ante aedificium earum quae | via erit, is eam viam arbitratu eius aed(ilis), quoi ea pars urbis h. l. obvenerit, tueatur; isque aed(ilis) curato, uti, quorum | ante aedificium erit, quamque viam h. l. quemque tueri oportebit, ei omnes eam viam arbitratu eius tueantur, neve eo | loco aqua consistat, quominus conmode populus ea via utatur. |

Aed(iles) cur(ules) aed(iles) pl(ebei), quei nunc sunt, queiquomque post h. l. r(ogatam) factei createi erunt eumve mag(istratum) in-ierint, iei in diebus v proxumeis, || quibus eo mag(istratu) designatei 25 erunt eumve mag(istratum) inierint, inter se paranto aut sortiunto, qua in partei urbis quisque | eorum vias publicas in urbe Roma, propiusve u(rbem) R(omam) p(assus) M, reficiundas sternendas curet, eiusque rei procurationem | habeat. Quae pars quoique aed(ilei) ita h. l. obvenerit, eius aed(ilis) in eis loceis quae in ea partei erunt viarum reficien|darum tuemdarum procuratio esto, utei h. l. opor-tebit. |

Quae via inter aedem sacram et aedificium locumve publicum et inter aedificium privatum est erit, eius || viae partem dimidiam is 30 aed(ilis), quoi ea pars urbis obvenerit, in qua parte ea aedis sacra erit seive aedificium | publicum seive locus publicus, tuemdam locato. |

Quemquomque ante suum aedificium viam publicam h. l. tueri oportebit, quei eorum eam viam arbitratu eius aed(ilis), | quoius oportuerit, non tuebitur, eam viam aed(ilis), quoius arbitratu eam tuerei oportuerit, tuemdam locato; | isque aed(ilis) diebus ne minus x, antequam locet aput forum ante tribunale suom propositum habeto, quam || viam tuendam et quo die locaturus sit, et quorum 35 ante aedificium ea via sit; eisque, quorum ante aedificium | ea via erit, procuratoribusve eorum domum denuntietur facito, se eam viam locaturum, et quo die locaturus | sit; eamque locationem palam in foro per q(uaestorem) urb(anum), eumve quei aerario praerit, facito. Quamta pecunia eam | viam locaverit, tamtae pecuniae eum eosque, quorum ante aedificium ea via erit pro

[289]

portioni, quamtum | quoiusque ante aedificium viae in longitudine
et in latitudine erit, q(uaestor) urb(anus), queive aerario praerit, in
40 tabulas || publicas pecuniae factae referundum curato. Ei quei eam
viam tuemdam redemerit, tamtae pecuniae eum eos|ve adtribuito
sine d(olo) m(alo). Sei is, quei adtributus erit, eam pecuniam diebus
xxx proxumeis, quibus ipse aut pro|curator eius sciet adtributionem
factam esse ei, quoi adtributus erit, non solverit neque satis fecerit,
is | quamtae pecuniae adtributus erit, tamtam pecuniam et eius
dimidium ei, quoi adtributus erit, dare debeto, | inque eam rem is,
quo quomque de ea re aditum erit, iudicem iudiciumve ita dato, utei
45 de pecunia credita || iudicem iudiciumve dari oporteret. |

Quam viam h. l. tuemdam locari oportebit, aed(ilis), quem eam
viam tuendam locare oportebit, is eam viam per | q(uaestorem)
urb(anum), queive aerario praerit, tuemdam locato, utei eam viam
arbitratu eius, quei eam viam locandam | curaverit, tueatur. Quam-
tam pecuniam ita quaeque via locata erit, t(amtam) p(ecuniam)
q(uaestor) urb(anus), queive aerario praerit, | redemptorei, quoi e
lege locationis dari oportebit, heredeive eius damdam adtribuendam
curato. ||
50 Quo minus aed(iles) et iiiivir(ei) vieis in urbem purgandeis,
iivir(ei) vieis extra propiusve urbem Rom(am) passus M | purgandeis,
queiquomque erunt, vias publicas purgandas curent eiusque rei
potestatem habeant, | ita utei legibus pl(ebei)ve sc(itis) s(enatus)ve
c(onsultis) oportet oportebit, eius h. l. n(ihilum) r(ogatur). |

Quoius ante aedificium semita in loco erit, is eam semitam, eo
aedificio perpetuo lapidibus perpetueis | integreis continentem, con-
stratam recte habeto arbitratu eius aed(ilis), quoius in ea parte h. l.
55 viarum || procuratio erit. |

Quae viae in u(rbe) R(oma) sunt erunt intra ea loca, ubi con-
tinenti habitabitur, ne quis in ieis vieis post k. Ianuar. | primas
plostrum interdiu post solem ortum, neve ante horam x diei ducito
agito, nisi quod aedium | sacrarum deorum inmortalium caussa
aedificandarum, operisve publice faciumdei causa advehei porta|ri
oportebit, aut quod ex urbe exve ieis loceis earum rerum, quae
60 publice demoliendae locatae erunt, publi||ce exportarei oportebit, et
quarum rerum caussa plostra h. l. certeis hominibus certeis de
causeis agere | ducere licebit. |

Quibus diebus virgines Vestales re*gem* sacrorum, flamines plos-
treis in urbe sacrorum publicorum p(opuli) R(omani) caussa | vehi
oportebit, quaeque plostra triumphi caussa, quo die quisque trium-
pha*b*it, ducei oportebit, quaeque | plostra ludorum, quei Romae aut
urbei Romae *p(ropius)* *p(assus)* M publice feient, inve pompam
ludeis circiensibus ducei agei opus || erit; qu*o* minus earum rerum 65
caussa eisque diebus plostra interdiu in urbe ducantur agantur,
e(ius) h(ac) l(ege) n(ihilum) r(ogatur). |

Quae plostra noctu in urbem inducta erunt, quo minus ea plostra
inania aut stercoris exportandei caussa | post solem ortum h(oris) x
diei bubus iumenteisve iuncta in u(rbe) R(oma) et ab u(rbe) R(oma)
p(assus) M esse liceat, e(ius) h. l. n(ihilum) rogatur. |

Quae loca publica porticusve *p*ublicae in u(rbe) R(oma) p(ropius)-
ve u(rbei) R(omae) p(assus) M sunt erunt, quorum locorum quoius-
que porticus | aedilium *e*orumve mag(istratuom), quei vieis loceisque
publiceis u(rbis) R(omae) p(ropius)ve u(rbei) R(omae) p(assus) M
purgandeis praerunt, legibus || procuratio est erit, nei quis in ieis 70
loceis inve ieis porticibus quid in aedificatum inmolit*u*mve habeto, |
neve ea loca porticumve quam possideto, neve eorum quod saeptum
clausumve habeto, quo minus eis | loceis porticibusque populus
utatur pateantve, nisi quibus uteique leg(ibus) pl(ebei)ve sc(itis)
s(enatus)ve c(onsultis) concessum permissumve es*t*. |

Quibus loceis ex lege locationis, quam censor aliusve quis mag-
(istratus) publiceis vectigalibus ultrove tributeis | fruendeis tuendeisve
dixet, dixerit, eis, quei ea fruenda tuendave condu*c*ta habebunt, ut
utei fruei liceat || *a*ut utei ea ab eis custodiantur, cautum est; ei 75
quo minus ieis loceis utantur fruantur ita, utei quoique eorum | *ex*
*lege loca*tionis ieis *sine d(olo) m(alo)* utei fruei licebit, ex h. l. n(ihilum)
r(ogatur). |

Quos lud(*os*) quisque Romae p(ropius)ve u(rbei) R(omae) p(assus)
M faciet, quo minus ei eorum ludorum caussa scaenam pulpitum
ceteraque, | quae ad eos ludos opus erunt, in loco publico ponere
statuere, eisque diebus, quibus eos faciet, loco publico utei | liceat,
e(ius) h. l. n(ihilum) r(ogatur). ||

Quei scribae librarei magistratibus apparebunt, ei quo minus 80
loceis publiceis, ubei is, *quoi* quisque eorum apparebunt, | iuserit,
apparendi caussa utantur, e(ius) h.l. n(ihilum) r(ogatur). |

Quae loca serveis publiceis ab cens(oribus) habitandei utendei caussa adtributa sunt, ei quo minus eis loceis utantur, e(ius) h. l. n(ihilum) r(ogatur). |

Queiquomque in municipieis coloneis praefectureis foreis conciliabuleis c(ivium) R(omanorum) iivir(ei) iiiivir(ei) erunt aliove | quo nomine mag(istratum) potestatemve sufragio eorum, quei
85 quoiusque municipi coloniae praefecturae || fori conciliabuli erunt habebunt: nei quis eorum quem in eo municipio colonia praefectura foro concilia|bulo in senatum decuriones conscriptosve legito neve sublegito neve coptato neve recitandos curato, | nisi in demortuei damnateive locum eiusve, quei confessus erit, se senatorem decurionem conscreiptumve | ibei h. l. esse non licere. |

Quei minor annos xxx natus est erit, nei quis eorum post k.
90 Ianuar. secundas in municipio colonia praefe||ctura iivir(atum) iiiivir(atum) neve quem alium mag(istratum) petito neve capito neve gerito, nisei quei eorum stipendia | equo in legione iii, aut pedestria in legione vi fecerit, quae stipendia in castreis inve provincia maiorem | partem sui quoiusque anni fecerit, aut bina semestria, quae ei pro singuleis annueis procedere oporteat, | aut ei vocatio rei militaris legibus pl(ebei)ve sc(itis) exve foidere erit, quocirca eum inveitum merere non | oporteat. Neve quis, quei praeconium dissignationem libitinamve faciet, dum eorum quid faciet, in muni-||
95 cipio colonia praefectura iivir(atum) iiiivir(atum) aliumve quem mag(istratum) petito neve capito neve gerito neve habeto, | neve ibei senator neve decurio neve conscriptus esto, neve sententiam dicito. Quei eorum ex eis, quei s(upra) s(criptei) s(unt), | adversus ea fecerit, is hs iↃↃↃ p(opulo) d(are) d(amnas) e(sto), eiusque pecuniae quei volet petitio esto. |

Queiquomque in municipio colonia praefectura post k. Quinct-(iles) prim(as) comitia iivir(eis) iiiivir(eis) aleive quoi mag(istratui) | rogando subrogandove habebit, is ne quem, quei minor anneis
100 xxx natus est erit, iivir(um), iiiivir(um), queive ibei || alium mag(istratum) habeat, renuntiato neve renuntiarei iubeto, nisi quei stipendia equo in legione iii, aut sti|pendia pedestria in legione vi fecerit, quae stipendia in castreis inve provincia maiorem partem sui | quoiusque anni fecerit, aut bina semestria, quae ei pro singuleis annueis procedere oporteat, cum eo | quod ei legibus pl(eibei)ve

sc(iteis) procedere oportebit, aut ei vocatio rei militaris legibus
pl(ebei)ve sc(iteis) exve foedere | erit, quo circa eum invitum merere
non oporteat. Neve eum, quei praeconium dissignationem libiti-
na*m*ve faciet, dum eorum quid || faciet, ɪɪvir(um) ɪɪɪɪvir(um), queive 105
ibei mag(istratus) sit, renuntiato, neve in senatum neve in de|curi-
onum conscriptorum*ve* numero legito, sublegito coptato neve sen-
tentiam rogato neve dicere neve | ferre iubeto sc(iens) d(olo) m(alo).
Quei adversus ea fecerit, is ʜꜱ ɪɔɔɔ p(opulo) d(are) d(amnas) esto,
eiusque pecuniae quei volet petitio esto. |

Quae municipia coloni*ae* praefectur*ae* fora conciliabula c(ivium)
R(omanorum) sunt erunt, nei quis in eorum quo municipio |
colonia praefectura *foro* conciliabulo *in* senatu decurionibus con-
screipteisque esto, neve quo*i* ibi in eo ordine || sente*m*tiam deicere 110
ferre liceto: quei furtei, quod *ipse* fecit fecerit, condemnatus pactusve
est erit; | queive iudicio fiduci*ae* pro socio, tutelae, mandatei, in-
iuriarum, deve d(olo) m(alo) condemnatus est erit; queive lege |
Plaetoria ob eamve rem, quod adversus eam legem fec*i*t fecerit,
condemnatus est erit; queive depugnandei | caussa auctoratus est
erit fuit fuerit; queive | in iure *bonam copiam abiuravit* abiuraverit,
bonamve copiam iuravit iuraverit; quei*ve* sponsoribus creditoribusve
sueis renuntiavit renuntiaverit, se soldum solvere non posse, aut
cum eis || pactus est erit, se soldum solvere non posse; prove quo 115
datum depensum est erit; quoiusve bona ex edicto | eius, qu*ei* i(*ure*)
d(eicundo) praefuit praefuerit, praeterquam sei quoius, quom pu-
pillus esset reive publicae caussa abesset, | neque d(olo) m(alo) fecit
fecerit quo magis r(ei) p(ublicae) c(aussa) a(besset), possessa pro-
scriptave sunt erunt; queive iudicio publico Romae | condemnatus
est erit, quo circa eum in Italia esse non liceat, neque in integrum
resti*tu*tus est erit; queive in eo | municipio colonia praefectura foro
conciliabulo, quoius erit, iudicio publico condemnatus est erit;
quemve || k(alumniae) praevaricationis caussa accussasse fecisseve 120
quod iudicatum est erit; quoive aput exercitum ingnominiae | caussa
ordo ademptus est erit; quemve imperator ingnominiae caussa ab
exer*c*itu decedere ius*i*t iuserit; | queive ob caput c(ivis) R(omanei)
referundum pecuniam praemium aliudve quid cepit ceperit; queive
corpor*e* quaestum | fecit fecerit; queive lanistaturam artemve ludi-
cram fecit fecerit; queive lenocinium faciet. Quei | adversus ea

[293]

in municipio colonia praefectur*a* foro conciliabulo *in senatu* de-
125 curionibus conscripteisve *f*uerit ‖ sentemtiamve dixerit, is HS IↃↃↃ
p(opulo) d(are) d(amnas) esto, eiusque pecuniae quei volet petitio esto. |
Quoi h. l. in municipio colonia praefectura foro conciliabulo
senatorem decurionem conscriptum esse, | inque eo ordine sentem-
tiam dicere ferre non licebit, nei quis, quei in eo municipio colonia
praefectura | foro conciliabulo senatum decuriones conscriptos
habebit, eum in senatum decuriones conscriptos | ire iubeto sc(iens)
d(olo) m(alo); neve eum ibei sentemtiam rogato neive dicere neive
130 ferre iubeto sc(iens) d(olo) m(alo); neve quis, que*i* ‖ in eo municipio
colonia praefectura foro conciliabulo sufragio eorum maxumam
potestatem habebit, | eorum quem ibei in senatum decuriones con-
scriptos ire, neve in eo numero esse n*e*ve sentemtiam ibei dicere |
ferreve sinito sc(iens) d(olo) m(alo); neve quis eius rationem comitieis conciliove *habeto, neive quis quem, sei adversus ea comitieis*
conciliove creatum est renuntiato; neve quis, | quei ibei mag(istratum)
potestatemve habebit, eum cum senatu decurionibus conscript*eis*
*ludo*s spectare neive in convivio | publico esse sin*i*to sc(iens) d(olo)
m(alo). ‖
135 Quibus h. l. in municipio colonia praefectura foro conciliabulo
in s*e*nat*u* decurionibus conscripteis esse | non licebit, ni quis eorum
in municipio colonia praefectura foro conciliabulo IIvir(atum)
IIIIvir(atum) aliamve | quam potestatem ex quo honore in eum
ordinem perveniat, petito neve capito; neve quis eorum ludeis, |
cumve gladiatores ibei pugnabunt, in loco senatorio decurionum
conscriptorum sed*e*to neve spectato | neve convivium publicum is
inito; neive quis, quei adversus ea creatu*s* renuntiatu*s* erit, ibei
140 IIvir IIIIvir ‖ esto, neve ibei m(agistratum) potestatemve habeto.
Qu*ei* adversus ea fecerit, is HS IↃↃↃ p(opulo) d(are) d(amnas) esto,
eiusque pecuniae quei | volet petitio esto. |
Quae municipia coloniae praefecturae c(ivium) R(omanorum) in
Italia sunt erunt, quei in eis municipieis coloneis | praefectureis
maximum mag(istratum) maxim*a*mve potestatem ibei habebit tum,
cum censor aliusve | quis mag(istratus) Romae populi c*e*nsum aget,
145 is diebus IX proxumeis, quibus sciet Romae censum populi ‖ agi,
omnium municipium colonorum suorum queique eius praefecturae
erunt, q(uei) c(ives) R(omanei) erunt, censum | ag*i*to, eorumque

[294]

nomina praenomina, patres aut patronos, tribus, cognomina, et quot
annos | quisque eorum habet, et rationem pecuniae ex formula
census, quae Romae ab eo, qui tum censum | populi acturus erit,
proposita erit, ab ieis iurateis accipito; eaque omnia in tabulas publicas
sui | municipi referunda curato; eosque libros per legatos, quos
maior pars decurionum conscriptorum || ad eam rem legarei mittei 150
censuerint tum, cum ea res consuleretur, ad eos, quei Romae censum
agent, | mittito; curatoque, utei quom amplius dies LX reliquei erunt,
ante quam diem ei, queiquomque Romae | censum aget, finem
populi censendi faciant, eos adeant librosque eius municipi coloniae
praefecturae | edant; isque censor, seive quis alius mag(istratus)
censum populi aget, diebus V proxumeis, quibus legatei eius |
municipi coloniae praefecturae adierint, eos libros census, quei ab
ieis legateis dabuntur, accipito || s(ine) d(olo) m(alo) exque ieis 155
libreis, quae ibei scripta erunt, in tabulas publicas referunda curato,
easque tabulas | eodem loco, ubei ceterae tabulae publicae erunt, in
quibus census populi perscriptus erit, condendas curato. |

Qui pluribus in municipieis coloneis praefectureis domicilium
habebit, et is Romae census erit, quo magis | in municipio colonia
praefectura h. l. censeatur, e(ius) h. l. n(ihilum) r(ogatur). |

Quei lege pl(ebeive) sc(ito) permissus est fuit, utei leges in muni-
cipio fundano municipibusve eius municipi daret, || sei quid is post 160
h. l. r(ogatam) in eo anno proxumo, quo h. l. populus iuserit, ad eas
leges *addiderit commutaverit conrexerit*, municipis fundanos | item
teneto, utei oporteret, sei eae res ab eo tum, quom primum leges
eis municipibus lege pl(ebei)ve sc(ito) dedit, | ad eas leges additae
commutatae conrectae essent; neve quis intercedito neve quid
facito, quo minus | ea rata sint, quove minus municipis fundanos
teneant eisque optemperetur.

l. 19. 1 *i.e.* singulos.
l. 29. via inter; viam per, *tablet.*
l. 64. ludorum, *sc.* caussa.
l. 92. oporteat; cum eo quod ei legibus plebeive sciteis procedere oportebit,
    omitted. Cf. ll. 102–103.
l. 117. abesset; *Mommsen and Dessau add* bona possessa proscriptave sunt
    erunt.

MUNICIPAL DOCUMENTS IN GREEK AND LATIN

A very large bronze tablet, with a more ancient Greek inscription on the back of it. It is broken into two parts. The lower part (ll. 76–163) was found near the site of Heraclea in 1732. The upper part was discovered in 1754. Both parts are now in the museum at Naples. The beginning of the law has been lost. The date of the inscription is fixed approximately or exactly from a letter of Cicero (*ad fam.* 6. 18. 1). In this letter he writes to Lepta, *simulatque accepi a Seleuco tuo litteras, statim quaesivi e Balbo per codicillos, quid esset in lege. Rescripsit eos, qui facerent praeconium, vetari esse in decurionibus; qui fecissent, non vetari.* The provision mentioned here is the exact point covered in our law (l. 94), and Cicero is evidently referring to this measure. He has obtained information in advance from an intimate friend of Caesar concerning the bill about to be submitted, which has not yet been promulgated. The date of Cicero's letter, Jan. 45 B.C., fixes the probable date of the law as 45 B.C. on Caesar's return from Spain (*cf.* Mommsen in Bruns, p. 102). For arguments in favor of the year 46, *cf.* Nissen, *Rh. Mus.* 45 (1890), 100 *ff.*, Hackel, *Wien. Stud.* 24 (1902), 552, and others. Since Savigny's time (*cf. Verm. Schr.* 3, 279 *ff.*) it has commonly been believed that this measure was intended to provide a normal charter for Italian towns. This conclusion was based largely upon certain apparent references in the Civil Law (*cf.* especially, *Cod. J.* 7. 9. 1; *Dig.* 50. 9. 3) to a general *lex municipalis*, which was identified with Caesar's measure, but most scholars have abandoned this identification (*cf.* however, Hardy, *Six Roman Laws*, 139 *ff.*, 165 *ff.*). Mommsen has gone so far (*Ges. Schr.* 1, 153) as to deny the existence of a model charter at any period whatsoever, but *cf.* pp. 185 *ff.*

The extant tablet covers four different matters, with a supplementary provision (ll. 159–163) ratifying such changes as the commissioners may make in the measure during the first year after its adoption. These four subjects are: (1) rules governing the distribution of corn in Rome (ll. 1–19); (2) regulations determining the duties of the aediles and other officials in Rome in repairing, cleaning, and policing the streets (ll. 20–82); (3) conditions governing the eligibility of candidates for the magistracies and the senate (ll. 83–141); (4) provisions regulating the taking of the census in the municipality (ll. 142–158). It is very difficult to account for the appearance, on a single tablet, of laws dealing with such diverse matters as the corn supply and the functions of the aedile, and concerning Rome as well as Italian municipalities (*cf.* Herzog, 2, 1, n. 1). Perhaps we have on the tablet parts of three different laws, *viz.* part of a municipal charter, and parts of two laws dealing with the corn supply and the aedile's duties in Rome. The theory that the law is a *lex satura* (Savigny, *op. cit.* 3, 327 *ff.*; de Petra, *Mon. ant. d. Lincei*, 6 (1895), 433 *ff.*) has been given up by most scholars. Still others believe that the law is a unit, being part of a comprehensive measure intended for Rome as well as for the Italian municipalities. Possibly, if we accept the first of these three theories mentioned above, we may surmise that we have on the tablet a municipal charter as the *pièce de résistance*, to which is added an article concerning the corn supply for the information of a municipality, and a chapter prescribing the duties of a Roman aedile to serve as a guide for the municipal magistracy (*cf.* Herzog, *loc. cit.*). Whatever relation the different parts of the inscription have to one another, from l. 83 on we have part of an early municipal charter which deals with the local executives and the local senate. *Cf.* no. 20. For the judicial powers of local magistrates, *cf.* no. 27.

It seems probable from a comparison of l. 83 with ll. 89–90 that *fora* and *conciliabula* had local magistrates, but that these magistrates did not bear the title of *duoviri* or of *quattuorviri*. On similar grounds we infer (*cf.* ll. 142 *ff.*) that the census was not taken in *fora* and *conciliabula*. (For another list of communities, *cf.* no. 27, chap. xxii.) Although criminal courts held in *fora* and *conciliabula* are mentioned in ll. 118–119, they cannot have been presided over by local magistrates (*cf.* Schulten, *R.E.* 7, 63), but must have been conducted by *praefecti* sent from larger communities. From ll. 83–88 it is clear that magistrates were to be elected in the popular assembly, and that decurions could be named by the magistrates. On the technical terms in l. 86, *cf.* Mommsen, *St. R.* 3, 855 *f.* and nn. Apparently decurions could also be elected in the popular assembly (*cf.* l. 132).

Rome required the census to be taken in Italian towns as early as 209 B.C. (Livy, 29. 15), but this is the earliest extended formula-

MUNICIPAL DOCUMENTS IN GREEK AND LATIN

tion which we have of the method of procedure. The charter of
Bantia (no. 11, chap. 4) bears witness to the taking of the census
in this Oscan town in the second century B.C., and prescribes a
penalty for those who fail to report themselves. Under the principate the census was also required in provincial towns (cf. Kubitschek,
R.E. 3, 1918 f.). We do not know whether the system outlined
here originated in Rome or was adopted from other Italian municipalities. The fact that a person might have a domicile in several
municipalities (l. 157) will be illustrated in concrete cases in later
inscriptions (cf. no. 94), in which we shall find certain men as
citizens in several *civitates*. The course of procedure which was
followed in granting this charter is indicated in l. 159. An enabling
act passed in the popular assembly authorized a commissioner or a
commission to frame a constitution and, a year after the passage
of the law, to make any necessary amendments. On the scope of
this article, cf. Elmore, *Trans. Am. Phil. Assoc.* 47 (1916), 40 ff.
For an extended commentary on the entire document, cf. Legras,
La table Latine d'Héraclée; Elmore, *Journ. Rom. Studies*, 5 (1915),
125 ff.; Hardy, *Class. Quart.* 11 (1917), 27 ff.; *Some Problems in
Roman History*, 239 ff.

25. SENATUS CONSULTUM ET EPISTULA
CAESARIS AD MYTILENAEOS
(45 a. Chr.)

IG. XII, 2, 35, ll. 14–37; Cagnat, *IGRR.* 4, 33; Ditt. *Syll.*³ 764
(in part).

[Περὶ ὧν π]ρεσβευταὶ Μυτιληναίων Ποτάμων Λεσβώνακτος,
Φαινίας Φαινίου τοῦ Καλλί[π]|που, Σέρφηος Διοῦς, Ἡρώδης
15 Κλέωνος, Διῆς Ματροκλέους, Δημήτριος Κλεωνύμου, ‖ Κρινα-
γόρας Καλλίππου, Ζωίλος Ἐπιγένους λόγους ἐποιήσαντο, χάριτα,
φιλίαν, συμμα|χίαν ἀνενεοῦντο, ἵνα τε ἐν Καπετωλίωι θυσ[ί]αν
ποιῆσαι ἐξῆι, ἅ τε αὐτοῖς | πρότερον ὑπὸ τῆς συγκλήτου συγκε-
χωρημ|[έ]να ἦν, ταῦτα ἐν δέλτωι χαλκῆι | γεγραμμένα προσ-
20 ηλῶσαι ἵνα ἐξῆι· περὶ τούτου τοῦ πράγματος οὕτως ‖ ἔδοξεν·
χάριτα, φιλίαν, συμμαχίαν ἀνενεώσασθαι, ἄνδρας ἀγαθοὺς καὶ
φί|λους προσαγορεῦσαι, ἐν Καπετωλίωι θυσίαν ποιῆσαι ἐξεῖναι, ἅ
τε αὐτοῖς πρό|τερον ὑπὸ τῆς συγκλήτου φιλάνθρωπα συγκεχωρη-

FROM ITALY AND THE PROVINCES

μένα ἦν, ταῦτα ἐν δέλ|τωι χαλκῆι γεγραμμένα προσηλῶσαι
ἐξεῖναι, ὅταν θέλωσιν· ἵνα τε Γάϊος | Καῖσαρ αὐτοκράτωρ, ἐὰν
αὐτῶι φαίνηται, τόπους χορήγια αὐτοῖς κατὰ τὸ || τῶν προγόνων 25
ἔθος ταμίαν μισθῶσαι κελεύσηι ο(ὕτ)ως ὡς ἂν αὐτῶι ἐκ τῶν
δη|μοσίων πραγμάτων πίστεώς τε τῆς ἰδίας φαίνηται. "Εδοξεν.
['Επ]εὶ δὲ καὶ | πρότερον ἐνετύχετέ μοι καὶ ἔγραψα πρὸς ὑμᾶς,
πάλιν ὑπέμ[ειν]αν οἱ | [ὑμέτεροι πρεσβευταὶ μη]δένα δεῖν
ἀτελῆ εἶ[ναι] παρ' ὑμῖν ἀκολούθ[ως τοῖς |..........καὶ τοῖς]
φιλανθρώποις ἃ ἔχετε παρ' ἡμῶν τοῖς τε [πρότε||ρον καὶ τοῖς 30
διὰ τούτου το]ῦ δόγματος δεδομένοις τὸ ἐξεῖναι ὑμῖ[ν...|...ταῖς]
τῆς πόλεως καὶ τῆς χώρας προσόδοις καθ' ἡ[συχίαν | χρῆσθαι.
Βούλομαι οὖν] ἀποφήνασθαι ὅτι οὐδενὶ συγχωρῶ οὐδὲ συγ[χω-
ρή|σω ἀτελεῖ παρ' ὑμῖν εἶναι. Ο]ὕτως οὖν πεπεισμένοι θαρ-
ροῦντες χρῆσθ[ε..|...ἀνεμποδ]ίστως· ἐγὼ ταῦτά τε ἡδέως
πεποίηκα ὑ[πὲρ || ὑμῶν καὶ εὔχομαι εἰς τ]ὸ μέλλον αἰεί τινος 35
ἀγαθοῦ παραίτιος ὑμῖν [γενέσθαι]. |

From Mytilene. The inscription contains the correspondence
and treaty between Rome and Mytilene. This city had been loyal
to Pompey, but after the battle of Pharsalia it had sent an embassy
to Caesar to sue for pardon (*cf.* Plutarch, *Pomp.* 75). A second
embassy was sent to Rome in 45 B.C. to ask for the renewal of the
old treaty of alliance. Their request was granted by the senate, and
Caesar sent this letter to the Mytileneans, of which we publish
a part. This part includes the decree of the senate renewing the
treaty and an edict of Caesar wherein he promises the city that no
resident of Mytilene shall enjoy the privilege of immunity. In spite
of the fact that this city enjoyed the status of an independent ally
of Rome, it is apparent that complete autonomy was not implied.
Since Roman citizens enjoyed special privileges of immunity in the
cities of the empire, it is probable that the edict of Caesar was
designed to subject them to the laws, customs, and duties of the
Mytileneans (*cf.* p. 192). Mytilene was a free city under Augustus
(Pliny, *N.H.* 5, 139). It may have lost its privileges under Vespasian
(Philostratus, *Apoll.* 5, 41), but they were restored by Hadrian.
Cf. Chapot, *La prov. rom. proc. d'Asie*, 118.

26. LEX COLONIAE GENITIVAE IULIAE SEU URSONENSIS
(44 a. Chr.)

CIL. II, *S.* 5439; Dessau, 6087; Bruns, 28; Girard, p. 89;
Riccobono, p. 142.

Tab. I,   *LXI.... Cui quis ita ma*|num inicere iussus erit, iudicati iure
col. III   ma|nus iniectio esto, itque ei s(ine) f(raude) s(ua) facere liceto.
Vin|dex arbitratu IIviri qui*v*e i(ure) d(icundo) p(raerit) locuples ‖
5 esto. Ni vindicem dabit iudicatum*v*e faci|et, secum ducito. Iure
civili vinctum habeto. | Si quis in eo vim faciet, ast eius vincitur,
du|pli damnas esto colonisq(ue) eius colon(iae) HS CCIƆƆ CCIƆƆ |
10 d(are) d(amnas) esto, eiusque pecuniae *q*ui vo‖let petitio, IIvir(o)
qui*v*e i(ure) d(icundo) p(raerit) exactio iudicati|oque esto. |

    LXII. IIviri quicumque erunt, *iis* IIviris in eos singulos | lictores
binos accensos sing(ulos), scribas bi|nos, viatores binos, librarium,
15 praeconem, ‖ haruspicem, tibicinem habere ius potestas|que esto.
Quique in ea colonia aedil(es) erunt, | iis aedil(ibus) in eos aedil(es)
sing(ulos) scribas sing(ulos), publi|cos cum cincto limo IIII, prae-
conem, haruspi|cem tibicinem habere ius potestasq(ue) esto. Ex eo ‖
20 numero, qui eius coloniae coloni erunt, habe|to. Iisque IIvir(is)
aedilibusque, dum eum mag(istratum) ha|bebunt, togas praetextas,
funalia, cereos ha|bere ius potestasq(ue) esto. Quos quisque eo|rum
25 ita scribas lictores accensos viatorem ‖ tibicinem haruspicem prae-
conem habebit, iis | omnibus eo anno, quo anno quisque eorum |
apparebit, militiae vacatio esto, neve quis e|um eo anno, quo
mag(istratibus) apparebit, invitum | militem facito neve fieri iubeto
30 neve eum ‖ cogito neve ius iurandum adigito neve a|digi iubeto
neve sacramento rogato neve | rogari iubeto, nisi tumultus Italici
Gallici|ve causa. Eisque merces in eos singul(os), qui IIvi|ris appare-
35 bunt, tanta esto: in scribas sing(ulos) ‖ HS ∞ CC, in accensos sing(ulos)
HS DCC, in lictores | sing(ulos) HS DC, in viatores sing(ulos) HS CCCC,
in libra|rios sing(ulos) HS CCC, in haruspices sing(ulos) HS D, prae|coni
HS CCC; qui aedilib(us) appareb(unt): in scribas | sing(ulos) HS DCCC,
col. IV in haruspices sing(ulos) HS C, in ti|bicines sing(ulos) HS CCC, in prae-
cones sing(ulos) HS CCC. | Iis s(ine) f(raude) s(ua) kapere liceto. |

    LXIII. IIviri, qui primi ad. pr. k. Ianuar. mag(istratum) habe-
bunt, appari|tores totidem habento *quot* sing(ulis) apparitores ex h(ac)

[300]

l(ege) ha‖bere lice*t*. Iisque apparitorib(us) merces tanta esto, │ 5
quantam esse oporteret, si partem IIII anni *appar*|uissent, ut pro
portione, quam diu apparuiss*e*nt, mer|cedem pro eo kaperent, itque
iis s(ine) f(raude) s(ua) c(apere) l(iceto). │

LXIIII. IIviri quicumque post colon(iam) deductam erunt, ii
in die‖bus x proxumis, quibus eum mag(istratum) gerere coeperint, 10
at │ decuriones referunto, cum non minus duae partes │ aderint, quos
et quot dies festos esse et quae sacra │ fieri publice placeat et quos
ea sacra facere place|at. Quot ex eis rebus decurionum maior pars,
qui ‖ tum aderunt, decreverint statuerint, it ius ratum|que esto, 15
eaque sacra eique dies festi in ea colon(ia) │ sunto. │

LXV. Quae pecunia poenae nomine ob vectiga*l*ia, quae │
colon(iae) G(enetivae) Iul(iae) erunt, in publicum redacta erit, eam ‖
pecuniam ne quis erogare neve cui dare neve attri|buere potestatem 20
habeto nisi at ea sacra, quae in │ colon(ia) aliove quo loco colonorum
nomine fia*n*t, │ neve quis aliter eam pecuniam s(ine) f(raude) s(u*a*)
kapito, n*e*ve quis │ de ea pecunia ad decuriones referundi neve quis ‖
de ea pecunia sententiam dicendi ius potestat(em)|que habeto. Eam-
que pecuniam ad ea sacra, quae │ in ea colon(ia) aliove quo loco 25
colonor*um* nomine │ fient, IIviri s(ine) f(raude) s(ua) dato attribuito
itque ei facere │ ius potestasq(ue) *e*sto. Eique cui ea *p*ecunia dabi‖tur 30
s(ine) f(raude) s(ua) kapere liceto. │

LXVI. Quos pontifices quosque augures G. Caesar, quive │
iussu eius colon(iam) deduxerit, fecerit ex colon(ia) Ge|net(iva), ei
pon*t*ifices eique augures c(oloniae) G(enetivae) I(uliae) sunto,
eiq(ue) │ pon*tifi*ces auguresque in pontificum augu‖rum conlegio 35
in ea colon(ia) sunto, ita uti qui │ optima lege optumo iure in quaque
colon(ia) │ pontif(ices) augures sunt erunt. Iisque pontificibus │
auguri*b*usque, qui in quoque eorum collegio │ erunt, liberisque eorum
militiae munerisq|ue publici vacatio sacrosanct*a* esto, uti pon|tifici col. v
Romano est erit, *ae*raque militaria ea omni|a merita sunto. De
auspiciis quaeque ad eas res per|tinebunt augurum iuris dictio iudi-
catio esto. Eis‖que pontificib(us) auguribusque ludis, quot publice 5
ma|gistratus facient, et cum ei pontific(es) augures sa|cra publica
c(oloniae) G(enetivae) I(uliae) facient, togas praetextas haben|di ius
potestasq(ue) esto, eisque pontificib(us) augurib(us)|q(ue) ludos
gladiatoresq(ue) inter decuriones specta‖re ius potestasque esto. │ 10

[301]

LXVII. Quicumque pontif(ex) quique augur c(oloniae) G(ene-
tivae) I(uliae) post h(anc) l(egem) da|tam in conlegium pontific(um)
augurumq(ue) in demor|tui damnative loco h(ac) l(ege) lectus co-
optatusve erit, | is pontif(ex) augurq(ue) in c(olonia) Iul(ia) in con-
15 legium [*sic*] pontifex ‖ augurq(ue) esto, ita uti qui optuma lege in
quaque | colon(ia) pontif(ices) auguresq(ue) sunt erunt. Neve quis |
quem in conlegium pontificum kapito suble|gito cooptato nisi tunc
cum minus tribus pon|tificib(us) ex iis, qui c(oloniae) G(enetivae)
20 sunt, erunt. Neve quis quem ‖ in conlegium augurum sublegito
cooptato ni|si tum cum minus tribus auguribus ex eis, qui | colon(iae)
G(enetivae) I(uliae) sunt, erunt. |

LXVII(I). IIviri praef(ectus)ve comitia pontific(um) augurum-
q(ue), quos h(ac) lege | facere oportebit, ita habeto, prodi*c*ito, ita
25 uti ‖ IIvir(um) creare facere sufficere h(ac) l(ege) o(portebit). |

LXIX. IIviri qui post colon(iam) deduc*t*am primi erunt, ei in
su|o mag(istratu) et quicumq(ue) IIvir(i) in colon(ia) Iul(ia) e*r*unt,
ii in | diebus LX proxumis, quibus eum mag(istratum) gerere coe|pe-
30 rint, ad decuriones referunto, cum non minus ‖ XX aderunt, uti
redemptori redemptoribusque, | qui ea redempta habebunt quae ad
sacra resq(ue) | divinas opus erunt, pecunia ex lege locationis |
adtribuatur solvaturq(ue). Neve quisquam rem ali|am at decuriones
35 referunto neve quot decuri‖onum decret(um) faciunto antequam
eis redemp|toribus pecunia ex lege locationis attribuatur | solvaturve
d(ecurionum) d(ecreto), dum ne minus XXX atsint, cum | e(a) r(es)
consulatur. Quot ita decreverint, ei IIvir(i) | redemptori redemptori-
bus attribuendum | solvendumque curato, dum ne ex ea pecunia |
solvant adtribuant, quam pecuniam ex h(ac) l(ege) | *ad e*a sacra, quae
5 in colon(ia) aliove quo loco pu‖blice fiant, dari adtribui oportebit. |

(L)XX. IIviri quicum*q*ue erunt praeter eos, qui primi | post
h(anc) l(egem) *fa*cti erunt, ⟨ei⟩ in suo mag(istratu) munus lu|dosve
scaenicos Iovi Iunoni Minervae deis | deabusq(ue) quadriduom
10 m(aiore) p(arte) diei, quot eius fie‖ri *pote*rit, arbitratu decurionum
faciun|to inque eis ludis eoque munere unusquis|que eorum de sua
pecunia ne minus HS ∞ ∞ | consumito et ex pecunia publica in
sing(ulos) | IIvir(os) d(um) t(axat) HS ∞ ∞ sumere consumere
15 liceto, it‖que eis s(ine) f(raude) s(ua) facere liceto, dum ne quis ex
ea | pecun(ia) sumat neve adtributionem faciat, | quam pecuniam

h(ac) l(ege) ad ea sacra, quae in co|lon(ia) aliove quo loco public*e* fient, dari | adtribui oportebit. ||

LXXI. Aediles quicumq(ue) erunt in suo mag(istratu) munus 20 lu|dos scaenicos Iovi Iunoni Minervae tri|duom maiore parte diei, quot eius fieri pote|rit, et unum diem in circo aut in foro Veneri | faciunto, inque eis ludis eoque munere unus||quisque eorum de sua 25 pecunia ne minus нs ∞ ∞ | consumito deve publico in sing(ulos) aedil(es) нs ∞ | sumere liceto, eamq(ue) pecuniam ıɪvir prae- f(ectusve) | dandam adtribuendam curanto itque iis | s(ine) f(raude) s(ua) c(apere) liceto. ||

LXXII. Quotcumque pecuniae stipis nomine in aedis | sacras 30 datum inlatum erit, quot eius pecuni|ae eis sacr*is* superfuerit, quae sacra, uti h(ac) l(ege) d(ata) | oportebit, ei deo deaeve, cuius ea aedes erit, fac|ta *fuerint*, ne quis facito neve curato neve interce||dito, quo 35 minus in ea aede consumatur, ad | quam aedem ea pecunia stipis nomine da|ta conlata erit, neve quis eam pecuniam alio | consumito ne*ve* quis facito, quo magis in | alia re consumatur. | col. ıı

LXXIII. Ne quis intra fines oppidi colon(iae)ve, qua aratro | circumductum erit, hominem mortuom | inferto neve ibi humato neve urito neve homi||nis mortui monimentum aedificato. Si quis | 5 adversus ea fecerit, is c(olonis) c(oloniae) G(enetivae) Iul(iae) нs ıɔɔ d(are) d(amnas) esto, | eiusque pecuniae *q*ui volet petitio persecu|tio ⟨exactioq(ue)⟩ esto. Itque quot inaedificatum | erit ɪɪvir aedil(is)ve dimoliendum curanto. Si || adversus ea mortuus 10 inlatus positusve erit, | expianto uti oportebit. |

LXXIV. Ne quis ustrinam novam, ubi homo mortuus | com- bustus non erit, pro*p*ius oppidum pas|sus ᴅ facito. Qui adversus ea fecerit, нs ıɔɔ c(olonis) || c(oloniae) G(enetivae) Iul(iae) d(are) 15 d(amnas) esto, eiusque pecuniae *q*ui volet peti|tio persecutioq(ue) ex h(ac) l(ege) esto. |

LXXV. Ne quis in oppido colon(ia) Iul(ia) aedificium detegito | neve demolito neve disturbato, nisi si praedes | ɪɪvir(um) arbitratu dederit se re*d*aedificaturum, aut || nisi decuriones decreverint, dum 20 ne minus ʟ ad|sint, cum e(a) r(es) consulatur. Si quis adversus ea fece(rit), | q(uanti) e(a) r(es) e(rit), t(antam) p(ecuniam) c(olonis) c(oloniae) G(enetivae) Iul(iae) d(are) d(amnas) e(sto), eiusq(ue) pecuniae qui volet pe|titio persecutioq(ue) ex h(ac) l(ege) esto. |

25   LXXVI. Figlinas teglarias maiores tegularum ccc tegu‖lariumq(ue) in oppido colon(ia) Iul(ia) ne quis habeto. Qui | habuerit *it* aedificium isque locus publicus | col(oniae) Iuli(ae) esto, eiusq(ue) aedificii quicumque in c(olonia) | G(enetiva) Iul(ia) i(ure) d(icundo) p(raerit), s(ine) d(olo) m(alo) eam pecuniam in publicum redi*g*ito. |

LXXVII. Si quis vias fossas cloacas ɪɪvir aedil(is)ve publice ‖
30   facere inmittere commutare aedificare mu|nire intra eos fines, qui colon(iae) Iul(iae) erunt, volet, | quot eius sine iniuria privatorum fiet, it is face|re liceto. |

LXXIIX. Quae viae publicae itinerave publica sunt fuerunt ‖
35   intra eos fines, qui colon(iae) dati erunt, quicumq(ue) | limites quaeque viae quaeque itinera per eos a|gros sunt erunt fueruntve, eae viae eique limites | eaque itinera publica sunto. |

40   LXXIX. Qui fluvi rivi fontes lacus aquae stagna paludes ‖ sunt
col. ɪɪɪ in agro, qui colon(is) h*ui*usc(e) colon(iae) divisus | erit, ad eos rivos fontes lacus aquas⟨que⟩ sta|gna paludes itus actus aquae haustus iis item | esto, qui eum agrum habebunt possidebunt, uti | iis fuit, qui eum
5   agrum habuerunt possederunt. ‖ Itemque iis, qui eum agrum habent possident ha|bebunt possidebunt, itineris aquarum lex ius|que esto. |

LXXX. Quot cuique negotii publice in colon(ia) de decu-
10   r(ionum) sen|tentia datum erit, is cui negotium datum erit e‖ius rei rationem decurionib(us) reddito referto|que in dieb(us) cʟ proxumis *quibus* it negotium confecerit | quibusve it negotium gerere desierit, quot eius | fieri poterit s(ine) d(olo) m(alo). |

LXXXI. Quicumque ɪɪvir(i) aed(iles)ve colon(iae) Iul(iae)
15   erunt, ii scribis ‖ suis, qui pecuniam publicam colonorumque | rationes scripturus erit, antequam tabulas | publicas scribet ⟨tractetve⟩ in contione palam | luci nundinis in forum ius iurandum
20   adigi|to per Iovem deosque Penates "sese pecuniam pu‖blicam eius colon(iae) concustoditurum rationes|que veras habiturum esse, u(ti) q(uod) r(ecte) f(actum) e(sse) v(olet) s(ine) d(olo) m(alo), ne|que se fraudem per litteras facturum esse sc(ientem) | d(olo) m(alo)." Uti quisque scriba ita iuraverit, in tabulas | publicas referatur facito.
25   Qui ita non iurave‖rit, is tabulas publicas ne scribito neve aes | apparitorium mercedemque ob e(am) r(em) kapito. | Qui ius iurandum non adegerit, ei ʜs ɪↃↃ mul|t*a* esto, eiusq(ue) pecuniae *q*ui volet petitio per|secutioq(ue) ex h(ac) l(ege) esto. ‖

LXXXII. Qui agri quaeque silvae quaeq(ue) aedificia c(olonis) 30
c(oloniae) G(enetivae) I(uliae) | quibus publice utantur, data ad-
tributa e|runt, ne quis eos agros neve eas silvas ven|dito neve locato
longius quam in quinquen|nium, neve ad decuriones referto neve
decu||rionum consultum facito, quo ei agri eaeve | silvae veneant 35
aliterve locentur. Neve si ve|nierint, itcirco minus c(oloniae)
G(enetivae) Iul(iae) sunto. Quique iis | rebus fruc*t*us erit, quot
se emisse dicat, is in | iuga sing(ula) inque annos sing(ulos) HS C
c(olonis) c(oloniae) G(enetivae) Iul(iae) d(are) d(amnas) || *esto,* 40
eiusque pecuniae qui volet petitio persecutioq(ue) ex h(ac) l(ege) esto.

(Deest tabulae pars dimidia)

XCI. Si quis ex hac lege decurio augur pontifex coloniae G(enetivae)
Iul(iae) factus creatusve | erit, tum quicumque decurio augur pon-   Tab. III,
tifex huiusque | col(oniae) domicilium in ea col(onia) oppido pro-   col. I
piusve it oppidum p(assus) ∞ | non habebit annis v proxumis, unde
pignus eius quot satis | sit capi possit, is in ea col(onia) augur ponti-
f(ex) decurio ne es||to qui*q*ue IIviri in ea col(onia) erunt, eius nomen 5
de decurio|nibus sacerdotibusque de tabulis publicis eximendum |
curanto, u(ti) q(uod) r(ecte) f(actum) e(sse) v(olent), idq(ue) eos
IIvir(os) s(ine) f(raude) s(ua) f(acere) l(iceto). |

XCII. IIviri quicumque in ea colon(ia) mag(istratum) habebunt,
ei de legatio|nibus publice mittendis ad decuriones referunto, cum ||
m(aior) p(ars) decurion(um) eius colon(iae) aderit, quotque de his 10
rebus | maior pars eorum qui tum aderunt constituerit, | it ius
ratumque esto. Quamque legationem ex h(ac) l(ege) exve | d(e-
curionum) d(ecreto), quot ex h(ac) l(ege) factum erit, obire opor-
tuerit | neque obierit qui lectus erit, is pro se vicarium ex eo ||
ordine, uti hac lege de(curionum)ve *decreto* d(ari) o(portet), dato. 15
Ni ita dederit, in | res sing(ulas) quotiens ita non fecerit, HS CCIƆ
colon(is) hu|iusque colon(iae) d(are) d(amnas) e(sto), eiusque pe-
cuniae *q*ui volet petitio | persecutioque esto. |

XCIII. Quicumque IIvir post colon(iam) deductam factus
creatusve || erit quive praef(ectus) ab IIvir(o) e lege huius coloniae 20
relic|tus erit, is de loco publico neve pro loco publico neve | ab
redempto*r*e mancipe praed(e)ve donum munus mercedem | aliutve
quid kapito neve accipito neve facito, quo | quid ex ea re at se

[305]

25 suorumve quem perveniat. Qui at‖versus ea fecerit, is нs ccɔɔ ccɔɔ c(olonis) c(oloniae) G(enetivae) Iul(iae) d(are) d(amnas) e(sto), eius|que pecuniae *q*ui vo*l*et petitio persecutioque esto. |

XCIIII. Ne quis in hac colon(ia) ius dicito neve cuius in ea colon(ia) | iuris dictio esto nisi ɪɪvir(i) aut quem ɪɪvi*r* praef(ectum) | reliquerit, aut aedil(is), uti h(ac) l(ege) o(portebit). Neve quis pro
30 eo ‖ imper(io) potestat(e)ve facito, quo quis in ea colonia | ius dicat, nisi quem ex h(ac) l(ege) dicere oporte*bit*. |

XCV. Qui reciperatores dati erunt, si eo die quo iussi erunt | non iudicabunt, ɪɪvir praef(ectus)ve ubi e(a) r(es) a(gitur) eos rec(i-
col. ɪɪ peratores) | eumque cuius res a(gitur) adesse iubeto diemque cer|tum dicito, quo die atsint, usque ateo, dum e(a) r(es) | iudicata erit, facitoque, uti e(a) r(es) in diebus xx | proxumis, quibus d(e) e(a) r(e) rec(iperatores) dati iussive e|runt iudicare, iudic(etur), u(ti) q(uod)
5 r(ecte) f(actum) e(sse) v(olet). Testibusque ‖ in eam rem publice dum ta*x*at h(ominibus) xx, qui colon(i) | incolaeve erunt, quibus *i*s qui rem quaere|*t* volet, denuntietur facito. Quibusq(ue) ita tes|ti- monium *d*enuntiatum erit quique in tes|timonio dicendo nominati
10 erunt, curato, ‖ uti at it iudicium atsint. Testimoniumq(ue) | si quis quit earum rer(um), quae res tum age|tur, sciet aut audierit, iuratus dicat faci|to, uti q(uod) r(ecte) f(actum) e(sse) v(olet), dum ne omnino amplius | h(omines) xx in iudicia singula testimonium
15 dice‖re cogantur. Neve quem invitum testimo|nium dicere cogito, *q*ui ei, *cuia* r(es) tum age|tur, gener socer, vitricus privignus, pa- tron(us) | lib(ertus), consobrinus sit propiusve eum ea cogna|tione
20 atfinitat*e*ve contingat. Si ɪɪvir ‖ praef(ectus)ve qui ea re colon(is) petet, non ade|rit ob eam rem, quot ei morbus sonticus, | vadimonium, iudicium, sacrificium, funus | familiare feriaeve de*n*icales erunt,
25 quo | minus adesse possit sive is propter magistra‖tus potestatemve p(opuli) R(omani) minus atesse poterit: | quo magis eo absente de eo cui *i*s negotium | facesset recip(eratores) sortiantur reiciantur res iu|dicetur, ex h(ac) l(ege) n(ihilum) r(ogatur). Si privatus petet
30 et is, cum | de ea re iudicium fieri oportebit, non aderit ‖ neque arbitratu ɪɪvir(i) praef(ecti)ve ubi e(a) r(es) a(getur) excu|sabitur e*i* harum quam causam esse, quo minus | atesse possit, morbum sonti- cum, vadimonium, | iudicium, sacrificium, funus familiare, ferias |
35 de*n*icales eumve propter mag(istratus) potestatemve ‖ p(opuli)

[306]

R(omani) atesse non posse: post ei earum *rerum*, quarum | h(ac) l(ege) quaestio erit, actio ne esto. Deq(ue) e(a) r(e) siremps | lex col. III resque esto, qu*asi* si neque iudices *d*electi neq(ue) recip(eratores) | in eam rem dati essent. |

XCVI. Si quis decurio eius colon(iae) ab IIvir(o) praef(ecto)ve postulabit | u*ti* ad decuriones referatur, de pecunia publica de‖que 5 multis poenisque deque locis agris aedificis | publicis quo facto qu*a*eri iudicarive oporteat: tum | IIvir qu*i*ve iure dicundo praerit d(e) e(a) r(e) primo | quoque die decuriones consulito decurionum|que consultum facito fiat, cum non minus m(aior) p(ars) ‖ decurionum 10 atsit, cum ea re*s* consuletur. Vti m(aior) p(ars) | decurionum, qui tum aderint, censuer(int), ita ius | ratumque esto. |

XCVII. Ne quis IIvir neve quis pro potestate in ea colon(ia) | facito neve ad decuriones referto neve d(ecurionum) d(ecretum) facito ‖ fiat, quo quis colon(is) colon(iae) patron(us) sit atoptetur|ve 15 praeter eum, *cu*i c(olonis) a(grorum) d(andorum) a(tsignandorum) i(us) ex lege Iulia est, eum|que, qui eam colon(iam) deduxerit, liberos posteros*q*ue | eorum, nisi de m(aioris) p(artis) decurion(um) *qui tum ad*erunt per tabellam | sentent*i*a, cum non minus L aderunt, cum e(a) r(es) ‖ consuletur. Qui atversus ea feceri*t*, HS IↃↃ colon(is) | 20 eius colon(iae) d(are) d(amnas) esto, eiusque pecuniae colon(is) eius | colon(iae) *q*ui volet petitio esto. |

XCVIII. Quamcumque munitionem decuriones huius|ce coloniae decreverint, si m(aior) p(ars) decurionum ‖ atfuerit, cum e(a) 25 r(es) consuletur, eam munitionem | fieri liceto, dum ne amplius in annos sing(ulos) in|que homines singulos puberes operas quinas et | in ⟨iumenta plaustraria⟩ iuga sing(ula) operas ter|nas decernant. Eique munitioni aed(iles) qui tum ‖ erunt ex d(ecurionum) d(ecreto) 30 praesunto. Vti decuriones censu|erint, ita muniendum curanto, dum ne in|vito eius opera exigatur, qui minor annor(um) XIIII | aut maior annor(um) LX natus erit. Qui in ea colon(ia) | intrave eius colon(iae) finis domicilium praedi‖umve habebit neque eius colon(iae) 35 colon(us) erit, is ei|dem munitioni uti colon(us) par*e*to. |

XCVIIII. Quae aquae publicae in oppido colon(iae) Gen(etivae) | adducentur, IIvir, qui tum erunt, ad decuriones, | cum col. IV duae partes aderunt, referto, per quos agros | aquam ducere liceat. Qua p*a*rs maior decurion(um), | qui tum aderunt, duci decreverint,

5 dum ne || per it aedificium, quot non eius rei causa factum | sit,
aqua ducatur, per eos agros aquam ducere | i(us) p(otestas)que esto,
neve quis facito, quo minus ita | aqua ducatur. |

10 C. Si quis colon(us) aquam in privatum caducam ducere || volet
isque at IIvir(um) adierit postulabit|*que*, uti ad decurion(es) referat,
tum is IIvir, a quo | ita postulatum erit, ad decuriones, cum non
mi|nus XXXX aderunt, referto. Si decuriones m(aior) p(ars) qui |
15 tum atfuerint, aquam caducam in privatum duci || censuerint, ita
ea aqua utatur, quot sine priva|*ti* iniuria fiat, i(us) potest(as)que e(sto). |

CI. Quicumque comitia magistrat*ibus* creandis subrogan|dis
habebit, is ne qu*em* eis comitis pro tribu acci|pito neve renuntiato
20 neve renuntiari iubeto, || qui *in* e*a*rum qu*a* causa erit, *e* qua *e*um
h(ac) l(ege) in colon(ia) | decurionem nominari creari inve decu-
rionibus | esse non oporteat non liceat. |

CII. IIvir qui h(ac) l(ege) quaeret iud(icium)*ve* exercebit, quod
iudicium | uti uno die fiat h(ac) l(ege) presti*tu*tum non est, ne quis ||
25 eorum ante h(oram) *I* neve post horam XI diei quaerito | neve
iudicium exerceto. Isque IIvir in singul(os) | accusatores, qui eorum
delator erit, ei h(oras) IIII, qui | subscriptor erit, h(oras) II accusandi
potest(atem) facito. Si | quis accusator de suo tempore alteri con-
30 cesserit, || quot eius cuique concessum erit, eo amplius cui | con-
cessum erit dicendi potest(atem) facito. Qui de suo | tempore alteri
concesserit, quot eius cuique conces|serit, eo minus ei dicendi
potest(atem) facito. Quot horas | omnino omnib(us) accusatorib(us)
35 in sing(ulas) actiones di||cendi potest(atem) fieri oporteb(it), totidem
horas et alter|um tantum reo quive pro eo dicet in sing(ulas)
col. v actiones **|** dicendi potest(atem) facito. |

CIII. Quicumque in col(onia) Genet(iva) IIvir praef(ectus)ve
i(ure) d(icundo) praerit, eum colon(os) | incolasque contributos*que*
quocumque tempore colon(iae) fin(ium) | *defen*dendorum causa
5 armatos educere decurion(es) censuerint, || quot m(aior) p(ars) qui
tum aderunt decreverint, id e(i) s(ine) f(raude) s(ua) f(acere) l(iceto).
Ei|que IIvir(o) aut quem IIvir armatis praefecerit idem | ius eadem-
que anim*a*dversio esto, uti tr(ibuno) mil(itum) p(opuli) R(omani)
in | exercitu p(opuli) R(omani) est, itque e(i) s(ine) f(raude) s(ua)
f(acere) l(iceto) i(us) p(otestas)que e(sto), dum it, quot | m(aior)
p(ars) decurionum decreverit, qui tum aderunt, fiat. ||

[308]

CIIII. Qui limites decumaniqu*e* intra fines c(oloniae) G(ene- 10
tivae) deducti facti|que erunt, quaecum(que) fossae limitales in eo
agro erunt, | qui iussu C. Caesaris dict(atoris) imp(eratoris) et lege
Antonia senat(us)que | c(onsultis) pl(ebi)que sc(itis) ager datus at-
signatus erit, ne quis limites | decumanosque opsaeptos neve quit
immolitum neve ‖ quit ibi opsaeptum habeto, neve eos arato, neve 15
eis fossas | opturato neve opsaepito, quo minus suo itinere aqua | ire
fluere possit. Si quis atversus ea quit fecerit, is in | res sing(ulas),
quotienscumq(ue) fecerit, HS ∞ c(olonis) c(oloniae) G(enetivae)
I(uliae) d(are) d(amnas) esto, | eiusq(ue) pecun(iae) *q*ui volet
petitio p(ersecutio)q(ue) esto. ‖

CV. Si quis quem decurion(um) indignum loci aut ordinis 20
de|curionatus esse dicet, praeterquam quot libertinus | erit, et ab
IIvir(o) postulabitur, uti de ea re iudici|um reddatur, IIvir, quo de
ea re in ius aditum erit, | ius dicito iudiciaque reddito. Isque
decurio, ‖ qui iudicio condemnatus erit, postea decurio | ne esto 25
neve in decurionibus sententiam dici|to neve IIvir(atum) neve aedili-
tatem petito neve | quis IIvir comitis suffragio eius rationem |
habeto neve IIvir(um) neve aedilem renunti‖ato neve renuntiari 30
sinito.

CVI. Quicumque c(olonus) c(oloniae) G(enetivae) erit, quae
iussu C. Caesaris dict(atoris) ded(ucta) | est, ne que*m* in ea col(onia)
coetum conventum coniu*rationem*. . .

(Deest tabula continens capita leg. CVI fin.
CVII–CXXII. CXXIII princ.)

*CXXIII. II*vir *ad* quem *d(e)* e(a) *r(e)* in ius aditum erit, ubi
iudicibus, apud quos *e(a)* r(es) agetur, maiori parti eorum planum
factum non erit, eum de quo iudicium datum est decurionis loco indignum
esse, eum* | qui accusabitur ab his iudicibus eo iudicio absolvi | iubeto. Tab. IV,
Qui ita absolutus erit, quod iudicium *pr*aevari|cation(is) causa col.
*f*actum non sit, is eo iudicio h(ac) l(ege) absolutus esto. |

CXXIIII. Si quis decurio c(oloniae) G(enetivae) decurionem
c(oloniae) G(enetivae) h(ac) l(ege) de indignitate ac‖cusabit, eum*que* 5
quem accusabit eo iudicio h(ac) l(ege) condemna|rit, is ⟨qui quem
eo iudicio ex h(ac) l(ege) condemnarit,⟩ si volet, | in eius locum
qui condemnatus erit sententiam dice|re, ex h(ac) l(ege) liceto itque

[309]

eum (sine) f(raude) s(ua) iure lege recteq(ue) fa|cere liceto, eiusque
10 is locus in decurionibus sen‖tentiae dicendae rogandae h(ac) l(ege)
esto. |

CXXV. Quicumque locus ludis decurionibus datus *at*signatus |
relictusve erit, ex quo loco decuriones ludos spectare | o(portebit),
ne quis in eo loco nisi qui tum decurio c(oloniae) G(enetivae) erit,
qui|ve tum magis*tr*atus imperium potestatemve colonor*(um)* ‖
15 suffragio ⟨geret⟩ iussuque C. Caesaris dict(atoris) co(n)s(ulis) prove |
co(n)s(ule) habebit, quive pro quo imperio potestateve tum | in
c(olonia) Gen(etiva) erit, quibusque loc*o*s in decurionum loco | ex
d(ecreto) d(ecurionum) col(oniae) Gen(etivae) d(ari) o(portebit),
quod decuriones de*c*r(everint), cum non minus | dimidia pars de-
20 curionum adfuerit cum e(a) r(es) consulta erit, ‖ ⟨ne quis praeter
eos, qui (supra) s(cripti) s(unt), qui locus decurionibus da|tus at-
signatus relictusve erit, in eo loco⟩ sedeto neve | quis alium in ea
loca sessum ducito neve sessum *d*uci | iubeto s*c*(iens) d(olo) m(alo).
Si quis adversu*s* ea sederit s(ciens) d(olo) m(alo) *sive* | quis atversus
25 ea sessum duxerit ducive iusserit s(ciens) d(olo) m(alo), ‖ is in res
sing(ulas), quotienscumque quit d(e) e(a) r(e) atv*er*sus ea | fecerit,
HS I⊃⊃ c(olonis) c(oloniae) G(enetivae) I(uliae) d(are) d(amnas)
esto, eiusque pecunia*e* *qu*i eorum | volet rec(iperatorio) iudicio aput
IIvir(um) praef(ectum)ve actio petitio perse|cutio ex h*(ac)* l*(ege)*
⟨i(us)⟩ potest(as)que⟩ e(sto). |

CXXVI. IIvir, aed(ilis), praef(ectus) quicumque c(oloniae)
30 G(enetivae) I(uliae) ludos scaenicos faciet, si‖ve quis alius c(oloniae)
G(enetivae) I(uliae) ludos scaenicos faciet, colonos Geneti|vos
incolasque hospites*que* atventoresque ita sessum du|cito, ⟨ita locum
dato distribuito atsignato,⟩ uti d(e) e(a) r(e) ⟨de | eo loco dando
atsignando⟩ decuriones, cum non min(us) | L ⟨decuriones⟩, cum
35 e(a) r(es) c(onsuletur), in decurionibus adfuerint, ‖ decreverint
statuerint s(ine) d(olo) m(alo). Quot ita ab decurionib(us) | ⟨de
loco dando atsignando⟩ statu*tum* decretum erit, | it h(ac) l(ege) i(us)
r(atum)q(ue) esto. Neve is qui ludos faciet aliter aliove | modo
sessum ducito neve duci iubeto neve locum dato | ne*ve* dari iubeto
40 neve locum attribuito neve attribui ‖ iubeto neve locum atsignato
neve atsignari iubeto ne|ve quit facito, qu*o* aliter aliove modo, adque
uti | locus datus atsignatus attributusve erit, sedeant, ne|ve facito,

[310]

quo quis alieno loco sedeat, sc(iens) d(olo) m(alo). Qui atver|sus
ea fecerit, is in res singulas, quotien*s*cumque quit ‖ atversus ea 45
fecerit, HS IƆƆ c(olonis) c(oloniae) G(enetivae) I(uliae) d(are)
d(amnas) e(sto), eiu*sque* pecuni|ae cui volet rec(iperatorio) iudicio
a*p*ut IIvir(um) pr*a*ef(ectum)ve actio pe|titio persecutioque h(ac)
l(ege) ⟨ius potestasque⟩ esto. |
   CXXVII. Quicumque ludi scaenici c(oloniae) G(enetivae)
I(uliae) fient, ne quis in or|chestram ludorum spectandor(um) causa col. II
praeter ma(gistratum) | prove mag(istratu) p(opuli) R(omani), quive
i(ure) d(icundo) p(raerit) *et* si quis senator p(opuli) R(omani) est
erit | fuerit, et si quis senatoris f(ilius) p(opuli) R(omani) est erit
fuerit, et si | quis praef(ectus) fabrum eius mag(istratus) prove
magistrat*u*, ‖ qui provinc(iarum) Hispaniar(um) ulteriorem ⟨Bae- 5
ticae pra|erit⟩ optinebit, er*i*t, et quos ex h(ac) l(ege) decurion(um)
loco | ⟨decurionem⟩ sedere oportet oportebit, ⟨praeter eos | qui supra
s(cripti) s(unt) ne quis in orchestram ludorum spectan|dorum causa⟩
sedeto, ⟨neve quisque mag(istratus) prove mag(istratu) ‖ p(opuli) 10
R(omani) q(ui) i(ure) d(icundo) p(raerit) ducito⟩, neve quem quis
sessum ducito, | neve in eo loco sedere sinito, uti q(uod) r(ecte)
f(actum) e(sse) *v*(olet) s(ine) d(olo) m(alo). |
   CXXVIII. II(vir) aed(ilis) pr*a*ef(ectus) c(oloniae) G(enetivae)
I(uliae) quicumque erit, is suo quoque anno mag(istratu) | im-
perioq(ue) facito curato, quod eius fieri poterit, | u(ti) q(uod) r(ecte)
f(actum) *e*(sse) v(olet) s(ine) d(olo) m(alo) mag(istri) ad fana templa
delubra, que*m* ‖ ad modum decuriones censuerin(*t*) ⟨suo qu*o*|que 15
anno⟩ fiant e*i*qu(*e*) ⟨d(ecurionum) d(ecreto)⟩ suo quoque anno |
ludos circenses, sacr*i*ficia pulvinariaque | facienda curent, que*m*
*a*d modum ⟨quitquit⟩ de iis | rebus, mag(istris) creandis, *lu*(dis)
circensibus facien‖dis, sacrificiis procu*r*andis, pulvinaribus fa|ciendis 20
decuriones statuerint decreverint, | ⟨ea omnia ita fiant⟩. Deque
iis omnibus rebus | quae s(upra) s(criptae) s(unt) quotcumque de-
curiones statuerint | decreverint, it ius ratumque esto, eiq(ue)
omnes, ‖ at quos ea res pertinebit, quot quemque eorum | ex h(ac) 25
l(ege) facere oportebit, faciunto s(ine) d(olo) m(alo). Si quis | at-
versus ea fecerit quotiens*cum*que quit atver|sus ea fecerit, HS CCIƆƆ
c(olonis) c(oloniae) G(enetivae) I(uliae) d(are) d(amnas) e(sto), eius-
que pecun(iae) | *q*ui eorum volet rec(iperatorio) iudic(io) aput

[311]

MUNICIPAL DOCUMENTS IN GREEK AND LATIN

30 IIvir(um) || praef(ectum)*ve* actio petitio persecutioq(ue) e(x) h(ac)
l(ege) | ⟨ius pot(estas)⟩ esto. |

CXXIX. IIvir(i) aediles praef(ectus) c(oloniae) G(enetivae)
I(uliae) quicumq(*u*)e erunt decurionesq(ue) c(oloniae) G(enetivae)
I(uliae) qui|cumq*ue* erunt, ii omnes d(ecurionum) d(ecretis) dili-
genter parento optemperanto s(ine) d(olo) m(alo) fa|ciuntoque uti
quot *que*mq(ue) eor(um) decurionum d(ecreto) agere facere o(porte-
35 bit) ea om||nia agant faciant, u(ti) q(uod) r(ecte) f(actum) e(sse)
v(olent) s(ine) d(olo) m(alo). Si quis ita non fecerit sive quit at-
ver|sus ea fecerit sc(iens) d(olo) m(alo), is in res sing(ulas) HS CCIƆ
c(*olonis*) c(oloniae) G(enetivae) I(uliae) d(are) d(amnas) e(sto),
eiusque pecuniae *q*ui | *e*or(um) volet rec(iperatorio) iudic(io) aput
IIvir(um) praef(ectum)ve actio petitio persecutioque ex h(ac) l(ege) |
⟨ius potestasque⟩ e(sto). |

CXXX. Ne quis IIvir aed(ilis) praef(ectus) c(oloniae) G(enetivae) I(uliae) quicunque erit ad decurion(es) c(oloniae) G(ene-
40 tivae) referto neve decurion(es) || consulito neve d(ecretum)
d(ecurionum) facito neve d(e) e(a) r(e) in tabulas p(ublicas) referto
neve referri iubeto | neve quis decur(io) d(e) e(a) r(e), q(ua) d(e)
r(e) a(getur), in decurionib(us) sententiam dicito neve d(ecretum)
d(ecurionum) scri|bito, neve in tabulas pu*b*licas referto, neve refe-
rundum curato, quo quis | senator senatorisve f(ilius) p(opuli)
R(omani) c(oloniae) G(enetivae) patronus atoptetur sumatur fiat
nisi de tri|um partium d(ecurionum) ⟨d(ecreto)⟩ senten*t(ia)* per
45 tabellam ⟨facito⟩ et nisi de eo homine, ⟨de quo || tum referetur con-
suletu*r*, *d(ecretum)* d(ecurionum) fiat⟩, qui, cum | e(a) r(es) a(getur),
in Italiam sine impe*r*io privatus | erit. Si quis adversus ea ad *decu*-
rion(es) rettulerit d(ecurionum)ve d(ecretum) fecerit faciendum*ve* |
curaverit inve tabulas pu*blicas* rettulerit referrive iusserit sive quis
in decurionib(us) | sententiam di*x*erit d(ecurionum)ve *d(ecretum)*
50 *scrips*erit in*ve* tabulas publicas rettulerit referendumve || curaverit,
in res sing(ulas), quo*tienscu*mque quit atversus ea fecerit, *is* HS CCCIƆƆ
c(*olonis*) c(oloniae) G(enetivae) I(uliae) | d(are) d(amnas) e(sto),
eiusque pecuniae *q*ui *eorum vole*t rec(iperatorio) iudi(cio) aput
IIvir(um) interregem praef(ectum) actio | petitio persecutioqu*e ex*
h(*ac*) l(*ege*) ⟨*i(us)* pot*est(as)*que⟩ e(sto). |

CXXXI. N*e* quis IIvir ⟨aed(ilis)⟩ praef(ectus) c(*oloniae*) G(*ene*-

[312]

tivae) I(*uliae*) *quicu*mque erit ad decuriones c(oloniae) G(enetivae) referto neve d(ecuriones) con|sulito neve d(ecretum) d(ecurionum) facito neve d(e) e(a) r(e) in tabulas publicas referto neve referri iubeto | neve quis decurio d(e) e(a) r(e) in decurionib(us) sententiam dicito neve d(ecretum) d(ecurionum) scribito ne|ve in tabulas publicas referto neve referundum curato, quo quis senator | senatorisve f(ilius) p(opuli) R(omani) c(oloniae) G(enetivae) I(uliae) hospes atoptetur, hospitium tesser*ave* hospi*talis* cum ‖ quo fi*at*, *n*isi 5 de maio*ris* p(artis) decurionum sententia per tabellam ⟨facito⟩ et nisi | de eo *h*omine, ⟨de quo tum referetur consuletur, d(ecretum) d(ecurionum) fiat⟩, qui, cum e(a) r(es) a(getur), in Italiam | sine imperio privatus erit. Si quis adversus ea ad decuriones rettulerit d(ecretum)ve | d(ecurionum) fe*c*erit faciendumve curaverit inve tabulas publicas rettulerit re|fer*ri*ve iusserit sive quis in decurionibus sententiam dixerit d(ecretum)ve d(ecurionum) ‖ scripserit in*v*e 10 tabul(as) public(as) rettulerit referendumve curaverit, | *i*s in res sing(ulas) quotienscumque quit adversus ea fecerit, HS CCIↃↃ c(olonis) c(oloniae) | G(enetivae) Iuliae d(are) d(amnas) e(sto), eiusque pecuniae *q*ui eorum volet recu(peratorio) iudic(io) | aput IIvir(um) pr*ae*f(ectum)ve actio petitio persecutioque h(ac) l(ege) ⟨ius potest(as)-que⟩ esto. |

CXXXII. Ne quis in c(olonia) G(enetiva) post h(anc) l(egem) datam petitor kandidatus, ‖ quicumque in c(olonia) G(enetiva) 15 I(ulia) mag(istratum) petet, *m*agistratus*ve* peten|di causa in eo anno, quo quisque anno petitor | kandidatus mag(istratum) petet petiturusve erit, ⟨mag(istratus) pe|tendi⟩ convivia facito neve at cenam que*m* | vocato neve convivium habeto neve facito s(ciens) d(*olo*) m(alo), ‖ quo qui*s* suae petitionis causa convi*vi*um habeat | 20 ad cenamve que*m* vocet, praeter ⟨dum⟩ quod ip|se kandidatus petitor in eo anno, *quo* mag(istratum) petat, | vocar*it* dum taxat *in* dies sing(ulos) h(ominum) VIIII ⟨convi*vi*um | habeto⟩, si volet, s(ine) d(olo) m(alo). Neve quis petitor kandidatus ‖ donum munus 25 aliudve quit det largiatur peti|tionis causa sc(iens) d(olo) m(alo). Neve quis alterius petitionis | causa convivia facito neve quem ad cenam voca|to neve convivium habeto, neve quis alterius pe|titionis causa cui quit d*on*um munus aliutve qu*it* ‖ dato donato largito 30 sc(iens) d(olo) m(alo). Si quis atversus ea | fecerit, HS IↃↃ c(olonis)

MUNICIPAL DOCUMENTS IN GREEK AND LATIN

c(oloniae) G(enetivae) I(uliae) d(are) d(amnas) e(sto), eiusque pe-
cuniae *qui* eor(um) volet | rec(iperatorio) iudic(io) aput IIvir(um)
praef(ectum)*ve* actio petitio per|sec(utio)que ex h(ac) l(ege) ⟨i(us)
potest(as)que⟩ esto. |

CXXXIII. Qui col(oni) Gen(etivi) Iul(ienses) h(ac) l(ege) sunt
35 erunt, eorum omnium uxo‖res, quae in c(olonia) G(enetiva) I(ulia)
h(ac) l(ege) sunt, ⟨eae mulieres⟩ legibus c(oloniae) G(enetivae)
I(uliae) vi|rique parento iuraque ⟨ex h(ac) l(ege)⟩, quaecumque |
in hac lege scripta sunt, omnium rerum ex h(ac) l(ege) hab*en*|to
s(ine) d(olo) m(alo). |

CXXXIV. Ne quis IIvir ⟨aedil(is)⟩ praefectus c(oloniae) G(ene-
40 tivae), quicumque erit, post ‖ h(anc) l(egem) ad decuriones c(oloniae)
G(enetivae) referto neve decuriones consu|lito neve d(ecretum)
d(ecurionum) facito n*e*ve d(e) e(a) r(e) in tabulas publicas re|ferto
neve referri iubeto neve quis decurio, cum e(a) | r(es) a(getur), in
decurionibus sententiam dicito neve d(ecretum) d(ecurionum) |
45 scribito neve in tabulas publicas referto nev*e* ‖ *re*ferendum curato,
quo cui pecunia publica a*liutve* | quid honoris habendi causa mune-
risve *dandi pol*|licendi *prove* statua danda ponenda detur do*netur*. . . .

Four bronze tablets found in 1870 and 1874 on the site of Urso
in Baetica, now in the museum at Madrid. Each tablet had originally five columns of text, as the third tablet, preserved in its
entirety, shows. From each of the other three extant tablets two
columns are missing. The tablets containing the early part of the
law, perhaps four in number, and the eighth tablet, have not been
found. Numbers added at a later date on the margins of the tablets
indicate the division into chapters. Probably these tablets were
not engraved until after Caesar's death, *cf.* Mommsen, *Ges. Schr.*
1, 208 *ff.*; Hübner, *Ex. scr. ep.* 805. Dessau places the date of
the engraving in the reign of Domitian. The letters on the fourth
tablet are smaller than those on the others and in it there are many
redundant words and phrases which we have enclosed in obtuse-
angled brackets. Some scholars think that this tablet takes the
place of one that had been lost. Gradenwitz (*Sitz. Ber. d. Heidelberger Akad.* 1920, Heft 17) explains the unevenness in form and
manner found in this law as well as in the charters of Malaca and
Salpensa on the theory that we have an *Urtext* and a *Beischrift*.

For a summary of the chapters, *cf.* Mommsen, *op. cit.* 1, 211 *ff.*, 247 *ff.* For a translation into English, *cf.* Hardy, *Three Spanish Charters*, 23 *ff.*

The law in its original form must have been drafted by Julius Caesar. In chap. 125 reference is made to any local magistrate holding office *iussu C. Caesaris dictatoris consulis prove consule* (*cf.* chap. 66), and similarly in chap. 106 we read *quae* (*i.e. colonia*) *iussu C. Caesaris dictatoris deducta est.* Caesar is nowhere called *divus*, so that the measure antedates the autumn of 43 B.C. (*cf.* Mommsen, *St. R.* 2, 756, n. 1). It probably belongs to the early part of the year 44 B.C. (*cf.* Mommsen, *Ges. Schr.* 1, 207), and may have been one of the bills which Antony found, or maintained that he found, among the papers of Caesar (*cf.* Cic. *Phil.* 5. 4. 10). The founding of the colony was authorized *iussu C. Caesaris dictatoris imperatoris et lege Antonia senatusque consultis plebique scitis* (chap. 104). This measure is then a *lex data* authorized by a *S.C.* and plebiscite, proposed by Antony.

The greater part of the document deals with strictly domestic matters, but certain chapters have to do with the relations which the municipality bore to the central government, or to Roman citizens, and only with those are we concerned here. The *legationes* referred to in chap. 92 would include embassies sent to Rome, to the provincial governor, or to the provincial council (*cf.* p. 150, n. 7 and no. 126). They sometimes played an important part in calling the grievances of a city or a province to the attention of the central government, but such missions were often useless and were expensive, and ultimately Vespasian limited the number of members to three (*Dig.* 50. 7. 5). In Urso, since the acceptance of an appointment was compulsory, probably *legati* met their own expenses.

For the part which *patroni* took in composing local difficulties and in representing a municipality in Rome, *cf.* Mommsen, *St. R.* 3, 1202 *ff.* and the documents in this book dealing with public arbitration. Chapp. 97 and 130 prescribe rules for the election of *patroni* at Urso. The man who led the colonists out and the man who assigned land to them, together with their descendants, are made patrons *ex officio.* Other patrons must be chosen in the senate when at least fifty members are present (*cf.* chap. 97). Mommsen believed (*Ges. Schr.* 1, 344 *ff.*) that the approval of the local popular assembly was also necessary for the choice of a patron, but *cf.* Hardy, *op. cit.* 108, n. 29. Chap. 130 requires the approval of seventy-five of the one hundred decurions, voting with secret ballots, for the election of a Roman senator or his son (*cf.* no. 64), and absolutely prohibits the election of such a person unless he is a private citizen in Italy *sine imperio.* All the governors of the provinces were at this time senators, and Rome wished to prevent municipalities from currying favour with the governor of their province by electing him to a position of honor. The same objection would attach in a less degree to the election of any senator, because he might at any time be put in charge of a province. The Album of Canusium of A.D. 223 (no. 136) has a list of thirty-nine *patroni,* of whom thirty-one are Roman senators and eight are knights. Mommsen finds (*Ges. Schr.* 1, 239) only three cases of patrons who were senators with the *imperium.* Perhaps they were elected after the termination of their *imperium* (*cf.* Marquardt, *St. Verw.* 1, 189, n. 1).

Patronatus and *hospitium* are often confused in the inscriptions (*cf.* Wilmanns, nos. 2850, 2852), but for the distinction between them, *cf.* Leonhard, *R.E.* 8, 2496. The fact that a senate could elect an *hospes* when only a majority of the decurions was present (chap. 131) shows that the position was held in less esteem than that of *patronus.* The same discrimination is made against Roman senators and their sons in this case as holds in the case of the patron.

Of the privileges granted to Roman officials and Roman senators the most noteworthy is the assignment to them of seats in the orchestra of the theatre (chap. 127).

The provision in chap. 103 which authorized the duovir, on receiving the approval of a majority of the decurions present at a meeting, "to call to arms colonists, resident aliens, and attributed persons" for the defense of the colony is surprising and without parallel in other charters, unless we accept Bormann's bold conjecture (*Jahreshefte d. öst. archäol. Inst.* 9 (1906), 315 *ff.*) for the *Fragm. legis Lauriscensis* (Bruns, 33*a*) and read *uter* (*i.e. ex* IIviris) *postea municipes incolasque....causa armatos educet.* There is no intimation even that the municipal senate required the authorization of the provincial governor in taking this step. Very likely this was a sovereign power granted to municipalities on the frontier or in unruly districts. Reference is made to the members of these armed forces in various inscriptions (*cf. hastiferi civitatis Mattiacorum, CIL.* XIII, 7317). They could be quickly summoned to repress an uprising and to hold an attacking enemy in check until the legions could arrive (*cf.* Cagnat, *De municipalibus et provincialibus militiis in imperio Romano,* 93), and perhaps the provincial militia (Hirschfeld, 392 *ff.*) was made up of these municipal levies (*cf.* Mommsen, *Ges. Schr.* 6, 154). It was in harmony with Roman practices in Italy to put this levy in charge of the local magistrate (*cf.* Mommsen, *St. R.* 3, 675, n. 3).

27. LEX DE GALLIA CISALPINA, VULGO LEX RUBRIA
DE GALLIA CISALPINA
(49–42 a. Chr.)

CIL. I, 205 = XI, 1146; Bruns, 16; Girard, p. 72; Riccobono, p. 135.

. . .iussum iudicatumve erit, id ratum ne esto; quodque quis|que Tab. I quomq(ue) d. e. r. decernet inter*d*eicetve seive sponsionem | fieri iudica*re*ive iubebit iudiciumve quod d. e. r. dabit, is | in id decretum interdictum sponsionem iudicium exceptio||nem addito addive 5 iubeto: "Q. d. r. operis novi nuntiationem | IIvir, IIIIvir praefectusve eius municipei non remeisserit." |

XX. Qua de re quisque, et a quo, in Gallia Cisalpeina damnei infectei | ex formula restipularei satisve accipere volet, et ab eo quei | ibei i(ure) d(eicundo) *p(raerit)* postulaverit, idque non k(alumniae) k(aussa) se facere iuraverit: tum is, quo || d. e. r. in ius aditum 10 erit, eum, quei in ius eductus erit, d. e. r. ex formu|la repromittere et, sei satis darei debebit, satis dare iubeto de|cernito. Quei eorum ita non repromeisserit aut non satis dede|rit, sei quid interim damni datum factumve ex ea re aut ob e(am) r(em) eo|ve nomine erit, quam ob rem, utei damnei infectei repromissio || satisve datio fieri 15 *iubeatur*, postulatum erit: tum mag(istratus) prove mag(istratu) IIvir | IIIIvir praefec(tus)ve, quoquomque d. e. r. in ius aditum erit, d. e. r. ita ius | deicito iudicia dato iudicareque iubeto cogito, proinde

atque sei | d. e. r., quom ita postulatum esset, damn*e*i infectei ex
formula | recte repromissum satisve datum esset. D. *e. r.* quod ita
20 iudicium || datum iudicareve iussum iudicatumve erit, ius ratumque
esto, | dum in ea verba, sei damnei infectei repromissum non erit,
iudi|cium det itaque iudicare iubeat: "I(udex) e(sto). S(ei), ante-
quam id iudicium | q. d. r. a(gitur) factum est, Q. Licinius damni
infectei eo nomine q. d. | r. a(gitur) eam stipulationem, quam is
25 quei Romae inter peregrei||nos ius deicet in albo propositam habet,
L. Seio repromeississet: | tum quicquid eum Q. Licinium ex ea
stipulatione L. Seio d(are) f(acere) opor|t*e*ret ex f(ide) b(ona) d(um)-
t(axat) ʜs e(ius) i(udex) Q. Licinium L. Seio, sei ex decreto ɪɪvir(ei) |
ɪɪɪɪvir(ei) praefec(tei)ve Mutinensis, quod eius *is* ɪɪvir ɪɪɪɪvir prae-
fec(tus)|ve ex lege Rubria, seive id pl(ebei)ve sc(itum) est, decre-
30 verit, Q. Licinius eo || nomine qua d. r. a(gitur) L. Seio damnei
infectei repromittere no|luit, c(ondemnato); s(ei) n(on) p(aret),
a(bsolvito)"; aut sei damnei infectei satis datum non erit, | in e*a* verba
iudicium det: "I(udex) e(sto). S(ei), antequam id iudicium q. d. r.
a(gitur) | *f*actum est, Q. Licinius damnei infectei eo nomine q. d. r.
a(gitur) ea | stipulatione, quam is quei Romae inter peregrinos ius
35 deicet || in albo propositam habet, L. Seio satis dedisset: tum q(uic)-
q(uid) eum | Q. Licinium e*x* ea stipulatione L. Seio d(are) f(acere)
oporteret ex f(ide) b(ona) d(um) t(axat), | e(ius) i(udex) Q. Liciniu*m*
L. Seio, sei ex decreto ɪɪvir(ei) ɪɪɪɪvir(ei) praef(ectei)ve Muti|nensis,
quod eius is ɪɪvir ɪɪɪɪvir praefect(us)*ve* ex lege Rubria, sei|ve id
pl(ebei)ve sc(itum) est, decreverit, Q. Licinius eo nomine q. d. r.
40 a(gitur) || L. Seio damnei infectei satis dare noluit, c(ondemnato);
s(ei) n(on) p(aret), a(bsolvito)"; dum ɪɪvir | ɪɪɪɪvir i(ure) d(eicundo)
praefec(tus)ve d. e. r. ius ita deicat curetve, utei ea no|mina et
municipium colonia locus in eo iudicio, quod ex ieis | quae proxsume
s(cripta) s(unt) accipi*e*tur, includ*a*ntur concipiantur, | quae includei
45 concipei s(ine) d(olo) m(alo) oporteret debebitve, ne quid || ei quei
d. e. r. aget petetve captionei ob e(am) r(em) aut eo nomine esse |
possit: neive ea nomina, qua*e* in earum qua formula quae s(upra) |
s(cripta) s(unt), aut Mutina*m* in eo iudicio includei concipei curet,
nise*i*, | iei, quos inter id iudicium accipietur leisve contestabitur, |
ieis nominibus fuerint, quae in earum qua formula s(upra) s(cripta)
50 s(*unt*), || et nisei sei Mutinae ea res agetur; neive quis mag(istratus)

[318]

prove mag(istratu), | neive quis pro quo imperio potestateve erit,
intercedito nei|ve quid aliud facito, quo minus de ea re ita iudicium
detur | iudiceturque. | Tab. II

XXI. A quoquomq(ue) pecunia certa credita, signata forma
p(ublica) p(opulei) R(omanei), in eorum quo o. m. c. p. | f. v. c. c.
t. ve, quae sunt eruntve in Gallia Cisalpeina, petetur, quae res non |
pluris HS XV erit, sei is eam pecuniam in iure apud eum, quei ibei
i(ure) d(eicundo) p(raerit), ei quei ‖ eam petet, aut ei quoius nomine 5
ab eo petetur, d(are) o(portere) debereve se confessus | erit, neque
id quod confessus erit solvet satisve faciet, aut se sponsione | iudicio-
que utei oportebit non defendet, seive is ibei d. e. r. in iure non |
responderit, neque d. e. r. sponsionem faciet neque iudicio utei
oportebit | se defendet: tum de eo, a quo ea pecunia peteita erit,
deque eo, quoi eam ‖ pecuniam d(arei) o(portebit), s(iremps) res 10
lex ius caussaque o(mnibus) o(mnium) r(erum) esto atque utei
esset esseve | oporteret, sei is, quei ita confessus erit, aut d. e. r.
non responderit aut se | sponsione iudicioque utei oportebit non
defenderit, eius pecuniae iei | quei eam suo nomine petierit quoive
eam d(arei) o(portebit), ex iudicieis dateis iudi|careve recte iusseis
iure lege damnatus esset fuisset. Queique quomque ‖ IIvir IIIIvir 15
praefec(tus)ve ibei i(ure) d(eicundo) p(raerit), is eum, quei ita quid
confessus erit | neque id solvet satisve faciet, eumve quei se sponsione
iudiciove utei | oportebit non defenderit aut in iure non responderit
neque id solvet | satisve faciet, t(antae) p(ecuniae), quanta ea pecunia
erit de qua tum inter eos am|bigetur, dum t(axat) HS XV s(ine)
f(raude) s(ua) duci iubeto; queique eorum quem, ad quem ‖ ea res 20
pertinebit, duxserit, id ei fraudi poenaeve ne esto: quodque ita
fac|tum actum iussum erit, id ius ratumque esto. Quo minus in
eum, quei ita | vadimonium Romam ex decreto eius, quei ibei i(ure)
d(eicundo) p(raerit), non promeisserit | aut vindicem locupletem
ita non dederit, ob e(am) r(em) iudicium recup(erationem) is, quei |
ibei i(ure) d(eicundo) p(raerit), ex h. l. det iudicareique d. e. r. ibei
curet, ex h. l. n(ihilum) r(ogatur). ‖

XXII. A quo quid praeter pecuniam certam creditam, signatam 25
forma p(ublica) p(opulei) R(omanei), | in eorum quo o. m. c. p.
f. v. c. c. t. ve quae sunt eruntve in Gallia cis Alpeis, | petetur,
quodve quom eo agetur, quae res non pluris HS XV erit, et sei | ea

res erit, de qua re omnei pecunia ibei ius deicei iudiciave darei ex
h. l. o(portebit), | sei is eam rem, quae ita ab eo petetur deve ea re
30 cum eo agetur, ei quei eam *rem* || petet deve ea re age*t*, aut iei quoius
nomine ab eo petetur quomve eo age|tur in iure apud eum, quei
ibei i(ure) d(eicundo) p(raerit), d(are) *f(acere)* p(raestare) restituereve
oportere aut | se debere, eiusve eam rem esse aut se eam habere,
eamve rem de | qua arguetur se fecisse obligatumve se eius rei
noxsiaeve esse confes|sus erit deixseritve neque d. e. r. satis utei
35 oportebit faciet aut, sei || sponsionem fierei oportebit, sponsionem
non faciet, *aut* non restituet, | neque se iudicio utei oportebit de-
fendet, aut sei d. e. r. in iure | nihil responderit, neque d. e. r. se
iudicio utei oportebit defendet: | tum de eo a quo ea res ita petetur
quomve eo d. e. r. ita agetur, deque | eo, quoi eam rem d(arei)
40 f(ierei) p(raestarei) restitui satisve d. e. r. fierei oportebit, || s(iremps)
l(ex) r(es) i(us) c(aussa)q(ue) o(mnibus) o(mnium) r(erum) e(sto),
atque utei esset esseve oporteret, sei is, quei ita | quid earum rerum
confessus erit aut d. e. r. non responderit neq(ue) | se iudicio utei
oportebit defenderit, de ieis rebus Romae apud pr(aetorem) | eumve
quei de ieis rebus Romae i(ure) d(eicundo) p(rae)esset in iure con-
fessus esset, | aut ibei d. e. r. nihil respondisset aut iudicio se non
45 defendisset; || p(raetor)q(ue) isve quei d(e) e(is) r(ebus) Romae i(ure)
d(eicundo) p(raerit) in eum et in heredem eius d(e) e(is) r(ebus)
om|nibus ita ius deicito decernito eosque duci bona eorum possideri |
proscreibeive ver·eireque iubeto, ac sei is heresve eius d. e. r. in |
iure apud eum pr(aetorem) eumve quei Romae i(ure) d(eicundo)
praesse*t*, confessus es|set aut d. e. r. nihil respondisse*t* neque se
50 iudicio utei oportuis||set defendisset; dum ne quis d. e. r. nisei
pr(aetor) isve quei Romae i(ure) d(eicundo) p(raerit) | eorum quoius
bona possiderei proscreibei veneire duceique | eum iubeat. |

XXIII. Queiquomque in eorum quo o. m. c. p. f. v. c. c. t. ve
quae in Gal|lia Cisalpeina sunt erunt, i(ure) d(eicundo) p(raerit), is
55 inter eos, quei de fami|||lia erceiscunda deividunda iudicium sibei
darei reddeive | in eorum quo o. m. c. p. f. v. c. c. t. ve, quae s(upra)
s(cripta) s(unt), postu|laverint, ita ius deicito decernito iudicia dato
iudicare | iubeto, utei in eo o. m. c. p. f. v. c .c. t. ve, in quo is,
quoius *de boneis agetur, domicilium habuerit* . . . . .

Bronze tablet found in 1760 in the ruins of Veleia, now in

Parma. The number (IIII) at the top of the tablet shows that three tablets which preceded it have been lost. Many scholars think that this law was passed after 42 B.C., when Gallia Cisalpina was incorporated into Italy. This is the view held by Savigny (*Verm. Schr.* 3, 319–326, 377–400), by Huschke (*Gaius, Beiträge,* 203–242), and by Karlowa (1, 440–443). Mommsen on the other hand maintains (*Ges. Schr.* 1, 175–191) that it belongs to the year 49 B.C. The reference to the region concerned in chap. xx as Gallia Cisalpina naturally points to a date earlier than 42 B.C. Mommsen holds also that the *fragmentum Atestinum* (no. 28) is a part of this law. Now in the second paragraph of this fragment a *lex rogata* of L. Roscius is cited by day and month, but the year is not mentioned. From this fact he concludes that the *lex de Gall. Cis.* must have been passed later in the same year. The *lex Roscia,* mentioned in the Atestine fragment, belongs, he thinks, to the year 49 B.C., in which year L. Roscius was one of the praetors (Caes. *B.C.* 1. 3). The validity of the principal argument rests, therefore, on the relation which the fragment of Este bears to our law, and on the attribution of the *lex Roscia* to the praetor, Roscius. For the serious difficulty which this explanation involves, *cf.* Pais, *Ricerche sulla storia e sul diritto pubblico di Roma, Serie terza,* 389. The theory of Nap, who ascribes the law to Sulla's dictatorship (*Themis,* 1913, 194 *ff.*), is adequately refuted by Hardy, *Some Problems in Roman History,* 207 *ff.*

For the connection between the Atestine fragment and our law, *cf.* Hardy, *Six Roman Laws,* 110–124, especially 123 *f.* Whether our law is identical with the *lex Rubria,* cited twice in the formulae in chap. xx, is a matter of high dispute. If it is identical with our law, it is a *lex rogata.* Mommsen, however, observes (*loc. cit.*) that the other laws promulgated for a similar purpose were *leges datae,* and that there are no formulae in our law to prove that it is a *lex rogata.* He is therefore inclined to think that it is a *lex data* and consequently distinct from the *lex Rubria.* For the opposite view, *cf.* Kipp, *Gesch. d. Quellen d. röm. Rechts*[3], 42, n. 10; Hardy, *op. cit.* 124.

This inscription is of great importance for two reasons: (1) It gives us the procedure at the beginning of the formulary period (on the *formulae, cf.* Wenger, *R.E.* 6, 2859 *ff.*); (2) It gives us the most precise information which we have of the lines of demarcation

MUNICIPAL DOCUMENTS IN GREEK AND LATIN

between the competence of the central government and of local magistrates in Italian communities, made up of Roman citizens, in judicial matters. We are concerned here with the second point only. The law applied to Gallia Cisalpina the same system long in vogue elsewhere in Italy. It was probably called forth by the grant of Roman citizenship to Gallia Cisalpina.

Following in part the system, as analyzed by Hardy (*op. cit.* 117–119), we find that it seems to cover the following points: (1) The municipal magistrate has full competence in matters involving 15,000 sesterces or less; (2) Even where larger amounts are at stake, he may take initial proceedings; (3) In certain cases he has jurisdiction irrespective of the amount claimed; (4) In the absence of a *cautio damni infecti* (*cf.* Leonhard, *R.E.* 3, 1816) the municipal magistrate may take action similar to that which would have been taken by the *praetor peregrinus* in like circumstances; (5) In certain cases of condemnation for debt, the municipal magistrate may provisionally arrest the debtor and make him *addictus* (*cf.* Leist, *R.E.* 1, 352). For the practice at Venafrum, *cf.* no. 33. The local magistrates mentioned are the *duoviri, quattuorviri*, and *praefecti* (chapp. XIX, XX). The *praefectus* is an official appointed in the absence of the regular magistrate. The duovirs were the usual magistrates in colonies, the quattuorvirs in *municipia* (*cf.* p. 59). For a description of the several communities mentioned in the early part of chap. XXI, *cf.* pp. 10 *ff.* The phrase *neive quis magistratus prove magistratu neive quis pro quo imperio potestateve erit*, etc. (chap. XX, end) seems to refer to the proconsul because Gallia Cisalpina continued to be a province until 42 B.C. Certain phrases indicated by abbreviations in this inscription are *d(e) e(a) r(e), qu(a) d(e) r(e), h(ac) l(ege)* or the grammatical forms needed in the connection, and *o(ppido) m(unicipio) c(olonia) p(raefectura) f(oro) v(eico) c(onciliabulo) c(astello) t(erritorio)* or the appropriate grammatical forms.

28. FRAGMENTUM ATESTINUM
(49–42 a. Chr.)

Notizie degli scavi, 1880, 213; Bruns, 17; Girard, p. 78; Riccobono, p. 140.

Quei post hanc legem rogatam in eorum quo oppido municipio colonia praefectura foro veico conciliabulo castello territoriove, quae in Gallia Cisalpeina sunt eruntve, ad IIvirum IIIIvirum praefectumve in iudi-ciumfiduciae aut pro socio aut mandati aut tutelae suo nomine quodve ipse earum rerum | quid gessisse dicetur, add*u*cetur, aut quod furti, quod ad ho|minem liberum liberamve pertinere deicatur, aut iniuri|-arum agatur: sei is, a quo petetur quomve quo agetur, d(e) ‖ e(a) 5 r(e) in eo municipio colonia praefectura iudicio certa|re *volet* et si ea res HS CCIƆƆ minorisve erit, quo minus ibei d(e) e(a) r(e) | iudex arbiterve addicatur detur, quove minus ibei d(e) e(a) r(e) iudi-cium ita | feiat, utei de ieis rebus, quibus ex h(ac) l(ege) iudicia | data erunt, iudicium fierei exerceri oportebit, ex h. l. n(ihilum) r(ogatur). ‖

Quoius rei in qu*o*que municipio colonia praefectura | quoiusque 10 IIvir(i) eiusve, qui ibei lege foedere pl(ebei)ve sc(ito) s(enatus)|ve c(onsulto) institutove iure dicundo praefuit, ante legem, sei|ve illud pl(ebei) sc(itum) est, quod L. Roscius a. d. v eid. Mart. populum | plebemve rogavit, quod privatim ambigetur, iuris dict*i*||o iudicis 15 arbitri recuperatorum datio addictiove *fuit* | quantaeque rei pequni-aeve fuit: eius rei pequn*iaeve* | quo magis privato Romae revocatio sit qu*o*ve |*mi*nus quei ibei i(ure) d(icundo) p(raerit) d(e) e(a) r(e) ius dicat iudice*m arbitrumve det* | utei ante legem, sive illud pl(ebei) sc(itum) est, *quod L. Roscius a. d.* ‖ v eidus Mart. populum plebe*mve* 20 *rogavit,* | *ab eo quei ibei i(ure) d(icundo) p(raerit) ius d*ici iu*dicem arbitrumve dari oportuit, ex h(ac) l(ege) n(ihilum) r(ogatur).*

Bronze tablet found in 1880 at Ateste in Cisalpine Gaul, now in the museum at Este. Mommsen held that it contained a fragment of the *lex de Gallia Cisalpina* (no. 27); cf. *Ges. Schr.* 1, 175–191. This view has been opposed by Alibrandi, *Opere giuridiche*, 1, 395 *ff.*; Karlowa, 1, 441; Krüger, *Gesch. d. Quellen*, 73; Esmein, *Mélanges d'histoire et du droit*, 269–292; Appleton, *Revue générale du droit*, 24 (1900), 193 *ff.*, and Kipp, *Gesch. d. Quellen*[3], 42, n. 10. The main objection to Mommsen's theory lies in the fact that the *lex de Gall. Cis.* grants municipal magistrates full competence in suits involving not more than 15,000 sesterces, whereas in this fragment, in certain cases, at least, the maximum is set at 10,000. The date is uncertain. Some editors think that it deals with the enfranchise-ment of all communities south of the Po after the Social war, in spite of the fact that the tablet was found in the Transpadane region, and they attribute the *lex Roscia*, mentioned in it, to Roscius, tribune in 67 B.C. Those who regard the fragment as part of the *lex de Gall. Cis.* put it in the year 49 B.C., while still others date it as not earlier than 49 or later than 42 B.C.

The purpose of the law was to make certain changes in competence necessitated by the granting of new rights. In some cases, at least, involving a sum not exceeding 10,000 sesterces, the accused has the option of bringing his case before the municipal magistrate, and *revocatio Romae* is limited, temporarily or permanently, in its application in some circumstances.

The nine classes of communities which are mentioned in no. 27, chap. XXI, and which Mommsen has included among the missing words at the beginning of this fragment, are reduced to three in the second paragraph of the fragment, because a local magistrate had judicial competence in a *municipium*, *colonia*, and *praefectura* only. The powers of a local magistrate may rest on any one of three different bases, according to the second paragraph of the fragment. They may be granted by a treaty (*foedere*), by an enactment of the popular assembly or senate (*lege, plebei scito, senatus consulto*), or traditional usage (*instituto*) may be continued in force without special legal authorization. The phrase *ante legem, seive illud plebei scitum est, quod L. Roscius...rogavit* implies that the Roscian law was a *plebiscitum*, and, consequently makes it difficult to connect this measure with the praetor L. Roscius of 49 B.C., but Mommsen believes that the bill in question was submitted to the plebeian assembly by the praetor (*St. R.* 3, 159, n. 2), and he calls attention to a parallel phrase in the *lex Bantina* (*CIL.* I, 197, ll. 7, 15).

29. EPISTULAE ANTONI ET CAESARIS AD PLARASENSES ET APHRODISIENSES
(39–35 a. Chr.)

CIG. 2737; Viereck, *Sermo Graecus*, 5; Bruns, 43; Ditt. *Or. Gr.* 453–455; Riccobono, p. 217.

[Μᾶρκος Ἀντώνιος Μάρκου υἱὸς αὐτοκράτωρ ὕπατος ἀπο-δεδει]‖γμένος τὸ β΄ καὶ [τὸ γ΄ | τῶν] τριῶν ἀνδρῶν τῆ[ς] | τῶν
5 δημοσίων πρα|γμάτων διατάξεως ‖ Πλαρασέων καὶ Ἀφρο|δει-σιέων ἄρχουσιν | βουλῆι δήμωι χαίρειν. | Εἰ ἔρρωσθε, εὖ ἂν

10 ἔ|χοι· ὑγιαίνω δὲ καὶ ‖ αὐτὸς μετὰ τοῦ στρα|τεύματος. Σόλων |
15 Δημητρίου ὑμέτερος | πρεσβευτής, ἐπι|μελέστατα πεφρον‖τικὼς
τῶν τῆς πό|λεως ὑμῶν πραγ|μάτων, οὐ μόνον | ἠρκέσθη ἐπὶ
20 τοῖς | γεγονόσιν οἰκονο‖[μή]μασιν, ἀλλὰ καὶ | ἡμᾶς παρεκά-
25 λεσ|εν εἰς τὸ τοῦ γεγο|νότος ὑμεῖν ἐπι|κρίματος καὶ δόγμα‖τος
καὶ ὁρκίου καὶ νό|μου ἀντιπεφωνημέ|να ἐκ τῶν δημοσίων |
30 δέλτων ἐξαποστεῖ|λαι ὑμεῖν τὰ ἀντίγρα‖φα. Ἐφ᾽ οἷς ἐπαινέ|σας
τὸν Σόλωνα μᾶλ|λον ἀπεδεξάμην ἔσ|χον τε ἐν τοῖς ὑπ᾽ ἐμοῦ |
35 γεινωσκομένοις,‖ ὧι καὶ τὰ καθήκοντα | ἀπεμέρισα φιλάν|θρωπα,
40 ἄξιον ἡγη|σάμενος τὸν ἄν|δρα τῆς ἐξ ἡμῶν τει|μῆς, ὑμεῖν τε
συ|νήδομαι ἐπὶ τῶι ἔχειν | τοιοῦτον πολείτην. | Ἔστιν δὲ ἀντί-
45 γραφα | τῶν γεγονότων ὑ‖μεῖν φιλανθρώπων | τὰ ὑπογεγραμ-
μένα· | ἃ ὑμᾶς βούλομαι | ἐν τοῖς δημοσίοις | τοῖς παρ᾽ ὑμεῖν ‖
50 γράμμασιν ἐντάξαι.

Γράμματα Καίσαρος

. . . .

[. . . . .| δί]καια ἐσθλά τε [πολλ]ὰ ἐλευθέρους εἶναι, τῶι
[τε] δικαίωι καὶ ταῖς [κρίσεσιν ταῖς ἰδίαις τὴν πό|λιν] τὴν
Πλαρασέων καὶ Ἀφροδεισιέων χρῆσθαι μήτε ἐγγύην ε[ἰς Ῥώμην
αὐτοὺς κατὰ δόγμα τι | κ]αὶ κέλευσιν ὁμολογεῖν· ἅ τέ τινα
ἔπαθλα τειμὰς φιλάνθρω[πα . . . . .τρεῖς ἄνδρες | ο]ἱ
τῆς τῶν δημοσίων πραγμάτων διατάξεως τῶι ἰδίωι ἐπικρίματι
5 Πλ[αρασεῦσι καὶ Ἀφροδισιεῦ‖σι] προσεμέρισαν προσμεριοῦσιν,
συνεχώρησαν συνχωρήσουσιν, τα[ῦτα πάντα κύρια εἶναι | γ]ενέ-
σθαι. Ὁμοίως τε ἀρέσκειν τῆι συγκλήτωι, τὸν δῆμον τὸν
Πλα[ρασέων καὶ Ἀφροδεισιέ|]ων τὴν ἐλευθερίαν καὶ τὴν ἀτέ-
λειαν αὐτοὺς πάντων τῶν πραγ[μάτων ἔχειν καρπίζεσθαι, |
καθ]άπερ καὶ τίς πολιτεία τῶι καλλίστωι δικαίωι καλλίστωι
τε νόμωι ἐστίν, [ἥτις παρὰ τοῦ | δήμο]υ τοῦ Ῥωμαίων τὴν
ἐλευθερίαν καὶ τὴν ἀτέλειαν ἔχει φίλη τε καὶ σύ[μμαχος γεγέ‖-
10 νηται. Ὅ τε] τέμενος θεᾶς Ἀφροδίτης ἐν πόλει Πλαρασέων
καὶ Ἀφροδεισιέω[ν καθιέρωται, τοῦτο | ἄσυλον ἔ]στω ταύτωι
⟨τῶι⟩ δικαίωι ταύτηι τε δεισιδαιμονίαι, ὧι δικαίωι καὶ ἧι δεισ[ι-
δαιμονίαι Ἀρτέμι|δος Ἐφε]σίας ἐστὶν ἐν Ἐφέσωι, κύκλωι τε
ἐκείνου τοῦ ἱεροῦ εἴτε τέμενος εἴτ[ε ἄλσος ἐστίν, οὗ|τος ὁ]
τόπος ἄσυλος ἔστω. Ὅπως τε ἡ πόλις καὶ οἱ πολεῖται
οἱ Πλαρασέων [καὶ Ἀφροδεισίεων | μεθ᾽ ὧ]ν κωμῶν χωρίων

MUNICIPAL DOCUMENTS IN GREEK AND LATIN

ὀχυρωμάτων ὁρῶν προσόδων πρὸς τὴν φιλίαν το[ῦ δήμου προσ-
15 ῆλθον, ταῦτα ‖ ἔχωσ]ιν κρατῶσιν χρῶνται καρπίζωνταί τε
πάντων πραγμάτων ἀτε[λεῖς ὄντες. Μηδέ τινα | φόρον δ]ιά τινα
αἰτίαν ἐκείνων διδόναι μηδὲ [σ]υνεισφέρειν ὀφείλωσιν, [ἀλλ'
αὐτοὶ πᾶ|σι τούτ]οις κατ' οὖσαν μετὰ ταῦτα ἐν ἑαυτοῖς κύρωσιν
χρῶν[ται καρπίζωνται κρατῶσιν. Ἔδοξεν].

From Aphrodisias in Caria. The union of two cities in a common
polity is not unusual. Plarasa and Aphrodisias issued coinage
jointly (Head, *Hist. Numm.* 530). The third document engraved
on the stone is the decree of the senate ratifying the acts of the
triumvirs. Aphrodisias is mentioned by Pliny (*N.H.* 5. 109) as
a free state. By this decree freedom was conferred, and exemption
from tribute granted. The citizens could not be compelled to give
bail for appearance before a court in Rome. The shrine of Aphrodite
enjoyed the same rights of asylum as that of Diana at Ephesus (*cf.*
Tac. *Ann.* 3. 61). The revenues from the *territorium* were granted
to the city without any liability to tribute. For the status of free
cities, *cf.* pp. 39 *ff.*

30. EPISTULA AUGUSTI AD MYLASENSES
(31 a. Chr.)

Viereck, *Sermo Graecus*, 6; Ditt. *Syll.*[3] 768.

Αὐτοκράτωρ Καῖσαρ θεοῦ Ἰουλίου | υἱὸς ὕπατός τε τὸ τρίτον
καθεσ|ταμένος Μυλασέων ἄρχουσι βου|λῆι δήμωι χαίρειν. Εἰ
5 ἔρρωσθε κ[α]‖λῶς ἂν ἔχοι· καὶ αὐτὸς δὲ μετὰ τ[οῦ] | στρατεύ-
ματος ὑγίαινον. Κα[ὶ πρό]‖τερον μὲν ἤδη περὶ τῆς κατ[ασχού]|-
σης ὑμᾶς τύχης προσεπέ[μψατέ] | μοι, καὶ νῦν παραγενομένω[ν
10 τῶν] ‖ πρεσβευτῶν, Οὐλιάδ[ου..]
..ς τῶν πολεμίων πταῖσαι καὶ πρατη[θεί]‖σης τῆς πόλεως,
πολλοὺς μὲν αἰχμαλώτο[υς] | ἀποβαλῖν πολίτας, οὐκ ὀλίγους
μὲν φονευθέ[ν]|τας, τινὰς δὲ καὶ συνκαταφλεγέ(ν τας τῇ πόλε[ι],‖
15 τῆς τῶν πολεμίων ὠμότητος οὐδὲ τῶν | ναῶν οὐδὲ τῶν ἱερῶν τῶν
ἁγιωτάτων ἀ|ποσχομένης· ὑπέδιξαν δέ μοι καὶ περὶ | τῆς χώρας
τῆς λελεηλατημένης καὶ τῶν | ἐπαύλεων τῶν ἐμπεπρησμένων,
20 ὥστε ἐμ ‖ πᾶσιν ὑμᾶς ἠτυχηκέναι· ἐφ' οἷς πᾶσιν συνε[ῖ]δον
παθόντας] ταῦτα πάσης τειμῆς καὶ χάρι|[τος ἀξίους ἄνδρας
γενομέν]ους ὑμᾶς πε[ρὶ Ῥωμαίους..]

From Mylasa. Unfortunately the major portion of the letter of Augustus is lost, and we cannot determine precisely its content, but it is probable that the Mylasans were given the rank of a free city (Pliny, *N.H.* 5. 108; *cf. CIG.* 2695*b*). The city of Mylasa had been occupied by the troops of Labienus nine years before. During a festival the soldiers were massacred by the citizens, who abandoned their homes when Labienus advanced against them. He rased the city to the ground (Cassius Dio, 48. 26; Strabo, 14. 2. 24, p. 660). *Cf.* nos. 32, 133.

31. TITULUS OPERIS PUBLICI
(31 a. Chr.)

Notizie degli scavi, 1915, 139; *An. ép.* 1916, no. 60.

Decuria | Q. Arrunti | Surai, cur(atoribus) | Q. Arruntio ‖ C. Sabello | Pig(neratore) T. Arrio. | Sum(ma) h(ominum) xciix. | 5 In sing(ulos) hom(ines) | op(eris) p(edes) xliii. S‖(umma) p(edum) 10 ∞ iↃↃccxiv.

Found at Saletto di Montagnana near Este in 1907. It refers to work performed by veterans, after the battle of Actium, in building levees along the river Atesis near Ateste. Another inscription from Ateste refers to the same matter (*CIL.* v, 2603). To carry out the work the soldiers were divided into squads, each one of them bearing the name of some leader. This squad took the name of Q. Arruntius Sura, who was also one of the overseers. In it were ninety-eight men, and to each man forty-three feet were assigned. This is one of the earliest of those great constructive works carried out by soldiers, from which the provincial cities profited so much under the empire, and of which we have so many records in Africa; *cf.* nos. 72 and 103.

32. EPISTULA IMPERATORIS, VEL PROCONSULIS, AD MYLASENSES
(ca. 30 a. Chr.)

Le Bas-Waddington, 3. 442–443; *CIG.* 2695*b*, 2700*e*.

...........................καὶ [τ]ὰς ὑπὲρ τῶν δημοσίων | [ἐπι]κτήσεις(?) εἴς τε τὸν κοινὸν [τῆς] πόλεως καρφισμὸν τινῶν ἀνα[σ|τά]σεις ὑπονοθεύειν, οἷς δὴ κἂν ἐπι[τρέ]πωμεν φορολογεῖν

MUNICIPAL DOCUMENTS IN GREEK AND LATIN

τὴν [Μυ]|λασέων πόλιν εἰς δουλικὴν περι[ου]σίαν, ἡμεῖν μὲν ἂν
5 ἴσως ἦι ἐφ[ορῶ]‖σιν αἰσχρά τε καὶ ἡμῶν ἀνάξιος, ἀ[δύ]νατος δὲ
ἂν ὅμως κἀκεί[ν]|οις γένοιτο πρά[σ]σουσι δημοσίαι τοὺς δημοσίαι
κυρίους, μ[ή]|τε χρημάτων μήτε προσόδω[ν] δημοσίων ὑποκει-
μέν[ω]|ν, εἰ μὴ κατὰ τελῶν ἐπίρειψιν λογ[ίζ]ειν τοὺς ἑνὸς
ἑκάστου. . . . .| υς τάς τε κεφαλὰς ἐπὶ τελῶν ει. . . θέλοιεν, τῆς
10 πόλεως οὐδ[ὲ τὴν] ‖ ἐπανόρθωσιν τῶν ἐκ τῆς Λαβιήνο[υ] ληστήας
ἐρειπίων ἑτοίμως ἀ[ν]‖αφερούσης, ὃ δὴ καὶ αὐτοὶ προϊδόμε[νοι]
προδανεισμοῖς ἰδιωτῶν [εἰς] | χρέα δημόσια τὴν πόλιν ὑπηγά-
γο[ν]το, οὐ διὰ τὸ καθ᾽ ὑπαλλαγὴ[ν ἀνα|λ]ωμάτων(?) τὴν
Καίσαρος ὑπὲρ Μυλασέ[ων. . . . .] |

From Mylasa. *Cf.* no. 30. This document appears to be a part
of a letter of some emperor or governor relative to the collection of
taxes or tribute, but the interpretation is exceedingly obscure. The
letter probably belongs to a period not much later than no. 30.

33. EDICTUM AUGUSTI DE AQUAEDUCTU VENAFRANO
(17–11 a. Chr.)

CIL. x, 4842; Bruns, 77; Girard, p. 186; Riccobono, p. 316;
Dessau, 5743.

*Ed*ictum *imp(eratoris) Caesaris Augusti (finis huius versus et prae-
terea sex fere toti evanuerunt)*— . . . .
Venafranorum nomin*e* . . . . *ius sit lice*atque.

Qui rivi specus saepta fon*tes* . . . . *que aquae ducend*ae
10 reficiundae ‖ causa supra infrave libram *facti aedi*ficati structi sunt,
sive quod | aliut opus eius aquae ducendae refi*ci*undae causa supra
infrave libram | factum est, uti quidquid earum *re*rum factum est,
ita esse habere itaque | reficere reponere restituere resarcire semel
saepius, fistulas canales | tubos ponere, aperturam committere, sive
15 quid aliut eius aquae ducen‖dae causa opus *er*it, facere placet: dum
qui locus ager in fundo, qui | Q. Sirini (?) L. f. Ter. *est esseve*
dicitur, et in fundo, qui L. Pompei M. f. Ter. Sullae | est esseve
dicitur, m*ace*ria saeptus est, per quem locum subve quo loco | specus
eius aquae p*erv*enit, ne ea maceria parsve quae eius maceriae | aliter
20 diruat*ur tollat*ur, quam specus reficiundi aut inspiciendi cau‖sa;
*neve quid ibi priv*ati sit, quominus ea aqua ire fluere ducive poss*it* |

[328]

...... Dextra sinistraque circa eum rivom circaque | ea o*pera, quae eius aqu*ae ducendae causa facta sunt, octonos pedes agrum | *vacuo*m *esse placet*, per quem locum Venafranis eive, qui Venafranorum | *nomine*......, iter facere eius aquae ducendae operumve eius aquae || *ductus faciendor*um reficiendorum *causa*, quod eius s(ine) 25 d(olo) m(alo) fiat, ius sit liceatque, | quaeque ea*rum rer*um cuius faciendae reficiendae causa opus erunt, quo | proxume poterit advehere adferre adportare, quaeque inde exempta erunt, | quam maxime aequaliter dextra sinistraque p. VIII iacere, dum ob eas res damn*i* | infecti iurato promittatur. Earumque rerum omnium ita habendarum || colon(is) (?) Ven*afra*nis ius potestatemque esse 30 placet, dum ne ob id opus domi|nus eorum cuius agri locive, per quem agrum locumve ea aqua ire fluere | ducive solet, invius fiat; neve ob id opus minus ex agro suo in partem agri | quam transire transferre transvertere recte possit; neve *c*ui eorum, per quo|rum agros ea aqua ducitur, eum aquae ductum corrumpere abducere aver||tere facereve, quo minus ea aqua in oppidum Venafranorum 35 recte duci | fluere possit, liceat. |

Quaeque aqua in oppidum Venafranorum it fluit ducitur, eam aquam | distribuere discribere vendundi causa, aut ei rei vectigal inponere consti|tuere, IIviro IIviris praefec(to) praefectis eius coloniae ex maioris partis decuri||onum decreto, quod decretum ita 40 factum erit, cum in decurionibus non | minus quam duae partes decurionum adfuerint; legemque ei dicere ex | decreto decurionum, quod ita ut supra scriptum est decretum erit, ius po|testatem*q*ue esse placet; dum ne ea aqua, quae ita distributa discripta deve qua | ita decretum erit, aliter quam fistulis plumbeis d(um) t(axat) ab rivo p(edes) L ducatur; neve || eae fistulae aut rivos nisi sub terra, 45 quae terra itineris viae publicae limi|tisve erit, ponantur conlocentur; neve ea aqua per locum privatum in|vito eo, cuius is locus erit, ducatur. Quamque legem ei aquae tuendae ope|ribusve, quae eius aquae ductus ususve causa facta sunt erunt, tuendis | II*viri praefecti* *ex* decurion(um) decreto, quod ita ut s(upra) s(criptum) e(st) factum erit, dixeri*nt,* || *eam*.....*fir*mam ratamque esset placet | (*undecim* 50 *versus evanidi facti*).................Venafranae s........ ......atio quam colono aut incola*e....|....*da......is cui ex decreto decurionum ita, ut supra comprensum est, ne||gotium datum 65

erit, agenti, tum, qui inter civis et peregrinos ius dicet, iudicium |
reciperatorium in singulas res HS. x reddere, testibusque dumtaxat x
denun|tiando quaeri placet; dum reciperatorum reiectio inter eum
qui aget et | eum quocum agetur ita fiet, *ut ex lege*, quae de iudicis
privatis lata est, | licebit oportebit.

On a block of marble at Venafrum. Venafrum is one of the
twenty-eight colonies established in Italy by Augustus (*cf.* Suet.
Aug. 46), as its name, *colonia Augusta Iulia* (*cf. CIL.* x, 4894, 4875;
Lib. colon. 239. 7) indicates. These colonies, Suetonius says (*Aug.*
46), (*Augustus*) *operibus ac vectigalibus publicis plurifariam instruxit.*
Very likely his gift to the colony was recorded in the first paragraph
of the inscription. There is no reference in it to the penalties
established by the *lex Quinctia de aquaeductibus* (*cf.* Bruns, 22) of
9 B.C., and the settlement of disputes is referred to the peregrine
praetor (*cf.* l. 65, *qui inter civis et peregrinos ius dicet*), and not to the
curatores aquarum, who took charge of such matters after 11 B.C.;
cf. Mommsen, *Ges. Schr.* 3, 97. On the other hand the *lex de
iudicis privatis* of the last paragraph is probably a *lex Iulia* of 17 B.C.
(*cf.* Wlassak, *Röm. Processgesetze*, 1, 173–188). Therefore the inscription falls between 17 and 11 B.C. The document is an edict.
No mention is made in it of the co-operation of the Roman senate;
cf. Mommsen, *op. cit.* 3, 81. From this document it is clear (*cf.*
l. 38, *vendundi causa*) that private persons did not receive water
free in the municipalities, as they did in Rome, but they were
charged a rental (*cf.* Mommsen, *op. cit.* 3, 91), and the proceeds
were covered into the local treasury; *cf.* p. 138. The distribution
of the water was under the control of the magistrates and decurions,
and the importance of the matter is indicated by the fact that the
presence of a quorum of two-thirds of the decurions was required
to make the action legal; *cf.* pp. 67 f. The most interesting point in
the inscription for us is the fact that the adjudication of offenses
is referred to Rome, not to the local magistrates. This is a logical
outcome of the fact that the aqueduct was given to the city by
Augustus. It is possible that cases involving a fine less than 10,000
sesterces were heard by the local magistrates. In the *lex de Gallia
Cisalpina* of 49–42 B.C., the municipal officials had full competence
in matters involving 15,000 sesterces or less; *cf.* no. 27. It is

FROM ITALY AND THE PROVINCES

probable, as Mommsen remarks (*op. cit.* 3, 96), that the Roman practice in this matter varied from place to place. With the establishment of the empire, gifts were more and more frequently made to the cities by the emperor, and this precedent shows us how these donations gave the central government the natural right to take part in the conduct of local affairs.

34. DECRETUM CONCILI ASIAE
DE FASTIS PROVINCIALIBUS
(ca. 9 a. Chr.)

Ditt. *Or. Gr.* 458, ll. 78 *ff.*; *Inschriften von Priene*, 105.

Ἔδοξεν τοῖς ἐπὶ τῆς ᾿Ασίας ῞Ελλησιν, γνώμηι τοῦ ἀρχιερέως 78
᾿Απολλωνίου τοῦ | Μηνοφίλου ᾿Αζεανείτου· ἐπεὶ τὴν νέαν νου-
μηνίαν ἀεὶ δεῖ ἑστάναι τὴν αὐτὴ[ν] || ἅπασιν τῆς εἰς τὰς ἀρχὰς 80
εἰσόδου κατά τε τὸ Παύλου Φαβίου Μαξίμου τοῦ ἀν|θυπάτου
διάταγμα καὶ τὸ τῆς ᾿Ασία(ς) ψήφισμα ἐνποδίζεται δὲ ἡ τοῦ
χρόνου | τάξις παρὰ τὰς ἐν τοῖς ἀρχαιρεσίοις ἐπικλήσεις, γεί-
νεσθαι τὰ κατὰ τὰ | ἀρχαιρέσια μηνὶ δεκάτωι, ὡς καὶ ἐν τῶι
Κορνηλίωι νόμωι γέγραπται, ἐντὸς | δεκάτης ἱσταμένου.

From Priene. We have omitted the first 77 lines of the inscription carved on this stone. Paullus Fabius Maximus, proconsul of Asia, wrote to the provincial assembly urging the council to adopt the natal day of Augustus as the beginning of the official year in the province, and to change from the lunar to the solar reckoning of the Julian calendar. The assembly adopted the recommendation enthusiastically as a means of conferring honor upon the deified emperor. Copies of the decree were ordered to be engraved and set up in the different cities. In addition to the copy from Priene, others have been found at Apamea (*CIG.* 3957), Dorylaeum (*CIL.* III, 13651), Eumenia (*CIG.* 3902*b*), and Maeonia (*Denkschriften der Wiener Akademie*, 54 (1911), 80 *ff.*). The part of the document which we have included in this collection is a second decree of the provincial assembly regulating the elections of municipal magistrates under the revised calendar according to the Sullan constitution. The Sullan era had been adopted by many of the cities of Asia, probably those whose constitutions he had remodelled. According

[331]

MUNICIPAL DOCUMENTS IN GREEK AND LATIN

to the Sullan law elections must be held fifty days before the beginning of the civil year. This arrangement was doubtless made to allow sufficient time for the settlement of appeals in the case of candidates who did not wish to serve in the office to which they had been elected. Very little is known of the Sullan constitution. It regulated the duties of the governor (Cic. *ad fam.* 1. 9. 25; 3. 6. 3, 6) and the administration of the municipalities (Cic. *ad fam.* 3. 10. 6), and apparently defined the privileges of free cities (*Ath. Mitth.* 24 (1899), 234, no. 74).

35. EPISTULA P. CORNELI SCIPIONIS, PROCONSULIS ASIAE, AD THYATIRENOS
(7–6 a. Chr.)

Cagnat, *IGRR.* 4, 1211; Viereck, *Sermo Graecus*, 8.

Πόπλιος Κορνήλιος Σ[κιπίων ἀνθύπατος Ῥωμαίων] | Θυατει-
ρηνοῖς ἄρχουσ[ι βουλῆι δήμωι χαίρειν]. | Δίκαιον εἶναι νομίζω
ὑ[μᾶς...........ὡς] | καὶ νόμιμόν ἐστιν τ[ὰς γενομένας ὑπὲρ
5 τῶν ἱε]||ρῶν χρημάτων κρίσε[ις........]|γης δικαστῶν κελευ-
[.........καὶ οὐ]||δὲν πλέον τοῖς ἐπικαλ[ουμένοις.......
ὑπε]||ρωνηθεῖσι τὸ παραβόλ[ιον.......ὁ|π]ό[σ]η τοῖς φυγοδι-
10 κοῦσ[ι........] | ||.....ἐμὴν ἅπαντα.........|[ε]ἰσηγησα-
μένου Αὔλου Ῥαυ(ί)ο[υ..........

The subject of this fragmentary letter of the provincial governor to the citizens of Thyatira is obscure. Apparently the temple-lands had been leased for a high rental and the lessees had brought suit for an abatement of the terms. It would seem that the decision of the court had been unacceptable to the Thyatirans and they had persisted in holding the lessees to their contract. The latter had appealed to the governor, and he urged the city to abide by the decision of the court or of the arbiters. *Cf.* Chapot, *La prov. rom. proc. d'Asie,* 128, n. 1.

36. EPISTULA IMPERATORIS AUGUSTI AD CNIDIOS
(6 a. Chr.)

Viereck, *Sermo Graecus*, 9; Cagnat, *IGRR.* 4, 1031; *IG.* xii,
3, 174; Ditt. *Syll.*³ 780.

[. . | . . δαμι]ωργοῦ δὲ Καιρογένεος Λευ[κα]θέου (?).

Αὐτοκράτωρ Καῖσαρ θεοῦ υἱὸς Σεβαστός, ἀρχιερεύς, | ὕπατος τὸ
δωδέκατον ἀποδεδειγμένος | καὶ δημαρχικῆς ἐξουσίας τὸ ὀκτωικαι-
δέκατον, ‖ Κνιδίων ἄρχουσι, βουλῆι, δήμωι χαίρειν. Οἱ πρέσ|βεις 5
ὑμῶν Διονύσιος β' καὶ Διονύσιος β' τοῦ Διονυ|σίου ἐνέτυχον ἐν
Ῥώμηι μοι, καὶ τὸ ψήφισμα ἀποδόντες | κατηγόρησαν Εὐβούλου
μὲν τοῦ Ἀναξανδρίδα τεθνει|ῶτος ἤδη, Τρυφέρας δὲ τῆς γυναικὸς
αὐτοῦ παρούσης ‖ περὶ τοῦ θανάτου τοῦ Εὐβούλου τοῦ Χρυσίππου. 10
Ἐγὼι | δὲ ἐξετάσαι προστάξας Γάλλωι Ἀσινίωι τῶι ἐμῶι φίλωι |
τῶν οἰκετῶν τοὺς ἐνφερομένους τῆι αἰτίᾳ διὰ βα|σάνων ἔγνων
Φιλεῖνον τὸν Χρυσίππου τρεῖς νύ|κτας συνεχῶς ἐπεληλυθότα
τῆι οἰκίαι τῆι Εὐβού‖λου καὶ Τρυφέρας μεθ' ὕβρεως καὶ τρόπωι 15
τινὶ πολι|ορκίας, τῆι τρίτηι δὲ συνεπηιγμένον καὶ τὸν ἀδελ|φὸν
Εὔβουλον, τοὺς δὲ τῆς οἰκίας δεσπότας Εὔβου|λον καὶ Τρυφέραν,
ὡς οὔτε χρηματίζοντες πρὸς | τὸν Φιλεῖνον οὔτε ἀντιφραττό-
μενοι ταῖς προσ‖βολαῖς ἀσφαλείας ἐν τῆι ἑαυτῶν οἰκίᾳ τυχεῖν 20
ἠδύναν|το, προστεταχότας ἑνὶ τῶν οἰκετῶν οὐκ ἀποκτεῖ|ναι, ὡς
ἴσως ἄν τις ὑπ' ὀργῆς οὐ[κ] ἀδίκου προήχθηι, ἀλ|λὰ ἀνεῖρξαι
κατασκεδάσαντα τὰ κόπρια αὐτῶν· τὸν | δὲ οἰκέτην σὺν τοῖς
καταχεομένοις εἴτε ἑκόντα ‖ εἴτε ἄκοντα—αὐτὸς μὲν γὰρ ἐνέ- 25
μεινεν ἀρνούμενο[ς] |—ἀφεῖναι τὴν γάστραν, [κα]ὶ τὸν Εὔβουλον
ὑποπεσεῖν δικαιό|[τ]ερον ἂν σωθέντα τἀδελφοῦ. Πέπονφα δὲ
ὑμεῖν καὶ α[ὐ|τ]ὰς τὰς ἀνακρίσεις. Ἐθαύμαζον δ' ἄν, πῶς εἰς
τόσον | ἔδεισαν τὴν παρ' ὑμεῖν ἐξετασίαν τῶν δούλων οἱ φ[εύ‖-
γοντες τὴν δίκην, εἰ μή ποι σφόδρα αὐτοῖς ἐδόξ[ατε] | χαλεποὶ 30
γεγονέναι καὶ πρὸς τὰ ἐναντία μισοπόνη[ροι], | μὴ κατὰ τῶν
ἀξίων πᾶν ὁτιοῦν παθεῖν, ἐπ' ἀλλο[τρίαν] | οἰκίαν νύκτωρ μεθ'
ὕβρεως καὶ βίας τρὶς ἐπεληλυ[θό]|των καὶ τὴν κοινὴν ἁπάντων
ὑμῶν ἀσφάλειαν [ἀναι]‖ρούντων ἀγανακτοῦντες, ἀλλὰ κατὰ τῶν 35
καὶ ἠν[ίκ' ἢ]|μύνοντο ἠτυχηκότων, ἠδικηκότων δὲ οὐδ' ἔστ[ιν ὅ,τι].
| Ἀλλὰ νῦν ὀρθῶς ἄν μοι δοκεῖτε ποιῆσαι τῆι ἐμῆι [περὶ τού]|των
γνώμηι προνοήσαντες καὶ τὰ ἐν τοῖς δημ[οσίοις] | ὑμῶν ὁμολο-
γεῖν γράμματα. Ἔρρωσθε.

MUNICIPAL DOCUMENTS IN GREEK AND LATIN

This inscription, containing the letter of Augustus to the Cnidians and the letter of Trajan to the Astypalaeans (no. 75), was found at Astypalaea. The letter of Augustus deals with the appeal of Eubulus and Tryphera to the emperor. They were residents of Cnidus, a free town, and a slave in their household had accidentally killed a Cnidian who had assailed their house. As public opinion was against them, they feared to submit themselves to the jurisdiction of the local court and they fled to Rome. The Cnidians sent an embassy to Augustus with a decree of the city accusing the fugitives and demanding their extradition or punishment. The emperor instructed the governor of Asia to investigate. When he made his report, Augustus rendered a decision acquitting the accused and rebuking the Cnidians for their attitude towards Eubulus and Tryphera (cf. Mommsen, *Roman Provinces*, I, 352, n. 1; Chapot, *La prov. rom. proc. d'Asie*, 126 f.). Free cities had jurisdiction over civil and criminal cases in their own courts, but the right of appeal to the emperor, granted to all citizens of the empire, marks the lessening of the power of local magistrates. This development was intensified, when, as at Cnidus, the local courts were swayed by partisan prejudice. *Cf.* nos. 25, 40.

37. IUSIURANDUM PAPHLAGONUM
(3 a. Chr.)

Cagnat, *IGRR.* 3, 137; Ditt. *Or. Gr.* 532.

Ἀπὸ Αὐτοκράτορος Καίσ[αρος] | θεοῦ υἱοῦ Σεβαστοῦ ὑπα-
τεύ[οντος τὸ] | δωδέκατον ἔτους τρίτου, π[ροτέραι] | νωνῶν
5 Μαρτίων ἐν Γάγγροις ἐν [τ]ἀ[γοραῖ] ὅρ‖κος ὁ τελεσθ[εὶς ὑ]πὸ
τῶ[ν] κατοικ[ούντων Πα]‖φλαγονία[ν καὶ τῶν πραγ]ματευο-
μ[ένων πα]‖ρ᾽ αὐτοῖς Ῥ[ωμαίων]. | Ὀμνύω Δία, Γῆν, Ἥλιον,
θεοὺς πάντα[ς καὶ πά]‖σας καὶ αὐτὸν τὸν Σεβασ[τ]όν, εὐνοή-
10 [σειν Καί]‖σαρι Σεβαστῶι καὶ τοῖς τ[έκ]νοις ἐγγό[νοις τε] |
αὐτοῦ πάν[τ]α [τ]ὸν τοῦ [βίου] χρόνον κ[αὶ λό]‖γωι [κ]αὶ ἔργωι
καὶ γνώμ[ηι, φί]λους ἡγού[μενος] | οὓς ἂν ἐκεῖνοι ἡγῶντα[ι]
ἐκχθροὺς τε ν[ομίζων] | οὓς ἂν αὐτοὶ κρίνωσιν, ὑπέρ τε τῶν τ[ού-
15 τοις] ‖ διαφερόντων μήτε σώματος φείσεσθ[αι μή]‖τε ψυχῆς
μήτε βίου μήτε τέκνων, ἀλ[λὰ παν]‖τὶ τρόπωι ὑπὲρ τῶ[ν]
ἐκείνοις ἀνηκό[ντων] | πάντα κίνδυνον ὑπομένειν· ὅτι τε ἄ[ν

[334]

FROM ITALY AND THE PROVINCES

αἴσ]‖θωμαι ἢ ἀκούσω ὑπεναντίον τούτ[οις λε]‖γόμενον ἢ βου- 20
λευόμενον ἢ πρασσό[μενον,] | τοῦτο ἐγμηνύσειν τε καὶ ἐχθρὸν
ἔσ[εσθαι τῶι] | λέγοντι ἢ βουλευομένωι ἢ πράσσο[ντί τι τού-|
των· οὕς τε ἂν ἐκχθροὺς αὐτ[ο]ὶ κρίν[ωσιν, τού]‖τους κατὰ γῆν
καὶ θάλασσαν ὅπλο[ις τε] ‖ καὶ σιδήρωι διώξειν καὶ ἀμυνεῖ- 25
σ[θαι.] | Ἐὰν δέ τι ὑπεναντίον τούτωι τ[ῶι ὅρκωι] | ποήσω ἢ
μὴ στοιχούντως καθὼ[ς ὤμο]‖σα, ἐπαρῶμαι αὐτός τε κατ' ἐμοῦ
καὶ σ[ώμα]‖τος τοῦ ἐμαυτοῦ καὶ ψυχῆς καὶ βίου κα[ὶ τέ]‖κνων 30
καὶ παντὸς τοῦ ἐμαυτοῦ γέν[ους] | καὶ συνφέροντος ἐξώλειαν
καὶ παν[ώλει]‖αν μέχρι πάσης διαδοχῆς τῆς ἐ[μῆς καὶ] | τῶν ἐξ
ἐμοῦ πάντων, καὶ μήτε σ[ώματα τὰ] | τῶν ἐμῶν ἢ ἐξ ἐμοῦ μήτε
γῆ μ[ήτε θάλασ]‖σα δέξαιτο μηδὲ καρποὺς ἐνέγ[κοι αὐτοῖς.] | 35
   Κατὰ τὰ αὐτὰ ὤμοσαν καὶ οἱ ἐ[ν τῆι χώραι] | πάντες ἐν τοῖς
κατὰ τὰς ὑ[παρχίας Σε]‖βαστήοις παρὰ τοῖς βωμοῖ[ς τοῦ]
Σεβαστοῦ·] | ὁμοίως τε Φαζιμωνεῖται οἱ [τὴν νῦν Νεάπο]‖λιν 40
λεγομένην κατοικοῦν[τες ὤμοσαν σύμ]‖παντες ἐν Σεβαστήωι
παρὰ τ[ῶι βωμῶι τοῦ] | Σεβαστοῦ.

From Phazimon (Neoclaudiopolis) in Paphlagonia. Paphlagonia
was organized as a province of the empire in 6 B.C. The oath of
loyalty to Augustus was taken three years later at Gangra, the seat
of provincial government, and the same oath was administered
throughout the province at the altars of Augustus. The restoration
ὑ[παρχίας] in l. 37 is due to Reinach, and is conditionally accepted
by Dittenberger. The hyparchy was the ancient satrapy (Hausoul-
lier, *Rev. Philol.* 25 (1901), 22 ff.). Dittenberger suggests that the
term may be applied to a *conventus* under the Roman administration.
For similar oaths, *cf.* nos. 47, 48. Phazimon was raised from a village
to a city by Pompey (Strabo, 12. 3. 38, p. 560).

38. RES GESTAE DIVI AUGUSTI
(28 a. Chr.–6 p. Chr.)

CIL. III, pt. II, pp. 769 *ff.*; Cagnat, *IGRR.* 3, 158.

Chap. 3 (= col. I, ll. 16 *ff.*).

Millia civium Roma*norum adacta* sacramento meo fuerunt cir-
citer *quingen*|ta. Ex quibus dedu*xi in coloni*as aut remisi in municipia
sua stipen*dis emeri*|tis millia aliquant*o plura qu*am trecenta et

[335]

iis omnibus agros a*dsignavi* | aut pecuniam pro p*raemis mil*itiae dedi.

_____

Chap. 15 (= col. III, ll. 17 *ff*.).

In colo*ni*s militum meorum consul quintum ex manibiis viritim| millia nummum singula dedi; acceperunt id triumphale congiarium | in colo*n*is hominum circiter centum et viginti millia.

Chap. 16 (= col. III, ll. 22 *ff*.).

Pecuniam *pro* agris, quos in consulatu meo quarto et postea consulibus | M. Cr*asso et* Cn. Lentulo augure adsignavi mili*t*ibus, solvi municipis. Ea | su*mma ses*tertium circiter sexsiens milliens
25 fuit, quam *p*ro Italicis || praed*is* numeravi, et cir*c*iter bis mil-li*ens* et sescentiens, quod pro agris | provin*c*ialibus solvi. Id primus et *s*olus omnium, qui *d*eduxerunt | colonias militum in Italia aut in provincis, ad memor*i*am aetatis | meae feci. Et postea Ti. Nerone et Cn. Pisone consulibus, item*q*ue C. Antistio | et D. Laelio cos., et C. Calvisio et L. Pasieno consulibus, et L. Le*ntulo et* M.
30 Messalla || consulibus, et L. Caninio et Q. Fabricio co*s*. mili*tibus*, *quos* eme|riteis stipendis in sua municip*i*a *dedux*i, praem*i*a nume-rato | persolvi, quam in rem seste*rtium q*uate*r m*illien*s l*ibente*r* | impendi. |

_____

Chap. 18 (= col. III, ll. 40 *ff*.).

40 *Inde ab eo anno, q*uo Cn. et P. Lentuli *cons*ules fuerunt, cum d*e*ficerent | *vectigalia, tum* centum millibus h*o*minum tu*m pl*uribus in*l*ato fru|*mento vel ad n*ummario*s tributus ex agro* et pa*t*ri*monio* meo *opem tuli*.

_____

Chap. 21 (= col. IV, ll. 26 *ff*.).

Auri coronari pondo triginta et quin|que millia municipiis et colonis Italiae conferentibus ad triumpho*s* | meos quintum consul remisi, et postea, quotienscumque imperator a*ppel*|latus sum, aurum
30 coronarium non accepi decernentibus municipii*s* || et coloni*s* aequ*e* benigne adque antea decreverant. |

Chap. 28 (= col. v, ll. 35 *ff.*).

Colonias in Africa Sicilia *M*acedonia utraque Hispania Achai*a* 35
Asia Syria | Gallia Narbonensi Pis*i*dia militum deduxi. Italia
autem xxviii *coloni*|as, quae vivo me celeberrimae et frequentis-
simae fuerunt, me*is auspicis* | deductas habet. |

Suppl., chap. 4.

[Δαπ]άναι δὲ | εἰς θέας καὶ μονομάχους καὶ ἀθλητὰς καὶ ναυ-
μα|χίαν καὶ θηρομαχίαν δωρεαί [τε] ἀποικίαις πόλεσιν | ἐν
Ἰταλία, πόλεσιν ἐν ἐπαρχείαις σεισμῷ κα[ὶ] ἐνπυ‖ρισμοῖς πεπο- 5
νηκυίαις ἢ κατ' ἄνδρα φίλοις καὶ συν|κλητικοῖς, ὧν τὰς τειμήσεις
προσεξεπλήρωσεν ἄ|πειρον πλῆθος. |

This document was originally cut on bronze tablets and placed
in front of the mausoleum of Augustus in Rome. Kornemann
(*Klio*, 15 (1917), 214 *ff.*) thinks that the period of composition
runs from 28 B.C. to A.D. 6, but *cf.* Koepp, *Sokrates*, 8 (1920),
289 *ff.* Kornemann's views are elaborated in his *Mausoleum u.
Tatenbericht d. Augustus* (1921). The extant copy comes from
Ancyra. It was discovered, and part of the Latin portion copied,
by Buysbecche in 1555. In 1746 Richard Pococke published a
few fragments of the Greek text. More of it was copied by Hamilton in 1832. The copy on which present-day editions are based
was made by Humann under the auspices of the Berlin Academy
in 1882. The text with a full commentary was published by Mommsen in 1865. A briefer commentary may be found in the editions
of Peltier (1886), Fairley (1898), Cagnat, *loc. cit.*, and Diehl (1918).
The Latin text has been republished by R. Wirz (1922), and the
entire text with commentary and English translation has been
edited by E. G. Hardy (1923).

The extracts which we have published from the *Res gestae* are
of interest because of the light which they throw on the colonizing
policy of the Romans under the early empire, on the provision
made for veterans at the time of their discharge from the army, on
the contributions offered to successful generals and to the emperor
on special occasions by municipalities, and on the assistance given
to needy cities in paying the *vectigalia*.

In his statement Augustus does not include the colonies founded by his colleagues in the triumvirate, but mentions only those established by himself. On the foundations in Italy a passage in Hyginus (*de lim.* p. 177, ed. Lachmann) furnishes an important commentary: Divus Augustus, in adsignata orbi terrarum pace, exercitus, qui aut sub Antonio aut sub Lepido militaverant, pariter et suarum legionum milites colonos fecit, alios in Italia, alios in provinciis; quibusdam, deletis hostium civitatibus, novas urbes constituit; quosdam in veteribus oppidis deduxit et colonos nominavit; illas quoque urbes, quae deductae a regibus aut dictatoribus fuerant, quas bellorum civilium interventus exhauserat, dato iterum coloniae nomine, numero civium ampliavit, quasdam et finibus.

In the case of Italian towns which had been hostile to him, he evidently followed somewhat the same policy which the Romans had adopted after the conquest of Sicily. Such places were turned over to the veterans and resettled by them. Other veterans were sent to established communities, which henceforth bore the title of colonies. Later in this record (chap. 28 = col. v, l. 36) Augustus can boast that twenty-eight of his Italian colonies were large and flourishing, and his boast is justified by the list of prosperous colonies in Italy bearing the title of Julia or of Augusta or both titles, such as Beneventum, Brixia, Minturnae, and Pisaurum. One might infer from chap. 16 (col. iii, l. 22) that the Italian and provincial settlements were both made in 30 B.C., but in fact the provincial settlements date from 14 B.C. The first sure case of a colony founded outside of Italy is that of Narbo Martius, settled in 118 B.C. (*cf.* p. 7), but this was a colony of civilians, whereas the ultramarine settlements of Augustus were military in character. In the last extract Augustus mentions ten different provinces in which he made these settlements, which in many cases served much the same purpose abroad as the Roman colonies had served in earlier days in pacifying and Romanizing Italy. This was the case especially with the military colonies planted in Galatia. The payments made to provincial municipalities for the lands occupied by soldiers (*cf.* chap. 16 = col. iii, ll. 22 *ff.*) would seem to be out of harmony with the legal theory that all the land in the provinces belonged to the Roman state (*cf.* p. 118). Whether this noteworthy precedent set by Augustus was followed by later emperors we do not know.

When Marius adopted the revolutionary policy of admitting the proletariat freely to the army, it was inevitable that some provision should be made for veterans at the end of their term of service. At first lands were assigned to them in colonies (*cf.* p. 7). Augustus, however, follows an alternative plan, not unlike the "adjusted compensation" proposal under discussion in the United States of America, of giving veterans either grants of land or money gratuities or both, as he did in 29 B.C. (*cf.* chap. 15 = col. III, ll. 17 *ff.*). The land-grant policy was given up after 14 B.C. (Cass. Dio, 54. 25), and from 7 B.C. a fixed money payment, probably of 12,000 sesterces, was made to each soldier on the completion of his term of service (Cass. Dio, 55. 23). To make these payments he spent 400,000,000 sesterces before the close of his reign (*cf.* chap. 16 = col. III, ll. 28 *ff.*). As the army became a more important factor in politics in the later years of the empire, great sums of money were given in the form of largesses to soldiers in active service, and this added heavily to the burden of taxes paid by the municipalities (*cf.* p. 219).

The contributions made by the cities of a province to provide golden crowns to be carried in the triumphal procession of its governor are well enough known under the republic. Augustus checked the development of this practice in Italy (chap. 21 = col. IV, ll. 26 *ff.*).

As Mommsen has observed, chap. 18 (col. III, ll. 40 *ff.*) is probably to be interpreted in the light of Cassius Dio's remark (54. 30) that: ἐπειδή τε ἡ Ἀσία τὸ ἔθνος ἐπικουρίας τινὸς διὰ σεισμοὺς μάλιστα ἐδεῖτο, τόν τε φόρον αὐτῆς τὸν ἔτειον ἐκ τῶν ἑαυτοῦ χρημάτων τῷ κοινῷ ἐσήνεγκε. Specifically Augustus doubtless has in mind the remission of the *vectigalia* in the case of cities which had suffered from earthquakes or experienced some other serious loss. This interpretation would harmonize with von Premerstein's emendation (*Phil. Wochenschr.* 1922, 135 *ff.*) of col. VI, l. 41 to read *donata pecunia...colonis, municipiis, oppidis terrae motu incendioque consumptis.* The results of these generous acts of Augustus and of some of his successors are noted in another connection (*cf.* pp. 147 *ff.*).

MUNICIPAL DOCUMENTS IN GREEK AND LATIN

39. EDICTUM PROCONSULIS ASIAE DE MURO EPHESIO
(ca. 11 p. Chr.)

I.B.M. 521; Viereck, *Sermo Graecus*, 7; Ditt. *Syll.*³ 784.

Μᾶρκος Ἑρέννιος Πίκης ἀνθ[ύπατος λέγει]. | ᾿Αφανοῦς γεγενη-
μένου τοῦ πα[ρατειχίσ]‖ματος, ὅπερ δημοσίαι κατασκε[υῆι ὑπὸ
5 τῶν] | ᾿Εφεσίων μεταξὺ τῆς ἀγορᾶς κα[ὶ τοῦ λιμέ]‖νος γεγονέναι
συνεφωνεῖτο, ε[ἴτε ἔν τινι] | τῶν καιρῶν ἢ τοῦ πολέμου πε[ρι-
στάσει, εἴ]‖τε διὰ τὴν τούτων ἀμέλειαν, οἳ τ[εταγμένοι | ἦσαν . . . .

From Ephesus. This edict of the proconsul refers to a wall erected
by the Ephesians for the convenience of exacting customs dues on
goods entering the city by sea. Unfortunately the major portion
of the inscription has disappeared, but, since the wall was built by
the city, it might be inferred that the *portorium* at Ephesus was a
municipal, and not an imperial tax (Cagnat, *Les impôts indirects chez
les Romains*, 4 *ff.*). The fact, however, that the wall had fallen into
decay, and that the governor issued the edict concerning it, leaves
the question of the control of this tax in uncertainty. The *portorium*
at Palmyra was a municipal tax, but elsewhere it seems to have
been imposed by the imperial authorities (*cf.* no. 89 and pp. 122 *ff.*).

40. EPISTULA PROCONSULIS ASIAE AD CHIOS
(5–14 p. Chr.)

CIG. 2222; Cagnat, *IGRR.* 4, 943; Ditt. *Syll.*³ 785.

. . | Σταφύλου ὑπαρχόντων πρὸς τοὺς Χείων πρέσβεις, ἀνα-
γεινωσ[κόν]‖των ἐπιστολὴν ᾿Αντιστίου Οὐέτερος τοῦ πρὸ ἐμοῦ
ἀνθυπάτ[ου], | ἀνδρὸς ἐπιφανεστάτου, κατακολουθῶν τῇ καθ-
5 ολικῇ μου [προ]‖θέ[σ]ει τοῦ [τ]η[ρ]εῖν τὰ ὑπὸ τῶν πρὸ ἐμοῦ
ἀνθυπάτων γραφέντ[α, φυ]‖λάττειν καὶ τὴν ὑπὲρ τούτων φερο-
μένην ἐπιστολὴν Οὐέτε[ρος] | εὔλογον ἡγησάμην· ὕστερον δὲ
ἑκατέρου μέρους ἐξ ἀντικα[τα]‖στάσεως περὶ τῶν κατὰ μέρος
ζητημάτων ἐν(τ)υγχόντος διή[κου]‖σα καὶ κατὰ τὴν ἐμὴν συνή-
10 θειαν παρ᾿ ἑκατέρου μέρους ἐπιμε[λέσ]‖τερα γεγραμμένα ᾔτησα
ὑπομνήματα· [ἃ λ]αβὼν καὶ κατὰ τὸ ἐπι[βάλ]‖λον ἐπιστήσας
εὗρον τοῖς μὲν χρόνο(ι)ς ἀρχαιοτάτου δόγμα[τος] | συνκλήτου

ἀντισ[φρ]άγισμα, γεγονότος Λουκίῳ Σύλλᾳ τὸ δε[ύτε]|ρον
ὑπάτωι, ἐν ᾧ μαρτυ[ρηθ]εῖσι τοῖς Χείοις, ὅσα ὑπὲρ Ῥωμαίων
δι[έθη]|κάν τε Μιθριδάτην ἀνδραγαθοῦντες καὶ ὑπ' αὐτοῦ ἔπαθον
ἡ σύν[κλη]|τος εἰδικῶς ἐβεβαίωσεν ὅπως νόμοις τε καὶ ἔθεσιν 15
καὶ δικαίοις [χρῶν]|ται, ἃ ἔσχον ὅτε τῇ Ῥωμαίων (φι)λίᾳ προσ-
ῆλθον, ἵνα τε ὑπὸ μηθ' ᾧτινι[οῦν] | τύπῳ ὦσιν ἀρχόντων ἢ
ἀνταρχόντων, οἵ τε παρ' αὐτοῖς ὄντες Ῥω[μαῖ]|οι τοῖς Χείων
ὑπακούωσιν νόμοις· Αὐτοκράτορος δὲ θεοῦ υἱοῦ Σ[ε]|βαστοῦ τὸ
ὄγδοον ὑπάτου ἐπιστολὴ(ν) πρὸς Χείους γράφοντ[ος || ..]ις.εν 20
τὴν πόλιν ἐπύθ[ετο ..]

From Chios. This letter confirms the Chians in their privileges
granted them by Sulla: the right of using their own laws, customs,
and courts. Resident Romans were subjected to the jurisdiction of
the Chian court. The latter concession is unusual, as Romans were
usually tried by the governor under the principles of Roman law.
Apparently some of the proconsuls had not observed the provisions
of the decree of the senate passed under Sulla's dictatorship, and
the emperor Augustus and the present proconsul had been memo-
rialized by the Chians who jealously guarded their privileges. This
letter, therefore, furnishes evidence of the encroachment of the
governors on the privileges which autonomous states enjoyed. It
is true that the action of Antistius Vetus is apparently reversed,
but it is evident that the governor is not instructed as to the varying
status of the cities under his jurisdiction. His administration tends,
accordingly, to be uniform in policy towards all the municipalities,
until some of them choose to protest. In such cases they are required
to furnish adequate proof for their claim to special treatment (cf.
Pliny, *Epp. ad Trai.* 47, 48, 92, 93). It is for this reason that
cities, cherishing their ancient privileges, send embassies to the
emperor on his inauguration asking for confirmation of their
charters (cf. nos. 75, 130). For the autonomy of Chios see Livy,
38. 39; Appian, *Mithr.* 25. 46; Pliny, *N.H.* 5. 136; Chapot,
La prov. rom. proc. d'Asie, 114, 125.

41. TITULUS HONORARIUS
(ca. 14 p. Chr.)

CIL. III, 1741; Dessau, 938.

P. Cornelio | Dolabellae cos. | VII viro epuloni, | sodali Titiensi, ||
5 leg. pro pr. divi Augusti | et Ti. Caesaris Augusti | civitates superioris | provinciae Hillyrici.

Found at Ragusa in Dalmatia, on the probable site of Epidaurus. This is the only extant inscription concerning a *concilium* in Dalmatia. Dolabella was consul in A.D. 10 and *legatus* from A.D. 14 on (*cf.* Vell. 2. 125).

42. TITULUS SEPULCHRALIS
(p. 14 p. Chr.)

CIL. III, 5232; Dessau, 1977.

C. Iulius Vepo donatus | civitate Romana viritim | et inmunitate
5 ab divo Aug., | vivos fecit sibi et || Boniatae Antoni fil. coniugi | et suis.

Found at Celeia in Noricum. On the grant of Roman citizenship to individuals, *cf.* no. 13. For similar cases under the empire, *cf.* Dessau, 1978–1980.

43. DECRETUM CENTUMVIRORUM
(26 p. Chr.)

CIL. XI, 3805; Dessau, 6579.

Centumviri municipii Augusti Veientis | Romae in aedem Veneris Genetricis cum convenis|sent, placuit universis, dum decretum conscriberetur, | interim ex auctoritate omnium permitti ||
5 C. Iulio divi Augusti l. Geloti, qui omni tempore | municip. Veios non solum consilio et gratia adiuverit | sed etiam inpensis suis et per filium suum celebrari | voluerit, honorem ei iustissimum de-
10 cerni, ut | Augustalium numero habeatur aeque ac si eo || honore usus sit, liceatque ei omnibus spectaculis | municipio nostro bisellio proprio inter Augus|tales considere cenisque omnibus publicis | inter centumviros interesse, itemque placere | ne quod ab eo liberisque
15 eius vectigal municipii || Augusti Veientis exigeretur. |

[342]

Adfuerunt | C. Scaevius Curiatius, | L. Perperna Priscus iivir., | M. Flavius Rufus q., || T. Vettius Rufus q., | M. Tarquitius 20 Saturnin., | L. Maecilius Scrupus, | L. Favonius Lucanus, | Cn. Octavius Sabinus, || T. Sempronius Gracchus, | P. Acuvius P. f. 25 Tro., | C. Veianius Maximus, | T. Tarquitius Rufus, | C. Iulius Merula. || Actum | Gaetulico et Calvisio Sabino cos. 30

Found at Veii. Only one other epigraphical case of the use of the title *centumviri* for the members of a municipal senate is known, viz. at Cures (*CIL.* ix, p. 472). For the usual titles, *cf.* p. 56. For municipal decrees of the second and third centuries after Christ, *cf. CIL.* v, 532 and no. 146.

44. TABULA PATRONATUS
(27 p. Chr.)

CIL. v, 4919; Dessau, 6100.

M. Crasso Frugi, L. Calpurnio | Pisone cos. | iii non. Febr. | civitas Themetra ex Africa hospitium || fecit cum C. Silio C. f. 5 Fab. Aviola *eu*m | liberos posterosque eius sibi liberis | posterisque suis patronum cooptave|runt. C. Silius C. f. Fab. Aviola civitatem Theme|trensem liberos posterosque eorum || sibi liberis posterisque 10 suis in fidem | clientelamque suam recepit. | Egerunt Banno Himilis f., sufes; Azdrubal Baisillecis f., | Iddibal Bos*t*haris f., leg.

A bronze tablet found near Brixia, apparently kept in the villa of Silius Aviola. Other extant tablets record the election of Aviola in two other cities; *cf.* Dessau, 6099, 6099a. On the other hand a single city might have several *patroni*; *cf.* no. 136. On the election of priests in the colonia Genitivae Iuliae, *cf.* no. 26. Azdrubal and Iddibal are deputies to announce his election to Aviola; *cf.* no. 135 and *CIL.* ix, 3429.

45. FASTI MAGISTRATUUM MUNICIPALIUM
(p. 33 p. Chr.)

CIL. x, 1233; Dessau, 6124.

. . . .

suf. A. Plautius, L. Nonius.
T. Salvius Parianus, A. Terentius iivir.;
Sex. Aponius Proculus, Q. Nolcennius aed.

MUNICIPAL DOCUMENTS IN GREEK AND LATIN

L. Cassius Longinus, M. Vinicius cos.,   *a. p. Chr.* 30

5   suf. C. Cassius Longinus, L. Naevius Surdinus.

M. Sentius Rufus, Q. Vibiedius Sedatus iivir.;

P. Subidius Pollio, Sex. Parianus Serenus aed.

Ti. Caesar Aug. v cos.   *a. p. Chr.* 31

     suf. vii id. Mai. Faustus Cornelius Sulla, Sex. Teidius

     Catull. cos.

10   suf. k. Iul. L. Fulcinius Trio cos.

T. Oppius Proculus, M. Staius Flaccus iivir. iter. q.;

M. Atinius Florens, A. Cluvius Celer aed.

     suf. k. Oct. P. Memmius Regulus cos.

Cn. Domitius Ahenobarbus cos.   *a. p. Chr.* 32

15   suf. k. Iul. A. Vitellius cos.

M. Valerius Postumus, Q. Luceius Clemens iivir.;

C. Sentius Severus, L. Ippellius Atticus aed.

Ser. Sulpicius Galba, L. Sulla Felix cos.   *a. p. Chr.* 33

. . . .

This document contains the names of the municipal magistrates at Nola from A.D. 29 to 33 inclusive. The inscription was probably cut subsequent to A.D. 33, because in that year Galba still retained the praenomen Lucius, which later he changed to Servius; *cf. Prosop.* 3, p. 284, no. 723. The appearance of the names of the magistrates of A.D. 31 after that of the *consul suffectus* named July 1, and before that of the *suffectus* named Oct. 1, probably points to July 1 as the date of election. This conforms to the practice in the col. Gen. Iul.; *cf.* no. 26, l. 98. Not infrequently in the inscriptions the names of the duovirs precede those of the consuls; *cf., e.g., CIL.* x, 1781. For a republican list of local magistrates, *cf. CIL.* ix, 422 = Dessau, 6123.

46. LITES INTER CIERENSES ET METROPOLITANOS
(11–35 p. Chr.)

IG. ix, 2, 261; de Ruggiero, *L'arbitrato pubblico*, 31; Tod, xli.

. . . . . . διαφέ]ρωνται πρὸς ἀ[λλή]λας οὐ|[. . . . .] ΙΗ αἰτεῖται, ὅπως μεθ' ὅρκου κρυφα[ί|ως . . . . Μητ]ροπολειτῶν κρινόντων, βραβεύον|[τος . . . . . . τ]ε παρ' ὑμεῖν ὀφίλοντος, καθ'

5 ἦν καὶ τῆς κρίσ[ε||ως . . . .]ν ἠνέχθησαν μεθ' ὅρκου ψῆφοι

Κιεριεῦσ[ι | διακόσιαι ἐνενήκοντα ὀκτώ, Μητρο]πολείταις τριά-
κοντα μία, ἄκυροι πέντε. |.... [Γαΐωι Ποππ]αίωι Σαβείνωι
πρεσβευτῆι Τιβερίου Καίσαρ[ος | ὁ δεῖνα τοῦ δεῖνος, γραμμα-
τε]ὺς τῶν συνέδρων πλεῖστα χαίρειν. Ἔγρα|[ψας ἡμῖν τὴν
Κιεριέων καὶ Μητ]ροπολειτῶν ὑπόθεσιν ἣν εἶχον περὶ ὅρων,
ὅ||[τι αὐτὴν ἠξίωσας τοὺς συνέδρου]ς κρῖναι οὓς καὶ ἐδήλους μοι 10
κατ' ὄψιν ἐν Αἰδε|[ψῶι· ἐμὲ δ' εὖ ἴσθι εὐθὺς οἴκαδε ἀ]ναγαγόντα
προθεῖναι τὴν κρίσιν ἐν τῶι ἐνε|[στηκότι Θεσσαλῶν τῶν ἐν
Λα]ρίσηι συνεδρίωι τῶι ἐν τῶι Θύωι μηνί· συνελθόντω[ν | δὲ
καὶ ἀμφοτέρων ἐπὶ τὴ]ν κρίσιν καὶ λόγων ὑπ' αὐτῶν γενομένων,
ἐνηνέ|[χθαι τὰς ψήφους κρυφαίως μεθ'] ὅρκου Κιεριεῦσιν μὲν
διακοσίας ἐνενήκον[τα || ὀκτώ, Μητροπολείταις δὲ τριάκοντ]α 15
μίαν, ἀκύρους πέντε. Ταῦτα ἐπιτήδειον ἡγη|[σάμεθα γράψαι.
Ἔρρωσο. Γαΐωι Ποπ]παίωι Σαβείνωι πρεσβευτῆι Τιβερίου
Καίσαρ[ος | ὁ δεῖνα τοῦ δεῖνος, στρατη]γὸς Θεσσαλῶν χαίρειν.
Ἔγραψας κἀμοὶ καὶ το[ῖς | συνέδροις τὴν Κιεριέων τε καὶ
Μ]ητροπολιτῶν ὑπόθεσιν, ἣν εἶχον περὶ ὅρων, ὅ|[τι τὸ συνέδριον
τὴν περὶ τούτων] διάγνωσιν ἀνέπεμψεν. Γείνωσκε οὖν εἰρη-
μ[έ||νους τοὺς συνέδρους τοὺς ἐν τῶι Θύ]ωι μηνὶ καὶ ἐνηνεγ- 20
μένους μεθ' ὅρκου κρυφαί|[ως τὰς ψήφους Κιεριεῦσιν] μὲν
διακοσίας ἐνενήκοντα ὀκτώ, Μητρ[ο|πο]λείταις δὲ τριάκοντα μίαν,
ἀκύρους πέ]ντε· ταῦτα οὖν ἐπιτήδειον ἡγησ[ά|με]θα γράψαι,
ὅπως.....]ον τὸ βέβαιον ἡ κρίσις ὑπό σου λάβηι ἐπι|....

From Cierium. Gaius Poppaeus Sabinus was governor of Moesia
from A.D. 11–35. In A.D. 15 the provinces of Achaea and Macedonia
were added to his jurisdiction, being transferred from the senate
to the emperor (Tac. *Ann.* 1. 80; 6. 39). In this document we
have an example of administrative arbitration (*cf.* pp. 158 *ff.*). The
dispute between the two cities was referred by the governor to the
κοινόν of Thessaly for decision. We learn that there were at least
334 members in this assembly, each casting a single vote. It is not
known whether the two cities Cierium and Metropolis were permitted to vote in a case which affected them, but if not, we may
assume that a larger number of votes could be cast at a full session
of all the members. It is evident that some of the cities in Thessaly
sent more than one delegate to the provincial assembly, as there
could not be three hundred cities in this κοινόν. *Cf.* pp. 166 *ff.*

47. IURIS IURANDI ARITIENSIUM IN PRINCIPEM FORMULA
(37 p. Chr.)

CIL. II, 172; Dessau, 190; Bruns, 101.

C. Ummidio Durmio Quadrato, | leg(ato) C. Caesaris Germanici imp(eratoris) | pro pr(aetore). |

Ius iurandum Aritiensium. ||

5 Ex mei animi sententia, ut ego iis inimicus | ero, quos C. Caesari Germanico inimicos esse | cognovero, et si quis periculum ei salutiq(ue) eius | infert inferetque armis bello internicivo | terra
10 mariq(ue) persequi non desinam, quoad || poenas ei persolverit: neq(ue) me neque liberos meos | eius salute cariores habebo, eosq(ue), qui in | eum hostili animo fuerint, mihi hostes esse | ducam: si sciens fallo fefellerove, tum me | liberosq(ue) meos Iuppiter optimus
15 maximus ac || divus Augustus ceteriq(ue) omnes di immortales | expertem patria incolumitate fortunisque | omnibus faxint.

A.d. v idus Maias in | Aritiense oppido veteri Cn. Acerronio |
20 Proculo, C. Petronio Pontio Nigrino cos., || mag(istris) | Vegeto Tallici,. . .ibio. . .arioni.

Bronze tablet found at Aritium in Lusitania. It contains an oath taken by the residents of communities throughout the Roman world on receiving news of the accession of Gaius. A similar oath was taken by civilians when Tiberius became *princeps* (Tac. *Ann.* 1. 7). Its general form was traditional; *cf.* Livy, 22. 53. The oath of allegiance which the people of Assos took to Gaius (no. 48) was preceded by a decree of the local senate and confirmed by the local Roman *conventus*. Among the *legati* sent to Rome were four Greeks and one Roman. For an oath of allegiance to Augustus of 3 B.C., *cf.* no. 37.

48. DECRETUM ET IUSIURANDUM ASSIORUM
(37 p. Chr.)

Bruns, 102; Cagnat, *IGRR.* 4, 251; Ditt. *Syll.*³ 797.

Ἐπὶ ὑπάτων Γναίου Ἀκερρωνίου | Πρόκλου καὶ Γαίου Ποντίου Πετρω|νίου Νιγρίνου. |

Ψήφισμα Ἀσσίων γνώμηι τοῦ δήμου. ||

5 Ἐπεὶ ἡ κατ’ εὐχὴν πᾶσιν ἀνθρώποις ἐλπισθεῖσα Γαίου | Καί-

σαρος Γερμανικοῦ Σεβαστοῦ ἡγεμονία κατήνγελται, | οὐδὲν δὲ
μέτρον χαρᾶς εὕρηκ[ε]ν ὁ κόσμος, πᾶσα δὲ πόλις | καὶ πᾶν
ἔθνος ἐπὶ τὴν τοῦ θεοῦ ὄψιν ἔσ[π]ευκεν, ὡς ἂν τοῦ | ἡδίστου
ἀνθρώποις αἰῶνο[ς] νῦν ἐνεστῶτος, ‖ ἔδοξεν τῇ βουλῇ καὶ τοῖς 10
πραγματευομένοις παρ' ἡμῖν | 'Ρωμαίοις καὶ τῶι δήμωι τῶι
'Ασσίων κατασταθῆναι πρεσ|βείαν ἐκ τῶν πρώτων καὶ ἀρίστων
'Ρωμαίων τε καὶ 'Ελλή|νων τὴν ἐντευξομένην καὶ συνησθη-
σομένην αὐτῶι, | δεηθησομένην τε ἔχειν διὰ μνήμης καὶ κηδε-
μονίας ‖ τὴν πόλιν, καθὼς καὶ αὐτὸς μετὰ τοῦ πατρὸς Γερμανικοῦ | 15
ἐπιβὰς πρώτως τῆι ἐπαρχείαι τῆς ἡμετέρας πόλεως | ὑπέσχετο. |
    "Ορκος 'Ασσίων. |
    "Ομνυμεν Δία Σωτῆρα καὶ θεὸν Καίσαρα Σεβαστὸν καὶ τὴν ‖
πάτριον ἁγνὴν Παρθένον, εὐνοήσειν Γαΐωι Καίσαρι Σεβασ|τῶι 20
καὶ τῶι σύμπαντι οἴκωι αὐτοῦ, καὶ φίλους τε κρινεῖν, | οὓς ἂν
αὐτὸς προαιρῆται, καὶ ἐχθρούς, οὓς ἂν αὐτὸς προβά|ληται.
εὐορκοῦσιν μὲν ἡμῖν εὖ εἴη, ἐφιορκοῦσιν δὲ τὰ ἐναν|τία. ‖
    Πρεσβευταὶ ἐπηνγείλαντο ἐκ τῶν ἰδίων· | Γάϊος Οὐάριος 25
Γαΐου υἱὸς Οὐολτινία Κάστος | 'Ερμοφάνης Ζωΐλου, | Κτῆτος
Πισιστράτου, | Αἰσχρίων Καλλιφάνους, ‖   'Αρτεμίδωρος 30
Φιλομούσου, | οἵτινες καὶ ὑπὲρ τῆς Γαΐου Καίσαρος Σεβαστοῦ
Γερμανικοῦ | σωτηρίας εὐξάμενοι Διὶ Καπιτωλίωι ἔθυσαν τῶι
τῆς πόλε|ως ὀνόματι.

A bronze tablet found at Assos. It contains the oath taken by
the city of Assos on the accession of Gaius. For similar oaths of
loyalty, cf. nos. 37, 47. The excessive flattery in which the Greek
cities indulged, when they sent their embassies to Rome, may be
clearly seen in the tone of this decree.

49. EDICTUM CLAUDI DE CIVITATE ANAUNORUM
(46 p. Chr.)

CIL. v, 5050; Dessau, 206; Bruns, 79; Girard, p. 188; Riccobono, p. 318; de Ruggiero, *L'arbitrato pubblico*, 39.

M. Iunio Silano, Q. Sulpicio Camerino cos. | idibus Martis,
Bais in praetorio, edictum | Ti. Claudi Caesaris Augusti Germanici
propositum fuit id | quod infra scriptum est. ‖

Ti. Claudius Caesar Augustus Germanicus pont. | maxim., trib.
potest. vi, imp. xi, p. p., cos. designatus iiii, dicit: |

[347]

Cum ex veteribus controversis pendentibus aliquamdiu etiam |
temporibus Ti. Caesaris patrui mei, ad quas ordinandas | Pinarium
10 Apollinarem miserat,—quae tantum modo || inter Comenses essent
(quantum memoria refero) et | Bergaleos,—isque primum apsentia
pertinaci patrui mei, | deinde etiam Gai principatu, quod ab eo
non exigebatur | referre, non stulte quidem, neglexserit; et posteac |
15 detulerit Camurius Statutus ad me, agros plerosque || et saltus mei
iuris esse: in rem praesentem misi | Plantam Iulium amicum et
comitem meum, qui | cum, adhibitis procuratoribus meis quique
in alia | regione quique in vicinia erant, summa cura inqui|sierit et
20 cognoverit, cetera quidem, ut mihi demons||trata commentario facto
ab ipso sunt, statuat pronun|tietque ipsi permitto. |

Quod ad condicionem Anaunorum et Tulliassium et Sinduno|rum
pertinet, quorum partem delator adtributam Triden|tinis, partem
25 ne adtributam quidem arguisse dicitur, || tametsi animadverto non
nimium firmam id genus homi|num habere civitatis Romanae
originem: tamen, cum longa | usurpatione in possessionem eius
fuisse dicatur et ita permix|tum cum Tridentinis, ut diduci ab is
sine gravi splendidi municipi | iniuria non possit, patior eos in eo
30 iure, in quo esse se existima||verunt, permanere beneficio meo, eo
quidem libentius, quod | plerique ex eo genere hominum etiam
militare in praetorio | meo dicuntur, quidam vero ordines quoque
duxisse, | nonnulli allecti in decurias Romae res iudicare. |

35 Quod benificium is ita tribuo, ut quaecunque tanquam || cives
Romani gesserunt egeruntque, aut inter se aut cum | Tridentinis
alisve, rata esse iubeam, nominaque ea, | quae habuerunt antea
tanquam cives Romani, ita habere is permittam.

Bronze tablet found in 1869 in the Val di Non, probably on the
site of the principal village of the Anauni, near Trent (Tridentum),
now in Trent. The date is fixed by the opening paragraphs. This
document takes the characteristic form of an edict (*cf.* pp. 236*f.*, and
Haberleitner, *Philol.* 68 (1909), 286 *ff.*). The introductory clauses
close with the conventional phrase *imperator . . . dicit*, and the verbs
which follow are in the first person singular. Claudius used the
form of the edict very freely for his constitutions (*cf.* Suet. *Claud.*
16, *uno die viginti edicta proposuit*).

Reference is made in the edict to two separate questions. One

[348]

question has arisen out of a dispute between Comum and the Bergalei. The other concerns the relations between Tridentum on the one hand and the Anauni (modern Non), the Tulliasses (Dolas), and the Sinduni (Saône) on the other. The body of the edict (ll. 22 *ff.*) deals only with certain aspects of the second question. Why is the first incident mentioned at all? Its inclusion may be due to the well-known interest of Claudius in historical and anti-quarian matters, but mention of it here is justified in part, at least, by the historical connection between the two incidents, and by the fact that several of the legal questions arising were common to the two cases. In both instances the relation which certain Alpine tribes bore to a neighboring municipality was the fundamental point at issue. The historical connection arose from the circumstance that the facts in the case of Comum and the Bergalei had been investigated by Pinarius Apollinaris, a commissioner sent out by Tiberius, probably at the instance of Comum (*cf.* Hardy, *Three Spanish Charters*, 127, n. 9) and that the report of Apollinaris had remained in abeyance until Claudius took up the matter again and appointed a new representative in the person of Camurius Statutus, whose investigation brought to light certain puzzling legal and political questions in the relation which three other Alpine tribes bore to the *municipium* of Tridentum. One matter involved in the case of the Anauni and the two other tribes concerns a claim to Roman citizenship. That can be decided only by the emperor, and to that question his edict (ll. 22 *ff.*) is devoted. Julius Planta, the commissioner of Claudius, is authorized to settle the other points, probably in the case of the Bergalei, as well as in that of the Anauni. It was the practice of the Roman people to put hamlets and people in the tribal state under the charge of the local magistrates of a neighboring *civitas* (*cf.* pp. 10 *ff.*). This practice had been followed in the Alpine region especially (*cf.* Hardy, *op. cit.* 130, n. 19; Marquardt, *St. Verw.* 1, 7, 14), and the Anauni seem to have taken it for granted that as *attributi* of Tridentum, they were citizens of Tridentum, and, consequently, Roman citizens (*cf.* Mommsen, *Ges. Schr.* 4, 300), or that they were actually in the *territorium* of Tridentum, and for that reason were Roman citizens (*cf.* Hardy, *op. cit.* 124). In point of fact it transpires that none of the Anauni are in the "territory" of Tridentum, that some of them are *attributi* and others have no connection with the municipality (ll. 23, 24), and that even those who are *attributi* do not have the full right of Tridentine citizenship (Mommsen, *op. cit.* 4. 304 *f.*), and therefore are not Roman citizens. However, in view of the fact that they have honestly exercised these rights for a long time, and that the people of Tridentum would be seriously inconvenienced by having their marriages with the Anauni declared illegal (*cf.* Mommsen, *op. cit.* 4. 307), the emperor allows them to continue in the status which they believed was theirs.

Tridentum is called a *municipium* in the edict (l. 28). With other Transpadane towns it received Roman citizenship from Caesar. Under the empire, but later than the time of Claudius, it was made a colony (*cf. CIL.* v, 5036).

In the question which arose between Genua and the Viturii (*cf.* no. 10) only the two communities mentioned were involved. The ownership of certain land was vested either in the one community or the other. The case was a simple one of arbitration by the Roman senate through its commissioners between two communities. But here there are certain districts which, as Claudius says (l. 15), are *mei iuris*. Such domains are subject to an impost, to be paid to the procurator (*cf.* Hirschfeld, 129 *f.*), and the state or the emperor is a party to the action. There are then three possibilities: (1) the Anauni may own the land in question; (2) they may be occupying land in the *territorium* of Tridentum. In this case they must pay tribute to Tridentum, or (3) their land may belong to Rome, in which case Rome has a claim on a part of the produce from it. Having settled the central question of citizenship, Claudius delegates the decision of the other points involved to his commissioner, Julius Planta, who is instructed to call into his *consilium* (*cf.* de Ruggiero, *L'arbitrato pubblico*, 350) the procurator of the neighboring province of Raetia and the procurators of the imperial domains near at hand (ll. 16–18). For *commentario* (l. 20), *cf.* Hirschfeld, 325, n. 1. The privilege which Claudius grants to the Anauni of retaining their Roman names (ll. 36, 37) would be implied in the gift of Roman citizenship. Perhaps the special mention of this matter reflects the fastidiousness of Claudius on this point (*cf.* Suet. *Claud.* 25, *peregrinae conditionis homines vetuit usurpare Romana nomina*).

50. ORATIO CLAUDI DE IURE HONORUM GALLIS DANDO
(48 p. Chr.)

CIL. XIII, 1668; Dessau, 212; Bruns, 52; Riccobono, p. 228; Nipperdey's *Tacitus*[10], 2, 317–322.

... | mae rerum no*strarum* sit u..........| Col. 1

Equidem primam omnium illam cogitationem hominum quam | maxime primam occursuram mihi provideo, deprecor, ne | quasi novam istam rem introduci exhorrescatis, sed illa ‖ potius cogitetis, 5 quam multa in hac civitate novata sint, et | quidem statim ab origine urbis nostrae in quo*t* formas | statusque res p(ublica) nostra diducta sit. |

Quondam reges hanc tenuere urbem, nec tamen domesticis succes|soribus eam tradere contigit. Supervenere alieni et quidam exter‖ni, ut Numa Romulo successerit ex Sabinis veniens, vicinus 10 qui|dem, sed tunc externus; ut Anco Marcio Priscus Tarquinius. *Is* | propter temeratum sanguinem, quod patre Demaratho Co|rinthio natus erat et Tarquiniensi matre generosa sed inopi, | ut quae tali marito necesse habuerit succumbere, cum domi re‖pelleretur a 15 gerendis honoribus, postquam Romam migravit, | regnum adeptus est. Huic quoque et filio nepotive eius (nam et | hoc inter auctores discrepat) insertus Servius Tullius, si nostros | sequimur, captiva natus Ocresia, si Tuscos, Caeli quondam Vi|vennae sodalis fidelis-simus omnisque eius casus comes, post‖quam varia fortuna exactus 20 cum omnibus reliquis Caeliani | exercitus Etruria excessit, montem Caelium occupavit et a duce suo | Caelio ita appellita*vit*, mutatoque nomine (nam Tusce Mastarna | ei nomen erat) ita appellatus est, ut dixi, et regnum summa cum rei | p(ublicae) utilitate optinuit. Deinde postquam Tarquini Superbi mores in‖visi civitati nostrae 25 esse coeperunt, qua ipsius qua filiorum ei*us*, | nempe pertaesum est mentes regni et ad consules, annuos magis|tratus, administratio rei p(ublicae) translata est. |

Quid nunc commemorem dictaturae hoc ipso consulari impe|rium valentius repertum apud maiores nostros, quo in a*s*‖perioribus bellis 30

[351]

aut in civili motu difficiliore uterentur? | aut in auxilium plebis
creatos tribunos plebei? quid a consu|libus ad decemviros translatum
imperium, solutoque postea | decemvirali regno ad consules rusus
reditum? quid in *plu*|ris distributum consulare imperium tribunosque
35 mil*itum* || consulari imperio appellatos, qui seni et saepe octoni
crearen|tur? quid communicatos postremo cum plebe honores, non
imperi | solum sed sacerdotiorum quoque? Iam si narrem bella, a
quibus | coeperint maiores nostri, et quo processerimus, vereor ne
nimio | insolentior esse videar et quaesisse iactationem gloriae
40 pro||lati imperi ultra oceanum. Sed illoc potius revertar. Civita-
tem | . . .

(nonnulla interciderunt)

Col. II   . . .*po*test. Sane | novo m*ore* et divus Aug*ustus* av*onc*ul*us* m*eus*
et patruus Ti. | Caesar omnem florem ubique coloniarum ac muni-
cipiorum, bo|norum scilicet virorum et locupletium, in hac curia
5 esse voluit. || Quid ergo? non Italicus senator provinciali potior
est? Iam | vobis, cum hanc partem censurae meae adprobare coe-
pero, quid | de ea re sentiam, rebus ostendam. Sed ne provinciales
quidem, | si modo ornare curiam poterint, reiciendos puto. |
   Ornatissima ecce colonia valentissimaque Viennensium, quam ||
10 longo iam tempore senatores huic curiae confert! Ex qua colo|nia
inter paucos equestris ordinis ornamentum L. Vestinum fa|miliaris-
sime diligo et hodieque in rebus meis detineo, cuius libe|ri fruantur
quaeso primo sacerdotiorum gradu, post modo cum | annis promo-
15 turi dignitatis suae incrementa; ut dirum nomen la||tronis taceam,
et odi illud palaestricum prodigium, quod ante in do|mum con-
sulatum intulit, quam colonia sua solidum civitatis Roma|nae beni-
ficium consecuta est. Idem de fratre eius possum dicere, | miserabili
quidem indignissimoque hoc casu, ut vobis utilis | senator esse non
possit. || —
20   Tempus est iam, Ti. Caesar Germanice, detegere te patribus
conscriptis, | quo tendat oratio tua; iam enim ad extremos fines
Galliae Nar|bonensis venisti. | —
   Tot ecce insignes iuvenes, quot intueor, non magis sunt paeni-
tendi | senatores, quam paenitet Persicum, nobilissimum virum,
25 ami||cum meum, inter imagines maiorum suorum Allobrogici
no|men legere. Quod si haec ita esse consentitis, quid ultra desi-

[352]

dera|tis, quam ut vobis digito demonstrem, solum ipsum ultra fines |
provinciae Narbonensis iam vobis senatores mittere, quando | ex
Luguduno habere nos nostri ordinis viros non paenitet. || Timide 30
quidem, p(atres) c(onscripti), egressus adsuetos familiaresque vobis
pro|vinciarum terminos sum, sed districte iam Comatae Galliae |
causa agenda est, in qua si quis hoc intuetur, quod bello per de|cem
annos exercuerunt divom Iulium, idem opponat centum | annorum
immobilem fidem obsequiumque multis trepidis re||bus nostris plus 35
quam expertum. Illi patri meo Druso Germaniam | subigenti
tutam quiete sua securamque a tergo pacem praes|titerunt, et quidem
cum *a* census novo tum opere et inadsue|to Gallis ad bellum advo-
catus esset; quod opus quam ar|duum sit nobis, nunc cum maxime,
quamvis nihil ultra, quam || ut publice notae sint facultates nostrae, 40
exquiratur, nimis | magno experimento cognoscimus.

On a bronze tablet found at Lugudunum, now in the museum
at Lyons. It is engraved in two columns. The upper part of the
tablet is lost. In the first column, which is not printed here, the
emperor seeks to show by many illustrations that changes in
political institutions have been frequent in Roman history, and that
the Romans of early days were liberal in their treatment of foreigners,
even taking some of their rulers from beyond the limits of the city.
Lines 20–22 are commonly regarded as an apostrophe addressed
by the emperor to himself. Mommsen regards them as *verba…
senatorum acclamantium et simul oratorem prolixum irridentium*
(*E.E.* 7, 394). A résumé of the speech of Claudius is given by
Tacitus (*Ann.* 11. 24), and from this summary a few additions may
be made to the speech as preserved on the tablet. The purpose of
the emperor was to secure to the people of Gallia Comata the right
to hold office in Rome and consequently to sit in the Roman senate
(col. II, l. 31). They had been Roman citizens for many years (Tac.
Ann. 11. 23), but under the Julio-Claudian emperors the grant of
Roman citizenship to provincial cities does not seem to have carried
with it of necessity the right to hold Roman magistracies (*cf.*
Mommsen, *St. R.* 1, 490 and nn.; *ibid.* 3, 876). The only Gallic
city outside Gallia Narbonensis having this fuller privilege was
Lugudunum (col. II, l. 29), which had been established as a colony
in 43 B.C. It had been also especially favored by Claudius (*cf.*

Kornemann, *R.E.* 4, 529). The policy of admitting to the senate provincials having Roman citizenship seems to have begun with Julius Caesar (*cf.* Willems, *Le sénat de la république rom.* 1, 594 *ff.*) and is mentioned by several Latin writers (*cf.* Suet. *Caes.* 76. 80; *Bell. Afr.* 28). It was continued by the triumvirs (*cf.* Willems, *op. cit.* 1, 613), and followed by Augustus and Tiberius (col. II, ll. 1–2). Eligibility to the Roman senate was probably granted to the people of Vienna in Gallia Narbonensis by Gaius in A.D. 39 or 40 (*cf.* Kornemann, *R.E.* 4, 542) out of regard to his Viennese favorite Valerius Asiaticus, to whom Claudius refers in the words *dirum nomen* (col. II, l. 14). On Valerius Asiaticus, *cf.* Tac. *Ann.* 11. 1–3, *Prosop.* 3, 352. The liberal policy of Claudius and his predecessors which tended to convert the Roman senate from an Italian into an imperial parliament was bitterly opposed in Rome (*cf.* Tac. *Ann.* 11. 23; Seneca, *Apocol.* 3). On the *oratio principis*, *cf.* pp. 234 *ff.*

Tacitus tells us (*Ann.* 11. 23) that the initiative in seeking *ius adipiscendorum in urbe honorum* was sought by the *primores Galliae*, which leads Hirschfeld (*Kleine Schr.* 132) to the interesting suggestion that the project originated in the Gallic *concilium* and that a formal request for the privileges here mentioned was transmitted to the emperor. There is an important article on this inscription by Grupe in *Zeitschr. d. Savigny-Stift., Roman. Abteil.* 42 (1921), 31–41; *cf.* also *Archiv*, 6 (1920), 153 *ff.*

51. EDICTUM CLAUDI DE CURSU PUBLICO
(49–50 p. Chr.)

CIL. III, *S.* 1, 7251; Dessau, 214.

Ti. Claudius Caesar Aug. | *Germ*anicus pontif. max., | trib. potest. VIIII, imp. XVI, p.p., | dicit: ||

5 Cum et colonias et municipia non solum | Ita*li*ae, verum etiam provinciarum, item | civita*t*ium cuiusque provinciae lebare oneribu*s* | veh*iculo*rum praebendorum saepe tem*p*ta*v*issem | *et* c*u*m sati*s* multa
10 remedia invenisse m*ihi viderer*, || *p*otu*it ta*men nequitiae hominum non satis per ea occurri . . . .

A marble tablet found at Tegea in Arcadia. The last part of

the inscription cannot be made out. *Trib. potest.* viiii shows that the document falls between Jan. 25, A.D. 49 and Jan. 25, A.D. 50. On the conventional form of an edict, *cf.* pp. 236 *ff.* The purpose of the edict is to relieve municipalities in Italy and in the provinces from the burdens put on them by the imperial post. On the *cursus publicus, cf.* Seeck, *R.E.* 4, 1846–1863; Hirschfeld, 190–204. Under the republic no system had been organized for the carriage of either private or official letters, but Augustus stationed runners, and later vehicles, at convenient intervals along the military roads (Suet. *Aug.* 49). These wagons served for the carriage of despatches and government officials. This inscription makes it clear that the cost of this service fell on the towns through which the post passed, that the burden was heavy, and that many attempts had been made to remedy abuses. What measures Claudius proposed, we do not know. Evidently they were not effective. Complaints in Italy led Nerva to relieve towns in the peninsula from the expense (Hirschfeld, 191, n. 2). Of Hadrian we are told (*Hist. Aug. Hadr.* 7. 5), *statum cursum fiscalem instituit, ne magistratus* (sc. *municipales*) *hoc onere gravarentur.* This reform would seem to have consisted in organizing the post under the *fiscus,* but towns were not relieved from meeting the expense of the service (*cf.* however, Seeck, *R.E.* 4, 1848). Hadrian's reform only meant that local magistrates were perhaps freed from the responsibility of providing teams and wagons. Septimius Severus was the first emperor to put the cost of maintaining the post on the *fiscus* (*Hist. Aug. Sev.* 14. 2), but it was soon transferred again to the *civitates* (Seeck, *R.E.* 4, 1849), and was the source of endless complaint through the third and fourth centuries, as we may infer from the Digest and from the Codes of Theodosius and Justinian. The cost included not only the furnishing of drivers, teams, vehicles, and fodder, but the maintenance of suitable *mansiones* at regular intervals to serve as inns for official travelers. One of the noteworthy things in this edict is the fact that the central government, even in this early period, could not always make effective its desire to right the wrongs done to the cities by its own officials. For the *cursus publicus* in the fourth century, *cf.* no. 156.

MUNICIPAL DOCUMENTS IN GREEK AND LATIN

52. DECRETUM RHODIORUM
(51 p. Chr.)

Cagnat, *IGRR.* 4, 1123; *IG.* XII, 1, 2, *et corrigenda*, p. 206.

.... [Ε]ὖ[χάρ]ης β', Μνασαῖο[ς ......, | ....]
Πύθωνος, Ἀριστογένης Πάπου, Ἀρ........|..........λο-
χου, Πείσαρχος Τειμασάρχου, Πολύχαρμος [Φίλωνος], ...|
.... τὰ εὐκταιότατα ἐνήνεκται τᾶι πόλει ἀποκρίματα ....||
5 [Ἀντί]πατρον καὶ Διονύσιον Ἀρτεμιδώρου [προ]τετείμακ[ε]ν
πάσ[ας τὰς τειμὰς..........,ἀνδριάν|των] ἀναθέσεις,δεδόχθαι
τᾶι βουλᾶι καὶ τῶι δάμωι,κυρωθέντος τοῦδε το[ῦ ψαφίσ]ματος,
[τὰ ὀνόματα ἀναγραφῆναι ὑπὸ τῶν | στρ]αταγῶν ἐπὶ βάσιος
λίθου λαρτίου ἐν τῶι τεμένει τοῦ Ἁλίου ὑπὲρ ...|....ου καὶ
Ἀντιπάτρου Ἀρτεμιδώρου καὶ Διονυσίου Ἀρτεμιδώρου ...|
.......στράτου, Κρατίδαν Φαρνάκευς, Ἀλεξινβροτίδαν Χρυ-
10 σίππου .||.. Δαμαγόραν β', Μοιραγένη Τειμοδίκου, Δαμόχαριν
Γοργία,.....|......, [Πολ]ύχαρμον Φίλωνος, Εὐκλῆ Ἀγη-
σάρχου, Εὐθρεπ[τ]ίδαν ...., [ἀποστα|λέντας ποτὶ]
Τιβέριον Κλαύδιον Καίσαρα Γερβανικὸν Αὐτοκράτορα....,
[ἀπο|δοθείσ]ας τᾶι πόλει τᾶς πατρίου πολιτείας καὶ τῶν νόμων
ὑπὸ τῶν ....[Νέ|ρω]νος Καίσαρος καὶ μαρτυρηθέντων
τῶν ἀνδρῶν τὰν ποτὶ τὰν πόλιν εὔν[οιαν]..........

This fragmentary inscription from Rhodes records the honors
conferred upon the ambassadors sent to Rome at the time when the
youthful Nero pleaded for the return of liberty to the Rhodians
(Suet. *Claud.* 25; *Nero*, 7).

53. TITULUS HONORARIUS
(p. 54 p. Chr.)

Compt. rend. de l'acad. d. inscr. et bel. lettr. 1915, 396; *An. ép.*
1916, no. 42.

   M. Val(erio), Bostaris | f(ilio), Gal(eria tribu), Severo, | aedili,
sufeti, IIvir(o), | flamini primo || in municipio suo, | praef(ecto)
5 auxilior(um) adversus Aedemo|nem oppressum bello. | Huic ordo
municipii Volub(ilitanorum), ob me|rita erga rem pub(licam) et
legatio||nem bene gestam, qua ab divo | Claudio civitatem Ro|manam
10 et conubium cum pere|grinis mulieribus immunitatem | annor(um)
15 x incolas, bona civium bel|||lo interfectorum quorum here|des non

extabant suis impetra|vit. | Fabia Bira, Izeltae f(ilia), uxor, indul-ge|ntissimo viro, honore usa, impensam || remisit | et d(e) s(ua) 20 p(ecunia) d(edit) d(e)dic(avit).

Found at Volubilis in Mauretania Tingitana. It is subsequent to A.D. 54 because Claudius is called *divus*. Towards the end of the reign of Caligula the people of Mauretania Tingitana rose in revolt under Aedemon because of the murder of their king by the emperor; *cf.* Pliny, *N.H.* 5. 1. 11. This uprising was suppressed by Severus. It was probably in recognition of this service that Claudius granted to the people of Volubilis the favors recorded here. The town is made a *municipium* with immunity from imperial taxation for ten years (*cf. Mus. Belge*, 28 (1924), 103 *ff.*). The citizens are given the right of intermarriage (*conubium*) with foreign women. Usually the right of *conubium* was granted to *peregrini*, and it is probable that this provision merely recognized marriages already contracted between citizens of Volubilis and women of other towns in order that their children may have the status of Roman citizens. The new municipality is given the property which had belonged to those of its citizens who had perished in the war and had died intestate. Ordinarily the estates of those who died without heirs and without leaving a will became imperial property (*cf.* Cuq, *Journal des savants*, 1917, 481 *ff.*). The interpretation of *incolas* in line 14 is uncertain. Most editors read *incolis* and assume that the benefits granted by Claudius were conferred upon aliens. De Sanctis (*Rivista di filologia*, 53 (1925), 372 *ff.*), however, retains the form as it occurs on the stone, and advances the theory that aliens resident in Volubilis were subject to a tax (*in-tributio*) which was now to be paid into the municipal treasury. For the *incolae attributi* in a Roman colony he refers to the charter of Urso (no. 26, chap. 103) where Mommsen reads incolaeque attributi*que*. The grant illustrates the Roman policy of encouraging the growth of the cities and of bringing indigenous peoples under Roman influence, as well as the generosity of Claudius in bestowing Roman citizenship. Severus had been sufes, duovir, and first flamen in Volubilis. As Cuq has shown, the introduction of the cult of the emperor, and the consequent appointment of a flamen, follow

[357]

MUNICIPAL DOCUMENTS IN GREEK AND LATIN

immediately on the erection of a *municipium* (*op. cit.* 497). Severus was probably sufes in the peregrine city, and became duovir and flamen when Volubilis was made a *municipium*. The title sufes accords with the Punic name of the father and father-in-law of Severus. On the sufes, cf. Gsell, *Histoire ancienne de l'Afrique du Nord*, 2, 193 *ff*. For similar *legationes*, cf. nos. 115, 126, and *An. ép.* 1916, no. 120. This inscription is also discussed in *Comptes rendus*, 1916, 261 *ff*., 284 *f.*; 1918, 227 *ff*.; 1920, 339 *ff*.; de Sanctis, *Atti della reale accademia delle scienze di Torino*, 53 (1918), 453 *ff*.; 54 (1919), 329 *ff*.; Weiss, *Zeitschr. d. Savigny-Stift.*, *Roman. Abteil.* 1921, 639 *ff*. Other inscriptions from Volubilis testify to the continued favor of the emperors, *e.g. An. ép.* 1916, no. 100.

54. EPISTULA IMPERATORIS NERONIS AD RHODIOS
(55 p. Chr.)

Cagnat, *IGRR.* 4, 1124; Ditt. *Syll.*³ 810.

['Επ' ἱερ]έως Δ[ιογέ]νευς, πρυτανίων τῶν σὺν | Μενεκλεῖ τῷ
'Α[ρ]χαγόρα, γραμμα[τε]ύοντος | βουλᾶς Νεικασιμάχου Δια-
[φ]άνου, καθ' ὑ(οθεσίαν δὲ) 'Αρχεδάμ[ου, ἁ] ἐπιστολὰ ἁ ἀπο-
5 σταλεῖσα ὑπὸ Νέρωνος ‖ Κλαυδίου Καίσαρος Πεταγειτνύου κζ'· |
[Νέρων] Κλαύδιος, θεοῦ Κλαυδίου υἱός, Τιβερίου Καίσ[α]‖ρος
Σεβαστοῦ καὶ Γερμανικοῦ Καίσαρος ἔγγονος, θε|οῦ Σεβαστοῦ
ἀπόγονος, Καῖσαρ Σ[εβ]αστὸς Γερμανι|κός, ἀρχιερεύς, δημαρ-
10 χικῆς ἐξουσίας, αὐτοκρά‖τωρ, 'Ροδίων ἄρχουσι βουλῇ [δή]μῳ
χαίρειν. |
Οἱ πρέσβεις ὑμῶν, οὓς ἐπὶ τῇ ψευδῶς ἐπι[σ]τολῇ | πρὸς ὑμᾶς
κομισθείσῃ τῷ τῶν ὑπάτων ὀνόματι | ταραχθέντες πρός με
ἐπέμψατε, καὶ τὸ ψήφισμα [ἁ]‖πέδοσαν καὶ περὶ τῶν θυσιῶν
15 ἐδήλωσαν ἃς ἐνετε[ί]‖λασθε αὐτοῖς ὑπὲρ τῆς πανοικίου μου ὑγείας
καὶ | τῆς ἐν τῇ ἡγεμ[ο]νίᾳ διαμονῆς ἐπιτελέσαι τῷ κατ' ἐ|ξοχὴν
παρ' ἡμεῖν τειμωμένῳ θεῷ Διὶ Καπετωλίῳ, | περί τ' ὧν ἐπεστάλ-
κειτε αὐτοῖς πρὸς τὴν τῆς πόλεως | δημοκρατίαν διαφερόντων
20 ἐνεφάνισαν διὰ Κ[λαυ]‖δίου Τειμοστράτου τοῦ ἀρχιπρεσβευτοῦ,
σπου|δαίῳ πάθει τοὺς ὑπὲρ ὑμῶν ἐπ' ἐμοῦ ποιησαμένων | λόγους,
ἀνδρὸς κ[ἀμ]οὶ ἐπὶ τῷ κρατ[ί]στῳ διὰ τ[ὴ]ν ἀνανέω|σιν τῶν πρὸς
ἡμᾶς αὐτῷ δικαίων ὑπαρχόντων γνωρί|μου καὶ παρ' ὑμεῖν ἐν τοῖς
25 ἐπιφανεστάτοις καταριθμου[μέ]‖νου. 'Εγὼ οὖν ἀπὸ τῆς πρώτης
ἡλικίας εὐνοϊκῶς πρὸς τὴ[ν πό]‖λιν ὑμῶν δι[α]κείμενος . .

From Rhodes. This letter is included because of the reference to the restoration of liberty to the Rhodians by Claudius when Nero pleaded their case before the senate (Suet. *Nero* 7; Tac. *Ann.* 12. 58). The Rhodians had, through internal dissensions or unwise alliances, suffered many changes in their relations to Rome. Tacitus says that their liberty had often been taken away or restored (*libertas saepe adempta aut firmata*). *Cf.* Chapot, *La prov. rom. proc. d'Asie,* 119 *f.*; no. 51.

55. DE PRAEDIIS PUBLICIS GORTYNIORUM
(64 p. Chr.)

Ἀρχαιολογικὸν Δελτίον, 2 (1916), 6.

Ex auctoritate | Neronis Cludi (*sic*) | Caesaris Aug. Ger|manici pontif. ‖ maxi., trib. pot. xi, | imp., cos iiii, p.p. et | ex s. c. | L. 5 Turpilius Dexter | proc. pr*aedia* *p*ublica ‖ Gortunio*rum* *p*leraqu|e 10 a privatis occupata | *restit*uit termin|avitque.

Found at Gortyn in Crete. The examination of the titles of Gortynian lands was authorized by the emperor in accordance with a decree of the senate. This procedure was probably due to the fact that Gortyn was in a senatorial province. The occupation of public lands by private citizens must have been of frequent occurrence, but this is the only inscription which bears directly upon the practice. The alienation of public lands was strictly forbidden in the charter of Urso (*cf.* no. 26, chap. 82).

56. ORATIO IMPERATORIS NERONIS DE GRAECORUM LIBERTATE
(67 p. Chr.)

IG. vii, 2713; Ditt. *Syll.*[3] 814.

Αὐτοκράτωρ Καῖσαρ λέγει. Τῆς εἴς με εὐνοί|ας τε καὶ εὐσε-βείας ἀμείψασθαι θέλων τὴν εὐγε|νεστάτην Ἑλλάδα κελεύω πλείστους καθ᾽ ὅ[σ]ο[ν] | ἐνδέχεται ἐκ ταύτης τῆς ἐπαρχείας παρῖναι ‖ ἱς Κόρινθον τῇ πρὸ τεσσάρων καλανδῶν Δε|κεμβρίων. | 5

Συνελθόντων τῶν ὄχλων ἐν ἐκκλησίᾳ προσεφώ|νησεν τὰ ὑπο-γεγραμμένα. |

Ἀπροσδόκητον ὑμεῖν, ἄνδρες Ἕλληνες, δωρεάν, ‖ εἰ καὶ μηδὲν 10 παρὰ τῆς ἐμῆς μεγαλοφροσύνης | ἀνέλπιστον χαρίζομαι τοσαύ-

MUNICIPAL DOCUMENTS IN GREEK AND LATIN

την ὅσην οὐκ ἐχωρή|σατε αἰτεῖσθαι· πάντες οἱ τὴν Ἀχαΐαν καὶ
τὴν ἕως | νῦν Πελοπόννησον κατοικοῦντες Ἕλληνες | λάβετε
15 ἐλευθερίαν, ἀνισφορίαν, ἣν οὐδ᾽ ἐν τοῖς εὐτυ||χεστάτοις ὑμῶν
πάντες χρόνοις ἔσχετε· | ἢ γὰρ ἀλλοτρίοις ἢ ἀλλήλοις ἐδουλεύ-
σατε. | Εἴθε μὲν οὖν ἀκμαζούσης τῆς Ἑλλάδος παρειχό|μην
ταύτην τὴν δωρεάν, ἵνα μου πλείονες ἀπολ|αύωσι τῆς χάριτος·
20 δι᾽ ὃ καὶ μέμφομαι τὸν αἰῶνα || προδαπανήσαντά μου τὸ μέγεθος
τῆς χάριτος· | καὶ νῦν δὲ οὐ δι᾽ ἔλεον ὑμᾶς, ἀλλὰ δι᾽ εὔνοιαν
εὐερ|γετῶ, ἀμείβομαι δὲ τοὺς θεοὺς ὑμῶν, ὧν καὶ διὰ | γῆς καὶ διὰ
θαλάττης αἰεί μου προνοουμένων πε|πείραμαι, ὅτι μοι τηλικαῦτα
25 εὐεργετεῖν παρέσχον· || πόλεις μὲν γὰρ καὶ ἄλλοι ἠλευθέρωσαν
ἡγεμόνες, | [Νέρων δὲ μόνος κα]ὶ ἐπαρχείαν.

From Acraephia (modern Karditza) in Greece. This document
includes the edict of Caesar summoning the Greeks to Corinth,
the proclamation which he issued there regarding the freedom of
Greece, and a decree passed by the Acraephians (omitted here),
dedicating an altar and offering sacrifices for the emperor. The
senate was given the province of Sardinia to compensate for the
loss of revenue derived from Greece, which was, by this proclamation,
relieved from the payment of tribute. The prodigal gift of Nero was
withdrawn by Vespasian (Pausanias, 7. 17. 2; Suet. *Vesp.* 8). The
gratitude of the Acraephians was short-lived, for they carefully
erased Nero's name on the inscription after his death.

57. DECRETUM PETRONI ET PUPI DE
FINIBUS SAGALASSENSIUM
(54–68 p. Chr.)

de Ruggiero, *L'arbitrato pubblico*, 40; Cagnat, *IGRR.* 3, 335;
Ditt. *Or. Gr.* 538.

Ἐξ ἐπιστολῆ[ς] θε|οῦ Σεβασ[τ]οῦ | Γερμανι[κοῦ Κα]ίσαρος |
5 Κόϊντος Πετρώνιο||ς Οὔμβ(ερ) πρεσβευτὴς | καὶ ἀντιστράτηγος
Νέρω|[ν]ος Κλαυδίου Καίσαρος | Σεβαστοῦ Γερμανικοῦ, | [καὶ]
10 Λο[ύκι]ος Πούπιος Πραί||ση[ς ἐπί]τροπος Ν[έρ]ωνος | Κλα[υ-
δ]ίου [Κ]αίσ[αρ]ος Σε|[βαστ]οῦ Γε[ρ]μανικοῦ ὡ|ροθέτησαν
15 τὰ μὲν ἐν | δεξιᾶι εἶναι Σαγαλασσέων, || τὰ δὲ ἐν ἀριστερᾶι
κώ|μης Τυμβριανασσο[ῦ..] | Νέρωνος Κλαυδίου Καίσαρος |
[Σεβαστοῦ Γ]ερμ[ανικοῦ ....]

[360]

"The stone containing this inscription was so placed that the reader, looking north, had on his right hand, eastward, Sagalassian territory, and on his left hand, westward, the imperial estate named Tymbrianassus" (Ramsay, *A.J.A.* 4 (1888), 267). The decision recorded on this stone settled a boundary dispute between the city of Sagalassus and an imperial estate to which the village of Tymbrianassus belonged. On instructions issued by the emperor, the *legatus* of the emperor in Galatia and the imperial procurator acted as arbiters. Sagalassus was once a *civitas foederata* (Marquardt, *St. Verw.* 1, 75; *cf.* Cagnat, *IGRR.* 3, 350, 352, 353), but was brought under Roman administration before the time of Strabo (Strabo, 12. 6. 5, p. 569). It is possible that her privileges had been abridged for the same reasons which had led to the change of status of the Rhodians (*cf.* no. 54). Petronius was *legatus* of Galatia early in the reign of Nero (*Prosop.* 3, no. 238) and Pupius was procurator of that province in the reign of both Claudius and Nero (*CIG.* 3991, *add.* p. 1108).

58. DECRETUM PROCONSULIS SARDINIAE DE FINIBUS PATULCENSIUM ET GALILLENSIUM
(69 p. Chr.)

CIL. x, 7852; Dessau, 5947; Bruns, 71*a*; Girard, p. 179; Riccobono, p. 256; Mommsen, *Ges. Schr.* 5, 325 *ff.*; de Ruggiero, *L'arbitrato pubblico*, 43.

Imp. Othone Caesare Aug. cos. xv k. Apriles | descriptum et recognitum ex codice ansato L. Helvi Agrippae procons(ulis), quem protulit Cn. Egnatius | Fuscus scriba quaestorius, in quo scriptum fuit it quod infra scriptum est tabula v c(apitibus) VIII | et VIIII et X: III idus Mart. L. Helvius Agrippa proco(n)s(ul) causa cognita pronuntiavit: || cum pro utilitate publica rebus iudicatis stare con- 5 veniat, et de causa Patulcensi|um M. Iuventius Rixa vir ornatissimus procurator Aug. saepius pronuntiaverit, fi|nes Patulcensium ita servandos esse, ut in tabula ahenea a M. Metello ordinati | essent, ultimoque pronuntiaverit, Galillenses frequenter retractantes controver|sia*m* nec parentes decreto suo se castigare voluisse, sed respectu clementiae optumi || maximique principis contentum esse 10 edicto admonere, ut quiescerent et rebus | iudicatis starent et intra

k. Octobres primas de praedis Patulcensium recederent vacuam|que possessionem traderent; quodsi in contumacia perseverassent, se in auctores | seditionis severe anim*a*dversurum; et post ea Caecilius Simplex vir clarissi|mus, ex eadem caussa aditus a Galillensibus
15 dicentibus: tabulam se ad eam rem || pertinentem ex tabulario principis adlaturos, pronuntiaverit, humanum esse | dilationem probationi dari, et in k. Decembres trium mensum spatium dederit, in|tra quam diem nisi forma allata esset, se eam, quae in provincia esset, secuturum. |

Ego quoque aditus a Galillensibus excusantibus, quod nondum forma allata esset, in | k. Februarias quae p(roximae) f(uerunt) spatium dederim, et mora*m* illis possessoribus intellegam esse iu-
20 cun||dam: Galilenses ex finibus Patulcensium Campanorum, quos per vim occupaverant, intra k. | Apriles primas decedant. Quodsi huic pronuntiationi non optemperaverint, sciant, | se longae contumaciae et iam saepe denuntiatae animadversioni obnoxios | futuros. In consilio fuerunt: M. Iulius Romulus leg. pro pr., T. Atilius Sabinus q. | pro pr., M. Stertinius Rufus f., Sex. Aelius Modestus,
25 P. Lucretius Clemens, M. Domitius || Vitalis, M. Lusius Fidus, M. Stertinius Rufus. | Signatores: Cn. Pompei Ferocis. Aureli | Galli. M. Blossi Nepotis. C. Cordi Felicis. L. Vigelli Crispini. L. Valeri Fausti. M. Luta|ti Sabini. L. Coccei Genialis. L. Ploti Veri. D. Veturi Felicis. L. Valeri Pepli.

On a bronze tablet found in 1866 in Sardinia. This is a decree of the proconsul L. Helvius Agrippa settling a dispute concerning land of two peoples of Sardinia. The quarrel had lasted from 114 B.C. to A.D. 69. Four steps in the adjudication of the matter are recorded in the document: the decisions, (1) of the proconsul Metellus in 114 B.C. (l. 7), (2) of M. Iuventius Rixa, procurator in A.D. 66–67 (ll. 12 *f.*), (3) of the proconsul Caecilius Simplex (ll. 13 *ff.*), and (4) of the proconsul L. Helvius Agrippa (ll. 20 *ff.*). Metellus had awarded the lands in dispute to the Patulcenses, but the Galillenses continued to hold them by force (l. 20). Rixa confirmed the decision of Metellus and ordered the Galillenses to vacate the territory in question before a fixed date, or to be adjudged *auctores seditionis* (ll. 12 *f.*). Simplex granted a delay of two months, from October 1 to December 1, in order that the Galillenses might obtain a copy

[362]

of the decree of Metellus from the *tabularium principis*. Agrippa continued the respite for two months more, but since the Galillenses did not submit the *forma* from Rome, he issued this decree, in accordance with the *forma* in the province, on Mar. 13 (l. 4), and a copy of it was furnished on Mar. 18 (l. 1) by Cn. Egnatius Fuscus, the *scriba quaestorius* of the provincial governor (Mommsen, *St. R.* 1, 348, n. 2; 349, n. 2), to the Patulcenses, who had it inscribed on this tablet. Sardinia was in charge of imperial procurators up to A.D. 67, when it was turned over to the senate (Pausanias, 7. 17. 3). Rixa, probably the last procurator, was succeeded by the proconsul Simplex, whom Agrippa followed. Mommsen is of the opinion that a governor did not have the power to settle a question like this one in Sardinia, but that it had to be referred to the emperor. However that may be, petitions seem to have been sent to the emperor, and probably the delay granted by Rixa was made at the suggestion of the emperor (ll. 8 *ff.*). Strangely enough the copy of the decree of Metellus in the *tabularium principis* is to be secured by the Galillenses, not by the governor. Agrippa has eight men in his *consilium* (ll. 23 *ff.*). At the head of the list stand his *legatus pro praetore* and his *quaestor pro praetore*. The copy is in tablet v, chapp. VIII–X, in the *codex ansatus* of Agrippa, which is produced for the purpose of making the copy by his *scriba quaestorius* (ll. 2 *ff.*). It is signed by eleven witnesses (ll. 25 *ff.*), whose names stand in the genitive on the bronze tablet, because on the copy they were probably preceded by seals. In ll. 8–9 the engraver should have cut *controversiam* and in l. 19 *moram*. Outside of the literature cited in the heading, *cf.* also Karlowa, 1, 818 *ff.* On the *decreta*, *cf.* p. 239, n. 4. On arbitration, *cf.* pp. 152 *ff.*

59. RESCRIPTUM VESPASIANI AD VANACINOS
(ca. 72 p. Chr.)

CIL. x, 8038; Bruns, 80; Girard, p. 190; Riccobono, p. 320.

Imp. Caesar Vespasianus Augustus | magistratibus et senatoribus | Vanacinorum salutem dicit. | Otacilium Sagittam, amicum et procu‖ratorem meum, ita vobis praefuisse, | ut testimonium vestrum 5 mereretur, | delector. | De controversia finium, quam ha|betis cum Marianis, pendenti ex ‖ is agris, quos a procuratore meo | Publilio 10

Memoriale emistis, ut | finiret Claudius Clemens procu|rator meus,
15 scripsi ei et mensorem | misi. || Beneficia tributa vobis ab divo |
Augusto post septimum consula|tum, quae in tempora Galbae re-
20 ti|nuistis, confirmo. | Egerunt legati || Lasemo Leucani f. sacerd(os)
Aug(usti), | Eunus Tomasi f. sacerd(os) Augusti, | C. Arruntio
Catellio Celere, M. | Arruntio Aquila cos. IIII idus Octobr. |

A bronze tablet found in Corsica. The letter of the emperor
not only provided for the settlement of a territorial dispute with
the colonia Mariana (*cf.* Abbott, *Class. Phil.* 10 (1915), 374), but
it also confirmed certain privileges granted by Augustus, which had
been allowed to lapse in the time of Galba. On the settlement of
territorial disputes, *cf.* pp. 154 *ff.* On the form of a rescript, *cf.*
pp. 237 *ff.*

60. TITULUS SACER
(76 p. Chr.)

CIL. II, 1610; Dessau, 1981.

Apollini Aug. | municip*es* Igabrenses | beneficio imp. Caesaris
5 Aug. Vespasiani | c. R. c. cum suis per h*o*n*o*rem || Vespasiano VI
cos., M. Aelius M. fil. Niger aed. | d. d.

Found on the site of Igabrum in Baetica. Vespasian showed
special favor to Spain, perhaps because of its early adherence to
his cause; *cf.* Tac. *Hist.* 2. 67, 86, 97; 3. 44. Probably in 74 he
conferred *Latium minus* on it. To certain individuals and to certain
communities he granted Roman citizenship; *cf.* Weynand, *R.E.*
6, 2659 *f.*, 2661, 2681. Furthermore, in the inscriptions there
are ninety cases in which the names of Spanish towns, the enrolment
of their citizens in the Flavian tribe, Quirina, or the application
of the epithet *municipium Flavium* probably indicate a remodelling
by Vespasian; *cf.* McElderry, *Journ. Rom. Studies*, 8 (1918), 68,
78. Altogether under Vespasian at least four hundred communities
received new charters; *cf.* McElderry, *loc. cit.* 78. On Vespasian's
grant to the Saborenses, *cf.* no. 61. His liberal policy in Spain was
followed by Domitian, who granted charters to several cities; *cf.*
nos. 64, 65. *C. R. c.* in our inscription is an abbreviation of *civitatem
Romanam consecuti.*

FROM ITALY AND THE PROVINCES

61. EPISTULA VESPASIANI AD SABORENSES
(78 p. Chr.)

CIL. II, 1423; Dessau, 6092; Bruns, 81; Girard, p. 190; Riccobono, p. 320.

Imp. Caes. Vespasianus Aug. pon|tifex maximus, tribuniciae | potestatis VIIII, imp. XIIX, consul | VIII, p. p., salutem dicit IIII viris et || decurionibus Saborensium. | Cum multis difficultatibus 5 infirmita|tem vestram premi indicetis, per|mitto vobis oppidum sub nomine meo, ut | voltis, in planum extruere. Vecti||galia, quae ab 10 divo Aug. accepisse dici|tis, custodio; si qua nova adicere vol|tis, de his procos. adire debebitis, ego | enim nullo respondente constitu|- ere nil possum. Decretum vestrum || accepi VIII ka*l.* August. 15 Legatos dimi|si IIII ka*l.* easdem. Valete. | IIviri C. Cornelius Severus et M. Septimi|us Severus publica pecunia in aere | ¡inci- derunt.

Bronze tablet found at Cañete in Baetica, Spain, in the sixteenth century, and now lost. The titles fix the date as in the latter half of A.D. 78. Vespasian permits the Saborenses to rebuild their town on a new site in the plain, with the title Flavia. The inscription is important as attesting imperial control over municipal taxation, and as showing the procedure which a town of this class must follow before laying new taxes. The central government required munici- palities to submit to it their plans for new imposts, for fear its own sources of revenue would be diminished by local taxation. Whether the *vectigalia* referred to here took the form of an octroi, as at Palmyra (*cf.* no. 89; p. 140, n. 2; Dessau, *Hermes*, 19 (1884), 486–533), or not, it is impossible to say (*cf.* Liebenam, *St. Verw.* 22; Marquardt, *St. Verw.* 1, 157, n. 5). To Stratonicea, a newly- founded city, Hadrian even turned over a tax which had previously been paid to the *fiscus* (*cf.* no. 83). The title Flavia follows about four years after the granting of Latin rights to all towns in Spain (*cf.* Plin. *N.H.* 3. 3. 30). On Vespasian's reconstruction of Spain, *cf.* no. 60.

62. LEX DE OFFICIIS ET HONORIBUS FLAMINIS
PROVINCIAE NARBONENSIS
(69–79 p. Chr.)

CIL. xii, 6038; Dessau, 6964; Riccobono, p. 159; Bruns, 29; Carette, *Les assemblées prov. de la Gaule rom.* 445 *ff.*

.........Narbone.............*flamen* | *cum rem divinam faciet sacrifica*bitque, lictores *qui magistratibus apparent, ei apparento.* |
..........*secundum lege*m iusque eius provinciae............
....|.........ei in decurionibus senatuve *sententiae dicendae*
5 *signandique...item* ‖............*inter decuriones* senatoresve subsellio primo spectan*di ludos publicos ius potestasque esto.* | ....
*uxor fla*minis veste alba aut purpurea vestita *festis diebus.*........
....|.......neve invita iurato neve corpus hominis mor*tui attingito neve* | ....*nisi necessa*rii hominis erit eique spectaculis publicis eius pr*ovinciae loco....interesse liceto.* |
10 De honoribus eius qui flamen *fuer*it. ‖ *Si qui flamen fu*erit adversus hanc legem nihil fecerit, tum is qui flamen erit *cum primum poterit ad legatos provinciae referto* | *iique per tabell*as iurati decernant, placeatne ei qui flamonio abierit permitti st*atuam sibi ponere. Cui ita decreverint* | *ius esse sta*tuae ponendae nomenque suum patrisque et unde sit et quo anno *flam*en *fuerit inscribendi, ei* | *Narbo*ne intra fines eius templi statuae ponendae ius esto, nisi cui imperator *Caesar Augustus interdixerit* (?). *Eidem* | in curia sua et concilio provinciae
15 Narbonesis inter sui ordinis secundum *legem*...... ‖ sententiae dicendae signandique ius esto, item spectaculo publico in provincia *edendo inter decuriones interesse prae*|textato eisque diebus, quibus, cum flamen esset, sacrificium fecerit, ea veste p*ublice uti, qua in eo faciendo usus est.* |
Si flamen in civitate esse des*ierit.* | Si flamen in civitate esse desierit, neque ei subrogatus erit, tum uti quis*que*...... | in triduo quo certior factus erit et poterit, Narbo*ne* sacra facito *omniaque*
20 *secundum hanc legem per reliquam* ‖ partem eius anni eo ordine habeto, quo annuorum flamin*um habentur, eique si ea fecerit per dies non minus* | xxx, siremps lex ius causaque esto, quae flamini Augus*tali ex hac lege facto erit.* |
Quo loco concilium *provinciae habendum sit.* | Qui in concilium

provinciae convenerint N*arbonem, ibi id habento. Si quid extra Narbonem finesve Narbone|*sium concilio habito actum erit, id ius rat*umque ne esto* (?) ||

De pecu*nia sacris destinata.* | Qui flamonio abierit, is ex ea pe- 25 cunia *quae sacris destinata erit, quod eius superfuerit, statu*|as imaginesve imperatoris Caes*aris Augusti*.......*arbitratu*(?) *eius qui eo anno pro*|vinciae praeerit intra idem t*emplum dedicato*...... *seque omnia sicut hac lege cautum est de* | ea re, fecisse apud eum qui rat*iones provinciae putabit*......*probato*. ||.....templ.......... 30

Bronze tablet found in 1888 at Narbonne, now in the Louvre. The upper left hand and the lower right hand corners are lost; see facsimile in Carette, *op. cit.* 445. Perhaps the inscription belongs to the reign of Vespasian; *cf.* Krascheninnikof, *Philol.* 53 (1894), 161 *ff.* Of most interest to one who is studying the *concilia* are the paragraphs beginning *de honoribus eius* and *quo loco concilium.* From the first paragraph it is clear that the *concilium* meets under the presidency of the flamen, who takes the initiative in laying the business of the meeting before the *legati,* or representatives of the several cities. In this important matter they vote by secret ballot, as the senators at Urso and Malaca did in similar circumstances (*cf.* nos. 26 and 64), and under oath. Probably on ordinary matters an oral vote was taken, without an oath. From the fact that the right of the emperor to interpose a veto in this case is set forth in the law, we may infer with probability that he rarely intervened (*cf.* no. 97). From the paragraph beginning *quo loco concilium* it seems highly probable that the assembly met in the temple of Rome and Augustus, remains of which have been found at Narbonne, and, if Mommsen's restoration at the end of this paragraph is correct, the *concilium,* like the Roman senate, could not legally meet outside the limits of the city.

63. EPISTULA DOMITIANI AD FALERIENSES
(82 p. Chr.)

CIL. IX, 5420; Bruns, 82; Girard, p. 191; Riccobono, p. 321.

Imp. Caesar divi Vespasiani f. | Domitianus Augustus | pontifex max., trib. potest., imp. II, | cos. VIII designat. VIIII, p. p., salutem dicit || IIII viris et decurionibus Faleriensium ex Piceno. | 5

Quid constituerim de subsicivis cognita causa | inter vos et Firmanos, ut notum haberetis, | huic epistulae subici iussi. |

10   P. Valerio Patruino.........cos. || xiiii k. Augustas. |

Imp. Caesar divi Vespasiani f. Domitianus | Aug. adhibitis utriusque ordinis splen|didis viris cognita causa inter Fale|rienses 15 et Firmanos pronuntiavi quod || suscriptum est. |

Et vetustas litis, quae post tot annos | retractatur a Firmanis adversus | Falerienses, vehementer me movet, | cum possessorum 20 securitati vel mi||nus multi anni sufficere possint, | et divi Augusti, diligentissimi et in|dulgentissimi erga quartanos suos | principis, 25 epistula, qua admonuit | eos, ut omnia subpsiciva sua collige||rent et venderent, quos tam salubri | admonitioni paruisse non dubito; | propter quae possessorum ius confirmo. | Valete.

D(atum) xi k. Aug. in Albano, | agente curam T. Bovio Vero, || 30 legatis P. Bovio Sabino, | P. Petronio Achille.—D(ecreto) d(ecurionum) p(ublice).

Bronze tablet found at Falerio in Picenum in 1595, now lost. Domitian's name in ll. 2 and 11 and that of the second consul in l. 9 have been cut off. The phrase *adhibitis utriusque ordinis splendidis viris* (ll. 12–13) implies that the *consilium*, or, as it was later called, the *consistorium* of the emperor was composed of both senators and knights, but that its composition had not become fixed, as it did under Hadrian (*cf.* Herzog, 2, 369 *ff.*, 757 *f.*; Mommsen, *St. R.* 2, 988 *ff.*; Hirschfeld, 340, n. 2; Seeck, *R.E.* 4, 927 *f.*; Cuq, *Mém. sur le consilium principis*). The letter settles the ownership of small parcels of land in the possession of Firmum, but claimed by Falerio. On the division of village lands, *cf.* Liebenam, *St. Verw.* 1–13. This inscription makes it highly probable that Falerio was a colony of veterans founded by Augustus (ll. 22 *ff.*; *cf.* Mommsen, *Hermes*, 18 (1883), 173; *CIL.* ix, p. 517). For the method of procedure before the emperor's *consilium*, *cf.* pp. 241 *ff.* For the concluding paragraph, *cf.* p. 238. For other cases of arbitration, *cf.* nos. 8, 10, 46, 57, 58, 59, 104, and pp. 152 *ff.*

64. LEX SALPENSA
(81–84 p. Chr.)

CIL. II, 1963; Dessau, 6088; Bruns, 30*a*; Girard, p. 108; Riccobono, p. 162.

R(ubrica). Vt magistratus civitatem Romanam consequantur. Col. 1

XXI. . . .Qui II*vir aedilis quaestor ex hac lege factus erit, cives Romani sunto, cum post annum magistratu* | abierint, cum parentibus coniugibusque *ac* liberi*s*, qui legitumis nuptis quae|siti in potestatem parentium fuer*i*nt, item nepotibus ac neptibus filio | nat*i*s *natabus*, qui quaeque in potestate parentium fuerint; dum ne plures c(ives) R(omani) | sint, qua*m* quod ex h(ac) l(ege) magistratus creare oportet. ||

R. Vt qui civitat(em) Roman(am) consequantur, maneant 5 in eorundem m(ancipio) m(anu) | potestate. |

XXII. Qui quae*v*e ex h. l. exve edicto imp(eratoris) Caesaris Aug(usti) Vespasiani, imp(eratoris)ve Titi | Caesaris Aug(usti), aut imp(eratoris) Caesaris Aug(usti) Domitiani p(atris) p(atriae), civitatem Roman(am) | consecutus consecuta erit: is ea in eius, qui c(ivis) R(omanus) h(ac) l(ege) factus erit, potestate || manu mancipio, 10 cuius esse deberet, si civitate Romana mutatus | mutata non esset, esto idque ius tutoris optandi habeto, quod | haberet, si a cive Romano ortus orta neq(ue) civitate mutatus mu|tata esset.

R. Vt qui c(ivitatem) R(omanam) consequentur, iura libertorum retineant. |

XXIII. Qui quaeve *ex* h(ac) l(ege) exve edicto imp(eratoris) Caes(aris) Vesp(asiani) Aug(usti), imp(eratoris)ve Titi Caes(aris) Vespasian(i) Au(gusti), || aut imp(eratoris) Caes(aris) Domitiani 15 Aug(usti), c(ivitatem) R(omanam) consecutus consecuta erit: is in | libertos libertasve suos suas paternos paternas, qui quae in c(ivitatem) | R(omanam) non | venerit, deque bonis eorum earum et is, quae libertatis causa inposita | sunt, idem ius eademque condicio esto, quae esset, si civitate mutat*u*s | mutat*a* non esset.

[369]

R. De praefecto imp(eratoris) Caesaris Domitiani Aug-
(usti). ||

20   XXIIII. Si eius municipi decuriones conscriptive municipesve
imp(eratori) Caesar*i* Domitian(o) | Aug(usto) p(atri) p(atriae)
iiviratum communi nomine municipum eius municipi de|tuler*i*nt
imp(erator)*q*ue Domitian*us* Caesa*r* Aug(ustus) p(ater) p(atriae) eum
iiviratum receperit | et loco suo praefectum quem esse iusserit: is
praefectus eo *iure* esto, quo | esset si eum iivir(um) i(ure) d(icundo)
ex h(ac) l(ege) solum creari oportuisset, isque ex h(ac) l(ege) solus ||
25 iivir i(ure) d(icundo) creatus esset.

R. De iure praef(ecti), qui a iivir(o) relictus sit. |

   XXV. Ex iiviris qui in eo municipio i(ure) d(icundo) p(rae-
erunt), uter postea ex eo municipio proficiscetur | neque eo die in
id municip*i*um esse se rediturum arbitrabitur, quem | praefectum
municipi non minorem quam annorum xxxv ex | decurionibus
30 conscriptisque relinquere volet, facito ut is iuret per || Iovem et
divom Aug(ustum) et div*o*m Claudium et divom Vesp(asianum)
Aug(ustum) et divom | Titum Aug(ustum) et Genium imp(era-
toris) Caesaris Domitiani Aug(usti) deosque Penates; | quae
iivir(um), qui i(ure) d(icundo) p(raeest), h(ac) l(ege) facere oporteat,
se, dum praefectus erit, d(um) *t(axat)* quae eo | tempore fieri possint
facturum, neque adversus ea *f*acturum scientem | d(olo) m(alo);
et cum ita iuraverit, praefectum eum eius municipi relinquito. *Ei* ||
35 qui ita praefectus relictus erit, donec in id municipium alteruter
ex iiviris | adierit, in omnibus rebus id ius *e*aque potestas esto, prae-
terquam de praefec|to relinquendo et de c(ivitate) R(omana) con-
sequenda, quod ius quaeque potestas h(ac) l(ege) | iivir*is qui* iure
dicundo praeerunt datur. Isque dum praefectus erit quo|tiensque
municipium egressus erit, ne plus quam singulis diebus abesto. ||

40 R. De iure iurando iivir(um) et aedil(ium) et q(uaes-
torum). |

   XXVI. Duovir(i) qui in eo municipio *i(ure)* d(icundo) p(rae-
sunt), item aediles *qui* in eo municipio sunt, item | quaestores qui
in eo muncipio sunt, eorum quisque in d*i*ebus quinq(ue) | proxumis
post h(anc) l(egem) datam; quique iivir(i) aediles quaestoresve postea

ex h(ac) l(ege) | creati erunt, eorum quisque in diebus quinque proxumis, ex quo IIvir ‖ aedil*is* quaestor esse coeperit, priusquam 45 decuriones conscriptive | habeantur, iuranto pro contione per Iovem Col. II et div*o*m Aug(ustum) et divom Claudi|um et divom Vespasianum Aug(ustum) et divom Titum Aug(ustum) et Genium Domitiani | Aug(usti) deosque Penates: se, quodqu*o*mque ex h(ac) l(ege) exqu*e* re communi m(unicipum) m(unicipi) Flavi | Salpensani censeat, recte esse facturum, ne*q*ue adversus h(anc) l(egem) remve commu‖ne*m* municipum eius municipi facturum scientem d(olo) m(alo), 5 quosque prohi|bere possit prohibiturum; neque se aliter consilium habiturum neq(ue) aliter | daturum neque sententiam dicturum, quam u*t ex* h(ac) l(ege) exque re communi | municipum eius municipi censeat fore. Qui ita non iuraverit, is HS x (milia) | municipibus eius municipi d(are) d(amnas) esto, eiusque pecuniae deque ea pecunia mu‖nicipum eius municipi cui volet, cuique per hanc legem 10 licebit, actio peti|tio persecutio esto.

R. De intercessione IIvir(um) et aedil(ium) *et* q(uaestorum). |

XXVII. Qui IIvir(i) aut aediles aut quaestores eius municipi erunt, his IIvir(is) inter | se et cum aliquis alterutrum eorum aut utrumque ab aedile aedilibus | aut quaestor*e* quaestoribus appellabit, item aedilibus inter se, *item quaestoribus inter se* inter‖cedendi, in 15 triduo proxumo quam appellatio facta erit poteritque | intercedi, quod eius adversus h(anc) l(egem) non fiat, et dum ne amplius quam semel | quisque eorum in eadem re appelletur, ius potestasque esto, neve quis | adversus ea qui*d*, qu*o*m intercessum erit, facito. |

R. De servis apud IIvir(um) manumittendis. ‖

XXVIII. Si quis municeps municipi Flavi Salpensani, qui 20 Latinus erit, aput IIvir(os), | qui iure dicundo praeerunt eius municipi, servom suom servamve suam | ex servitute in libertate*m* manumiserit, liberum liberamve esse iusserit, | dum ne quis pupillus neve quae virgo mulierve sine tutore auctore | quem quamve manumittat, liberum liberamve esse iubeat: qui ita ‖ manumissus liberve 25 esse iussus erit, liber esto, quaeque ita manumissa | liberave *esse* iussa erit, libera esto, uti qui optumo iure Latini libertini li|beri sunt erunt; *d*um is qui minor xx annorum erit ita manumittat, |

si causam manumittendi iusta*m* esse is numerus decurionum, per quem | decreta h(ac) l(ege) facta rata sunt, censuerit.

R. De tutorum datione. ||

30   XXIX. Cui tutor non erit incertusve erit, si is e*a*ve municeps municipi Flavi Salpensani | erit, et pupilli pupillaeve non erunt, et ab iiviris, qui i(ure) d(icundo) p(raeerunt) eius municipi, postu-| laverit, uti sibi tutorem det, *et* eum, quem dare volet, nominaverit: *t*um is, | a quo postulatum erit, sive unum sive plures collegas habebit, de omnium colle|garum sententia, qui tum in eo municipio 35 intrave fines municipi eius er*u*nt, || causa cognita, si ei videbitur, eum qui nominatus erit tutorem dato. Sive | is e*a*ve, cuius nomine ita postulatum erit, pupil(lus) pupillave erit, sive is, a quo | postulatum erit, non habebit collegam, *collega*ve eius in eo municipio intrave | fines eius municipi nemo erit: *t*um is, a quo ita postulatum erit, causa co|gnita in diebus x proxumis, ex decreto decurionum, 40 quod cum duae partes || decurionum non minus adfuerint, factum erit, eum, qui nominatus | erit, quo ne ab iusto tutore tutela *a*beat, ei tutorem dato. Qui tutor h(ac) l(ege) | datus erit, is ei, cui datus erit, quo ne ab iusto tutore tutela *a*beat, tam iustus | tutor esto, quam si is c(ivis) R(omanus) et *ei* adgnatus proxumus c(ivis) R(o-manus) tutor esset. |

In 1851 two bronze tablets, one with five columns, the other with two columns of text, were found near Malaga. They were protected from injury by a cloth wrapping and a casing of tiles, so that they had evidently been buried deliberately, perhaps to escape seizure. (For other theories, *cf.* Dessau, *Wien. Stud.* 24 (1902), 240; Mommsen, *Ges. Schr.* 1, 283.) The tablet with two columns contains a part of the charter of Salpensa, the other, a part of the charter of Malaca (no. 65). The provision made for choosing Domitian duovir (chap. xxiv) and the form of oath to be taken by magistrates (chapp. xxii, xxiii) show that the charter of Salpensa was granted by Domitian, and consequently subsequent to Sept. A.D. 81. A similar conclusion may be drawn for Malaca (no. 65, chap. lix). The document antedates A.D. 84 because Domitian does not bear the cognomen Germanicus. To confine our attention to the political relations which these two towns bore to the outside world, it is clear that Salpensa, at least, had only *Latium minus,* because only local magistrates with their families and with the members of the second generation in the male line acquired Roman citizenship (chap. xxi, *cf.* p. 192). Evidently decurions who had not held a magistracy did not enjoy this privilege. Nothing is said about the acquisition of Roman citizenship in the extant fragments of the *lex Malacitana,* but in all probability the two towns had the same political status, and it is proper to take it for granted that the same provisions held good for both municipalities. The phrase, "if any citizen of the *mun. Flav. Salp. qui Latinus erit*" (chap. xxviii), shows that there were Roman citizens, as well as Latins, in Salpensa, and they had the right to vote both in Salpensa and in Rome, and in the *lex Malacitana* (chap. liii) provision is made for their assignment to a particular *curia.*

Up to the time of Vespasian Malaca was a *civitas foederata,* and Salpensa probably a *civitas stipendiaria* (Mommsen, *Ges. Schr.* 1, 293 *ff.*). This emperor gave them Latin rights (Pliny, *N.H.* 3. 3. 30). That this gift of Latin rights was made by Vespasian in the case of Salpensa, at least, is evident from the reference to this emperor in the charter (chapp. xxii, xxiii). It is confirmed by Titus and Domitian. Since these privileges emanate from the Flavian emperors, the two towns are *municipia Flaviana,* like so many other Spanish municipalities (*CIL.* ii, *S.* p. 1160).

In the *lex Salpensa* provision is made for the election of Domitian to the duovirate. Under the early empire other members of the imperial family might receive this honor. Tiberius seems to have restricted the privilege to the emperor (p. 63). In Salpensa the prefect representing the emperor is chosen by him, but in other municipalities the power to make the choice could be delegated to the local senate (*CIL.* ix, 3044), in which case the prefect bore the title *praefectus imperatoris ex senatus consulto.*

The article in the *lex Malacitana* which governs the election of *patroni* prescribes a quorum of two-thirds of the members of the senate and secret balloting, but it does not expressly forbid the election of a Roman senator *cum imperio* (chap. lxi; *cf.* no. 26).

That many of the provisions in these charters were adopted from the corresponding usages in the city of Rome seems to be clear from the *lex Malacitana*, chap. LXIV.

Unfortunately chap. LXIX which deals with the judiciary is incomplete. A minimum of 1000 sesterces and a maximum, not named, are certainly fixed. Perhaps in suits involving less than 1000 sesterces, the aedile was competent (Mommsen, *Ges. Schr.* 1, 335), while actions involving more than 1000 sesterces and less than the unnamed maximum went before the duovir. Cases running beyond the maximum were probably heard by the proconsul (*cf.* commentary on no. 27). So far as we can infer, this local jurisdiction applied to all citizens, whether Romans or Latins.

For the earlier literature on these charters, *cf.* Riccobono, p. 163. For the text with a commentary, cf. Mommsen, *Ges. Schr.* 1, 267 *ff.* A translation of the two charters and a commentary on them may be found in Hardy, *Three Spanish Charters*, 61 *ff.*

65. LEX MALACITANA
(81–84 p. Chr.)

CIL. II, 1964; Dessau, 6089; Bruns, 30*b*; Girard, p. 112; Riccobono, p. 168.

Col. I. *R(ubrica). De nominatione candidatorum.*

LI. Si ad quem diem professio | fieri oportebit, nullius nomine aut | pauciorum, quam tot quod creari opor|tebit, professio facta
5 er*it* sive ex his, | quorum nomine professio facta erit, ‖ pauciores erunt quorum h(ac) l(ege) comitiis ra|tionem habere oporteat, quam tot *quot* cre|ari oportebit: tum is qui comitia ha|bere debebit proscribito, ita u(t) d(e) p(lano) r(ecte) l(egi) p(ossint), | tot nomina
10 eorum, quibus per h. l. ‖ eum honorem petere licebit, quod de|runt ad eum numerum, ad quem crea|ri ex h. l. oportebit. Qui ita proscripti | erunt, ii, si volent, aput eum, qui ea co|mitia habiturus
15 erit, singuli singu‖los eiiusdem condicio*n*is nominato, | ique item, qui tum ab is nominati erunt, si | volent, singuli singulos aput eun|dem e*a*demque condicione nomina|to; isque, aput quem ea
20 nominatio fac‖ta erit, eorum omnium nomina pro|ponito ita u. d. p. r. l. p., deque is om|nibus item comitia habeto, perinde | ac si eorum quoque nomine ex h. l. de | petendo honore professio facta

esset || intra praestitutum diem, peterque | eum honorem sua sponte 25
coepissent ne|que eo proposito destitissent. |

R. De comitiis habendis. |

LII. Ex ɪɪviris qui nunc sunt, item ex is, qui || deinceps in eo 30
municipio ɪɪviri erunt, | uter maior natu erit, aut, si ei causa qu|ae
inciderit q(uo) m(inus) comitia habere pos|sit, tum alter ex his
comitia ɪɪvir., item | aedilibus, item quaestoribus rogandis || sub- 35
rogandis h. l. habeto; utique ea dis|tributione curiarum, de qua supra
con|prehensum est, suffragia ferri debe|bunt, ita per tabellam feran-
tur facito. | Quique ita creati erunt, ii annum unum || aut, si in 40
alterius locum creati erunt, | reliqua parte eiius anni in eo honore |
sunto, quem suffragis erunt consecuti. |

R. In qua curia incolae suffragia | ferant. ||

LIII. Quicumque in eo municipio comitia ɪɪviris, | item aedili- 45
bus, item quaestoribus rogan|dis habebit, ex curiis sorte ducito
unam, | in qua incolae, qui cives R. Latinive cives | erunt, suffra-
gium ferant, eisque in ea cu||ria suffragi latio esto. | 50

R. Quorum comitis rationem habe|ri oporteat. |

LIIII. Qui comitia habere debebit, is primum ɪɪvir. | qui iure
dicundo praesint ex eo genere in||genuorum hominum, de quo h. l. 55
cau|tum conprehensumque est, deinde proxi|mo quoque tempore
aediles item quaesto|res ex eo genere ingenuorum hominum, | de
quo h. l. cautum conprehensumque est, || creandos curato; dum ne 60
cuiius comi|tis rationem habeat, qui ɪɪviratum pe|tet qui minor
annorum xxv erit, qui|ve intra quinquennium in eo honore |
fuerint; item qui aedilitatem quaesturam||ve petet, qui minor quam 65
annor. xxv erit, | quive in earum qua causa erit, propter | quam, si Col. ɪɪ
c. R. esset, in numero decurio|num conscriptorumve eum esse non
lice|ret.

R. De suffragio ferendo. |

LV. Qui comitia ex h. l. habebit, is municipes cu||riatim ad 5
suffragium ferendum voca|to ita, ut uno vocatu omnes curias in |
suffragium vocet, eaeque singulae in | singulis consaeptis suffragium
per ta|bellam ferant. Itemque curato, ut ad cis||tam cuiusque curiae 10
ex municipibus | eiius municipi terni sint, qui eiius cu|riae non sint,

qui suffragia custodiant | diribeant, et uti antequam id faciant
15 qu|isque eorum iurent, se rationem suffra||giorum fide bona habi-
turum relaturum|que. Neve prohibeto, q. m. et qui hono|rem
petent singulos custodes ad singu|las cistas ponant. Iique custodes
20 ab eo | qui comitia habebit, item ab his positi || qui honorem petent,
in ea curia quis|que eorum suffragium ferto, ad cuiius cu|riae cistam
custos positus erit, eorum|que suffragia perinde iusta rataque sun|to
25 ac si in sua quisque curia suffragium || tulisset.

R. Quid de his fieri oporteat, qui | suffragiorum numero
    pares erunt. |

    LVI. Is qui ea comitia habebit, uti quisque curiae | cuiius plura
quam alii suffragia habue|rit, ita priorem ceteris eum pro ea curia ||
30 factum creatumque esse renuntiato, | donec is numerus, ad quem
creari opor|tebit, expletus sit. Qua in curia totidem | suffragia duo
pluresve habuerint, ma|ritum, quive maritorum numero erit, ||
35 caelibi liberos non habenti qui mari|torum numero non erit; ha-
bentem libe|ros non habenti; plures liberos haben|tem pauciores
habenti praeferto priorem|que nuntiato ita, ut bini liberi post
40 no||men inpositum aut singuli puberes amis|si virive potentes amissae
pro singulis | sospitibus numerentur. Si duo pluresve to|tidem suf-
fragia habebunt et eiiusdem | condicionis erunt, nomina eorum in ||
45 sortem coicito, et uti quiiusque (sic) nomen sor|ti ductum erit, ita
eum priorem alis renunti|ato.

R. De sortitione curiarum et is, qui cu|riarum numero
    pares erunt. |

50   LVII. Qui comitia h. l. habebit, is relatis omnium || curiarum
tabulis nomina curiarum in sor|tem coicito, singularumque curiarum
no|mina sorte ducito, et ut cuiiusque curiae | nomen sorte exierit,
quos ea curia fecerit, | pronuntiari iubeto; et uti quisque prior ||
55 maiorem partem numeri curiarum con|fecerit, eum, cum h. l. iura-
verit caverit|que de pecunia communi, factum crea|tumque renun-
tiato, donec tot magistra|tus sint quod h. l. creari oportebit. Si
60 toti||dem curias duo pluresve habebunt, | uti supra conprehensum
est de is qui | suffragiorum numero pares essent, ita | de is qui totidem
65 curias habebunt fa|cito, eademque ratione priorem quem||que
creatum esse renuntiato. |

[376]

R. Ne quid fiat, quo minus comitia ha|beantur. |

LVIII. Ne quis intercedito neve quit aliut fa|cito, quo minus in eo muncipio (*sic*) h. l. || comitia habeantur perficiantur. | Qui 70 aliter adversus ea fecerit sciens | d(olo) m(alo), is in res singulas Col. III HS x̄ mu|nicipibus municepii (*sic*) Flavi Malacitani | d(are) d(amnas) e(sto), eiiusque pecuniae deque ea pecun. | municipi eius municipii, qui volet, cuique || per h. l. licebit, actio petitio persecutio esto. | 5

R. De iure iurando eorum, qui maiorem | partem numeri curiarum expleverit. |

LIX. Qui ea comitia habebit, uti quisque eorum, | qui IIviratum aedilitatem quaesturam||ve petet, maiiorem partem numeri curia|rum 10 expleverit, priusquam eum factum | creatumque renuntiet, ius-iurandum adi|gito in contionem (*sic*) palam per Iovem et di|vom Augustum et divom Claudium et divom || Vespasianum Aug. et 15 divom Titum Aug. | et Genium imp. Caesaris Domitiani Aug. | deosque Penates: se e*a* qu*ae* ex h. l. facere|oportebit facturum, neque adversus | h. l. fecisse aut facturum esse scientem || d. m. 20

R. Ut de pecunia communi munici|pum caveatur ab is, qui IIviratum | quaesturamve petet. |

LX. Qui in eo municipio IIviratum quaesturam|ve petent quique propter ea, quod pauciorum || nomine quam oportet professio facta | 25 esset, nominatim in eam condicionem | rediguntur, ut de his quoque suffragi|um ex h. l. ferri oporteat: quisque eorum, | quo die comitia habebuntur, ante quam || suffragium feratur arbitratu eius qui ea | 30 comitia habebit praedes in commune mu|nicipum dato pecuniam communem eo|rum, quam in honore suo tractaverit, | salvam is fore. Si d. e. r. is praedibus minus || cautum esse videbitur, praedia 35 subsignato | arbitratu eiiusdem. Isque ab iis praedes prae|diaque sine d. m. accipito, quoad recte cau|tum sit, uti quod recte factum esse volet. | Per quem eorum, de quibus IIvirorum quaes||torumve 40 comitiis suffragium ferri opor|tebit, steterit, q. m. recte caveatur, eius qu*i* co|mitia habebit rationem ne habeto. |

R. De patrono cooptando. |

LXI. Ne quis patronum publice municipibus muni||cipii Flavi 45 Malacitani cooptato patrocini|umve cui deferto, nisi ex maioris

partis de|curionum decreto, quod decretum factum | erit, cum duae
50 partes non minus adfue|rint et iurati per tabellam sententiam tu||le-
rint. Qui aliter adversus ea patronum | publice municipibus muni-
cipii Flavi Ma|lacitani cooptaverit patrociniumve cui | detulerit,
is HS x̄ n. in *p*ublicum munici|pibus municipii Flavi Malacitani
55 d. d. e.; *et* is || qu*i* adversus h. l. patronus cooptatus cui|*ve* patrocinium
delatum erit, ne magis | ob eam rem patronus municipium (*sic*)
muni|cipii Flavi Malacitanitanii (*sic*) esto. |

60 R. Ne quis aedificia, quae restitutu||rus non erit, destruat.|

LXII. Ne quis in oppido municipii Flavi Malacita|ni quaeque
ei oppido continentia aedificia | erunt, aedificium detegito destruito
demo|liundumve curato, nisi *de* decurionum con|scriptorumve sen-
65 tentia cum maior pars || eorum adfuerit, quod restiturus (*sic*) intra
proxi|mum annum non erit. Qui adversus ea fece|rit, is quanti
e(a) r(es) e(rit), t(antam) p(ecuniam) municipibus municipi | Flavi
Malacitani d. d. e., eiusque pecuniae | deque ea pecunia municipi
70 eius municipii || qui volet, cuique per h. l. lice*b*it, actio petitio |
Col. IV persecutio esto. |

R. De locationibus legibusque locatio|num proponendis
et in tabulas mu|nicipi referendis. ||

5 LXIII. Qui IIvir i(ure) d(icundo) p(raeerit), vectigalia ultroque
tributa, | sive quid aliut communi nomine munici|pum eiius
municipi locari oportebit, lo|cato. Quasque locationes fecerit quas-
10 que | leges dixerit, quanti quit locatum sit et *qui* prae||des accepti
sint quaeque praedia subdita | subsignata obligatave sint quique
prae|diorum cognitores accepti sint, in tabu|las communes muni-
cipum eius (*sic*) municipi | referantur facito et proposita habeto
15 per || omne reliquom tempus honoris sui, ita ut | d. p. r. l. p., quo
loco decuriones conscripti|ve proponenda esse censuerint. |

R. De obligatione praedum praediorum | cognitorum-
que. ||

20 LXIV. Quicumque in municipio Flavio Malacitano | in com-
mune municipum eiius municipi | praedes facti sunt erunt, quaeque
praedia | accepta sunt erunt, quique eorum prae|diorum cognitores
25 facti sunt erunt: ii om||nes et quae cuiiusque eorum tum *fuerunt*

[378]

erunt, cum | praees (*sic*) cognitorve factus est erit, quaeque pos|tea esse, cum ii obligati esse coeper*u*nt c*o*e|perint, qui eorum soluti liberatique non sunt | non erunt aut non sine d. m. sunt erunt, ea||que 30 omnia, qua*e* eorum soluta liberata|que non sunt non erunt aut non sine | d. m. sunt erunt, in commune municipum | eiius municipii item obligati obli|gataeque (*sic*) sunto, uti ii e*a*ve p. R. obligati obli||gatave essent, si aput eos, qui Romae aera|rio praessent, ii 35 praedes *i*ique cognito|res facti eaque praedia subdita subsigna|ta obligatave essent. Eosque praedes eaque | praedia eosque cognitores, si quit eorum, in || quae cognitores facti erunt, ita non erit, | qui 40 quaeve soluti liberati soluta libera|taque non sunt non erunt aut non sine | d. m. sunt erunt, iiviris, qui ibi i. d. prae|runt, ambobus alter*i*ve eorum ex de||curionum conscriptorumque decreto, qu|od 45 decretum cum eorum partes tertiae | non minus quam duae adessent factum | erit, vendere legemque his vendundis dicere | ius potestasque esto; dum e*a*m legem is re||bus vendundis dicant, quam 50 legem eos, | qui Romae aerario praeerunt, e lege prae|diatoria praedibus praedisque vendun|dis dicere oporteret, aut, si lege praedia|toria emptorem non inveniet, quam le||gem in vacuom vendendis dicere 55 opor|teret; et dum ita legem dicant, uti pecu|niam infore municipi Flavi Malacitani | referatur luatur solvatur. Quaeque lex | ita dicta *e*rit, iusta rataque esto. ||

R. Ut ius dicatur e lege dicta praedibus | et praedis 60
    vendundis. |

    LXV. Quos praedes quaeque praedia quosque cog|nitores iiviri municipii Flavi Malaci|tani h. l. vendiderint, de iis quicumque || i(ure) d(icundo) p(raeerit), ad quem de ea re in ius aditum erit, | 65 ita ius dicito iudiciaque dato, ut ei, qui | eos praedes cognitores ea praedia mer|cati erunt, praedes socii heredesque eorum | *i*ique, ad quos ea res pertinebit, de is rebus || agere easque res petere persequi 70 re|cte possit.

R. De multa, quae dicta erit. |

    LXVI. Multas in eo municipio ab iiviris prae|fectove dictas, Col. v item ab aedilibus quas ae|diles dixisse se aput iiviros ambo alter|ve ex is professi erunt, iivir, qui i. d. p., in | tabulas communes municipum eiius mu||nicipi referri iubeto. Si cui ea multa dicta | erit 5

aut nomine eiius alius postulabit, ut | de ea ad decuriones con-
scriptosve refe|ratur, de ea decurionum conscriptorum|ve iudicium
10 esto. Quaeque multae non || erunt iniustae a decurionibus con|-
scriptisve iudicatae, eas multas IIviri | in publicum municipum eiius
muni|cipii redigunto. |

15 R. De pecunia communi municipum || deque rationibus
   eorundem. |

   LXVII. Ad quem pecunia communis municipum | eiius muni-
cipi pervenerit, heresve ei|ius, isve ad quem ea res pertinebit, in
20 die|bus xxx proximis, quibus ea pecunia || ad eum pervenerit, in
publicum muni|cipum eiius municipi eam referto. Qui|que rationes
communes negotiumve qu|od commune municipum eius munici|pi
25 gesserit tractaverit, is, heresve eiius || isve ad quem ea res pertinebit,
in diebus xxx | proximis, quibus ea negotia easve ratio|nes gerere
tractare desierit quibusque | decuriones conscriptique habebuntur, |
30 rationes edito redditoque decurioni||bus conscriptisve cuive de his
accipi|endis cognoscendis ex decreto decurio|num conscriptorumve,
quod decretum | factum erit cum eorum partes non mi|nus quam
35 duae tertiae adessent, nego||tium datum erit. Per quem steterit, q. |
m. ita pecunia redigeretur referre|tur quove minus ita rationes
redde|rentur, is, per quem steterit q. m. rationes | redderentur quove
40 minus pecunia redige||retur referretur, heresque eius isque ad qu|em
ea res qua de agitur pertinebit, q(uanti) e(a) r(es) | erit, tantum et
alterum tantum munici|pibus eiius municipi d. d. e., eiusque pe-
45 cuni|ae deque ea pecunia municipum muni||cipii Flavi Malacitani
⟨eius ea pecunia | municipum Flavi Malacitani⟩ qui volet, cuique
per h. l. licebit, actio pe|titio persecutio esto. |

   R. De constituendis patronis causae, cum | rationes
   reddentur. ||

50   LXVIII. Cum ita rationes reddentur, IIvir, qui decurio|nes
conscriptosve habebit, ad decuriones | conscriptosve referto, quos
placeat publi|cam causam agere, iique decuriones con|scriptive per
55 tabellam iurati d. e. r. decer||nunto, tum cum eorum partes non
minus | quam duae tertiae aderunt, ita ut tres, qu|os plurimi per
tabellam legerint, causam | publicam agant, iique qui ita lecti erunt

[380]

tem|pus a decurionibus conscriptisve, quo cau||sam cognoscant 60
actionemque suam or|dinent, postulanto, eoque tempore quod is |
datum erit transacto eam causam uti quod | recte factum esse volet
agunto. |

R. De iudicio pecuniae communis. ||

LXIX. Quod m(unicipum) m(unicipii) Flavi Malacitani no- 65
mine pe|tetur ab eo, qui eius municipi municeps incolave erit,
quodve cum eo agetur | quod pluris HS CIƆ sit neque tanti sit, ut |
de ea re proconsulem ius dicere iudiciaque dare ex hac lege oporteat:
de ea re IIvir praefectusve, qui iure dicundo praeerit eius municipii,
ad quem de ea re in ius aditum erit, ius dicito iudiciaque dato....

LXIV. 1. 56. pecuniam infore municipi, *tablet*; *perhaps* pecunia in publicum municipum.

LXVII, l. 45. eius ea....Malacitani, *dittography.*

See no. 64 and commentary.

65*a*. EDICTUM L. ANTISTI RUSTICI, LEGATI DOMITIANI,
DE ANNONA COLONIAE ANTIOCHIAE
(ca. 93 p. Chr.)

Trans. Am. Phil. Assoc. 55 (1924), 5 *ff.*; *Journ. Rom. Studies,*
14 (1924), 180.

L. Antistius Rusticus leg(atus) | imp(eratoris) Caesar(i)s Domi-
tiani | Aug(usti) Germ(anici) pro pr(aetore), dic(it): | Cum IIvir(i)
et decurion(es) || splendidissim(ae) col(oniae) Ant(iochensis) | 5
scripserint mihi propter | hiemis asperitatem an|nonam frumenti
ex|arsisse petierintque ut || pleps copiam emendi haberet, | b. *f.* 10
omnes, qui Ant(iochensis) col(oniae) aut | coloni aut incolae
sunt, | profiteantur apud IIviros col(oniae) | Antiochensis intra
tri||censimum diem quam | hoc edictum meum pro|positum fuerit 15
quantum | quisque et quo loco fru|menti habeat et quan||tum in 20
semen aut in | cibaria annua familiae | suae deducat, et reliqui |
omnis frumenti copiam | emptoribus col(oniae) Antiochens(is) ||
faciat. Vendendi au(t)em | tempus cons(t)ituo in k(alendas) 25
Aug(ustas) | primas. Quod si quis non | paruerit, sciat me, quid|quid
contra edictum me||um retentum fuerit, | in commissum vindica-| 30
turum, delatoribus prae|mi nomine octava por|tione constituta.

35 Cum ‖ autem adfirmatur mihi ante | hanc hibernae asperitatis
per|severantiam octonis et | novenis assibus modium fru|menti in
40 colonia fuisse ‖ et iniquissimum sit famem | civium suorum prae-
dae cui|quam esse, excedere sing(ulos) | (denarios) sing(ulos) modios
pretium | frumenti veto.

l. 11. b(ono) te(mpori), *Robinson*: B (*in margin*), et, *Ramsay.*

This inscription was discovered at Pisidian Antioch. The second
column, containing the edict of Antistius Rusticus, is reproduced
above. Prior to publication Professor D. M. Robinson kindly
furnished us with the text and notes on the document. He
believes that the famine referred to in the edict may be associated
with that referred to in *Revelation* VI. 6, *cf.* Reinach, *Rev. Arch.*
39 (1901), 350 *ff.*

The local magistrates of Antioch had been unable to meet the
situation caused by the famine and consequent hoarding of grain by
farmers and speculators. They appealed to the governor for legislation to compel the merchants and producers to sell. The edict is an
early example of imperial interference in the regulation of prices
in provincial towns. Although the famine must have been widespread, it may be noted that the edict does not apply to the whole
province, but deals only with conditions in the city which presented
the petition. Similarly in the reign of Trajan, Pliny and the emperor
dealt with each city in Bithynia individually. The confession of
impotence on the part of the magistrates of Antioch may have been
a factor in the development of the policy of appointing *curatores
rei publicae* to deal with problems of municipal government a few
years later. For regulations in regard to control of local markets,
cf. nos. 90 and 91.

Antioch was probably founded as a Roman colony prior to 27 B.C.
although Ramsay favors a later date (*cf. R.E.* 4, 531 *f.*; Ramsay,
Journ. Rom. Studies, 6 (1916), 83 *ff.*). In the proclamation of the
governor the chief magistrates and members of the local senate are
styled by titles current in the West rather than by the Greek equiva-
lents. The use of the Latin language in the eastern provinces for
the edict of governors is rare (*cf.* no. 22). The Roman calendar
and the Roman system of weights and coinage were also used. It
may be noted that a distinction is made between *coloni*, who were

FROM ITALY AND THE PROVINCES

probably descendants of the veterans settled there by Augustus, and the *incolae*, who probably represent the original members of Antioch. In the time of Domitian the two classes had not yet been placed on an equal footing politically, *cf. Journ. Rom. Studies*, 8 (1918), 107 ff.

66. TITULUS HONORARIUS
(81–96 p. Chr.)

CIL. II, 1945; Dessau, 1982.

Imp. Domitiano | Caesari | Aug. Germanico | L. Munius Quir. || Novatus et | L. Munius Quir. | Aurelianus | . f. c. R. per h*ono*rem | 5
II vir. consecuti || d. s. p. d.d.   10

Found at Iluro in Baetica. On the grant of Roman citizenship on election to a local magistracy (*civitatem Romanam per honorem duoviratus*), *cf.* pp. 191 ff.

67. TITULUS HONORARIUS
(96–97 p. Chr.)

B.C.H. 44 (1920), 73; *An. ép.* 1922, no. 30.

Ὁ δῆμος ἐτείμησεν ταῖς δευτέραις | τιμαῖς Μᾶρκον Κοκκήιον Νέρουαν | τὸν αὐτοκράτορα ὕπατόν τε ἀποδεδει|γμένον, εὐεργέτην καὶ πάτρωνα καὶ σω||τῆρα γεγονότα τῆς πόλεως, ἀποκαθεστα-| 5
κότα δὲ ἡμῖν καὶ τὴν πάτριον ἐλευθερί|αν τε καὶ πολειτείαν, ἐπαίνωι, χρυσῶι | στεφάνωι ἀριστείωι, εἰκόνι χαλκῆι ἐφίπ|πωι, προεδρίαι ἐν τοῖς ἀγῶσιν, ἀρετῆς || ἕνεκα καὶ εὐνοίας καὶ εὐερ- 10
γεσίας τῆς | εἰς ἑαυτόν.

From Lagina in Caria. Lagina (Stratonicaea) was given freedom and autonomy by a decree of the Roman senate in 81 B.C. (no. 17). The city still enjoyed these privileges in the time of Pliny the Elder (*N.H.* 5. 109), and probably lost them as a result of the fiscal reforms of Vespasian. From this document we learn that Nerva restored the former privileges. It may be doubted whether Vespasian made any change in the municipal constitution when he cancelled the immunity from tribute, and the restoration of the ancestral πολιτεία ascribed to Nerva probably means nothing more than a return to the former status of Stratonicaea in the empire.

[383]

MUNICIPAL DOCUMENTS IN GREEK AND LATIN

68. EPISTULAE LABERI MAXIMI ET ALIORUM
DE FINIBUS HISTRIANORUM
(43–100 p. Chr.)

An. ép. 1919, no. 10; *Annales de l'académie Roumaine*, 38, no. 15; Wilhelm, *Anzeiger der Akad. der Wissen. in Wien*, 59 (1922), 78 *ff.*; *Suppl. Ep. Gr.* 1, 329.

'Οροθεσία Λαβερίου Μαξίμου. |
Fines Histrianorum hos esse constitui...........*Pe*|ucem
lacum Halmyridem a do*minio*.............. | Argamensium inde
5 iugo summo..............*ad c*||onfluentes rivorum Picusculi et
Ga*brani inde ab im*|o Gabrano ad capud eiusdem inde.... *iuxta
rivum* | Sanpaeum inde ad rivum Turgiculum.......... | a rivo
Calabaeo milia passuum circit*er* D. VI...... |

'Επιστολὴ Σαβείνου. ||

10 Φλάβιος Σαβεῖνος 'Ιστριανῶν ἄρχουσ[ιν], βουλῆι, δήμωι | χαίρειν. Τὸ περὶ Πεύκην ὑμεῖν δίκαιο[ν ὅπως] ἀκέραιον δι|ατηρηθῆι, ἔσται ἐπιμελὲς 'Αρουντίωι Φλά[μμαι] τῶι ἐπάρχωι. Οὕ|τως γὰρ αὐτῶι ἐπέστειλα. Λαλήσω δὲ καὶ Αἰμιλιανῶι διαδόχωι |
15 μου καὶ εἰς τὸ παντελὲς συστήσω ὑμᾶς. ῎Αλλη ἐπιστολὴ || τοῦ αὐτοῦ Σαβείνου. Φλα. Σαβεῖνος π[ρεσβευτὴς] 'Ιστρι|ανῶν ἄρχουσιν, βουλῆι, δήμωι χαίρειν. Καὶ εἰ καὶ [τ]ὸ τῆς κατὰ τὸν | ῎Ιστρον ὄχθης τέλος μέχρις θαλάσσης διήκει καὶ ἐκ το|σούτου διαστήματος ἀφέστηκεν ἡ πόλις ἀπὸ τῶν τοῦ | ποταμοῦ στο-
20 μάτων ὅμως ἐπεὶ καὶ οἱ πρέσβεις ὑμῶν || διεβεβαιοῦντο καὶ 'Ασιατικὸς ὁ ἔπαρχος ἔλεγε σχεδὸν | ἐκείνην μόνην εἶναι τῆς πόλεως πρόσοδον τὴν ἐκ τοῦ | ταρειχευομένου ἰχθύος, ἔδοξα δεῖν ὑμεῖν κατὰ τὴν [ὑμετέ]|ραν συνήθιαν μένειν τὴν αὐτὴν ἄδειαν τοῦ τε ἁλιεύ[ειν] | ἐν τῶι Πεύκης στόματι καὶ τοῦ παρα-
25 φέρειν τὴν δᾶδα || εἰς τὴν ἑνὸς ἑκάστου χρείαν δίχα τέλους· περὶ | γὰρ τῶν τῆς ὕλης χρειῶν ἀναμφισβήτητα ἔχετε ὅρια | καὶ τὴν ἐξ ἐκείνων χρῆσιν πᾶσαν τῶι τέλλει [ἀν]υπεύθυνον. |

'Επιστολὴ Πομπωνίου Πείου. |

Πομπώνιος Πεῖος 'Ιστριανῶν ἄρχουσιν, [βουλῆι, δήμωι χα]ί-
30 ρειν. || Καὶ ἐκ τῶν γεγραμμένων ὑμεῖν ὑπὸ Φλ. Σαβείνου [καὶ Αἰμιλι]|ανοῦ ἀνδρῶν ἐπισημοτάτων [καὶ ἐ]μοὶ τειμιω[τάτων ἦν ἀντι]||λαβέσθαι ὅτι ἡ ἀσθένια τῆς πόλεως ὑμῶ[ν προνοίας

[384]

τυγχάνει· πρὸ οὖν] | πάντων φροντίζοντος τοῦ θειοτάτου [Καί-
σαρος καὶ ὡς ἀληθῶς σωτῆ]|ρος ἡμῶν, ἵνα μὴ μόνον διαφυλαχθῆι
ἀλ[λὰ καὶ αὐξηθῆι] || τὰ τῶν πόλεων δίκαια, ἐπέκρεινα τὴν τ[ῶ]ν 35
κ[ατὰ στόμ]α Πε[ύκη]ς ἁλι|ευομένων ἰχθύων πρόσοδον ὑμετέραν
εἶναι, [ὧι] δικαίωι ταῦ|τα τὰ τέλη οἱ πρόγονοι ὑμῶν καὶ πατέρες
[τῆι] χάριτι τῶν Σε[βαστῶ]ν | ἀδιαλείπτως ἔσχον. ᾿Αλλη ἐπι-
στολὴ Πλαυτί[ου Αἰλι]ανοῦ. | Πλαύτιος Αἰλιανὸς ᾿Ιστριανῶν
ἄρχουσιν [χ]αίρειν. || Τὸ ψήφισμα ὑμῶν ἀπέδοσάν μοι οἱ πρέσ- 40
βει[ς Κ]αλλίστρατος | Δημητρίου καὶ Μειδίας ᾿Αρτεμιδώρου.
᾿Ηξιοῦτε δὲ διὰ τοῦ ψη|φίσματος παραπεμφθῆναι τὴν εὐχα-
ριστοῦ[σ]αν [τῶι] τειμιωτάτωι | ἡμῶν Σαβείνωι πρεσβείαν, ὃ
καὶ δι᾽ αὐτὸν μόνον τὸν Σαβεῖνον [ἀ]||σμένως ἂν ἐποίησα.
᾿Ηξιοῦτε δὲ καὶ τὰ τῆς Πεύκης ὑμε[ῖν] ἄθραυσ||τα τηρεῖν δίκαια. 45
᾿Εγὼ δὲ τοσοῦτον ἀπέχ[ω] τοῦ θραῦσαί τι τῶν ἐκ | χρόνου φυλασ-
σομένων ὑμεῖν δικαίων, ὡς καὶ παρευρεῖν ἂν ἡδέ|ως δι᾽ ὧν ἐνέσται
κοσμεῖν ἀρχέαν πόλιν καὶ ῾Ελληνίδα καὶ εἰς τὸν Σ[ε]βα|στὸν
εὐσεβῆ καὶ πρὸς ἡμᾶς αὐτοὺς οὖσαν εὐσ[ε]βῆ. |

᾿Επιστολὴ Τουλλίου Γεμίνου. ||

Τούλλιος Γέμινος πρεσβευτὴς καὶ ἀντιστράτηγος Τιβ. Κλα(υ)- 50
δί|ου Καίσαρος Σεβ. Γερμανικοῦ ᾿Ιστριανῶν ἄρχουσιν, βουλῆι,
δήμωι | χαίρειν. Οἱ πρέσβεις ὑμῶν Δημήτριος Χαβρίας Χαιρή-
μων Δημήτριος Αἰσχρίων Τα.[. . .] [Με]ιδίας | Διονυσόδωρος
῾Ηγησαγόρας ᾿Αρισταγόρας Μ[ητρόδωρ]ος ἐν|τυχόντες μοι ἐν
Τόμει τὸ ψήφισμα ὑμῶν ἐπέδοσαν καὶ εἰς τὸν Σ[εβα]σ||τὸν ἡμῶν 55
ἐπιδειξάμενοι εὔνοιαν συνήσθησαν ἐ[πὶ τῆι] ἡμετέραι ὑ[γιεί]|αι
καὶ παρουσίαι σπουδεστάτην ποιησάμενοι τὴν [περὶ ὧν ἐνετεί-
λασ]||θε αὐτοῖς ὁμειλίαν. ᾿Επιγνοὺς οὖν (τ)ὴν καὶ πρὸς [ἡμᾶς
αὐτοὺς τῆς] | πόλεως ὑμῶν διάθεσιν πειράσομαι ἀεί τινος ὑ[μεῖν
ἀγαθοῦ] | γενέσθαι παραίτιος. Περὶ δὲ Πεύκης καὶ τῶν στομ[ά-
των διδαχ]θε||ὶς ὑπὸ τῶν πρέσβεων ὑμῶν ἐδικαίωσα τηρῖσθαι 60
ὑμεῖν τ[ὰ τῶν προ]||γόνων ὑμῶν ὅρια.

Exemplum epistulae | Mari Laberi Maximi, leg. Aug. pr. pr. |
Imp. Caesari Traiano Aug. Germanico III Iulio Fron|tino III cos.
VIII ka. Novembres. Descriptum || et recognitum factum ex comm. 65
Mari Laberi | Maximi leg. Aug. pr. pr. Permitt. . . . .| Fabio
Pompeiano. Quae iam era .scri. . . . . . .| Charagonio Phicora-

laestro con*ductore publici por*|tori ripae Thraciae postulante u*t vectigal*
70 *Hal*‖myridis et Peuci daretur secund*um veterem legem?* | . . . . . . bit.
Ius exigendi port*ori* . . . .| . . . . . .arum dimensium usque
ad . . . .|

This document contains the letters of several governors of Moesia
to the officials of the town of Histria. Laberius Maximus was
governor in 100, Tullus Geminus in 54, Plautus Aelianus in
52–53, Pomponius Pius in 51, Aemilianus in 50, and Flavius
Sabinus in 43–49. From the frequency of the letters, we may
infer that the privileges of the city in regard to their monopoly
of salt fish, their forest rights, and even the extent of their *territorium*, were being constantly called in question, probably by the
agents of the imperial *fiscus*. From this document we also learn
that the chief source of revenue of the city came from its fishing
privileges, but there is no evidence to prove that these were a
municipal monopoly, leased out to its residents.

69. DECRETUM CHIORUM DE PECUNIA ADMINISTRANDA
(saec. 1 p. Chr.)

Cagnat, *IGRR.* 4, 948.

. . . . [εἶναι τὴν δάνεισιν | τοῦ χρήματος] ἄπα[ντο]ς, [οὐ-
δενὸς ἔχοντ]|ος ἐξουσίαν τῶν δαν[ειστῶν] . . . . . . | καταβολὴ[ν]
5 ποιήσασθαι οὐδ[εμίαν τοῦ] ἀργ‖[υ]ρίου καὶ τῶν ἐπακ[ο]λου-
[θ]ούντων τόκ[ων πρὶν ἢ | τ]ὸ διελθεῖν τὴν πενταετίαν. Αἱρε-
[θῆναι | δὲ] ἄνδρας ὀκτὼ ἐν ταῖς ἀρχαιρεσίαις [ἐπὶ] τ[ὸ|ν]
δανει[σ]μὸν τῶν χρημάτων μετὰ τὴν αἵρεσιν τοῦ | ἀγω]νοθέτου
10 τῶν Σεβαστῶν ἀγώνων. Ἔπειτα δ]ὲ ‖ τὴν μεταπαράδοσιν γεί-
νεσθαι ὑπὸ τῶν τετε[λε]|[κ]ότων τὴ[ν] χρείαν ἀνδρῶν διὰ ἀπο-
γραφῆς τῆ(ι) ἐνά|[τη](ι) τῆ(ι) τοῦ Ποσειδεῶνος, [ἐ]σομένης
ἀ[ντ]απ[ο|γ]ρα[φῆς] ὑπ[ὸ τῶν] παραλα[μβαν]όντ[ω]ν, πα[ντὸ]ς |
15 τοῦ χ[ρή]ματος ἐσομένης τῆς δ[ανείσ]εως κα‖[θ]ότι π[ρογέ-
γ]ραπτ[αι, προ]καταβαλούντων τούτ[ων] | καὶ τῶ[ν ἀ]εὶ
χειρ[ο]τ[ο]νη[θ]ησομένων ἀ[νδρ]ῶν τ[ὴν | τ]οῦ πρώ[του ἔ]τους
π[ρόσο]δον πρ[ὸ ἡμερ]ῶν τρ[ιῶν | τῆς] τοῦ Σ[εβαστ]οῦ Γερμανι-
κο[ῦ Καίσα]ρος ἡμέ[ρας | γε]νεθλί[ο]υ δει[νά]ρια θχ΄· κα[ί, ἐ]ὰν
20 ἐμβόλιμος ἄγη‖[ται] μήν, καὶ τ[ού]του προσκαταβαλλό⟨ν⟩ντων
. . . .

[386]

FROM ITALY AND THE PROVINCES

This inscription from Chios is important for the regulation of endowment funds given to the city. Eight men are chosen to administer the trust, which is to accumulate for four years. Then the accumulated interest is to be paid to the proper officials. In the case of similar endowments, *e.g.* that of Salutaris at Ephesus (no. 71), the consent of the provincial governor was sometimes secured. Such a provision may have been found in the portion of the decree which has disappeared.

70. SMYRNAEORUM PORTARIA
(saec. fere I vel II p. Chr.)

I.B.M. 1021; Ditt. *Syll.*³ 1262; Cagnat, *IGRR.* 4, 1427.

....τη[ιε]ι.........δια..... | [τ]οὺς πολλοὺς κω[λύο]υσι
[κοι|ν]ωνεῖν τῆς πορθμείας, πρ[ὸς] | δὲ τούτοις ἀντὶ δύο ὀβο-
λ[ῶν] ‖ δύο ἀσσάρια πεποιήκασι τ[ὸν] | ναῦλον, δι' αὐτὸ τοῦτο 5
καὶ σ[υν]‖εστηκότες καὶ κωλύοντες | τὸν βουλόμενον πορθμεύ-
[ειν, | ὅ]πως ἐπάν[αγ]κες αὐτοῖς οἱ [δε‖ό]μενοι τῆς πορ[θμ]είας 10
χρῶ[ν|τ]αι· ὁμοίως δὲ κ[αὶ] περὶ τὰς ἄ[λ|λ]ας πορθμείας κα-
κουργοῦσ[ι κ|α]τὰ ταὐτά· ἔδοξε τῆι βουλῆι κ[αὶ | τ]ῶι δήμωι,
καθὰ εἰσηγή[σατο].............

From Smyrna. The document is apparently a decree of the city regulating the ferry traffic across the Hermus. Not enough of the inscription is preserved to enable us to determine whether the city was concerned in the regulation of the traffic because of a possible loss of revenue (*cf.* no. 128 where the ferry was a civic monopoly), or from a desire to keep the peace.

71. EPISTULA AQUILI PROCULI, PROCONSULIS
ASIAE, AD EPHESIOS
(104 p. Chr.)

I.B.M. 481 (pt. IV, p. 246, ll. 336 *ff.*); Laum, *Stiftungen*, 74.

['Ακουίλλιος Πρόκλος, ὁ λαμπρό]τατος, Ἐφεσ[ί]ων ἄρχ[ουσι, |
βουλῆι, δήμωι] χαίρειν. | [Οὐείβιον Σαλουτάριον ὄντ]α τοῖς τε
ἄλ[λο]ις πᾶσι[ν | πολείτην ἄριστον καὶ πρό]τερον ἐν πολ[λοῖ]ς
τῆς ἑαυ‖[τοῦ φιλοτειμίας πολλά τε καὶ οὐ]χ ὡς ἔτυχεν π[αρε]- 340
σχημένον | [παραδείγματα εἰδώς, ὥσπερ] ἦν ἄξιον, ἐν τοῖς

[387]

MUNICIPAL DOCUMENTS IN GREEK AND LATIN

[οἰκ]ειοτάτ[οις | ἡμῶν εἶχον φίλοις· νῦν δέ, ἐ]πεὶ τὴν μὲν πό[λιν
προῄρ]ηται | [μεγίστοις τε καὶ ἀξιολογω]τάτοις δώροι[ς κοσ]-
μῆσαι με||[γαλοπρεπῶς εἰς τειμὴν τῆς] τε ἐπιφαν[εστάτη]ς καὶ
345 μεγίσ||[της θεᾶς ᾿Αρτέμιδος καὶ τοῦ] οἴκο[υ τῶν Σεβαστ]ῶν καὶ
τῆς | [ὑμετέρας πόλεως, τοῖς δὲ πολείταις εἰς διανο]μὰς καὶ
κλή|[ρους καθιέρωκε δην. δισμύρια, νομίζω καὶ ὑμᾶς,] ἐφ᾿ οἷς ἤδη |
[πεποίηκεν ὑμεῖν καὶ νῦν ἐπανγέλλεται ἀγαθοῖ]ς, χρῆναι τῆι τε |
[φιλοτειμίαι αὐτοῦ ἀνταποδοῦναι καὶ τῆι εὐμεν]είαι, ἃ πρὸς ||
350 [τειμὴν αὐτοῦ ἐψηφίσατε. Συνήδομαι δ᾿ ὑμεῖν εἰς τὸ ἐπαι]νέσαι
τε τὸν | [ἄνδρα καὶ ἀξιῶσαι αὐτὸν δικαίας παρ᾿ ἡμεῖν] μαρτυ-
ρίας | [πρὸς τὸ καὶ πλείους γενέσθαι τοὺς κατὰ τὰ] δύνατα
προ|[θυμουμένους εἰς τὰ ὅμοια. Τὰ δὲ ὑπ᾿ αὐτοῦ καθιε]ρούμενα
χρή|[ματα καὶ τὰ ἀπεικονίσματα τῆς θεοῦ καὶ τὰς] εἰκόνας η
355 τισ||[. . . . . | . . . .]χε[. . . . .]αισ [. . . . . . | .] εταιονδε
[. . . . . .]εχρησ[. . . . . . | .]ε οὐδένα β[ούλομαι νυ]νὶ τρόπ[ωι
οὐδενὶ οὔτε παρευρέσει οὐ|[δ]εμιᾶι μετ[αβαλεῖν ἢ π]αραλλά[ξαι
360 τι τῶν ὑπ᾿ αὐτοῦ διατεταγμέ||ν]ων· εἰ δ[έ τις ἐπι]χειρή[σ]ει ἢ
λῦσ[αι ἢ παραλλάξαι τι τῶν | ὑ]φ᾿ ὑμῶ[ν διὰ το]ύτου τ[οῦ
ψηφίσματος κυρωθησομένων | ἢ] εἰσ[ηγή]σασθαί τι τοιο[ῦτον
πειράσει, ὑποκείσθω εἰς προσ|κ]όσ[μ]ησιν τῆς κυρίας ᾿Αρτέ-
μιδ[ος δη. Β̄ μ(υρίοις) ε̄ καὶ εἰς τὸν ἱερ|]ώτατον φίσκον ἄλλοις
365 δη. [δισμυρίοις πεντακισχειλίοις καὶ || οὐ]δὲν ἔλαττον ἔστω
ἄκυρον [ἅπαν τὸ παρὰ τὴν] καθιέ[ρωσιν. Συν|ή]δο(ι)μ[α]ι δὲ
αὐτῶι εἰς τὸ πᾶσιν [νῦν φανερὰν γενέ]σθαι τ[ήν | τ]ε πρὸς τὴν
θεὸν εὐσέβεια[ν καὶ τὴν πρὸς τοὺς Σε]βαστο[ὺς | κ]αὶ τὴν πρὸς
τὴν πόλιν ε[ὐμένειαν αὐτοῦ ἐν τῶι] θεάτρωι. | ῎Ερρ[ωσθε].

From Ephesus. Of the great inscription which records the endowment founded by Vibius Salutaris for the benefit of his fellow-
citizens at Ephesus, we have given only the letter of the governor
ratifying the gift and naming the penalty imposed on anyone who
should seek to void or disregard the provisions of the foundation.
We rarely find a record of such ratifications by imperial officials
(cf. Laum, op. cit. nos. 19b, 162, 206), and the act was probably
unnecessary, but the submission of the terms of the gift to the
emperor or to the governor was inspired by motives of vanity and
by a desire to bring the individual or the city to the notice of the
central government. This procedure gave an excellent opening for

[388]

imperial interference in municipal matters, and undoubtedly led to the development of paternalistic tendencies. In general, endowments which provided for the distribution of money to citizens were deprecated (*cf.* no. 101; Pliny, *Epp. ad Trai.* 116, 117). Since Salutaris provided that 450 denarii should be distributed annually to the senators at the rate of a denarius apiece, we learn that the Ephesian senate normally had 450 members at this period (*cf.* the commentary of the editors of the *I.B.M. ad loc.*). Laum points out that fully half of the endowment assigned to provide a dole to the six tribes at Ephesus had disappeared or had been diverted to other uses within a few years after the foundation (*op. cit.* 1, 222 *f.*).

72. TITULUS OPERIS PUBLICI
(111 p. Chr.)

An. ép. 1904, no. 59.

Imp. Caesar | *divi Nervae f.* | *Nerva Tra*ianus | *Aug. Ger*-manicus || *Dacicus pont.* maximus | *trib. pot. xv imp. vi cos. v* | 5
*p. p. redacta in form*am | *provincia* Arabia | *Viam N*ovam a finibus ||
Syriae usque ad | *Mare Rubru*m aperuit | *et stravit per* C. | *Claudium* 10
Sever*um* | leg. pro pr. || CLXVI. 15

This inscription and no. 103 record the completion of public works under the order of the emperor for the benefit of provincial communities. For a similar inscription of an earlier date, *cf.* no. 31.

73. SENATUS CONSULTUM ET EPISTULA TRAIANI
AD PERGAMENOS DE LUDIS INSTAURANDIS
(112–117 p. Chr.)

CIL. III, *S.* 7086; Cagnat, *IGRR.* 4, 336; *Alterthümer von Pergamon*, VIII, 2, 269.

(Primi versus omissi sunt)

['Επὶ . . . . στρατηγοῦ καὶ . | . .]ο[υ] Κλαυδίου Σειλα- 15
νοῦ ἀρχιερέως | . . . . . cos. . . . . .ias s. c. factum de postulatione
Pergamenorum(?) | *placere ut certamen illud,* quod in honorem templi
Iovis amicalis et | *Imp. Caes. divi Nervae f. N*ervae Traiani Augusti Germanici Dacici || *pontificis maximi est const*itutum εἰσελασ- 20
τικὸν in civitate | *Pergamenorum, eiusdem cond*icionis sit, cuius

est quod in honorem Romae | et Divi Aug. ibi agitur, ita ut ea
impendia, quae propter id certamen | fieri oportebit, cedant in onus
Iuli Quadrati clarissimi viri. | . . . . eorumque ad quos ea res
25 pertinebit. || [Κεφαλαῖον ἐκ τ]ῶν Καίσαρος ἐντολῶν. | Cum
secundum meam constitutionem certamen in civitate | Pergamenorum
ab Iulio Quadrato amico clarissimo viro quinquennale, | quod dicitur
εἰσελαστικόν, constitutum sit idq. amplissimus ordo | eiusdem iuris
30 esse decreverit, cuius est quod in eadem civitate || in honorem Romae
et divi Aug. institutum est, huius quoq. ise(l)as|tici idem quod in
altero certamine custoditur dare oportebit | victoribus praemium. |
[Αὐτοκράτωρ Καῖσαρ Θεοῦ Νερούα υἱ]ὸς Νέρουας Τραϊανὸς
Ἄριστος | [Σεβαστὸς Γερμανικὸς Δακικός, ἀρ]χιερεὺς μέγιστος,
35 δημαρχικῆς || [ἐξουσίας τὸ ι., αὐτοκράτωρ τὸ . ., ὕπα]τος τὸ
ϛ´, πατὴρ πατρίδος, | [Περγαμηνῶν τῆι βουλῆι καὶ τῶ]ι δήμωι
χαίρειν. | [Ἐλθούσης ὑμῶν πρεσβείας, ἀποδεξά]μενος αὐτῆς τό
τε ἀξίωμα | [καὶ τὰ συγγράμματα, περὶ πάντων ἃ ἐν αὐτ]οῖς
ἠξιώσατε συγκατεθέμην | [. . . . . μ]ε[τ]άσχοιτε,
40 ἐπιτρέπω οὖν ὑ||[μῖν. . . . .]λόντων ἐν ἀγοραίοις |
[. . . . .] τῶν θεωριῶν ὡρισμένον |. . . . .
. . . . . ὁρῶ [δ]ὲ καὶ τὰς ὑπο . . . .

From Pergamum. This inscription deals with the relations of a
senatorial province to the emperor and senate. When Julius Quadratus wished to establish games in honor of Trajan in Pergamum,
the emperor was apparently consulted first. He referred the matter
to the senate, and when they approved the request, the emperor
issued the edict instead of the senate (secundum meam constitutionem).
He also confirmed the senate's action in making the games equal
in rank to those in honor of Augustus. The letter of Trajan in
Greek is too fragmentary to permit an accurate interpretation, but
it apparently deals with some remission of the market-tax during
the games. If so, the tax was probably an imperial one levied in a
senatorial province. For Julius Quadratus, cf. Waddington, Fastes
des provinces asiatiques, 114.

74. EPISTULA PROCURATORUM AD
COLONOS VILLAE MAGNAE
(116–117 p. Chr.)

Bruns, 114; Girard, p. 870; Riccobono, p. 352.

*Pro sal*ute | Aug(usti) n(ostri) imp(*eratoris*) Caes(aris) Traiani Col. 1
princ(*ipis*) | totiusque domus divine | *o*ptimi Germanici Parthici.
Data a Licinio || *Ma*ximo et Feliciore Aug(usti) lib(erto) procc(ura- 5
toribus) ad exemplu*m* | *leg*is Manciane. Qui eorum *i*ntra fundo
villae Mag|ne Variani id est Mappalia Siga *habitabunt*, eis eos agros
qui su|*b*cesiva sunt excolere permittitur lege Manciana | . . .ita
ut eas qui excoluerit usum proprium habe||at. Ex fructibus qui eo 10
loco nati erunt, dominis au*t* | conductoribus vilicisve eius f(undi)
partes e lege Ma|nciana prestare debebunt hac condicione: coloni |
fructus cuiusque culture quos ad aare*m* deportare | et terere debe-
bunt, summas de*fer*ant arbitratu || *s*uo conductoribus vilicis*ve* eius 15
f(undi) et si conducto|res vilic*iv*e eius f(undi) in assem p*artes*
c*ol*(on)icas datur|as renuntiaverint tabellis*que obsignatis*. . .f s ca-
vea|nt eius fructus partes, qu*as presta*re debent, | conductores vili-
c*iv*e eius *f(undi) col*oni colonic||as partes prestare debeant. Qui in 20
f(undo) villae Mag|nae sive Mappalia Siga villas habent habebunt |
dominicas *dominis* eius f(undi) aut conductoribus vilicis*v*e | eorum
in assem partes fructuu*m* et vinea*rum* ex | consuetudine Manciane
cu*i*usque gene||ris habet prestare debebunt; tritici ex a|ream partem 25
tertiam, hordei ex aream | *part*em tertiam, fabe ex aream partem
qu|*ar*tam, vinu de laco partem tertiam, ol|*ei co*acti partem tertiam,
mellis in alve||*is* mellaris sextarios singulos. Qui supra | quinque 30
alveos | habebit in tempore quo vin|demia mellaria fu*it fuerit*, | Col. II
dominis aut conduct*oribus vili*||cisve eius f(undi) qui in assem *par*- 5
tem. . . | d(are) d(ebebit). Si quis alveos, examina, apes, *vasa* |
mellaria ex f(undo) villae Magne sive M|appalie Sige in octonarium
agru*m* | transtulerit, quo fraus aut dominis au*t* || conductoribus vili- 10
cisve eis quam fiat, alv|*ei*, exam*in*a, apes, vasa mellaria, mel qui
in *eo f(undo)* | erunt conductor*um vil*icorumve in assem e*ius* | f(undi)
erunt. Ficus aride arbor*esve aliaeq*ue extra poma|rio erunt, qua
pomariu*m in*tra villam ipsam || sit, ut non amplius iu*sta vindemia* 15
*fi*at, colon|us arbitrio suo co*actorum fructuu*m conduc*to*|ri vilicisve

[391]

eius f(undi) par*tem tantam d(are) d(ebebit)*. Ficeta vete|ra et oliveta,
que ante ha*nc lege*m *sata sunt, ex* consuetu|din*e* fructum conductori
20 vilicisve eius prestar*e* || debea*nt*. Si quod ficetum postea factum erit,
eius fic*eti* | fruc*t*um per continuas ficationes quinque | arbitrio suo
e*i* qui serverit percipere permittitur, | post quintam ficationem eadem
leg*e* qua s(upra) s(criptum) est | conductoribus vilicisve eius f(undi)
25 p(restare) d(ebebit). Vineas serere || colere loco veterum permittitur
ea condicione *ut* | ex ea satione proxumis vindemi*s* quinque fructu*m* |
earum vinearum is qui ita *secuerit* suo arbitr*i*o per|cip*i*at itemque
post quinta(m) vindemia(m) quam ita sata | erit, fructus partes
30 tertias e lege Manciana conduc||toribus | vi*licisve* eius in assem dare
Col.III debe|*bit*. Olivetum serere colere in | eo loc*o* qua quis incultum
5 excolu|erit permittitur ea condicione u||t ex ea satione eius fructus
oliveti q|uid ita satum est per olivationes pro|ximas decem arbitrio
suo *percipe*|re debeat, item post olivationes (decem) ole*i* | coacti
10 partem tertiam *c*onducto||ribus vilicisve eius f(undi) d(are) d(ebebit).
Qui inserue|rit oleastra post *olivationes qui*nque par|tem tertiam
d(are) d(ebebit).......in f(undo) | ville Magne Var*i*ani siv*e*
15 Mappaliae | Sige sunt eruntve ex*tra eo*s agros qui || vicias habent,
eorum a*g*rorum fruct|*u*s conductoribus vilicisv*e e*ius d(are) d(ebe-
bunt); custodes e|xigere debebu*nt*. Pro pecora*que i*ntra f(undum)
ville M|agne sive Mappalie Sig*e* pascentur, in pectora sin|gula aera
20 quattus conductoribus vilicisve do||minorum eius f(undi) prestari
debebu*nt*. Si quis ex f(undo) ville | Magne *sive* Mappalie Sige
fructus stantem pen|dentem, maturum inmaturum caec*i*derit, ex-
cider|it, exportaverit deportaverit conbuserit desequer|it sequ*entis*
Col.IV *bi*enii detrimentum conductoribus vilicisve eius f(undi) | coloni erit
ei cui de.... | tantum prestare d(ebebit). *Si qui in f(undo) ville
Mag*|ne siv(e) Mappalie Sige *arbores frugiferas se*|verunt severint *iis*
5 *eius superficiei usum* || qui e legitimo.......| testamen..........
sup|erficies...hoc tempus lege M*anciana* | ritu...fiducieve data
sunt dabuntur...*id* | ..ve ius fiduciae lege Manciana serva*bitur*...
10 *Qui* || superficiem ex inculto excoluit excolu*erit ibique* | ...aedi-
ficium deposuit posuerit *i*sve qui *coluit colere* | desierit perdesierit eo
tempore, quo ita ea super*ficies* | coli desit desierit, ea quo fuit fuerit
ius colendi dumtaxa|d bienn*i*o proximo ex qua die colere desierit
15 servatu*r* || servabitur; post biennium conductores vilic*i*ve eoru*m*... |

[392]

Ea superficies que proxumo anno *c*ulta fuit et coli *desi*|erit con-
ductor vilicusve eius f(undi) *ei cuius* ea superficies esse dicit|ur
denuntiet superficiem cultam...... | denuntiationem denuntiatur
...testa....— || o itemque in sequentem annum per*s*istat ea sine 20
que*re*|*l*a eius f(undi) post biennium conductor vilicusve co*lere de-*|
beto. Ne quis conductor vilicus*ve eoru*m inquilinum *eius* | f(undi).
Coloni qui intra f(undum) ville Magne *sive* Mappalia Sige habit-|
abunt dominis aut conduct*oribus vilicisve* in assem *qu*||odannis in 25
hominibus *singulis in arati*ones ope|ras n(umero) 11 et in messem
op........generis | singulas operas bin*as* p*r*estare *debebunt*. Co-
loni | inquilini eius f(undi) intra...anni n|omina sua conductor*ibus
vilicisve*....*i*n custo||dias singulas qu.............nent | ratam 30
seorsu*m*...um. | Stipendiari*orum qui in f*(*undo*) *ville Magne sive
M*appa|lie Sige habita*bunt*....uas c|onductoribus vil*icisve*...cust-||
odias f(undi) servis dominic...nit est | (*quae sequuntur quinque lineae* 35
legi non possunt.) *H*ec lex scripta a Luro Victore Odilonis magistro,
et Flavio Gem|inio defensore; Felice Annobalis Birzilis.

I, ll. 16–17. daturas; daturos se, *Rostowzew.*
I, l. 17. sine fraude sua; f s, *tablet.*
II, l. 10. eis quam; usquam *or* eis qu(i) (in) a(sse)m, *Gradenwitz.*
II, l. 13. arboresve aliae que, *Schulten*; arborum earum quaeque, *Ros-
towzew, taking* ficus aride *as a genitive.*
III, l. 12. in fundo, *tablet*; Qui agri herbosi in fundo, *Rostowzew.*
III, l. 23. desequerit = desecuerit, *Toutain.*
III, l. 24. fundi, *tablet*; *perhaps* fundi prestare debebit, *Schulten.*
IV, l. 1. coloni, *tablet*; Si culpa coloni, *Schulten.*
IV, l. 1. ei cui de...; ei cui debet partes colonicas alterum, *H. Krüger.*
IV, ll. 5–6. *Gradenwitz remarks that the sense requires* qui e legitimo iure
ad hereditatem eius venient vel testamento instituti heredes erunt.
IV, l. 8. ritu...; pignori(s) t(itulo), *Gradenwitz and Dessau; Schulten
gives sense of passage*: Si quae aedificia superficiesve post hoc tempus
e lege Manciana pignori obligata fiducieve data sunt dabuntur eorum
in biennium colono heredi eius fiducia e lege Manciana servabitur.
IV, ll. 16–22. *Schulten restores the sense as follows*: Ea superficies que
proximo anno culta fuit et coli desierit conductor vilicusve eius fundi
ei cuius ea superficies esse dicitur denuntiet superficiem cultam colen-
dam esse; si post hanc denuntiationem denuntiatas cessare pergat
itemque insequentem annum persistat, ea superficies sine querela eius
post triennium conductor vilicusve eius fundi colere debeto.
IV, l. 19. *after* denuntiatur *Schulten finds on stone* essegabit *or* essechatis.
IV, l. 21. *Schulten thinks* eius fundi *belongs after* conductor vilicusve.

MUNICIPAL DOCUMENTS IN GREEK AND LATIN

IV, l. 23. *after* fundi *Schulten conjectures that* plus quam...prestare cogat *has fallen out.*

IV, l. 26. *after* messem *Schulten proposes* operas n...et in sarritiones cuiusque.

IV, l. 29. *after* vilicisve *the words* eius fundi edere et operas *have been suggested.*

IV, l. 30. *after* singulas *the words* quas agris prestare debent *have been proposed.*

IV, l. 33. *after* vilicisve *the words* eius fundi prestare debeant *have been suggested. The words* Hec lex, *etc., stand at the bottom of the first column.*

An altar found in 1896 at Henchir Mettich in Tunis. The inscription is written on all four sides of it. For list of articles bearing on it, *cf.* Bruns, Girard, Riccobono, and Rostowzew, *Gesch. d. röm. Kol.* 322 *ff.* Trajan's title of Parthicus fixes its date. It contains, after a dedication of the altar to the emperor (ll. 1–4), a letter of the procurators. At the bottom of the first column stand the words *hec lex scripta,* etc., here printed at the end. The letter is addressed to the *coloni* of the villa Magna Variani sive Mappalia Siga (*cf.* col. 1, ll. 6–7), and settles certain disputes between them and the *conductor.* There are three main points at issue: What part of the produce is due from the tenants? How many days' labor do they owe to the *conductor* each year? What rights have they in new land put under cultivation? Perhaps the general regulations of the *lex Manciana* (*cf.* pp. 17 *ff.*) on these points are at variance with local usage, and need to be modified. More probably, however, as in the case of the *saltus Burunitanus* (*cf.* no. 111), the *conductor* has been demanding more than the law allowed. At all events the procurators settle the dispute in this letter, in which they set forth, in a form adapted to the purpose and perhaps modified for the locality, the pertinent regulations of the law mentioned above. This document is engraved by the local representatives of the *coloni,* the *magister* and the *defensor* (*cf.* p. 19). The *lex Manciana,* being intended for all the estates within a given district, covers both imperial domains and such private estates as still exist. The *domini,* to whom frequent reference is made, are probably private owners, or possibly head-tenants (*cf.* Heitland, *Agricola,* 343). The *conductores* are agents in charge of imperial or private estates. The *vilici* are subordinate overseers. Outside of the administrative classes

[394]

the document speaks of *coloni*, or regular tenants, *inquilini*, possibly landless residents on the estates (*cf.* Rostowzew, *op. cit.* 341; *cf.* however, Seeck, *R.E.* 4, 496), and *stipendiarii*, perhaps occupants of an *ager stipendiarius* within the limits of the *fundus* (*cf.* Rostowzew, *op. cit.* 341). This *ager stipendiarius* may be identical with the *ager octonarius* (II, l. 8), *i.e.* the land upon which eight *denarii* were to be paid for each acre (*cf.* Rostowzew, *op. cit.* 341). Licinius Maximus (I, ll. 4–5) seems to be the *procurator tractus Karthaginiensis*, and Felicior, the freedman, is procurator of the local *saltus*. Of the names mentioned at the bottom of the first column, Lurius Victor, the son of Odilo, is the local headman. The full title of *defensor* would probably be *defensor gentis*, although this official is not to be identified with the later *defensor civitatis* (*cf.* Toutain, *Nouv. rev. hist. d. droit fr. et étr.* 21 (1897), 389 *f.*). Whether Flavius Geminius or Felix, son of Birzil, and grandson of Annobal, holds this position is uncertain (*cf.* Toutain, *op. cit.* 23 (1899), 411–412; Schulten, *Abh. d. königl. Ges. d. Wiss. zu Göttingen, phil.-hist. Klasse, Neue Folge,* II, no. 3, p. 36). The main provisions of the document are these: The *coloni* may put under cultivation the *subseciva*, or small tracts of land not already cultivated (I, ll. 6–9). In return they are to pay the part of the produce fixed by the *lex Manciana* (I, ll. 10–20). Those who occupy farms, orchards, or vineyards, or keep bees must pay according to the *consuetudo Manciana* (I, l. 20–II, l. 6). Honey fraudulently taken to the *ager octonarius* (to avoid the usual payment?) will be confiscated (II, ll. 6–13). The rental in the case of dried figs and olives is determined by usage (II, ll. 17–20). Those who set out an orchard of fig trees or a vineyard may have all the figs or grapes for five years, but after that they must pay rental (II, ll. 20–30). An olive orchard planted on uncultivated ground is free for ten years (III, ll. 2–10); wild olive trees, put under cultivation, for five years (III, ll. 10–12). For each head of cattle four *denarii* are to be paid (III, ll. 17–20). If anyone damage or take away property, a penalty is fixed (III, ll. 20–24). Transfer of land is allowed on certain conditions (IV, ll. 2–9). After two years abandoned property goes to the overseers (IV, ll. 9–21). The *coloni* must render a certain number of days' work free, probably six, each year (IV, ll. 23–27). The *inquilini*, and

MUNICIPAL DOCUMENTS IN GREEK AND LATIN

probably the *stipendiarii*, must register (IV, ll. 27 ff.). From the fact that farms could be abandoned (IV, ll. 9–21), it would seem to follow that at the beginning of the second century tenants were free to leave an estate. The rental, including, as it did in most cases, one-third of the produce of the land (I, ll. 25 ff.) and six days' labor on the private land of the contractor, seems rather high, but on the other hand the privilege granted to sub-tenants of bringing waste land under cultivation and of enjoying the entire return from it for a period of five or ten years, seems to show a desire to keep the *coloni* on the land and confirms the conclusion that they were at liberty to give up their holdings.

The small number of days' labor exacted of the tenants each year seems to indicate that slave labor was freely employed on this estate, although there is only one reference to slaves in the document (IV, l. 35), and although we should naturally suppose that there must have been a scarcity of slaves at this time in consequence of the comparatively small number of prisoners taken in foreign wars. For a fragmentary inscription dealing with the imperial domains, cf. *An. ép.* 1913, no. 72.

75. EPISTULA IMPERATORIS TRAIANI
AD ASTYPALAEENSES
(117 p. Chr.)

Cagnat, *IGRR*. 4, 1031; *IG*. XII, 3, 175.

Αὐτοκράτωρ Καῖσαρ θεοῦ Τραϊανοῦ [Παρθικοῦ] | υἱός, θεοῦ Νερούα υἱωνός, Τραϊανὸς ['Αδριανὸς] | Σεβαστός, ἀρχιερεὺς μέγι- στος, δημ[αρχικῆς | ἐξ]ουσίας, ὕπατος τὸ β΄, 'Αστυπαλ[αιέων τοῖς ||
5 ἄρχο]υσι καὶ τῆι βουλῆι καὶ τῶι δήμωι χαίρ[ειν. | Καὶ πα]ρὰ τοῦ πρεσβευτοῦ ὑμῶν Πε[τρωνίου τοῦ | 'Ηράκω]ντος καὶ ἐκ τοῦ ψηφίσματ[ος ὑμῶν | ἔμαθον] ὅπως ἤσθητε διαδεξαμέν[ου ἐμοῦ |
10 τὴν πατ]ρώιαν ἀρχήν, ἐπαινέσας δ[ὲ ὑμᾶς || εἰ ἀληθ]ῶς τὴν ἐλευθερίαν ὑ[μῖν ὁ πατήρ μου ἔδωκεν, αὐτὴν κατακυρώσας...

This inscription is engraved on the same stone as no. 36, and comes from Astypalaea. We have adopted the restoration proposed by Domaszewski (Ditt. *Syll.*³ 832, note). Apparently the privileges

FROM ITALY AND THE PROVINCES

granted to a state by any emperor were valid only during his reign, and had to be confirmed by his successors (*cf.* nos. 40, 130). Astypalaea had once been an ally of Rome (Chapot, *La prov. rom. proc. d'Asie*, 114), but it seems that its freedom and immunity from taxation had been curtailed (*cf.* no. 76).

76. EPISTULA IMPERATORIS HADRIANI
AD ASTYPALAEENSES
(118 p. Chr.)

Lafoscade, 19; Cagnat, *IGRR.* 4, 1032 *c*; *IG.* XII, 3, 176; Ditt. *Syll.*[3] 832.

Αὐτοκράτωρ Καῖσαρ, θεοῦ Τραϊανοῦ Παρθικ[οῦ] | υἱός, θεοῦ Νερούα υἱωνός, Τραϊανὸς Ἁδριανὸς | Σεβαστός, ἀρχιερεὺς μέγιστος, δημαρχικῆς | ἐξουσίας, ὕπατος τὸ β', Ἀσστυπαλαιέων || ἄρχουσι καὶ τῆι βουλῆι καὶ τῶι δήμωι χαίρειν. | Ἐντυχὼν ὑμῶν 5 τῶι ψηφίσματι, ὅτι μὲν ἀπο|ρεῖν φατε καὶ οὐ δύνασθαι τελεῖν τὸ ἐπαγγελ|τικὸν ἀργύριον ἐμάνθανον· οὐ μὴν ὁπό|σον τε τοῦτο οὐδὲ ἐκ πότε φέρειν αὐτὸ ἤρξασ[θε. . . .

From Astypalaea. The liberty of the Astypalaeans had been taken away by the Flavian emperors and restored by Trajan (*cf* no. 75). From this document we learn that the *aurum coronarium* was paid by free cities as well as by others. This tax had been remitted by Hadrian in Italy and lessened in provincial cities (*Hist. Aug. Vit. Hadr.* 6). Apparently the payment of the tax had been a serious burden for the Astypalaeans, and they sent an embassy to the emperor to ask for its remission. *Cf. Ath. Mitt.* 48 (1923), 99 *ff.*

77. EPISTULA LEGATI AD POMPAELONENSES
(119 p. Chr.)
CIL. II, 2959.

Claudius Quartinus | II viris Pomp*el*(*onensibus*) salutem. | Et ius magistratibus vestri | exequi adversus contumaces || potestis et 5 nihilominus, qui | cautionibus accipiendis de|sunt, sciant futurum ut non | per hoc tuti sint. Nam et | non acceptarum cautionum peri-|| culum ad eos respiciet et quid|quid praesentes quoque egerint, | 10 id communis oneris erit. Bene | valete. Dat(um) non(is) Octubri-

MUNICIPAL DOCUMENTS IN GREEK AND LATIN

15 (bus) Ca|*l*lagori imp(eratore) Caes(are) Traiano ‖ Hadriano Aug-
(usto) III co(n)s(ule).

Bronze tablet from Pompaelo in Tarraconensis. The last sentence
fixes the date as A.D. 119. The writer's name in full is Ti. Claudius
Ti. f. Pal. Quartinus (*cf.* Boissieu, *Inscr. de Lyon*, 284, no. 38). He
was at this time *legatus* of Tarraconensis. The letter is written at
Calaguris (or Callagoris) Nasica, the birthplace of Quintilian. Its
interest lies in the fact that it seems to confirm the judicial competence of the local magistrates in the matter of requiring a *cautio*
(*cf.* no. 27). Mommsen would correct *quoque* to *quique*.

78. EPISTULA IMPERATORIS HADRIANI AD EPHESIOS
(120 p. Chr.)

Lafoscade, 23; Ditt. *Syll.*[3] 833.

[Αὐτοκράτωρ] Κα[ῖ]σαρ, θεοῦ Τραϊ(α)νοῦ Παρθικοῦ υἱός, |
[θεοῦ Νερούα υ]ἰωνός, Τραϊανὸς ᾿Αδριανὸς Σεβαστός, | [ἀρχιερεὺς
μ]έγιστος, δημαρχικῆς ἐξουσίας τὸ δ΄, | [ὕπατος τ]ὸ γ΄, ᾿Εφεσίων
5 τῆι γερουσίαι χαίρειν. ‖ [Μέττιος] Μόδεστος ὁ κράτιστος εὖ
ἐποίησεν τὰ δίκ|[αια ὑμῖν κατα]νείμας ἐν τῆι κρίσει· ἐπεὶ δὲ
πολλοὺς ἐδηλ[ώσατε] | σφ[ετερί]ζεσθαι χρήματα ὑμέτερα, οὐσίας
τῶν δεδανισ[μέ]‖νω[ν κ]ατέχοντας, οὐ φάσκοντας δὲ κληρονο-
μεῖν, τοὺς [δὲ] | καὶ [αὐ]τοὺς χρεώστας ὄντας, πέπομφα ὑμῶν
10 τὸ ἀντ[ίγραφον] ‖ τοῦ ψηφίσματος Κορνηλίωι Πρείσκωι τῶι
κρατίστωι | ἀνθυπάτωι, ἵνα εἴ τι τοιοῦτον εἴη ἐπιλέξηταί τινα, |
ὃς κρινεῖ τε τἀμφισβητούμενα καὶ εἰσπράξει πάντα | ὅσα ἂν
ὀφείληται τῆι γερουσίαι. ῾Ο πρεσβεύων ἦν | Κασκέλλιος Π[ον]-
15 τικός, ὧι τὸ ἐφόδιον δοθήτω, εἴ γε μὴ ‖ προῖκα ὑπέ[σχε]το
πρεσβεύσειν. Εὐτυχεῖτε. Πρ(ὸ) ε΄ κ(αλανδῶν) ᾿Οκτωβρίων. |
[Γραμματεύοντος Πο]πλίου ῾Ρουτειλίου Βάσσου.

From Ephesus. The members of the *gerusia* at Ephesus had lost
money by bad investments and appealed to the governor for assistance
in solving their financial difficulties. The former governor of the
province had given them some help in this matter, but the properties
of certain debtors had passed into the hands of new owners, and
these claimed that they did not inherit the obligations of the former
owners, as they were not their heirs-at-law. The emperor instructed

the present governor to appoint a judge to settle these cases and exact the amounts due to the *gerusia*. The right of πρωτοπραξία, or first lien on property, was thus granted to the *gerusia* by the emperor. Trajan refused to grant this privilege to Bithynian towns to the detriment of private individuals, unless the city already had acquired the right from former emperors, who, apparently, had granted it freely (Pliny, *Epp. ad Trai.* 108, 109).

79. EPISTULA IMPERATORIS HADRIANI (?)
AD HERACLEOTAS
(121–125 p. Chr.)

B.C.H. 21 (1897), 162.

. ʌ . . . οι λειτουργείτωσαν· οἱ δὲ κεκτημένοι μόνον ταῖς τῆι |
[πόλει ἐ]πιβαλλομέναις λειτουργίαις ὑπεύθυνοι ἔστωσαν· τίνα |
[δὲ δεῖ τρ]όπον στόρνυσθαι τὰς ὁδούς, κοινῶι διατάγματι ἐδή-
λωσα· | [κε]λεύω καὶ ΑΝΤΑΝΟΤΣ συντελεῖν ὑμεῖν εἰς τὰ
ἀναλώματα, || τὸ τρίτον συνεισφέροντας· ἡ δὲ συνεισφορὰ γε-
νέσθω ἀπὸ | τῶν ἐν Μακεδονίαι ὄντων ΑΝΤΑΝΩΝ. Εὐτυχεῖτε. |
Πρὸ ιγ´ καλανδῶν Ἰουνίων· ἀπὸ Δυρραχίου.   5

This inscription is said to have been found on the site of Heraclea in Macedonia. Heraclea was a free state (Caesar, *B.C.* 3. 34; Strabo, 7. 7, p. 326). From this letter we learn that the citizens of this city, who owned property, were responsible for the maintenance of that part of the Egnatian Way which lay within their *territorium*, or, possibly, of the roads which led from the main highway through their district, since the plural form ὁδούς is used. It is probable that the *civitates liberae* were required to keep in repair the state roads which passed through their domains (*cf.* Le Bas-Waddington, 2806). In the case of Heraclea the citizens were helped by the ANTANOI who were required to contribute a third of the expense. Perdrizet thinks that the reading of this word is incorrect, but offers no emendation. He assumes that it refers to some corporation of traders in Macedonia who were concerned in the proper upkeep of the roads (*B.C.H.* 21 (1897), 162 f.). The reading Ἀτιντανοί is suggested by Holleaux (*Rev. d. ét. gr.* 11 (1898), 273 ff.).

[399]

MUNICIPAL DOCUMENTS IN GREEK AND LATIN

80. EPISTULA LEGATI LYCIAE, VALERI SEVERI,
AD RHODIAPOLITANOS
(125 p. Chr.)

Cagnat, *IGRR*. 3, 739, c. 16; Lafoscade, 104.

Οὐαλήριος Σεουῆρ[ος, π]ρεσβευτὴς Σεβαστοῦ | 'Ροδιαπολει-
τῶν [ἄρ]χουσι, βουλῆι, δήμωι | χαίρειν. Ὡς ἀξιοῦ[τε], 'Οπραμόαι
5 'Α[π]ολλωνί|ου δὶς τοῦ Καλλ[ιάδο]υ, ὄντι καλῶι καὶ ἀ∥γαθῶι
πολείτηι κα[ὶ οὐ] μόνον τῆς ἀ|φ' ὑμῶν μαρτυρί[ας, ἀλ]λὰ καὶ
τῆς ἀπὸ | τοῦ ἔθνους ἐπι[βοήσεως τυχόντι τειμὰς] | ὑμᾶς ψηφί-
ζεσ[θαι ἡδέως ἐπιτρέπω. | 'Ερρῶσθαι ὑμ]ᾶς εὔχομαι. 'Α[νε-
10 γρ]άφ[η] ∥ ἐπὶ ἀρχι(ερέος) 'Αττάλου τοῦ Φανίου, Δείου α'.

We have included a few (nos. 84, 87, 97, 99, 102) of the inscriptions engraved on the walls of the mausoleum of Opramoas,
a distinguished citizen of Rhodiapolis in Lycia. Before his death,
Opramoas collected a series of honorary decrees and letters from the
emperor and provincial governors and had them engraved on the
tomb which he had erected. They constitute an important record
for the study of the relation of the central government to the
municipalities of the province and to the κοινόν. From them we
learn that honorary decrees were submitted to the governor or to
the emperor by the κοινόν and by the cities, that the governor
had the right of vetoing such decrees, and that an appeal could be
made to the emperor over the veto of the governor. This is the case
with decrees conferring unusual honors. It was, apparently, the
practice of cities to refer honorary decrees to the governor or
emperor, probably through motives of vainglory or servility, for
many of the documents on the monument of Opramoas are mere
acknowledgments by the officials, and there is no indication that
their sanction of the action of the city was required. In the document which we have given above, the Rhodiapolitani ask for the
approval of the governor in conferring honors upon Opramoas.

[400]

FROM ITALY AND THE PROVINCES

81. RESCRIPTUM IMPERATORIS HADRIANI (?)
AD PERGAMENOS DE COLLYBO
(125 p. Chr.?)

Ditt. *Or. Gr.* 484; *Alterthümer von Pergamon*, VIII, 2, 279.

...... λοῦμεν τω.......... | .... μετεπεμ]-
ψάμην, βουληθεὶς μὲ[ν] φαί|[νεσθαι δίκαιος κατὰ τὴν ἐμαυτοῦ
συν]ήθειαν, μόνα δὲ ταῦτα ἐξετάσαι | [τὰ ἐγκλήματα τῶν ἐργα-
ζομένων ἐπ]ὶ τῆς πόλεως (ὑ)μῶν ἀνδρῶν, περὶ ὧν ‖ [ὁ ἀποσταλεὶς 5
ὑφ' ὑμῶν πρεσβευτὴς Κ]αλουίσιος Γλύκων ἐδίδαξεν ἡμᾶς.
Πα|[ρεῖναι δ' ἐκέλευσα αὐτούς, ἵνα δῆλ]ον ἦν εἴ τι λέγειν
ἐβούλοντο. Ὁ οὖν τῆς ἀ|[μείψεως τρόπος οὐ νόμιμος ἦν, ἀ]λ(λ)ὰ
παρὰ τὸ δίκαιον καὶ παρὰ τὴν συναλλαγὴν | [πράττειν αὐτοῖς
ἐ]πέτρεπον. Παρὰ γὰρ τῶν ἐργαστῶν καὶ καπήλων καὶ τῶν
ὀ|[ψαριοπωλῶν ε]ἰς τὸν λεπτὸν ἐμπολᾶν εἰωθότων χαλκὸν
δεκαοκτὼ ἀσσάρια ‖ [τὸ δη]νάρ[ιον] λαμβάνειν ὀφείλοντες καὶ 10
τοῖς τὸ δηνάριον διαλλάσσειν βου|[λ]ομένοι[ς πρὸ]ς [δ]ε[κα]επτὰ
διδόναι οὐκ ἠρκοῦντο τὴν τῶν ἀσσαρίων ἄμει|ψιν, ἀλλ[ὰ κ]αὶ
ἐὰν δηναρίων ἀργυρῶν τις ἀγοράσηι τὸ ὀψάριον, καθ' ἕκα|στον
δηνάριον εἰσέπρασσον ἀσσάριον ἕν. Ἔδοξεν οὖν ἡμεῖν καλῶς
ἔχειν | εἰς [τ]ὸ λοιπὸν τοῦτο διορθῶσθαι, ἵνα μὴ συμβαίνηι τοῖς
ὠνηταῖς ὑπ' αὐτῶν ‖ τελωνεῖσθαι, καθ' ὧν οὐδεμίαν αὐτοῖς ἐξου- 15
σίαν δεδόσθαι συμβέβηκεν. | Ὅσα μέντοι τῶν λεπτῶν ὀψαρίων
σταθμῶι πιπρασκόμενα τιμᾶται ὑπὸ | τῶν ἀγορανόμων, τούτων,
κἂν πλείονας μνᾶς ὠνήσωνταί τινες, ἤρε|σεν ἡμεῖν τὴν τιμὴν
αὐτοὺς διδόναι πρὸς κέρμα, ὥστε ἀπ' αὐτῶν σώσ|ζεσθαι τῆι
πόλει τὴν ἐκ τοῦ κολλύβου πρόσοδον. Ὁμοίως καὶ ἐὰν πλείο‖νες 20
συνθέμενοι ἀργυρῶν δηναρίων δόξωσιν ἠγορακέναι εἶτα διαι-|
ρῶνται, καὶ τούτους λεπτὸν διδόναι χαλκὸν τῶι ὀψαριοπώληι,
ἵνα ἀνα|φέρηται ἐπὶ τὴν τράπεζαν· διδόναι δὲ πρὸς δεκαεπτὰ
ἀσσάρια, ἐπει|δὴ ἡ τῆς ἀμειπτικῆς ἐργασία(ς) δοκεῖ μόνοις τοῖς
ἐργασταῖς διαλέγεσ|θαι. Ἠ(λ)έ(γ)χθησαν μετὰ τοῦτο καὶ ἕτερά
τινα συνκεχωρηκότες ἑαυ‖τοῖς κερδῶν ὀνόματα ἀσπρατούραν τε 25
καὶ τὸ καλούμενον παρ' αὐτοῖς | προσφάγιον, δι' ὧν ἐπηρέαζον
μάλιστα τοὺς τὸν ἰχθὺν πιπράσκοντας. | Καὶ ταῦτα οὖν ἐδοκι-
μάσαμεν διορθῶσθαι· πλεονεκτεῖσθαι γὰρ τοὺς | ὀλίγους ὑπ'
αὐτῶν ἀνθρώπους δ(ῆλ)ον ἦν, συνέβαινεν δὲ πᾶσιν αἰσθη|τὴν
γείνεσθαι τοῖς ὠνουμένοις τὴν ἄδικον τῶν πιπρασκόντων ζη‖μίαν. 30

[401]

Ἠτιάθησαν καὶ ὡς ἐνεορτάδια παρὰ τῶν ἐργαστῶν εἰσπράσ-
σον|τες, ἅπερ ἀρνουμένων αὐτῶν ἡδέως ἐπίστευον, τοῦ μὴ ὀφεί-
λειν | γείνεσθαι τὸ τοιοῦτο λαμβάνων καὶ τὴν παρ' αὐτῶν
συνκατάθεσιν. | Μόνον μέντοι ὡμολόγουν τῶι Ὑπερβερεταίωι
μηνὶ δίδοσθαι ἑαυ|τοῖς τὸ εἰς τὸν Ἑρμῆ λεγόμενον ἐκ τοιαύτης
35 ἀφορμῆς· ὅρκον ἑαυτοῖς ‖ ἀπαιτεῖν συνκεχωρῆσθαι παρὰ τῶν
ἐνπολώντων τὸ λεπτὸν καὶ | πρὸς αὐτοὺς ἀναφερόντων περὶ τοῦ
μηδὲν αὐτοὺς παρὰ τὴν διά|ταξιν πεποιηκέναι. Τοὺς οὖν διὰ τὸ
συνειδὸς ὀμνύναι μὴ δυναμέ|νους διδόναι τι αὐτοῖς, ὥστε μὴ τὴν
τοῦ ὀμνύναι ἀνάγκην ὑπομέ|νειν· ὃ οὐκ ἔδοξεν ἄλογον. Ἀντομ-
40 νύναι μέντοι καὶ αὐτοὺς τοῖς ἐργ[ασ]‖ταῖς περὶ τοῦ μηδὲν αὐτοὺς
ἠδικηκέναι ἐν τῆι τοῦ ἀργυροῦ νομίσ[μα]|τος δόσει καὶ αὐτὸ
δίκαιον ἡγησάμην. Ἐλέγοντο καὶ ἐνεχυρα[σί]|ας ἑαυτοῖς ποιεῖ-
σθαι⟨ν⟩ ἐπιτρέπειν ὅλας τε τῶν ἐργαστῶν ἔσ[θ' ὅτε] | κρατεῖν
τὰς ἐμπολάς, τῆς συναλλαγ[ῆ]ς οὐ τοῦτο συνχωρού[σης], | ἀλλὰ
ἐπὶ τοὺς ταμίας αὐτοὺς παραγείνεσθαι κελευούση[ς, ἐὰν] ‖
45 αἰτιάσωνταί τινα, καὶ παρ' ἐκείνων δημόσιον λαμβάν[ειν δοῦ]|-
λον, ἵνα νομίμως ποιῶνται τὴν ἐνεχυρασίαν, ὥστε [τὸ πρὸ τῆς] |
κρίσεως τούτωι τῶι τρόπωι ληφθὲν μένειν το[ῖς ὀφείλουσ]ι. | Καὶ
τοῦτο οὖν ἔδοξεν ἡμεῖν οὕτως ὀφείλειν γείν[εσθαι, ὅπ]ως
πε|ριεῖχεν ἡ ἔκδοσις, καὶ διὰ τοῦ δημοσίου μέντοι [δούλου μὴ
50 σύ]μμε‖τρον εἶναι τὴν ἐνεχυρασίαν, ἀλλὰ ἢ τὸ ἱκαν[ὸν πρὸ κρίσ]εως
λ[α]μβά|νεσθαι, ἢ ἐὰν δοῦναί τις μὴ δύνηται τὸ σ[υμβόλα]ιον,
εἶνα[ι τ]ὸ ἐ|νέχυρον ὅσου ἂν τὸ πρᾶγμα καὶ τὸ ἐπ' αὐτῶι
[πρόσ]τιμον ἦι. [Τὰς μέντ]οι κρί|σεις γείνεσθαι μὴ ἐπὶ τῶν
ταμιῶ[ν, ἀλλ]ὰ ἐπὶ τῶν ἐστρατη[γηκ]ότων | ἀνδρῶν ἐξ ἀπολογῆς
55 εὔλο[γον εἶ]ναι νομίζω, ἔτι δὲ το[ὺ]ς μὲν τα‖μίας μετέχειν τῆς
χρε[ίας κ]αθῆκον, το[ὺ]ς δὲ ἐσ[τρα]τη[γηκ]ότας | καὶ ἐμπείρους
εἶνα[ι καὶ ......]ο]υς τῶν πραγμάτ[ω]ν [κα]ὶ με....μον|τας τὸ
τῆς περ[ιγιγνομένης] οὐσίας αὐτοὺς ἀπο[στ]ε[ρε]ῖν δυνάμε|νον,
τὸν δὲ ....ε.κεν καὶ οἷς ἂν ἄλλ[οις]
τελώναις | ἐφε[δ]ρεύοντας ἔγνωμεν ποιε[ῖ]σθαι αὐτοὺς τὴν ἐνεχυ-
60 ρασίαν κα[ὶ ‖ ....] ταῖς ἀγοραίοις πιπρασκο-
μένων ι..|[.................]ως δίδοσθαι τέλος, ἀλλ'
ἐὰν λ...|[.............]να.ερεινε..ιτη........

From Pergamum. This rescript is assigned by von Prott (*Ath.
Mitt.* 27 (1902), 78 ff.) to the emperor Hadrian. The city of Per-

gamum issued bronze coins and the right of exchanging them for the Roman denarius was given to contractors at a fixed rate of exchange on condition that a certain percentage of their profits should be paid to the municipal treasury. The contractors had changed the rate arbitrarily, so that both they and the city gained an increased revenue. The merchants protested by appealing to the emperor who summoned both parties to give evidence. In his rescript he reviews the evidence and gives his decision in favor of the merchants and traders. In this document we have evidence of a municipal monopoly. The Greek cities which retained the privilege of issuing coins apparently compelled local traders to conduct business in the local currency, and the exchange of foreign money was regulated by municipal laws. From the exchange a certain amount of revenue was derived (*cf. CIG.* 2053). The right of exchange was either let to contractors, as in this case, or was conducted by the city with officials appointed for the purpose (*cf.* Reinach, *B.C.H.* 20 (1896), 523 *ff.*, where the evidence for public and private bankers in the Greek states is collected). *Cf.* nos. 133, 199. For a full commentary, *cf.* von Prott, *loc. cit.*

82. EPISTULA AVIDI QUIETI, PROCONSULIS ASIAE, AD AEZANITAS
(125–126 p. Chr.)

CIG. 3835; Le Bas-Waddington, 860–863; Lafoscade, 93; Ditt. *Or. Gr.* 502; Cagnat, *IGRR.* 4, 571; *CIL.* III, 355 and *S.* 7003; de Ruggiero, *L'arbitrato pubblico*, 57.

Ἀουίδιος Κουιῆτος Αἰζανειτῶν ἄρχουσι βουλῆι | δήμωι χαί- 1
ρειν. Ἀμφισβήτησις περὶ χώρας ἱερᾶς, ἀνα|τεθείσης πάλαι τῶι
Διί, τρειβομένη πολλῶν ἐτῶν, τῆι προνοίαι τοῦ | μεγίστου
αὐτοκράτορος τέλους ἔτυχε. Ἐπεὶ γὰρ ἐπέστειλα αὐτῶι δη‖λῶν 5
τὸ πρᾶγμα ὅλον, ἠρόμην τε ὅτι χρὴ ποιεῖν, δύο τὰ | μάλιστα
τὴν | διαφορὰν ὑμεῖν κεινοῦντα καὶ τὸ δυσεργὲς καὶ δυσεύρετον
τοῦ | πράγματος παρεχόμενα, μείξας τῶι φιλανθρώπωι τὸ δίκαιον
ἀκολού|θως τῆι περὶ τὰς κρίσεις ἐπιμελείαι τ[ὴ]ν πολυχ[ρ]όνιον
ὑμῶν μάχην καὶ ὑποψί‖αν πρὸς ἀλλήλους ἔλυσεν, καθὼς ἐκ τῆς 10
ἐπιστολῆς ἣν ἔπεμψεν πρός με | μαθήσεσθε, ἧς τὸ ἀντίγραφον
ὑμεῖν πέπομφα. Ἐπέστειλα δὲ Ἑσπέρωι τῶι ἐπι|τρόπωι τοῦ

Σεβαστοῦ, ὅπως γεομέτρας ἐπιτη(δ)[είους] λεξάμενος ἐκείνοις |
προσχρήσηται τὴν χώραν διαμετρῶν κἀκ [τούτου ἀγαθὸ]ν ὑμεῖν
γενήσεται. | Καὶ ἐκ τῶν ἱερῶν τοῦ Καίσαρος γραμμάτω[ν ὑμεῖν
15 δ]εδήλωκα ὅτι⟨ο⟩ δεῖ τε‖λεῖν ὑπὲρ ἑκάστου κλήρου κατὰ τὴν
[τοῦ Καίσαρος ἀπό]φασιν ἐξ ἧς ἂν ἡ|μέρας λάβητε τὴν ἐπιστο-
λήν. "Εκαστ[ος δὲ τὸ τέλος τῶι] ἱερο[ταμίαι τῆς] | χώρας τελέσει,
ἵνα μὴ πάλιν τινὲς ἀ[μφισβητοῦντες περὶ αὐτῆς τοῦ] | βράδειον
ἀπολαῦσαι τὴν πόλιν τῆς [προσηκούσης προσόδου παραίτιοι] |
γένωνται· ἀρκεῖ γὰρ αὐτοῖς τὸ μέχρι ν[ῦν ἀπολελαυκέναι τούτων.
20 Πέπομ]‖φα δὲ καὶ τῆς πρὸς "Εσπερον ἐπιστο[λῆς τὸ ἀντίγραφον
καὶ ἧς "Εσπερος ἐ]|μοὶ γέγραφεν. 'Ερρῶσθαι ὑμᾶς εὔχο[μαι].

II Exempl(ar) epistulae Caesaris scriptae ad | Quietum. | Si in
quantas particulas, quos cleros appellant, ager Aezanen|si Iovi dicatus
5 a regibus divisus sit, non apparet, optimum est, ‖ sicut tu quoque
existimas, modum qui in vicinis civitatibus | clerorum nec maximus
nec minimus est observari. Et si, cum | Mettius Modestus con-
stitueret, ut vectigal pro is pendere|tur, constitit qui essent cleruchici
agri aequum est ex hoc | tempore vectigal pendi. Si non constitit,
10 iam ex hoc tempo‖re vectigal pendendum est. At si quae morae
quaerantur | usque dum pendant integrum, dentur.

III Exempl(ar) epistulae Quieti scriptae ad | Hesperum. | Cum
variam esse clerorum mensuram | cognoverim, et sacratissimus
5 imp(erator) con‖stitutionis suae causa neq(ue) maximi neq(ue) |
minimi mensuram iniri iusserit in ea re|gione, quae Iovi Aezanitico
dicata dicitur, | mando tibi, Hesper(e) carissime, explores qu|ae
10 maximi cleri mensura, quae minimi in ‖ vicinia et in ipsa illa regione
sit, et id | per litteras notum mihi facias.

IV Exempl(ar) epistulae scriptae Quie|to ab Hespero. | Quaedam
5 negotia, domine, non ali|ter ad consummationem perduci ‖ possunt,
quam per eos qui usu sunt | eorum periti. Ob hoc, cum mihi in-
iunxisses ut tibi renuntiarem, quae | mensura esset clerorum circa
re|gionem Aezaniticam, misi in rem | praesentem ei...

From Aezani. In this group of documents we have an example
of administrative arbitration. Lands sacred to Jupiter had been
confiscated by the Greek kings and parcelled out in allotments. The
holders paid a rental to the municipality and also to the imperial
fiscus. For this reason the governor refers the dispute, not to the

FROM ITALY AND THE PROVINCES

senate, but to the emperor. The dispute which had arisen is not clear, but apparently the tenants had acquired larger holdings in the course of time and continued to pay the same rental as on the original smaller leasehold. The emperor instructs the governor to find out the average size of such leaseholds in neighboring states and regulate those of Aezani accordingly. In the governorship of Mettius Modestus the question had arisen as to what lands were cleruchic. Apparently, some tenants had ceased to pay rental and had held the land as if entitled to absolute ownership (cf. no. 55). Mettius had been called upon by the city to reestablish the title of the state to the confiscated property.

83. EPISTULA IMPERATORIS HADRIANI AD STRATONICENSES
(127 p. Chr.)

Cagnat, *IGRR.* 4, 1156a; Lafoscade, 23; Ditt. *Syll.*[3] 837; Riccobono, p. 325.

Αὐτοκράτωρ Καῖσαρ, θεοῦ Τραϊαν[οῦ] | Παρθικοῦ υἱός, θεοῦ
Νερούα υἱωνό[ς], | Τραϊανὸς Ἁδριανὸς Σεβαστός, ἀρ[χιε]|ρεὺς
μέγιστος, δημαρχικῆς ἐξο[υσί]||ας τ(ὸ) ια', ὕπατος τ(ὸ) γ', Ἁδριανο-   5
π[ο]|λειτῶν Στρατονεικέ[ω]ν τοῖς ἄρχ[ου]|σι καὶ τῆι βουλῆι καὶ
τῶι δήμωι χαίρει[ν]. | Δίκαια ἀξιοῦν μοι δοκεῖτε καὶ ἀναγκαῖα
ἄ[ρ]|τι γεινομένηι πόλει· τά τε οὖν τέλη τὰ ἐ[κ] || τῆς χώρας δίδωμι   10
ὑμεῖν, καὶ τὴν οἰκίαν Τι[β.] | Κλαυδίου Σωκράτους τὴν οὖσαν
ἐν τῆι [πό]|λει ἢ ἐπισκευαζέτω Σωκράτης ἢ ἀποδό[σ]||θω τινὶ
τῶν ἐπιχωρίων, ὡς μὴ χρόνωι [καὶ | ἀ]μελίαι καταριφθείη.
Ταῦτα ἐπέστειλα καὶ [τῶι || κρ]ατίστωι ἀνθυπάτωι Στερτινίωι   15
Κουαρ[τίνωι] | καὶ τῶι ἐπιτρόπωι μου [Πο]μπηΐωι Σεου[ήρωι]. |
Ἐπρέσβευσεν Κλ. Κάνδιδος, ὧι τὸ ἐφόδι[ον] | δοθήτω, εἰ μὴ
προῖκα ὑπέσχηται. | Εὐτυχεῖτε. Καλάνδαις Μαρτίαις ἀπὸ
Ῥώ||[μ]ης. Κλ. Κάνδιδος ἀπέδωκα τὴν ἐπιστο|[λ]ὴν Λολλίωι   20
Ῥουστικῶι ἄρχοντι τῆι πρὸ α' ἰδῶ[ν] | Μαίων ἐν τῆι ἐκκλησίαι.

From Stratonicea-Hadrianopolis. This city had been founded by Hadrian himself by the grant of civic status to a village on the site. The form of government is that usually found in Greek states, with archons, senate, and popular assembly. The calendar, however, was Roman. The city was unable to support itself and pay the requisite tribute to Rome. On appeal to the emperor, Hadrian remitted the taxes—τὰ τέλη τὰ ἐκ τῆς χώρας. It is possible that the mention of the imperial procurator in this connection should be interpreted as a reference to rents from public lands of the emperor (Weber, *Unters. Gesch. Hadr.* 136 *f.*), which he assigns to the new municipality. On the policy of creating new municipalities in Asia, *cf.* Chapot, *La prov. rom. proc. d'Asie,* 100 *ff.* The second request of the embassy is an interesting example of the petty problems referred to Rome by the cities in this period. The house of Socrates had fallen into disrepair, and the emperor gives orders that the owner should restore the building or sell it to some citizen of Stratonicea. There is no evidence that this house had been converted into a shrine because Hadrian may have resided there during his visit to the city (*cf.* Weber, *op. cit.* 138).

84. EPISTULA LEGATI LYCIAE, POMPONI VETTONIANI, AD COMMUNE LYCIORUM
(128 p. Chr.)

Cagnat, *IGRR.* 3, 739, c. 14; Lafoscade, 103.

[Π]ομπών[ιος Ἀ]ν[τ]ισ[τιανὸς Φουνισουλανὸ]ς [Οὐ]|εττωνι-
ανὸς πρεσβε[υτὴς καὶ] ἀντι[στράτ]η|γος, τῆι κοινῆι τοῦ ἔθνους
ἀρχαιρεσιακῆι ἐκ|κλησίαι χαίρειν. Τὸ τειμᾶν τοὺς ἀγαθοὺς ‖
5 ἄνδρας καλόν ἐστιν· μάλ[ι]στα ἐξαιρέτ[ω]ς | ἀναφαίνετε·
ὥσπερ καὶ ν[ῦ]ν Ἀπολλω|νίωι δὶς τοῦ Καλλιάδου, ὃ[ς] ὑμεῖν
ἀρχιερέα | τὸν υἱὸν ἐθελόντ[ω]ς παρ[έσχ]ηται, καὶ αὐ|τὸς παρα-
10 γενόμενος φιλο[τειμο]υμένωι καὶ ‖ ἀνιέντι ὑμεῖν τὸν ἑαυτ[οῦ
πλοῦτο]ν, εἰς κόσ|μον τῆς τοῦ ἔθνους ἀξί[ας μαρ]τυρῶ | τ[α]ῖς
τειμαῖς ταῖς εἰς αὐτὸ[ν ὑφ᾽ ὑμῶν] δο|θησομέναις τήν τε προ-
εδ[ρίαν ἐπιτρέ]πω | κυρωθῆναι αὐτῶι τόν τ[ε εἰσιόντα (?) ἀρχιε]-
15 ρέα ‖ υἱὸν [αὐ]τοῦ Ἀπολλώνι[ον . . . . .

See note on no. 80. In this letter the governor approves in advance the honors which the provincial assembly proposes to confer upon Opramoas, and apparently ratifies the election of his son to the chief priesthood of the province. There is no evidence that the provincial assembly was required to submit their action in either

FROM ITALY AND THE PROVINCES

case to the governor or that he exercised veto powers in the elections of provincial officials. For the veto of the governor on provincial decrees *cf.* no. 97.

85. EPISTULA IMPERATORIS HADRIANI AD EPHESIOS
(129 p. Chr.)

Lafoscade, 26; *I.B.M.* 3, 487; Ditt. *Syll.*³ 838.

Αὐ[το]κράτωρ Καῖσαρ, θεοῦ [Τραϊανοῦ] | Παρθ[ι]κοῦ υἱός,
θεοῦ Νερ[ο]ύα υ[ἱ]ων[ός], | Τραϊα[ν]ὸς Ἁδριαν[ὸ]ς Σεβασ[τός,
ἀρ]χιερεὺ[ς] | μέγισ[το]ς, δημαρχ[ικῆ]ς ἐξουσί[ας τὸ ι]γ´, ὕπατος
τὸ γ´, ‖ πατὴ[ρ πατ]ρίδος, Ἐφ[εσί]ων τοῖς ἄ[ρ]χουσ[ι καὶ τῆι 5
β]ουλῆι χαίρειν· | Λ. Ἔ[ρ]αστος καὶ πολ[εί]της ὑ[μ]ῶν [ε]ἶναί
φ[ησιν κ]αὶ πολλ[άκις] | πλ[εῦσ]αι τ[ὴ]ν θάλασ[σαν, καὶ ὅ]σα
ἀπὸ τού[του δυν]ατὸς | χρήσιμ[ο]ς γενέσ[θαι τῆι πατρ]ίδι, καὶ
τοῦ ἔθν[ους τ]ο[ὺ]ς ἡγε|μόνας ἀεὶ δι[α]κομ[ίσαι], ἐ[μ]οὶ δὲ δ[ὶς]
ἤδη συ[νέπλευ]σεν, ‖ τὸ μὲν πρῶτον εἰς Ῥόδον ἀπὸ τῆς 10
Ἐ[φέ]σου κο[μιζ]ομέ[νωι], | νῦν δὲ ἀπὸ Ἐλευσεῖνος πρὸς ὑμᾶς
ἀφικ[ν]ουμέν[ωι, βούλ]εται[ι] | δὲ βουλευτὴς γενέσθαι· κἀγὼ τ[ὴν]
μὲν [δοκι]μασία[ν ἐ]φ᾽ ὑμεῖν | ποιοῦμαι, εἰ δὲ μηδὲν ἐνποδών
[ἐστι καὶ δοκεῖ τῆς τι]μῆς ἄξ[ι]ος, | τὸ ἀργύριον, ὅσον διδόασιν
οἱ βουλεύοντες, [δώσω τῆς ἀρχαι]ρεσίας [ἕ]νεκα. ‖ Εὐτυχεῖτε. 15

From Ephesus. Hadrian requests the Ephesians to elect Erastus to the municipal senate. The scrutiny of the qualifications of the candidate is placed in the power of the city, while the emperor promises to pay the requisite *summa honoraria* (*cf.* Pliny, *Ep. ad Trai.* 112, 113). Nothing is known of the method of election to the senate at Ephesus in this period beyond the indications given in this letter. If the word ἀρχαιρεσίας is properly restored in l. 14, it may indicate that senators were elected at the special meeting of the senate or assembly at which the usual magistrates were elected (*cf.* Chapot, *La prov. rom. proc. d'Asie*, 199).

86. PRIVILEGIA CONCESSA DIANAE EPHESIAE
AB IMPERATORE HADRIANO
(129 p. Chr.)

Ditt. *Syll.*³ 839.

Αὐτοκράτορα Καίσαρα, θεοῦ | Τραϊανοῦ Παρθικοῦ υἱόν, θεοῦ |
Νερούα υἱωνόν, Τραϊανὸν Ἁδριανὸν | Σεβαστὸν καὶ Ὀλύμπιον,

MUNICIPAL DOCUMENTS IN GREEK AND LATIN

5 δημαρ‖χικῆς ἐξουσίας τὸ (ι)γ΄, ὕπατον | τὸ γ΄, πατέρα πατρίδος, |
ἡ βουλὴ καὶ ὁ δῆμος ὁ Ἐφεσίων | τὸν ἴδιον κτιστὴν καὶ σωτῆρα,
10 διὰ | τὰς ἀνυπερβλήτους δωρεὰς Ἀρτέ‖μιδι, διδόντα τῇ θεῷ τῶν
κληρο|νομιῶν καὶ βεβληκότων τὰ δίκαια | καὶ τοὺς νόμους
αὐτῆς, σειτοπομ[πίας δὲ] | ἀπ᾽ Αἰγύπτου παρέχοντα, καὶ τοὺς
15 λιμένας | πο[ιήσαν]τα πλωτούς, ἀποστρέψαντά τε ‖ καὶ τὸν
βλά[πτοντα τοὺς] λιμένας ποταμὸν | Κάϋστρον διὰ τὸ . .

From Ephesus. In visiting this city, Hadrian granted to the priests of the goddess Diana the right of receiving inheritances in the name of the divinity. *Cf.* Ulpian, *Frag.* XXII, 6: deos heredes instituere non possumus, praeter eos, quos senatus consultis constitutionibusve principum instituere concessum est, sicuti Iovem Tarpeium, Apollinem Didymaeum Mileti, Martem in Gallia, Minervam Iliensem, Herculem Gaditanum, Dianam Efesiam, Matrem deorum Sipylenen, Nemesim, quae Smyrnae colitur, et Caelestem Salinsem Carthigini. Apparently those who violated the laws of the sanctuary were liable to condemnation, and their property was confiscated for the benefit of the temple's treasury.

87. EPISTULA SUFENATIS VERI, LEGATI LYCIAE, AD LYCIARCHAM
(131 p. Chr.)

Cagnat, *IGRR.* 3, 739, c. 18; Lafoscade, 105.

[Ἐπὶ] ἀρχιερέο[ς Κλαυδίου Μαρκιανοῦ | . . . . Σου]φ[ήνα
Οὐῆ]ρ[ος] Ἰο[. . . . . . | Λυκ]ιάρχηι χαίρειν. Ὀπραμόαν Ἀπο[λ-
5 λω]‖νίου δὶς τοῦ Καλλιάδου καὶ αὐτὸς ἀ[πο]‖δέχομαι ἐπὶ τῆι
φιλοτειμίαι, ἣν πρὸς τὸ λα[μ]‖πρότατον ἔθνος ὑμῶν ἐπεδείξατο,
δω|ρησάμενος αὐτῶι δηνάρια πεντάκις μύ|ρια πρὸς οἷς πέρυσι
ὑπέσχητο εἰς τὴν κα|ταλλαγὴν τοῦ νομίσματος δηναρίοις ‖
10 πεντάκις χειλίοις. Τὴν οὖν προδηλουμέ|νην αὐτοῦ δωρεὰν βε-
βαιῶ ἐπί τε τῶι ἀσάλευ|τον καὶ ἀμετάθετον εἰς τὸν ἀεὶ χρόνον
εἶ|ναι καὶ ἐπὶ ταῖς ἄλλαις αἱρέσεσιν, αἷς ἐπην‖[γείλ]ατο.
15 Ἐρρῶσθαί σε εὔχομαι. Ἐδόθη ‖ πρὸ [. . .] εἰδῶν Ὀκτωνβρίων.

See note on no. 80. The governor ratifies the establishment of an endowment fund of fifty-five thousand denarii, the income of which is to be devoted to an annual distribution to the officials and members of the provincial assembly (Cagnat, *IGRR*. 3, 739, c. 20). The gift of five thousand denarii, made in the previous year for the exchange of money, is interesting. The exchange of local and imperial money was a form of taxation (*cf.* nos. 81, 133), and this gift was designed to relieve the people who attended the assembly and had to make purchases at the fair held in connection therewith (*cf.* no. 73). It appears, however, that his help had not been needed, and this sum is now included in the endowment fund.

88. TITULUS HONORARIUS
(132 p. Chr.)

CIL. III, *S.* 1, 7282; Dessau, 315.

Imp. Caesari divi Traiani | Parthici f., divi Nervae nep., | Traiano Hadriano Aug. p. m., | tr. p. XVI, cos. III, p. p., Olympio ob || multa beneficia quae viritim | quae publice praestitit, resti-| 5 tutori coloniae suae, Troadenses | per legatos M. Servilium Tu- tilium | Paulum et L. Vedumnium Aulum. || Τρωαδέων.   10

A square base found in 1886 at Athens probably on the site of the *gymnasium Hadriani*. Lines 8–9 were added by another hand. The colonia Alexandria Troas was founded between 27 and 12 B.C. (*cf.* Kornemann, *R.E.* 4, 550). This inscription celebrates the restoration of the colony by Hadrian. For other inscriptions cut at the same time in similar circumstances, *cf. CIL.* III, *S.* 1, 7281, 7283, and *IG.* III, 472–486.

89. LEX PALMYRENORUM
(137 p. Chr.)

Ditt. *Or. Gr.* 629; Cagnat, *IGRR.* 3, 1056, ll. 1–16.

['Ἐπὶ Αὐτοκράτορος Καίσαρος, θεοῦ Τραϊανοῦ Παρθι]κοῦ υἱο[ῦ, θε]οῦ [Νερούα υἱωνοῦ, Τραϊανοῦ Ἀδριανοῦ Σεβαστοῦ, δημαρχικῆς | ἐξουσίας τὸ κα', αὐτοκράτορος τὸ β', ὑπ]άτου τὸ γ', πατρὸς πατρίδος, ὑπάτω[ν Λ(ουκίου) Αἰλίου Καίσαρος τὸ β' Π(οπλίου) Κοιλίου Βαλβίνου]. | Ἔτους ημυ', μηνὸς Ξανδικοῦ ιη',

[409]

MUNICIPAL DOCUMENTS IN GREEK AND LATIN

δόγμα βουλῆς. | Ἐπὶ Βωννέους Βωννέους τοῦ Αἰράνου προέδρου,
5 Ἀλεξάνδρου τοῦ Ἀλεξάνδρου τοῦ || Φιλοπάτορος γραμματέως
βουλῆς καὶ δήμου, Μαλίχου Ὀλαιοῦς καὶ Ζεβείδου Νεσᾶ
ἀρχόν|των, βουλῆς νομίμου ἀγομένης, ἐψηφίσθη τὰ ὑποτεταγ-
μένα. Ἐπειδὴ [ἐν τ]οῖς πάλαι χρόνοις | ἐν τῶι τελωνικῶι νόμωι
πλεῖστα τῶν ὑποτελῶν οὐκ ἀνελήμφθη, ἐπράσ[σετ]ο δὲ ἐκ
συνηθείας, ἐν|γραφομένου τῆι μισθώσει τὸν τελωνοῦντα τὴν
πρᾶξιν ποιεῖσθαι ἀκολούθως τῶι νόμωι καὶ τῆι | συνηθείαι,
συνέβαινεν δὲ πλειστάκις περὶ τούτου ζητήσεις γείνεσθ[αι
10 με]ταξὺ τῶν ἐνπόρων || πρὸς τοὺς τελώνας· δεδόχθαι, τοὺς
ἐνεστῶτας ἄρχοντας καὶ δεκαπρώτους διακρείνοντας | τὰ μὴ
ἀνειλημμένα τῶι νόμωι ἐνγράψαι τῆι ἔνγιστα μισθώσει καὶ
ὑποτάξαι ἑκάστωι εἴδει τὸ | ἐκ συνηθείας τέλος, καὶ ἐπειδὰν
κυρωθῆι τῶι μισθουμένωι, ἐνγραφῆναι μετὰ τοῦ πρώτου νό|μου
στήληι λιθίνηι τῆι οὔσηι ἀντικρὺς [ἱ]ερ[οῦ] λεγομένου Ῥαβα-
σείρη, ἐ[πι]μελεῖσθαι δὲ τοὺς τυγχά|νοντας κατὰ καιρὸν ἄρχον-
τας καὶ δεκαπρώτους καὶ συνδίκ[ους τοῦ] μηδὲν παραπράσσειν ||
15 τὸν μισθούμενον.

From Palmyra. We omit the Aramaic version recorded on the
stone, and the register of taxes imposed by the decree, which is
recorded in both Greek and Aramaic. The customs were usually
under imperial control (Cagnat, *Les impôts indirects chez les
Romains*), but Palmyra, in the midst of a desert, had no other
revenue except that which she derived from her position as a way-
station on the trade-route to the Orient. There is no evidence that
the Romans collected *portoria* in Syria (Mommsen, *E.E.* 5, 18).
This law is proposed by the Palmyran senate which authorizes the
magistrates and *decaproti* to draw up the tariff in those particulars
not specified in the existing law. After their proposed tariff was
ratified by the firm of *publicani* which collected the tax, the schedule
was to be posted in a public place where the traders could refer to
it in case of a dispute with the collectors. Mylasa in Caria also
had control of the tax on goods entering that port (*CIL.* III, *S.* 1,
7151; Dessau, *Hermes*, 19 (1884), 436 *ff.*; *cf.* p. 140).

90. LEX DE CERTA OLEI PORTIONE
REI PUBLICAE VENDENDA
(117–138 p. Chr.)

IG. ii and iii (*editio minor*), 1100; de Ruggiero, *L'arbitrato pubblico*, 36.

Κε. νο. θε. Ἀδριανοῦ. | Οἱ τὸ ἔλαιον γεωργοῦντες τὸ τρίτον | καταφερέτωσαν, ἢ τὸ ὄγδοον οἱ τὰ | Ἱππάρχου χωρία τὰ ὑπὸ τοῦ φίσκου ‖ πραθέντα κεκτημένοι· μόνα γὰρ ἐ|κεῖνα τὸ δίκαιον 5 τοῦτο ἔχει· καταφε|ρέτωσαν δὲ ἅμα τῶι ἄρξασθαι συνκο‖[μιδῆς κ]ατὰ μέρος, πρὸς λόγον το[ῦ | συνκομιζ]ομένου, τοῖς ἐλεώναι[ς, ‖ οἵτινες ἀεὶ] προνοοῦσιν τῆ[ς | δημοσίας χρεία]ς· ἀπογραφέσθω- 10 [σαν δὲ | . . . .] τῆς συνκομιδῆς πρὸ[ς | τοὺς ταμίας κα]ὶ τὸν κήρυκα δύο | [. . . . .]ιδόντες ὑπογρα‖φήν· [ἡ] δὲ 15 ἀπ[ογραφ]ὴ ἔστω μετὰ ὅρκου | καὶ πόσον συνεκόμισεν τὸ πᾶν, | καὶ ὅτι διὰ δούλου τοῦδε ἢ ἀπελευ|θέρου τοῦδε· ἐὰν δὲ πωλήσηι τὸν | καρπὸν ὁ δεσπότης τοῦ χωρίου, ἢ ὁ ‖ γεωργὸς ἢ ὁ καρ- 20 πώνης, ἀπογραφέ|σθω δὲ πρὸς τοὺς αὐτοὺς καὶ ὁ ἐπ᾽ ἐξα|γωγῆι πιπράσκων, πόσον πιπράσκει | καὶ τίνι καὶ ποῦ ὁρμ[ε]ῖ τὸ [π]λοῖον. Ὁ δ[ὲ] | ἀπογραφῆς χωρὶς π[ιπράσκων] ἐπ᾽ ἐξα-‖ γωγῆι, κἂν ὃ ὤφειλεν ἦι κα[τενηνοχὼς] | τῆι πόλει, στερέσθω 25 τοῦ πραθ[έντος]. | Ὁ δὲ ψευδεῖς ἀπογραφὰς ποιήσα[ς] | ἢ τὰς περὶ τῆς συνκομιδῆς [ἢ τ]ὰ[ς περὶ | τῆς ἐξαγωγῆς ἢ ὑπὲρ χωρίου, [ὃ μὴ πα]‖ρὰ φίσκου ἐπρίατο μὴ Ἱππάρχ[ειο]ν [ὃ]ν 30 ὄγδοον κατενεγκών, σ[τερέ|σθω, τὸ δὲ ἥμισυ ὁ μη]νύσας λαμ[βα]νέτω. | Ὃς δ᾽ ἂν ἐπ᾽ ἐξαγω]γὴν ἀναπόγ[ραπτα | πρίηται . . . . .] ειρεειμ . . . . . . ‖ . . . . των ἀπ[ο]στερ . . . . . 35 . . . . . ος αὐτὸς ἢ ὅν[τινα | ἂν ἕληται, πιπρασκέ]τω μὲν ἐξ ἀπ[ο- γρα|φῆς . . . . . . τ]ῆς δὲ τειμῆς τὸ [μὲν ἥ]|μισυ κατεχέτω, εἰ μήπω δέδωκεν ἢ λαμ‖βανέτω, τὸ δὲ ἥμισυ ἔστω δημόσιον. | Γραφέσθω 40 δὲ καὶ ὁ ἔμπορος, τί ἐξάγει | καὶ πόσον παρ᾽ ἑκάστου· ἐὰν δὲ μὴ ἀπο|γραψάμενος φωραθῆι ἐκπλέων, στερέ|σθω· ἐὰν δὲ ἐκπλεύ- σας φθάσηι καὶ μηνυ‖θῆι, γραφέσθω καὶ τῆι πατρίδι αὐτοῦ ὑπὸ 45 τοῦ | δήμου κἀμοί. Τὰς δὲ περὶ τούτων δίκας | μέχρι μὲν πεντή- κοντα ἀμφορέων ἡ βου|λὴ μόνη κρεινέτω, τὰ δὲ ὑπὲρ τοῦτο μετὰ | τοῦ δήμου. Ἐὰν δὲ τῶν ἐκ τοῦ πλοίου τις ‖ μηνύσηι, 50 ἐπάναγκες ὁ στρατηγὸς τῆι ἑξῆς | ἡμέραι βουλὴν ἀθροισάτω, εἰ

[411]

MUNICIPAL DOCUMENTS IN GREEK AND LATIN

δ' ὑπὲρ τοὺς | πεντήκοντα ἀμφορεῖς εἴη τὸ μεμηνυ|μένον, ἐκ-
κλησίαν· καὶ διδόσθω τῶι ἐλέγ|ξαντι τὸ ἥμισυ. Ἐὰν δὲ ἐκκαλέ-
55 σηταί τις ἢ || ἐμὲ ἢ τὸν ἀνθύπατον, χειροτονείτω συν|δίκους ὁ
δῆμος. Ἵνα δὲ ἀπαραίτητα ἦι τὰ | κατὰ τῶν κακουργούντων
ἐπι[τ]είμι[α], τει|μῆς ἰς τὸ δημόσιον καταφερέσθω τὸ ἔλαι|ον,
60 ἥτις ἂν ἐν τῆι χώραι ἦι. Εἰ δέ ποτε εὐφορ[ί]||ας ἐλαίου γενο-
μένης πλέον εἴη τὸ ἐκ τῶν | τρίτων ἢ ὀγδόων καταφερόμενον τῆς
εἰς | ὅλον τ[ὸ]ν ἐνιαυτὸν δημοσίας χρείας, ἐξέ|στω τοῖς μ[ὲν
γεωρ]γοῦσιν τὸ ἔλαιον ἢ πᾶν | ἢ μέρος δευτέραν ἀπογραφὴν
65 ποιησαμέ||νοις καὶ δημόσιον τό τε ὀφειλόμενον | πόσον ἐστὶν
. . . .ὃ οἱ ἐλαιῶναι ἢ ο[ἱ] ἀργυ|ροταμία[ι] οὐ βούλονται παρ' αὐ-
70 τῶν λαβεῖν, | φυλά[ττειν. . . . .]|ξετα. . . . .||σκ. . . .

From Athens. In the first line Dittenberger proposed the restoration κε(λεύει) νό(μος) θε(οῦ) and dated the document after
the death of Hadrian. Premerstein proposed κε(φάλαιον) νό(μου)
θε(οῦ) Ἀδριανοῦ and would date the law in 124–125, the year
of Hadrian's first visit to Athens (cf. Weber, Unters. Gesch. Hadr.
165). Although Athens was a free city, allied to Rome, and free
to enact her own laws, Hadrian was asked to devise new laws which
he modelled on those given by Solon and Draco (Hieron., Chr., ab
Abr. 2137). As Solon is said to have restricted the exportation of
olives from Attica, it is possible that this document may contain
one of the clauses of Hadrian's legislation, although it seems to
be a separate enactment. The law stipulated that the olive-growers
must reserve one-third of their supply to be sold to the Athenian
state at the market price, with the proviso that tenants on the estate
of Hipparchus, formerly owned by the imperial fiscus, should
reserve one-eighth only. Failure to declare the amount of oil produced, or the amount bought or sold for export, or a false declaration, led to confiscation. The Athenian senate had jurisdiction over
cases in which less than fifty amphorae were involved. Where
greater quantities were in question, the case came before the popular
assembly. Appeals could be taken to the emperor or to the governor,
and in such cases the city was represented by advocates elected by
popular vote.

The special consideration shown to those on the estate of Hipparchus is noteworthy. Hipparchus was the grandfather of Herodes

Atticus and his lands had been confiscated by the *fiscus* because he had been suspected of revolutionary designs (Philostratus, *Vit. Soph.* 2. 1. 2). If these lands had been sold outright, as seems to be implied, it is difficult to understand why the purchasers should be entitled to such favorable consideration in comparison with other landowners in Attica. We suspect, however, that the verb πραθέντα is used here in the same sense as in the law concerning the disposal of the public lands of Thisbe (*cf.* no. 129 and commentary), and that the lands of Hipparchus formed an imperial estate within the territory of Attica in spite of the fact that Athens was in possession of the status of a *civitas foederata et libera*.

Although the law implied that the city must pay the prevailing market price (ll. 58–59), it is difficult to understand why there should be any difficulty in securing an adequate supply of oil in the open market under such circumstances. It is probable that the city fixed a price lower than that prevailing in the export trade, and this law virtually imposes a tax upon the olive-growers in so far as the price paid by the city for the third of their produce is below the current market quotations.

91. EPISTULA IMPERATORIS HADRIANI (?)
AD ATHENIENSES
(117–138 p. Chr.)

IG. ii and iii (*editio minor*), 1103.

. . . . . λ . ει μετρη[ς . . . .]‖δε τὴν διοβελίαν . . . .
. . . . a μηδὲ[. . . . . . . τοῖς] | δὲ ἐν Ἐλευσεῖνι ἁλιεῦσιν ἀτέλειαν
ἰχθύ[ων εἶναι ὅταν ἐν Ἐλευ]‖σεῖνι ἐν τῆι ἀγορᾶι πιπράσκωσιν,
ὡς μένηι [. . . . . . ἵνα τὸ διὰ τὰ] ‖ εἰσαγώγια ὄφελος εἰς μέγα τι 5
ἀπαντήσηι· τ[οὺς δὲ . . . .] | καὶ τοὺς πάλιν καπηλεύοντας
πεπαυσθ[αι . . . .] | βούλομαι ἢ ἔνδειξιν αὐτῶν γείνεσθαι
πρ[ὸς τ]ὸν κ[ή]ρυκα τῆς ἐξ Ἀ|ρείου πάγου βουλῆς· τὸν δὲ
εἰσάγειν εἰς το[ὺς Ἀ]ρεοπαγείτας, τοὺς δὲ | τειμᾶν ὅτι χρὴ
παθεῖν ἢ ἀποτεῖσαι· πιπρασκέ[τω]σαν δὲ πάντα ἢ αὐτοὶ οἱ ‖
κομίζοντες ἢ οἱ πρῶτοι παρ᾽ αὐτῶν ὠνού[με]νοι· τὸ δὲ καὶ τρίτους 10
ὠ|νητὰς γεινομένους τῶν αὐτῶν ὠνίων με[τα]πιπράσκειν ἐπι-
τείνει | τὰς τειμάς. Ταύτην τὴν ἐπιστολὴν στήληι ἐ[γ]γράψαντες
ἐν Πειραεῖ | στήσατε πρὸ τοῦ δείγματος. Εὐτυχεῖτε. |

[413]

MUNICIPAL DOCUMENTS IN GREEK AND LATIN

Ἐπιμελητεύοντος τῆς πόλεως Τ. Ἰουλίου Ἡρωδιαν[οῦ] Κολλυτέως.

From Athens. In this letter there appears to be an interesting attempt on the part of the writer of the letter to reduce the high cost of living in Athens by suppressing the middleman. Merchandise brought into the city must be retailed by the importer, or by the first purchaser. Possibly the law dealt only with the importation of fish. The arrogance of the fishermen at Athens was proverbial, and it is possible that the dealers in the fishmarket had combined to compel higher prices; *cf.* Wilhelm, *Jahreshefte d. öst. arch. Inst.* 12 (1909), 146 *f.* Athens, though a free city, was unable to cope with her own problems, and appealed to the emperor (?), probably through the *curator rei publicae*, to devise legislation which would prevent speculation and consequent advancement in the cost of food supplies (*cf.* no. 65a). For a list of *curatores* at Athens, *cf.* *R.E. s.v. curator.* On the importance of the Areopagus as a court in Roman times, *cf.* Mitteis, *Reichsrecht und Volksrecht,* 86, n. 4.

92. EDICTUM IMPERATORIS HADRIANI (?)
DE VECTIGALIBUS
(117–138 p. Chr.)

IG. ii and iii (*editio minor*), 1104.

........δέχονται τὸ ἀργύριον, ἐπιτίμιον ὁριζέτωσαν | αὐτοῖς
κατὰ τὴν τῆς ἀπε[ι]θίας ἀξίαν· ἐ[ὰν] δ[ὲ] οἱ πα|ραδο[θέ]ντες
εἰσφέρειν μὴ βούλωνται, [εἶ]τα | ὑπεύθυνοι ἔστωσαν πρῶτον
5 μὲν ἑκατοστιαίων τόκω[ν], ‖ ἀφ᾽ οὗ δέον ποιήσασθαι τὴν εἴσοδον
οὐκ ἐποιήσαν|το, μέχρι μηνῶν ἄλλων δύο τῆς τελευταίας ἀπο-|
δόσεως, μετὰ δὲ τοὺς μῆνας τούτους εἰ μένοιεν | μὴ πειθόμενοι,
ἀποδόσθωσαν οἱ ἀργυροταμίαι μετὰ | τοῦ κήρυκος τὰς ὑποθήκας,
10 ἐ[χόν]των αὐτὰς ἐξουσίαν ‖ λύσασθαι ἑξήκοντα ἡμερῶν πρῶτον
μὲν τῶν δεδωκότ|ων, εἶτα καὶ τῶν ἐγγυητῶν οἵτινες ὑπεύθυνοι
τῶν | ἐνδεησάν[τω]ν ΟΦΕΛΟΥΥΠΕΤΘΑΝΟΕΙΤΩΝΕΝΔΕΗ-
ΣΑΤΩΝ | Οφ ἑξήκοντα ἡμαιρῶν ὀφίλουσιν ἐκτεῖσαι.

This inscription from Athens is assigned by Boeckh (*CIG.* 354) to the time of Hadrian. The document appears to be an imperial edict regulating the collection of taxes. These were farmed out to contractors who were required to furnish securities for the proper fulfilment of their obligations. Those who failed to comply with the terms of their contract were fined. In case of refusal to pay the fine, interest was charged on the amount due on the defaulted payment. If, after two months, the contractor was still recalcitrant, the securities must be sold at public auction under the privilege of redemption.

93. SERMO ET EPISTULAE PROCURATORUM DE TERRIS VACUIS EXCOLENDIS
(117–138 p. Chr.)

Carcopino, *Mélanges de l'école franç. de Rome*, 26 (1906), 365–481; *An. ép.* 1907, no. 196; Bruns, 116; Girard, p. 874; Riccobono, p. 357.

Coloni. . .tuani rogamus, procurato|*res*, *per* providentiam ves- Col. I
tram, quam | *nomine Ca*esaris praestatis, velitis nobis | *et utilitati*
illius consulere, dare no||*bis eos agros* qui sunt in paludibus et | in 5
silvestribus instituendos olivetis | et vineis, lege Manciana con-
dicione | *s*altus Neroniani vicini nobis. Cu*m* | *e*deremus hanc
pe*titi*onem nostr*am* || *fu*ndum suprascriptum N|*eronianum* | incre- 10
mentum habit*atorum*. . . . .|

(Desunt versus circa octo)

. . . . . .iubeas. Sermo procurato*rum im*|p(eratoris) *C*aes(aris) Col. II
Hadriani Aug(usti). Quia Caes*ar n(oster) pro* | infatigabili cura sua,
per qu*am adsi*|due *pro* humanis utili*t*atibus excu*bat, om*||nes partes 5
agrorum, *qua*e *tam oleis* aut | vineis quam frumentis aptae sunt
ex|coli iubet, itcirco permissu prov*id*|*e*ntiae eius, potestas fit omnibus
etia|m eas partes occupandi, quae in *cent*||*u*ris elocatis saltus Blan- 10
diani e*t* U|*de*nsi*s et in illi*s partibus sunt q*uae ex* | *saltu Lamiano et*
Domitiano iunctae | *Thusdritano sunt nec a conductoribus* | *ex*ercentur
cet.

F*ructuum* quam *coloni* ob summ*am Caes. cle*|*mentiam is qui lo*ca Col. III
neglecta a *conduc*|*toribus* occupaverit, quae *da*|*ri sol*ent, tertias partes
fructuum || *dabit*; *de* eis quoq(ue) regionibus qu|*ae ex* Lamiano et 5
Domitiano | *saltu* iunctae Tuzritano sunt | *tantundem* dabit. De
oleis quas quis*que* | *aut in scrobibu*s *p*osuerit aut oleast*r*||*is* inseruerit, 10
c*apto*rum fruct*uum* | *nulla pars decem proximis annis exige*|*tur* cet.

Col. IV   *E*arinus et Dory*phor*us Primige*nio* | *s*uo salutem. Exemplum
epistulae scrip|tae nobis a Tutilio Pudente egregio viro | ut notum
5 haberes et it quod subiectum est || *ce*leberrimis locis propone. Verri-
dius | Bassus et Ianuarius Martiali suo salut*em*. | Si qui agri cessant
et rudes sunt, *si qui sil*|vestres aut palustres in eo sal*tuum trac*|*tu*,
*v*olentis lege Mancia*na colere ne prohibeas.*

        III, ll. 1–2. fructuum...qui, *Schulten, from the letters remaining.*

    A stone inscribed on all four sides found at Aïn-el-Djemala in
Tunis in 1906. The upper and lower parts of the stone are lacking.
The principal commentaries on it are those of Carcopino, *loc. cit.*;
Mispoulet, *Nouv. rev. hist. d. droit fr. et étr.* 31 (1907), 5–48;
Schulten, *Klio*, 7 (1907), 188–212; Carcopino, *Klio*, 8 (1908),
154–185.

    The inscription belongs to the time of Hadrian; *cf.* col. ii, l. 2.
Different explanations have been given of the contents of the
document by different commentators. To follow the analysis of
Rostowzew (*cf. Gesch. d. röm. Kol.* 334 *ff.*), which seems the most
convincing, of the officials mentioned in the document, Earinus (or
Carinus) is probably procurator of the *saltus* or *regio* concerned;
Doryphorus, his *adiutor*; Verridius Bassus, *procurator tractus*; Janu-
arius, his subordinate; Martialis, perhaps a secretary; Tutilius Pudens
is one of the predecessors of Verridius Bassus in the office of
procurator tractus. The document then seems to be made up of the
following parts: (1) a petition addressed to the *procurator tractus
Carthaginiensis (tuani... incrementum habit.*) by the *coloni* of a certain
saltus; (2) a letter from Tutilius Pudens, a former *procurator tractus*,
to Primigenius, of which only the word *iubeas* is extant. This letter
Primigenius had neglected to publish; (3) the *sermo procuratorum*,
extending through *exigetur cet.* The *sermo procuratorum* recited the
apposite parts of the general statute, known as the *lex Manciana*,
with the proper adaptation to the *saltus* concerned; (4) a letter of
the *procurator saltus* and his assistant to Primigenius, and (5) a
letter to Martialis. Earinus and Doryphorus speak of sending a
copy of a letter by Tutilius Pudens and a document appended to it
(*it quod subiectum est*). The appended document is of course no. 3
(*cf.* Rostowzew, *op. cit.* 334). The *lex Manciana*, to which the

[416]

petitioners refer, was a Flavian statute, drawn up perhaps by a legate of Vespasian (*cf.* Rostowzew, *op. cit.* 336). This law was modified in some respects by the *lex Hadriana*. To the later law, however, the petitioners make no reference. In the general statute the *maxima* and *minima* of the contributions (*partes*) and the days' work (*operae*) required of *coloni* were probably fixed. In the *sermo procuratorum*, within the ranges fixed by the law, the contributions and services required of the *coloni* of the *saltus* concerned were established. This became the *lex saltus*, and, since it was under the protection of the *numen* of the emperor, it was inscribed on an altar; *cf. ara legis Hadrianae* (Bruns, 115). By comparing the extant portions of the *ara legis Hadrianae* with those of our inscription, we are able to fill out large lacunae in both documents. In this way the long italicized passages in cols. II and III of this inscription have been restored. In their petition the *coloni* ask permission to bring waste land under cultivation. Their request is granted not only for land never before cultivated but also for land which has been out of cultivation for ten years, with the further concession, that, for a fixed term of years, the tenants shall not be obliged to pay a part of the produce as rental (*cf.* col. III). Whether the provisions of the *lex Hadriana*, upon which the procurator bases his decision (*cf.* col. II), applied only to a specified number of imperial domains, to all those in Africa, or to imperial domains, wherever situated, is a matter of dispute. Probably the regulations applied to Africa only. For the organization of a *saltus*, *cf.* pp. 17 *ff*.

94. TITULUS HONORARIUS
(117–138 p. Chr.)

CIL. II, 5941; Dessau, 6954.

L. Aemil. M. f. M. nep. Quirina Rectus domo Roma, qui et Karth. | et Sicellitanus et Assotanus et Lacedaemonius et Baste-tanus | et Argius, scriba quaestorius, scriba aedilicius, donatus equo publ. | ab imp. Caesare Traiano Hadriano Aug., aedilis coloniae Karthagi., patronus rei publicae Assotanor. testamento suo || rei 5 pub. Assotan. fieri iussit, epulo annuo adiecto.

Set up at Asso near Caravaca in Spain. Rectus was a Roman

citizen and also a citizen of five other municipalities, one in Africa, two in Spain and two in Greece (*cf.* no. 24), a municipal official in Carthage and patron of Asso. He probably owed these honors to the favor of Hadrian.

95. TITULUS HONORARIUS
(119–138 p. Chr.)

CIL. II, 3239.

Imp. Caesari divi | Trai*ani Parthici* | f. divi *Nervae n.* | Traia*no*
5 *Hadri*‖ano *Aug., pont. max.,* | trib. *pot......cos.* | III, p. p., im*p. II*
10 *opt. max.* | q. pri*ncipi restitu*|tori m*unicipii* ‖ Ilugo*nenses d. d.*

Found at Ilugo in Tarraconensis. Whether we should restore *restitutori, fundatori* or *conditori* Mommsen considers uncertain. The importance of the inscription for us lies in the fact that it seems to record the elevation by Hadrian of a *civitas stipendiaria* to the position of a *municipium.*

96. SENATUS CONSULTUM DE NUNDINIS SALTUS BEGUENSIS
(138 p. Chr.)

CIL. VIII, 270 = VIII, *S.* 11451; Bruns, 61; Riccobono, p. 236.

S.C. de nundinis saltus Beguensis in t(erritorio) | Casensi, descriptum et recognitum ex libro sen|tentiarum in senatu dictarum Kari Iuni Nigri, C. Pompo|ni Camerini cos., in quo scripta erant
5 A*f*ricani iura et id ‖ quod i(nfra) s(criptum) est. Idibus Oct.... In comitio in curia Iu*l*(*ia*) | adfuerunt Q. Gargilius Q. f. Antiq(u)us, Ti. Cl. Ti....Pa*l*. Quar*t*inus, | C. Oppius C. f. Vel. Severus, C. Herennius C. f. Pa*l*. Caecilianus, M. Iu*l*. | M. f. Quir. Clarus, P. Cassius P. f. Cla. Dexter q(uaestor), P. Nonius M. f. Ou*f*. Mac|rinus q. In senatu fuerunt c. ‖
10 S.C. per discessionem factum. Quod P. Cassius Se|cundus, P. Delphius Peregrinus Aleius Alennius Maxi|mus Curtius Valerianus Proculus M. Nonius Mucianus | coss. verba fecerunt de desiderio amicorum Lucili Afri|cani c. v., qui petunt: ut ei permittatur in
15 provincia Afric(a), regione ‖ Beguensi, territorio Musulamiorum, ad Casas, nundinas | IIII nonas Novemb. et XII k. Dec., ex eo omnibus mensibus IIII non. | et XII k. sui cuiusq(ue) mensis instituere habere, quid fieri | placeret,

de ea re ita censuerunt: permittendum Lu|cilio Africano, c. v., in provincia Afric(a), regione Beguensi, || territorio Musula- 20 miorum, ad Casas, nundinas IIII non. | Novemb. et XII k. De-cembr. et ex eo omnibus mensibus IIII non. et XII k. | sui cuiusq(ue) mensis instituere et habere, eoque vicinis | advenisq(ue) nundinandi dumtaxat causa coire conve|nire sine iniuria et incommodo cuius-quam liceat. ||

Actum idibus Octobr. P. Cassio Secundo, M. Nonio Muciano. | 25 Eodem exemplo de eadem re duae tabellae signatae sunt. | Signatores: T. Fl(avi) Comini scrib(ae), C. Iuli Fortunati scrib(ae), | M. Caesi Helvi Euhelpisti, Q. Metili Onesimi, C. Iuli Peri|blepti, L. Verati Phile(rotis), T. Fl(avii) Crescentis.

Two stones, upon each of which the entire inscription was cut, were found in 1860 and 1879 respectively in Henschir Begar in Tunis. For a commentary on the inscription, *cf. E.E.* 2, 271 *ff.* The inscriptions were perhaps cut in the third or fourth century. Permission to establish markets was granted sometimes by the senate (*cf.* Plin. *Epp.* 5. 4; Suet. *Claud.* 12) and sometimes by the emperor (*cf. Dig.* 50. 11. 1). The *liber sententiarum in senatu dictarum,* from which this document was copied, is known more commonly as the *acta senatus* (*e.g.* Suet. *Iul.* 20; *Aug.* 5. 36) or *acta patrum* (Tac. *Ann.* 5. 4) or *commentarii senatus* (Tac. *Ann.* 15. 74). On the senatorial archives *cf.* p. 233, n. 7. It is interesting to notice that parliamentary forms are still followed rather strictly, even in the manner of voting, of requiring a quorum, and of appointing a committee to draft the motion.

97. EPISTULA CORNELI PROCULI, LEGATI LYCIAE, AD COMMUNE LYCIORUM
(139 p. Chr.)

Cagnat, *IGRR.* 3, 739, c. 28; Lafoscade, 108.

Ἐπὶ ἀρχιερέος Ἰάσον[ος τ]οῦ Νεικοστράτου, | Πανήμο[υ] κα΄, [Κορνήλ]ιος Πρόκλος, | πρεσβευτὴς ἀντισ[τράτηγος α]ὐτο-κράτορος, τῶι κοιν[ῶι Λυκίων χαίρει]ν. Καὶ | παρὼν ἔ[γνωκα, ὅτι ἃς μετὰ πλείστης (?)] || σπουδῆ[ς πρ]ὸς Ὀπραμόαν ['Απολ- 5 λ]ωνίου | δὶς το[ῦ] Καλλιάδου καὶ ὅ[τε ἀντέτ]αττον | τειμὰς

[419]

MUNICIPAL DOCUMENTS IN GREEK AND LATIN

ἐψηφίσασθε, ταύτας νῦν καὶ ἡνίκα | ἔξεστιν ἀποδοῦναι βούλεσθε,
10 τοῦτο συν|χωρήσαντος τοῦ μεγίστου πάντων αὐτο||κράτορος, ὃς
Ξανθίοις ἀνῆκε τὴν ἐπίκλησιν | τὴν ἀντικρὺς τούτων γενομένην.
Καὶ ἐμοὶ | δὲ δοκεῖ καὶ Ὀπραμόας πάντων ἔνεκεν ἄ|ξιος ἐπαι-
νεῖσθαι καὶ τειμᾶσθαι πρὸς ὑμῶν, | καὶ φιλότειμος ὢν καὶ περὶ
15 πᾶσαν πόλιν ὡς || πατρίδα ἐσπουδακὼς καὶ τοῖς ἰδίοις ὡς κοι-|
νοῖς χρώμενος· ἐπαινῶ δὲ καὶ ὑμᾶς αὐ|τοὺς τοὺς τὰς τειμὰς
διδόντας ὅτι ασ|.......(septem versus maxime mutili; in fine:)
Ἐρρῶσθαι [ὑμᾶς βο]ύλο|[μαι. Ἐδ]όθη πρὸ ια′ κα(λανδῶν)
Ὀ[κτω]υβρ[ίων] | ἐν Παττάροις.

See note on no. 80. In A.D. 137 the governor had vetoed the
proposal of the provincial assembly to confer unusual honors on
Opramoas (Cagnat, *IGRR.* 3, 739, c. 24, 26). In the following
year (c. 26) the Xanthians appealed to the emperor, and the provincial assembly supported their action by passing a decree and
sending an embassy to Rome. From the document which we have
printed above, we learn that the emperor reversed the action of
the governor in 137, and instructed the present governor to inform
the assembly of his consent to grant the desired honors.

98. EPISTULA PROCONSULIS ASIAE L. VENULEI
APRONIANI AD EPHESIOS
(ca. 138–139 p. Chr.)
Lafoscade, 94.

Οὐενουλήιος Ἀπρωνιανὸς ἀνθύπατο[ς] | Ἐφεσίων ἄρχουσι,
βουλῆι, δήμωι χαίρε[ιν]. | Ἀεὶ καὶ μᾶλλον ἐπιδείκνυσθε τὴν
5 πρ[ὸς τὸν] | μέγιστον αὐτοκρ[ά]τορα ἡμῶν [Α]ἴλ[ιον] || Ἀν-
τωνεῖνον Σ[εβ]αστὸν εὐ[σέβειαν | πάσηι τε (?) γν]ώμηι τῆς
λαμπ[ροτάτης | πόλεως ὑμ]ῶν καὶ νῦν ψηφισά[μενοι ἐν | ταῖς
ἐπιφανε]στάταις ἡμεῖν καὶ αἰων[ίοις] | αὐτο[ῦ γενε]θλίαις ἡμέραις
10 καὶ θέας ἡ[μερῶν] || πέντε ἐπιτελεῖν καὶ διανομὴν τοῖς | πολεί-
ταις ἐκ τῶν καλουμένων εἰς τὰς | θυσίας ἑκάστωι δηνάριον
διδόναι. Καὶ | ταῦτα μὲν ὑμεῖν ὀρθῶς καὶ καλῶς ὥσπερ | ε(ἰ)
15 αὐτὸς εἰσηγησάμενος ἔτυχ[ο]ν || νενομοθετήσθω. Ἐρρῶσθαι
ὑμᾶς εὔχομαι.

An edict of Trajan had forbidden *donationes* from the municipal
treasury to citizens (Pliny, *Epp. ad Trai.* 110), but in this document

[420]

from Ephesus we see that, in the age of the Antonines, the town council proposed a distribution of a denarius to each citizen present at the sacrifices in honor of the emperor on his birthday, if his name was on the roll of invited guests. Endowments for such distributions were common in antiquity (Laum, *Stiftungen*, 1, 103 *ff.*; *cf.* nos. 69, 71), but we seldom find record of a direct distribution of municipal funds as proposed at Ephesus. The approval of the governor was required, and we infer from his answer that he had the right to propose legislation in the municipal council, at least in matters dealing with the finances of the city.

99. EPISTULA CORNELI PROCULI, LEGATI LYCIAE, AD SCRIBAM PUBLICUM MYRORUM
(140 p. Chr.)

Cagnat, *IGRR.* 3, 739, c. 34; Lafoscade, 110.

Κορνήλιος Πρόκλος, | πρεσβευτὴς ἀντι|στράτηγος αὐ[το-
κρά]||το[ρος], ᾿Ιουλίωι Κα[πετω]||λείνωι [Μ]υρέων γραμμα|τεῖ 5
χαίρειν. [Ο]ἷς ἡ βου|λὴ καὶ ὁ δῆμος ὀνόμα|σιν ἐτε[ί]μησεν
᾿Οπραμό|αν ᾿Απολλωνίου δὶς || τοῦ Καλλιάδου, τού|τοις κἀγὼ 10
τοῦτον | προσαγορεύεσθαι | συνχωρῶ, εἰ μὴ τοῦτ᾿ ἔ[σ]||τιν ὑπε-
ναντίον ἢ τοῖς || νόμοις ἢ τοῖς ἔθεσ[ι]ν | [τοῖς πα]ρ᾿ ὑμε[ῖ]ν. 15
[᾿Ερρῶσ]||θαί σε εὔχομαι. ᾿Αναγέ|γραπται ἐπὶ ἀρχι(ερέως) |
[Πολ]υχάρμ[ου].

Cf. no. 80. The city of Myra proposed to confer certain honors on Opramoas, but first asked the provincial legate if he would sanction their decree. He replied that the city could do so, if their act was not contrary to their laws or customs. In submitting their proposal to the legate, the municipal authorities were probably animated by motives of vanity, but in this way they invited the interference of the imperial authorities in local affairs (*cf.* nos. 71, 114). To some extent the powers of cities were limited by the laws of the commissioners or governor in organizing the province. Edicts were also issued by various emperors regulating the internal affairs of the municipalities. For example, Trajan issued an edict forbidding the payment of money from municipal treasuries to private individuals as gifts (Pliny, *Epp. ad Trai.* 110). Treaties made between Rome and various cities also contained clauses which gave Romans special privileges and apparently restricted the freedom of the city in giving similar rights to other aliens (*cf. IG.* VII, 20 (Tanagra) [δεδόσθαι].. καὶ τ[ἄλλ]α πάντ[α] ... [πλὴν εἴ τινα ἄλλως] προστέτ[ακται ἡμῖν ἐν ταῖς σ]υν[θήκαις τ]αῖ[ς γενομέναις πρὸς] ᾿Ρωμαίους: Dio Chrys. 41, 10; *cf.* no. 19).

100. EPISTULA ANTONINI PII AD EPHESIOS
(140–144 p. Chr.)

Lafoscade, 51; Ditt. *Syll.*[3] 849.

Αὐτοκρ[άτωρ Καῖσαρ, θεοῦ ᾿Αδ]ριανοῦ | υἱός, θεο[ῦ Τραιανοῦ Παρθικοῦ υἱων]ός, | θεοῦ Νερ[ούα ἔκγονος, Τίτος Αἴλιος ᾿Αδρι]-
5 ανὸς | ᾿Αντωνεῖν[ος Σεβαστός, ἀρχιερεὺς μέ]γιστος, || δημαρχικῆ[ς ἐξουσίας τὸ.., αὐτοκράτωρ τὸ β′], ὕπατος | τὸ γ′, πατὴρ πα[τρί-δος, ᾿Εφεσίων τ]οῖς [ἄρχουσι καὶ τῆι] βουλῆι | [καὶ τῶι δή]μωι χαίρ[ειν]. | Περγαμηνο[ὺς ἀπεδε]ξάμην ἐν τοῖς π[ρὸς ὑμᾶς γ]ράμμασιν | χρησαμένο[υς το]ῖς ὀνόμ[α]σιν οἷς ἐγὼ χρῆσθαι
10 τὴν πόλιν || τὴν ὑμετέραν [ἀπ]εφ[η]νάμην. Οἶμαι δὲ καὶ Σμυρναί-ους κατὰ | τύχην παραλ[ελ]οιπέναι ταῦτα ἐν τῶ περὶ τῆς συνθυσίας | ψηφίσματι, τοῦ λοιποῦ δὲ ἑκόντας εὐγνωμονήσειν, ἐὰν | καὶ ὑμεῖς ἐν τοῖς πρὸς αὐτοὺς γράμμασιν ὃν [π]ροσήκει |
15 τρόπον καὶ κέκριται τῆς πόλεως αὐτῶν [φαίνησθ]ε μεμνη||[μ]ένοι. Τὸ ψήφισμα ἔπεμψεν Σουλπίκιος ᾿Ιου[λια]νὸ[ς ἐπίτ]ροπός μου. | Εὐτυχεῖτε. | [Τὸ] δὲ ψήφισμα ἐποίησεν γραμματεύων Πό. Οὐήδιος ᾿Αν[τωνε]ῖνο[ς].

From Ephesus. This letter illustrates the rivalry between Greek cities in Asia Minor for preeminence which was characteristic at this period (Cassius Dio, 52. 37. 10; Dio Chrys. 34. 48). The emperor had determined the proper rank and titles for the three cities, Ephesus, Smyrna, and Pergamum. Neither Smyrna nor Ephesus accepted his decision, and in their communications to each other had neglected to use the proper titles of honor. The Ephesians complained to the emperor, and in his reply he attempts to allay their wrath with a mild rebuke, suggesting that they also use the proper titles of honor in addressing Smyrna. This dispute raged again some years later, and was once more referred to the emperor (Aristides, περὶ ὁμονοίας ταῖς πόλεσιν; *cf.* Chapot, *La prov. rom proc. d'Asie*, 144 f.; Ditt. *Syll.*[3] 849, n. 2).

FROM ITALY AND THE PROVINCES

101. EPISTULA IMPERATORIS ANTONINI PII AD EPHESIOS
(145 p. Chr.)

Lafoscade, 54; Ditt. *Syll.*³ 850; *I.B.M.* 3, 491.

[Αὐτοκράτω]ρ Καῖσ[α]ρ, θε[οῦ ᾿Αδ]ρι[ανο]ῦ | [υἱός, θεοῦ
Τραϊ]ανο[ῦ Παρθ]ικο[ῦ υἱω]νός, | [θεοῦ Νερούα ἔ]κγον[ος, Τίτος]
Αἴλιο[ς ᾿Αδρι]ανὸς | [᾿Αντωνεῖνος Σεβα]στό[ς, ἀρχιερεύ]ς μ[έ-
γιστος, δη]μαρ‖[χι]κ[ῆς ἐξουσίας] τὸ η΄, α[ὐτοκράτωρ τ]ὸ β΄, 5
ὕπα[τ]ος [τὸ δ΄, πα]‖τὴρ π[ατρίδος, ᾿Εφεσί]ων τοῖς [ἄρ]χουσι
καὶ τ[ῇ] βουλῇ καὶ | [τῷ δήμῳ χ]αίρε[ιν. Τ]ὴν φιλοτιμίαν ἣν
φιλοτιμ[εῖται | πρὸς ὑμ]ᾶς Ο[ὐήδιο]ς ᾿Αντωνεῖνος ἔμαθον οὐχ
οὕτω[ς] ἐκ | τῶν ὑμετέρω[ν γραμ]μάτων ὡς ἐκ τῶν [ἐκ]είνου·
βουλόμε‖νος γὰρ παρ᾿ ἐμοῦ τυχεῖν βοηθείας [εἰς τὸ]ν κόσμον 10
τῶν | ἔργων, ὧν ὑμεῖν ἐπηνγείλατο, ἐδήλ[ωσεν ὅσα κα]ὶ ἡλίκα
οἰ‖κοδομήματα προστίθησιν τῇ πόλ[ει, ἀλλ᾿ ὑμ]εῖς ο[ὐκ] ὀρ|θῶς
ἀποδέχεσθε αὐτόν· κἀγὼ καὶ συ[νεχώρησα α]ὐτῷ[ι ὅσ]|α ᾐτή-
σατ[ο], καὶ ἀπεδεξάμην ὅτι [οὐ] τὸν [συνήθη τῶ]ν πο‖λειτευο- 15
μένων τρόπον, οἳ τοῦ [παρ]αχρῆμ[α εὐδοκιμ]εῖν χά|[ρ]ιν εἰς
θέα[ς κ]αὶ διανομὰς καὶ τὰ τῶ[ν ἀγώνων θέματα δαπαν]ῶ[σι |
τὴ]ν φι[λοτιμ]ίαν, ἀλλὰ δι᾿ οὗ πρὸς τὸ [μέλλον ἐλπίζει σ]εμνο|-
[τέραν ποιή]σειν τὴν πόλιν προῄρ[ηται. Τὰ γράμματα ἔπε]μψεν |
[Κλ. ᾿Ιου]λιανὸς ὁ κράτιστος ἀνθύ[πατος. Εὐτυχεῖτ]ε.

From Ephesus. This letter reveals the undercurrents of municipal
life at this period. Vedius Antoninus had secured assistance from
the emperor in building the Odeum at Ephesus, and had contributed
generously from his own purse. The emperor rebukes the city for
their lukewarmness in giving honor to Vedius because he had
spent his wealth in an enduring monument instead of giving games
or distributing doles to the citizens. (*Cf.* Hicks, *I.B.M.* 3, 492,
493.)

102. EPISTULA RUPILI SEVERI, LEGATI LYCIAE,
AD LYCIARCHAM
(150 p. Chr.)

Cagnat, *IGRR.* 3, 739, c. 45; Lafoscade, 114.

᾿Ρουπίλιος Σεουῆ[ρ]ος ᾿Αν[δ]ροβίωι Λυκιάρχηι χαίρε[ιν.
᾿Επε]ὶ ἡ κρα|τίστ[η] τοῦ ἔθνους βουλὴ ἐπεβοήσατο τὸ ψήφισμα
δι[αγ]ρα|φῆναι ὑπὲρ ᾿Οπραμόα ᾿Απολλωνίου πρὸς τὸν μέγιστον

MUNICIPAL DOCUMENTS IN GREEK AND LATIN

αὐ[τ]ο|κράτορα, δύνασαι ποιεῖν ὃ βούλονται. Ἐρρῶσθαί σε
εὔχομ[αι].

Cf. no. 80. The provincial assembly of Lycia requests permission
of the governor to send a copy of an honorary decree to the emperor.
The lyciarch is given authority to carry out the wish of the assembly.

103. TITULUS OPERIS PUBLICI
(152 p. Chr.)

An. ép. 1904, no. 21.

Imp. Caesar | *T. Aelius Hadrianus* | *Antoninus Aug. Pius* | *pont.*
5 *max. tribu‖ni*cia potestate xv cos. iiii | viam per Alpiis | Numidicas,
10 ve|tustate inter|ruptam, ponti‖*b*us denuo fac|*ti*s, paludibus | sic-
15 catis, labibus | confirmatis, | restituit, ‖ curante M. Valerio |
Etrusco leg. suo | pr. pr.

For similar inscriptions, *cf.* nos. 31 and 72.

104. TRES EPISTULAE ANTONINI PII AD
CORONENSES ET THISBENSES
(140–155 p. Chr.)

IG. vii, 2870.

I ......δί]|καιον, ὁπότε ὑμεῖς οὐκ [ἐ]πείθεσθε τοῖς κριθεῖσιν,
ἀλλὰ εἰσήιειτε εἰς τὴν ἐκείνων χώρα[ν], | κἀκείνους (ε)ἰς τὸ μὴ
περ[ι]ορᾶν ὑμᾶς νέμοντας τρέπεσθαι. Πόσον δέ ἐστιν τὸ ὀφει-
λόμ[ε]|νον τέλος ἢ τίνα εἰσὶν ἃ κατεσχήκασιν ὑμῶν Κορωνεῖς
5 ἐνέχυρα, Ἀριστώνυμος ‖ ὁ αὐτὸς κρινεῖ. Εὐτυχεῖτε.

II Αὐτοκράτωρ Καῖσαρ, θεοῦ Ἀδριανοῦ υἱός, θεοῦ Τραϊανοῦ
Παρθι|κοῦ υἱωνός, θεοῦ Νερούα ἔκγονος, Τίτος Αἴλιος Ἀδριανὸς
Ἀντωνεῖνος Σεβαστός, ἀρχιερεὺς μέγιστος, | δημαρχικῆς ἐξου-
σίας τὸ γ′, ὕπατος γ′, πατὴρ πατρίδος, Κορωνέων τοῖς ἄρχουσι
καὶ τῆι βουλῆι καὶ τῶι δή|μωι χαίρειν. Καὶ τοῦ θεοῦ πατρός
μου δικαίως μεμνημένοι καὶ τῆς ἐμῆς ἀρχῆς κατὰ τὸ προσῆκον ‖
5 ἐπηισθημένοι καὶ ὑπὲρ τοῦ υἱοῦ μου προθύμως συνηδόμενοι πρέ-
ποντα Ἕλλησιν ἀνθρώποις ποιεῖ|τε. Ἐπρέσβευεν Δημήτριος
Διονυσίου, ὧι τὸ ἐφόδιον δοθήτω, εἰ μὴ προῖκα ὑπέσχετο. Εὐτυχεῖτε.

III Αὐτοκράτωρ Καῖσαρ, θεοῦ Ἀδ[ρι]ανοῦ υἱός, θεοῦ Τραϊανοῦ
Παρθικοῦ υἱωνός, θεοῦ Νερούα ἔκγονος, Τί|τος Αἴλιος Ἀδριανὸς

[424]

FROM ITALY AND THE PROVINCES

Ἀντων[εῖ]νος Σεβαστός, ἀρχιερεὺς μέγιστος, δημαρχικῆς ἐξου-
σίας τὸ ιη΄, αὐτο|κράτωρ τὸ β΄, ὕπατος τὸ δ΄, πατὴρ πατρίδος,
Κορωνέων τοῖς ἄρχουσι καὶ τῆι βουλῆι καὶ τῶι δήμωι χαί|ρειν.
Τῆς ἀποφάσεως ἣν ἐ[π]οιησάμην μεταξὺ ὑμῶν καὶ Θισβέων
ἀπόγραφον ὑμεῖν ἔπενψα, ἐ||πέστειλα δὲ καὶ Μεστρίωι Ἀρι-   5
σ[τ]ωνύμωι ἀπομετρῆσαι τὰ πλέθρα Θισβεῦσιν, ἃ προσέταξεν
αὐτοῖς ὁ | θεὸς πατήρ μου παραδοθῆ[ναι], τῆς δὲ ἔξωθεν χώρας
εἴ τινα Θισβεῖς ἐπινέμοιεν πείθοντες ὑμᾶς, | δώσουσιν μὲν νόμιον
τέλ[ος, ἂν] δὲ καὶ ἀποδῶσιν, ὅσον ἂν ὑπὲρ τοῦ χρόνου τοῦ
παρελθόντος ὀφ[εί]|λειν αὐτοὺς κριθῆι, δηλονό[τι] ὑμεῖς τὰ
ἐνέχυρα αὐτοῖς ἀποδώσετε. Ἐπρέσβευον Αἴλιος Γλύκω[ν] | καὶ
Διονύσιος Διονυσοδώρου, [οἷς τὸ] ἐφόδιον δοθήτω, εἰ μὴ προῖκα
ὑπέσχηνται. Εὐτυχεῖτε.

From Coronea. The people of Thisbe had been encroaching on
the territory of Coronea. The dispute had been referred to Hadrian
and a decision rendered, but the aggressions continued. Antoninus
appointed Aristonymus to survey the land, ordering both Thisbans
and Coroneans to pay the taxes to the respective cities to which
the disputed lands might be awarded.

105. EDICTUM PROCONSULIS ASIAE DE FESTIS
DIEBUS EPHESIORUM
(ca. 160 p. Chr.)

I.B.M. 482; *CIG.* 2954; Ditt. *Syll.*³ 867.

[..Πο]πίλλιος Κᾶρος Πέδω[ν] | ἀνθύπατος λέγει. | [Ἔ]μαθον ἐκ
τοῦ πεμφθέντος [εἰς ἐ]|μὲ ψηφίσματος ὑπὸ τῆς λαμπροτ[ά]||της   5
Ἐφεσίων βουλῆς τοὺς πρὸ ἐμ[οῦ] | κρατίστους ἀνθυπάτους
ἱε[ρὰς] | νομίσαι τὰς ἡμέρας τῆς [πα]νη[γύρεως | τ]ῶν Ἀρτ[ε-
μισίων] καὶ τοῦτο διατά|γματι δεδηλωκέναι· ὅθεν ἀναγκαῖ||ον   10
ἡγησάμην καὶ αὐτὸς ἀποβλέ|πων εἴς τε τὴν εὐσέβειαν τῆς θεοῦ |
καὶ εἰς τὴν τῆς λαμπροτάτης Ἐφε|σίων πόλεως τειμὴν φανερὸν
ποι|ῆσαι διατάγματι ἔσεσθαι τὰς ἡμέρας || ταύτας ἱερὰς καὶ τὰς   15
ἐπ᾽ αὐταῖς ἐκε|χειρίας φυλαχθήσεσθαι· προεστῶ|τος τῆς πανη-
γύρεως | Τίτου Αἰλίου Μαρκιανοῦ Πρίσκου | τοῦ ἀγωνοθέτου,
υἱοῦ Αἰλίου || Πρίσκου, ἀνδρὸς δοκιμωτάτου καὶ | πάσης τειμῆς   20
καὶ ἀποδοχῆς ἀξίου.

From Ephesus. The governor of Asia had, apparently, given offence to the citizens of this city by transacting public business—possibly holding court—on days sacred to Diana. The Ephesians lodged a protest, citing the edicts of former governors regarding their holy days. The second part of the inscription, omitted here, contains a decree of the city making the whole of the month Artemision sacred to the goddess.

106. SENATUS CONSULTUM DE CYZICENIS
(138–160 p. Chr.)

CIL. III, *S.* 7060; *E.E.* 3, 156; Dessau, 7190; Bruns, 62; Riccobono, p. 237.

*S.C. de p*ostulatione Kyzicenor. ex Asia, | qui dicunt ut corpus quod appellatur ne|on et habent in civitate sua auctoritate | *am-*
5 *plissimi* ordinis confirmetur. Scri||*bendo adfue*runt M. Aelius imp. Titi Aeli | *Hadriani An*tonini *f.* Pap. Aurelius Ve|*rus,*....s M. f. Gal. Verus, M. Hosidius | M. *f.* A...*Geta*, M. Annius M. f. Gal. Libo, Q. | Pomp*eius* Q. f. Hor. Bassianus, L. Fl. L. f. ||
10 Quir. Iulianus, L. Gellius L. f. Ter. Severus, | q(uaestores). Sententia dicta ab Appio Galio | cos. desig. relatione IIII concedente | imp. Caes*are Tito A*elio Hadriano An|*tonino Aug. Pio*...IIII re-
15 latione sua || ....*Kyziceno*s ex Asia | ....*quos neos a*ppellant....

A stone tablet found in 1876 on the site of Cyzicus, now in the British Museum. Cyzicus was a *civitas libera* (*cf.* Chapot, *La prov. rom. proc. d'Asie,* 115) in the senatorial province of Asia. As Kornemann has shown (*R.E.* 4, 408 *ff.*), the imperial policy in the matter of associations was determined by the *lex Iulia* of Augustus (*cf. CIL.* VI, 2193). Under this law only useful organizations were allowed, and a new association must secure the consent of the senate and the approval of the emperor. Under the early empire the senate took action even on requests from cities in imperial provinces (*cf. CIL.* V, 7881), but gradually its competence was restricted to Italy and the senatorial provinces, as in this case, and in the course of time, even in senatorial provinces, the consent of the emperor was the determining factor. In the cities of the East particularly the central government was chary of allowing the

[426]

formation of clubs, because of their tendency to develop into political organizations (*cf.* Plin. *Epp. ad Trai.* 33, 34). On the danger attending the formation of *corpora neon* (= *iuvenum*), Mommsen cites *Dig.* 48. 19. 28, 3, from the third century, *solent quidam, qui volgo se iuvenes appellant, in quibusdam civitatibus turbulentis se adclamationibus popularium accommodare.* The emperor had the right to present the first four motions at a meeting of the senate, but in this case he conceded his right to the fourth motion (*cf.* l. 12) to the *consul designatus* (*cf.* Mommsen, *St. R.* 2, 898, n. 4). The words *sententia dicta* show that the stone gives an extract from the *Acta Senatus* rather than the *S.C.* itself. After 11 B.C. the *Acta Senatus* were in charge of the quaestors.

107. TITULUS HONORARIUS
(138–161 p. Chr.)

CIL. XII, 594; Dessau, 6988.

Pagani pagi Lucreti, qui sunt fini|bus Arelatensium loco Gargario, Q. Cor. | Marcelli lib. Zosimo IIIIIIvir Aug. col. Iul. | Paterna Arelate ob honorem eius, qui notum (*sic*) fecit || iniuriam nostram 5 omnium saec*ulor*um sacra|tissimo principi T. Aelio Antonino *Pio*, . . r Romae | misit per multos annos ad praesides pro*vinci*ae per-se|cutus est iniuriam nostram suis in*pendiis e*t ob hoc | donavit nobis inpendia quae fecit, ut omnium saecu||lorum sacratissimi principis 10 imp. Caes. Antonini Aug. Pii | beneficia durarent permanerentque quibus frueremur | . . . .et balineo gratuito quod ablatum erat paganis | *pagi Lucreti,* quod usi fuerant amplius annis xxxx.

Found at St Jean de Garguier near Massilia. The *pagus Lucretius* was an *oppidum attributum,* which had probably been taken from Massilia and given to Arelate, because of the resistance which Massilia offered to Caesar in 49 B.C., *cf.* Marquardt, *St. Verw.* 1, 263 *f.*; Herzog, *Gallia Narbonensis,* 171 and no. 358. On *oppida attributa* and their disputes with their suzerain states, *cf.* nos. 10 and 49; pp. 10 *ff.*, 138 *ff.* In ll. 6–7 Hirschfeld would read *patienter Romae mansit.*

MUNICIPAL DOCUMENTS IN GREEK AND LATIN

108. EPISTULA IMPERATORIS ANTONINI AD MINOETAS
(138–161 p. Chr.)

IG. XII, 7, 242; Cagnat, *IGRR.* 4, 1010.

[Μεινωητῶν τῆι βου]|λῆι καὶ [τῶι δήμωι χαίρειν]..... |
5 πολλῶν........[τὴν ὑμετέραν πό]||λιν· καὶ γὰρ α.....||ων
ἐπιφανῶ[ς.....πρὸς τὸν ʿΡω]||μαίων δῆμον........ | δὲ τῆς
πρὸς τὸν....... | εὐνοίας, μάλιστα [δὲ πρὸς τὸν πατέρα
10 ʿΑδριανὸν] | Θεὸν Σεβα(σ)τόν, ὃς........... || διατρείψας
παρ᾽ ὑμε[ῖν πολλῶν....... ἀγαθῶν] | καὶ φιλανθρώπων
ε.........|τα· ὅθεν καὶ τῶι ψηφίσ[ματι τῶι ὑμετέρωι ἐνέ]|-
τυχον ἡδέως, καὶ το[ῖς παρ᾽ ὑμῶν πρεσβευταῖς] | Θεοπόμπωι
15 ʾΑνόκνο[υ]......... || στράτωι ἐχρημάτισα· [διὰ ταῦτα οὖν
ὑμῖν ἐλευ]||θερίαν καὶ αὐτονομί[αν καὶ ἀτέλειαν, καθὼς] | παρὰ
τῶν πρόσθεν α[ὐτοκρατόρων ἐλάβε]||τε, ἐβεβαίωσα, ετ....
......

From Minoa in the island Amorgus. The emperor, presumably
Antoninus Pius, ratifies the gift of freedom, independence, and
immunity, which the city had received from former emperors.
The visit of Hadrian to the islands in the Aegean was made in
123 (Weber, *Unters. Gesch. Hadr.* 142 *ff.*). Cf. nos. 40, 75.

109. EPISTULA PRAEFECTORUM PRAETORIO
(168–172 p. Chr.)

CIL. IX, 2438; Bruns, 71*b*; Riccobono, p. 260.

(1) Bassaeus Rufus et Macrin*i*us Vindex mag|(istratibus)
　　　　Saepinat(ibus)　　　　　salutem. |
Exemplum epistulae scriptae nobis a Cosmo Aug(usti) lib(erto) |
5 a rationibus cum his quae iuncta erant subiecimus, et admonem||us
abstineatis iniuris faciendis conductoribus gregum oviarico|rum cum
magna fisci iniuria, ne necesse sit recognosci de hoc | et in factum,
si ita res fuerit, vindicari. |
(2) Cosmi Aug(usti) lib(erti) a rationibus scriptae ad Basseum
Rufum et ad | Macrin*i*um Vindic(em) pr(aefectos) pr(aetorio)
10 e(minentissimos) v(iros).—Exemplum epistul(ae) scriptae mihi || a
Septimiano colliberto et adiutore meo subieci, et peto tanti | faciatis

scribere mag(istratibus) Saepin(atibus) et Bovian(ensibus), uti desinant iniuriam | conductoribus gregum oviaricorum qui sunt sub cura mea facere, | ut beneficio vestro ratio fisci indemnis sit.

(3) Script(ae) a Septimiano ad Co|smum.—*Cum* conductores gregum oviaricorum, qui sunt sub cura tua, in re presenti ‖ subinde 15 mihi quererentur per itinera callium frequenter iniuriam | se accipere a stationaris et mag(istratibus) Saepino et Boviano eo, quod in transitu | iumenta et pastores, quos conductos habent *retineant* dicentes fugitivos esse et | iumenta abactia habere et sub hac specie oves quoque dominicae | *sibi pe*reant in illo tumultu: necesse habebamus etiam *et etiam* scribere, quietius ag‖erent, ne res dominica 20 detrimentum pateretur; et cum in eadem contumacia | perseverent, dicentes non curaturos se neque meas litteras neque si tu eis | scripseris haut fieri rem, rogo, domine, si tibi videbitur, indices Basseo Rufo | et Macrinio Vindici pr(aefectis) pr(aetorio) e(minentissimis) v(iris), ut epistulas emittant ad eosdem mag(istratus) et stati|onarios. . . . .*t*andiu t*e*m*e*re (?) *i*rritum (?) factum est.

Found on a stone at Saepinum. The *cursus honorum* of M. Bassaeus Rufus is given in *CIL.* VI, 1599 (= Dessau, 1326). He was probably prefect of Egypt from 166 to 168 (*cf.* v. Rohden in *R.E.* 3, 103 *f.*; Meyer, *Hermes,* 32 (1897), 226). Subsequently he was made praetorian prefect. M. Macrinius Vindex was killed in 172 probably (*cf. Prosop.* 2, p. 313). Their joint incumbency of the praetorian prefecture therefore probably fell between 168 and 172. The situation which calls forth this letter is clear. The officials of Saepinum and Bovianum have illtreated the keepers of the imperial herds and wrongfully taken some of their animals. The attention of Cosmus, *a rationibus,* is called to this state of things by his *adiutor,* Septimianus, in a letter (ll. 10–24). Cosmus sends this letter with a brief superscription of his own (ll. 8–10) to the praetorian prefects, who in turn prefix a warning (ll. 1–7) to the document and send it to the magistrates of Saepinum. Our interest in the document lies primarily in the fact that it deals with a quarrel between municipal magistrates and imperial employees, and shows how such a difficulty was settled. The prefects take the action which they do in this case not as fiscal officers, but as officials charged with the maintenance of order in Italy, and this is one of the earliest known instances of the exercise by the praetorian prefect of this function; *cf.* Mommsen, *St. R.* 2, 969, 1120.

The *stationarii* (l. 16) are in this case of course members, not of the imperial, but of the municipal police force; *cf.* Lécrivain, *Dict. Dar.* 4, 1469. For the functions of the *scrinium a rationibus*, *cf.* pp. 240 *ff.* For its organization, *cf.* Hirschfeld, 31 *ff.* On the imperial domains, *cf.* pp. 17 *ff.*

110. SENATUS CONSULTUM DE SUMPTIBUS LUDORUM GLADIATORUM MINUENDIS
(176–177 p. Chr.)

CIL. ii, *S.* 6278; Dessau, 5163; Bruns, 63; Riccobono, p. 238.

.....tantam illam pestem nulla medicina sanari posse. Nec poterat: verum nostri principes quibus omne studium est quanto li|bet morbo salutem publicam mersam et enectam refovere et integrae valuetudini reddere, in primis anima adverterunt quae | causa illi morbo vires daret, unde foeda et inlicita vectigalia ius haberent, quis auctor et patronus esset usurpandis quasi | legitimis, quae omnibus legibus et divinis et humanis prohibentur. ||

5   Fiscus dicebatur: fiscus non sibi, set qui lanienae aliorum prae-texeretur, tertia vel quarta parte ad licentiam foedae rapinae invi|ta-tus. Itaque fiscum removerunt a tota harena. Quid enim Marci Antonini et *Luci Commodi* cavendum fisco cum hare|na? Omnis pecunia horum principum *p*ura est, nulla cruoris humani adspergine contaminata, nullis sordibus foedi quae|stus inquinata, et quae tam sanctae paratur quam insumitur. Itaque facessat sive illut ducen-tiens annu*u*m seu trecenties | est; satis amplum patr*i*m*o*nium imperio parati*s* ex parsimonia vestra. Quin etiam ex reliquis lanistarum, quae
10 (sestertium) quingenties su||pra sunt, pars lanistis condonetur. Ob quae, oro vos, merita? Nulla sane, inquiunt, merita, set prohibiti talibus grassaturis sola|cium ferant et in posterum tanto pretio in-vitentur ad opsequium humanitatis. |

O magni impp., qui scitis altius fundari remedia, quae etiam malis consulunt, qui se etiam necessarios fecerint! Et iam fructus tan|tae vestrae providentiae emerg*i*t. Legebatur etiam nunc apud nos oratio; sed ubi rumore delatu*m e*st questus lanistarum recisos, fis|cum

omnem illam pecuniam quasi contaminatam reliquisse, statim sacerdotes fidelissimarum Galliarum vestrarum ‖ concursare, gaudere, 15
inter se loqui. |

Erat aliquis, qui deploraverat fortunas suas creatus sacerdos, qui
auxilium sibi in provocatione ad principes facta constituerat. Sed |
ibidem ipse primus et de consilio amicorum: quid mihi iam cum
appellatione? Omne onus, quod patrimonium meum opprimebat,
sanc|tissimi impp. remiserunt; iam sacerdos esse et cupio et opto
et, editionem muneris quam olim detestabamur, amplector. |

Itaque gratiae appellationis non solum ab illo, verum et a ceteris
petitae; et quanto plures petentur! Iam hoc genus causarum di-
versam formam ‖ habebit, ut appellet qui non sunt creati sacerdotes, 20
immo populus. |

Quae igitur tantis tam salutarium rerum consilis vestris alia
prima esse sententia potest, quam ut, quod singuli sentiunt, quod
universi | de pectore intimo clamant, ego censeam? |

Censeo igitur in primis agendas maximis impp. gratias, qui salu-
taribus remedis, fisci ratione post habita, labentem civitatium statum
et prae|cipitantes iam in ruinas principalium virorum fortunas
restituerunt: tanto quidem magnificentius, quod, cum excusatum
esset reti‖nerent quae ali instituissent et quae longa consuetudo con- 25
firmasset, tamen olli peraeque nequaquam sectae suae congruere
arbitra|ti sunt male instituta servare et quae turpiter servanda essent
instituere. |

Quamquam autem non nulli arbitrentur de omnibus, quae ad
nos maximi principes rettulerunt, una et succincta sententia cen-
sendum, | tamen, si vos probatis, singula specialiter persequar, verbis
ipsis ex oratione sanctissima ad lucem sententiae translatis, ne qua
ex parte pravis in|terpretationibus sit locus.

Itaque censeo, uti munera, quae assiforana appellantur, in sua
forma maneant nec egrediantur sump‖tu (sestertium) xxx (milia). 30
Qui autem supra (sestertium) xxx (milia) ad lx (milia) usque munus
edent, is gladiatores tripertito praebeantur numero pari. Summum
pre|tium sit—(v. 31–34 *sequuntur pretia gladiatorum*).

Et haec sit summo ac formonso gladiatori defi‖nita quantitas. 35
Utique in omnibus muneribus quae generatim distincta sunt, lanista
dimidiam copiam universi numeri promisque multitu|dinis praebeat

exque his qui gregari appellantur, qui melior *l*acertat*u*s erit duobus
milibus sub signo pugnet, nec quisquam ex eo numero | mille
nummum minore. Lanistas etiam promovendos vili studio questus:
sibi copiam dimidiae partis praebenda*e negantes* esse ex nu|mero
gregariorum uti sciant inpositam sibi necessitatem de ceteris quos
meliores opinabuntur transferre tantisper plendi nu|meri grega-
riorum gratia. Itaque is numerus universae familiae aequis partibus
40 in singulos dies dispartiatur, *ne*que ullo die minus quam || dimidia
pars gregariorum sit ibi eo die dimicabunt. Utque ea opservat*i*o
a lanistis quam diligentissime exigatur, iniungendum | his qui pro-
vinciae praesidebunt et legatis vel quaestoribus vel legatis legionum
vel iis qui ius dicunt c(larissimis) v(iris) aut procurator*ibus* maxi-
morum | principum quibus provinciae rector mandaverit; is etiam
procurator*ibus* qui provinciis praesidebunt. Trans Padum autem
perque omnes Italiae | regiones arbitrium iniungendum praefectis
alimentorum ⟨dandis⟩, si aderunt, vel viae curatori aut, si nec is
praesens erit, iuridico vel | tum classis praetoriae praefecto. ||
45   Item censeo de exceptis ita opservandum, ut praecipuum mer-
cedes gladiator sibi quisque paciscatur, eius pecuniae quae ob hanc
causam excipi|ebatur, quartam portionem liber, ser*v*us autem quin-
tam excipiat. De pretis autem gladiatorum opservari paulo ante
censui secundum praescrip|tum divinae orationis, sed ut ea pretia
ad eas civitates pertine*n*t, in quibus ampliora gladiatorum pretia
flagrabant. Quod si quibus civitatibus | res publica tenuior est, non
eadem serventur quae aput fortiores civitates scripta sunt, nec supra
modum virium onerent, sed hactenus in eundem, | ut qu*a*e in
publicis privatisque rationibus repperientur pretia summa ac media
ac postrema, si quidem provinciarum eae civitates sunt, ab eo ||
50 qui praesidebit provinciae opserventur, ceterarum autem iuridico
vel curatori provinciae vel classis praetoriae praefecto vel procura-
tori | maxumorum principum, uti cuiusque civitatis potestasque ibi
prima erit. Atque ita rationibus decem retroversum annorum in-
spectis, exemplis | munerum in quaque civitate edito*rum* conside-
ratis, conserventur ab eo cuius arbitrium erit de tribus pretis: vel si
melius ei videbitur | ex eo modo quem persequitur effici*a*t et tri-
fariam pretia deducantur eaque forma etiam in posterum servetur.
Sciantque v(iri) c(larissimi), qui procon|sules paulo ante profecti

sunt, intra suum quisque annum it negotium exsequi se oportebit, ii etiam, qui non sortito provincias ‖ regant, intra annum. | 55

Ad Galliam sed et princeps........, qui in civitatibus splendidissimarum Galliarum veteri more et sacro ritu expectantur, ne ampliore pretio | lanistae praebeant, quam binis milibus. Cum maximi principes oratione sua praedixerint fore, ut damnatum ad gladium | procurator eorum.........nisi plure quam sex aureis et nisi iuraverit. |

Sacerdotes quoque provinciarum quibus nullum cum lanistis negotium erit, gladiatores a prioribus sacerdotibus sus‖ceptos vel 60 sibimet auctoratos recipiunt, at post editionem eodem pretio in succedentes tramittunt; neque singulatim aliquem | rei gladiatoriae causa vendat plure quam lanistis est pretium persolutum. |

Is autem qui aput tribunum plebei c(larissimum) v(irum) sponte ad dimicandum profitebitur, cum habeat ex lege pretium duo milia, liberatus si discri|men instauraverit, aestimatio eius post hac (sestertium) xii (milia) non excedat. Is quoque qui senior atque inabilior operam suam denuo......

l. 50. provinciae; viae, *Hirschfeld*.
l. 54. oportebit ii *for* oportere eos.
l. 56. ad Galliam...civitatibus; ad Gallicas editiones quae in civitatibus, *Hirschfeld*.
l. 58. *after* procurator eorum *some words have been lost.*

At several points in this inscription, indicated by italics, emendations of scholars have been admitted into the text. Mere orthographical or grammatical errors which do not obscure the sense have usually been allowed to stand.

A bronze tablet, found in 1888 near Italica in Baetica, now in Madrid. Commodus was named imperator in Nov. 176. He was therefore the colleague of M. Aurelius until the latter's death in 180. The inscription consequently falls between these dates (*cf.* l. 6), but since M. Aurelius was absent from Rome on a campaign against the Marcomanni from 178 to 180, this document probably falls in the year 176 or 177.

The plays and games which were given annually in all the principal towns of the empire and the yearly games at the meetings of the *concilia* (*cf.* no. 155) constituted a heavy charge on the municipal budget. At Urso in Spain in the first century B.C., each duovir and aedile was called on to contribute at least 2000 sesterces, and the city added from the public treasury 2000 for each duovir and 1000 for each aedile (*cf.* no. 26, chapp. 70–71). Pliny's letters to Trajan refer frequently to the large sums which were being spent by the cities in his province on theatres, amphitheatres, and baths (*cf. Epp.* 23, 39). The gifts and bequests made by private citizens (*cf.* Liebenam, *St. Verw.* 118, n. 7; 119, n. 1) added materially to the sums spent each year. Some records of the cost of these entertainments are given by Guiraud, *Les assemblées prov.* 130. The central government was aware of the heavy financial burden which these festivals laid on the municipalities, and Cassius Dio (52. 30) makes Maecenas advise Augustus to forbid them outside of Rome, but this document contains the earliest formal action looking to economy in such matters of which we have any record. How serious the matter has become is indicated by ll. 23–24, *labentem civitatium statum et praecipitantes iam in ruinas principalium virorum fortunas.* The subject is brought before the senate in the form of an *oratio principum* (*cf.* ll. 13, 28, 47, 57). This would probably be read by the quaestor, and immediately put to vote by the presiding officer (*cf.* Mommsen, *St. R.* 2, 899; Abbott, 350). The speech which Claudius made in a similar way *de iure honorum Gallis dando* has come down to us (*cf.* no. 50 and Tac. *Ann.* 11. 24–25). This inscription contains a speech made by a senator sometime after the reading of the *oratio principum* (*cf. ubi rumore delatum est,* l. 13). The proposal of M. Aurelius and Commodus, like the speech of Claudius, and like the messages of the President of the United States, was probably cast in the form of a general recommendation. One of the senators, on the basis of this recommendation, proceeds to formulate a bill. His motion, following the preamble (ll. 1–22), consists of two parts: (1) a vote of thanks to the emperors (ll. 23–29), and (2) certain articles limiting the amount of money which may be spent on gladiatorial contests (ll. 29–63). The provisions of the measure are to be enforced by imperial officials (ll. 41–44, 50–55). On these officials, *cf.* Mommsen, *Ges. Schr.* 8, 509–511. To make the new arrangement easier for those who give the games, the emperors have already provided for the remission of the tax paid to the *fiscus* of one-third or one-fourth of the gains made by the *lanistae* (*cf.* ll. 5–6). The sum of 2,000,000 or 3,000,000 sesterces which the senator estimates (*cf.* l. 8) will be lost annually by the *fiscus*, in consequence of the remission of this tax, gives us some conception of the large amounts spent on these games. To the *sacerdotes Romae et Augusti*, upon whom fell the duty of arranging the games held at the annual meeting of the *concilium*, the imperial proposal appealed very strongly (*cf.* ll. 13–20). It is interesting to notice incidentally that M. Aurelius had apparently urged in support of the imperial measure the inhumanity of the gladiatorial contests (*cf.* ll. 3–8). On the salaries to be paid the gladiators, *cf.* Mommsen, *Ges. Schr.* 8, 521–531.

III. RESCRIPTUM COMMODI DE SALTU BURUNITANO
(180–183 p. Chr.)

CIL. VIII, 10570; *cf. S.* 14464; Dessau, 6870; Bruns, 86; Girard, p. 199; Riccobono, p. 361.

........*intellegis praevaricationem* quam non mod*o* cum Allio Col. II
Maximo adver|sario nostro, set cum omnibus fere *con*|ductoribus
contra fas atq. in perniciem | rationum tuarum sine modo exercuit, ||
ut non solum cognoscere per tot retro | annos instantibus ac supli- 5
cantib*us* | vestramq. divinam subscriptionem | adlegantibus nobis
supersederit, ve|rum etiam hoc eiusdem Alli Maximi || conductoris 10
artibus gratiosissimi | *ult*imo indulserit, ut missis militib. | *in* eundem
saltum Burunitanum ali|*os no*strum adprehendi et vexari, ali|*os*
vinc*iri*, nonullos, cives etiam Ro||*manos*, virgis et fustibus effligi 15
iusse|*rit, scilic*et eo solo merito nostro, qu|*od venientes* in tam gravi
pro modulo me|*diocritat*is nostrae tamq. manifesta | *iniuria* im-
ploratum maiestatem tu||*am acerbiore* epistula usi fuissemus. Cu|*ius* 20
*nostrae in*iuriae evidentia, Caes., | *inde profec*to potest aestimari,
qu|*od*......quidem, quem maiesta|*t*.....*ex*sistimamus vel pro ||
..........t omnino cognos |..........plane gratificati | 25
..........mum invenerit |.........nostris, quibus |......
...bamus cogni ||.........beret inte|.......*praestare* operas | 30
..........ret ita tot re|*tro*.....t tu....(*deficiunt quaedam*).

*Quae res c*ompulit nos miserrimos homi|*nes iam rur*sum divinae Col. III
providentiae | *tuae supl*icare, et ideo rogamus, sa|cratissime imp.,

5 subvenias. Ut kapite le‖gis Hadriane, quod supra scriptum est, ad|emptum est, ademptum sit ius etiam proccb., | nedum conductori, adversus colonos am|pliandi partes agrarias aut operar. prae|bi-

10 tionem iugorumve et ut se habent littere ‖ procc. quae sunt in ta*b*ulario tuo tractus Kar|thag., non amplius annuas quam binas | aratorias, binas sartorias, binas messo|rias operas debeamus, itq. sine

15 ulla contro|versia sit, utpote cum in aere inciso et ab ‖ omnib. omnino undiq. versum vicinis nost. | perpetua in hodiernum forma prae*stitu*|tum et procc. litteris quas supra scripsimus | ita confir-matum. Subvenias, et cum homi|nes rustici tenues man*u*um nos-

20 trarum ope‖ris victum tolerantes conductori profusis | largitionib. gratiosismo (*sic*) impares aput | procc. tuos simu*s*, quib. *per* vices successi|on. per condicionem conductionis notus est, | mis*erearis*

25 ac sacro rescripto tuo n. ampli‖us praestare nos, quam ex lege Hadriana et | ex litteras procc. tuor. debemus, id est ter | binas operas, praecipere digneris, ut bene|ficio maiestatis tuae rustici tui vernulae |

30 et alumni salt*u*um tuorum n. ultr. a conduc‖torib. agror. fiscalium inquietem*ur* (*deficiunt quaedam*).

Col. iv   *Imp. Ca*es. M. Aurelius Commodus An|*toni*nus Aug. Sarmat. Germanicus | Maximus Lurio Lucullo et nomine a|liorum. Procc.

5 contemplatione dis‖cipulinae et instituti mei ne plus | quam ter binas operas curabunt, | ne quit per iniuriam contra perpe|tuam formam a vobis exigatur. | Et alia manu: scripsi. Recognovi. ‖

10 Exemplum epistulae proc. e. v. | Tussanius Aristo et Chrysanthus | Andronico suo salutem. Secundum | sacram subscriptionem domini

15 n. | sanctissimi imp., quam ad libellum ‖ suum datam Lurius Lu-cullus *accepit*. . . . . . (*deficiunt versus sex*) *et ali*|a manu: *opt*amus te feli|cissimum be*ne vive*re. Vale. Dat. | pr. idus Sept. Karthagini. ‖

25 Feliciter | consummata et dedicata | idibus M*a*is Aureliano et Corne|liano cos. Cura agente | C. Iulio P*e*lope Salaputi, mag(istro).

Engraved on a stone found in 1879 at Souk-el-Khmis, the ancient saltus Burunitanus, in northern Africa. The inscription is in four columns. Of these the first is almost entirely lost; on the lower part of the second column, the lines are broken on the left side; the third and fourth columns are intact. Commodus took the title of Pius in 183. The inscription therefore falls between 180 and 183. The most important commentaries on it and on related subjects are those of Mommsen, *Ges. Schr.* 3, 153 *ff.*; Esmein, *Mélanges d'hist. et du droit*, 293 *ff.*; Fernique and Cagnat, *Rev. arch.* 41 (1881), 94 *ff.*, 138 *ff.*; Karlowa, 1, 616, 656 *f.*, 924 *ff.*; Fustel de Coulanges, *Recherches sur quelques problèmes d'histoire*, 33 *ff.*; Schulten, *Die römischen Grundherrschaften*; Beaudouin, *Les grands domains dans l'empire romain*; Schulten, *Klio*, 7 (1907), 195 *f.*; Hirschfeld, 122 *ff.*; Rostowzew, *Gesch. d. röm. Kol.* 332 *ff.* The inscription is made up of four parts: (1) the *libellus* of the *coloni* of the saltus Burunitanus (col. I, II, III); (2) the *subscriptio* of Commodus (IV, 1 *ff.*); (3) the *epistula procuratoris tractus Carthaginiensis* (IV, 10 *ff.*), addressed to Andronicus, the *procurator saltus Burunitani*; (4) the date of publication and name of the communal official. Of the people mentioned in the document, Allius Maximus (II, 2) is a *conductor*; Lurius Lucullus (IV, 2) represents the petitioners; Tussanius Aristo (IV, 11) is the *procurator tractus Carth.*; Chrysanthus is his assistant; Andronicus (IV, 12) is *procurator saltus Burunitani*; and Salaputis (IV, 29) the *magister* of the *saltus*, who probably superintends the construction of the altar on which the stone containing the inscription is cut. The tenants complain that the procurators have been unduly influenced and bribed by the contractors, that soldiers have been brought in, that they themselves have been seized and punished, and that their annual contributions of produce and labor have been raised beyond the limits fixed in the *lex Hadriana*. Heitland (*Agricola*, 347) thinks that the phrase, *alumni saltuum tuorum*, implies that their holdings had descended to the present tenants from their fathers.

Not far from the place where this inscription was found, and probably within the limits of the saltus Burunitanus, a fragment of another rescript of Commodus, addressed to Lurius Lucullus, has been discovered (*CIL.* VIII, *S.* 14451). This document is also a reply to the complaints of the *coloni*. In another *libellus* (*CIL.* VIII, *S.* 14428), addressed to the same emperor, the tenants on an imperial domain complain of the wrongs done them, and refer to the fact that they are required to furnish twelve days' work each year. Apparently there was concerted action among the *coloni* in Africa under Commodus. For similar complaints from the Orient, *cf.* nos. 141 and 142.

MUNICIPAL DOCUMENTS IN GREEK AND LATIN

For an imperial reply to a similar complaint from an imperial domain in Phrygia, *cf.* Bruns, 93. The appeal to the emperor in the document before us, probably through the *procurator saltus* (II, 20), was made by Lurius Lucullus, the representative of the tenants, and the emperor's rescript is addressed to Lucullus. A copy of it is sent to the *procurator tractus*, who communicates it to the *procurator saltus* (*cf. quam...accepit*, IV, 15). In their appeal the tenants rely on three documents, viz. the *lex Hadriana* (III, 5), the *litterae procuratorum* (III, 9 *f.*), and the *perpetua forma* (III, 16). For the first two documents, *cf.* no. 93 and p. 16. The *forma perpetua* is the *lex Hadriana* (*cf.* Rostowzew, *op. cit.* 332 *f.*). The *coloni* have not yet been reduced to serfdom. Some of them are Roman citizens (II, 14 *f.*). For the history of the imperial domains, their political organization, and the decline in the status of the *coloni, cf.* pp. 16 *ff.* For the form of an imperial *subscriptio, cf.* pp. 242 *ff.* The petition would go to the *scrinium a libellis.*

112. EPISTULA IMPERATORIS COMMODI AD CHERSO-
NESITANOS DE CAPITULO LENOCINII
(185–186 p. Chr.)

Latyschev, 4, 81; *CIL.* III, *S.* 13750; Cagnat, *IGRR.* 1, 860, ll. 32 *ff.*

E(xemplum) e(pistulae). Τίνα ἐπέστειλα Ἀτειλίωι Πρειμι-|
[ανῶι καὶ ἄλλοις περὶ τοῦ πορνικοῦ τέλ]ους, ὑποταγῆναι ἐκέλευσα
προνοῶν μήτε ὑμᾶς παρὰ τὰ δεδογμένα ἐνοχλί|[ζεσθαι, μήτε
τοὺς ἡμεῖν ὑπηρ]ετοῦντας ὑπερβαίνειν τὸν περιγεγραμμένον
ὅρον. E(xemplum) e(pistulae). ||

35 *Ut scias quae sint officia militum* agentium in vexillatione Cher-
sonessitana de capitulo lenocini quod su*b.* | . . . . , *misi tibi exem-*
plum sententiae Arri Alcibiadis tunc trib(uni) praepositi eiusdem
vexill*a|tionis* . . . . . . us tam intentionem eius quam manifeste de-
terminatam partem ad ius per|tinentem . . . . . et quoniam idem Alci-
biades videri non ⟨po⟩potest sub tempus vent*urum*(?) . | . . . . . . *recu-*
*p*erandae vectigalis quantitatis sponte suscepisse, cum sententiam sub
40 iu*di*||*cii forma* . . . . . . .pridem et dixerit et proposuerit et omnibus
annis fisco pariaverit, dubium n*on* est | *debere et circa vectigalis*

[438]

quantitatem et circa discipulina(e) ratione(m) et observare et ob-
tine*re* | *volo, eius sententiae* exemplum aperta manu scriptum, unde
de plano recte legi possit iuxta | . . . . positum esse cura.

E(xemplum) e(pistulae). Quid scripserim Atilio Primiano tr*ibuno* |
. . . . . . rio commilitionum, quod ad me⟨e⟩ idem tribunus propter
capitulum le*no*||*cini* . . . . . . *s*ecundum formam sententiae Arri Alci- 45
biadis tunc trib(uni) dictae om.. | . . . . . *causas ne quid adve*rs*us*
discipulinam vel cum iniuria aut contumelia paganorum commit-
tatur. |

E(xemplum) e(pistulae). Quid ad decretum Chersonessitanorum
rescripserim, *co*|*gnoscetis ex iis quae* . . . . . . .es subici praecipi, et
rursum admoneo caveatis ne sub obtentu hu*ius*|*modi inquisitionis
milites ordinata*m iam pridem placitam ac custoditam cum dispendio
vestrae exsist*ima*||*tionis* . . . .*i*nquietent vel innovare quid 50
temptent.

['Aνεστάθη(?) . . . . . .] ἐπὶ ἀρχόντων τῶν περὶ Μ. Αὐρ. Βασι-
λειδιανὸν 'Αλεξάνδρον· ['Επρέσβευον(?). . . .] Φλ. 'Αρίστων καὶ
Οὐαλέριος Γερμανός.

From the Tauric Chersonesus. We have omitted the fragmentary
beginning of this bilingual document (ll. 1–31). The citizens of
Chersonesus had appealed to the emperor Commodus in regard to
the collection of the tax on prostitutes (ll. 13–31 in the part omitted).
This was an imperial tax first instituted by Gaius (Suet. *Gai.* 40),
and collected by officers of the army. The evidence for this tax
under the empire is collected by Domaszewski in editing the inscription (*CIL.* III, *S.* 13750). Apparently there had been some
dispute between the municipality and the officials who collected
the tax. The emperor, in his letter to Primianus the chiliarch and
Valerius Maximus the centurion, bids them to collect the tax without
offence to the citizens and without exceeding the amount prescribed. For the exactions of the soldiery, *cf.* pp. 136*f.*, and
nos. 68, 139–144.

MUNICIPAL DOCUMENTS IN GREEK AND LATIN

113. EPISTULA IULI SATURNINI, LEGATI
SYRIAE, AD PHAENESIOS
(185–186 p. Chr.)

Cagnat, *IGRR*. 3, 1119; Ditt. *Or. Gr.* 609; Lafoscade, 117.

5 Ἰούλιος Σα|τουρνῖνο|ς Φαινησί|οις μητρο||κωμίαι τοῦ | Τρά-
10 χωνος |χαίρειν. | Ἐάν τις ὑμῖν | ἐπιδημήσηι || βιαίως στρα|τιώτης
15 ἢ | καὶ ἰδιώτης, | ἐπιστείλαν|τές μοι ἐκ||δικηθήσεσ|θαι· οὔτε |
20 γὰρ συνεισ|φοράν τι|να ὀφείλε||τε τοῖς ξέ|νοις, καὶ ξε|νῶνα
25 ἔχον|τες οὐ δύ|νασθε ἀνα||νκασθῆ|ναι δέξασ|θαι ταῖς οἰ|κίαις
30 τοὺς | ξένους. Ταῦ||τά μου τὰ | γράμματα | ἐν προδήλ|ωι τῆς
35 μη|τροκωμί||ας ὑμῶν χ|ωρίωι πρόθ|ετε, μή τις | ὡς ἀγνοή|σας
40 ἀπολο||γήσηται.

The date of this inscription from Phaena in Syria is determined
by Harrer (*Studies in the History of the Roman Province of Syria*, 40).
The villagers complained to the governor that they had been compelled to furnish *hospitium* to soldiers and others, although there
was an official hostel in their village. For similar complaints, *cf.*
nos. 139, 141–144.

114. EPISTULA PROCONSULIS LYCIAE ET
PAMPHYLIAE AD SIDYMEOS
(185–192 p. Chr.)

Cagnat, *IGRR*. 3, 582; *T.A.M.* 2, 175.

Ἐπὶ ἀ[ρχ]ιερέος τ[ῶν Σεβα]στῶν Διογέν[ους] γʹ τοῦ Μητρο-
δώρου, Δείου βʹ, εἰσηγησ[α]μένου τοῦ γραμ|ματέως τῆς βο[υλῆς
Δη]μοσθένους το[ῦ Ἀν]δροβίου, ἐπιψηφισαμένου δὲ τοῦ ἱερέος
τῶν Σεβαστῶν Ἀλεξάν|δρου τοῦ Λύσω[νος]. Ἐπεὶ διὰ τοὺς
[εὐ]τυχεστάτους καιροὺς τοῦ θειοτάτου Αὐτοκράτορος Καίσα-
ρος | . . . . Σεβαστοῦ Εὐσεβοῦς Εὐτυχοῦς, καὶ διὰ τὴν τοῦ
5 κρατίστου || ἀνθυπάτου Γαίου Πομπωνίου Βά[σ]σου Τερεντιανοῦ
περὶ τὰς πόλεις αὔξησιν, καὶ ἡ ἡμετέρα | πόλις ἐψηφίσατο
σύστημα γεροντικὸν κατὰ τὸν νόμον, ἐννόμου βουλῆς καὶ ἐκλη-
σίας ἀγομέ|νης, ἔδοξεν γραφῆναι ψήφισμα τῶ κρατίστω ἀνθυ-
πάτω δι᾽ οὗ παρακληθῆναι καὶ αὐτὸν συνεπικυρῶσαι | τὴν τῆς
βουλῆς καὶ τοῦ δήμου κρίσιν Χ δι᾽ ἃ τύχῃ ἀγαθῇ δεδόχθαι
Σιδυμέων τῇ βουλῇ καὶ τῷ δήμῳ | συνγεγράφθαι τόδε τὸ

FROM ITALY AND THE PROVINCES

[ψ]ήφισμα ὃ καὶ ἀναδοθῆναι αὐτῷ ὑπὸ τοῦ ἀξιολογωτάτου
Λυκιάρχου, πολεί‖του ἡμῶν, Τι. Κλ. Τηλεμάχου Ξαν[θ]ίου καὶ   10
Σιδυμέος. Πομπώ(νιος) Βάσσος ἀνθύ(πατος) Σιδυμέων | ἄρχουσι
βουλῇ δήμῳ χαίρειν. Τὰ καλῶς γεινόμενα ἐπαινεῖσθαι μᾶλλον
προσ|ήκει ἢ κυροῦσθαι, ἔχει γὰρ τὸ βέβαιο[ν] ἀφ' ἑαυτῶν.
Ἐρρῶσθαι ὑμᾶς εὔχομαι. Ἐκομίσθη ἐπὶ τοῦ αὐτοῦ | Λυκιάρχου
Ἀπελλαίου κγ', ἐνεγράφη ὑπὸ Εὐέλθοντος τοῦ καὶ Εὐτυχέους
Τελεσίου Σιδυμέος | γυμνασιαρχήσαντος τῆς γερουσίας [π]ρώ-
του.

From Sidyma in Lycia. The name of the emperor, erased in
antiquity, was that of Commodus. He received the title of Felix
in 185. The city of Sidyma had decreed the formation of a *gerusia*,
in accordance with the laws which regulated such association. This
action was submitted to the provincial governor for approval and
ratification. The proconsul replied that their action was more
worthy of praise than of ratification; for worthy achievements
carry their own confirmation. The phrase κατὰ τὸν νόμον (l. 6)
seems to imply that the action of the city required the sanction of
the governor before the decree was valid, but it is also possible that
the request for his approval was inspired by motives of vanity. The
different theories of the purpose of the *gerusia* are discussed by
Chapot, *La prov. rom. proc. d'Asie*, 216 ff. The senate passed a decree
authorizing the establishment at Cyzicus of a *neon*, or organization of young men (138–160 p. Chr., *cf.* no. 106). It may be
noted that, in the later period, the Sidymeans did not think it necessary to refer the proposal for the formation of the *gerusia* to the
senate. *Cf. Suppl. Ep. Gr.* 1, 327, 330.

115. TITULUS HONORARIUS
(150–200 p. Chr.)

An. ép. 1902, no. 164; *Compt. rend. de l'acad. d. inscr. et bel.
lettr.* 1902, 38; Dessau, 6780.

M. Servilio P. f. Quir. | Draconi Albuciano | II viro, flam.
perp., | quod super multa in remp. ‖ merita et amplissimum | muni-   5
ficentiae studium le|gationem urbicam gratui|tam ad Lat*ium* maius
pe|tendum duplicem susce‖perit tandemq. feliciter | renuntiaverit,   10

ordo publi|ce ponendam censuit, et | cum is honore contentus |
15 pecuniam rei p. remisis||set, populus de suo posuit.

Found at Bou-Ghara (ancient Gigthi) in Tunis. The double
cognomen and the form of the inscription make it probable that it
belongs to the latter half of the second century. On Gigthi, *cf.*
Reid, *Municipalities of the Roman Empire*, 293, and Constans,
Nouv. arch. des missions, fasc. 14, 1916. On *Latium minus* and
maius, cf. pp. 191 *ff.* and Reid, *op. cit.* 242. The legal distinction between the two classes of rights was perhaps made by Hadrian. This
inscription, with no. 95, illustrates the stages through which a
village passed in its progress toward Roman citizenship. Gigthi,
at first probably a *civitas stipendiaria*, had already been made a
municipium, since it had duovirs. Now it receives *Latium maius*.
For another inscription from Gigthi, *cf.* no. 161.

116. TITULUS HONORARIUS
(saec. I vel II p. Chr.)

Cagnat, *IGRR.* 3, 634; *T.A.M.* 2, 291.

Σέξστον Μάρκιον | ᾿Απολλωνίδου υἱὸν Κυρείναι | ᾿Απολ-
5 λωνίδην [᾿Ρ]ωμαῖον καὶ | Ξάνθιον, τετε[ι]μημένον ‖ ὑπὸ τῆς
[β]ουλῆς καὶ τοῦ δήμο[υ], | οἱ ἀνειμένοι τοῦ ἐνκυκλίου | τοπικοῦ
τέλους ἀνέστησαν | ἐκ τοῦ ἰδίου κατὰ τὴν διαθήκην | ἀπολι-
10 πόντος αὐ[τοῦ] εἰς τὸν ‖ τῆς ἀτελείας λόγον ἀργυρίου | δηνάρια
τρισμύρια.

From Xanthus in Lycia. Sextus Marcius Apollonides, a Roman
citizen and a Xanthian, left thirty thousand denarii as an endowment to provide funds for the *munera* or for some form of local tax
in his native city. In Egypt we find τὸ ἐγκύκλιον τέλος as a ten
per cent. tax on sales, and it is possible that a similar tax is mentioned
here. Those released from this burden set up a statue in honor of
Sextus, and it is probable that a guild of merchants would render
this honor, rather than hypothetical incumbents of a liturgy which
might never be imposed. The sales-tax in the empire was usually
one per cent. *Cf.* Hirschfeld, 73 *ff.*

117. HIERAPOLITANORUM DECRETUM
DE PARAPHYLACIBUS
(saec. I vel II p. Chr.)

Ditt. *Or. Gr.* 527.

. . . . *ον* |

['Επὶ στρατηγοῦ Θεοφ]ίλου τοῦ β' νεωτέρου, μηνὸς δεκάτο[υ
. . . ., | ἔδοξε τῶ]ν Ἱεραπολειτῶν τῆι βουλῆι ἐπὶ τῶν ἀρχα[ι]-
ρεσιῶν· [τοὺς παραφύλα|κας τὸ λοιπ]ὸν ἀπ' ἑαυτῶν ἐν ταῖς
κώμαις ποιεῖσθαι ἐπιδη[μίαν, ἐφ' ὥιτε || μηδὲν ἔτερ]ον αὐτοῖς 5
παρέχειν ἢ μόνον ξύλα καὶ ἄχυρα καὶ μον[ήν, ἄλλο δὲ μηδὲν |
μηδενὶ ἄ]λλωι ὧι ἄν ποτε τρόπωι. Ἐὰν δέ τις παρὰ ταῦτα
ποιήσηι ἢ ἑ[τέρωι ποιοῦντι συμ|πράξηι, ἐ]λενχθέντα πεποιη-
κέναι προστείμου ὀνόματι εἰς [τὸ δημόσιον | κατατιθ]έναι αὐτὸν
ὅσα ἂν ἐλενχθῆι εἰληπφὼς παρά τινος, ἄτι[μον δὲ | εἶναι. Καὶ
τοὺς] ἐλενχθέντας παραφύλακας μὴ λαμβάνειν τὰς παρὰ τῆ[ς
κώμης τιμάς || . . . .] ἢ κωμάρχας ἄκοντας στεφανοῦν 10
παραφ[ύλακα, ἀποδοῦναι | αὐτὸν τὸ] ἀργύριον, ἥτις [δ'] ἂν κώμη
βουληθῆι στεφανῶσαι παρα[φύλακα, ... |. . . . . . .
παρὰ ταῦ]τα μηθὲν [γ]είνεσθαι· εἰ δὲ μή, τὸν ὑπεναντίως ποιήσ-
[αντα μὴ τιθέναι | εἰς τὸ τοῦ Ἀπ]όλλωνος ἀναθήματα, ὄντος
τούτου τοῦ ψηφίσματο[ς κυρίου | καὶ] ἐπέχοντος.

From a village near Hierapolis. This document contributes some
information on village-government under the municipalities. The
villages of Hierapolis were provided with officials called comarchs.
In addition police officers were sent from the city who had been
guilty of making illegal exactions from the villagers. By this decree
the *paraphylaces* are placed under more strict control, and are forbidden to exact anything beyond a supply of wood for fuel, chaff
for bedding, and housing during their stay. Other expenses must
be met out of their own pocket. Honors must not be conferred by
the village, especially under compulsion, and, apparently, if money
is voted by the village to crown one of these officers, this sum must
be restored.

MUNICIPAL DOCUMENTS IN GREEK AND LATIN

118. EDICTUM AUCTORIS INCERTI AD BEROIAEOS
(saec. ι–ιι p. Chr.)

B.C.H. 37 (1913), 90 *f.*

```
........ Οὐα[λ]εριαν[ὸς (?)..|........]να Ἰ[ουλ(?)]ιανῶι
[Φ]λανίωι......|......λε[ιν] τὸν ἐργολάβον ὡς ὅτι μά-
λιστ[α....|...] ἐὰν μὴ κα(τὰ) τὴν ἐν τῆι συγγραφῆι σύμπ-
```
5 ```
[νοιαν (?)...||...συ]μφώνου πρὸς ἔκτη(ξ)ιν, ἔνοχος ἔσται οὐ
πρ[ὸς (?)..|...τῶ]ν Σεβαστῶν εἰκόνας ἐστεφανουμέν[ας] ΦΛΙ-
PAMN[...|...τὴ]ν χρημάτων ἔξοδον τῆι πατρίδι διοικήσει
ὑπ[ὲρ (?)...|..(?) καὶ τῶν τῆι] πόλει συμφερόντων, καταλιπεῖν
δίκην τὴν [....|... ἔδοξέ μοι (?) τοῦτ]ωι τῶι διατάγματι διορ-
```
10 ```
θῶσαι· ἐπεὶ τοίνυν κατ[....||......]ατην προσόδωι μεγάλα
λυποῦσαν, κελεύω τοὺ[ς...|..τὴν] πρόρρησιν ἀρθῆναι, εἴτε
λέγεται, δέκα δύο δι[αιτητὰς (?)...|......] συντηρήσεως, διαι-
ρουμένου τοῦ ἐνιαυτοῦ [.....|...διατ]ελῆ τὴν φροντίδα τοῦ
πράγματος εἶναι πρὸς [...|... τ]ὸν ἴδιον χρόνον ἐπιμελείας,
```
15 ```
ἐὰν κατὰ τὴν εἰ[.....||....] τῶι δὲ ἐπαφέντι κηπουρῶι καὶ
ὀχετηγοῦντι δι[ὰ...|...] ἀποτάσσω εἰς τὴν τοῦ καινοῦ βαλα-
νείου ἐπι[μέλειαν (?)...|...]ον οὐκ ὀφέ(λ)ηι μὴ γενέσθαι· εἰ γὰρ
τολμήσει ἐν τ[ῶι...|....]ακισχειλίοις εἰς τὸ γυμνασιαρχικόν·
περὶ μὲ[ν οὖν (?)...|... δαπ]ανῶν μὴ πλέον πράττεσθαι τοῦ
```
20 ```
συνήθους ὑ[πὲρ (?)...||... α]ὐταῖς ὑμῶν πλέονα σύνοδον ἐν
ἑκάστωι μην[ὶ....|.....]των ξυλείας· εἰ μὲν ὁ χρόνος ἔτι μοι
συνεχωρε[ῖτο....|... ἐπεὶ οὖν] ἁρπάζεται τῆι ἐπείξει μου,
κελεύω τοὺς γερ[ουσιαστὰς (?)..|...]ειας, μηδὲ διὰ ταύτης τῆς
αὐθαδίας, καὶ ἐνε[ργεῖν (?)..|.... τῆς τῶν] ξύλων χρήσεως ὡς
```
25 ```
ἐνδεεστάτην ὕλης, πόλε[ι...||...] μὲν γὰρ τάχα περὶ τούτου
με, καὶ ἐς ἅπαν ἐπεί[γω (?)...|... τ]ὰς τειμίας ἄξια ὡς τῶι
δήμωι....τὴν ἔκτη[ξιν (?)..|...] αὐτὸν συνκεχωρῆσθαι· ἐπεὶ
οὖν τὰ ἄλλ[α διέταξα (?)....| καὶ ἐτιμωρησ]άμην τοὺς τοῦτο τολ-
μῶντας ποιεῖν, ἀναγρ[άψαι (?)...|.....] ταμεῖον· ὀχυρώτατα
```
30 ```
τοῦτο τὸ διάταγμα βε[βαιῶ(?)..||....ἱκανὸν] ἔσται πᾶσιν εὐδίαν
ἐσανάγειν. Εὐτυχεῖτε. |
```

(*vacat*)

Τῆι πόλει

```
[......Ἰ]ουλιανὸς διὰ τῆς ἐπ[αρχείας (?)...|.....τῆς ἐπι-
μ]ελείας τὴν στήλλην χα[ράξας ἀνέθηκεν ἐκ τῶν] ἰδίων.
```

[444]

FROM ITALY AND THE PROVINCES

This inscription was found at Beroia in Macedonia. The marble is broken on the right and left sides, and the restoration of the document is extremely problematical. The editors of the inscription suggest that it is an edict of an emperor, or the letter of a provincial governor. In brief, their interpretation of the contents is as follows: It treats of the friendly annulment of a contract which had been entered into between the city and a contractor who had undertaken some public work in which he had failed to fulfil the conditions. The suit is to be abandoned (l. 9), and apparently provision is made for some form of arbitration of claims (l. 12). The letter then takes up the case of a gardener who has diverted water from the New Baths, who is required to make amends or pay a fine to the gymnasiarch. Finally, hasty regulations are devised in regard to the supply of wood, which is becoming scarce, and the fines which are to be imposed for the violation of these provisions. It is unfortunate that the document is so fragmentary, for this might give us some information on the important question of deforestation in ancient times.

119. EPISTULA PROCONSULIS ASIAE AD COOS
(saec. I–II p. Chr.)

Cagnat, *IGRR.* 4, 1044; Paton and Hicks, *Inscriptions of Cos*, 26.

[.....πυθόμενος ἐκ τοῦ ὑμετ]έρου ψηφίσμα|[τος ὅτι.....τὴν
ἔκκ]λησιν ἔθετο ἐπὶ | [τὸν Σεβαστόν, ἱκανῶς ἠισ]θόμην ἐπη-
ρείας | [χάρι]ν αὐτὸν [το]ῦτο πεποιηκέναι· δε||[ὸν τ]οίνυν, εἰ μὲν   5
ἐπὶ τὸν Σεβαστὸν | [ἡ ἔκ]κλησις γείνεται, πρότ[ε]ρον ἐμὲ |
[ἐξετ]άσαι τὴν αἰτίαν· εἰ δὲ ἐπ' ἐμέ, τὸ | [παρὸ]ν ἀξιόχρεως λα-
βεῖν τοὺς ἀ[ρ|ρα]βῶν]ας δηναρίων δισχειλίων π[ε]ν||[τακο(σίων)   10
κατὰ] τὸ προτε[θ]ὲν ὑπ' ἐ[μ]ο[ῦ] σ[ύν|ταγ]μα διὰ τοὺς φυγοδ[ι]-
κοῦντας· | [ἐὰν δ]ὲ πρὸς ταῦτα μὴ γ.....

This inscription from Cos deals with the right of appeal. A citizen of Cos had lost his case in the local court, and threatened to appeal. The Coans sent a memorial to the governor, and his reply is recorded in this document. If the appeal is to the emperor, the governor must first examine the case to decide whether it should be forwarded to Rome. If the appeal is made to the court of the

MUNICIPAL DOCUMENTS IN GREEK AND LATIN

provincial governor, the appellant must provide a *cautio* of 2500 denarii, which was required by an edict of the governor in order to guard against unwarranted appeals (*cf.* Hicks, *loc. cit.*; Mommsen, *Zeitschr. d. Savigny-Stift.*, *Roman. Abteil.* 24 (1890), 34 *ff.*; nos. 36, 40, 90, 121). Nothing in this document implies that Cos was a *civitas libera* at this time, but the fact that appeals could be taken from the local court to the governor does not necessarily imply that Cos was a part of the province of Asia (*cf.* no. 90). On the status of Cos, see Chapot, *La prov. rom. proc. d'Asie*, 115.

120. EPISTULA IMPERATORIS INCERTI AD PRO-CONSULEM SEU LEGATUM ASIAE
(saec. II p. Chr.)

Rev. d. ét. grec. 19 (1906), 83.

(*Primi versus, maxime mutili, omissi sunt.*)

.........δε..ας τὰ μετὰ | [τῆ]ς σοι προσηκούσης ἐπι|[με]-
5 λείας, ἅμα προνοούμε|νος καὶ τοῦ τὰ ὀφειλόμενα ‖ τῶν χρημάτων
εἰσπράττεσ|θαι τῆι πόλει, κατεπέμψα|μεν δέ σοι καὶ τὰς παρ'
ἡμῶν | ἐν[το]λὰς ἵνα καὶ τὴν ἡμετέ|ραν | [συ]μβουλὴν ἐν τοῖς
10 πρα‖[χθ]ησομένοις ἔχ[ηι]ς. Ἔρρωσο.

From Aphrodisias. This letter seems to refer to the collection of certain sums due to the city. Since Aphrodisias was a *civitas libera* (*cf.* no. 29), the governor could not interfere in her internal affairs without the consent of the civic authorities or the authorization of the emperor (*cf.* Pliny, *Epp. ad Trai.* 47–48). Reinach, who published the inscription, suggests that the document may also be interpreted as a letter from a governor to an agonothete as in *CIG.* 2742.

121. RESCRIPTUM IMPERATORIS AD LACEDAEMONIOS
(saec. II p. Chr.)

IG. v, 21.

Col. 1 .....δὲ [τ]ού[τ]ων ἑκα[στ.....|... οὐδεπ]ώποτε περὶ τῆς
ἐμαυτο[ῦ....|...] πότερον πραθῆναι ἢ μισθοῦσθαι καὶ [π]ό|-
[τερον σύμπαντας..τ]οὺς ἀγροὺς ἢ κατὰ μέρος, παραινῶι ‖
5 [....προσ]όδους μέμνημαι πολλῶι μείζονας | [.......]ν καὶ

δεδωρημένον ὑμῖν αἴτ[η]σιν | [...προσόδ]ους ἔσεσθαι, εἰ ἑτέρα
μίσθωσις γ[έν]οι|[το......π]οιεῖν ὑμᾶς, κ[αὶ ἐ]ὰν τὸ τρίτον
τῆς νῦν | [......τοῦ] τρίτου.......ς ἑτέ[ρας] ||
................λε[α] | (vacat) ο[ὔτε τὴν ἐκ] τῶν [ἐπ]ι-   Col.
κλήσεων βοήθειαν [τ]οὺς ἀδικουμέ|νους οἴομαι δῖν ἀφειρῆσθαι
οὔτε ἀφορμὴν ταύτην γείνε|σθαι τοῖς συκοφαντοῦσιν ὡς τά τε
δημόσια καὶ ἰδιωτικὰ || μὴ τελεῖσθαι κατὰ τοὺς νόμους· διὸ δὴ 5
περὶ μὲν τῶν ἀμφι|σβητήσεων, αἵτινες ἂν ὦσιν ἐλάττους ‚α
δηναρίων καὶ μή|τε κριτήριον ἢ πρόκριμα κεφαλικῆς δίκης
ἢ ἐπιτιμίας ἔξου|σιν, ἐπικαλεῖσθαί με ἢ πείθ[ε]σθαι τοῖς
ἐπικαλεσαμένοις κω|[λ]ύωι· τὰς δὲ ἐπικλήσεις, ἃς [γ]είνεσθαι
ἐπιτρέπωι, διακρινέτω||[σαν οἱ σύνεδ]ροι, πότερον δ(ι)καίως 10
γείνονται ἢ ἐπὶ τῶι τ[ὰ]ς δί|[κας....τάς τε π]ροβολὰς ποιεῖσθαι
εἰς τὸ μὴ κριθῆ|[ναι...........οἱ σύνε]δροι τῶι πατρίωι
ἔ|[θει(?)..............ἡ]μέρα ᾗ ἐντ[ὸς |...............
κριν]έτωσαν.

From Mistra near Sparta. The inscription is engraved in two
columns, but the content of col. I can only be determined in a
general way owing to the fragmentary condition of the stone. The
document appears to deal with different problems. In col. I there
is a reference to the rental or sale of public lands owing to a depreciation in local revenues. In col. II the subject of appeal is
considered. The emperor forbade appeals to his jurisdiction in cases
involving less than a thousand denarii, and those which do not
involve the death penalty or loss of civic rights. All appeals must
be submitted to a board of synedri, who shall determine whether
the appellant has just grounds for his petition or whether he is
merely attempting to delay justice (cf. nos. 36, 90, 119). At Athens
syndics, elected by the people, heard appeals before they were forwarded to the emperor (cf. no. 90), while at Cos the governor decided
such questions (cf. no. 119). It is evident that the emperors were
seeking to discourage the practice of appealing to Rome on trivial
questions, but uniform legislation had not yet been devised in regard
to procedure. A comparison of this document with no. 90 shows
that the free cities received laws from Rome, and appeals from their
local courts to the emperor had already become an established
practice (cf. Mitteis, *Reichsrecht und Volksrecht*, 87 f.).

MUNICIPAL DOCUMENTS IN GREEK AND LATIN

122. TITULUS HONORARIUS POGLENSIS
(saec. I vel II p. Chr.)

Cagnat, *IGRR.* 3, 409.

[Π]ό[πλι]ο[ν] Καίλ[ι]ον [Λ]ουκ[ιανὸν ...]ο[... ἀγω]‖νοθε-
τήσαντα ἀγῶνα πεντ[αετηρικὸν σύν | τε] ἀνδριάσιν καὶ βραβείοις
καὶ τειμη[θέντα β(?), | δ]εδωκότα διανομὰς ἔτεσιν πολ[ιτείας] ‖
5 βουλευταῖς τε καὶ ἐκλησιασταῖς [καὶ πᾶ]‖σι πολείταις, κτίζοντα
ἔργα τῆι πόλει, κρεί|νοντα τοπικὰ δικαστήρια ἔτεσιν κοινω|ν[ίας],
πέμψαντα ἀννῶναν εἰς τὸ Ἀλεξαν|δρέων ἔθνος, προη[γ]ορ[ή-
10 σαντ]α καὶ ‖ [πρεσβεύσα]ντα ὑπὲ[ρ τῆς πό]λεως, | [γένους τ]οῦ
πρω[τεύοντ]ος ἐν | [τῆι πα]τρίδι.

This inscription from Pogla in Pisidia was first published by
Rostowzew in *Jahreshefte d. öst. arch. Inst.* 4 (1901), *Beiblatt*,
38 *ff.* The document is important because it marks the development
of a village on an imperial estate into a municipal organization.
The reference in ll. 6–8: κρείνοντα τοπικὰ δικαστήρια ἔτεσιν
κοινωνίας, shows that Publius Caelius Lucianus acted as local
judge when the community was still a κοινόν. On the quasi-
municipal organization of the imperial villages and their development into towns, *cf.* Ramsay, *Studies in the History and Art of
Asia Minor*, 305 *ff.*; Rostowzew, *Gesch. d. röm. Kol.* 288 *ff.* *Cf.*
nos. 139, 140–142; pp. 23 *f.* It should be noted that the citizens
of the new city are divided into βουλευταί, ἐκκλησιασταί and
πολῖται (*cf.* Levy, *Rev. d. ét. grec.* 8 (1895), 209).

123. TITULUS HONORARIUS
(saec. II p. Chr.)

Cagnat, *IGRR.* 4, 788; Ramsay, *Cities and Bishoprics*, 2, 462.

Ἡ βουλὴ καὶ ὁ δῆμος καὶ οἱ κατοικοῦντες Ῥωμαῖοι | ἐτείμησαν
Τιβέριον Κλαύδιον Τιβερίου Κλαυδίου Μι|θριδάτου υἱὸν Κυρεί-
ναι Πείσωνα Μιθριδατιανόν, ἱερέα | διὰ βίου Διὸς Κελαινέως,
5 γυμνασιαρχήσαντα δι' ἀγο‖ραίας καὶ ἀγορανομήσαντα δι' ἀγο-
ραίας, καὶ ἐφηβαρχήσαντα, | καὶ ὑποσχόμενον ὑπὲρ Κλαυδίου
Γραν⟨ν⟩ιανοῦ τοῦ υἱοῦ | γυμνασιαρχίαν δι' ἀγοραίας ἐκ τῶν ἰδίων
καὶ χαρισάμενον | τῆι πόλει τὸν ἐξ ἔθους διδόμενον ὑπ' αὐτῆς

[448]

τῶι γυμνα|σιαρχοῦντι πόρον δηνάρια μύρια πεντακισχείλια καὶ
τῆι μὲν ‖ πρώτηι ἑξαμήνωι, ἐν ἧι καὶ ἡ ἀγόραιος ἤχθη, θέντα τὸ | 10
ἔλαιον, ὑπὲρ δὲ τῶν λοιπῶν μηνῶν ἐξ δεδοκότα, | καθὼς ἡ πόλις
ἠξίωσεν, δηνάρια μύρια ἐνακισχεί|λια, ὥστε προστεθέντα καὶ
τοῦτον τὸν πόρον | τοῖς μυρίοις πεντακισχειλίοις δηναρίοις σώζειν ‖
τόκον δραχμιαῖον εἰς τὸ τῶν κουρατόρων ἐπι|ζήμιον τὸ κατὰ ἔτος 15
ὑπ' αὐτῶν διδόμενον, ὥσ|τε τοῦ λοιποῦ χρόνου μηκέτι εἶναι
κουρατό|ρας, καθὼς ἡ πόλις ἐψηφίσατο, δι' ὅλου | τοῦ αἰῶνος,
τὴν ἀνάστασιν ποιησαμένων ‖ ἐκ τῶν ἰδίων τῶν ἐν τῆι Θερμαίαι 20
πλατείαι.

From Apamea in Phrygia. The nature and purpose of the endowment has been the subject of considerable dispute. Mommsen
(*E.E.* 7, 436 *ff.*) believed that the city was enabled to dispense with
the *curator conventus Romanorum,* but this is unlikely, for the city
probably had no jurisdiction over this organization. Ramsay (*loc.
cit.*) believed that Apamea used the endowment to get rid of the
curator rei publicae. This official, however, was always styled λογιστής
in the East, and there is no evidence that more than one ever held
office in any city at the same time. Nor is it likely that a city which
could spend so lavishly would need a curator. It is possible that an
explanation may be found in a document from Cibyra (Cagnat,
IGRR. 4, 914; *cf. ibid.* 4, 259), where Quintus Veranius secured
from the emperor the removal of Tiberius Nicephorus who exacted
three thousand denarii annually from the city. It is, however,
more probable that the endowment was devoted to defraying the
liturgical expenses of certain officials in connection with the gymnasiarchy, and that *curator* is here used as an equivalent of liturgy
(*cf.* Bérard, *B.C.H.* 17 (1893), 312). For similar endowments,
cf. nos. 116, 150, 189.

124. EDICTUM SEU EPISTULA PROCONSULIS AD EPHESIOS
(saec. II p. Chr.)

B.C.H. 7 (1883), 504; *Inschriften von Magnesia,* 114.

. . . . δὲ καὶ κατὰ συνθήκ[ας . . . . . . αντων . . . . . . λικ . . . .
. . . . ὥστε συμ|βαί]νειν ἐνιότε τὸν δῆμον ἰς ταραχὴν καὶ θορύ-
βους ἐνπίπτιν διὰ τὴν σ[καιο(?)|λ]όγον κα(τ)α(θ)ρασίαν τῶν

MUNICIPAL DOCUMENTS IN GREEK AND LATIN

ἀρτοκόπων ἐπὶ τῇ ἀγορᾷ στάσεων, ἐφ᾽ οἷς ἐχρῆν [αὐ|]τοὺς μετα-
πεμφθέντας ἤδη δίκην ὑποσχεῖν· ἐπεὶ δὲ τὸ τῇ πόλει συμφέ[ρον]‖
5 τῆς τούτων τιμωρίας μᾶλλον προτιμᾶν ἀναγκαῖον, ἡγησάμην
διατάγ[ματι] | αὐτοὺς σωφρονίσαι. Ὅθεν ἀπαγορεύω μήτε
συνέρχεσθαι τοὺς ἀρτοκ[ό]|πους κατ᾽ ἑταιρίαν μήτε προεστη-
κότας θρασύνεσθαι, πειθαρχεῖν δὲ π[άν]|τως τοῖς ὑπὲρ τοῦ κοινῇ
συμφέροντος ἐπιταττομένοις καὶ τὴν ἀ[ναγ]|καίαν τοῦ ἄρτου
10 ἐργασίαν ἀνενδεῆ παρέχειν τῇ πόλει. Ὡς ἂν ἁλῶ τι[ς αὐ]‖τῶν
τὸ ἀπὸ τοῦδε ἢ συνιὼν παρὰ τὰ διηγορευμένα ἢ θορύβου τινὸς
[καὶ στά]|σεως ἐξάρχων, μεταπεμφθεὶς τῇ προσηκούσῃ τειμωρίᾳ
κολασθή[σεται]· | ἐὰν δέ τις τολμήσῃ τὴν πόλιν ἐνεδρεύων
ἀποκρύψαι αὐτόν, "δεκνειρ[ίας]" ἐπὶ πο]|δὸς προσσημιωθήσεται,
καὶ ὁ τὸν τοιοῦτον δὲ ὑποδεξάμενος [τῇ] | αὐτῇ τιμωρίᾳ ὑπεύθυνος
15 γενήσεται. ‖ Ἐπὶ πρυτάνεως Κλ(αυδίου) Μοδέστου, μηνὸς Κλα-
ρεῶνος δ᾽ ἰσ(ταμένου), βουλῆς ἀγομέ[νης κατ᾽ (?)] | ἄλλο μέρος,
Μαρκελλεῖνος εἶπεν· τῆς δὲ ἀπονοίας τῶν ἐργαστηριαρχῶ[ν
μέγι]‖στον δεῖγμα χθὲς Ἑρμείας ὁ πρὸς τῇ ΓΑΜΙΛΩΜΕΤ....
................ANTH

From Ephesus. The first part of this inscription contains the
proclamation of the provincial governor who had been compelled
to settle an outbreak and riot of the members of the bakers' guild
at Ephesus. The subject of strikes in Asia Minor is discussed by
Buckler, *Anatolian Studies in Honour of Sir W. M. Ramsay*, 27 *ff*.
The municipal authorities were unable to deal with the situation
and were compelled to appeal to the governor. Similarly in Pergamum (Cagnat, *IGRR.* 4, 444) the proconsul interfered in a strike
of the builders. *Cf. Acts* 19, 24 *ff*., where the riot of the silversmiths
at Ephesus inspired fear of being called to account by the governor.

125. TITULUS HONORARIUS
(150–200 p. Chr.)

CIL. VIII, *S.* 17899 = *E.E.* 5, 698.

C. Annio Arminio Do*nato*, *claris*simo puero C. An|ni Flaviani,
proc. *patrimoni* tractus Kar|thaginiensis, *filio Anni* Armini Do|nati,
5 flaminis *perpetui* nepoti, ‖ concilium pro*vinciae* Africae.

Found at Thamugadi. C. Annius Flavianus took part in one

[450]

of the wars under M. Aurelius and Commodus (*cf. CIL.* VIII, *S.* 17900), so that his son probably flourished toward the end of the second century. A *tractus* included several *saltus,* or imperial estates, and a *procurator tractus* held a post as important as that of a provincial procurator; *cf.* p. 19. This *concilium prov. Africae* seems to have been composed of representatives from the *civitates* of both Africa Proconsularis and Numidia; *cf.* Kornemann, *R.E.* 4, 808.

126. TITULUS HONORARIUS
(saec. II p. Chr.)

Rev. arch. 3 (1916), 339; *An. ép.* 1916, no. 120.

Sacerdoti omnium Caesar, T. Vetuiro T. fil. Gol. Campestir auguir II viro II vir q. q. II vir III panec rgrati anuon sacerdoti da.. lrcuri condtoir patriat H II misso lecmo...a colonai nurbemsikeviatco...semelouidemardivom Hadrianum....III auem adoptimum maximum oue...bisimpcaesar T. Aelium Hadrianum... Antoninum Auc Pium ex d. d. vicuscopdy.

Transcription

Sacerdoti omnium Caesarum, T. Veturio T. fil. Collina Campestri, auguri, II viro, II viro quinquennali, II viro tertium....et curatori annonae, sacerdoti Dei Mercuri, conditori patriae, quater misso legato a colonia in Urbem sine viatico, semel quidem ad divum Hadrianum, ter autem ad optimum maximumque...Imperatorem Caesarem T. Aelium Hadrianum Antoninum Aug. Pium ex decreto decurionum vicus......

On a marble column, found at Sinope, on which had stood a statue. The mistakes in the text are due to the difficulty which the Greek copyist had with the Latin letters and words. That the position of *sacerdos omnium Caesarum* ranked higher even than the chief magistracy in Sinope is shown by the place which it has at the beginning of the inscription. Veturius like many other Asiatics belonged to the tribus Collina. The particular point of interest for us is the fact that Veturius represented his native city four times on missions to Rome. For similar cases, *cf.* nos. 53 and 115.

MUNICIPAL DOCUMENTS IN GREEK AND LATIN

127. EPISTULA IMPERATORUM SEVERI ET CARACALLAE AD SMYRNAEOS
(198–210 p. Chr.)

CIG. 3178; Lafoscade, 72; Ditt. *Syll.*³ 876; Cagnat, *IGRR.* 4, 1402.

Οἱ θειότατοι αὐτοκράτορες Σεουῆρος καὶ Ἀντωνεῖνος Καίσαρες
Σμυρναίοις. | Εἰ Κλαύδιος Ῥουφῖνος ὁ πολείτης ὑμῶν ὁ διὰ τὴν
προαίρεσιν | ᾗ σύνεστιν ἐπὶ παιδείᾳ καὶ τὸν ἐν λόγοις συνεχῆ
βίον τὴν | προκειμένην τοῖς σοφισταῖς κατὰ τὰς θείας τῶν προ-
5 γόνων ‖ ἡμῶν διατάξεις ἀτέλειαν τῶν λειτουργιῶν καρπούμενος |
ὑμῶν αὐτὸν ἑκουσίῳ ἀνάγκῃ προκαλουμένων ὑφέστη τὴν | στρατη-
γίαν κατὰ τὸ πρὸς τὴν πατρίδα φίλτρον· τὴν γοῦν εἰς τὰ | ἄλλα
μένειν ἀπραγμοσύνην ἀκείνητον αὐτῷ δικαιότατόν | ἐστιν· οὐ
10 γὰρ ἄξιον τῷ ἀνδρὶ τὴν εἰς ὑμᾶς φιλοτειμίαν γενέ‖σθαι ζημίαν,
καὶ μάλιστα ταύτην ὑμῶν αἰτούντων ὑπὲρ | αὐτοῦ τὴν χάριν.
Εὐτυχεῖτε. | Ἐπρέσβευον Αὐρ. Ἀντωνεῖνος καὶ Αἴλιος Σπηρᾶτος.

From Smyrna. The cities of Asia were classified in three groups
according to wealth and population. A letter of Antoninus Pius
to the provincial assembly gave permission to the cities in each group
to grant immunity to a specified number of doctors, rhetoricians,
and philosophers (*Dig.* 27. 1. 6). Apparently the Asiatic cities had
been too lavish in their grants of immunity to the professions, and
the emperor curtailed their power in this respect. The case of
Rufinus is not clear. Apparently he had enjoyed the privilege of
immunity, but had forfeited it by undertaking a liturgy voluntarily.
The city, apparently, had not the power to renew the grant at this
period and sent an embassy to the emperor asking for the reinstate-
ment of Rufinus in his former privileges.

128. MYRENSIUM DECRETUM DE NAVIGATIONE
(saec. II vel III p. Chr.)

Le Bas-Waddington, 1311; *CIG.* 4302a (*Add.* p. 1136); Ditt.
Or. Gr. 572.

Ἀγαθῆι τύχηι. | Ἔδοξε τῆι βουλῆι | καὶ τῶι δήμωι, | πρυτά-
5 νεων γνώ‖μη· ἐπεὶ διὰ τὸ | μὴ ἐξευρίσ|κειν τὴν ἐπὶ Λί|μυρα
10 πορθμι|κὴν ὠνὴν τὴν ἀξί‖αν συνβαίνει ἐ(λα)σ|σοῦσθαι τὰς

προσ|όδους, μὴ ἐξεῖναι | ἕτερον παραπορ|θμεῦσαι μηδὲν ‖ μήτε 15
ἀπὸ τῆς Δασ[εί]|ας μήτε ἀπὸ τοῦ στό|ματος τῆς λίμνης | ἢ ἀπὸ
'Ανδριακῆς, | ἢ ὀφειλήσει τῶι δή‖μωι ὑπὲρ ἑκάστου | πλοὸς Ⅹ 20
ατ', ἐξου|σίαν ἔχοντος σ(τ)έ|ρ(η)σιν ἀπογράφεσ|θαι ‖ τοῦ τὴν 25
ὠ|νὴν ἔχον|τος τοῦ τε πλοί|ου καὶ τῶν σκευ|ῶν αὐτοῦ. ‖ Πλεύσει 30
δὲ | μόνα τὰ ἀπο|γεγραμμένα | πλοῖα καὶ οἷς | ἂν συνχωρή‖σηι 35
ὁ τὴν ὠνὴν | ἔχων, λαμβά|νοντος παντὸς | ναύλου τὸ δ' | καὶ
τῶν ἐνβαλ‖λομένων. Ἐὰν | δέ τις αὐτόστο|λον ναυλώσηι, | 40
προσφωνείτω | καὶ διδότω παντὸς ‖ τοῦ ναύλου τὸ δ', | ἢ ὑπο- 45
κείσεται τῶι | προγεγραμμένωι | προστείμωι.

From Myra in Lycia. The right to ferry across the river Limyra
was leased by the city to contractors, and considerable revenue was
derived from this source. Private boatmen, however, had entered
into competition against the company holding the lease from the
city, and by offering lower rates made the municipal lease so unat-
tractive that the city could find no bidders and was thus in danger
of losing a profitable source of revenue. In this law the municipality
creates a monopoly by forbidding private carriers the use of certain
routes over which most of the traffic was carried. For similar
monopolies, *cf.* no. 70; *CIL.* III, 7151, 7152.

129. EDICTUM M. ULPI PROCONSULIS. EPISTULA GEMINI MODESTI PROCONSULIS ACHAIAE AD THISBENSES
(saec. II vel III. in. p. Chr.

IG. VII, 2226, 2227, *Add.* p. 747; Ditt. *Syll.*³ 884.

Μᾶρκος Οὔλπιος [. . ἀνθύπατος λέγει]. | Ὁ βουλόμενος
Θισβαίων χωρίον δη[μόσιον ἢ ἱερὸν . . φυ|τεῦσαι] τῶν ἐπ' ἐμοῦ
γεωργουμένων [παραδότω τοῖς στρατηγοῖς τῆς πόλεως] | βιβλίον,
γράψας ἐν αὐτῶι τόπον τε ὂν βο[ύ]λεται λαβεῖν καὶ φόρον ὂν
δώσει κατ' ‖ ἐ͜ν]ιαυτὸν ὑπὲρ ἑκάστου πλέθρου[. .| βου]λῆς ἢ 5
ἐκκλησίας κατὰ τὸ δεδογμένον . .| . . ῳν· κ[αὶ] εἰ μέν τις . .| . . τῆ
ἐκκ[λησία . .| . . σ]θω εἰς . .

. . υ‖σκοι καὶ α[. .| . . κ]οιναί· γραφέτω [δ]' ἐν ε[. .| κ]αὶ τὴν 10
ποσότητα τοῦ φόρου [. .| . . τοῖ]ς τε ἄρχουσιν καὶ δεκατ[ευταῖς]
κα[ὶ . .| . .] τ[ὴ]ν πρόσοδον τὴν ἐκ [τούτ]ων καὶ [. .| . . .τ]α τοῦ 15
τόπου. [Λήψε]τε δὲ [ὑ]πὲρ ἑκά[στου χωρίου ὁ καταλαβὼν] |

MUNICIPAL DOCUMENTS IN GREEK AND LATIN

ἄνεσιν τοῦ φόρου τῶν πρώτων [ἐτ]ῶν πέντ[ε· ἔπειτα δὲ καθ᾽
ἕκαστον ἐνιαυτὸν] | δώσει τὸν φόρον τὸν ἐτήσιον το[ῦ κ]ατα-
λαμβανομ[ένου χωρίου τοῦ μηνὸς τοῦ] | ᾽Αλαλκομεναίου τ[ῇ]
πεντεκαιδεκ[άτῃ]· οἱ δὲ μὴ πράξαντες σ[τρατηγοὶ τὴν πρόσο]|δον
ὑπεύθυνοι ἔσονται ὧν οὐκ ἔ[πρ]αξαν. Εἰ δέ τις λαβὼν [ἐν]τὸς
20 [τῆς πεν]‖ταετίας μὴ φυτεῦσαι, τό τε χωρίον [με]ταπωλήσουσιν
οἱ καταλαμβάν[οντες] | στρατηγοὶ (κ)αὶ ὃν ὑπέστη τελέσει[ν
φό]ρον πράξουσιν παρ᾽ αὐτοῦ τῆς [πενταετί]|ας. Εἰ δὲ φυτεύσει
ἐν μέρος ὡς ε[ἶναι] ἄξιον τοῦ φόρου τῶν πέντε ἐτ[ῶν, τὸν μὲν] |
φόρον μὴ πραττέσθω, πιπρασκέσθω [δὲ] τὸ χωρίον πολείτῃ,
καὶ τὸ ἀργὸν κα[ὶ τὸ πεφυ]‖τευμένον, ἐπὶ τῷ τὴν μὲν τειμὴν τ[οῦ
25 π]εφυτευμένου εἰσκομισθῆναι τῇ πόλ[ει, τὸν] ‖ δὲ φόρον παντὸς
τελεῖσθαι καθ᾽ ἕκαστο[ν] ἐνιαυτόν, ὅσον τελέσ[ε]ιν καὶ ὁ πρότερο[ς ὠμο]‖λόγησεν, συγχωρουμένου τῷ πρια[μέν]ῳ τοῦ φόρου τῆς
πενταετίας ὑπὲρ [τοῦ ἀρ]‖γοῦ μόνου. Λαμβανέτω δὲ [ὁ πολεί]της
ἕκαστος μὴ πλέον πλέθρω[ν . .]· | εἰ μέντοι τις φωραθείη φυτεύ-
σας τ[ού]τοις πλέον, πωλήσουσιν [οἱ στρατηγοὶ | τῷ βουλ]ομένῳ
30 τῶν πολειτῶν ἐπὶ τῷ καὶ ἐκ τούτου σώζεσθαι τ[ῇ πόλει ‖ . .
φόρον] τοσοῦτον ὅσον τ[ελέσειν] ὡμολόγησεν ὑπὲρ ἑκάστο[υ
πλέθρου. ῾Ην δὲ μηδεὶς | βούληται πρίασθαι, πράξουσ]ιν παρὰ
το[ῦ πρώτου λαβό]ντος τὸν γεινόμε[νον φόρον, | ὅσον ὑπὲρ
ἑκάστου πλέθρου τελέσειν ὑπεδέ]ξατο. |
35 [. . πλέ]θρον το[ῦ . .|. .]άμενος καὶ . .‖. .ου ἐξ ὅσου τ[. .|. .
π]αρὰ τῆς πόλεω[ς . .|. .]ίῳ καὶ τὰ ἄλλα κα[. .|. . πραττ]ο-
40 μένου τοῦ φόρου [. .|. . πολ]είτῃ δανειστῇ, ὡς κα[ὶ . .‖. . δημ]ο-
σίου χωρίου ἢ δ[. .| δ]ημοσίου καθ᾽ ἡμ[. .|. . α]ὐτὸς γραφέτω
45 . .|. .ντ. .οι εκα. .|. . πόσον ἢ ὅτ. .‖. .ατος υ. . . . . . . |
[. . . . τ]ό τε ὄνομα [τ]ο[ῦ . .|. .] εἰ δέ τις ἐξαπατήσα[ς τῶν]
ὀφειλόν[των ξένῳ ὑποθείη | τι τῶν χωρίων τῶ]ν δημοσίων καὶ
τοῦτο ἐλενχθείη, ἀφαιρε[ίσθω αὐτὸν τὸ | χωρίον τὸ ὑποτεθὲν] ἢ
50 πόλις, ὁ δὲ δανειστὴς ὁ ξένος ἐκ τῶν ἄλλ[ων κτημάτων ‖ τῶν
τοῦ ὑποθ]έντος τὴν εἴσπραξιν ποιείσθω τοῦ ὀφειλομέ[νου. Εἰ
δέ τις | διαθήκ]αις καταλίποι ξένῳ συνγενεῖ ἢ φίλῳ τούτων τι
τῶν [χωρίων, ἄκυρος | ἔστω α]ὐτοῦ ἡ δωρεά, ἔστω δὲ τῆς πόλεως
τὸ χωρίον. Εἰ δ[έ τις μὴ καταλι|πὼν δια]θήκας τελευτήσαι, ᾧ
μή εἰσιν νόμιμοι κληρονόμοι, [ὑ]π[αρχέτω | κατ᾽ ἀμφ]ότερα
κληρονόμος τοῦ ἑαυτῆς κτήμ[ατ]ος ἡ πόλις. ‖

FROM ITALY AND THE PROVINCES

[Γε]μίνιος Μόδεστος ἀνθύπατος Θισβ[έων τοῖς τε 55
ἄρχουσι καὶ] τῇ βουλῇ καὶ τῷ δήμῳ χαίρειν. Ἱκανὸν
[μὲν οὖν .. | εἶναι] κύρια τὰ δόξαντα ὑμεῖν περὶ τῆς πρότε[ρον
.. | ..] γεγενημένης, καὶ τὸ τοῦ ἀξιολ[ογωτάτου .. | ..ἐ]π' [α]ὐ-
τῶν ἐπιχωρίου καὶ ..

From Thisbe. Dittenberger dates the document in the beginning
of the third century, while Rostowzew is inclined to ascribe it to
the reign of Hadrian, or a little later. In accordance with this edict
of the provincial governor, the public (and sacred?) lands of Thisbe
are to be sold in small lots to the citizens of the town subject to
the payment of an annual tax (φόρος), which, however, is to be
remitted for the first five years of occupancy. The purchaser is
under obligation to plant (φυτεῦσαι) in vineyard or orchard during
this period. If he fails to do so, the magistrates shall sell the property
and exact the tax for the first five years. If only a part of the land
is brought under cultivation according to the contract, the magistrates shall sell the allotment to a citizen, the price of the cultivated
portion being paid into the treasury in lieu of the yearly tax, while
the new purchaser shall pay the stipulated tax for the whole plot
annually thereafter. If any farmer occupies more than the legal
allotment, the magistrates shall sell the portion held illegally, safeguarding the payment of the annual tax. If, however, a purchaser
cannot be found, they shall exact from the first farmer the amount
of tax which he agreed to pay for his original assignment. The
tenant may mortgage or bequeath his holdings, but not to a non-
resident of the city. If he dies without heirs, the property reverts
to the city. This document belongs to the class known as νόμος
πωλητικός (Rostowzew, *Gesch. d. röm. Kol.* 386 *ff.*), and the
form of perpetual leasehold instituted in the municipal territory
of Thisbe is similar in all respects to that prevalent in Egypt.
Several points of interest may be noted. The magistrates (στρατηγοί) are responsible personally for the exaction of the φόρος.
The doctrine of *origo* is implied in forbidding any lease to be granted
to aliens, and in the restrictions applied to mortgages and bequests
to non-residents. The legislation of the governor is, furthermore,
in the interest of the small proprietor, and every attempt is made to
prevent the encroachment of the capitalist and his *latifundia*.

Finally, it may be noted that the central government at this period does not hesitate to regulate in minute detail the internal affairs of the municipalities in the provinces. For a discussion of the legislation regarding similar tenure of land on the imperial domains, *cf.* pp. 15 *ff.*, and nos. 90, 111.

130. EPISTULA IMPERATORUM SEVERI ET CARACALLAE AD TYRANOS
(201 p. Chr.)

CIL. III, 781; Cagnat, *IGRR.* 1, 598; Bruns, 89; Dessau, 423; Riccobono, p. 332.

Exemplum epistulae ad Tertullum.

Misimus tibi epistulam ad Heraclitum, unde intelleges quid statuerimus de immunitate, quam Tyrani sibi concessam contendunt. Quam licet admittere non soleamus nisi privile|gii auct*oritate perpensa et origine immu*|nitatis inspecta, quod us*u receptum esse qua*|qua ratione videbatur, cum iusta *moderati*|one servavimus, ut neque ipsi
5 con*suetudi*||ne diuturna pellerentur et in poster*um* | decreta civium adsumendorum consi*liis* | praesidis provinciae c(larissimi) v(iri) perpenderetu*r.* | Exemplum epistulae ad Heraclitum. | Quamquam
10 Tyranorum civitas or*i*ginem || dati beneficii non ostendat, nec facile, quae | per errorem aut licentiam usurpata sunt, prae|scriptione temporis confirmentur, tamen, | quoniam divi Antonini parentis nostri litte|ras, sed et fratrum imperatorum cogitamus, item ||
15 Antonii Hiberi gravissimi praesidis, quod attinet | ad ipsos Tyranos quique ab iis secundum leges | eorum in numerum civium adsumpti sunt, ex pri|stino more nihil mutari volumus. Retineant | igitur
20 quaqua ratione quaesitam sive possessam || privilegii causam in promercalibus quoque re|bus, quas tamen pristino more professionibus | ad discernenda munifica mercimoniorum eden|das esse meminerint. Sed cum Illyrici fructum | per ambitionem deminui
25 non oporteat, sciant || eos, qui posthac fuerint adsumpti, fructum | immunitatis ita demum habituros, si eos legatus | et amicus noster v(ir) c(larissimus) iure civitatis dignos esse de|creto pronuntiaverit. Quos credimus satis a|bundequ*e* sibi consultum, si grati fuerint,
30 exi||stimaturos, quod origine beneficii non quaesi|ta dignos honore cives fieri praeceperimus. |

FROM ITALY AND THE PROVINCES

'Οουίνιος Τέρτυλλος ἄρχουσι, βουλῆι, δή|μωι Τυρανῶν χαί-
ρειν. | 'Αντίγραφον τῶν θείων γραμμάτων, πεμ||φθέντων μοι ὑπὸ 35
τῶν κυρίων ἡμῶν ἀνει|κήτων καὶ εὐτυχεστάτων αὐτοκρατόρων, |
τούτοις μου τοῖς γράμμασιν προέταξα, ὅ|πως γνόντες τὴν θείαν
εἰς ὑμᾶς μεγαλο|δωρίαν τῆι μεγάληι αὐτῶν τύχηι εὐχαριστή||-
σητε. 'Ερρῶσθαι ὑμᾶς καὶ εὐτυχεῖν πολ|λοῖς ἔτεσιν εὔχομαι. 40
'Απεδόθη πρὸ | ιγ' καλανδῶν Μαρτίων Ληνεῶνος η'. | 'Ανεστάθη
ἐπὶ Μουκιανοῦ καὶ Φαβιανοῦ | ὑπάτων, ἐν τῶι εμπ' ἔτει, ||
ἀρχῆς Π. Αἰλίου Καλπουρνίου. 45

From Tyra in Lower Moesia. Tertullus was the provincial
governor, and Heraclitus the *procurator vectigalis Illyrici*. The importance of the document lies in the fact that the Tyrans claimed
immunity from certain taxes, especially the *portorium* (Cagnat, *Les
impôts indirects chez les Romains*, 20 ff.), and, since had been
rather liberal in granting citizenship to aliens, the imperial revenues
had suffered. The procurator, apparently, had complained to the
governor and to the emperors, with the result that the Tyrans were
asked to submit the evidence on which they based their claim of
immunity. This they were able to do only in part, and from the
letter of the emperors we may infer that certain cities in the empire
had claimed similar privileges without any right to do so. These
claims had apparently been disallowed, unless the city had been
able to show the reason for the gift and the original charter. The
Tyrans had only been able to produce the letters of Antoninus Pius,
and his successors; the letters of the governor, Antoninus Hiberus,
had also been submitted. Accordingly the emperors confirm the
privileges which the Tyrans claim, but the grant of citizenship
conferred by the city is hereafter subject to the approval of the
provincial governor. Since citizenship in a community which enjoyed any form of immunity would be highly prized, it is probable
that Tyra had been guilty of increasing her revenues by this means.
Similarly Athens, enjoying the status of a free city, had bestowed
citizenship so lightly in return for a small payment in money that
Augustus took away the right to make the grant (*cf.* p. 139).
Tarsus sold the grant of citizenship for 500 drachmae (Dio Chrys.
34, 23).

MUNICIPAL DOCUMENTS IN GREEK AND LATIN

131. EDICTUM LEGATI IMPERATORUM, Q. SICINI
CLARI, DE PIZO CONDENDA
(202 p. Chr.)

Cagnat, *IGRR.* 1, 766; Ditt. *Syll.*³ 880; Kalinka, *Ant. Denk.
Bulgar.* 34.

Ἀγαθῇ τύχῃ. | Ὑπὲρ τῆς τῶν μεγίστων καὶ θειοτάτων αὐτο-
κρα|τόρων Λ. Σεπτιμίου Σευήρου Περτίνακος κὲ Μ. Αὐρη. |
5 Ἀντωνείνου Σεββ. κὲ [Π. Σεπτ. Γέτα Καίσαρος] κὲ || Ἰουλίας
Δόμνης μητρὸς κάστρων νείκης καὶ αἰωνίου | διαμονῆς καὶ τοῦ
σύμπαντος αὐτῶν οἴκου καὶ ἱερᾶς συν|κλήτου καὶ δήμου τοῦ
Ῥωμαίων καὶ ἱερῶν στρατευμάτων, | ἐκτίσθη κατὰ δωρεὰν τῶν
κυρίων ἐνπόριον Πίζος, ἐπὶ | ὑπάτων τῶν κυρίων αὐτοκρατόρων
10 Λ. Σεπ. Σεουήρου Περ||τίνακος κὲ Μ. Αὐρ. Ἀντωνείνου Σεββ.,
καὶ μετῴκισαν εἰς αὐτὸ | οἱ ὑποτεταγμένοι. |
Κ(όϊντος) Σικίννιος Κλᾶρος | πρεσβ(ευτὴς) Σεβ(αστῶν) ἀντι-
στρά|τηγος λέγει. ||
15 Τῇ προόψει τῶν σταθμῶν ἠσθέ[ν]||τες ο[ἱ] κύριοι ἡμῶν μέ-
γιστοι | καὶ θειότατοι αὐτοκράτορες | διὰ παντός τε τοῦ ἑαυτῶν
20 αἰῶ|νος βουληθέντες ἐν τῇ αὐτῇ εὐπρε||πείᾳ διαμεῖναι τὴν αὐτῶν|
ἐπαρχείαν, προσέταξαν τὰ ὄν|τα ἐνπόρια ἐπιφανέστερα ὑπ[άρ]|-
25 ξαι, καὶ τὰ μὴ πρότερον ὄντα | γενέσθ[α]ι· καὶ γέγονεν. || [Ἐ]πεὶ
οὖν δεῖ τὰ ἐκ θείας δωρε|ᾶς ὁρμώμενα εὐτυχέστε|ρα εἶναι καὶ ἐκ
τῆς τῶν ἐφε|στώτων τάξεως, οὐκ ἐνπορι|ακοὺς δημότας, ἀλλὰ
30 τοπάρ||χους βουλευτὰς ἐκέλευσα | ἐκπέμπεσθαι εἰς ταῦτα τὰ |
[ἐ]νπ[όρ]ια, δοὺς αὐτοῖς καὶ δι' ἐπιστο[λῆς] σημαντῆρα καὶ
35 δικαιοδοσίαν | [καὶ ἐντεί]λας μὴ ὕβρει μηδὲ βίᾳ, || [δικα]ιοσύνῃ δὲ
καὶ ἐπεικείᾳ | [κρ]α[τ]εῖν τοὺς ἐνοικοῦντας καὶ | [μὴ μό]νον αὐτοὺς
ταῦτα πράσσ|[ειν, ἀλλ]ὰ [κ]αὶ ἀπὸ τῶν ἄλλων τῷ ἀδικεῖν | ν[εω-
40 τε]ρίζειν προῃρημένων ῥύε||σθ[αι χρ]είας καὶ πολυπληθείας. |
Πρὸς τοῦ εἶναι εὐδαιμονέστερα | ταῦτα ἐμπόρια ἐπε(ι)θόμην,
ἀνδρά|σιν [ἐπι]πα[ρ]ευρεῖν εὐδοκιμούντω[ν] ἐ[κ] | τ[ῶν πέ]ριξ
45 κωμῶν, πείθοντας δὲ || ο .. καὶ μετοικίζειν εἰς ταῦ|τα [τ]ὰ ἐν-
πόρια, καὶ αὐτὸς δὲ προ|τ[ιθ]έ[μεν]ος καὶ τοὺς βουλομένους |
ἑκοντὴν τοῦτο ποιεῖν ἔξοντας | θείας τύχης τῶν Σεβαστῶν ||
50 μεγάλας δωρεάς, τουτέστιν | πολειτικοῦ σείτου ἀνεισφορίαν |
καὶ συν[τελ]είας βουργαρίων καὶ | [φ]ρουρῶν καὶ ἀνγαρειῶν

ἄνεσιν. | Καὶ ταῦτα μὲν περὶ τῆς τάξεως || [τ]οῦ τοπάρχου καὶ 55
περὶ τῆς ἀλειτουρ|[γησ]ίας τῶν ἐνοικούντων ἢ ἐνοικη|[σό]ντων.
Περὶ δὲ τῶν οἰκοδομη|[μά]των, ὅπως ἐπιμελείας τυν|χάνοντα
εἰς ἀεὶ διαμένοι, || κελεύω τοὺς τοπάρχους καὶ τοὺς | ἐπιστάθ- 60
μους στρατιώτας | [π]α[ρ]ὰ τῶν ἐπιμελητῶν παραλα[ν|β]ά[νι]ν
τὰ πραιτώρια καὶ τὰ βα|λανεῖα πανταχόθεν ὁλόκλη||ρα, τουτέστιν 65
ἐν τοῖς οἰκοδομικοῖς | καὶ ἐν τοῖς λεπτουργικοῖς καὶ ἐν | τοῖς
χρηστικοῖς, παραδιδόντας | τοῖς μεθ᾽ ἑαυτοὺς ἐγγράφ[ω]ς, ὥσ-
περ | παραλαμβάνουσιν. ["Ο]πως δ]ὲ ἐπι||μελεστέρους αὐτοὺς 70
παρασκευ|άσω πρὸς τὴν παρά[λη]μψιν, | καὶ τὴν παράδοσιν,
π[αρακε]λεύ|ω ἀπὸ τοῦ χρόνου τῆς [πα]ραλήμ|ψεως μέχρι τῆς
παρα[δόσ]εω[ς] || τὰ ὑπάρχοντα τῶν τοπάρχων | καὶ τῶν ἀρχόν- 75
των οὓς ἐκέλευσα | τῷ ἰδίῳ κινδύνῳ αὐτοὺς προβάλ|λεσθαι,
ὑπεύθυνα εἶναι τῷ | δημοσίῳ τῶν πόλεων, πρὸς δὲ δ[ια||λύ]σωσ[ι] 80
αὐτὰ τὰ ἐνπόρια εἰς τὸ | [τε]τραπλάσιον τοῦ ἐνδεήσον|τος.

From Pizus in Thrace. We have omitted in our text the names
of the colonists who were settled in the new foundation. These are
arranged in four columns under the villages from which they were
drawn. In the fourth column there are nine names under the title
ὕπατοι οἰκήτορες, probably one from each of the nine villages,
who were chosen to act as magistrates in the new community
(Seure, *B.C.H.* 22 (1898), 472 *ff.*, 520 *ff.*). The number of colonists
is 181. Pizus had the rank of an *emporium* or *forum*, and was
established as a *statio* (σταθμός) on the imperial highway which
led from Philippopolis towards Hadrianopolis. The edict was issued
after a visit of the emperors to Thrace, and it apparently formed a
model for the creation of similar stations along the highway and
throughout the province. The settlers were drawn from nearby
villages, and they were induced to settle in the new foundation under
the promise of remission of various liturgies, the *annona*, the provision of troops recruited for service in the *burgi* and garrisons, and
angary, or the supply of animals and labor in the service of the
public post. The residents are not called citizens but ἐνοικοῦντες.
The duty of administration and of dispensing justice is entrusted to
a member of the senate from the toparchy, or administrative district
in which Pizus is founded (*cf. Cod. Th.* 12. 1. 21). Apparently the
government of *fora* had been given hitherto to ordinary residents

of the station (ll. 25 ff.). The chief magistrate has the title τόπαρχος, and is assisted in his administrative duties by the nine ὕπατοι οἰκήτορες mentioned above. These officials are responsible for the care of the public buildings provided by the emperors, and their property is held as security by the municipality or toparchy, which is entrusted with the administration of the station. The management of the buildings is shared with the troops stationed at the post, but the soldiers are not placed under a similar bond. On the *fora* in the Roman empire, *cf.* pp. 10 ff. The reading συν[τελ]είας in l. 52 is suggested by Rostovtseff, *Journ. Rom. Studies*, 8 (1918), 26 ff., where he also discusses the liturgy of providing recruits for military service.

132. EDICTUM IMPERATORUM SEVERI ET CARACALLAE DE HOSPITIO
(204 p. Chr.)

Lafoscade, 74; Ditt. *Syll.*³ 881; *CIL.* III, *S.* 14203⁸,⁹; *IG.* XII, 5, 132.

I ʿΙερὰ γράμματα. | [Δ]οκεῖς ἡμεῖν τὸ δόγμα | [τ]ῆς συγκλήτου
5 ἀγνο|[εῖ]ν, ὅς, ἐὰν μετ᾽ ἐμπεί|[ρ]ων συναντιβάληις, | [ε]ἴσηι μὴ
εἶναι ἐπάναγ|[κ]ες συγκλητικῶι | [δ]ήμου ʿΡωμαίων ἄκον|[τι]
10 ξένον ὑποδέχε||[σ]θαι. ᾽Εδόθη | α᾽ καλ. ᾽Ιουνι. ʿΡώμηι, | [Φα]βίωι
Κείλωνι τὸ β᾽ καὶ | [᾽Α]ννίωι Λίβωνι ὑπάτοις]. |

II Sacrae *litt*erae⟨s⟩. | Videris *nobi*s s. co. | ignor*are qui* si cum |
5 peritis *cont*ul*eris* ‖ scies *sen*atori p. R. | necess*e non* esse | invito
10 *hosp*item | suscip*ere.* | Dat. pri*d. kal.* Iun. *Rom*a*e* ‖ *Fab*io *Cil*on*e* II
et | *Ann*io *Libo*ne coss.

From the island of Paros. This edict was issued in answer to a complaint lodged by a magistrate or private citizen on the island. The inscription seems to have been set up on the wall of the house owned by the senator who claimed immunity from the service of lodging officials or soldiers. There is no other record of the decree of the senate to which the emperors refer. The liturgy of furnishing *hospitium* was most severe, and complaints of the abuses which were inflicted by the members of the bureaucracy and army characterize most of the documents of the third century. *Cf.* nos. 113, 139, 141–144. On the character of this document, *cf.* pp. 236 ff. On immunity, *cf.* pp. 101 ff.

[460]

133. DECRETUM MYLASENSIUM DE TRAPEZITIS

(209–211 p. Chr.)

Ditt. *Or. Gr.* 515.

```
. . . . . . . ην . . . φ . . . |  . . . . . . . . . . γα . . . . . . | . . . . . εσειν
. . . . . . δ . ονετ . . . . . . . . | τὴν βουλὴ[ν κ]α[ὶ τὸν δῆμον . . . . . .
. . . || . . . . . . . κο]ινὴν ὁμόφρονα γνώ[μην . . . . . . . | . . . . . . ] ἐν 5
ταῖς νομίμοις ἡ[μέραις . . . . . . | . . . . . . . . ]ων ἐπανορθῶ[σαι
. . . . . . . . | . . . . . ] ἀφορήτου πᾶσιν ὄντος το[ῦ . . . . . . . | . ., οὐ
φαίν]ηται δὲ δύνασθ[αι ἰαθῆναι || πλ]ὴ[ν] διὰ [τὴν τ]ῶν μεγίστων 10
[καὶ θειοτάτων κυρ|ί]ων ἡμῶν Αὐτοκρατόρων Λο[υκίου Σεπτι-
μίου Σεου|ή]ρου Εὐσεβοῦς Περτίνακος κ[αὶ Μάρκου Αὐρηλίου
Ἀν|τω]νίνου [Εὐσεβοῦς καὶ Ποπλίου Σεπτιμίου Γέτα Σεβα|σ]-
τῶν τύχην, ψηφίσματι τῆς β[ουλῆς καὶ τοῦ δήμου ἐπ||α]νορθω- 15
θέντα· δεδόχθαι τῆι[βουλῆι καὶ τῶι δήμωι. Ἐ|ά]ν τις οἱοιδητινιοῦν
τρόπωι, [εἴτε ἐλεύθερος εἴτε | δ]οῦλος, ἔξωθεν τοῦ μεμισθωμ[ένου
καὶ ἐργαζ|ο]μένου τὴν τράπεζαν, ἀμειβόμεν[ος ἁλῶι νόμισμα
ἢ | πρι]άμενος, πρὸς τὸν τραπεζείτην [τοῦτον ἄγεσθαι || γεν]ο- 20
μένης προσαγγελίας τῆι βουλῆι [ὑπὸ τοῦ βουλομέ|νου τ]ῶν
πολειτῶν, καὶ ἐλενχθέντα ἐπ[ὶ τῶν ἀρχόντων καὶ | τῆς] βουλῆς,
εἰ μὲν ἄνευ κολλύβου τοῦτ[ο ἐποίησε, τοῦ ἀργυρίου | πρᾶξ]ιν
εἶναι τῶι τραπεζείτηι καὶ τῶι μηνύσ[αντι καὶ ἑλόν|τι, ἔ]χοντος
τοῦ τραπεζείτου καὶ κατ᾽ αὐτὸν ἐξο[υσίαν πράττε||σθαι κα]θὰ 25
ἠσφάλισται, εἰ δὲ ἐπὶ κολλύβωι, τὸν [μὲν ἐλεύθερον ἀπο|τίνει]ν
(ε)ἰς τὸ ἱερώτατον ταμεῖον τῶν κυρίω[ν ἡμῶν θειοτά|των] αὐτο-
κρατόρων ✕ φ᾽, τῶι δὲ δήμωι ✕ σν᾽, κ[αὶ τῶι μηνύ|σαντ]ι καὶ ἑλόντι
✕ ρ᾽, καὶ τὸ φωραθὲν ἀργυροῦ[ν νόμισ|μα πρ]ασσόμενον εἶναι
στερέσιμον τῶι τραπεζε[ίτηι· τὸν δὲ δοῦλ||ον ἐλ]ενχθέντα ὡς προ- 30
γέγραπται, παραδοθέν[τα δὲ ὑπὸ τοῦ δεσ|πότου] τοῖς ἄρχουσι
ἐπὶ [τῆ]ς βουλῆς, μαστειγοῦσθα[ι ν᾽ πληγὰς | καὶ] ἐμβάλλεσθαι
(ε)ἰς τὸ πρακτόρειον καὶ εἶναι [αὐτὸν | ἐπὶ] τῆς (ε)ἱρκτῆς τασ-
σόμενον μῆνας ἕξ· ἐὰν δὲ [ὁ δεσπότης μὴ | ποι]ήσ[ε]ιε ταῦτα
τὸν δοῦλον, ὀφείλειν αὐτὸν τὰ [γεγραμμένα || ἐπί]τειμα τῶι 35
ἱερωτάτωι ταμείωι καὶ τῶι δήμωι [καὶ τῶι μηνύσαντι καὶ | ἑλό]ντι.
Τὰς δὲ τοιαύτας προσαγγελίας εἰσδέ[χεσθαι τὸν γραμματέα |
τῶν] ἀρχόντων, γενομένης μετὰ τὸ ἐπιδ[οθῆναι τὴν προσ|αγγε-
λ]ίαν προγραφῆς ἐφεξῆς ἐπὶ τρεῖς ἡμέ[ρας ἐν ἱεροῖς | καὶ δη]-
μοσίοις τόποις, ῥητῶς τῆς προγραφῆς [λεγούσης ὅτι || συνάγ]εται 40
```

[461]

MUNICIPAL DOCUMENTS IN GREEK AND LATIN

ἡ βουλὴ διὰ τοῦτο. Ἐὰν δὲ οἱ ἄρχοντε[ς ἢ ὁ γραμματεὺς | τῶν
ἐψη]φισμένων τι παραλίπωσιν ἢ οἱ βουλευταὶ [μὴ συν|έλθω]σιν
δυνατοὶ ὄντες καὶ ἐπίδημοι, τοὺς μὲν [ἄρχοντας καὶ | τὸν γραμ]-
ματέα ἀποτεῖσαι ἕκαστον αὐτῶν (ε)ἰς τὸ [ἱερώτατον ταμεῖον | τῶν
45 Σεβα]στῶν ἀνὰ ✗ τ', τοὺς δὲ βουλευτὰς [ἀνὰ ✗ .. ἀναγρά||ψαι δὲ
τό]δε τὸ ψήφισμα ἐν στήληι, ἣν καὶ ἀνα[σταθῆναι | δεήσει ἐν τῆι]
ἀγορᾶι ἐν τῶι ἐπισημοτάτωι τόπωι, ὥσ[περ νόμον εἰς τὸν πάν|τα
χρόνο]ν καταστῆσον· σαλεύει γὰρ ὡς ἀλη[θῶς ἡ σωτηρία | τῆς
πόλε]ως ἐκ κακουργίας καὶ πανουργίας ὀλί[γων τινῶν | αὐτῆι
50 ἐπεμβα]ινόντων καὶ ἀπονοσφιζομένων τ[ὰ κοινά, ὧν ὑπὸ || τῆς
δυνάμ]εως κόλλυβός τις ἐνπεφοίτηκεν εἰς [τὴν ἀγοράν, | κωλύων
τὴν πό]λιν τὰ ἐπιτήδ(ε)ια ἔχειν, ἀπορούντων [τῶν πολλῶν | καὶ
τοῦ κοινοῦ σ]πανίζοντος. Καὶ διὰ τοῦτο καὶ ἡ εὐ[πορία ἡ | πρὸς
τοὺς κυρίους αὐ]τοκράτορας τῶν φόρων βραδύνει . . . . |
. . . . μεγάλης ἡγεμονίας τοῦτο πᾶσα ἡ. . . .
55 . . . . . . || . . . . ἐπανορθῶσαι. Succlam(atum) est.
(E)ἰς αἰῶ[να . . . . | . . . .]ων ἀνεικήτοις τοῖς κυ-
ρίοις, ναοῖς [. . . . . . | . . . . κόλλ]υβον. Τὸ ζῆν οὐκ ἔχομεν,
ἀλλ᾽ ἡ πό[λις . . . . | . . . . πονη]ρευόμενοί τινες ἐνπο-
ρείας ταρ[άσσουσιν καὶ | τὸ νόμισμα . . . .]ουσιν τὸ ἀργυροῦν,
60 καὶ τοῦτο [. . . . . || . . . . τ]οὺς νόμους πολλάκις ἡ
βο[υλὴ. . . . . | . . . .] π . . . . . . πολειτ . . . .

From Mylasa. As was the case at Pergamum (*cf.* no. 81),
Mylasa derived a certain revenue from the exchange of local and
foreign currency. The right of exchange was leased to a firm of
bankers. Apparently private individuals had also engaged in the
business to such an extent that trade had been demoralized and the
revenues of the municipality seriously impaired. The document is
of interest because the fines and penalties are imposed by the city,
and the local magistrates and senate administer the law. This is
the latest evidence for the independent powers of municipal governments in initiating legislation in the imperial period (*cf.* Mommsen,
Röm. Strafrecht, 114). The court is constituted by the magistrates
and senate of the city. The secretary is empowered to summon the
court on giving three days' notice. A fine, payable to the imperial
fiscus, is imposed on any member of the court who fails to attend the
session when he is able to do so.

Reinach (*B.C.H.* 20 (1896), 523 *ff.*) offers the following ex-

[462]

FROM ITALY AND THE PROVINCES

planation of the monetary crisis. The municipal laws probably required the use of local coinage in the transaction of business within the city. As at Pergamum the rate of exchange was fixed. With the rapid depreciation of imperial coinage, traders and speculators purchased the undepreciated local currency and by holding it or by hoarding, it disappeared from circulation. There was a consequent rise in local prices and trade was seriously hampered. The law attempted to remedy conditions by confining all transactions in exchange to the municipal bank or to the firm which leased the privilege of exchange from the city (*cf.* nos. 81, 199).

134. EPISTULA IMPERATORIS CARACALLAE
AD PHILADELPHENOS
(213–214 p. Chr.)

Ditt. *Syll.*³ 883; Lafoscade, 78; Cagnat, *IGRR*. 4, 1619.

Ἀντωνεῖνός σ᾽ ἔκτιζε. | Αὐτοκράτωρ | Καῖσαρ Μᾶρκος | Αὐρήλιος Ἀντωνεῖ‖νος Εὐσεβὴς Σεβασ᾽τὸς Παρθικὸς μέγισ᾽τος 5 Βρεταννικὸς μέ|γιστος Γερμανικὸς | μέγιστος Αὐρηλίωι ‖ Ἰο[υ- 10 λιανῶ]ι τῶι τιμι|ωτάτωι χαίρειν. | Εἰ καὶ μηδεὶς αἱρεῖ | λόγος τὸν Φιλαδελ|φέα Ἰουλιανὸν ἀ‖πὸ τῶν Σαρδιανῶν | εἰς τὴν τῆς 15 πατρί|δος μεταθεῖναι φι|λοτειμίαν, ἀλλ᾽ ὅμως | σὴν χάριν ἡδέως ‖ τοῦτο ποιῶ, δι᾽ ὃν καὶ | τὴν νεωκορίαν αὐ|τὴν τοῖς Φιλαδελ|φεῦ- 20 σ[ιν δέ]δωκα. | Ἔρρωσο Ἰουλι[ανὲ]‖| τιμιώτατέ μοι καὶ φίλ|τατε. | 25 Ἀνεγνώσθη ἐν τῶι | θεάτρωι ἔτους σμέ, μη|νὸς Ἀπελλαίου ε᾽.

From Philadelphia. The letter is addressed to Aurelius Julianus who must not be confused with the Julianus about whom the letter is written. The latter was a native of Philadelphia who had become a resident of Sardis. Apparently he wished to undertake some liturgy for his native city—possibly in connection with the imperial cult—when the Sardians protested. Their motive was doubtless due to the rivalries and civic jealousies which so thoroughly inspired many of the cities of Asia under Roman rule. The Sardians had no legal claim to the exclusive services of Julianus, for by law the city of his birth took precedence over his place of residence (*Dig.* 50. 1. 1, 6, 16, 17; *Cod. J.* 10. 39. 1). When the Philadelphians took up the dispute with the emperor he replied that he would gladly fulfil the request of his friend Julianus, even if he had no legal right to do so.

[463]

135. TABULA PATRONATUS
(222 p. Chr.)

CIL. vi, 1454; Dessau, 6109.

Imp. Caes. M. Aur. Severo Alexandro | cos. eidib. Aprilibus |
concilium conventus Clunien*s*. | G. Marium Pudentem Cornelia-||
5 num leg. leg., c. v., patronum | sibi liberis posterisque suis | co-
optavit ob multa et egregia | eius in singulos universos|que merita,
10 per legatum || Val. Marcellum | Cluniensem.

Bronze tablet found at Rome. The patron in this case, Cor-
nelianus, a *legatus legionis*, belongs, as most patrons do, to the
senatorial order. In Pliny's time Hispania Citerior was divided into
seven *conventus* (*N.H.* 3. 3. 18), one of which had its seat at Clunia;
cf. Kornemann, *R.E.* 4, 805, 1177; Schulten, *R.E.* 8, 2037. The
election of a *patronus* by this *concilium conventus* seems to show that
the *conventus* of Hispania Citerior was a political as well as a judicial
division of the province. For a general treatment of the *concilia*,
cf. pp. 162 *ff.*

136. ALBUM DECURIONUM
(223 p. Chr.)

CIL. ix, 338; Dessau, 6121.

L. Mario Maximo II, L. Roscio Aeliano cos.,

M. Antonius Priscus, L. Annius Secundus iivir. quinquenn.

nomina decurionum in aere incidenda curaverunt.

patroni cc. vv.:	quinquennalicii:	aedilicii:
App. Claudiu s Iulianu s	T. Ligeriu s Postuminu s	T. Flaviu s Crocalianu s
T. Loreniu s Celsu s	T. Annaeu s Rufu s	(*et alia nomina duo-*
M. Aediniu s Iulianu s	L. Abucciu s Proculu s	*deviginti, in his*)
L. Didiu s Marinu s	T. Aeliu s Rufu s	L. Faeniu s Merop s iun.
(*et alia nomina viginti*	T. Aeliu s Flavianu s	quaestoricii:
septem, in his)	M. Antoniu s Priscu s	L. Ceiu s Asclepiodotianu s
M. Statiu s Longinu s	L. Anniu s Secundu s	(*et alia nomina octo*)
C. Petroniu s Magnu s	allecti inter quinq.:	pedani:
M. Statiu s Longinus iun.	C. Galbiu s Soterianu s	Q. Fabiu s Fabianu s
patroni eeqq. RR.:	L. Abucciu s Iulianu s	(*et alia nomina tri-*
P. Gerellanu s Modestu s	C. Siliu s Ant*h*u s	*ginta et unum*)
T. Ligeriu s Postuminu s	P. Aeliu s Victorinu s	praetextati:
T. Munatiu s Feli x	iiviralicii:	T. Flaviu s Frontinu s
T. Flaviu s Crocalianu s	A. Caeselliu s Proculu s ii	C. Iuliu s Hospitali s iun.
C. Galbiu s Soterianu s	L. Faeniu s Merop s ii	L. Abucciu s Proculu s iun.
T. Aeliu s Rufu s	L. Abucciu s Maximianu s	(*et alia nomina vi-*
T. Aeliu s Flavianu s	Q. Iuniu s Alexande r ii	*ginti duo*)
Q. Coeliu s Sabinianu s	(*et alia nomina viginti*	
	quinque)	

[464]

A bronze tablet found at Canusium, now in Florence. Such lists were drawn up by the *quinquennales*. The regulations governing the revision of the list were usually stated in the *lex municipii*. For the early period, *cf.* no. 24, ll. 83 *ff.* In the later period the interference of the emperor is evident (*Dig.* 50. 3. 2, *qui dignitates principis iudicio consecuti sunt*). This album shows the normal number of one hundred decurions (*cf.* no. 151). In it also appear the names of thirty-nine *patroni* and twenty-five *praetextati*. In the album of Thamagudi (*CIL.* VIII, 2403; *S.* 17824; Dessau, 6122), of the middle of the fourth century, there are twelve *patroni* and fifty-nine decurions, and of the decurions a majority have been *flamines perpetui*, *i.e.* they have been priests of the imperial cult and consequently officially connected with the central government (Jullian, *Dict. Dar. s.v. flamen*, pp. 1180 *ff.*). On M. Aedinius Julianus in the album of Canusium, *cf.* no. 140. On *patroni*, *cf.* nos. 42 and 135. The groups of active decurions are arranged in the order of their rank. At the end come the *pedani* who have held no magistracy, and the *praetextati*, who were probably, for the most part, sons of decurions. However, all the sons of regular decurions cannot have been of age to wear the *praetexta*. Consequently the decurionship cannot have become hereditary as early as A.D. 223. Otherwise the names of minors would naturally appear in the list (Mommsen, *Festschrift zu Hirschfeld*, 4). The acceptance of the hereditary principle probably became the usage in the times of Diocletian and Constantine. It is explicitly laid down as a principle (Mommsen, *op. cit.* 5, n. 4) by Theodosius in *Cod. Th.* 12. 1. 20: *Is vero ratio diversa est qui statim ut nati sunt curiales esse coeperunt.* One group, whose presence in the album of Thamagudi a century and a half later and whose absence here is significant of a decline in municipal prosperity and of a desire to avoid the burdens which were being laid on the decurions as time went on, is that of the *excusati*. They were excused from the *munera* of the office. On the *munera*, *cf.* pp. 84 *ff.* The name of C. Petronius Magnus has been erased from the album, but may still be read. Dessau conjectures that he was put to death by Maximinus; *cf.* Herodian, 7. 1. 5; *Hist. Aug. Maximin.* 10. 1.

MUNICIPAL DOCUMENTS IN GREEK AND LATIN

137. EPISTULA PROCONSULIS ASIAE AD APHRODISIENSES
(222–235 p. Chr.)

Rev. d. ét. grec. 19 (1906), 86 *f.*

```
.κε........ |
```
 .εὐτ]υχεῖς δηλ[αδὴ ἀ]κόλουθόν ἐσ[τι | πάσ]ας πόλεις τὰς
5 καθωσιωμένας | [τ]ῆ μεγάλη αὐτοῦ τύχη φιλεῖν τε || καὶ τειμᾶν,
ὅπερ με ποιεῖν ἡδέως | κ[α]ὶ αὐτοὶ ἴστε, ἐξαιρέτως δὲ τὰς
τει|μηθείσας τῆ ἐλευθερία ὑπὸ τῶν προ|γόνων τοῦ κυρίου ἡμῶν
10 αὐτοκράτορο[ς] | ('Αλεξάνδρου) βεβαιοῦντος αὐτο[ῦ || αὐτ]ὴν
καὶ αὔξοντος τὰ δίκαια οἶ[ς | εὐθυ]μεῖσθε καὶ ἡδέως ἐλεύσομα[ι |
πρὸς] ὑμᾶς καὶ ἐπιδημήσω ἐν τῆ λαμ|[προτ]άτη πόλει ὑμῶν καὶ
τῆ πατρίω ὑμῶν | [θεᾶ] θύσω ὑπέρ τε τῆς σωτηρίας καὶ αἰω||-
15 [ν]ίου διαμονῆς τοῦ τε κυρίου ἡμῶν αὐ|τοκράτορος ('Αλεξάνδρου)
καὶ τῆς κυρ|[ίας] ἡμῶν Σεβαστῆς (Μαμαίας) μητρὸς | τοῦ κυρίου
20 ἡμῶν καὶ στρατοπέδων, | εἰ μήτε νόμος τῆς πόλεως ὑμῶν || [μ]ήτε
δόγμα συνκλήτου μήτε διάτα|ξις μήτε θεία ἐπιστολὴ κωλύει
τὸν | [ἀ]νθύπατον ἐπιδημεῖν τῆ πόλει [ὑμῶν]. | [E]ἰ γάρ τι
κωλύει τῶν προγεγρα[μμένων], | θύων, ὡς ἔθος μοί ἐστιν, τοῖς
25 [ἄλλοις || θε]οῖς ὑπέρ τε τῆς τύχης κα[ὶ σωτηρίας | κ]αὶ αἰωνίου
διαμονῆς τοῦ κυ[ρίου ἡμῶν] | αὐτοκράτορος ('Αλεξάνδρου) [καὶ
τῆς] | μητρὸς αὐτοῦ (Μαμαίας) Σεβαστῆ[ς, κυρίας] | δὲ ἡμῶν,
30 καὶ τὴν πάτριον ὑμῶν [θεὰν ἐγ||κ]αλέσομαι. Ταῦτα δὲ ἀπεκρι-
[νάμην..|.... τοῖς πρώτοις τῆς λαμπροτάτης] | ὑμῶν πόλεως. |
['Ερρῶσ]θαι ὑμᾶς εὔχομαι.

Since Aphrodisias was a *civitas libera*, whose privileges had been
confirmed and extended by Alexander (l. 10), it could not be subjected to the expense of entertaining the provincial governor and
his staff. In free towns this immunity was secured either by the
municipal laws, a decree of the senate, or an imperial edict or letter
(ll. 18–22). The governor is evidently Sulpicius Priscus (*cf.* no. 138).
The name of the emperor has been erased on the stone.

[466]

FROM ITALY AND THE PROVINCES

138. TITULUS HONORARIUS
(222–235 p. Chr.)

Rev. d. ét. grec. 19 (1906), 84.

Ὁ δῆμος | τῆς λαμπροτάτης | Ἀφροδεισιέων | πόλεως Σουλ
πίκιον ‖ Πρεῖσκον τὸν δια|σημότατον ἀνθύ|πατον κατὰ τὰς τοῦ | 5
μεγίστου καὶ θειο|τάτου κυρίου ἡμῶν ‖ αὐτοκράτορος Σεου|[ή]ρου 10
(Ἀλεξάνδρου) [ἐντολάς (?)].

This inscription was recorded on the base of a statue set up in
honor of the governor. The name of the emperor had been erased
in antiquity. Although the restoration of the last word is uncertain, it is clear that the Aphrodisians had asked the emperor for
permission to erect this statue. Augustus forbade provincials to
pass honorary decrees for a governor until sixty days after his
departure from his office (*cf.* p. 164). The erection of an honorary
statue to provincial officials seems to have required special permission, but this is the only example in Greek lands known to us.

139. RESCRIPTUM GORDIANI AD SCAPTOPARENOS
(238 p. Chr.)

CIL. III, *S.* 12336; Cagnat, *IGRR.* I, 674; Ditt. *Syll.*[3] 888;
Riccobono, p. 371; Girard, p. 205.

Bona Fortuna. Fulvio Pio et Pontio Proculo cons. XVII kal. I
Ian. descriptum et recognitum factum | ex libro libellorum rescriptorum a domino n(ostro) imp. Caes. M. Antonio Gordiano
Pio Felice Aug. | et propositorum Romae in porticu thermarum
Traianarum in verba q(uae) i(nfra) s(cripta) s(unt); | dat(um) per
Aure(lium) Purrum mil(item) coh(ortis) x pr(aetoriae) P(iae)
F(elicis) Gordianae Proculi convicanum et conpossessorem.

Αὐτοκράτορι Καίσαρι Μ. Ἀντωνίῳ | Γορδιανῷ Εὐσεβεῖ II
Εὐτυχεῖ Σεβ. δέησις | παρὰ κωμητῶν Σκαπτοπαρηνῶν τῶν καὶ |
Γρησειτῶν· ἐν τοῖς εὐτυχεστάτοις καὶ αἰωνίοις ‖ σοῦ καιροῖς 5
κατοικεῖσθαι καὶ βελτι|οῦσθαι τὰς κώμας ἤπερ ἀναστάτους |
γίγνεσθαι τοὺς ἐνοικοῦντας πολλά|κ(ις) ἀντέγραψας· ἔστιν γε
καὶ ἐπὶ τῇ τῶν | ἀνθρώπων σωτηρίᾳ τὸ τοιοῦτο καὶ ἐπὶ ‖ τοῦ 10
ἱερωτάτου σου ταμείου ὠφελείᾳ. | Ὅπερ καὶ αὐτοὶ ἔννομον ἱκε
σίαν | τῇ θειότητί σου προσκομί[ζ]ομεν, εὐ|χόμενοι ἱλέως ἐπι

[467]

15 νεῦσαι ἡμεῖν | δεομένοις τὸν τρόπον τοῦτον. Οἰκοῦ‖μεν καὶ
κεκτήμεθα ἐν τῇ προγεγραμ|μένῃ κώμῃ οὔσῃ εὐεπεράστῳ διὰ
τὸ | ἔχειν ὑδάτων θερμῶν χρῆσιν καὶ κεῖ|σθαι μέσον δύο στρατο-
20 πέδων τῶν ὄν|των ἐν τῇ σῇ Θράκῃ· καὶ ἐφ' οὗ μὲν τὸ ‖ πάλ⟨λ⟩αι
οἱ κατοικοῦντες ἀόχλητοι | καὶ ἀδειάσειστοι ἔμενον, ἀνενδεῶς |
τούς τε φόρους καὶ τὰ λοιπὰ | ἐπιτάγματα συνετέλουν· ἐπεὶ δὲ
κατὰ καιροὺς εἰς | [ὔ]β[ρι]ν προχωρεῖν τινες καὶ βιάζεσθαι ‖
25 ἤρξαντο, τηνικαῦτα ἐλαττοῦσθαι | καὶ ἡ κώμη ἤρξατο. Ἀπό γε
μειλίων | δύο τῆς κώμης ἡμῶν πανηγύρεως | ἐπιτελουμένης δια-
30 βοήτου οἱ ἐκεῖσε | τῆς πανηγύρεως εἵνεκεν ἐπιδημοῦν‖τες ἡμέρας
πεντεκαίδεκα ἐν τῷ | τόπῳ τῆς πανηγύρεως οὐ καταμέ|νουσιν,
ἀλλ' ἀπολιμπάνοντες ἐπέρ|χονται εἰς τὴν ἡμετέραν κώμην | καὶ
35 ἀναγκάζουσιν ἡμᾶς ξενίας ‖ αὐτοῖς παρέχειν καὶ ἕτερα πλεῖστα
εἰς | ἀνάλημψιν αὐτῶν ἄνευ ἀργυρίου χο|ρηγεῖν· πρὸς δὲ τούτοις
καὶ στρατιῶται | ἀλλαχοῦ πεμπόμενοι καταλιμπά|νοντες τὰς
40 ἰδίας ὁδοὺς πρὸς ἡμᾶς πα‖ραγείνονται καὶ ὁμοίως κατεπείγουσιν |
παρέχειν αὐτοῖς τὰς ξενίας καὶ τὰ ἐπι|τήδια μηδεμίαν τιμὴν
καταβαλόντες· | ἐπιδημοῦσι δὲ ὡς ἐπὶ τὸ πλεῖστον | διὰ τὴν
45 τῶν ὑδάτων χρῆσιν οἵ τε ἡγού‖μενοι τῆς ἐπαρχίας, ἀλλὰ καὶ οἱ
ἐπί|τροποί σου· καὶ τὰς μὲν ἐξουσίας συ|ν(εχ)έστατα δεχόμεθα
κατὰ τὸ ἀναγκαῖον, | τοὺς (δὲ) λοιποὺς ὑποφέρειν μὴ δυνάμεν|οι
50 ἐνετύχομεν πλειστάκις τοῖς ἡγε‖μόσι τῆς Θράκης, οἵτινες ἀκο-
λούθως | ταῖς θείαις ἐντολαῖς ἐκέλευσαν ἀοχλή|τους ἡμᾶς εἶναι·
ἐδηλώσαμεν γὰρ μη|κέτι ἡμᾶς δύνασθαι ὑπομένειν, ἀλ|λὰ καὶ
55 νοῦν ἔχειν ἐνγκαταλιπεῖν καὶ τοὺς ‖ πατρῴους θεμελίους διὰ τὴν
τῶν | ἐπερχομένων ἡμεῖν βίαν· καὶ γὰρ | ὡς ἀληθῶς ἀπὸ πολλῶν
οἰκοδεσπο|τῶν εἰς ἐλαχίστους κατεληλύθα|μεν. Καὶ χρόνῳ μέν
60 τινι ἴσχυσεν ‖ τὰ προστάγματα τῶν ἡγουμένων | καὶ οὐδεὶς
ἡμεῖν ἐνόχλησεν οὔτε | ξενίας [αἰτή]ματι οὔτε παροχῆς ἐπι|τη-
δείων, προϊόντων δὲ τῶν χρόνων | πάλιν ἐτόλμησαν ἐπιφύεσθαι
65 ἡ‖μεῖν πλεῖστοι ὅσοι τῆς ἰδιωτίας | ἡμῶν καταφρονοῦντες. Ἐπεὶ
οὖν οὐ|κέτι δυνάμεθα φέρειν τὰ βάρη | καὶ ὡς ἀληθῶς κινδυ-
70 νεύομεν ὅπερ | οἱ λοιποὶ [ὧ]δε καὶ ἡμεῖς προλιπεῖν ‖ τοὺς προ-
γονικοὺς θεμελίους, τού|του χάριν δεόμεθά σου, ἀνίκητε | Σεβαστέ,
(ὅ)πως διὰ θείας σου ἀντιγρα|φῆς κελεύσῃ(ς) ἕκαστον τὴν ἰδίαν
75 πο|ρεύεσθαι ὁδὸν καὶ μὴ ἀπολιμπάνοντας ‖ αὐτοὺς τὰς ἄλλας
κώμας ἐφ' ἡμᾶς | ἔρχεσθαι μήτε καταναγκάζειν | ἡμᾶς χορηγεῖν

αὐτοῖς προῖκα τὰ | ἐπιτήδια, ἀλλὰ μηδὲ ξενίαν αὐτοῖς | παρέχειν
οἷς μή ἐστιν ἀνάγκη—ὅτι ‖ γὰρ οἱ ἡγούμενοι πλεονάκις ἐκέ|- 80
λευσαν μὴ ἄλλοις παρέχεσθαι ξε|νίαν εἰ μὴ τοῖς ὑπὸ τῶν
ἡγουμέ|νων καὶ ἐπιτρόπων πεμ|πομένοις εἰς ὑπηρεσίαν, ἐάν τε ‖
βαρ[ώ]μεθα, φευξόμεθα ἀπὸ τῶν | οἰκείων καὶ μεγίστην ζημίαν τὸ | 85
ταμεῖον περιβληθήσεται—ἵνα | ἐλεηθέντες διὰ τὴν θείαν σου |
πρόνοιαν καὶ μείνα(ντε)ς ἐν ‖ τοῖς ἰδίοις τούς τε ἱεροὺς φόρους | 90
καὶ τὰ λοιπὰ τελέσματα παρέχειν | δυνησόμεθα· συμβήσεται
δὲ | τοῦτο ἡμεῖν ἐν τοῖς εὐτυχεστά|τοις σου καιροῖς, ἐὰν κελεύ-
σῃς ‖ τὰ θεῖά σου γράμματα ἐν στή|λῃ ἀναγραφέντα δημοσίᾳ 95
π(ρ)ο|κεῖσθαι, ἵνα τούτου τυχόντες | τῇ τύχῃ σου χάριν ὁμο-
λογεῖν | δυνησόμεθα, ὡς καὶ νῦν κα...‖ώμενοι σοῦ ποιούμεν. | 100

Διογένης ὁ Τύριος ὁ π[ραγμα|τικὸς] ἀπὸ θείας φιλανθρω|πίας   III
ἐπὶ τὴν ἔντευξιν ταύ|την ἐλήλυθεν· δοκεῖ δέ ‖ μοι θεῶν τις   105
προνοήσασθαι | τῆς παρούσης ἀξιώσεως· | τὸ γὰρ τὸν θειότατον
αὐτο|κράτορα περὶ τούτων πέμ|ψαι τὴν ἰδίαν γνῶσιν ἐπὶ ‖ σέ,   110
δ[ν] ἤδε[ι] ἤ[δ]η φθάσαντα | περὶ τούτου καὶ προγράμ|μασιν
καὶ διατάγμασιν | δεδωκέναι, τοῦτο ἐμοὶ δο|κεῖ τῆς ἀγαθῆς
τύχης ἔργον ‖ εἶναι. Ἡ(ν) δὲ ἡ ἀξίωσις· ἡ κώ|μη ἡ τοῦ βοηθου-   115
μένου στρα|τιώτου ἐσ[τὶν] ἐν τῷ καλλί|στῳ τῆς πολειτίας τῆς
ἡμε|τέρας τῶν Πανταλιωτῶν ‖ κειμένη, καλῶς μὲν τῶν ὁρῶν | 120
καὶ τῶν πεδίων ἔχουσα, | πρὸς δὲ τούτοις καὶ θερ|μῶν ὑδάτων
λουτρὰ οὐ μό|νον πρὸς τρυφὴν ἀλλὰ καὶ ‖ ὑγείαν καὶ θεραπείαν | 125
σωμάτων ἐπιτηδειότατα, | πλησίον δὲ καὶ πανήγυρις | πολλάκις
μὲν ἐν τῷ ἔτει | συναγομένη, περὶ δὲ [κ]α[λ]. ‖ Ὀκτωμβρίας   130
καὶ εἰς πεντε|καίδεκα ἡμερῶν ἀτ[έλειαν]· | συμβέβηκεν τοίνυν τὰ
δοκοῦν|τα τῆς κώμης ταύτης πλεον|εκτήματα τῷ χρόνῳ περι‖-
εληλυθέναι αὐτῆς εἰς ἐλ[ατ|τ]ώματα· διὰ γὰρ τὰς | προειρημένας   135
ταύτας | προφάσεις πολλοὶ πολλά|κις στρατιῶται ἐνεπιδη‖-
μοῦντες ταῖς τε ἐπιξενώ|σεσι καὶ ταῖς βαρήσεσιν | ἐνοχλοῦσι   140
τὴν κώμην· | διὰ ταύτας τὰς αἰτίας πρό|τερον αὐτὴν καὶ πλου-
σιο‖τέραν καὶ πολυάνθρωπον | [μᾶλλον] οὖσαν νῦν εἰς ἐσχά|την   145
ἀπορίαν ἐληλυθέναι. | Ἐπεὶ τούτων ἐδεήθη|σαν πολλάκις καὶ
τῶν ἡγου‖μένων, ἀλλὰ καὶ μέχρις τι|νὸς ἴσχυσεν αὐτῶν τὰ | 150
προστάγματα, μετὰ δὲ | ταῦτα κατωλιγορήθη | διὰ τὴν συνήθειαν
τῆς ‖ τοιαύτης ἐνοχλήσεως· | διὰ τοῦτο ἀναγκαίως κατ|έφυγον ἐπὶ   155
τὸν θειότατον | [αὐτοκράτορα..

[469]

MUNICIPAL DOCUMENTS IN GREEK AND LATIN

IV   Imp. Caesar M. Antonius Gordianu*s Pius* Felix Au*g. vi*kanis
*p*er Pyrrum mil(item) con*p*osses|sorem: id genus qu*ae*rellae prae-
cibus intentum an*te* iustitia pr*ae*s*i*dis | *p*oti*us s*uper his quae adlega-
buntur instructa discin*ge qu*am rescripto principali | certam formam
reportare debeas. Rescripsi. Recognovi. Signa.

From Scaptopara in Thrace. The village was within the territory
of the city Pataulia. The residents of Scaptopara had frequently
complained to the governors of Thrace of the exactions made by
soldiers, visitors, and especially officials of the province who demanded the right of being entertained at the expense of the community, although an imperial edict had exempted them from the
liturgy of *hospitium*, or of furnishing supplies except on a requisition
from the governor or procurator. This edict had been respected for
a time, but the exactions had been renewed; the residents of Scaptopara had been reduced from affluence to poverty, and now threaten
to abandon their property with consequent loss to the imperial
treasury. After appealing in vain to the provincial authorities, the
villagers presented their petition direct to the emperor through one
of their number, Pyrrhus, who is also called a member of the
praetorian cohort. He was probably a veteran who, on his discharge,
had taken up his residence in this village. The emperor replied that
petitions of this kind should be directed to the provincial governor,
and Pyrrhus was sent back to this official with a copy of the petition
and a recommendation to the governor that he enforce the edicts
(ll. 110 *ff.*). The action taken by the authorities is indicated in the
statement of Diogenes, although the villagers did not take the trouble
to engrave the whole of his letter upon the stone. It is therefore
impossible to determine the nature of the remedies promised, but
the answer must have been satisfactory or it would not have been
engraved on stone.

The position held by Diogenes is uncertain. The editors of the
inscription have restored π[ραγματικός] in l. 101 but it is also
possible to restore π[ραγματευτής], which is a Greek rendering of
the Latin *actor* (Ramsay, *Cities and Bishoprics*, 1, 281). The term
π[ραγματικός] is extremely rare in Greek inscriptions, and is
found only in Magnesia where the magistracy was apparently important (Kern, *Inschriften von Magnesia*, 189). Diogenes, however,

[470]

was a Tyrian and probably an imperial freedman in charge of the imperial estates in Thrace. If we restore π[ραγματευτής] as the title of Diogenes, we must assume that Scaptopara formed part of an imperial property within the territory of Pataulia. *Cf.* no. 90 where the estates of Hipparchus had been confiscated by the emperor and held for a time before being sold. Thus imperial estates might exist even within the territory of a free city. It is evident that the Pataulians were not concerned in the petition in any way, and Scaptopara acted on its own initiative without reference to the municipal authorities within whose territory the village lay. On the other hand the villagers do not call themselves tenants of the emperor, but property-owners in their own right, and Pyrrhus is styled as a *conpossessor*. It is possible that the imperial estates in Thrace were organized on a different basis from those in other parts of the empire. In l. 116 Scaptopara is called the village of the soldier Pyrrhus and it is possible that he held some sort of a grant as a reward for his military service. In ll. 10 and 86 the villagers call attention to the peril of the imperial *fiscus* which was threatened if further exactions were permitted. In this respect the complaint is similar to the petitions from Asia which clearly come from imperial estates (*cf.* nos. 113, 141–144, Bruns, 93). In ll. 3 *ff.* of the petition the villagers appeal to the emperors recalling their great concern in the depopulation and desertion of village-communities which they had already observed and had attempted to remedy by their edicts. For the interpretation of the terms *rescripsi, recognovi*, see pp. 242 *ff.*

Rostovtseff has recently put forward a new and interesting theory concerning the policy of the imperial government in the third century towards the municipalities and villages of the empire (*Mus. Belge*, 27 (1923), 233 *ff.*). In his opinion the reigns of Commodus and Septimius Severus marked a struggle, not between the imperial power and the senate, but between the army and the wealthier classes in the municipalities. The edict of Caracalla aimed at a political and social levelling of the classes. The emperor Maximinus, chosen by the soldiers, acted as their representative in systematically persecuting the privileged classes especially in the municipalities, and the counter-revolution provoked in Africa was led by the proprietors or wealthy residents of the towns. The army and the military emperors had one aim—the levelling, politically, socially, economically, and intellectually, of the privileged classes. One of the prime factors in this policy was the change in the character of the army at the end of the second century. The citizen-soldiery had disappeared, and the army was composed largely of peasants drawn from provinces least Romanized or Hellenized, and the troops were conscripted largely from the most warlike and least civilized classes.

The peasants resident in the country villages (*pagani*) were usually despised by the urban population and regarded, not as members of the body politic, but as subjects to be exploited. In the second century the emperors sought to create a sturdy class of peasantry in order to strengthen the dying municipalities. They only succeeded in intensifying the antagonism of town and country and in making the peasant realize his importance, for he now regarded the emperor as his protector against the urban population. Moreover the peasant now had the army to enforce his will.

Rostovtseff finds proof of his argument in the number of petitions addressed by villagers direct to the emperor instead of to the provincial governor. Almost all of these complaints are directed against the system of requisitions and contain accusations charging the governors with indifference to the interests of the people. Finally, most of the appeals were transmitted by soldiers.

While the author promises fuller proof of his theory in a forthcoming work, the evidence seems to contradict the main points of his argument. In the third century most, if not all, complaints of this character come from tenants on imperial estates, not from municipal villages, and are directed for the most part against the very soldiers who are supposed to have the interests of the peasants at heart. Besides the soldiers, the chief offenders are the imperial agents who might naturally be supposed to represent the policy of the government in their treatment of the provincials. In view of the fact that the provincial governors were powerless to control the undisciplined bands of soldiers scattered throughout their district, the tenants on imperial estates would naturally direct their appeals to the emperor when they found that the governors were powerless or incompetent, or even conniving with other imperial agents in illegal acts.

While we would agree with Rostovtseff in his claim that the army and military leaders exploited the wealthier classes, we believe that this was done through no higher motive than the need of raising money to replenish an exhausted treasury and to support a greedy and clamorous army. There does not seem to be any evidence for the theory that the army or the emperors were concerned in the elevation of the peasantry as a means of supporting the city or infusing new strength into the municipalities. The foundations in the early part of the second century were devoted to checking the decline in native stock, but the charitable endowments were neither far-reaching nor widely extended geographically, and most of them must have been dissipated as a result of the depreciation of money and the ravages of civil wars. In the third century the records of legislative achievement have disappeared for the most part, but the general tendency of the peasant class was not in the direction of social or economic regeneration but rather downward, for the agricultural laborer appears in the legislation of Constantine bound by laws which regard him as a virtual serf. To attribute to the peasants of the empire any stirring of class-consciousness is anachronistic.

140. TITULUS HONORARIUS
(238 p. Chr.)

CIL. XIII, 3162; Desjardins, *Géographie de la Gaule romaine,* 3, planches VII, VIII, IX.

I

T(ito) Sennio Sollemni, Sollem|nini fil(io), duumvir(o)...| (*deficiunt tres versus*) | ...genus spec|taculorum...gladia|...quibus per qua|...mission...| (*deficiunt tres versus*) Cons...| in perp... staur...Sollemnis, ‖ amicus Tib(erii) Claud(ii) Paulin(i), leg(ati) 15 Aug(usti) pro pr(aetore) pro|vinc(iae) Lugd(unensis) et cliens fuit; cui, postea, | *l*eg(ato) Aug(usti) pr(opraetore) in Britan(nia), ad legionem sex(tam) | adsedit, *q*uique et salarium militiae | *i*n auro aliaque munera longe pluris miss*it*. ‖ Fuit cliens probatissimus 20 Aedini*i* Iuliani, | leg(ati) Aug(usti) prov(inciae) Lugd(unensis), qui postea praef(ectus) praet(orio) | fuit, sicut epistula, quae ad latus

scripta est, | declaratur; adsedit etiam, in provincia Num(idia) |
Lambense, M(arco) Valerio Floro, trib(uno) mil(itum) leg(ionis)
25 tertiae Aug(ustae), || iudici arcae ferrar(iarum). | TRES PROVINCIAE
GALLIAE | primo umquam, in sua civitate, posuerunt. | Locum ordo
civitatis Viducass(ium) liber(ae) d(e)d(it). | P(ositum) decimum
30 septimum k(alendas) Ian(uarias), Pio et Proculo || co(n)s(ulibus). |

II

*E*xemplum epistulae Cl(audii) | *P*aulini, leg(ati) Aug(usti)
pr(o)pr(aetore) prov(inciae) | *B*ritanniae, ad Sennium Sol*lem*|nem,
5 —a Tampio. || "Licet plura merenti, tibi, h*aec*, | a me, pauca tamen,
quonia*m* | honoris causa offeruntu*r*, | velim accipias libente*r*: |
10 chlamidem Canusinam, || dalmaticam Laodiceam, fibulam | *au*ream,
cum gemmis, rachanas | duas, tossiam Brit(annicam), pellem vit*uli* |
*m*arini.—Semestris autem epistulam, | ubi propediem vacare coe-
15 per*im*, || mittam, cuius militiae salarium, | *i*d est; sestertium viginti
quinque millia n(ummum), in auro, suscipe. | *D*is faventibus et
maiestate sancta | *i*mp(eratoris), deinceps, pro meritis | *a*dfectionis
20 magis digna || consecuturus. Concordia." |

III

*E*xemplum epistul(ae) Aedin*ii* | Iuliani, praefecti praet(orio), |
ad Badium Comnianum, pro|cur(atorem) et vice⟨s⟩ praesidis agen-
5 t(em). || "Aedinius Iulianus, Badio | Comniano, sa(lutem).—In
provincia | Lugduness(i), quinque fascal(ia) | cum agerem, pleros-
10 q(ue) bonos | viros perspexi, inter quos || Sollemnem istum, oriun-
dum | ex civitate Viduc(assium), sacerdotem, | quem, propter
sectam, gravitat(em) | et honestos mores, amare coep*i*. | His accedit
15 quod, cum Cl(audio) Paulin*o*, || decessori meo, in Concilio | Gal-
liarum, instinctu quorund*am*, | qui, ab eo, propter merita sua, lae*di* |
videbantur, quasi ex consensu provin*c*(iae), | accussationem instituere
20 tentar*ent*, || Sollemnis iste meus proposito eor*um* | restitit, provo-
catione scilicet interpo|sita, quod patria eius, cum, inter ce*teros*, |
legatum eum creasset, nihil de accussa|*t*ione mandassent, immo,
25 contra, laudass*e*||nt; qua ratione effectum est ut o*mnes* | ab accussa-
tione desisterent: que*m* | magis, magisque amare et compro*bare* |
coepi. Is, certus honoris mei er*ga* | se, ad videndum me, in Urbem
30 venit. || Proficiscens, petit ut eum tibi *com*|memdarem: recte itaque
feceris, s*i* | d*eside*rio illius adnueris. . .—et r(eliqua). . ." |

FROM ITALY AND THE PROVINCES

Found in the sixteenth century at Vieux in Normandy, on the site of Araegenuae, the chief village of the Viducasses. The stone was transported to Thorigny, where it remained for many years, and the document is commonly known as the inscription of Thorigny. It is cut on three sides of a block of marble which formed the pedestal of a statue. On the front of the monument there is a record (styled I here), somewhat fragmentary, of the offices and benefactions of Sollemnis, of his relations with distinguished men, of the action of the three provinces, Lugdunensis, Aquitania, and Belgica, in authorizing the statue and of the Viducasses in providing a place for it, and the date. The right hand side (II) contains a copy of a letter to Sollemnis from Claudius Paulinus, propraetor of Britain, written at an unknown place, Tampium, mentioning certain gifts which Paulinus makes to Sollemnis. On the left side of the pedestal (III) there is a copy of a letter from Aedinius Julianus, praetorian prefect, to Badius Comnianus, procurator, and therefore the interim governor of Lugdunensis, recommending Sollemnis to the good offices of Comnianus particularly because of a service which Sollemnis had rendered Paulinus at a meeting of the assembly of the Gauls. Aedinius Julianus was praetorian prefect about A.D. 235. This fact dates his letter as probably between A.D. 235 and 238. He had been governor of Lugdunensis about 230. His immediate predecessor in this province had been Cl. Paulinus, who, at the time of writing the letter on the left side, was propraetor of Britain. Therefore, after being governor of Lugdunensis and before receiving the post in Britain, he must have been consul, since the governorship of Britain was a consular office (Marquardt, *St. Verw.* 1, 287). According to *CIL.* VII, 1045, he was probably in Britain about 232 (Desjardins, *op. cit.* 3, 204, n. 1), and the stormy scene in the *concilium* at Lugdunum occurred three years or more before this date. He is one of the *patroni* in the album of Canusium (no. 136). Sollemnis was *sacerdos Romae et Augusti* at Lugdunum, the place of meeting of the *concilium*, but the statue was set up in his native village. All the cities of the three provinces, fifty-seven in number at the beginning of the empire (Carette, *Les assemblées prov. de la Gaule rom.* 119 *ff.*), had the right to send deputies. From the expression *cum inter ceteros legatum eum creasset*, it may be

[475]

MUNICIPAL DOCUMENTS IN GREEK AND LATIN

inferred with some probability that certain cities had more than one deputy. This *concilium* could evidently inquire into the conduct of a governor, and draw up an accusation against him. We have no other epigraphical record of the exercise of such power by a *concilium* unless indirect reference is made to it in no. 161. However, Tacitus and other writers mention nineteen cases in which such charges were made by *concilia* (Guiraud, *Les assemblées prov.* 173 *f.*). Several inscriptions mention resolutions passed in honor of a retiring governor (*cf. CIL.* III, 1412; X, 1430–1432). For another possible instance of the exercise of important political functions by a Gallic *concilium*, *cf.* no. 50. Probably *ex consensu provinciae* (III, 18) means the same as *universi censuerunt* (*CIL.* II, 4248). This conclusion seems to be confirmed by the addition of *quasi* here (*cf.* Guiraud, *op. cit.* 109). On the legal meaning of *consensus*, *cf.* Leonhard, *R.E.* 4, 906. The deputies would seem in some cases to have come with instructions from their native cities; *cf. nihil mandassent*, III, 23–24. For the use of *et reliqua* at the end, *cf. Hist. Aug. Firmi*, 5.

141. RESCRIPTUM IMPERATORUM DE QUERELLIS ARAGUENORUM
(244–247 p. Chr.)

Ditt. *Or. Gr.* 519; Cagnat, *IGRR.* 4, 598; *Röm. Mitth.* 13 (1898), 231 *ff.*; Riccobono, p. 373; Bruns, 93; *CIL.* III, *S.* 14191; Girard, p. 207.

Ἀγαθῆι τύχηι |

Imp(erator) Caes(ar) M. *Iul(ius)* Phil*ippus* *Aug(ustus)* et M. *Iul(ius) Philippu*s nobi*l*issimus Caes(ar) M. Au*relio Eglecto* | pe(r) Didymum miugenerum. Proco*n*sule v. c. perspecta fide eorum quae *scribis, ne* | quid iniuriose geratur, ad sollicitudinem suam revocabit.

5 xa. || Αὐτοκράτορι Καίσαρι Μ(άρκωι) Ἰουλίωι Φιλίππωι Εὐσεβεῖ Εὐτυχεῖ Σεβ(αστῶι) κ[αὶ Μ(άρκωι) Ἰουλίωι] | Φιλίππωι ἐπιφανεστάτωι Καίσαρι δέησις παρὰ Αὐρηλίου Ἐγλέκτ[ου ὑπὲρ τοῦ κοι]||νοῦ τῶν Ἀραγουηνῶν παροίκων καὶ γεωργῶν τῶν ὑμετέρων, [πρεσβείας γενομένης δαπ]||άνηι δήμου κοινο(ῦ Τ)ο[τ]τεανῶν Σοηνῶν τῶν κατὰ Φρυγίαν τόπων διὰ Τ(ίτου) Οὐ[ινίου Διδύμου] | στρατιώτου.—Πάντων ἐν τοῖς μακαριωτάτοις ὑμῶν 10 καιροῖς, εὐσεβέσ[τατοι καὶ ἀλυ]||πότατοι τῶν πώποτε βασιλέων,

[476]

ἤρεμον καὶ γαληνὸν τὸν βίον δια[γόντων, πο]‖νηρίας καὶ δια-
σεισμῶν πε[π]αυμένων, μόνοι ἡμεῖς ἀλλότρια τ[ῶ]ν ε[ὐτυχεστά-
των] | καιρῶν πάσχοντες τήνδε τὴν ἱκετεί[αν ὑ]μεῖν προσάγομεν
ἐχέ[γγυοι τοῦ δικαίου τῆς δε]‖ήσεως ἐν τούτοις.

Χωρίον ὑμέτερόν ἐσμεν ἱερώτατ[ον καὶ ὡσπερεὶ δὴ]‖μος ὁλό-
κληρος, οἱ καταφεύγοντες καὶ γενόμενοι τῆς ὑμετέρας [θειότητος
ἱκέται, δια]‖σειόμεθα δὲ παρὰ τὸ ἄλογον καὶ παραπρασσόμεθα 15
ὑπ᾽ ἐκείνων ο[ὓς ἥκιστα ἀδικεῖν τὸν πλη]‖σίον ὀφ(ε)ίλει.—
Μεσόγειοι γὰρ τυγχάνοντες καὶ μ(ή)τε παρὰ στρατά[ρχου μήτε
παρ᾽ ἄλλου κακὰ παθόντες νῦν πάσ]‖χομεν ἀλλότρια τῶν
ὑμετέρων μακαριωτάτων καιρῶν· [πιέζουσι γὰρ ἡμᾶς οἱ διοδεύ-
οντες] | τὸ Ἀππιανῶν κλίμα παραλιμπάνοντες τὰς λεωφόρους
ὁ[δοὺς στρατάρχαι τε καὶ στρατ]‖ιῶται καὶ δυνάσται τῶν
προυχόντων κ[ατ]ὰ τὴν πόλιν [Καισαριανοί τε ὑ]‖μέτεροι ἐπεισ- 20
ε[ρ]χόμενοι καταλιμπάνοντες τὰς λε[ωφόρους ὁδοὺς καὶ ἀπὸ
τῶν] | ἔργων ἡμᾶς ἀφιστάντες καὶ τοὺς ἀροτῆρας βόας ἀνγ[α-
ρεύοντες τὰ μὴ ὀφει]‖λόμενα αὐτοῖς παραπράσσουσιν, καὶ συν-
βαίνει ο[ὐ τὰ τυχόντα ἡμᾶς ἐκ τ]‖ούτου ἀδικεῖσθαι διασειομένους·
περὶ ὧν ἀπά[ντων ἐγράφη πρὸς τὸ σόν,] | Σεβαστέ, μέγεθος, ὁπότε
τὴν ἔπαρχον διεῖπε[ν ἐξουσίαν . . . .]‖νος, καὶ ὅπως περὶ 25
τούτων ἐκειν(ή)θη σοῦ ἡ θε[ιότης, ἡ ἀντιγραφὴ δηλοῖ ἡ ἐνταῦθα] |
ἐντεταγμένη· Quae libello complexi estis *ut examinet praesidi
mandavi,* | qui da(b)it operam ne di*u*tiuis querell*i*s *locus sit.* |
Ἐπειδὴ οὖν οὐδὲν ὄφελο[ς ἡ]μεῖν ἐκ ταύτης τῆ[ς ἀντιγραφῆς
ἐγένετο, συμβέ]‖βηκεν δὲ ἡμᾶς κατὰ τὴν ἀγροικίαν τὰ μὴ ὀφει-
[λόμενα παραπράσσεσθαι, ἐ]‖πενβαινό[ν]των τινῶν καὶ συμπα- 30
τούντων ἡμᾶς [παρὰ τὸ δίκαιον, ἐπειδὴ δ]ὲ ὑπὸ τῶν Καισαριανῶν
οὐ τὰ τυχόντα δι[ασ]είεσ[θαι ἡμᾶς συνέβη καὶ τὰ ἡμέτερα |
ἐξαναλί]σκεσθαι καὶ τὰ χωρία ἐρημοῦσθαι καὶ . . αν . . . .
. . | . . . . . ς καὶ οὐ παρὰ τ[ὴν ὁ]δὸν κατοικούντ[ων . . . . |
. . . .] δυνάμενα . . . . ταυτι . . ει . . . .

From Aragua, a village on one of the imperial estates in Phrygia.
The tenants in this community were too poor to send an embassy
to the emperor, but the expenses of the delegation were borne by
the κοινόν, apparently a union of the villages on the estate in a
quasi-municipal organization. Aurelius Eclectus was probably
magister vici of Aragua, who acts as spokesman for the community.

MUNICIPAL DOCUMENTS IN GREEK AND LATIN

Didymus was the ambassador sent to Rome. The title *miugenerum* (l. 2) may stand for *mili(tem) (f)rum(entarium)*, although this interpretation is rejected by Dittenberger. The complaint of the Aragueni is similar to that of other villages in the third century (*cf.* nos. 113, 139, 142–144). They suffered from the exactions of soldiers and public officials, here especially the Caesariani (*cf. R.E. s.v.*), who demanded the services of the villagers and their oxen for transport duty (Rostowzew, *Klio*, 6 (1906), 249 *ff.*). The villagers had appealed once before to the emperors, and their complaint had been referred to the provincial governor with instructions to remedy the matter. Apparently the latter was powerless to curb the licence of the imperial officials and soldiery, or he may have connived at their exactions. At any rate, it may be observed that the bureaucratic officials and soldiery could not be effectively controlled at this period either by imperial mandates or by provincial governors. *Cf.* pp. 15 *ff.*; *J.H.S.* 17 (1897), 417 *ff.*; 18 (1898), 340 *ff.*; *Röm. Mitth.* 13 (1898), 231 *ff.*; Rostowzew, *Gesch. d. röm. Kol.* 303 *f.*; *Klio*, 6 (1906), 249 *ff.*; *Mus. Belge*, 27 (1923), 233 *ff.*

142. EPISTULA COLONORUM AD IMPERATORES
(ca. 200–250 p. Chr.)

Keil and Premerstein, *Denkschriften der Wiener Akademie*, 57 (1914–15), 37 *f*.

...ντας ἰδεῖν κατὰ δίοδον τὴν ω.........οι....|..ντος καὶ
ἵνα δόξῃ τις τῆς τοιαύτης αὐτοῖς θ[ρα|σύτ]ητος ἀπολογία κατα-
λιμπάνεσθαι, ἐνέα σ[υλ|λαβό]ντες καὶ ἐν δεσμοῖς ποιήσαντες
5 ἔφασκ[ον ‖ παραπ]έμπειν ἐπὶ τοὺς κρατίστους ἐπιτρόπο[υς |
τοὺς ὑμ]ετέρους διέποντ(ο)ς Αἰλίου Ἀγλαοῦ [τοῦ | κρατίσ]του
καὶ τὰ τῆς ἀνθυπατείας μέρη· κα[ὶ | τὸ]ν μὲν ἕνα τῶν ἐννέα ἀρ-
10 γύριον ἐκπρα|[ξ]άμενοι ὑπὲρ τὰς χειλίας Ἀττικὰς λύτρον ‖ [τ]ῆς
σωτηρίας ἀφῆκαν, τοὺς δὲ λοιποὺς κατ[έ]|σχαν ἐν τοῖς δεσμοῖς,
καὶ οὐκ ἴσμεν σαφῶς, | θειότατοι τῶν αὐτοκρατόρων, ὁπότερον
ζῶν|τας τούτους παραπέμψουσιν παρὰ τ(ὸ)ν κράτισ|τον Ἀγλαὸν
15 ⟨ἢ⟩ καὶ αὐτοὺς διαθῶνται παραπλήσι‖ον τοῖς φθάνουσιν. Ἡμε[ῖ]ς
οὖν, ὅπερ ἦν δυνατὸν | ἀθλίοις ἀν[θ]ρώποις ἀφῃρημένοις καὶ
βίου καὶ | συνγενῶν οὕτως ὠμῶς, ὃ δυνατὸν ἡμεῖν ἦν, ἐ|δηλώ-

[478]

σαμεν ταῦτα καὶ τῶ τῆς τάξεως ἐπιτρό|πω ὑμῶν Αὐ[ρ(ηλίω)]
Μαρκιανῶ καὶ τοῖς ἐν 'Ασία κρατ[ίσ]||τοις ἐπιτρόποις ὑμῶν· 20
ἱκέται δὲ τῆς ὑμετέ|ρας γεινόμεθα, θειότατοι τῶν πώποτε αὐτο-
κρα|[τ]όρων, θείας καὶ ἀνυπερβλήτου βασιλείας, καὶ | [το]ῖς τῆς
γεωργίας καμάτοις προσέχειν κεκωλυ|[μ]ένοι τῶν κολλητιώνων
καὶ τῶν ἀντικαθεστώ||των ἀπειλούντων καὶ ἡμεῖν τοῖς καταλει- 25
πομέ|νοις τὸν περὶ ψυχῆς κίνδυνον καὶ μὴ δυνάμενοι⟨ς⟩ | ἐκ τοῦ
κωλύεσθαι τὴν γῆν ἐργάζεσθαι μηδὲ ταῖς δε|[σ]ποτικαῖς ἐπα-
κούειν ἀποφοραῖς καὶ ψήφοις πρὸς | [τ]ὰ ἑξῆς, καὶ δεόμεθα
εὐμενῆ (sic) ὑμᾶς προσέσθαι τὴν || δέησιν ἡμῶν καὶ ἐπιθέσθαι τῶ 30
ἐξηγουμένω τοῦ | ἔθνους καὶ τοῖς κρατίστοις ἐπιτρόποις ὑμῶν
ἐκ|δικῆσαι τὸ τετολμημένον, κωλῦσαι δὲ τὴν εἰς τὰ | χωρία τὰ
δεσποτικὰ ἔφοδον καὶ τὴν εἰς ἡμᾶς ἐν[ό]|χλησιν γεινομένην ὑπό
(τ)ε τῶν κολλητιώνων || καὶ τῶν ἐπὶ προφάσει ἀρχῶν ἢ λειτουρ- 35
γιῶν τοὺς ὑ|μετέρους ἐνοχλούντων καὶ σκυλλόντων (sic) γεω[ρ]|-
γοὺς τῶ πάντα τὰ ἡμέτερα ἐκ προγόνων προυπε[ύ]|θυνα εἶναι τῶ
ἱερωτάτω ταμείω τῶ τῆς γεωργί[ας] | δικαίω· τἀληθῆ γὰρ πρὸς
τὴν ὑμετέραν θειότητα || ἤρηται (sic). ('Ω)ν ἐὰν μὴ ὑπὸ τῆς ὑμε- 40
τέρας οὐρανίου δε|ξιᾶς ἐκδικία τις ἐπὶ τοῖς τοσούτοις τετολμη-
μέ|νοις ἐπαχθῆ καὶ βοήθια εἰς τὰ μέλλοντα, ἀνάγ|κη τοὺς
καταλελειμμένους ἡμᾶς, μὴ φέροντας | τὴν τῶν κολλητιώνων καὶ
τῶν ἐναντιας (sic), ἐφ' αἷς || προειρήκαμεν προφάσεσιν, πλεονεξίαν, 45
κατα|λείπειν καὶ ἑστίας πατρώας καὶ τάφους προγονικο[ὺ]ς |
μετελθεῖν τε εἰς ἰδιωτικὴν γῆν πρὸς τὸ διασωθῆναι— | φείδονται
γὰρ μᾶλλον τῶν ἐκεῖ κατοικούντων οἱ τὸ[ν] | πονηρὸν ζῶντες
βίον ἢ τῶν ὑμετέρων γεωργῶν— || φυγάδας ⟨τε⟩ γενέσθαι τῶν 50
δεσποτικῶν χωρίων, ἐν οἷς | (κ)αὶ ἐγεννήθημεν καὶ ἐτράφημεν
καὶ ἐκ προγόνων | διαμένοντες γεωργοὶ τὰς πίστεις τηροῦμεν τῶ |
δεσποτικῶ λόγω.

This inscription comes from the modern village, Aga Bey, in
the province of Lydia. It contains the complaint of the villagers
on an imperial estate protesting against the exactions of imperial
officials and municipal magistrates. The first part of the petition is
lost, but it is apparent that the immediate cause of complaint was
the arrest of nine of the tenants by officers who claimed to be acting
under the authority of the procurator. One of the nine had been
released under a heavy ransom, but the fate of the remainder could

MUNICIPAL DOCUMENTS IN GREEK AND LATIN

not be ascertained, and an appeal to Aurelius Marcianus had been ineffectual. The petitioners now set forth the fact that they had been tenants on the imperial estate on hereditary leasehold (ll. 38, 47, 51 *ff.*): that they were oppressed by *collationes* (*cf.* Garroni, *Accademia dei Lincei*, 25 (1916), 66 *ff.*) and by municipal magistrates who sought to compel them to perform liturgies and to hold office in the neighboring cities. Apparently residents of the cities had sought to escape their municipal obligations by taking up leases on the imperial estates (*cf.* Ramsay, *Studies in the History and Art o the Eastern Provinces*, 356 *ff.*; Rostowzew, *Gesch. d. röm. Kol.* 229, 398 *ff.*). Such tenants were exempt from municipal charges (*Dig.* 50. 6. 6, 11), but this method of evasion had become so common in the fourth century that Constantine issued an edict forbidding *curiales* the right to hold leases on imperial estates except under very strict regulation (*Cod. Th.* 12. 1. 33). The petitioners also threaten to abandon the imperial leaseholds and to take refuge on private estates, where, they claim, the villainous officials do less harm. This document is most important as it reveals the flight from the cities; the oppression of officials even on tenants of the imperial estates; and, finally, the power of patronage exerted by great land-owners at this time, who were able to protect their tenants where the emperor could not. *Cf.* pp. 214 *f.*, nos. 113, 139, 141, 143, 144; *Zeitschr. der Savigny-Stift., Roman. Abtheil.* 36 (1915), 157 *ff.* The editors of this document are inclined to limit its date between A.D. 198–222.

143. EPISTULA VICANORUM AD IMPERATORES
(ca. 200–250 p. Chr.)

Keil and Premerstein, *Denkschriften der Wiener Akademie*, 57 (1914), 25.

.... [τη]ν προαίρεσιν αὐτῶν λογιζομένων ν[ομοθε|σίαν (?)]
μήτε νομίμου κατηγόρου τινὸς ἐξιστ[αμέ|νου, μ]ήτε ὑποκειμένης
αἰτίας, μηδὲ φανεροῦ τι[νος ἐγ|κλήματ]ος ἰδίου τινὸς ὄντος,
5 ἐπιτρέχουσιν οἱ τοιοῦτοι μόν[οι ἢ μετὰ τῶν (?) ‖ σεσημ]ειομένων
τάξεων ἰς διασεισμὸν τῆς κώμης· μόνη[ν ἐν φ]όβῳ τῷ[δε ταύ|την
βο]ήθιαν ἐπενόησεν ἡ προδηλουμένη κώμη συν[δε|ηθεῖ]σα δι'
ἐμοῦ τῆς μεγάλης ὑμῶν καὶ οὐρανίου κα[ὶ ἱερω|τάτη]ς βασιλείας,

ἰς τοῦτό με προχειρισαμένη καὶ τὴ[ν ἱκε|τεία]ν προσενενκεῖν.
Καὶ τοῦτο δεόμεθ' ἀπιδόντας ὑμ[ᾶς, μέ‖γιστ]οι καὶ θειότατοι τῶν   10
πώποτε αὐτοκρατόρων, πρός τε τοὺ[ς | ὑμετέ]ρους νόμους τῶν τε
προγόνων ὑμῶν καὶ πρὸς τὴν εἰρηνικὴ[ν | ὑμῶ]ν περὶ πάντας δικαιο-
σύνην, μεισήσαντας δέ, οὓς ἀεὶ με[ι|σήσ]ατε αὐτοί τε καὶ πᾶν
τὸ τῆς βασιλείας προγονικὸν ὑμ[ῶν | γένο]ς, τοὺς τὴν τοιαύτην
προαίρεσιν ἔχοντας κολλητίωνα[ς, κε‖κωλ]υμένους μὲν ἀεὶ καὶ   15
κολάζεσθαι κελευομένους, οὐ[κ ἀπο|δεξα]μένους δέ, ἀλλὰ ἀεὶ
βαρύτερον ἀντιμαχομένου[ς | ταῖ]ς ὑμετέραις νομοθεσίαις, εἴτε
φρουμενταρίοις προμ[ε|μήνυν]το, εἴτε ὁμοίαις τάξεσιν, κελεῦσαι
καὶ χρηματίσαι νόμῳ τι[νί, | ὡς τὴν ἀν]αίδιαν αὐτῶν αὐτοῖς ⟨ἡ⟩
ἡγεμονεία προσάγει· εἰ δέ τις, ἔξω τῶ[ν ‖ τοι]ούτων λέγων εἶναι,   20
προφάσει κατηγορίας τινὸς ἐπὶ (ἐ)σκ[εμ|μένη]ν τὴν κακουργίαν
ἐπιτρέχοι, μὴ διὰ τῆς ἡγεμονίας, ἀ[λλὰ | διὰ τῶν] τάξεων
βασανίζων, ὡς οἱ νόμοι θέλουσιν ὑμῶν τ[ε καὶ | τῶν προγόνων
εἰ μὴ νόμιμος κατήγορος, μὴ προσέ[ρχων|ται πρὸς τοῦτο αἱ] τῆς
τάξεως ἐξουσίαι καὶ........

This inscription comes from Mendechora (Πέντε χωρία) in
Lydia. The editors (*loc. cit.*) believe that this village lay within the
territorium of, and belonged to, the ancient city of Philadelphia.
It is also possible that the village may have become part of an imperial estate before the petition was forwarded to the emperor, since
there is no reference to the city officials, and the appeal appears
to have been presented by someone designated by the village (*cf.*
Rostovtseff, *Mus. Belge*, 27 (1923), 233 *ff.*). As in similar documents of this period the villagers protest against the exactions of
officials; the *collationes* (*cf.* no. 142), the *frumentarii*, and similar
agents (ὁμοίαις τάξεσιν). The villagers complain especially of
illegal arrests by officials, apparently, without lodging any formal
accusation (*cf.* no. 142). Such arrests were contrary to the law
(*Dig.* 48. 18. 22), but the village-authorities were powerless. On
the interpretation of the legal principles involved *cf.* Keil and
Premerstein, *loc. cit.*; Weiss, *Zeitschr. der Savigny-Stift., Roman.
Abteil.* 36 (1915), 157 *ff.*; Garroni, *Accademia dei Lincei*, 25 (1916),
66 *ff.*; Rostovtseff, *Jour. Rom. Studies*, 8 (1918), 26 *ff.*; *cf.* nos. 113,
139, 141–144.

MUNICIPAL DOCUMENTS IN GREEK AND LATIN

144. QUERELLAE VICANORUM
(ca. 200–250 p. Chr.)

Keil and Premerstein, *Denkschriften der Wiener Akademie*, 57 (1914–15), 11.

(*Versus* 1–9, 26 *seqq.*, *maxime mutili, omissi sunt.*)

10 εἰωθότω[ν] ταῖς [. . . . .? στατιωνα]‖ρίων [κ(αὶ)]
φρουμε[νταρίω]ν ων . . . . .φ. .| σιν αν. . . . .| νοι . . . .
15 . . . .| τ. . . . . .νχα. . . .‖ [ταῖς κ]ώμαις ἐπισείοντες
ἐνε. . . . .| ἀγαθοῦ μὲν οὐδενὸς γεινόμενοι αἴτι|οι, ἀνυποίστοις δὲ
φορτίοις κ(αὶ) ζημιώμα|σιν ἐνσείοντες τὴν κώμην, ὡς συμβαί|νειν
20 ἐξαναλουμένην αὐτὴν εἰς τὰ ἄμε‖τρα δαπανήματα τῶν ἐπι[δη]-
μούντων | κ(αὶ) ε[ἰς τ]ὸ πλῆθος τῶν κολλητιώνων ἀ|πο[στειρεῖ-
σθ(?)]α[ι] μὲν λουτροῦ δι' ἀπορίαν, | ἀποστειρεῖσ[θ]ε [δὲ κ(αὶ)]
τῶν πρὸς τὸν βί|ον ἀ[ν]ανκέ[ω]ν ἀ[π]α[γ]ο[ρ]ενε . . ε . . πρὸς ‖
25 τὰς . . . . .εκ . . . . . .ουμεν . . . | κατοίκων.

This fragmentary inscription was found in the modern village of Ekiskuju in Asia Minor. As in nos. 113, 142–143, the villagers are harassed by the exactions of officials, the *stationarii, frumentarii,* and others. Unbearable fines and burdens are imposed upon them, and the villagers have been ruined by the cost of entertaining officials and by *collationes.* The document seems to record the reply of the governor to the petition of the residents. The editors suggest that Aurelius Marinus, whose name appears in the first line of the inscription, is the provincial governor. For similar complaints, *cf.* nos. 113, 139, 141–143.

145. EPISTULA IMPERATORUM TRAIANI DECI ET HERENNI ETRUSCI AD APHRODISIENSES
(251 p. Chr.)

Le Bas-Waddington, 3, 1624; *CIG.* 2743.

Αὐτοκράτωρ Καῖσαρ [Γάιος Μέσσιος Κύιντος Τραιανὸς |
Δέκιος], Εὐσεβής, Εὐτυχής, Σεβαστός, δημαρχικῆς | ἐξουσίας
τὸ γ', ὕπατος τὸ β', ἀποδεδειγμένος τὸ τρίτον, | πατὴρ πατρίδος,
5 ἀνθύπατος, καὶ ['Ερέννιος Τραιανὸς ‖ Δέκιος Καῖσαρ], ἀρχιερεὺς
μέγιστος, δημαρχικῆς ἐξουσίας | τὸ πρῶτον, ὕπατος ἀποδεδειγ-
μένος, 'Αφροδεισιέων τοῖς | ἄρχουσιν καὶ τῆι βουλῆι καὶ τῶι

δήμωι χαίρειν. | Εἰκὸς ἦν ὑμᾶς καὶ διὰ τὴν ἐπώνυμον τῆς πόλεως
θεὸν καὶ | διὰ τὴν πρὸς ῾Ρωμαίους οἰκειότητά᾿τε καὶ πίστιν
ἠσθῆναι ‖ μὲν ἐπὶ τῆι καταστάσει τῆς βασιλείας τῆς ἡμετέρας, | 10
θυσίας δὲ καὶ εὐχὰς ἀποδοῦναι δικαίας. Καὶ ἡμεῖς δὲ | τήν τε
ἐλευθερίαν ὑμεῖν φυλάττομεν τὴν ὑπάρχουσαν | καὶ τὰ ἄλλα δὲ
σύνπαντα δίκαια, ὁπόσων παρὰ τῶν πρὸ ἡ|μῶν αὐτοκρατόρων
τετυχήκατε, συναύξειν ἑτοίμως ‖ ἔχοντες ὑμῶν καὶ τὰς πρὸς τὸ   15
μέλλον ἐλπίδας. | ᾿Επρέσβευον Αὐρήλιοι Θεόδωρος καὶ ᾿Ονήσι-
μος. | Εὐτυχεῖτε.

From Aphrodisias in Caria. The names of the emperors, erased
in antiquity, were restored by Boeckh as those of Diocletian and
Maximian. The difficulties of this restoration were pointed out
by Waddington, and we have followed the text which he adopted.
The title of *pontifex maximus*, ascribed to the son instead of the
father, is undoubtedly an error on the part of the stonecutter.
Aphrodisias is recorded as a free city by Pliny (*N.H.* 5. 29), and
retained this privilege as late as the reign of Gordian (Waddington,
note *ad loc.*). Reinach corrects the readings of Waddington (*Rev. d.
ét. grec.* 19 (1906), 82). *Cf.* nos. 137, 138, 153.

146. DECRETUM DECURIONUM ET POSSESSORUM
(256 vel fortasse 186 p. Chr.)

An. ép. 1903, no. 202; *cf. ibid.* 1894, no. 61.

. . . .*M.*' Acilio
Glabrione II cos. . .pr(idie). . .Ianuarias(?). . .*in civitate*. . .*in curia
cum conventus haberetur decurionum* et possessorum civium ibi Victor
Gallitios(i) f. et Honor*atus* | . . .*f(ilius) sufetes verba fecerunt: cum
audivissemus L. Titium et C. Sei*um questos quod agri suorum
pecoribus ovium devas|*tarentur et in re praesenti constitisset et agros
vastatos et arbores magnam part*em conrosas esse quod ipsum initium
honoris nostri | *instabat dominis pecorum ut servos iniuria prohibeant
denuntiavimus*. . . .i. . .sit facta etiam mentione sacrarum litte-
rarum ‖ . . .*illi responderunt servos sua sponte iniuriam fecisse*. . .   5
on. . .*n*ostramque denuntiationem initium honoris | *nostri ante-
cessisse*. . .*cum*. . .t ne. .eat eis contu. . .rum prodesse et aliter ea
res | . . .*et contra talem iniuriam iam pri*. . .ss. . .*undum sacras*

[483]

co...ones actum fuerit quae | ...*rem vestro decre*to *s*ubiciendam existimavi*mus.* | *Exemplum epistulae datae ab imp....ad.*.cum
10 mihi desiderium vestrum videtur et exemplo adiuva‖*ri anteriorum legum*...*et per se iustum esse. Itaque veto quemquam in agru*m vestrum invitis vobis pecora pascendi gratia indu|*cere*...re quod si ignorante domino servus induxe*rit* pecora | ...*in ip*sum servum procos. severe constituet si iusso domini | ....*induxerit non solum servum ipsum sed e*tiam praetium servi ex form*a* censoria ✕ d. dominus|....*praestare debebit. Servi si sciente quidem domino sed*
15 *s*ua sponte id admiserint a procos. flectentur ita ut in ‖ *posterum nemo audeat*...elegentur...quit fieri placeret de ea re universi cen|*suere* ...passim in territorio uniuscuiu*scum*que pecora pascendi | ...iniu et *c*um etiam post ea *con*stitut*i*one...nu....

Fragment found at Henchir-Snobbeur. The inscription has been restored and interpreted by Schulten, *Festschrift zu Hirschfeld*, 171 *ff.* It belongs perhaps to the year A.D. 256, when M.' Acilius Glabrio was consul. The use of *cognomina* in place of *nomina* in the names of the two magistrates, and the peregrine patronymic of Victor, show that the place was a peregrine *civitas*. Its magistrates would therefore be *sufetes*. It would appear that the flocks of certain residents of this village have been driven on the land of other citizens, and that the aggrieved citizens have laid the case before the local magistrates, who have forbidden further trespass. But the trespassers have persisted. In these circumstances the magistrates call a meeting of the decurions and *possessores* (l. 2). No parallel to such a meeting is known. The stone records the result. The *relatio* of the magistrates begins with *ibi*, and is given in the first person plural. It includes an imperial rescript beginning with *mihi desiderium* and ending with *ita ut...audeat*. The decree of the decurions, of which only a few words are left, begins with *quit fieri*. The ordinary price of a slave in Italy was 2500 denarii; *cf.* Kübler, *Festschrift f. Vahlen*, 561. The proconsul referred to is the proconsul of Africa Proconsularis, in whose territory the village lay. Our interest in the document lies in the fact that we find local magistrates, in settling a local legal question, applying a principle laid down in an imperial constitution drawn up for the guidance of a proconsul in a similar situation.

FROM ITALY AND THE PROVINCES

147. EDICTUM IMPERATORUM VALERIANI ET GALLIENI
(253–259 p. Chr.)

Le Bas-Waddington, 3, 2720*a*; Ditt. *Or. Gr.* 262; *CIG.* 4474.

Imp. Caesar | Publius Licin|nius Valerianus | Pius Felix Aug.   I
et imp. || Caesar Publius Licinius | Gallienus Pius Fel(ix) Aug. et   5
Licin|nius Cornelius Saloninus | Valerianus nobilissimus Caesar |
Aurelio Mareae *et* aliis: || Regum antiqua beneficia consuetu|dine   10
etiam insecuti temporis adpro|bata is qui provinciam regit remota |
violentia part*i*s adversae incolumia | vobis manere curabit.

         Ἐπιστολὴ Ἀντιόχου βασιλέως. | II
Βασιλεὺς Ἀντίοχος Εὐφήμωι χαίρειν. Ἐδόθη ὁ κατακεχω-
ρισ|μένος ὑπομνηματισμός· γενέσθω οὖν καθότι δεδήλωται περὶ
ὧν δεῖ διὰ σοῦ | συντελεσθῆναι. Προσενεχθέντος μοι περὶ τῆς
ἐνεργείας θεοῦ Διὸς Βαιτοκαίκης || ἐκρίθη συγχωρηθῆναι αὐτῶι   5
εἰς ἄπαντα τὸν χρόνον, ὅθεν καὶ ἡ δύναμις τοῦ | θεοῦ κατάρχεται,
κώμην τὴν Βαιτοκαι[κη]νήν, ἣν πρότερον ἔσχεν Δημήτριος |
Δημητρίου τοῦ Μνασαίου ἐντουρίωνα τῆς περὶ Ἀπάμιαν σατρα-
πείας, σὺν τοῖς | συνκυροῦσι καὶ καθήκουσι πᾶσι κατὰ τοὺς
προϋπάρχοντας περιορισμοὺς | καὶ σὺν τοῖς τοῦ ἐνεστῶτος ἔτους
γενήμασιν, ὅπως ἡ ἀπὸ ταύτης πρόσοδος || ἀναλίσκηται εἰς τὰς   10
κατὰ μῆνας συντελουμένας θυσίας καὶ τἆλλα τὰ πρὸς αὔξησ|ιν
τοῦ ἱεροῦ συντείνοντα ὑπὸ τοῦ καθισταμένου ὑπὸ τοῦ θεοῦ ἱερέως,
ὡς εἴ|θισται· ἄγωνται δὲ καὶ κατὰ μῆνα πανηγύρεις ἀτελεῖς τῆι
πεντεκαιδεκάτηι καὶ | τριακάδι· καὶ εἶναι τὸ μὲν ἱερὸν ἄσυλον,
τὴν δὲ κώμην ἀνεπίσ[ταθ]μον μηδεμιᾶς | ἀπορρήσεως προσενε-
χθείσης, τὸν δὲ ἐναντιωθησόμενόν τισι τῶν προγε||γραμμένων   15
ἔνοχον εἶναι ἀσεβείαι. Ἀναγραφῆναί τε καὶ τὰ ἀντίγραφα ἐν |
στήληι λιθίνηι καὶ τεθῆναι ἐν τῶι αὐτῶι ἱερῶι. Δεήσει οὖν
γραφῆναι οἷς εἴ|θισται, ἵνα γένηται ἀκολούθως τοῖς δηλουμένοις. |

     Ψήφισμα τῆς πόλεως πεμφθὲν θεῶι Αὐγούστωι. | III
     Ἐπάνανκες δὲ ἀνέρχεσθαι πάντα τὰ ὤνεια διὰ τῶν ἐνταῦθα
καὶ ἐπὶ χώρας | ἀγορητῶν πραθησόμενα καθ᾽ ἑ[κ]άστην ἱερο-
μηνίαν πρὸς τὸ ἀδιάλε(ι)π[τα] | ὑπάρχιν | πᾶσι τοῖς ἀνιοῦσει
προσκυνηταῖς, ἐπιμελομένου τοῦ τῆς πόλεως ἀγο||ρητοῦ μηδὲ   5
ἐπιχειροῦντος ἢ ὀχλοῦντος προφάσει παροχῆς καὶ τέλους | καὶ
ἐπηρείας τινος ἢ ἀπαιτήσαιως· ἀνδράποδα δὲ καὶ τετράποδα | καὶ

MUNICIPAL DOCUMENTS IN GREEK AND LATIN

λοιπὰ ζῶα ὁμοίως πωλείσθω ἐν τῶι τόπωι χωρὶς τέλους ἢ ἐπη|ρείας
τινος ἢ ἀπαιτήσαιως. Οἱ κάτοχοι ἁγίου οὐρανίου Διὸς τῆς ὑπὸ τῶν
10 Σε|βάστων εἴς τε τὸν θεὸν εὐσεβείας καὶ τὸν τόπον ἐλευθε||ρε[ί]ας
τὴν θείαν ἀντιγραφὴν ὑπὸ πάντων προσκυνουμένην προέταξαν.

This inscription, from Baetocaece in Syria, is of interest because
of the regard for tradition shown by the Roman emperors even in
the third century. King Antiochus had assigned the village to the
temple of Zeus with the privilege of holding regular markets where
the traders were not subject to the regular taxes imposed on the
sale of goods, and the villagers were exempted from the obligation
to provide hospitality (*hospitium*) for soldiers or officials. In later
times the village was part of a municipal *territorium* (possibly belonging to Apamea), but it still enjoyed its old privileges of immunity.
These were in danger of being lost, and the city appealed on behalf
of the village to the emperors who confirmed the grant made by
Antiochus hundreds of years before. *Cf.* Ditt. *Or. Gr.* 483.

148. EPISTULA PROCONSULIS ASIAE DE
NUNDINIIS CONSTITUENDIS
(260–270 p. Chr.)

Cagnat, *IGRR.* 4, 1381, ll. 1–17.

. . . . .ος Μαξιμιλλιανὸς [ἀνθ]ύπατος | [τῆς Ἀσίας] Δομ-
νί[ν]ωι Ῥούφωι υἱῶι Ἀσιά[ρχο]υ [εὐε]ρ[γ]έτου | καὶ Ἀσιάρχηι
χα[ίρειν. | Τῆι σ]ῆι πρὸς τοὺς θεούς, ο[ὓ]ς ἱδρῦσθαί φης [ἐν ||
5 τῆι Τ]ετραπυ[ρ]γίαι, [θρη]σκείαι [καὶ τ]ῆι το[ῦ γ]ένους ἐνδόξ[ου
λαμπρότη[τ]ι καὶ τῆι σ[ῆι μ]ετὰ τῆς εὐγεν|εί[α]ς τῶν τρό[π]ων
κοσμι[ό]τητι π[αν]τὶ ἡγοῦ|μαι δῆλον ὡς τ[ειμ]ᾶσθε δίκαιος
ὑπ[άρ]χεις . . . . | . .τω γοῦν τοῖς τῆς ἀγοραίου ἀπο[ρο]ῦσιν [βοη-
10 θεῖν . || . . . . Τ]ετραπυργί[α δ]ιὰ τὴν ε[ἴς] σε τον . αμεα . . . . |
. . . .τα τειμὴν ἀγέτω τ[ὴν] ἀγορα[ῖο]ν | [ἑκάσ]τηι πεν[τ]εκαι-
δεκά[τηι] ὁ τῶν . . . | . . . . [Τετρα]πυργειτ[ῶ]ν δῆμος . . . αιστα,
μ[η]δεμιᾶς [τῶν | πόλεων] τῶν κατ[ὰ] τὴν Μαιο[νί]αν φθ[αν]ου-
15 σῶν . . . . . || . . . . [ἐν τ]αύτηι τῆι ἡμέραι ἀγο[ρα]ῖον ἀγούση[ς,
καὶ γειν|ήσεται τ]οῦτο καθ' ἕκαστον [μῆ]να ἀν[επι]κωλύτως. |
Ἔ[ρρ]ωσο. |

(We have omitted parts *b* and *c* of the document as published by
Cagnat.)

[486]

FROM ITALY AND THE PROVINCES

From Koula in Lydia. From this inscription we learn that a city or village must make application to the governor of the province for the privilege of establishing a market-fair in its district. *Cf.* Besnier, *Dict. Dar.* IV, p. 122; nos. 96, 147.

149. DECRETUM XV VIRUM DE SACRIS FACIUNDIS
(289 p. Chr.)

CIL. x, 3698; Dessau, 4175; Bruns, 75; Riccobono, p. 262.

M. Magrio Basso, L. Ragonio | Quintiano cos., k. Iunis, | Cumis in templo divi Vespa|siani, in ordine decurionum, || quem M. Mal- 5 lonius Undanus | et Q. Claudius Acilianus praet. | coegerant, scribundo sorte | ducti adfuerunt Caelius Pan|nychus, Curtius Votivos, Considi||us Felicianus, referentibus pr. | de sacerdote 10 faciendo Matris | deae Baianae in locum Restituti | sacerdotis defuncti, placuit uni|versis Licinium Secundum || sacerdotem fieri. | 15 —xv viri sac(ris) fac(iundis) pr(aetoribus) | et magistratibus Cuman. sal. | Cum ex epistula vestra cognove|rimus creasse vos sacerdotem || Matris deum Licinium Secundum | in locum Claudi Restituti 20 defunc|ti, secundum voluntatem vestra (*sic*) | permisimus ei occavo et | corona, dumtaxat intra || fines coloniae vestrae, uti. | Optamus 25 vos bene valere. | Pontius Gavius Maximus | promagistro suscripsi XVI kal. | Septembres, M. Umbrio Primo, || T. Fl. Coeliano cos. 30

Stone found near Baiae in 1785. It contains a decree of the decurions of Cumae announcing the election of a new *sacerdos Matris deae* to fill a vacancy and a letter of the *quindecimviri sacris faciundis* of Rome confirming the election. The interest of the inscription for us lies in the fact that, with the rapid extension of the cult of Magna Mater in the period following the Antonines, and with the admission of Roman citizens to its priesthood (*cf.* Wissowa, *Religion u. Kultus d. Römer*, 265 ff.), the chapters in the cities were brought under the control of the *xv viri* of the city of Rome. Cf. also *CIL.* x, 3699, *ex s. c. dendrophori creati qui sunt sub cura xv virorum, s. f.*

[487]

MUNICIPAL DOCUMENTS IN GREEK AND LATIN

150. TITULUS HONORARIUS
(saec. III p. Chr.)

Keil and Premerstein, *Denkschriften der Wiener Akademie*, 57 (1914), 87.

᾽Αγαθῆι Τύχηι. | ᾽Επὶ πρυτάνεως Λ. Σεπτ(ιμίου) Αὐρ(ηλίου) |
᾽Αχιλλείδη νε(ωτέρου) μη(νὸς) ε´ Αὐρ(ήλιος) ῾Ερμόλαος | ῾Ρου-
5 στίκου ἔδωκεν ὑπὲρ ἀρχῆς ‖ λογιστείας καθὼς ἔδοξε τοῖς |
κωμήταις (δηνάρια) διακόσια πεντή|κοντα προσχωρήσαντα εἰς
τὴν τῶν τειρώνων συντέλειαν.

This inscription from Lydia is important for the study of village administration and for the history of recruiting in the third century. The sum of two hundred and fifty denarii was exacted as an initiation fee for the office of λογιστής and, by a decree of the villagers, the whole amount was devoted to the payment of the *aurum tironicum* in the village. For the history of this tax, *cf.* Mitteis, *P. Leipzig*, 54 (*cf. ibid.* no. 35); *P. Oxy.* 1103, and Rostovtseff *Jour. Rom. Studies*, 8 (1918), 26 *ff.*

151. EPISTULA IMPERATORUM INCERTORUM DE CONSTITUTIONE CIVITATIS TYMANDENORUM
(saec. III p. Chr.)

CIL. III, *S.* 6866; Dessau, 6090; Bruns, 34; Riccobono, p. 338.

....ovi penitus.....|......Tymandenis item | ....ad
5 scientiam nostram | .....tua pertulit, contemplati sumus ‖ *Tyman-*
denos voto praecipuo, summo etiam | studio optare, ut ius et digni-
tatem civita|tis praecepto nostro consequantur, Lepide | carissime.
Cum itaque ingenitum nobis | sit, ut per universum orbem nostrum
10 civi‖tatum honor ac numerus augeatur eos|que eximie *c*upere
videamus, ut civitatis | nomen honestatemque percipiant, isdem |
maxime pollicentibus quod apud se decu|rionum sufficiens futura
15 sit copia, cre‖didimus adnuendum. Quare volumus, | ut eosdem
Tymandenos hortari cu|res, ut voti sui conpotes redditi⟨s⟩ | cum
ceteris civitatibus nostris ea que | ipsos consecutos ius civitatis con-
20 pe‖tit recognoscere, obsequio suo nitan|tur inplere. Ut autem sic
uti ceteris | civitatibus ius est coeund*i in* curiam, | faciendi etiam
25 decreti et gerend*i* ce|tera que iure permissa sunt, ipsa quo‖que per-

missu nostro agere possit, et | magistratus ei itemque aediles, quaes-| tores quoque et si qua alia necessaria | facienda sunt, creare debebunt. Quem | ordinem agendarum rerum perpetuo || pro civitatis merito 30 custodiri conve|niet. Numerum autem decurionum | interim quinquaginta hominum in|stituere debebis. Deorum autem in|mortalium favor tribuet, ut auctis || eorum viribus adque numero maior e|orum 35 haberi copia possit.

This inscription was found by Sterrett (*cf. Papers of the Am. School of Class. Studies at Athens*, 3 (1884–1885), p. 384, no. 558) on the site of Tymandus in Pisidia. The names of the emperors at the beginning are lacking, but the script seems to belong to the close of the third or the early part of the fourth century. The words *deorum immortalium* (ll. 33 f.) seem to fix the date before Constantine. As in no. 154 the reply to the petition is addressed to an official. Whether Lepidus (l. 7) was governor of Pisidia, *vicarius* of Asia, or *praef. praet. Or.* (Mommsen, *Ges. Schr.* 5, 550), we cannot say. Like the people of Orcistus the Tymandeni ask for the *ius et dignitas civitatis* (ll. 6 f.; *cf.* 11 f.). The granting of their request carries with it the privilege of establishing a *curia*, passing *decreta*, and the election of duovirs, aediles, and quaestors (ll. 22 ff.). A normal municipal senate comprised one hundred members, but we find instances of smaller and larger numbers (*cf.* no. 136). The emperors plan to increase the number of members as Tymandus grows (ll. 34 ff.). The statement *isdem maxime pollicentibus, quod apud se decurionum sufficiens futura sit copia* (ll. 12 ff.) is a significant reference to the comparatively large fortune required for a decurionship, and perhaps to the entrance fee exacted in many cities (*cf.* pp. 142 f.). It would be interesting to know whether the imperial writers have in mind also the responsibility of the *curiales* for the taxes due to the central government. The fact that Tymandus wished to have a *curia* would seem to show that membership in it was still prized; *cf.* pp. 113 ff.

152. RESCRIPTUM DE OFFICIALIUM
EXACTIONIBUS INLICITIS
(saec. III p. Chr.)

CIL. VIII, *S.* 17639.

....et onerari se inlic*itis*...|*militu*m atq(ue) oficialium exa|*cti-*
*onibus ratione habita d*ecreti concili, quod su*sci*|*tavit has querelas* cum
5   magno animi mei || *dolore audivi*; temporum illorum quorum | ...
fuit ad nunc quis aequo animo | *ferat e*xactionibus inlicitis quibus |
*i*mponunt fortunis alienis immi|*nere ruina*m exauriant compendis
o   su||*is* ....uam populi vel fisci debiti | *r*eciproce requi*es* non et
mi|*lites* parentium ac liberorum | *summ*a excipit oficiales munifi-|
15 *centia*...*n*e quasi quodam more consti||*tuto p*ublici vectigalis pa-
terentur | *n*e posthac admittant | *aut poenae iis p*ro delicti qualitate
in|*rogentur*...s de qua re et pro(curatoribus) meis | *litteras misi*
20 *et rescriptum meum etiam pr*ovincialibus innotescere vo||*lui*....ciant
L. Apronius Pius leg. Aug.....
*Benevole*ntia eius circa provinciam suam hic.

An inscription painted in red letters on a stone tablet found at
Aïn Zui in the ancient province of Numidia. The left edge of the
stone is broken off. Probably the last line begins the second part
of the inscription which was continued on another stone. The
uncertainty of some of the restorations made by Mommsen leaves
us in doubt of the exact meaning at various points, but the main
purpose of the emperor is plain. The document is an imperial
rescript or edict from about the middle of the third century. The
emperor intervenes to put a stop to the unlawful exactions made
from the provincials by imperial officials and soldiers. Since his
efforts to this end have been ineffective in the past, he does not
content himself with giving instructions to his procurators, but he
causes this rescript to be published (l. 19) in Numidia, probably
by the legate L. Apronius Pius (l. 20), of whom we hear in other
inscriptions (*cf. E.E.* 5, 669; 7, 793; 7, 395 = Dessau, 1196;
CIL. VIII, 8782).

153. TITULUS OPERIS PUBLICI
(ca. 312 p. Chr.)

CIL. VIII, 210 = VIII, *S.* 11299.

(*a*)

Coloniae Cillitanae |

Q. Manlius Felix C. filius Papiria receptus post alia arcum quoque cum insignibus colo*niae* | solita in patriam libertate erexit ob cuius dedicationem decurionibus sportulas curiis epu*las ded.*

(*b*)

Clementia temporis et virtute | divina D*D. NN.* Constantini *et Licini* inuc (*sic*) | semp. Aug. ornamenta *liberta.* restituta et vetera civi|tatis insignia curante Ceionio Aproniano c. v. || patro. civitatis. 5

Two inscriptions found on an arch at colonia Flavia Cillium or colonia Cillitana. Inscription (*b*) is in smaller letters and of a later date than (*a*). The arch was probably thrown down when Maxentius invaded Africa in 311 and was restored after the victory of Constantine and Licinius in 312. In l. 2 of (*b*) *D.N.* and *et Licini,* according to Mommsen, were originally on the stone, erased in consequence of the quarrel between Constantine and Licinius, and restored later. *Ornamenta liberta(tis) restituta* would naturally imply that the town was restored to the status of a *civitas libera. Cf.,* however, Henze, *De civitatibus liberis,* 80 *f.*

154. EPISTULA ABLABI PRAEFECTI PRAETORIO ET CONSTANTINI IMPERATORIS DE IURE CIVITATIS ORCISTANORUM
(323–326; 331 p. Chr.)

CIL. III, *S.* 7000; Dessau, 6091; Bruns, 35; Riccobono, p. 341.

Ut alia *s*ic haec quae in precem con*tuli*stis *et nominis* | et digni- Col. 1 tatis reparationem iure quae*runt obtine*|re. Proinde vicari intercessione quae *fuerant mut*|ilata ad integrum prisci honoris *reduxit imp(erator) super omnes re*||*tr*o pius, ut et vos oppidumque dilig*entia* 5 *vestra tui*|*t*um expetito legum adque appellationis *s*plendore *iure decreti* | perfruamini infrascribti. |

[491]

Have Ablabi carissime nobis. | Incole Orcisti, iam nunc oppidi
10 et || civitatis, iucundam munificien|tiae nostrae materiem prae-
bue|runt, Ablabi carissime et iucundissi|me. Quibus enim studium
15 est urbes vel no|vas condere vel longaevas erudire vel in||termortuas
reparare, id quod petebatur acce|ptissimum fuit. Adseruerunt enim
vicum suum | spatiis prioris aetatis oppidi splendore floru|isse, ut
et annuis magistratuum fascibus orna|retur essetque curialibus ce-
20 lebre et populo || civium plenum. Ita enim ei situ adque ingenio |
locus opportunus esse perhibetur, ut ex qu|attuor partibus eo
totidem in sese congruant | viae, quibus omnibus publicis mansio
25 ea medi|alis adque accommoda esse dicatur. Aquarum || ibi abun-
dantem afluentiam, labacra quoque | publica privataque eorum,
istatuis veterum | principum ornata, et populum commanentium |
adeo celebrem.......ali ibidem sunt, | facile compleantur provisa
30 ex decursibus || praeterfluentium aquarum,........|rum numerum
copiosum. Quibus cum omni|bus memoratus locus abundare di-
catur, con|tigisse adseruerunt, ut eos Nacolenses sibi | adnecti ante
35 id temporis postularent. Quod || est indignum temporibus nostris,
ut tam op|portunus locus civitatis nomen amittat, | et inutile com-
manentibus, ut depraeda|tione potiorum omnia sua commoda
40 utilita|tesque deperdant. Quibus omnibus quasi || quidam cumulus
accedit, quod omnes | ibidem sectatores sanctissimae religi|onis
habitare dicantur. Qui cum praeca|rentur, ut sibi ius antiquum
45 nomenque | civitatis concederet nostra clementia, || sicuti adnota-
tionis nostrae subiecta | cum precibus exempla testantur, huiusmo|di
sententiam dedimus. Nam haec quae in pre|cem contulerunt, et
Col. II nominis et dignitatis | reparationem iure quae|runt obtinere.
5 Proinde gra|vitatis tuae intercessione | quae fuerant mutilata || ad
integrum prisci honoris | reduci sancimus, ut et ipsi | oppidumque
10 diligentia sua | tuitum expetito legum ad|que appellationis splen||dore
perfruantur. Par est | igitur sinceritatem tuam | quod promptissime
15 pro tempo|ris nostri dignitate concessi|mus, erga supplicantes fes||ti-
nanter implere. Vale, Ablabi, | carissime et iucundissime nobis. |

Exemplum Precum. |

Ad auxilium pietatis vestrae | confugimus, domini impp. Con-
20 stantine || Maxime victor semper Aug. et Crispe, | Constantine et
Constanti nobb. Caes. |

*Patri*a nostra Orcistos vetust*is*|*simum* oppidum fuit et ex anti-
quis*si*|*mis* temporibus, ab origine etiam||*civi*tatis dignitatem obtinuit. | 25
Id in medio confinio Galatiae p*erbe*|*na*e situm est. Nam quattuor
via*rum* | *tra*nsitus ex*hi*bet: id est civita*tis* | *P*essinuntesium, quae
civita*s dis*||*tat* a patria nostra tricensim*o fe*|*re l*apide; nec non etiam 30
civita*tis Mi*|*d*aitanorum, quae et ipsa est a *patria* | nostra in tri-
censimo miliario; *et civi*|tatis Amorianorum, quae posita... *(re-
liqua desiderantur).*

　　*A*ct. prid. | kal. Iulias | *C*onstantinopoli. |　　　　　　Col. III

　　*I*mp. Caes. Constantinus || maximus Guth. victor ac trium|*f*ator 5
Aug. et Fl. Cla. Constantinus | Alaman. et F*l*. *I*ul. Constantius
nnbb. | *C*aess. salutem dicunt | ordini civit. Orcistanorum. || Actum 10
est indulgentiae nos|trae munere, ius vobis civita|tis tributum non
honore modo | verum libertatis etiam privi|legium custodire. Itaque
Na||colensium iniuriam ultra in|dulgentiae nostrae beneficia | per- 15
durantem praesenti re|scribtione removemus, idque | oratis vestris
petitionique || deferimus, ut pecuniam, quam | pro cultis ante 20
solebatis in|ferre, minime deinceps dependa|tis. Hoc igi*t*ur ad virum
praesta|ntissimum rationalem Asia||nae dioeceseos lenitas nostra | 25
perscribsit, qui secutus for|mam indulgentiae concessae | vobis
pecuniam deinceps pro | supra dicta specie expeti a vo||bis postu- 30
larique prohibebit. | Bene valere vos cupimus. | *B*asso et Abla*bi*o
cons.

A large stone, with an inscription on three sides of it, which was
copied in part by Pococke in 1752, by Hamilton in 1839, and in
its entirety by Ramsay in 1886 (*cf.* Mommsen, *Ges. Schr.* 5, 542–
544). It was found on the site of Orcistus in Phrygia Salutaris.
The stone bears inscriptions of two different dates. In the first
place we have three inscriptions of the same year containing (*a*) the
last part of the letter of Ablabius to the Orcistani (col. I, ll. 1–7);
(*b*) the rescript of Constantine to Ablabius (col. I, 8–11, 16);
(*c*) the beginning of the petition of the Orcistani to Constantine
and his sons. In the second place we have a rescript (*d*) of Constantine at a later date to the Orcistani (col. III, 1–32). The date
of (*a*), (*b*), and (*c*) falls between A.D. 323, when Constantius became
Caesar, and 326, when Crispus died (Mommsen, *op. cit.* 5, 548).
The last inscription (*d*) is dated June 30, A.D. 331. The first

[493]

MUNICIPAL DOCUMENTS IN GREEK AND LATIN

petition of the people of Orcistus (*c*) was given to the *vicarius dioceseos Asianae* (*cf.* I, 3), transmitted by him to Ablabius, *praef. praet. per Orientem*, and then sent to the emperor. The emperor sends his answer (*b*) to the prefect, who in turn communicates it to the Orcistani with a letter of his own (*a*). In the second instance we have only the rescript of the emperor (*d*) addressed to the *ordo civitatis Orcistanorum* (III, 9). The *Dioecesis Asiana* (*cf.* III, 25) in which Orcistus lay was in direct charge of a *vicarius* (*cf.* I, 3), who in turn was subordinate to the *praefectus praetorio Orientis* (*cf.* Abbott, 338; Kornemann, *R.E.* 5, 729). Ablabius was in high favor with Constantine for many years, and held the post of *praef. praet.* for at least six years (*cf.* Seeck, *R.E.* I, 103). During one of these years (A.D. 331) he was also consul (*cf.* col. III, 32; *Palladii Historia Lausiaca* (ed. Butler), 2, 230, n. 102).

What the people of Orcistus asked is clear from the two imperial rescripts. They begged (I, 43–44) *ut sibi ius antiquum nomenque civitatis concederet*. This position the town had held in earlier days (*cf. nominis et dignitatis reparationem*, I, 1–2; *ad integrum prisci honoris reduxit*, I, 4 and II, 5–6; *cf.* II, 22–25). The town is now claimed as a *vicus* (*cf.* I, 16) by the neighboring *civitas* of Nacolia (I, 33–34). It has lost the right of self-government, and tribute for the *aerarium* is apportioned among the people of Orcistus by the *curiales* of Nacolia (III, 14–23), and Orcistus probably has to pay a disproportionate share (*cf. depraedatione potiorum*, I, 37–38). A decline in the prosperity of Orcistus may well have led to this change in her political status (*cf.* Isidore, *Orig.* 15, 2, 11, *vici et castella et pagi sunt, quae nulla dignitate civitatis ornantur, sed vulgari hominum conventu incoluntur et propter parvitatem sui maioribus civitatibus attribuuntur*). Mommsen in his comments on *CIL.* III, 352 cites the similar case of Equus Tuticus (*CIL.* IX, 2165) which lost its independent status and was attributed to Beneventum. It was probably with a view to proving the prosperity of Orcistus that its people descant on its roads (II, 27), aqueducts, baths, and statues (I, 20–31). Furthermore they were ardent Christians (I, 39–42), and this fact may have enlisted for them the favor of Ablabius, who was a strong supporter of the new faith (*cf. R.E.* I, 103). *Oppidum* and *civitas* are used in all these documents in a semi-technical way

[494]

of a self-governing community (*cf.* I, 5; I, 17; I, 36; I, 43–44 II, 23; II, 25; III, 11), whose characteristics are defined in I, 18–20. *Civitas* came to be the generic name for such a city and, after the promulgation of the *constitutio Antoniana*, crowded out *colonia* and *municipium* (*cf.* Kornemann, *R.E., Suppl.* 303). *Legum . . .splendore* (I, 6; II, 8–9) suggests the phrase *uti suis legibus*, used of the grant of autonomy, and *libertatis privilegium* (III, 13–14) suggests the same right, but the designation *civitas libera* would probably not have its old characteristic meaning at this time. It is interesting to notice that the Orcistani themselves in speaking of their town in its present status use the colorless word, *patria* (II, 22, 30, 32).

Five years or more after the prayer of the Orcistani had been granted, Orcistus was still under the control of Nacolia. This situation called forth the second rescript, which, to make the *ius civitatis* of Orcistus effective, instructed the *rationalis Asianae Dioeceseos* (Hirschfeld, 35 *ff.*) to forbid Nacolia to require the payment of taxes from Orcistus. These taxes, payable in kind in any form of produce receivable at the public granaries (*species, cf.* Mommsen, *CIL.* III, 352), were commuted by a payment of money (*cf.* III, 28–29).

On the general form which these documents take, *cf.* pp. 237 *ff.* The first three, viz. the *preces* of the Orcistani, the *decretum* of the emperor, and the *epistula* of Ablabius, are quite unconventional. No one of them bears a date. The letter of Ablabius has no *inscriptio* or salutation at the end. If Mommsen's conjecture, *decreti* (I, 6), is accepted, we must take the word in a broad way of all kinds of imperial documents, rather than in the technical sense (*cf.* Hesky, *R.E.* 2289 *f.*). For *adnotationis* (I, 45), *cf.* p. 241. Mommsen (*CIL.* III, *S.* 7000) surmises that the emperor's *adnotatio* was on a stone now lost. In its contents the *decretum* follows very closely the *preces* of the people of Orcistus. The last document is more systematic, with its *inscriptio* (III, 1–9), the text proper (III, 10–30), and the *subscriptio* (III, 31). Rather exceptionally the place and the precise date are given at the beginning (III, 1–3).

MUNICIPAL DOCUMENTS IN GREEK AND LATIN

155. EDICTUM CONSTANTINI AD UMBROS
(326–337 p. Chr.)

CIL. xi, 5265; Dessau, 705; Mommsen, *Ges. Schr.* 8, 25.

E. S. R. |

Imp. Caes. Fl. Constantinus | max. Germ. Sarm. Got. victor |
5 triump. Aug. et Fl. Constantinus || et Fl. Iul. Constantius et Fl. |
Constans. | Omnia quidem, quae humani gene|ris societate(m)
tuentur, pervigilium cu|ra*rum* cogitatione conplectimur; sed pro-||
10 visionum nostrarum opus maximus (*sic*) | est, ut universae urbes,
quas in luminibus provin|ciarum *a*c regionum omnium species et
forma dis|tingui*t*, non modo dignitate(m) pristinam teneant, | sed
15 etiam ad meliorem statum beneficentiae nos||trae munere *prove-
hantur.* Cum igitur ita vos Tusci|ae adsereretis esse coniunctos, ut
instituto | consuetudinis priscae per singulos (*sic*) annorum vi|ces
a vobis *a*dque praedictis sacerdotes creentur, | qui aput Vulsinios
20 Tusciae civitate(m) ludos || schenicos et gladiatorum munus exhi-
beant, | sed propter ardua montium et iti|nerum saltuosa inpendio
posceretis, ut indulto | remedio sacerdoti vestro ob editiones cele-|
25 brandas Vulsinios pergere necesse non esset, || scilicet ut civitati,
cui nunc Hispellum nomen | est quamque Flaminiae viae confinem
adque con|tinuam esse memoratis, de nostro cognomine | nomen
daremus, in qua templum Flaviae gentis | opere magnifico nimirum
30 pro amplitudinem (*sic*) || nuncupationis exsurgere*t*, ibidemque *i*s |
sacerdos, quem anniversaria vice Umbria de|disset, spectaculum
tam scenicorum ludorum | quam gladiatorii muneris exhibere*t*,
35 manente | per Tuscia (*sic*) ea consuetudine, ut indidem cre||atus
sacerdos aput Vulsinios ut solebat | editionum antedictarum spec-
tacula fre|quentare*t*: precationi ac desiderio vestro | facilis accessit
noster adsensus. Nam civi|tati Hispello aeternum vocabulum
40 nomenq. || venerandum de nostra nuncupatione conces|simus, sci-
licet ut in posterum praedicta urbs | Flavia Constans vocetur; in
cuius gremio | aedem quoque Flaviae, hoc est nostrae gen|tis, ut
45 desideratis, magnifico opere perfici || volumus, ea observatione per-
scripta, ne ae|dis nostro nomini dedicata cuiusquam con|tagiose
superstitionis fraudibus polluatur; | consequenter etiam editionum
50 in prae|dicta civitate exhibendorum (*sic*) vobis || licentiam dedimus

[496]

scilicet ut, sicuti | dictum est, per vices temporis sollem|nitas editionum Vulsinios quoque non de|serat, ubi creatis e Tuscia sacerdotibus memo|rata celebritas exhibenda est. Ita quippe nec || veteribus institutis plurimum videbitur | derogatum, et vos, qui ob 55 praedictas causas | nobis supplices extitistis, ea quae inpen|dio postulastis, impetrata esse gaude|bitis.

1. 21. et difficultates itinerum: *tablet*.

Marble slab found at Hispellum in Umbria in 1733. For more than a century this inscription was regarded as a forgery, based in part on *CIL*. xi, 5283 (Dessau, 6623), another document found on the site of Hispellum. In 1850, however, Mommsen removed all doubt of its authenticity (*Ges. Schr.* 8, 24 *ff.*), and published a long commentary on it. Its authenticity was established largely by a comparison with Constantine's epistle to Orcistus (no. 154) which it resembles in language, in form, and in the titles employed, by the appearance of such archaic forms as *conplectimur* (l. 8), *aput* (l. 19), and *inpendio* (l. 22), as well as by the nature of the request and Constantine's reply to it.

It is of course a rescript, as the initial letters (*E.S.R.* = *exemplum sacri rescripti*) indicate, and is a reply to a petition, or, as Mommsen prefers to characterize it (*op. cit.* 8, 33 *ff.*), "ein rescriptähnliches Edict" or *lex edictalis*. It bears no date, and therefore seems to violate Constantine's own law of 322 (*Cod. Th.* I. I. I), which rendered an edict without a date invalid, but the date may well have stood on the dedicatory stone (Mommsen, *op. cit.* 8, 29). From internal evidence it was evidently composed between A.D. 326, the date of the death of Crispus, and before Constantine's death in 337 (Mommsen, *op. cit.* 8, 32). Strangely enough the names of the persons addressed do not appear in the *inscriptio*, but the document is evidently intended for the Umbrians.

At this time Tuscia and Umbria had a common government under a *corrector* (*cf.* Marquardt, *St. Verw.* 1, 236, n. 2), and from this inscription it would appear that the province had a *concilium* at Volsinii, although there is no direct reference to such a body (*cf.* Kornemann, *R.E.* 4, 821 *f.*). At the annual meeting in Volsinii priests were elected, and plays and gladiatorial games given (ll. 17–20), but for the Umbrians the journey to Volsinii was hard

and costly (l. 21). They therefore ask the emperor that they may
not be required to go to Volsinii in the future (l. 24), that the
emperor will give his name to Hispellum in Umbria, that they may
found there a *templum Flaviae gentis*, choose a priest, and hold
their annual plays and games, without interrupting the annual
festival at Volsinii (ll. 27–34). The emperor grants their petition
(ll. 36, 37) and allows Hispellum henceforth to bear the name Urbs
Flavia Constans (ll. 41, 42). In Constantine's decision concerning the proposed temple (ll. 44, 45) his half-Christian, half-
pagan state of mind is evident. His tolerant attitude in this case is
paralleled, as Mommsen observes (*op. cit.* 8, 37), by his permission
to Africa to establish a *templum gentis Flaviae*. For the policy of
his successors in such matters, *cf. op. cit.* 8, 21 *ff.* In defining *gens
Flavia* as *gens nostra*, the emperor is of course distinguishing his
own line from the Flavian emperors of the first century

The particular interest which this document has for us lies in
the fact that it illustrates the gradual substitution of the province
for the municipality as the political and social unit in the empire,
and may well bear evidence to the decline of municipal life. Under
the republic and the early empire the city had been the recognized
political unit, and it was with a city, or with a league of cities, that
the senate or the emperor dealt. But from Constantine's time on
we see a distinct effort being made to establish direct relations
between the provincials, especially through their assemblies, and
the central government. The *Codex* of Justinian contains edicts of
Constantine addressed *ad Afros* (12. 57. 1) of A.D. 315, *ad Bithynos*
(11. 8. 1) of 317, *ad Lusitanos* (1. 23. 4) of 322, *ad Afros* (10. 21. 1)
of 327, and *ad concilium provinciae Africae* (2. 12. 21) of 315. There
are three more addressed *ad provinciales*, one, *provincialibus suis*,
two, *ad universos provinciales*, of which the earliest (8. 16. 7) is
of the year 315, and eight *ad populum*. It is probable that every
province was required to establish a *concilium*. At least this seems
to have been the situation at the close of the fourth century (*cf.
Cod. Th.* 12. 12. 13). The increase in the number of provinces
from forty-five in A.D. 117 to one hundred and eight at the close
of the fourth century (*cf.* Marquardt, *St. Verw.* 1, 489 *ff.*) meant
a corresponding decrease in the size of each province, which made

[498]

FROM ITALY AND THE PROVINCES

it possible for the residents of a province to have interests in common and take common action to further them, and Diocletian and his successors may well have had this consideration in mind in decreasing the size of the provinces (*cf.* Mommsen, *op. cit.* 8, 32–33; Kornemann, *R.E.* 4, 822 *f.*).

156. TITULUS HONORARIUS
(362–363 p. Chr.)

CIL. v, 8987; Dessau, 755.

Ab insignem singula|remque erga rem publicam | suam faborem | d(ominus) n(oster) Iulianus invictissimus prin||ceps remota provin- 5
cialibus cura | cursum fiscalem breviatis mutationum spa|tiis fieri iussit, | disponente Claud*i*o Mamertino v(iro) c(larissimo) per Ita|liam et Inlyricum praefecto praetorio, || curante Vetulenio Praenestio 10
v(iro) p(erfectissimo) corr(ectore) | Venet(iae) et Histr(iae).

l. 1. ab *for* ob.

Found at Concordia, north-east of Venice. Cl. Mamertinus was praetorian prefect of Illyricum and Italy under Julian in 362 and 363; *cf.* Gensel, *R.E.* 3, 2730. On the *cursus publicus* in the early empire, *cf.* no. 51. The wrongs which the municipalities in the fourth century suffered at the hands of those who managed the post are graphically described by Libanius (*Orat.* 20), cited by Hudemann in *Gesch. d. röm. Postwesens,* 34. Draught animals were commandeered for the service; they were exhausted by long journeys, ill-fed, and sometimes turned loose on the highway. The accuracy of his statements is confirmed by the sixty-six constitutions of Title 5 of Bk 8 of the *Theodosian Code.* From constitutions, nos. 12, 13, 14, and 16, addressed to Mamertinus by Julian, we learn that he limited the number of passes (*diplomata* or *evectiones*) granted, and restricted to the emperor, the praetorian prefect, and the governor of a province the right to give them. In the *Itinerarium Hierosolymitanum* of A.D. 333 there were thirty points at which the animals were changed (*mutationes*) in a journey of 371 miles, and the distances covered by a single team varied from five to twenty-four miles; *cf.* Seeck, *R.E.* 4, 1855. Although the post is called the *cursus fiscalis,* it would seem from the constitutions

MUNICIPAL DOCUMENTS IN GREEK AND LATIN

of the period that the cities were still obliged to furnish fodder for
the animals, pay for the construction and repair of the *mansiones*
and *stabula*, and meet the expenses of the cross roads; *cf.* Humbert,
Dict. Dar. 1, 1660.

157. RESCRIPTUM VALENTINIANI VALENTIS GRATIANI DE
MOENIBUS INSTAURANDIS ET DE REDITIBUS FUNDO-
RUM CIVITATIUM ASIAE

(371 p. Chr.)

Anzeiger der Akad. der Wissen. in Wien, 1905, no. 10; *Jahreshefte d. öst. archäol. Inst.* 8 (1905), *Beiblatt*, 71 *ff.*; *ibid.* 9 (1906),
40 *f.*; Bruns, 97 *a*; Riccobono, p. 374.

D.D.D. n.n.n. Auggg. Valentini*anus, Valens*, Gratianus. Hab(e),
Eutropi car(issim)e nobis. |

*Quod ex red*itibus fundorum iuris re*i publicae quo*s intra Asiam
diversis quibusque civitatibus ad instaurand*am mo*enium fac*iem*,....
...*pro* certis | *partibu*s habita aestimatione concensimus capere
quidem urb*es* singulas beneficii nostri uberem fructum et pro *temporum*
*r*efers felici*tate nostro*rum a foedo | *prioru*m squalore ruinarum in
antiquam sui faciem nova reparatione consurgere, verum non in-
5 tegram gra*tiam con*cessi ad *ur*bes singulas beneficii || *perv*enire si
quidem pro partibus praestitis reditus civitatibus potius q*ua*m ipsi
cum reditibus fundi fuerint restitu*end*i et ministrandi, idem reditus
ab actor*i*bus | *pr*ibatae rei nostrae et diu miserabiliterque poscantur
et vix aegr*e*que tribuantur adque id quod amplius e*x i*sdem fundis
super statutum canonem | *c*olliga*t*ur, et isdem civitatibus pereat
eorundemqu*e* actorum fraudibus devoratum nihil tamen aerario
nostro adiciat augmenti possitque | a curialibus vel excultione maiore
vel propensiore diligentia nonnullus praestitionis cumulus ad gratiam
concessionis accedere, igitur cuncta diligenti coram investigatione
perspeximus. | —Et primum Efesenae urbi, quae Asiae caput est,
10 missa ad nos dudum legatione poscen*ti* || *p*artem reditum non
fundorum advertimus fuisse concessam; unde illi interim quam esse
omnium maximam nulla dubitatio est, in parte con|cessa cum eo
fundo quem Leucem nomine nostra iam liberalitate detentat, tra*di*
centum iuga promulgata sanctione mandavimus, ut eius exemplo
quid adhoc | ista in reparandis moenibus profecerit intuentes an

[500]

FROM ITALY AND THE PROVINCES

reliquis praestandum sit similia, decernamus. Hac sane quia ratione plenissima, quod intra Asiam rei publicae | iuga esse videantur cuiusque qualitatis quantumve annua praestatione dependant, mansuetudo nostra instructa cognovit, offerendam experientiae tuae | credidimus optionem, ut, si omnem hanc iugationem quae est per omnem diffusa provinciam, id est sex milia sentingenta triginta sex semis opima || adque idonea iuga, quae praeter vinum solidorum ad fixum semel canonem trea milia extrinsicus solidorum annua praestare referuntur, sed et septingenta tria deserta | et iam defecta ac sterilia iuga quae per illa quae idonea diximus sustinentur, suscipere propria praestatione non abnuis, petitis maiestas nostra consentiat, | scilicet ut arbitrio tuo per curias singulas omni iugatione dispersa retracto eo redituum modo quem unicuique civitatum propria largitate concensimus | reliquam summam per officium tuum rei privatae nostrae inferre festines, ut et omnem usuram diligentia avidis eripiamus actoribus et si quid extrinsicus | lucri est cedat rationibus civitatum. Sane quia rerum omnium integram cupimus habere notitiam et ex industria nobis tuam expertam diligentiam || pollicemur, plena te volumus ratione disquirere per omnem Asiam provinciam fundos iugationemque memoratam, qui in praesentem diem habita | licitatione possideant et quantum per iuga singula rei privatae nostrae annua praestatione dependant, qui etiam opimi adque utiles fundi | fisco grati singulis quibusque potentissimis fuerint elocati et qui contra infecundi ac steriles in damnum rei nostrae paenes actores | fuerint derelicti scilicet ut omni per idoneos ratione discussa ac (?) confectis quam diligentissime brevibus mansuetudini nostrae veri | fidem nunties, ut instructi super omnibus amplissimum efficacis industriae praestantiae tuae testimonium deferamus.

    Eutropius, to whom this rescript was addressed, was governor of Asia in A.D. 371 (cf. Ammianus, 29. 1. 36, and Schulten, *Jahreshefte d. öst. archäol. Inst.* 9 (1906), 43 f.). The cities in Asia had suffered severely from earthquakes in 358 and 365 (Ammianus 17. 7. 1; Libanius, 1, 621 (Reiske); Schulten, *op. cit.* 52). Furthermore much of their land had been confiscated or reverted to the emperors and had been converted into imperial domains; cf. Declareuil, *Quelques problèmes d'histoire des institutions municipales,*

[501]

332 *f.* Probably reference is made to the recent earthquakes in ll. 3–4. The setting of the rescript is thus explained by Heberdey (*Jahreshefte d. öst. archäol. Inst.* 9 (1906), 192). In 365 Valens arranged that certain cities of Asia should receive a part of the returns from some of the *fundi rei publicae* for the purpose of rebuilding their walls. The dishonesty of the managers of the domains led the governor of Asia to propose that the cities should be allowed to manage these properties themselves. The plan was first tried in Ephesus, and finally this rescript was sent to Eutropius directing him to collect the revenue and divide it between the cities and the *res privatae* of the emperor; *cf. arbitrio tuo...festines* (ll. 17 *ff.*). For a somewhat different explanation, *cf.* Schulten, *loc. cit.* The *actores* in Asia were evidently as venal as the procurators in Africa; *cf.* no. 111. The emperors complain that most of the revenue from the public lands goes, not to the cities, nor into the public treasury, but into the pockets of the officials (*cf.* l. 7). Schulten notes (*loc. cit.* 58 *f.*) that Valentinian had already issued two edicts (*Cod. Th.* 4. 13. 7; 15. 1. 18), in one of which he directed Constantius, the proconsul of Africa, to devote a third part of the revenues from the *fundi rei publicae* to public works in the cities, and in 395 a constitution of Arcadius and Honorius (*Cod. Th.* 15. 1. 33) refers to the assignment of one third to the cities for the repair of their walls. Before Valentinian, Alexander Severus (*Hist. Aug. Alex. Sev.* 22, 44) and Constantius (*Cod. Th.* 4. 13. 5) had given a part of the *vectigalia*, in Africa one fourth, to the repair of the walls and public works of provincial cities. The central government took up the matter of repairing the walls of cities on the borders of the empire because of the barbarian invasions which began about this time; *cf.* Ammianus, 26. 4. 5. For the *canon*, *cf.* Leonhard, *R.E.* 3, 1486; for the *iugatio* and *iuga*, *cf.* pp. 130 *ff.* In l. 15 probably vi or vii has been corrupted into *vinum*.

158. RESCRIPTUM IMPERATORUM VALENTINIANI VALENTIS
GRATIANI AD FESTUM PROCONSULEM ASIAE DE LUDIS
PROVINCIALIBUS

(375 p. Chr.)

Bruns, 97*b*.

D.D.D. n.n.n. Auggg. Valen*t*inianus, Valens, Gratia*n*us. *Habe*(?) I
Feste *car(issime)* *n*ob(is). |

Honorem Asiae ac totius provinci*ae* dignitatem, quae ex iudi-
cantis pendebat arbitrio, *ex*emplo Illyri*ci* a*d*que *It*alarum urbium
recte pe*r*spexi*mus* | esse firmatum. Nec enim utile videbatur, u*t*
*p*o*n*pa conventus publici unius arbitrio gereretur, qu*a*m consuet*u*-
dinis instaurata deberet solemnitas | exhibere. Ex sententiis deni*q*ue
factum est, quod divisis officiis per quattuor civitates, quae met*r*o-
polis apu*d* Asiam nominantur, lustrali̠s cernitur edi*tio* (?) || consti- 5
tuta, ut, dum a singulis ex*h*ibitio postulatur, non desit provinciae
coronatus nec gr*a*vis cuiquam erogatio sit futura, cum servatis
vicibus qu*in*|to anno civitas praebeat editorem. Nam et *illu*d quoque
libenter admisimus quod in minoribus m*u*nicipiis generatis, quos
popularis animi gloria maior | attollit, facultatem tribui edendi
mu*n*er*i*s postulasti, videlicet ut in metropoli Efesena *a*l*i*a e civit*a*te
asiarchae sive alytarchae pro*ceda*n*t* a*c* s*ic* | officiis melioribus nobili-
tate contend*ant*. Unde qui desideriis sub seculi nostri felicitate
ferv*en*ti*b*us gaudiorum debeamus *f*o*men*ta *p*rae*s*tare cele|brandae
editionis dedimus potestat*e*m, adversum id solum voluntatem con-
trariam ref*er*en*tes, ne suae civitatis obliti e*i*us in qua edideri*nt* ||
munera cu*ria*e socientur, Feste carissime ac iucundissime. Lauda*t*a 10
ergo experientia tua n*os*t*ri potius praecepta sequatur arbitrii, ut
omn*es* | qui ad hos ho*n*ores transire festinant, c*u*nctas primitus civi-
tatis suae restituant functiones, u*t* *p*eractis curiae muneribus a*d*
*h*onorem totiu*s* | provinciae debito fabore festinent p*er*cepturi
postmodum, si tamen voluerint, senato*r*iam dignitatem, *ita tam*en,
ut satisfacien*t*es legi in locis s*uis* | alteros deser*a*nt substitutos.
Ceterum nequaquam ad commodum credimus esse iustitiae, ut
expensis rebus suis laboribusque transactis | veluti novus tiro ad
curiam transeat alienam, cum rectius honoribus fultus in sua debeat
vivere civitate.

Τὴν τειμὴν τῆς Ἀσίας καὶ ὅλης τῆς ἐπαρχίας τὸ ἀξίωμα, ὅπερ II

MUNICIPAL DOCUMENTS IN GREEK AND LATIN

καὶ ἐκ τῆς ἐπικρίσεως ἤρτητο τοῦ ἄρχοντος, ἐξ ὑποδίγματος τοῦ
Ἰλλυρικοῦ καὶ τῶν [τ]ῆς Ἰταλίας | πόλεων ὀρθῶς λείαν κατε-
νοήσαμεν διακεκρίσθαι. Οὔτε γὰρ λυσιτελὲς ἐνομίζετο τὴν
πομπὴν τῇ[ς] συνόδου τῆς δημοσίας ἑνὸς γνώμη πράτ[τε]σθαι, |
ἢ[ν] ἐκ συνηθίας ἐπαντρέχοντες οἱ χρόνοι ἀπήτουν. Ἀκολούθως
τοίνυν γεγένηται ἐπιμε[ρ]ισθῆναι τοὺς χρόνους εἰς τὰς τέσσαρας
πόλεις, αἵτινες | μητροπόλεις ἐν Ἀσίᾳ ψηφίζονται, ὡς τὴν τῆς
πενταετηρίδος ἔκδοσιν τοιαύτην ἔχειν τὴν κατάστασιν καὶ μηδε-
5 πώποτε δύνασθαι λείπειν ‖ τὸν κοσμούμενον ὑπὸ τοῦ τῆς Ἀσίας
στεφάνου. Ἀλλ' οὔτε ἐπιφορτίζεσθαί τις δύναται ὑπὸ τοῦ δαπανή-
ματος, ἐπὰν μάλιστα ἀμοιβαδὸν τρεχόντων | τῶν χρόνων ἑκάστη
τῶν μ.ητροπόλεων μετὰ πενταετῆ τὸν χρόνον δίδωσιν τὸν λιτουρ-
γή[σ]οντα. Καίτοι ἡδέως προσηκάμεθα ἐπί περ τοὺς τε|χθέντας
ἐν ταῖς μικραῖς πόλεσιν, ἐπὰν δημοτικωτέρας γενάμενοι ψυχῆς
τὸν ἔπαινον τὸν ἐκ τοῦ δήμου φαντάζωντε, ἐξουσίαν αὐτοῖς |
παρέχεσθαι τοῦ ἐν τῇ Ἐφεσίων μητροπό[λ]ει μόνη τὴν ἀσιαρχίαν
ἢ τὴν ἀλυταρχίαν αὐτὸν ἀνύειν καὶ τοῖς καθήκοις τοῖς καλλίοσιν
ἐκ τῆς ἐπιφανοῦς | λειτουργίας φαίνεσθαι. Ὅθεν, ἐπειδὴ ἐκ τῆς
εὐμοιρίας τῶν καιρῶν τῶν ἡμετέρων αἱ ἐπιθυμίαι αἱ πλίονα τὴν
10 ἑορτὴν ἔχουσαι ὀφίλουσιν αὔξεσθαι ‖ καὶ παρ' ἡμῶν αὐτῶν ἔχειν
τὴν σπουδήν, βουλομένοις αὐτοῖς λειτουργεῖν παρέχομεν ἄδιαν,
εἰς τοῦτο μόνον διασφαλιζόμενοι τοὺς τοιούτους, ἵνα μ[ὴ] | τῶν
ἰδίων πόλεων ἐπιλανθανόμενοι πάντη ἑαυτοὺς μεταγράφουσιν,
Φῆστε τιμιώτατε καὶ προσφιλέστατε. Ἡ ἐπαινετὴ ἐνπειρία σου
τοῦ ἡμετέρου θ[ε]σ|πίσματος ἀκολουθησάτω τῇ γνώμη καὶ πάντας
τοὺς εἰς ταύτην τὴν τιμὴν ἐπιτρέχοντας πάσας πρότερον τὰς
λιτουργίας τῇ ἑαυτοῦ πόλει ἀποπληροῦν | προσταξάτω, πληρω-
θέντων δὲ τῶν λιτουργημάτων εἰς τὴν τιμὴν τὴν μίζονα, τουτέστιν
ὅλης τῆς [ἐ]παρχίας σπεύδουσιν αὐτοῖς ἄδιαν παρεχέτω, δυνα-
μένοις μ[ετὰ] | ταῦτα καὶ τὸ τῶν λαμπροτάτων ἀξίωμα
κ[α]τ[αδ]έχεσθαι, οὕτως μέντοι, ὡς πρότερον αὐτοὺς τὸ ἱκανὸν
ποιοῦντας τῷ νόμῳ εἰς τὸν ἑαυτῶν τόπον ὑποκαθίσταν(ται)
15 τα[ῖς] ‖ ἑαυτῶν πατράσιν ἑτέρους. Οὔτε δὲ ἑτέρο[θι λ]υσιτελεῖν
νενομίκαμεν αὐτοῖς, ἵνα ἀναλώσ(α)ντες τὰ ἑαυτῶν μετὰ τοὺς
πόνους τῶν λειτουργημάτων ἀπα[χθεὶς] | ὡς νεαρὸς τίρων εἰς
ἕτερον βο[υλευτ]ή[ριο]ν ἑαυτὸν μεταγράφει ὀφίλων ἐν τῇ (ἑ)αυτοῦ
(μᾶ)λλον ζῆ[ῇ]ν τε καὶ φαίνεσθαι πόλει.

[504]

FROM ITALY AND THE PROVINCES

The provincial games at this period were held in four cities in the province of Asia, and the liturgy of asiarch or alytarch could legally be held only by residents of those cities. Citizens of other cities in the province were ambitious to attain these honors, and by this rescript the emperors gave them permission to hold these offices on condition that they first perform all the regular liturgies of their place of origin (*cf. Cod. Th.* 15. 5. 1). The performance of these liturgies in a metropolitan city did not confer citizenship in that city, and these aspirants for provincial honors from the smaller towns could not renounce their allegiance to their local curia (*cf. Cod. Th.* 12. 1. 106). In this period it is evident that citizens sought this method of escape from the obligations of their native place (*Cod. Th.* 12. 1. 176). *Cf. Jahreshefte d. öst. arch. Inst.* 8 (1905), *Beiblatt,* 74 ff.

159. TITULUS HONORARIUS
(376 p. Chr.)

CIL. vi, 1736; Dessau, 1256.

Hymetii. — | . . . Iulio Festo Hymetio c. v., | correctori Tusciae et Umbriae, praetori urbano, | consulari Campaniae cum Samnio, || vicario urbis Romae aeternae, proconsuli | provinciae Africae, ob 5 insignia eius | in rempublicam merita et ob depulsam | ab eadem provincia famis et inopiae vastitatem | consiliis et provisionibus, et quod caste || in eadem provincia integreque versatus est, | *qu*od neque 10 aequitati in cognoscendo | neque iustitiae defuerit, quod studium | sacerdotii provinciae restituerit | ut nunc a conpetitoribus adpetatur || quod antea formidini fuerit: ob quae eadem | provincia Africa, 15 decretis ad divinos principes | dominos nostros missis | Valentem Gratianum et Valentinianum | perpetuos Augustos, || statuam unam 20 apud Carthaginem sub auro, | alteram quoque Romae eidem sub auro | postulandam esse credidit, quod nulli | proconsulum vel ex proconsulibus | statuendam (*sic*) antea postularit. (*In latere*) dd. nn. Val*en*te *V et Valentiniano coss.* . . . . .

Found in Rome. Hymetius' proconsulship in Africa began in 366 (*cf. Cod. J.* 3. 61. 1; *Cod. Th.* 9. 19. 3). This inscription furnishes proof of a *concilium* in Africa Proconsularis in the fourth century. Several other references to this *concilium* are found in the *Codices, e.g. Cod. J.* 2. 12. 21; *Cod. Th.* 11. 30. 15. The steps which Augustus (*cf.* Cass. Dio, 56. 25) and Nero took (*cf.* Tac. *Ann.* 15. 22) to prevent provinces from passing complimentary decrees in honor of a governor were evidently ineffective. Several such decrees are extant, *e.g. CIL.* x, 1430–1432, 3853; iii, 1412, 1741. On the *concilia, cf.* pp. 162 *ff.*

160. INDEX SODALIUM FAMILIAE PUBLICAE
(saec. iv p. Chr.?)

CIL. xiv, 255; Dessau, 6153.

Familia Publica:

Ost. Herme	s tab.	Onesimu	s
Dionysiu	s ark.	Ost. Callistu	s
Euaristu	s ark.	Geminius Trophimianus	
5 Ost. Eutychu	s	Ost. Appianu	s
Ost. Asclepiade	s	Vetulenius Primion	
Ost. Liberali	s	Mamidia Hygia	
Ost. Primio	n	Ost. Sabinu	s
Ost. Polygonu	s	Mumius Luciu	s
10 Faustu	s	Onesimu	s
Ost. Epafroditu	s	Ost. Sanctu	s

(*sequuntur alia nomina sexaginta et unum*).

Found at Ostia. Into this college even freemen (*e.g.* Geminius Trophimianus) were admitted. For the *tabularius* and *arkarius* of *collegia, cf.* Kornemann, *R.E.* 4, 423 *f.*

161 DECRETUM PROVINCIAE AFRICAE
(saec. iv p. Chr.?)

CIL. viii, *S.* 11017.

5 *Geni*o senatus | ob *repar*atam | iustitiam, | servata defen‖saqu*e* p(rovincia) A(frica), | Gigth*e*nses | publice ex | d(ecreto) p(rovinciae) A(fricae).

Found at Gigthi in the provincia Tripolitana. It records the passage of a resolution in the *concilium*, probably of Africa Proconsularis, expressing gratitude to the Roman senate, probably for the conviction and punishment of an unjust governor, against whom the province had made charges. On Gigthi, *cf.* no. 115.

[506]

II. DOCUMENTS FROM EGYPT

162. EDICTUM L. AEMILI RECTI DE ANGARIA
(42 p. Chr.)

P. Br. Mus. 1171; Wilcken, *Chrestomathie*, 439.

Λεύκιος Αἰμίλλις Ῥῆκτος λέγει. | Μηδενὶ ἐξέστω ἐνγαρεύειν
τοὺς ἐπὶ τῆς χώρας | μηδὲ ἐφόδια ἢ ἄλλο τι δωρεὰν αἰτεῖν ἄτερ
τοῦ | ἐμο[ῦ] διπλώματος, λαμ[β]άνειν δὲ ἕκασ[το]ν τῶν ‖ ἐχ[όν- 5
τ]ων ἐμὸν δίπλωμα τὰ αὐταάρκει ἐπιδήτια | τιμὴν ἀποδιδόντας
αὐτῶν. Ἐὰν δέ τις | μηνυθῆι ἢ τῶν στρατευομένων ἢ τῶν
μαχαιροφόρω(ν) | ἢ ὅστις οὖν τῶν ὑπηρετῶν τῶ[ν ἐν τ]αῖς
δημοσ[ίαις] | χρήαις παρ[ὰ τ]ὸ ἐμὸν διάτα[γμ]α [π]εποηκὼς ἢ
βεβιασ‖μένος τινὰ τῶν ἀπὸ τῆς χώρας ἢ ἀργυρολογήσας, | κατὰ 10
τούτου τῆι ἀνωτάτωι χρήσομαι τειμωρίαι. | (Ἔτους) β Τιβερίου
Κλαυδίου Καίσαρος Σεβαστοῦ Αὐτοκράτορος | Γερμανικοῦ δ.

l. 3. ἄτερ τοῦ is a correction made by the scribe for ἄτερ.
l. 5. αὐταάρκει Wilcken; αὐτὰ ἃ ἀρκεῖ Grenfell-Hunt, *Archiv*, 4, 539.
ἐπιδήτια = ἐπιτήδεια.

Beginning with the edict of Germanicus in A.D. 19 (Preisigke,
Sammelbuch, 3924), we find a number of edicts issued by various
prefects of Egypt designed to check the extortions practised by
soldiers and officials in the villages. *Cf.* nos. 163, 165. In spite
of the fact that Egypt was under the direct supervision of the
emperor, it is evident that the control of the soldiery in the outlying
regions was a difficult problem in the very beginning of the empire.
Although the severest penalties are threatened, the frequent repetition of similar edicts shows that the penalties were not inflicted,
and the abuses remained unchecked. It is probable that the imperial
provinces where soldiers were stationed suffered in the same way,
but documentary evidence is lacking until the third century. *Cf.*
nos. 139, 141–144; Rostowzew, *Klio*, 6 (1906), 249 *ff.*

DOCUMENTS FROM EGYPT

163. EDICTUM CN. VERGILI CAPITONIS PRAEFECTI
(49 p. Chr.)

CIG. 3, 4956 (cf. Add., p. 1236); Lafoscade, 119; Ditt. Or. Gr.
665.

Ποσιδώνιος στρατηγός. | Τῆς πεμφθείσης μοι ὑπὸ τοῦ κυρίου
ἡγεμόνος | ἐπιστολῆς σὺν τῶι ὑποτεταγμένωι προστάγ|ματι τὰ
5 ἀντίγραφα ὑμεῖν ὑποτέταχα, ἵν᾽ εἰδό‖[τες] αὐτὰ καὶ [εὐπ]ειθῆτε
καὶ μηδὲν ὑπεναντίον τοῖς προσ|[τεταγμένο]ις ποιῆ[τε]. Ἐπὶ
ἔτο[υς] ἐνάτου Τιβερίου Κλαυδίου Καίσαρος | [Σεβαστοῦ Γερ-
μανι]κοῦ Αὐτοκράτορος Μεχεὶρ ζ΄. |
Γν[(αῖος) Ο]ὐεργίλιος Κ]απίτων Ποσειδωνίωι, στρατηγῶι
Ὀάσε[ως | Θηβαΐδος, χαίρειν. Ὁ ἐπὶ] τῆς πόλεως [πρ]οέθηκα
10 διάταγμα, ‖ [τούτου ἀντίγραφον] ἔπεμψά σ[οι]. Βούλομαι οὖν
[σ]ε ἐν | [τάχει ἔν] τε τῆι μητροπόλει τοῦ νομοῦ καὶ καθ᾽
ἕ[κ|ασ]τον τόπο]ν αὐτὸ προθεῖναι σαφέσι καὶ εὐσήμοις | [γράμ-
μασιν], ἵνα [παν]τὶ [ἔκ]δηλα γένηται τὰ ὑπ᾽ ἐμοῦ [σταθέντα]. |
15 Γναῖος Οὐ[εργί]λιος Καπίτων λέγει. ‖ Καὶ πάλαι μὲν ἤκουόν
τινας δαπάνας ἀδίκους καὶ παραλογισ[θεί|σ]ας ὑπὸ τῶν πλεο-
νεκτικῶς καὶ ἀναιδῶς ταῖς ἐξουσίαις ἀπο|χρωμένων γείνεσθαι,
καὶ νῦν δὲ ἐν τῆι τῶν Λιβύων μάλιστα | ἔγνων ὑποθέσει, ὅτι
ἀναλίσκεταί τινα ἁρπαζόντων ἀδε|ῶς τῶν ἐπὶ ταῖς χρείαις ὡς
20 ὑποκείμενα εἰς δαπάνας ‖ καὶ ξένια (ἑ)αυτῶν τὰ μήτε ὄντα μήτε
ὀφείλοντα εἶναι, | ὁμοίως δὲ καὶ ἀνγαρειῶν ὀνόματι. Διὸ κελεύω⟨ι⟩
τοὺς | διοδεύοντας διὰ τῶν νομῶν στρατιώτας καὶ ἱππεῖς καὶ |
στάτορας καὶ ἑκατοντάρχας καὶ χειλιάρχους καὶ τοὺς ⟨λο⟩ι|ποὺς
25 ἅπαντας μηδὲν λαμβάνειν μηδὲ ἀνγαρεύειν εἰ μή ‖ τινες ἐμὰ
διπλώματα ἔχουσιν· καὶ τούτους δὲ στέγηι μόνον δέ|χεσθαι
τοὺς διερχομένους, ὑποκείμενόν τε μηδένα μηδὲν πράτ|τειν ἔξω
τῶν ὑπὸ Μαξίμου σταθέντων. Ἐὰν δέ τις δῶι ἢ ὡς δε|δομένον
λογίσηται καὶ εἰσπράξηι δημοσίαι, τοῦτον τὸ δεκαπλοῦν |
ἐγὼ⟨ι⟩ ἐκπράξω⟨ι⟩ οὗ αὐτὸς ἔπραξεν τὸν νομόν, καὶ τῶι μηνύ-
30 σαντι ‖ τὸ τετραπλάσιον μέρος δώσω⟨ι⟩ ἐκ τῆς τοῦ κατακριθέντος
οὐσίας. | Ο[ἱ μὲν οὖν β]ασιλικοὶ γραμματεῖς καὶ κωμογραμ-
ματεῖς καὶ τοπογραμ|[ματ]εῖς κατὰ νομὸν πάντα ὅσα δαπανᾶται
ἐκ τοῦ νομοῦ, εἴ τινα | πέπρακται παραλόγως ἢ ἄλλο τι ἀνα-
γραφ[έσ]θωσαν καὶ ἐ[ν ἡμέραις] | ἐξήκοντα ἐπιδότωσαν οἱ δ᾽

ἐ[ν]τὸς Θηβαΐδος διὰ τετραμήνου, [εἰς τὰ] ‖ λογιστήρια καὶ πρὸς 35
Βασιλείδην τὸν Καίσαρος ἀπελεύθερον τὰ ἐξ ἑκάσ|του λογι-
στηρίου, καὶ τοὺς ἐκλογιστὰς πεμπέτωσαν, ἵν' ἐάν τι παρὰ τὸ
δί|καιον λελογευμένον ἢ πεπραγμένον ἦι, τοῦτο διορθώσομαι·
Ὁμοίως | δ[ὲ] βούλομαι δηλοῦσθαι . . . . (reliqui versus,
maxime mutili, omissi sunt.)

This inscription is engraved on the great temple at Girgeh. The
prefect sent a copy of the edict to the strategus in command of
the Thebaid with instructions to publish it in various places. The
tenor of the edict is similar to that of nos. 113, 139, 141, 162, 165;
cf. P.S.I. 446. Here we have the confession of the prefect that
complaints of the exactions of soldiers and officials had long been
known to him, but apparently no action had been taken until the
Libyans had appealed to him. In this edict the punishment is more
explicit than that prescribed in no. 162. The prefect promises to
exact tenfold from anyone who makes exactions without a requisition, and a reward of fourfold is to be given to the informer.

164. EDICTUM L. LUSI GETAE DE
IMMUNITATE SACERDOTUM
(54 p. Chr.)

Lafoscade, 120; Ditt. Or. Gr. 664; Milne, Greek Inscriptions,
p. 11.

Λούσιος [Γέτας] Κλαυδίωι Λυσα|νίαι στρατηγῶι Ἀρσινοεί-
του | χαίρειν. Τὸ ὑπογεγραμμένον | ἔκθεμα πρόθες ἐν οἷς καθήκει ‖
τοῦ νομοῦ τόποις, ἵνα πάντες | (ε)ἰδῶσι τὰ ὑπ' ἐμοῦ κελευόμενα. | 5
Ἔρρωσο. | Λούκιος Λούσιος [Γέτας] λέγει. | Ἐπεὶ Ἀρσινοείτου
ἱερεῖς θεοῦ ‖ Σοκνοπαίου ἐνέτυχόν μοι | λέγοντες εἰς γεωργίας 10
ἄγεσθαι, | τούτους μὲν ἀπολύω(ι)· ἐὰν | δέ τις ἐξελεγχθῆι τὰ
ὑπ' ἐμοῦ | ἅπαξ κεκριμένα ἢ προστα‖χθέντα κεινήσας ἢ βου- 15
ληθεὶς | ἀμφίβολα ποιῆσαι, κατὰ [π]ᾶν | ἢ ἀργυρικῶς ἢ
σωματικῶς | κολασθήσεται. L ιδ' Τιβερίου | Κλαυδίου Καίσαρος
Σεβαστοῦ, ‖ Φαρμουθὶ ι'.   20

This inscription is carved on a stone now in the Museum of
Cairo. The edict of the prefect indicates the desire of the government to control the license of subordinates who had apparently

DOCUMENTS FROM EGYPT

been guilty of disregarding the orders issued from the office of the prefect (*cf.* nos. 162, 163, 165). On the position of the priesthood in Egypt under the empire see the commentary on no. 178; Otto, *Priester und Tempel, passim.*

165. EDICTUM TIBERI IULI ALEXANDRI PRAEFECTI
(68 p. Chr.)

Ditt. *Or. Gr.* 669; *CIG.* 4957 (*cf.* vol. 3, *Add.* p. 1236); Riccobono, p. 253; Girard, p. 174.

Ἰούλιος Δημήτριος, στρατηγὸς Ὀάσεως Θηβαΐδος. Τοῦ πεμφθέντος μοι διατάγματος ὑπὸ τοῦ κυρίου ἡγεμόνος | Τιβερίου Ἰουλίου Ἀλεξάνδρου τὸ ἀντίγραφον ὑμεῖν ὑπέταξα, ἵν᾿ εἰδότες ἀπολαύητε τῶν εὐεργεσιῶν. L β΄ Λουκίου Λιβίου Σεβαστοῦ Σουλπικίου | Γάλβα Αὐτοκράτορος Φαωφὶ α΄ Ἰουλίαι Σεβαστῆι.

Τιβέριος Ἰούλιος Ἀλέξανδρος λέγει. Πᾶσαν πρόνοιαν ποιούμενος τοῦ διαμένειν τῶι προσήκοντι κα|ταστήματι τὴν πόλιν ἀπολαύουσαν τῶν εὐεργεσιῶν ἃς ἔχει παρὰ τῶν Σεβαστῶν καὶ τοῦ τὴν Αἴγυπτον ἐν εὐσταθείαι διάγουσαν εὐθύμως ὑπηρετεῖν
5 τῆι τε εὐθηνίαι καὶ τῆι μεγίσ‖τηι τῶν νῦν καιρῶν εὐδαιμονίαι, μὴ⟨ι⟩ βαρυνομένην καιναῖς καὶ ἀδίκοις εἰσπράξεσι· σχεδὸν δὲ ἐξ οὗ τῆς πόλεως ἐπέβην καταβοώμενος ὑπὸ τῶν ἐντυγχανόντων καὶ κατ᾿ ὀλίγους καὶ κα|τὰ πλήθη⟨ι⟩ τῶν τε ἐνθάδε εὐσχημονεστάτων καὶ τῶν γεωργούντων τὴν χώραν μεμφομένων τὰς ἔγγιστα γενομένας ἐπηρείας, οὐ διέλιπον μὲν κατὰ τὴν ἐμαυτοῦ δύναμιν τὰ ἐπείγοντα | ἐπανορθούμενος· ἵνα δὲ εὐθυμότεροι πάντα ἐλπίζητε παρὰ τοῦ ἐπιλάμψαντος ἡμεῖν ἐπὶ σωτηρίαι τοῦ παντὸς ἀνθρώπων γένους εὐεργέτου Σεβαστοῦ Αὐτοκράτορος Γάλβα τά τε πρὸς σωτηρίαν | καὶ τὰ πρὸς ἀπόλαυσιν, καὶ γινώσκητε ὅτι ἐφρόντισα τῶν πρὸς τὴν ὑμετέραν βοήθειαν ἀνηκόντων, προέγραψα ἀναγκαίως περὶ ἑκάστου τῶν ἐπιζητουμένων, ὅσα ἔξεστί μοι κρεί|νειν καὶ ποιεῖν, τὰ δὲ μείζονα καὶ δεόμε⟨να⟩ τῆς τοῦ αὐτοκράτορος δυνάμεως καὶ μεγαλειότητος αὐτῶι δηλώσω⟨ι⟩ μετὰ πάσης
10 ἀληθείας, τῶν θεῶν ταμιευσαμένων εἰς τοῦτον τὸν ‖ ἱερώτατον
§1 καιρὸν τὴν τῆς οἰκουμένης ἀσφάλειαν. Ἔγνων γὰρ πρὸ παντὸς εὐλογωτάτην οὖσαν τὴν ἔντευξιν ὑμῶν ὑπὲρ τοῦ μὴ⟨ι⟩ ἄκοντας ἀνθρώπους εἰς τελωνείας ἢ⟨ι⟩ ἄλ|λας μισθώσεις οὐσιακὰς παρὰ τὸ κοινὸν [ἔ]θος τῶν ἐπαρχειῶν πρὸς βίαν ἄγεσθαι, καὶ ὅτι οὐκ

[510]

ὀλ[ίγ]ω[ι] ἔβλαψε τὰ πράγματα τὸ πολλοὺς ἀπείρους ὄντας
τῆς τοιαύ|της πραγματείας ἀχθῆναι μετ' ἀνάγκης ἐπιβληθέντων
αὐτοῖς τῶν τελῶν. Διόπερ καὶ αὐτὸς οὔτε ἤγαγόν τινα εἰς
τελωνείαν ἢ⟨ι⟩ μίσθωσιν οὔτε ἄξω⟨ι⟩ εἰδὼς τοῦτο | συμφέρειν
καὶ ταῖς κυριακαῖς ψήφοις τὸ μετὰ προθυμίας ἑκόντας πραγμα-
τεύεσθαι τοὺς δυνατούς. Πέπεισμαι δὲ ὅτι οὐδ' εἰς τὸ μέλλον
ἄκοντάς τις ἄξει τελώνας | ἢ⟨ι⟩ μισθωτάς, ἀλλὰ διαμισθώσει
τοῖς βουλομένοις ἑκουσίως προ(σ)έρχεσθαι, μᾶλλον τὴν τῶν
προτέρων ἐπάρχων αἰώνιον συνήθειαν φυλάσσων ἢ⟨ι⟩ τὴν πρόσ-
καιρόν τινος ἀδικίαν ‖ μειμησάμενος.   Ἐπειδὴ⟨ι⟩ ἔνιοι 15
προφάσει τῶν δημοσίων καὶ ἀλλότρια δάνεια παραχωρούμενοι §2
εἴς τε τὸ πρακτόρειόν τινας παρέδοσαν καὶ εἰς ἄλλας φυλακάς,
ἃς καὶ δι' αὐτὸ τοῦτο | ἔγνων ἀναιρεθείσας, ἵνα αἱ πράξεις τῶν
δανείων ἐκ τῶν ὑπαρχόντων ὦσι καὶ μὴ⟨ι⟩ ἐκ τῶν σωμάτων,
ἑπόμενος τῆι τοῦ θεοῦ Σεβαστοῦ βουλήσει κελεύω⟨ι⟩ μηδένα τῆι
τῶν δημοσίων προφά|σει παραχωρεῖσθαι παρ' ἄλλων δάνεια ἃ
μὴ⟨ι⟩ αὐτὸς ἐξ ἀρχῆς ἐδάνεισεν, μὴ⟨ι⟩ δ' ὅλως κατακλείεσθαί
τινας ἐλευθέρους εἰς φυλακὴν ἡντινοῦν, εἰ μὴ⟨ι⟩ κακοῦργον, μηδ'
εἰς τὸ πρακ|τόρειον, ἔξω⟨ι⟩ τῶν ὀφειλόντων εἰς τὸν κυριακὸν
λόγον.................'Ενετεύχθην δὲ καὶ περὶ τῶν ἀτε- §4
λειῶν καὶ κουφοτελειῶν, ἐν αἷς ἐστιν καὶ τὰ προσοδικά, ἀξιούντων
αὐτὰς φυλαχθῆναι, ὡς ὁ θεὸς Κλαύδιος | ἔγραψεν Ποστόμωι
ἀπολύων, καὶ λεγόντων ὕστερον κατακεκρίσθαι τὰ ὑπὸ ἰδιωτῶν
πραχθέντα ἐν τῶι μέσωι χρόνωι μετὰ τὸ Φλάκκον κατακρεῖναι
καὶ πρὸ τοῦ τὸν θεὸν | Κλαύδιον ἀπολῦσαι. Ἐπεὶ οὖν καὶ
Βάλβιλλος καὶ Οὐηστεῖνος ταῦτα ἀπέλυσαν, ἀμφοτέρων τῶν
ἐπάρχων ἐπικρίματα φυλάσσω⟨ι⟩ καὶ ἐκείνων κατηκολουθηκότων
τῆι | τοῦ θεοῦ Κλαυδίου χάριτι, ὥστε ἀπολελύσθαι τὰ μηδέπω⟨ι⟩
ἐξ αὐτῶν εἰσπραχθέντα, δηλονότι εἰς τὸ λοιπὸν τηρουμένης
αὐτοῖς τῆς ἀτελείας καὶ κουφοτελείας..................... §6
Ἀκόλουθον δέ ἐστιν ταῖς τῶν Σεβαστῶν | χάρισι καὶ τὸ τοὺς
ἐνγενεῖς Ἀλεξανδρεῖς καὶ ἐν τῆι [χώ]ραι διὰ φιλεργίαν κατοι-
κοῦντας εἰς μηδεμίαν [λειτουργίαν ἄγεσθαι, ὃ ὑμεῖς] | πολλάκις
μὲν ἐπεζητήσατε, καὐτὸς δὲ φυλάσσω⟨ι⟩, ὥστε μηδένα τῶν
ἐνγενῶν Ἀλεξανδρέων εἰς λειτουργίας χωρικὰς ἄγεσθαι. Μελήσει §7
δέ ‖ μοι καὶ τὰς στρατηγίας μετὰ διαλογισμὸν πρὸς τριετίαν 35
ἐνχ(ε)ιρίζειν τοῖς κατασταθησομένοις.................‖.Οὐκ 45
                                                              §10

DOCUMENTS FROM EGYPT

ἀγνοῶ⟨ι⟩ δ' ὅτι πολλὴν πρόνοιαν ποιεῖσθε καὶ τοῦ τὴν
Αἴγυπτον ἐν εὐσταθείαι δια[μένειν,] ἐξ ἧς [ἃς εἰς τὸν βίον
ἅπαντα] | χορηγίας ἔχετε, ὅσα οἷόν τε ἦν ἐπηνωρθωσάμην.
Ἐνέτυχον γάρ μοι πολλάκις οἱ καθ' ὅλην τὴν χώραν γεωρ-
γοῦντες καὶ ἐδήλωσαν ὅτι πολλὰ καινῶς κατεκρίθησα[ν, καίπερ
δῆλον ὂν ὅσα δεῖ | φέρειν] τελέσματα σιτικὰ καὶ ἀργυρικά,
καὶ οὐκ ἔξον τοῖς βουλομένοις εὐχερῶς καθολικόν τι καινίζειν.
Ταῦτα δὲ καὶ τὰ τοιαῦτα κατακρίματα οὐκ ἐπὶ τὴν Θηβαΐδα
μόνην [εὖρον ἐκτεινόμενα | οὐ]δὲ ἐπὶ τοὺς πόρρω⟨ι⟩ νομοὺς τῆς
κάτω⟨ι⟩ χώρας, ἀλλὰ καὶ τὰ προάστια τῆς πόλεως ἔφθασεν
τήν τε Ἀλεξανδρέων καλουμένην χώραν καὶ τὸν Μαρεώτην
[λαβεῖν. Διὸ κελεύω | το]ῖς κατὰ νομὸν στρατηγοῖς ἵνα εἴ
τινα καινῶς τῆι ἔγγιστα πενταετίαι τὰ μὴ⟨ι⟩ πρότερον τελούμενα
καθολικῶς ἢ⟨ι⟩ πληθικῶς νομῶν ἢ⟨ι⟩ τοπαρ[χιῶν ἢ κωμῶν
50 . . . . || κα]τεκρίθη⟨ι⟩, ταῦτα εἰς τὴν προτέραν τάξιν
ἀποκαταστήσωσιν, παρέντες αὐτῶν τὴν ἀπαίτησιν, ἃ καὶ ἐπὶ
τὸν διαλογισμὸν ἀχθέντα ἐκ τῶν [. . . . . ἐξαιρεθήτω. |
§ 11 Ἐξήτ]ασα δ' ἔτι καὶ πρότερον καὶ τὴν ἄμετρον ἐξουσίαν τῶν
ἐγλογιστῶν διὰ τὸ πάντας αὐτῶν καταβοᾶν ἐπὶ τῶι παρα-
γράφειν αὐτοὺς πλεῖστα ἐκ τῆ[ς ἰδίας ἐπιθυ|μίας·] ἐξ οὗ συνέ-
βαινεν αὐτοὺς μὲν ἀργυρίζεσθαι, τὴν δὲ Αἴγυπτον ἀνάστατον
γείνεσθαι. Καὶ νῦν τοῖς αὐτοῖς παραγγέλλω μηδὲν ἐξ ὁμοιώ-
μα[τος | ἐπι]γράφειν ἀλ[λ]αχῆι ἄλλο τι τῶν καθόλου χωρὶς τοῦ
κρεῖναι τὸν ἔπαρχον. Κελεύω⟨ι⟩ δὲ καὶ τοῖς στρατηγοῖς μηδὲν
παρὰ ἐγλογιστῶν μεταλαμβάνειν χωρὶς τῆ[ς ἀδείας | τοῦ]
ἐπάρχου. Καὶ οἱ ἄλλοι δὲ πραγματικοί, ἐάν τι εὑρεθῶσι ψευδὲς
ἢ⟨ι⟩ παρὰ τὸ δέον παραγεγραφότες, καὶ τοῖς ἰδιώταις ἀποδώ-
55 σουσιν ὅσον ἀπηιτήθησαν καὶ τὸ [ἴσον] || ἀποτ(ε)ίσουσιν εἰς τὸ
δημοσιον. . . . . (reliqui versus omissi sunt.)

From Khargeh. This inscription is most important for a study
of the policy of the imperial administration in attempting to correct
abuses in the government of Egypt. The large number of similar
edicts found in Egypt show that the problem of good administration
was difficult even in a country under the direct supervision of the
emperor. The edict is published in fifteen sections each dealing
with a specific problem. In § 1 the prefect forbids the practice of
compulsion in contracting for the collection of taxes and in the

DOCUMENTS FROM EGYPT

leasing of public lands (γῆ οὐσιακή). For the difficulty in securing contractors for farming the taxes, see no. 167. A similar law prevailed in other parts of the empire (*Dig.* 39. 4. 9, 1; 49. 14. 3, 6), although in cases where no bidders were forthcoming former contractors were compelled to take the contract on the same terms as their original bid (*Dig.* 39. 4. 11, 5). In § 2 the prefect corrects an abuse which had developed in the capitals of the nomes where the local magistrates had been guilty of seizing the property of debtors and confining them in the public prisons, although the law forbade the distraint of a person for debt, unless he owed the imperial treasury. In § 4 we find that those who enjoyed immunity of various kinds and those who occupied lands such as the γῆ προσόδου, on which there was a lighter tax than on other imperial property, were deprived of their privileges by former governors. To citizens of these classes Julius confirms their former rights. In § 6 we learn that citizens of Alexandria resident in other parts of Egypt were exempt from local liturgies. The full liturgical system was not introduced into Egypt until later, and it is probable that, when it finally became a part of the Egyptian administrative policy, the Alexandrians were released from all local, but not from imperial, liturgies (*cf.* no. 173; p. 103). In §§ 10 and 11 the prefect forbids the superexactions imposed by officials in the nomes. The legal assessment and the quota of taxation was determined every fourteen years. Officials had arbitrarily increased the quota and had grown rich by appropriating the excess. They are ordered to restore the amount of their illegal extortions for the five years preceding the publication of the edict and to pay an equal sum to the public treasury.

166. DE CENSU δωδεκαδράχμων
(86–87 p. Chr.)

P. Oxy. 258, ll. 4–26; Wilcken, *Chrestomathie*, 216.

. . . .

Διδύμου τῶν ἀπ᾿ Ὀξυρύγχ[ων πόλεως] ‖ ἐπ᾿ ἀμβόδου Πυμενικῆς. 5
Κατὰ τὰ | κριθέντα ἐπὶ τῶν προσβεβηκότων | ἰς τρισκαιδεκα-
ετεῖς, εἰ ἐξ ἀμφοτέ|ρων γονέων μη[τ]ροπολειτῶν δω|δεκαδράχμων
ε[ἰσ]ίν, ἐτάγη ἐπὶ ‖ τοῦ αὐτοῦ ἀμφόδου ὁ υ[ἱός μ]ου . . . . |ος 10

[513]

μητρὸς Θεψεῖτος τῆς [Δι]δύμου | προσβέβηκεν εἰς τρισκαι-
δεκα[ετεῖ]ς | τῶι ἐνεστῶτι. (ἔτει) Αὐτοκράτ[ορος] | Καίσαρος
15 Δομιτιανοῦ Σεβαστοῦ ‖ Γερμανικοῦ. Ὅθεν πα[ρ]α[γενόμε]‖νος
ἰς τὴν τούτου ἐπ[ίκρισιν ⟨δηλῶ⟩ εἶ]‖ναι ἐμὲ κατὰ τ..........
... | καὶ τὸν τῆ[ς μη]τ[ρὸς αὐτοῦ πατέ]‖ρα Δίδυμον ......
20 .... ‖ ἀναγραφόμενον ενο........ | ἐπ’ ἀμφόδου
[........ος καὶ τε]‖τελεύτηκε τ[ῶι ...... ἔτει Νέρω]‖νος καὶ
ὀμνύ[ω Αὐτοκράτορα Καίσαρα] | Δομιτιανὸν Σε[βαστὸν Γερ-
25 μανικὸν] ‖ ἀληθῆ εἶναι [τὰ προγεγραμμένα]. | Ἔτους ἕκ[τ]ου
[Αὐτοκράτορος Καίσαρος] Δομιτι[ανοῦ Σεβαστοῦ Γερμανικοῦ
.....]‖

From Oxyrhynchus. The documents which deal with the registration of citizens, especially with the *epicrisis*, or scrutiny of those who claim more favored treatment, are important for the study of the different gradations in the status of the residents of Egypt. Distinctions of a similar kind are traceable in Asiatic towns (*cf.* pp. 75 f.), but little is known of the status of the various classes outside of Egypt. The present state of our information in regard to the *epicrisis* is summarized by Grenfell-Hunt (*P. Oxy.* 1451, 1452. See the references to previous literature on the subject cited by them). The favored classes were veterans, Roman citizens with their freedmen and slaves, Alexandrians, and Graeco-Egyptians. The *epicrisis* in the case of Romans was held before the prefect or some official delegated by him for the purpose. It was not confined to the question of remission of poll-tax, but was a determination of the legal status of the individual. From the document which we publish here we learn that certain citizens of Oxyrhynchus enjoyed a lower rate of poll-tax (twelve drachmae) than that exacted from the rest of the citizens (forty drachmae). In this declaration the lad is thirteen years old, and he was registered at this age because the poll-tax was levied at fourteen. Both parents were citizens of Oxyrhynchus, and the father and maternal grandfather belonged to the twelve-drachmae class. In other towns the rate of poll-tax for the privileged class varied (Wilcken, *Grundzüge*, 199). From *P. Oxy.* 1452 it seems probable that οἱ ἐκ τοῦ γυμνασίου, or those belonging to a gymnasium, formed a larger class, and within this group the members who paid twelve drachmae were those who received a special remission for some reason which cannot at present be determined. The *epicrisis* of this class may be held before the strategus, the royal scribe, or others (*P. Oxy.* 1452, l. 2). *Cf.* Bell, *Archiv*, 6 (1920), 107 *ff*.

167. DE VECTIGALIBUS LOCANDIS
(ca. 81–96 p. Chr.)

P. Oxy. 44; Wilcken, *Chrestomathie*, 275.

[Πα]νίσκος ....λας στρατηγὸς Ὀξυρυ[γ]χ(ίτου) |
['Ασ]κληπιάδ[ηι βασιλικῶ]ι γραμμα(τεῖ) τοῦ αὐτοῦ νομοῦ |
χαίρειν. | Ἐπὶ τῆς γενομένης διαπράσεως τῶν τελωνι‖κῶν ὑπὸ 5
τοῦ τε ἐμοῦ καὶ σοῦ ἐπὶ παρόντων καὶ | τῶν εἰωθότων, δυσπειθούν-
των τῶν τὸ ἐν|κύκλιον ἀσχολουμένων καὶ ⟨⟨τοῦ⟩⟩ τὸ ἀγο|ρανόμιον
δημοσιωνῶν ὡς ἱκανὰ βλαπτο|μένων καὶ κινδυνευόντων μετ-
αναστῆ‖ναι, δόξαν ἡμεῖν ἔγραψα τῶι κρατίστωι | ἡγεμόνι περὶ 10
τοῦ πράγματος. Ἀντιγράψαν|τος οὖν αὐτοῦ μοι περὶ τοῦ ἐφ-
ιδόντα τὰς|π[ρο]τέρας μισθώσεις κατὰ τὸ δυνατὸν | [ἀνα]κουφίσαι
τοὺς τελώνας ὑπὲρ τοῦ μὴ ‖ φυγ[ά]δας γενέσθαι τ[ο]ὺς πρὸς 15
β[ίαν] ἀ[γο]‖μένους, καὶ πρότερόν σοι τὸ ἀντίγρ[αφο]ν | τῆς
ἐπιστολῆς μετέδωκα, ἵν᾽ εἰδῆις, καὶ | ὅτι ἀποδημοῦντός σου καὶ
τῶν ὠνῶν | μὴ ἐπιδεδεγμένων ὑπὸ τῶν τελωνῶν ‖ μηδὲ μὴν ἄλλων 20
προσερχ[ομ]ένων αὐ|τοῖς [[πολλάκις]] πολλάκις προκηρυχθει-
σῶν | ἔλαβον χειρογραφείας τῶν τε τὸ ἐν⟨⟨κυ⟩⟩|κύκλιον καὶ τὸ
γραφεῖον ἀσχολουμένων........

l. 15. πρὸς β[ίαν] ἀ[γο]μένους, Wilcken; προσβ[ιβ]α[ζο]μένους,
Grenfell-Hunt.

From Oxyrhynchus. This document furnishes a commentary on the edict of Tiberius Julius Alexander. The tax on sales, which amounted to ten per cent., and the fee to the agoranomus for his services in drawing up contracts, etc. were farmed out to contractors. These had suffered such losses that they were likely to abscond when they were urged to renew their contract, since no bidders had appeared at the last offering. These contracts were let by the strategus and the royal scribe in conjunction. The strategus had written to the prefect concerning the present situation, and the latter had authorized him to examine the former contracts with a

DOCUMENTS FROM EGYPT

view to lightening the conditions in order that those who took the contract under compulsion might not be constrained to avoid the rigorous terms by voluntary exile (*cf.* no. 165).

168. EDICTUM GAI VIBI MAXIMI, PRAEFECTI
(104 p. Chr.)

P. Br. Mus. 3, 904, ll. 18–38; Wilcken, *Chrestomathie*, 202.

Γ[άϊο]ς Οὐί]βιο[ς Μάξιμος ἔπα]ρχ[ος] | Αἰγύπτ[ου λέγει.] ||
20 Τῆς κατ᾽ οἰ[κίαν ἀπογραφῆς ἐ]νεστώ[σης] | ἀναγκαῖόν [ἐστιν
πᾶσιν τοῖ]ς καθ᾽ ἥ[ντινα] | δήποτε αἰτ[ίαν ἀποδημοῦσιν ἀπὸ
τῶν] | νομῶν προσα[γγέλλε]σθαι ἐπα[νελ]|θεῖν εἰς τὰ ἑαυ[τῶν
25 ἐ]φέστια, ἵν[α] || καὶ τὴν συνήθη [οἰ]κονομίαν τῆ[ς ἀπο]|γραφῆς
πληρώσωσιν καὶ τῆι προσ[ηκού]|σηι αὐτοῖς γεωργίαι προσκαρ-
τερήσω[σιν]. | Εἰδὼς μέντο[ι ὅ]τι ἐνίων τῶν [ἀπὸ] | τῆς χώρας
30 ἡ πόλις ἡμῶν ἔχει χρε[ίαν] || βούλομ[αι] πάντα[ς τ]οὺς εὔ[λ]ογον
δο[κοῦν]|τα[ς] ἔχειν τοῦ ἐνθάδε ἐπιμένιν [αἰ]|τίαν ἀπογράφε-
σ[θ]αι παρὰ βουλ...... | Φήστωι ἐπάρχω[ι] εἴλης, ὃν ἐπὶ
35 το[ύτωι] | ἔταξα, οὗ καὶ τὰς [ὑ]πογραφὰς οἱ ἀποδ[εί]||ξαντες
ἀναγκ[αίαν α]ὐτῶν τὴν παρου[σίαν] | λήψοντα[ι κατὰ τ]οῦ[τ]ο
τὸ παράγγελμ[α] | ἐντὸς [τῆς τριακάδος τοῦ ἐν]εσ[τ]ῶτος
μη|νὸς Ἐ[πεὶφ............ ἐ]πανελθεῖν | μεθ᾽ ἧ[ς.......
.... *(reliqui versus omissi sunt.)*

l. 20. [ἐ]νεστώ[σης], Wilcken; [συ]νεστώ[σης], Kenyon-Bell.
l. 34. [ὑ]πογραφάς, Wilcken; [ἀ]πογραφάς, Kenyon-Bell.

From Alexandria. In this edict the prefect orders all those absent from the place of their nativity to return for registration since the census was about to be taken. Many of these absentees were peasants, who had abandoned their farms and had gone to join the urban mob at Alexandria. They are ordered to return to their farms. An exception is made for a few whose services were needed in the city and these are permitted to register with Festus. *Cf.* no. 193; Rostowzew, *Gesch. d. röm. Kol.* 205 *ff.*; Wilcken, *Grundzüge*, 26 *ff.*, 65. Other documents which deal with this subject are *P. Gen.* 16; *P. Fay.* 24; nos. 174, 193, 194. *Cf.* Luke, 2, 3, for a similar law in Judaea at the time of the birth of Christ. This document is not only important for its bearing on the doctrine of *origo*

[516]

DOCUMENTS FROM EGYPT

(ἰδία), but also furnishes our earliest evidence for the urban movement in Egypt under Roman rule.

169. DE SUMPTIBUS γυμνασιαρχίας MINUENDIS
(114–117 p. Chr.)

P. Amh. 2. 70, col. 1; Wilcken, Chrestomathie, 149.

Col. 1, Fragment A

Φήλικι Κλανδίωι Οὐίνδικι τῶι κρατίστωι ἐπ[ιστρ(ατήγωι)]
παρὰ ἀρχόντων | Ἑρμοῦ πόλ(εως). Τοῦ κρατίστου ἡγεμόνος
Ῥουτιλ[ίου Λο]ύπ(ου) κελεύσαντος | συσταλῆναι τὰ πολλὰ τῶν
ἀναλωμάτων τῆ[ς γυ]μνασιαρχίας, ἵν[α οἱ] | καθιστ[α]νάμενοι
προθυμότερον ὑπομέ[νωσ]ι τὸ ἀνάλωμα, || καὶ σοῦ δημοσίαι 5
ἐπιτρέψαντος τοῦ ἀ[ναλώ]μα[τ]ος, ἃ ἐνεδέ|χετο, [σ]υσταλῆναι
καὶ ταῦτα εκου..ι.......ς τοὺς νῦν | γυμνασιαρχεῖν μέ[λ]-
λοντας παρ.........λημμα καὶ τ[ὸ] | βαλανεῖον καὶ τὸ
συνήθω[ς] διδόμ[ε]ν[ο]ν ὑ[π]ὲρ τιν...να.[ἀ]|πὸ τοῦ γυμνασίου
εἰς τὸ δημ[ό]σιο(ν) χῶμα τ.....σδ..ων.. || λυχναψίας, ἅσπερ 10
ὁ κατὰ το[ὺ]ς γυμνασι....ρ...εκαυ..... | κατὰ τὸ καθῆκον
συσταλ[ῆναι] τὰ π[λε]ίω τῶν ὑπὸ του .. | ἐλάσσονος γινομένου
αυτ.........τατος αν..ω ε.| ἑτέρας χρείας ἐδίδου ἀπὸ......
.........ιθ...υ.. |.........στ...α..τουσ............||

Fragment B

] (δραχμαὶ) ξ ἀνθ' (ὧν) ἱκαναί εἰσιν [...   15
]τους (δραχμαὶ) τξ, μουσ[ικῶν?...
].ησαι ὡς ἐπιμελητ( ) .α[...
]ωρατι. νεωκορ.ιας ουδ.[...
] (δραχμαὶ) τ...λης αλ( ) λέγομε[ν ||
] ἱκαναὶ (δραχμαὶ) τ. [Λο]ιπ(αὶ) (δραχμαὶ) [...   20
] λοιπ(αὶ) (δραχμαὶ) σξ, καὶ ὑπὸ τοῦ.[...
] (δραχμαὶ) Ἀ, αιτινε...συ φι[..
] ὑπὸ τοῦ ε.....του[..

From Hermopolis. The gymnasiarch was a member of the college of archons in the metropolis. Evidently the cost of the office had become so great that it was difficult to fill it. Accordingly Rutilius issued an edict defining the amounts which should be

DOCUMENTS FROM EGYPT

spent in the various duties connected with the position. Unfortunately the papyrus is so badly mutilated that it is only possible to decipher references to the baths and to torch-lighting. At this period the office was probably held for one year and was shared by two or more who took the duties alternately (Oertel, *Die Liturgie*, 316 *ff.*). In the third century the office was held for a longer period, but each member of the college served only for short periods of a few days at a time (*P. Oxy.* 1413, 1418; Wilcken, *Chrestomathie*, 39. *Cf.* Oertel, *loc. cit.*; Preisigke, *St. Beamtenw.* 53 *ff.*; Jouguet, *Vie munic.* 166, 292 *ff.*, 318 *ff.*, 399 *ff.*).

170. EPISTULAE PETRONI MAMERTINI ET STATILI MAXIMI
DE IMMUNITATE CIVIUM ANTINOOPOLITANORUM
(135, 156 p. Chr.)

Wilcken, *Chrestomathie*, 26.

I

15 Πετρώνιος Μαμερτεῖνος Ὡρείωνι στρατηγῶι Θεινείτου χαίρειν. | Ἀντίγραφο[ν ἐπ]ιστολῆς γραφείσης [μ]οι ὑπὸ Δημητρίου .ο..... τῶν ἰς | τὴν Ἀντι[νόο]υ κεκληρωμένων [ἐκ τ]ῆς Π[το]λεμαέω[ν] πόλεως τού|τοις τοῖς γρ[άμ]μασιν ὑπέταξα βουλόμενός σε φροντίσ[αι, ὅ]πως ο[ἵ] τε αὐ|τοῦ καὶ οἱ τῶν
20 ἄλλων τῶν ἰς τὴν Ἀντινόου ἀπωικισ[μέ]νων ἀ[νύ]βρισ‖τοι καὶ ἀνεπ[ηρ]έαστοι διάγωσιν ἐν τῶι νομῶι. (Ἔτους) ιθ θεοῦ [Ἁ]δριανοῦ Φαρμοῦ|θι ιθ.

II

Στατείλιος Μάξιμος Ὁρείωνι στρατηγῶι Θεινείτου χαίρειν. | Ἔντυχε βιβλειδίωι δοθέντι μοι παρὰ Κάστορος Ἀφροδισίου, δι
30 ἐγ‖γέγραπ[τ]αι καὶ ἐπιστολὴ τοῦ κρατίστης μνήμης Μαμερτείνου, δι᾽ ἧς | οὐχ ὅπως τοὺς Ἀντινοέας, ἀλλὰ καὶ τοὺς αὐτῶν ἠθέλησεν [ἀν]υβρίσ|τους εἶν[αι, κ]αὶ ἴσθι, ε[ἰ το]ιοῦτον κλό[π]ι[ον (?) πρ]άξαις, δηλώσαντά με τῶι κρα|τίστωι ἡγεμόνι. (Ἔτους ιθ θεοῦ Αἰλίου Ἀντωνίνου Μεσορὴ | ἐπαγομένων ᾱ. (2nd H.)
35 Σεμπρώνιος ἐπι⟨δέ⟩δωκα. ‖ (3rd H.) Εἴ τινα δίκαια ἔχεις, τῶι στρατηγῶι παραθοῦ | καὶ τὰ δέοντα ποιήσει. (4th H.) Ἀπόδος.

On the founding of Antinoopolis, *cf.* Jouguet, *Vie munic.* 115 *ff.* From this document we learn that citizens of Ptolemais were drafted by Hadrian for the settlement of Antinoopolis, and that the

DOCUMENTS FROM EGYPT

selection was made by lot. As compensation for this compulsory
change of residence, not only the Antinoopolitans, but their parents,
were exempt from liturgies which might be imposed upon them
outside of their place of residence. Both letters imply that there
was a disposition on the part of local officials to forget the grant
made by Hadrian, probably because the pressure to secure available
candidates for liturgies was already becoming severe. It is also
evident that Ptolemais, although a Greek city, did not enjoy the
favored position in Egypt which Alexandria had, nor is there any
evidence that the administration of Ptolemais differed in any way
from that of the ordinary Egyptian metropolis (Wilcken, *Grundzüge*, 48). At any rate its citizens were subject to the strategus of
the nome in the matter of liturgies, as this document clearly indicates. *Cf.* no. 184.

171. DE VECTIGALIBUS EXIGENDIS
A SENIORIBUS VICI
(136 p. Chr.)

P. Br. Mus. 2, 255; Wilcken, *Chrestomathie*, 272.

Σοκμῆνις Σοκμήνεως καὶ Ἀπίων | Ἡρακλείδου [καὶ] Ἀτρῆς
Πεθέως καὶ Ἀπολ|λώνιος Διοδώρου καὶ Πασόξις Ἡρᾶτος | καὶ
Ὡρίων Ὡρίωνος καὶ Πτολλίων ‖ Χαιρήμονος καὶ Ἥρων Καλ- 5
λίου | καὶ Ἥρων Ἡρακλείδου καὶ Σαραπᾶς | Μύσθου καὶ οἱ
λοιπ(οὶ) πρεσ(βύτεροι) κώμης | Καρ(ανίδος) τοῦ κ (ἔτους)
Ἀδριανοῦ Καίσαρος | τοῦ κυρίου Ὡρίωνι Ὡρίωνος χα(ίρειν). ‖
Ἐπὶ συνεστάκαμέν σοι ἀνθ' ὑμῶ[ν] | πρακτορεύιν καὶ χιρίζιν 10
τήν δε | ζυτηρὰν καὶ φόρου προβάτων καὶ ἄλ|λων εἰδῶν τῆς
αὐτῆς κώμης, | ἐπρακτόρευσας καὶ ἐχίρισας μέ‖[χ]ρι ἕως Φαῶφι 15
μηνὸς τοῦ κα (ἔτους) | καὶ αὐτοῦ τοῦ Φαῶφι, [τ]ὰς μὲν τῆς |
ζυτηρᾶς ἐπὶ τὴν δημοσίαν τράπε|ζαν, τὰς δὲ τοῦ φόρου τῶν
προβά|των εἰς [τ]ὴν ἐπὶ τούτοις τράπεζα[ν], ‖ καὶ οὐδέν [σ]οι 20
ἐνκαλοῦμεν περὶ | τούτων. Πασόξις Ἡρᾶτος διὰ τοῦ | πατρ[ὸς]
Ἡρ[ᾶ]ς οὐδὲν ἐκαλῶ καθὼς π[ρόκ(ειται)]. | Ἀπ[ολ]λ[ώ]ν[ι]ος
Διοδώρου οὐδὲ[ν] | ἐν[κ]αλ[ῶ]. Ἀπίων Ἡρακλείδου ‖ οὐδ[ὲν] 25
ἐνκαλῶ καθὼς πρό|[κ]ειται.

l. 10. Ἐπὶ=Ἐπεὶ; ὑμῶν=ἡμῶν. l. 11. δε=τε.

[519]

DOCUMENTS FROM EGYPT

From the Fayûm. This document shows us that the elders of the village were required to collect certain taxes. In this case they have contracted with Horion to gather the tax on beer and the sheep-tax. At the end of his term he is given a formal release as prescribed by law. It is probable that the three men who give the release were those to whom the liturgy was assigned by the whole body of elders (Oertel, *Die Liturgie*, 146 *ff.*; Jouguet, *Vie munic.* 217 *ff.*). The assignment of the duties of a liturgy is frequently recorded in Egypt (Wenger, *Die Stellvertretung im Rechte der Papyri*, 75 *ff.*; *cf.* Wilcken, *Chrestomathie*, 263, 264), but in certain cases it seems to have been forbidden, *cf. P. Fior.* 382; p. 101.

172. DE CIVIBUS AD MUNERA SUBEUNDA NOMINATIS
(ca. 137 p. Chr.)

BGU. 235; Wilcken, *Chrestomathie*, 399.

[Oὐ]εγέτωι στρ(ατηγῶι) ['Aρ]σι(νοΐτου) Ἡρ[ακλ(είδου) μερί-
δος] | παρ[ὰ] Π[ε]θέως [κω]μογ[ρ(αμματέως)] . . . . . καὶ ἄλλων] |
5 κωμῶν. | 'Aν[τὶ] 'Aφροδᾶ ἐπικ[αλουμένου . . . . .]||ἔν[γι]στα πλη-
ροῦντος εἰς Φαμενὼθ κθ | καὶ Π[α]σ[ί]ων[ος] 'Aφροδισίου ἐπι-
κ(αλουμένου) Κέννις | καὶ Σ[α]βίνου 'Aρπάλου τ[ῶ]ν β̄ | ἔνγιστα
πληρούντων εἰς Παῦν[ι..] | καὶ 'Iσχυρίωνος Πετεσ[ούχου καὶ
10 . . . .] || κουρ[έ]ως τετελ(ευτηκότων) τῶν [β̄..]α· ἀπ[ὸ] | κώμ(ης)
Πτολεμαΐδος Νέ[ας ἀναδίδω]μι τοὺ[ς] | ὑπογεγρ(αμμένους) ὄντας
εὐπόρους καὶ ἐπιδηδίο[υς] | γνώμηι καὶ κινδύ[ν]ων τῶν ἀπὸ τῆς |
15 κώμης τῶν καὶ ἐνγνομέ[νο]υς κατὰ τὸ ἔ[θος] || πεμπθησομένους
τῶι κρα[τ(ίστωι) ἐπιστρ(ατήγωι) εἰς κλ(ῆρον)]. | Εἰσὶ δέ· |
Σαραπάμμων Τεβούλου ἔχ[ων πόρον . . . . . .] | Προπελᾶς Προ-
20 πελάου[ ] | Εἰσχυρᾶς Πεθ[έ]ως..[ ] || . . . . .
. . . . . . .ωνο[ς . . . . . .] | Πα. . .

l. 13. *lege* κινδύνωι.   l. 14. *lege* ἐγγνομένων.

From the Fayûm. This document reveals the method of appointment to liturgies in the villages at this period. Candidates were chosen by the elders, who were legally bound as sureties for their nominees. The list was drawn up by the village-scribe, who forwarded it to the strategus. From the latter official the names were forwarded to the epistrategus, who chose the candidates for the

DOCUMENTS FROM EGYPT

various offices by lot. It may be noted that Petheus serves as secretary for several villages. For the capital required for various liturgies, *cf.* Oertel, *Die Liturgie*; Wilcken, *Gr. Ostraka*, 1, 507 *ff.*; *P. Giess.* 58. In some cases we find the liturgists appointed by the prefect (*P. Amh.* 64; *P. Br. Mus.* 1220).

173. DE STATU CIVIUM ROMANORUM
ET ALEXANDRINORUM
(139 p. Chr.)

BGU. 747; Wilcken, *Chrestomathie*, 35.

Col. 1

Ἀυϊδίωι Ἡλ[ιοδ]ώρωι τῶι κρατίστωι ἡγεμόν(ι) | Πτολεμαῖος
[σ]τ[ρ]ατηγὸς Κοπτ[εί]του χαίρειν. | Τῶν κυριακῶν πραγμάτων,
ἡγεμὼν μέγιστε, | ἐπιζητούντων ἐξαίρετον φροντίδα καὶ συνε‖χῇ   5
ἐπιμέλ[ι]αν καὶ δεδομένων εἰς τοῦ[τ]ο οὐ μ[ό]νον | ἀξιοχρέω[ν],
ἀλλὰ καὶ ἀπιθηνίων μάλιστα ἀν|θρώπων, [οὐ] διέλιπον, κύριε,
τοῖς ἐν ταῖς δημοσίαις | χρείαις το[ῦ ν]ομοῦ οὖσι Ῥωμαίοις καὶ
Ἀλε[ξα]νδρεῦσι | κα[ὶ] πάλ[α]ι στρατιώταις ἀντιστατοῦσι τοῖς
πράγ[μ]ασιν ‖ παραινῶν πείθε[σθ]αι τοῖς κελευομένοις, καὶ οἱ|ό-   10
[μ]ενος με[τ]ανοή[σι]ν ἡμεῖν ἐπῖχό[ν] σοι τῶι κυ|ρίωι δηλῶσαι.
Ἐπ[έ]μ[ε]νον δὲ [α]ὐτῶν κατὰ τὸ [ἀ]ναγ|καῖον ἐπιγόμενος ὑπὸ
τῆς χρείας ἀναφέρ[ε]σθαι. | Τῶν γὰρ πραγμάτων τὸ μέγι[σ]τόν
ἐστιν καὶ γνη‖σ[ι]ώτερον [π]ολλῆς τε προε[δ]ρίας δεομένων | [αἱ   15
ἀ]παιτή[σε]ις τῶν ὀφιλομέ[ν]ων τῶι κυριακῶι | λ[ό]γωι. Δι'ὅ[π]ερ
ἐπα[γ]ρυπνῶ προσφ[ε]ρόμενος | τῆι ἐκπράξει καὶ [ὑ]πὸ χέρα
καὶ πρ[ὸ]ς τὸ[ν ..].ι | .....ισμ[ὸ]ν κα[τὰ] μῆνα μετα[π]εμπό-
μ[εν]ος ‖ [τ]οὺς πράκτορας δ[ι]ακρείνω π[ρ]ὸς τὸν ε[ἰ]σ[ι]όν[τ]α   20
ὑπὲρ [τ]ῆς ἰδί[α]ς πρακτωρί[α]ς λόγο[ν] α[ἰ|τ]ούμ[ε]να π[λ]η-
[ρ]οφορε[ῖ]ν ἐπ. κ....υτ...ος | [ὁ]φείλω το[..... ἐ]ξ αὐτῶ[ν.
Ἐπ]ιχωρι. [π]ρ[ο]τρέπ.....υ..μ...

Col. II

ἄλλου χρείαι δημοσίαι | ἐνχιρισθέντες | ἧι ὑπακούσειν ὀφίλουσιν
κἀμοὶ | ἀπαιτοῦντι πίθεσται χαιρησάμενοι | ἑαυτο[ὺ]ς μὴ εἶναι
ὑπὸ τὴν στρατηγίαν ‖ μηδέ[π]ω κατὰ τὸ ἴσα τοῖς ἐνχωρίοις | 5
πράκτωρσιν ὀφείλειν ἵστασθαι κἂν | ἐπιτιμητοι(?) αὐτοὶ εἶναι
λέγοντες | τὸ ὅσον ὅτι αὐτοῖς τὰς ἐκπράξεις ἐν|ποδίζουσιν,
ἐνιαχοῦ δὲ καὶ τολμῶσιν ‖ ἀντίστασθαι καὶ καθόλου ὅσοι εἰσὶν | 10

[521]

τοιοῦτοι ἐν ταῖς λιτουργίαις μέχρι αὐ|θαδίας ἐπ[ι]χειροῦσιν
φθάνειν ὡς | κα[ὶ τ]οῖς ἀπὸ τοῦ νομοῦ ὑπόδιγμα τῆς | ἀπειθίας
15 δοκε[ῖ]ν ὑποτίθεται. Ἐπὶ οὖν ‖ οὕτως τὰ κυριακὰ πράγματα
ἐνπο|δίζεται, δέομαι, κύριε, οὐχ ὀλίγων | ἐκ τούτου κινδυνευο-
μένων, ἐάν | σοι δόξῃ, διαλαβεῖν περὶ αὐτῶν καὶ ὃ ἂν | δοκιμά-
20 [σηι]ς στῆσαι, τῶι τρόπωι προσ‖έρχεσθαι αὐτοῖ[ς] δέον ἐστὶν εἰς
τὸ μήτε | τ[ὴ]ν ἀπαίτησιν τῶν δημοσίων ἐμ|[ποδ]ί[ζ]ε[σ]θαι τ..
να κυριακ[ὰπ]ράγμ[ατα.|...κ]αιρῶι αν....ι κ[α]ι....ι.|.....

Verso

Τῶν ἰς τὰς δημοσίας χρείας κατιστανομένων | καὶ μὴ βουλο-
μένους ὁμοίως τοῖς ἄλλοις πρα|γματικοῖς ὑπακούειν δύνασαι
παραστῆσαι | τῶι κρατίστωι ἐπιστρατήγωι, ὃς ἐπ[α]ναγκάσει ‖
5 αὐτοὺς τὰ προσήκοντα αὐτοῖς ἐκτελεῖν. | (Ἔτους) β̅ Φαρμοῦθι δ̅.

From Coptus. The Alexandrians were exempt from χωρικαὶ
λειτουργίαι (no. 165). It is evident that Romans resident in
Egypt were also freed from similar liturgies, and their privileged
position led these two classes to claim exemption from the imperial
liturgies as well. Apparently Ptolemaeus was unable to compel them
to undertake the duty of collecting the taxes due to the imperial
fiscus, and their disobedience was demoralizing to the discipline of
the nome. The prefect instructed the strategus to send the names
of those nominated to liturgies to the epistrategus, who will compel
them to discharge their duties. The only evidence for a Roman
citizen discharging a liturgy in Egypt is found in BGU. 1062. In
this case, however, he takes over the collection of a tax as a business
contract from the holder of the liturgy. In P. Fior. 57 an Alexandrian owning property in Hermopolis claims immunity on the
ground of his age and not on the basis of his Alexandrian origin.
His petition is dated in 223–225, or later than the edict of Caracalla, and it is probable that the grant of Roman citizenship may
have done away with the favored position which the Alexandrians
held. The citizens of Antinoopolis, however, retained their privileges until later (Wilcken, Chrestomathie, 397 (A.D. 254). Cf.
Wilcken, Grundzüge, 345 f.).

DOCUMENTS FROM EGYPT

174. DE IMMUNITATE MEDICORUM
(140 p. Chr.)

P. Fay. 106; Wilcken, *Chrestomathie*, 395.

.... ὑπομνη]|μ[α]τισμ[ὸ]ν Σεπ[τιμίου Μάρκωνος
ἐπι]|στρατήγου κεχρον[ι]σμένον [εἰς .. (ἔτος)] | Ἀντωνίν[ο]υ
τοῦ κυρίου Φαρμοῦ[θι..], || Ἡλιόδωρος εἶπεν· Κέκρικε[ν....] | 5
ἀπολύσας. |

Γαΐωι Ἀουιδίωι Ἡλιοδώρωι ἐ[πάρχ(ωι) Αἰγ(ύπτου)] | παρὰ
Μάρ(κου) Οὐαλερ[ί]ου Γεμέλλου [ἰατροῦ]. | Παρὰ τὰ ἀπηγο-
ρευμένα ἀχθ[εὶς εἰς ἐπι]||τήρησιν γε[ν]ημα[τ]ογραφουμ[ένων] | 10
ὑπαρχόντ[ων πε]ρὶ κώμα[ς Βακχ(ιάδα)] | καὶ Ἡφαιστιάδα τῆς
Ἡρακλ[είδου] | μερίδος τοῦ Ἀρσινοΐτου τ[ετραε]|τεῖ ἤδη χρόνωι
ἐν τῆι χρ[είαι] || πονούμενος ἐξησθένησα [ὅλως(?)], | κύριε, ὅθεν 15
ἀξιῶ σαὶ τὸν σω[τῆρα] | ἐλεῆσαί με καὶ κελεῦσαι ἤ[δη με] |
ἀπολυθῆναι τῆς χρείας, ὅπ[ως δυ]|νηθῶ ἐμαυτὸν ἀνακτήσα[σθαι
ἀ]||πὸ τῶν καμάτων, οὐδὲν δ[ὲ δεῖ.(?).] | τὸν καὶ ὁμοιώμ[ατα] 20
ὑποτάξα[ι, ὅτι] | τέλεον ἀπολύονται τῶν [λειτουρ]|γιῶν οἱ τὴν
ἰατρικὴν ἐπιστή[μην] | μεταχειριζόμενοι, μάλ[ι]στα [δὲ οἱ δε]||-
δοκιμασμένοι ὥσπερ κἀγ[ώ, ἵν'] | ὦ εὐεργετημένος. Διευτύ[χει]. 25

From the Fayûm. The petition of the physician Gemellus is
directed to the prefect. Wilcken infers that the edict of Antoninus
conferring immunity on a certain number of physicians in each
town had not yet been promulgated (*Dig.* 27. 1. 6, 2; Wilcken,
Chrestomathie, 395), but Gemellus points out that he had been
assigned to the liturgy contrary to law (παρὰ τὰ ἀπηγορευμένα),
and in ll. 29 *ff.* he adds that there is no need for him to submit
copies of the law(?) that physicians, if registered (δεδοκιμασμένοι),
are absolutely exempt from liturgies (*cf.* P. Oxy. 40; Oertel, *Die
Liturgie*, 391). It may be noted that the liturgy of guardian of the
confiscated lands was held by Gemellus for four years instead of
one, which was apparently the period of tenure of liturgies in other
parts of the empire, and that the liturgy had cost him the loss of
his personal fortune (ἐξησθένησα). For a general sketch of the
classes which enjoyed immunity, *cf.* Jouguet, *Vie munic.* 98 *ff.*

DOCUMENTS FROM EGYPT

175. EDICTUM M. SEMPRONI LIBERALIS,
PRAEFECTI AEGYPTI
(154 p. Chr.)

BGU. 372; Wilcken, *Chrestomathie,* 19.

Col. i

[Μᾶ]ρκος [Σεμπρώνιος] Λιβερ[άλι]ς ἔπαρ[χος] | Αἰγύπ[του
λέγ]ει. | Πυνθάνομ[αί τινας] διὰ τὴν γενομένην δυσ|χέρειαν
5 [τ]ῶ[ν] ..... [τὴν] οἰκείαν ἀπ[ολε]λοιπέναι ἀλλα‖χ.ει (?) τὰ
προσ[.....]πορίζοντας, ἑτέρους δὲ λιτουρ|[γεία]ς τινὰς ἐ[κφυ-
γόντας] διὰ τὴν [τ]ότε περὶ αὐ|τοὺς ἀσθένειαν ἐν ἀλλοδαπῆι ἔτι
καὶ νῦν διατρεί|βειν φόβωι τῶν γενομένων παραυτίκα προ|-
10 γρ[α]φῶν. Προτρέ[πομαι] οὖν πάντας ἐπαν[ελθ]εῖν ‖ ἐπὶ τὰ
ἴδια καὶ τὸ[ν μὲν π]ρῶτον καὶ μέγιστ[ον] | κ[α]ρπὸν τῆς εὐε-
τ[ηρίας κ]αὶ τῆς τοῦ κυρίου ἡμῶν | Α[ὐτο]κράτορος περὶ πάντας
ἀνθρώπους κη[δε]‖μονίας ἀποφέρεσθαι [καὶ] μὴ ἀνεστίους καὶ
15 ἀο[ί]|κ[ου]ς ἐπὶ ξένης ἀλᾶσθα[ι. Ἵνα δὲ τοῦτο προθυμ[ότ]ε‖[ρο[ν]
κα[ὶ] ἥδιο[ν π]ο[ιή]σω[σιν, ἵ]στωσαν [μ]ὲν τ[ὸ]ν π...ι | τ..ἐκ
ταύτ[ης] τῆς αἰτ[ίας ἔ]τι κατεχόμενον α[ἰσ]‖θήσεσθαι τῆ[ς] τοῦ
μ[εγίσ]του Αὐτοκράτορος εὐ[μ]ε|ν[εί]ας καὶ χρη[σ]τότητος,
ἐ[πι]τρεπούσης καὶ μ[ηδ]ε|μίαν πρὸς α[ὐ]τοὺς ζήτησιν ἔσεσθαι,
20 ἀλλὰ μηδ[ὲ] ‖ πρὸς τοὺς ἄλ[λο]υς τοὺς ἐ[ξ] ἧς δήποτε αἰτίας
ὑπὸ | τῶν στρατη[γῶν] προγραφέντας· καὶ τούτους γὰρ |
.... κατέρχ[εσθαι] εἰς τ[οὺς τό]πους ... reliqui versus,
maxime mutili, omissi sunt.

Col. ii

...ουτω... δὲ ἑκό[ν]τας ἀπ[ο]δρᾶσι πονη|ρ[ὸν κ]α[ὶ] ληισ[τ]ρι-
κὸν βίον [ἑ]λομ[έ]νοις μείγνυσ|θ[αι]. Ἵνα δὲ μὴ μόνον το[ύτ]οις,
ἀλλὰ [κ]αὶ ἑτέ[ρ]οις | ταὐτά με παραινεῖν καὶ πράσσειν μάθωσι, ‖
5 ἴστωσαν, ὅτ[ι] κ[α]ὶ τοῖς κρατίστοι[ς] ἐπιστρατήγοις | καὶ τοῖς
σ[τ]ρατηγοῖς καὶ τοῖς πε[μ]φθεῖσι ὑπ᾽ ἐμ[οῦ] | πρὸς τὴν τῆς
χώρας ἀσφάλειαν καὶ ἀμεριμνίαν | στρατιώταις παρήγγελ[τ]αι,
τὰς μὲν ἀρχομένας | ἐφόδους κ[ω]λύειν, προορῶντας καὶ προ-
10 απαν‖τῶντας, τὰς [δὲ γ]ενομένας παρ[α]υτίκα ἐπιδιώ|κειν κα[ὶ]
το[ὺ]ς λημφθέντας ἐπ᾽ αὐτ[ο]φ[ώρ]ωι κα|κούργους μ[η]δὲν
περαιτέρω τῶν ἐν αὐτῆι τῆι | ληιστείαι γενο[μ]ένων ἐξετάζειν,
ἄλλοις δὲ τῶν πο|τε προγραφ[έ]ντων ἡσυχάζουσι καὶ ἐν τῆι
15 οἰ‖κείαι τῆι γεω[ργ]ίαι προσκαρτεροῦσι μὴ ἐνοχλεῖν. | Κατερχέ-

DOCUMENTS FROM EGYPT

[σ]θωσαν οὖν ἀμ[έ]ριμνοι καὶ ἔστω | π[ρο]θεσμία [αὐτο]ῖς, ἐξ
οὗ ἂν τοῦτ[ό] μου τὸ διάτα|γ[μ]α ἐν ἑκά[στ]ωι νομῶι προτεθῆι,
μῆνες γ. | Ἐ[ἀ]ν δέ τις [με]τὰ τὴν τοσαύτην μου φιλαν||θ[ρ]ωπίαν   20
[ἐ]πὶ ξένης πλανώμενος φανῆι, | οὗτος οὐκέ[τι] ὡς ὕποπτος,
ἀλλὰ ὡς ὁμόλογος | κακοῦργος σ[υ]νλημφθεὶς πρός με ἀνα-
πεμ|φ[θήσε]ται. | ("Ετους) [ι]η Ἀντωνίνου τοῦ κυρίου. || Θὼθ α.   25

l. 16. Καρτερχέ[σ]θωσαν, in original copy.

From the Fayûm. This edict was issued after the revolt of the
Egyptians in A.D. 153–154 had been crushed (Meyer, *Klio*, 7
(1907), 124 *f.*). Some had left their homes because of the political
upheaval, others had been driven forth because of the severity of
the liturgies. The latter had been proscribed (προγραφέντων),
since they were liable to imprisonment (cf. no. 194). The document
reveals the oppressiveness of the liturgies at this early period, since
property-holders were abandoning their property and living in exile
rather than face the burdens imposed upon them, *cf.* Rostowzew,
Gesch. d. röm. Kol. 206 *ff.*

176. DE IMMUNITATE PATRIBUS ANTINOO-
POLITANORUM CONCESSA
(159 p. Chr.)

Compt. rend. de l'acad. d. inscr. et bell. lett. 1905, 160 *ff.*;
Wilcken, *Chrestomathie*, 28.

Ἀντίγρα(φον) ἐπιστολ(ῆς) ἐπιστρα(τήγου) Θηβαΐδος. | Αἴλιος
Φαυστεῖνος στρα(τηγῶι) Λυκοπ(ολίτου) | χαίρειν. | Βιβλίδιον
Ἀπολλοφάνους Ὡρί⟨⟨ω⟩⟩||ωνος σημιωσάμενος πεμφ|θῆναί σοι   5
ἐκέλευσα. Ἐπεὶ | οὖν φησιν πατέρα ἑαυτὸν | ὄντα παίδων
Ἀντινοϊτικῶν | κα[ὶ ο]ὗ τὰ [ἐ]πικεφάλια τελοῦν||τα κεκληρῶσθαι   10
κατ᾽ ἄγνοι|αν ὑπὸ Ξεινοκράτους εἰς πρα|κτορείαν κα[τ]ακριμά-
[τω]ν | καὶ νῦν ἐπιδημήσαντα ... | πρὸς διώρθωσιν δημοσίω||ν   15
κατεσχῆσθ[αι..]τοε... | χρείαι. Φρόντισον, εἰ ταῦτα [οὕ|τως
ἔχει, καθ᾽ ἃ παρέθετ[ο] | ἐφ᾽ ὁμοίων κεκρίσθαι, τ[οῦ] | ἕτερα
ὀνόματα ἀντ᾽ αὐτοῦ || εἰς τὴν χρέαν πέμψαι. | Ἐρρῶσθ(αί σε)   20
εὔχο(μαι). | ("Ετους) κβ Ἀντωνείνου Καίσαρος | τ[οῦ] κυρίου
Παχὼν δ̄.

[525]

DOCUMENTS FROM EGYPT

This document shows that parents of the settlers in Antinoopolis were exempt from the poll-tax and from liturgies which might be imposed on them in villages where they held property outside the limits of their native place (*cf.* nos. 170, 183).

177. DE IMMUNITATE VETERANORUM
(172 p. Chr.)

BGU. 180; Wilcken, *Chrestomathie*, 396.

. . . .

παρὰ [Γα]ΐου Ἰ[ου]λ[ίου Ἀπολ]ινα[ρίο]υ οὐ[ε]‖τρανοῦ γε[ο]υ-
χ[ο]ῦ[ντος ἐν] κώμηι Κα[ρα]‖νίδι. [Δ]ιατέτακ[ται, κ]ύριε, τού⟨ς⟩
5 οὐετρα|νοὺς ἔχειν μετὰ τ[ὴν ἀπό]λυσιν πεντ[α]‖ετῆ χρό[ν]ον
ἀναπ[αύσε]ως. Παρὰ δὴ ταύ|την τὴν [δι]άτ[α]ξιν ἐ[γὼ] ἐπη-
ρεάσθην | μ[ε]τὰ διετίαν τῆς [ἀπο]λύσεως κα[ὶ] | ἀ[ν]εδόθην
κατ᾽ ἐπή[ρια]ν εἰς λειτουργίαν | καὶ μέχρι τοῦ δεῦρο [κ]ατὰ τὸ
10 ἑξῆς ‖ ἐν λειτουργίαι εἰμ[ὶ] ἀδιαλεί[πτ]ως. | Τοῦ τοιούτου παντ[ὶ]
ἀπηγορευ|μένου [ἐ]πὶ τῶν ἐν[χ]ωρίων πολλῶι | πλεῖον ἐπ᾽ ἐμοῦ
15 συντηρεῖσθαι | ὀφείλι τοῦ ὑπηρετήσαντος τὸν ‖ τοσοῦ[το]ν τῆς
στρατείας χρόνον. | Διόπερ προσφεύγειν σοι ἠναγκήσ|θην δικαίαν
δέ[ησ]ιν ποιούμενος | καὶ ἀξιῶ συντηρῆσαί μοι τὸν τῆς | ἀνα-
20 παύσεως ἴσον χρόνον κατὰ ⟨τὰ⟩ ‖ περὶ τούτου διατεταγμένα, ἵνα
δυνηθῶ | κἀαγὼ τ[ὴ]ν ἐπιμέλειαν τῶν ἰδίων | ποιεῖσθαι, ἄ[ν]-
θρ[ω]πος πρεσβύ[τη]ς καὶ | μόνος τυγχ[άν]ων, [κ]αὶ τῆι τύχηι
25 σου | εἰς ἀεὶ εὐχαριστῶ. Διευτύχει. ‖ (2nd H.) Γάϊος Ἰούλιος
Ἀπολινάριος ἐπιδέδωκ|α. | (3rd H.) (Ἔτους) ιβ′′ Μεχεὶρ κθ. |
(4th H.) Τῶι σ[τρατη]γ[ῶι] ἔντυχ[ε] καὶ τὰ | πρ[οσήκο]ντα
30 ποιήσει. ‖ (5th H.) Ἀ[πόδος].

From the Fayûm. An edict of Octavian (Wilcken, *Chresto-mathie*, 462) and of Domitian (*ibid.* 463) granted immunity to veterans apparently without restrictions. From the petition of Apolinarius we learn that veterans in Egypt at this period only enjoyed immunity for five years after their discharge. In his case, he had been beguiled into taking a liturgy two years after his release from the army and he had held it continuously without any *vacatio* such as the natives had (*Cod. J.* 10. 41. 1; *P. Giess.* 59, where *vacationes* of three and seven years are recorded). There is no

DOCUMENTS FROM EGYPT

other evidence in any part of the empire for limitation of the period of immunity to five years. By an edict of Severus veterans were forever freed from all liturgies except those imposed upon their patrimony (*Dig.* 50. 5. 7). It is probable that Apolinarius, being a property-holder, enjoyed immunity from *munera patrimoniorum* for a period of five years. Under Severus this privilege was withdrawn (*cf.* pp. 106 *f.*).

178. DE MUNERIBUS SACERDOTUM
(177 p. Chr.)

BGU. 194; Wilcken, *Chrestomathie*, 84.

Φλα[υ]εί[ω]ι ᾿Απολ[λ]ωνίωι | ᾿Αρσινοείτου ῾Ηρακ(λείδου)
μερίδος | παρὰ ῾Ηρᾶ κωμογρα(μματέως) Νείλου πόλεως. | ᾿Αντὶ
῎Ωπεως ᾿Ενούπεως κλη[ρ]ωθ(έντος) ‖ ἐκ τῆς τῶν εὐσχημόνων 5
γραφῆς | εἰς πρακτορίαν ἀργυρικῶν τῆς κώμης | γνωσθέντος μοι
εἶναι ἱερέως τοῦ ὄντος | ἐν τῆι κώμηι ἱεροῦ καὶ τῶν λειτουργιῶ[ν] |
ἀφεθέντων, καθὰ ἠξίωσαν οἱ ἀπὸ τῆς κώ‖μης ἀναδεξάμενοι ἐκ 10
συνκαταθέσεως τὰς | λειτουργείας ἐπιβαλλούσας αὐτοῖς ἐκτε-
λέσειν, ἀ[κ]ολούθως | τῶι παρακομισθ[έ]ντι σοι βιβλιδίωι μ[ου]
ἐπὶ ὑπο|γραφῆς τοῦ κρατίστου ἐπιστρα(τήγου), ὧι ἐνπεριεί|-
λημπται ἀντίγρ(αφα) ἐπιστολῶν δύο, μειᾶς μὲν ‖ Σκουτίωι 15
᾿Ασκληπιαδότωι, τὴν δὲ ἑτέραν σου, | καθ᾿ ἃς ἀντὶ ἑτέρου ἱερέως
ἀπολυθέντο(ς) | ἕτεροι εἰς κλῆρον πεμφθέντος ἐκλη|ρώθησαν,
καὶ τοῦ ἐκ συνκαταθέσεως τῶν | ἀπὸ [τ]ῆς κώμης γενομένου ἐπὶ
Ποτάμωνος ‖ στρατηγήσαντος ὑπομνηματισμοῦ δίδωμει | τοὺς 20
ὑπογεγρ(αμμένους) ὄντος εὐπόρους καὶ ἐπι|τηδείους πεμφθη-
σομένους εἰς κλῆρον τῶι | κρατίστωι ἐπιστρ(ατήγωι). Εἰσὶ δέ·
Σαραπίων Καλ...υ Α, | Διόσκορος Νείλ(ου) ἐπικαλ(ουμένου)

O[. . . .] Α· ‖ (῎Ετους) ιη᾿ ο̅ ᾿Αθὺρ α[   ].   25

l. 17. πεμφθέντος=πεμφθέντες. l. 21. ὄντος=ὄντας.

From the Fayûm. Rostowzew (*G.G.A.* 1909, 639 *ff.*) has pointed out that, under the Roman administration, the privileges of the priestly hierarchy were steadily reduced. From this document we learn that the priests were subject to certain liturgies, but they had made a private agreement with the village-officials of Neilopolis whereby the latter had consented to release them from

[527]

DOCUMENTS FROM EGYPT

certain burdens. The terms of the agreement are not stated, but we must assume that the priests had secured it by offering some form of compensation. Opeus had been included in the annual list of citizens submitted for the collection of tribute, and when the appointment had been made by the usual method his name had been drawn for the office. The matter was brought to the attention of the village-scribe, who wrote this letter to the strategus, notifying him of the error and submitting the names of two other men having an annual income of a thousand drachmae, one of whom was to be chosen by lot for the post vacated by Opeus. On the liturgy πρακτορία ἀργυρικῶν, cf. Oertel, *Die Liturgie*, 195 ff., and for the immunity of priests, cf. *ibid.* 392, n. 3; Otto, *Priester und Tempel*, 2, 250 ff.

179. DE IMMUNITATE MULIERUM
(ca. 180 p. Chr.)

P. Teb. 327; Wilcken, *Chrestomathie*, 394.

[Οὐ]εττίωι Τού[ρβων]ι τῶι | κρατίστωι [ἐ]πιστρατ[ήγωι] |
παρὰ Κρονοῦτο[ς] Ζωίλ[ου] | τ[ο]ῦ Πετεσούχου ἀπὸ κώμης ‖
5 [Τε]βτύνεως Πολέμωνος | με[ρίδος] τοῦ Ἀρ[σ]ινοείτου. | Ἔτι
πάλαι, κύριε, τοῦ προγεγραμ|μένου μου πατρὸς ἀναδο|θέντος εἰς
10 ἐπιτήρησιν γε‖[ν]ηματογραφου[μέ]νων | [ὑ]παρχόντων καὶ μετὰ
τὸν | [ὡ]ρισμένον χρόνον τῆς | [ἐ]πιτηρήσεως τετελευτη|κότος
15 ἀπ[όρου] μηδὲ ἐν κα‖ταλείπ[οντο]ς ἔτι ἀπὸ τοῦ | τρισκαιδεκάτου
ἔτους | θεοῦ Αὐρηλίου Ἀντωνίν[ου] | αὐτὴ ἔκτοτε οὐ δεόντως |
20 ἀπαιτοῦμα[ι] τὰ ὑπὲρ τῶν ‖ ὑπαρχόν[τω]ν τελούμενα | δημόσια.
[Κε]κελευσμένου | οὖν, κύριε, γ[υ]ναῖκας ἀφεῖ|σθαι τῶν τ[οιο]ύ-
25 των χρειῶν | ἀναγκαίω[ς] [γ]υνὴ οὖσα ἀβοή‖θητος πο[λλο]ῖς
ἔτεσι βεβα|ρημένη [καὶ] κινδυνεύουσα | διὰ τοῦτ[ο κατ]αλείπειν
τὴν | [ἰ]δίαν [ἐπὶ σὲ] καταφεύγω | [ἀξιοῦσά σε κ]ελεῦσαι ἤδη ‖
30 [τὰ ἐν ὀνόμ]ατι τοῦ πατρὸς | . . . . θῆναι εἰς τὴν | . . . . ν
καὶ ἐπὶ ζῶν | [τ. . . . . . .]ους χρόνου ον| . . . . μενου τοῖς ἐν ‖
35 . . . . ε. Διευτύχει. | (2nd H.) (Ἔτους) [. . . . Μ]εσορὴ ι. |
Μηδενὸς [ἐπε]χομένου | τῶι στρατ[ηγ]ῶι ἔντυχε. | (3rd H.)
Ἀπόδος.

From the Fayûm. The father of the petitioner had been appointed to the post of superintendent of confiscated property, and in the

[528]

DOCUMENTS FROM EGYPT

discharge of this liturgy his fortune had been seriously impaired. His daughter Cronous, as his heiress, complained to the epistrategus that continual demands had been made upon her since her father's death for moneys to be paid in connection with this liturgy. It is not clear whether she was actually holding the liturgy, or whether these sums were exacted from her estate as obligations which her father had not fulfilled before his death. For the liability of heirs, *cf.* Wilcken, *Chrestomathie*, 278, where the estate of a decaprotus is certainly liable for the obligations of the holder of the liturgy (*cf.* Oertel, *Die Liturgie*, 374, n. 4). It is probable that Cronous was purposely obscuring the issue in her petition, and that she was not actually discharging the liturgy, since she claimed that there was an edict which forbade the assignment of such liturgies to women. Women, however, were not exempt from *munera patrimoniorum* (*Cod. J.* 10. 42. 9; 10. 64. 1).

180. DE FUGA EORUM QUI MUNERIBUS OBNOXII SUNT
(186 p. Chr.)

P. Geneva, 37; Wilcken, *Chrestomathie*, 400.

Ἀπολλωτᾶι στρα(τηγῶι) Ἀρσι(νοΐτου) Ἡρακ(λείδου) | μερί-
δος | παρὰ Σωτηρίχου Σώτου καὶ τῶν | λοιπ(ῶν) πρεσβ(υτέρων)
διαδεχο(μένων) καὶ τὰ κατὰ τὴν || κωμογρα(μματείαν) κώ(μης) 5
Σοκνοπ(αίου) Νήσου. | Ἀντὶ Τρύφωνος Σεμπρωνίου | [κ]αὶ
Παουῆτις Πεκᾶτος καὶ Πνεφερῶτο(ς) | Σώτου καὶ Ἁρπαήσεως
Ἁρπαγάθου | [τ]ῶν δ ἐ[ν] κλ[ή]ρωι πρακ(τορίας) ἀργυρι(κῶν) ||
[τ]ῆς προκει(μένης) κώ(μης) μὴ φαινομένων | δίδομεν τοὺς ὑπο- 10
γεγρα(μμένους) ὄντας εὐπό|ρους καὶ ἐπιτηδείους, πεμφθησομέ-
νους | εἰς κλῆρον τῶι κρατίστωι ἐπιστρα(τήγωι). |

Εἰσὶ δέ· ||

Σάτυρος Ἀσκληπιάδου ἔχω(ν) πό(ρον) (δραχμῶν) ω 15
Σώτας Σώτο¬ ἐπικαλ(ούμενος) Ἀσίαρξ ὁ(μοίως) δραχμῶν) ω
Παβοῦς Παβοῦτος ὁμοίως (δραχμῶν) ψ
Στοτοῆτις Σώτου λαξὸς ὁ(μοίως) δραχμῶν) ψ
(2nd H.) Σωτήριχος (ἐτῶν) ν´ οὐλ(ὴ) μετώπ(ωι) ||
ἐξ ἀριστ(ερῶν) 20
(1st H.) (Ἔτους) κϛ´ Μάρκου Αὐρηλίου Κομμόδου
Ἀντωνίνου Καίσαρος τοῦ κυρ(ίου). Ἐπεὶφ κϛ´.

[529]

DOCUMENTS FROM EGYPT

From the Fayûm. This document reveals the great distress caused by the imposition of liturgies. Four men, chosen by lot for the collection of taxes in the village of Socnopaei Nesus, had fled to escape the liturgy. The village-elders submitted the names of four others to be sent to the epistrategus. It may be noted that no choice by lot is possible, and it is probable that the elders were unable to submit enough names to permit a choice (*cf.* pp. 112 *ff.*; Rostowzew, *Gesch. d. röm. Kol.* 206 *ff.*; nos. 189, 194).

181. DE NOMINATIONE MAGISTRATUUM
(192 p. Chr.)

P. Ryl. 77, ll. 32–52.

32 Καὶ ἀντίγ[ραφον ὑπο]μνήματος· με[. . . . . δη]μόσια πρὸς τῶι
β[ήματι] παρόντων τῶ[ν ἐνάρ]χων Δίου γυμ[ν]ασιάρχου Διο-
νυσίου|[το]ῦ καὶ . . . νθεου ἐξηγήτου, Ὀλυμ[πιο]δώρου προδίκου,
Ἀπολ[λων]ί[ο]υ Ἡρακλαπόλλων[ος γυ]μνασιαρχ(ήσαντος) καὶ
Ἀχιλ[λέως] Κορνηλίου, τῶν π[αρ]εστώτων ἀπὸ τῆς πόλεως
ἐπιφωνη|[σ]άντων· στεφέσθω Ἀχιλλεὺς κοσμητείαν· μιμοῦ τὸν
πα[τ]έρα τὸν φιλότιμον τὸν [γ]έροντα φῶτα. Ἀχιλλε[ὺ]ς εἶπεν·
35 πειθόμενος τῆι ἐμαυτοῦ πατρίδι ἐπιδέχομαι στεφα‖[νη]φόρον ἐξηγητείαν ἐπὶ τῶι ἐτήσια εἰσφέρειν με τάλαντα δύο καὶ ἀπαλλα-
γῆναι ἐπιτηρήσεως διαμισθουμένης γῆς. Ὀλυμπιόδωρος εἶπ(εν)· ἡ
τύχη τοῦ κυρίου ἡμῶν | Αὐ[το]κράτορος ἀφθόνως ἀρχὰ[ς] παρέχει
καὶ τῆς πόλ(εως) αὐξάνε[ι] τὰ πράγματα, τί τ' οὐκ ἤμελλεν ἐπὶ
τῆι ἐπαφροδείτωι ἡγεμονίαι Λαρκίου Μέμορος; Εἰ μὲν οὖν ὁ
Ἀχιλλεὺς | βούλεται στεφανωθῆναι ἐξηγητείαν, εἰσενεγκάτω τὸ
ἰσητήριον ἐντεῦθεν, εἰ δὲ μή, ⟨οὐχ⟩ ἧττον ἑαυτὸν ἐχειροτόνησεν
εἰς τὴν κατεπείγουσαν ἀρχὴν κοσμητεί|αν. Ἀχιλλεὺς εἶπ(εν)·
ἐγὼ ἀνεδεξάμην ἐξηγητείαν ἐπὶ τῶι κατ' ἔτος δύο τάλαντα
εἰσφέρειν, οὐ γὰρ δύναμαι κοσμητείαν. Ὀλυμπιόδωρος εἶπ(εν)·
ἀναδεξάμενος | τὴν μείζονα ἀρχὴν οὐκ ὀφείλει τὴν ἐλάττον'
ἀποφεύγειν. Ἀμμωνίων Διοσκόρου ὑποτυχὼν εἶπ(εν)· πάσης
40 τῆς ἐνεστώσης ἔτυψέ με ὁ Ἀχιλλεὺς καὶ αὐτὰ ταῦτα ‖ ἀσφαλί-
σομαι διὰ τῶν σῶν ὑπομνημάτων ὅτι καὶ ἐντυγχάνω τῶι λαμπρο-
τάτωι ἡγεμόνι περὶ τῆς ὕβρεως. Ἀχιλλεὺς εἶπ(εν)· οὔτε ἔτυψα
αὐτὸν οὔτε ὕβρισα. | Σαραπίων ὁ καὶ Ἀπολλώνιος στρ(ατηγὸς)
εἶπ(εν)· ἃ μὲν εἰρήκατε γέγραπται, μεταπεμφθήσονται δὲ καὶ οἱ

DOCUMENTS FROM EGYPT

κοσμηταὶ ἵνα ἐπὶ παροῦσι αὐτοῖς αὐτὰ ταῦτα εἴπητε. Μετ᾽
ὀλίγον | πρὸς τῶι Καισαρείωι Διογένης καὶ Διόσκορος καὶ
⟨οἳ⟩ σὺν αὐτοῖς κοσμηταὶ προελθόντες παρόντος τοῦ Ἀχιλλέως
διὰ τοῦ ἑνὸς αὐτῶν, Διογένης εἶπ(εν)· ἐμάθομεν τὸν Ἀχιλ|λέα
προβαλόμενον ἑαυτὸν εἰς ἐξηγ(ητείαν) ἀπόντων ἡμῶν, τοῦτο
δὲ οὐκ ἐξῆν, ὁ γὰρ θειότατος Ἀντωνῖνος διὰ ⟨δια⟩τάγματος
ἐκέλευσεν μὴ συγχωρῖσθαι ἄνευ τριῶν ἐπιλόγ|χων εἰς ἐξηγ(η-
τείαν)· πολλῶν οὖν ἐπιλόγχων ⟨ὄντων⟩ ὀφείλει εἰς τὴν κατεπεί-
γο[υσα]ν ἀρχὴν παραβαίνειν, ὡς ἀναγνώσομαί σοι τὸ διάταγμα.
Καὶ ἀναγνόντος ἀντίγρα(φον) διατάγματος ‖ Μάρκου Αὐρηλίου   45
Ἀντωνίνου Καίσαρος, Ἀσπιδᾶς πατὴρ Ἑρμᾶ κοσμητ[ε]ύ-
(σαντος) παρὼν εἶπ(εν)· ἰδίωι κινδύνωι στέφω τὸν Ἀχιλλέα τὴν
κοσμητείαν. Ὀλυμπιόδωρος εἶπ(εν)· | ἔχομεν δὴ φωνὴν τοῦ
Ἀσπιδᾶ ὅτι ἰδίωι κινδύνωι αὐτὸν στέφει. Κα[ὶ] ὀφείλει στεφῆναι,
ἤδη γὰρ ἡ ἀρχὴ ἀδιάπτωτός ἐστιν τῆι πόλ(ει). Ὁ στρα(τηγὸς)
εἶπ(εν)· τὰ εἰρημένα ὑπομνηματισθῆ|ναι. Ἀνέγνων. Καὶ ἑτέρου
ἐπιστάλματος τὸ ἀντίγρα(φον). Ἄρχον[τ]ες Ἑρμοῦ πόλ(εως)
τῆς μεγάλ(ης) Σαραπίωνι τῶι καὶ Ἀπολλωνίωι στρα(τηγῶι)
Ἑρμοπολ(ίτου) τῶι φιλ(τάτωι) χαίρειν. | Ἀχιλλεὺς Νεαρχίδου
τοῦ καὶ Κορνηλίου ἀγορανομήσαντος ἀγόμενος [ε]ἰς κοσμητείαν
ὑπό τινων κοσμητῶν ὑπέσχετο ἐπὶ σοῦ ἐξηγ(ητεύσειν). Ἡμῶν
δὲ προτρεπομέ|νων αὐτὸν ἀναδέξασθαι τὴν κοσμητείαν διὰ τὸ
μὴ πολλοὺς ἔχειν τὴν πόλ(ιν) κοσμητὰς πλειόνων ὄντων ἐπιλόγχων ἐξηγητῶν Ἀσπιδᾶς πατὴρ Ἑρμᾶ‖κοσμητεύσαντος ἔστε-   50
ψεν αὐτὸν ἰδίωι κινδύνωι τὴν κοσμητ(είαν), καθὰ δι᾽ ὑπομνημάτων
σου ἀνείλημπται. Τῆς οὖν ἀρχῆς τῆι πόλ(ει) ἀδιαπτώτου οὔσης
ἐξ ὁποτέ|ρου αὐτῶν ἐπιστέλλεταί σοι ὅπως ἀκόλουθα τοῖς ἐπὶ
σοῦ γενομένοις προνοήσαι πρᾶξαι, εἰς τὸ τὴν πόλιν ἀπολαβεῖν
τὴν ἀρχήν. (Ἔτους) λβ Φαρμοῦθι ιγ. Ὑπέγρα(ψαν) | ἐξηγητὴς
καὶ γυμνασίαρχος.

From Hermopolis. The first part of this document, which we
have omitted from our text, apparently dealt with a recalcitrant
nominee to public office, but the fragmentary character of the
papyrus makes it impossible to determine whether it treated of the
nomination of Achilleus, or whether it cited precedents dealing
with his case (cf. no. 183). It is probable that the two cases were
not related. That part of the text which we have included in this

collection is our most important source of information on the obscure subject of appointments to public office in the Egyptian metropolis prior to the establishment of the municipal organization. The problems which are presented in this document are discussed by the editors of the Rylands papyri in their commentary, by Jouguet (*Rev. d. ét. grec.* 30 (1917), 294 *ff.*), by Méautis (*Hermoupolis-la-Grande*, 118 *ff.*), and by Van Groningen (*Mnemosyne*, 51 (1923), 421 *ff.*).

Achilleus, a wealthy citizen of Hermopolis, was nominated by the board of cosmetae to a vacancy in the college. The strategus was notified, and on a stated day certain officials of the metropolis, a group of citizens, and Achilleus appeared at the tribunal of the governor. When the citizens by their acclamations signified their approval of the candidate, Achilleus sought to evade the office by making a counter-proposal, offering to accept the position of exegete, to which he would contribute two talents annually if he were released from the liturgy of superintending lands under lease. Olympiodorus, the advocate of Hermopolis, protested against the action of Achilleus, claiming that, if the latter were permitted to enter the higher office, he should pay the entrance fee which was apparently exacted from those who entered the more advanced positions without going through the regular *cursus* (if this is the proper interpretation of ἐντεῦθεν). Olympiodorus added that Achilleus, by offering himself for exegete, could not decline the lower office where there was greater need for his services. When Achilleus persisted in his refusal on the plea that he was unable to bear the expense of the office, the strategus summoned the board of cosmetae to the hearing. They refused to withdraw their nomination, and when they heard of the counter-proposal of Achilleus, they cited a decree of the emperor Antoninus to the effect that, when there were sufficient members in a higher office, a candidate should accept office in a magistracy where the board was weaker in numbers and where his services were more urgently required. At this point Aspidas, father of Hermas who was an ex-cosmete, intervened by offering himself as guarantor for Achilleus. This ended the proceedings before the strategus at this time. Apparently an interval was allowed Achilleus in case he wished to appeal. When he took no action, the board of archons wrote to the strategus to take the proper steps to have the nomination and appointment of Achilleus or his surety confirmed. A copy of this letter was included in the minutes along with the records bearing on the hearing before the strategus. It may be noted that the strategus crowns the candidate for the gymnasiarchy at Elephantine (Wilcken, *Chrestomathie*, 4).

The edict of Antoninus is important as there is no record of a similar law elsewhere. Unfortunately it is cited so concisely that its meaning is not absolutely certain, and the word ἐπιλόγχους appears nowhere else in this connection and its interpretation is obscure. Apparently there were two classes of members in the various colleges of the official *cursus*. Of these, one is known as ἔναρχοι or στεφανηφόροι, who are actively engaged in the duties of the office. The term ἐπίλογχοι is apparently applied to supernumeraries of an honorary character who share the expenses of the office with the working members of the board. It is probable that wealthy and patriotic citizens were willing to share the burdens in return for the glory of enjoying the distinction of a title, and if there were a large number of such honorary members the expenses of the magistracy would be considerably lightened. Naturally there would be a desire to enter the higher offices, and apparently there was a high entrance fee exacted as a *summa honoraria*. The edict of Antoninus provided a remedy for those communities where some boards were excessively large, while others suffered from a lack of regular candidates. If we understand the law aright, it provided that a citizen could voluntarily present himself for membership in a board if not more than three supernumeraries were already attached to that office. If there were four or more, the candidate should accept membership in that board where his services were required and where the burdens were disproportionately severe because they were distributed among a smaller number.

The procedure in nominating a cosmete or exegete in Hermopolis at this period may be thus summarized. A suitable candidate is coopted by the existing college and the nomination is sent to the board of archons who transmit it to the strategus. On a day appointed there appear before the tribunal of the strategus representatives of the college of archons, citizens of Hermopolis, and the nominee. Van Groningen (*loc. cit.*) believes that the presence of the citizens indicates that the imperial government gave them a fictitious show of power in the election of magistrates, but we are inclined to believe that they had no formal or official purpose in being present at the tribunal. When the citizens signified their approval of the candidate, he might signify his acceptance at once. In that case the strategus transmitted the notice of nomination and acceptance to his superior, the epistrategus, who makes the formal appointment, or instructs the strategus to do so. If, however, the candidate refused the nomination, the board which made the nomination was summoned. In the case of Achilleus, the cosmetae defend their action. The nominee might now appeal to the epistrategus or prefect on the ground of some illegality, or he might offer to surrender his property to his nominators, who would administer it for the term of appointment and discharge the expenses of the office from the revenue of the estate, possibly reserving a certain proportion of the income for the owner (*cf.* nos. 185, 198). Before Achilleus could act in either way, Aspidas offered to crown him as cosmete, thereby presenting himself as guarantor for Achilleus and liable to the obligations of the office in case Achilleus defaulted for any reason. According to law Achilleus became a cosmete-elect, and when the legal period for appeal had expired without any further action on his part the officials of the metropolis request the strategus to take the proper steps to confirm the appointment.

It may be noted that, while the board of cosmetae makes the nomination, it is not responsible at this period for the obligations of the nominee, for these are voluntarily undertaken by Aspidas, who is a private citizen. Van Groningen advances the plausible theory that he offered himself as surety in order to relieve his son (who, however, is called ex-cosmete) from the burdens of office by ensuring the addition of another wealthy member to the board. If this is the case, it is possible that the board was responsible for their nominee and only escaped by the action of Aspidas. Van Groningen's theory leads to the further implication that the separate boards were constituted by acting members, honorary members, and ex-members who had not yet advanced to a higher grade in the *cursus*,

DOCUMENTS FROM EGYPT

since Aspidas acts to relieve his son, Hermas, who is still an ex-cosmete, and, therefore, still liable for his share as a member of the college. It is clear that there were more than one in the membership of the boards of cosmetae and exegetae, and that the cost of these offices to the incumbents was very great. Achilleus voluntarily offered two talents as his share in the college of exegetae and sought to escape the lower office because of the greater expense. Since he offered this sum as an annual contribution, it may be inferred that the office was held for more than a year at a time, unless we accept Van Groningen's theory that ex-officials remained as members of the board until they entered the higher grade.

This document furnishes conclusive evidence that a citizen could hold a higher magistracy without having filled the lower (cf. pp. 85 ff.). Voluntary candidacy for office was probably not unusual (cf. Wilcken, *Chrestomathie*, 38), but the abuse of such candidacy, which we may infer from the edict of Antoninus, is a new and curious phase of ancient municipal history. Incidentally the law could not have been issued unless public liturgies had become so burdensome that the wealthy class had sought this method of escape. For the office of cosmete, cf. Oertel, *Die Liturgie*, 329 ff.

182. DE MUNERIBUS VICANORUM
(194 p. Chr.)

BGU. 15, col. 1; Wilcken, *Chrestomathie*, 393.

Ἐξ ὑπομνηματισμῶν Ἰουλίου Κουιντιανοῦ τοῦ κρατίστου |
ἐπιστρατήγου ἔτους δευτέρου Λουκίου | Σεπτιμίου Σεουήρου
Περτείνακος Σεβαστοῦ Μεσορὴ β̄· Μεθ' (ἕτερα). | Κληθέντος
Πεκύσις Ἀπύγχεως καὶ ὑπακούσαντος Διαδέλ‖φος ῥήτωρ εἶπεν. 5
Ἐάν σοι δοκῆι, κάλεσον τὸν τῆς Νείλου | πόλεως κωμογραμματέα,
ὧι ὁ ἡμέτερος ἐγκαλεῖ. Κλη|θέντος καὶ μὴ ὑπακούσαντος Ἀρτεμί-
δωρος εἶπ[ε]ν. | Κωμογραμματέα οὐκ ἔχι ἡ Νείλου πόλις, ἀλλὰ
πρεσβυτέρους | διαδεχομένους. Διάδελφος ῥήτωρ εἶπεν. Κεκέ-
λευσται ὑπὸ ‖ τῶν κατὰ καιρὸν ἡγεμόνων ἕκαστον ἰς τὴν ἑαυτοῦ 10
κώ|μην καὶ μὴ ἀπ' ἄλλης κώμης εἰς ἄλλην μεταφαίρεσθαι. |
Ὅτι νῦν κωμογραμματεὺς ἐπηρεάζει τῶι συνηγορου|μ[έ]νωι,
ἀνέδωκεν αὐτὸν πράκτορα ἀργυρικῶν τῆς ἰδίας | κώμης εἰς ἄλλην
λειτουργείαν. Ἀξιοῖ ἀναγεινώσκων τὰ κε‖κελευσμένα μὴ ἀφέλ- 15

[535]

DOCUMENTS FROM EGYPT

κεσθαι ἀπὸ τῆς ἰδίας εἰς ἀλλοτρίαν. | Κοιντινιανὸς εἶπεν.
Στρατηγὸς διαλήμψεται, ὃ τῶν ἐμῶν | μερῶν καταλάβηται, ἐπ᾽
ἐμὲ ἀναπέμψιν.

From the Fayûm. In this document the procedure in cases of
appeals from liturgies is shown. The appeal is heard before the
epistrategus. The strategus is present, and the village-scribe is
summoned to defend his nomination. Pekysis has an advocate,
Diadelphus. The advocate cites a law, which he says had been
regularly proclaimed by the prefects, to the effect that villagers
should not be drawn from one village to another, but should
remain in their own community. Wilcken points out that the law
was imperfectly expressed, because there is no objection to a
villager performing a liturgy in another district where he happens
to have some property, but when he has already been assigned to a
liturgy in his native village, he cannot be called upon to perform a
liturgy in another district at the same time (*Dig.* 50. 1. 17, 4).
Cf. P. Giess. 58.

183. DE IMMUNITATE ANTINOOPOLITANORUM
(196 p. Chr.)

BGU. 1022; Wilcken, *Chrestomathie,* 29.

Τῆι κρατίστηι βουλῆι Ἀντινοέων | Νέων Ἑλλήνων | παρὰ
Λουκίου Οὐαλερίου Λουκρη|τιανοῦ Ματιδείου τοῦ καὶ Πλωτι-
5 νί∥ου καὶ Λ[ουκίο]υ Λογγείνου Ἑρεννίου | Παυλεινίου τοῦ καὶ
Μεγαλεισίου. Οὐκ ἀ|[γ]νοεῖτε, ἄνδρες κράτιστοι, ὅτι πασῶν |
[λει]τουργιῶ[ν] ἀφ⟨⟨θ⟩⟩είθημεν τῶν ἀλλαχοῦ | [κατ]ὰ διάταξιν
10 θεοῦ Ἁδριανοῦ ⟨τοῦ⟩ καὶ οἰκιστοῦ ∥ [τ]ῆς ἡμετέρα[ς πό]λ[ε]ως.
Ἐπεὶ οὖν γενόμε|[νο]ι [ε]ἰς Φειλα[δ]ελφίαν κ[ώ]μην τοῦ Ἀρσι-
νο|[εί]τ[ο]υ τῆς [Ἡρα]κλείδου μερίδος, ἔνθα γεου|[χο]ῦμεν, ἐπ[ὶ]
τῆς διορθ[ώσ]εως δημ[οσ]ίων | ..... λοτων, ὁ τῆς προκ[ει]μένης
15 κώμης ∥ [κωμ]ογραμματεὺς Ἀφροδᾶς Θέωνος κατ᾽ ἐπή|[ρια]ν
ἐπέδωκεν ἡμᾶς ἐπὶ τῆς καταγωγῆς | τοῦ σείτου παρὰ τὰ διατε-
ταγμένα, κατὰ τὸ ἀναγ|[καῖο]ν, κύριοι, [τ]ὴν πρόσοδο[ν] πρὸς
20 ὑμᾶς ποι|[οῦ]μεν ἀξιοῦντες, ἐὰν ὑμῖν δόξῃι, ἀνε∥νεγκεῖν τῶι
κρατίστωι ἐπιστρατήγωι | Καλπουρνίωι Κονκέσσωι περὶ τούτου,
ὅπως | κατὰ τὰ ὑπάρχοντα ἡμῖν δίκαια κελεῦσαι | ἑτέρ[ο]υς

DOCUMENTS FROM EGYPT

ἀνθ᾽ ἡμῶν κατασταθῆναι καὶ | λόγον αὐτὸν ὑποσχεῖν τῶν τετολ-
μημέ‖νων καὶ εἰς τὸ πέραν ἐπκρεάστους (sic) φυλα|χθῆναι. 25
(2nd H.) Διευ[τυ]χεῖτε. (Ἔτους) δ᾽ Αὐτοκράτορος | Καίσαρος
Λουκίου Σε[πτι]μίο[υ | Σε]ουήρου Εὐσεβοῦς Περτίνακος |
Σεβαστοῦ ᾽Αραβικ(οῦ) ᾽Αδιαβηνικ[(οῦ) Μεσ]ορὴ κ̄. (3rd H.)
Λούκιος ‖ [Ο]ὐαλέριος Λ[ο]υκ[ρ]ητιανὸς ἐπιδέδοκα | καὶ ἔγραψα 30
ὑπὲρ ῾Ερεννίου μὴ [εἰ]δότος | γρά[μμα]τα.

From Antinoopolis. This appeal of citizens of Antinoopolis is of
interest because of its mode of procedure. It is directed to the senate
of their native city with the request that this body transmit their
appeal to the epistrategus. Ordinarily an appeal was forwarded
directly to the epistrategus. For the immunity enjoyed by the
Antinoopolitans, cf. nos. 170, 176; Wilcken, *Chrestomathie*, 397.

184. DE CONNUBIO ANTINOOPOLITANORUM
ET AEGYPTORUM
(saec. II p. Chr.)

Compt. rend. de l'acad. d. inscr. et bell. lett. 1905, 160 ff.;
Wilcken, *Chrestomathie*, 27.

Εἰ τοῖς ἀναγνωσθεῖσι ψηφίσ|μα[σ]ι ὑπεναντίον τί ἐστιν κα|τὰ
νόμον ἢ κατὰ διάταξιν. | Ε[ἰ γὰ]ρ ὑπεναντίον ἐστὶν τὸ ‖ πα[ρά]- 5
δειγμα οὐκ ἰσχυρόν, προ|κρεί[ν]ονται γὰρ παντὸς οὑτινοσ|οῦν
οἱ νόμοι καὶ διατάξεις. | ῾Ερμόδωρος Εὐτυχίδους βου|λευτὴς
εἶπεν. ᾽Αναγνωσθέ‖τω ἡ διάταξις Πρόκλου. ᾽Ανα|γνωσθεί- 10
σ(ης) "᾽Επὶ τοῦ θ (ἔτους) θεοῦ | Αἰλίου ᾽Αντ[ω]νείνου ᾽Αθὺρ
κ̄ᾱ." Νε|μεσίων ᾽Αμμωνίου βουλευ|[τὴς] εἶπεν. Περὶ τούτου
ὡς ἔδο‖ξε[ν], προσφωνησάτω ἡμεῖν | ὁ πρυτανικός. Λούκιος 15
᾽Απολινά|ριος πρυτανικὸς εἶπεν. ῾Η ἐπι|γαμία ἐδόθη ἡμεῖν
πρὸς | Αἰγυπ[τί]ου[ς] κατ᾽ ἐξαίρετον ‖ ὑπὸ τοῦ θεοῦ ῾Αδριανοῦ, 20
ἤν|περ ⟨⟨ου⟩⟩ οὐκ ἔχουσι Ναυκρα⟨⟨τι⟩⟩|τεῖται, ὧν τοῖς νόμοις
χρώ|μεθα, καὶ τὰ περὶ τῆς ἐπιγα|μίας πάλιν ἀναγεινώσκω. ‖
Καὶ ἀναγνόντος μετὰ τὴν ⟨⟨α⟩⟩|ἀνάγνωσιν. ᾽Αρισταῖος βου- 25
⟨⟨λε[υ]⟩⟩|λευτὴς εἶπεν. Τοῦτο οὐχ ἅπα|ξ ἐνν...... κεκεί-
νηται, | ἀλλὰ καὶ πλεονάκις, ἰδί‖ως ἔπ[ρ]επε[ν] ἡμῶν τῶι | 30
῾Ελληνικ[ῶι λό(?)]γωι. ᾽Ηθέλη|σα....ν περιτροπὴν ε|τ.υσεπ.
κ....ἡμῖν...

[537]

DOCUMENTS FROM EGYPT

From this document we learn that Antinoopolis received the same code of laws as Naucratis on the occasion of its foundation by Hadrian. The Antinoopolitans, however, enjoyed the rights of intermarriage with citizens of other Egyptian towns—a privilege which the people of Naucratis did not possess. It is evident that the former city had a senate and prytanies of a form usual in other Greek cities.

185. DE MUNERE EORUM QUI VECTIGALIA EXIGUNT
(200 p. Chr.?)

P. Oxy. 1405.

. . . . .ρ. . . . παρεχώρ[η|σας . . . .] εὔδηλόν ἐστιν
μὴ τῶι | [ταμεί]ωι ἡμῶν τὴν παραχώρησιν | [γενέσ]θαι ἀλλὰ
5 τῶι εἰς τὴν λειτουργίαν ‖ . . . .μένωι, ὃς ἀναλαβὼν σοῦ
τὰ | ὑπάρχον[τ]α τὸ λοι[πὸν τοῦ . .]πο. . .ι|τικο[ῦ] παρέξει
καὶ τὴν λειτουργίαν ἀπο|πληρώσει. Τὸ γὰρ ταμεῖον ἡμῶν | τῶν
10 τοιούτων παραχωρήσεων ‖ οὐκ ἐφείεται. Ἡ δὲ ἐπιτειμία σου
ἐ|κ τούτου οὐδὲν βλαβήσεται, οὐδὲ εἰς τὸ | σῶμα ὑβρεισθήσει.
Προετέθη ἐν Ἀλεξαν|δρείαι η' (ἔτους) Φαρμοῦθι. |
15 Αὐρηλίωι Λεωνίδηι στρα(τηγῶι) Ὀξυρυγχ(ίτου) ‖ παρὰ Αἰμι-
λίου Στεφάνου Ἀτρῆτος μη|τρὸς Τασορ[ά]πι[ος] ἀπὸ κώμης
Σιγκέφα. | Τῆι ἐνεστώσηι ἡμέραι ἔμαθον ἀντωνο|μάσθαι με ὑπὸ
Αὐρηλίου Ἀμόϊτος Πατᾶτος | μητρὸς Δημητροῦτος ἀπὸ τῆς
20 αὐτῆς κ[ώ]‖|μης εἰς πρακτορείαν ἀργυρικῶν κωμ[η]‖|τικῶν λημ-
μάτων τῆς αὐτῆς Σιγκέφα τοῦ | ἐνεστῶτος γ (ἔτους) ὡς εὔπορον
καὶ ἐπιτή|δειον. Οὐκ ἀνὰ λόγων οὖν οὐδὲ πρὸς [τὸ(?)] | μέρος τῆς
25 λειτουργίας, ἀλλ' ἐξιστανόμενο[ς] ‖ αὐτῷ κα⟨τὰ⟩ τὴν προκειμένην
θείαν | [διάταξιν] δη[λ]ῶ ἔχειν με πόρου ἐπὶ δι. . . . .

From Oxyrhynchus. The first part of this document appears to be an edict of the prefect issued in answer to an appeal from an Egyptian who offered to cede his property to the imperial *fiscus* for the year in lieu of his performing a liturgy to which he had been nominated. The prefect states that the government does not administer such estates, but that it goes to the man who nominated him for the office, and he administers the estate and defrays the expenses of the liturgy from the revenue. The recipient of this rescript is guaranteed against loss of status and corporal punishment.

Unfortunately the document is badly mutilated and almost un-decipherable in ll. 5–6 (*cf.* commentary of Grenfell-Hunt, *loc. cit.*), and the exact details of the law cannot be determined. It is evident, however, that liturgies as well as magistracies could be avoided in Egypt by appealing to the prefect with an offer to cede one's property to the nominator. If we read [δεχο]μένωι in l. 5 (although the editors, who proposed [δεδο]μένωι, note that the traces of the first letter do not suit this reading), we may have proof of the existence of a form of ἀντίδοσις or exchange of properties similar to the earlier Athenian custom. In this connection a rescript of Antoninus may be cited (*Cod. J.* 10. 67. 1), which instructs a certain Basilides to plead his case (before the governor), if he thinks that some one else is more capable of performing the liturgy. *Cf.* no. 181, where there is, apparently, reference to a similar cession of an estate to avoid a liturgy or magistracy. *Cf.* Mitteis, *Chresto-mathie,* 375, for a copy of the edict dealing with this question, and no. 198, where, in a later period, the law appears to require that, in cases where the estate is surrendered by a nominee to the nominators, two-thirds of the revenue may be devoted to the expense of the magistracy, and the remainder is returned to the owner.

The second part of the document is an appeal from a villager to the strategus. He had been nominated to the office of tax-collector of the village by his predecessor in that office as a suitable candidate and financially able to support the liturgy. Stephanus cites the proclamation of the prefect and offers to cede his property on the same terms as expressed in the edict on the ground, apparently, that his income is insufficient. The document is important because the method of nomination is different from the earlier practice, whereby nominations were made by the comarchs or other village-officials who sent a list of candidates to the strategus, and he in turn for-warded it to the epistrategus who selected the candidates by lot. We also learn that the villager sent his appeal to the strategus, although in the first document which he had cited the appeal was apparently forwarded to the prefect. *Cf.* pp. 99 *ff.*

The document is dated in the eighth year of some emperor and the editors assign it to A.D. 200. It is contemporary with no. 188,

DOCUMENTS FROM EGYPT

which must belong to the period after the introduction of the municipal organization and it is possible that both documents may belong to a later period, either to the eighth year of Alexander Severus or of Gallienus. *Cf.* Wilcken, *Archiv*, 6 (1920), 420 *f.*

186. DE VICIS DEMINUENDIS
(ca. 200 p. Chr.)

Preisigke, *Sammelbuch*, 8; *Festschrift Hirschfeld*, 125.

λ| . . . . θ γ(ίνονται) . . | . . . . (δραχμαὶ) μθϜϛ χ(αλκοῦς) |
εἰδῶ[ν .]. δ . . . . . (δραχμαὶ) λθ, γ(ίνονται) (δραχμαὶ) πηϜϛ
5 χ(αλκοῦς), ‖ T . αγ . . . , ἐφ᾽ ἧς ὁ κωμογρα(μματεὺς) ἐδήλ(ωσεν)
τοὺς | ἐπ᾽ αὐτῆς ἀναγρα(φομένους) ἄνδρας ἐκ το[ῦ] | πλείστου
ἐγλελοιπέναι, γεγονέναι | γὰρ τὴν κώμην τὸ πάλαι, ὅτε κεφ[ά-
10 λ(αιά)] | φησιν ἐστάθη ὑπὸ αὐτῶν [δί]‖δοσθαι, ἀπὸ ἀνδρῶν ρ̅κ̅η̅,
νῦν [δὲ] | κατηντηκέναι εἰς μόνους . . , | ἀφ᾽ ὧν ἀνακεχωρηκέναι
. . . , | καὶ ὀφείλειν τὸ ἐπιβάλλον | κουφισθῆναι δ[ιοικ(ήσεως)] ‖
15 ὑποκει(μένων) κωμογρ(αμματείαι) ἐφ . . | λογισμο . . . .
. . |γ(ίνεται) . . | ἐπιστάτει φυλ . . (δραχμαὶ) φ . . | παρανα . λ . .
20 (πυροῦ) (ἀρτάβαι) . . . . ‖ ἱερ . . . . | προ(σδιαγραφόμενα)
(δραχμαὶ) γρ χ(αλκοῖ) γ, | εἰδῶν . . . . . ει . . .

The origin of this fragment of papyrus is unknown. While there are numerous documents in the third century and in the Byzantine period which portray the decline of village communities (Rostowzew, *Gesch. d. röm. Kol.* 206 *ff.*), there are a few from the second century which reveal the same tendency (Wilcken, *Festschrift Hirschfeld*, 125 *ff.*). Wilcken connects the subject-matter of this document with the plague which was brought back from the Orient by the armies of Marcus and Verus. In *BGU.* 902, which apparently belongs to the same period, the village had decreased from eighty-five to ten. Here the original census had been one hundred and twenty-five, and of the remainder after the plague a number had deserted the village. The document is an appeal for a lightening of the taxes (*cf.* Wilcken, *loc. cit.*). *Cf.* for similar documents of the same period, *P.S.I.* 101, 102, 105.

DOCUMENTS FROM EGYPT

187. DE MUNERIBUS OXYRHYNCHI
(201 p. Chr.)
P. Oxy. 54.

Σαραπίωνι τῶι καὶ Ὡρίωνι ἐν[άρ]χωι | γυμνασιάρχωι κατα-
δεοῦς τὴν ἡλι|κίαν διὰ τοῦ κατὰ πατέρα πάππου | Ἀπίωνος
γυμνασιαρχήσαντος, ‖ καὶ Ἀχιλλίωνι ἐνάρχωι ἐξηγητῆι | διὰ 5
Ἀχιλλίωνος τοῦ καὶ Σαραπάμ|μωνος υἱοῦ καὶ διαδόχου, | παρὰ
Διογένους Σαραπίωνος καὶ Λου|κίου Ἑρμίου, ἀμφοτέρων ἀπ'
Ὀξυ‖ρύγχων πόλεως, εἰσδοθέντων ὑ|πὸ τοῦ τῆς πόλεως γραμ- 10
ματέως | γνώμηι τοῦ κοινοῦ τῶν ἀρχόντων | εἰς ἐπιμέλειαν
ἐπισκευῆς καὶ κα|τασκευῆς Ἀδριανῶν θερμῶν. ‖ Αἰτούμεθα 15
ἐπισταλῆναι ἐκ τοῦ | τῆς πόλεως λόγου εἰς τειμὴν γε|νῶν ἐπὶ
λόγου ἀργυρίου τάλαντα | τρία, γί(νεται) Ἀγ, ὧν λόγον τάξομεν |
[ὡς] δέον ἐστίν. (Ἔτους) θ ‖ Α[ὐ]τοκρατόρων Καισάρων | 20
Λουκίου Σεπτιμίου Σεουήρου | Εὐσεβοῦς Περτίνακος Ἀραβικοῦ |
Ἀδιαβηνικοῦ Παρθικοῦ Μεγίστου | καὶ Μάρκου Αὐρηλίου
Ἀντωνίνου ‖ Εὐσεβοῦς Σεβαστῶν [[καὶ | Πουβλίου Σεπτιμίου 25
Γέτα]] | Καίσαρος Σεβαστοῦ, Φαρμοῦθι. | (2nd H.) Διογένης
Σαραπ[ί]ωνος αἰτοῦ|μαι τὰ τ[ο]ῦ ἀργυρίου τάλαν‖τα τρία ὡς 30
πρόκιται. (3rd H.?) Λ[ού]|κιος Ἑρμίου συναιτοῦμαι | τὰ τοῦ
ἀργυρίου τάλαντα τρία | ὡ[ς πρό]κιται.

From Oxyrhynchus. This document is our chief source of information about the method of appointment to metropolitan liturgies before the civic organization was introduced. The names of
candidates were given in (εἰσδοθέντων) by the secretary of the
metropolis after consultation with the council of archons (*cf.*
pp. 27 *ff.*; 99 *ff.*). It is probable that the lists were forwarded to the
strategus and from his office to the epistrategus who made the
appointments by lot as in the villages. In some cases, however,
appeals were directed to the prefect, and he also received names of
candidates for certain offices (*cf. P. Amh.* 64; *P. Br. Mus.* 1220,
dated A.D. 202–207).

DOCUMENTS FROM EGYPT

188. DE VECTIGALIBUS
(ca. 202 p. Chr.)

P. Oxy. 890; Wilcken, *Chrestomathie,* 280.

Λούκιος Σεπτίμιος Αὐρήλιος | Σαραπίων ὁ καὶ Ἀπολινάριος
καὶ ὡς | χρηματίζω ἔναρχος πρύτανις τῆς | Ὀξυρυγχειτῶν
5 πόλεως Αὐρηλίωι ‖ Λεωνίδηι στρατηγῶι τῶι φιλ|τάτωι χαίρειν. |
Τοὺς ἀπαιτεῖσ[θα]ι μέλλοντας ἀφ' ὧν | [ὀ]φ[είλ]ουσι τῆι π[όλει]
10 χωρούντων | [εἰς δι]αγραφὴν τῶν ἐκ λόγου τῆς ‖ [πόλε]ως
διαγραφομένων καὶ νῦν | [γράφομέν] σοι πρὸς τὸ μὴ ἐμποδί|-
[ζεσθαι τὴ]ν εἴσπραξιν τοῦ ἱερωτάτου | [ταμείου.] Εἰσὶ δέ·
15 Αὐρήλιοι | [. . . . . καὶ Ἀ]πολλώνιος καὶ Δομιττια‖[νὸς οἱ τρεῖς
Σ]αραπίωνος τοῦ καὶ | [. . . . . . . ἀγορ]ανομήσαντος (δραχμὰς)
υ, | [. . . . . Ἡρ]ακλᾶς ὀνόματος | . . . .
. . . ατ . . . .

From Oxyrhynchus. The prytanis of Oxryhynchus forwards to
the strategus a list of citizens owing the city treasury. This was
apparently a necessary preliminary to the proceedings about to be
instituted against the defaulters. It would seem that the city paid
a certain amount to the imperial treasury as tribute. There is no
indication that the city council was liable for the deficiency at this
period, but unfortunately we cannot determine where the liability
would fall in case the proceedings against the defaulters failed. This
document may have some bearing on the interpretation of no. 202.
Cf. pp. 99 *ff.* The document is contemporary with no. 185, and
therefore dates ca. A.D. 202, or immediately on the introduction
of the municipal organization. The unique character of the document is probably due to the fact that it comes from the transitional
period. The strategus Aurelius Leonides served both before and
after the reconstruction if this date is correct. It is, however,
possible that he was in office ca. 230 (*cf.* no. 185, note) as he bears
the name Aurelius in both periods.

DOCUMENTS FROM EGYPT

189. EPISTULA IMPERATORIS SEPTIMI SEVERI
AD AURELIUM HORIONEM
(202 p. Chr.)

P. Oxy. 705, ll. 54–79; Wilcken, *Chrestomathie,* 407.

Αὐτοκράτωρ Καῖσαρ Λ[ο]ύκιος [Σ]επτίμ[ιος Σ]ε[ου]ῆρος ‖
Εὐσεβ[ὴ]ς Περτίναξ Σεβαστὸς Ἀραβικοῦ Ἀδιαβηνικὸς | Παρθι- 55
κοῦ Μεγίσ[το]υ [κ]αὶ Αὐτοκράτωρ Καῖσαρ | Μᾶρκο[ς] Αὐρήλιος
Ἀντωνῖνος Εὐσεβὴς Σεβαστὸς | Αὐρηλίωι Ὡρείωνι χαίρειν. |
Ἀποδεχόμεθά σε καὶ ταύτης τῆς ἐπιδόσεως ἣν ‖ ἀξιοῖς ἐπιδοῦναι 60
ταῖς κώμαις τῶν Ὀξυρυγχειτῶν | ἀποδιδοὺς ἀμοιβὴν ἐνκτήσεως.
Τ[ὸ] ὅμοιον δὴ καὶ | ἐ[π]ὶ τούτου φυλαχθήσεται καὶ καθότ[ι
ἠ]θέλησας ἀμε|τάστρεπτον εἰς ἕτερόν τι δαπανήσ[εσ]θαι τὴν
χάριν. | Ἔστιν δὲ ἡ ἀξίωσις. ‖ Τοῖς εὐμενεστάτοις Αὐτοκρά- 65
τ[ο]ρσι Σε[ουήρ]ωι καὶ Ἀντωνίωι | τοῖς πάντων ἀνθρώπων
σωτῆρσιν [κ]αὶ εὐεργέταις | Αὐρήλιος Ὡρείων γενόμενος στρα-
τη[γ]ὸς καὶ ἀρχιδικασ|τὴς τῆς λαμ[π]ροτάτης πόλεως τῶν
Ἀλεξανδρέων χαίρειν. | Κῶμαί τινες τοῦ Ὀξυρυγχείτου νομοῦ,
ὧ φιλανθρωπότα‖τοι Αὐτοκράτορες, ἐν αἷς ἐγώ τε ⟨καὶ⟩ οἱ υἱοί 70
μου χωρία κεκτήμε|θα, σφ[ό]δρα ἐξησθένησαν ἐνοχλούμεναι ὑπὸ
τῶν κατ᾿ ἔτος | λειτουργιῶν τοῦ τε ταμείου καὶ τῆς παρα[φ]υ-
[λ]ακῆς τῶν | τόπων, κινδυνεύουσί τε τῶι μὲν ταμείωι παραπο-
λέ|σθαι, τὴν δὲ ὑμετέραν γῆν ἀγεώργητον καταλιπεῖν. ‖ Ἐγὼ 75
[ο]ὖν καὶ τοῦ φιλανθρώπου καὶ τοῦ χρησίμου στοχα|ζ[όμε]νος
βούλομαι εἰς ἀνάκτησιν αὐτῶν ἐπίδοσίν | τ[ινα] βραχεῖαν
ἑκάστηι ποιήσασθαι εἰς συνωνὴν | χ[ωρί]ου, οὗ ἡ πρόσοδος
κατατεθήσεται εἰς τροφὰς καὶ | δ[απά]νας τῶν κατ᾿ ἔτος λειτουρ-
γησόντων ἐπὶ τῶι . . . .

l. 78. χ[όρτ]ου Grenfell-Hunt; χ[ωρί]ου Wilcken.

From Oxyrhynchus. This is one of the few endowments known
from Egypt, and is of interest because the consent of the emperors
was obtained. The endowment was made to relieve villages in the
region of Oxyrhynchus which had become impoverished because
of the pressure of imperial liturgies. In l. 77 the expression συνωνήν
is noteworthy, as it implies that Horion was contributing a certain
sum to each village for the purchase of property whose income would
be used to defray the expenses of the liturgies, and the remainder

DOCUMENTS FROM EGYPT

of the purchase price would be paid by the village. The endowment
of a school at Como by Pliny was made along similar lines, and
Horion apparently made his gift, actuated by the same motives as
Pliny.

190. QUERELLAE VICANORUM CONTRA POSSESSORES
(207 p. Chr.)

Preisigke, *Sammelbuch*, 4284, ll. 1–17.

Διονυσίωι στρ(ατηγῶι) Ἀρσιν(οΐτου) Ἡρακλ(είδου) μερίδ(ος) |
παρὰ Ἐριέως Στοτοήτεως πρεσβυτέρου καὶ Παβοῦτος [Π]αβοῦ-
[τ]ος μητρὸς Σεγάθιος ἀρχεφόδου καὶ Ἐριέω[ς Πα]κύσεως καὶ
Ἀπύγχεως Ὡρίωνος καὶ Ἐσούρεως Παουιτῆτος | καὶ Δημᾶ
Δημᾶτος καὶ Ὀρσενούφεως Ἐριέ[ως] καὶ Πετ[ε]σούχου Σώτου
καὶ Ὥρου μητρὸς Θαισᾶτος καὶ Σωτηρίχου ἀπάτορος μητρὸς
Θερμούθεως καὶ Πκᾶτος Πεκύ|σεως καὶ Πατῆτος Σαταβοῦτος καὶ
Παβοῦτος Παβοῦτος καὶ Καννεῖτος Πατῆτος καὶ Σωτᾶ Παβοῦτος
καὶ Παεῖτος Σαταβοῦτος καὶ Πεκύσεως Ψενήσιος καὶ Ἀπύγχεως
5 Ἀπύγ‖χεως καὶ Ἀβοῦτος Σαταβοῦτος καὶ Π[ακύ]σεως Ἐριέως
κ[αὶ] Πογσεῖτος Ματάϊτος καὶ Πακύσεως ⟨⟨Ματάϊτος καὶ
Πακύσεως⟩⟩ Ἀπύγχεως καὶ Μέλανος Πακύσεως καὶ Ἀεί|ετος
Καν[εῖ]τος καὶ Ἀπύγχεως Σαραπίωνος τῶν κε καὶ τ[ῶ]ν λοιπῶν
δημοσίων γεωργῶν κώμης Σοκνοπαίου Νήσου. Οἱ κύριοι ἡμῶν
θιότατοι καὶ ἀήτ'ητοι | Αὐτοκράτορες Σεουῆρος καὶ Ἀντωνεῖνος
ἀνατείλαντες [ἐ]ν ⟨τῆι⟩ ἑα[υ]τῶν Αἰγύπτωι, μεθ' ὧν πλεῖσ⟨τ⟩ων
ἀγαθῶν ἐδωρήσαντο, ἠθέλησαν καὶ τοὺς ἐν ἀλλοδαπῆι διατρί-
βοντας πάν|τας κατιέναι εἰς τὴν ἰδίαν οἰκείαν ἐκ'κόψαντες τὰ
βίαια [καὶ ἄν]ομα, καὶ κατὰ τὰς ἱερὰς αὐτῶν ἐν[κελεύ]σεις
κατεισήλθαμεν. Ἐχομένων οὖν ἡμῶν [τῆι] κατεργασίαι | τῆι
ἀποκαλυφθείσηι αἰγιαλίτι⟨δι⟩ γῆι ἑκάστον καθὸ δύναμις, Ὀρσεύς
τις ἀνὴρ βίαιος καὶ αὐθάδης τυ[γχάν]ων ἐπῆλθεν ἡμῖν σὺν ἀδελ-
10 φοῖς αὐτοῦ τέτρασι κ[ω]λύων τὴν κα|τεργασίαν καὶ κατασπορὰν
ποεῖσθαι καὶ ἐκφοβῶν ἡμᾶς, ἵν' [ἐκ το]ύ[το]υ κατὰ τὸ πρότερον εἰς
τ[ὴν] ἀλλο[δ]απὴν φύγωμεν καὶ μόνοι ἀντιποιήσονται [τ]ῆς γῆς,
δηλοῦ|μεν δέ σοι, κύριε, τὴν τούτων βίαν. Οὔτε γὰρ συνείσφοροι
γ[ε]ίνονται τῶν κατὰ μῆνα γει[νο]μένων ἐν τῆι κώμηι ἐπιμερισμῶν
τε καὶ ἐπιβολῶν σι[τ]ικῶν τε καὶ ἀρ|γυρικῶν τελεσμάτων, ἀλλὰ
καὶ οὐσία ἐστὶν ὑπὲρ ἧς κατ' ἔτος διαγράφ[ομε]ν μόνοι ἡμεῖς
δραχμὰς δισχειλίας τετρακοσίας καὶ μόνων τούτων τὰ τετράποδα

[544]

DOCUMENTS FROM EGYPT

πλεῖ|στα ὄντα τὰς ν[ο]μὰς ποιεῖται. Καὶ οὐδεπώποτε ἐλιτο[ύ]ρ-
[γησ]αν ἐ[κ]φοβοῦντες τοὺς κατὰ χρόνους κωμογραμματέως.
῞Οθεν κατὰ τὸ ἀναγκαῖον τὴν [ἐπί] σε καταφυ|γὴν ποιούμεθα καὶ
ἀξιοῦμεν, ἐάν σου τῆι τύχηι δόξηι, κελεῦσαι, ἀχθῆναι αὐτο[ὺς] ἐπί
σ[ο]υ καὶ διακοῦσαι ἡμῶν πρὸς αὐτὸν πρὸς τὸ ἐκ τῆς σῆς βοηθείας
ἐκδικηθέντες δυνη||θῶμεν τῆι γῆι σχολάζειν καὶ ταῖς ἐπιβα[λ]- 15
λούσαις ἡμε[ῖν] χρείαις προσκαρτερεῖν, τὸν δὲ 'Ορσέα καὶ τοὺς
ἀδελφ[ο]ὺς συνεισφόρας εἶναι τοῖς δημοσίοις τελέσμασι καὶ |
λιτ[ο]υργεῖν τ[ὰς] ἁρμοζούσας αὐτοῖς λιτουργίας καὶ ἔχ[εσθαι
ἐξ] ἴσου [ἡ]μᾶς πάντας τῆς σπορᾶς τῆς ἀποκαλυφ(θ)είσης γῆς,
ἵν' ὦμεν ἐν τῆι ἰδίαι συμμένοντες τῆι τύχηι σου | εὐχαριστεῖν.
Διευτύχει.

l. 9. ἑκάστον = ἑκάστων.
l. 13. κωμογραμματέως = κωμογραμματέας.
l. 15. συνεισφόρας = συνεισφόρους.

From the Fayûm. The relations of the great landlords to the small proprietor and to the village community are clearly indicated in this petition. These villagers had fled from their homes and engaged in a life of brigandage. On the issuance of the edict of Severus and Antoninus granting amnesty to all fugitives, they had returned to the village of Socnopaei Nesus and taken up leases in the public lands along the shore. Thereupon a certain Orseus and his brothers attempted to drive the fugitives away, as apparently they had done before, in order that they might continue to pasture their flocks on the lands thus vacated. Furthermore these men were so powerful that the village-secretary was always terrified. As a result Orseus and the members of his family paid no tribute or taxes and never performed any of the liturgies. Nor had they taken their due share of waste land to be cultivated which had been assigned to them. The petitioners apply to the strategus to bring these men to judgement in order that they themselves may not be forced to flee from their homes again and that Orseus and his party may be compelled to take their due share of public liturgies. This is the earliest documentary evidence for the encroachment of the wealthy landed proprietor on the holdings of the peasants and of the defiance of the local authorities by the rich (cf. pp. 203, 216 ff.; Wilcken, *Chrestomathie*, 354, 355; *Archiv*, 3 (1906), 548 ff.).

DOCUMENTS FROM EGYPT

191. DE TRIBUBUS METROPOLEOS
(212 p. Chr.)

P. Oxy. 1030; Wilcken, *Chrestomathie*, 36.

(5th H.) πε. | (1st H.) Σερήνωι ἀμφοδογρα(μματεῖ) α φυλ(ῆς)
β περιόδ(ου) | παρὰ Διογένους. (2nd H.) Παποντῶτος | τοῦ
5 Σπαρτᾶ μητρὸς Τερεῦτος ‖ ἀπ' Ὀξυρύγχων πόλεως. Ὁ | ἐμοῦ
καὶ τῆς ὁμοπατρίας μου | ἀδελφῆς Θαήσιος δοῦλος Ἱστόρη|τος
ὑπερετὴς ἄτεχ(νος) ἀναγραφό|μενος ἐπ' ἀμφόδου Παμμένους ‖
10 Παραδείσου ἐτελ(εύτησε) τῶι διελ(θόντι) ἔτει. | Διὸ ἐπιδίδωμι
τὸ ὑπόμνημα | ἀξιῶν α[ὐ]τὸν ἀναγραφῆναι ἐν | τῆι τῶν [ὁ]μοίων
15 τάξει, καὶ | ὀμνύω τὴν τοῦ κυρίου Μάρκου ‖ Αὐρηλίου [Σ]εουήρου
Ἀντωνίνου | τύχην μὴ ἐψεῦσθαι. (Ἔτους) κα | Αὐτοκράτ[ο]ρος
Καίσαρος Μάρκου | Αὐρηλίου [Σε]ουήρου Ἀντωνίνου | Παρθικοῦ
20 Μεγίστου Βρεταννικοῦ ‖ Μεγίστου Εὐσεβοῦς Σεβαστοῦ | [[μηνὸς
Ἀδριανοῦ]] κ. (3rd H.) Διογένης | Παποντῶτος ἐπιδέδωκα καὶ
ὀμώ|μεκα τὸν ὅρκον. | (4th H.) Σερῆνος ἀμφοδογρα(μματεὺς)
25 ἔσχον τού‖του τὸ ἴσον.

From Oxyrhynchus. This declaration is dated shortly after the
introduction of the municipal organization into Egypt by Severus.
Oxyrhynchus was divided into tribes and circuits numbered
numerically. The *amphodon* is a geographical division, each including a tribe (*P. Oxy.* 1119; Wilcken, *Grundzüge*, 348 f.). The
tribe had an archon and a secretary, and apparently there was a
cycle according to which each tribe took the municipal liturgies in
rotation (Wilcken, *loc. cit.*). The tribal secretary also received the
registrations of deaths, and probably all similar records connected
with the census in his particular district. In *P. Br. Mus.* 2, 281,
the death certificates from the villages are forwarded to the village-
secretary. Sometimes the royal scribe receives these declarations
(*cf.* note *ad loc.*).

[546]

DOCUMENTS FROM EGYPT

192. EDICTUM CARACALLAE DE CIVITATE PEREGRINIS DANDA
(212 p. Chr.)

P. Giess. 40, col. 1 (vol. III, p. 164); Mitteis, *Chrestomathie*, 377; Segré-Beltrami, *Rivista di Filologia*, 45 (1917), 16 *ff.*; Meyer, *Juristische Papyri*, 1; Girard, p. 203.

[Αὐτοκράτωρ Καῖσαρ Μᾶ]ρκος Αὐρήλι[ος Σεουῆρος] Ἀντωνῖνο[ς] Σ[εβαστὸ]ς λέγει. | [Νυνὶ δὲ νικήσαντα χρ]ὴ μᾶλλον ἀν[αβαλόμενον τὰ]ς αἰτίας κ[α]ὶ το[ὺ]ς λ[ιβ]έλλου[ς | ζητεῖν, ὅπως ἂν τοῖς θ]εοῖς τ[οῖ]ς ἀθ[αν]άτοις εὐχαριστήσαιμι, ὅτι τῆι τοιαύτηι | [νίκηι ἐτίμησαν καὶ σῶο]ν ἐμὲ συν[ετή]ρησαν. Τοιγαροῦν νομίζω [ο]ὕτω με‖[[γαλοπρεπῶς καὶ εὐσεβ]ῶς δύ[να]σθαι 5 τῆι μεγαλει[ό]τητι αὐτῶν τὸ ἱκανὸν ποι|[εῖν, εἰ τοὺς ξένους, ὁσ]άκις ἐὰν ὑ[π]εισέλθ[ωσ]ιν εἰς τοὺς ἐμοὺς ἀν[θρ]ώπους, | [εἰς τὰ χαριστήρια τῶ]ν θεῶν συνεπενέγ[κοι]μι. Δίδωμι τοί[ν]υν ἄπα|[σιν ξένοις τοῖς κατὰ τ]ὴν οἰκουμένην π[ολιτ]είαν Ῥωμαίων, [μ]ένοντος | [παντὸς γένους πολιτευμ]άτων χωρ[ὶς] τῶν [δεδ]ειτικίων. Ὀ[φ]είλει [γ]ὰρ τὸ ‖ [πλῆθος πρόπαν οὐ μόνον συμπο]νεῖν 10 πάντα ἀ[λλ]ὰ ἤδη κ[α]ὶ τῆι νίκηι ἐνπεριει[λῆφθαι. Ἔτι δὲ καὶ τοῦτο τὸ διάτ]αγμα ὁ[μ]αλώσει [τὴν] μεγαλειότητα [το]ῦ Ῥωμα[ί]ων δήμου διὰ τὸ τὴν αὐτὴν ἀξίαν] περὶ τοὺς [ξένο]υς γεγενῆσθαι. (*Reliqui versus omissi sunt.*)

l. 2. νικήσαντα, Segré.   l. 4. ἐτίμησαν καί, Segré.
l. 7. τὰ χαριστήρια, Segré.   l. 9. πολιτευμ]άτων, χωρίς, Meyer.
l. 10. [πρόπαν οὐ μόνον συμπο]νεῖν, Segré.
l. 11. [λῆφθαι. Ἔτι δὲ καὶ τοῦτο τὸ διάτ]αγμα ὁ[μ]αλώσει, Segré;
     [λεῖσθαι. Ἔτι δὲ καὶ τοῦτο τὸ πρ]άγμα ἐ[..] . λωσει, Meyer.
l. 12. [διὰ τὸ τὴν αὐτὴν ἀξίαν] περὶ τοὺς [ξένο]υς, Segré.

The origin of this document is unknown, but it probably came from Heptacomia. The papyrus is unfortunately preserved in a seriously mutilated condition, and its restoration is an exceedingly difficult problem. We have followed the text adopted by Beltrami incorporating the restorations proposed by Segré (*loc. cit.*). The document presents to us the only copy of the edict of Caracalla whereby he conferred Roman citizenship on the *peregrini* in the empire. This version is manifestly a Greek translation of the original edict published in Latin. The translator retained the Latin word *dediticii*, apparently because there is no adequate phrase to express the meaning in Greek, and the discussion of the edict depends almost entirely on the interpretation of the word. Meyer, whom Wilcken follows, interprets *dediticii* as λαογραφούμενοι or those subject to the poll-tax (Meyer, *loc. cit.*; Wilcken, *Grundzüge*, 55 ff.). Wilcken estimates the population of Egypt at this period at about seven millions, and assumes that those possessing a fortune of 100,000 sesterces, or about two millions, received citizenship by this edict. It is probable that his estimate of the wealthy class is entirely too high, and if the same proportion prevailed in the rest of the empire, the use of the word ἄπασι is a travesty (*Archiv*, 5, 426 ff.). Rostowzew (*Gesch. d. röm. Kol.* 222 ff.) identifies the λαογραφούμενοι with the ὁμόλογοι, and assumes that the latter is a translation of *dediticii*. However, the terms ὁμόλογοι and λαογραφούμενοι must have been perfectly familiar to the translator, and the scribe would undoubtedly have used one or other of them if they expressed the meaning required. The definition of *dediticii* in the legal language is also contrary to this interpretation, for Gaius (*Inst.* 1, 14) explains the term as applied to those who had fought against Rome and who had surrendered on defeat. It could not, therefore, be applied to the Egyptians without great difficulty. Moreover Justinian does not recognize the class of *dediticii*, and certainly does not apply the term to payers of poll-tax (*Cod. J.* 7. 5. 1; 7. 6. 1). The interpretation of Segré (*Atti della soc. it. per il progresso delle scienze*, Settima Riunione, Siena, 1913, 1013 ff.) seems worthy of consideration. He joins the phrase χωρὶς τῶν δεδειτικίων with the genitive absolute construction to which it logically belongs and explains δεδειτικίων as *civitates stipendiariae*. The edict, according to this view, preserved the privileged position of federated states and colonies with Latin rights, etc., but conferred Roman citizenship on members of tribute-paying states, and removed the legal disabilities under which these people labored in the eyes of the law (Mitteis, *Reichsrecht und Volksrecht*, 90 ff., 159 ff.). Latin rights were finally abolished by Justinian (*Cod. J.* 7. 6. 1, 6) as no longer having any meaning (*supervacua adiectio Latinitas aboleatur*).

Wilcken properly discounts the motive for the edict cited by Dio (*Archiv*, 5, 426 ff.), but his own theory that the edict was promulgated to foster the imperial cult seems equally wide of the mark. This cult first originated in the provinces where the gift of Roman citizenship was rarely enjoyed, and was especially fostered by the non-Roman element (*cf*. pp. 163 *ff*). His theory might be true for Egypt, but not for any of the provinces. In our opinion the edict was designed to relieve the peculiar situation which had developed in the municipalities at this period. In Egyptian cities both Romans and Alexandrians enjoyed a general immunity from local liturgies (*cf*. nos. 165, 173), and it is very probable that in the non-Roman communities throughout the rest of the empire the Romans enjoyed similar privileges. The veterans on discharge were granted Roman citizenship and general immunity from liturgies (*cf*. pp. 106 *f*.; no. 38) in the cities where they took up their residence. In many cities we find guilds of Roman citizens who form a corporation distinct from the general mass of the citizens, although there is occasionally cooperation. Most important, however, is the fact that in the great number of inscriptions which record liturgies, there are very few cases which indicate that a Roman discharged these duties for the municipality in which he resided. He was first and foremost a citizen of Rome, and by the law of *origo* this took precedence over any claim which the city in which he lived might exercise. In the few cases where Romans undertook liturgies, it is probable that such duties were discharged voluntarily or before the grant of citizenship was received. Under the empire Roman citizenship was granted freely to individuals and especially to ex-magistrates in communities which enjoyed major or minor Latin rights (*cf*. pp. 88, 191 *f*.). The gift was hereditary, and there was, therefore, a constantly increasing class of residents in every non-Roman community which could claim immunity from local liturgies. This class usually consisted of the wealthy members of the community, and the burdens of the city, which were constantly increasing, fell with greater severity upon a narrower circle of the community whose members were less able to undertake them. Under these conditions the municipal organization was in grave danger of complete disruption, and the imperial treasury was consequently faced with a serious problem. The legislation of Caracalla gave the municipalities a new lease of life by distributing the burdens of residents in a more equable manner. The immunity of veterans was reduced to a period of five years, at least for a time (*cf.* no. 177). The guilds of Roman citizens disappeared in the non-Roman states, and the only class which enjoyed exemption from local liturgies were the members of the imperial nobility (*cf.* pp. 103 *ff.*). The edict of Caracalla was a piece of wise and just legislation, and might have been followed by far-reaching results had not the empire been swept by famine, plague, and civil war in the third century. The disastrous effect of these evils was augmented to such an extent by a great increase in the burdens of taxation and by the development of the bureaucratic system that the municipalities were unable to recover financially, and their political development was stifled (*cf.* pp. 190 *ff.*; 228 *ff.*).

193. EDICTUM CARACALLAE DE REDITU AEGYPTIORUM IN AGROS
(215 p. Chr.)

P. Giess. 40, col. II, ll. 16–29; Wilcken, *Chrestomathie*, 22.

Αἰ[γύπτι]οι πάντες, οἵ εἰσιν ἐν Ἀλεξανδρείαι, καὶ μάλιστα
ἄ[γ]ροικοι, οἵτινες πεφε[ύγασιν] | ἀλ[λοθεν κ]αὶ εὐμαρῶς ε[ὑ]ρί-
σ[κε]εσθαι δύναντα[ι], πάντηι πάντως ἐγβλήσιμοί εἰσιν, ο[ὐχ]ὶ |
μ[έν]τοι γε χοιρέμπο[ρ]οι καὶ ναῦται ποτά[μ]ιοι ἐκεῖνοί τε οἵτινες
κάλαμον πρ[ὸ]ς τὸ | ὑποκαίειν τὰ βαλα[νεῖ]α καταφέρουσι.
20 Τοὺς δὲ ἄλλους ἔγβ[α]λλε, οἵτινες τῶι πλήθε[ι] τῶι ‖ ἰδίωι κα[ὶ
οὐ]χὶ χρήσει ταράσσουσι τὴν πόλιν. Σαραπείοις καὶ ἑτέραις τισὶν
ἑορ|τασί[μοις ἡ]μέραις εἰωθέναι κατάγειν θυσίας εἵνεκεν ταύρους
καὶ ἄλλα τινὰ | ἔνψ[υ]χα ἢ καὶ ἄλλαις ἡ[μ]έραις Αἰγυπτίους
μανθάνω· διὰ τοῦτο οὔκ εἰσι κωλυτέοι. | Ἐ[κεῖνοι] κωλ[ύ]εσθαι
ὀφε[ί]λουσιν, οἵτινες φεύγουσι τὰς χώρας τὰς ἰδίας, ἵνα μὴ |
ε.... ἄγροικον ποιῶσι, οὐχὶ μέντοι, ⟨οἵτινες⟩ τὴν πόλ[ι]ν τὴν
25 Ἀλεξανδρέων τὴν λαμπρο‖τάτ[ην] ⟨⟨ἦν⟩⟩ ἰδεῖν θέλον[τ]ες εἰς
αὐτὴν συνέρχονται ἢ πολειτικωτέρας ζωῆς ἕνε|κεν [ἢ πρ]αγμα-
τείας προ[σ]καίρου ἐνθάδε κ[α]τέρχονται. Μεθ' ἕτ]ερα. Ἐπι-
γεινώσκε|σθαι γὰ[ρ] εἰς τοὺς λ[ι]νούφ[ο]υς οἱ ἀληθινοὶ Αἰγύπτιοι
δύναντ[α]ι εὐμαρῶς φωνῆι, ἢ | ἄλλων [δηλ]οῖ ⟨αὐτοὺς⟩ ἔχειν

DOCUMENTS FROM EGYPT

ὄψεις τε καὶ σχῆμα· ἔτι τε καὶ ζω[ὴ] δεικνύει ἐναντία ἤθη | ἀπὸ ἀναστροφῆς [πο]λειτικῆς εἶναι ἀγροίκους Α[ἰ]γυπτίους.

This edict of Caracalla is part of a letter addressed to the prefect of Egypt. Cassius Dio refers to the driving of foreigners out of Alexandria by Caracalla excepting only the merchants (77. 23). From the edict we learn that the terms were not as severe as the historian maintains. Dio finds the motive for this legislation in the hatred of the emperor and the extreme lawlessness of the city mob, but it is probable that the urban movement and the desertion of the leaseholds and farms by the peasants were the cause (*cf.* no. 168; Rostowzew, *Gesch. d. röm. Kol.* 211 *ff.*).

194. DE SEVERITATE MUNERUM
(216 p. Chr.)

BGU. 159; Wilcken, *Chrestomathie*, 408.

. . . . .αστω. . .τε του πυ. . . . . καὶ ἀπὸ |
τ. . . . . . .[λαχανο]σπέρμου ἀρτ[αβῶ]ν τριῶν . . .τομ. . . .γδ. . .
γραμ|μ[ατ. . . . . ο]ὐκ ἐξέδετό μοι. Μετὰ δὲ ταῦτα ἀναδο[θέντο]ς
μου | εἰς δη[μοσ]ί[α]ν λειτουργίαν βαρυτάτην οὖσαν ἀπέστ[η]ν
τῆς κώμης ‖ οὐ δυνόμενος ὑποστῆναι τὸ βάρος τῆς λειτουργίας. 5
Τοῦ οὖν | λαμπροτάτου ἡγεμόνος Οὐαλερίου Δάτου κελεύσ[αν]-
το[ς] ἅπαντας τοὺς | ἐπὶ ξένης διατρείβοντας εἰς τὰς ἰδίας
κατεισέρχεσθαι, κατεισῆλθον. | Ἐπεὶ οὖν ὁ τούτου υἱὸς Αὐρήλιος
Σωτήριχος [ἐ]ξηγητεύσας τῆς αὐτῆς | πόλεως ἐπῆλθέν μοι
ἐκπράσσων τὸ τριπλοῦν τοῦ ὀφειλομένου, ‖ ἐπιδίδωμει καὶ ἀξιῶ 10
ἀκοῦσαί μου πρὸς αὐτοὺς καὶ τὸ δοκοῦν σοι κελεύσῃς | γενέ-
σθαι. Διευτύχει. | Α[ὐρ]ήλιος Πακῦσις ὡς (ἐτῶν) ν οὐλ(ὴ) γόνατι
ἀριστερῶι. | . . . .ου | (Ἔτους) κδ Αὐτο[κράτορ]ος Καίσαρος
Μάρκου Αὐρηλίου Σεουήρου Ἀντωνείνου Παρθικοῦ ‖ Μεγίστου 15
Β[ρεταννικοῦ Μεγ]ίστου Γερμανι[κοῦ Με]γίστου Εὐσεβοῦς
Σεβαστοῦ Παῦνι ια.

From the Fayûm. The severity of the liturgy imposed upon Pakysis was so great that he fled from the village. When Valerius Datus published his edict in 216 promising amnesty, Pakysis returned. He was immediately requested to forfeit threefold the cost of the liturgy which he had defaulted. This appears to have

DOCUMENTS FROM EGYPT

been the legal penalty in Egypt and if so, it was much higher than in other parts of the empire (*cf. Cod. Th.* 12. 1. 16). Since the penalty was exacted by an ex-official of the metropolis, it is probable that Pakysis had been nominated to a liturgy in the city, although it is possible that, after the reorganization of Severus, the municipal officials may have been authorized to enforce the performance of the liturgies in the villages of the nome. Wilcken points out that the petitioner states the cause of his flight as if it were the customary method of escape from the burdens of public service (*cf.* pp. 112 *ff.*; nos. 180, 186, 189, 190).

195. EDICTUM CARACALLAE DE SENATORIBUS
(213–217 p. Chr.)

P. Oxy. 1406.

Αὐτοκράτωρ Καῖσαρ Μ[ᾶρκος Αὐρήλιος] | Σεουῆρος Ἀντω-
νῖνο[ς Παρθικὸς Μέγιστος] | Βρεταν⟨ν⟩ικὸ[ς Μέγιστος Γερμανι-
5 κὸς] | Μέγιστος Ε[ὐσ]εβ[ὴς Σεβαστὸς] ‖ λέγει. | Ἐὰν βουλευτὴς
τὸν [πρύτανιν ἢ βουλευ]|τὴν τύψηι ἢ μέμψ[ητα]ι ....
..., | ὁ μὲν βουλ[ε]υτὴς τῆς βουλείας ἀ[παλλά]|ξεται καὶ εἰς
10 ἄτιμον χώραν [καταστή]‖σεται. Προετέθη ἐν Β[αβυλῶνι(?)] |
ὑπὸ στ[ο]ᾶι δημοσία ἐν[άρχου ἄρ]|χοντος Αὐρηλ(ίου) Ἀλεξάν-
δρ[ου . . . . .] | ἀπὸ Ἡλίου [π]όλεως

From Oxyrhynchus. This edict gives an interesting sidelight on the proceedings of the municipal councils in Egypt. It would seem that Severus had introduced municipal government before the Egyptians were ready for the responsibilities of it. The meetings of the town councils were marred by unseemly brawls and quarrels, and the emperor was forced to impose the serious penalty of exile on those members who forgot senatorial courtesy so far as to strike the presiding officer or a fellow-member. This document may throw some light on no. 181, ll. 39 *ff.*, where the proceedings in a case of appeal are curiously interrupted by a charge of assault.

196. EDICTUM AURELI SERENISCI, στρατηγοῦ, DE CENSU
(226 p. Chr.)

P. Teb. 288; Wilcken, *Chrestomathie*, 266.

[Αὐρ]ήλιος Σερηνίσκος ὁ καὶ Ἑρμησίας [στ]ρα(τηγὸς) Ἀρσι-
(νοΐτου) Θε(μίστου) [καὶ] Πολ(έμωνος) μερίδος. | Παραγ⟨γ⟩έλλεται

[552]

DOCUMENTS FROM EGYPT

τοῖς πράκ[τ]ορσι τοῦ ε (ἔτους) τῶν [γε]ωργ(ῶν) | καὶ κληρούχων
ἐπακολουθῆσαι τῆι γεινομένηι ἐπ᾽ ἀ|[γ]αθοῖς ἀναμετρήσει τοῦ
σπόρου καὶ ἀναγράψασθαι ‖ πᾶσαν τὴν ἐσπαρμένην γῆν ἔν τε 5
πυρῶι καὶ ἄλλοις | γ[ένεσ]ι καὶ τὰ [ὀνό]ματα τῶν κατὰ φύσιν
⟨γε⟩γεωργη|κ[ότ]ων δημοσίων γεωργῶν καὶ κληρ[ο]ύ|χων πρὸς
τὸ μηδὲν ἐπὶ ⟨περι⟩γραφῆι τοῦ ἱερωτάτου | ταμείου γενέσθαι
ὑπὸ τῶν λαογράφων ‖ ἢ πραγματικῶν, ὡς τοῦ κινδύνου καὶ 10
ὑμεῖν | [αὐ]τοῖς ἅμα ἐκείνοις διοίσοντος, ἐάν τι φανῆι | [κε]κα-
κουργημέ[νο]ν ἢ οὐ δεόντως πεπρ[α]γ|μένον, μηδεμειᾶς προφάσεως
ὑμεῖν | ὑπολειπομένης ἐπὶ τῆς ἀπαιτήσεως ‖ ἕνεκεν γνωρισμοῦ· 15
καὶ τῆς μέντοι γει|[ν]ομένης ὑφ᾽ ὑμῶν ἀναγραφὴν τὴν | ἴσην
ἐπίδοτε. | (Ἔτους) ε Αὐ[τοκρά]τορος Καίσαρος Μάρκου | [Αὐ]-
ρηλί[ου] Σεουήρ[ου Ἀλε]ξάνδρου Εὐσεβοῦς‖Εὐτυχοῦς Σεβαστοῦ 20
Μεχεὶρ θ.

l. 16. *lege* ἀναγραφῆς.

From the Fayûm. The instructions issued to the collectors of
the taxes in kind by the strategus of the district show that these
officials had also to make a record of the seed distributed and of the
land sown by the tenants on the public lands and by the cleruchi.
Furthermore the collectors, the λαογράφοι, and πραγματικοί seem
to share joint liability if the treasury suffers any loss. The λαογράφοι
are officials connected with the collection of the poll-tax. The
πραγματικοί occur but rarely in the Egyptian records and their
duties are usually in connection with the allotment of the tax in
grain. *Cf. P. Ryl.* 85; *P. Amh.* 107, 108, 109. In *P. Giess.* 58
the title is used as a general term for officials (A.D. 116). Oertel
omits this group in his study of the liturgy.

197. DE MUNERE DECAPROTORUM
(post 242 p. Chr.)

P. Oxy. 62, verso; Wilcken, *Chrestomathie*, 278.

....ας (ἑκατόνταρ)χ(ος) ἐπὶ κτήσ(εων) | [θεο(ῦ)(?)] Τ]ίτου
Σύρωι διαδε|[χο]μένωι στρατηγίαν χαί(ρειν). | [Ἐξα]υτῆς λαβών
μου τὰ ‖ [γρ]άμματα πέμψον | [το]ὺς κληρονόμους Ἀπο[λ]]- 5
λωνίου τοῦ δεκαπρώτ[ο]υ | τῆς Θμοισεφὼ τοπαρχ(ίας), | ἵνα
μὴ ἐκ τῆς σῆς ἀμε‖λείας ἐνέδρα περὶ τὴν | ἐμβολὴν γένηται. 10

[553]

Ἔ|πεμψα δὲ εἰς τοῦτο τὸν | στατιωνάριον ἀλλὰ | καὶ τοὺς
15 λοιποὺς δεκα||πρώτους, ἵνα δυνη|θῶμεν, ὅθεν ἐὰν δ⟨έ⟩ηι, | τὴν
ἐμβολὴν ποιῆσαι | διὰ τάχους. (2nd H.) Ἐρρῶσθέ σε εὔχομαι.

From Oxyrhynchus. From this letter of the centurion in charge
of the imperial estates we learn that the heirs of a decaprotus were
liable for the obligations of the liturgy during the remainder of the
term of the deceased. This office was introduced into Egypt after
the reorganization by Severus. There were normally two for each
toparchy. There is some doubt as to whether they were members of
the local senate or not (cf. Wilcken, *Grundzüge*, 218; *Klio*, 1,
147 ff.; Jouguet, *Vie munic.* 366 ff.; Oertel, *Die Liturgie*, 211 ff.;
R.E. s.v.; *P. Oxy.* 1410), but they were apparently nominated by
the senate. The liturgy, however, is not municipal but imperial
(Jouguet, *op. cit.* 369), and in this respect it apparently differs from
its counterpart in the rest of the empire. Grenfell is of the opinion
that the office was usually held for five years (*P. Oxy.* 1410), and
the evidence seems to support the view that the office was held for
a number of years in the later period, but this was not because of
the normal tenure of the liturgy. The edict of Magnius Rufus
(*P. Oxy.* 1410) merely forbids reappointment, and there is no
implication that the legal period of the liturgy was longer than a
year.

198. DE CESSIONE BONORUM EORUM
QUI MUNERA DECLINANT
(250 p. Chr.)

C.P.R. 20; Wilcken, *Chrestomathie*, 402.

Col. 1

[Αὐρήλιος Ἑρμόφι]λος Ὠρίωνος κοσμητεύσας Ἑρμοῦ πόλεως
τῆς μεγάλης ἀρχαίας καὶ λαμπρᾶς καὶ σεμνοτάτης | [Αὐρηλίωι
Εὐδαίμ]ονι τῶι καὶ Θεοδότωι γυμνα[σι]αρχήσαντι καὶ ἀρχιερα-
τεύσαντι βουλευτῆι διαδεχομένωι τὴν πρυ|[τανείαν τῆς αὐτ]ῆς
πόλεως τῶι τιμιωτάτ[ωι] χαίρειν. Φθά[σ]ας μὲν ἐπέστειλα τῆι
κρατίστηι βουλῆι διὰ σοῦ | [τὰ διὰ τοῦ ἐ]πιστάλματος τοῦ τοῦ
νομοῦ στρατηγοῦ Αὐρηλίου Ἱέρωνος διὰ Αὐρηλίου Ἑ[ρ]μοῦ στρα-
5 τηγικ[ο]ῦ || [ὑπηρέτου ἀ]ντιγραφέντα μοι ὑπὸ τοῦ λαμπροτάτου
ἡμῶν ἡγεμόνος Ἀππίου Σαβείνου, πρὸς ἃ ἠξί|[ουν παρ'] αὐτοῦ

ἐξιστανόμενος πάντων ὧν ἔχω τοῖς προβαλομένοις τὸν ἡμέτερον
υἱὸν | [Αὐρήλιον Ὠρίω]να τὸν καὶ Ἑρμαῖον εἰς κοσμητείαν τῆς
αὐτῆς πόλεως μεθ' ἣν ὑπογύως | [ἐξετέλεσα ὑπὲρ] ἐμαυτοῦ ἐξανα-
λωθείς, δι' ὧν ἠθέλησεν τὸν κίνδυνον τῆς προβολῆς εἶναι πρὸς |
[τοὺς ὀνομάσαντ]ας, τὸν δὲ [τ]οῦ νομοῦ στρα⟨τη⟩γὸν βίαν γεινο-
μένην κωλῦσαι, εἰ γείνο[ι]το παρὰ τὰ ὑπ' αὐτοῦ ‖ [σωτηρίως   10
διηγορευθ]έντα, ἅπερ ἐπενήνεκται ἀκολούθως τῆι ἐκδοθείσηι μοι
ὑπὸ τοῦ εἰς τοῦτο ἐπισταλέν|[τος ὑπηρέτου ὑ]πογραφῆι ἐπὶ τῆς
μ[ι]ᾶς καὶ εἰκάδος τοῦ ὄντος μηνὸς Ἐπείφ. Ἐχθὲς δὲ ἥτις ἦν κ̄β̄ |
[Ἐπείφ, ἐξεδόθη μοι] διὰ βουλευτ[ι]κοῦ ὑπηρ⟨έτ⟩ου ἐπίσταλμά
σου τοῦ Εὐδαίμ[ο]νος τοῦ καὶ Θεοδότου αὐτο|[προσώπως ἀντ-
επ]ισταλέντ[ο]ς περὶ τῆ[ς α]ὐτῆς ἀρχῆς μετ' ἔκστασιν καὶ
παραμορισθέντα ἐκ τῶν νόμων | [καὶ] τῆς [ὑπογρα]φῆ[ς] ἐπι-
φ[θ]όνως τινὰ δηλώσαντος κατὰ τὸ ἀναγκαῖον. Καὶ νῦν ἀντ-
επιστέλλω σοι, ‖ ἐπ[ε]ιδ[ήπερ τῶι] ἐκστάντ[ι] καὶ τῶν ἰδ[ί]ων   15
ἀφισταμένωι ὑπάρχει ἐκ τῶν νόμων καὶ τῶν θείων διατά|[ξ]εων
. . . . . η . [. . . βο]ήθεια τὸ μηδεμίαν βίαν πάσχειν [ο]ἷς ἁρμοζό-
μενος ὁ λαμπρότατος ἡγεμὼν καὶ | [κ]αθοσιο[ύμ]εν[ος] ἠθέλησεν
[τὸ]ν στρατηγὸν βίαν κωλῦσαι, προσθεὶς τὸν κίνδυνον τῆς
προβολῆς εἶναι περὶ | [τοὺ]ς ὀνομ[ά]σαντας. Εἰ δὲ οἴει, σὺ
[αὐ]τὸς τὰ πάντα μου λαβὼ[ν] ἀντὶ τοῦ νενομισμένου τρίτου τὰ
τῆι ἀρχῆι [δ]ιαφέροντα | [π]άντα ἀ[π]οπληρώσεις καὶ [μ]ὴ
ἐνεδρεύειν μή[[δ]]τε τὴν πόλιν μήδε τὴν κρατίστην βουλήν. Ἀρ-
κεσθή‖[σο]μαι γὰρ τῶιδ[ε] τῶι ἀντεπι[σ]τάλματι ἐ[ν] μεγίστωι   20
δικαιώματι. Αὐρήλιος Ἑρμόφιλος Ὠρίων[ος] κοσμητεύσας |
[ἐρρῶσθ]αί σε εὔχ[ομ]αι, φίλτατε. | [(Ἔτους)] α' Αὐτοκρά[το]ρος
Καίσαρος Γαΐου Μεσσίου Κυίντου Τραιανοῦ Δεκίου Εὐσεβοῦς
Εὐτυχοῦς Σεβαστοῦ Ἐφεὶπ κ̄γ̄.

Col. II

Αὐρηλίωι Ἀππίωι Σαβείνωι τῶι λαμπροτάτωι ἡγεμόνι | παρὰ
Αὐρηλίου Ἑρμοφίλου Ὠρίωνος κοσμητεύσαντος Ἑρμοῦ πόλεως
τῆς μεγάλης ἀρχαίας | καὶ λαμπρᾶς καὶ σεμν[ο]τάτης. Ἐπί-
σταλμα δισσὸν γραφὲν ὑπ' ἐμοῦ πρὸς τὸν τὴν πρυτα|νείαν
διαδεχόμενον Αὐρή[λ]ιον Εὐδαίμονα τὸν καὶ Θεοδότον γυμνασιαρχήσαντα βουλευτὴν ‖ τῶν [α]ὐτ(ῶν) Ἑρ(μοπολιτῶν) πρὸς ἃ   5
αὐτὸς ἀ[ντ]ε[π]έστειλέν μοι αὐτοπροσώπως μόνος περὶ κοσμη-

DOCUMENTS FROM EGYPT

τείας | εἰς ἣν ὠνομάσθη οὐ δεόντως ὁ ἡμέτερος υἱὸς Αὐρήλιος
'Ωρίων ὁ καὶ 'Ερμαῖος μεθ' ἣν ἐξε|τέλεσα ὑπὲρ ἐμαυτοῦ προ-
τέ[ρ]αν ὑπογύως φθάσαντός μου ἐπιστείλαντος τῆι κρατίστηι |
βουλῆι δι' αὐτοῦ τὰ ἀντιγραφέντα μοι ὑπὸ τοῦ λαμπροτάτου
ἡγεμόνος σοῦ τοῦ δεσπότου | δηλαδὴ [ἐ]ξ ἀξιώσεώς μου μ[ε]τ'
10 ἐκστάσεως πάντων τῶν ὑπαρχόντων μου πρὸς τὴν ἄνο‖μον
ὀνομασίαν καὶ μὴ δε[χο]μένου αὐτὰ ὡς περιέχει ἀποτίθεμαι ἐν
τῶι ἐνταῦθα | Σεβαστείωι παρὰ τοῖς εἴ[χ]νεσι τοῦ κυρίου ἡμῶν
καὶ θεοφιλεστάτου Αὐτοκράτορος | Γαΐου Μεσσ[ί]ου Κυΐντου
Τραιανοῦ Δεκίου Εὐσεβοῦς Εὐτυχοῦς Σεβαστοῦ καὶ 'Ερεννίας |
Κουπρεσσήνας 'Ετρουσκίλλας Σεβαστῆς ἅμα τῶιδε τῶι μαρτυ-
ροποιήματι πρὸς τὸ μηδὲν | τὸ σὸν μέγεθος λανθάνειν, ἀσφαλιζό-
15 μενος τὴν περὶ ἐμὲ φρουρὰν διὰ ὑπηρέτου βουλευ‖τικοῦ καὶ
φύλακος τῆς πρυτανείας ἔτι ἀπὸ εἰκάδος τοῦ ὄντος μηνὸς 'Επεὶφ
παρὰ τὰ | ὑπὸ σοῦ σωτηρίως διηγορευμένα, φυλασσομένων μοι
ὧν ἔχω παντοίων δι[κ]αί|ων. | ("Ετους) α' Αὐτοκράτορος Καίσαρος
Γαΐου Μεσσίου Κυΐντου Τραιανοῦ Δεκίου Εὐσεβοῦς Εὐτυχοῦς |
Σεβαστοῦ 'Επεὶφ κγ̄. Αὐρήλιος 'Ερμόφιλος 'Ωρίωνος κοσμη-
20 τεύσας ἀπεθέμην ‖ ὡς πρόκειται. | (2nd H.) Α(ὐρήλιος) 'Ηρωδίων
ἔσχον ἴσον. ("Ετους) α' 'Επεὶφ κγ̄. Τούτων τὰ ἴσα ἀπέθου.

From Hermopolis. The petition of Hermophilus is most important for the study of municipal administration in Egypt after
the reforms of Severus. Hermophilus had recently held the office
of cosmete and claims to have been almost ruined by the expenses
attached to this magistracy. His son was now nominated for the same
office without his father's consent and Hermophilus appealed to the
prefect offering to cede all his property to the nominators according
to the law. The prefect accepted his proposal and sent instructions
accordingly to the strategus that Hermophilus should not suffer loss
of citizenship or corporal restraint (cf. no. 185). This acceptance had
been forwarded by Hermophilus to the civic council and he had
surrendered his property according to law. The council, however,
was apparently free to accept or reject the proposal and it proceeded
to order the arrest of Hermophilus in order to compel him to accept
the liability for his son's proper performance of the magistracy.
Thereupon Hermophilus writes to the prytanis or presiding officer
of the council offering the whole of his income, without reserving

the customary third, to the prytanis if the latter will relieve him from the burden of undertaking the magistracy on behalf of his son, and will administer his estate on behalf of the liturgy. From this it is probable that the nomination had been made by the prytanis, though this inference is not absolutely necessary. In the second column Hermophilus lodges a copy of the correspondence in the shrine of the Augusti and appeals again to the prefect. In this case he characterizes the nomination as illegal although there is no implication of this charge in his previous correspondence. It is assumed that Horion was a senator although he is not designated by any official title in the petition. However, it is probable, although not certain, that only members of the council could be nominated to magistracies (cf. pp. 89 f.). The illegality may rest in the nomination to office of members in the same family without due regard to the law of vacatio (cf. no. 177 and p. 88).

The law whereby two-thirds of the revenues of a surrendered estate were appropriated for the liturgy which the owner had refused to accept, and one-third was reserved for the use of the owner by the nominator or nominators who administered the estate for the benefit of the liturgy which they were compelled to undertake, is unknown elsewhere. Mitteis has brought together all the evidence which bears on this problem in his excellent commentary on the legal aspects of this petition (C.P.R. 20), although Grenfell has cast some doubt on his interpretation of the document (P. Oxy. 1405). Cf. pp. 89 f., nos. 181, 185; P. Ryl. 77 notes; Hermes, 32 (1897), 651 ff.; 55 (1920), 21 ff.

199. DE TRAPEZITIS OXYRHYNCHI

(260 p. Chr.)

P. Oxy. 1411.

Αὐρήλιος Πτολεμαῖος ὁ καὶ Νεμεσιανὸς,| στρατηγὸς 'Οξυρυγ-
χείτου. Τῶν δημοσίων εἰς | ἐν συναχθέντων καὶ αἰτιασαμένων |
τοὺς τῶν κολλυβιστικῶν τραπεζῶν ‖ τραπεζείτας ὡς ταύτας 5
ἀποκλεισάν|τ[ω]ν τῶι μὴ βούλεσθαι προσ⟨⟨σ⟩⟩ίεσθαι | τὸ θεῖον
τῶν Σεβαστῶν νόμισμα, ἀ[νάγ]‖κη γεγένηται παραγγέλματι
π[αραγ]‖γελῆναι πᾶσει τοῖς τὰς τραπέζας κεκτ[ημέ]‖‖ν[οι]ς ταύτας 10
ἀνοῖξαι καὶ πᾶ[[η]]ν[[π]]νόμι|σ[μ]α προσίεσθαι πλὴν μάλισ[τα]‖

[557]

παρατύπου καὶ κιβδήλου καὶ κατακ[ερμα]|τίζειν, οὐ μόνοις δὲ
15 αὐτοῖς ἀλλὰ [τοῖς] | καθ᾽ ὅντινα δὴ τρόπον τὰς συνα[λλα]||γὰς
ποιουμένοις, γεινώσκουσι[ν] | ὡς, εἰ μὴ πειθαρχήσιαν τῆιδε τ[ῆι
παρ]|αγγελίαι, πειραθήσονται ὧν τὸ [μέ]||γεθος τῆς ἡγεμονίας
20 καὶ ἔτι ἄνω[θεν] | ἐπ᾽ αὐτοῖς [[το με]]γε[[θοσ]]νέσθαι πρ[οσ]||έ-
ταξεν. Ἐσημειωσάμην. Ἔτου[ς πρώ]|το[υ] Ἀθὺρ[[ι]] ὀγδόη
κ[[ει]]αὶ εἰκάς.

l. 5. *lege* ἀποκλείσαντας.

From Oxyrhynchus. The officials of the city accused the bankers
of the city, who dealt in exchange, of closing their doors and refusing to accept the new imperial coinage. The strategus ordered the
banks to open and to accept and exchange all coin except the
spurious and counterfeit on the pain of suffering the penalties already
prescribed in the past by the prefect for similar acts. For the banking
problem in Roman Egypt, *cf.* Preisigke, *Girowesen.* The importance
of this document lies in its value in the economic history of the
period rather than in its bearing on municipal institutions. The
depreciation of the currency by successive emperors was apparently
accompanied by laws compelling banks under state control to
accept the new issue at the same value as the old, or at a value fixed
above its real worth. Accordingly when a new issue came into
circulation there was a rush to exchange it for the older and purer
coinage. The banks of exchange would close their doors or refuse
to part with their reserves, but they were again and again compelled
to open and exchange money by the edicts of the prefects. *Cf.*
nos. 81, 133.

200. DE NOMINATIONE EORUM QUI MUNERA SUBEUNT
(265 p. Chr.)

P. Fior. 2, VII, ll. 166–201; Wilcken, *Chrestomathie*, 401.

(4th H.) [Φλάυιος Πα]νί[σκ]ος ὁ καὶ Λό[γγο]ς στρα(τηγὸς)
Ἑρμοπολ(είτου). | [Τοῦ δοθέν]το[ς] μοι προσ[αγγ]έλματος ὑπὸ
κωμαρχῶν | [κώμης Ἐν]σεῦ διὰ τῶν ληισ[τοπ]ιαστῶν εἰσδιδόν|-
170 [των] τοὺς δι᾽ αὐτοῦ ἐγ[γεγ]ραμμένους εἰς τὴν || [ἀν]θ᾽ ἑαυτῶν
κωμαρχίαν [ἴσ]ον δημοσίαι | [πρ]όκειται, ἵνα πάντες ε[ἰδ]ῶσι
καὶ οἱ εἰσαγ᾽|γελέντες ἔχωνται τῶν [ἐγχει]ρισθέντων αὐτοῖς |

[558]

DOCUMENTS FROM EGYPT

ὑγιῶς καὶ πιστῶς εἰς τὸ ἔ[ν μηδ]ενὶ μεμφ[θῆ]ναι. | (5th H.)
Ἐσημει[ωσά]μην. ||
(4th H.) (Ἔτους) ιβ΄ τοῦ κυρίου ἡμῶν Γαλ[λι]ηνοῦ Σεβαστοῦ | 175
Ἐπεὶφ γ̅. |
(1st H.) Φλανίωι Πανίσκωι τῶι καὶ Λόγγωι [στ]ρατηγῶι
Ἑρμοπολείτου | π[αρὰ] Αὐρηλίων Τυράννου Ἑρμα[πό]λλωνος
καὶ Παθώτου | . . . . ἀμφοτέρων κωμαρχῶ[ν κ]ώμης Ἐνσεῦ
δι᾽ ἡμῶν, || Αὐ[ρη]λίων Πόλλωνος Παθώ[του κ]αὶ Ὥρου Ἀτρῆτος 180
ἀμφοτέ|ρων λῃστοπιαστῶν [κα]ὶ τῶν [λοιπ]ῶν δι᾽ ἡμῶν τῶν
πα|ρόντων. Δίδομεν καὶ προσα[γγ]έλλομεν τοὺς ὑπογε|γραμ-
μένους κωμάρχας, ἐφ᾽ ὧι α[ὐτ]οὺς ἀντιλα[βέσθ]αι τῆς | χρείας
ἀπὸ σήμερον, ἥτις ἐστὶν [γ΄ τ]οῦ Ἐπεὶφ το[ῦ ἐνεστ]ῶτος || ιβ΄ 185
(ἔτους), ὄντας εὐπόρους καὶ ἐπι[τη]δείους κινδύ[ν]ωι ἡμῶν | καὶ
πάντων τῶν καταμενόν[τ]ων ἐν τῆι αὐτῆι κώ|μηι ἐξ ἀλληλεγ-
γύης, οὓς καὶ ἡμ[εῖ]ς ἐγγυώμεθα. Εἰσὶ δέ. | Παῆσις Κολλούθου
μητ(ρὸς) . . . . ης | ὡς (ἐτῶν) με΄, πόρ[ον ἔ]χ(ων) (δραχμῶν
δισχιλίων) || Ποτάμων Παήσιος μητ[ρὸς . . . . .]ήσιος | ὡς (ἐτῶν) 190
λε΄, πόρ[ον ἔ]χ(ων) (δραχμῶν δισχιλίων). | Διευτ[ύχει]. | (Ἔτους)
ιβ΄ Αὐτοκράτορος Καίσαρ[ος Πουπλί]ου Λικιννίου | Γαλλιηνοῦ
Γερμανικοῦ Μεγίστ[ου Εὐσε]β[οῦς Εὐτυχοῦς || Σεβαστοῦ 195
Ἐπεὶφ γ΄. (2nd H.) Οἱ π[ροκείμενοι κω]μάρχαι | δι᾽ ἡμῶν τῶν
παρόντ[ων λῃστοπια]στῶ(ν) | ἐπιδεδώκαμεν. Α[ὐρήλιος . . . .
. . . . |. .]ος ἔγραψα ὑπὲρ αὐτ(ῶν) [γράμματα μὴ εἰδότων] |.
(3rd H.?) Ἐσημ(ειωσάμην). || (6th H.) Τύρανν[ος ὑπηρέτης δημο- 200
σίαι προθεὶς κα|τε]χώρ(ισα).

From Hermopolites. This document is important for the history
of the liturgy of the comarch. This official replaced the village-elders
in the control of the affairs of the village after the municipal reorganization. There were usually two in each village and they
were nominated by their predecessors in office. It is noteworthy
that, in this period, not only the nominators, but also the citizens
and the residents of the village were bound as sureties for the proper
fulfilment of the liturgy (cf. Wilcken, loc. cit. note on l. 186; Oertel,
Die Liturgie, 153 ff.; nos. 171, 196; pp. 99 ff.). The epistrategus had no longer any connection with the appointment of
officials in the villages as this document was issued by the strategus
(cf. Wilcken, Grundzüge, 349).

DOCUMENTS FROM EGYPT

201. DE CONDUCTIONE AGRORUM PUBLICORUM
(266 p. Chr.)

C.P.H. 119, recto, col. vii; *C.P.R.* 39; Wilcken, *Chrestomathie,* 377·

[Τ]ῆι κρατίστηι βουλῆι Ἑρμοῦ πόλεως τ[ῆς μεγάλης] | ἀρχαίας καὶ λαμπρᾶς καὶ σεμνοτάτ[ης διὰ Αὐρηλίου] | Κορελλίου Ἀλεξάνδρου ἱππικοῦ ἀπὸ στρ[ατιῶν] | γυμνασιάρχου βουλευτοῦ
5 ἐνάρχου πρυτάνεως ‖ τῆς αὐτῆς πόλεως καὶ ὡς χρηματίζει | [πα]ρὰ Αὐρηλίου Μενελάου Πασχειοῦτος μητρὸς | Ἐγεῦτος ἀπὸ κώμης Θελβώνθεως. Βούλομαι | [ἑ]κουσίως μισθώσασθαι ἐκ τοῦ π[ο]λειτικοῦ λόγου | ἐπὶ χρόνον ἔτη τέσσαρα ἀπὸ τοῦ
10 ἐνεστῶτος ιδ΄ (ἔτους) ‖ περὶ τὴν α[ὐ]τὴν Θελβῶνθιν ἐκ τοῦ Φιλοκράτους | κλήρου ἀρούρας ἓξ εἰς ⟨σ⟩πορὰν πυροῦ καὶ ἀναπαυ|ματικῶν γενῶν κατ᾽ ἔτος κατὰ τὸ ἥμισυ, ἐκφορί|ου καὶ φόρου κατ᾽ ἔτος ἀποτά[κ]του τῶ[ν ὅλων] | ἀρουρῶν πυροῦ ἀρτα-
15 βῶν δέκα ὀκτὼ καὶ ἀργυ‖ρίου δραχμῶν ἑβδομήκοντα δύο, ἃς ἀποδώσω | καὶ μετρήσω ἐν τῶι Παῦνι καὶ Ἐπεὶφ μησὶ κατ᾽ ἔτος, | τὸ μὲν ἀργύρι[ο]ν δόκιμον, τὸν δὲ πυρὸν εἰς τὸ δη|μόσιον πρώτηι μετρήσει μία[ν] δοχικῶι ἀντὶ | μιᾶς Ἀθηναίου καὶ ᾽ποίσω
20 μέτρησιν κα[θ]αρὰν εἰς τὸ ‖ . . ασταλῆναι, τῶν δημοσίων πάντων τῆς γῆς | καὶ ἐπιμερισμῶν ὄντων πρὸς τὸν τῆς πόλεως | λόγον. Ἐὰν δὲ ὃ μὴ γείνοιτο ἄβροχος γένηται ἀπὸ το[ῦ] | ἑξῆς ἔτου[ς], ἐπάναγ᾽κες ἐπαντλήσω κ[αὶ] τελέσω | τῶν προκειμένων φόρων
25 τὸ ἥμισυ, ἐπιθαί‖ματος δὲ γεινομένου ἐξὸν ἑτέροις μεταμισθοῦν | ἢ καὶ αὐτουργ[ῖ]ν καὶ ἐπερωτ(ηθεὶς) ὡμολ(όγησα.) (Ἔτους) ιδ΄ Αὐτοκράτορο[ς] | Καίσαρος Πουπλίου Λικιννίου Γαλλιηνοῦ | Γερμανικοῦ Μεγίστου Περσικοῦ Μεγίστου Εὐσεβοῦς | Εὐτυχοῦς
30 Σε[β]αστοῦ Χοίακ γ΄. ‖ [Α(ὐρήλιος)] Μενέλα[ος Πασχειοῦτ]ος μεμίσθωμαι ὡς πρόκ(ειται). | Α(ὐρήλιος) Κοπρῆ[ς ἔγρ(αψα) ὑ(πὲρ) αὐτ(οῦ) μ]ὴ εἰδ(ότος) γρ(άμματα).

From Hermopolis. This document gives the terms of a lease of the public lands of the city from the municipal council for a term of four years. The rental is paid partly in kind, partly in money. It is noteworthy that the lessee states that his contract is voluntary on his part, implying that compulsory leaseholds were not unknown at this period. In case of lack of water in any season the lessee pays

DOCUMENTS FROM EGYPT

half the stipulated rental, but in case the city receives a better offer for the lease of the land during the term of the leasehold, it has the right to cancel the lease. From this document it is apparent that the municipality now controlled a certain amount of land in the nome, and it is probable that Severus transferred some if not all of the state lands in the nome to the municipality when he instituted the new organization (*cf.* pp. 29 *f.*; Wilcken, *Grundzüge*, 308).

202. EPISTULA SENATUS HERMOPOLITANI AD στρατηγόν
(266–267 p. Chr.)

C.P.H. 52; Wilcken, *Chrestomathie*, 38.

['Ερμοῦ πόλεως τῆς μεγάλης] ἀρχαίας [καὶ λαμπροτάτης] |
[καὶ σεμνοτάτης ἡ κρατίστη βου]λὴ Αὐ[ρηλίωι | . . . .
στρ]ατηγῶι Ἑρμ[οπολίτου | τῶι φιλτά]τωι [χαίρειν· ‖ 5
. . . .]τα τοῦ κυρίου . . . . | . . . . .ς
πᾶσι καὶ π . . . . | . . . . .ν μέρος τῶν αρ[. . . . .
. . . . | . . . . .φο]ρολογίας και π . . . . | . . . .
ερου ταύτης ἐγδ[. . . . . ‖ . . . . ὁ λαμ]πρότατος 10
ἡγεμὼ[ν . . . . | . . . .]ταγμα ἀπειλ . . . . |
. . . . καὶ δεκάπρωτον ὡς ἐπιχειρησ . . . . | . . . .
. . . . . . ἀπαιτ[εῖ]ν τὸ ὑποπείπτον τρίτον μέρος . . . . . . | .ρας
ἀναγκαίως ἐψηφισάμεθα ⟨καταφυγεῖν⟩ πρὸς τὸ μέγεθο[ς] ‖ αὐτοῦ 15
[ἀ]ξιοῦντες παραδεχθῆναι ἡμῖν τὰ μ[ὴ] | δεόντως ἀπῃτημένα
εἰς ἄλλα ἡμῶν ὀφλήμα|τα καὶ [πι]στεύομεν κατὰ τὴν ἔμφυτον
αὐτοῦ | πρὸς το[ὺς ὑπ]ηκόους φιλανθρωπίαν καὶ πρὸς τὰ θεῖ[α] |
εὐσέβε[ιαν] ἐπινεύσειν τῆι δεήσει τοῦ κοινοῦ ἡμῶν ‖ συνεδρίου. 20
Ἐπειδὴ δὲ ἀναγκαῖον ἦν δε καὶ σὲ ἐπιστέλ|λεσθαι κάτω καὶ
ἀπόσχηι τοιαύτης | εἰσπράξεως, ἣν παρὰ τὰ θείως διηγορευμένα |
γεινομένην ἐμέμψατο ἡ μεγαλειότης τοῦ | λαμπροτάτου ἡγεμόνος,
ἀκολούθως τοῖς ἐν ἡ‖μῖν δόξασιν ἐπιστέλλομέν σοι ε[ἰδ]ότι ὡς 25
οὐ|δενὶ ἀκίνδυνον Αὐτοκρατόρων χάριτι | [ἀ]ντι[βλ]έπειν, λόγου
φυλασσομένο[υ τ]ῆι πόλει | καὶ τῆι βουλῆι περὶ οὗ ἔχουσι
παντὸς δικαίου· ‖ ἀκολ(ούθως) τοῖς ἐν ἡμ(ῖν) δόξ(ασι) ἐπιστέλ- 30
[λομέν] σοι αὐτὰ ταῦ|τα, ἵν᾽ εἰδῆις κ(αὶ) π(ερι)μείνης τὸν τ(ῆς)
ἡγ(εμονίας) ὅρον | ὡς οὐδὲν ἀκίνδυνον αὐτοκρατορικαὶ χάρι|τι
[ἀντι]βλέπειν. | (Ἔτους) ιδ´ [Αὐ]τοκράτορος Καίσαρος Που-

DOCUMENTS FROM EGYPT

35 πλίου ‖ Λικιννίου Γαλλιηνοῦ Γερμανικοῦ Μεγίστου | Περσικοῦ
Μεγίστου Εὐσεβοῦς Εὐτυχοῦς Σεβάστου | ...

l. 14. καταφυγεῖν supplied by Wilcken.
l. 20. Ἐπειδὴ δ' corrected by scribe to Ἐπειδὴ δέ: ἦν καὶ to ἦν δε καί.
l. 21. κατ' ειδηο κάτω corrected by scribe to κάτω.
l. 29. καὶ μείνηις τὸν τῆς ἡγεμονίας ὅρον erased by scribe.
l. 30. εἰδότι τα corrected by scribe to αὐτὰ ταῦτα.

From Hermopolis. Unfortunately this piece of papyrus is very
fragmentary and its meaning can only be made out in part. It is
evident, however, that the city was heavily in arrears in its quota
of tribute, and the senators appealed to the prefect to have certain
sums illegally exacted credited to their indebtedness. The strategus
had paid no heed to their protests and had continued his exactions
in spite of the law—apparently an edict which forbade the strategus
to collect arrears by confiscation or by fines until appeals were
decided. The senate hereby warns the strategus to desist until the
prefect visits Hermopolis on his next judicial circuit.

203. ACTA SENATUS OXYRHYNCHI
(270–275 p. Chr.)

P. Oxy. 1413.

..... η καὶ ψήφισμα αὐτῶι ἐπὶ τούτοις γινέσθω εἰς ἡμιχώριον
τ..........υδ..... | .....ας δὲ εἰσηγοῦμαι. Σεπτίμιος
Σερῆνος ὁ καὶ Ἰσχυρίων ἐξηγητὴς εἶ[π(εν)]........ρ......
.... καὶ ω[....|...ἐπὶ τού]τοις τοῖς ὅροις. Οἱ βουλευταὶ
εἶπ(ον)· ὠκεανέ, ἐξηγητά. | [ὁ πρύτανις εἶπεν· τὸ μεγα]λῖον τοῦ
κυρίου ἡμῶν Αὐρηλιανοῦ Σεβαστοῦ. Ὀνομάσατε οὖν καὶ βουλευ-
5 τὰς ἵνα τὰ στεπτικὰ αὐτῶν εἰσ[...... ‖ οἱ βουλευταὶ εἶπον·
.....]ι. Ὁ πρύτανις εἶπ(εν)· προτρέψασθε οἱ ἐξηγηταί τινας. Οἱ
ἐξηγηταὶ εἶπ(ον)· προτραπήτω [Σ]ερῆνος εἰς ἐξηγητείαν. Ὁ πρύ-
τανις εἶπ(εν)· ...|... Σα]βεῖνος καὶ ὡς χρημα(τίζει) πρυτανεύ-
σας εἶπ(εν)· ὁ Πλουτίων στεπτικὸν ἔτι ὀφείλει ἧς ἀνεδέξατο ἀπὸ
τιμῶν ἐξηγητείας. Ὁ πρύτ[ανις | εἶπ(εν)· .... γ]ραμματεὺς
πολειτικῶν εἶπ(εν)· ναί. Ἰουλιανὸς ὁ καὶ Διοσκουρίδης ἐξηγητὴς
εἶπ(εν)· Πλουτίων ὀφείλει στεπτι[κόν], οὔκουν [...|... Οἱ
βουλευτ]αὶ εἶπ(ον)· ὁ ὀνομασθεὶς ἐπὶ τῶι ἰδίωι πόρωι ὠνομάσθη.
Σεπτίμιος Διογένης ὁ καὶ Ἀγαθὸς Δαίμων γενόμενος ὑπομνημα-
τογρ[ά]φος καὶ .... | ... [ὡς χρημα(τίζει) σύνδικος εἶπ(εν)·

Σερῆνό(?)]ς ἐστιν γυμνασίαρχος. Ὁ πρύτανις εἶπ(εν)· ὀνομάσατε
ἄλλους, ἵνα κἂν τὸ ἐξηγητικὸν συσταθῆι. Οἱ ἐξηγηταὶ εἶπ(ον)·
προτραπήτω Ἴων υἱὸς ...‖.... [εἰς τὴν ἐξηγητεί]αν τοῦ πάπ-   10
που. Σεκοῦνδος Σεκούνδου ἀρχιερεὺς εἶπ(εν)· ἐπιτηρείσθω οὖν
ὁ ὀνομασθείς. Ὁ πρύτανις εἶπ(εν)· αἱροῦμαι εἰς ἐπιτή|[ρησιν
...... Φιλέαν καὶ] Πλουτεῖνον ἵνα τὴν πίστιν ἀποπληρώσωσιν
τῆι βουλῆι. Οἱ βουλευταὶ εἶπ(ον)· ἁγνὲ πιστὲ Φιλέα, ἁγνὲ πιστὲ
Πλο[υ]τεῖνε. Τούτων [..|... ὑπερτεθέντων εἰς τὴν]ἑξῆς βουλήν, ὁ
πρύτανις εἶπ(εν)· καὶ αἱ ἄλλαι ἀρχαὶὀνομασάτωσαν. Ὀνομάσατε
δὲ καὶ βουλευτάς. Οἱ ἀπὸ τῆς τρίτης φυλῆς εἶπ(ον)·....|...[Ὁ
πρύτανις εἶπ(εν)· ἐπι]τηρήσει Νεῖλος βουλευτής. Οἱ βουλευταὶ
εἶπ(ον)· ἁγνὲ πιστὲ Νεῖλε, ἀεὶ καλῶς Νεῖλος, βοήθειαν αὐτῶι.
Οἱ ἀπὸ τῆ[ς τ]ρίτης φυλῆ[ς | εἶπ(ον)· Σεπτίμιος Διογένης ὁ καὶ
Ἀγαθὸς Δαίμων γενόμενος ὑπομνηματογράφος καὶ ὡς χρημα-
(τίζει) σύνδικος εἶπ(εν)· ...]κατείληφα πόρον, τουτέστιν γενή-
ματα ἀποκείμενα ἐν τῶι Μονίμου, καὶ ὅταν γνωσθῆι ἡ ποσότης,
παρατε[θ]ήσεται ὑμῖ[ν. ... ‖ ....]φος καὶ ὡς χρημα(τίζει)   15
εἶπ(εν)· ὅσοι νῦν ὠνομάσθησαν ὑπὸ Φελέου καὶ Ἡρακλιδίωνος
ὠνομάσθησαν. Οἱ βουλευτ[α]ὶ εἶπ(ον)· ἀπὸ ὅλης .... | [τῆς
φυλῆς(?).... ἁγνὲ πισ]τὲ Ὠρίων γεουχῶν ἐν Νεσμείμι, ἁγνὲ
πιστὲ Λεωνίδη γεουχῶν ἐν Δωσιθέου, ἁγνὲ πιστὲ Βη[σ]αρίων
γεου|[χῶν ἐν........ Σεπτίμιος Διογένης ὁ καὶ Ἀγαθὸς Δαίμων
γενόμενος ὑπομνηματογράφος καὶ ὡς χ]ρημα(τίζει) σύνδικος
εἶπ(εν)· ἵνα προτράπωσιν καὶ ἄρχωσιν οἱ ὀνομαζόμενοι, τὸ
πρωτενίαυτον τῆς λιτουργησία[ς .....|.........|........
Πτολεμαῖος γυμνασίαρχος εἶπ(εν)· .... ε]ἰς τὴ[ν τρια]κάδα
τοῦ Μεσορὴ χρεῖσαι. Τῆι μὲν τριακάδι οὐκ ἔχρεισεν, ἀλλὰ τῆι
ἑξῆς νεομηνίαι δι' ἐμοῦ ἔ[χρεισε]ν, παραδεχ[......., ‖β......]ς   20
ὁ τοῦ Φιλοσόφου, γ ἐπεστάτει Θεόδωρος υἱὸς Πτολεμαίου καὶ
οὐκ ἔχρεισεν, ἀλλ' ἐγὼ ἐκ προχρείας [ἔχρεισ]α. Ἐὰν οὖν
[.....|..... οἱ βουλευταὶ εἶπ(ον)·] ὠκεανὲ Πτολεμαῖε, ὠκεανὲ
γυμνασίαρχε. ια Διονύσιος ὁ καὶ Ἀρτεμίδωρος, ιβ Ἀριστίων ὁ
καὶ Ἀνδ[ρόνει]κος Ἀσ[υ]γκρί[του .... | ...... γυμνασίαρχος
εἶπ(εν)· ...] ἡ ἐναλλαγὴ τῶν ἡμερῶν. Οἱ βουλευταὶ εἶπ(ον)·
κύρια τὰ ψηφίσματα. ιγ Ξενικὸς καὶ οἱ μέλλοντες γυμ[νασι-
αρχεῖν, ... | ....] Σερῆνος Ἀμμωνίου γυμνασίαρχος
εἶπ(εν)· μὴ βλαπτέτω μου τὸ ψήφισμα ἡ ἐναλλαγὴ τῆς ἡ[μ]έ[ρας

DOCUMENTS FROM EGYPT

............|...... εἰ] καὶ μὴ ἔχρεισεν. κη Σεουῆρος καὶ
Ἐπίμαχος οἱ τοῦ Φιλοσόφου. Οἱ βουλευταὶ εἶπ(ον)· ὠκε[ανὲ
25 Σερῆνε, ὠκεανὲ γυμνασίαρχε ......||.... ὁ πρύτανις εἶπ(εν)·
.....] ὁ ἐπείκτης χρυσοῦ στεφάνου καὶ νείκης τοῦ κυρίου ἡμῶν
Αὐρηλιανοῦ Σεβ(αστ)οῦ Ἰο[υλι........ |...... τοῦ κυρίου
ἡμῶν Αὐρηλια]νοῦ Σεβαστοῦ καὶ ὅτι καὶ ὁ στέφανος αὐτοῦ ἤδη
ἐγένετο, καὶ εἰ μὴ οἱ τεχνεῖται [.............|...τὰ σκ]εύη
ταῦτα κατ' εὐχὴν γείνεται. Ἄλλα δώδεκα τάλαντα δοθήτω τοῖς
τεχνείτα[ι]ς ....|...... Οἱ βουλευταὶ εἶπ(ον)· οἱ αὐτοὶ
ἀπαιτείτωσαν. Θέων ὁ καὶ Ὠριγένης Χ[αιρήμον(?)]ος καὶ ὡς
χρ[ημα(τίζει) εἶπ(εν)· ....|..... δύν]ασθε αὐτοὺς ἀπαι-
τῆσαι. Οἱ βουλευταὶ εἶπ(ον)· ἀγνοὶ πιστοὶ ἀπαιτηταί. Εὔπορ[ος]
30 ὁ καὶ Ἀγα[θὸς Δαίμων καὶ ὡς χρημα(τίζει) εἶπ(εν)·....||...]ναι,
ἐὰν [μ]ὴ τελειωθῆι τὸ ἔργον. Ὁ πρύτανις εἶπ(εν)· καὶ ὁ κράτι-
σ[τος] ἐπιστράτηγος δ[....|....... Εὔπορος ὁ καὶ Ἀγαθὸς
Δαίμων κ]αὶ ὡς χρημα(τίζει) εἶπ(εν)· ὅταν οὖν εὐθέως ἔλθηι,
ἐπειχθήσεται τ[ὸ ἔ]ργον. Οἱ βουλε[υταὶ ε]ἶ[π(ον)· ....|
.....]τε Εὔπορε, εὐδιοίκητε Εὔπορε. Σεπτίμιος Διογένης ὁ καὶ
Ἀγαθὸς Δαίμων γενόμ[ενος ὑπομνηματογράφος | καὶ ὡς χρημα-
(τίζει) σύνδικος εἶπ(εν)· εἴ τι τοῖ]ς τεχνείταις ἐν πίστι ἀναλί-
σκεται, παρατεθήσεται ὑμῖν. |..... [Ὁ πρύτανις εἶπ(εν)·
......] πον ἦν καὶ ἐπεστάλη τότε τὸ κοινὸν τῶν κοσμητ[ῶν διὰ
35 Κ]ορνηλιανοῦ καὶ Παυσαν[ίου ....||.....]ος δεδη[λωκέν]αι
πρὶν ἂν τὸ πᾶν ἀνάλωμα δοθ[ῆι ....] Μάξιμον εν...δ[..
..|............ λιτουργ(?)]ησίαν ..... ἕως τοῦ Παχὼν α....
........|........τον.........ο.ς αἰτησω........

From Oxyrhynchus. This record of the proceedings in the senate
at Oxyrhynchus was written on an unusually broad sheet of papyrus.
More than eighty letters have been lost from the beginning of the
lines, and the part of the document still preserved can be interpreted
only in part. Sufficient remains, however, to give valuable information in regard to the organization of the senate, the procedure
in appointment to magistracies and liturgies, and details in regard
to municipal administration. The first three lines give the conclusion of a discussion about filling an official post, probably that
of exegetes. The prytanis apparently brings the proposal before the
senate in each case. In ll. 4–18 the topic is the appointment of

[564]

municipal magistrates, particularly the exegetae and their ἐπιτηρηταί. The latter are evidently official guardians of the officials
elected, and apparently the senators are more interested in them
than in the nominees to office. The relations of these guardians or
supervisors to the exegetae are uncertain. They may have administered the duties of the office while the exegetae provided the
funds, but is more probable that they were responsible in some
way for the ⁀erson of the candidate, and were appointed to prevent
his flight or avoidance of the liturgy and its obligations. Supervisors
of gymnasiarchs (*P. Oxy.* 471) and of the office of agoranomus
(Oertel, *Die Liturgie*, 239 *f.*) are also known, and the latter sometimes replaces the agoranomus (*P. Oxy.* 1413, l. 10 note). The
relation of the magistrate, his supervisor, and his nominators becomes a complicated problem which cannot be solved with the
scanty evidence available. In l. 4 the prytanis opened the debate
with a reference to honoring the emperor by the nomination of
senators to magistracies in order that their payments for crowns of
office should be available for the state. Evidently, at this period,
only senators were available for magistracies (*cf.* pp. 89 *f.*). The
exegetae were asked to nominate candidates to succeed themselves
or possibly to fill a vacancy in the college. They suggested a certain
Serenus (?) for the post. The remarks of the prytanis, probably a
request for more names, are lost. Sabinus now called attention to
the fact that Plution had not paid his fee for the crown on entering
the college of exegetae. This statement was confirmed by the
secretary of the municipal treasury and the debate was continued,
probably with a warning that the precedent should not be followed
by Serenus. The senators made the statement that the nominee
(Plution or Serenus) was named on the security of his own property.
The syndic then apparently closed the discussion about Serenus
with a remark of which the point is obscure, but which perhaps
implied that Serenus was ineligible because he already held the post
of gymnasiarch. The exegetae then nominated Ion and, on the
proposal of the chief-priest, Phileas and Plutinus were named as
Ion's supervisors. Next comes a reference to business, probably
concerning the supervisors, which is deferred to the next meeting.
The prytanis then calls upon the other colleges to make nominations

[565]

DOCUMENTS FROM EGYPT

for office, and he also asks for nominations to the senate. The third tribe, whose turn it was, apparently, to make nominations for liturgies during the following year (cf. no. 191; Jouguet, *Vie munic.* 410 f.), now made a nomination for some office and the prytanis named a supervisor. In this case only one supervisor is named, and the office must be different from that to which Ion was nominated, as two ἐπιτηρηταί were named for the exegetes. The third tribe then made another nomination, but the syndic intervened explaining that he had impounded the property of some individual (probably the person whose name had just been mentioned) and would report on its value later. The meaning of ll. 15–17 is obscure. Grenfell thinks that objection was made to the previous nomination because only two names supported it. This was followed by the selection of candidates on the nomination of the senate collectively, and chosen from the whole body of the tribe or of the senate. The debate concluded with some remarks concerning the first year of their liturgy. This may imply that liturgies were now held for a longer term than one year which has hitherto been regarded as the normal tenure of office. In ll. 19–24 we find some new information about the gymnasiarchs. They took turns in providing the oil, each furnishing the requisite amount for one day. The gymnasiarchs-elect also were required to share this burden, but in a body, not singly. From *P. Oxy.* 1418 (A.D. 247) we learn further that the office was often held for longer terms than a year, although the incumbent may have only been called upon to serve for short periods of a few days each time. In ll. 25 ff. the debate deals with the preparation of a gold crown due from the city, and the method of raising money to pay for it.

204. ACTA SENATUS OXYRHYNCHI

(270–275 p. Chr.)

P. Oxy. 1414.

[.....ὀ]φίλε[τα]ι [κ]αὶ τάλ[α]ντα δεκατέσσαρα. Ἡ τιμὴ τῶν ρ σ[τι]χ[α]ρίων τάλαντα ἑκατὸν τεσσαρ[άκοντα|.......]ἀπέχω τὰ διαφέροντα τῶι νομῶι εἰς τὸ μέρος τῆς πόλεως ἐξ ἥμισοι. Μηνιαῖοι ἀποδοῦναι ἐκ τῆς ἰδίας ἀπαιτείσθωσαν ἑ[πτὰ ἥμισυ..| ....]χίζεται. |....[Ὁ πρύτανις εἶπ(εν)· τὴ]ν τοῦ ἱεροῦ

[566]

γραφ[ὴ]ν κ[ατ]εσκέψασθαι καὶ ὅρον δεδώκατε καὶ ἐπεστάλη⟨ν⟩
τὰ δόξαντα ὑμεῖν τῶι στρατηγῶι, ἀλλὰ [οἱ ἱερεῖς μὴ ‖ . . . . .τοὺς 5
τὸ ἔρ]γον τοῦτο μεταχειρισαμένους μηδὲ τὰ[ς] γυναῖκας αὐτῶν
δύνασθαι κλώθειν τὸ λείνον προεβάλοντο . .| . . . . .α. . . .ὅπως
καὶ περὶ τοῦτο ὅρον δῶτε· ὀλίγε γὰρ κῶ[μα]ί εἰσιν αἱ ἐν τῶι
νομῶι ὑμῶν τοῦτο τὸ εἶδος ἔχουσιν. Οἱ βου[λ]ε[υταὶ εἶπ(ον)·
. . .| . . . . . .]ναι. Σεπτίμιος Διογένης ὁ καὶ Ἀγαθὸς Δαίμων
γενόμενος ὑπομνηματογράφος καὶ ὡς χρημα(τίζει) σύν[δικος
εἶπ(εν)· οἱ λινέμποροι(?). .| . . . . . .]σαι καὶ ἐ[κ] τεσσαράκοντα
ἐννέα δηναρίων εἶναι τὸ λείνον τὸ στημονικόν, ἔνδεκα δὲ δηνάρια
αὐτοῖς ἐξωδιάσθη ἀπ[ὸ τοῦ ταμιακοῦ λόγου | . . . .γ]ενέσθαι.
[Οἱ βο]υλευταὶ εἶπ(ον)· [δε]καεννέα δηναρίοις ἀρκείσθωσαν οἱ
λεινένποροι⟨⟨ς⟩⟩ μετὰ τὸ ἐξωδιαζ[ό]μενον ἀπὸ τοῦ τα[μ]ι[ακοῦ
λόγου. Σεπτίμιος Διογένης ὁ καὶ Ἀγαθὸς Δαίμων γενόμενος ‖
ὑπομνηματογρά]φος καὶ ὡς χρημα(τίζει) σύνδικος εἶπ(εν)· εἰ 10
τοῦτο ὑμ[ῖ]ν [ἔ]δοξεν ἐπὶ τοῦ στημονικοῦ, πεῖραν προσενεγκοῦ-
μ[ε]ν καὶ τοῖς μέλλουσι[ν ὑφαίνειν | . . . . .] ταξάτωσάν τινα οἱ
λινόϋφοι οἱ μέλλοντες ὑφαίνειν τὴν ὀθόνην τοῦ ἱεροῦ ἀνα. . . .|
. . .[ἀναγνωσθείσης ἀξ]ιώσεως τῶ[ν τῆ]ς πόλεως λινούφων περὶ
τοῦ μετὰ τὰς πέρυσιν ἐξοδιασθεῖσαν αὐτοῖς [ὑπὲρ. . .δραχμὰς
δοθῆναι ἄλλας δραχμὰς | . . . . . .δι]ὰ [τὴ]ν πλεοτιμίαν [τῶ]ν
εἰδῶν καὶ τὴν πλεομισθίαν τῶν ὑπουργ[ῶ]ν, μετὰ τὴν ἀνάγνωσιν
ὁ π[ρύτανις εἶπ(εν)· δοθήτωσαν τοῖς λινούφοις ἄλλαι δραχμαὶ |
. . . .κο]ντα εἰς [σ]υνπλήρωσιν δραχμῶν διακοσίων διὰ τὴν
πλεοτιμίαν τῶν εἰδῶν. Τοῦτο ψηφ[ίσασθε ‖ . . .συντε]τιμημένου 15
τοῦ κρίκου καὶ αὐται προσγενέσθωσαν. Οἱ τελοῦντες τὴν τιμὴν
τοῦ [λίνου(?) | . . . . . .]π[α]ρατεθήσεται ὑμῖν τῆι ἑξῆς βουλῆι.
Οἱ βουλευταὶ εἶπ(ον)· οὕτω. | . . . . . .[ἀναγ]νωσθέντος ἐπιστάλ-
ματος Τερεντίου Ἀρίου στρα(τηγοῦ) περὶ τοῦ αἱρεθῆναι εκα[. . . .|
ἔδοξεν ὑπερτεθῆνα]ι [ε]ἰς τὴν ἑξῆς βουλήν. | . . .[ἀναγνωσθέντος
ἐπιστά]λματος τ[οῦ] στρατηγοῦ περὶ αἱρέσεως ἄλλω[ν κατα]-
πομπῶν ζώιων με[τὰ τὴν ἀνάγνωσιν ὁ πρύτανις εἶπ(εν)· ‖
. . . .] μάλιστα [δὲ] τῶν κ[ατ]απομπῶν τῶν καταφε[ρομέν]ων 20
ζώιων τοῖς ἅμα τ[ο]ῖς καταφ[ερομένοις. .| . . . . . .]υπον συνάξας
τινὰς τοὺς παρ[ό]ντας ἀπὸ τῆς βουλῆς ὠ[ν]ομάσαμεν ἕνα
Σαραπ[ίωνα . . . ἵνα μὴ | . . . . . .] γ[έ]νηται. Οἱ βουλευταὶ
εἶπ(ον)· ἀτίμητε πρύτανι, σώζου ἡμῖν, πρύτανι, καλῶς ἄρχις

DOCUMENTS FROM EGYPT

κα[λῶς ......ὁ πρύτανις εἶπ(εν)· ...|.......] ἐν τῶι λογισ-
τηρίωι ἐστίν. Οἱ βουλευταὶ εἶπ(ον)· ἐπιεικῶς ὁ πρύτανις. |
....[Ὁ πρύτανις εἶπ(εν)· ὁ νόμ]ος κ[ε]λεύει πρὸ ἑξαμήνου τὸν
μελλοπρύτανιν ὀνομάζεσθαι. Ὑπομιμνήσκ[ω ὑ]μᾶς τ..... ||

25 ....[οἱ] β[ουλευ]ταὶ εἶπ(ον)· μετὰ σκέψεως ἡ ὀνομασία
γείν[ε]ται τ[..... ὁ πρύτανις εἶπ(εν)· |.......]υ γὰρ ἐ⟨ν⟩
νόσωι εἰμὶ καὶ τῆς πλευρᾶς [ῥ]έγχομαι, ὡς ἐπίστασθαι, καὶ
.........|...[Οἱ βουλευταὶ εἶπ(ον)· ....]δυπε πρύτανι,
εὐγεν[ὲς] πρύ[τ]ανι, ἔτι κάμε ὑπὲρ ἡμῶν, κάμε ἄξια τοῦ ἐπάν[ω
χρόνου. ...|....Ὁ πρύτανις εἶπ(εν)· ....] ἐστίν, καὶ οἱ
ἥμι[σ]υ τούτ[ου] τοῦ μέρους [ὁ]φε[ί]λ[ον]τες....εουτιν...
δεω......[Οἱ βουλευταὶ εἶπ(ον)·........|.............ὁ]
πρύτανις εἶπ(εν)· ἐπειδὴ σ[ή]μερον πρόσκλητον βου[λὴν ||

30 ....]αι π[ρόνο]ιαν ποιήσηται ἅπαν το...

From Oxyrhynchus. This document is similar to no. 203. About
sixteen letters are lost from the beginning of the lines and about
fifty from the ends. The first question discussed deals with the
textile industry which was apparently a municipal monopoly (*cf.*
Grenfell-Hunt, Introduction to their commentary, and the references cited there). In ll. 1–4 some statement is made about debts
and the value of garments. The receipt of six talents and a half of
the fourteen talents from the nome on account of the city's share is
acknowledged. In ll. 4–11 Grenfell's interpretation is as follows:
The topic is the supply of yarn required for making the vestments
of a local temple, which was under municipal jurisdiction, and the
amount to be paid to the yarn-merchants. Owing to the difficulty
of securing yarn the previous budget had to be modified. The village
spinners had either refused or had been unable to carry out their
engagements, and it had apparently been necessary to apply to the
city yarn-merchants for the supply. Their price was considered too
high by the senators and they reduced it from 49 to 30 denarii. In
ll. 12–16 the weavers, who are organized in a guild, present a
petition for higher remuneration in consideration of the increased
cost of raw materials and the rise in wages of their assistants. The
presentation of the petition to the local senate implies that the city
controlled the industry rather than the state.

In ll. 17 *ff.* reference is made to a communication from the strategus concerning the election of some official. Action on this was deferred until the next meeting. A further communication from the strategus dealt with the nomination of some one to convoy animals. The prytanis informed the senate that he had already nominated Sarapion with the approval of some senators who were with him at the time the communication was received in order that there might be no delay. The senate approved his appointment. From this it is clear that the prytanis did not make nominations on his own responsibility, but that he could act in an emergency and have the nomination approved at the next meeting of the senate (*cf.* pp. 89 *f.*; *P. Oxy.* 1412). In ll. 24 *ff.* the prytanis calls attention to the fact that nominations for his office must be made six months in advance, and apparently asks for nominations from the senate. Apparently he was renominated by acclamation, but declined on the ground of ill-health. In this case the prytanis did not nominate his successor as was the case in certain other magistracies. Later the prefect appointed the prytanis (*cf.* no. 206), on the favorable vote of the senate.

205. DE EXACTIONE TRIBUTI
(saec. III p. Chr.)

P. Br. Mus. 2, 213; Wilcken, *Chrestomathie*, 267.

.... εια................τατα | ....νοι..τε
καὶ ...εσως καὶ | ...δηλῶσαί μοι α...τεκ...ενουσαν |
.....ν διάθε[σι]ν ἀλλὰ κ[αὶ] τ[ὴ]ν περι‖[γ]ενομένην ἀπ' 5
αὐτῶν πρόσοδον | κα[ὶ τὸ] καθ' ἓν δηλῶσαί μοι. Εἰ γὰρ |-
δ....ωσει τι πρὸς χάριν πραχθὲν | ἐλέγχθη, αὐτὸς ἐπ[ὶ] τῶ[ν]
τόπων | γενόμενος ὅτι ἂν καταλάβοιμι ἐπὶ ‖ περιγραφῆι τοῦ 10
ταμείου πραχθέν, | τοῦτο κατὰ τοὺς τοῦ ταμείου νόμους | ἔκ τε
[[ἐκ]] τῶν σῶν ὑπαρχόντων | καὶ ⟨τῶν⟩ ὑπευθύνων κελεύσω ἀπο-
κατα|σ[τ]αθῆναι. Ἐρρῶ(σθαί σε) εὔχο(μαι). ‖('Έτους) β Μεχεὶρ ζ. 15

The origin of this piece of papyrus is unknown. It contains part of a rescript or edict of a strategus to the collector of taxes in one of the districts under his supervision. It is expressly stated that the law of the treasury rendered the property of a collector and of his guarantors liable for any fraud practised by him in the collection of the imperial revenues. *Cf. Dig.* 50. 6. 6, 10.

DOCUMENTS FROM EGYPT

206. DE MUNERE εὐθηνιαρχίας
(ca. saec. III fin. p. Chr.)

P. Oxy. 1252, verso, col. II.

[Παρὰ τοῦ π]ρυτάνε[ω]ς. | [Δεῖ,] ἡγεμὼν δέσποτ[ά] μ[ο]υ,
πᾶσαν εὐθένιαν ὑπάρχειν το[ῖς πολίταις,] | μάλιστα δὲ τὴν τοῦ
ἄρτου χορηγίαν. Καὶ νῦν εὐτυχῶς ἡμῖν [........] | κατὰ τὸν
προεληλυθότα ἐνιαυτὸν ἀνανέωσιν πεποίησαι τοῦ στε[φάνου
5 τοῦ] ‖ εὐθηνιαρχικοῦ καὶ ἀγορανομικοῦ πολλῶι χρόνωι τούτων
[ἐπιλελοι]‖πότων. Αὐτὸς τοίνυν ἐγώ, ἡγ[ε]μὼν κύριε, ὑ[πογύω]ς
χειροτονη[θεὶς διὰ] | τῆς εὐτυχοῦς σου δεξιᾶς εἰς τὴν παρὰ
Ὀξυρυγχ[είταις] πρυτανείαν ἀ[σμένως (?)] | παρελθὼν ἐπὶ τὸ
ἀναδήσασθαι τὸν στέφανον τοῦτον φροντίδ[α οὐδεμί]‖αν ἄλλην
10 πεποίημαι καίτοι....να ἔχων τὰ ἐπικείμενά μοι ἀν[αλώμα]‖τα
εἴς τε τὴν διοίκησιν τῶν δημοσίων λουτρῶν καὶ εἰς τὰ λ[οιπὰ
πολι]‖τικὰ δαπανήματα καὶ τὸ συνεχῶς τῆι βουλῆι περὶ τῆς
τῶν ἀρχόντω[ν ἀποδεί]‖ξεως. Καὶ δὴ τὸ τάγμα τὸ τῶν γυμνα-
σιάρχων ἀπέδειξεν [ε]ὐθη[νιάρχας] | τέως ἀπὸ τριῶν τῶν
ἐτησίως ζητουμένων μόνους δύο [........] | Ἡράκλειον υἱὸν
15 Πλουτάρχου καὶ Σαραπάμμωνα υἱὸν ....ρ..[......οἵ]‖τινες
κατὰ μὲν τὴν προτροπὴν τῆς βουλῆς παρελθόντες α[ὐ]τ[ίκα
τὴν] | ἀρχὴν παρηιτήσαντο, ὕστερον δὲ πεισθέντες καὶ ...οντες
ἀνελ[άβοντο] | καὶ ἐκ μέρους ἐχορήγησαν τὴν εὐθηνιαρχείαν ἣν
ἔδει πᾶσα[ν.....ἐκ] | κλήρου ἀποδοθῆναι τῆι πόλει. Τετραμ-
μένος γὰρ ἐφ᾽ ἑκάστου τέτακται [ἐκ κλήρου] | ὑπὲρ τοῦ αὐτοὺς
20 μὴ ἀθρόως τὴν τετράμηνον χορηγήσαντας ὑ[.......] ‖ ἐπιτρί-
βεσθαι. Προετρεψάμην Ἀμμώνιον Πτολλαρίω[νος ἔναρχον] |
γυμνασίαρχον γνωσθέντα ὀφείλειν λοιπὸν μῆνα τῆς εὐθη[νιαρ-
χείας] | ἑαυτοῦ ἐν τῶι μεταξὺ ἀποδοῦναι ὑπὲρ τοῦ τούτους
ἀνάκτησιν σ[τήσαντας] | εὐμαρῶς καὶ τὸ ὑπόλοιπον τῆς ἀρχῆς
ἀμέμπτως ἀποδοῦναι. Ἀ[λλὰ ἐπεὶ] | ἐπισταλέντες οὗτοι
25 χορηγῆσαι τὰς τροφὰς τῆι πόλει τοῦ ὑπολοίπου [χρόνου] ‖ τῆς
ἀρχῆς αὐτῶν ἀντιλέγοντες ἔρρωνται, κατὰ τὸ ἀναγκαῖον [προσ-
φεύγω] | ἐπὶ τὴν σὴν ἰλεικρίνειαν ἀξιῶν διὰ τοῦ στρατηγοῦ
αὐτοὺ[ς] του.....

From Oxyrhynchus. This document belongs strictly to the
Byzantine period, but it has been included in this collection because

[570]

we learn that the office of eutheniarch and agoranomus had been discontinued in Oxyrhynchus before the beginning of the Byzantine period and had only recently been revived by the prefect. At the end of the second century Oxyrhynchus had nine and probably twelve eutheniarchs. The office had lapsed like many of the other municipal offices in the third century as the increasing cost of the liturgies attached to the magistracies made all positions in the municipality undesirable and so burdensome that citizens sought to avoid public service at any cost, even by going into exile or surrendering their property (*cf.* pp. 112 *ff.*; nos. 180, 194, 198). In the period of Diocletian's reign it is evident that many changes in organization had taken place. The appointment of the prytanis was ratified by the prefect. The order of gymnasiarchs nominated the eutheniarchs, apparently on their own risk; for they had only nominated two out of the three required. These two had sought to evade the office, but were finally persuaded to undertake the position. Each served four months in order that the difficulties of collective liability might be avoided. The two appointees, having filled the first two terms in a somewhat dilatory fashion, refused to act in the third period of four months, and the prytanis asked the prefect to instruct the strategus to compel them to fulfil their term.

ABBREVIATIONS

Works frequently cited are designated by the following abbreviations:

Abbott = Abbott, *Roman Political Institutions.*

An. ép. = *L'année épigraphique.*

Archiv = *Archiv für Papyrusforschung.*

Beaudouin = Beaudouin, *Les grandes domaines dans l'Empire romain.*

BGU. = *Aegyptische Urkunden aus den königlichen Museum zu Berlin Griechische Urkunden.*

Bruns = Bruns, *Fontes iuris Romani antiqui.*

B.C.H. = *Bulletin de correspondance hellénique.*

Cagnat, *IGRR.* = Cagnat, *Inscriptiones Graecae ad res Romanas pertinentes.*

CIG. = *Corpus inscriptionum Graecarum.*

CIL. = *Corpus inscriptionum Latinarum.*

C.P.R. = *Corpus papyrorum Raineri.*

C.P.H. = *Corpus papyrorum Hermopolitanorum.*

Cod. J. = *Codex Justinianus.*

Cod. Th. = *Codex Theodosianus.*

Dessau = Dessau, *Inscriptiones Latinae selectae.*

Dict. Dar. = Daremberg-Saglio, *Dictionnaire des antiquités grecques et romaines.*

Dig. = *Digesta corporis iuris civilis.*

Ditt. *Or. Gr.* = Dittenberger, *Orientis Graecae inscriptiones selectae.*

Ditt. *Syll.*[3] = Dittenberger, *Sylloge inscriptionum Graecarum,* ed. ter.

E.E. = *Ephemeris epigraphica, CIL. supplementum.*

Girard = Girard, *Textes de droit romain.*

Herzog = Herzog, *Geschichte und System der römischen Staatsverfassung.*

Hirschfeld = Hirschfeld, *Die kaiserliche Verwaltungsbeamten bis auf Diocletian.*

I.B.M. = *Ancient Greek Inscriptions in the British Museum.*

IG. = *Inscriptiones Graecae.*

Jouguet, *Vie munic.* = Jouguet, *La vie municipale dans l'Égypte romaine.*

Karlowa = Karlowa, *Römische Rechtsgeschichte.*

Lafoscade = Lafoscade, *De epistulis imperatorum magistratuumque Romanorum.*

Latyschev = Latyschev, *Inscriptiones antiquae orae Septentrionalis Ponti Euxini, Graecae et Latinae.*

[573]

ABBREVIATIONS

Le Bas-Waddington = Le Bas-Waddington, *Voyage archéologique en Grèce et en Asie Mineure: Inscriptions.*

Liebenam, *St. Verw.* = Liebenam, *Städteverwaltung im römischen Kaiserreiches.*

Madvig, *Verf. u. Verw.* = Madvig, *Die Verfassung und Verwaltung des römischen Staats.*

Marquardt, *St. Verw.* = Marquardt, *Römische Staatsverwaltung.*

Mitteis, *Chrestomathie; Grundzüge* = Mitteis-Wilcken, *Grundzüge und Chrestomathie der Papyruskunde, Zweiter Band: Juristicher Teil. Erste Hälfte; Grundzüge. Zweite Hälfte; Chrestomathie.*

P. Amh. = *Amherst Papyri.*

P. Br. Mus. = *Greek Papyri in the British Museum.*

P. Fay. = *Fayûm Towns and their Papyri.*

P. Fior. = *Papiri Fiorentini.*

P. Giess. = *Griechische Papyri im Museum d. Oberhess. Geschichtsvereins zu Giessen.*

P. Oxy. = *Oxyrhynchus Papyri.*

P. Ryl. = *Catalogue of the Greek Papyri in the Rylands Library.*

P.S.I. = *Papiri della Società Italiana.*

P. Teb. = *Tebtunis Papyri.*

Prosop. = *Prosopographia imperii Romani.*

R.E. = Pauly-Wissowa-Kroll, *Realencyclopädie der classischen Altertumswissenschaft.*

Riccobono = Riccobono, *Fontes iuris Romani anteiustiniani.*

Rostowzew, *Gesch. d. röm. Kol.* = Rostowzew, *Studien zur Geschichte der römischen Kolonats.*

Supp. Ep. Gr. = *Supplementum Epigraphicum Graecum.*

T.A.M. = *Tituli Asiae Minoris.*

Tod = Tod, *International Arbitration.*

Wilcken, *Chrestomathie; Grundzüge* = Mitteis-Wilcken, *Grundzüge und Chrestomathie der Papyruskunde, Erster Band: Historische Teil. Erste Hälfte; Grundzüge. Zweite Hälfte; Chrestomathie.*

Wilmans = Wilmans, *Exempla inscriptionum Latinarum.*

LIST OF DOCUMENTS

I. DOCUMENTS FROM ITALY AND THE PROVINCES

1. Epistula Flaminini ad Chyretienses (196–194 a. Chr.).
   IG. IX, 2, 338; *CIG.* 1770; Ditt. *Syll.*³ 593; Viereck, *Sermo Graecus*, 1.

2. Decretum proconsulis Hispaniae Ulterioris (189 a. Chr.).
   CIL. II, 5041; Dessau, 15; Bruns, 70; Riccobono, p. 248.

3. Epistula Spuri Postumi, praetoris, ad Delphos (189 a. Chr.).
   Viereck, *Sermo Graecus*, 10; Ditt. *Syll.*³ 612.

4. Epistula consulis ad Heracleotas (ca. 189–188 a. Chr.).
   CIG. 3800; Viereck, *Sermo Graecus*, 3; Ditt. *Syll.*³ 618; *Rev. ét. an.* 19 (1917), 237 *ff.*

5. Senatus consulta de Thisbensibus (170 a. Chr.).
   IG. VII, 2225; Ditt. *Syll.*³ 646; Viereck, *Sermo Graecus*, 11; Riccobono, p. 199; Bruns, 37.

6. Senatus consultum de Delo (164 a. Chr.).
   Ditt. *Syll.*³ 664.

7. Senatus consultum de Tiburtibus (ca. 159 a. Chr.).
   CIL. I, 201 = XIV, 3584; Dessau, 19; Bruns, 39; Riccobono, p. 204.

8. Senatus consultum de Narthaciensibus et Melitaeensibus (159–147 a. Chr.).
   IG. IX, 2, 89; Ditt. *Syll.*³ 674; de Ruggiero, *L' arbitrato pubblico*, 8; Tod, XXXIV; Viereck, *Sermo Graecus*, 12.

9. Epistula Q. Fabi Maximi ad Dymaeos (ca. 139 a. Chr.).
   CIG. 1543; Ditt. *Syll.*³ 684; Viereck, *Sermo Graecus*, 4.

10. Sententia Q. M. Minuciorum inter Genuates et Viturios (117 a. Chr.).
    CIL. I¹, 199 = V, 7749; Dessau, 5946; Bruns, 184.

11. Lex Osca Tabulae Bantinae (150–100 a. Chr.).
    Bruns, 8; Girard, p. 26; Riccobono, p. 130; Buck, *Oscan and Umbrian Grammar*, p. 230; v. Planta, *Gramm. d. osk.-umbr. Dial.* 2, 599; Conway, *Exempla Selecta*, 2.

12. Senatus consultum de controversia inter publicanos et Pergamenos (in. saec. I a. Chr.).
    E.E. 4, 213 *ff.*; Viereck, *Sermo Graecus*, 15.

13. Decretum Cn. Pompei Strabonis (90 a. Chr.).
    CIL. I², 709; Dessau, 8888; Girard, p. 61; *An. ép.* 1911, no. 126; *Bull. arch. com.* 38 (1910), 275.

14. Ilienses honorant Lucium Iulium Caesarem (89 a. Chr.).
    Ditt. *Or. Gr.* 440.

[575]

LIST OF DOCUMENTS

15. Tabulae ad memoriam libertatis restitutae servandam aptae (81 a.Chr.).
    CIL. I, 587, 588, 589.

16. Senatus consultum de Tabenis (82 a. Chr.).
    Ditt. *Or. Gr.* 442.

17. Senatus consultum de Stratonicensibus (ca. 81 a. Chr.).
    Ditt. *Or. Gr.* 441, ll. 1–129; Viereck, *Sermo Graecus*, 16.

18. Senatus consultum de Amphiarai Oropi agris (73 a. Chr.).
    IG. VII, 413; Viereck, *Sermo Graecus*, 18; Ditt. *Syll.*³ 747; Bruns, 42;
    Riccobono, p. 209; de Ruggiero, *L' arbitrato pubblico*, 25.

19. Lex Antonia de Termessibus (ca. 71 a. Chr.).
    CIL. I, 204; Bruns, 14; Dessau, 38; Girard, pp. 68–70; Riccobono,
    pp. 105–107.

20. Lex municipi Tarentini (ca. 88–62 a. Chr.?).
    Dessau, 6086; Bruns, 27; Riccobono, p. 132; Girard, p. 61.

21. Lex Gabinia Calpurnia de Deliis (58 a. Chr.).
    Dürrbach, *Choix d'inscr. Délos*, 163; *Suppl. Ep. Gr.* I, 335.

22. Epistula proconsulis Asiae ad provinciales (ca. 56–50 a. Chr.).
    Knackfuss, *Das Rathaus von Milet*, p. 101, ll. 38 *ff.*

23. Pergameni honorant Publium Servilium Isauricum (ca. 46 a. Chr.).
    Ditt. *Or. Gr.* 449; Fraenkel, *Alterthümer von Pergamon*, 413.

24. Tabula Heracleensis, vulgo Lex Iulia Municipalis (45 a. Chr.).
    CIL. I, 206; Bruns, 18; Dessau, 6085; Girard, p. 80; Riccobono,
    p. 109.

25. Senatus consultum et epistula Caesaris ad Mytilenaeos (45 a. Chr.).
    IG. XII, 2, 35, ll. 14 *ff.*; Cagnat, *IGRR.* 4, 33; Ditt. *Syll.*³ 764.

26. Lex coloniae Genitivae Iuliae seu Ursonensis (44 a. Chr.).
    CIL. II, *S.* 5439; Dessau, 6087; Bruns, 28; Girard, p. 89; Riccobono,
    p. 142.

27. Lex de Gallia Cisalpina, vulgo Lex Rubria de Gallia Cisalpina
    (49–42 a. Chr.).
    CIL. I, 205=XI, 1146; Bruns, 16; Girard, p. 72; Riccobono, p. 135.

28. Fragmentum Atestinum (49–42 a. Chr.).
    Notizie degli scavi, 1880, 213; Bruns, 17; Girard, p. 78; Riccobono,
    p. 140.

29. Epistulae Antoni et Caesaris ad Plarasenses et Aphrodisienses (39–
    35 a. Chr.).
    CIG. 2737; Viereck, *Sermo Graecus*, 5; Bruns, 43; Ditt. *Or. Gr.* 453–
    455; Riccobono, p. 217.

30. Epistula Augusti ad Mylasenses (31 a. Chr.).
    Viereck, *Sermo Graecus*, 6; Ditt. *Syll.*³ 768.

[576]

31. Titulus operis publici (31 a. Chr.).
    Notizie degli scavi, 1915, 139; *An. ép.* 1916, no. 60.

32. Epistula imperatoris, vel proconsulis, ad Mylasenses (ca. 30 a. Chr.).
    Le Bas-Waddington, 3. 442–443; *CIG.* 2695*b*, 2700*e*.

33. Edictum Augusti de aquaeductu Venafrano (17–11 a. Chr.).
    CIL. x, 4842; Bruns, 77; Girard, p. 186; Riccobono, p. 316; Dessau, 5743.

34. Decretum concili Asiae de fastis provincialibus (ca. 9 a. Chr.).
    Ditt. *Or. Gr.* 458, ll. 78 *ff.*; *Inschriften von Priene*, 105.

35. Epistula P. Corneli Scipionis, proconsulis Asiae, ad Thyatirenos (7–6 a. Chr.).
    Cagnat, *IGRR.* 4, 1211; Viereck, *Sermo Graecus*, 8.

36. Epistula imperatoris Augusti ad Cnidios (6 a. Chr.).
    Viereck, *Sermo Graecus*, 9; Cagnat, *IGRR.* 4, 1031; *IG.* XII, 3, 174; Ditt. *Syll.*³ 780.

37. Iusiurandum Paphlagonum (3 a. Chr.).
    Cagnat, *IGRR.* 3, 137; Ditt. *Or. Gr.* 532.

38. Res gestae divi Augusti (28 a. Chr.–6 p. Chr.).
    CIL. III, pt. II, pp. 769 *ff.*; Cagnat, *IGRR.* 3, 158.

39. Edictum proconsulis Asiae de muro Ephesio (ca. 11 p. Chr.).
    I.B.M. 521; Viereck, *Sermo Graecus*, 7; Ditt. *Syll.*³ 784.

40. Epistula proconsulis Asiae ad Chios (5–14 p. Chr.).
    CIG. 2222; Cagnat, *IGRR.* 4, 943; Ditt. *Syll.*³ 785.

41. Titulus honorarius (ca. 14 p. Chr.).
    CIL. III, 1741; Dessau, 938.

42. Titulus sepulchralis (p. 14 p. Chr.).
    CIL. III, 5232; Dessau, 1977.

43. Decretum centumvirorum (26 p. Chr.).
    CIL. XI, 3805; Dessau, 6579.

44. Tabula patronatus (27 p. Chr.).
    CIL. v, 4919; Dessau, 6100.

45. Fasti magistratuum municipalium (p. 33 p. Chr.).
    CIL. x, 1233; Dessau, 6124.

46. Lites inter Cierenses et Metropolitanos (11–35 p. Chr.).
    IG. IX, 2, 261; de Ruggiero, *L' arbitrato pubblico*, 31; Tod, XLI.

47. Iurisiurandi Aritiensium in principem formula (37 p. Chr.).
    CIL. II, 172; Dessau, 190; Bruns, 101.

48. Decretum et iusiurandum Assiorum (37 p. Chr.).
    Bruns, 102; Cagnat, *IGRR.* 4, 251; Ditt. *Syll.*³ 797.

49. Edictum Claudi de civitate Anaunorum (46 p. Chr.).
    CIL. v, 5050; Dessau, 206; Bruns, 79; Girard, p. 188; Riccobono, p. 318; de Ruggiero, *L' arbitrato pubblico*, 39.

LIST OF DOCUMENTS

50. Oratio Claudi de iure honorum Gallis dando (48 p. Chr.).

    CIL. XIII, 1668; Dessau, 212; Bruns, 52; Riccobono, p. 228; Nipperdey's *Tacitus*[10], 2, 317–322.

51. Edictum Claudi de cursu publico (49–50 p. Chr.).

    CIL. III, *S.* I, 7251; Dessau, 214.

52. Decretum Rhodiorum de libertate (51 p. Chr.).

    IG. XII, 1, 2, *et corrigenda*, p. 206; Cagnat, *IGRR.* 4, 1123.

53. Titulus honorarius (p. 54 p. Chr.).

    Compt. rend. de l'acad. d. inscr. et bel. lettr. 1915, 396; *An. ép.* 1916, no. 42.

54. Epistula imperatoris Neronis ad Rhodios (55 p. Chr.).

    Cagnat, *IGRR.* 4, 1124; Ditt. *Syll.*[3] 810.

55. De praediis publicis Gortyniorum (64 p. Chr.).

    Ἀρχαιολογικὸν Δελτίον, 2 (1916), 6.

56. Oratio imperatoris Neronis de Graecorum libertate (67 p. Chr.).

    IG. VII, 2713; Ditt. *Syll.*[3] 814.

57. Decretum Petroni et Pupi de finibus Sagalassensium (54–68 p. Chr.).

    de Ruggiero, *L' arbitrato pubblico*, 40; Cagnat, *IGRR.* 3, 335; Ditt. *Or. Gr.* 538.

58. Decretum proconsulis Sardiniae de finibus Patulcensium et Galillensium (69 p. Chr.).

    CIL. X, 7852; Dessau, 5947; Bruns, 71a; Girard, p. 179; Mommsen, *Ges. Schr.* 5, 325 ff.; Riccobono, p. 256; de Ruggiero, *L' arbitrato pubblico*, 43.

59. Rescriptum Vespasiani ad Vanacinos (ca. 72 p. Chr.).

    CIL. X, 8038; Bruns, 80; Girard, p. 190; Riccobono, p. 320.

60. Titulus sacer (76 p. Chr.).

    CIL. II, 1610; Dessau, 1981.

61. Epistula Vespasiani ad Saborenses (78 p. Chr.).

    CIL. II, 1423; Dessau, 6092; Bruns, 81; Girard, p. 190; Riccobono, p. 320.

62. Lex de officiis et honoribus flaminis provinciae Narbonensis (69–79 p. Chr.).

    CIL. XII, 6038; Dessau, 6964; Riccobono, p. 159; Bruns, 29; Carette, *Les assemblées prov. de la Gaule rom.* 445 ff.

63. Epistula Domitiani ad Falerienses (82 p. Chr.).

    CIL. IX, 5420; Bruns, 82; Girard, p. 191; Riccobono, p. 321.

64. Lex Salpensa (81–84 p. Chr.).

    CIL. II, 1963; Dessau, 6088; Bruns, 30a; Girard, p. 108; Riccobono, p. 162.

LIST OF DOCUMENTS

65. Lex Malacitana (81–84 p. Chr.).

    CIL. II, 1964; Dessau, 6089; Bruns, 30*b*; Girard, p. 112; Riccobono, p. 168.

65*a*. Edictum L. Antisti Rustici, legati Domitiani, de annona coloniae Antiochiae (ca. 93 p. Chr.).

    Trans.Am.Phil.Assoc. 55 (1924), 5 *ff.*; *Journ.Rom.Studies*, 14 (1924), 180.

66. Titulus honorarius (81–96 p. Chr.).

    CIL. II, 1945; Dessau, 1982.

67. Titulus honorarius (96–97 p. Chr.).

    B.C.H. 44 (1920), 73; *An. ép.* 1922, no. 30.

68. Epistulae Laberi Maximi et aliorum de finibus Histrianorum (43–100 p. Chr.).

    An. ép. 1919, no. 10; *Annales de l'académie Roumaine*, 38, no. 15; Wilhelm, *Anzeiger der Akad. der Wissen. in Wien*, 59 (1922), 78 *ff.*; *Suppl. Ep. Gr.* I, 329.

69. Decretum Chiorum de pecunia administranda (saec. I p. Chr.).

    Cagnat, *IGRR.* 4, 948.

70. Smyrnaeorum Portaria (saec. fere I vel II p. Chr.).

    I.B.M. 1021; Ditt. *Syll.*[3] 1262; Cagnat, *IGRR.* 4, 1427.

71. Epistula Aquili Proculi, proconsulis Asiae, ad Ephesios (104 p. Chr.).

    I.B.M. 481 (pt. IV, p. 246, ll. 336 *ff.*); Laum, *Stiftungen*, 74.

72. Titulus operis publici (111 p. Chr.).

    An. ép. 1904, no. 59.

73. Senatus consultum et epistula Traiani ad Pergamenos de ludis instaurandis (112–117 p. Chr.).

    CIL. III, *S.* 7086; Cagnat, *IGRR.* 4, 336; Fraenkel, *Alterthümer von Pergamon*, VIII, 2, 269.

74. Epistula procuratorum ad colonos Villae Magnae (116–117 p. Chr.).

    Bruns, 114; Girard, p. 870; Riccobono, p. 352.

75. Epistula imperatoris Traiani ad Astypalaeenses (117 p. Chr.).

    Cagnat, *IGRR.* 4, 1031; *IG.* XII, 3, 175.

76. Epistula imperatoris Hadriani ad Astypalaeenses (118 p. Chr.).

    Lafoscade, 19; Cagnat, *IGRR.* 4, 1032 *c*; *IG.* XII, 3, 176; Ditt. *Syll.*[3] 832.

77. Epistula legati ad Pompaelonenses (119 p. Chr.).

    CIL. II, 2959.

78. Epistula imperatoris Hadriani ad Ephesios (120 p. Chr.).

    Lafoscade, 23; Ditt. *Syll.*[3] 833.

79. Epistula imperatoris Hadriani (?) ad Heracleotas (121–125 p. Chr.).

    B.C.H. 21 (1897), 162.

80. Epistula legati Lyciae, Valeri Severi, ad Rhodiapolitanos (125 p. Chr.).

    Lafoscade, 104; Cagnat, *IGRR.* 3, 739, c. 16.

81. Rescriptum imperatoris Hadriani (?) ad Pergamenos de collybo (125 p. Chr. ?).

Ditt. *Or. Gr.* 484; Fraenkel, *Alterthümer von Pergamon*, VIII, 2, 279.

82. Epistula Avidi Quieti, proconsulis Asiae, ad Aezanitas (125–126 p. Chr.).

CIG. 3835; Le Bas-Waddington, 860–863; Lafoscade, 93; Ditt. *Or. Gr.* 502; Cagnat, *IGRR.* 4, 571; *CIL.* III, 355, *S.* 7003; de Ruggiero, *L' arbitrato pubblico*, 57.

83. Epistula imperatoris Hadriani ad Stratonicenses (127 p. Chr.).

Lafoscade, 23; Cagnat, *IGRR.* 4, 1156a; Ditt. *Syll.*³ 837; Riccobono, p. 325.

84. Epistula Pomponi Vettoniani, legati Lyciae, ad commune Lyciorum (128 p. Chr.).

Cagnat, *IGRR.* 3, 739, c. 14; Lafoscade, 103.

85. Epistula imperatoris Hadriani ad Ephesios (129 p. Chr.).

Lafoscade, 26; *I.B.M.* 3, 487; Ditt. *Syll.*³ 838.

86. Privilegia concessa Dianae Ephesiae ab imperatore Hadriano (129 p. Chr.).

Ditt. *Syll.*³ 839.

87. Epistula Sufenatis Veri, legati Lyciae, ad lyciarcham (131 p. Chr.).

Lafoscade, 105; Cagnat, *IGRR.* 3, 739, c. 18.

88. Titulus honorarius (132 p. Chr.).

CIL. III, *S.* I, 7282; Dessau, 315.

89. Lex Palmyrenorum (137 p. Chr.).

Ditt. *Or. Gr.* 629; Cagnat, *IGRR.* 3, 1056, ll. 1–16.

90. Lex de certa olei portione rei publicae vendenda (117–138 p. Chr.).

IG. II and III (ed. min.), 1100; de Ruggiero, *L' arbitrato pubblico*, 36.

91. Epistula imperatoris Hadriani (?) ad Athenienses (117–138 p. Chr.).

IG. II and III (ed. min.), 1103.

92. Edictum imperatoris Hadriani (?) de vectigalibus (117–138 p. Chr.).

IG. II and III (ed. min.), 1104.

93. Sermo et epistulae procuratorum de terris vacuis excolendis (117–138 p. Chr.).

Carcopino, *Mélanges de l'école franç. de Rome*, 26 (1906), 365–481; *An. ép.* 1907, no. 196; Bruns, 116; Girard, p. 874; Riccobono, p. 357.

94. Titulus honorarius (117–138 p. Chr.).

CIL. II, 5941; Dessau, 6954.

95. Titulus honorarius (119–138 p. Chr.).

CIL. II, 3239.

96. Senatus consultum de nundinis saltus Beguensis (138 p. Chr.).

CIL. VIII, 270 = VIII, *S.* 11451; Bruns, 61; Riccobono, p. 236.

LIST OF DOCUMENTS

97. Epistula Corneli Proculi, legati Lyciae, ad commune Lyciorum (139 p. Chr.).
    Cagnat, *IGRR.* 3, 739, c. 28; Lafoscade, 108.

98. Epistula proconsulis Asiae, L. Venulei Aproniani, ad Ephesios (ca. 138–139 p. Chr.).
    Lafoscade, 94.

99. Epistula Corneli Proculi, legati Lyciae, ad scribam publicum Myrorum (140 p. Chr.).
    Cagnat, *IGRR.* 3, 739, c. 34; Lafoscade, 110.

100. Epistula imperatoris Antonini Pii ad Ephesios (140–144 p. Chr.).
     Lafoscade, 51; Ditt. *Syll.*³ 849.

101. Epistula imperatoris Antonini Pii ad Ephesios (145 p. Chr.).
     Lafoscade, 54; Ditt. *Syll.*³ 850; *I.B.M.* 3, 491.

102. Epistula Rupili Severi, legati Lyciae, ad lyciarcham (150 p. Chr.).
     Lafoscade, 114; Cagnat, *IGRR.* 3, 739, c. 45.

103. Titulus operis publici (152 p. Chr.).
     An. ép. 1904, no. 21.

104. Tres epistulae Antonini Pii ad Coronenses et Thisbenses (140–155 p. Chr.).
     IG. vii, 2870.

105. Edictum proconsulis Asiae, Popili Cari, de diebus festis Ephesiorum (ca. 160 p. Chr.).
     I.B.M. 482; *CIG.* 2954; Ditt. *Syll.*³ 867.

106. Senatus consultum de Cyzicenis (138–160 p. Chr.).
     CIL. iii, *S.* 7060; Dessau, 7190; *E.E.* 3, 156; Bruns, 62; Riccobono, p. 237.

107. Titulus honorarius (138–161 p. Chr.).
     CIL. xii, 594; Dessau, 6988.

108. Epistula imperatoris Antonini Pii ad Minoetas (138–161 p. Chr.).
     IG. xii, 7, 242; Cagnat, *IGRR.* 4, 1010.

109. Epistula praefectorum praetorio (168–172 p. Chr.).
     CIL. ix, 2438; Bruns, 71*b*; Riccobono, p. 260.

110. Senatus consultum de sumptibus ludorum gladiatorum minuendis (176–177 p. Chr.).
     CIL. ii, *S.* 6278; Dessau, 5163; Bruns, 63; Riccobono, p. 238.

111. Rescriptum Commodi de saltu Burunitano (180–183 p. Chr.).
     CIL. viii, 10570; *cf. S.* 14464; Dessau, 6870; Bruns, 86; Girard, p. 199; Riccobono, p. 361.

112. Epistula imperatoris Commodi ad Chersonesitanos de capitulo lenocinii (185–186 p. Chr.).
     Latyschev, 4, 81; *CIL.* iii, *S.* 13750; Cagnat, *IGRR.* 1, 860, ll. 32 *ff.*

[581]

LIST OF DOCUMENTS

113. Epistula Iuli Saturnini, legati Syriae, ad Phaenesios (185–186 p. Chr.).
     Lafoscade, 117; Cagnat, *IGRR.* 3, 1119; Ditt. *Or. Gr.* 609.

114. Epistula proconsulis Lyciae et Pamphyliae ad Sidymeos (185–192 p. Chr.).
     Cagnat, *IGRR.* 3, 582; *T.A.M.* 2, 175.

115. Titulus honorarius (150–200 p. Chr.).
     An. ép. 1902, no. 164; Dessau, 6780; *Compt. rend. de l'acad. d. inscr. et bel. lettr.* 1902, 38.

116. Titulus honorarius (saec. I vel II p. Chr.).
     Cagnat, *IGRR.* 3, 634; *T.A.M.* 2, 291.

117. Decretum Hierapolitanorum de paraphylacibus (saec. I vel II p. Chr.).
     Ditt. *Or. Gr.* 527.

118. Edictum vel epistula auctoris incerti ad Beroiaeos (saec. I–II p. Chr.).
     B.C.H. 37 (1913), 90 *f.*

119. Epistula proconsulis Asiae ad Coos (saec. I–II p. Chr.).
     Cagnat, *IGRR.* 4, 1044; Paton and Hicks, *Inscriptions of Cos,* 26.

120. Epistula imperatoris incerti ad proconsulem seu legatum Asiae (saec. II p. Chr.).
     Rev. d. ét. gr. 19 (1906), 83.

121. Rescriptum imperatoris ad Lacedaemonios (saec. II p. Chr.).
     IG. v, 21.

122. Titulus honorarius Poglensis (saec. I vel II p. Chr.).
     Cagnat, *IGRR.* 3, 409.

123. Titulus honorarius (saec. II p. Chr.).
     Cagnat, *IGRR.* 4, 788; Ramsay, *Cities and Bishoprics,* 2, 462.

124. Edictum seu epistula proconsulis ad Ephesios (saec. II p. Chr.).
     B.C.H. 7 (1883), 504; *Inschriften von Magnesia,* 114.

125. Titulus honorarius (150–200 p. Chr.).
     CIL. VIII, *S.* 17899 = *E.E.* 5, 698.

126. Titulus honorarius (saec. II p. Chr.).
     Rev. arch. 3 (1916), 339; *An. ép.* 1916, no. 120.

127. Epistula imperatorum Severi et Caracallae ad Smyrnaeos (198 210 p. Chr.).
     CIG. 3178; Lafoscade, 72; Ditt. *Syll.*³ 876; Cagnat, *IGRR.* 4, 1402.

128. Decretum Myrensium de navigatione (saec. II vel III p. Chr.).
     Le Bas-Waddington, 1311; *CIG.* 4302a (*Add.* p. 1136), Ditt. *Or. Gr.* 572.

129. Edictum M. Ulpi proconsulis et epistula Gemini Modesti proconsulis Achaiae ad Thisbenses (saec. II vel III in. p. Chr.).
     IG. VII, 2226, 2227, *Add.* p. 747; Ditt. *Syll.*³ 884.

LIST OF DOCUMENTS

130. Epistula imperatorum Severi et Caracallae ad Tyranos (201 p. Chr.).
    CIL. III, 781; Cagnat, *IGRR.* 1, 598; Bruns, 89; Dessau, 423; Riccobono, p. 332.

131. Edictum legati imperatorum, Q. Sicini Clari, de Pizo condenda (202 p. Chr.).
    Cagnat, *IGRR.* 1, 766; Ditt. *Syll.*[3] 880; Kalinka, *Ant. Denk. Bulgar.* 34.

132. Edictum imperatorum Severi et Caracallae de hospitio (204 p. Chr.).
    Lafoscade, 74; Ditt. *Syll.*[3] 881; *CIL.* III, *S.* 14203[8,9]; *IG.* XII, 5, 132.

133. Decretum Mylasensium de trapezitis (209–211 p. Chr.).
    Ditt. *Or. Gr.* 515.

134. Epistula imperatoris Caracallae ad Philadelphenos (213–214 p. Chr.).
    Lafoscade, 78; Ditt. *Syll.*[3] 883; Cagnat, *IGRR.* 4, 1619.

135. Tabula patronatus (222 p. Chr.).
    CIL. VI, 1454; Dessau, 6109.

136. Album decurionum (223 p. Chr.).
    CIL. IX, 338; Dessau, 6121.

137. Epistula proconsulis Asiae ad Aphrodisienses (222–235 p. Chr.).
    Rev. d. ét. grec. 19 (1906), 86 f.

138. Titulus honorarius (222–235 p. Chr.).
    Rev. d. ét. grec. 19 (1906), 84.

139. Rescriptum imperatoris Gordiani ad Scaptoparenos (238 p. Chr.).
    CIL. III, *S.* 12336; Cagnat, *IGRR.* 1, 674; Ditt. *Syll.*[3] 888; Riccobono, p. 371; Girard, p. 205.

140. Titulus honorarius (238 p. Chr.).
    CIL. XIII, 3162; Desjardins, *Géographie de la Gaule rom.* planches VII, VIII, IX.

141. Rescriptum imperatorum de querellis Araguenorum (244–247 p. Chr.).
    CIL. III, *S.* 14191; Ditt. *Or. Gr.* 519; Cagnat, *IGRR.* 4, 598; Bruns, 93; Girard, p. 207; Riccobono, p. 373; *Röm. Mitth.* 13 (1898), 231 ff.

142. Epistula colonorum ad imperatores (ca. 200–250 p. Chr.).
    Denkschriften der Wiener Akademie, 57 (1914–1915), 37 f.

143. Epistula vicanorum ad imperatores (ca. 200–250 p. Chr.).
    Denkschriften der Wiener Akademie, 57 (1914–1915), 25.

144. Querellae vicanorum (ca. 200–250 p. Chr.).
    Denkschriften der Wiener Akademie, 57 (1914–1915), 11.

145. Epistula imperatorum Traiani Deci et Herenni Etrusci ad Aphrodisienses (251 p. Chr.).
    Le Bas-Waddington, 3, 1624; *CIG.* 2743.

[583]

LIST OF DOCUMENTS

146. Decretum decurionum et possessorum (256, vel fortasse 186, p. Chr.).
An. ép. 1903, no. 202; *cf. ibid.* 1894, no. 61.

147. Edictum imperatorum Valeriani et Gallieni de nundinis (253–259 p. Chr.).
Le Bas-Waddington, 3, 2720*a*; Ditt. *Or. Gr.* 262; *CIG.* 4474.

148. Epistula proconsulis Asiae de nundinis constituendis (260–270 p. Chr.).
Cagnat, *IGRR.* 4, 1381.

149. Decretum xv virum de sacris faciundis (289 p. Chr.).
CIL. x, 3698; Dessau, 4175; Bruns, 75; Riccobono, p. 262.

150. Titulus honorarius (saec. iii p. Chr.).
Denkschriften der Wiener Akademie, 57 (1914–1915), 87.

151. Epistula imperatorum incertorum de constitutione civitatis Tymandenorum (saec. iii p. Chr.?).
CIL. iii, *S.* 6866; Dessau, 6090; Bruns, 34; Riccobono, p. 338.

152. Rescriptum de officialium exactionibus inlicitis (saec. iii p. Chr.).
CIL. viii, *S.* 17639.

153. Titulus operis publici (ca. 312 p. Chr.).
CIL. viii, 210=viii, *S.* 11299.

154. Epistula Ablabi praefecti praetorio et Constantini imperatoris de iure civitatis Orcistanorum (323–326; 331 p. Chr.).
CIL. iii, *S.* 7000; Dessau, 6091; Bruns, 35; Riccobono, p. 341.

155. Edictum Constantini ad Umbros (326–337 p. Chr.).
CIL. xi, 5265; Dessau, 705; Mommsen, *Ges. Schr.* 8, 25.

156. Titulus honorarius (362–363 p. Chr.).
CIL. v, 8987; Dessau, 755.

157. Rescriptum Valentiniani Valentis Gratiani de moenibus instaurandis et de reditu fundorum civitatium Asiae (371 p. Chr.).
Anzeiger der Akad. der Wissen. in Wien, 1905, no. 10; *Jahreshefte d. öst. archaeol. Inst.* 8 (1905), *Beiblatt*, 71 *f.*; *ibid.* 9 (1906), 40 *f.*; Bruns, 97*a*; Riccobono, p. 374.

158. Rescriptum imperatorum Valentiniani Valentis Gratiani ad Festum proconsulem Asiae de ludis provincialibus (375 p. Chr.).
Bruns, 97*b*.

159. Titulus honorarius (376 p. Chr.).
CIL. vi, 1736; Dessau, 1256.

160. Index sodalium familiae publicae (saec. iv p. Chr.?).
CIL. xiv, 255; Dessau, 6153.

161. Decretum provinciae Africae (saec. iv p. Chr.?).
CIL. viii, *S.* 11017.

LIST OF DOCUMENTS

II. DOCUMENTS FROM EGYPT

162. Edictum L. Aemili Recti de angaria (42 p. Chr.).
P. Br. Mus. 1171; Wilcken, *Chrestomathie*, 439.

163. Edictum Cn. Vergili Capitonis praefecti (49 p. Chr.).
CIG. 3, 4956, *Addenda*, p. 1236; Lafoscade, 119; Ditt. *Or. Gr.* 665.

164. Edictum L. Lusi Getae de immunitate sacerdotum (54 p. Chr.).
Lafoscade, 120; Ditt. *Or. Gr.* 664; Milne, *Greek Inscriptions*, p. 11.

165. Edictum Tiberi Iuli Alexandri praefecti (68 p. Chr.).
Ditt. *Or. Gr.* 669; *CIG.* 4957 (*cf.* vol. 3, *Add.* p. 1236); Riccobono, p. 253; Girard, p. 174.

166. De censu δωδεκαδράχμων (86–87 p. Chr.).
P. Oxy. 258; Wilcken, *Chrestomathie*, 216.

167. De vectigalibus locandis (ca. 81–96 p. Chr.).
P. Oxy. 44; Wilcken, *Chrestomathie*, 275.

168. Edictum Gai Vibi Maximi, praefecti (104 p. Chr.).
P. Br. Mus. 3, 904; Wilcken, *Chrestomathie*, 202.

169. De sumptibus γυμνασιαρχίας minuendis (114–117 p. Chr.).
P. Amh. 2, 70; Wilcken, *Chrestomathie*, 149.

170. Epistulae Petroni Mamertini et Statili Maximi de immunitate civium Antinoopolitanorum (135, 156 p. Chr.).
Wilcken, *Chrestomathie*, 26.

171. De vectigalibus exigendis a senioribus vici (136 p. Chr.).
P. Br. Mus. 2, 255; Wilcken, *Chrestomathie*, 272.

172. De civibus ad munera subeunda nominatis (ca. 137 p. Chr.).
BGU. 235; Wilcken, *Chrestomathie*, 399.

173. De statu civium Romanorum et Alexandrinorum (139 p. Chr.).
BGU. 747; Wilcken, *Chrestomathie*, 35.

174. De immunitate medicorum (140 p. Chr.).
P. Fay. 106; Wilcken, *Chrestomathie*, 395.

175. Edictum M. Semproni Liberalis, praefecti (154 p. Chr.).
BGU. 372; Wilcken, *Chrestomathie*, 19.

176. De immunitate patribus Antinoopolitanorum concessa (159 p. Chr.).
Compt. rend. de l'acad. d. inscr. et bell. lettr. 1905, 160 *ff.*; Wilcken, *Chrestomathie*, 28.

177. De immunitate veteranorum (172 p. Chr.).
BGU. 180; Wilcken, *Chrestomathie*, 396.

178. De muneribus sacerdotum (177 p. Chr.).
BGU. 194; Wilcken, *Chrestomathie*, 84.

LIST OF DOCUMENTS

179. De immunitate mulierum (ca. 180 p. Chr.).
   P. Teb. 327; Wilcken, *Chrestomathie*, 394.

180. De fuga eorum qui muneribus obnoxii sunt (186 p. Chr.).
   P. Geneva, 37; Wilcken, *Chrestomathie*, 400.

181. De nominatione magistratuum (192 p. Chr.).
   P. Ryl. 77, ll. 32 *ff.*

182. De muneribus vicanorum (194 p. Chr.).
   BGU. 15, col. 1; Wilcken, *Chrestomathie*, 393.

183. De immunitate Antinoopolitanorum (196 p. Chr.).
   BGU. 1022; Wilcken, *Chrestomathie*, 29.

184. De connubio Antinoopolitanorum et Aegyptorum (saec. II p. Chr.).
   Compt. rend. de l'acad. d. inscr. et bell. lettr. 1905, 160 *ff.*; Wilcken, *Chrestomathie*, 27.

185. De munere eorum qui vectigalia exigunt (200 p. Chr.?).
   P. Oxy. 1405.

186. De vicis deminuendis (ca. 200 p. Chr.).
   Preisigke, *Sammelbuch*, 8; *Festschrift Hirschfeld*, 125.

187. De muneribus Oxyrhynchi (201 p. Chr.).
   P. Oxy. 54.

188. De vectigalibus (ca. 202 p. Chr.).
   P. Oxy. 890; Wilcken, *Chrestomathie*, 280.

189. Epistula imperatoris Septimi Severi ad Aurelium Horionem (202 p. Chr.).
   P. Oxy. 705, ll. 54 *ff.*; Wilcken, *Chrestomathie*, 407.

190. Querellae vicanorum contra possessores (207 p. Chr.).
   Preisigke, *Sammelbuch*, 4284, ll. 1–17.

191. De tribubus metropoleos (212 p. Chr.).
   P. Oxy. 1030; Wilcken, *Chrestomathie*, 36.

192. Edictum Caracallae de civitate peregrinis danda (212 p. Chr.).
   P. Giess. 40 (*cf.* vol. III, p. 164); Mitteis, *Chrestomathie*, 377; Segré-Beltrami, *Rivista di Filologia*, 45 (1917), 16 *ff.*; Meyer, *Juristische Papyri*, 1; Girard, p. 203.

193. Edictum Caracallae de reditu Aegyptiorum in agros (215 p. Chr.
   P. Giess. 40, col. II, ll. 16–29; Wilcken, *Chrestomathie*, 22.

194. De severitate munerum (216 p. Chr.).
   BGU. 159; Wilcken, *Chrestomathie*, 408.

95. Edictum Caracallae de senatoribus (213–217 p. Chr.).
   P. Oxy. 1406.

196. Edictum Aureli Serenisci de censu (226 p. Chr.).
   P. Teb. 288; Wilcken, *Chrestomathie*, 266.

LIST OF DOCUMENTS

197. De munere decaprotorum (post 242 p. Chr.).
   P. Oxy. 62, verso; Wilcken, *Chrestomathie*, 278.

198. De cessione bonorum eorum qui munera declinant (250 p. Chr.).
   C.P.R. 20; Wilcken, *Chrestomathie*, 402.

199. De trapezitis Oxyrhynchi (260 p. Chr.).
   P. Oxy. 1411.

200. De nominatione eorum qui munera subeunt (265 p. Chr.).
   P. Fior. 2, VII, ll. 166–201; Wilcken, *Chrestomathie*, 401.

201. De conductione agrorum publicorum (266 p. Chr.).
   C.P.H. 119, recto, col. VII; *C.P.R.* 39; Wilcken, *Chrestomathie*, 377.

202. Epistula senatus Hermopolitani ad στρατηγόν (266–267 p. Chr.).
   C.P.H. 52; Wilcken, *Chrestomathie*, 38.

203. Acta senatus Oxyrhynchi (270–275 p. Chr.).
   P. Oxy. 1413.

204. Acta senatus Oxyrhynchi (270–275 p. Chr.).
   P. Oxy. 1414.

205. De exactione tributi (saec. III p. Chr.).
   P. Br. Mus. 2, 213; Wilcken, *Chrestomathie*, 267.

206. De munere εὐθηνιαρχίας (ca. saec. III fin. p. Chr.).
   P. Oxy. 1252, verso, col. II.

INDEX

absentes rei publicae causa, 105
Achaea, 163, 166, nos. 8, 9, 46
Acraephia, no. 56
acta senatus, nos. 203, 204
actor, nos. 139, 157
adiectio, 37, 211
adlectio of citizens, 58
adnotationes, 237
Adramyttus, no. 22
aediles, 59, 63, 89, nos. 20, 24, 26, 45, 63, 64, 65
Aemilius Paullus, 70, no. 2
Aetolia, nos. 1, 3
Aezani, no. 82
Africa, 15 f., 85, 119, 123, 182, 186, 210, nos. 96, 125, 146, 159, 161
Aga Bey, no. 142
ager Dentheliates, 156
ager privatus, no. 10
ager publicus, 31 f., 47, 179, 181, nos. 1, 3, 5, 10: alienation forbidden, nos. 26, 55: disputes concerning, nos. 55, 57, 58, 59, 63, 68, 82, 104: sale regulated, nos. 121, 129: confiscated, no. 157: octonarius and stipendiarius, no. 74
agoranomus, 25, 28, no. 206
Aïn-el Djemela, no. 93
Aïn Zui, no. 152
Alabanda, no. 22
album: of senate, 65, 202: of Canusium, no. 136
Alexandria, 71, 83, 103, 244 f., nos. 165, 166, 168, 173, 192, 193
Amastris, 150
Ambracia, 45 n. 1
Amisus, 43 n. 2, 146, 160
amphodon, no. 191
Anauni, no. 49
Ancyra, 147, no. 38
angary, no. 131
Antinoopolis, 103, 192, nos. 170, 173, 176, 183, 184
Antioch, 24, 144: in Pisidia, no. 65 a
Antiochus, nos. 1, 147
Antium, 3, 5, 177

Antony, 5, 39, nos. 26, 29, 38
Apamea, 52, 68, 151, nos. 34, 123, 147
Aphrodisias, 39, 41 n. 4, nos. 29, 120, 137, 138, 145
Apollonides, 40 n. 3
appeals: from imperial estates, nos. 139, 141, 142, 143, 144: from provincial assemblies to Rome, 172: regulated by law, nos. 90, 121: to Rome, 79, nos. 12, 14, 21, 36, 63, 78, 81, 97, 100, 119, 121: to governor, nos. 35, 68, 90, 104, 112, 113, 139, 141: from nomination to office in Egypt, nos. 181, 182, 183, 185: from exactions of strategus, no. 202. *See also under* embassies
Appius Claudius, 154
Apulum, 14
Aquincum, 14
Araegenuae, no. 140
Aragueni, 53 n. 3, no. 141
a rationibus, no. 109
arbitration, 152 ff., nos. 8, 10, 15, 18, 46, 57, 58, 82, 104
archephodus, 28
archiereus, 28
archiphylax, 170
archives, 244 n. 8, 245 n. 5, nos. 9, 22, 24, 26, 29, 36, 65, 96
archon, 56
Arelate, no. 107
Areopagus, 77, no. 91
Argos, 22
Aricia, 8
Aritium, no. 47
Arpinum, 138
Asculum, no. 13
Asia, 48, 119, 163 ff., 167, 168, 183, 185, nos. 157, 157, 158
asiarch, no. 158
assemblies: local, 199; *see also under* comitia: provincial, 162 ff.; influence in provincial government, 165; relation to municipalities, 166 ff.; of Africa, nos. 125, 159, 161; of Asia, nos. 34, 158; of Dalmatia, no.

INDEX

assemblies (*cont.*)
41; of Gaul, nos. 50, 62, 140; of
Lycia, nos. 15, 84, 87, 97; of Thessaly, no. 46: privileges of flamen,
no. 62: veto power of emperor, no.
62: method of voting and procedure,
no. 62: asks governor for permission
to forward copy of decree to emperor, no. 102: cost of shows regulated, no. 110: regulation of liturgies
of festival in Asia, no. 158
Assos, nos. 48, 94
Astypalaea, 41 n. 4, 130 n. 3, 161,
nos. 75, 76
asylum, nos. 3, 17, 29
ἀτέλεια, 101, nos. 29, 139. *See also
under* immunity
Ateste, nos. 28, 31
Athens, 75, 139, 154 f., nos. 6, 21, 90,
91, 92, 130
Attalus, no. 12
attributi, nos. 2, 10, 16, 17, 25, 29, 49,
53, 107
augurs, nos. 26, 126
Augustales, no. 43
autonomy, 40 n. 1, 82, nos. 3, 4, 11,
16, 17, 19, 25, 40, 67, 108. *See*
civitas libera

Baetica, 48, nos. 60, 61, 66
Baetocaece, no. 147
Baiae, no. 149
banking, 139, nos. 81, 199
Bantia, no. 11
Beneventum, nos. 38, 154
Bergalei, no. 49
Beroia, no. 118
billeting of troops, nos. 19, 113, 139,
141, 152
Bithynia and Pontus, 74, 76, 150, 160,
163, 166, 182, 189
Bovianum, no. 109
brabeutae, 25
Britain, no. 140
Brixia, nos. 38, 154
buildings in municipalities: destruction forbidden, nos. 20, 65, 83
bureaucracy, 151, 165, 186, 219 f.,
228 f.: in Egypt, 36
bureaus: names and duties, 240 f.
burgi, no. 128
Byzantium, 24, 68, 150

Caesariani, no. 141
Calaguris, no. 77
Calama, 142
Camerinum, 161
canabae, 10, 13 f., 65: magister and
curatores, 13
candidacy of magistrates: at Urso,
no. 26: at Malaca, no. 65
Canusium, 65, no. 136
Cappadocia, 73, 185
Capua, 11
caput, unit of taxation, 130
Caranis, no. 177
Carnuntum, 14
Carteia, 7, 184
Carthage, 11, 46, 47, 66, 156 f., 184
Casae, no. 96
Casinum, 66 n. 4
castellum, 10 ff., 65, no. 27: prefect of,
12: Carcassonne, 13 n. 1
cautio: magistrates, nos. 20, 65, 77:
tax-gatherers, no. 92: in appeals,
no. 119
Celeia, no. 42
censor: in East, 76: in West, 59 f.:
Bantia, no. 11: in Italy, no. 24
census: in Egypt, no. 166, 196: of
Augustus, 120: of Diocletian, 132
centumviri, no. 43
Centuripae, 47, 138
Cercina, 45, n. 5
cessio bonorum, nos. 181, 185, 198.
See liturgies
charities: municipal, 208, 218. *See*
endowments
charters, nos. 11, 20, 24, 25, 26, 64, 65,
151: number granted by Vespasian,
no. 60
Chersonese, no. 112
Chios, 40 n. 3, 82, nos. 40, 69
Chrysopolis, 24
Church Councils, 176: and municipal
institutions, 224 f.
Chyretiae, no. 1
Cibyra, no. 123
Cicero, 50 f., 80, 121, 136, 149, 187, 202
Cierium, no. 46
Cilicia, 50 ff., 80, 119, 136, 149, 187,
202
citizenship: various classes in Asia,
nos. 65 a, 122: how attained, 58:
decrees submitted to governor, 97,

[589]

INDEX

courts: local, 43, 60 f., *see also* jurisdiction: ecclesiastical, 205: of provincial assemblies, 172: of fora and conciliabula, no. 24

Crete, 73, 167, 170, no. 55

Cumae, 11, no. 149

curator rei publicae: origin, 63 powers, 92 ff.: history, 90 ff.: general, 78, 81 f., 112, 151, 188 f., 193, 201, 204, 229: nominated to liturgies, 98: title in Orient, 91, nos. 91, 123

Cures, 65, no. 43

curia, 85, 94, 207, 216 f., 225, 229: at Tymandus, no. 151: in villages, 23: elected officials, 85: responsibility for liturgies, 98: deserted, 110 ff., 198 ff. *See also* curiales, senate

curiales, 113 f., 194 f., 202 f., 206 ff., 215 f., 222, 225, 229 ff.: escape from liturgies, 106, *see also* liturgies: Jews and Christians in membership, 110 f. *See also* decurions, senate

cursus fiscalis, no. 156

cursus honorum, 59, 78, 84, 85, no. 10

cursus publicus, 137, 149, no. 156. *See also* post

Cyzicus, no. 106

decaproti and decemprimi, 94, 113, 170, 222, no. 89: in Egypt, no. 197

decemviri, 56

decentralization, 185

decline: municipal institutions, 198 ff., 226 ff.: village communities, no. 186: of democratic institutions, 186 ff.

decreta, 235, 236, 239: of Roman magistrates, nos. 2, 13, 57, 58: of cities, nos. 14, 23, 43, 48, 52, 66, 67, 69, 70, 72, 88, 94, 95, 115, 117, 122, 123, 126, 128, 133, 138, 146, 149, 156, 159: of provincial assemblies, nos. 34, 125, 161

decumae, 39, 118, 127

decurions: in West, 65 ff.: in East, 76 ff.: honorary, 77: album, 65, no. 136: named by magistrates, no. 24: elected by comitia, no. 24: removal from office, no. 26: eligibility, 65 f., no. 24: in documents,

nos. 20, 24, 26, 33, 43, 61, 63, 65 a, 126, 136, 146, 149. *See also* curiales, senate

dediticii, no. 192

defense, permission to levy local troops, no. 26

defensor: plebis, 78, 90, 92 ff., 112, 195, 201, 205, 229: on imperial estates, no. 74

deforestation, 212, no. 118

Delos, nos. 6, 21

Delphi, 39, 155, no. 3

demarch, 25

Demetrias, 21

democracy, 70, 75, 182, 186 f., 195, 199, 227 ff.: 'restored' at Pergamum, no. 23

δημοσιῶναι, nos. 12, 14, 17, 18

dictator in Italian towns, 56

diplomata, no. 156

domicile: required of municipal magistrates, no. 26. *See also* origo

dominium, 9

Dorylaeum, no. 34

duoviri, 11, 12, 56, 59, 60, 89, nos. 24, 26, 27, 28, 33, 45, 53, 64, 65, 65 a, 66, 77, 115, 126, 136, 140: election of emperor, no. 64

ecclesia: in villages, 25: in towns, 75

ecdicus, 25, 167

economic conditions, 209 ff. *See also* decline

edicts, 232 f., 235 ff., 242, nos. 33, 39, 49, 51, 56, 92, 105, 118, 124, 129, 131, 132, 147, 155, 162–165, 167, 168, 175, 177, 181, 185, 190, 192–195: provincial, 48 ff., 199: Cilician, 50 ff.: e. Siciliense, 50: tralaticium, 50: perpetuum, 239: Caracalla, 53, 57, 77, 103, 125, 161, 191 f., no. 192

Egypt, 27 ff., 33 ff., 83, 89 ff., 99 ff., 102, 118, 132 ff., 139, 185, 213, 244 ff., nos. 162–206

Ekiskuju, no. 144

election of magistrates: fifty days before beginning of year, no. 34: by popular assembly, nos. 24, 26: at Nola on July 1, no. 45: at Malaca, no. 65 in the East, 78 f.: in Africa, 85: in local senate, 186 f. *See* honores, candidacy, appeals

INDEX

INDEX

ferries a municipal monopoly, 139, nos. 70, 128
Fidenae, 187
finances, municipal, 138 ff. *See under* monopolies, vectigalia, taxes
fines: a source of revenue, 141 ff., nos. 24, 26, 64, 65, 128
Firmum, no. 63
fisheries, 139, no. 68
flamens: of municipality, 64, nos. 53, 62, 115, 136: of province, 166, no. 62, 84, 87, 102, 110, 158, 159
Flamininus, 69, nos. 1, 5, 8
foedus aequum, 160 f. *See* civitas foederata
fora, 10, nos. 24, 27, 131. *See* emporium
Formiae, 8
Forum: Livi, 12: Populi, 12
freedom, nos. 15, 34. *See* civitates liberae
frumentarii, nos. 142, 144
Fundi, 8

Gabinius, 72, no. 21
Galatia, 73, 163, nos. 38, 57, 154
Galillenses, no. 58
Gallia, 15, 119, 123, 164, 170, 185, 204, 210, nos. 27, 50, 110, 140
games and shows, 145, nos. 26, 73, 110, 155, 158, 169
gens, 10, 15
Genua, 11, 139, no. 10
gerusia, 25, 77, nos. 78, 114
gifts, 142. *See* endowments
Gigthi, nos. 115, 161
Girgeh, no. 163
Gortyna, 154, no. 55
governor: appeals, 99, *see under* appeals: approved municipal decrees, nos. 80, 98, 99, 114: veto, 168, nos. 84, 97: veto power overruled by emperor, no. 97: edict, *see* edicts: powers, 202 ff.; defined in Asia by lex Cornelia, no. 34: ratifies endowment, no. 71: regulates prices, no. 65 a: judicial power, 204 ff., nos. 64, 78: regulates municipal taxes, 130, no. 61: nominates to liturgies, 98: establishes market, no. 148: settles strikes, no. 124: oversight of municipal finances, 151, no. 98.

See lex provinciae, assemblies, epistulae
Gracchi, 7, 122, 179, 183 f., 210, no. 20
guilds, 77: immunity from liturgies, 103, 107 ff., 207 f.: local and imperial, 107 ff.: purpose, 194: hereditary, 208: navicularii, 108: municipal, nos. 124, 204. *See also* collegiality, gerusia, conventus c. R., neon
gymnasiarch, 28, nos. 169, 181, 187, 198, 203, 206

Halaesa, 47
Haliartus, no. 5
Halicyae, 47
Hastenses, no. 2
Helvetii, 15
Henchir-Snobbeur, no. 146
Heptacomia, no. 192
Heraclea: at Latmos, no. 4: in Macedonia, no. 79
Heracleia, 49, no. 24
Hermopolis, nos. 169, 181, 198, 201, 202
Hermopolites, no. 200
Hierapolis, 24, no. 117
Hierapytna, 154
Hispellum, no. 155
Histria, no. 68
honores, 84 ff. *passim*: in West, 56 ff.: in East, 77 f.: fasti, no. 45: in municipal charters, nos. 11, 20, 24, 26, 64, 65: election in Asia, no. 34: ius honorum granted to Gauls, no. 50: honores flaminum, no. 62. *See also* candidacy, election, *and titles of various offices*
hospes, no. 26
hospitium, nos. 26, 113, 132, 137, 138, 147
hyparchy, no. 37
hypomnematographus, 28, nos. 203, 204

ἰδία, *see* origo
Igabrum, no. 60
Ilium, 24, 41 n. 2, 138, nos. 12, 14
illustres, 105
Illyria, 123, 185, no. 130
Ilugo, no. 95

INDEX

immunity: from liturgies, 101 ff., 205 f.: of philosophers, no. 127: granted by emperor, nos. 42, 158: by decree of local assembly, no. 43: from imperial taxation, no. 53; to Delphi, no. 3; to Mitylene, no. 25; to Delos, no. 21; *see also under* civitas libera et immunis: Tyrans, no. 130: settlers in Pizus, no. 131: pontiffs and augurs, no. 26: citizens of Antinoopolis, nos. 170, 176, 183: Alexandrians and Romans in Egypt, nos. 165, 173, 192: physicians, no. 174: veterans, nos. 177, 192: women, no. 179: priests, no. 178. *See also* appeals, liturgies, honores
incolae, 58, nos. 26, 53, 65, 65 a
indictio, 129
inscriptio, 238
intercessio, nos. 11, 64
interrex, 56
intributio, 97
irenarch, 99, 170
Italica, no. 110
Itanus, 154
iudex as title of governor, 204
iugatio, no. 157
iugum as unit of taxation, 130, no. 157
iuridici, 204
ius civitatis, nos. 151, 154
ius conubii, 6, nos. 53, 184
ius Italicum, 9, 72, 188, 192
ius iurandum, nos. 37, 47, 48
ius Latii, 7, 88, 188: maius, minus, 9, 192, nos. 60, 61, 64, 66, 115, 192

Jerusalem, 23
Jews, 110, 134
Julius Caesar, 5, 7, 14, 15, 59, 66, 68, 121, 146, 156, 184 f., 210, nos. 24 (lex Iulia municipalis), 25, 26, 29, 50
jurisdiction: civil and criminal, 61, 64, 82, 183, 204 f., nos. 10, 11, 25, 26, 27, 28, 33, 36, 40, 58, 64, 65, 65 a, 77, 131, 133. *See also* law, courts, appeals

Khargeh, no. 165
κοινόν: of villages, 21 ff., no. 141: of magistrates, 28, nos. 169, 181: of provinces, *see* assemblies

Koula, no. 148

Lagina, nos. 17, 67
Lambaesis, 14
land: classification in Egypt, 33 ff. *See* ager publicus, estates, saltus, territoria
Langensis, 139, no. 10
Lanuvium, 8
Laodicaea, 39, no. 15
λαογραφούμενοι, no. 192
latifundia, 203, 213, 216, 228, no. 129. *See* saltus, estates, land
Latin rights, *see* ius Latii
law: given to Athens by Hadrian, no. 90: alimentary, 211, 223, no. 65 a: administration in East, 82: Greek and Oriental versus Roman, 81 f., 204: extension of R. law, 179 f., 188, 193: autonomy, local, *s.v. See* jurisdiction, courts
League, Latin, 177 f.
leases: of public lands, nos. 5, 10, 24, 26, 55, 65, 82, 121, 129, 157: of temple land, no. 35: disputes concerning, no. 58: in Egypt, no. 201
Lepidus, 5
Lesbos, 130 n. 3
lex: Aemilia, 49 n. 2: Antonia, no. 26: Antonia de Termessibus, 42 ff., no. 19: Atestina, no. 28: Bantina, no. 11: coloniae Genitivae Iuliae, 59 f., 67, no. 26: Cornelia, 72, no. 34: data, 233, nos. 11, 13, 20, 26, 27: de certa portione olei vendunda, no. 90: de imperio Vespasiani, 161: de iudiciis privatis, no. 33: de officio flaminum, no. 62: Gabinia Calpurnia, no. 21: Hadriana, 17 f., nos. 93, 111: Hieronica, 47: Iulia, no. 13, 111: Iulia agraria, 60, 118: Iulia et Plautia Papiria, 8: Iulia municipalis, 59 f., 86 f., 180, 185, no. 26: Malacitana, 17 f., 58 f., 67, no. 65: Manciana, 17 f., nos. 74, 93: Metelli, 49 n. 2: organizing colony, 4 f.: Palmyrenorum, no. 89: Plaetoria, no. 24: Pompeia, 47, 72, 74, 76: Porcia, 44, no. 19: provinciae, 17, 48 f., 52, 72, 82, 162, 181, 183, 202, 204, 233, 240: Quinctia de aquaeductibus, no. 33: rogata, 232, nos.

INDEX

lex *(cont.)*
13, 19, 24, 27: Roscia, nos. 27, 28:
Rubria de Gallia Cisalpina, 10, 60,
184, nos. 27, 33: Rupilia, 49, 159:
Salpensa, no. 64: saltus, no. 93:
Sempronia, 46, 118 n. 3, 122: Tarentina, no. 20: Villia annalis, no. 11
libellus colonorum, no. 111
liturgies, 84 ff. *passim*: classification,
79, 94 f.: exemption, 101 ff., *see also*
immunity *and* appeals: flight of
incumbents, nos. 180, 189, 190, 194:
provincial, no. 158: in Egypt, 37,
83, 99 ff., *see* documents from Egypt
(nos. 165 ff.), *passim*: imperial, 189,
see angary, post, appeals
logistae, 25, no. 150
Lucullus, 146
Lugudunum, 164, nos. 50, 140
Lusitania, 48, no. 47
Lycaonia, 164
Lycia, 164, 166, 169 ff., nos. 80, 128
Lydia, nos. 142, 148, 150

Macedonia, 117, 128, 171, no. 1
Maeonia, no. 34
magister: canabae, 13: saltus, 15, no.
74: vicus, 15, no. 141
magistrates, *see* honores
Magnesia, 40 n. 3, 154
Malaca, 8, 58, 62, 67, 112, nos. 64, 65
mandata, 236 ff., 239
mansiones, nos. 51, 156
Mantinea, 22
Marius, 7, 184, no. 38
markets, 139 n. 9, *see* emporium,
fora: in villages, nos, 147, 148:
in saltus, no. 96: during games at
Pergamum, no. 73
Massilia, 41, 138, 146, no. 107
Melitaea, no. 8
Mendechora, no. 143
Messana, 47
Messene, 156
metrocomia, 22 f., no. 113
Metropolis, no. 46
metropolis, 28 f.
Miletus, 156, no. 22
Minturnae, no. 38
Mithradates, nos. 16, 17, 19, 21, 40
Mitylene, 42
Moesia, no. 130

monopolies: municipal, 139, 209, 224:
banking, no. 81: ferry, nos. 71,
128: fishing, no. 68: weaving, no.
204
Mucius Scaevola, 158, 163
Mummius, 70, 156, 163, nos. 8, 9
munera, *see* liturgies
municeps, 58
municipia: definition, 8 f.: in Italy,
177 f., 180: in provinces, 9: fundana,
9, no. 24: charters, 8, *see* lex Iulia
municipalis, Bantia, Tarentina: Flavia, nos. 60, 61, 64, 65: developed
from praefecturae, 11; from colonies,
etc., nos. 20, 95, 115: at Volubilis,
no. 53
Municipium Augustum, 58
Mutina, 7
Mylasa, 139, 154 f., nos. 22, 30, 32,
89, 133
Myra, nos. 99, 128

Nacoleia, 24, no. 154
Narbo, no. 62
Narbo Martius, 7, 184, no. 38
Narthacium, no. 8
Naucratis, 83, no. 184
Neaetum, 41 n. 4
Neapolis, 148
negotiatores, 131
Neilopolis, nos. 178, 182
Nemausus, 138
neocorate, 81
neon, 77, no. 106
Neptunia, no. 20
Netum, 47
Nicaea, 68, 144, 150
Nicomedia, 68, 143, 150
Nola, no. 45
nomarch, 29
nomination of officials, 59 ff., 78 f.,
85 ff., 202, nos. 24, 34, 65: in Egypt,
nos. 172, 173, 181, 185, 198, 200,
203
νομογραφεύς, 172
νόμος πωλητικός, no. 129
Nuceria, 158, no. 11
Numidia, nos. 125, 140, 152
nundinae, no. 96. *See* emporia, fora

Oath: of loyalty, nos. 37, 38, 47, 48:
of magistrates, nos. 64, 65

[595]

INDEX

octroi, 139. *See* portoria
oligarchy: favoured by governors, 72, 182, 183, 186 f., 229 f.: pro-Roman party in power, nos. 5, 9
ὁμόλογοι, no. 192
ὁμόνοια, 161
oppida: definition, 4, 10: attributa, 138, nos. 16, 17, 27, 33, 107, 154
Opramoas, nos. 80, 84, 87, 97, 99, 102
oratio principum, 234 ff., 244, nos. 50, 56, 110
Orcistus, 13, 24, no. 154
Orientalism, 26, 193, 227 ff.
origo, 194, 208, 211, 216, 226, nos. 129, 158, 168, 182, 192, 193
Oropus, 154 f., nos. 12, 18
Ostia, 3, no. 160
Oxyrhynchus, nos. 166, 167, 185, 187–189, 191, 195, 197, 199, 203, 204, 206

pagani, no. 107. *See also* villages
pagus, 10, 14 f.
Pagus Apollinaris, Lucretius, Martius, Valerius, Veronensis, 14
Palmyra, 44 n. 7, 140, no. 89
Panormus, 47
Paphos, 148
paraphylaces, no. 117
Parma, 7
Paros, no. 132
particularism, 195
Passala, 140
paternalism, 80, 189, 200, no. 71
Patrae, 42
patronage, patrocinium, 26, 113, 203, 215, 217, no. 142
patroni: of senate, 65: at Asso, no. 94: at Brixia, no. 44: at Canusium, no. 136: at Clunia, no. 135: at Genua, no. 10: at Malaca, no. 65: at Stratonicea, no. 67: at Urso, no. 26
Patulcenses, no. 58
Pautalia, no. 139
peculation of municipal funds, no. 20
pedani, no. 136
peregrini: given Roman citizenship, no. 192: peregrine city made a municipium, no. 53
perfectissimi, 105

Pergamum, 163, nos. 12, 22, 23, 73, 81, 100, 124, 133
Phaenae, no. 113
Phazimon, no. 37
Philadelphia, nos. 134, 143: in Egypt, no. 183
Philip of Macedon, no. 1
Phrygia, nos. 123, 141, 154
phylaces, 28
phylarch, 21
Pisaurum, no. 38
Pisidia, nos. 19, 65 a, 122, 151
Pizus, 26, no. 131
Plasara, no. 29
plebiscite, no. 19
Pliny, 53, 65, 68, 80, 136, 150 ff., 202, 215
Pogla, 23, no. 122
Pompaelo, no. 77
Pompeii, 143, 144, 158 f.
Pompey, 23, 42, 49, 72, 76, 86, nos. 13, 20, 21, 25, 37
pontiff, 64, no. 26
populus: in West, 57: in East, 75
portoria, nos. 19, 39, 89, 130. *See* taxes
possessores, 131, no. 146
post, imperial, 129, 136, no. 51. *See* angary, liturgies
praefectura, 10 ff., nos. 24, 27, 28
praefectus: iure dicundo in municipalities, 11, 15, 17, 59, 62 f., nos. 24, 26–28, 33, 64: of emperor in municipalities, 62 f., no. 64: pagorum, 15: praetorio, 60, 130, nos. 109, 140, 154, 156: urbi, 61: of Egypt, nos. 162 ff.
praetextati, 65, no. 136
praetor in municipalities, 56
πραγματευτής, no. 139
πραγματικός, nos. 139, 196
prices regulated, nos. 65 a, 90, 91
Priene, 154 f., nos. 8, 14, 34
priesthoods: elected, 64: sold, 79: honor, 93: exemption, 109 f., nos. 164, 178. *See also under* augurs, flamens, pontiff
primus curiae, 94
princeps, 234. *See* emperors
principales, 94, 99
private ownership developed in Egypt, 37

INDEX

INDEX

Stratonicea, 146, nos. 17, 67
Stratonicea-Hadrianopolis, no. 83
strikes, no. 124
subscriptio, 236 ff., 244, nos. 111, 154
sufes, 56, nos. 44, 45, 53, 146
Sufes, 13
Sulla, 5, 72, 146, 159, 180, 184, nos.
    15–18, 22, 34, 40
summa honoraria, 62, 76, 79, 87, nos.
    85, 151, 181, 203: in villages, 25,
    no. 150
summa legitima, 142
susceptores, 131 f.
syndicus, no. 203
Syria, 163, 213, no. 147

Tabae, 42 n. 1, nos. 15, 16
tabularii, 131
tabularium principis, no. 58
Tampium, no. 140
Tanagra, no. 99
Tarentum, 8, no. 20
Tarraco, 164
Tarsus, 75, 139 n. 6, no. 130
Tauromenium, 41 n. 4, 47
taxes, 117 ff. See vectigalia
Teanum Sidicinum, no. 11
Tebtunis, no. 179
Tegea, no. 51
temple-lands, 33, 35, 135, nos. 12, 14,
    18, 35, 82, 129
temple-states, 22 f., 32
tenancy, 31, 33, 34, 37, 217. See
    estates, latifundia, saltus, coloni
Teos, 50, no. 3
Termessus, 42 ff., no. 19
territoria, 10, 26, 73, 134, 138, 182,
    210, 214, nos. 27, 49, 59, 68, 82.
    See also ager publicus
Tetrapurgia, no. 148
Thamagudi, 65, 91, 143, nos. 125, 136
Thebaid, no. 163
Thera, 130 n. 3
Thessaly, 168, nos. 1, 8
Thisbe, 50, nos. 5, 104, 129
Thorigny, 167, no. 140
Thrace, 185, no. 131
Thurreion, 40
Thyatira, no. 35
Tibur, no. 7
toparchies, 21, 36, no. 131
tractus, 17 ff., no. 125

Tralles, 130 n. 3, no. 122
transportation, 214. See angary, post
treaties, 160 f., no. 99. See civitas
    foederata
tresviri, 56
tribes, 178, nos. 10, 191
tribute, 39 ff., 117 ff.: t. capitis, soli,
    119. See vectigalia
Tridentinum, no. 49
Tripolitana, no. 161
Troas, no. 88
Troezen, 40 n. 5
Tulliasses, no. 49
Turris Lascutana, no. 2
Tuscia, nos. 155, 159
Tymanda, 24, 74, no. 151
Tymbrianassus, no. 57
Tyra, 97, no. 130
Tyre, 41 n. 1, 42
Tyrus, 41 n. 4

Umbria, 155, 159
uniformity in legislation, 188, 193,
    nos. 22, 40
urban movement, 209, 211, 223, 228,
    nos. 168, 193
Urso, 5, 8, 66 ff., 95, 139, no. 26
Utica, 39

vacatio, no. 177. See immunity
Vanacini, no. 59
vectigalia: annona, 122, 127 ff.: au-
    rum: coronarium, 221, nos. 38, 76,
    150; negotiatorum, 131; oblaticium,
    131, 221; tironicum, 221, no. 150:
    capitatio plebeia, 119, 122, 128, 131,
    209, 221; paid by officer of pro-
    vincial assembly, 171: capitulum
    lenocinii, 122, 127, no. 112: cen-
    tesima rerum venalium, 122, 124;
    endowment for, no. 116: collatio
    lustralis, 122, 131: gladiatorial, 122,
    no. 110: house, 120: land, 117, see
    iugum: portoria, s.v.: salt, no. 14:
    vicesima hereditatis, 122, 124, 167,
    no. 192: vicesima libertatis, 122,
    124, 142; municipal, 140: vicesima
    quinta venalium mancipiorum, 122,
    125: in Egypt, 132 f.; beer, no. 171;
    poll, nos. 166, 176, 196; sales, no.
    167; sheep, no. 171; collection, nos.
    165, 167, 171, 185, 188, 196, 202,

[598]

INDEX

vectigalia (*cont.*)

205: Diocletian's reforms, 127, 221: Hiero's system, 121: Sempronian law, 182 f.: paid in kind, 120, 221; in money, 120: remitted by Augustus, no. 38; by Hadrian, no. 83: applied to building of walls, no. 157: levy of new taxes by municipality approved by provincial governor, no. 61: disputes re territorial tax, nos. 10, 82: collection at Athens, no. 92: Delos, no. 21: Aphrodisias free from any tax, no. 29: Greece freed from tribute, no. 56: Antani (?) at Heraclea, no. 79: Histriani, no. 68: Mitylene, no. 25: Mylasa, no. 32: Sulla determines amount paid by attributi to Stratonicea, no. 17: Thisbe, nos. 5, 104, 129: water rates at Venafrum, no. 33: remission of imperial taxes for ten years at Volubilis, no. 53. *See also* ager publicus, banking, civitas stipendiaria, endowments, finances, fines, publicani, summa honoraria

Veii, 65, no. 43

Veleia, no. 27

Venafrum, 140, no. 33

Verres, 202

veterans: colonies, 7, 13, 184, 211, nos. 33, 38: privileges, 106 f., no. 166

vicarii, 130

vicus, 10 f., 14, 21 ff., 65

Viducasses, no. 140

villages: attributi, nos. 10, 17, 29, 117, 147, 154: on imperial estates, *see* saltus, estates: complaints from, *see* embassies, exactions: development into cities, 24, 32 f., 73 f., nos. 37, 83, 115, 122: depopulation, nos. 139, 141, 154: government, 21 ff., nos. 117, 131: officials, 25 ff., no. 150: Egyptian, 27 ff.: taxes, 26 f., nos. 110, 154: cities reduced to villages, 24 ff., no. 154: markets, nos. 96, 147, 148: privileges conferred by Antiochus ratified by later emperors, no. 147. *See also* territoria, pagus, vicus

Villa magna Variana, no. 74

Villa Mappalia Siga, no. 74

Viturii, no. 10

Vocontii, 15, 41 n. 4

Volsinii, no. 155

Volubilis, no. 53

voting in municipal elections, no. 65

Vulceii, 130

walls, no. 157

waste lands, no. 93

Xanthus, nos. 97, 116

Zela, 23